Henry Van Dyke, Complete Collection

In this book:
The Story of the Other Wise Man
The Mansion
The First Christmas Tree
The Spirit of Christmas
The Lost Word
The Sad Shepherd, A Christmas Story
Fighting For Peace
Fisherman's Luck
The Valley of Vision
The Americanism of Washington
The Unruly Sprite
Days Off And Other Digressions
Little Rivers, A Book of Essays
in Profitable Idleness
The complete Poems
of Henry Van Dyke
The house of Rimmon

Henry Jackson van Dyke (1852 –1933) was an American author, educator, and clergyman. Among his popular writings are the two Christmas stories, "The Other Wise Man" (1896) and "The First Christmas Tree" (1897). Various religious themes of his work are also expressed in his poetry, hymns and the essays collected in Little Rivers (1895) and Fisherman's Luck (1899). He wrote the lyrics to the popular hymn, "Joyful, Joyful We Adore Thee" (1907), sung to the tune of Beethoven's "Ode to Joy". He compiled several short stories in The Blue Flower (1902), named after the key symbol of Romanticism introduced first by Novalis.

In this book:
The Story of the Other Wise Man………………Pag. 3
The Mansion……………………………………Pag. 11
The First Christmas Tree……………………..Pag. 21
The Spirit of Christmas………………………..Pag. 29
Fighting For Peace…………………...……….Pag. 35
The Valley of Vision…………..………………..Pag. 71
The Sad Shepherd, A Christmas Story……...Pag. 121
The Lost Word………………………………….Pag. 128
The Americanism of Washington…………..Pag. 137
The Unruly Sprite……………………………..Pag. 143
Days Off And Other Digressions………..…..Pag. 146
Little Rivers, A Book of
Essays in Profitable Idleness…..…………….Pag. 197
Fisherman's Luck………………..…………Pag. 250
The complete Poems
of Henry Van Dyke………....................…..…Pag. 294
The house of Rimmon...Pag. 371

The Story of the Other Wise Man

YOU know the story of the Three Wise Men of the East, and how they traveled from far away to offer their gifts at the manger-cradle in Bethlehem. But have you ever heard the story of the Other Wise Man, who also saw the star in its rising, and set out to follow it, yet did not arrive with his brethren in the presence of the young child Jesus? Of the great desire of this fourth pilgrim, and how it was denied, yet accomplished in the denial; of his many wanderings and the probations of his soul; of the long way of his seeking, and the strange way of his finding, the One whom he sought—I would tell the tale as I have heard fragments of it in the Hall of Dreams, in the palace of the Heart of Man.

THE SIGN IN THE SKY

IN the days when Augustus Caesar was master of many kings and Herod reigned in Jerusalem, there lived in the city of Ecbatana, among the mountains of Persia, a certain man named Artaban, the Median. His house stood close to the outermost of the seven walls which encircled the royal treasury. From his roof he could look over the rising battlements of black and white and crimson and blue and red and silver and gold, to the hill where the summer palace of the Parthian emperors glittered like a jewel in a sevenfold crown.

Around the dwelling of Artaban spread a fair garden, a tangle of flowers and fruit trees, watered by a score of streams descending from the slopes of Mount Orontes, and made musical by innumerable birds. But all color was lost in the soft and odorous darkness of the late September night, and all sounds were hushed in the deep charm of its silence, save the plashing of the water, like a voice half sobbing and half laughing under the shadows. High above the trees a dim glow of light shone through the curtained arches of the upper chamber, where the master of the house was holding council with his friends.

He stood by the doorway to greet his guests—a tall, dark man of about forty years, with brilliant eyes set near together under his broad brow, and firm lines graven around his fine, thin lips; the brow of a dreamer and the mouth of soldier, a man of sensitive feeling but inflexible will—one of those who, in whatever age they may live, are born for inward conflict and a life of quest.

His robe was of pure white wool, thrown over a tunic of silk; and a white, pointed cap, with long lapels at the sides, rested on his flowing black hair. It was the dress of the ancient priesthood of the Magi, called the fire-worshippers. "Welcome!" he said, in his low, pleasant voice, as one after another entered the room—"welcome, Abdus; peace be with you, Rhodaspes and Tigranes, and with you my father, Abgarus. You are all welcome, and this house grows bright with the joy of your presence."

There were nine of the men, differing widely in age, but alike in the richness of their dress of many-colored silks, and in the massive golden collars around their necks, marking them as Parthian nobles, and in the winged circles of gold resting upon their breasts, the sign of the followers of Zoroaster.

They took their places around a small black altar at the end of the room, where a tiny flame was burning. Artaban, standing beside it, and waving a barsom of thin tamarisk branches above the fire, fed it with dry sticks of pine and fragrant oils. Then he began the ancient chant of the Yasna, and the voices of his companions joined in the beautiful hymn to Ahura-Mazda:

> We worship the Spirit Divine,
>
> all wisdom and goodness possessing,
>
> Surrounded by Holy Immortals,
>
> the givers of bounty and blessing,
>
> We joy in the works of His hands,
>
> His truth and His power confessing.
>
> We praise all the things that are pure,
>
> for these are His only Creation;
>
> The thoughts that are true, and the words
>
> and deeds that have won approbation;
>
> These are supported by Him
>
> and for these we make adoration.

Hear us, O Mazda! Thou livest
in truth and in heavenly gladness;

Cleanse us from falsehood, and keep us

from evil and bondage to badness;

Pour out the light and the joy of Thy life

on our darkness and sadness.

Shine on our gardens and fields,

Shine on our working and weaving;

Shine on the whole race of man,
Believing and unbelieving;

Shine on us now through the night,

Shine on us now in Thy might,
The flame of our holy love

and the song of our worship receiving.

The fire rose with the chant, throbbing as if it were made of musical flame, until it cast a bright illumination through the whole apartment, revealing its simplicity and splendor.

The floor was laid with tiles of dark blue veined with white; pilasters of twisted silver stood out against the blue walls; the clearstory of round-arched windows above them was hung with azure silk; the vaulted ceiling was a pavement of sapphires, like the body of heaven in its clearness, sown with silver stars. From the four corners of the roof hung four golden magic-wheels, called the tongues of the gods. At the eastern end, behind the altar, there were two dark-red pillars of porphyry; above them a lintel of the same stone, on which was carved the figure of a winged archer, with his arrow set to the string and his bow drawn.

The doorway between the pillars, which opened upon the terrace of the roof, was covered with a heavy curtain of the color of a ripe pomegranate, embroidered with innumerable golden rays shooting upward from the floor. In effect the room was like a quiet, starry night, all azure and silver, flushed in the east with rosy promise of the dawn. It was, as the house of a man should be, an expression of the character and spirit of the master.

He turned to his friends when the song was ended, and invited them to be seated on the divan at the western end of the room.

"You have come to-night," said he, looking around the circle, "at my call, as the faithful scholars of Zoroaster, to renew your worship and rekindle your faith in the God of Purity, even as this fire has been rekindled on the altar. We worship not the fire, but Him of whom it is the chosen symbol, because it is the purest of all created things. It speaks to us of one who is Light and Truth. Is it not so, my father?"

"It is well said, my son," answered the venerable Abgarus. "The enlightened are never idolaters. They lift the veil of the form and go in to the shrine of the reality, and new light and truth are coming to them continually through the old symbols."

"Hear me, then, my father and my friends," said Artaban, very quietly, "while I tell you of the new light and truth that have come to me through the most ancient of all signs. We have searched the secrets of nature together, and studied the healing virtues of water and fire and the plants. We have read also the books of prophecy in which the future is dimly foretold in words that are hard to understand. But the highest of all learning is the knowledge of the stars. To trace their courses is to untangle the threads of the mystery of life from the beginning to the end. If we could follow them perfectly, nothing would be hidden from us. But is not our knowledge of them still incomplete? Are there not many stars still beyond our horizon—lights that are known only to the dwellers in the far south-land, among the spice-trees of Punt and the gold-mines of Ophir?"

There was a murmur of assent among the listeners.

"The stars," said Tigranes, "are the thoughts of the Eternal. They are numberless. But the thoughts of man can be counted, like the years of his life. The wisdom of the Magi is the greatest of all wisdoms on earth, because it knows its own ignorance. And that is the secret of power. We keep men always looking and waiting for a new sunrise. But we ourselves know that the darkness is equal to the light, and that the conflict between them will never be ended."

"That does not satisfy me," answered Artaban, "for, if the waiting must be endless, if there could be no fulfilment of it, then it would not be wisdom to look and wait. We should become like those new teachers of the Greeks, who say that there is no truth, and that the only wise men are those who spend their lives in discovering and exposing the lies that have been believed in the world. But the new sunrise will certainly dawn in the appointed time. Do not our own books tell us that this will come to pass, and that men will see the brightness of a great light?"

"That is true," said the voice of Abgarus; "every faithful disciple of Zoroaster knows the prophecy of the Avesta and carries the word in his heart. 'In that day Sosiosh the Victorious shall arise out of the number of the prophets in the east country. Around him shall shine a mighty brightness, and he shall make life everlasting, incorruptible, and immortal, and the dead shall rise again.'"

"This is a dark saying," said Tigranes, "and it may be that we shall never understand it. It is better to consider the things that are near at hand, and to increase the influence of the Magi in their own country, rather than to look for one who may be a stranger, and to whom we must resign our power."

The others seemed to approve these words. There was a silent feeling of agreement manifest among them; their looks responded with that indefinable expression which always follows when a speaker has uttered the thought that has been slumbering in the hearts of his listeners. But Artaban turned to Abgarus with a glow on his face, and said: "My father, I have kept this prophecy in the secret place of my soul. Religion without a great hope would be like an altar without a living fire. And now the flame has burned more brightly, and by the light of it I have read other words which also have come from the fountain of Truth, and speak yet more clearly of the rising of the Victorious One in his brightness."

He drew from the breast of his tunic two small rolls of fine linen, with writing upon them, and unfolded them carefully upon his knee.

"In the years that are lost in the past, long before our fathers came into the land of Babylon, there were wise men in Chaldea, from whom the first of the Magi learned the secret of the heavens. And of these Balaam the son of Beor was one of the mightiest. Hear the words of his prophecy: 'There shall come a star out of Jacob, and a sceptre shall arise out of Israel.'"

The lips of Tigranes drew downward with contempt, as he said:

"Judah was a captive by the waters of Babylon, and the sons of Jacob were in bondage to our kings. The tribes of Israel are scattered through the mountains like lost sheep, and from the remnant that dwells in Judea under the yoke of Rome neither star nor sceptre shall arise."

"And yet," answered Artaban, "it was the Hebrew Daniel, the mighty searcher of dreams, the counsellor of kings, the wise Belteshazzar, who was most honoured and beloved of our great King Cyrus. A prophet of sure things and a reader of the thoughts of God, Daniel proved himself to our people. And these are the words that he wrote." (Artaban read from the second roll:) "'Know, therefore, and understand that from the going forth of the commandment to restore Jerusalem, unto the Anointed One, the Prince, the time shall be seven and threescore and two weeks.'"

"But, my son," said Abgarus, doubtfully, "these are mystical numbers. Who can interpret them, or who can find the key that shall unlock their meaning?"

Artaban answered: "It has been shown to me and to my three companions among the Magi—Caspar, Melchior, and Balthazar. We have searched the ancient tablets of Chaldea and computed the time. It falls in this year. We have studied the sky, and in the spring of the year we saw two of the greatest stars draw near together in the sign of the Fish, which is the house of the Hebrews. We also saw a new star there, which shone for one night and then vanished. Now again the two great planets are meeting. This night is their conjunction. My three brothers are watching at the ancient Temple of the Seven Spheres, at Borsippa, in Babylonia, and I am watching here. If the star shines again, they will wait ten days for me at the temple, and then we will set out together for Jerusalem, to see and worship the promised one who shall be born King of Israel. I believe the sign will come. I have made ready for the journey. I have sold my house and my possessions, and bought these three jewels—a sapphire, a ruby, and a pearl—to carry them as tribute to the King. And I ask you to go with me on the pilgrimage, that we may have joy together in finding the Prince who is worthy to be served."

While he was speaking he thrust his hand into the inmost fold of his girdle and drew out three great gems—one blue as a fragment of the night sky, one redder than a ray of sunrise, and one as pure as the peak of a snow mountain at twilight—and laid them on the out-spread linen scrolls before him.

But his friends looked on with strange and alien eyes. A veil of doubt and mistrust came over their faces, like a fog creeping up from the marshes to hide the hills. They glanced at each other with looks of wonder and pity, as those who have listened to incredible sayings, the story of a wild vision, or the proposal of an impossible enterprise. At last Tigranes said: "Artaban, this is a vain dream. It comes from too much looking upon the stars and the cherishing of lofty thoughts. It would be wiser to spend the time in gathering money for the new fire-temple at Chala. No king will ever rise from the broken race of Israel, and no end will ever come to the eternal strife of light and darkness. He who looks for it is a chaser of shadows. Farewell."

And another said: "Artaban, I have no knowledge of these things, and my office as guardian of the royal treasure binds me here. The quest is not for me. But if thou must follow it, fare thee well."

And another said: "In my house there sleeps a new bride, and I cannot leave her nor take her with me on this strange journey. This quest is not for me. But may thy steps be prospered wherever thou goest. So, farewell."

And another said: "I am ill and unfit for hardship, but there is a man among my servants whom I will send with thee when thou goest, to bring me word how thou farest."

But Abgarus, the oldest and the one who loved Artaban the best, lingered after the others had gone, and said, gravely: "My son, it may be that the light of truth is in this sign that has appeared in the skies, and then it will surely lead to the Prince and the mighty brightness. Or it may be that it is only a shadow of the light, as Tigranes has said, and then he who follows it will have only a long pilgrimage and an empty search. But it is better to follow even the shadow of the best than to remain content with the worst. And those who would see wonderful things must often be ready to travel alone. I am too old for this journey, but my heart shall be a companion of the pilgrimage day and night, and I shall know the end of thy quest. Go in peace."

So one by one they went out of the azure chamber with its silver stars, and Artaban was left in solitude. He gathered up the jewels and replaced them in his girdle. For a long time he stood and watched the flame that flickered and sank upon the altar. Then he crossed the hall, lifted the heavy curtain, and passed out between the dull red pillars of porphyry to the terrace on the roof.

The shiver that thrills through the earth ere she rouses from her night sleep had already begun, and the cool wind that heralds the daybreak was drawing downward from the lofty, snow-traced ravines of Mount Orontes. Birds, half awakened, crept and chirped among the rustling leaves, and the smell of ripened grapes came in brief wafts from the arbors.

Far over the eastern plain a white mist stretched like a lake. But where the distant peak of Zagros serrated the western horizon the sky was clear. Jupiter and Saturn rolled together like drops of lambent flame about to blend in one. As Artaban watched them, behold, an azure spark was born out of the darkness beneath, rounding itself with purple splendors to a crimson sphere, and spiring upward through rays of saffron and orange into a point of white radiance. Tiny and infinitely remote, yet perfect in every part, it pulsated in the enormous vault as if the three jewels in the Magian's breast had mingled and been transformed into a living heart of light.

He bowed his head. He covered his brow with his hands.

"It is the sign," he said. "The King is coming, and I will go to meet him."

BY THE WATERS OF BABYLON

A LL night long Vasda, the swiftest of Artaban's horses, had been waiting, saddled and bridled, in her stall, pawing the ground impatiently, and shaking her bit as if she shared the eagerness of her master's purpose, though she knew not its meaning.

Before the birds had fully roused to their strong, high, joyful chant of morning song, before the white mist had begun to lift lazily from the plain, the other wise man was in the saddle, riding swiftly along the high-road, which skirted the base of Mount Orontes, westward.

How close, how intimate is the comradeship between a man and his favorite horse on a long journey. It is a silent, comprehensive friendship, an intercourse beyond the need of words.

They drink at the same wayside springs, and sleep under the same guardian stars. They are conscious together of the subduing spell of nightfall and the quickening joy of daybreak. The master shares his evening meal with his hungry companion, and feels the soft, moist lips caressing the palm of his hand as they close over the morsel of bread. In the gray dawn he is roused from his bivouac by the gentle stir of a warm, sweet breath over his sleeping face, and looks up into the eyes of his faithful fellow-traveller, ready and waiting for the toil of the day. Surely, unless he is a pagan and an unbeliever, by whatever name he calls upon his God, he will thank Him for this voiceless sympathy, this dumb affection, and his morning prayer will embrace a double blessing—God bless us both, and keep our feet from falling and our souls from death!

And then, through the keen morning air, the swift hoofs beat their spirited music along the road, keeping time to the pulsing of two hearts that are moved with the same eager desire—to conquer space, to devour the distance, to attain the goal of the journey.

Artaban must, indeed, ride wisely and well if he would keep the appointed hour with the other Magi; for the route was a hundred and fifty parasangs, and fifteen was the utmost that he could travel in a day. But he knew Vasda's strength, and pushed forward without anxiety, making the fixed distance every day, though he must travel late into the night, and in the morning long before sunrise.

He passed along the brown slopes of Mount Orontes, furrowed by the rocky courses of a hundred torrents.

He crossed the level plains of the Nisaeans, where the famous herds of horses, feeding in the wide pastures, tossed their heads at Vasda's approach, and galloped away with a thunder of many hoofs, and flocks of wild birds rose suddenly from the swampy meadows, wheeling in great circles with a shining flutter of innumerable wings and shrill cries of surprise.

He traversed the fertile fields of Concabar, where the dust from the threshing-floors filled the air with a golden mist, half hiding the huge temple of Astarte with its four hundred pillars.

At Baghistan, among the rich gardens watered by fountains from the rock, he looked up at the mountain thrusting its immense rugged brow out over the road, and saw the figure of King Darius trampling upon his fallen foes, and the proud list of his wars and conquests graven high upon the face of the eternal cliff.

Over many a cold and desolate pass, crawling painfully across the wind-swept shoulders of the hills; down many a black mountain-gorge, where the river roared and raced before him like a savage guide; across many a smiling vale, with terraces of yellow limestone full of vines and fruit trees; through the oak groves of Carine and the dark Gates of Zagros, walled in by precipices; into the ancient city of Chala, where the people of Samaria had been kept in captivity long ago; and out again by the mighty portal, riven through the encircling hills, where he saw the image of the High Priest of the Magi sculptured on the wall of rock, with hand uplifted as if to bless the centuries of pilgrims; past the entrance of the narrow defile, filled from end to end with orchards of peaches and figs, through which the river Gyndes foamed down to meet him; over the broad rice-fields, where the autumnal vapors spread their deathly mists; following along the course of the river, under tremulous shadows of poplar and tamarind, among the lower hills; and out upon the flat plain, where the road ran straight as an arrow through the stubble-fields and parched meadows; past the city of Ctesiphon, where the Parthian emperors reigned, and the vast metropolis of Seleucia which Alexander built; across the swirling floods of Tigris and the many channels of Euphrates, flowing yellow through the corn-lands—Artaban pressed onward until he arrived, at nightfall of the tenth day, beneath the shattered walls of populous Babylon.

Vasda was almost spent, and he would gladly have turned into the city to find rest and refreshment for himself and for her. But he knew that it was three hours' journey yet to the Temple of the Seven Spheres, and he must reach the place by midnight if he would find his comrades waiting. So he did not halt, but rode steadily across the stubble-fields. A grove of date-palms made an island of gloom in the pale yellow sea. As she passed into the shadow Vasda slackened her pace, and began to pick her way more carefully.

Near the farther end of the darkness an access of caution seemed to fall upon her. She scented some danger or difficulty; it was not in her heart to fly from it—only to be prepared for it, and to meet it wisely, as a good horse should do. The grove was close and silent as the tomb; not a leaf rustled, not a bird sang.

She felt her steps before her delicately, carrying her head low, and sighing now and then with apprehension. At last she gave a quick breath of anxiety and dismay, and stood stock-still, quivering in every muscle, before a dark object in the shadow of the last palm-tree.

Artaban dismounted. The dim starlight revealed the form of a man lying across the road. His humble dress and the outline of his haggard face showed that he was probably one of the poor Hebrew exiles who still dwelt in great numbers in the vicinity. His pallid skin, dry and yellow as parchment, bore the mark of the deadly fever which ravaged the marsh-lands in autumn. The chill of death was in his lean hand, and, as Artaban released it, the arm fell back inertly upon the motionless breast.

He turned away with a thought of pity, consigning the body to that strange burial which the Magians deemed most fitting—the funeral of the desert, from which the kites and vultures rise on dark wings, and the beasts of prey slink furtively away, leaving only a heap of white bones in the sand.

But, as he turned, a long, faint, ghostly sigh came from the man's lips. The brown, bony fingers closed convulsively on the hem of the Magian's robe and held him fast.

Artaban's heart leaped to his throat, not with fear, but with a dumb resentment at the importunity of this blind delay.

How could he stay here in the darkness to minister to a dying stranger? What claim had this unknown fragment of human life upon his compassion or his service? If he lingered but for an hour he could hardly reach Borsippa at the appointed time. His companions would think he had given up the journey. They would go without him. He would lose his quest.

But if he went on now, the man would surely die. If he stayed, life might be restored. His spirit throbbed and fluttered with the urgency of the crisis. Should he risk the great reward of his divine faith for the sake of a single deed of human love? Should he turn aside, if only for a moment, from the following of the star, to give a cup of cold water to a poor, perishing Hebrew?

"God of truth and purity," he prayed, "direct me in the holy path, the way of wisdom which Thou only knowest." Then he turned back to the sick man. Loosening the grasp of his hand, he carried him to a little mound at the foot of the palm-tree.

He unbound the thick folds of the turban and opened the garment above the sunken breast. He brought water from one of the small canals near by, and moistened the sufferer's brow and mouth. He mingled a draught of one of those simple but potent remedies which he carried always in his girdle—for the Magians were physicians as well as astrologers—and poured it slowly between the colorless lips. Hour after hour he labored as only a skilful healer of disease can do; and, at last, the man's strength returned; he sat up and looked about him.

"Who art thou?" he said, in the rude dialect of the country, "and why hast thou sought me here to bring back my life?"

"I am Artaban the Magian, of the city of Ecbatana, and I am going to Jerusalem in search of one who is to be born King of the Jews, a great Prince and Deliverer of all men. I dare not delay any longer upon my journey, for the caravan that has waited for me may depart without me. But see, here is all that I have left of bread and wine, and here is a potion of healing herbs. When thy strength is restored thou canst find the dwellings of the Hebrews among the houses of Babylon."

The Jew raised his trembling hand solemnly to heaven.

"Now may the God of Abraham and Isaac and Jacob bless and prosper the journey of the merciful, and bring him in peace to his desired haven. But stay; I have nothing to give thee in return—only this: that I can tell thee where the Messiah must be sought. For our prophets have said that he should be born not in Jerusalem, but in Bethlehem of Judah. May the Lord bring thee in safety to that place, because thou hast had pity upon the sick."

It was already long past midnight. Artaban rode in haste, and Vasda, restored by the brief rest, ran eagerly through the silent plain and swam the channels of the river. She put forth the remnant of her strength, and fled over the ground like a gazelle.

But the first beam of the sun sent her shadow before her as she entered upon the final stadium of the journey, and the eyes of Artaban, anxiously scanning the great mound of Nimrod and the Temple of the Seven Spheres, could discern no trace of his friends.

The many-colored terraces of black and orange and red and yellow and green and blue and white, shattered by the convulsions of nature, and crumbling under the repeated blows of human violence, still glittered like a ruined rainbow in the morning light.

Artaban rode swiftly around the hill. He dismounted and climbed to the highest terrace, looking out towards the west.

The huge desolation of the marshes stretched away to the horizon and the border of the desert. Bitterns stood by the stagnant pools and jackals skulked through the low bushes; but there was no sign of the caravan of the wise men, far or near. At the edge of the terrace he saw a little cairn of broken bricks, and under them a piece of parchment. He caught it up and read: "We have waited past the midnight, and can delay no longer. We go to find the King. Follow us across the desert."

Artaban sat down upon the ground and covered his head in despair.

"How can I cross the desert," said he, "with no food and with a spent horse? I must return to Babylon, sell my sapphire, and buy a train of camels, and provision for the journey. I may never overtake my friends. Only God the merciful knows whether I shall not lose the sight of the King because I tarried to show mercy."

FOR THE SAKE OF A LITTLE CHILD

T HERE was a silence in the Hall of Dreams, where I was listening to the story of the Other Wise Man. And through this silence I saw, but very dimly, his figure passing over the dreary undulations of the desert, high upon the back of his camel, rocking steadily onward like a ship over the waves.

The land of death spread its cruel net around him. The stony wastes bore no fruit but briers and thorns. The dark ledges of rock thrust themselves above the surface here and there, like the bones of perished monsters. Arid and inhospitable mountain ranges rose before him, furrowed with dry channels of ancient torrents, white and ghastly as scars on the face of nature. Shifting hills of treacherous sand were heaped like tombs along the horizon. By day, the fierce heat pressed its intolerable burden on the quivering air; and no living creature moved on the dumb, swooning earth, but tiny jerboas scuttling through the parched bushes, or lizards vanishing in the clefts of the rock. By night the jackals prowled and barked in the distance, and the lion made the black ravines echo with his hollow roaring, while a bitter, blighting chill followed the fever of the day. Through heat and cold, the Magian moved steadily onward. Then I saw the gardens and orchards of Damascus, watered by the streams of Abana and Pharpar, with their sloping swards inlaid with bloom, and their thickets of myrrh and roses. I saw also the long, snowy ridge of Hermon, and the dark groves of cedars, and the valley of the Jordan, and the blue waters of the Lake of Galilee, and the fertile plain of Esdraelon, and the hills of Ephraim, and the highlands of Judah. Through all these I followed the figure of Artaban moving steadily onward, until he arrived at Bethlehem. And it was the third day after the three wise men had come to that place and had found Mary and Joseph, with the young child, Jesus, and had lain their gifts of gold and frankincense and myrrh at his feet.

Then the other wise man drew near, weary, but full of hope, bearing his ruby and his pearl to offer to the King. "For now at last," he said, "I shall surely find him, though it be alone, and later than my brethren. This is the place of which the Hebrew exile told me that the prophets had spoken, and here I shall behold the rising of the great light. But I must inquire about the visit of my brethren, and to what house the star directed them, and to whom they presented their tribute."

The streets of the village seemed to be deserted, and Artaban wondered whether the men had all gone up to the hill-pastures to bring down their sheep. From the open door of a low stone cottage he heard the sound of a woman's voice singing softly. He entered and found a young mother hushing her baby to rest. She told him of the strangers from the far East who had appeared in the village three days ago, and how they said that a star had guided them to the place where Joseph of Nazareth was lodging with his wife and her new-born child, and how they had paid reverence to the child and given him many rich gifts.

"But the travellers disappeared again," she continued, "as suddenly as they had come. We were afraid at the strangeness of their visit. We could not understand it. The man of Nazareth took the babe and his mother and fled away that same night secretly, and it was whispered that they were going far away to Egypt. Ever since, there has been a spell upon the village; something evil hangs over it. They say that the Roman soldiers are coming from Jerusalem to force a new tax from us, and the men have driven the flocks and herds far back among the hills, and hidden themselves to escape it."

Artaban listened to her gentle, timid speech, and the child in her arms looked up in his face and smiled, stretching out its rosy hands to grasp at the winged circle of gold on his breast. His heart warmed to the touch. It seemed like a greeting of love and trust to one who had journeyed long in loneliness and perplexity, fighting with his own doubts and fears, and following a light that was veiled in clouds.

"Might not this child have been the promised Prince?" he asked within himself, as he touched its soft cheek. "Kings have been born ere now in lowlier houses than this, and the favorite of the stars may rise even from a cottage. But it has not seemed good to the God of wisdom to reward my search so soon and so easily. The one whom I seek has gone before me; and now I must follow the King to Egypt."

The young mother laid the babe in its cradle, and rose to minister to the wants of the strange guest that fate had brought into her house. She set food before him, the plain fare of peasants, but willingly offered, and therefore full of refreshment for the soul as well as for the body. Artaban accepted it gratefully; and, as he ate, the child fell into a happy slumber, and murmured sweetly in its dreams, and a great peace filled the quiet room.

But suddenly there came the noise of a wild confusion and uproar in the streets of the village, a shrieking and wailing of women's voices, a clangor of brazen trumpets and a clashing of swords, and a desperate cry: "The soldiers! the soldiers of Herod! They are killing our children."

The young mother's face grew white with terror. She clasped her child to her bosom, and crouched motionless in the darkest corner of the room, covering him with the folds of her robe, lest he should wake and cry.

But Artaban went quickly and stood in the doorway of the house. His broad shoulders filled the portal from side to side, and the peak of his white cap all but touched the lintel.

The soldiers came hurrying down the street with bloody hands and dripping swords. At the sight of the stranger in his imposing dress they hesitated with surprise. The captain of the band approached the threshold to thrust him aside. But Artaban did not stir. His face was as calm as though he were watching the stars, and in his eyes there burned that steady radiance before which even the half-tamed hunting leopard shrinks, and the fierce blood-hound pauses in his leap. He held the soldier silently for an instant, and then said in a low voice:

"I am all alone in this place, and I am waiting to give this jewel to the prudent captain who will leave me in peace." He showed the ruby, glistening in the hollow of his hand like a great drop of blood.

The captain was amazed at the splendor of the gem. The pupils of his eyes expanded with desire, and the hard lines of greed wrinkled around his lips. He stretched out his hand and took the ruby.

"March on!" he cried to his men, "there is no child here. The house is still."

The clamor and the clang of arms passed down the street as the headlong fury of the chase sweeps by the secret covert where the trembling deer is hidden. Artaban re-entered the cottage. He turned his face to the east and prayed: "God of truth, forgive my sin! I have said the thing that is not, to save the life of a child. And two of my gifts are gone. I have spent for man that which was meant for God. Shall I ever be worthy to see the face of the King?" But the voice of the woman, weeping for joy in the shadow behind him, said very gently:

"Because thou hast saved the life of my little one, may the Lord bless thee and keep thee; the Lord make His face to shine upon thee and be gracious unto thee; the Lord lift up His countenance upon thee and give thee peace."

IN THE HIDDEN WAY OF SORROW

THEN again there was a silence in the Hall of Dreams, deeper and more mysterious than the first interval, and I understood that the years of Artaban were flowing very swiftly under the stillness of that clinging fog, and I caught only a glimpse, here and there, of the river of his life shining through the shadows that concealed its course. I saw him moving among the throngs of men in populous Egypt, seeking everywhere for traces of the household that had come down from Bethlehem, and finding them under the spreading sycamore-trees of Heliopolis, and beneath the walls of the Roman fortress of New Babylon beside the Nile—traces so faint and dim that they vanished before him continually, as footprints on the hard river-sand glisten for a moment with moisture and then disappear. I saw him again at the foot of the pyramids, which lifted their sharp points into the intense saffron glow of the sunset sky, changeless monuments of the perishable glory and the imperishable hope of man. He looked up into the vast countenance of the crouching Sphinx and vainly tried to read the meaning of the calm eyes and smiling mouth. Was it, indeed, the mockery of all effort and all aspiration, as Tigranes had said—the cruel jest of a riddle that has no answer, a search that never can succeed? Or was there a touch of pity and encouragement in that inscrutable smile—a promise that even the defeated should attain a victory, and the disappointed should discover a prize, and the ignorant should be made wise, and the blind should see, and the wandering should come into the haven at last?

I saw him again in an obscure house of Alexandria, taking counsel with a Hebrew rabbi. The venerable man, bending over the rolls of parchment on which the prophecies of Israel were written, read aloud the pathetic words which foretold the sufferings of the promised Messiah—the despised and rejected of men, the man of sorrows and the acquaintance of grief.

"And remember, my son," said he, fixing his deep-set eyes upon the face of Artaban, "the King whom you are seeking is not to be found in a palace, nor among the rich and powerful. If the light of the world and the glory of Israel had been appointed to come with the greatness of earthly splendor, it must have appeared long ago. For no son of Abraham will ever again rival the power which Joseph had in the palaces of Egypt, or the magnificence of Solomon throned between the lions in Jerusalem. But the light for which the world is waiting is a new light, the glory that shall rise out of patient and triumphant suffering. And the kingdom which is to be established forever is a new kingdom, the royalty of perfect and unconquerable love.

"I do not know how this shall come to pass, nor how the turbulent kings and peoples of earth shall be brought to acknowledge the Messiah and pay homage to Him. But this I know. Those who seek Him will do well to look among the poor and the lowly, the sorrowful and the oppressed."

So I saw the other wise man again and again, travelling from place to place, and searching among the people of the dispersion, with whom the little family from Bethlehem might, perhaps, have found a refuge. He passed through countries where famine lay heavy upon the land, and the poor were crying for bread. He made his dwelling in plague-stricken cities where the sick were languishing in the bitter companionship of helpless misery. He visited the oppressed and the afflicted in the gloom of subterranean prisons, and the crowded wretchedness of slave-markets, and the weary toil of galley-ships. In all this populous and intricate world of anguish, though he found none to worship, he found many to help. He fed the hungry, and clothed the naked, and healed the sick, and comforted the captive; and his years went by more swiftly than the weaver's shuttle that flashes back and forth through the loom while the web grows and the invisible pattern is completed.

It seemed almost as if he had forgotten his quest. But once I saw him for a moment as he stood alone at sunrise, waiting at the gate of a Roman prison. He had taken from a secret resting- place in his bosom the pearl, the last of his jewels. As he looked at it, a mellower lustre, a soft and iridescent light, full of shifting gleams of azure and rose, trembled upon its surface. It seemed to have absorbed some reflection of the colors of the lost sapphire and ruby. So the profound, secret purpose of a noble life draws into itself the memories of past joy and past sorrow. All that has helped it, all that has hindered it, is transfused by a subtle magic into its very essence. It becomes more luminous and precious the longer it is carried close to the warmth of the beating heart.

Then, at last, while I was thinking of this pearl, and of its meaning, I heard the end of the story of the Other Wise Man.

A PEARL OF GREAT PRICE

T HREE-and-thirty years of the life of Artaban had passed away, and he was still a pilgrim, and a seeker after light. His hair, once darker than the cliffs of Zagros, was now white as the wintry snow that covered them. His eyes, that once flashed like flames of fire, were dull as embers smouldering among the ashes.

Worn and weary and ready to die, but still looking for the King, he had come for the last time to Jerusalem. He had often visited the holy city before, and had searched through all its lanes and crowded hovels and black prisons without finding any trace of the family of Nazarenes who had fled from Bethlehem long ago. But now it seemed as if he must make one more effort, and something whispered in his heart that, at last, he might succeed.

It was the season of the Passover. The city was thronged with strangers. The children of Israel, scattered in far lands all over the world, had returned to the Temple for the great feast, and there had been a confusion of tongues in the narrow streets for many days.

But on this day there was a singular agitation visible in the multitude. The sky was veiled with a portentous gloom, and currents of excitement seemed to flash through the crowd like the thrill which shakes the forest on the eve of a storm. A secret tide was sweeping them all one way. The clatter of sandals, and the soft, thick sound of thousands of bare feet shuffling over the stones, flowed unceasingly along the street that leads to the Damascus gate.

Artaban joined company with a group of people from his own country, Parthian Jews who had come up to keep the Passover, and inquired of them the cause of the tumult, and where they were going.

"We are going," they answered, "to the place called Golgotha, outside the city walls, where there is to be an execution. Have you not heard what has happened? Two famous robbers are to be crucified, and with them another, called Jesus of Nazareth, a man who has done many wonderful works among the people, so that they love him greatly. But the priests and elders have said that he must die, because he gave himself out to be the Son of God. And Pilate has sent him to the cross because he said that he was the 'King of the Jews.'"

How strangely these familiar words fell upon the tired heart of Artaban! They had led him for a lifetime over land and sea. And now they came to him darkly and mysteriously like a message of despair. The King had arisen, but He had been denied and cast out. He was about to perish. Perhaps He was already dying. Could it be the same who had been born in Bethlehem thirty-three years ago, at whose birth the star had appeared in heaven, and of whose coming the prophets had spoken?

Artaban's heart beat unsteadily with that troubled, doubtful apprehension which is the excitement of old age. But he said within himself: "The ways of God are stranger than the thoughts of men, and it may be that I shall find the King, at last, in the hands of His enemies, and shall come in time to offer my pearl for His ransom before He dies."

So the old man followed the multitude with slow and painful steps towards the Damascus gate of the city. Just beyond the entrance of the guard-house a troop of Macedonian soldiers came down the street, dragging a young girl with torn dress and dishevelled hair. As the Magian paused to look at her with compassion, she broke suddenly from the hands of her tormentors, and threw herself at his feet, clasping him around the knees. She had seen his white cap and the winged circle on his breast.

"Have pity on me," she cried, "and save me, for the sake of the God of Purity! I also am a daughter of the true religion which is taught by the Magi. My father was a merchant of Parthia, but he is dead, and I am seized for his debts to be sold as a slave. Save me from worse than death."

Artaban trembled.

It was the old conflict in his soul, which had come to him in the palm-grove of Babylon and in the cottage at Bethlehem—the conflict between the expectation of faith and the impulse of love. Twice the gift which he had consecrated to the worship of religion had been drawn from his hand to the service of humanity. This was the third trial, the ultimate probation, the final and irrevocable choice.

Was it his great opportunity, or his last temptation? He could not tell. One thing only was clear in the darkness of his mind—it was inevitable. And does not the inevitable come from God?

One thing only was sure to his divided heart—to rescue this helpless girl would be a true deed of love. And is not love the light of the soul?

He took the pearl from his bosom. Never had it seemed so luminous, so radiant, so full of tender, living lustre. He laid it in the hand of the slave.

"This is thy ransom, daughter! It is the last of my treasures which I kept for the King."

While he spoke, the darkness of the sky thickened, and shuddering tremors ran through the earth, heaving convulsively like the breast of one who struggles with mighty grief.

The walls of the houses rocked to and fro. Stones were loosened and crashed into the street. Dust clouds filled the air. The soldiers fled in terror, reeling like drunken men. But Artaban and the girl whom he had ransomed crouched helpless beneath the wall of the Praetorium.

What had he to fear? What had he to live for? He had given away the last remnant of his tribute for the King. He had parted with the last hope of finding Him. The quest was over, and it had failed. But, even in that thought, accepted and embraced, there was peace. It was not resignation. It was not submission. It was something more profound and searching. He knew that all was well, because he had done the best that he could, from day to day. He had been true to the light that had been given to him. He had looked for more. And if he had not found it, if a failure was all that came out of his life, doubtless that was the best that was possible. He had not seen the revelation of "life everlasting, incorruptible and immortal." But he knew that even if he could live his earthly life over again, it could not be otherwise than it had been.

One more lingering pulsation of the earthquake quivered through the ground. A heavy tile, shaken from the roof, fell and struck the old man on the temple. He lay breathless and pale, with his gray head resting on the young girl's shoulder, and the blood trickling from the wound. As she bent over him, fearing that he was dead, there came a voice through the twilight, very small and still, like music sounding from a distance, in which the notes are clear but the words are lost. The girl turned to see if some one had spoken from the window above them, but she saw no one. Then the old man's lips began to move, as if in answer, and she heard him say in the Parthian tongue:

"Not so, my Lord: For when saw I thee an hungered and fed thee? Or thirsty, and gave thee drink? When saw I thee a stranger, and took thee in? Or naked, and clothed thee? When saw I thee sick or in prison, and came unto thee? Three-and- thirty years have I looked for thee; but I have never seen thy face, nor ministered to thee, my King."

He ceased, and the sweet voice came again. And again the maid heard it, very faintly and far away. But now it seemed as though she understood the words:

"*Verily I say unto thee, Inasmuch as thou hast done it unto one of the least of these my brethren, thou hast done it unto me.*"

A calm radiance of wonder and joy lighted the pale face of Artaban like the first ray of dawn on a snowy mountain-peak. One long, last breath of relief exhaled gently from his lips.

His journey was ended. His treasures were accepted. The Other Wise Man had found the King.

THE END

The Mansion

THERE was an air of calm and reserved opulence about the Weightman mansion that spoke not of money squandered, but of wealth prudently applied. Standing on a corner of the Avenue no longer fashionable for residence, it looked upon the swelling tide of business with an expression of complacency and half-disdain.

The house was not beautiful. There was nothing in its straight front of chocolate-colored stone, its heavy cornices, its broad, staring windows of plate glass, its carved and bronze-bedecked mahogany doors at the top of the wide stoop, to charm the eye or fascinate the imagination. But it was eminently respectable, and in its way imposing. It seemed to say that the glittering shops of the jewelers, the milliners, the confectioners, the florists, the picture-dealers, the furriers, the makers of rare and costly antiquities, retail traders in luxuries of life, were beneath the notice of a house that had its foundations in the high finance, and was built literally and figuratively in the shadow of St. Petronius' Church.

At the same time there was something self-pleased and congratulatory in the way in which the mansion held its own amid the changing neighborhood. It almost seemed to be lifted up a little, among the tall buildings near at hand, as if it felt the rising value of the land on which it stood.

John Weightman was like the house into which he had built himself thirty years ago, and in which his ideals and ambitions were incrusted. He was a self-made man. But in making himself he had chosen a highly esteemed pattern and worked according to the approved rules. There was nothing irregular, questionable, flamboyant about him. He was solid, correct, and justly successful.

His minor tastes, of course, had been carefully kept up to date. At the proper time, pictures by the Barbizon masters, old English plate and portraits, bronzes by Barye and marbles by Rodin, Persian carpets and Chinese porcelains, had been introduced to the mansion. It contained a Louis Quinze reception-room, an Empire drawing-room, a Jacobean dining-room, and various apartments dimly reminiscent of the styles of furniture affected by deceased monarchs. That the hallways were too short for the historic perspective did not make much difference. American decorative art is *capable de tout*, it absorbs all periods. Of each period Mr. Weightman wished to have something of the best. He understood its value, present as a certificate, and prospective as an investment.

It was only in the architecture of his town house that he remained conservative, immovable, one might almost say Early-Victorian-Christian. His country house at Dulwich-on-the-Sound was a palace of the Italian Renaissance. But in town he adhered to an architecture which had moral associations, the Nineteenth-Century-Brownstone epoch. It was a symbol of his social position, his religious doctrine, and even, in a way, of his business creed.

"A man of fixed principles," he would say, "should express them in the looks of his house. New York changes its domestic architecture too rapidly. It is like divorce. It is not dignified. I don't like it. Extravagance and fickleness are advertised in most of these new houses. I wish to be known for different qualities. Dignity and prudence are the things that people trust. Every one knows that I can afford to live in the house that suits me. It is a guarantee to the public. It inspires confidence. It helps my influence. There is a text in the Bible about 'a house that hath foundations.' That is the proper kind of a mansion for a solid man."

Harold Weightman had often listened to his father discoursing in this fashion on the fundamental principles of life, and always with a divided mind. He admired immensely his father's talents and the single-minded energy with which he improved them. But in the paternal philosophy there was something that disquieted and oppressed the young man, and made him gasp inwardly for fresh air and free action.

At times, during his college course and his years at the law school, he had yielded to this impulse and broken away—now toward extravagance and dissipation, and then, when the reaction came, toward a romantic devotion to work among the poor. He had felt his father's disapproval for both of these forms of imprudence; but it was never expressed in a harsh or violent way, always with a certain tolerant patience, such as one might show for the mistakes and vagaries of the very young. John Weightman was not hasty, impulsive, inconsiderate, even toward his own children. With them, as with the rest of the world, he felt that he had a reputation to maintain, a theory to vindicate. He could afford to give them time to see that he was absolutely right.

One of his favorite Scripture quotations was, "Wait on the Lord." He had applied it to real estate and to people, with profitable results.

But to human persons the sensation of being waited for is not always agreeable. Sometimes, especially with the young, it produces a vague restlessness, a dumb resentment, which is increased by the fact that one can hardly explain or justify it. Of this John Weightman was not conscious. It lay beyond his horizon. He did not take it into account in the plan of life which he made for himself and for his family as the sharers and inheritors of his success.

"Father plays us," said Harold, in a moment of irritation, to his mother, "like pieces in a game of chess."

"My dear," said that lady, whose faith in her husband was religious, "you ought not to speak so impatiently. At least he wins the game. He is one of the most respected men in New York. And he is very generous, too."

"I wish he would be more generous in letting us be ourselves," said the young man. "He always has something in view for us and expects to move us up to it."

"But isn't it always for our benefit?" replied his mother. "Look what a position we have. No one can say there is any taint on our money. There are no rumors about your father. He has kept the laws of God and of man. He has never made any mistakes."

Harold got up from his chair and poked the fire. Then he came back to the ample, well-gowned, firm-looking lady, and sat beside her on the sofa. He took her hand gently and looked at the two rings—a thin band of yellow gold, and a small solitaire diamond—which kept their place on her third finger in modest dignity, as if not shamed, but rather justified, by the splendor of the emerald which glittered beside them.

"Mother," he said, "you have a wonderful hand. And father made no mistake when he won you. But are you sure he has always been so inerrant?"

"Harold," she exclaimed, a little stiffly, "what do you mean? His life is an open book."

"Oh," he answered, "I don't mean anything bad, mother dear. I know the governor's life is an open book—a ledger, if you like, kept in the best bookkeeping hand, and always ready for inspection—every page correct, and showing a handsome balance. But isn't it a mistake not to allow us to make our own mistakes, to learn for ourselves, to live our own lives? Must we be always working for 'the balance,' in one thing or another? I want to be myself—to get outside of this everlasting, profitable 'plan'—to let myself go, and lose myself for a while at least—to do the things that I want to do, just because I want to do them."

"My boy," said his mother, anxiously, "you are not going to do anything wrong or foolish? You know the falsehood of that old proverb about wild oats."

He threw back his head and laughed. "Yes, mother," he answered, "I know it well enough. But in California, you know, the wild oats are one of the most valuable crops. They grow all over the hillsides and keep the cattle and the horses alive. But that wasn't what I meant—to sow wild oats. Say to pick wild flowers, if you like, or even to chase wild geese—to do something that seems good to me just for its own sake, not for the sake of wages of one kind or another. I feel like a hired man, in the service of this magnificent mansion—say in training for father's place as majordomo. I'd like to get out some way, to feel free—perhaps to do something for others."

The young man's voice hesitated a little. "Yes, it sounds like cant, I know, but sometimes I feel as if I'd like to do some good in the world, if father only wouldn't insist upon God's putting it into the ledger."

His mother moved uneasily, and a slight look of bewilderment came into her face.

"Isn't that almost irreverent?" she asked. "Surely the righteous must have their reward. And your father is good. See how much he gives to all the established charities, how many things he has founded. He's always thinking of others, and planning for them. And surely, for us, he does everything. How well he has planned this trip to Europe for me and the girls—the court-presentation at Berlin, the season on the Riviera, the visits in England with the Plumptons and the Halverstones. He says Lord Halverstone has the finest old house in Sussex, pure Elizabethan, and all the old customs are kept up, too—family prayers every morning for all the domestics. By-the-way, you know his son Bertie, I believe."

Harold smiled a little to himself as he answered: "Yes, I fished at Catalina Island last June with the Honorable Ethelbert; he's rather a decent chap, in spite of his ingrowing mind. But you?—mother, you are simply magnificent! You are father's masterpiece." The young man leaned over to kiss her, and went up to the Riding Club for his afternoon canter in the Park.

So it came to pass, early in December, that Mrs. Weightman and her two daughters sailed for Europe, on their serious pleasure trip, even as it had been written in the book of Providence; and John Weightman, who had made the entry, was left to pass the rest of the winter with his son and heir in the brownstone mansion.

They were comfortable enough. The machinery of the massive establishment ran as smoothly as a great electric dynamo. They were busy enough, too. John Weightman's plans and enterprises were complicated, though his principle of action was always simple—to get good value for every expenditure and effort. The banking-house of which he was the chief, the brain, the will, the absolutely controlling hand, was so admirably organized that the details of its direction took but little time. But the scores of other interests that radiated from it and were dependent upon it— or perhaps it would be more accurate to say, that contributed to its solidity and success—the many investments, industrial, political, benevolent, reformatory, ecclesiastical, that had made the name of Weightman well known and potent in city, church, and state, demanded much attention and careful steering, in order that each might produce the desired result. There were board meetings of corporations and hospitals, conferences in Wall Street and at Albany, consultations and committee meetings in the brownstone mansion.

For a share in all this business and its adjuncts John Weightman had his son in training in one of the famous law firms of the city; for he held that banking itself is a simple affair, the only real difficulties of finance are on its legal side. Meantime he wished the young man to meet and know the men with whom he would have to deal when he became a partner in the house. So a couple of dinners were given in the mansion during December, after which the father called the son's attention to the fact that over a hundred million dollars had sat around the board.

But on Christmas Eve father and son were dining together without guests, and their talk across the broad table, glittering with silver and cut glass, and softly lit by shaded candles, was intimate, though a little slow at times. The elder man was in rather a rare mood, more expansive and confidential than usual; and, when the coffee was brought in and they were left alone, he talked more freely of his personal plans and hopes than he had ever done before.

"I feel very grateful to-night," said he, at last; "it must be something in the air of Christmas that gives me this feeling of thankfulness for the many divine mercies that have been bestowed upon me. All the principles by which I have tried to guide my life have been justified. I have never made the value of this salted almond by anything that the courts would not uphold, at least in the long run, and yet—or wouldn't it be truer to say and therefore?—my affairs have been wonderfully prospered. There's a great deal in that text 'Honesty is the best'—but no, that's not from the Bible, after all, is it? Wait a moment; there is something of that kind, I know."

"May I light a cigar, father," said Harold, turning away to hide a smile, "while you are remembering the text?"

"Yes, certainly," answered the elder man, rather shortly; "you know I don't dislike the smell. But it is a wasteful, useless habit, and therefore I have never practised it. Nothing useless is worth while, that's my motto—nothing that does not bring the reward. Oh, now I recall the text, 'Verily I say unto you they have their reward.' I shall ask Doctor Snodgrass to preach a sermon on that verse some day."

"Using you as an illustration?"

"Well, not exactly that; but I could give him some good material from my own experience to prove the truth of Scripture. I can honestly say that there is not one of my charities that has not brought me in a good return, either in the increase of influence, the building up of credit, or the association with substantial people. Of course you have to be careful how you give, in order to secure the best results—no indiscriminate giving—no pennies in beggars' hats! It has been one of my principles always to use the same kind of judgment in charities that I use in my other affairs, and they have not disappointed me."

"Even the check that you put in the plate when you take the offertory up the aisle on Sunday morning?"

"Certainly; though there the influence is less direct; and I must confess that I have my doubts in regard to the collection for Foreign Missions. That always seems to me romantic and wasteful. You never hear from it in any definite way. They say the missionaries have done a good deal to open the way for trade; perhaps—but they have also gotten us into commercial and political difficulties. Yet I give to them—a little—it is a matter of conscience with me to identify myself with all the enterprises of the Church; it is the mainstay of social order and a prosperous civilization. But the best forms of benevolence are the well-established, organized ones here at home, where people can see them and know what they are doing."

"You mean the ones that have a local habitation and a name."

"Yes; they offer by far the safest return, though of course there is something gained by contributing to general funds. A public man can't afford to be without public spirit. But on the whole I prefer a building, or an endowment. There is a mutual advantage to a good name and a good institution in their connection in the public mind. It helps them both. Remember that, my boy. Of course at the beginning you will have to practise it in a small way; later, you will have larger opportunities. But try to put your gifts where they can be identified and do good all around. You'll see the wisdom of it in the long run."

"I can see it already, sir, and the way you describe it looks amazingly wise and prudent. In other words, we must cast our bread on the waters in large loaves, carried by sound ships marked with the owner's name, so that the return freight will be sure to come back to us."

The father laughed, but his eyes were frowning a little as if he suspected something irreverent under the respectful reply.

"You put it humorously, but there's sense in what you say. Why not? God rules the sea; but He expects us to follow the laws of navigation and commerce. Why not take good care of your bread, even when you give it away?"

"It's not for me to say why not—and yet I can think of cases—" The young man hesitated for a moment. His half-finished cigar had gone out. He rose and tossed it into the fire, in front of which he remained standing—a slender, eager, restless young figure, with a touch of hunger in the fine face, strangely like and unlike the father, at whom he looked with half-wistful curiosity.

"The fact is, sir," he continued, "there is such a case in my mind now, and it is a good deal on my heart, too. So I thought of speaking to you about it to-night. You remember Tom Rollins, the Junior who was so good to me when I entered college?"

The father nodded. He remembered very well indeed the annoying incidents of his son's first escapade, and how Rollins had stood by him and helped to avoid a public disgrace, and how a close friendship had grown between the two boys, so different in their fortunes.

"Yes," he said, "I remember him. He was a promising young man. Has he succeeded?"

"Not exactly—that is, not yet. His business has been going rather badly. He has a wife and little baby, you know. And now he has broken down,—something wrong with his lungs. The doctor says his only chance is a year or eighteen months in Colorado. I wish we could help him."

"How much would it cost?"

"Three or four thousand, perhaps, as a loan."

"Does the doctor say he will get well?"

"A fighting chance—the doctor says."

The face of the older man changed subtly. Not a line was altered, but it seemed to have a different substance, as if it were carved out of some firm, imperishable stuff.

"A fighting chance," he said, "may do for a speculation, but it is not a good investment. You owe something to young Rollins. Your grateful feeling does you credit. But don't overwork it. Send him three or four hundred, if you like. You'll never hear from it again, except in the letter of thanks. But for Heaven's sake don't be sentimental. Religion is not a matter of sentiment; it's a matter of principle."

The face of the younger man changed now. But instead of becoming fixed and graven, it seemed to melt into life by the heat of an inward fire. His nostrils quivered with quick breath, his lips were curled.

"Principle!" he said. "You mean principal—and interest too. Well, sir, you know best whether that is religion or not. But if it is, count me out, please. Tom saved me from going to the devil, six years ago; and I'll be damned if I don't help him to the best of my ability now."

John Weightman looked at his son steadily. "Harold," he said at last, "you know I dislike violent language, and it never has any influence with me. If I could honestly approve of this proposition of yours, I'd let you have the money; but I can't; it's extravagant and useless. But you have your Christmas check for a thousand dollars coming to you tomorrow. You can use it as you please. I never interfere with your private affairs."

"Thank you," said Harold. "Thank you very much! But there's another private affair. I want to get away from this life, this town, this house. It stifles me. You refused last summer when I asked you to let me go up to Grenfell's Mission on the Labrador. I could go now, at least as far as the Newfoundland Station. Have you changed your mind?"

"Not at all. I think it is an exceedingly foolish enterprise. It would interrupt the career that I have marked out for you."

"Well, then, here's a cheaper proposition. Algy Vanderhoof wants me to join him on his yacht with—well, with a little party—to cruise in the West Indies. Would you prefer that?"

"Certainly not! The Vanderhoof set is wild and godless—I do not wish to see you keeping company with fools who walk in the broad and easy way that leads to perdition."

"It is rather a hard choice," said the young man, with a short laugh, turning toward the door. "According to you there's very little difference—a fool's paradise or a fool's hell! Well, it's one or the other for me, and I'll toss up for it to-night: heads, I lose; tails, the devil wins. Anyway, I'm sick of this, and I'm out of it."

"Harold," said the older man (and there was a slight tremor in his voice), "don't let us quarrel on Christmas Eve. All I want is to persuade you to think seriously of the duties and responsibilities to which God has called you—don't speak lightly of heaven and hell—remember, there is another life."

The young man came back and laid his hand upon his father's shoulder.

"Father," he said, "I want to remember it. I try to believe in it. But somehow or other, in this house, it all seems unreal to me. No doubt all you say is perfectly right and wise. I don't venture to argue against it, but I can't feel it—that's all. If I'm to have a soul, either to lose or to save, I must really live. Just now neither the present nor the future means anything to me. But surely we won't quarrel. I'm very grateful to you, and we'll part friends. Good-night, sir."

The father held out his hand in silence. The heavy portière dropped noiselessly behind the son, and he went up the wide, curving stairway to his own room.

Meantime John Weightman sat in his carved chair in the Jacobean dining-room. He felt strangely old and dull. The portraits of beautiful women by Lawrence and Reynolds and Raeburn, which had often seemed like real company to him, looked remote and uninteresting. He fancied something cold and almost unfriendly in their expression, as if they were staring through him or beyond him. They cared nothing for his principles, his hopes, his disappointments, his successes; they belonged to another world, in which he had no place. At this he felt a vague resentment, a sense of discomfort that he could not have defined or explained. He was used to being considered, respected, appreciated at his full value in every region, even in that of his own dreams.

Presently he rang for the butler, telling him to close the house and not to sit up, and walked with lagging steps into the long library, where the shaded lamps were burning. His eye fell upon the low shelves full of costly books, but he had no desire to open them. Even the carefully chosen pictures that hung above them seemed to have lost their attraction. He paused for a moment before an idyll of Corot—a dance of nymphs around some forgotten altar in a vaporous glade—and looked at it curiously. There was something rapturous and serene about the picture, a breath of spring-time in the misty trees, a harmony of joy in the dancing figures, that wakened in him a feeling of half-pleasure and half-envy. It represented something that he had never known in his calculated, orderly life. He was dimly mistrustful of it.

"It is certainly very beautiful," he thought, "but it is distinctly pagan; that altar is built to some heathen god. It does not fit into the scheme of a Christian life. I doubt whether it is consistent with the tone of my house. I will sell it this winter. It will bring three or four times what I paid for it. That was a good purchase, a very good bargain."

He dropped into the revolving chair before his big library table. It was covered with pamphlets and reports of the various enterprises in which he was interested. There was a pile of newspaper clippings in which his name was mentioned with praise for his sustaining power as a pillar of finance, for his judicious benevolence, for his support of wise and prudent reform movements, for his discretion in making permanent public gifts—"the Weightman Charities," one very complaisant editor called them, as if they deserved classification as a distinct species.

He turned the papers over listlessly. There was a description and a picture of the "Weightman Wing of the Hospital for Cripples," of which he was president; and an article on the new professor in the "Weightman Chair of Political Jurisprudence" in Jackson University, of which he was a trustee; and an illustrated account of the opening of the "Weightman Grammar-School" at Dulwich-on-the-Sound, where he had his legal residence for purposes of taxation.

This last was perhaps the most carefully planned of all the Weightman Charities. He desired to win the confidence and support of his rural neighbors. It had pleased him much when the local newspaper had spoken of him as an ideal citizen and the logical candidate for the Governorship of the State; but upon the whole it seemed to him wiser to keep out of active politics. It would be easier and better to put Harold into the running, to have him sent to the Legislature from the Dulwich district, then to the national House, then to the Senate. Why not? The Weightman interests were large enough to need a direct representative and guardian at Washington.

But to-night all these plans came back to him with dust upon them. They were dry and crumbling like forsaken habitations. The son upon whom his complacent ambition had rested had turned his back upon the mansion of his father's hopes. The break might not be final; and in any event there would be much to live for; the fortunes of the family would be secure. But the zest of it all would be gone if John Weightman had to give up the assurance of perpetuating his name and his principles in his son. It was a bitter disappointment, and he felt that he had not deserved it.

He rose from the chair and paced the room with leaden feet. For the first time in his life his age was visibly upon him. His head was heavy and hot, and the thoughts that rolled in it were confused and depressing. Could it be that he had made a mistake in the principles of his existence? There was no argument in what Harold had said—it was almost childish—and yet it had shaken the elder man more deeply than he cared to show. It held a silent attack which touched him more than open criticism.

Suppose the end of his life were nearer than he thought—the end must come some time—what if it were now? Had he not founded his house upon a rock? Had he not kept the Commandments? Was he not, "touching the law, blameless"? And beyond this, even if there were some faults in his character—and all men are sinners—yet he surely believed in the saving doctrines of religion—the forgiveness of sins, the resurrection of the body, the life everlasting. Yes, that was the true source of comfort, after all. He would read a bit in the Bible, as he did every night, and go to bed and to sleep.

He went back to his chair at the library table. A strange weight of weariness rested upon him, but he opened the book at a familiar place, and his eyes fell upon the verse at the bottom of the page.

"Lay not up for yourselves treasures upon earth."

That had been the text of the sermon a few weeks before. Sleepily, heavily, he tried to fix his mind upon it and recall it. What was it that Doctor Snodgrass had said? Ah, yes—that it was a mistake to pause here in reading the verse. We must read on without a pause—*Lay not up treasures upon earth where moth and rust do corrupt and where thieves break through and steal*—that was the true doctrine. We may have treasures upon earth, but they must not be put into unsafe places, but into safe places. A most comforting doctrine! He had always followed it. Moths and rust and thieves had done no harm to his investments.

John Weightman's drooping eyes turned to the next verse, at the top of the second column.

"But lay up for yourselves treasures in heaven."

Now what had the Doctor said about that? How was it to be understood—in what sense—treasures—in heaven?

The book seemed to float away from him. The light vanished. He wondered dimly if this could be Death, coming so suddenly, so quietly, so irresistibly. He struggled for a moment to hold himself up, and then sank slowly forward upon the table. His head rested upon his folded hands. He slipped into the unknown.

How long afterward conscious life returned to him he did not know. The blank might have been an hour or a century. He knew only that something had happened in the interval. What it was he could not tell. He found great difficulty in catching the thread of his identity again. He felt that he was himself; but the trouble was to make his connections, to verify and place himself, to know who and where he was.

At last it grew clear. John Weightman was sitting on a stone, not far from a road in a strange land.

The road was not a formal highway, fenced and graded. It was more like a great travel-trace, worn by thousands of feet passing across the open country in the same direction. Down in the valley, into which he could look, the road seemed to form itself gradually out of many minor paths; little footways coming across the meadows, winding tracks following along beside the streams, faintly marked trails emerging from the woodlands. But on the hillside the threads were more firmly woven into one clear band of travel, though there were still a few dim paths joining it here and there, as if persons had been climbing up the hill by other ways and had turned at last to seek the road.

From the edge of the hill, where John Weightman sat, he could see the travelers, in little groups or larger companies, gathering from time to time by the different paths, and making the ascent. They were all clothed in white, and the form of their garments was strange to him; it was like some old picture. They passed him, group after group, talking quietly together or singing; not moving in haste, but with a certain air of eagerness and joy as if they were glad to be on their way to an appointed place. They did not stay to speak to him, but they looked at him often and spoke to one another as they looked; and now and then one of them would smile and beckon him a friendly greeting, so that he felt they would like him to be with them.

There was quite an interval between the groups; and he followed each of them with his eyes after it had passed, blanching the long ribbon of the road for a little transient space, rising and receding across the wide, billowy upland, among the rounded hillocks of aerial green and gold and lilac, until it came to the high horizon, and stood outlined for a moment, a tiny cloud of whiteness against the tender blue, before it vanished over the hill.

For a long time he sat there watching and wondering. It was a very different world from that in which his mansion on the Avenue was built; and it looked strange to him, but most real—as real as anything he had ever seen. Presently he felt a strong desire to know what country it was and where the people were going. He had a faint premonition of what it must be, but he wished to be sure. So he rose from the stone where he was sitting, and came down through the short grass and the lavender flowers, toward a passing group of people. One of them turned to meet him, and held out his hand. It was an old man, under whose white beard and brows John Weightman thought he saw a suggestion of the face of the village doctor who had cared for him years ago, when he was a boy in the country.

"Welcome," said the old man. "Will you come with us?"

"Where are you going?"

"To the heavenly city, to see our mansions there."

"And who are these with you?"

"Strangers to me, until a little while ago; I know them better now. But you I have known for a long time, John Weightman. Don't you remember your old doctor?"

"Yes," he cried—"yes; your voice has not changed at all. I'm glad indeed to see you, Doctor McLean, especially now. All this seems very strange to me, almost oppressive. I wonder if—but may I go with you, do you suppose?"

"Surely," answered the doctor, with his familiar smile; "it will do you good. And you also must have a mansion in the city waiting for you—a fine one, too—are you not looking forward to it?"

"Yes," replied the other, hesitating a moment; "yes—I believe it must be so, although I had not expected to see it so soon. But I will go with you, and we can talk by the way."

The two men quickly caught up with the other people, and all went forward together along the road. The doctor had little to tell of his experience, for it had been a plain, hard life, uneventfully spent for others, and the story of the village was very simple. John Weightman's adventures and triumphs would have made a far richer, more imposing history, full of contacts with the great events and personages of the time. But somehow or other he did not care to speak much about it, walking on that wide heavenly moorland, under that tranquil, sunless arch of blue, in that free air of perfect peace, where the light was diffused without a shadow, as if the spirit of life in all things were luminous.

There was only one person besides the doctor in that little company whom John Weightman had known before—an old bookkeeper who had spent his life over a desk, carefully keeping accounts—a rusty, dull little man, patient and narrow, whose wife had been in the insane asylum for twenty years and whose only child was a crippled daughter, for whose comfort and happiness he had toiled and sacrificed himself without stint. It was a surprise to find him here, as care-free and joyful as the rest.

The lives of others in the company were revealed in brief glimpses as they talked together—a mother, early widowed, who had kept her little flock of children together and labored through hard and heavy years to bring them up in purity and knowledge—a Sister of Charity who had devoted herself to the nursing of poor folk who were being eaten to death by cancer—a schoolmaster whose heart and life had been poured into his quiet work of training boys for a clean and thoughtful manhood—a medical missionary who had given up a brilliant career in science to take the charge of a hospital in darkest Africa—a beautiful woman with silver hair who had resigned her dreams of love and marriage to care for an invalid father, and after his death had made her life a long, steady search for ways of doing kindnesses to others—a poet who had walked among the crowded tenements of the great city, bringing cheer and comfort not only by his songs, but by his wise and patient works of practical aid—a paralyzed woman who had lain for thirty years upon her bed, helpless but not hopeless, succeeding by a miracle of courage in her single aim, never to complain, but always to impart a bit of her joy and peace to every one who came near her. All these, and other persons like them, people of little consideration in the world, but now seemingly all full of great contentment and an inward gladness that made their steps light, were in the company that passed along the road, talking together of things past and things to come, and singing now and then with clear voices from which the veil of age and sorrow was lifted.

John Weightman joined in some of the songs—which were familiar to him from their use in the church—at first with a touch of hesitation, and then more confidently. For as they went on his sense of strangeness and fear at his new experience diminished, and his thoughts began to take on their habitual assurance and complacency. Were not these people going to the Celestial City? And was not he in his right place among them? He had always looked forward to this journey. If they were sure, each one, of finding a mansion there, could not he be far more sure? His life had been more fruitful than theirs. He had been a leader, a founder of new enterprises, a pillar of Church and State, a prince of the House of Israel. Ten talents had been given him, and he had made them twenty. His reward would be proportionate. He was glad that his companions were going to find fit dwellings prepared for them; but he thought also with a certain pleasure of the surprise that some of them would feel when they saw his appointed mansion.

So they came to the summit of the moorland and looked over into the world beyond. It was a vast, green plain, softly rounded like a shallow vase, and circled with hills of amethyst. A broad, shining river flowed through it, and many silver threads of water were woven across the green; and there were borders of tall trees on the banks of the river, and orchards full of roses abloom along the little streams, and in the midst of all stood the city, white and wonderful and radiant.

When the travelers saw it they were filled with awe and joy. They passed over the little streams and among the orchards quickly and silently, as if they feared to speak lest the city should vanish.

The wall of the city was very low, a child could see over it, for it was made only of precious stones, which are never large. The gate of the city was not like a gate at all, for it was not barred with iron or wood, but only a single pearl, softly gleaming, marked the place where the wall ended and the entrance lay open.

A person stood there whose face was bright and grave, and whose robe was like the flower of the lily, not a woven fabric, but a living texture. "Come in," he said to the company of travelers; "you are at your journey's end, and your mansions are ready for you."

John Weightman hesitated, for he was troubled by a doubt. Suppose that he was not really, like his companions, at his journey's end, but only transported for a little while out of the regular course of his life into this mysterious experience? Suppose that, after all, he had not really passed through the door of death, like these others, but only through the door of dreams, and was walking in a vision, a living man among the blessed dead. Would it be right for him to go with them into the heavenly city? Would it not be a deception, a desecration, a deep and unforgivable offense? The strange, confusing question had no reason in it, as he very well knew; for if he was dreaming, then it was all a dream; but if his companions were real, then he also was with them in reality, and if they had died then he must have died too. Yet he could not rid his mind of the sense that there was a difference between them and him, and it made him afraid to go on. But, as he paused and turned, the Keeper of the Gate looked straight and deep into his eyes, and beckoned to him. Then he knew that it was not only right but necessary that he should enter.

They passed from street to street among fair and spacious dwellings, set in amaranthine gardens, and adorned with an infinitely varied beauty of divine simplicity. The mansions differed in size, in shape, in charm: each one seemed to have its own personal look of loveliness; yet all were alike in fitness to their place, in harmony with one another, in the addition which each made to the singular and tranquil splendor of the city.

As the little company came, one by one, to the mansions which were prepared for them, and their Guide beckoned to the happy inhabitant to enter in and take possession, there was a soft murmur of joy, half wonder and half recognition; as if the new and immortal dwelling were crowned with the beauty of surprise, lovelier and nobler than all the dreams of it had been; and yet also as if it were touched with the beauty of the familiar, the remembered, the long-loved. One after another the travelers were led to their own mansions, and went in gladly; and from within, through the open doorways, came sweet voices of welcome, and low laughter, and song.

At last there was no one left with the Guide but the two old friends, Doctor McLean and John Weightman. They were standing in front of one of the largest and fairest of the houses, whose garden glowed softly with radiant flowers. The Guide laid his hand upon the doctor's shoulder.

"This is for you," he said. "Go in; there is no more pain here, no more death, nor sorrow, nor tears; for your old enemies are all conquered. But all the good that you have done for others, all the help that you have given, all the comfort that you have brought, all the strength and love that you have bestowed upon the suffering, are here; for we have built them all into this mansion for you."

The good man's face was lighted with a still joy. He clasped his old friend's hand closely, and whispered: "How wonderful it is! Go on, you will come to your mansion next, it is not far away, and we shall see each other again soon, very soon."

So he went through the garden, and into the music within. The Keeper of the Gate turned to John Weightman with level, quiet, searching eyes. Then he asked, gravely:

"Where do you wish me to lead you now?"

"To see my own mansion," answered the man, with half-concealed excitement. "Is there not one here for me? You may not let me enter it yet, perhaps, for I must confess to you that I am only—"

"I know," said the Keeper of the Gate—"I know it all. You are John Weightman."

"Yes," said the man, more firmly than he had spoken at first, for it gratified him that his name was known. "Yes, I am John Weightman, Senior Warden of St. Petronius' Church. I wish very much to see my mansion here, if only for a moment. I believe that you have one for me. Will you take me to it?"

The Keeper of the Gate drew a little book from the breast of his robe and turned over the pages.

"Certainly," he said, with a curious look at the man, "your name is here; and you shall see your mansion if you will follow me."

It seemed as if they must have walked miles and miles, through the vast city, passing street after street of houses larger and smaller, of gardens richer and poorer, but all full of beauty and delight. They came into a kind of suburb, where there were many small cottages, with plots of flowers, very lowly, but bright and fragrant. Finally they reached an open field, bare and lonely-looking. There were two or three little bushes in it, without flowers, and the grass was sparse and thin. In the center of the field was a tiny hut, hardly big enough for a shepherd's shelter. It looked as if it had been built of discarded things, scraps and fragments of other buildings, put together with care and pains, by some one who had tried to make the most of cast-off material. There was something pitiful and shamefaced about the hut. It shrank and drooped and faded in its barren field, and seemed to cling only by sufferance to the edge of the splendid city.

"This," said the Keeper of the Gate, standing still and speaking with a low, distinct voice—"this is your mansion, John Weightman."

An almost intolerable shock of grieved wonder and indignation choked the man for a moment so that he could not say a word. Then he turned his face away from the poor little hut and began to remonstrate eagerly with his companion.

"Surely, sir," he stammered, "you must be in error about this. There is something wrong—some other John Weightman—a confusion of names—the book must be mistaken."

"There is no mistake," said the Keeper of the Gate, very calmly; "here is your name, the record of your title and your possessions in this place."

"But how could such a house be prepared for me," cried the man, with a resentful tremor in his voice—"for me, after my long and faithful service? Is this a suitable mansion for one so well known and devoted? Why is it so pitifully small and mean? Why have you not built it large and fair, like the others?"

"That is all the material you sent us."

"What!"

"We have used all the material that you sent us," repeated the Keeper of the Gate.

"Now I know that you are mistaken," cried the man, with growing earnestness, "for all my life long I have been doing things that must have supplied you with material. Have you not heard that I have built a school-house; the wing of a hospital; two—yes, three—small churches, and the greater part of a large one, the spire of St. Petro—"

The Keeper of the Gate lifted his hand.

"Wait," he said; "we know all these things. They were not ill done. But they were all marked and used as foundation for the name and mansion of John Weightman in the world. Did you not plan them for that?"

"Yes," answered the man, confused and taken aback, "I confess that I thought often of them in that way. Perhaps my heart was set upon that too much. But there are other things—my endowment for the college—my steady and liberal contributions to all the established charities—my support of every respectable—"

"Wait," said the Keeper of the Gate again. "Were not all these carefully recorded on earth where they would add to your credit? They were not foolishly done. Verily, you have had your reward for them. Would you be paid twice?"

"No," cried the man, with deepening dismay, "I dare not claim that. I acknowledge that I considered my own interest too much. But surely not altogether. You have said that these things were not foolishly done. They accomplished some good in the world. Does not that count for something?"

"Yes," answered the Keeper of the Gate, "it counts in the world—where you counted it. But it does not belong to you here. We have saved and used everything that you sent us. This is the mansion prepared for you."

As he spoke, his look grew deeper and more searching, like a flame of fire. John Weightman could not endure it. It seemed to strip him naked and wither him. He sank to the ground under a crushing weight of shame, covering his eyes with his hands and cowering face downward upon the stones. Dimly through the trouble of his mind he felt their hardness and coldness.

"Tell me, then," he cried, brokenly, "since my life has been so little worth, how came I here at all?"

"Through the mercy of the King"—the answer was like the soft tolling of a bell.

"And how have I earned it?" he murmured.

"It is never earned; it is only given," came the clear, low reply.

"But how have I failed so wretchedly," he asked, "in all the purpose of my life? What could I have done better? What is it that counts here?"

"Only that which is truly given," answered the bell-like voice. "Only that good which is done for the love of doing it. Only those plans in which the welfare of others is the master thought. Only those labors in which the sacrifice is greater than the reward. Only those gifts in which the giver forgets himself."

The man lay silent. A great weakness, an unspeakable despondency and humiliation were upon him. But the face of the Keeper of the Gate was infinitely tender as he bent over him.

"Think again, John Weightman. Has there been nothing like that in your life?"

"Nothing," he sighed. "If there ever were such things, it must have been long ago—they were all crowded out—I have forgotten them."

There was an ineffable smile on the face of the Keeper of the Gate, and his hand made the sign of the cross over the bowed head as he spoke gently:

"These are the things that the King never forgets; and because there were a few of them in your life, you have a little place here."

The sense of coldness and hardness under John Weightman's hands grew sharper and more distinct. The feeling of bodily weariness and lassitude weighed upon him, but there was a calm, almost a lightness, in his heart as he listened to the fading vibrations of the silvery bell-tones. The chimney clock on the mantel had just ended the last stroke of seven as he lifted his head from the table. Thin, pale strips of the city morning were falling into the room through the narrow partings of the heavy curtains.

What was it that had happened to him? Had he been ill? Had he died and come to life again? Or had he only slept, and had his soul gone visiting in dreams? He sat for some time, motionless, not lost, but finding himself in thought. Then he took a narrow book from the table drawer, wrote a check, and tore it out.

He went slowly up the stairs, knocked very softly at his son's door, and, hearing no answer, entered without noise. Harold was asleep, his bare arm thrown above his head, and his eager face relaxed in peace. His father looked at him a moment with strangely shining eyes, and then tiptoed quietly to the writing-desk, found a pencil and a sheet of paper, and wrote rapidly:

"My dear boy, here is what you asked me for; do what you like with it, and ask for more if you need it. If you are still thinking of that work with Grenfell, we'll talk it over to-day after church. I want to know your heart better; and if I have made mistakes—"

A slight noise made him turn his head. Harold was sitting up in bed with wide-open eyes.

"Father!" he cried, "is that you?"

"Yes, my son," answered John Weightman; "I've come back—I mean I've come up—no, I mean come in—well, here I am, and God give us a good Christmas together."

THE END

The First Christmas Tree

I
THE CALL OF THE WOODSMAN
I
THE **day before Christmas, in the year of our Lord 722.**

Broad snow-meadows glistening white along the banks of the river Moselle; pallid hill-sides blooming with mystic roses where the glow of the setting sun still lingered upon them; an arch of clearest, faintest azure bending overhead; in the center of the aerial landscape of the massive walls of the cloister of Pfalzel, gray to the east, purple to the west; silence over all,—a gentle, eager, conscious stillness, diffused through the air like perfume, as if earth and sky were hushing themselves to hear the voice of the river faintly murmuring down the valley.

In the cloister, too, there was silence at the sunset hour. All day long there had been a strange and joyful stir among the nuns. A breeze of curiosity and excitement had swept along the corridors and through every quiet cell. The elder sisters,—the provost, the deaconess, the stewardess, the portress with her huge bunch of keys jingling at her girdle,—had been hurrying to and fro, busied with household cares. In the huge kitchen there was a bustle of hospitable preparation. The little bandy-legged dogs that kept the spits turning before the fires had been trotting steadily for many an hour, until their tongues hung out for want of breath. The big black pots swinging from the cranes had bubbled and gurgled and shaken and sent out puffs of appetizing steam.

St. Martha was in her element. It was a field-day for her virtues.

The younger sisters, the pupils of the convent, had forsaken their Latin books and their embroidery-frames, their manuscripts and their miniatures, and fluttered through the halls in little flocks like merry snow-birds, all in black and white, chattering and whispering together. This was no day for tedious task-work, no day for grammar or arithmetic, no day for picking out illuminated letters in red and gold on stiff parchment, or patiently chasing intricate patterns over thick cloth with the slow needle. It was a holiday. A famous visitor had come to the convent. It was Winfried of England, whose name in the Roman tongue was Boniface, and whom men called the Apostle of Germany. A great preacher; a wonderful scholar; he had written a Latin grammar himself,—think of it,—and he could hardly sleep without a book under his pillow; but, more than all, a great and daring traveller, a venturesome pilgrim, a high-priest of romance.

He had left his home and his fair estate in Wessex; he would not stay in the rich monastery of Nutescelle, even though they had chosen him as the abbot; he had refused a bishopric at the court of King Karl. Nothing would content him but to go out into the wild woods and preach to the heathen.

Up and down through the forests of Hesse and Thuringia, and along the borders of Saxony, he had wandered for years, with a handful of companions, sleeping under the trees, crossing mountains and marshes, now here, now there, never satisfied with ease and comfort, always in love with hardship and danger.

What a man he was! Fair and slight, but straight as a spear and strong as an oaken staff. His face was still young; the smooth skin was bronzed by wing and sun. His gray eyes, clear and kind, flashed like fire when he spoke of his adventures, and of the evil deeds of the false priests with whom he had contended.

What tales he had told that day! Not of miracles wrought by sacred relics; nor of courts and councils and splendid cathedrals; though he knew much of these things, and had been at Rome and received the Pope's blessing. But to-day he had spoken of long journeyings by sea and land; of perils by fire and flood; of wolves and bears and fierce snowstorms and black nights in the lonely forest; of dark altars of heaven gods, and weird, bloody sacrifices, and narrow escapes from wandering savages.

The little novices had gathered around him, and their faces had grown pale and their eyes bright as they listened with parted lips, entranced in admiration, twining their arms about one another's shoulders and holding closely together, half in fear, half in delight. The older nuns had turned from their tasks and paused, in passing by, to hear the pilgrim's story. Too well they knew the truth of what he spoke. Many a one among them had seen the smoke rising from the ruins of her father's roof. Many a one had a brother far away in the wild country to whom her heart went out night and day, wondering if he were still among the living.

But now the excitements of that wonderful day were over; the hours of the evening meal had come; the inmates of the cloister were assembled in the refectory.

On the dais sat the stately Abbess Addula, daughter of King Dagobert, looking a princess indeed, in her violet tunic, with the hood and cuffs of her long white robe trimmed with fur, and a snowy veil resting like a crown on her snowy hair. At her right hand was the honoured guest, and at her left hand her grandson, the young Prince Gregor, a big, manly boy, just returned from school.

The long, shadowy hall, with its dark-brown raters and beams; the double rows of nuns, with their pure veils and fair faces; the ruddy flow of the slanting sunbeams striking upwards through the tops of the windows and painting a pink glow high up on the walls,—it was all as beautiful as a picture, and as silent. For this was the rule of the cloister, that at the table all should sit in stillness for a little while, and then one should read aloud, while the rest listened.

"It is the turn of my grandson to read to-day," said the abbess to Winfried; "we shall see how much he has learned in the school. Read, Gregor; the place in the book is marked."

The tall lad rose from his seat and turned the pages of the manuscript. It was a copy of Jerome's version of the Scriptures in Latin, and the marked place was in the letter of St. Paul to the Ephesians,—the passage where he describes the preparation of the Christian as the arming of a warrior for glorious battle. The young voice rang out clearly, rolling the sonorous words, without slip or stumbling, to the end of the chapter.

Winfried listened, smiling. "My son," said he, as the reader paused, "that was bravely read. Understandest thou what thou readest?"

"Surely, father," answered the boy; "it was taught me by the masters at Treves; and we have read this epistle clear through, from beginning to end, so that I almost know it by heart."

Then he began again to repeat the passage, turning away from the page as if to show his skill.

But Winfried stopped him with a friendly lifting of the hand.

"No so, my son; that was not my meaning. When we pray, we speak to God; when we read, it is God who speaks to us. I ask whether thou hast heard what He has said to thee, in thine own words, in the common speech. Come, give us again the message of the warrior and his armour and his battle, in the mother-tongue, so that all can understand it."

The boy hesitated, blushed, stammered; then he came around to Winfried's seat, bringing the book. "Take the book, my father," he cried, "and read it for me. I cannot see the meaning plain, though I love the sound of the words. Religion I know, and the doctrines of our faith, and the life of priests and nuns in the cloister, for which my grandmother designs me, though it likes me little. And fighting I know, and the life of warriors and heroes, for I have read of it in Virgil and the ancients, and heard a bit from the soldiers at Treves; and I would fain taste more of it, for it likes me much. But how the two lives fit together, or what need there is of armour for a clerk in holy orders, I can never see. Tell me the meaning, for if there is a man in all the world that knows it, I am sure it is none other than thou."

So Winfried took the book and closed it, clasping the boy's hand with his own.

"Let us first dismiss the others to their vespers," said he, "lest they should be weary."

A sign from the abbess; a chanted benediction; a murmuring of sweet voices and a soft rustling of many feet over the rushes on the floor; the gentle tide of noise flowed out through the doors and ebbed away down the corridors; the three at the head of the table were left alone in the darkening room.

Then Winfried began to translate the parable of the soldier into the realities of life.

At every turn he knew how to flash a new light into the picture out of his own experience. He spoke of the combat with self, and of the wrestling with dark spirits in solitude. He spoke of the demons that men had worshipped for centuries in the wilderness, and whose malice they invoked against the stranger who ventured into the gloomy forest. Gods, they called them, and told strange tales of their dwelling among the impenetrable branches of the oldest trees and in the caverns of the shaggy hills; of their riding on the wind-horses and hurling spears of lightning against their foes. Gods they were not, but foul spirits of the air, rulers of the darkness. Was there not glory and honour in fighting with them, in daring their anger under the shield of faith, in putting them to flight with the sword of truth? What better adventure could a brave man ask than to go forth against them, and wrestle with them, and conquer them? "Look you, my friends," said Winfried, "how sweet and peaceful is this convent to-night, on the eve of the nativity of the Prince of Peace! It is a garden full of flowers in the heart of winter; a nest among the branches of a great tree shaken by the winds; a still haven on the edge of a tempestuous sea. And this is what religion means for those who are chosen and called to quietude and prayer and meditation.

"But out yonder in the wide forest, who knows what storms are raving to-night in the hearts of men, though all the woods are still? who knows what haunts of wrath and cruelty and fear are closed to-night against the advent of the Prince of Peace? And shall I tell you what religion means to those who are called and chosen to dare and to fight, and to conquer the world for Christ? It means to launch out into the deep. It means to go against the strongholds of the adversary. It means to struggle to win an entrance for their Master everywhere. What helmet is strong enough for this strife save the helmet of salvation? What breastplate can guard a man against these fiery darts but the breastplate of righteousness? What shoes can stand the wear of these journeys but the preparation of the gospel of peace?" "Shoes?" he cried again, and laughed as if a sudden thought had struck him. He thrust out his foot, covered with a heavy cowhide boot, laced high about his leg with thongs of skin.

"See here,—how a fighting man of the cross is shod! I have seen the boots of the Bishop of Tours,—white kid, broidered with silk; a day in the bogs would tear them to shreds. I have seen the sandals that the monks use on the highroads,—yes, and worn them; ten pair of them have I worn out and thrown away in a single journey. Now I shoe my feet with the toughest hides, hard as iron; no rock can cut them, no branches can tear them. Yet more than one pair of these have I outworn, and many more shall I outwear ere my journeys are ended. And I think, if God is gracious to me, that I shall die wearing them. Better so than in a soft bed with silken coverings. The boots of a warrior, a hunter, a woodsman,—these are my preparation of the gospel of peace."

"Come, Gregor," he said, laying his brown hand on the youth's shoulder, "come, wear the forester's boots with me. This is the life to which we are called. Be strong in the Lord, a hunter of the demons, a subduer of the wilderness, a woodsman of the faith. Come!"

The boy's eyes sparkled. He turned to his grandmother. She shook her head vigorously.

"Nay, father," she said, "draw not the lad away from my side with these wild words. I need him to help me with my labours, to cheer my old age."

"Do you need him more than the Master does?" asked Winfried; "and will you take the wood that is fit for a bow to make a distaff?"

"But I fear for the child. Thy life is too hard for him. He will perish with hunger in the woods."

"Once," said Winfried, smiling, "we were camped by the bank of the river Ohru. The table was spread for the morning meal, but my comrades cried that it was empty; the provisions were exhausted; we must go without breakfast, and perhaps starve before we could escape from the wilderness. While they complained, a fish-hawk flew up from the river with flapping wings, and let fall a great pike in the midst of the camp. There was food enough and to spare. Never have I seen the righteous forsaken, nor his seed begging bread."

"But the fierce pagans of the forest," cried the abbess,—"they may pierce the boy with their arrows, or dash out his brains with their axes. He is but a child, too young for the dangers of strife."

"A child in years," replied Winfried, "but a man in spirit. And if the hero must fall early in the battle, he wears the brighter crown, not a leaf withered, not a flower fallen."

The aged princess trembled a little. She drew Gregor close to her side, and laid her hand gently on his brown hair. "I am not sure that he wants to leave me yet. Besides, there is no horse in the stable to give him, now, and he cannot go as befits the grandson of a king."

Gregor looked straight into her eyes.

"Grandmother," said he, "dear grandmother, if thou wilt not give me a horse to ride with this man of God, I will go with him afoot."

II
THE TRAIL THROUGH THE FOREST

II

TWO years had passed, to a day, almost to an hour, since that Christmas eve in the cloister of Pfalzel. A little company of pilgrims, less than a score a men, were creeping slowly northward through the wide forest that rolled over the hills of central Germany.

At the head of the band marched Winfried, clad in a tunic of fur, with his long black robe girt high about his waist, so that it might not hinder his stride. His hunter's boots were crusted with snow. Drops of ice sparkled like jewels along the thongs that bound his legs. There was no other ornament to his dress except the bishop's cross hanging on his breast, and the broad silver clasp that fastened his cloak about his neck. He carried a strong, tall staff in his hand, fashioned at the top into the form of a cross.

Close beside him, keeping step like a familiar comrade, was the young Prince Gregor. Long marches through the wilderness had stretched his limbs and broadened his back, and made a man of him in stature as well as in spirit. His jacket and cap were of wolfskin, and on his shoulder he carried an axe, with broad, shining blade. He was a mighty woodsman now, and could make a spray of chips fly around him as he hewed his way through the trunk of spruce-tree.

Behind these leaders followed a pair of teamsters, guiding a rude sledge, loaded with food and the equipage of the camp, and drawn by two big, shaggy horses, blowing thick clouds of steam from their frosty nostrils. Tiny icicles hung from the hairs on their lips. Their flanks were smoking. They sank above the fetlocks at every step in the soft snow.

Last of all came the rear guard, armed with bows and javelins. It was no child's play, in those days, to cross Europe afoot.

The weird woodland, sombre and illimitable, covered hill and vale, tableland and mountain-peak. There were wide moors where the wolves hunted in packs as if the devil drove them, and tangled thickets where the lynx and the boar made their lairs. Fierce bears lurked among the rocky passes, and had not yet learned to fear the face of man. The gloomy recesses of the forest gave shelter to inhabitants who were still more cruel and dangerous than beasts of prey,—outlaws and sturdy robbers and mad were-wolves and bands of wandering pillagers.

The pilgrim who would pass from the mouth of the Tiber to the mouth of the Rhine must travel with a little army of retainers, or else trust in God and keep his arrows loose in the quiver.

The travellers were surrounded by an ocean of trees, so vast, so full of endless billows, that it seemed to be pressing on every side to overwhelm them. Gnarled oaks, with branches twisted and knotted as if in rage, rose in groves like tidal waves. Smooth forests of beech-trees, round and gray, swept over the knolls and slopes of land in a mighty ground-swell. But most of all, the multitude of pines and firs, innumerable and monotonous, with straight, stark trunks, and branches woven together in an unbroken Hood of darkest green, crowded through the valleys and over the hills, rising on the highest ridges into ragged crests, like the foaming edge of breakers.

Through this sea of shadows ran a narrow stream of shining whiteness,—an ancient Roman road, covered with snow. It was as if some great ship had ploughed through the green ocean long ago, and left behind it a thick, smooth wake of foam. Along this open track the travellers held their way,—heavily, for the drifts were deep; warily, for the hard winter had driven many packs of wolves down from the moors.

The steps of the pilgrims were noiseless; but the sledges creaked over the dry snow, and the panting of the horses throbbed through the still, cold air. The pale-blue shadows on the western side of the road grew longer. The sun, declining through its shallow arch, dropped behind the tree-tops. Darkness followed swiftly, as if it had been a bird of prey waiting for this sign to swoop down upon the world.

"Father," said Gregor to the leader, "surely this day's march is done. It is time to rest, and eat, and sleep. If we press onward now, we cannot see our steps; and will not that be against the word of the psalmist David, who bids us not to put confidence in the legs of a man?"

Winfried laughed. "Nay, my son Gregor," said he, "thou hast tripped, even now, upon thy text. For David said only, 'I take no pleasure in the legs of a man.' And so say I, for I am not minded to spare thy legs or mine, until we come farther on our way, and do what must be done this night. Draw the belt tighter, my son, and hew me out this tree that is fallen across the road, for our campground is not here."

The youth obeyed; two of the foresters sprang to help him; and while the soft fir-wood yielded to the stroke of the axes, and the snow flew from the bending branches, Winfried turned and spoke to his followers in a cheerful voice, that refreshed them like wine.

"Courage, brothers, and forward yet a little! The moon will light us presently, and the path is plain. Well know I that the journey is weary; and my own heart wearies also for the home in England, where those I love are keeping feast this Christmas eve. But we have work to do before we feast to-night. For this is the Yuletide, and the heathen people of the forest have gathered at the thunder-oak of Geismar to worship their god, Thor. Strange things will be seen there, and deeds which make the soul black. But we are sent to lighten their darkness; and we will teach our kinsmen to keep a Christmas with us such as the woodland has never known. Forward, then, and let us stiffen up our feeble knees!" A murmur of assent came from the men. Even the horses seemed to take fresh heart. They flattened their backs to draw the heavy loads, and blew the frost from their nostrils as they pushed ahead.

The night grew broader and less oppressive. A gate of brightness was opened secretly somewhere in the sky; higher and higher swelled the clear moon-flood, until it poured over the eastern wall of forest into the road. A drove of wolves howled faintly in the distance, but they were receding, and the sound soon died away. The stars sparkled merrily through the stringent air; the small, round moon shone like silver; little breaths of the dreaming wind wandered whispering across the pointed fir-tops, as the pilgrims toiled bravely onward, following their clue of light through a labyrinth of darkness.

After a while the road began to open out a little. There were spaces of meadow-land, fringed with alders, behind which a boisterous river ran, clashing through spears of ice.

Rude houses of hewn logs appeared in the openings, each one casting a patch of inky blackness upon the snow. Then the travellers passed a larger group of dwellings, all silent and unlighted; and beyond, they saw a great house, with many outbuildings and enclosed courtyards, from which the hounds bayed furiously, and a noise of stamping horses came from the stalls. But there was no other sound of life. The fields around lay bare to the moon. They saw no man, except that once, on a path that skirted the farther edge of a meadow, three dark figures passed by, running very swiftly.

Then the road plunged again into a dense thicket, traversed it, and climbing to the left, emerged suddenly upon a glade, round and level except at the northern side, where a swelling hillock was crowned with a huge oak-tree. It towered above the heath, a giant with contorted arms, beckoning to the host of lesser trees. "Here," cried Winfried, as his eyes flashed and his hand lifted his heavy staff, "here is the Thunder-oak; and here the cross of Christ shall break the hammer of the false god Thor."

III
THE SHADOW OF THE THUNDER-OAK

III

WITHERED leaves still clung to the branches of the oak: torn and faded banners of the departed summer. The bright crimson of autumn had long since disappeared, bleached away by the storms and the cold. But to-night these tattered remnants of glory were red again: ancient bloodstains against the dark-blue sky. For an immense fire had been kindled in front of the tree. Tongues of ruddy flame, fountains of ruby sparks, ascended through the spreading limbs and flung a fierce illumination upward and around. ward and around. The pale, pure moonlight that bathed the surrounding forests was quenched and eclipsed here. Not a beam of it sifted down-ward through the branches of the oak. It stood like a pillar of cloud between the still light of heaven and the crackling, flashing fire of earth. But the fire itself was invisible to Winfried and his companions. A great throng of people were gathered around it in a half-circle, their backs to the open glade, their faces towards the oak. Seen against that glowing background, it was but the silhouette of a crowd, vague, black, formless, mysterious.

The travellers paused for a moment at the edge of the thicket, and took counsel together.

"It is the assembly of the tribe," said one of the foresters, "the great night of the council. I heard of it three days ago, as we passed through one of the villages. All who swear by the old gods have been summoned. They will sacrifice a steed to the god of war, and drink blood, and eat horse-flesh to make them strong. It will be at the peril of our lives if we approach them. At least we must hide the cross, if we would escape death."

"Hide me no cross," cried Winfried, lifting his staff, "for I have come to show it, and to make these blind folk see its power. There is more to be done here to-night than the slaying of a steed, and a greater evil to be stayed than the shameful eating of meat sacrificed to idols. I have seen it in a dream. Here the cross must stand and be our rede." At his command the sledge was left in the border of the wood, with two of the men to guard it, and the rest of the company moved forward across the open ground. They approached unnoticed, for all the multitude were looking intently towards the fire at the foot of the oak.

Then Winfried's voice rang out, "Hail, ye sons of the forest! A stranger claims the warmth of your fire in the winter night."

Swiftly, and as with a single motion, a thousand eyes were bent upon the speaker. The semicircle opened silently in the middle; Winfried entered with his followers; it closed again behind them.

Then, as they looked round the curving ranks, they saw that the hue of the assemblage was not black, but white,—dazzling, radiant, solemn. White, the robes of the women clustered together at the points of the wide crescent; white, the glittering byrnies of the warriors standing in close ranks; white, the fur mantles of the aged men who held the central place in the circle; white, with the shimmer of silver ornaments and the purity of lamb's-wool, the raiment of a little group of children who stood close by the fire; white, with awe and fear, the faces of all who looked at them; and over all the flickering, dancing radiance of the flames played and glimmered like a faint, vanishing tinge of blood on snow.

The only figure untouched by the glow was the old priest, Hunrad, with his long, spectral robe, flowing hair and beard, and dead-pale face, who stood with his back to the fire and advanced slowly to meet the strangers. "Who are you? Whence come you, and what seek you here?" His voice was heavy and toneless as a muffled bell.

"You kinsman am I, of the German brotherhood," answered Winfried, "and from England, beyond the sea, have I come to bring you a greeting from that land, and a message from the All-Father, whose servant I am."

"Welcome, then," said Hunrad, "welcome, kinsman, and be silent; for what passes here is too high to wait, and must be done before the moon crosses the middle heaven, unless, indeed, thou hast some sign or token from the gods. Canst thou work miracles?"

The question came sharply, as if a sudden gleam of hope had flashed through the tangle of the old priest's mind. But Winfried's voice sank lower and a cloud of disappointment passed over his face as he replied: "Nay, miracles have I never wrought, though I have heard of many; but the All-Father has given no power to my hands save such as belongs to common man."

"Stand still, then, thou common man," said Hunrad, scornfully, "and behold what the gods have called us hither to do. This night is the death-night of the sun-god, Baldur the Beautiful, beloved of gods and men. This night is the hour of darkness and the power of winter, of sacrifice and mighty fear. This night the great Thor, the god of thunder and war, to whom this oak is sacred, is grieved for the death of Baldur, and angry with this people because they have forsaken his worship. Long is it since an offering has been laid upon his altar, long since the roots of his holy tree have been fed with blood. Therefore its leaves have withered before the time, and its boughs are heavy with death. Therefore the Slavs and the Wends have beaten us in battle. Therefore the harvests have failed, and the wolf-hordes have ravaged the folds, and the strength has departed from the bow, and the wood of the spear has broken, and the wild boar has slain the huntsman. Therefore the plague has fallen on our dwellings, and the dead are more than the living in all our villages. Answer me, ye people, are not these things true?"

A hoarse sound of approval ran through the circle. A chant, in which the voices of the men and women blended, like the shrill wind in the pine-trees above the rumbling thunder of a waterfall, rose and fell in rude cadences.

O Thor, the Thunderer,
Mighty and merciless,
Spare us from smiting!
Heave not thy hammer,
Angry, against us;
Plague not thy people.
Take from our treasure
Richest of ransom.
Silver we send thee,
Jewels and javelins,
Goodliest garments,
All our possessions,
Priceless, we proffer.
Sheep will we slaughter,
Steeds will we sacrifice;

> Bright blood shall bathe thee,
> O tree of Thunder,
> Life-floods shall lave thee,
> Strong wood of wonder.
> Mighty, have mercy,
> Smite us no more,
> Spare us and save us,
> Spare us, Thor! Thor!

With two great shouts the song ended, and a stillness followed so intense that the crackling of the fire was heard distinctly. The old priest stood silent for a moment. His shaggy brows swept down over his eyes like ashes quenching flame. Then he lifted his face and spoke.

"None of these things will please the god. More costly is the offering that shall cleanse your sin, more precious the crimson dew that shall send new life into this holy tree of blood. Thor claims your dearest and your noblest gift." Hunrad moved nearer to the handful of children who stood watching the red mines in the fire and the swarms of spark-serpents darting upward. They had heeded none of the priest's words, and did not notice now that he approached them, so eager were they to see which fiery snake would go highest among the oak branches. Foremost among them, and most intent on the pretty game, was a boy like a sunbeam, slender and quick, with blithe brown eyes and laughing lips. The priest's hand was laid upon his shoulder. The boy turned and looked up in his face.

"Here," said the old man, with his voice vibrating as when a thick rope is strained by a ship swinging from her moorings, "here is the chosen one, the eldest son of the Chief, the darling of the people. Hearken, Bernhard, wilt thou go to Valhalla, where the heroes dwell with the gods, to bear a message to Thor?"

The boy answered, swift and clear:

"Yes, priest, I will go if my father bids me. Is it far away? Shall I run quickly? Must I take my bow and arrows for the wolves?"

The boy's father, the Chieftain Gundhar, standing among his bearded warriors, drew his breath deep, and leaned so heavily on the handle of his spear that the wood cracked. And his wife, Irma, bending forward from the ranks of women, pushed the golden hair from her forehead with one hand. The other dragged at the silver chain about her neck until the rough links pierced her flesh, and the red drops fell unheeded on the snow of her breast. A sigh passed through the crowd, like the murmur of the forest before the storm breaks. Yet no one spoke save Hunrad:

"Yes, my Prince, both bow and spear shalt thou have, for the way is long, and thou art a brave huntsman. But in darkness thou must journey for a little space, and with eyes blindfolded. Fearest thou?"

"Naught fear I," said the boy, "neither darkness, nor the great bear, nor the were-wolf. For I am Gundhar's son, and the defender of my folk."

Then the priest led the child in his raiment of lamb's-wool to a broad stone in front of the fire. He gave him his little bow tipped with silver, and his spear with shining head of steel. He bound the child's eyes with a white cloth, and bade him kneel beside the stone with his face to the east. Unconsciously the wide arc of spectators drew inward toward the centre, as the ends of the bow draw together when the cord is stretched. Winfried moved noiselessly until he stood close behind the priest.

The old man stooped to lift a black hammer of stone from the ground,—the sacred hammer of the god Thor. Summoning all the strength of his withered arms, he swung it high in the air. It poised for an instant above the child's fair head—then turned to fall.

One keen cry shrilled out from where the women stood: "Me! take me! not Bernhard!"

The flight of the mother towards her child was swift as the falcon's swoop. But swifter still was the hand of the deliverer.

Winfried's heavy staff thrust mightily against the hammer's handle as it fell. Sideways it glanced from the old man's grasp, and the black stone, striking on the altar's edge, split in twain. A shout of awe and joy rolled along the living circle. The branches of the oak shivered. The flames leaped higher. As the shout died away the people saw the lady Irma, with her arms clasped round her child, and above them, on the altar-stone, Winfried, his face shining like the face of an angel.

IV
THE FELLING OF THE TREE

IV

A SWIFT mountain-flood rolling down its channel; a huge rock tumbling from the hill-side and falling in midstream; the baffled waters broken and confused, pausing in their flow, dash high against the rock, foaming and murmuring, with divided impulse, uncertain whether to turn to the right or the left.

Even so Winfried's bold deed fell into the midst of the thoughts and passions of the council. They were at a standstill. Anger and wonder, reverence and joy and confusion surged through the crowd. They knew not which way to move: to resent the intrusion of the stranger as an insult to their gods, or to welcome him as the rescuer of their darling prince.

The old priest crouched by the altar, silent. Conflicting counsels troubled the air. Let the sacrifice go forward; the gods must be appeased. Nay, the boy must not die; bring the chieftain's best horse and slay it in his stead; it will be enough; the holy tree loves the blood of horses. Not so, there is a better counsel yet; seize the stranger whom the gods have led hither as a victim and make his life pay the forfeit of his daring.

The withered leaves on the oak rustled and whispered overhead. The fire flared and sank again. The angry voices clashed against each other and fell like opposing waves. Then the chieftain Gundhar struck the earth with his spear and gave his decision.

"All have spoken, but none are agreed. There is no voice of the council. Keep silence now, and let the stranger speak. His words shall give us judgment, whether he is to live or to die."

Winfried lifted himself high upon the altar, drew a roll of parchment from his bosom, and began to read.

"A letter from the great Bishop of Rome, who sits on a golden throne, to the people of the forest, Hessians and Thuringians, Franks and Saxons. *In nomine Domini, sanctae et individuae trinitatis, amen!*"

A murmur of awe ran through the crowd. "It is the sacred tongue of the Romans: the tongue that is heard and understood by the wise men of every land. There is magic in it. Listen!"

Winfried went on to read the letter, translating it into the speech of the people.

"'We have sent unto you our Brother Boniface, and appointed him your bishop, that he may teach you the only true faith, and baptize you, and lead you back from the ways of error to the path of salvation. Hearken to him in all things like a father. Bow your hearts to his teaching. He comes not for earthly gain, but for the gain of your souls. Depart from evil works. Worship not the false gods, for they are devils. Offer no more bloody sacrifices, nor eat the flesh of horses, but do as our Brother Boniface commands you. Build a house for him that he may dwell among you, and a church where you may offer your prayers to the only living God, the Almighty King of Heaven.'"

It was a splendid message: proud, strong, peaceful, loving. The dignity of the words imposed mightily upon the hearts of the people. They were quieted as men who have listened to a lofty strain of music.

"Tell us, then," said Gundhar, "what is the word that thou bringest to us from the Almighty. What is thy counsel for the tribes of the woodland on this night of sacrifice?"

"This is the word, and this is the counsel," answered Winfried. "Not a drop of blood shall fall to-night, save that which pity has drawn from the breast of your princess, in love for her child. Not a life shall be blotted out in the darkness tonight; but the great shadow of the tree which hides you from the light of heaven shall be swept away. For this is the birth-night of the white Christ, son of the All-Father, and Saviour of mankind. Fairer is He than Baldur the Beautiful, greater than Odin the Wise, kinder than Freya the Good. Since He has come to earth the bloody sacrifices must cease. The dark Thor, on whom you vainly call, is dead. Deep in the shades of Niffelheim he is lost forever. His power in the world is broken. Will you serve a helpless god? See, my brothers, you call this tree his oak. Does he dwell here? Does he protect it?"

A troubled voice of assent rose from the throng. The people stirred uneasily. Women covered their eyes. Hunrad lifted his head and muttered hoarsely, "Thor! take vengeance! Thor!"

Winfried beckoned to Gregor. "Bring the axes, thine and one for me. Now, young woodsman, show thy craft! The king-tree of the forest must fall, and swiftly, or all is lost!"

The two men took their places facing each other, one on each side of the oak. Their cloaks were flung aside, their heads bare. Carefully they felt the ground with their feet, seeking a firm grip of the earth. Firmly they grasped the axe-helves and swung the shining blades.

"Tree-god!" cried Winfried, "art thou angry? Thus we smite thee!"

"Tree-god!" answered Gregor, "art thou mighty? Thus we fight thee!"

Clang! clang! the alternate strokes beat time upon the hard, ringing wood. The axe-heads glittered in their rhythmic flight, like fierce eagles circling about their quarry.

The broad flakes of wood flew from the deepening gashes in the sides of the oak. The huge trunk quivered. There was a shuddering in the branches. Then the great wonder of Winfried's life came to pass.

Out of the stillness of the winter night, a mighty rushing noise sounded overhead.

Was it the ancient gods on their white battle-steeds, with their black hounds of wrath and their arrows of lightning, sweeping through the air to destroy their foes?

A strong, whirling wind passed over the tree-tops. It gripped the oak by its branches and tore it from its roots. Backward it fell, like a ruined tower, groaning and crashing as it split asunder in four great pieces.

Winfried let his axe drop, and bowed his head for a moment in the presence of almighty power.

Then he turned to the people, "Here is the timber," he cried, "already felled and split for your new building. On this spot shall rise a chapel to the true God and his servant St. Peter.

"And here," said he, as his eyes fell on a young fir-tree, standing straight and green, with its top pointing towards the stars, amid the divided ruins of the fallen oak, "here is the living tree, with no stain of blood upon it, that shall be the sign of your new worship. See how it points to the sky. Let us call it the tree of the Christ-child. Take it up and carry it to the chieftain's hall. You shall go no more into the shadows of the forest to keep your feasts with secret rites of shame. You shall keep them at home, with laughter and song and rites of love. The thunder-oak has fallen, and I think the day is coming when there shall not be a home in all Germany where the children are not gathered around the green fir-tree to rejoice in the birth-night of Christ."

So they took the little fir from its place, and carried it in joyous procession to the edge of the glade, and laid it on the sledge. The horses tossed their heads and drew their load bravely, as if the new burden had made it lighter. When they came to the house of Gundhar, he bade them throw open the doors of the hall and set the tree in the midst of it. They kindled lights among the branches until it seemed to be tangled full of fire-flies. The children encircled it, wondering, and the sweet odour of the balsam filled the house.

Then Winfried stood beside the chair of Gundhar, on the dais at the end of the hall, and told the story of Bethlehem; of the babe in the manger, of the shepherds on the hills, of the host of angels and their midnight song. All the people listened, charmed into stillness.

But the boy Bernhard, on Irma's knee, folded by her soft arm, grew restless as the story lengthened, and began to prattle softly at his mother's ear.

"Mother," whispered the child, "why did you cry out so loud, when the priest was going to send me to Valhalla?"

"Oh, hush, my child," answered the mother, and pressed him closer to her side.

"Mother," whispered the boy again, laying his finger on the stains upon her breast, "see, your dress is red! What are these stains? Did some one hurt you?"

The mother closed his mouth with a kiss. "Dear, be still, and listen!"

The boy obeyed. His eyes were heavy with sleep. But he heard the last words of Winfried as he spoke of the angelic messengers, flying over the hills of Judea and singing as they flew. The child wondered and dreamed and listened. Suddenly his face grew bright. He put his lips close to Irma's cheek again.

"Oh, mother!" he whispered very low, "do not speak. Do you hear them? Those angels have come back again. They are singing now behind the tree."

And some say that it was true; but others say that it was only Gregor and his companions at the lower end of the hall, chanting their Christmas hymn:

<blockquote>
All glory be to God on high,
And to the earth be peace!
Good-will, henceforth, from heaven to men
Begin, and never cease.
</blockquote>

The Spirit of Christmas

A DREAM-STORY
THE CHRISTMAS ANGEL

It was the hour of rest in the Country Beyond the Stars. All the silver bells that swing with the turning of the great ring of light which lies around that land were softly chiming; and the sound of their commotion went down like dew upon the golden ways of the city, and the long alleys of blossoming trees, and the meadows of asphodel, and the curving shores of the River of Life.

At the hearing of that chime, all the angels who had been working turned to play, and all who had been playing gave themselves joyfully to work. Those who had been singing, and making melody on different instruments, fell silent and began to listen. Those who had been walking alone in meditation met together in companies to talk. And those who had been far away on errands to the Earth and other planets came homeward like a flight of swallows to the high cliff when the day is over.

It was not that they needed to be restored from weariness, for the inhabitants of that country never say, "I am tired." But there, as here, the law of change is the secret of happiness, and the joy that never ends is woven of mingled strands of labour and repose, society and solitude, music and silence. Sleep comes to them not as it does to us, with a darkening of the vision and a folding of the wings of the spirit, but with an opening of the eyes to deeper and fuller light, and with an effortless outgoing of the soul upon broader currents of life, as the sun-loving bird poises and circles upward, without a wing-beat, on the upholding air.

It was in one of the quiet corners of the green valley called Peacefield, where the little brook of Brighthopes runs smoothly down to join the River of Life, that I saw a company of angels, returned from various labours on Earth, sitting in friendly converse on the hill-side, where cyclamens and arbutus and violets and fringed orchids and pale lady's-tresses, and all the sweet-smelling flowers which are separated in the lower world by the seasons, were thrown together in a harmony of fragrance. There were three of the company who seemed to be leaders, distinguished not only by more radiant and powerful looks, but by a tone of authority in their speech and by the willing attention with which the others listened to them, as they talked of their earthly tasks, of the tangles and troubles, the wars and miseries that they had seen among men, and of the best way to get rid of them and bring sorrow to an end.

"The Earth is full of oppression and unrighteousness," said the tallest and most powerful of the angels. His voice was deep and strong, and by his shining armour and the long two-handed sword hanging over his shoulder I knew that he was the archangel Michael, the mightiest one among the warriors of the King, and the executor of the divine judgments upon the unjust. "The Earth is tormented with injustice," he cried, "and the great misery that I have seen among men is that the evil hand is often stronger than the good hand and can beat it down.

"The arm of the cruel is heavier than the arm of the kind. The unjust get the better of the just and tread on them. I have seen tyrant kings crush their helpless folk. I have seen the fields of the innocent trampled into bloody ruin by the feet of conquering armies. I have seen the wicked nation overcome the peoples that loved liberty, and take away their treasure by force of arms. I have seen poverty mocked by arrogant wealth, and purity deflowered by brute violence, and gentlenes and fair-dealing bruised in the winepress of iniquity and pride.

"There is no cure for this evil, but by the giving of greater force to the good hand. The righteous cause must be strengthened with might to resist the wicked, to defend the helpless, to punish all cruelty and unfairness, to uphold the right everywhere, and to enforce justice with unconquerable arms. Oh, that the host of Heaven might be called, arrayed, and sent to mingle in the wars of men, to make the good victorious, to destroy all evil, and to make the will of the King prevail!

"We would shake down the thrones of tyrants, and loose the bands of the oppressed. We would hold the cruel and violent with the bit of fear, and drive the greedy and fierce-minded men with the whip of terror. We would stand guard, with weapons drawn, about the innocent, the gentle, the kind, and keep the peace of God with the sword of the angels!"

As he spoke, his hands were lifted to the hilt of his long blade, and he raised it above him, straight and shining, throwing sparkles of light around it, like the spray from the sharp prow of a moving ship. Bright flames of heavenly ardour leaped in the eyes of the listening angels; a martial air passed over their faces as if they longed for the call to war.

But no silver trumpet blared from the battlements of the City of God; no crimson flag was unfurled on those high, secret walls; no thrilling drum-beat echoed over the smooth meadow. Only the sound of the brook of Brighthopes was heard tinkling and murmuring among the roots of the grasses and flowers; and far off a cadence of song drifted down from the inner courts of the Palace of the King.

Then another angel began to speak, and made answer to Michael. He, too, was tall and wore the look of power. But it was power of the mind rather than of the hand. His face was clear and glistening, and his eyes were lit with a steady flame which neither leaped nor fell. Of flame also were his garments, which clung about him as the fire enwraps a torch burning where there is no wind; and his great wings, spiring to a point far above his head, were like a living lamp before the altar of the Most High. By this sign I knew that it was the archangel Uriel, the spirit of the Sun, clearest in vision, deepest in wisdom of all the spirits that surround the throne.

"I hold not the same thought," said he, "as the great archangel Michael; nor, though I desire the same end which he desires, would I seek it by the same way. For I know how often power has been given to the good, and how often it has been turned aside and used for evil. I know that the host of Heaven, and the very stars in their courses, have fought on the side of a favoured nation; yet pride has followed triumph and oppression has been the first-born child of victory. I know that the deliverers of the people have become tyrants over those whom they have set free, and the fighters for liberty have been changed into the soldiers of fortune. Power corrupts itself, and might cannot save.

"Does not the Prince Michael remember how the angel of the Lord led the armies of Israel, and gave them the battle against every foe, except the enemy within the camp? And how they robbed and crushed the peoples against whom they had fought for freedom? And how the wickedness of the tribes of Canaan survived their conquest and overcame their conquerors, so that the children of Israel learned to worship the idols of their enemies, Moloch, and Baal, and Ashtoreth?

"Power corrupts itself, and might cannot save. Was not Persia the destroyer of Babylon, and did not the tyranny of Persia cry aloud for destruction? Did not Rome break the yoke of the East, and does not the yoke of Rome lie heavy on the shoulders of the world? Listen!"

There was silence for a moment on the slopes of Peacefield, and then over the encircling hills a cool wind brought the sound of chains clanking in prisons and galleys, the sighing of millions of slaves, the weeping of wretched women and children, the blows of hammers nailing men to their crosses. Then the sound passed by with the wind, and Uriel spoke again:

"Power corrupts itself, and might cannot save. The Earth is full of ignorant strife, and for this evil there is no cure but by the giving of greater knowledge. It is because men do not understand evil that they yield themselves to its power. Wickedness is folly in action, and injustice is the error of the blind. It is because men are ignorant that they destroy one another, and at last themselves.

"If there were more light in the world there would be no sorrow. If the great King who knows all things would enlighten the world with wisdom—wisdom to understand his law and his ways, to read the secrets of the earth and the stars, to discern the workings of the heart of man and the things that make for joy and peace—if he would but send us, his messengers, as a flame of fire to shine upon those who sit in darkness, how gladly would we go to bring in the new day!

"We would speak the word of warning and counsel to the erring, and tell knowledge to the perplexed. We would guide the ignorant in the paths of prudence, and the young would sit at our feet and hear us gladly in the school of life. Then folly would fade away as the morning vapour, and the sun of wisdom would shine on all men, and the peace of God would come with the counsel of the angels."

A murmur of pleasure followed the words of Uriel, and eager looks flashed around the circle of the messengers of light as they heard the praise of wisdom fitly spoken. But there was one among them on whose face a shadow of doubt rested, and though he smiled, it was as if he remembered something that the others had forgotten. He turned to an angel near him.

"Who was it," said he, "to whom you were sent with counsel long ago? Was it not Balaam the son of Beor, as he was riding to meet the King of Moab? And did not even the dumb beast profit more by your instruction than the man who rode him? And who was it," he continued, turning to Uriel, "that was called the wisest of all men, having searched out and understood the many inventions that are found under the sun? Was not Solomon, prince of fools and philosophers, unable by much learning to escape weariness of the flesh and despair of the spirit? Knowledge also is vanity and vexation. This I know well, because I have dwelt among men and held converse with them since the day when I was sent to instruct the first man in Eden."

Then I looked more closely at him who was speaking and recognised the beauty of the archangel Raphael, as it was pictured long ago:

> "A seraph winged; six wings he wore to shade
> His lineaments divine; the pair that clad
> Each shoulder broad came mantling o'er his breast,
> With regal ornament; the middle pair
> Girt like a starry zone his waist, and round
> Skirted his loins and thighs with downy gold
> And colours dipped in Heav'n; the third his feet
> Shadowed from either heel with feathered mail,
> Sky-tinctured grain. Like Maia's son he stood
> And shook his plumes, that Heavenly fragrance filled
> The circuit wide."

"Too well I know," he spoke on, while the smile on his face deepened into a look of pity and tenderness and desire, "too well I know that power corrupts itself and that knowledge cannot save. There is no cure for the evil that is in the world but by the giving of more love to men. The laws that are ordained for earth are strange and unequal, and the ways where men must walk are full of pitfalls and dangers. Pestilence creeps along the ground and flows in the rivers; whirlwind and tempest shake the habitations of men and drive their ships to destruction; fire breaks forth from the mountains and the foundations of the world tremble. Frail is the flesh of man, and many are his pains and troubles. His children can never find peace until they learn to love one another and to help one another.

"Wickedness is begotten by disease and misery. Violence comes from poverty and hunger. The cruelty of oppression is when the strong tread the weak under their feet; the bitterness of pride is when the wise and learned despise the simple; the crown of folly is when the rich think they are gods, and the poor think that God is not.

"Hatred and envy and contempt are the curse of life. And for these there is no remedy save love—the will to give and to bless—the will of the King himself, who gives to all and is loving unto every man. But how shall the hearts of men be won to this will? How shall it enter into them and possess them? Even the gods that men fashion for themselves are cruel and proud and false and unjust. How shall the miracle be wrought in human nature to reveal the meaning of humanity? How shall men be made like God?"

At this question a deep hush fell around the circle, and every listener was still, even as the rustling leaves hang motionless when the light breeze falls away in the hour of sunset. Then through the silence, like the song of a far-away thrush from its hermitage in the forest, a voice came ringing: "I know it, I know it, I know it."

Clear and sweet—clear as a ray of light, sweeter than the smallest silver bell that rang the hour of rest—was that slender voice floating on the odorous and translucent air. Nearer and nearer it came, echoing down the valley, "I know it, I know it, I know it!"

Then from between the rounded hills, among which the brook of Brighthopes is born, appeared a young angel, a little child, with flying hair of gold, and green wreaths twined about his shoulders, and fluttering hands that played upon the air and seemed to lift him so lightly that he had no need of wings. As thistle-down, blown by the wind, dances across the water, so he came along the little stream, singing clear above the murmur of the brook.

All the angels rose and turned to look at him with wondering eyes. Multitudes of others came flying swiftly to the place from which the strange, new song was sounding. Rank within rank, like a garden of living flowers, they stood along the sloping banks of the brook while the child-angel floated into the midst of them, singing:

"I know it, I know it, I know it! Man shall be made like God because the Son of God shall become a man."

At this all the angels looked at one another with amazement, and gathered more closely about the child-angel, as those who hear wonderful news.

"How can this be?" they asked. "How is it possible that the Son of God should be a man?"

"I do not know," said the young angel. "I only know that it is to be."

"But if he becomes a man," said Raphael, "he will be at the mercy of men; the cruel and the wicked will have power upon him; he will suffer."

"I know it," answered the young angel, "and by suffering he will understand the meaning of all sorrow and pain; and he will be able to comfort every one who cries; and his own tears will be for the healing of sad hearts; and those who are healed by him will learn for his sake to be kind to each other."

"But if the Son of God is a true man," said Uriel, "he must first be a child, simple, and lowly, and helpless. It may be that he will never gain the learning of the schools. The masters of earthly wisdom will despise him and speak scorn of him."

"I know it," said the young angel, "but in meekness will he answer them; and to those who become as little children he will give the heavenly wisdom that comes, without seeking, to the pure and gentle of heart."

"But if he becomes a man," said Michael, "evil men will hate and persecute him: they may even take his life, if they are stronger than he."

"I know it," answered the young angel, "they will nail him to a cross. But when he is lifted up, he will draw all men unto him, for he will still be the Son of God, and no heart that is open to love can help loving him, since his love for men is so great that he is willing to die for them."

"But how do you know these things?" cried the other angels. "Who are you?"

"I am the Christmas angel," he said. "At first I was sent as the dream of a little child, a holy child, blessed and wonderful, to dwell in the heart of a pure virgin, Mary of Nazareth. There I was hidden till the word came to call me back to the throne of the King, and tell me my name, and give me my new message. For this is Christmas day on Earth, and to-day the Son of God is born of a woman. So I must fly quickly, before the sun rises, to bring the good news to those happy men who have been chosen to receive them."

As he said this, the young angel rose, with arms outspread, from the green meadow of Peacefield and, passing over the bounds of Heaven, dropped swiftly as a shooting-star toward the night shadow of the Earth. The other angels followed him—a throng of dazzling forms, beautiful as a rain of jewels falling from the dark-blue sky. But the child-angel went more swiftly than the others, because of the certainty of gladness in his heart.

And as the others followed him they wondered who had been favoured and chosen to receive the glad tidings.

"It must be the Emperor of the World and his counsellors," they thought. But the flight passed over Rome.

"It may be the philosophers and the masters of learning," they thought. But the flight passed over Athens.

"Can it be the High Priest of the Jews, and the elders and the scribes?" they thought. But the flight passed over Jerusalem.

It floated out over the hill country of Bethlehem; the throng of silent angels holding close together, as if perplexed and doubtful; the child-angel darting on far in advance, as one who knew the way through the darkness.

The villages were all still: the very houses seemed asleep; but in one place there was a low sound of talking in a stable, near to an inn—a sound as of a mother soothing her baby to rest.

All over the pastures on the hillsides a light film of snow had fallen, delicate as the veil of a bride adorned for the marriage; and as the child-angel passed over them, alone in the swiftness of his flight, the pure fields sparkled round him, giving back his radiance.

And there were in that country shepherds abiding in the fields, keeping watch over their flocks by night. And lo! the angel of the Lord came upon them, and the glory of the Lord shone round about them, and they were sore afraid. And the angel said unto them: "Fear not; for behold I bring you glad tidings of great joy which shall be to all nations. For unto you is born this day, in the city of David, a Saviour, which is Christ the Lord. And this shall be a sign unto you; ye shall find the babe wrapped in swaddling clothes, lying in a manger."

And suddenly there was with the angel a multitude of the heavenly host, praising God and saying: "Glory to God in the highest, and on earth peace, good-will toward men." And the shepherds said one to another: "Let us now go, even to Bethlehem, and see this thing which is come to pass."

So I said within myself that I also would go with the shepherds, even to Bethlehem. And I heard a great and sweet voice, as of a bell, which said, "Come!" And when the bell had sounded twelve times, I awoke; and it was Christmas morn; and I knew that I had been in a dream.

Yet it seemed to me that the things which I had heard were true.

A LITTLE ESSAY
CHRISTMAS-GIVING AND CHRISTMAS-LIVING

I

The custom of exchanging presents on a certain day in the year is very much older than Christmas, and means very much less. It has obtained in almost all ages of the world, and among many different nations. It is a fine thing or a foolish thing, as the case may be; an encouragement to friendliness, or a tribute to fashion; an expression of good nature, or a bid for favour; an outgoing of generosity, or a disguise of greed; a cheerful old custom, or a futile old farce, according to the spirit which animates it and the form which it takes.

But when this ancient and variously interpreted tradition of a day of gifts was transferred to the Christmas season, it was brought into vital contact with an idea which must transform it, and with an example which must lift it up to a higher plane. The example is the life of Jesus. The idea is unselfish interest in the happiness of others.

The great gift of Jesus to the world was himself. He lived with and for men. He kept back nothing. In every particular and personal gift that he made to certain people there was something of himself that made it precious.

For example, at the wedding in Cana of Galilee, it was his thought for the feelings of the giver of the feast, and his wish that every guest should find due entertainment, that lent the flavour of a heavenly hospitality to the wine which he provided.

When he gave bread and fish to the hungry multitude who had followed him out among the hills by the Lake of Gennesaret, the people were refreshed and strengthened by the sense of the personal care of Jesus for their welfare, as much as by the food which he bestowed upon them. It was another illustration of the sweetness of "a dinner of herbs, where love is."

The gifts of healing which he conferred upon many different kinds of sufferers were, in every case, evidences that Jesus was willing to give something of himself, his thought, his sympathy, his vital power, to the men and women among whom he lived. Once, when a paralytic was brought to Jesus on a bed, he surprised everybody, and offended many, by giving the poor wretch the pardon of his sins, before he gave new life to his body. That was just because Jesus thought before he gave; because he desired to satisfy the deepest need; because in fact he gave something of himself in every gift. All true Christmas-giving ought to be after this pattern.

Not that it must all be solemn and serious. For the most part it deals with little wants, little joys, little tokens of friendly feeling. But the feeling must be more than the token; else the gift does not really belong to Christmas.

It takes time and effort and unselfish expenditure of strength to make gifts in this way. But it is the only way that fits the season.

The finest Christmas gift is not the one that costs the most money, but the one that carries the most love.

II

But how seldom Christmas comes—only once a year; and how soon it is over—a night and a day! If that is the whole of it, it seems not much more durable than the little toys that one buys of a fakir on the street-corner. They run for an hour, and then the spring breaks, and the legs come off, and nothing remains but a contribution to the dust heap.

But surely that need not and ought not to be the whole of Christmas—only a single day of generosity, ransomed from the dull servitude of a selfish year,—only a single night of merry-making, celebrated in the slave-quarters of a selfish race! If every gift is the token of a personal thought, a friendly feeling, an unselfish interest in the joy of others, then the thought, the feeling, the interest, may remain after the gift is made.

The little present, or the rare and long-wished-for gift (it matters not whether the vessel be of gold, or silver, or iron, or wood, or clay, or just a small bit of birch bark folded into a cup), may carry a message something like this:

"I am thinking of you to-day, because it is Christmas, and I wish you happiness. And to-morrow, because it will be the day after Christmas, I shall still wish you happiness; and so on, clear through the year. I may not be able to tell you about it every day, because I may be far away; or because both of us may be very busy; or perhaps because I cannot even afford to pay the postage on so many letters, or find the time to write them. But that makes no difference. The thought and the wish will be here just the same. In my work and in the business of life, I mean to try not to be unfair to you or injure you in any way. In my pleasure, if we can be together, I would like to share the fun with you. Whatever joy or success comes to you will make me glad. Without pretense, and in plain words, good-will to you is what I mean, in the Spirit of Christmas."

It is not necessary to put a message like this into high-flown language, to swear absolute devotion and deathless consecration. In love and friendship, small, steady payments on a gold basis are better than immense promissory notes. Nor, indeed, is it always necessary to put the message into words at all, nor even to convey it by a tangible token. To feel it and to act it out—that is the main thing.

There are a great many people in the world whom we know more or less, but to whom for various reasons we cannot very well send a Christmas gift. But there is hardly one, in all the circles of our acquaintance, with whom we may not exchange the touch of Christmas life.

In the outer circles, cheerful greetings, courtesy, consideration; in the inner circles, sympathetic interest, hearty congratulations, honest encouragement; in the inmost circle, comradeship, helpfulness, tenderness,—

"*Beautiful friendship tried by sun and wind
Durable from the daily dust of life.*"

After all, Christmas-living is the best kind of Christmas-giving.

A SHORT CHRISTMAS SERMON
KEEPING CHRISTMAS

ROMANS, xiv, 6: *He that regardeth the day, regardeth it unto the Lord.*

It is a good thing to observe Christmas day. The mere marking of times and seasons, when men agree to stop work and make merry together, is a wise and wholesome custom. It helps one to feel the supremacy of the common life over the individual life. It reminds a man to set his own little watch, now and then, by the great clock of humanity which runs on sun time.

But there is a better thing than the observance of Christmas day, and that is, keeping Christmas.

Are you willing to forget what you have done for other people, and to remember what other people have done for you; to ignore what the world owes you, and to think what you owe the world; to put your rights in the background, and your duties in the middle distance, and your chances to do a little more than your duty in the foreground; to see that your fellow-men are just as real as you are, and try to look behind their faces to their hearts, hungry for joy; to own that probably the only good reason for your existence is not what you are going to get out of life, but what you are going to give to life; to close your book of complaints against the management of the universe, and look around you for a place where you can sow a few seeds of happiness—are you willing to do these things even for a day? Then you can keep Christmas.

Are you willing to stoop down and consider the needs and the desires of little children; to remember the weakness and loneliness of people who are growing old; to stop asking how much your friends love you, and ask yourself whether you love them enough; to bear in mind the things that other people have to bear on their hearts; to try to understand what those who live in the same house with you really want, without waiting for them to tell you; to trim your lamp so that it will give more light and less smoke, and to carry it in front so that your shadow will fall behind you; to make a grave for your ugly thoughts, and a garden for your kindly feelings, with the gate open—are you willing to do these things even for a day? Then you can keep Christmas.

Are you willing to believe that love is the strongest thing in the world—stronger than hate, stronger than evil, stronger than death—and that the blessed life which began in Bethlehem nineteen hundred years ago is the image and brightness of the Eternal Love? Then you can keep Christmas.

And if you keep it for a day, why not always?

But you can never keep it alone.

TWO CHRISTMAS PRAYERS

A CHRISTMAS PRAYER FOR THE HOME

Father of all men, look upon our family,
Kneeling together before Thee,
And grant us a true Christmas.
With loving heart we bless Thee:
For the gift of Thy dear Son Jesus Christ,
For the peace He brings to human homes,
For the good-will He teaches to sinful men,
For the glory of Thy goodness shining in His face.

With joyful voice we praise Thee:
For His lowly birth and His rest in the manger,
For the pure tenderness of His mother Mary,
For the fatherly care that protected Him,
For the Providence that saved the Holy Child
To be the Saviour of the world.
With deep desire we beseech Thee:
Help us to keep His birthday truly,
Help us to offer, in His name, our Christmas prayer.
From the sickness of sin and the darkness of doubt,
From selfish pleasures and sullen pains,
From the frost of pride and the fever of envy,
God save us every one, through the blessing of Jesus.
In the health of purity and the calm of mutual trust,
In the sharing of joy and the bearing of trouble,
In the steady glow of love and the clear light of hope,
God keep us every one, by the blessing of Jesus.
In praying and praising, in giving and receiving,
In eating and drinking, in singing and making merry,
In parents' gladness and in children's mirth,
In dear memories of those who have departed,
In good comradeship with those who are here,
In kind wishes for those who are far away,
In patient waiting, sweet contentment, generous cheer,
God bless us every one, with the blessing of Jesus.
By remembering our kinship with all men,
By well-wishing, friendly speaking and kindly doing,
By cheering the downcast and adding sunshine to daylight,
By welcoming strangers (poor shepherds or wise men),
By keeping the music of the angels' song in this home,
God help us every one to share the blessing of Jesus:

In whose name we keep Christmas:
And in whose words we pray together:
Our Father which art in heaven, hallowed be Thy name.
Thy kingdom come. Thy will be done in earth, as it is in heaven.
Give us this day our daily bread. And forgive us our debts, as we forgive our debtors.
And lead us not into temptation, but deliver us from evil:
For Thine is the kingdom, and the power, and the glory, forever. Amen.

A CHRISTMAS PRAYER FOR LONELY FOLKS

Lord God of the solitary,
Look upon me in my loneliness.
Since I may not keep this Christmas in the home,
Send it into my heart.
Let not my sins cloud me in,
But shine through them with forgiveness in the face of the child Jesus.
Put me in loving remembrance of the lowly lodging in the stable of Bethlehem,
The sorrows of the blessed Mary, the poverty and exile of the Prince of Peace.

For His sake, give me a cheerful courage to endure my lot,
And an inward comfort to sweeten it.
Purge my heart from hard and bitter thoughts.
Let no shadow of forgetting come between me and friends far away:
Bless them in their Christmas mirth:
Hedge me in with faithfulness,
That I may not grow unworthy to meet them again.
Give me good work to do,
That I may forget myself and find peace in doing it for Thee.
Though I am poor, send me to carry some gift to those who are poorer,
Some cheer to those who are more lonely.
Grant me the joy to do a kindness to one of Thy little ones:
Light my Christmas candle at the gladness of an innocent and grateful heart.
Strange is the path where Thou leadest me:
Let me not doubt Thy wisdom, nor lose Thy hand.
Make me sure that Eternal Love is revealed in Jesus, Thy dear Son,
To save us from sin and solitude and death.
Teach me that I am not alone,
But that many hearts, all round the world,
Join with me through the silence, while I pray in His name:

Our Father which art in heaven, hallowed be Thy name.
Thy kingdom come. Thy will be done in earth, as it is in heaven.
Give us this day our daily bread. And forgive us our debts, as we forgive our debtors.
And lead us not into temptation, but deliver us from evil:
For Thine is the kingdom, and the power, and the glory, forever. Amen.

Fighting For Peace
FOREWORD

This brief series of chapters is not a tale
 "Of moving accidents by flood and field,
  Of hair-breadth 'scapes i' the imminent deadly breach."
Some dangers I have passed through during the last three years, but nothing to speak of.

Nor is it a romance in the style of those thrilling novels of secret diplomacy which I peruse with wonder and delight in hours of relaxation, chiefly because they move about in worlds regarding which I have no experience and little faith.

There is nothing secret or mysterious about the American diplomatic service, so far as I have known it. Of course there are times when, like every other honestly and properly conducted affair, it does not seek publicity in the newspapers. That, I should suppose, must always be a fundamental condition of frank and free conversation between governments as between gentlemen. There is a certain kind of reserve which is essential to candor.

But American diplomacy has no picturesque meetings at midnight in the gloom of lonely forests; no confabulations in black cellars with bands of hireling desperadoes waiting to carry out its decrees; no disguises, no masks, no dark lanterns—nothing half so exciting and melodramatic. On the contrary, it is amazingly plain and straightforward, with plenty of hard work, but always open and aboveboard. That is the rule for the diplomatic service of the United States.

Its chief and constant aims are known to all men. First, to maintain American principles and interests, and to get a fair showing for them in the world. Second, to preserve and advance friendly relations and intercourse with the particular nation to which the diplomat is sent. Third, to promote a just and firm and free peace throughout the world, so that democracy everywhere may live without fear.

It was the last of these three aims that acted as the main motive in my acceptance of President Wilson's invitation to go out as American Minister to the Netherlands and Luxembourg in the summer of 1913. It was pleasant, of course, to return for a while to the land from which my ancestors came so long ago. It seemed also that some useful and interesting work might be done to forward the common interests and ideals of the United States and the Netherlands—that brave, liberty-loving nation from which our country learned and received so much in its beginnings—and in particular that there might be opportunity for co-operation in the Far East, where the Dutch East Indies and the Philippines are next-door neighbors. But the chief thing that drew me to Holland was the desire to promote the great work of peace which had been begun by the International Peace Conferences at The Hague. This indeed was what the President especially charged me to do.

Two conferences had already been held and had accomplished much. But their work was incomplete. It lacked firm attachments and sanctions. It was left to a certain extent "hanging in the air." It needed just those things which the American delegates to the Conference of 1907 had advocated—the establishment of a Permanent Court of Arbitral Justice; an International Prize Court; an agreement for the protection of private property at sea in time of war; the further study and discussion of the question of the reduction of armaments by the nations; and so on. Most of these were the things of which Germany had hitherto prevented the attainment. A third International Peace Conference was necessary to secure and carry on the work of the first two. The President told me to do all that I properly could to forward the assembling of that conference in the Palace of Peace at the earliest possible date.

So I went to Holland as an envoy of the world-peace founded on justice which is America's great desire. For that cause I worked and strove. Of that cause I am still a devoted follower and servant. I am working for it now, but with a difference. It is evident that we cannot maintain that cause, as the world stands to-day, without fighting for it. And after it is won, it will need protection. It must be Peace with Righteousness and Power.

The following chapters narrate some of the experiences—things seen and heard and studied during my years of service abroad—which have forced me to this conclusion. To the articles which were published in Scribner's Magazine for September, October, and November, 1917, I have added two short chapters on the cause of the war and the kind of peace America is fighting for.

The third peace conference is more needed, more desirable, than ever. But we shall never get it until the military forces of Germany are broken, and the predatory Potsdam gang which rules them is brought low.

Chapter I
FAIR-WEATHER AND STORM SIGNS
I

It takes a New England farmer to note and interpret the signs of coming storm on a beautiful and sunny day. Perhaps his power is due in part to natural sharpness, and in part to the innate pessimism of the Yankee mind, which considers the fact that the hay is cut but not yet in the barn a sufficient reason for believing that "it'll prob'ly rain t'morrow."

I must confess that I had not enough of either of these qualities to be observant and fearful of the presages of the oncoming tempest which lurked in the beautiful autumn and winter of 1913-14 in Europe. Looking back at them now, I can see that the signs were ominous. But anybody can be wise after the event, and the role of a reminiscent prophet is too easy to be worth playing.

Certainly all was bright and tranquil when we rolled through the pleasant land of France and the rich cities of Belgium, and came by ship-thronged Rotterdam to The Hague in the first week of October, 1913. Holland was at her autumnal best. Wide pastures wonderfully green were full of drowsy, contented cattle. The level brown fields and gardens were smoothly ploughed and harrowed for next year's harvest, and the vast tulip-beds were ready to receive the little gray bulbs which would overflow April with a flood-tide of flowers. On the broad canals innumerable barges and sloops and motor-boats were leisurely passing, and on the little side-canals and ditches which drained the fields the duckweed spread its pale-emerald carpet undisturbed. In the woods—the tall woods of Holland—the elms and the lindens were putting on frosted gold, and the massy beeches glowed with ruddy bronze in the sunlight. The quaint towns and villages looked at themselves in the waters at their feet and were content. Slowly the long arms of the windmills turned in the suave and shimmering air. Everybody, in city and country, seemed to be busy without haste. And overhead, the luminous cloud mountains—the poor man's Alps—marched placidly with the wind from horizon to horizon.

The Hague—that "largest village in Europe," that city of three hundred thousand inhabitants set in the midst of a park, that seat of government which does not dare to call itself the capital because Amsterdam is jealous—was in especially good form and humor, looking forward to a winter of unhurried gayety and feasting such as the Hollanders love. The new Palace of Peace, given by Mr. Andrew Carnegie for the use of the Permanent Court of Arbitration and its auxiliary bodies, had been opened with much ceremony in September. Situated before the entrance of that long, tree-embowered avenue which is called the Old Scheveningen Road, the edifice has an imposing exterior although a mixture of architects in the process of building has given it something the look of a glorified railway station. But the interior is altogether dignified and splendid, more palatial, in fact, than any of the royal residences. It is lined with costly marbles, rare Eastern woods, wonderful Japanese tapestries, and adorned with gifts from all the nations, except the United States, which had promised to give a marble statue representing "Peace through Justice," to be placed on the central landing of the great Stairway of Honor, the most conspicuous position in the whole building. The promise had been standing for some years, but not the statue. One of my first minor tasks at The Hague was to see to it that active steps were taken at Washington to fulfil this promise, and to fill this empty place which waits for the American sculpture.

Meantime the rich collection of books on international law was being arranged and classified in the library under the learned direction of M. Alberic Rolin. The late roses were blooming abundantly in the broad gardens of the palace. Thousands of visitors were coming every day to see this new wonder of the world, the royal house of "Vrede door Recht."

Queen Wilhelmina was still at her country palace, Het Loo, in Gelderland. It was about the middle of October that I was invited there to lunch and to have my first audience with Her Majesty, and to present my letter of credence as American Minister.

The journey of three or four hours was made in company with the Dutch Minister of Foreign Affairs, Jonkheer Loudon, who represented the Netherlands at Washington for several years and is an intelligent and warm friend of the United States, and the Japanese Minister, Mr. Aimaro Sato, a very agreeable gentleman (and, by the way, an ardent angler), who now represents Japan at Washington. He talked a little, and with great good sense and feeling, of the desirability of a better understanding and closer relations between the United States and Japan. I liked what he said and the way he said it. But most of our conversation on that pleasant journey, it must be confessed, was personal and anecdotic—fish-stories not excluded.

The ceremony of presenting the letter of credence, which I had rather dreaded, was in fact quite simple and easy. I handed to Her Majesty the commendatory epistle of the President (beginning, as usual, "Great and good friend") and made a short speech in English, according to the regulations. The Queen, accepting the letter, made a brief friendly reply in French, which is the language of the court, and passed at once into an informal conversation in English. She speaks both languages fluently and well. Her first inquiry, according to royal custom, was about family matters; the number of the children; the health of the household; the finding of a comfortable house to live in at The Hague, and so on. There is something very homely and human in the good manners of a real court. Then the Queen asked about the Dutch immigrants in America, especially in recent times—were they good citizens? I answered that we counted them among the best, especially strong in agriculture and in furniture-making, where I had seen many of them in the famous shops of Grand Rapids, Michigan. The Queen smiled, and said that the Netherlands, being a small country, did not want to lose too many of her good people.

The impression left upon me by this first interview, and deepened by all that followed, was that Queen Wilhelmina is a woman admirably fit for her task. Her natural shyness of temperament is sometimes misinterpreted as a haughty reserve. But that is not correct. She is, in fact, most sincere and straightforward, devoted to her duty and very intelligent in doing it, one of the ablest and sanest crowned heads in Europe, an altogether good ruler for the very democratic country of the Netherlands.

We settled down in the home which I had rented at The Hague. It was a big, dignified house on the principal street, the Lange Voorhout, which is almost like a park, with four rows of trees down the middle. Our house had once been the palace of the Duchess of Saxe-Weimar, a princess of the Orange-Nassau family. But it was not at all showy, only comfortable and large. This was fortunate for our country when the rush of fugitive American tourists came at the beginning of the war, for every room on the first floor, and the biggest room on the second floor, were crowded with the work that we had to do for them.

But during the first winter everything went smoothly; there was no hurry and no crowding. The Queen came back to her town palace. The rounds of ceremonial visits were ground out. The Hague people and our diplomatic colleagues were most cordial and friendly. There were dinners and dances and court receptions and fancy-dress balls—all of a discreet and moderate joyousness which New York and Newport, perhaps even Chicago and Hot Springs, would have called tame and rustic. The weather, for the first time in several years, was clear, cold, and full of sunshine. The canals were frozen. Everybody, from grandparents to grandchildren, including the Crown Princess Juliana, went on skates, which greatly added to the gayety of the nation.

At the same time there was plenty of work to do. The affairs of the legation had to be straightened out; the sending of despatches and the carrying out of instructions speeded up; the arrangements for a proposed international congress on education in the autumn of 1914, forwarded; the Bryan treaty for a year of investigation before the beginning of hostilities—the so-called "Stop-Look-Listen" treaty—modified and helped through; and the thousand and one minor, unforeseen jobs that fall on a diplomatic chief carefully attended to.

II

Through all this time the barometer stood at "Set Fair." The new Dutch Ministry, which Mr. Cort van der Linden, a wise and eloquent philosophic liberal, had formed on the mandate of the Queen, seemed to have the confidence of the Parliament. Although it had no pledged majority of any party or bloc behind it, the announcement of its simple programme of "carrying out the wishes of the majority of the voters as expressed in the last election," met with approval on every side. The "Anti-Revolutionary" lion lay down with the "Christian-Historical" lamb; the "Liberal" bear and the "Clerical" cow fed together; and the sucking "Social-Democrat" laid his hand on the "Reactionary" adder's den. It was idyllic. Real progress looked nearly possible.

The international sky was clear except for the one big cloud, which had been there so long that the world had grown used to it. The Great Powers kept up the mad race of armaments, purchasing mutual terror at the price of billions of dollars every year.

Now the pace was quickened, but the race remained the same, with Germany still in the lead. Her new army bill of 1912 provided for a peace strength of 870,000 men, and a war strength of 5,400,000 men. Russia followed with a bill raising the term of military service from three to three and a half years; France with a bill raising the term of service from two to three years (but this was not until in June, 1913). Great Britain, with voluntary service, still had a comparatively small army: in size "contemptible," as Kaiser Wilhelm called it later, but in morale and spirit unsurpassed. Evidently the military force of Germany, which lay like a glittering sword in her ruler's hand, was larger, better organized and equipped, than any other in the world.

But might it not still be used as a make-weight in the scales of negotiation rather than as a weapon of actual offense? Might not the Kaiser still be pleased with his dramatic role of "the war-lord who kept the peace"? Might he not do again as he did successfully in 1909, when Austria violated the provisions of the Congress of Berlin (1878) by annexing Bosnia and Herzegovina, and Germany protected the theft; and with partial success at Algeciras in 1906, and after the Agadir incident in 1911, when Germany gained something she wanted though less than she claimed? Might he not still be content with showing and shaking the sword, without fleshing it in the body of Europe? It seemed wiser, because safer for Germany, that the Kaiser should follow that line. The methodical madness of a forced war looked incredible.

Thus all of us who were interested in the continuance and solidification of the work of the peace conferences at The Hague reasoned ourselves into a peaceful hope. We knew that no other power except Germany was really prepared for war. We knew that the effort to draw Great Britain into an offensive and defensive alliance with Germany had failed, although London was willing to promise help to Berlin if attacked. We remembered Bismarck's warning that a war against Russia and Great Britain at the same time would be fatal, and we trusted that it had not been forgotten in Berlin. We knew that Germany, under her policy of industrial development and pacific penetration, was prospering more than ever, and we thought she might enjoy that enough to continue it. We hoped that a third peace conference would be assembled before a general conflict of arms could be launched, and that some things might be done there which would make wilful and aggressive war vastly more dangerous and difficult, if not impossible. So we were at ease in Zion and worked in the way which seemed most promising for the peace of the world.

But that way was not included in the German plan. It was remote from the Berlin-Baghdad-Bahn. It did not lead toward a dominant imperial state of Mittel-Europa, with tentacles reaching out to ports on every sea and strait. The plan for another Hague conference failed to interest the ruling clique at Berlin and Potsdam because they had made "other arrangements."

Very gradually slight indications of this fact began to appear, though they were not clearly understood at the time. It was like watching a stage-curtain which rises very slowly a little way and then stops. Through the crack one could see feet moving about and hear rumbling noises. Evidently a drama was in preparation. But what it was to be could hardly be guessed. Then, after a long wait, the curtain rose swiftly. The tragedy was revealed. Flames burst forth from the stage and wrapped the whole house in fire. Some of the spectators were the first victims. The conflagration still rages. It will not be put out until the flame-lust is smothered in the hearts of those who kindled and spread the great fire in Europe.

III

I must get back from this expression of my present feelings and views to the plain story of the experiences which gradually made me aware of the actual condition of affairs in Europe and the great obstacle to a durable peace in the world.

The first thing that disquieted me a little was the strange difficulty encountered in making the preliminary arrangements for the third peace conference. The final resolution of the second conference in 1907, unanimously recommended, first, that the next conference, should be held within a period of eight years, and second, that a preparatory committee should be appointed two years beforehand, to consider the subjects which were ripe for discussion, and to draw up a programme which could be examined in advance by the countries interested. That, of course, was necessary. No sensible government will go into a conference blindfold, without knowing what is to be talked about.

But in 1914, when the matter came into my hands, the lapse of time and the negligence of the nations (the United States included) had made it too late to fulfil both of these recommendations. If one was carried out the other must be modified or disregarded. The then Secretary of State, Mr. Bryan, instructed me to endeavor to have the conference called in 1915, that is, within the period of eight years. After careful investigation and earnest effort, I reported that it could not be done at that date. The first thing was to get the preparatory committee, which would require at least two years for its formation and work. Toward this point, then, with the approval of the President, I steered and rowed hard, receiving the warmest sympathy and most effective co-operation from Jonkheer Loudon, the Netherlands Minister of Foreign Affairs. Indeed the entire Dutch Government, with the Queen at the head, were favorable. Holland naturally likes to have the peace conferences at The Hague. They add to the dignity of the country. The honor is well-deserved, for Holland may fairly be called the fountainhead of modern international law, and has produced many of its best expounders, from Grotius and Bynkershoek to Asser. Moreover, as a side consideration, these meetings bring a multitude of visitors to the country, some famous and many profitable, and this is not bad for business. So the movement is generally popular.

My own particular suggestion toward getting the required "preparatory committee" seemed to its author to have the double advantage of practical speed and representative quality. It was to make use, at least for the first steps, of a body already in existence and in which all the nations were represented. But there is no need of describing it, because it did not go through. I was not so much stuck upon it that any other fair and speedy plan would not have received my hearty backing.

But the trouble was that, push as hard as we would, there was no plan that would move beyond a certain point. There it stood still. Washington and The Hague were earnest and enthusiastic. St. Petersburg was warmly interested, but showed a strong preference for its own plan, and a sense of its right to a leading place as the proposer of the first conference. London and Paris seemed favorable to the general idea, and took an expectant attitude toward any proposal of organization that would be on the level and fair for everybody. Berlin was singularly reserved and vague. It said little or nothing. It did not seem to care about the matter.

I talked informally with my German friends at The Hague. They were polite and attentive. They may have had a real interest in the subject, but it was not shown so that you could notice it. They expressed opinions on the value of peace conferences in general which I am not at liberty to repeat. The idea of a third conference at The Hague may have seemed beautiful to them, but it looked as if they felt that it was lacking in actuality. Possibly I did not understand them. That was just the trouble—I could not. It was all puzzling, baffling, mysterious.

It seemed as if all our efforts to forward the calling of the next conference in the interest of permanent peace brought up dead against an invisible barrier, an impassable wall like the secret line drawn in the air by magic, thinner than a cobweb, more impenetrable than steel. What was it? Indifference? General scepticism? Preoccupation with other designs which made the discussion of peace plans premature and futile? I did not know. But certainly there was something in the way, and the undiscovered nature of that something was food for thought.

The next jolt that was given to my comfortable hope that the fair weather in Europe was likely to last for some time was a very slight incident that happened in the Grand Duchy of Luxembourg, to which small sovereign state I was also accredited as American Minister.

The existence and status of Luxembourg in Europe before the war are not universally understood in America, and it may be useful to say a few words about it. The grand duchy is a tiny independent country, about 1,000 square miles of lovely hills and dales and table-lands, clothed with noble woods, watered by clear streams, and inhabited by about 250,000 people of undoubted German-Keltic stock and of equally undoubted French sympathies. The land lies in the form of a northward-pointing triangle between Germany, Belgium, and France. The sovereign is the Grand Duchess Marie Adelheid (of Nassau), a beautiful, sincere, high-spirited girl who succeeded to the crown on her father's death. The political leader for twenty-five years was the Minister-President Paul Eyschen, an astute statesman and a devoted patriot, who nursed his little country in his arms like a baby and brought it to a high degree of prosperity and contentment.

Like Belgium, Luxembourg was a neutralized country—the former by the Treaty of 1831; the latter by the Treaty of 1867; both treaties were signed and guaranteed by the Great Powers. But there was a distinct difference between the two neutralities. That of Belgium was an armed neutrality; her forts and her military forces were left to her. That of Luxembourg was a disarmed neutrality; her only fortress was dismantled and razed to the ground, and her army was reduced and limited to one company of gendarmes and one company of infantry. Thus Belgium had the right, the duty, and the power to resist if her territory were violated by the armed forces of a belligerent. But Luxembourg was made powerless to resist; she could only protest.

Remember this when you consider the fates which fell on the two countries. Remember how the proud and independent little duchy must have felt beforehand, standing without a weapon amid the mighty armed powers of Europe.

It was in February or early in March, 1914, that the Grand Duchess sent out an invitation to the Diplomatic Corps to attend a court function. We all went gladly because of the pleasantness of the land and the good hospitality of the palace. There were separate audiences with Her Royal Highness in the morning, a big luncheon given by the Cabinet and the city authorities at noon, a state dinner in the old Spanish palace at night, and after that a gala concert. It was then that the incident occurred. I had heard in the town that thirty military officers from the German garrison at Trier, a few miles away on the border, were coming, invited or self-invited, to the concert, and the Luxembourgers did not like the idea at all. Well, the Germans came in a body, some of them courteous and affable, the others stiff, wooden, high-chinned, and staring—distinctly a foreign group. They were tactless enough to propose staying over the next day. A big crowd of excited Luxembourgers filled the streets in the morning and gave every sign of extreme dissatisfaction. "What were these Prussian soldiers doing there? Had they come to spy out the land and the city in preparation for an invasion? Was there a stray prince or duke among them who wanted to marry the Grand Duchess? The music was over. These Kriegs-Herren had better go home at once—at once, did they understand?" Yes, they understood, and they went by the next train, which took them to Trier in an hour.

It was a very trivial affair. But it seemed to throw some light on the mentality of the German army. It also made me reflect upon the state of mind of this little unarmed country living next door to the big military machine and directly on the open way to France. Yet we all laughed and joked about the incident on the way back to Holland in the train. Only the French, German, Italian, and Belgian Ministers were not with us, for these countries have separate missions in Luxembourg.

At The Hague everything pursued its tranquil course as usual. Golf set in. The tulips bloomed in a sea of splendor. I strove at the footless task of promoting the third peace conference. It was not until the season of Pentecost, 1914, that I went to Luxembourg again, intending to gather material for a report on the flourishing steel industry there, which had developed some new processes, and to get a little trout-fishing on the side. During that pleasant journey two things happened which opened my eyes.

The first was at a luncheon which Prime Minister Eyschen gave me. It was a friendly foursome: our genial host; the German Minister, Von B.; the French Minister, M.; and myself. Mr. Eyschen's wine-cellar was famous, and his old Luxembourg cook was a wonder; she served a repast which made us linger at table for three hours. The conversation rambled everywhere, and there were no chains or padlocks on it. It was in French, English, and German, but mostly in French. One remark has stuck in my memory ever since. Mr. Eyschen said to me: "You have heard of the famous 'Luxembourger Loch'? It is the easiest military road between Germany and France." Then he continued with great good humor to the two gentlemen at the ends of the table: "Perhaps one of your two countries may march an army through it before long, and we certainly cannot stop you." Then he turned to Herr von B., still smiling: "Most likely it will be your country, Excellenz! But please remember, for the last ten years we have made our mining concessions and contracts so that they will hold, whatever happens. And we have spent the greatest part of our national income on our roads. You can't roll them up and carry them off in your pocket!" Of course we all laughed. But it was serious. Two months later the French Minister had to make a quick and quiet flight along one of those very roads.

A couple of days after the luncheon, at the beginning of June, I saw a curious confirmation of Eyschen's hint. Having gone just over the German border for a bit of angling, I was following a very lovely little river full of trout and grayling. With me were two or three Luxembourgers and as many Germans, to whom fishing with the fly—fine and far off—was a new and curious sight. Along the east bank of the stream ran one of the strategic railways of Germany, from Koln to Trier. All day long innumerable trains rolled southward along that line, and every train was packed with soldiers in field-gray—their cheerful, stolid bullet-heads stuck out of all the windows. "Why so many soldiers," I asked, "and where are they all going?" "Ach!" replied my German companions, "it is Pfingstferien (Pentecost vacation), and they are sent a changing of scene and air to get." My Luxembourg friends laughed. "Yes, yes," they said. "That is it. Trier has a splendid climate for soldiers. The situation is kolossal for that!"

When we passed through the hot and dusty little city it was simply swarming with the field-gray ones—thousands upon thousands of them—new barracks everywhere; parks of artillery; mountains of munitions and military stores. It was a veritable base of operation, ready for war.

Now the point is that Trier is just seven miles from Wasserbillig on the Luxembourg frontier, the place where the armed German forces entered the neutral land on August 2, 1914.

The government and the "grande armee" of the Grand Duchess protested. But—well, did you ever see a wren resist an eagle? The motor-van (not the private car of Her Royal Highness, as rumor has said, but just an ordinary panier-a-salade), which was drawn up across the road to the capital, was rolled into the ditch. The mighty host of invaders, having long been ready, marched triumphantly into the dismantled fortress, and along their smooth, unlawful way to France. I had caught, in June, angling along the little river, a passing glimpse of the preparation for that march.

But what about things on the French side of the border in that same week of June, 1914? Well, I can only tell what I saw. Returning to Holland by way of Paris, I saw no soldiers in the trains, only a few scattered members of the local garrisons at the railway stations, not a man in arms within ten kilometres of the frontier. It seemed as if France slept quietly at the southern edge of Luxembourg, believing that the solemn treaty, which had made Germany respect the neutrality of that little land even in the war of 1870, still held good to safeguard her from a treacherous attack in the rear, through a peaceful neighbor's garden. Longwy—the poor, old-fashioned fortress in the northeast corner of France—had hardly enough guns for a big rabbit-shoot, and hardly enough garrison to man the guns. The conquering Crown Prince afterward took it almost as easily as a boy steals an apple from an unprotected orchard. It was the first star in his diadem of glory. But Verdun, though near by, was not the second.

From this little journey I went home to The Hague with the clear conviction that one nation in Europe was ready for war, and wanted war, and intended war on the first convenient opportunity. But when would that be? Not even the most truculent government could well venture a bald declaration of hostilities without some plausible pretext, some ostensible ground of quarrel. Where was it? There was none in sight. Of course the danger of a homicidal crisis in the insanity of armaments was always there. And of course the ambition of Germany for "a place in the sun" was as coldly fierce as ever. The Pan-Germanists were impatient. But they could hardly proclaim war without saying what place and whose place they wanted. Nor was there any particular grievance on which they could stand as a colorable ground of armed conflict. The Kaiser had prepared for war, no doubt. The argument and justification of war as the means of spreading the German Kultur were in the Potsdam mind. But the concrete and definite occasion of war was lacking. How long would that lack hold off the storm? Could the precarious peace be maintained until measures to enforce and protect it by common consent could be taken?

These questions were answered with dreadful suddenness. The curtain which had half-concealed the scene went up with a rush, and the missing occasion of war was revealed in the flash of a pistol.

IV

On June 28, 1914, the Archduke Franz Ferdinand, heir apparent to the Austro-Hungarian crowns, and his wife, the Duchess of Hohenburg, were shot to death in the street at Serajevo, the capital of the annexed provinces of Bosnia and Herzegovina, to which they were paying a visit of ceremony. The news of this murder filled all thoughtful people in Europe with horror and dismay. It was a dark and sinister crime. The Crown Prince and his wife had not been "personae gratae" with the Viennese court, but the brutal manner of their taking off aroused the anger of the people. Vengeance was called for. The two wretched murderers were Austrian subjects, but they were Servian sympathizers, and in some kind of connection with a society called Narodna Obrana, whose avowed object was to work for a "Greater Servia," including the southern Slavic provinces of Austria. The Government of Austria-Hungary, having conducted a secret inquiry, declared that it had proofs that the instructions and the weapons for the crime came from Servia. On the other hand, it has not been denied that the Servian Minister at Vienna had conveyed a warning to the Government there, a week before the ceremonial visit to Serajevo, to the effect that it would be wise to give the visit up, as there were grounds for believing that an assassination had been planned. We knew little or nothing of all this at the time, in The Hague. Anxiously we waited for light under the black cloud. It came like lightning in the Austro-Hungarian note to Servia of July 23, 1914.

It was made public the next day. I remember coming home that evening from a motor-drive through the dead cities of the Zuyder Zee. Taking up the newspaper in the quiet library, I read the note. The paper dropped from my hand, and I said to my son: "That means an immense war. God knows how far it will go and how long it will last."

This Austrian ultimatum was so severe in matter and in manner as to justify the comment of Sir Edward Grey: "Never have I seen one state address to another independent state a document of so formidable a character." It not only dictated a public confession of guilt; it also made a series of ten sweeping demands on Servia, one of which (No. 5) seemed to imply a surrender of independent sovereignty; and it allowed only forty-eight hours for an unqualified, complete acceptance.

Russia promptly declared that she would not object to the punishment of Servians for any proved offense, but that she must defend the territorial integrity and independence of Servia. Italy and France suggested an extension of time for the answer. France and Russia advised Servia to make a general acceptance of the ultimatum. She did so in her reply of the 25th, reserving demand No. 5, which she said she did not understand, and offering to submit that point, or the whole matter, to the tribunal at The Hague. Austria had instructed her minister at Belgrade to reject anything but a categorical submission to the ultimatum. When the Servian reply was handed to him he said that it was not good enough, demanded his passports, and left the capital within half an hour. Germany, vowing that she had no knowledge of the text of the Austrian note before it was presented and had not influenced its contents (which seems incredible, as I shall show later), nevertheless announced that she approved and would support it.

Verily this was "miching mallecho," as Hamlet says. It meant mischief. Austria was inflexible in her purpose to make war on Servia. Russia's warning that in such a case she could not stand aside and see a small kindred nation subjugated, and her appeals for arbitration or four-power mediation, which Great Britain, France, and Italy supported, were disregarded. Behind Austria stood Germany, proud, menacing, armed to the teeth, ready for attack, supporting if not instigating the relentless Austrian purpose. Something vast and very evil was impending over the world.

That was our conviction at The Hague in the fateful week from July 24 to August 1, 1914. We who stood outside the secret councils of the Central Powers were both bewildered and dismayed. Could it be that Europe of the twentieth century was to be thrust back into the ancient barbarism of a general war? It was like a dreadful nightmare. There was the head of the huge dragon, crested, fanged, clad in glittering scales, poised above the world and ready to strike. We were benumbed and terrified. There was nothing that we could do. The monstrous thing advanced, but even while we shuddered we could not make ourselves feel that it was real. It had the vagueness and the horrid pressure of a bad dream.

If it seemed dreamlike to us, so near at hand, how could the people in America, three thousand miles away, feel its reality or grasp its meaning? They could not do it then, and many of them have not done it yet.

But we who were on the other side of the sea were suddenly and rudely awakened to know that the bad dream was all too real. On July 28 Austria declared war on Servia. On the 29th Russia ordered a partial mobilization of troops on the Austrian frontier. On the same night the Austrian troops entered Servia and bombarded Belgrade. On the 31st Austria and Russia ordered a general mobilization.

Then Germany, already coiled, struck.

On August 1 Germany declared war on Russia. On the 2d Germany invaded Luxembourg and France. On the 3d Germany declared war on France. On the 4th Germany invaded Belgium, in violation of her solemn treaty. On the 5th Great Britain, having given warning to the Kaiser that she meant to keep her promise to protect the neutrality of Belgium, severed diplomatic relations, and on the 6th Parliament, by a vote of extraordinary supply, formally accepted a state of war with Germany, the invader.

So the storm signs, foreshadowed in fair weather, were fulfilled in tempest, more vast and cruel than the world had ever known.

The Barabbas of war was preferred to the Christ of righteous judgment.

The hope of an enduring peace through justice receded and grew dim. We knew that it could not be rekindled until the ruthless military power of Germany, that had denied and rejected it, was defeated and brought to repentance.

Thus those who loved true peace—peace with equal security for small and great nations, peace with law protecting the liberties of the people, peace with power to defend itself against assault—were forced to fight for it or give it up forever.

Chapter II
APOLOGUE

The man who was also a Werwolf sat in his arbor, drinking excellent beer.

He was not an ill-looking man. His fondness for an out-of-door life had given him a ruddy color. He was tall and blond. His eyes were gray. But there was a shifty look in them, now dreamy, now fierce. At times they contracted to mere slits. His chin sloped away to nothing. His legs were long and thin, his movements springy and uncertain.

The philosopher who came to pay his respects to the man who was also a
Werwolf (whom we shall henceforth call MWAW for short) was named
Professor Schmuck. He was a globular man, with protruding china-blue
eyes, much magnified by immense spectacles. The fame of his book on
"Eschatological Problems among the Hivites and Hittites" was world-wide.
But his real specialty was universal knowledge.

Yet on entering the arbor where MWAW was sitting, this world-renowned Learned One made three deep obeisances, as if he were approaching an idol, and stammered in a husky voice: "Highly Exalted!—dare I—?"

"Ah, our good Schmuck!" said MWAW, turning in his chair and recrossing his legs. "Come in. Take place. Take beer. Take breath. Speak out."

The professor, thus graciously reassured, set forth his errand.

"I have come to you, Highly Exalted, to inquire your exalted views on the subject of Lycanthropy. Your Exaltedness knows—"

"Yes, yes," broke in MWAW, "old Teutonic legend. Men become wolves. Strongest and fiercest breed. Eat people up. Frighten everybody. Ravage countryside. Beautiful myth! Teaches power is greatest thing. Might gives right. Force over all!"

"Certainly, Highly Exalted," said Schmuck humbly, "it is a wonder-beautiful myth, full of true idealism. But what if it lost its purely mythical quality and became historical, actual, contemporaneous? Would it not change its aspect? Would not people object to it? Might not the Werwolf get himself disliked?"

"Perhaps," answered MWAW, smiling till his eyes almost disappeared. "But what difference? Ignorant people, weak people, no account. Werwolf is stronger race, therefore superior. Objections silly."

"True, Exaltedness," said Schmuck. "It is the first duty of every ideal to realize itself. Yet in this particular matter the complaints are very bitter. It is said that great numbers of helpless men and women have been devoured, their children torn in pieces, their farms and gardens ravaged, and their houses destroyed by Werwolves quite recently. Shall I deny it?"

"No," growled MWAW. "Don't be a fool. It is too well known. We know it ourselves. We are the wolf-pack. Don't deny it. Justify it. That's your business. Earn your salary."

Schmuck was as nearly embarrassed as it is possible for a professor to be.

"Willingly, Exaltedness," he stammered. "But the trouble is to find the basic arguments. Even among the Hivites and the Hittites, I have not yet discovered any traces—"

"Nonsense," snapped MWAW. "Hivites and Hittites are dead. WE are alive.

Justify US. Think!"

"Pardon, Highly Exalted," said Schmuck, "I was trying to think. The first justification that occurs to me is the plea of necessity—biological necessity."

"It sounds good," grunted MWAW. "But vague. Explain."

"A biological necessity is a thing that knows no law. It is the inward urge of every living creature to expand its own life without regard to the lives of others. It is above morality, because whatever is necessary is moral."

"Excellent," exclaimed MWAW. "We have felt that ourselves. Continue."

"Now, doubtless, the Highly Exalted are often hungry."

"Always," interrupted MWAW, "say always!"

"Always being hungry," droned Schmuck, "the Highly Exalted may feel at certain times the craving for a certain kind of food in order to obtain a more perfect expansion. To need is to take. Is it not so?"

"It is," said MWAW, "and we do. Find another argument."

"Self-defense," replied Schmuck.

"Too old," said MWAW. "Worn out. Won't go any more."

"But as I shall put it, Highly Exalted will see a newness in it. The best way to defend oneself is by injuring others. Sheep, for example, when gathered in sufficient numbers are the most dangerous animals in the world. The only way to be safe from them is to attack them and scatter them. Especially the small flocks, for that prevents their growing larger and becoming more dangerous. Particularly should the sheep with horns be attacked. Sheep have no right to have horns. Wolves have none. But even the hornless sheep and the lambs should not be spared, for by rending them you may frighten and discourage the horned ones."

"Capital," cried MWAW, springing up and pacing the arbor in excitement. "Just our own idea. Frightfulness increases force. We like to make people afraid. We feel stronger. Essence of Werwolfery. Give another argument, excellent Schmuck. Think once more."

"The Highly Exalted will forgive me. I cannot, momentarily, bring forth another."

"What!" snarled an angry voice above the trembling professor. "Not think of the best argument of all! Forget your creed! Deny your faith! Wretched Schmuck! Who gave you a place? Who feeds you? Who are WE?"

"The Lord's Anointed!" murmured Schmuck, falling on his knees.

MWAW drew himself up, stiff as steel. His eyes blazed through their slits like coals of fire.

"Right!" he cried. "Right at last. That is the great argument. Use it. WE are the Chosen of God. WE are his weapon, his vicegerent. Whatever WE do is a brave act and a good deed. Woe to the disobedient!"

He held out his hand and lifted the professor to his feet.

"Stand up, Schmuck. You are forgiven. Take more beer. To-night I follow biological necessity. More work to do. But you go and tell people the truth."

So Schmuck went. Whether he told the truth or not is uncertain. At all events, it was in different words. And the Werwolfery continued.

Chapter III
THE WERWOLF AT LARGE
I

In the days immediately before and after the breaking of the war-tempest, the servants of the United States Government in Europe were suddenly overwhelmed by a flood of work and care. The strenuous, incessant toil in the consulates, legations, and embassies acted somewhat as a narcotic. There was so much to do that there was no time to worry.

The sense of an unmeasured calamity was present in the background of our thoughts from the very beginning. But it was not until later that the nature of the disaster grew clear and poignant. As month after month hammered swiftly by, the meaning and portent of the catastrophe emerged more sharply and penetrated our minds more deeply, stinging us awake.

A mighty nation which "rejected the dream of universal peace throughout the world as non-German" (the Crown Prince, Germany in Arms); a nation trained for war as a "biological necessity in which Might proves itself the supreme Right" (Bernhardi, Germany and the Next War); a nation which had been taught that "frightfulness" is a lawful and essential weapon in war (Von Clausewitz); and whose generals said, "Frankly, we are and must be barbarians" (Von Diefurth, Hamburger Nachrichten), while their philosophers declared that "The German is the superior type of the species homo sapiens" (Woltmann); a nation whose Imperial Head commended to his soldiers the example of the Huns, and proclaimed, "It is to the empire of the world that the German genius aspires" (Kaiser Wilhelm, Speech at Aix-la-Chapelle, June 20, 1902)—a nation thus armed, instructed, disciplined, and demoralized had broken loose. Another Attila had come, with a new horde behind him to devastate and change the face of the world. In the tumult and darkness which enfolded Europe, the Werwolf was at large. We could hear his ululations in the forest. The cries of his victims grew louder, piercing our hearts with pity and just wrath.

II

But even when the most dreadful things are happening around you, the regular and necessary work of the world must be carried on. Your own particular "chore" must be done as well as you can do it.

As the trouble drew near and suddenly fell upon the world, the burden of enormously increased and varied duties pressed heavily upon the American representatives abroad. The first thing that we had to do was to make provision for taking care of our own people in Europe who were caught out in the storm and the danger.

That was a practical job with unlimited requirements. No one, except those who had the distracting privilege of being in the American diplomatic and consular service in the summer of 1914, knows how much work and how many kinds of work rushed down upon us in a moment. Banking, postal, and telegraph service, transportation, hotel and boarding-house business, baggage express, the recovery of missing articles and persons, the reunion of curiously separated families, confidential inquiries, medical service (mainly mind-healing), and free consultation on every subject under the sun—all these different occupations, trades, and professions were not set down in our programme when we came to Europe, nor covered by the slim calf-bound volume of Instructions to Diplomatic Officers which was our only guide-book. But we had to learn them at short notice and practise them as best we could. No doubt we often acted in a way that was not strictly protocolaire. Certainly we made mistakes. But it was better to do that than to sit like bumps on a log doing nothing. The immediate affair in hand was to help our own folks who were in distress and difficulty and who wanted to get home as quickly and as safely as possible. So we tried to do it, making use of the best means available, and praying that heaven and our diplomatic colleagues would forgive any errors or gaffes that we might make. We preserved a profound respect for etiquette and regularity. But our predominant anxiety was to get the things done that had to be done.

Take an illustration. Excuse the personal references in it.

From the very beginning it seemed clear to me that one of the greatest difficulties in the first days of war would be to secure a supply of ready money for American travellers in flight. As a rule they carried little hard cash with them. Paper money would be at a discount; checks and drafts difficult, if not impossible, to negotiate in Holland. Moratoriums were falling everywhere as thick as leaves in Vallombrosa.

So I went directly to my friend Foreign Minister Loudon, and asked him a plain question.

"Would your Government be willing to help us in getting American travellers' checks and drafts on letters of credit cashed if I should indorse them as American Minister?"

He answered as promptly as if the suggestion had already been formed in his own mind—as perhaps it had.

"Certainly, and gladly! Those pieces of paper would be the best securities in the world—short-term notes of the American Government. If you will get the authority from Washington to indorse, the Bank of the Netherlands will honor the checks and drafts; and if the Bank hesitates the National Treasury will cash them."

I cabled to the Department of State asking permission to make the indorsements (a thing hitherto expressly forbidden by the instructions to diplomatic officers), and explaining that I would take in each case the best security obtainable, whether in the form of a draft on a letter of credit or a personal note of hand with satisfactory references, and that no money should be drawn except for necessary living expenses and the cost of the journey home. The answer came promptly: "You have the authority to indorse."

So a system of international banking between two Governments was introduced. I believe it was absolutely a new plan. But it worked.

Then another idea occurred to me. The letters of credit were usually drawn on London or Paris. In both cities a moratorium was on. Why not make the drafts directly on New York? Why not call on the signer of the letter of credit for the money instead of calling on the addressee? This would cut out any possibility of difficulty from the moratorium.

This also was a new method. But it seemed reasonable. We tried it. And it worked. A visiting committee of New York bankers to whom I related this experience later laughed immensely. They also made some remarks about "amateurs" and "audacity" which I would rather not repeat. But upon the whole they did not seem shocked beyond recovery.

So it happened, by good fortune, that there was never a day in The Hague when an American fugitive from the war, homeward bound, could not obtain what cash he needed for him to live and to get to the United States. But not money to buy souvenir spoons, or old furniture and pictures. "Very sorry," we explained, "but our Government is not dealing in antiquities at present. It is simply helping you to get home as quickly and comfortably as possible. Please tell us how much money you need for board and passage-money and you shall have it."

Except three or four chronic growlers and a few passionate antiquarian ladies, everybody took it good-humoredly and cheerfully. I think they understood, though not always clearly, that our Government was doing more for its citizens caught out in a tempest than any other government in the world would have done.

When the Tennessee arrived in the latter part of August with $2,500,000 in gold for the same purpose, it was another illustration of our Government's parental care and forethought. We received our share of this gold at The Hague. The first use we made of part of it was to take up the American checks and drafts on which the Bank of the Netherlands had advanced the money. Then we sent the paper to America for collection and repayment to the National Treasury. I have not the accounts here and cannot speak by the book, but I think I am not far out in saying that our loss on these transactions was less than five per cent of the total amount handled. And we banked for some very poor people, too!

I never had any idea, before the war broke out, how many of our countrymen and countrywomen there are roaming about Europe every summer, and with what a cheerful trust in Providence and utter disregard of needful papers and precautions some of them roam! There were young women travelling alone or in groups of two or three. There were old men so feeble that one's first thought on seeing them was: "How did you get away from your nurse?" There were people with superfluous funds, and people with barely enough funds, and people with no funds at all. There were college boys who had worked their way over and couldn't find a chance to work it back. There were art-students and music-students whose resources had given out.

There was a very rich woman, plastered with diamonds, who demanded the free use of my garage for the storage of her automobile. When I explained that, to my profound regret, it was impossible, because three American guest cars were already stored there and the place could hold no more, she flounced out of the room in high dudgeon.

There was a lady of a different type who came to say, very modestly, that she had a balance in a bank at The Hague which she wanted to leave to my order for use in helping people who were poor and deserving. "Please make as sure as you can of the poverty," said she, "but take a chance, now and then, on the deserts. We can't confine our kindness to saints." This gift amounted to two or three thousand dollars, and was the foundation of the Minister's private benevolence fund, which proved so useful in later days and of which a remnant has been left for my successor.

An American wrote to us from a little village in a remote province of the Netherlands saying that his remittances from home had not arrived and that he was penniless. He added by way of personal description: "My social position is that of a Catholic priest with nervous prostration." We helped him and he proved to be all right.

A rising comic-opera star, of engaging appearance and manners (American), who was under a temporary financial obscuration because her company in Holland had broken up, came to ask us to assist her in getting to Germany, where she had friends and hoped to find work. We did it with alacrity. Then she wrote asking us to forward certain legal papers in connection with a divorce which she contemplated. We did it. Then she sent us some of her newspaper articles and a lot of clippings from German journals, requesting us to transmit them in the Legation pouch to America. This we politely declined, with the plea of "non possumus". Whereupon she was furious and denounced us to the German authorities and the German-American press.

An American lady whose husband was dying in Hamburg came in desperate distress with her daughter, to beg us to aid them in getting to him. We found the only way that was open, a little-known route through the northeast corner of Holland, procured the necessary permits, and enabled the wife and daughter to reach his bedside before he died.

A poor woman (with a nice little baby), husband, a naturalized American, was "somewhere in Argentina," wanted to go to his family in one of the northwestern States. She had no money. We paid her expenses in The Hague until we could get into communication with the family, and then sent her home rejoicing.

These are a few examples of the ever-recurring humor and pathos which touched our incessant grind of peace work in war times at The Hague. Thousands and thousands of Americans, real or presumptive, passed through the Legation—all sorts and conditions of men, asking for all kinds of things.

Our house was transformed into an Inquiry Office and a Bureau for First Aid to the Injured. There was often a dense throng outside the front door, filling the street and reaching over into the park. Two Dutch boy scouts, capital fellows in khaki, volunteered their assistance in keeping order, and stood guard at the entrance giving out numbered tickets of admission so that the house would not be choked and all the work stopped.

You see, Holland was the narrow neck of the bottle, and the incredible multitudes of Americans who were scattered about in Germany, Austria, Russia, and parts of Switzerland, came pouring out our way. There was no end to the extra work. Many a night I did not get my clothes off, but took a bath and breakfast in the morning and went ahead with the next day's business. No eight-hour day in that establishment!

It would have been impossible to hold on and keep going but for the devotion and industry of the entire Legation staff, and the splendid aid of the volunteers who came to help us through. Professor George Grafton Wilson, of Harvard, was our Counsellor in International Law. Professor Philip M. Brown, of Princeton, former Minister to Honduras, gave his valuable service. Professor F. J. Moore, of the Massachusetts Institute of Technology, took charge of the registration bureau. Hon. Charles H. Sherrill, former Ambassador to the Argentine, and Charles Edward Russell, the Socialist, and his wife, were among our best workers. Alexander R. Gulick was at the head of the busy correspondence department. Van Santvoord Merle-Smith, Evans Hubbard, and my son ran the banking department. These are only a few names among the many good men and women who helped their country for love.

My library was the Diplomatic Office, to which the despatches and the passports came; the Conference Chamber, where all vexed questions were discussed and decided; the Court of Appeal, where people who thought they had not received fair treatment could present their complaints; and the Consolation Room, where the really distressed, as well as the slightly hysterical, came to tell their troubles. Some of them were tragic and some comic. The most agitated and frightened persons were among the fat commercial men. The women, as a rule, were fine and steady and cheerful, especially the American-born. They met the adventure with good sense and smiling faces; asked with commendable brevity for the best advice or service that we could give them; and usually took the advice and were more grateful for the service than it deserved.

So the days rolled on, full of infinitely varied cares and labors; and every afternoon, about five o'clock, the whole staff with a dozen or a score of our passing friends, went out under the spreading chestnut-tree in the back garden for a half-hour of tea and talk. It was all very peaceful and democratic. We were in neutral, friendly Holland. The big, protecting shield of "Uncle Sam" was over us, and we felt safe.

III

Yet how near, how fearful, was the fierce reality of the unpardonable war! Belgium was invaded by the Germans, an hour or two away from us. At any moment their troops might be tempted to take the short cut through the narrow strip of Dutch territory which runs so far down into Belgium; and then the neutrality of Holland would be gone! The little country would be part of the battle-field. Holland has always been resolved to fight any invader.

All through August and September, 1914, that fear hung over the Dutch people. It recurred later again and again—whenever a movement of German troops came too close to the borders of Holland; whenever a newspaper tale of impending operations transpired from Berlin or London. Once or twice the anxiety rose almost to a popular panic. But I noticed that even then the stock-market at Amsterdam remained calm. Now, the Dutch are a very prudent folk, especially the bankers. Therefore I concluded that somebody had received strong assurances both from Germany and Great Britain that neither would invade the Netherlands provided the other abstained.

But all the time there was that dreadful example of the "scrap of paper"—the treaty which had been no protection for Belgium—to shake confidence in any pledge of Germany. And all the time the news from just beyond the border grew more and more horrible. Towns and villages were looted and burned. Civilians were massacred; women outraged; children brought to death. Heavy fines and ransoms were imposed for slight or imaginary offenses. (They amounted to more than $40,000,000 in addition to the "war contribution" exacted, which by August, 1917, had reached $288,000,000.) Churches were ruined. Priests were shot. The country was stripped and laid waste. All the scruples and rules by which men had sought to moderate the needless cruelties of war were mocked and flung aside. Ruin marked the track of the German troops, and terror ran before their advance.

On August 19 Aerschot was sacked and 150 of its inhabitants killed. On the 20th Andenne met the same fate and the number of the slain was 250. On the 23d Dinant was wrecked and more than 600 men and women were murdered. On the 25th the university library at Louvain was set on fire and burned. The pillage and devastation of the city and its environs continued for ten days. More than 2,000 houses were destroyed, and more than 100 civilians were butchered. Time would fail me to tell of the industrious little towns and the quaint Old World hamlets that were wrecked, or of the men and women and young children who were tortured, and had trial of mockings and bonds and imprisonment, and were slain by the sword and by fire. Is it not all set down by sworn witnesses in the great gray book of the Kingdom of Belgium, and in the blue book of the committee of which Lord Bryce was the head? Have I not heard with my own ears the agony of those whose parents were shot down before their eyes, whose children were slain or ravished, whose wives or husbands were carried into captivity, whose homes were made desolate, and who themselves barely escaped with their lives?

Find an explanation for these Belgian atrocities if you can. What if a few shots were fired by ignorant and infuriated civilians from the windows of houses? It has not been proved. But even if it were, it would be no reason for the martyrdom of a whole population, for the destruction of distant and unincriminated towns, for the massacre of evidently innocent persons.

Was it the drink found in the cellars of the houses that made the German officers and soldiers mad? Perhaps so. But that makes the case no better. It was stolen drink.

Was it the carrying out of the cold-blooded policy of "frightfulness" as a necessary weapon of war? That is the wickedest excuse of all. It is really an accusation. The probable truth of it is supported by what happened later, when the Germans came to Poland, and when the Turks, their allies and pupils in the art of war, slaughtered 800,000 Armenians or drove them to a slow, painful death. It means just what the title of this article says. The Werwolf was at large.

The first evidence of this spirit in the German conduct of the war that came to my personal knowledge was on August 25. Two or three days before, our American Consul-General in Antwerp, which was still the temporary seat of the Belgian Government, had written to me saying that he was absolutely destitute and begging me to send him some money for the relief of his family and other Americans who were in dire need. The Tennessee was lying off the Hook of Holland at that time, and there were several of our splendid army officers ready and eager for any service. One of the best of them, Captain Williams, offered himself as messenger, and I sent him in to Antwerp, with three thousand dollars in gold in a belt around his waist, on August 24. He had a hard, slow journey, but he went through and delivered the money.

That very night, while he was in the city, a Zeppelin air-ship, the first of its devilish tribe to get into action, sailed over sleeping Antwerp dropping bombs. No military damage was done. But hundreds of private houses were damaged and sixty destroyed. One bomb fell on a hospital full of wounded Belgians and Germans. Scores of innocent civilians, mostly women and children, were killed. "In a single house," writes an eye-witness, "I found four dead: one room was a chamber of horrors, the remains of the mangled bodies being scattered in every direction."

Mark the exact nature of this crime. The dropping of bombs from aircraft is not technically illegal. The agreement of the nations to abandon and prohibit this method of attack for five years unfortunately expired by limitation of time in 1912 and was not renewed. But the old-established rules of war among civilized nations have forbidden and still forbid the bombardment of populous towns without due notice, in order that the non-combatants may have a chance to find refuge and safety. This German monster of the air came unannounced, in the dead of night, and, having wrought its hellish surprise, vanished into the darkness again. This was a crime against international law as well as a sin against humanity.

My captain returned to The Hague the next morning, bringing his report. He had seen the horror with his own eyes. More: with the care of a true officer he had made a map of the course taken by the air-ship in its flight over the city. That map showed beyond a doubt that the aim of the marauder was to destroy the principal hospital, the hotel where the Belgian Ministers lived, and the palace in which the King and Queen with their children were sleeping.

I cabled the facts to Washington at once, and sent the map with a fuller report the next day. I felt deeply (and ventured to express my feeling) that the United States could, and ought to, protest against this clear violation of the law of nations—this glaring manifestation of a spirit which was going to make this war the most cruel and atrocious known to history. The foreboding of a return to barbarism has been fulfilled, alas, only too abominably!

In every step of that downward path Germany has led the way, by the perfection of her scientific methods applied to a devilish purpose.

Take, for example, the use of poisonous gas in warfare. This was an ancient weapon, employed long before the beginning of the Christian era. It had been abandoned by civilized nations, and was prohibited by one of the Hague conventions, for a period of five years. But that period having expired, and the convention being only a "scrap of paper," Germany revived the ancient deviltry in a more scientific form. On April 22, 1915, she sent the yellow clouds of death rolling down upon the trenches of Ypres, where the British defended the last city of outraged Belgium. The suffocating horrors of that hellish method of attack are beyond description. The fame of this achievement of spectacled barbarism belongs to the learned servants of the predatory Potsdam gang. But we cannot blame the Allies if they were forced reluctantly to take up the same weapon in self-defense.

IV

The real character and the inhuman effect of the German invasion were brought home to us, and made painfully clear to our eyes and our hearts, by the amazing tragic spectacle of the flood of refugees pouring out of Belgium.

It began slowly. When the quaint frontier town of Vise, surrounded by its goose-farms, was attacked and set on fire on August 4, there were many families from the neighborhood who fled to Holland. When Liege was captured on the 7th after a brave defense, and its last fort fell on the 15th, there were more fugitives. When Brussels was occupied without resistance on the 20th there were still more. As the invasion spread westward and southward, engulfing city after city in widening waves of blood, the tide of terror and flight rose steadily. It reached its high-water mark when Antwerp, after the Germans had pounded its outer and inner circle of forts for nine days, was bombarded on October 7 and captured on the 18th.

Nothing like that sad, fear-smitten exodus has been seen on earth in modern times. There was something in it at once fateful, trembling, and irresistible, which recalled De Quincey's famous story of The Flight of a Tartar Tribe. No barrier on the Holland border could have kept that flood of Belgian refugees out. They were an enormous flock of sheep and lambs, harried by the Werwolf and fleeing for their lives.

But Holland did not want a barrier. She stood with open doors and arms, offering an asylum to the distressed and persecuted.

I do not believe that any country has ever made a better record of wise, steady, and true humanitarian work than Holland made in this matter. It is not necessary to exaggerate it. Naturally, Belgium and Great Britain bore by far the largest part of the financial burden of caring for the refugees. Regular subsidies were guaranteed for this purpose. But Holland gave freely and generously what was more important: a prompt and sufficient welcome and shelter from the storm; abundant supplies of money for immediate needs, food and clothing, a roof and a fire; personal aid and care, nursing, medical attendance—all of which these bewildered exiles needed desperately and at once.

This is not the place, nor the time, in which to attempt a full report of the humane task which was suddenly thrown upon Holland by the deadly doings of the German Werwolf in Belgium, nor of the way in which that task was accepted and carried out. I shall note only a few things of which I have personal knowledge.

Going along the railway line which leads to Antwerp, I saw every train literally packed with fugitives. They had come, not in organized, orderly companies, but in droves—tens of thousands, hundreds of thousands. They were dazed and confused, escaping from they knew not what, carried they knew not whither. It is well for the poet to say:

"Be not like dumb, driven cattle";

but what can you do in a case like this except run from hell as fast as you can and take the first open road?

The station platforms were crowded with folks in motley garments showing signs of wear and tear. Their possessions were done up in bags and shapeless bundles, rolled in pieces of sacking, old shawls, red-and-white-checkered table-cloths. The men, with drawn and heavy faces, waited patiently. The women collected and watched their restless flocks. The baby tugged at its mother's breast. The little sister carried the next-to-baby in her arms. The boys, as usual, wandered everywhere undismayed and peered curiously into everything.

The crowds were not disorderly or turbulent; there was no shrieking or groaning. There were, of course, some of the baser sort in the vast multitude that fled to Holland—street rowdies and other sons of Belial from the big towns, women of the pavements, and other wretched by-products of our social system. How could it be otherwise in a throng of about a million, scooped up and cast out by an evil chance? But the great bulk of the people were decent and industrious—no more angels than the rest of us can show per thousand.

I remember a very respectable old couple, cleanly though plainly clad, waiting at the station of a small village, looking in vain for a chance to board the train. Everything was full except the compartment reserved for us. We opened the door and asked them to get in. The old gentleman explained that he was a landscape-gardener, living in a small villa with a small garden, in a suburb of Antwerp.

"It was a beautiful garden, monsieur," he said with glistening eyes. "It was arranged with much skill and care. We loved every bush, every flower. But one evening three German shells fell in it and burst. The good wife and I" (here a wan smile) "thought the climate no longer sanitary. We ran away that night on foot. Much misery for old people. Last night we slept in a barn with hundreds of others. But some day we go back to restore that garden. N' est-ce pas vrai, cherie?"

Rosendaal, the Dutch custom-house town on the way to Antwerp, claims 15,000 inhabitants. In two nights at least 40,000 refugees poured into that place. Every house from the richest to the poorest opened its doors in hospitality. The beds and the floors were all filled with sleepers. A big vacant factory building was fitted with improvised bunks and straw bedding. Two thousand five hundred people were lodged there. Open-air kitchens were set up. The burgomaster and aldermen and doctors and all the other "leading citizens" took off their coats and worked. The best women in the place were cooking, serving tables, nursing, making clothes, doing all they could for their involuntary guests.

In the picturesque old city of Bergen-op-Zoom—famous in history—I saw the same thing. There a large tent-camp had been set up for the overflow from the houses. It was like a huge circus of distress. The city hall was turned into an emergency storehouse of food: the vaulted halls and chambers filled with boxes, bags, and barrels. When I went up to the bureau of the burgomaster, his wife and daughters were there, sewing busily for the refugees.

I visited the main hospital and the annexes which had been established in the schoolhouses. Twice, as we climbed the steep stairs, we stood aside for stretchers to be carried past. They bore the bodies of people who had died from exposure and exhaustion.

In one ward there were a score of the most ancient women I have ever seen. They had made the flight on foot. God knows how they ever did it. One of them was so weak that she could not speak, so short of breath that she could not lie down. As she sat propped with pillows, rocking slowly to and fro and coughing, coughing, feebly coughing her life out, she looked a thousand years old. Perhaps she was, if suffering measures years.

Another room was for babies born in the terror and the flight. A few were well-looking enough; but most of them were pitiful scraps and tatters of humanity. They were tenderly nursed and cared for, but their chance was slender. While I was there one of the little creatures shuddered, breathed a tiny sigh, and slipped out of a world that was too hard for it.

It was part of my unofficial duty to visit as many as possible of the private shelters and hospitals and workrooms and the public camps, because the Belgian Relief Committee and other friends in New York had sent me considerable sums of money to use in helping the refugees. In the careful application of these funds I had the advice of Mr. Th. Stuart, President of the "Netherlands Relief Committee for Belgian and Other Victims of War," and of Baron F. van Tuyll van Serooskerken, a great friend of mine, whom the Queen had appointed as General Commissioner to oversee all the public refugee camps.

Three of these, Nunspeet, Ede, and Uden, were improvised villages, with blocks of long community houses, separate dormitories for the unmarried men and for the single women, a dining-hall, a chapel, one or two schoolhouses, a recreation-hall, a house of detention for refractory persons, one hospital for general cases, and another for infectious diseases. It was all built of wood, simple and primitive, but as comfortable as could be expected under the conditions. The chief danger of the camps was idleness. In providing work to combat this peril the Rockefeller Foundation and the committee of the English "Society of Friends" were of great assistance. Each of these camps had accommodation for about 10,000 people.

The fourth camp was at the ancient city of Gouda, famed for its great old church with stained-glass windows and for its excellent cheese and clay pipes. This camp was the earliest and one of the most interesting that I visited. It was established in a series of exceptionally large and fine greenhouses, which happened to be empty when the emergency came. Somebody—I think it was the clever Burgomaster Yssel de Scheppe and his admirable wife—had the good idea of utilizing them for the refugees. It seemed a curious notion, to raise human plants under glass. But it worked finely. The houses were long and lofty; they had concrete floors and broad concrete platforms where the "cubicles" for the separate families could easily be erected; steam heat, electric light, hot and cold water were already "laid on"; it was quite palatial in its way. A few wooden houses, a laundry, a kitchen, a carpenter-shop for the men, and so on, were quickly run up. There was a bowling-alley and a playground and a schoolhouse. The people could go to church in the town. Soon twenty-five hundred exiles were living in this queer but comfortable camp.

But it was evident that this refugee life, even under the best conditions that could be devised, was abnormal. There was not room in the industrial life of Holland for all these people to stay there permanently. Besides, they did not want to stay, and that counts for something in human affairs. The question arose whether it might not be wise to let them go home. Not to send them home, you understand. That was never even contemplated. But simply to allow them to return to their own country, at least in the regions where the fury of war had already passed by. I suggested to Mr. Stuart that before you allow poor folks to "go home," you ought to know whether they have a "home" to go to. So we took my motor in October and made a little tour of investigation in Belgium.

That was a strange and memorable journey. The long run in the dripping autumn afternoon along the Antwerp Road, where the miserable fugitives were still trudging in thousands; the search for lodgings in the stricken city, where most of the streets were silent and deserted as if the plague had passed there, and the only bustling life was in the central quarter, where "the field-gray ones" abounded; the closed shops, the house-fronts shattered by shells, the great cathedral standing in the moonlight, unharmed as far as we could see, except for one shell which had penetrated the south transept, just where Rubens's "Descent from the Cross" used to hang before it was carried away for safety—I shall never forget those impressions.

The next morning, provided with permits which the German Military Commandant had very courteously given us, we set out on our tour. The journey became still more strange. The beautiful trees of the suburbs were razed to the ground, the little villas stood empty, many of them half-ruined. (Perhaps one of them belonged to our friend the landscape-gardener.) We could see clearly the emplacements for the big German guns, which had been secretly laid long before the war began, concealed in cellars and beneath innocent-looking tennis-courts. The ring-forts surrounding Antwerp were knocked to pieces, their huge concrete gateways, their stone facings, their high earthworks, all battered out of shape.

Town after town through which we passed lay half-destroyed or in complete ruins. Wavre, Waelhem, Termonde, Duffel, Lierre, and many smaller places were in various stages of destruction, burned or shattered by shell fire and explosives. The heaps of bricks and stones encumbered the streets so that it was hard to pick our way through. The smell of decaying bodies tainted the air. The fields had been inundated in the valleys; the water was subsiding; here and there corpses lay in the mud. Old trenches everywhere; thousands of rudely heaped graves, marked by two crossed sticks; miles on miles of rusty barbed-wire defenses, with dead cows or horses entangled in them, slowly rotting, haunted by the carrion crows.

Yet there were some people in the countryside. Now and then we saw a woman or an old man digging in field or garden. We stopped at the front yard of a little farmhouse, where the farmer's wife stood, and asked her some directions about the road. She gave them cheerfully, though the house at her back was little more than a mass of ruins.

"Were you here in the fighting?" we asked.

"But no, messieurs," she answered with a short laugh. "If I had been here, I should not be here. I ran away to Holland and returned yesterday to my house. But how shall I creep in?" She pointed over her shoulder to the pile of bricks. "I am not a cat or a rat."

They are indomitable, those Flemish people. At Lierre we were very hungry and searched vainly for an inn or a grocery. At last in one of the streets we saw a little baker-shop. The upper story was riddled and broken. But the shop was untouched, the window-shade half up, and underneath we could see two loaves of bread. We went in. The bare-armed baker met us.

"Can you sell us a little bread?"

"But certainly, messieurs, that is what I am here for. Not the window loaves, however; I have a fresh loaf, if you please. Also a little cheese, if you will."

"Were you here in the fighting?"

"Assuredly not! It was impossible. But I hurried back after three days. You see, messieurs, some people were returning, and me—I am the Baker of Lierre."

He said it as if it were a title of nobility.

At Malines (Mechelen) the devastation appeared perhaps more shocking because we had known the russet and gray old city so well in peaceful years. Many of the streets were impassable, choked with debris. One side of the great Square was knocked to fragments. The huge belfry, Saint Rombaud's Tower, wherein hangs the famous carillon of more than thirty bells, was battered but still stood firm. The vast cathedral was a melancholy wreck of its former beauty and grandeur. The roof was but a skeleton of bare rafters; the side wall pierced with gaping rents and holes; the pictured windows were all gone; the sunlight streamed in everywhere upon the stone floor, strewn with an indescribable confusion of shattered glass, fallen beams, fragments of carved wood, and broken images of saints.

A little house behind the Church of Saint Peter and Saint Paul, the roof and upper story of which had been pierced by shells, seemed to be occupied. We knocked and went in. The man and his wife were in the sitting-room, trying to put it in order. Much of the furniture was destroyed; the walls were pitted with shrapnel-scars, but the cheap ornaments on the mantel were unbroken. In the ceiling was a big hole, and in the floor a pit in which lay the head and fragments of a German shell. I asked if I might have them. "Certainly," answered the man. "We wish to keep no souvenirs of that wicked thing."

V

I do not propose to describe the magnificent work of the "Commission for Relief in Belgium." It is too well known. Besides, it is not my story; it is the story of Herbert Hoover, who made the idea a reality, and of the crew of fine and fearless young Americans who worked with him. England and France furnished more money to buy food; but the United States, in addition to money and wheat, gave the organization, the personal energy and toil and tact, the assurance of fair play and honest dealing, without which that food could never have gotten into Belgium or been distributed only to the civil population.

Holland was the door through which all the supplies for the C. R. B. had to pass. The first two cargoes that went in I had to put through personally, and nearly had to fight to do it. My job was to keep the back of the United States against that door and hold it open. It was not always easy. I was obliged to make protests, remonstrances, and polite suggestions about what would happen if certain things were not done.

Once the Germans refused to give any more "safe-conduct passes" for relief ships on the return voyage. Of course, that would have made the work impossible. A German aircraft bombed one of these ships. I put the matter mildly but firmly to the German Minister. "This work is in your interest. It relieves you from the burden of feeding a lot of people whom you would otherwise be bound to feed. You want it to go on?" "Yes, certainly, by all means." "Well, then, you will have to stop attacking the C. R. B. ships or else the work will have to stop. The case is very simple. There is only one thing to do." He promised to take the matter up with Berlin at once. In a couple of days the answer came: "Very sorry. Regrettable mistake. Aviator could not see markings on side and stern of ship. Advise large horizontal signs painted on top deck of ships, visible from above. Safe-conducts will be granted."

When this was told to Captain White, a clever Yankee sea-captain who had general charge of the C. R. B. shipping, he laughed considerably and then said: "Why, look-a-here, I'll paint those boats all over, top, sides, and bottom, if that'll only keep the —— Germans from sinkin' 'em."

From a million and a half to two million men, women, and children in Belgium and northern France were saved from starving to death by the work of the C. R. B. The men who were doing it had a chance to observe the conditions in those invaded countries. They came to the Legation at The Hague and told simply what they knew. We got the real story of Miss Cavell, cruelly done to death by "field-gray" officers. We got full descriptions of the system of deporting the civil population—a system which amounted to enslavement, with a taint of "white slavery" thrown in. When the Belgian workmen were suddenly called from their homes, herded before the German commandant, and sent away, they knew not whither, to work for their oppressor, as they were entrained they sang the "Marseillaise." They knew they would be punished for it, kept without food, put to the hardest labor. But they sang it. They knew that France, and England too, were fighting for them, for their rights, for their liberty. They believed that it would come. They were not conquered yet.

Here I must break off my story for a month. It has not been well told. Words cannot render the impression of black horror that lay upon us, the fierce indignation that stirred us, during all those months while we were doing the tasks of peace in peaceful Holland.

We were bound to be neutral in conduct. That was the condition of our service to the wounded, the prisoners, the refugees, the sufferers, of both sides. We lived up to that condition at The Hague without a single criticism from anybody—except the subsidized German-American press in the United States.

But to be neutral in thought and feeling—ah, that was beyond my power. I knew that the predatory Potsdam gang had chosen and forced the war in order to realize their robber-dream of Pan-Germanism. I knew that they were pushing it with unheard-of atrocity in Belgium and northern France, in Poland and Servia and Armenia. I knew that they had challenged and attacked the whole world of peace-loving nations. I knew that America belonged to that imperilled world. I knew that there could be no secure labor and no quiet sleep in any land so long as the Potsdam Werwolf was at large.

Chapter IV
GERMANIA MENDAX
I

The truth about the choosing, beginning, and forcing of this abominable war has never been told by official Germandom.

Now and then an independent German like Maximilian Harden is brave enough to blurt it out: "Of what use are weak excuses? We willed this war, ... willed it because we were sure we could win it." (Zukunft, August, 1914.) But in general the official spokesmen of Germany keep up the claim that their country was attacked and forced to fly to arms to protect herself.

"Gentlemen," said the Imperial Chancellor to the members of the Reichstag on August 4,1914, "we are now acting in self-defense. Necessity knows no law. Our troops have occupied Luxembourg and have possibly already entered on

Belgian soil. A little earlier in the speech he confessed that they had also invaded France. Gentlemen, that is a breach of international law. The French Government has notified Brussels that it would respect Belgian neutrality as long as the adversary respected it. But we know that France stood ready for an invasion. France could wait. We could not .... The injustice we commit—I speak openly—we will try to make good as soon as our military aims have been attained. He who is menaced as we are, and is fighting for his all, can only consider the one and best way to strike."

It was against such weak excuses as this, against the vain pretext that the German war-lords were the attacked instead of the attackers, that Herr Harden made the frank protest which I have quoted above.

Meantime the falsehood of the tales of French preparation for invasion and of actual violations of German territory has been exposed by the evidence of Germans themselves. General Freytag-Loringhoven, in his essay on "The First Victories in the West," has shown that the French high command was taken off its guard by the swift stab through Luxembourg and Belgium, and could not get the Fifth Army Corps to the Douai-Charleroi line until August 22. The municipal authorities of Nuremburg have declared that they have no knowledge of the dropping of bombs on that city by French aviators.

The falsehood of the Chancellor's promise that Germany would "make good her injustice" to Belgium after attaining her military aims is foreshadowed to-day. (September 27.) The newspapers of this morning contain a semi-official press statement in regard to a note verbale handed by the Foreign Secretary to the Papal Nuncio at Berlin. Germany, if this statement is correct, now proposes to spoil the future of Belgium by splitting the nation into two administrative districts, Flemish and Walloon, thus injecting the poison-germ of disunion into the body politic. She also demands "the right to develop her economic interests freely in Belgium, especially in Antwerp," and a guarantee that "any such menace as that which threatened Germany from Belgium! in 1914 shall be excluded." This is the German idea of making good an injustice by committing a fresh injury. It is in the style of a highwayman who says to his victim: "I will reward you by letting you go. But I must keep the big pearl, and you must permit me to break both your arms.

"History now shows us that, neither prior to, nor at the outset of hostilities, were people able to rely to any great extent on a neutral Belgium, and, should we attach a certain importance to these historic truths, we shall not, however, on the conclusion of peace, suffer ourselves to allow of the revival of Belgium as a neutral state and country. An independent or neutral Belgium, or a Belgium whose status would be fixed by treaties of another kind, will be, as before the war, under the inauspicious influence of England and France, as well as the prey of America, who is seeking to utilize Belgian securities. There is only one way to prevent this, viz.: by the policy of force, and it is force that should achieve the result that the population, at present still hostile, should become used to German rule and submit to it. Moreover, it will be necessary, through a peace assuring us the annexation of Belgium, that we should be able to protect, as we are now compelled to do, the German subjects who have settled in this country, and the protection we shall be enabled to afford them will be of special service to us in the struggle about to take place in the world's market. It is only by reigning over Belgium that we shall be able to utilize (verwerten), with a view to German interests, Belgian capital in savings and the numerous Belgian joint-stock companies already existing in enemy countries. We ought to have control over the important enterprises that Belgian capital has founded in Turkey, the Balkans, and China. . . ."

II
THE AUSTRIAN ULTIMATUM TO SERVIA

In the latter part of 1916 the New York Times published an admirable series of articles, signed "Cosmos," on The Basis of Durable Peace With almost every statement of this learned and able writer I found myself in thorough accord. But the fourth sentence of the first article I could not accept.

"The question as to who or what power," writes Cosmos, "is chiefly responsible for the last events that immediately preceded the war has become for the moment one of merely historical interest."

On the contrary, it seems to me a question of immediate, vital, decisive interest. It certainly determined the national action of France, Great Britain, and Italy. They did not believe that Germany and Austria were acting in self-defense. If that had been the case, Italy at least would have been bound by treaty to come to the aid of her partners in the Triple Alliance, which was purely a defensive league. But she formally declined to do so, on the ground that "the war undertaken by Austria, and the consequences which might result, had, in the words of the German Ambassador himself, a directly aggressive object." The same ground was taken in the message of the President of the French Republic to the Parliament on August 4, 1914 and in the speech of the British Prime Minister, August 6, the day on which the Parliament passed the first appropriation for expenses arising out of the existence of a state of war (British Blue Book).

The conviction that the ruling militaristic party in Germany, abetted by Austria, bears the moral guilt of thrusting this war upon the world as the method of settling international difficulties which could have been better settled by arbitration or conference, is a very real thing at the present moment. It is shared by the Entente Allies and the United States. It is one of those "imponderables" which, as Bismarck said long ago, must never be left out of account in estimating national forces. It will hold the Allies and the United States together. It will help them to win the war for peace under conditions for Germany which may not be "punitive," but which certainly must be "reformatory".

Understand, I do not imagine or maintain that the primary or efficient causes of this war are to be found in any things that happened in 1914 or 1913. They are inherent in false methods of government, in false systems of so-called national policy, in false dealing with simple human rights and interests, in false attempts to settle natural problems on an artificial basis.

All nations have a share in them. They go back to Austria's annexation of Bosnia and Herzegovina in 1908; to the Congress of Berlin in 1878; to the Franco-Prussian War in 1870; to the Prusso-Austrian War in 1866; to the conquest of Constantinople by the Turks in 1453. Yes, they go back further still, if you like, to the time when Cain killed Abel! That was the first assertion of the doctrine that "might makes right."

But the "occasional cause" of this war, the ground on which it was brought to a head and let loose by Germany, was the Austrian ultimatum to Servia, presented on July 23, 1914, at 6 P. M.

This remarkable state-paper, so harsh in its tone, so imperious in its demands, that it called forth the disapproval even of a few bold German critics, was apparently meant to be impossible of acceptance by Servia, and thus to serve either as the instrument for crushing the little country which stood in the way of the "Berlin-Baghdad-Bahn," or as a torch to kindle the great war in Europe. I do not propose to trace its history and consequences in detail. I propose only to show, by fuller proofs than have hitherto been available, that Germany must share the responsibility for this flagitious and incendiary document.

On July 25, 1914, the German Ambassador at Petrograd handed an official "note verbale" to the Russian Minister for Foreign Affairs which stated that "The German Government had no knowledge of the text of the Austrian note before it was presented, and exercised no influence upon its contents." Similar communications were presented in France and England.

This barefaced denial that the German Government knew what would be in the Austrian ultimatum, or had anything to do with the framing of it, was a palpable falsehood. It was discredited at the time. The antecedent incredibility of the statement has been well set forth by Mr. James N. Beck, in his vigorous book, The Evidence in the Case New evidence has come in. I intend here to present briefly and arrange in a new order the facts which prove to a moral certainty that the German Government knew beforehand what the content and intent of the Austrian ultimatum would be, and what consequences it would probably entail.

(1) Austria was the most intimate ally of Germany, admittedly dependent upon her big friend for backing in all international affairs. The German Ambassador in Vienna, Herr von Tschirsky, and the Austrian Ambassador in Berlin, Count Szogyeny, were in close consultation with the Governments to which they were accredited during the weeks that followed the crime of Serajevo, June 28-July 23. It is absolutely incredible that Austria should not have consulted her big friend in regard to the momentous step against Servia, altogether impossible that Germany should not have insisted upon knowing what her smaller friend was doing in a matter of such importance to them both. You might as well imagine that the board of managers of a subsidiary railway would block out a new policy without consulting the directors of the main line.

(2) On July 5, 1914, it appears that a secret conference was held at Potsdam at which high officials of the German and Austrian Governments were present. It is not possible to give their names with certainty—not yet, perhaps never—because these gentlemen come and go in the dark. But the fact of the meeting was brought out publicly in the speech of Deputy Haase in the Reichstag, July 19, 1917, and not contradicted. Whatever may have been the ostensible object of this conference, it is impossible to believe that the most important affairs in the world for Austria and Germany at that moment, namely the nature of the ultimatum to Servia and the possible eventuality of a European war, were not discussed, and perhaps decided.

(3) On July 15, 1914, the Italian Ambassador to Turkey, Signor Garroni, had an interview with the German Ambassador to Turkey, Baron Wangenheim, who had just come back from a visit to Berlin. The German diplomat said that he had been present at a conference where it had been decided that the ultimatum to Servia was to be made of such a nature that it could not be accepted, and that this would be the provocation of the war which would probably ensue. Shortly afterward these statements were narrated by Signor Garroni to Mr. Lewis Einstein, attache of the American Embassy at Constantinople, who carefully noted them in his diary.

(4) On July 22, 1914, the British Ambassador in Berlin sent a despatch to his Government which indicated for the first time clearly the attitude which the German Government had decided to take. I therefore quote it in full.

"Last night I met Secretary of State for Foreign Affairs, and the forthcoming Austrian demarche at Belgrade was alluded to by his Excellency in the conversation that ensued. His Excellency was evidently of opinion that this step on Austria's part would have been made ere this. He insisted that the question at issue was one for settlement between Servia and Austria alone, and that there should be no interference from outside in the discussions between those two countries. He had therefore considered it inadvisable that the Austro-Hungarian Government should be approached by the German Government on the matter. He had, however, on several occasions, in conversation with the Servian Minister, emphasized the extreme importance that Austro-Servian relations should be put on a proper footing.

"Finally, his Excellency observed to me that for a long time past the attitude adopted toward Servia by Austria had, in his opinion, been one of great forbearance."

This shows that Germany knew what Austria was doing, approved her plan, and had resolved that there "should be no interference from outside in the discussion"—in other words, Germany would allow no other nation to prevent Austria from doing what she liked to Servia. Could Germany have taken this absolutely "committal" position if she had been ignorant of what Austria intended to do?

(5) On July 23, 1914, the crushing Austrian ultimatum, having been prepared in the dark, was sent to Servia and delivered in Belgrade at 6 P. M. On the same day, and almost certainly at an earlier hour, the German Chancellor

prepared a circular confidential telegram to the Ambassadors at Paris, London, and Petrograd, instructing them to tell the Governments to which they were accredited that "the action as well as the demands of the Austro-Hungarian Government can be viewed only as justifiable. . . . If the demands were refused nothing would remain for it, but to enforce the same by appeal to military measures, in regard to which the choice of means must be left to it."

Is it credible that the German Government would have pronounced a judgment so important, so far-reaching in its foreseen consequences, if it had had no previous knowledge of the "action and demands" of Austria?

(6) On July 23, 1914, the French Minister at Munich telegraphed his Government as follows: "The President of the Council said to me to-day that the Austrian ultimatum, the contents of which were known to him, seemed to him couched in terms which Servia could accept, but that, nevertheless, the actual situation appeared to him serious."

How did this gentleman in Munich come to know about the ultimatum, while the gentlemen in Berlin professed ignorance?

(7) On July 25, 1914, the Russian Government was officially informed that: "Germany as the ally of Austria naturally supports the claims made by the Vienna Cabinet against Servia, which she considers justified."

This was a very grave declaration, in view of the public announcement which the Russian Government had made on the same day: "Recent events and the despatch of an ultimatum to Servia by Austria-Hungary are causing the Russian Government the greatest anxiety. The Government are closely following the course of the dispute between the two countries, to which Russia cannot remain indifferent."

Certainly Germany would not have come to the serious decision of giving unqualified support to the claims of Austria as against the expressed interests of Russia, unless she had long known and had full time to consider those claims and what they would involve.

(8) On July 30, 1914, the British Ambassador in Vienna telegraphed to his Government: "I have private information that the German Ambassador knew the text of the Austrian ultimatum to Servia before it was despatched, and telegraphed it to the German Emperor. I know from the German Ambassador himself that he indorses every line of it."

(9) Count Bernstorff, German Ambassador at Washington, published an article in The Independent, New York, September 7, 1914. In this article he answered, officially, several questions. The first question was: Did Germany approve in advance the Austrian ultimatum to Servia? The answer was: "Yes. Germany's reasons for doing so are the following, &c."

(10) The German Government has itself acknowledged that it was consulted by Austria in regard to the attitude to be taken toward Servia, and the possibility of ensuing war if Russia intervened to protect the life of her little sister state. Germany accepted the responsibility and pledged support. "With all our heart we were able to agree with our ally's estimate of the situation, and assure him that any action considered necessary to end the movement directed against the conservation of the monarchy would meet with our approval."

This is a carte blanche of a kind which no great government could possibly give to another without a definite understanding of what it involved.

Here the summary of the evidence that Austria was not playing "a lone hand" ends—at least until further confidential documents and information about secret meetings are dug up.

Meantime the Imperial German Government maintains its plea of "not guilty." It still denies all previous knowledge of, and all part in, the nefarious Austrian ultimatum to Servia which precipitated the world war.

The denial is both impudent and mendacious.

"Credat Judaeus Apella!"

III
THE RUSSIAN MOBILIZATION

It has been loudly asserted and persistently maintained by the Potsdam gang that the cause of this abominable war was the mobilization of Russia in preparation to maintain the sovereignty of her little sister state Servia if necessary. "Germany," it is said, "earnestly desired, from the purest of motives, to 'localize the conflict'"—which means in plain words to let Austria deal with Servia as she liked, without interference—rather a one-sided proposition, considering the relative size of the two parties in the benevolently urged single combat. "But Russia rashly interfered with this beautiful design by declaring that she could not remain indifferent to the fate of a small nation of kindred blood, and by calling up troops to prevent any wiping out of Servia by Austria, to whom Germany had already given carte blanche and promised full support. This was a wicked threat against the life and liberty of Germany. This was an action which rendered the great war inevitable." So say the German authorities.

The subtitle of the official German White Book reads: "How Russia and Her
Ruler Betrayed Germany's Confidence and Thereby Made the European War."

This is the Potsdam contention in regard to the cause of the war. The documents indicate that it is a false contention, based upon suppressions of the truth. This is what I intend to show.

I hold no brief for the late Imperial Russian Government. Doubtless it was shady in its morals and tricky in its ways.

The telegrams recently discovered by an excellent American journalist, Mr. Herman Bernstein, and published in the "New York Herald," show that the late Czar Nicolas and the still Kaiser Wilhelm were plotting together, a very few years ago, to make a secret "combine" which should control the world. When that plan failed, no doubt the vast power and resources of Russia, under an absolute imperial Government, were regarded by the equally autocratic Government of Germany with jealousy and distrust, not to say fear. No doubt Russia was an actual and formidable obstacle to the Pan-German purpose of getting Servia out of the path of the "Berlin-Baghdad-Bahn".

Grant all this. Pass over, also, the interminable and inextricable dispute about the precise meaning and application of the terms "mobilization," "partial mobilization," "complete mobilization," "precautionary measures," "Kriegsgefahr," an so on. That is an unfathomable morass wherein many deceptions hide. In that controversy each opponent always charges the other with lying, and a wise neutral doubts both. It seems to be true—mark you, I only say it seems—that the first great European Power to order partial mobilization was Austria, July 26, 1914. On July 28 the order for complete mobilization was signed, war was declared against Servia

On July 29 Russia ordered partial mobilization in the districts of Odessa, Kief, Moscow, and Kasan, and declared that she had no aggressive intention against Germany. The Russian preparations obviously had relation only to Austria's war on Servia which was already under way.

On July 30 Germany had effected her "covering dispositions" of troops along the French border, from Luxembourg to the Vosges, part of which by chance I saw in June and on the same day the Berlin semi-official press announced that a complete mobilization had been ordered. This announcement was contradicted and withdrawn later on the same day by government orders.

On July 31, at 1 a.m., the Austrian order of complete mobilization, which was signed on the 28th, was issued. Later in the same day the Russian Government ordered complete mobilization and the German Government proclaimed a state of Kriegsgefahr, "wardanger.".) At seven o'clock in the evening of the same day Germany sent an ultimatum to France, and at midnight an ultimatum to Russia.

On August 1 she declared war on Russia, and on August 3 she declared war on France, having previously invaded French territory and sent her army through neutral Luxembourg.

Now in all this the German Government tries to make it appear that it was simply acting on the defensive, taking necessary steps to guard against the peril threatened by the military measures of Russia.

The falsity of this pretense is easily shown from two facts: First, the Russian Government was all the time pleading for a peaceful settlement of the Austro-Servian dispute, by arbitration, or by a four-power conference. Second, definite offers were made to halt the Russian military measures at once on conditions most favorable to Austria, if Austria and Germany would agree to an examination by the Great Powers of Austria's just claims on Servia.

On the first point, I do not propose to retell the long story of the efforts supported by France, England, Italy, and Russia herself, to get Germany to consent to some plan, any plan, which might avert war by an appeal to reason and justice. To these efforts Germany answered in effect that she could not "coerce" her ally Austria.

But one document in this line seems to me particularly interesting—even pathetic. It is a telegram sent by the late Czar Nicolas to his Imperial Cousin, Kaiser Wilhelm. It is dated July 29, 1914, and reads as follows:

"Thanks for your telegram which is conciliatory and friendly, whereas the official message presented to-day by your Ambassador to my Minister was conveyed in a very different tone. I beg you to explain this divergency. It would be right to give over the Austro-Servian problem to The Hague Tribunal. I trust in your wisdom and friendship." "NICOLAS."

This telegram is not contained in the "German White Book." But Professor von Mach gives it in his "Official Diplomatic Documents" (p. 596).

I have been unable to find in any book, pamphlet, or collection of papers a trace of the Kaiser's answer. Probably he did not send one.

On the second point I propose to quote only the three definite proposals which were before the German Government on July 31, 1914.

Sir Edward Grey, the British Secretary for Foreign Affairs, had been trying with the cordial help of the Russian Foreign Minister, Sazonof, and the President of the Council of France, M. Viviani, to formulate a plan of averting general hostilities which would meet the approval of Germany.

(1) On July 29 Sir E. Grey had an official conversation with the German Ambassador in London and laid before him a proposal in regard to the halting of military measures, described in the following words:

"It was of course too late for all military operations against Servia to be suspended. In a short time, I supposed, the Austrian forces would be in Belgrade, and in occupation of some Servian territory. But even then it might be possible to bring some mediation into existence if Austria, while saying that she must hold the occupied territory until she had complete satisfaction from Servia, stated that she would not advance further, pending an effort of the Powers to mediate between her and Russia." This proposal was telegraphed to Berlin on the same day, and from there to Vienna. So far as I know no answer to it has ever been received, though King George V warmly supported the proposal in a personal telegram (July 30) to Prince Henry of Prussia, and begged him to urge it upon the Kaiser.

(2) On July 30 Sazonof in the name of the Czar presented to the German Ambassador at Petrograd, and telegraphed for delivery to the Foreign Offices at Berlin and Vienna, the following proposal:

"If Austria, recognizing that the Austro-Servian question has assumed the character of a question of European interest, declares herself ready to eliminate from her ultimatum points which violate the sovereign rights of Servia, Russia undertakes to stop her military preparations."

The German Foreign Minister von Jagow, without waiting to consult Vienna, replied "that he considered it impossible for Austria to accept the proposal." Austria said nothing at all!

(3) On July 31 practically the same proposal, modified on the suggestion of Sir E. Grey and M. Viviani, was renewed by Russia. As presented to Berlin and Vienna it read as follows:

"If Austria consents to stay the march of her troops on Servian territory; and if, recognizing that the Austro-Servian conflict has assumed the character of a question of European interest, she admits that the Great Powers may examine the satisfaction which Servia can accord to the Austro-Hungarian Government without injury to her rights as a sovereign State or her independence, Russia undertakes to maintain her expectant attitude."

No answer from Austria, who had ordered a general mobilization at one o'clock in the morning of that day!

No answer from Germany, except the prompt proclamation of Kriegsgefahr, and the declaration of war on Russia on August 1!

Thus three successive opportunities of putting a stop to further military preparations of Russia on the simple condition that Austria would go no further, but be content with what she already had occupied as a guarantee for reparation from Servia—three golden occasions of preserving the peace of Europe—were brushed aside by Germany practically without consideration.

Yet the marvellous people at Potsdam go on saying that it was the Russian military preparation that brought this war down on the world!—that Germany always wanted peace, and worked for it!

Why then did she not accept the proffered chance of staying the progress of Russian preparations when it lay within her power to do so by lifting a finger?

Because she did not wish the chance. Because she wished Austria to go on with the subjugation of Servia. Because she wished Russia to be forced to go on with her measures to intervene for the rescue of Servia from extinction. Because she wished herself to go on with her design of putting her own incomparable military machine at work to force her will on Europe. Because she wished to have a false excuse to cover her own guilt in making the war by saying: "Russia did it."

The Potsdam gang forgot one thing. Most liars forget something.

They forgot that by refusing the opportunity for peaceful settlement which would have removed their excuse for making war, they would furnish the proof that their excuse was false.

Chapter V
A DIALOGUE ON PEACE BETWEEN
A HOUSEHOLDER AND A BURGLAR

The house was badly wrecked by the struggle which had raged through it. The walls were marred, the windows and mirrors shattered, the pictures ruined, the furniture smashed into kindling-wood.

Worst of all, the faithful servants and some of the children were lying in dark corners, dead or grievously wounded.

The Burglar who had wrought the damage sat in the middle of the dining- room floor, with his swag around him. It was neatly arranged in bags, for in spite of his madness he was a most methodical man. One bag was labelled silverware; another, jewels; another, cash; and another, souvenirs. There was blood on his hands and a fatuous smile on his face.

"Surely I am a mighty man," he said to himself, "and I have proved it! But I am very tired, as well as kind-hearted, and I feel that it is now time to begin a Conversation on Peace."

The Householder, who was also something of a Pacifist on appropriate occasions, but never a blind one, stood near. Through the brief lull in the rampage he overheard the mutterings of the Burglar.

"'Were you speaking to me?" he asked. "As a matter of fact," answered the Burglar, "I was talking to myself. But it is the same thing. Are we not brothers? Do we not both love Peace? Come sit beside me, and let us talk about it."

"What do you mean by Peace," said the Householder, looking grimly around him; "do you mean all this?"

"No, no," said the Burglar; "that is—er—not exactly! 'All this' is most regrettable. I weep over it. If I could have had my way unopposed it would never have happened. But until you sit down close beside me I really cannot tell you in particular what I mean by that blessed word Peace. In general, I mean something like the status quo ante bel-"

"In this case," interrupted the Householder, "you should say the status quo ante furtum—not bellum the state of things before the burglary, not before the war, You are a mighty robber—not a common thief, but a most uncommon one. Do you mean to restore the plunder you have grabbed?"

"Yes, certainly," replied the Burglar, in a magnanimous tone; "that is to say, I mean you shall have a part of it, freely and willingly. I could keep it all, you know, but I am too noble to do that. You shall take the silverware and the souvenirs, I will take the jewels and the cash. Isn't that a fair division? Peace must always stand on a basis of equality between the two parties. Shake hands on it."

The Householder put his hand behind his back.

"You insult me," said he. "If I were your equal I should die of shame. Waive the comparison. What about the damage you have done here? Who shall repair it?"

"All the world," cried the Burglar eagerly; "everybody will help—especially your big neighbor across the lake. He is a fool with plenty of money. You cannot expect me to contribute. I am poor, but as honest as my profession will permit. This damage in your house is not wilful injury. It is merely one of the necessary accompaniments of my practice of burglary. You ought not to feel sore about it. Why do you call attention to it, instead of talking politely and earnestly about the blessings of Peace?"

"I am talking to you as politely as I can," said the Householder, moistening his dry lips, "but while I am doing it, I feel as if I were smeared with mud. Tell me, what have you to say about my children and my servants whom you have tortured and murdered?"

"Ah, that," answered the Burglar, shrugging his shoulders and spreading out his hands, palms upward, so that he looked like a gigantic toad, "—that indeed is so very, very sad! My heart mourns over it. But how could it be avoided? Those foolish people would not lie down, would not be still. Their conduct was directly contrary to my system; see section 417, chapter 93, in my 'Great Field-Book of Burglary,' under the title 'Schrecklichkeit.' Perhaps in the excitement of the moment I went a little beyond those scientific regulations. The babies need not have been killed—only terrified. But that was a mere error of judgment which you will readily forgive and forget for the sake of the holy cause of Peace. Will you not?"

The Householder turned quickly and spat into the fireplace.

"Blasphemer," he cried, "my gorge rises at you! Can there be any forgiveness until you repent? Can there be any Peace in the world if you go loose in it, ready to break and enter and kill when it pleases you? Will you lay down your weapons and come before the Judge?"

The Burglar rose slowly to his feet, twisting up his mustache with bloody brass-knuckled hands.

"You are a colossal ass," he growled. "You forget how strong I am, how much I can still hurt you. I have offered you a chance to get Peace. Don't you want it?"

"Not as a present from you," said the Householder slowly. "It would poison me. I would rather die a decent man's death."

He went a step nearer to the Burglar, who quickly backed away.

"Come," the Householder continued, "let us bandy compliments no longer. You are where you have no right to be. You can talk when I get you before the Judge. I want Peace no more than I want Justice. While there is a God in heaven and honest freemen still live on earth I will fight for both."

He took a fresh grip on his club, and the Burglar backed again, ready to spring.

Through the dead silence of the room there came a loud knocking at the door. Could it be the big neighbor from across the lake?

Chapter VI
STAND FAST, YE FREE!
I

From the outset of this war two things have been clear to me.

First, if the war continued it was absolutely inevitable that the United States would be either drawn into it by the impulse of democratic sympathies or forced into it by the instinct of self-preservation.

Second, the most adequate person in the world to decide when and how the
United States should accept the great responsibility of fighting beside
France and Great Britain for peace and for the American ideal of freedom
was President Wilson.

His sagacity, his patience, his knowledge of the varied elements that are blended in our nationality, his sincere devotion to pacific conceptions of progress, his unwavering loyalty to the cause of liberty secured by law, national and international, made him the one man of all others to whom this great decision could most safely be confided.

The people of the United States believed this in the election of 1916. They trusted him sincerely then because "he kept us out of the war" until the inevitable hour. No less sincerely do they trust him now when he declares that the hour has come when we must "dedicate our lives and our fortunes, everything that we are and everything that we have" (President's Message to Congress, April 2, 1917), to defend ourselves and the world from the Imperial German Government, which is waging "a warfare against mankind."

In the quiet, but never idle, American Legation at The Hague there was an excellent opportunity to observe and study the incredible blunders by which Germany led us, and the unspeakable insults and injuries by which she compelled us, to enter the war.

Our adherence to the Monroe Doctrine was, at first, an obstacle to that entrance. Believing that European governments ought not to interfere in domestic affairs on the American continents, we admitted the converse of that proposition, and held that America should not meddle with European controversies or conflicts. But we soon came to a realizing sense of the ominous fact that Germany was the one nation of Europe which openly despised and flouted the Monroe Doctrine as an outworn superstition. Her learned professors (followed by a few servile American imitators) had poured ridicule and scorn upon it in unreadable books. Her actions in the West Indies and South

America showed her contempt for it as a "bit of American bluff." Gradually it dawned upon us that if France were crushed and England crippled our dear old Monroe Doctrine would stand a poor chance against a victorious and supercilious Imperial German Government. As I wrote to Washington in August, 1914, their idea was to "lunch in Paris, dine in London, and spend the night somewhere in America."

Another real barrier to our taking any part in the war was our sincere, profound, traditional love of peace. This does not mean, of course, that America is a country of pacifists. Our history proves the contrary. Our conscientious objections to certain shameful things, like injustice, and dishonor, and tyranny, and systematic cruelty, are stronger than our conscientious objection to fighting. But our national policy is averse to war, and our national institutions are not favorable to its sudden declaration or swift prosecution.

In effect, the United States is a pacific nation of fighting men.

What was it, then, that forced such a nation into a conflict of arms?

It was the growing sense that the very existence of this war was a crime against humanity, that it need not and ought not to have been begun, and that the only way to put a stop to it was to join the Allies, who had tried to prevent its beginning, and who are still trying to bring it to the only end that will be a finality.

It was also the conviction that the Monroe Doctrine, so far from being an obstacle, was an incentive to our entrance. The real basis of that doctrine is the right of free peoples, however small and weak, to maintain by common consent their own forms of government. This Germany and Austria denied. The issue at stake was no longer merely European. It was worldwide.

The Monroe Doctrine could not be saved in one continent if its foundation was destroyed in another. The only way to save it was to broaden it.

The United States, having grown to be a World Power, must either uphold everywhere the principles by which it had been begotten and made great or sink into the state of an obese, helpless parasite. Its sister republics would share its fate.

But more than this: it was the flagrant and contemptuous disregard of all the principles of international law and common humanity by the Imperial German Government that alarmed and incensed us. The list of crimes and atrocities ordered in this war by the mysterious and awful power that rules the German people—which I prefer to call, for the sake of brevity and impersonality, the Potsdam gang—is too long to be repeated here. The levying of unlawful tribute from captured cities and villages; the use of old men, women, and children as a screen for advancing troops; the extortion of military information from civilians by cruel and barbarous methods; the burning and destruction of entire towns as a punishment for the actual or suspected hostile deeds of individuals, and the brutal avowal that in this punishment it was necessary that "the innocent shall suffer with the guilty" (see the letter of General von Nieber to the burgomaster of Wavre, August 27, and the proclamation of Governor-General von der Goltz, September 2, 1914); the introduction of the use of asphyxiating gas as a weapon of war (at Ypres, April 22, 1915); the poisoning of wells; the reckless and needless destruction of priceless monuments of art like the Cathedral of Reims; the deliberate and treacherous violation of the Red Cross, which is the sign of mercy and compassion for all Christendom; the bombardment of hospitals and the cold-blooded slaughter of nurses and wounded men; the sinking of hospital ships with their helpless and suffering company—all these, and many other infamies committed by order of the Potsdam gang made the heart of America hot and angry against the power which devised and commanded such brutality. True, they were not, technically speaking, crimes directed against the United States. They did not injure our material interests. They injured only our souls and the world in which we have to live. They were vivid illustrations of the inward nature of that German Kultur whose superiority, the German professors say, "is rooted in the unfathomable depths of its moral constitution."

But there were two criminal blunders—or perhaps it would be more accurate to call them two series of obstinate and stupid offenses against international law—by which the Potsdam gang directly assailed the sovereignty and neutrality of the United States and forced us to choose between the surrender of our national integrity and a frank acceptance of the war which Germany was waging, not only against our principles and interests, but against the things which in our judgment were essential to the welfare of mankind and to the existence of honorable and decent relations among the peoples of the world.

The first of these offenses was the cynical and persistent attempt to take advantage of the good nature and unsuspiciousness of the United States for the establishment of an impudent system of German espionage; to use our territory as a base of conspiracy and treacherous hostilities against countries with which we were at peace; and to lose no opportunity of mobilizing the privileges granted by "these idiotic Yankees" (quotation from the military attache of the Imperial German Embassy at Washington)—including, of course, the diplomatic privilege—to make America unconsciously help in playing the game of the Potsdam gang.

The second of these offenses was the illegal, piratical submarine warfare which the Potsdam gang ordered and waged against the merchant shipping of the world, thereby destroying the lives and the property of American citizens and violating the most vital principle of our steadfast contention for the freedom of the sea.

The message of the President to Congress on April 2, 1917, marked these two offenses as the main causes which made it impossible for the United States to maintain longer an official attitude of neutrality toward the German Government, which "did what it pleased and told its people nothing." The President generously declared that the source of these offenses "lay not in any hostile feeling or purpose of the German people toward us." That was a magnanimous declaration, and we sincerely hope it may prove true.

But practically the difficulty lies in the fact that at the present hour several millions of the German people stand in arms, on land that does not belong to them, to maintain the purpose and continue the practices of the Potsdam gang. It is a pity, but it is true. The only way to get at the gang which chose and forced this atrocious war is to go through the armed people who still defend that choice and the atrocities which have emphasized it.

Forgiveness must wait upon repentance. Repentance must be proved by restitution and reparation. Any other settlement of this world conflict would be a world calamity. For America and for all the Allies who are fighting for a peace worth having and keeping, the watchword must be: Stand fast, ye free!

II

The offenses against the neutrality of the United States which were instigated and financed by the Potsdam gang were enumerated by the Committee on Foreign Affairs of the House of Representatives in the first week of April, 1917, and amounted to at least twenty-one distinct crimes or unfriendly acts, including the furnishing of bogus passports to German reservists and spies, the incitement of rebellion in India and in Mexico, the preparation of dynamite outrages against Canada, the placing of bombs in ships sailing from American ports, and many other ill-judged pleasantries of a similar character.

The crown was put on this series of blundering misdeeds by the note of January 19, 1917, sent from the German Foreign Office (under cover of our diplomatic privilege, of course) to the German Minister in Mexico, directing him to prepare an alliance with that country against the United States in the event of war, urging him to use Mexico as an agent to draw Japan into that alliance, and offering as a bribe to the Mexicans the possession of American territory in Texas, New Mexico, and Arizona.

The fact is, we have only just begun to understand the real nature of the German secret service, which works with, and either under or over, the diplomatic service.

It is certainly the most highly organized, systematic, and expensive, and at the same time probably the most bone-headed and unscrupulous, secret service in the world.

Its powers of falsification and evasion are only exceeded by its capacity for making those mistakes which spring from a congenital contempt for other people.

At The Hague I had numerous opportunities of observing and noting the workings of this peculiar system. The story of many of them cannot be publicly told without violating that reserve which I prefer to maintain in regard to confidential communications and private affairs in which the personal reputation of individuals is involved. But there are two or three experiences of which I may write freely without incurring either self-reproach or a just reproach from others. They are not at all sensational. But they seemed at the time, and they seem still, to have a certain significance as indications of the psychology of the people with whom we were then in nominal friendship.

Three requests were made to me for the forwarding of important communications to Brussels under cover of the diplomatic privilege of the American Legation. The memoranda of the dates and so on are in the Chancellery at The Hague, so I cannot refer to them. But it is certain that the requests came shortly after the beginning of the war, in the first or second week of August, 1914, and the content and purport of them are absolutely clear in my memory.

The first request was from Berlin for the transmission of a note to the Belgian Government, renewing the proposition which the Potsdam gang had made on August 2: namely, that Belgium should permit the free passage of German troops through her neutral ground on condition that Germany would pay for all damage done and that Belgian territory would not be annexed. King Albert had already replied, on August 3, to this proposition, saying that to permit such a passage of hostile troops against France would be "a flagrant violation of international law" and would "sacrifice the honor of the nation." After such an answer it did not seem to me that the renewal of the dishonorable proposal was likely to have a good effect. Yet the Berlin note was entirely correct in form. It merely offered a chance for Belgium to choose again between peace with the friendship of Germany and dishonor attached, and war in defense of the neutrality to which she was bound by the very treaties (1831, 1839) which brought her into being. I had no right to interpose an obstacle to the repetition of Belgium's first heroic choice. I pointed out that, not being accredited to the Belgian Government, I was not in a position to transmit any communication to it. But I was willing to forward the note to my colleague the American Minister in Brussels, absolutely without recommendation, but simply for such disposal as he thought fit. Accordingly the note was transmitted to him.

What Whitlock did with it I do not know. What answer, if any, Belgium made I do not know. But I do know that she stood to her guns and kept her honor intact and immortal.

The second request was of a different quality. It came to me from the Imperial German Legation at The Hague. It was a note for transmission to the Belgian Government, beginning with a reference to the fall of Liege and the hopeless folly of attempting to resist the German invasion, and continuing with an intimation of the terrible consequences which would follow Belgium's persistence in her mad idea of keeping her word of honor. In effect the note was a curious combination of an insult and a threat. I promptly and positively refused to transmit it or to have anything to do with it.

"But why," said the German counsellor, sitting by my study fire—a Prussian of the Prussians—"why do you refuse? You are a neutral, a friend of both parties. Why not simply transmit the note to your colleague in Brussels as you did before? You are not in any way responsible for its contents."

"Quite so," I answered, "and thank God for that! But suppose you had a quarrel with a neighbor in the Rheinland, who had positively declined a proposition which you had made to him. And suppose, the ordinary post-boy services being interrupted, you asked me to convey to your neighbor a note which began by addressing him as a 'silly s— of a b——,' and ended by telling him that if he did not agree you would certainly grind him to powder. Would you expect me to play the post-boy for such a billet-doux on the ground that I was not responsible for its contents and was a friend of both parties?"

"Well," replied the counsellor, laughing at the North American directness of my language, "probably not." So he folded up the note and took it away. What became of it I do not know nor care.

The third request was of still another quality. It came from the Imperial Austro-Hungarian Legation, which very politely asked me to transmit a message in the American diplomatic code to my colleague in Brussels for delivery to the Austro-Hungarian Legation, which still lingered in that city. The first and last parts of the message were in plain language, good English, quite innocent and proper. But the kernel of the despatch was written in the numerical secret cipher of Vienna, which of course I was unable to read. I drew attention to this, and asked mildly how I could be expected to put this passage into our code without knowing what the words were. The answer was that it would not be necessary to code this passage; it could be transmitted in numbers just as it stood; the Austro-Hungarian charge d'affaires at Brussels would understand it.

"Quite so," I answered, "but you see the point is that I do not understand it. My dear count, you are my very good friend, and it grieves me deeply to decline any requests of yours. But the simple fact is that our instructions explicitly forbid us to send any message in two codes."

The count—who, by the way, was an excellent and most amiable man— blushed and stammered that he was only carrying out the instructions of his chief, but that my point was perfectly clear and indisputable. I was glad that he saw it in that light, and we parted on the most friendly terms. What became of the message I do not know nor care.

It was about the 1st of September, 1915, that I came into brief contact with the case of Mr. J. F. J. Archibald. This gentleman was an American journalist, and a very clever and agreeable man. We had met some months before, when he was on his way back to America from his professional work in Germany, and he had been a welcome guest at my table. But the second meeting was different.

This time Mr. Archibald was returning toward Germany on the Holland-America steamship Rotterdam. When the boat touched at Falmouth, on August 30, the British authorities examined his luggage and found that he was carrying private letters and official despatches from Doctor Dumba the Austrian Ambassador at Washington, from Count Bernstorff the German Ambassador, and from Captain von Papen his military attache. Not only was the carrying of these letters by a private person on a regular mail route a recognized offense against the law, but the documents themselves contained matter of an incriminating and seditious nature, most unfriendly to the United States. The egregious Doctor Dumba, for example, described how it would be possible to "disorganize and hold up for months if not entirely prevent," the work of American factories; and the colossal Captain von Papen, in a letter referring to the activities of German secret agents in America, gave birth to his eloquent and unforgettable phrase, "these idiotic Yankees." The papers, of course, were taken from Mr. Archibald at Falmouth, but he was allowed to continue his voyage to Rotterdam en route for Berlin.

Before his arrival, however, a cablegram came from the Department of State at Washington instructing me to take up his regular passport which was made out to cover travel in Germany; to give him an emergency passport valid for one month and good only for the return to the United States; and to use all proper means to get him back to New York at the earliest possible date.

Having found out that he was lodged at a certain hotel I sent him a courteous invitation to call at the Legation on business of importance. He came promptly and we sat down in the library for a conversation which you will admit had its delicate points.

He began by saying that he supposed I had seen the newspaper accounts of what happened to him at Falmouth; that he was greatly surprised and chagrined about the matter; that he had been entirely ignorant of the contents of the documents found in his possession; that he had imagined—indeed he had been distinctly told—that they were innocent private letters relating to personal and domestic affairs; that he did not know there was any impropriety in conveying such letters; that if he had suspected their nature or known that they included official despatches he would never have taken them.

I replied that his personal statement was enough for me on that point, but that it seemed to throw rather a dark shadow on the character and conduct of his friends in the German and Austrian Embassies who had knowingly exposed his innocence to such a risk. I added that it was probably with a view to obtaining his help in clearing up the matter that the Department of State had instructed me to take up his passport.

"But have you the legal right to do that?"

"Under American law, yes, unquestionably."

"But under Dutch law?"

"Probably not. But I hope it will not be necessary to invoke that law.

Simply to inform the Dutch Foreign Minister of the presence of an

American whose passport had been revoked but who refused to give it up, would be sufficient for my purpose."

He reflected for a moment, and then said, smiling:

"I don't refuse to give it up. Here it is. Now tell me what I shall do without a passport.

"Thank you. Fortunately I have authority to give you an emergency passport, good for a month, and covering the return voyage to America."

"But I don't want to go there. I want to go on to Berlin."

"Unfortunately I fear that will be impossible. Your old passport is invalid and will not carry you over the Dutch border. Your new passport cannot be made out for Germany. Your best course is to return home."

"I see. But have you any right to arrest me and send me to America?"

"None whatever, my dear sir. Please don't misunderstand me. This is just a bit of friendly advice. 'Your country needs you.' You naturally want an early chance to tell Washington what you have told me. The Rotterdam is a very comfortable ship, and she sails for New York the day after to-morrow. I have already bespoken an excellent room for you. Do you accept?"

"Yes, and thank you for the way you have put the matter. But do you think they will arrest me when I get to New York?"

"Probably not. But to help in forestalling that unpleasant possibility I will cable Washington that you are coming at once, of your own free will, and anxious to tell the whole story."

So he went, and I saw him off on the Rotterdam, a pallid and downcast figure. I pitied him. It seemed strange that any one should ever trust that unscrupulous, callous, thick-pated diplomatic-secret-service machine which is always ready to expose a too confiding and admiring friend to danger or disgrace in order to serve its imperious necessities.

Holland, of course, owing to its geographical situation, was a regular nest of German espionage. Other spies were there, too, but they were much less in evidence than the Germans. Of the tricks and the manners of the latter I had some picturesque experiences which I do not feel at liberty to narrate. The Department of State has been informed of them, and has no doubt put the information safely away with a lot of other things which it knows but does not think it expedient or necessary to tell until the proper time.

But there is no reason why the simple little tale of the futile attempt to plant two German spies in my household at The Hague should not be told. One of the men in our domestic service, a Hollander, had been obliged to leave and we wanted to fill his place. This was difficult because the requirements of the Dutch army service claimed such a large number of the younger men.

The first who applied for the vacant place professed to be a Belgian. Perhaps he was. On demand he produced his "papers"—birth-certificate, baptismal registry, several Passier-scheine, and so forth. But down in a corner on the back of one of the papers was a dim blue stamp—"Imperial German Marine." What was the meaning of this? What had the Potsdam High-Sea Fleet to do with this peaceable overland traveller from Belgium? Voluble excuses, but no satisfactory explanation. I told him that I feared he was too experienced for the place.

The second who applied was an unquestionable Dutchman, young, good-looking, intelligent. Papers in perfect order. Present service with a well-known pro-German family. Previous service of one year with a lady who was one of my best friends—the wife of a high government official. I rang her up on the telephone and asked if she could tell me anything about A. B., who had been in service with her for a year. A second of silence, then the answer: "Yes, a good deal, but not on the telephone, please. Come around to tea this afternoon." Madame L. then told me that while the young man was clean, sober, and industrious, he had been found rummaging among her husband's official papers, in a room which he was forbidden to enter, and had been caught several times listening at the keyhole of doors while private conferences were going on.

It seemed to me that a young man with such an uncontrollable thirst for knowledge would not be suited for the very simple service which would be required of him in our household.

Afterward, traces of both of these men were found which led unmistakably to the lair of the chief spider of the German secret service at The Hague. The incident was a very small one. But, after all, life is made up of small incidents with a connected meaning.

At the time when I am writing this (September 24, 1917) the moral character of the tools of the Potsdam gang has again been stripped naked by the disclosure of the treachery by which the German Legation in Argentina has utilized the Swedish Legation in that country to transmit, under diplomatic privilege, messages inciting to murder on the high seas. Argentina has already taken the action to be expected from an American Republic by dismissing the German Minister. What Sweden will do to vindicate her honor remains to be seen. Her attitude may affect our opinion of her as a victim or a vassal of Potsdam.

There are two points in the disclosures made on September 23 by the Department of State which bear directly upon this simple narrative of experiences at The Hague.

The fetching female comic-opera star, Ray Beveridge, discreetly alluded to in the third chapter (p. 71), was secretly paid three thousand dollars by the Imperial German Embassy in Washington to finance her artistic activities. So, you see, I was not far wrong in forwarding her divorce papers to Germany and refusing to transmit her newspaper correspondence to America. She was a paid soubrette in the Potsdam troupe.

The affable and intelligent Mr. Archibald, alluded to in this chapter (p. 169), received on April 21, 1915, according to these disclosures, five thousand dollars from the Imperial German Embassy in Washington for "propaganda" services. If I had known this when he came to me in September, it is possible that I should have been less careful to spare his feelings.

III

The record of the German submarine warfare on merchant shipping is one of the most extraordinary chapters in history. Americans have read it with appropriate indignation, but not always with clear understanding of the precise issues involved. Let me try to make those issues plain, since the submarine campaign was one of the causes which forced this war upon the United States. (President's Message to Congress, April 2, 1917, paragraphs 2-10.)

In war all naval vessels, including of course submarines, have the right to attack and destroy, by any means in their power, any war-ship of the enemy. In regard to merchant-ships the case is different, according to international law. (See G. G. Wilson, International Law, paragraphs 114, 136, New York, 1901-1909.)

The war-vessel has the right of "visit and search" on all merchant-ships, enemy or neutral. It has also the right, in case the cargo of the merchant-ship appears to include more than a certain percentage of contraband, to capture it and take it into a port for adjudication as a prize. The war-vessel has also the right to sink a presumptive prize under conditions (such as distance, stress of weather, and so forth) which make it impossible to take it into port.

But here the right of the war-vessel stops. It has absolutely no right to sink the merchant-ship without warning and without making efficient provision for the safety of the passengers and crew. That is the common law of civilized nations. To break it is to put one's self beyond the pale.

Some Germanophile critics have faulted me for calling the Teutonic submarines "Potsdam pirates." A commissioned vessel, these critics say, which merely executes the orders of its government, cannot properly be called a pirate.

Why not? Take the definition of piracy given in the New Oxford Dictionary: "The crime of robbery or depredation on the sea by persons not holding a commission from an established civilized state."

There's the point! Is a nation which orders its servants to commit deeds forbidden by international law, a nation which commands its naval officers to commit deliberate, wanton, dastardly murder on the high seas (case of Belgian Prince, July 31, 1917, and others), is such a nation to be regarded as "an established civilized state"?

Were Algiers and Tunis and Tripoli "civilized states" when they sent out the Barbary pirates in the eighteenth and early nineteenth centuries? We thought not, and we sent our war-ships to whip the barbarism out of them.

Commodore Stephen Decatur, in 1815, forced the cruel and cowardly Dey of Algiers to sign a deed of renunciation and a promise of good conduct, on the deck of an American frigate, under the Stars and Stripes.

A hundred years ago the glory of the American navy was made clear to the world in the suppression of the pirates of North Africa. To-day that glory must be maintained by firm, fearless, unrelenting war against the pirates of North Germany.

A commission to do a certain thing which is in itself unlawful does not change the nature of the misdeed. No nation has a right to commission its officers to violate the law of nations.

But the Germans say their submarines are such wonderful, delicate, scientific machines that it is impossible for them to give warning of an attack, or to do anything to save the helpless people whose peaceful vessel has been sunk beneath their feet. The precious, fragile submarine cannot be expected to observe any law of humanity which would imperil its further usefulness as an instrument of destruction.

Marvellous argument—worthy of the Potsdam mind in its highest state of Kultur! By the same reasoning any assassin might claim the right to kill without resistance because he proposed to commit the crime with a dagger so delicately wrought, so frail, so slender, that the slightest struggle on the part of his victim would break the costly, beautiful, murderous weapon.

Again, these extraordinary Germans say that merchant-ships ought not to carry weapons for defense; it is too dangerous for the dainty U-boat; every merchantman thus armed must be treated as a vessel of war. But the law of nations for more than two centuries has sanctioned the carrying of defensive armament by merchant-ships, and precisely because they might need it to protect themselves against pirates.

Shall the United States be asked to rewrite this article of international law, in the midst of a great war on sea and land? Shall the government at Washington be seduced by cajolery, or compelled by threats, to rob the merchantmen of the poor protection of a single gun in order that they may fall absolutely helpless into the black hands of the prowling Potsdam pirates? That would be neutrality with a vengeance! Yet that is just what the Imperial German Government tried to persuade or force the United States to do. Thank God the effort was vain.

These were the matters under discussion when I was called to Washington in February, 1916, for consultation with the President. The long and wearing controversy had been going on for months. Every month notes were coming from Berlin, each more evasive and unsatisfactory than the last. Every week Count Bernstorff and his aides were coming to the State Department with new excuses, new subterfuges, and the same old lies. The President and Secretary Lansing, both of whom are excellent international lawyers, found their patience tried to the uttermost by the absurdity of the arguments presented to them and by the veiled contempt in the manner of the presentation. But they kept their tempers and did their best to keep the peace.

On two points they were firm as adamant. First, the law of nations should not and could not be changed in the midst of a war to suit the need of one of the parties. Second, "the use of submarines for the destruction of commerce is of necessity, because of the very character of the vessels employed and the very methods of attack which their employment of course involves, incompatible with the principles of humanity, the long-established and incontrovertible rights of neutrals, and the sacred immunities of non-combatants." (President Wilson's Address to Congress, April 19, 1916.)

It was on my return from this visit to Washington that I had an opportunity of observing at close range the crooked methods of the Potsdam gang in regard to the U-boat warfare. Arriving at The Hague on March 24, 1916, I found Holland aflame with helpless rage over the recent sinking of the S.S. Tubantia, the newest and best boat of the Netherlands-Lloyd merchant-fleet. She was torpedoed by an unseen submarine on March 15.

An explanation was promptly demanded from the German Government, which denied any knowledge of the affair. Holland, lacking evidence as to the perpetrator of the crime, would have had to swallow this denial but for an accident which furnished her with the missing proof. One of the Tubantia's small boats drifted ashore. In the boat was a fragment of a Schwarzkopf torpedo—a type manufactured and used only by Germany. This fragment was forwarded to Berlin, with another and more urgent demand for explanation, apology, and reparation.

The German newspapers coolly replied with the astounding statement that there had been two or three Schwarzkopf torpedoes in naval museums in England, and that this particular specimen had probably been given to a British submarine and used by her to destroy the good ship Tubantia.

Again Holland would have been left helpless, choking with indignation, but for a second accident. Another of the lost steamship's boats was found, and in it there was another fragment of the torpedo. This fragment bore the mark of the German navy, telling just when the torpedo was made and to which of the U-boats it had been issued.

With this bit of damning evidence in his bag a Dutch naval expert was sent to Berlin to get to the bottom of the crime and to demand justice. He got there, but he found no justice in that shop.

The German navy is very systematic, keeps accurate books, makes no accidental mistake. The pedigree and record of the Schwarzkopf were found. It was issued to a certain U-boat on a certain date. Undoubtedly it was the missile which unfortunately sank the Tubantia. All this was admitted and deeply regretted. But Germany was free from all responsibility for the sad occurrence. The following amazing reason was given by the Imperial German Government.

This certain U-boat had fired this certain torpedo at a British war-vessel somewhere in the North Sea ten days before the Tubantia was sunk. The shot missed its mark. But the naughty, undisciplined little torpedo went cruising around in the sea on its own hook for ten days waiting for a chance to kill somebody. Then the Tubantia came along, and the wandering-Willy torpedo promptly, stupidly, ran into the ship and sank her. This was the explanation. Germany was not to blame. (See the official report in the Orange Books of the Netherlands Government, July, 1916, December, 1916.)

This stupendous fairy-tale Holland was expected to believe and to accept as the end of the affair. She did not believe it. She had to accept it. What else could she do? Fight? She did not want to share Belgium's dreadful fate. The Dutch Government proposed that the whole Tubantia incident be submitted to an international commission. The German Government accepted this proposal en principe, but said it must be deferred until after the war.

I wonder why some of the Americans who blame Holland for not being in arms against Germany never think of that stern and awful deterrent which stands under her eyes and presses upon her very bosom. She is still independent, still neutral, still unravaged. Five-sixths of her people, I believe, have no sympathy with the German Government in its choice and conduct of this war. At least this was the case while I was at The Hague. But the one thing that Holland is, above all else, is pro-Dutch. She wants to keep her liberty, her sovereignty, her land untouched. To defend these treasures she will fight, and for no other reason. I have heard Queen Wilhelmina say this a score of times. She means it, and her people are with her.

Seven Dutch ships were sunk in a bunch in the English Channel by the Potsdam pirates on February 22, 1917. Holland was furious. She stated her grievance, protested, remonstrated—and there she stopped. If she had tried to do anything more she stood to lose a third of her territory in a few days and the whole in a few weeks—lose it, mark you, to the gang that ruined Belgium.

But the position, and therefore the case, of America in regard to the German submarine warfare was quite different. She was one of the eight "Big Powers" of the world. She was the mightiest of the neutrals.

Her rights at sea were no greater than theirs. But her duties were greater, just because she was larger, more powerful, better able to champion those rights not only for herself but also for others.

She would not have to pay such an instant, awful, crushing penalty for armed resistance to the brutalities of the Potsdam gang as would certainly be inflicted upon the little northern neutrals if they attempted to defend themselves against injustice and aggression.

Their part was to make protest, and record it, and wait for justice until the war was ended. America's part was to make protest, and then—her protest being mocked, scorned, disregarded—to stand up in arms with France and Great Britain and help to end the war by a victory of righteous peace.

But did we not also have objections to some of the measures and actions of the British blockade—as, for instance, the seizure and search of the mails? Certainly we did, and Secretary Lansing stated them clearly and maintained them firmly. But here is the difference. These objections concerned only the rights of neutral property on the high seas. We knew by positive assurance from England, and by our experience with her in the Alabama Claims Arbitration, that she was ready to refer all such questions to an impartial tribunal and abide by its decision. Our objections to the conduct of the German navy concerned the far more sacred rights of "life, liberty, and the pursuit of happiness."

The murder of one American child at sea meant more to us than the seizure of a thousand cargoes of alleged contraband.

No one has ever accused the British or French or Italian sailors in this war of sinking merchant-ships without warning, leaving their crews and passengers to drown. On the contrary, British seamen have risked and lost their lives in a chivalrous attempt to save the lives even of their enemies after the fair sinking of a German war-ship.

But the hands of the Potsdam pirates are red with innocent blood. The bottom of the sea is strewn with the wrecks they have made. "The dark unfathom'd caves of ocean" hide the bones of their helpless victims, who shall arise at the judgment-day to testify against them.

On May 7, 1915, the passenger liner Lusitania, unarmed, was sunk without warning by a German U-boat off the Irish coast. One hundred and fourteen Americans—men, women, and little children, lawful and peaceful travellers— were drowned—

"Butchered to make a German holiday."

The holiday was celebrated in Germany. The schools were let out. The soldiers in the reserve camps had leave to join in the festivities. The towns and cities were filled with fluttering flags and singing folks. A German pastor preached: "Whoever cannot bring himself to approve from the bottom of his heart the sinking of the Lusitania—him we judge to be no true German." (Deutsche Reden in Schwerer Zeit) A medal was struck to commemorate the great achievement. It is a very ugly medal. I keep a copy of it in order that I may never forget the character of a nation which was not content with rejoicing over such a crime but desired to immortalize it in bronze.

The three strong and eloquent notes of President Wilson in regard to the Lusitania are too well known to be quoted here. The practical answer from Potsdam (passing over the usual subterfuges and falsehoods) was the sinking of the Arabic August 19 and the murder of three more Americans. Then the correspondence languished until the torpedoing (March 24, 1916) of the Sussex, a Channel ferry-boat, crowded with passengers, among whom were many Americans. Then the President sent a flat message calling down the Potsdam pirates and declaring that unless they abandoned their nefarious practices "the United States had no choice but to sever diplomatic relations with the German Empire altogether" (April 18, 1916).

This brought a grudging promise from Germany that she would henceforth refrain from sinking merchant-vessels "without warning and without saving human lives, unless the ship attempted to escape or offer resistance." How this promise was kept may be judged from the sinking of the Marina (October 28), with the loss of eight American lives, and of the Russian (December 14), with the loss of seventeen American lives, and other similar sinkings.

During all this time Germany had been building new and larger submarines with wonderful industry. She had filled up her pack of sea-wolves. On January 31, 1917, she revoked her flimsy pledge, let loose her wolf-pack, and sent word to all the neutral nations that she would sink at sight all ships found in the zones which she had marked "around Great Britain, France, Italy, and in the Eastern Mediterranean." (Why We Are at War,, New York, 1917.) The President promptly broke off diplomatic relations (February 3), and said that we should refrain from hostilities until the commission of "actual overt acts" by Germany forced us to the conviction that she meant to carry out her base threat.

The overt acts came quickly. Between February 3 and April 1 eight American merchant-ships were sunk, and more than forty American lives were destroyed by the Potsdam pirates.

The die was cast. On April 2, 1917, the President advised Congress that the United States could no longer delay the formal acceptance of "the status of belligerent which had been thrust upon it." On April 6 Congress took the necessary action. On the same day the President proclaimed that "a state of war exists between the United States and the Imperial German Government."

Back of this momentous and noble decision, in which the hearts of the immense majority of Americans are with the President, there are undoubtedly many strong and righteous reasons. Some of these I have tried to set forth in the first part of this article. But we must never forget that the specific reason given by the President, the definite cause which forced us into the war, is the German method of submarine warfare, which he has repeatedly denounced as illegal, immoral, inhuman—a direct and brutal attack upon us and upon all mankind. These words cannot be forgotten, nor is it likely that the President will retract them.

They set up at least one steadfast mark in the midst of the present flood of peace talk. There can be no parley with a criminal who is in full and exultant practice of his crime. Unless the U-boat warfare is renounced, repented of, and abandoned by the Potsdam pirates, an honorable peace is unattainable except by fighting for it and winning it.

Hospital ships sunk: Britannic (probably but not certainly torpedoed); Asturias, March 24. 1917; Gloucester Castle, March 30; Donegal, April 17; Lanfranc, April 17 (with British wounded and German wounded prisoners).

Among the neutral nations Norway alone has lost more than six hundred ships by mines and torpedoes of German origin. The dance of death still goes on.

IV

Only a little space is left for writing of my retirement from the post at The Hague and my experiences thereafter in England and France.

The reader may have gathered from the tenor of these chapters that the work at the legation was hard and that the situation was trying to a man with strong convictions and the habit of expressing them frankly. My resignation was tendered in September, 1916, with the request that it should not be made public until after the re-election of President Wilson, which I earnestly desired and expected. My reasons for resigning were partly of a domestic nature. But the main reason was a personal wish to get back to my work as a writer, "with full freedom to say what I thought and felt about the war."

The German-American press has tried to start a rumor that I was recalled to Washington to explain my action on a certain point. That is absolutely and entirely false. The government never asked for an explanation of anything in my conduct while in office, or afterward. On the contrary, the President has been kind enough to express his approval of my services in terms too friendly to be quoted here.

In November, after President Wilson had been triumphantly chosen for a second term, I ventured to recall his attention to my letter of September. He answered that he would "reluctantly yield" to my wishes, but would appreciate my remaining at The Hague until a successor could be found for the post. Of course I willingly agreed to this.

In December the name of this successor was cabled to me with instructions to find out whether he would be acceptable to the Queen and the Government of Holland. Her Majesty said that this gentleman would certainly be persona grata, and I cabled to Washington to this effect.

Early in January a message came from the Secretary of State saying that, as all was arranged except the final confirmation of the appointment, I might feel free to leave at my convenience. Having cleaned up my work and left everything in order for my successor (including the lease of my house), I took ship from Flushing for England on January 15, 1917.

The voyage through the danger zone was uneventful. The visit to England was unforgettable.

Everywhere I saw the evidences that Great Britain was at war, in earnest, and resolved to "carry on" with her Allies until the victory of a real peace was won.

Women and girls were at work in the railway stations, on the trams and omnibuses, in the munition factories, in postal and telegraph service, doing the tasks of men. We shall have to revise that phrase which speaks of "the weaker sex."

By night London was
"Dark, dark, dark, irrecoverably dark."
But it was not still, nor terrified by the instant danger of Zeppelin raids. Every time a German vulture passed over England dropping bolts of indiscriminate death, it woke the heart of the people to a new impulse, not of fear but of hot indignation.

By day the great city swarmed with eager life. Business was going on at full swing, though not "as usual." Women were driving trucks, carrying packages, running ticket-offices. Men in khaki outnumbered those in civilian dress. Wounded soldiers hobbled cheerfully along the streets. The parks were adorned with hospitals. Mrs. Pankhurst spoke from a soap-box near the Marble Arch; not now for woman-suffrage—"That will come," she said, "but the great thing to-day is to carry on the war to a victory for freedom!"

Oxford—gray city of the golden dream, Learning's fairest and most lovely seat in all the world—Oxford was transformed into a hospital for the wounded, a training-camp for new soldiers, a nursery of noble manhood equipped for the stern duties of war.

Every family that I knew was in grief for a dear one lost on the field of glorious strife. But not one was in mourning. The great sacrifice was bravely accepted as a part of the greater duty.

The friends with whom I talked most—men like Lord Bryce, Sir Sydney Lee, Sir Herbert Warren, Sir Robertson Nicoll, Sir William Osler—were lovers of peace, tried and well-known. All were of one mind in holding that Britain's faith and honor bound her to accept the war when Germany violated Belgium, and that it must be fought through until the Prussian military autocracy which began it was broken.

There were restricted rations in England; but no starvation and no sign of it. There were partisan criticisms and plenty of "grousing." The Britisher is never contented unless he can grumble—especially at his own government. But there was no lack of a real unity of purpose, nor of a solid, cheerful, bull-dog determination to hang on to the enemy until he came down. It is this spirit that has enabled a nation, which was almost ignorant of what military preparedness meant, to put between three and four million troops into the field in defense of justice and liberty.

At the end of January I went to France, eager to see with my own eyes the great things that were doing there and to taste with my own lips the cup of danger. That at least I was bound to do before I could come home and urge my countrymen to face the duty and brave the peril of a part in this war.

Paris was not so dark as London but more tragic. After Belgium and
Servia the heaviest brunt of this dreadful conflict has fallen upon
France. She has suffered most. Yet on the faces of her women I saw no
tears and in the eyes of her men no fear nor regret.

If Britain was magnificent, France was miraculous! Loving and desiring peace she accepted the cross of war without a murmur. Her women were no less brave than her men. She wears the hero-star of Roland and the saintly halo of Joan of Arc.

After meeting many men in Paris—statesmen, men of letters, generals—and after visiting the splendid American Ambulance at Neuilly and other institutions in which our boys and girls were giving their help to France in the chivalric spirit of Lafayette, I went out toward the front.

The first visit was under the escort of Captain Francois Monod to a chateau beyond Compiegne, where Rudyard Kipling with his family and I with my family had passed the Christmas week of 1913 together, as joyous guests of the American chatelaine Mrs. Julia Park. She has given the spacious, lovely house for a military hospital. And there, while the German guns thundered a few kilometres away from us and a German sausage balloon floated in the sky, I watched the skilful ministrations of French and American doctors and nurses to the wounded.

One thought haunted me—the memory of Kipling's only son, nineteen years old, who was with us in that happy Christmastide. The lad was reported "missing" after one of the battles between Loos and Hulluch. For six months I sought, with the help of Herr von Kuhlmann, German Minister at The Hague, to find a trace of the brave boy. But never a word could we get.

The second visit was to the battle-field of the Marne under the escort of Captain the Count de Ganay. We motored slowly through the ruined towns and villages. Those which had been wrecked by shellfire were like mouthfuls of broken teeth—chimneys and fragments of walls still standing. Those which had been vengefully burned by the retreating Germans were mere heaps of ashes. Most of our time was spent around the Marais de St. Gond, where the French General Foch held the Thermopylae of Europe.

Four times he advanced across that marsh and was driven back, but not beaten. The fifth time he advanced and stayed, and Paris was forever lost to the Germans. Think of the men who made that last advance and saved Europe from the Potsdam gang. Their graves, carefully marked and tended, lie thickly strewn along the lonely ridges of all that region—humble but immortal reminders of glorious heroism.

The third visit was with the same escort to the fighting front at
Verdun.

The long, bare, rolling ridges between Bar-le-Duc and the Meuse; the high-shouldered hills along the river and around the ruined little city; the open fields, the narrow valleys, the wrecked villages, the shattered woodlands—all were covered with dazzling snow. The sun was bright in a cloudless sky. A bitter, biting wind poured fiercely, steadily out of the north, driving the glittering snow-dust before it. Every man had put on all the clothes he possessed, and more; pads of sheepskin over back and breast; gunny sacks tied around the shoulders. The troops of cavalry, the teams of mules and horses dragging munition-wagons or travelling kitchens or long "75" guns, clattered along the iron surface of the Via Sacra—that blessed road which made the salvation of Verdun possible after the only railway was destroyed. Endless trains of motor-lorries lumbered by. The narrow trenches were coated with ice. The hillside trails were slippery as glass. In the deep dugouts small sheet-iron stoves were burning, giving out a little heat and a great deal of choking smoke. The soldiers sat around them playing cards or telling stories.

But there! What I saw in that shell-pitted, snow-covered, hard-frozen amphitheatre of heroism cannot be described in these brief paragraphs. The serenity, cheerfulness, courtesy, and indomitable courage of the French poilus defending their own land; the scenes in the trenches with the German shells breaking around us and the wounded men being carried past us; the luncheon in the citadel with the commandant and officers in a subterranean room where the motto on the wall, above the world-renowned escutcheon of Verdun, was "On ne passe pas"—"They don't get by"; the dinner with the general and staff of the Verdun army, in a little village "somewhere in France," and their last words to me, "On les aura! Ca peut etre long, mais on les aura!"—"It may take long, but we shall get them!"—all these and a thousand more things are vivid in my memory but cannot be told now.

One scene sticks in my mind and asks to be recorded.

The hospital was just back of the Verdun lines. Its roofs were marked with the Red Cross. Twenty-four hundred beds, all clean and quiet. Wards full of German wounded, cared for as tenderly as the French. "Will you see an operation?" said the proud little commandant who was showing me through his domain. "Certainly." A big, husky fellow was on the operating-table, unconscious, under ether. One of the best surgeons in France was performing the operation of trepanning. I could see the patient's brain, bare and beating, while the surgeon did his skilful work. Other doctors stood around, and three nurses, one an American girl, Miss Cowen, of Pittsburgh. "Will the man get well?" I asked the surgeon. "I hope so," he answered. "At all events, we shall do our best for him. You know, he is a German—c'est un Boche!"

On August 20, 1917, that very hospital, marked with the Red Cross, was bombed by German aeroplanes. One wing was set on fire. While the nurses and helpers were trying to rescue the patients, the bloody Potsdam vultures flew back and forth three times over the place, raking it with machine guns. More than thirty persons were killed, including doctors, German wounded, and one woman nurse. God grant it was not the American girl! Yet why would not the killing of a French sister under the Red Cross be just as wicked?

Here I break off—uncompleted—my narration of the evil choice of war and the crimes in the conduct of war which have made the name of Germany abhorred.

The Allies, from the beginning, have pleaded for peace and fought for peace. America, obeying her conscience, has joined them in the conflict.

But what do we mean now by peace? We mean more than a mere cessation of hostilities. We mean that the burglar shall give back all that he has grabbed. We mean that the marauder shall make good all the damage that he has done.

We mean that there shall be an open league of free democratic states, great and small, to guard against the recurrence of such a bloody calamity as the autocratic, militaristic Potsdam gang precipitated upon the world in 1914.

In the next chapter I shall discuss briefly the practical significance of this kind of peace and the absolute preconditions which must be realized before any conference on the subject will be profitable or even safe.

The duty of the present is to fight on beside France, Great Britain,

Italy, Belgium, Servia, Roumania, and, we hope, Russia, "to bring the

Government of the German Empire to terms and end the war."

To talk of any other course is treason, not only to our country but to the cause of true Peace.

Chapter VII
PAX HUMANA
I

The trouble with the ordinary or garden variety of pacifist is that he has a merely negative idea of peace.

The true idea of peace is positive, constructive, forward-looking. It is not content with a mere cessation of hostilities at any particular period of the world's history. It aims at the establishment of reason and justice as the rule of the world's life. It proposes to find the basis of this establishment in the freely expressed will of the peoples of the world.

The men and women who do the world's work are the sovereigns who must guarantee this real peace of the world.

That is what we are fighting for. Not pax Romana, nor pax Germanica, nor pax Britannica, but pax Humana—a peace which will bring a positive benefit to all the tribes of humanity.

Since the choice by the Imperial German Government, in August, 1914, of war as the means of settling international disputes, the Allies have been fighting against that choice and its bloody consequences. Every one of them—Great Britain, France, Italy, Russia—had pleaded for arbitration, conference, consultation, to avert this fearful conflict of arms. But it was in vain.

The United States of America, forced by the flagrant violation of its neutral rights to take an active part in the war, and led by its vital sympathies to the side of the Allies, committed by honor and conscience to the duty of fighting for a real peace of mankind, must carry on this war until its humane and democratic object is attained. To do less than that would be to renounce our place as a great nation, to deny our faith as Americans, and to expose our country to incalculable peril and disaster.

But now that all the nations of the earth have begun to realize the horror of this abominable German war, and to desire its ending, it is necessary for us, in conjunction with our friends of peaceful and democratic purpose, to consider, first, the conditions under which peace may be discussed with the Imperial German Government, and, second, the terms on which a peace may possibly be concluded.

II THE CONDITIONS OF A PEACE CONFERENCE

We should distinguish clearly between the conditions which must be fulfilled before we can honorably enter into any talk of peace with our adversary, the begetter and beginner of this war; and the terms which the Allies and the United States and the other nations at war with Germany would put forward in such a conversation as a just and durable basis for the establishment of peace.

This distinction is essential. The conditions are antecedent and indispensable. Until they are fulfilled we cannot talk with the enemy, except in the language which he has chosen and forced upon us—the stern tongue of battle by land and sea.

Germany grandiloquently claims to be the first to propose a peace-conference as a substitute for the horrors of war. (See the Kaiser's note of December 12, 1916.

She forgets the many proposals for such a conference which were made to her in the fateful month of July, 1914, by Servia, France, Great Britain, Italy, and Russia—all of which she contemptuously brushed aside in her scornful will to war. She forgets the offenses against international law and against the plain precepts of humanity which she has committed since that time and which have earned for her the indignation and mistrust of mankind. She forgets that her so-called proposal for a peace conference contained no suggestion of the terms of peace which she was willing to discuss. She forgets that such a proposal is a mere hypocritical mockery. No sane person, no intelligent nation, would enter into a conference without knowledge of the things to be considered.

This last point lies at the base of President Wilson's note of December 18, 1916, suggesting that the belligerent powers, on both sides, should "avow their respective views as to the terms upon which the war might be concluded and the arrangements which would be deemed satisfactory as a guarantee against its renewal or the kindling of any similar conflict in the future." This note, I believe, was sent to all the American Ambassadors and Ministers in Europe, with instructions to communicate it to the Governments to which they were accredited, whether belligerent or neutral.

Here is a point at which I can throw a little new light upon the situation. I handed the note, as I was ordered to do, to the Dutch Minister, without comment or recommendation. Almost immediately the German-subsidized press in Holland began to assail the Dutch Government for refusing to support President Wilson's note. It seemed to me that this was a falsehood, unjust to Holland, injurious to our Government, which had not asked for support. Therefore I made the following statement to the press on January 9, 1917:

"The Dutch Minister of Foreign Affairs is absolutely correct in saying that I handed him President Wilson's note of December 18 without any request or suggestion that the Netherlands Government should support it. I did so because I was so instructed by my Government. I was told to transmit the President's note simply as a matter of information. No request was added. The reason for this is because America understands the delicate and difficult position of the Netherlands Government, in the midst of the present war, and will not urge nor even ask it to do anything which it does not judge to be wise and prudent and helpful. I have done my best to promote this right understanding of the position of Holland in the United States, and I shall continue to do so. I have no knowledge of any instructions from Washington in regard to the manner of delivering the President's note in Spain.

"What I cannot understand is the general misunderstanding of that note. It expressly declared that it was not an offer of mediation nor a proposal of peace. It was simply a suggestion that the belligerents on both sides should state the terms on which they would be willing to consider and discuss peace. The Entente Powers have already done this with some clearness, and will probably soon do so even more clearly. The Central Powers have politely, even affectionately, but very practically, declined the President's invitation to state their terms. There is the deadlock on peace talk at present. When both sides are equally frank the world can judge whether the peace which all just men desire is near or far away."

The accuracy and propriety of this statement have never been questioned by the Department of State. On the contrary, it was practically affirmed by the President in his address to the Senate on January 22, 1917, when he said:

"On the 18th of December last I addressed an identic note to the Governments of the nations now at war, requesting them to state, more definitely than they had yet been stated by either group of belligerents, the terms upon which they would deem it possible to make peace. I spoke on behalf of humanity and of the rights of all neutral nations like our own, many of whose most vital interests the war puts in constant jeopardy.

"The Central Powers united in a reply which stated merely that they were ready to meet their antagonists in conference to discuss terms of peace.

"The Entente Powers have replied much more definitely and have stated, in general terms indeed, but with sufficient definiteness to imply details, the arrangements, guarantees, and acts of reparation which they deem to be indispensable conditions of a satisfactory settlement." Here, then, we come within sight of the first of the conditions which are absolutely precedent, at least so far as America is concerned, to any discussion of peace.

1. Germany must answer President Wilson's note of December 18, 1916. She must state her terms of peace, maximum or minimum, frankly and unequivocally.

Germany asserts that she is waging a defensive war. She must tell the world what she is defending. That she has never been willing to do.

Germany asserts that she is victorious thus far. She must say what she thinks her "victories" mean, and what they entitle her to claim and keep.

In brief, Germany must lay her cards on the table. If she wants peace—and certainly she needs it,—she must be willing to say what she means by it.

2. The second condition precedent to any discussion of peace terms with Germany has been clearly defined by President Wilson in his reply to the note issued by His Holiness Pope Benedict.

That reply was thoroughly sympathetic and conciliatory. Among its frank and strong paragraphs there was one which must be particularly noted:

"We cannot take the word of the present rulers of Germany as a guarantee of anything that is to endure unless explicitly supported by such conclusive evidence of the will and purpose of the German people themselves as the other peoples of the world would be justified in accepting. Without such guarantees treaties of settlement, agreements for disarmament, covenants to set up arbitration in the place of force, territorial adjustments, reconstitutions of small nations, if made with the German Government, no man, no nation, could now depend on."

Understand—this is not a flat refusal to treat with the House of Hohenzollern in any circumstances, which the more rabid and less thoughtful newspapers of England have urged. It is merely a statement that the rulers of Germany must have behind them a sufficient and explicit mandate and guarantee of the people of Germany before we can trust them.

We do not presume to interfere in the internal affairs of the German Empire. The people of that empire have a right to say how they shall be ruled. If they like the Hohenzollerns, good!

All that we ask is some clear, democratic guarantee of the German people behind the word of its chosen Government.

Does this mean a complete reformation of the German Empire, which in effect now consists of twenty-two hereditary kings, princes, dukes, and grand dukes, with the Kaiser at the head? Does it mean a constitutional remoulding of the empire?

That would be a long process. The people of Germany are well disciplined. There is small prospect of a revolution in that country unless war compels it.

What is it that we are pledged by President Wilson's statement to insist upon as a precondition of any peace conference with Germany? Simply this—that behind the word of the Kaiser there must be the word of the German people.

That word must be given in advance and in a way which will satisfy both the Allies and the United States. It is for the German people to find the way.

We cannot honorably talk peace with Germany until that way is found.

3. The third condition antecedent to a conference on peace is the renunciation and abandonment of the German submarine warfare upon merchant shipping.

On this point I do not speak with any kind of authority or official sanction. What I say is based, indeed, upon words uttered with the highest authority. But the conclusion drawn from them is merely my own judgment and has no force beyond that of the reasoning that has led me to it.

The American position in regard to this submarine warfare—its illegality, its inhumanity—has been clearly and eloquently defined by our Government again and again.

"The Government of the United States has been apprised that the Imperial German Government considered themselves to be obliged, by the extraordinary circumstances of the present war and the measures adopted by their adversaries in seeking to cut Germany off from all commerce, to adopt methods of retaliation which go much beyond the ordinary methods of warfare at sea, in the proclamation of a war zone from which they have warned neutral ships to keep away. This Government has already taken occasion to inform the Imperial German Government that it cannot admit the adoption of such measures or such a warning of danger to operate as in any degree an abbreviation of the rights of American shipmasters or of American citizens bound on lawful errands as passengers on merchant ships of belligerent neutrality; and that it must hold the Imperial German Government to a strict accountability for any infringement of those rights, intentional or incidental. It does not understand the Imperial German Government to question those rights. It assumes, on the contrary, that the Imperial German Government accept, as of course, the rule that the lives of non-combatants, whether they be of neutral citizenship or citizens of one of the nations at war, cannot lawfully or rightfully be put in jeopardy by the capture or destruction of an unarmed merchantman, and recognize also, as all other nations do, the obligation to take the usual precaution of visit and search to ascertain whether a suspected merchantman is in fact of belligerent nationality or is in fact carrying contraband of war under a neutral flag." (The Secretary of State, Washington, D. C., to the German Minister for Foreign Affairs, May 13, 1915.)

"The fact that more than one hundred American citizens were among those who perished" (reference to the sinking of the Lusitania) "made it the duty of the Government of the United States to speak of these things and once more, with solemn emphasis, to call the attention of the Imperial German Government to the grave responsibility which the Government of the United States conceives that it has incurred in this tragic occurrence, and to the indisputable principle upon which that responsibility rests. The Government of the United States is contending for something much greater than mere rights of property or privileges of commerce. It is contending for nothing less high and sacred than the rights of humanity, which every government honors itself in respecting and which no government is justified in resigning on behalf of those under its care and authority." (The Secretary of State, Washington, D. C., to the German Minister for Foreign Affairs, June 9, 1915.)

"If a belligerent cannot retaliate against an enemy without injuring the lives of neutrals as well as their property, humanity, as well as justice and a due regard for the dignity of neutral powers, should dictate that the practice be discontinued. If persisted in it would in such circumstances constitute an unpardonable offense against the sovereignty of the neutral nation affected. . . . The rights of neutrals in time of war are based upon principle, not upon expediency, and the principles are immutable. It is the duty and obligation of belligerents to find a way to adapt the new circumstances to them." (The Secretary of State, Washington, D. C., to the German Minister for Foreign Affairs, July 21, 1915.)

"The law of nations in these matters, upon which the Government of the United States based that protest" (i.e., against the German declaration of February, 1915, declaring the danger zone around Great Britain and Ireland) "is not of recent origin or founded upon merely arbitrary principles set up by convention. It is based, on the contrary, upon manifest principles of humanity and has long been established with the approval and by the express assent of all civilized nations. . . . It has become painfully evident to it (the Government of the United States) that the position which it took at the very outset is inevitable, namely—the use of submarines for the destruction of an enemy's commerce is, of necessity, because of the very character of the vessels employed and the very methods of attack which their employment of course involves, utterly incompatible with the principles of humanity, the long-established and incontrovertible rights of neutrals, and the sacred immunities of non-combatants." (The Secretary of State, Washington, D. C., to the German Minister for Foreign Affairs, April 18, 1916.)

But we cannot forget that we are in some sort and by the force of circumstances the responsible spokesmen of the rights of humanity, and that we cannot remain silent while those rights seem in process of being swept away in the maelstrom of this terrible war. We owe it to a due regard for our own rights as a nation, to our sense of duty as a representative of the rights of neutrals the world over, and to a just conception of the rights of mankind to take this stand now with the utmost solemnity and firmness." (President Wilson's Address to Congress, April 19, 1916.)

"The present German warfare against commerce is a warfare against mankind. It is a war against all nations. American ships have been sunk, American lives taken, in ways which it has stirred us very deeply to learn of, but the ships and people of other neutral and friendly nations have been sunk and overwhelmed in the waters in the same way. There has been no discrimination. The challenge is to all mankind. Each nation must decide for itself how it will meet it." (President Wilson's Message to Congress, April 2, 1917.)

The United States cannot go back on these words. They are fundamental in our position. I do not know whether the Allies have formally indorsed them or not. But that makes no difference. It seems to me that for America, with her traditional, unalterable devotion to the doctrine of Mare Liberum, as Grotius stated it, there can be no peace conference with a Government which is in active and flagrant violation of that principle.

I think that for us at least—we do not venture to speak for the Allies, though we believe they sympathize with our point of view—there can be no peace parley with Germany until she renounces and abandons her atrocious method of submarine warfare on merchant shipping.

Here, then, are the three conditions which ought to be fulfilled before we can honorably enter a conference on peace with the Imperial German Government. The first is a legitimate inference from the statements of the President. The second has been positively laid down by the President. The third is drawn, purely on my own responsibility, from his words.

First, Germany should frankly declare the aims with which she began this war, and the purposes with which she continues it on the territories which she has invaded.

Second, Germany must offer adequate guarantees that in any peace negotiations her rulers shall speak only and absolutely with the voice of the people behind them—in other words, with a democratic, not an autocratic, sanction.

Third, Germany ought to give a pledge of good faith by the abandonment of her illegal and inhuman submarine warfare on the merchant shipping of the world.

Is it likely that the predatory Potsdam gang will be willing to accept these three conditions soon?

I frankly confess that I do not know. Germany is in sore straits. That I know from personal observation. But I know also that she is magnificently organized, trained, and disciplined for obedience to the imperial will. She will carry her fight for world empire to the last limit.

When that limit is reached, when the German people know that the attempt of their rulers to dominate the world by war has failed, then it will be time to talk with them about the terms of peace.

III
THE TERMS OF PEACE

This is a long subject; and for that reason I mean to make it a short chapter.

1. A discussion of peace terms with our enemy, the Imperial German Government, is neither desirable nor safe under the present conditions.

Until that Government is disabused of the delusion that it has won, is winning, or will win a substantial victory in this war, it is not likely to say anything sane or reasonable about peace. A pax Germanica is what it is willing to discuss.

But that is just what we do not want. To enter such a discussion now would be both futile and perilous.

It would probably postpone the coming of that real pax humana for which the Allies have already made such great sacrifices, and for which we have pledged ourselves to fight at their side.

But meantime it is wise and right and useful to let the German people know, by such means as we can find, that we have not entered this war in the spirit of revenge or conquest, and that their annihilation or enslavement is not among the ends which we contemplate.

An admirable opportunity to give this humane and prudent assurance was offered by the Pope's proposal of a Peace Conference (August, 1917). President Wilson, with characteristic acuteness and candor, made good use of this opportunity. While declining the proposal clearly and firmly, as impossible under the present conditions, he added the following statement of the peace purposes of the United States—a statement which approaches a definition by the process of exclusion:

"Punitive damages, the dismemberment of empires, the establishment of selfish and exclusive economic leagues, we deem inexpedient, and in the end worse than futile, no proper basis for a peace of any kind, least of all for an enduring peace, that must be based upon justice and fairness and the common rights of mankind." (President Wilson's Note to His Holiness the Pope, August 27, 1917.)

Thus far (and in my judgment no farther) we may go in an indirect, third-personal discussion of the terms of peace with our enemy.

2. On the other hand, a full discussion of the terms of peace with our friends, the allied nations, will be most profitable—indeed, it is absolutely necessary.

The sooner it comes—the more frank, thorough, and confidential it is—the better!

The Allies, as President Wilson said in the address already quoted (January 22, 1917), have stated their terms of peace "with sufficient definiteness to imply details."

These terms have been summed up again and again in three general words:

RESTITUTION, REPARATION, GUARANTEES FOR THE FUTURE.

It is for us to discuss the details which are implied in these terms, not with our enemy, but with our friends who have borne the brunt of this German war against peace.

Nothing which would make their sacrifice vain could ever satisfy the heart and conscience of the United States.

We cannot honorably accept a peace which would leave Belgium, Luxembourg, Servia, Montenegro, Roumania crushed and helpless in the hands of their captors.

We cannot honorably accept a peace which would leave our sister-republic France hopelessly exposed to the same kind of an assault which Germany made upon her in 1870 and in 1914.

We cannot honorably accept a peace which would leave Great Britain crippled and powerless to work with us in the maintenance of the freedom of the sea.

We cannot honorably accept a peace which would leave the Italian demand for unity unsatisfied, and the new Russian Republic helpless before its foes. Such, it seems to me, are the principles which must guide and govern us in the coming conference with our friends about the terms of peace.

In regard to the right of the peoples of the world, small or great, to determine their own form of government and their own action, we are fully committed. This principle is fundamental to our existence as a nation. President Wilson has reaffirmed it again and again, never more clearly or significantly than in his address to the Senate on January 22, 1917.

"And there is a deeper thing involved than even equality of rights among organized nations. No peace can last which does not recognize and accept the principle that governments derive all their just powers from the consent of the governed, and that no right anywhere exists to hand people about from sovereignty to sovereignty as if they were property.

"I take it for granted, for instance, if I may venture upon a single example, that statesmen everywhere are agreed that there should be a united, independent, and autonomous Poland, and that henceforth inviolable security of life, of worship, and of industrial and social development should be guaranteed to all peoples who have lived hitherto under the power of governments devoted to a faith and purpose hostile to their own."

This "example" must be interpreted in its full bearing upon all the questions which are likely to come up in the conference in regard to the terms of peace.

There is one more fixed point in the terms of a peace which the United States and the Allies can accept with honor. That is the formation, after this war is ended, of a compact, an alliance, a league, a union—call it what you will—of free democratic nations, pledged to use their combined forces, diplomatic, economic, and military, against the beginning of war by any nation which has not previously submitted its cause to international inquiry, conciliation, arbitration, or judicial hearing.

Here, again, experience enables me to throw a little new light upon the situation. In November, 1914, on my way home to America for surgical treatment, I had the privilege of conveying a personal, unofficial message to Washington from the British Minister of Foreign Affairs, Sir Edward (now Viscount) Grey. Remember, at this time America was neutral, and the "League to Enforce Peace" had not been formed.

This was the substance of the message: "The presence and influence of America in the council of peace after the war will be most welcome to us provided we can be assured of two things: First, that America stands for the restoration of all that Germany has seized in Belgium and France. Second, that America will enter and support, by force if necessary, a league of nations pledged to resist and punish any war begun without previous submission of the cause to international investigation and judgment."

This was the message that I took to Washington in 1914. Since that time the "League to Enforce Peace" has been organized in America (June 17, 1915). In my opinion it would be better named the "League to Defend Peace." But the name makes little difference. It is the principle, the idea, that counts.

This idea has been publicly approved by the leading spokesmen of all the allied nations, and notably by President Wilson in his speech at the League banquet, May 27, 1916, and in his address to the Senate, January 22, 1917, in which he said:

"Mere terms of peace between the belligerents will not satisfy even the belligerents themselves. Mere agreements may not make peace secure. It will be absolutely necessary that a force be created as a guarantor of the permanency of the settlement so much greater than the force of any nation now engaged in any alliance hitherto formed or projected that no nation, no probable combination of nations, could face or withstand it. If the peace presently to be made is to endure it must be a peace made secure by the organized major force of mankind."

Consider for a moment what such an organization would mean.

It would mean, first of all, the strongest possible condemnation of the attitude and action of Germany and her assistants in plotting, choosing, beginning, and forcing the present war upon the world.

It is precisely because she disdained and refused to submit the Austro-Servian quarrel, and her own secret plans and purposes to investigation, conference, judicial inquiry, that her blood-guiltiness is most flagrant, and her criminal assault upon the world's peace cries to Heaven for punishment.

Moreover, such an organization of free democratic states would mean a practical step toward a new era of international relations. It would amount, in effect, to what Premier Ribot, in his recent address at the anniversary of the battle of the Marne, called "a league of common defense." It would be a new kind of treaty of alliance—open, not secret—made by peoples, not by monarchs—an alliance against wars of aggression and conquest—an alliance against all wars whose beginners are unwilling to submit their cause to the common judgment of mankind. Such an open treaty of defense would practically condemn and cancel all secret treaties for offensive war as treasonable conspiracies against the commonwealth of the world.

But would the organization of such a league of nations to defend peace make war henceforward impossible?

No sane man, who knows the ignorance, the imperfection, the passionate frailty of human nature entertains such a wild dream or makes such an extravagant claim.

All that the league can hope to do is to make an aggressive war, such as Germany thrust upon the world in 1914, more difficult and more dangerous. All that it purposes is to set up a new safeguard of peace, based upon justice, and supported by the common faith, the collective force, and the mutual trust of democratic peoples.

That is one of the things—yes, I think it is the most important thing—for which we are now fighting with the Allies against Germany and her assistants:

PEACE WITH POWER.

These pages have been written as a voluntary contribution to the cause of our country in this righteous war against war. I should have been happier if my active service at the front could have been accepted. But since my age made that impossible I have tried, and shall go on trying, to do what I can in other ways to help our fight for real peace.

I close this bit of work with the noble lines of Tennyson:

"I would that wars should cease,
I would the globe from end to end
Might sow and reap in peace,
And some new Spirit o'erbear the old,
Or Trade refrain the Powers
From war with kindly links of gold,
Or Love with wreaths of flowers.
Slav, Teuton, Kelt, I count them all
My friends and brother souls,
With all the peoples, great and small,
That wheel between the poles.
But since our mortal shadow, Ill,
To waste this earth began—
Perchance from some abuse of Will
In worlds before the man
Involving ours—he needs must fight
To make true peace his own,
He needs must combat might with might,
Or Might would rule alone."

The Valley of Vision

PREFACE

"Why do you choose such a title as *The Valley of Vision* for your book," said my friend; "do you mean that one can see farther from the valley than from the mountain-top?"

This question set me thinking, as every honest question ought to do. Here is the result of my thoughts, which you will take for what it is worth, if you care to read the book.

The mountain-top is the place of outlook over the earth and the sea. But it is in the valley of suffering, endurance, and self-sacrifice that the deepest visions of the meaning of life come to us.

I take the outcome of this Twentieth Century War as a victory over the mad illusion of world-dominion which the Germans saw from the peak of their military power in 1914. The united force of the Allies has grown, through valley-visions of right and justice and human kindness, into an irresistible might before which the German "will to power" has gone down in ruin.

There are some Half-Told Tales in the volume—fables, fantasies—mere sketches, grave and gay, on the margin of the book of life,

"Where more is meant than meets the ear."

Dreams have a part in most of the longer stories. That is because I believe dreams have a part in real life. Some of them we remember as vividly as any actual experience. These belong to the imperfect sleep. But others we do not remember, because they are given to us in that perfect sleep in which the soul is liberated, and goes visiting. Yet sometimes we get a trace of them, by a happy chance, and often their influence remains with us in that spiritual refreshment with which we awake from profound slumber. This is the meaning of that verse in the old psalm: "He giveth to His beloved in sleep."

The final story in the book was written before the War of 1914 began, and it has to do with the Light of the World, leading us through conflict and suffering towards Peace.

AVALON, November 24, 1918.

A REMEMBERED DREAM

This is the story of a dream that came to me some five-and-twenty years ago. It is as vivid in memory as anything that I have ever seen in the outward world, as distinct as any experience through which I have ever passed. Not all dreams are thus remembered. But some are. In the records of the mind, where the inner chronicle of life is written, they are intensely clear and veridical. I shall try to tell the story of this dream with an absolute faithfulness, adding nothing and leaving nothing out, but writing the narrative just as if the thing were real.

Perhaps it was. Who can say?

In the course of a journey, of the beginning and end of which I know nothing, I had come to a great city, whose name, if it was ever told me, I cannot recall.

It was evidently a very ancient place. The dwelling-houses and larger buildings were gray and beautiful with age, and the streets wound in and out among them wonderfully, like a maze.

This city lay beside a river or estuary—though that was something that I did not find out until later, as you will see—and the newer part of the town extended mainly on a wide, bare street running along a kind of low cliff or embankment, where the basements of the small houses on the water-side went down, below the level of the street, to the shore. But the older part of the town was closely and intricately built, with gabled roofs and heavy carved facades hanging over the narrow stone-paved ways, which here and there led out suddenly into open squares.

It was in what appeared to be the largest and most important of these squares that I was standing, a little before midnight. I had left my wife and our little girl in the lodging which we had found, and walked out alone to visit the sleeping town.

The night sky was clear, save for a few filmy clouds, which floated over the face of the full moon, obscuring it for an instant, but never completely hiding it—like veils in a shadow dance. The spire of the great cathedral was silver filigree on the moonlit side, and on the other side, black lace. The square was empty. But on the broad, shallow steps in front of the main entrance of the cathedral two heroic figures were seated. At first I thought they were statues. Then I perceived they were alive, and talking earnestly together.

They were like Greek gods, very strong and beautiful, and naked but for some slight drapery that fell snow-white around them. They glistened in the moonlight. I could not hear what they were saying; yet I could see that they were in a dispute which went to the very roots of life.

They resembled each other strangely in form and feature—like twin brothers. But the face of one was noble, lofty, calm, full of a vast regret and compassion. The face of the other was proud, resentful, drawn with passion. He appeared to be accusing and renouncing his companion, breaking away from an ancient friendship in a swift, implacable hatred. But the companion seemed to plead with him, and lean toward him, and try to draw him closer.

A strange fear and sorrow shook my heart. I felt that this mysterious contest was something of immense importance; a secret, ominous strife; a menace to the world.

Then the two figures stood up, marvellously alike in strength and beauty, yet absolutely different in expression and bearing, the one serene and benignant, the other fierce and threatening. The quiet one was still pleading, with a hand laid upon the other's shoulder. But he shook it off, and thrust his companion away with a proud, impatient gesture.

At last I heard him speak.

"I have done with you," he cried. "I do not believe in you. I have no more need of you. I renounce you. I will live without you. Away forever out of my life!"

At this a look of ineffable sorrow and pity came upon the great companion's face.

"You are free," he answered. "I have only besought you, never constrained you. Since you will have it so, I must leave you, now, to yourself."

He rose into the air, still looking downward with wise eyes full of grief and warning, until he vanished in silence beyond the thin clouds.

The other did not look up, but lifting his head with a defiant laugh, shook his shoulders as if they were free of a burden. He strode swiftly around the corner of the cathedral and disappeared among the deep shadows.

A sense of intolerable calamity fell upon me. I said to myself:

"That was Man! And the other was God! And they have parted!"

Then the multitude of bells hidden in the lace-work of the high tower began to sound. It was not the aerial fluttering music of the carillon that I remembered hearing long ago from the belfries of the Low Countries. This was a confused and strident ringing, jangled and broken, full of sudden tumults and discords, as if the tower were shaken and the bells gave out their notes at hazard, in surprise and trepidation.

It stopped as suddenly as it began. The great bell of the hours struck twelve. The windows of the cathedral glowed faintly with a light from within.

"It is New Year's Eve," I thought—although I knew perfectly well that the time was late summer. I had seen that though the leaves on the trees of the square were no longer fresh, they had not yet fallen.

I was certain that I must go into the cathedral. The western entrance was shut. I hurried to the south side. The dark, low door of the transept was open. I went in. The building was dimly lighted by huge candles which flickered and smoked like torches. I noticed that one of them, fastened against a pillar, was burning crooked, and the tallow ran down its side in thick white tears.

The nave of the church was packed with a vast throng of people, all standing, closely crowded together, like the undergrowth in a forest. The rood-screen was open, or broken down, I could not tell which. The choir was bare, like a clearing in the woods, and filled with blazing light.

On the high steps, with his back to the altar, stood Man, his face gleaming with pride.

"I am the Lord!" he cried. "There is none above me! No law, no God! Man is power. Man is the highest of all!"

A tremor of wonder and dismay, of excitement and division, shivered through the crowd. Some covered their faces. Others stretched out their hands. Others shook their fists in the air. A tumult of voices broke from the multitude—voices of exultation, and anger, and horror, and strife.

The floor of the cathedral was moved and lifted by a mysterious ground-swell. The pillars trembled and wavered. The candles flared and went out. The crowd, stricken dumb with a panic fear, rushed to the doors, burst open the main entrance, and struggling in furious silence poured out of the building. I was swept along with them, striving to keep on my feet.

One thought possessed me. I must get to my wife and child, save them, bring them out of this accursed city.

As I hurried across the square I looked up at the cathedral spire. It was swaying and rocking in the air like the mast of a ship at sea. The lace-work fell from it in blocks of stone. The people rushed screaming through the rain of death. Many were struck down, and lay where they fell.

I ran as fast as I could. But it was impossible to run far. Every street and alley vomited men—all struggling together, fighting, shouting, or shrieking, striking one another down, trampling over the fallen—a hideous melee. There was an incessant rattling noise in the air, and heavier peals as of thunder shook the houses. Here a wide rent yawned in a wall—there a roof caved in—the windows fell into the street in showers of broken glass.

How I got through this inferno I do not know. Buffeted and blinded, stumbling and scrambling to my feet again, turning this way or that way to avoid the thickest centres of the strife, oppressed and paralyzed by a feeling of impotence that put an iron band around my heart, driven always by the intense longing to reach my wife and child, somehow I had a sense of struggling on. Then I came into a quieter quarter of the town, and ran until I reached the lodging where I had left them.

They were waiting just inside the door, anxious and trembling. But I was amazed to find them so little panic-stricken. The little girl had her doll in her arms.

{Illustration with caption: The cathedral spire... was swaying and rocking in the air like the mast of a ship at sea.}

"What is it?" asked my wife. "What must we do?"

"Come," I cried. "Something frightful has happened here. I can't explain now. We must get away at once. Come, quickly."

Then I took a hand of each and we hastened through the streets, vaguely steering away from the centre of the city.

Presently we came into that wide new street of mean houses, of which I have already spoken. There were a few people in it, but they moved heavily and feebly, as if some mortal illness lay upon them. Their faces were pale and haggard with a helpless anxiety to escape more quickly. The houses seemed half deserted. The shades were drawn, the doors closed.

But since it was all so quiet, I thought that we might find some temporary shelter there. So I knocked at the door of a house where there was a dim light behind the drawn shade in one of the windows.

After a while the door was opened by a woman who held the end of her shawl across her mouth. All that I could see was the black sorrow of her eyes.

"Go away," she said slowly; "the plague is here. My children are dying of it. You must not come in! Go away."

So we hurried on through that plague-smitten street, burdened with a new fear. Soon we saw a house on the riverside which looked absolutely empty. The shades were up, the windows open, the door stood ajar. I hesitated; plucked up courage; resolved that we must get to the waterside in some way in order to escape from the net of death which encircled us.

"Come," I said, "let us try to go down through this house. But cover your mouths."

We groped through the empty passageway, and down the basement-stair. The thick cobwebs swept my face. I noted them with joy, for I thought they proved that the house had been deserted for some time, and so perhaps it might not be infected.

We descended into a room which seemed to have been the kitchen. There was a stove dimly visible at one side, and an old broken kettle on the floor, over which we stumbled. The back door was locked. But it swung outward as I broke it open. We stood upon a narrow, dingy beach, where the small waves were lapping.

By this time the "little day" had begun to whiten the eastern sky; a pallid light was diffused; I could see westward down to the main harbor, beside the heart of the city. The sails and smoke-stacks of great ships were visible, all passing out to sea. I wished that we were there.

Here in front of us the water seemed shallower. It was probably only a tributary or backwater of the main stream. But it was sprinkled with smaller vessels—sloops, and yawls, and luggers—all filled with people and slowly creeping seaward.

There was one little boat, quite near to us, which seemed to be waiting for some one. There were some people on it, but it was not crowded.

"Come," I said, "this is for us. We must wade out to it."

So I took my wife by the hand, and the child in the other arm, and we went into the water. Soon it came up to our knees, to our waists.

"Hurry," shouted the old man at the tiller. "No time to spare!"

"Just a minute more," I answered, "only one minute!"

That minute seemed like a year. The sail of the boat was shaking in the wind. When it filled she must move away. We waded on, and at last I grasped the gunwale of the boat. I lifted the child in and helped my wife to climb over the side. They clung to me. The little vessel began to move gently away.

"Get in," cried the old man sharply; "get in quick."

But I felt that I could not, I dared not. I let go of the boat. I cried "Good-by," and turned to wade ashore.

I was compelled to go back to the doomed city. I must know what would come of the parting of Man from God!

The tide was running out more swiftly. The water swirled around my knees. I awoke.

But the dream remained with me, just as I have told it to you.

ANTWERP ROAD

{OCTOBER, 1914}

Along the straight, glistening road, through a dim arcade of drooping trees, a tunnel of faded green and gold, dripping with the misty rain of a late October afternoon, a human tide was flowing, not swiftly, but slowly, with the patient, pathetic slowness of weary feet, and numb brains, and heavy hearts.

Yet they were in haste, all of these old men and women, fathers and mothers, and little children; they were flying as fast as they could; either away from something that they feared, or toward something that they desired.

That was the strange thing—the tide on the road flowed in two directions.

Some fled away from ruined homes to escape the perils of war. Some fled back to ruined homes to escape the desolation of exile. But all were fugitives, anxious to be gone, striving along the road one way or the other, and making no more speed than a creeping snail's pace of unutterable fatigue. I saw many separate things in the tide, and remembered them without noting.

A boy straining to push a wheelbarrow with his pale mother in it, and his two little sisters trudging at his side. A peasant with his two girls driving their lean, dejected cows back to some unknown pasture. A bony horse tugging at a wagon heaped high with bedding and household gear, on top of which sat the wrinkled grandmother with the tiniest baby in her arms, while the rest of the family stumbled alongside—and the cat was curled up on the softest coverlet in the wagon. Two panting dogs, with red tongues hanging out, and splayed feet clawing the road, tugging a heavy-laden cart while the master pushed behind and the woman pulled in the shafts. Strange, antique vehicles crammed with passengers. Couples and groups and sometimes larger companies of foot-travellers. Now and then a solitary man or woman, old and shabby, bundle on back, eyes on the road, plodding through the mud and the mist, under the high archway of yellowing leaves.

{Illustration: All were fugitives, anxious to be gone, ... and making no more speed than a creeping snail's pace of unutterable fatigue.}

All these distinct pictures I saw, yet it was all one vision—a vision of humanity with its dumb companions in flight—infinitely slow, painful, pitiful flight!

I saw no tears, I heard no cries of complaint. But beneath the numb and patient haste on all those dazed faces I saw a question.

"What have we done? Why has this thing come upon us and our children?"

Somewhere I heard a trumpet blown. The brazen spikes on the helmets of a little troop of German soldiers flashed for an instant, far down the sloppy road. Through the humid dusk came the dull, distant booming of the unseen guns of conquest in Flanders.

That was the only answer.

A CITY OF REFUGE

In the dark autumn of 1914 the City sprang up almost in a night, as if by enchantment.

It was white magic that called it into being—the deep, quiet, strong impulse of compassion and protection that moved the motherly heart of Holland when she saw the hundreds of thousands of Belgian fugitives pouring out of their bleeding, ravaged land, and running, stumbling, creeping on hands and knees, blindly, instinctively turning to her for safety and help.

"Come to me," she said, like a good woman who holds out her arms and spreads her knees to make a lap for tired and frightened children, "come to me. I will take care of you. You shall be safe with me."

All doors were open. The little brick farmhouses and cottages with their gayly painted window-shutters; the long rows of city houses with their steep gables; the prim and placid country mansions set among their high trees and formal flower-gardens—all kinds of dwellings, from the poorest to the richest, welcomed these guests of sorrow and distress. Many a humble family drained its savings-bank reservoir to keep the stream of its hospitality flowing. Unused factories were turned into barracks. Deserted summer hotels were filled up. Even empty greenhouses were adapted to the need of human horticulture. All Holland was enrolled, formally or informally, in a big *Comite voor Belgische Slachtoffers.*

But soon it was evident that the impromptu methods of generosity could not meet the demands of the case. Private resources were exhausted. Poor people could no longer feed and clothe their poorer guests. Families were unhappily divided. In the huge flock of exiles driven out by the cruel German Terror there were goats as well as sheep, and some of them bewildered and shocked the orderly Dutch homes where they were sheltered, by their nocturnal habits and negligible morals. Something had to be done to bring order and system into the chaos of brotherly love. Otherwise the neat Dutch mind which is so close to the Dutch heart could not rest in its bed. This vast trouble which the evil of German militarism had thrust upon a helpless folk must be helped out by a wise touch of military organization, which is a good thing even for the most peaceful people.

So it was that the City of Refuge (and others like it) grew up swiftly in the wilderness.

It stands in the heathland that slopes and rolls from the wooded hills of Gelderland to the southern shore of the Zuider Zee—a sandy country overgrown with scrub-oaks and pines and heather—yet very healthy and well drained, and not unfertile under cultivation. You may see that in the little neighbor-village, where the trees arch over the streets, and the kitchen-gardens prosper, and the shrubs and flowers bloom abundantly.

The small houses and hotels of this tiny summer resort are of brick. It has an old, well-established look; a place of relaxation with restraint, not of ungirdled frivolity. The plain Dutch people love their holidays, but they take them serenely and by rule: long walks and bicycle-rides, placid and nourishing picnics in the woods or by the sea, afternoon tea-parties in sheltered arbors. One of their favorite names for a country-place is *Wel Teweden,* "perfectly contented."

The commandant of the City of Refuge lives in one of the little brick houses of the village. He is a portly, rosy old bachelor, with a curly brown beard and a military bearing; a man of fine education and wide experience, seasoned in colonial diplomacy. The ruling idea in his mind is discipline, authority. His official speech is abrupt and final, the manner of a martinet covering a heart full of kindness and generous impulses.

"Come," he says, after a good breakfast, "I want you to see my camp. It is not as fine and fancy as the later ones. But we built it in a hurry and we had it ready on time."

A short ride over a sandy road brings you to the city gate—an opening in the wire enclosure of perhaps two or three square miles among the dwarf pines and oaks. The guard-house is kept by a squad of Dutch soldiers. But it is in no sense a prison-camp, for people are coming and going freely all the time, and the only rules within are those of decency and good order.

"Capacity, ten thousand," says the commandant, sweeping his hand around the open circle, "quite a city, *niet waar?* I will show you the various arrangements."

All the buildings are of wood, a mushroom city, but constructed with intelligence to meet the needs of the sudden, helpless population. You visit the big kitchen with its ever-simmering kettles; the dining-halls with their long tables and benches; the schoolhouses full of lively, irrepressible children; the wash-house where always talkative and jocose laundresses are scrubbing and wringing the clothes; the sewing-rooms where hundreds of women and girls are busy with garments and gossip; the chapel where religious services are held by the devoted pastors; the recreation-room which is the social centre of the city; the clothing storerooms where you find several American girls working for love.

Then you go through the long family barracks where each family has a separate cubicle, more or less neat and comfortable, sometimes prettily decorated, according to the family taste and habit; the barracks for the single men; the barracks for the single women; the two hospitals, one general, the other for infectious diseases; and last of all, the house where the half-dozen disorderly women are confined, surrounded by a double fence of barbed wire and guarded by a sentry.

Poor, wretched creatures! You are sorry for them. Why not put the disorderly men into a house of confinement, too?

"Ah," says the commandant bluntly, "we find it easier and better to send the disorderly men to jail or hospital in some near town. We are easier with the women. I pity them. But they are full of poison. We can't let them go loose in the camp for fear of infection."

How many of the roots of human nature are uncovered in a place like this! The branches and the foliage and the blossoms, too, are seen more clearly in this air where all things are necessarily open and in common.

The men are generally less industrious than the women. But they work willingly at the grading of roads and paths, the laying out and planting of flower-beds, the construction of ornamental designs, of doubtful taste but unquestionable sincerity.

You read the names which they have given to the different streets and barracks, and the passageways between the cubicles, and you understand the strong, instinctive love which binds them to their native Belgium. "Antwerp Avenue," "Louvain Avenue," "Malines Street," "Liege Street," and streets bearing the names of many ruined towns and villages of which you have never heard, but which are forever dear to the hearts of these exiles. The names of the hero-king, Albert, and of his brave consort, Queen Elizabeth, are honored by inscriptions, and their pictures, cut from, newspapers, decorate the schoolrooms and the little family cubicles.

The brutal power which reigns at Berlin may drive the Belgians out of Belgium by terror and oppression. But it cannot drive Belgium out of the hearts of the Belgians. While they live their country lives, and Albert is still their King.

But think of the unnatural conditions into which these thousands of human beings—yes, and hundreds of thousands like them, torn from their homes, uprooted, dispersed, impoverished—are forced by this bitter, cruel war. Think of the cold and ruined hearthstones, the scattered families, the shelterless children, the desolate and broken hearts. This is what Germany has inflicted upon mankind in order to realize her robber-dream!

Yet the City of Refuge, being human, has its bright spots and its bits of compensation. Here is one, out of many.

The chief nurse, a young Dutch lady of charming face and manners, serving as a volunteer under the sacred sign of the Red Cross, comes in, one morning, to make her report to the commandant.

"Well," he says, disguising in his big voice of command the warm admiration which he feels for the lady, "what is the trouble to-day? Speak up."

"Nothing, sir," she answers calmly. "Everything is going on pretty well. No new cases of measles—those in hospital improving. The only thing that bothers me is the continual complaint about that Mrs. Van Orley—you remember her, a thin, dark little person. She is melancholy and morose, quarrels all the time, says some one has stolen her children. The people near her in the barracks complain that she disturbs them at night, moans and talks aloud in her sleep, jumps up and runs down the corridor laughing or crying: 'Here they are!' They don't believe she ever had any children. They think she is crazy and want her put out. But I don't agree with that. I think she has had children, and now she has dreams."

"Send her away," growls the commandant; "send her to a sanatorium! This camp is not a lunatic asylum."

"But," interposes the nurse in her most discreet voice, "she is really a very nice woman. If you would allow me to take her on as a housemaid in the general hospital, I think I could make something out of her; at least I should like to try."

"Have your own way," says the commandant, relenting; "you always do. Now tell me the next trouble. You have something more up your sleeve, I'm sure."

"Babies," she replies demurely; "two babies from Amsterdam. Lost, somehow or other, in the flight. No trace of their people. A family in Zaandam has been taking care of them, but can't afford it any longer. So the Amsterdam committee has sent them here."

The commandant has listened, his cheeks growing redder and redder, his eyes rounder and more prominent. He springs up and paces the floor in wrath.

"Babies!" he cries stormily. "By all the gods, da—those Amsterdammers! Excuse me, but this is too much. Do they think this is a foundling asylum? or a nursing home? Babies! What in Heaven's name am I to do with them? Babies! Where are those babies?"

"Just outside, and very nice babies indeed," says the nurse, opening the hall door and giving a soft call.

Enter a slim black-haired boy of about three and a half years and a plump golden-haired girl about a year younger. They toddle to the nurse and snuggle against her blue dress and white apron.

Smiling she guides them toward the commandant and says: "Here they are, sir. How do you like them?"

That terrific personage has been suddenly transformed from haircloth into silk. He beams, and pulling out his fat gold watch, coos like a hoarse dove: "Look here, *kinderen*, come and hear the bells in my tick-tock!"

Presently he has one of them leaning against the inside of each knee, listening ardently to the watch.

"What do you think of that!" he says. "What is your name, youngster?"

"Hendrik," answers the boy, looking up.

"Hendrik *what*? You have another name, haven't you?"

The boy shakes his head and looks puzzled, as if the thought of two names were too much for him. *"Hendrik,"* he repeats more clearly and firmly.

"And what is her name?" asks the commandant, patting the little girl.

"Sooss," answers the boy. "Mama say *'ickle angel.'* Hendrik say *Sooss.*"

All effort to get any more information from the children was fruitless. They were too small to remember much, and what they did remember was of their own size—only very little things, of no importance except to themselves. The commandant looks at the nurse quizzically.

"Now, miss, you have unloaded these vague babies on me. What do you propose that I should do with them? Adopt them?"

"Not yet, anyhow," she answers, smiling broadly. "Let us take them up to the camp. I'll bet we can find some one there to look after them. What do you say, sir?"

"Well, well," he sighs, "have your own way as usual! Just ring that bell for the automobile, *als't-Ublieft.*"

In the busy sewing-room the two children are standing up on one of the tables. The commandant has an arm around each of them, for they are a little frightened by so much noise and so many eyes looking at them. The chatter dies down, as he speaks in his gruff authoritative voice, but with a twinkle in his eyes, rather like a middle-aged Santa Claus.

"Look here! I've got two fine babies."

A titter runs through the room.

"Ja, Men'eer," says one of the women, "congratulations! They are *lievelingen*—darlings!"

"Silence!" growls the commandant amiably. "None of your impudence, you women. Look here! These two children—I want somebody to adopt them, or at least to take care of them. I will pay for them. Their names are Hendrik and—"

A commotion at the lower end of the room. A thin, dark little woman is standing up, waving her piece of sewing like a flag, her big eyes flaming with excitement.

"Stop!" she cries, hurrying and stumbling forward through the crowd of women and girls. "Oh, stop a minute! They are mine—I lost them—mine, I tell you—lost—mine!"

She reaches the head of the table and flings her arms around the boy, crying: "My Hendrik!"

The boy hesitates a second, startled by the sudden wildness of her caress. Then he presses his hot little face in her neck.

"Lieve moeder!" he murmurs. "Where was you? I looked."

But the thin, dark little woman has fainted dead away.

The rest we will leave, as the wise commandant does, to the chief nurse.

A SANCTUARY OF TREES

The Baron d'Azan was old—older even than his seventy years. His age showed by contrast as he walked among his trees. They were fresh and flourishing, full of sap and vigor, though many of them had been born long before him.

The tracts of forest which still belonged to his diminished estate were crowded with the growths native to the foothills of the Ardennes. In the park around the small chateau, built in a Belgian version of the First Empire style, trees from many lands had been assembled by his father and grandfather: drooping spruces from Norway, dark-pillared cypresses from Italy, spreading cedars from Lebanon, trees of heaven from China, fern-leaved gingkos from Japan, lofty tulip-trees and liquidambars from America, and fantastic sylvan forms from islands of the Southern Ocean. But the royal avenue of beeches! Well, I must tell you more about that, else you can never feel the meaning of this story.

The love of trees was hereditary in the family and antedated their other nobility. The founder of the house had begun life as the son of a forester in Luxemburg. His name was Pol Staar. His fortune and title were the fruit of contracts for horses and provisions which he made with the commissariat of Napoleon I. in the days when the Netherlands were a French province. But though Pol Staar's hands were callous and his manners plain, his tastes were aristocratic. They had been formed young in the company of great trees.

Therefore when he bought his estate of Azan (and took his title from it) he built his chateau in a style which he considered complimentary to his imperial patron, but he was careful also to include within his domain large woodlands in which he could renew the allegiance of his youth. These woodlands he cherished and improved, cutting with discretion, planting with liberality, and rejoicing in the thought that trees like those which had befriended his boyhood would give their friendly protection to his heirs. These are traits of an aristocrat—attachment to the past, and careful provision for posterity. It was in this spirit that Pol Staar, first Baron d'Azan, planted in 1809 the broad avenue of beeches, leading from the chateau straight across the park to the highroad. But he never saw their glory, for he died when they were only twenty years old.

His son and successor was of a different timber and grain; less aristocratic, more bourgeois—a rover, a gambler, a man of fashion. He migrated from the gaming-tables at Spa to the Bourse at Paris, perching at many clubs between and beyond, and making seasonal nests in several places. This left him little time for the Chdteau d'Azan. But he came there every spring and autumn, and showed the family fondness for trees in his own fashion. He loved the forests so much that he ate them. He cut with liberality and planted without discretion. But for the great avenue of beeches he had a saving admiration. Not even to support the gaming-table would he have allowed them to be felled.

When he turned the corner of his thirty-first year he had a sharp illness, a temporary reformation, and brought home as his wife a very young lovely actress from the ducal theatre at Saxe-Meiningen. She was a good girl, deeply in love with her handsome husband, to whom she bore a son and heir in the first year of their marriage. Not many moons thereafter the pleased but restless father slid back into his old rounds again. The forest waned and the debts waxed. Rumors of wild doings came from Spa and Aix, from Homburg and Baden, from Trouville and Ostend. After four years of this the young mother died, of no namable disease, unless you call it heart-failure, and the boy was left to his grandmother's care and company among the trees.

Every day when it was fair the old lady and the little lad took their afternoon walk together in the beech-tree avenue, where the tips of the branches now reached the road. At other times he roamed the outlying woods and learned to know the birds and the little wild animals. When he was twelve his grandmother died. After that he was left mainly to the housekeeper, his tutors, and the few friends he could make among the children of the neighborhood.

When he had finished his third year at the University of Louvain and attained his majority, his father returned express-haste from somewhere in Bohemia, to attend the coronation of Leopold II, that remarkable King of Belgium and the Bourse. But by this time the gay Baron d'Azan had become stout, the pillar of his neck seemed shorter because it was thicker, and the rose in his bold cheek had the purplish tint of a crimson rambler. So he died of an apoplexy during the festivities, and his son brought him back to the Chateau d'Azan, and buried him there with due honor, and mourned for him as was fitting. Thus Albert, third Baron d'Azan, entered upon his inheritance.

It seemed, at first, to consist mainly of debts. These were paid by the sale of the deforested lands and of certain detached woodlands. By the same method, much as he disliked it, he made a modest provision of money for continuing his education and beginning his travels. He knew that he had much to learn of the world, and he was especially desirous of pursuing his favorite study of botany, which a wise old priest at Louvain had taught him to love. So he engaged an intelligent and faithful forester to care for the trees and the estate, closed the house, and set forth on his journeys.

They led him far and wide. In the course of them no doubt he studied other things than botany. It may be that he sowed some of the wild oats with which youth is endowed; but not in the gardens of others; nor with that cold self-indulgence which transforms passionate impulse into sensual habit. He had a permanent and regulative devotion to botanical research; and that is a study which seems to promote modesty, tranquillity, and steadiness of mind in its devotees, of whom the great Linnaeus is the shining exemplar. Young Albert d'Azan sat at the feet of the best masters in Europe and America. He crossed the western continent to observe the oldest of living things, the giant Sequoias of California. He went to Australasia and the Dutch East Indies and South America in search of new ferns and orchids. He investigated the effect of ocean currents and of tribal migrations in the distribution of trees. His botanical monographs brought him renown among those who know, and he was elected a corresponding member of many scientific societies. After twenty years of voyaging he returned to port at Azan, richly laden with observation and learning, and settled down among his trees to pursue his studies and write his books.

The estate, under the forester's care, had improved a little and promised a modest income. The house, though somewhat dilapidated, was easily made livable. But the one thing that was full of glory and splendor, triumphantly prosperous, was the great avenue of beeches. Their long, low aisle of broad arches was complete. They shimmered with a pearly mist of buds in early spring and later with luminous green of tender leafage. In mid-summer they formed a wide, still stream of dark, unruffled verdure; in autumn they were transmuted through glowing yellow into russet gold; in winter their massy trunks were pillars of gray marble and the fan-tracery of their rounded branches was delicately etched against the sky.

"Look at them," the baron would say to the guests whom the fame of his learning and the charm of his wide-ranging conversation often brought to his house. "Those beeches were planted by my grandfather after the battle of Wagram, when Napoleon whipped the Austrians. After that came the Beresina and Leipsic and Waterloo and how many battles and wars of furious, perishable men. Yet the trees live on peaceably, they unfold their strength in beauty, they have not yet reached the summit of their grandeur. We are all *parvenus* beside them."

"If you had to choose," asked the great sculptor Constantin Meunier one day, "would you have your house or one of these trees struck by lightning?"

"The house," answered the botanist promptly, "for I could rebuild it in a year; but to restore the tree would take three-quarters of a century."

"Also," said the sculptor, with a smile, "you might change the style of your house with advantage, but the style of these trees you could never improve."

"But tell me," he continued, "is it true, as they say, that lightning never strikes a beech?"

"It is not entirely true," replied the botanist, smiling in his turn, "yet, like many ancient beliefs, it has some truth in it. There is something in the texture of the beech that seems to resist electricity better than other trees. It may be the fatness of the wood. Whatever it is, I am glad of it, for it gives my trees a better chance."

"Don't be too secure," said the sculptor, shaking his head. "There are other tempests besides those in the clouds. When the next war comes in western Europe Belgium will be the battle-field. Beech-wood is very good to burn."

"God forbid," said the baron devoutly. "We have had peace for a quarter of a century. Why should it not last?"

"Ask the wise men of the East," replied the sculptor grimly.

When he was a little past fifty the baron married, with steadfast choice and deep affection, the orphan daughter of a noble family of Hainault. She was about half his age; of a tranquil, cheerful temper and a charm that depended less on feature than on expression; a lover of music, books, and a quiet life. She brought him a small dowry by which the chateau was restored to comfort, and bore him two children, a boy and a girl, by whom it was enlivened with natural gayety. The next twenty years were the happiest that Albert d'Azan and his wife ever saw. The grand avenue of beeches became to them the unconscious symbol of something settled and serene, august, protective, sacred.

On a brilliant morning of early April, 1914, they had stepped out together to drink the air. The beeches were in misty, silver bloom above them. All around was peace and gladness.

"I want to tell you a dream I had last night," he said, "a strange dream about our beeches."

"If it was sad," she answered, "do not let the shadow of it fall on the morning."

"But it was not sad. It seemed rather to bring light and comfort. I dreamed that I was dead and you had buried me at the foot of the largest of the trees."

"Do you call that not sad?" she interrupted reproachfully.

"It did not seem so. Wait a moment and you shall hear the way of it. At first I felt only a deep quietness and repose, like one who has been in pain and is very tired and lies down in the shade to sleep. Then I was waking again and something was drawing me gently upward. I cannot exactly explain it, but it was as if I were passing through the roots and the trunk and the boughs of the beech-tree toward the upper air. There I saw the light again and heard the birds singing and the wind rustling among the leaves. How I saw and heard I cannot tell you, for there was no remembrance of a body in my dream. Then suddenly my soul—I suppose it was that—stood before God and He was asking me: 'How did you come hither?' I answered, 'By Christ's way, by the way of a tree.' And He said it was well, and that my work in heaven should be the care of the trees growing by the river of life, and that sometimes I could go back to visit my trees on earth, if I wished. That made me very glad, for I knew that so I should see you and our children under the beeches. And while I was wondering whether you would ever know that I was there, the dream dissolved, and I saw the morning light on the tree-tops. What do you think of my dream? Childish, wasn't it?"

She thought a little before she answered.

"It was natural enough, though vague. Of course we could not be buried at the foot of the beech-tree unless Cardinal Mercier would permit a plot of ground to be consecrated there. But come, it is time to go in to breakfast."

She seemed to dismiss the matter from her mind. Yet, as women so often do, she kept all these sayings and pondered them in her heart.

The promise of spring passed into the sultry heat of summer. The storm-cloud of the twentieth century blackened over Europe. The wise men of Berlin made mad by pride, devoted the world not to the Prince of Peace but to the lords of war. In the first week of August the fury of the German invasion broke on Belgium. No one had dared to dream the terrors of that tempest. It was like a return of the Dark Ages. Every home trembled. The pillars of the tranquil house of Azan were shaken.

The daughter was away at school in England, and that was an unmixed blessing. The son was a lieutenant in the Belgian army; and that was right and glorious, but it was also a dreadful anxiety. The father and mother were divided in mind, Whether to stay or take flight with their friends. At last the father decided the hard question.

"It is our duty to stay. We cannot fight for our country, but we can suffer with her. Our daughter is in safety; our son's danger we cannot and would not prevent. How could we really live away from here, our home, our trees? I went to consult the cardinal. He stays, and he advises us to do so. He says that will be the best way to show our devotion. As Christians we must endure the evil that we cannot prevent; but as Belgians our hearts will never consent to it."

That was their attitude as the tide of blood and tears drew nearer to them, surrounded them, swept beyond them, engulfed the whole land. The brutal massacres at Andenne and Dinant were so near that the news arrived before the spilt blood was dry. The exceeding great and bitter cry of anguish came to them from a score of neighboring villages, from a hundred lonely farmhouses. The old botanist withered and faded daily; his wife grew pale and gray. Yet they walked their *via crucis* together, and kept their chosen course.

They fed the hungry and clothed the naked, helped the fugitives and consoled the broken-hearted. They counselled their poor neighbors to good order, and dissuaded the ignorant from the folly and peril of violence. Toward the invading soldiery their conduct was beyond reproach. With no false professions of friendship, they fulfilled the hard services which were required of them. Their servants had been helped away at the beginning of the trouble—all except the old forester and his wife, who refused to leave. With their aid the house was kept open and many of the conquerors lodged there and in the outbuildings. So good were the quarters that a departing Saxon chalked on the gate-post the dubious inscription: *"Gute Leute-nicht auspliin-dern."* Thus the captives at the Chateau d'Azan had a good name even among their enemies. The baron received a military pass which enabled him to move quite freely about the district on his errands of necessity and mercy, and the chateau became a favorite billet for high-born officers.

In the second year of the war an evil chance brought two uninvited guests of very high standing indeed—that is to say in the social ring of Potsdam. Their names are well known. Let us call them Prince Barenberg and Count Ludra. The first was a major, the second a captain. Their value as warriors in the field had not proved equal to their prominence as noblemen, so they were given duty in the rear.

They were vicious coxcombs of the first order. Their uniforms incased them tightly. Like wasps they bent only at the waist. Their flat-topped caps were worn with an aggressive slant, their swords jingled menacingly, their hay-colored mustaches spoke arrogance in every upturned hair. When they bowed it was a mockery; when they smiled it was a sneer. For the comfortable quarters of the Chateau d'Azan they had a gross appreciation, for the enforced hospitality of its owners an insolent condescension. They took it as their due, and resented the silent protest underneath it.

"Excellent wine, Herr Baron," said the prince, who, like his comrade, drank profusely of the best in the cellar. "Your Rudesheimer Berg '94 is *kolossal*. Very friendly of you to save it for us. We Germans know good wine. What?"

"You have that reputation," answered the baron.

"And say," added the count, "let us have a couple of bottles more, dear landlord. You can put it in the bill."

"I shall do so," said the baron gravely. "It shall be put in the bill with other things."

"But why," drawled the prince, "does *la Baronne* never favor us with her company? Still very attractive—musical probably—here is a piano—want good German music—console homesickness."

"Madame is indisposed," answered the baron quietly, "but you may be sure she regrets your absence from home."

The officers looked at each other with half-tipsy, half-angry eyes. They suspected a jest at their expense, but could not quite catch it.

"Impudence," muttered the count, who was the sharper of the two when sober.

"No," said the prince, "it is only stupidity. These Walloons have no wit."

"Come," he added, turning to the baron, "we sing you a good song of fatherland—show how *gemuthlich* we Germans are. You Belgians have no word for that. What?"

He sat down to the piano and pounded out *"Deutschland ueber Alles,"* singing the air in a raucous voice, while Ludra added a rumbling bass.

"What do you think of that? All Germans can sing. *Gemuthlich*. What?"

"You are right," said the baron, with downcast eyes. "We Belgians have no word for that. It is inexpressible—except in German. I bid you good night."

For nearly a fortnight this condition of affairs continued. The baron endured it as best he could, obeying scrupulously the military regulations which necessity laid upon him, and taking his revenge only in long thoughts and words of polite sarcasm which he knew would not be understood. The baroness worked hard at the housekeeping, often cooking and cleaning with her own hands, and rejoicing secretly with her husband over the rare news that came from their daughter in England, from their boy at the front in West Flanders. Sometimes, when the coast was clear, husband and wife walked together under the beech-trees and talked in low tones of the time when the ravenous beast should no more go up on the land.

The two noble officers performed their routine duties, found such amusement as they could in neighboring villages and towns, drank deep at night, and taxed their ingenuity to invent small ways of annoying their hosts, for whom they felt the contemptuous dislike of the injurer for the injured. They were careful, however, to keep their malice within certain bounds, for they knew that the baron was in favor with the commandant of the district.

One morning the baron and his wife, looking from their window in a wing of the house, saw with surprise and horror a score or more of German soldiers assembled beside the beech-avenue, with axes and saws, preparing to begin work.

"What are they going to do there?" cried he in dismay, and hurried down to the dining-room, where the officers sat at breakfast, giving orders to an attentive corporal.

"A thousand pardons, Highness," interrupted the baron; "forgive my haste. But surely you are not going to cut down my avenue of beeches?"

"Why not?" said the prince, swinging around in his chair. "They are good wood."

"But, sir," stammered the baron, trembling with excitement, "those trees—they are an ancient heritage of the house—planted by my grandfather a century ago—an old possession—spare them for their age."

"You exaggerate," sneered the prince. "They are not old. I have on my hunting estate in Thuringia oaks five hundred years old. These trees of yours are mere upstarts. Why shouldn't they be cut? What?"

"But they are very dear to us," pleaded the baron earnestly. "We all love them, my wife and children and I. To us they are sacred. It would be harsh to take them from us."

"Baron," said the prince, with suave malice, "you miss the point. We Germans are never harsh. But we are practical. My soldiers need exercise. The camps need wood. Do you see? What?"

"Certainly," answered the poor baron, humbling himself in his devotion to his trees. "Your Highness makes the point perfectly clear—the need of exercise and wood. But there is plenty of good timber in the forest and the park—much easier to cut. Cannot your men get their wood and their exercise there, and spare my dearest trees?"

Ludra laughed unpleasantly.

"You do not yet understand us, dear landlord. We Germans are a hard-working people, not like the lazy Belgians. The harder the work the better we like it. The soldiers will have a fine time chopping down your tough beeches."

The slender old man drew himself up, his eyes flashed, he was driven to bay.

"You shall not do this," he cried. "It is an outrage, a sacrilege. I shall appeal to the commandant. He will protect my rights."

The officers looked at each other. Deaf to pity, they had keen ears for danger. A reproof, perhaps a punishment from their superior would be most unpleasant. They hesitated to face it. But they were too obstinate to give up their malicious design altogether with a good grace.

"Military necessity," growled the prince, "knows no private rights. I advise you, baron, not to appeal to the commandant. It will be useless, perhaps harmful."

"Here, you," he said gruffly, turning to the corporal, "carry out my orders. Cut the two marked beeches by the gate. Then take your men into the park and cut the biggest trees there. Report for further orders to-morrow morning."

The wooden-faced giant saluted, swung on his heels, and marched stiffly out. The baron followed him quickly.

He knew that entreaties would be wasted on the corporal. How to get to the commandant, that was the question? He would not be allowed to use the telephone which was in the dining-room, nor the automobile which belonged to the officers; nor one of their horses which were in his stable. The only other beast left there was a small and very antique donkey which the children used to drive. In a dilapidated go-cart, drawn by this pattering nag, the baron made such haste as he could along twelve miles of stony road to the district headquarters. There he told his story simply to the commandant and begged protection for his beloved trees.

The old general was of a different type from the fire-eating dandies who played the master at Azan. He listened courteously and gravely. There was a picture in his mind of the old timbered house in the Hohe Venn, where he had spent four years in retirement before the war called him back to the colors. He thought of the tall lindens and the spreading chestnuts around it and imagined how he should feel if he saw them falling under the axe.

Then he said to his petitioner:

"You have acted quite correctly, *Monsieur le Baron,* in bringing this matter quietly to my attention. There is no military necessity for the destruction of your fine trees. I shall put a stop to it at once."

He called his aide-de-camp and gave some instructions in a low tone of voice. When the aide came back from the telephone and reported, the general frowned.

"It is unheard of," he muttered, half to himself, "the way those titled young fools go beyond their orders."

Then he turned to his visitor.

"I am very sorry, *Monsieur le Baron,* but two of your beeches have already fallen. It cannot be helped now. But there shall be no more of it, I promise you. Those young officers are—they are—let us call them overzealous. I will transfer them to another post to-morrow. The German command appreciates the correct conduct of you and *Madame la Baronne.* Is there anything more that I can do for you?"

"I thank your Excellency sincerely," replied the baron. Then he hesitated a moment, as if to weigh his words. "No, *Herr General,* I believe there is nothing more—in which you can help me."

The old soldier's eyelids flickered for an instant. "Then I bid you a very good day," he said, bowing.

The baron hurried home, to share the big good news with his wife. The little bad news she knew already. Together they grieved over the two fallen trees and rejoiced under the golden shadow of their untouched companions. The officers had called for wine, and more wine, and yet more wine, and were drinking deep and singing loud in the dining-room.

In the morning came an orderly with a despatch from headquarters, ordering the prince and the count to duty in a dirty village of the coal region. Their baggage was packed into the automobile, and they mounted their horses and went away in a rage.

"You will be sorry for this, dumbhead," growled the prince, scowling fiercely. "Yes," added Ludra, with a hateful grin, "we shall meet again, dear landlord, and you will be sorry."

Their host bowed and said nothing.

Some weeks later the princely automobile came to the door of the chateau. The forester brought up word that the Prince Barenberg and the Count Ludra were below with a message from headquarters; the commandant wished the baron to come there immediately; the automobile was sent to bring him. He made ready to go. His wife and his servant tried hard to dissuade him: it was late, almost dark, and very cold—not likely the commandant had sent for him—it might be all a trick of those officers—they were hateful men—they would play some cruel prank for revenge. But the old man was obstinate in his resolve; he must do what was required of him, he must not even run the risk of slighting the commandant's wishes; after all, no great harm could come to him.

When he reached the steps he saw the count in the front seat, beside the chauffeur, grinning; and the prince's harsh voice, made soft as possible, called from the shadowy interior of the car:

"Come in, baron. The general has sent for you in a hurry. We will take you like lightning. How fine your beeches look against the sky. What?"

The old man stepped into the dusky car. It rolled down the long aisle, between the smooth gray columns, beneath the fan-tracery of the low arches, out on to the stony highway. Thus the tree-lover was taken from his sanctuary.

He did not return the next day, nor the day after. His wife, tortured by anxiety, went to the district headquarters. The commandant was away. The aide could not enlighten her. There had been no message sent to the baron—that was certain. Major Barenberg and Captain Ludra had been transferred to another command. Unfortunately, nothing could be done except to report the case.

The brave woman was not broken by her anguish, but raised to the height of heroic devotion. She dedicated herself to the search for her husband. The faithful forester, convinced that his master had been killed, was like a slow, sure bloodhound on the track of the murderers. He got a trace of them in a neighboring village, where their car had been seen to pass at dusk on the fatal day. The officers were in it, but not the baron. The forester got a stronger scent of them in a wine-house, where their chauffeur had babbled mysteriously on the following day. The old woodsman followed the trail with inexhaustible patience.

"I shall bring the master's body home," he said to his mistress, "and God will use me to avenge his murder."

A few weeks later he found his master's corpse hidden in a hollow on the edge of the forest, half-covered with broken branches, rotting leaves, and melting snow. There were three bullets in the body. They had been fired at close range.

The widow's heart, passing from the torture of uncertainty to the calm of settled grief, had still a sacred duty to live for. She had not forgotten her husband's dream. She went to the cardinal-archbishop to beg the consecration of a little burial-plot at the foot of the greatest of the beeches of Azan. That wise and brave prince of the church consented with words of tender consolation, and promised his aid in the pursuit of the criminals.

"Eminence," she said, weeping, "you are very good to me. God will reward you. He is just. He will repay. But my heart's desire is to follow my husband's dream."

So the body of the old botanist was brought back to the shadow of the great beech-trees, and was buried there, like the bones of a martyr, within the sanctuary.

Is this the end of the story?

Who can say?

It is written also, among the records of Belgium, that the faithful forester disappeared mysteriously a few weeks later. His body was found in the forest and laid near his master.

Another record tells of the trial of Prince Barenberg and Count Ludra before a court martial, The count was sentenced to ten years of labor *on his own estate.* The death-sentence of the prince was commuted to imprisonment *in some unnamed place.* So far the story of German justice.

But of the other kind of justice—the poetic, the Divine—the record is not yet complete.

I know only that there is a fatherless girl working and praying in a hospital in England, and a fatherless boy fighting and praying in the muddy trenches near Ypres, and a lonely woman walking and praying under certain great beech-trees at the Chateau d'Azan. The burden of their prayer is the same. Night and day it rises to Him who will judge the world in righteousness and before whose eyes the wicked shall not stand.

September, 1918.

THE KING'S HIGH WAY

In the last remnant of Belgium, a corner yet unconquered by the German horde, I saw a tall young man walking among the dunes, between the sodden lowland and the tumbling sea.

The hills where he trod were of sand heaped high by the western winds; and the growth over them was wire-grass and thistles, bayberry and golden broom and stunted pine, with many humble wild flowers—things of no use, yet beautiful.

The sky above was gray; the northern sea was gray; the southern fields were hazy gray over green; the smoke of shells bursting in the air was gray. Gray was the skeleton of the ruined city in the distance; gray were the shattered spires and walls of a dozen hamlets on the horizon; gray, the eyes of the young man who walked in faded blue uniform, in the remnant of Belgium. But there was an indomitable light in his eyes, by which I knew that he was a King.

"Sir," I said, "I am sure that you are his Majesty, the King of Belgium."

He bowed, and a pleasant smile relaxed his tired face.

"Pardon, monsieur," he answered, "but you make the usual mistake in my title. If I were only 'the King of Belgium,' you see, I should have but a poor kingdom now—only this narrow strip of earth, perhaps four hundred square miles of debris, just a *'pou sto,'* a place to stand, enough to fight on, and if need be to die in."

His hand swept around the half-circle of dull landscape visible southward from the top of the loftiest dune, the *Hooge Blikker*. It was a land of slow-winding streams and straight canals and flat fields, with here and there a clump of woods or a slight rise of ground, but for the most part level and monotonous, a checker-board landscape—stretching away until the eyes rested on the low hills beyond Ypres. Now all the placid charm of Flemish fertility as gone from the land—it was scarred and marred and pitted. The shells and mines had torn holes in it; the trenches and barbed-wire entanglements spread over it like a network of scars and welts; the trees were smashed into kindling-wood; the farmhouses were heaps of charred bricks; the shattered villages were like mouths full of broken teeth. As the King looked round at all this, his face darkened and the slight droop of his shoulders grew more marked.

"But, no," he said, turning to me again, "that is not my kingdom. My real title, monsieur, is *King of the Belgians.* It was for their honor, for their liberty, that I was willing to lose my land and risk my crown. While they live and hold true, I stand fast."

Then ran swiftly through me the thought, of how the little Belgian army had fought, how the Belgian people had suffered, rather than surrender the independence of their country to the barbarians. The German cannonade was roaring along the Yser a few miles away; the air trembled with the overload of sound; but between the peals of thunder I could hear the brave song of the skylark climbing his silver stairway of music, undismayed, hopeful, unconquerable. I remembered how the word of this quiet man beside whom I stood had been the inspiration and encouragement of his people through the fierce conflict, the long agony: *"I have faith in our destiny; a nation which defends itself does not perish; God will be with us in that just cause."*

"Sir," I said, "you have a glorious kingdom which shall never be taken away. But as for your land, the fates have been against you. How will you ever get back to it? The Germans are strong as iron and they bar the way. Will you make a peace with them and take what they have so often offered you?"

"Never," he answered calmly; "that is not the way home, it is the way to dishonor. When God brings me back, my army and my Queen are going with me to liberate our people. There is only one way that leads there—the King's high way. Look, *monsieur,* you can see the beginning of it down there. I hope you wish me well on that road, for I shall never take another."

So he bade me good afternoon very courteously and walked away among the dunes to his little cottage at La Panne.

Looking down through the light haze of evening I saw a strip of the straight white road leading eastward across the level land. At the beginning of it there was a broken bridge; in places it seemed torn up by shells; it disappeared in the violet dusk. But as I looked a vision came.

The bridge is restored, the road mended and built up, and on that highway rides the King in his faded uniform with the Queen in white beside him. At their approach ruined villages rejoice aloud and ancient towns break forth into singing.

In Bruges the royal comrades stand beside the gigantic monument in the centre of the Great Market, and above the shouting of the multitude the music of the old belfry floats unheard. Ghent and Antwerp have put on their glad raiment, and in their crooked streets and crowded squares joy flows like a river surging as it goes. Into Brussels I see this man and woman ride through a welcome that rises around them like the voice of many waters—the welcome of those who have waited and suffered, the welcome of those to whom liberty and honor were more dear than life. In the *Grande Place,* the antique, carven, gabled houses are gay with fluttering banners; the people delivered from the cruel invader sing lustily the *Marseillaise* and the old songs of Belgium.

In the midst, Albert and Elizabeth sit quietly upon their horses. They have come home. Not by the low road of cowardly surrender; not by the crooked road of compromise and falsehood; not by the soft road of ease and self-indulgence; but by the straight road of faith and courage and self-sacrifice—the King's High Way.

HALF-TOLD TALES
THE TRAITOR IN THE HOUSE

The Guest, who came from beyond the lake, had lived in the house for years and had the freedom of it, so that he had become quite like a member of the family. He was friendly treated and well lodged. Indeed, some thought he had the best room of all, for though it was in the wing, it was spacious and well warmed, and had a side door, so that he could go in and out freely by day or night.

It must be said that he had earned his living on the place, being industrious and useful, a very handy man about the house; and the children had a liking for him because he sang merry songs and told beautiful fairy-tales.

So he was all the more surprised and aggrieved when the Master of the house said to him one night, as they sat late by the fire:

"I suspect you."

"But of what?" cried the Guest.

"Of caring more for the house that you came from than for the house that you live in."

"But you know I was at home there once," said the Guest, "would you have me forget that? Surely you will not deny me the freedom of my thoughts and memories and fond feelings. Would you make me less than a man?"

"No," said the Master, "but I will ask you to choose between your old home and your new home now. The house in which you lived formerly is become our enemy—a nest of brigands and bloody men. They have killed a child of ours on the highway. They threaten us to-night with an attack in force. Tell me plainly where you stand."

The Guest looked down his nose toward the smouldering embers of the fire. He knocked out the dottle of his pipe on one of the andirons. Two fat tears rolled down his cheeks; he was very sentimental.

"I am with you," he said.

"Good," said the Master, "now let us make the house fast!" {Illustration with caption: 'I will ask you to choose between your old home and your new home now'}

So they closed and barred the shutters and locked and bolted the front door.

Then they lighted their bedroom candles and bade each other good night.

But as the Guest went along his dim corridor, the Master turned and followed him very softly on tiptoe, watching.

Outside the house, in the darkness, there was a sound of many shuffling feet and whispering voices.

When the Guest came to the side door he tried the latch, to see that it was working freely. He moved the bolt, not forward into its socket, but backward so that it should be no hindrance. In the window beside the doorway he set his candle. So the house was ready for late-comers.

Then the Guest sighed a little. "They are my old friends," he murmured, "my dear old friends! I could not leave them out in the cold. I am not responsible for what they do. Only I must my old affection prove." So he sighed again and turned softly to his bed.

But as he turned the Master stood before him and took him by the throat.

"Traitor!" he cried. "You would betray the innocent. Already your soul is stained with my sleeping children's blood." And with his hands he choked the false Guest to death.

Then he shot the bolt of the side door, and barred the window, and called the servants, and made ready to defend the house.

Great was the fighting that night. In the morning, when the robbers were driven off, the false Guest was buried, outside the garden, in an unmarked grave.

February 2, 1918.

JUSTICE OF THE ELEMENTS

So the Criminal with a Crown came to the end of his resources. He had told his last lie, but not even his servants would believe it. He had made his last threat, but no living soul feared it. He had put forth his last stroke of violence and cruelty, but it fell short.

When he saw his own image reflected in the eyes of men, and knew what he had done to the world and what had come of his evil design, he was afraid, and cried, "Let the Earth swallow me!" And the Earth opened, and swallowed him.

But so great was the harm that he had wrought upon the Earth, and so deeply had he drenched it with blood, that it could not contain him. So the Earth opened again, and spewed him forth.

Then he cried, "Let the Sea hide me!" And the waves rolled over his head.

But the Sea, whereon he had wrought iniquity, and filled the depths thereof with the bones of the innocent, could not endure him and threw him up on the shore as refuse.

Then he cried, "Let the Air carry me away!" And the strong winds blew, and lifted him up so that he felt exalted.

But the pure Air, wherein he had let loose the vultures of hate, dropping death upon helpless women and harmless babes, found the burden and the stench of him intolerable, and let him fall.

And as he was falling he cried, "Let the Fire give me a refuge!" So the Fire, wherewith he had consumed the homes of men, rejoiced; and the flames which he had compelled to do his will in wickedness leaped up as he drew near.

"Welcome, old master!" roared the Fire. "Be my slave!"

Then he perceived that there was no hope for him in the justice of the elements. And he said, "I will seek mercy of Him against whom I have most offended."

So he fled to the foot of the Great White Throne. And as he kneeled there, broken and abased, the world was silent, waiting for the sentence of the Judge of All.

August, 1918.

ASHES OF VENGEANCE

Dun was a hard little city, proud and harsh; but impregnable because it was built upon a high rock. The host of the Visigoths had besieged it for months in vain. Then came a fugitive from the city, at midnight, to the tent of Alaric, the Chief of the besiegers.

The man was haggard and torn. His eyes were wild, his hands trembling. The Chief held and steadied him with a look.

"Who are you?" he asked. "Your name, the purpose that brings you here?"

"My name," said the man, "is the Avenger. For thirty years I have lived in Dun, and the people have been unjust and cruel to me. They persecuted my family, because they hated me. My wife died of a broken heart, my children of starvation. I have just escaped from the prison of Dun, and come to tell you how the city may be taken. There is a secret pathway, a hidden entrance. I know it and can reveal it to you."

"Good," said the Chief, measuring the man with tranquil eyes, "but what is your price?"

"Vengeance," said the man, "I ask only the right to revenge my sufferings upon those who have inflicted them, when you have taken the city."

Alaric bent his head and was silent for a moment. "It is a fair price," he said, "and I will pay it. Tell me the way to take the city, and I will leave at your command a troop of soldiers sufficient to work your will on it afterward."

II

The trumpet sounded the capture of the city in the morning. The Avenger, waking late from his troubled sleep, led his soldiers through the open gate.

It was like a city of the dead, and the bodies of those who had been killed in the last defense, lay where they had fallen. Empty and silent were the streets where lie had so often walked in humiliation. Gone were the familiar faces that had frowned on him and mocked him. The houses at whose doors he had often knocked were vacant. His wrath sank within him, and the arrow of solitude pierced him to the heart.

Then he came to the belfry, and there was the bell-ringer, one of the worst of his ancient persecutors, standing at the entrance of the tower.

"Why are you here?" said the Avenger.

"By the orders of King Alaric," answered the bell-ringer, "to ring the bells when peace comes to the city."

"Ring now," said the Avenger, "ring now!"

Then, at the sound of the bells, the people who had concealed themselves at Alaric's command came trooping forth from the cellars and caves where they had been hiding,—old men and women and children, a motley throng of sufferers.

The Avenger looked at them and the tears ran down his cheeks, because he remembered.

"Listen," he said, "don't be afraid. These soldiers are going on to join their army. You have done me great wrong. But the fire of hatred is burnt out, and in the ashes of vengeance we are going to plant the seeds of peace."

December, 1918.

THE BROKEN SOLDIER AND THE MAID OF FRANCE
I. THE MEETING AT THE SPRING

Along the old Roman road that crosses the rolling hills from the upper waters of the Marne to the Meuse a soldier of France was passing in the night.

In the broader pools of summer moonlight he showed as a hale and husky fellow of about thirty years, with dark hair and eyes and a handsome, downcast face. His uniform was faded and dusty; not a trace of the horizon blue was left, only a gray shadow. He had no knapsack on his back, no gun on his shoulder. Wearily and doggedly he plodded his way, without eyes for the veiled beauty of the sleeping country. The quick, firm military step was gone. He trudged like a tramp, choosing always the darker side of the road.

He was a figure of flight, a broken soldier.

Presently the road led him into a thick forest of oaks and beeches, and so to the crest of a hill overlooking a long open valley with wooded heights beyond. Below him was the pointed spire of some temple or shrine, lying at the edge of the wood, with no houses near it. Farther down he could see a cluster of white houses with the tower of a church in the centre. Other villages were dimly visible up and down the valley on either slope. The cattle were lowing from the barnyards. The cocks crowed for the dawn. Already the moon had sunk behind the western trees. But the valley was still bathed in its misty, vanishing light. Over the eastern ridge the gray glimmer of the little day was rising, faintly tinged with rose. It was time for the broken soldier to seek his covert and rest till night returned.

So he stepped aside from the road and found a little dell thick with underwoods, and in it a clear spring gurgling among the ferns and mosses. Around the opening grew wild gooseberries and golden broom and a few tall spires of purple foxglove. He drew off his dusty boots and socks and bathed his feet in a small pool, drying them with fern leaves. Then he took a slice of bread and a piece of cheese from his pocket and made his breakfast. Going to the edge of the thicket, he parted the branches and peered out over the vale.

Its eaves sloped gently to the level floor where the river loitered in loops and curves. The sun was just topping the eastern hills; the heads of the trees were dark against a primrose sky.

In the fields the hay had been cut and gathered. The aftermath was already greening the moist places. Cattle and sheep sauntered out to pasture. A thin silvery mist floated here and there, spreading in broad sheets over the wet ground and shredding into filmy scarves and ribbons as the breeze caught it among the pollard willows and poplars on the border of the stream. Far away the water glittered where the river made a sudden bend or a long smooth reach. It was like the flashing of distant shields. Overhead a few white clouds climbed up from the north. The rolling ridges, one after another, enfolded the valley as far as eye could see; dark green set in pale green, with here and there an arm of forest running down on a sharp promontory to meet and turn the meandering stream.

"It must be the valley of the Meuse," said the soldier. "My faith, but France is beautiful and tranquil here!"

The northerly wind was rising. The clouds climbed more swiftly. The poplars shimmered, the willows glistened, the veils of mist vanished. From very far away there came a rumbling thunder, heavy, insistent, continuous, punctuated with louder crashes.

"It is the guns," muttered the soldier, shivering. "It is the guns around Verdun! Those damned Boches!"

He turned back into the thicket and dropped among the ferns beside the spring. Stretching himself with a gesture of abandon, he pillowed his face on his crossed arms to sleep.

A rustling in the bushes roused him. He sprang to his feet quickly. It was a priest, clad in a dusty cassock, his long black beard streaked with gray. He came slowly treading up beside the trickling rivulet, carrying a bag on a stick over his shoulder.

"Good morning, my son," he said. "You have chosen a pleasant spot to rest."

The soldier, startled, but not forgetting his manners learned from boyhood, stood up and lifted his hand to take off his cap. It was already lying on the ground. "Good morning, Father," he answered, "I did not choose the place, but stumbled on it by chance. It is pleasant enough, for I am very tired and have need of sleep."

"No doubt," said the priest. "I can see that you look weary, and I beg you to pardon me if I have interrupted your repose. But why do you say you came here 'by chance'? If you are a good Christian you know that nothing is by chance. All is ordered and designed by Providence."

"So they told me in church long ago," said the soldier coldly; "but now it does not seem so true—at least not with me."

The first feeling of friendliness and respect into which he had been surprised was passing. He had fallen back into the mood of his journey—mistrust, secrecy, resentment.

The priest caught the tone. His gray eyes under their bushy brows looked kindly but searchingly at the soldier and smiled a little. He set down his bag and leaned on his stick. "Well," he said, "I can tell you one thing, my son. At all events it was not chance that brought me here. I came with a purpose."

The soldier started a little, stung by suspicion. "What then," he cried, roughly, "were you looking for me? What do you know of me? What is this talk of chance and purpose?"

"Come, come," said the priest, his smile spreading from his eyes to his lips, "do not be angry. I assure you that I know nothing of you whatever, not even your name nor why you are here. When I said that I came with a purpose I meant only that a certain thought, a wish, led me to this spot. Let us sit together awhile beside the spring and make better acquaintance."

"I do not desire it," said the soldier, with a frown.

"But you will not refuse it?" queried the priest gently. "It is not good to refuse the request of one old enough to be your father. Look, I have here some excellent tobacco and cigarette-papers. Let us sit down and smoke together. I will tell you who I am and the purpose that brought me here."

The soldier yielded grudgingly, not knowing what else to do. They sat down on a mossy bank beside the spring, and while the blue smoke of their cigarettes went drifting under the little trees the priest began:

"My name is Antoine Courcy. I am the curé of Darney, a village among the Reaping Hook Hills, a few leagues south from here. For twenty-five years I have reaped the harvest of heaven in that blessed little field. I am sorry to leave it. But now this war, this great battle for freedom and the life of France, calls me. It is a divine vocation. France has need of all her sons to-day, even the old ones. I cannot keep the love of God in my heart unless I follow the love of country in my life. My younger brother, who used to be the priest of the next parish to mine, was in the army. He has fallen. I am going to replace him. I am on my way to join the troops—as a chaplain, if they will; if not, then as a private. I must get into the army of France or be left out of the host of heaven."

The soldier had turned his face away and was plucking the lobes from a frond of fern. "A brave resolve, Father," he said, with an ironic note. "But you have not yet told me what brings you off your road, to this place."

"I will tell you," replied the priest eagerly; "it is the love of Jeanne d'Arc, the Maid who saved France long ago. You know about her?"

"A little," nodded the soldier. "I have learned in the school. She was a famous saint."

"Not yet a saint," said the priest earnestly; "the Pope has not yet pronounced her a saint. But it will be done soon. Already he has declared her among the Blessed Ones. To me she is the most blessed of all. She never thought of herself or of a saint's crown. She gave her life entire for France. And this is the place that she came from! Think of that—right here!"

"I did not know that," said the soldier.

"But yes," the priest went on, kindling. "I tell you it was here that the Maid of France received her visions and set out to her work. You see that village below us—look out through the branches—that is Domremy, where she was born. That spire just at the edge of the wood—you saw that? It is the basilica they have built to her memory. It is full of pictures of her. It stands where the old beech-tree, 'Fair May,' used to grow. There she heard the voices and saw the saints who sent her on her mission. And this is the Gooseberry Spring, the Well of the Good Fairies. Here she came with the other children, at the festival of the well-dressing, to spread their garlands around it, and sing, and eat their supper on the green. Heavenly voices spoke to her, but the others did not hear them. Often did she drink of this water. It became a fountain of life springing up in her heart. I have come to drink at the same source. It will strengthen me as a sacrament. Come, son, let us take it together as we go to our duty in battle!"

Father Courcy stood up and opened his old black bag. He took out a small metal cup. He filled it carefully at the spring. He made the sign of the cross over it.

"In the name of the Father, the Son, and the Holy Spirit," he murmured, "blessed and holy is this water." Then he held the cup toward the soldier. "Come, let us share it and make our vows together."

The bright drops trembled and fell from the bottom of the cup. The soldier sat still, his head in his hands.

"No," he answered heavily, "I cannot take it. I am not worthy. Can a man take a sacrament without confessing his sins?"

Father Courcy looked at him with pitying eyes. "I see," he said slowly; "I see, my son. You have a burden on your heart. Well, I will stay with you and try to lift it. But first I shall make my own vow."

He raised the cup toward the sky. A tiny brown wren sang canticles of rapture in the thicket. A great light came into the priest's face—a sun-ray from the east, far beyond the treetops.

"Blessed Jeanne d'Arc, I drink from thy fountain in thy name. I vow my life to thy cause. Aid me, aid this my son, to fight valiantly for freedom and for France. In the name of God, Amen."

The soldier looked up at him. Wonder, admiration, and shame were struggling in the look. Father Courcy wiped the empty cup carefully and put it back in his bag. Then he sat down beside the soldier, laying a fatherly hand on his shoulder.

"Now, my son, you shall tell me what is on your heart."

II. THE GREEN CONFESSIONAL

For a long time the soldier remained silent. His head was bowed. His shoulders drooped. His hands trembled between his knees. He was wrestling with himself.

"No," he cried, at last, "I cannot, I dare not tell you. Unless, perhaps"—his voice faltered—"you could receive it under the seal of confession? But no. How could you do that? Here in the green woods? In the open air, beside a spring? Here is no confessional."

"Why not?" asked Father Courcy. "It is a good place, a holy place. Heaven is over our heads and very near. I will receive your confession here."

The soldier knelt among the flowers. The priest pronounced the sacred words. The soldier began his confession:

"I, Pierre Duval, a great sinner, confess my fault, my most grievous fault, and pray for pardon." He stopped for a moment and then continued, "But first I must tell you, Father, just who I am and where I come from and what brings me here."

"Go on, Pierre Duval, go on. That is what I am waiting to hear. Be simple and very frank."

"Well, then, I am from the parish of Laucourt, in the pleasant country of the Barrois not far from Bar-sur-Aube. My word, but that is a pretty land, full of orchards and berry-gardens! Our old farm there is one of the prettiest and one of the best, though it is small. It was hard to leave it when the call to the colors came, two years ago. But I was glad to go. My heart was high and strong for France. I was in the Nth Infantry, We were in the centre division under General Foch at the battle of the Marne. *Fichtre!* but that was fierce fighting! And what a general! He did not know how to spell 'defeat.' He wrote it 'victory.' Four times we went across that cursed Marsh of St.-Gond. The dried mud was trampled full of dead bodies. The trickling streams of water ran red. Four times we were thrown back by the boches. You would have thought that was enough. But the general did not think so. We went over again on the fifth day, and that time we stayed. The Germans could not stand against us. They broke and ran. The roads where we chased them were full of empty wine-bottles. In one village we caught three officers and a dozen men dead drunk. *Bigre!* what a fine joke!"

Pierre, leaning back upon his heels, was losing himself in his recital. His face lighted up, his hands were waving. Father Courcy bent forward with shining eyes.

"Continue," he cried. "This is a beautiful confession—no sin yet. Continue, Pierre."

"Well, then, after that we were fighting here and there, on the Aisne, on the Ailette, everywhere. Always the same story—Germans rolling down on us in flood, green-gray waves. But the foam on them was fire and steel. The shells of the barrage swept us like hailstones. We waited, waited in our trenches, till the green-gray mob was near enough. Then the word came. *Sapristi!* We let loose with mitrailleuse, rifle, field-gun, everything that would throw death. It did not seem like fighting with men. It was like trying to stop a monstrous thing, a huge, terrible mass that was rushing on to overwhelm us. The waves tumbled and broke before they reached us. Sometimes they fell flat. Sometimes they turned and rushed the other way. It was wild, wild, like a change of the wind and tide in a storm, everything torn and confused. Then perhaps the word came to go over the top and at them. That was furious. That was fighting with men, for sure—bayonet, revolver, rifle-butt, knife, anything that would kill. Often I sickened at the blood and the horror of it. But something inside of me shouted: 'Fight on! It is for France. It is for "L'Alouette" thy farm; for thy wife, thy little ones. Will you let them be ruined by those beasts of Germans? What are they doing here on French soil? Brigands, butchers, apaches! Drive them out; and if they will not go, kill them so they can do no more shameful deeds. Fight on!' So I killed all I could."

The priest nodded his head grimly. "You were right, Pierre; your voice spoke true. It was a dreadful duty that you were doing. The Gospel tells us if we are smitten on one cheek we must turn the other. But it does not tell us to turn the cheek of a little child, of the woman we love, the country we belong to. No! that would be disgraceful, wicked, un-Christian. It would be to betray the innocent! Continue, my son."

"Well, then," Pierre went on, his voice deepening and his face growing more tense, "then we were sent to Verdun. That was the hottest place of all. It was at the top of the big German drive. The whole sea rushed and fell on us—big guns, little guns, poison-gas, hand-grenades, liquid fire, bayonets, knives, and trench-clubs. Fort after fort went down. The whole pack of hell was loose and raging. I thought of that crazy, chinless Crown Prince sitting in his safe little cottage hidden in the woods somewhere—they say he had flowers and vines planted around it—drinking stolen champagne and sicking on his dogs of death. He was in no danger. I cursed him in my heart, that blood-lord! The shells rained on Verdun. The houses were riddled; the cathedral was pierced in a dozen places; a hundred fires broke out. The old citadel held good. The outer forts to the north and east were taken. Only the last ring was left. We common soldiers did not know much about what was happening. The big battle was beyond our horizon. But that General Petain, he knew it all. Ah, that is a wise man, I can tell you! He sent us to this place or that place where the defense was most needed. We went gladly, without fear or holding back. We were resolute that those mad dogs should not get through. *'They shall not pass'!* And they did not pass!"

"Glorious!" cried the priest, drinking the story in. "And you, Pierre? Where were you, what were you doing?"

"I was at Douaumont, that fort on the highest hill of all. The Germans took it. It cost them ten thousand men. The ground around it was like a wood-yard piled with logs. The big shell-holes were full of corpses. There were a few of us that got away. Then our company was sent to hold the third redoubt on the slope in front of Port de Vaux. Perhaps you have heard of that redoubt. That was a bitter job. But we held it many days and nights. The boches pounded us from Douaumont and from the village of Vaux. They sent wave after wave up the slope to drive us out. But we stuck to it. That ravine of La Caillette was a boiling caldron of men. It bubbled over with smoke and fire. Once, when their second wave had broken just in front of us, we went out to hurry the fragments down the hill. Then the guns from Douaumont and the village of Vaux hammered us. Our men fell like ninepins. Our lieutenant called to us to turn back. Just then a shell tore away his right leg at the knee. It hung by the skin and tendons. He was a brave lad. I could not leave him to die there. So I hoisted him on my back. Three shots struck me. They felt just like hard blows from a heavy fist. One of them made my left arm powerless. I sank my teeth in the sleeve of my lieutenant's coat as it hung over my shoulder. I must not let him fall off my back. Somehow—God knows how—I gritted through to our redoubt. They took my lieutenant from my shoulders. And then the light went out."

The priest leaned forward, his hands stretched out around the soldier. "But you are a hero," he cried. "Let me embrace you!"

The soldier drew back, shaking his head sadly. "No," he said, his voice breaking—"no, my Father, you must not embrace me now. I may have been a brave man once. But now I am a coward. Let me tell you everything. My wounds were bad, but not desperate. The *brancardiers* carried me down to Verdun, at night I suppose, but I was unconscious; and so to the hospital at Vaudelaincourt. There were days and nights of blankness mixed with pain. Then I came to my senses and had rest. It was wonderful. I thought that I had died and gone to heaven. Would God it had been so! Then I should have been with my lieutenant. They told me he had passed away in the redoubt. But that hospital was beautiful, so clean and quiet and friendly. Those white nurses were angels. They handled me like a baby. I would have liked to stay there. I had no desire to get better. But I did. One day several officers visited the hospital. They came to my cot, where I was sitting up. The highest of them brought out a Cross of War and pinned it on the breast of my nightshirt. 'There,' he said, 'you are decorated, Pierre Duval! You are one of the heroes of France. You are soon going to be perfectly well and to fight again bravely for your country.' I thanked him, but I knew better. My body might get perfectly well, but something in my soul was broken. It was worn out. The thin spring had snapped. I could never fight again. Any loud noise made me shake all over. I knew that I could never face a battle—impossible! I should certainly lose my nerve and run away. It is a damned feeling, that broken something inside of one. I can't describe it."

Pierre stopped for a moment and moistened his dry lips with the tip of his tongue.

"I know," said Father Courcy. "I understand perfectly what you want to say. It was like being lost and thinking that nothing could save you; a feeling that is piercing and dull at the same time, like a heavy weight pressing on you with sharp stabs in it. It was what they call shell-shock, a terrible thing. Sometimes it drives men crazy for a while. But the doctors know what to do for that malady. It passes. You got over it."

"No," answered Pierre, "the doctors may not have known that I had it. At all events, they did not know what to do for it. It did not pass. It grew worse. But I hid it, talking very little, never telling anybody how I felt. They said I was depressed and needed cheering up. All the while there was that black snake coiled around my heart, squeezing tighter and tighter. But my body grew stronger every day. The wounds were all healed. I was walking around. In July the doctor-in-chief sent for me to his office. He said: 'You are cured, Pierre Duval, but you are not yet fit to fight. You are low in your mind. You need cheering up. You are to have a month's furlough and repose. You shall go home to your farm. How is it that you call it?' I suppose I had been babbling about it in my sleep and one of the nurses had told him. He was always that way, that little Doctor Roselly, taking an interest in the men, talking with them and acting friendly. I said the farm was called *'L'Alouette'*—rather a foolish name. 'Not, at all,' he answered; 'it is a fine name, with the song of a bird in it. Well, you are going back to *"L'Alouette"* to hear the lark sing for a month, to kiss your wife and your children, to pick gooseberries and currants. Eh, my boy, what do you think of that? Then, when the month is over, you will be a new man. You will be ready to fight again at Verdun. Remember they have not passed and they shall not pass! Good luck to you, Pierre Duval.' So I went back to the farm as fast as I could go."

He was silent for a few moments, letting his thoughts wander through the pleasant paths of that little garden of repose. His eyes were dreaming, his lips almost smiled.

"It was sweet at *'L'Alouette,'* very sweet, Father. The farm was in pretty good order and the kitchen-garden was all right, though, the flowers had been a little neglected. You see, my wife, Josephine, she is a very clever woman. She had kept up the things that were the most necessary. She had hired one of the old neighbors and a couple of boys to help her with the ploughing and planting. The harvest she sold as it stood. Our yoke of cream-colored oxen and the roan horse were in good condition. Little Pierrot, who is five, and little Josette, who is three, were as brown as berries. They hugged me almost to death. But it was Josephine herself who was the best of all. She is only twenty-six, Father, and so beautiful still, with her long chestnut hair and her eyes like stones shining under the waters of a brook. I tell you it was good to get her in my arms again and feel her lips on mine. And to wake in the early morning, while the birds were singing, and see her face beside me on the white pillow, sleeping like a child, that was a little bit of Paradise. But I do wrong to tell you of all this, Father."

"Proceed, my big boy," nodded the priest. "You are saying nothing wrong. I was a man before I was a priest. It is all natural, what you are saying, and all according to God's law—no sin in it. Proceed. Did your happiness do you good?" Pierre shook his head doubtfully. The look of dejection came back to his face. He frowned as if something puzzled and hurt him. "Yes and no. That is the strange thing. It made me thankful—that goes without saying. But it did not make me any stronger in my heart. Perhaps it was too sweet. I thought too much of it. I could not bear to think of anything else. The idea of the war was hateful, horrible, disgusting. The noise and the dirt of it, the mud in the autumn and the bitter cold in the winter, the rats and the lice in the dugouts, And then the fury of the charge, and the everlasting killing, killing, or being killed! The danger had seemed little or nothing to me when I was there. But at a distance it was frightful, unendurable. I knew that I could never stand up to it again. Besides, already I had done my share—enough for two or three men. Why must I go back into that hell? It was not fair. Life was too dear to be risking it all the time. I could not endure it. France? France? Of course I love France. But my farm and my life with Josephine and the children mean more to me. The thing that made me a good soldier is broken inside me. It is beyond mending."

His voice sank lower and lower. Father Courcy looked at him gravely.

"But your farm is a part of France. You belong to France. He that saveth his life shall lose it!"

"Yes, yes, I know. But my farm is such a small part of France. I am only one man. What difference does one man make, except to himself? Moreover, I had done my part, that was certain. Twenty times, really, my life had been lost. Why must I throw it away again? Listen, Father. There is a village in the Vosges, near the Swiss border, where a relative of mine lives. If I could get to him he would take me in and give me some other clothes and help me over the frontier into Switzerland. There I could change my name and find work until the war is over. That was my plan. So I set out on my journey, following the less-travelled roads, tramping by night and sleeping by day. Thus I came to this spring at the same time as you by chance, by pure chance. Do you see?"

Father Courcy looked very stern and seemed about to speak in anger. Then he shook his head, and said quietly: "No, I do not see that at all. It remains to be seen whether it was by chance. But tell me more about your sin. Did you let your wife, Josephine, know what you were going to do? Did you tell her good-by, parting for Switzerland?"

"Why, no! I did not dare. She would never have forgiven me. So I slipped down to the post-office at Bar-sur-Aube and stole a telegraph blank. It was ten days before my furlough was out. I wrote a message to myself calling me back to the colors at once. I showed it to her. Then I said good-by. I wept. She did not cry one tear. Her eyes were stars. She embraced me a dozen times. She lifted up each of the children to hug me. Then she cried: 'Go now, my brave man. Fight well. Drive the damned boches out. It is for us and for France. God protect you. *Au revoir!*' I went down the road silent. I felt like a dog. But I could not help it."

"And you were a dog," said the priest sternly. "That is what you were, and what you remain unless you can learn to help it. You lied to your wife. You forged; you tricked her who trusted you. You have done the thing which you yourself say she would never forgive. If she loves you and prays for you now, you have stolen that love and that prayer. You are a thief. A true daughter of France could never love a coward to-day."

"I know, I know," sobbed Pierre, burying his face in the weeds. "Yet I did it partly for her, and I could not do otherwise."

"Very little for her, and a hundred times for yourself," said the priest indignantly. "Be honest. If there was a little bit of love for her, it was the kind of love she did not want. She would spit upon it. If you are going to Switzerland now you are leaving her forever. You can never go back to Josephine again. You are a deserter. She would cast you out, coward!"

The broken soldier lay very still, almost as if he were dead. Then he rose slowly to his feet, with a pale, set face. He put his hand behind his back and drew out a revolver. "It is true," he said slowly, "I am a coward. But not altogether such a coward as you think, Father. It is not merely death that I fear. I could face that, I think. Here, take this pistol and shoot me now! No one will know. You can say you shot a deserter, or that I attacked you. Shoot me now, Father, and let me out of this trouble."

Father Courcy looked at him with amazement. Then he took the pistol, uncocked it cautiously, and dropped it behind him. He turned to Pierre and regarded him curiously. "Go on with your confession, Pierre. Tell me about this strange kind of cowardice which can face death."

The soldier dropped on his knees again, and went on in a low, shaken voice: "It is this, Father. By my broken soul, this is the very root of it. I am afraid of fear."

The priest thought for an instant. "But that is not reasonable, Pierre. It is nonsense. Fear cannot hurt you. If you fight it you can conquer it. At least you can disregard it, march through it, as if it were not there."

"Not this fear," argued the soldier, with a peasant's obstinacy. "This is something very big and dreadful. It has no shape, but a dead-white face and red, blazing eyes full of hate and scorn. I have seen it in the dark. It is stronger than I am. Since something is broken inside of me, I know I can never conquer it. No, it would wrap its shapeless arms around me and stab me to the heart with its fiery eyes. I should turn and run in the middle of the battle. I should trample on my wounded comrades. I should be shot in the back and die in disgrace. O my God! my God! who can save me from this? It is horrible. I cannot bear it."

The priest laid his hand gently on Pierre's quivering shoulder. "Courage, my son!"

"I have none."

"Then say to yourself that fear is nothing."

"It would be a lie. This fear is real."

"Then cease to tremble at it; kill it."

"Impossible. I am afraid of fear."

"Then carry it as your burden, your cross. Take it back to Verdun with you."

"I dare not. It would poison the others. It would bring me to dishonor."

"Pray to God for help."

"He will not answer me. I am a wicked man. Father, I have made my confession. Will you give me a penance and absolve me?"

"Promise to go back to the army and fight as well as you can."

"Alas! that is what I cannot do. My mind is shaken to pieces. Whither shall I turn? I can decide nothing. I am broken. I repent of my great sin. Father, for the love of God, speak the word of absolution."

Pierre lay on his face, motionless, his arms stretched out. The priest rose and went to the spring. He scooped up a few drops in the hollow of his hand. He sprinkled it like holy water upon the soldier's head. A couple of tears fell with it.

"God have pity on you, my son, and bring you back to yourself. The word of absolution is not for me to speak while you think of forsaking France. Put that thought away from you, do penance for it, and you will be absolved from your great sin."

Pierre turned over and lay looking up at the priest's face and at the blue sky with white clouds drifting across it. He sighed. "Ah, if that could only be! But I have not the strength. It is impossible."

"All things are possible to him that believeth. Strength will come. Perhaps Jeanne d'Arc herself will help you."

"She would never speak to a man like me. She is a great saint, very high in heaven."

"She was a farmer's lass, a peasant like yourself. She would speak to you, gladly and kindly, if you saw her, and in your own language, too. Trust her."

"But I do not know enough about her."

"Listen, Pierre. I have thought for you. I will appoint the first part of your penance. You shall take the risk of being recognized and caught. You shall go down to the village and visit the places that belong to her—her basilica, her house, her church. Then you shall come back here and wait until you know—until you surely know what you must do. Will you promise this?"

Pierre had risen and looked up at the priest with tear-stained face. But his eyes were quieter. "Yes, Father, I can promise you this much faithfully."

"Now I must go my way. Farewell, my son. Peace in war be with you." He held out his hand.

Pierre took it reverently. "And with you, Father," he murmured.

III. THE ABSOLVING DREAM

Antoine Courcy was one of those who are fitted and trained by nature for the cure of souls. If you had spoken to him of psychiatry he would not have understood you. The long word would have been Greek to him. But the thing itself he knew well. The preliminary penance which he laid upon Pierre Duval was remedial. It belonged to the true healing art which works first in the spirit.

When the broken soldier went down the hill, in the blaze of the mid-morning sunlight, toward Domremy, there was much misgiving and confusion in his thoughts. He did not comprehend why he was going, except that he had promised. He was not sure that some one might not know him, or perhaps out of mere curiosity stop him and question him. It was a reluctant journey.

Yet it was in effect an unconscious pilgrimage to the one health-resort that his soul needed. For Domremy and the region round about are saturated with the most beautiful story of France. The life of Jeanne d'Arc, simple and mysterious, humble and glorious, most human and most heavenly, flows under that place like a hidden stream, rising at every turn in springs and fountains. The poor little village lives in and for her memory. Her presence haunts the ridges and the woods, treads the green pastures, follows the white road beside the river, and breathes in the never-resting valley-wind that marries the flowers in June and spreads their seed in August.

At the small basilica built to her memory on the place where her old beech-tree, "Fair May," used to stand, there was an ancient caretaker who explained to Pierre the pictures from the life of the Maid with which the walls are decorated. They are stiff and conventional, but the old man found them wonderful and told with zest the story of *La Pucelle*—how she saw her first vision; how she recognized the Dauphin in his palace at Chinon; how she broke the siege of Orleans; how she saw Charles crowned in the cathedral at Rheims; how she was burned at the stake in Rouen. But they could not kill her soul. She saved France.

In the village church there was a priest from the border of Alsace, also a pilgrim like Pierre, but one who knew the shrine better. He showed the difference between the new and the old parts of the building. Certain things the Maid herself had seen and touched.

"Here is the old holy-water basin, an antique, broken column hollowed out on top. Here her fingers must have rested often. Before this ancient statue of St. Michel she must have often knelt to say her prayers. The cure of the parish was a friend of hers and loved to talk with her. She was a good girl, devout and obedient, not learned, but a holy and great soul. She saved France."

In the house where she was born and passed her childhood a crippled old woman was custodian. It was a humble dwelling of plastered stone standing between two tall fir-trees, with ivy growing over the walls, lilies and hollyhocks blooming in the garden. Pierre found it not half so good a house as *"L'Alouette."* But to the custodian it was more precious than a palace. In this upper room with its low mullioned window the Maid began her life. Here, in the larger room below, is the kneeling statue which the Princess Marie d'Orleans made of her. Here, to the right, under the sloping roof, with its worm-eaten beams, she slept and prayed and worked.

"See, here is the bread-board between two timbers where she cut the bread for the *croute au pot.* From this small window she looked at night and saw the sanctuary light burning in the church. Here, also, as well as in the garden and in the woods, her heavenly voices spoke to her and told her what she must do for her king and her country. She was not afraid or ashamed, though she lived in so small a house. Here in this very room she braided her hair and put on her red dress, and set forth on foot for her visit to Robert de Baudricourt at Vaucouleurs. He was a rough man and at first he received her roughly. But at last she convinced him. He gave her a horse and arms and sent her to the king. She saved France."

At the rustic inn Pierre ate thick slices of dark bread and drank a stoup of thin red wine at noon. He sat at a bare table in the corner of the room. Behind him, at a table covered with a white cloth, two captains on furlough had already made their breakfast. They also were pilgrims, drawn to Domremy by the love of Jeanne d'Arc. They talked of nothing else but of her. Yet their points of view were absolutely different.

One of them, the younger, was short and swarthy, a Savoyard, the son of an Italian doctor at St. Jean de Maurienne. He was a sceptic; he believed in Jeanne, but not in the legends about her.

"I tell you," said he eagerly, "she was one of the greatest among women. But all that about her 'voices' was illusion. The priests suggested it. She had hallucinations. Remember her age when they began—just thirteen. She was clever and strong; doubtless she was pretty; certainly she was very courageous. She was only a girl. But she had a big, brave idea which possessed her—the liberation of her country. Pure? Yes. I am sure she was virtuous. Otherwise the troops would not have followed and obeyed her as they did. Soldiers are very quick about those things. They recognize and respect an honest woman. Several men were in love with her, I think. But she was *une nature froide.* The only thing that moved her was her big, brave idea—to save France. The Maid was a mother, but not of a mortal child. Her offspring was the patriotism of France."

The other captain was a man of middle age, from Lyons, the son of an architect. He was tall and pale and his large brown eyes had the tranquillity of a devout faith in them. He argued with quiet tenacity for his convictions.

"You are right to believe in her," said he, "but I think you are mistaken to deny her 'voices.' They were as real as anything in her life. You credit her when she says that she was born here, that she went to Chinon and saw the king, that delivered Orleans. Why not credit her when she says she heard God and the saints speaking to her? The proof of it was in what she did. Have you read the story of her trial? How clear and steady her answers were! The judges could not shake her. Yet at any moment she could have saved her life by denying the 'voices.' It was because she knew, because she was sure, that she could not deny. Her vision was a part of her real life. She was the mother of French patriotism—yes. But she was also the daughter of true faith. That was her power."

"Well," said the younger man, "she sacrificed herself and she saved France. That was the great thing."

"Yes," said the elder man, stretching his hand across the table to clasp the hand of his companion, "there is nothing greater than that. If we do that, God will forgive us all."

They put on their caps to go. Pierre rose and stood at attention. They returned his salute with a friendly smile and passed out.

After a few moments he finished his bread and wine, paid his score, and followed them. He watched them going down the village street toward the railway station. Then he turned and walked slowly back to the spring in the dell.

The afternoon was hot, in spite of the steady breeze which came out of the north. The air felt as if it had passed through a furnace. The low, continuous thunder of the guns rolled up from Verdun, with now and then a sharper clap from St. Mihiel.

Pierre was very tired. His head was heavy, his heart troubled. He lay down among the ferns, looking idly at the foxglove spires above him and turning over in his mind the things he had heard and seen at Domremy. Presently he fell into a profound sleep.

How long it was he could not tell, but suddenly he became aware of some one near him. He sprang up. A girl was standing beside the spring.

She wore a bright-red dress and her feet were bare. Her black hair hung down her back. Her eyes were the color of a topaz. Her form was tall and straight. She carried a distaff under her arm and looked as if she had just come from following the sheep.

"Good day, shepherdess," said Pierre. Then a strange thought struck him, and he fell on his knees. "Pardon, lady," he stammered. "Forgive my rudeness. You are of the high society of heaven, a saint. You are called Jeanne d'Arc?"

She nodded and smiled. "That is my name," said she. "Sometimes they call me *La Pucelle*, or the Maid of France. But you were right, I am a shepherdess, too. I have kept my father's sheep in the fields down there, and spun from the distaff while I watched them. I know how to sew and spin as well as any girl in the Barrois or Lorraine. Will you not stand up and talk with me?"

Pierre rose, still abashed and confused. He did not quite understand how to take this strange experience—too simple for a heavenly apparition, too real for a common dream. "Well, then," said he, "if you are a shepherdess, why are you here? There are no sheep here."

"But yes. You are one of mine. I have come here to seek you."

"Do you know me, then? How can I be one of yours?"

"Because you are a soldier of France and you are in trouble."

Pierre's head drooped. "A broken soldier," he muttered, "not fit to speak to you. I am running away because I am afraid of fear."

She threw back her head and laughed. "You speak very bad French. There is no such thing as being afraid of fear. For if you are afraid of it, you hate it. If you hate it, you will have nothing to do with it. And if you have nothing to do with it, it cannot touch you; it is nothing."

"But for you, a saint, it is easy to say that. You had no fear when you fought. You knew you would not be killed."

"I was no more sure of that than the other soldiers. Besides, when they bound me to the stake at Rouen and kindled the fire around me I knew very well that I should be killed. But there was no fear in it. Only peace."

"Ah, you were strong, a warrior born. You were not wounded and broken."

"Four times I was wounded," she answered gravely. "At Orleans a bolt went through my right shoulder. At Paris a lance tore my thigh. I never saw the blood of Frenchmen flow without feeling my heart stand still. I was not a warrior born. I knew not how to ride or fight. But I did it. What we must needs do that we can do. Soldier, do not look on the ground. Look up."

Then a strange thing took place before his eyes. A wondrous radiance, a mist of light, enveloped and hid the shepherdess. When it melted she was clad in shining armor, sitting on a white horse, and lifting a bare sword in her left hand.

"God commands you," she cried. "It is for France. Be of good cheer. Do not retreat. The fort will soon be yours!"

How should Pierre know that this was the cry with which the Maid had rallied her broken men at Orleans when the fort of *Les Tourelles* fell? What he did know was that something seemed to spring up within him to answer that call. He felt that he would rather die than desert such a leader.

The figure on the horse turned away as if to go.

"Do not leave me," he cried, stretching out his hands to her. "Stay with me. I will obey you joyfully."

She turned again and looked at him very earnestly. Her eyes shone deep into his heart. "Here I cannot stay," answered a low, sweet, womanly voice. "It is late, and my other children need me."

"But forgiveness? Can you give that to me—a coward?"

"You are no coward. Your only fault was to doubt a brave man."

"And my wife? May I go back and tell her?"

"No, surely. Would you make her hear slander of the man she loves? Be what she believes you and she will be satisfied."

"And the absolution, the word of peace? Will you speak that to me?"

Her eyes shone more clearly; the voice sounded sweeter and steadier than ever. "After the penance comes the absolution. You will find peace only at the lance's point. Son of France, go, go, go! I will help you. Go hardily to Verdun."

Pierre sprang forward after the receding figure, tried to clasp the knee, the foot of the Maid. As he fell to the ground something sharp pierced his hand. It must be her spur, thought he.

Then he was aware that his eyes were shut. He opened them and looked at his hand carefully. There was only a scratch on it, and a tiny drop of blood. He had torn it on the thorns of the wild gooseberry-bushes.

His head lay close to the clear pool of the spring. He buried his face in it and drank deep. Then he sprang up, shaking the drops from his mustache, found his cap and pistol, and hurried up the glen toward the old Roman road.

"No more of that damned foolishness about Switzerland," he said, aloud. "I belong to France. I am going with the other boys to save her. I was born for that." He took off his cap and stood still for a moment. He spoke as if he were taking an oath. "By Jeanne d'Arc!"

IV. THE VICTORIOUS PENANCE

It never occurred to Pierre Duval, as he trudged those long kilometres toward the front, that he was doing a penance.

The joy of a mind made up is a potent cordial.

The greetings of comrades on the road put gladness into his heart and strength into his legs.

It was a hot and dusty journey, and a sober one. But it was not a sad one. He was going toward that for which he was born. He was doing that which France asked of him, that which God told him to do. Josephine would be glad and proud of him. He would never be ashamed to meet her eyes. As he went, alone or in company with others, he whistled and sang a bit. He thought of *"L'Alouette"* a good deal. But not too much. He thought also of the forts of Douaumont and Vaux.

"Dame!" he cried to himself. "If I could help to win them back again! That would be fine! How sick that would make those cursed boches and their knock-kneed Crown Prince!"

At the little village of the headquarters behind Verdun he found many old friends and companions. They greeted him with cheerful irony.

"Behold the prodigal! You took your time about coming back, didn't you? Was the hospital to your taste, the nurses pretty? How is the wife? Any more children? How goes it, old man?"

"No more children yet," he answered, grinning; "but all goes well. I have come back from a far country, but I find the pigs are still grunting. What have you done to our old cook?"

"Nothing at all," was the joyous reply. "He tried to swim in his own soup and he was drowned."

When Pierre reported to the officer of the day, that busy functionary consulted the record.

"You are a day ahead of your time, Pierre Duval," he said, frowning slightly.

"Yes, sir," answered the soldier. "It costs less to be a day ahead than a day too late."

"That is well," said the officer, smiling in his red beard. "You will report to-morrow to your regiment at the citadel. You have a new colonel, but the regiment is busy in the old way."

As Pierre saluted and turned to go out his eye caught the look of a general officer who stood near, watching. He was a square, alert, vigorous man, his face bronzed by the suns of many African campaigns, his eyes full of intelligence, humor, and courage. It was Guillaumat, the new commander of the Army of Verdun.

"You are prompt, my son," said he pleasantly, "but you must remember not to be in a hurry. You have been in hospital. Are you well again? Nothing broken?"

"Something was broken, my General," responded the soldier gravely, "but it is mended."

"Good!" said the general. "Now for the front, to beat the Germans at their own game. We shall get them. It may be long, but we shall get them!"

That was the autumn of the offensive of 1916, by which the French retook, in ten days, what it had cost the Germans many months to gain.

Pierre was there in that glorious charge at the end of October which carried the heights of Douaumont and took six thousand prisoners. He was there at the recapture of the Fort de Vaux which the Germans evacuated in the first week of November. In the last rush up the slope, where he had fought long ago, a stray shell, an inscrutable messenger of fate, coming from far away, no one knows whence, caught him and ripped him horribly across the body.

It was a desperate mass of wounds. But the men of his squad loved their corporal. He still breathed. They saw to it that he was carried back to the little transit hospital just behind the Fort de Souville.

It was a rude hut of logs, covered with sand-bags, on the slope of the hill. The ruined woods around it were still falling to the crash of far-thrown shells. In the close, dim shelter of the inner room Pierre came to himself.

He looked up into the face of Father Courcy. A light of recognition and gratitude flickered in his eyes. It was like finding an old friend in the dark.

"Welcome!—But the fort?" he gasped.

"It is ours," said the priest.

Something like a smile passed over the face of Pierre. He could not speak for a long time. The blood in his throat choked him. At last he whispered:

"Tell Josephine—love."

Father Courcy bowed his head and took Pierre's hand. "Surely," he said. "But now, my dear son Pierre, I must prepare you—"

The struggling voice from the cot broke in, whispering slowly, with long intervals: "Not necessary.... I know already.... The penance. ... France.... Jeanned'Arc.... It is done."

A few drops of blood gushed from the corner of his mouth. The look of peace that often comes to those who die of gunshot wounds settled on his face. His eyes grew still as the priest laid the sacred wafer on his lips. The broken soldier was made whole.

THE HEARING EAR

There were three American boys from the region of Philadelphia in the dugout, "Somewhere in France"; and they found it a snug habitation, considering the circumstances.

The central heating system—a round sheet-iron stove, little larger than a "topper" hat—sent out incredible quantities of acrid smoke at such times as the rusty stovepipe refused to draw. But on cold nights and frosty mornings the refractory thing was a distinct consolation. The ceiling of the apartment lacked finish. When wet it dropped mud; when dry, dust. But it had the merit of being twenty feet thick—enough to stop any German shell except a "Jack Johnson" full of high explosive. The beds were elegantly excavated in the wall, and by a slight forward inclination of the body you could use them as *fauteuils*. The rats approved of them highly.

There were two flights of ladder-stairs leading down from the trench into the dugout, and the holes at the top which served as vestibules were three or four yards apart. It was a comfort to think of this architectural design; for if the explosion of a big shell blocked up one of the entrances, the other would probably remain open, and you would not be caught in a trap with the other rats.

The main ornament of the *salon* was a neat but not gaudy biscuit-box. The top of it was a centre-table, illuminated by a single, guttering candle; the interior was a "combination" wardrobe and sideboard. Around this simple but satisfying piece of furniture the three transient tenants of the dugout had just played a game of dummy bridge, and now sat smoking and bickering as peacefully as if they were in a college club-room in America. The night on the front was what the French call *"relativement calme."* Sporadic explosions above punctuated but did not interrupt the debate, which eddied about the high theme of Education—with a capital "E"—and the particular point of dispute was the study of languages.

"Everything is going to change after the war," said Phipps-Herrick, a big Harvard man from Bryn Mawr and a member of the Unsocial Socialists' Club. "We are going to make a new world. Must have a new education. Sweep away all the old stuff—languages, grammar, literature, philosophy, history, and all that. Put in something modern and practical. Montessori system for the little kids. Vocational training for the bigger ones. Teach them to make a living. Then organize them politically and economically. You can do what you like, then, with England, France, and America together. Germany will be shut out. Why study German? From a practical point of view, I ask you, why?"

"Didn't you take it at Harvard?" sarcastically drawled Rosenlaube, a Princeton man from Rittenhouse Square. (His grandfather was born at Frankfort-on-the-Main, but his mother was a Biddle, and he had penetrated about an inch into the American diplomatic service when the war summoned him to a more serious duty.) "I understood that all you Harvard men were strong on modern languages, especially German."

Phipps-Herrick grunted.

"Certainly I took it. It was supposed to be a soft-snap course. What do you think we go to Harvard for? But that little beast, Professor von Buch, gave me a cold forty-minus on examination. So I dropped it, and thank God I've forgotten the little I ever knew of German! It will be absolutely useless in the new world."

"Right you are," said Rosenlaube. "My grandfather used to speak it when he was angry—a sloppy, slushy language, extremely ugly. At Princeton, you know, we stand by the classics, Latin and Greek, the real thing in languages. You ought to hear Dean Andy West talk about that. Of course a fellow forgets his Virgil and his Homer when he gets out in the world. But, then, he's had the benefit of them; they've given him real culture and literature. There's nothing outside of the classics, except perhaps a few things in French and Italian. Thank God I never studied German!"

The third man, who had kept silence up to this point, now gently butted in. It was little Phil Mitchell, of Overbrook, a University of Pennsylvania man, who had been stopped in his junior year by a financial catastrophe in the family, and had gone out to Idaho to earn his living as third assistant bookkeeper in a big mining concern. He took a few real books with him, besides those that he was to "keep." Double entry was his business; reading, his recreation; thinking, his vocation. From all this the great war called him as with a trumpet.

"Look here, you fellows," he said quietly, "in spite of this war and all the rest of it, there are some good things in German."

"What," they cried, "you, a fire-eater, stand up for the Kaiser and his language? Damn him!"

"With all my heart," assented Mitchell. "But the language isn't his. It existed a long while before he was born. It isn't very pretty, I'll admit. But there are lots of fine things in it. Kant and Lessing, Goethe and Schiller and Heine—they all loved liberty and made it shine out in their work. Do you mean to say that I must give them up and throw my German overboard because these modern Potsdammers have acted like brutes?"

"Yes," cried Phipps-Herrick and Rosenlaube, nodding at each other, "that's what we mean, and that's what America means. The German language must go!"

"Look here," said Phipps-Herrick, "you admit that modern education must be useful? Well, there won't be any more use for German, because we are going to shut Germany out of the international trades-union. She has betrayed the principles of the new era. We are going to boycott her."

"Won't that be rather difficult?" queried Mitchell, shaking his head. "Seventy or eighty million people—hard to shut them out of the world, eh?"

"Nonsense, dear Phil," drawled Rosenlaube; "it will be easy enough. But I don't agree with Phipps-Herrick about the reason or method. We are going to have a new era after the war. But it will not be a utilitarian age. It will be a return to beauty and form and culture—not with a 'k.' First of all, we are going to kill a great many Germans. Then we are going to Berlin to knock down all the ugly statues in the *Sieges-Allee* and smash the parvenu German Empire. Then we shall have a new age on classic lines. People will still use French and English and Italian because there is some beauty in those languages. But nobody outside of Germany will speak or read German. It is a barbarous tongue—shapeless and hideous—used by barbarians who gobble and snort when they talk. Sorry for Kant and Goethe and Heine and all that crowd, but their time is up; they've got to go out with their beastly language!"

"Yes," said Phipps-Herrick, "out with them, bag and baggage. Think what the German spies and propagandists have done in America. Schools full of pacifist and pro-German teachers; text-books full of praise of the German Empire and the Hohenzollern Highbinders; newspapers full of treason, printed in the German language. Why, it's only a piece of self-defense to clean it all out, root and branch. No more German taught or spoken, printed or read, in the United States. Forget it! Twenty-three for the Hun language!"

"Noble," gently murmured Mitchell, shaking his head again; "very noble! But not very easy and perhaps not entirely wise. Why should I throw away something that has been useful to me, and may be again? Why forget the little German that I know and burn my Goethe and refuse to listen to Beethoven's music? I won't do it, that's all."

"Our little friend is a concealed Kaiserite," said Rosenlaube. "He wants to Germanize America."

"No, Rosy," said Mitchell, thoughtfully running his hand over some nicks on the butt of his rifle in the corner; "you know I'm not a Kaiserite of any kind. I've got seven scored against him already, and I'm going to get some more.

But the language question seems to me different. Cut out the German newspapers and the German schools in America by all means! No more teaching of the primary branches in any language but English! Make it absolutely necessary for everybody in the U. S. A. to learn the language of the country the first thing. Then in the high schools and universities let German be studied like any other foreign language, by those who want it—chemists, and philosophers, and historians, and electrical engineers, and so on. We could censor the text-books and keep out all complimentary allusions to the Hohenzollern family."

"Oh, shut up, Phil," growled Phipps-Herrick. "You're too soft, you old easy-mark! You don't go half far enough. We may not decide to exterminate the Hun race in Europe. But we have decided to exterminate their language in America."

His hand was groping inside the biscuit-box. He pulled out a little ditty-bag and carefully extracted a bit of newspaper.

"Listen to this, you fellows. This is from the National Obscurity Society. You know a chap with a German name is president of it, but he's a real patriot, hundred per cent, not fifty-fifty, Philly. 'The following States have abolished the teaching of German: Massachusetts, Connecticut, New York, New Jersey, Pennsylvania, Maryland, Virginia, Georgia, Mississippi, Indiana, Ohio, Illinois, Nebraska, Missouri, Kansas, Iowa, Arkansas, Arizona, Colorado, Montana, California, and Oregon.' *Abolished*, mind you! What do you think of that?"

"Most excellent Phippick," nodded Rosenlaube, "I opine, as Horace said to Cicero, 'That's the stuff,' or words to that effect. What saith the senator from Mitchellville?"

"Noble," grinned Phil, "unmistakably noble! Those Obscurity fellows are a fiery lot. It reminds me that during the late war with Spain, when I was a little, tiny boy, but brimful of ferocity, I refused to eat my favorite dessert because it was called *Spanish* cream. I felt sure at the time that my heroic conduct was of distinct assistance to Dewey in the battle of Manila Bay."

"Well, then," said Phipps-Herrick, grabbing him by the shoulders and shaking him good-humoredly, "you murderous little pacifist with seven nicks on your gun, will you give up your German? Will you forget it?"

Mitchell chuckled and shook his head,

"As far as requisite under military orders. But no further, not by a—"

A pair of muddy boots was heard and seen descending one of the ladders, followed by the manly and still rather neat form of Lieutenant Barker Bunn, a Cornell man from West Philadelphia. The three men sprang to their feet and saluted smartly, for the lieutenant was very stiff about all the preliminary forms.

"Too loud talking here," he said gruffly. "I heard you before I came down. Who is here? Oh, I see, Sergeant Phipps-Herrick, Privates Rosenlaube and Mitchell. It's your turn to go out on listening post to-night, sergeant. Twelve sharp, stay three hours, go as far as you can, come back and report, take Mitchell or Rosenlaube with you. Captain's orders."

The sergeant saluted again, and the two men looked at each other.

"Why not both of us, sir?" said Mitchell.

The lieutenant regarded him with some surprise. Listening post is not a detail passionately desired by the men. It is always dirty, frequently dangerous, generally obscure, and often fatal. Hence there is no keen competition for it.

"Two is the usual number for a listening post," said Barker Bunn thoughtfully. "But there is no regulation about it, and the captain did not specify any number. Well, yes, I suppose you can all three go, if you are set on it. In fact, I give the order to that effect."

"Thank you, sir," said Rosenlaube and Mitchell. Phipps-Herrick, feeling that the strict etiquette of the preliminaries had been fully observed and the time to be human had come, held out a box of "Fierce Fairies."

"Have a cigarette, Bunn, and take a chair, do. Time for a little talk this quiet night? Tell us what's doing up above."

"Nothing particular," said Barker Bunn, lighting and relaxing. "But the old man has a hunch that the Fritzies are grubbing a mine—a corker—to get our goat. Hence this business of ears forward. The old man thinks the Fritzies have a strong grouch against this little alley, and since they couldn't take it top side last week they're going to try to bust it out bottom side with a big bang some day soon. Maybe so—maybe just greens—but, anyway, you've got to go on the Q. T. with this job—no noise, don't even whisper unless you have to; just listen for all you're worth. P'r'aps you'll hear that little tap-tap-tapping that tells where Fritzie Mole is at work. Then if you come back and tell the old man where it is, he'll give you all the cigarettes you want. But say, do you want me to give you a pointer on the way to go, the method of procedure, as the old man would call it?"

They agreed that they were thirsting for information and instruction.

"Well, it's this way," continued Barker Bunn. "You know I had a bit of experience in listening post while I was with the Canadians down around 'Wipers'; and I noticed that most of the troubles came from a bad method of procedure. Fellows went out any old way; followed each other in the dark, and then hunted for each other and came to grief; all those kind of silly fumbles. Now, what you need is *formation*—see? Must have some sort of formation for advance. Must keep in touch. For two men a tandem is right. For three men, what you want is a spike-team—middle man crawls ahead, other men follow on each side just near enough to touch his left heel with right hand and right heel with left hand—a triangle, see? Keep touching once every thirty seconds. If you miss it, leader crawls back, side men crawl in, sure to meet, nobody gets lost. Go as far *as* you can, then spread out like a fan, fold together *when* you can, come back *if* you can—that's the way to cover the most possible ground on a listening post. Do you get me?"

"We get you," they nodded. "It's a wonderful scheme." And Rosenlaube added in his most impressive literary manner: "Plato, it *must* be so, thou reasonest well."

"But tell me," said the lieutenant, "what were you fellows chattering about so loud when I came down?"

So they told him, and, according to the habit of college boys, they skirmished over the ground of debate again, and Barker Bunn vigorously supported the majority opinion, and Mitchell was left in a hopeless minority of one, clinging obstinately to his faith that there had been, and still might be, some use for the German language.

Midnight came, and with it the return of the lieutenant's official manner. He saw the trio slide over the top, one by one, vanishing in the starless dark. "Good luck going and coming," he whispered; and it sounded almost like an unofficial prayer.

In single file they crept through the prepared opening in the barbed-wire entanglement, and so out into No Man's Land, where they took up their spike-team formation. Phipps-Herrick was the leader, the other men were the wheelers. They had agreed on a code of silent signals: One kick with the heel or one pinch with the hand meant "stop"; two meant "back"; three meant "get together." They carried no rifles, because the rifle is an awkward tool for a noiseless crawler to lug. But each man had a big trench-knife and a pair of automatic pistols, with plenty of ammunition.

The space between the two front lines of barbed wire in this region was not more than four or five hundred yards. In the murk of that unstarred, drizzling night, where every inch must be felt out, it seemed like a vast, horrible territory. There was nothing monotonous about it but the blackness of darkness. To the touch it was a *paysage accidente*, a landscape full of surprises. Dead bodies were sprinkled over it. It was pockmarked with small shell-holes and pitted with large craters, many of them full of water, all slimy with mud. Phipps-Herrick nearly slipped into one of the deepest, but a lively kick warned his followers of the danger, and they pulled him back by the heels.

Now and then a star-shell looped across the spongy sky, casting a lurid illumination over the ghastly field. When the three travellers caught the soft swish of its ascent, they "froze"—motionless as a shamming 'possum—mimicking death among the dead.

It was a long, slow, silent, revolting crawl. Sounds which did not concern them were plenty—distant cannonade, shells exploding here and there, scattered rifle-shots. All these they unconsciously eliminated, listening for something else, ears pressed to the ground wherever they could find a comparatively dry spot. From their point of hearing the night was still as the grave—no subterranean tapping and scraping could they hear anywhere under the sea of mud.

Once Rosenlaube caught a faint metallic sound, and signalled through Phipps-Herrick's left leg to Mitchell's left arm, "Stop!" All three listened tensely. They crawled toward the faint noise. It was made by a loose end of wire swaying in the night-wind and tapping on a broken helmet.

They were getting close to the German barbed wire. The leader had swung around to the west, following what he judged to be the line of the front trench, perhaps forty yards away. He was determined to hear something before he went back. And he did!

Just as he had made up his mind to call up the other fellows for the final spreadout in fan formation, his groping right hand touched something round and smooth and hard. It seemed to be made fast to a string or wire, but he pulled it toward him and gave the "stop" signal to his followers.

The thing he had picked up was a telephone receiver. How it came to be there he did not know. Perhaps a German listening post had carried it out last night, in order to receive directions from the trench; perhaps the mining party—man killed, receiver dropped, wire connection not cut, or tangled up with other wires—who can tell? One thing is sure—here is the receiver, faintly buzzing. Phipps-Herrick joyfully puts it to his ear. He hears a voice and words, but it is all gibberish to him. With a look of desperation on his face he gives the "get together" signal.

Rosenlaube crawls up first and takes hold of the cylinder, puts it to his ear. He hears the sound, but it says absolutely nothing to him. It is like being at the door of the secret of the universe and unable to get over the threshold.

Then comes Mitchell, slowly, a little lame, and almost "all in." Phipps-Herrick thrusts the receiver into his hand. As he listens a beatific expression spreads over his face. It lasts a long time, and then he lays down the cylinder with a sigh.

The three heads are close together, and Mitchell whispers under his breath:

"Got 'em—got the whole thing—line of mine changed—raiders coming out now—twelve men—rough on us, but if we can get back to our alley we've got 'em! Crawl home quick."

{Illustration with caption: "I'm going to carry you in, spite of hell"}

They crawled together in a bunch, formation ignored. Presently steps sounded near them. A swift light swept the hole where they crouched, a volley of rifle-shots crashed into it. The Americans answered with their pistols, and saw three or four of the dark forms on the edge of the hole topple over. The rest disappeared. But Rosenlaube had a rifle-ball through his right hip and another through his shoulder. Mitchell and Phipps-Herrick started to carry him.

"Drop it," he whispered. "I'm safe here till dawn—you get home, quick! Specially Phil. He's the one that counts. Cut away, boys!"

Meantime the American trench had opened fire and the German trench answered. The still night broke into a tempest of noise. A bullet or a bit of shell caught Mitchell in the knee and crumpled him up. Phipps-Herrick lifted him on his back and stood up.

"Come on," he said, "you little cuss. You're the only one that has the stuff we went out after. I'm going to carry you in, 'spite of hell."

And he did it.

Mitchell told the full story of the change in the direction of the German mine and the plan of the next assault, as he had heard it through that lost receiver. The captain said it was information of the highest value. It counted up to a couple of hundred German prisoners and three machine-guns in the next two days.

Rosenlaube, still alive, was brought in just before daybreak by a volunteer rescue-party under the guidance of Phipps-Herrick. All three were cited in the despatches. Phipps-Herrick in due time received the Distinguished Service Cross for gallantry on the field. But Mitchell had the surplus satisfaction of the hearing ear.

"Look here, old man," Rosenlaube said to him as they lay side by side in the hospital, "'member our talk in the dugout just before our big night? Well, I allow there was something in what you said. There are times when it is a good thing to know a bit of that barbarous German language. And you never can tell when one of those times may hit you."

SKETCHES OF QUEBEC

If you love a certain country, for its natural beauty, or for the friends you have made there, or for the happy days you have passed within its borders, you are troubled and distressed when that country comes under criticism, suspicion, and reproach.

It is just as it would be if a woman who had been very kind to you and had done you a great deal of good were accused of some unworthiness. You would refuse to believe it. You would insist on understanding before you pronounced judgment. Memories would ask to be heard.

That is what I feel in regard to French Canada, the province of Quebec, where I have had so many joyful times, and found so many true comrades among the *voyageurs*, the *habitants*, and the *coureurs de bois*.

People are saying now that Quebec is not loyal, not brave, not patriotic in this war for freedom and humanity.

Even if the accusation were true, of course it would not spoil the big woods, the rushing rivers, the sparkling lakes, the friendly mountains of French Canada. But all the same, it hurts me to hear such a charge against my friends of the forest.

Do you mean to tell me that Francois and Ferdinand and Louis and Jean and Eugene and Iside are not true men? Do you mean to tell me that these lumbermen who steer big logs down steep places, these trappers who brave the death-cold grip of Winter, these canoe-men who shout for joy as they run the foaming rapids,—do you mean to tell me that they have no courage?

I am not ready to credit that. I want to hear what they have to say for themselves. And in listening for that testimony certain little remembrances come to me—not an argument—only a few sketches on the wall. Here they are. Take them for what they are worth.

I

LA GRANDE DECHARGE

September, 1894

In one of the long stillwaters of the mighty stream that rushes from *Lac Saint Jean* to make the Saguenay—below the *Ile Maligne* and above the cataract of Chicoutimi—two birch-bark canoes are floating quietly, descending with rhythmic strokes of the paddle, through the luminous northern twilight.

The chief guide, Jean Morel, is a *coureur de bois* of the old type—broad-shouldered, red-bearded, a fearless canoeman, a good hunter and fisherman—simple of speech and deep of heart: a good man to trust in the rapids.

"Tell me, Jean," I ask in the comfortable leisure of our voyage which conduces to pipe-smoking and conversation, "tell me, are you a Frenchman or an Englishman?"

"Not the one, nor the other," answers Jean in his old-fashioned *patois*. "M'sieu' knows I am French-Canadian."

A remarkable answer, when you come to think of it; for it claims a nationality which has never existed, and is not likely to exist, except in a dream.

"Well, then," I say, following my impulse of psychological curiosity, of which Jean is sublimely ignorant, "suppose a war should come between France and England. On which side would you fight?"

Jean knocks the dottle out of his pipe, refills and relights. Then, between the even strokes of his paddle, he makes this extraordinary reply:

"M'sieu, I suppose my body would march under the flag of England. But my heart would march under the flag of France."

Good old Jean Morel! You had no premonition of this glorious war in which the Tricolor and the Union Jack would advance together against the ravening black eagle of Germany, and the Stars and Stripes would join them.

How should you know anything about it? Your log cabin was your capitol. Your little family was your council of state. Even the rest of us, proud of our university culture, were too blind, in those late Victorian days, to see the looming menace of Prussian paganism and the conquer-lust of the Hohenzollerns, which has plunged the whole world in war.

II

OXFORD

February, 1917

The "Schools" building, though modern, is one of the stateliest on the Main Street. Here, in old peaceful times, the university examinations used to be held. Now it is transformed into a hospital for the wounded men from the fighting front of freedom.

Sir William Osier, Canadian, and world-renowned physician, is my guide, an old friend in Baltimore, now Regius Professor of Medicine in Oxford.

"Come," he says, "I want you to see an example of the Carrel treatment of wounds."

The patient is sitting up in bed—a fine young fellow about twenty years old. A shrapnel-shell, somewhere in France, passed over his head and burst just behind him. His bare back is a mass of scars. The healing fluid is being pumped in through the shattered elbow of his right arm, not yet out of danger.

"Does it hurt," I ask.

"Not much," he answers, trying to smile, "at least not too much, M'sieu'."

The accent of French Canada is unmistakable. I talk to him in his own dialect.

"What part of Quebec do you come from?"

"From *Trois Rivieres*, M'sieu', or rather from a country back of that, the Saint Maurice River."

"I know it well—often hunted there. But what made you go to the war?"

"I heard that England fought to save France from the damned Germans. That was enough, M'sieu', to make me march. Besides, I always liked to fight."

"What did you do before you became a soldier?"

"I was a lumberjack."

(What he really said was, *"J'allais en chantier,"* "I went in the shanty." If he had spoken in classic French he would have said, *"J'etais bucheron.'* How it brought back the smell of the big spruce forest to hear that word *chantier*, in Oxford!)

{Illustration: "I was a lumberjack."}

"Well, then, I suppose you will return to the wood-cutting again, when this war is over."

"But no, M'sieu', how can I, with this good-for-nothing arm? I shall never be capable of swinging the axe again."

"But you could be the cook, perfectly. And you know the cook gets the best pay in the whole shanty."

His face lights up a little.

"Truly," he replies; "I never thought of that, but it is true. I have seen a bit of cooking at the front and learned some things. I might take up that end of the job. *But anyway, Im glad I went to the war."*

So we say good-by—*"bonne chance!"*

Since that day the good physician who guided me through the hospital has borne without a murmur the greatest of all sacrifices—the loss of his only son, a brave and lovely boy, killed in action against the thievish, brutal German hordes.

III

SAINTE MARGUERITE August, 1917

The wild little river *Sainte Marguerite* runs joyously among the mountains and the green woods, back of the Saguenay, singing the same old song of liberty and obedience to law, as if the world had never been vexed and tortured by the madness of war-lords.

A tired man who has a brief furlough from active service is lucky if he can spend it among the big trees and beside a flowing stream. The trees are ministers of peace. The stream is full of courage and adventure as it rushes toward the big sea.

We are coming back to camp from the morning's fishing, with a brace of good salmon in the canoe.

"Tell me, Iside," I ask of the wiry little bowman, the best hunter and fisher on the river, "why is it that you are not at the war?"

"But, M'sieu', I am too old. A father of family—almost a grandfather—the war is not for men of that age. Besides, it does not concern us here in Quebec."

"Why not? It concerns the whole world. Who told you that it does not concern you?"

"The priest at our village of *Sacre Coeur,* M'sieu'. He says that it is only right and needful for a good Christian to fight in defense of his home and his church. Let those Germans attack us here, *chez nous*, and you shall see how the men of *Sacre Coeur* will stand up and fight."

It was an amazing revelation of a state of mind, absolutely simple, perfectly sincere, and strictly imprisoned by the limitations of its only recognized teacher.

"But suppose, Iside, that England and France should be beaten down by Germany, over there. What would happen to French Canada? Do you think you could stand alone then, to defend your home and your church? Are you big enough, you French-Canadians?"

"M'sieu', I have never thought of that. Perhaps we have more than a million people—many of them children, for you understand we French-Canadians have large families—but of course the children could not fight. Still, we should not like to have them subject to a German Emperor. We would fight against that, if the war came to us here on our own soil."

"But don't you see that the only way to keep it from coming to you on your own soil is to fight against it over there? Hasn't the English Government given you all your liberties, for home and church?"

"Yes, M'sieu', especially since Sir Wilfred Laurier. Ah, that is a great man! A true French-Canadian!"

"Well, then, you know that he is against Germany. You know he believes the freedom of Canada depends on the defeat of Germany, over there, on the other side of the sea. You would not like a German Canada, would you?"

"Not at all, M'sieu', that would be intolerable. But I have never thought of that."

"Well, think of it now, will you? And tell your priest to think of it, too. He is a Christian. The things we are fighting for belong to Christianity—justice, liberty, humanity. Tell him that, and tell him also some of the things which the Germans did to the Christian people in Belgium and Northern France. I will narrate them to you later."

"M'sieu'," says Iside, dipping his paddle deeper as we round the sharp corner of a rock, "I shall remember all that you tell me, and I shall tell it again to our priest. You know we have few newspapers here. Most of us could not read them, anyway. I am not well convinced that we yet comprehend, here in French Canada, the meaning of this war. But we shall endeavor to comprehend it better. And when we comprehend, we shall be ready to do our duty—you can trust yourself to the men of *Sacre Coeur* for that. We love peace—we all about here *(nous autres d'icite)*—but we can fight like the devil when we know it is for a good cause—liberty, for example. Meanwhile would M'sieu' like to stop at the pool *'La Pinette'* on the way down and try a couple of casts? There was a big salmon rising there yesterday."

That very evening a runner comes up the river, through the woods, to tell Iside and Eugene, who are Selectmen of the community of *Sacre Coeur,* that they must come down to the village for an important meeting at ten o'clock the next morning.

So they set off, quite as a matter of course, for their thirty-five mile tramp through the forest in the dark. They are good citizens, as well as good woodsmen, you understand. On the second day they are back again at their work in the canoe.

"Well, Iside," I ask, "how was it with the meeting yesterday? All correct?"

"All correct, M'sieu'. It was an affair of a new schoolhouse. We are going to build it. All goes well. We are beginning to comprehend. Quebec is a large corner of the world. But it is only a corner, after all, we can see that. And those damned Germans who do such terrible things in France, we do not love them at all, no matter what the priest may say about Christian charity. They are Protestants, M'sieu', is it not?"

"Well," I answer, hiding a smile with a large puff of smoke, "some of them call themselves Protestants and some call themselves Catholics. But it seems to me they are all infidels, heathen—judging by what they do. That is the real proof."

"*C'est b'en vrai, M'sieu',*" says Iside. "It is the conduct that shows the Christian."

IV

BELOW CAPE DIAMOND March, 1818

The famous citadel of Quebec stands on top of the steep hill that dominates the junction of the Saint Charles River with the Saint Lawrence. That is Cape Diamond—a natural stronghold. Indians and French, and British, and Americans have fought for that coign of vantage. For a century and a half the Union Jack has floated there, and under its fair protection the Province of Quebec, keeping its quaint old language and peasant customs, has become an important part of the British Empire.

The Upper Town, on the high shoulders of Cape Diamond, with its government buildings, convents, hospitals, showy new shops, and ancient gardens, its archiepiscopal palace, trim theological seminary, huge castle-like hotel, and placid ramparts dominating the *Ile d'Orleans* with rows of antiquated, harmless cannon around which the children play—the Upper Town belongs distinctly to the citadel. The garrison is in evidence here. A regimental band plays in the kiosk on Dufferin Terrace on summer evenings. There is a good mixture of khaki in the coloring of the street crowd, and many wounded soldiers are seen, invalided home from the front. They are all very proud of the glorious record that Canada has made in the battle for freedom. Most of them, it seems to me, are from English-speaking families. But by no means all. There are many of unmistakable French-Canadian stock; and they tell me proudly of the notable bravery of a certain regiment which was formed early from volunteers of their own people—hunters, woodsmen, farmers, guides. The war does not seem very far away, up here in the region of the citadel.

The Lower Town, with its narrow streets, little shops, gray stone warehouses, dingy tenements, and old-fashioned markets, is quite a different place. It belongs to the slow rivers on whose banks it drowses and dreams. The once prosperous lumberyards are half empty now. The shipping along the wharfs has been dwindling for many years. The northern winter puts a quietus on the waterside. Troops, munitions, supplies, must go down by rail to an ice-free port. The white river-boats are all laid up. But a way is kept open across the river to Levis, and the sturdy, snub-nosed little ice-breaking ferry-boats buffet back and forth almost without interruption. There is a plenty of nothing to do, now, in the Lower Town; pipe-smoking and heated discussion of parish politics are incessant; an inconsiderate quantity of bad liquor is imbibed, *pour faire passer le temps.*

Suddenly—if anything can be said to happen suddenly in Quebec—bad news comes from the Lower Town. A riot has broken out, an insurrection of the French-Canadians against the new military service act, an armed resistance to the draft. Windows have been smashed, shops looted. A mob, not very large perhaps, but extremely noisy, has marched up the steep curve of Mountain Hill Street, into the Upper Town. Shots have been exchanged. People have been killed. The revolution in Quebec has begun.

That is the disquieting rumor which comes to us, carefully spread and magnified by those agencies which have an interest in preventing, or at least obstructing the righteous punishment of the German criminals in this war. Can it possibly be true? Have the French-Canadians gone crazy, as the Irish did in 1916, under the lunatic incantations of the Sinn-Feiners? Are they also people without a country, playing blindly into the hands of the Prussian gang who have set out to subjugate the world?

No! This riot in the old city is not an expression of the spirit of French Canada at all. It is only a shrewdly stupid trick in local politics, planned and staged by small-minded and loud-voiced politicians who are trying to keep their hold upon the province. The so-called revolutionists are either imported loafers and trouble-makers, or else they are drawn from that class of "hooligans" who have always made a noise around the Quebec hotels at night. They shout much: they swear abominably: but they have no real fight in them. They can be hired and used—up to a certain point—but beyond that they are worthless. It is a waste of money to employ them. The trouble below Cape Diamond froths up and goes down as quickly as the effervescence on a bottle of ginger beer. Before you can find out what it is all about, it is all over. It has not even touched the real French-Canadians, the men of the forests and the farms. They are loyal by nature, and slow by temperament. You have got to give them time, and light.

What is happening in Quebec now? Just what ought to happen. The draft is going forward smoothly and steadily, without resistance. Sons of the best French-Canadian families are volunteering for the war. Recruits from Laval University are coming in, stirred perhaps by the knowledge that forty thousand Catholic priests in France have entered the army which fights against the Prussian paganism.

The petty politicians who have sought to serve their own ends by putting forward the mad notion of secession and an independent "Republic of Quebec" have gone to cover under a storm of ridicule and indignation. M. Bourassa's iridescent dream of French-Canadian nationalism has disappeared like a soap-bubble. M. Francoeur's motion in the Quebec legislature, carrying a vague hint that the province might withdraw from the Dominion if the other provinces were not particularly nice to it, was snowed under by an overwhelming vote. The patriotic and eloquent speech of the provincial Premier, M. Gouin, was received with every sign of approval. The political cinema has shown its latest film, and the title is evidently *"Fidelite de Quebec."*

Meantime a Catholic missioner has been in the province. The visit of Archbishop Mathieu of Saskatchewan was probably made on the invitation, certainly with the consent, of the hierarchy of Quebec. That intelligent and fearless preacher brought with him a clear and ringing gospel, a call to all Christian folk to stand up together and "resist even unto blood, striving against sin"—the sin of the German war-lords who have plunged the world in agony to enforce their heresy that Might makes Right.

Such a message, at this time, must be of inestimable value to the humble and devout people of the province, attached as they are to their church, and looking patiently to her for guidance. The parish priests, devoted to their lonely tasks in obscure hamlets, may get a new and broader inspiration from it. They may have a vision of the ashes of Louvain University, the ruin of Rheims Cathedral, wrought by ruthless German hands. Then the church in Quebec will measure up to the church in Belgium and in France. Then the village cure will say to his young men: "Go! Fight! It is for the glory of God and the good of the world. It is for the Christian religion and the life of free Canada."

"Well, then," says the gentle reader, of a sociological turn of mind, who has followed me thus far, "what have you got to say about the big political problem of Quebec? Is a French-speaking province a safe factor in the Dominion of Canada, in the British Empire? Why was Quebec so late in coming into this world war against Germany?"

Dear man, I have nothing whatever to say about what you call the big political problem of Quebec. I told you that at the beginning. That is a question for Canada and Great Britain to settle. The British colonial policy has always been one of the greatest liberality and fairness, except perhaps in that last quarter of the eighteenth century, when the madness of a German king and his ministers in England forced the United States to break away from her, and form the republic which has now become her most powerful friend.

The perpetuation of a double language within a state, an *enclave*, undoubtedly carries with it an element of inconvenience and possibly of danger. Yet Belgium is bilingual and Switzerland is quadrilingual. If any tongue other than that of the central government is to be admitted, what could be better than French—the language of culture, which has spoken the large words, *liberte, egalite, fraternite?* The native dialect of French Canada is a quaint and delightful thing—an eighteenth-century vocabulary with pepper and salt from the speech of the woodsmen and hunters. I should be sorry if it had to fade out. But evidently that is a question for Canada to decide. She has been a bilingual country for a long time. I see no reason why the experiment should not be carried on.

Quebec has been rather slow in waking up to the meaning of this war for world-freedom. But she has been very little slower than some of the United States, after all.

The Church? Well, the influence of the Church always has depended and always must depend upon the quality of her ministers. In France, in Belgium, they have not fallen short of their high duty. The Archbishop of Saskatchewan, who came to Quebec, preached a clear gospel of self-sacrifice for a righteous cause.

But the plain people of Quebec—the *voyageurs*, the *habitants*, my old friends in the back districts—that is what I am thinking about. I am sure they are all right. They are very simple, old-fashioned, childish, if you like; but there is no pacifist or pro-German virus among them. If their parochial politicians will let them alone, if their priests will speak to them as prophets of the God of Righteousness, they will show their mettle. They will prove their right to be counted among the free peoples of the world who are willing to defend peace with arms.

That is what I expect to find if I ever get back to my canoemen on the *Sainte Marguerite* again.

SYLVANORA, July 10, 1918.

A CLASSIC INSTANCE

"Latin and Greek are dead," said Hardman, lean, eager, absolute, a fanatic of modernity. "They have been a long while dying, and this war has finished them. We see now that they are useless in the modern world. Nobody is going to waste time in studying them. Education must be direct and scientific. Train men for efficiency and prepare them for defense. Otherwise they will have no chance of making a living or of keeping what they make. Your classics are musty and rusty and fusty. *Heraus mit——*"

He checked himself suddenly, with as near a blush as his sallow skin could show.

"Excuse me," he stammered; "bad habit, contracted when I was a student at Kiel—only place where they really understood metallurgy."

Professor John De Vries, round, rosy, white-haired, steeped in the mellow lore of ancient history, puffed his cigar and smiled that benignant smile with which he was accustomed joyfully to enter a duel of wits. Many such conflicts had enlivened that low-ceilinged book-room of his at Calvinton.

"You are excused, my dear Hardman," he said, "especially because you have just given us a valuable illustration of the truth that language and the study of language have a profound influence upon thought. The tongue which you inadvertently used belongs to the country that bred the theory of education which you advocate. The theory is as crude and imperfect as the German language itself. And that is saying a great deal."

Young Richard De Vries, the professor's favorite nephew and adopted son, whose chief interest was athletics, but who had a very pretty side taste for verbal bouts, was sitting with the older men before a cheerful fire of logs in the chilly spring of 1917. He tucked one leg comfortably underneath him and leaned forward in his chair, lighting a fresh cigarette. He foresaw a brisk encounter, and was delighted, as one who watches from the side-lines the opening of a lively game.

"Well played, sir," he ejaculated; "well played, indeed. Score one for you, Uncle."

"The approbation of the young is the consolation of the aged," murmured the professor sententiously, as if it were a quotation from Plutarch. "But let us hear what our friend Hardman has to say about the German language and the Germanic theory of education. It is his turn."

"I throw you in the German language," answered Hardman, rather tartly. "I don't profess to admire it or defend it. But nobody can deny its utility for the things that are taught in it. You can learn more science from half a dozen recent German books than from a whole library of Latin and Greek. Besides, you must admit that the Germans are great classical scholars too."

"Rather neat," commented Dick; "you touched him there, Mr. Hardman. Now, Uncle!"

"I do not admit," said the professor firmly, "that the Germans are great classical scholars. They are great students, that is all. The difference is immense. Far be it from me to deny the value of the patient and laborious researches of the Germans in the grammar and syntax of the ancient languages and in archaeology. They are painstaking to a painful degree. They gather facts as bees gather pollen, indefatigably. But when it comes to making honey they go dry. They cannot interpret, they can only instruct. They do not comprehend, they only classify. Name me one recent German book of classical interpretation to compare in sweetness and light with Jowett's 'Dialogues of Plato' or Butcher's 'Some Aspects of the Greek Genius' or Croiset's 'Histoire de la Litterature Grecque.' You can't do it," he ended, with a note of triumph.

"Of course not," replied Hardman sharply. "I never claimed to know anything about classical literature or scholarship. My point at the beginning—you have cleverly led the discussion away from it, like one of your old sophists—the point I made was that Greek and Latin are dead languages, and therefore practically worthless in the modern world. Let us go back to that and discuss it fairly and leave the Germans out."

"But that, my dear fellow, is precisely what you cannot do. It is partly because they have insisted on treating Latin and Greek as dead that the Germans have become what they are—spectacled barbarians, learned Huns, veneered Vandals. In older times it was not so bad. They had some perception of the everlasting current of life in the classics. When the Latin spirit touched them for a while, they acquired a sense of form, they produced some literature that was good—Lessing, Herder, Goethe, Schiller. But it was a brief illumination, and the darkness that followed it was deeper than ever. Who are their foremost writers to-day? The Hauptmanns and the Sudermanns, gropers in obscurity, violent sentimentalists, 'bigots to laxness,' Dr. Johnson would have called them. Their world is a moral and artistic chaos agitated by spasms of hysteria. Their work is a mass of decay touched with gleams of phosphorescence. The Romans would have called it *immunditia*. What is your new American word for that kind of thing, Richard? I heard you use it the other day."

"Punk," responded Dick promptly. "Sometimes, if it's very sickening, we call it pink punk."

"All right," interrupted Hardman impatiently. "Say what you like about Hauptmann and Sudermann. They are no friends of mine. Be as ferocious with them as you please. But you surely do not mean to claim that the right kind of study and understanding of the classics could have had any practical influence on the German character, or any value in saving the German Empire from its horrible blunders."

"Precisely that is what I do mean."

"But how?"

"Through the mind, *animus*, the intelligent directing spirit which guides human conduct in all who have passed beyond the stage of mere barbarism."

"You exaggerate the part played by what you call the mind. Human conduct is mainly a matter of heredity and environment. Most of it is determined by instinct, impulse, and habit."

"Granted, for the sake of argument. But may there not be a mental as well as a physical inheritance, an environment of thought as well as of bodily circumstances?"

"Perhaps so. Yes, I suppose that is true to a certain extent."

"A poor phrase, my dear Hardman; but let it pass. Will you admit that there may be habits of thinking and feeling as well as habits of doing and making things?"

"Certainly."

"And do you recognize a difference between bad habits and good habits?"

"Of course."

"And you agree that this difference exists both in mental and in physical affairs? For example, you would call the foreman of a machine-shop who directed his work in accordance with the natural laws of his material and of his steam or electric power a man of good habits, would you not?"

"Undoubtedly."

"And you would not deny him this name, but would rather emphasize it, if in addition he had the habit of paying regard to the moral and social laws which condition the welfare and efficiency of his workmen; for example, self-control, cheerfulness, honesty, fair play, honor, human kindness, and so on. If he taught these things, not only by word but by deed, you would call him an excellent foreman, would you not?"

"Without a question. That machine-shop would be a great success, a model."

"But suppose your foreman had none of these good mental and moral habits. Suppose he was proud, overbearing, dishonest, unfair, and cruel. Do you not believe he would have a bad influence upon his men? Would not the shop, no matter what kind of work it turned out, become a nest of evil and a menace to its neighbors?"

"It surely would."

"What, then, would you do with the foreman?"

"I would try to teach him better. If that failed, I would discharge him."

"In what method and by what means would you endeavor to teach him?"

"By all the means that I could command. By precept and by example, by warning him of his faults and by showing him better ways, by wholesome books and good company."

"And if he refused to learn; if he remained obstinate; if he mocked you and called you a hypocrite; if he claimed that his way was the best, in fact the only way, divinely inspired, and therefore beyond all criticism, then you would throw him out?"

"Certainly, and quickly! I should regard him as morally insane, and try my best to put him where he could do no more harm. But tell me why this protracted imitation of Socrates? Where are you trying to lead me? Do you want me to say that the German Kaiser is a very bad foreman of his shop; that he has got it into a horrible mess and made it despised and hated by all the other shops; that he ought to be put out? If that is your point, I am with you in advance."

"Right you are!" cried Dick joyously. "Can the Kaiser! We all agree to that. And here the bout ends, with honors for both sides, and a special prize for the Governor."

The professor smiled, recognizing in the name more affection than disrespect. He leaned forward in his chair, lighting a fresh cigar with gusto.

"Not yet," he said, "O too enthusiastic youth! Our friend here has not yet come to the point at which I was aiming. The application of my remarks to the Kaiser—whom I regard as a gifted paranoiac—is altogether too personal and limited. I was thinking of something larger and more important. Do you give me leave to develop the idea?"

"Fire away, sir," said Dick.

Hardman nodded his assent. "I should like very much to hear in what possible way you connect the misconduct of Germany, which I admit, with your idea of the present value of classical study, which I question."

"In this way," said the professor earnestly. "Germany has been living for fifty years with a closed mind. Oh, I grant you it was an active mind, scientific, laborious, immensely patient. But it was an ingrowing mind. Sure of its own superiority, it took no counsel with antiquity and scorned the advice of its neighbors. It was intent on producing something entirely new and all its own—a purely German *Kultur*, independent of the past, and irresponsible to any laws except those of Germany's interests and needs. Hence it fell into bad habits of thought and feeling, got into trouble, and brought infinite trouble upon the world."

"And do you claim," interrupted Hardman, "that this would have been prevented by reading the classics? Would that have been the only and efficient cure for Germany's disease? Rather a large claim, that!"

"Much too large," replied the professor. "I did not make it. In the first place, it may be that Germany's trouble had gone beyond any cure but the knife. In the second place, I regard the intelligent reading of the Bible and the vital apprehension of the real spirit of Christianity as the best of all cures for mental and moral ills. All that I claim for the classics—the works of the greatest of the Greek and Roman writers—is that they have in them a certain remedial and sanitary quality. They contain noble thoughts in noble forms. They show the strength of self-restraint. They breathe the air of clearness and candor. They set forth ideals of character and conduct which are elevating. They also disclose the weakness and the ugliness of things mean and base. They have the broad and generous spirit of the true *literae humaniores*. They reveal the springs of civilization and lead us—

'To the glory that was Greece,
To the grandeur that was Rome.'

Now these are precisely the remedies 'indicated,' as the physicians say, for the cure, or at least the mitigation, of the specific bad habits which finally caused the madness of Germany."

"Please tell us, sir," asked Dick gravely, "how you mean us to take that. Do you really think it would have done any good to those brutes who ravaged Belgium and outraged France to read Tacitus or Virgil or the Greek tragedies? They couldn't have done it, anyhow."

"Probably not," answered the professor, while Hardman sat staring intently into the fire, "probably not. But suppose the leaders and guides of Germany (her masters, in effect, who moulded and *kultured* the people to serve their nefarious purpose of dominating the world by violence), suppose these masters had really known the meaning and felt the truth of the Greek tragedies, which unveil reckless arrogance—*Hybris*—as the fatal sin, hateful to the gods and doomed to an inevitable Nemesis. Might not this truth, filtering through the masters to the people, have led them to the abatement of the ruinous pride which sent Germany out to subjugate the other nations in 1914? The egregious General von der Goltz voiced the insane arrogance which made this war when he said, 'The nineteenth century saw a German Empire, the twentieth shall see a German world.'

"Or suppose the Teutonic teachers and pastors had read with understanding and taken to heart the passages of Csesar in which he curtly describes the violent and thievish qualities of the ancient Germans—how they spread desolation around them to protect their borders, and encouraged their young men in brigandage in order to keep them in practice. Might not these plain lessons have been used as a warning to the people of modern Germany to discourage their predatory propensities and their habits of devastation and to hold them back from their relapse into the *Schrecklichkeit* of savage warfare? George Meredith says a good thing in 'Diana of the Crossways': 'Before you can civilize a man, you must first de-barbarize him.' That is the trouble with the Germans, especially their leaders and masters. They have never gotten rid of their fundamental barbarism, the idolatry of might above right.

They have only put on a varnish of civilization.
It cracks and peels off in the heat.

"Take one more illustration. Suppose these German thought-masters and war-lords had really understood and assimilated the true greatness of the conception of the old Roman Empire as it is shown, let us say, by Virgil. You remember that splendid passage in the Sixth Book of the AEneid where the Romans are called to remember that it is their mission 'to crown Peace with Law, to spare the humbled, and to subdue and tame the proud.' Might not sucn a noble doctrine have detached the Germans a little from their blind devotion to the Hohenzollern-Hollweg conception of the modern pinchbeck German Empire—a predatory state, greedy to gain new territory but incapable of ruling it when gained, scornful of the rights of smaller peoples, oppressing them when subjugated, as she has oppressed Poland and Schleswig-Holstein and Alsace-Lorraine, a clumsy and exterminating tyrant in her own colonies, as she has shown herself in East and West Africa? I tell you that a vital perception of what the Roman Empire really meant in its palmy days might have been good medicine for Germany. It might have taught her to make herself fit for power before seeking to grasp it."

"Granted, granted," broke in Hardman, impatiently poking the fire. "You can't say anything about Germany too severe to suit me. Whatever she needed to keep her from committing the criminal blunder of this war, it is certain that she did not get it. The blunder was made and the price must be paid. But what I say now, as I said at the beginning, is that Latin and Greek are dead languages. For us, for the future, for the competitions of the modern industrial and social era, the classics are no good. For a few ornamental persons a knowledge of them may be a pleasing accomplishment. But they are luxuries, not necessaries. They belong to a bygone age. They have nothing to tell us about the things we most need to know—chemistry and physics, engineering and intensive agriculture, the discovery of new forms and applications of power, the organization of labor and the distribution of wealth, the development of mechanical skill and the increase of production—these are the things that we must study. I say they are the only things that will count for success in the new democracy."

"That is what *you* say," replied Professor De Vries dryly. "But the wisest men of the world have said something very different. No democracy ever has survived, or ever will survive, without an aristocracy at the heart of it. Not an aristocracy of birth and privilege, but one of worth and intelligence; not a band of hereditary lords, but a company of well-chosen leaders. Their value will depend not so much upon their technical knowledge and skill as upon the breadth of their mind, the clearness of their thought, the loftiness of their motives, the balance of their judgment, and the strength of their devotion to duty. For the cultivation of these things I say—pardon the apparent contradiction of what *you* said—I say the study of the classics has been and still is of the greatest value."

"What did George Washington know about the classics?" Hardman interrupted sharply. "He was one of your aristocrats of democracy, I suppose?"

"He was," answered the professor blandly, "and he knew more about the classics than, I fear, you do, my dear Hardman. At all events, he understood what was meant when he was called 'the Cincinnatus of the West'—and he lived up to the ideal, otherwise we should have had no American Republic.

"But let us not drop to personalities. What I maintain is that Latin and Greek are not dead languages, because they still convey living thoughts. The real success of a democracy—the production of a finer manhood—depends less upon mechanics than upon morale. For that the teachings of the classics are excellent. They have a bracing and a steadying quality. They instil a sense of order and they inspire a sense of admiration, both of which are needed by the people—especially the plain people—of a sane democracy. The classics are fresher, younger, more vital and encouraging than most modern books. They have lessons for us to-day—believe me—great words for the present crisis and the pressing duty of the hour."

"Give us an example," said Dick; "something classic to fit this war."

"I have one at hand," responded the professor promptly. He went to the book-shelves and pulled out a small brown volume with a slip of paper in it. He opened the book at the marked place. "It is from the Eighth Satire of Juvenal, beginning at line 79. I will read the Latin first, and afterward a little version which I made the other day."

The old man rolled the lines out in his sonorous voice, almost chanting:

> *"'Esto bonus miles, tutor bonus, arbiter idem*
> *Integer; ambiguae si quando citabere testis*
> *Incertaeque rei, Phalaris licet imperet ut sis*
> *Falsus et admoto dictet periuria tauro,*
> *Summum crede nefas, animam praeferre pudori*
> *Et propter vitam vivendi perdere causas.'"*

"Please to translate, sir," said Dick, copying exactly the professor's classroom phrase and manner.

"To gratify my nephew," said the professor, nodding and winking at Hardman. "But, understand, this is not a real translation. It is only a paraphrase. Here it is:

> *"Be a good soldier, and a guardian just;*
> *Likewise an upright judge. Let no one thrust*
> *You in a dubious cause to testify,*
> *Through fear of tyrant's vengeance, to a lie.*
> *Count it a baseness if your soul prefer*
> *Safety above what Honor asks of her:*
> *And hold it manly life itself to give,*
> *Rather than lose the things for which we live.*

It is not half as good as the Latin. But it gives the meaning. How do you like it, Richard?"

"Fine!" answered the young man quickly; "especially the last lines. They are great." He hesitated slightly, and then went on. "Perhaps I ought to tell you now, sir, that I have signed up and got my papers for the training-school at Madison Barracks. I hope you will not be angry with me."

The old man put both hands on the lad's shoulders and looked at him with a suspicious moisture in his eyes. He swallowed hard a couple of times. You could see the big Adam's apple moving up and down in his wrinkled throat.

"Angry!" he cried. "Why, boy, I love you for it."

Hardman, who was a thoroughly good fellow at heart, held out his hand.

"Good for you, Dick! But I must be going now. I am putting up at the Ivy. Will you walk up with me? I'd like to have a word with you."

The two men walked in silence along the shady, moon-flecked streets of the tranquil old university town. Then the elder one spoke.

"You have done the right thing, I am sure. That officers' training-school is a good place to get a practical education. When you are through, how would you like to have a post in the Ordnance Department at Washington? I have some influence there and believe I could get you in without difficulty."

"Thanks, a lot," answered the lad modestly. "You're awfully kind. But, if you don't mind my saying so, I think I'd rather have service at the front—that is, if I can qualify for it."

There was another long silence before Hardman spoke again, with an apparent change of subject:

"I wish you would tell me what you really think of your uncle's views on the classics, you and the other fellows of your age in the university."

Dick hesitated a moment before he replied:

"Well, personally, you know, I believe what Uncle says is usually about right. He has the habit of it. But I allow when he gets on his hobby he rides rather hard. Most of the other fellows have given up the classics—they like the modern-language course with sciences better—perhaps it's softer. They say not; but I know the classics are hard enough. I flunked out on my Greek exam junior year. So, you see, I'm not a very good judge. But, anyhow, wasn't the bit he read us from Juvenal simply fine? And didn't he read it well? I've felt that a hundred times, but never knew how to say it."

It was in the early fall of 1918, more than a year later, that Hardman came once more into the familiar library at Calvinton. He had read the casualty list of the last week of August and came to condole with his friend De Vries.

The old man sat in the twilight of the tranquil book-lined room, leaning back in his armchair, with an open letter on the table before him. He gave his hand cordially to Hardman and thanked him for his sympathetic words. He talked quietly and naturally about Dick, and confessed how much he should miss the boy—as it were, his only son.

"Yes," he said quietly. "I am going to be lonely, but I am not forsaken. I shall be sad sometimes, but never sorry—always proud of my boy. Would you like to see this letter? It is the last that he wrote."

It was a young, simple letter, full of cheerful joking and personal details and words of affection which the shy lad would never have spoken face to face. At the end he wrote:

"Well, dear Governor, this is a rough life, and some parts are not easy to bear. But I want you to know that I was never happier in all my days. I know that we are fighting for a good cause, justice, and freedom, and a world made clean from this beastly German militarism. The things that the Germans have done to France and Belgium must be stopped, and they must never be done again. We want a decent world to live in, and we are going to have it, no matter what it costs. Of course I should like to live through it all, if I can do it with honor. But a man never can tell what is going to happen. And I certainly would rather give up my life than the things we are fighting for—the things you taught me to believe are according to the will of God. So good-night for the present, Uncle, and sleep well.

"Your loving nephew and son,

"DICK."

Hardman's hand shook a little as he laid the paper on the table.

"It is a beautiful letter," he said.

"Yes," nodded the old professor, putting his hand upon it; "it is a classic; very clear and simple and high-minded. The German Crown Prince says our American soldiers do not know what they are fighting for. But Richard knew. It was to defend 'the things for which we live' that he gladly gave his life."

September, 1918.

HALF-TOLD TALES
THE NEW ERA AND CARRY ON

The Commandant of the Marine Hospital was at his desk, working hard, when the door of the room was flung open and the Officer of the Day rushed in.

"Sir," he exploded, "the New Era has come."

"Very likely, Mr. Corker," answered the Commandant. "It has been coming continually since the world began. But is that any reason why you should enter without knocking, and with your coat covered with bread-crumbs and cigarette-ashes?"

So the Officer of the Day went outside, brushed his coat, knocked at the door, and awaited orders.

"Mr. Corker," said the Commandant, "have the kindness to bring me your report on the condition of yesterday's cases, and let me know what operations are indicated for to-day. Good morning. Orderly, my compliments to the Executive Officer, and I wish to see him at once."

When the Executive Officer arrived, he began:

"Sir, the New Era—"

"Quite so, Mr. Greel, but you understand this Hospital has to carry on as required in any kind of an era. How many patients did we receive yesterday? Good. Have we enough bedding and provisions? Bad. Attend to it immediately, and let me know the result of your efforts to remedy a situation which should never have arisen. The Navy cannot be run on hot air."

As the Executive Officer went out he held the door open for the Head Nurse to pass in. She was a fine, upstanding creature, tremulous with emotion.

"Oh, Doctor," she cried, "I simply must tell you about the New Era. Woman Suffrage is going to save the world."

"I hope so, Miss Dooby, it certainly needs saving. Meantime how are things in the pneumonia ward?"

"Two deaths last night, sir, three new cases this morning. Oxygen is running short: no beef-tea or milk. Five of my nurses have gone to attend conventions of woman—"

"Slackers," interrupted the Commandant. "Put them on report for leaving the ship without permission. I shall attend to their cases. Fill their places from the volunteer list. Be so good as to send the head steward here immediately."

"I'm very sorry, Sir," said the steward, "but ye see it's just this way. The mess-boys was holdin' a New Era mass-meetin', and the cook he forgot—"

"Milk and beef-tea!" growled the Commandant as if they were swear-words. "What the devil is this new influenza that has struck the hospital? Steward, you will provide what the head nurse requires at once. Orderly, my cap, and call Mr. Greel to accompany me on inspection."

In the galley the fires were out, the ovens cold, the soup-kettles empty, and all the cooks, dish-washers, and scrubbers were absorbing the eloquence of the third assistant pie-maker, who stood on an empty biscuit-box and explained the glories of the one-hour day in the New Era.

"'Ten*shun!*'" yelled the Orderly, and the force of habit brought the men up, stiff and silent. The Commandant looked around the circle, grinning.

"My word!" he cried, "what a beautiful sight! What do you think this is—a blooming debating society? Wrong! It's a hospital, with near a thousand sick and wounded to take care of. And it's going to be done, see? And you're going to help do it, see? No work—no pay and no food! Neglect of orders means extra duty and no liberty—perhaps a couple of twenty-four-hour days in the brig. That's the rule in all eras, see? Now get busy, all of you. Chow at twelve as usual. Carry on, men."

"Aye, aye, sir," they answered cheerily, for they were weary of the third assistant pie-maker's brand of talk and felt the pangs of healthy hunger.

Then came the second engineer, out of breath with running, followed by two or three helpers.

"Fire, captain," he gasped, "fire in the fuel-room—awful blaze—started in the wood box—cigarette—we were just settin' round talkin' over what we were goin' to do in the New Era, an' the first thing we knew it was burnin' like—"

"The New Era," snapped the Commandant, "and be damned to it! Sound the fire-call. All hands to quarters. Lead along the hose. Follow me," he cried, hurrying forward through the gathering smoke, "this ship must be saved."

And so it was—strictly in conformity with the old laws that fire burns, water quenches, and every man must do his duty promptly. On these ancient principles, and others equally venerable, the hospital carried on its good work. But the Commandant made one new rule. It cost five dollars to mention the New Era within its walls.

THE PRIMITIVE AND HIS SANDALS

"I am sick of all this," said the Great Author, sweeping his hand over the silver-laden dinner-table. He seemed to include in his gesture the whole house and the broad estate surrounding it. "It bores me, and I don't believe it can be right."

His wife, at the other end of the table, shining in her low-necked dress with diamonds on her breast and in her hair, leaned forward anxiously, knowing her husband's temperament.

"But, Nicholas," she said, "what do you mean? You have earned all this by your work as a writer. You are the greatest man in the country. You are entitled to a fine house and a large estate."

He gravely nodded his big head with its flamboyant locks, and lit a fresh cigarette.

"Quite right, my dear," said he, "you are always right on practical affairs. But, you see, this is an artistic affair. My books are realistic and radical. They teach the doctrine of the universal level, that no man can be above other men. They have made poverty, perhaps not exactly popular, but at least romantic. My villains are always rich and my heroes poor. The people like this; but it is rather a strain to believe it and keep on believing it. If my work is to hold the public it must have illustrations—moving pictures, you know! Something in character! Nobody else can do that as well as I can. It will be better than many advertisements. I am going to become a virtuous peasant, a son of the soil, a primitive."

His wife laughed, with a slight nervous tremor in her voice. She knew her husband's temperament, to be sure, but she never knew just how far it would carry him.

"I think you must be a little crazy, Nicholas," she said.

"Thank you, Alexandra," he answered, "thank you for the temperate flattery. Evidently you have heard the old proverb about genius and madness. But why not make the compliment complete and say 'absolutely crazy'?"

"Well," she replied, "because I do not understand just what you propose to do. Are you going to impoverish yourself and the whole family? Are you thinking of turning over your farms to these stupid peasants who will let them go to rack and ruin? Will you give your property to the village council who will drink it up in a month? You know how much money Peter needs; he is a member of twelve first-class clubs. And Olga's husband is not earning much. Are you going to starve your children and grandchildren for the sake of an idea of consistency in art?"

The Great Author was now standing in front of the fireplace, warming himself and filling a pipe. The flames behind him made an aureole in his extravagant white hair and beard. He smiled and puffed slowly at his pipe. At last he answered.

"My dear, you go too fast and too far. You know I am enthusiastic, but have you ever known me to be silly? It would be wrong to make you and the children suffer. I have no right to do that."

{Illustration: I am going to become a virtuous peasant, a son of the soil, a primitive}

She nodded her head emphatically, and a look of comprehension spread over her face. "Suppose," he continued, "suppose that I should make over the real estate and farms to you—you are an excellent manager. And suppose that I should put the personal estate, including copyrights, into a trust, the income to be paid to you and the children. You would take care of me while I became a primitive, wouldn't you?"

"I would," she answered, "you know I would. But think how uncomfortable it will be for you. While we are living in luxury, you—"

"Don't worry about that," he interrupted with a laugh. "I shall have all the luxury I want: flannel shirts, loose around the neck, instead of these infernal stiff collars; velveteen trousers and jacket instead of this waiter's uniform; and I shall go barefoot when the weather is suitable—do you understand? Barefoot in the summer grass—it will be immense."

"But your food," she asked, "how will you manage that on a primitive basis?"

"You will manage it," he replied, "you know I have always preferred beefsteak and onions to any French dish. Champagne does not agree with me. I'd rather have a glass of the straight stuff, without any gas in it."

"But your sleeping arrangements," she murmured, "are you going to leave the house? Our bedroom is not exactly primitive."

"No fear of it," he answered. "There is a little room beyond your bathroom. Put an iron cot in there, with a soft mattress, linen sheets, and light blankets. I'll do my morning wash at the pump in the yard, for the sake of the picture. When I want a bath you'll leave the door of the room open if you are not actually in the tub."

"Nicholas," she said, with a Mona Lisa smile, "for an author you have a very clever way of putting things. But suppose we have guests at the house, you can't come to dinner in dirty clothes and with bare feet."

"Certainly not," he answered. "I shall put on clean flannels, clean velveteens, and sandals."

"Sandals," she murmured, "sandals for dinner are simply wonderful. Do you think I could—"

"Not at all, my dear," said the Great Author firmly. "Your present style of dress becomes you amazingly. I am the only one who has to do the primitive."

So the arrangements were completed. The interviewers who came to the house described the Great Author in his loose flannels and velveteens, with bare feet, returning from labor in the fields. The moving pictures were full of him. But the sandals did not appear. There were no flash-lights permitted at the part-primitive dinner-table.

DIANA AND THE LIONS

In the darkest hour before the dawn, Diana floated away from her Garden Tower and came down between the Lions on the Library Steps.

At first, she did not know they were Lions. She thought they were Cats, and so she was afraid. For she was very lightly clad; and (except in Egypt) Cats are terrible to undomesticated goddesses. Diana shivered as she strung her bow for defense. She felt that she was divine, but she knew that she had cold feet.

In truth, the Library Steps were wet and glistening, for there had been a shower after midnight. But now the gibbous moon was giving a silent imitation of an arc-light high in the western heaven. Her beams silver-plated the weird architecture of the shrines of Commerce which face the great Temple dedicated to the Three Muses of New York—Astor, Lenox, and Tilden.

But on the awful animals guarding the steps the light was florid, like a flush of sunburn discovered by the ablution of a warranted complexion cream. They were wonderfully pink, and Diana hastened to draw an arrow from her quiver, for it seemed to her as if her feline neighbors were beginning to glow with rage.

"Do not shoot," said the ruddier one; "we are not angry, we are only blushing." And he glanced at her costume.

Diana was astonished to hear a masculine voice utter such a modest sentiment. But being a woman, she knew that the first word does not count.

"Cats never blush," she answered boldly, "no matter how big they are."

"But we are not Cats," they cried, ramping suddenly like crests on a millionaire's note-paper. "We are Lions!"

Diana smiled at this, for now she felt safe, remembering that when a male begins to boast he is not dangerous.

"Roar a little for me, please," she said, laying down her unconcealed weapon.

"Impossible," said the Northern Lion, "a city ordinance forbids unnecessary noise."

"Nonsense!" interrupted the Southern Lion. "Who would not break a law to oblige a lady?"

"Let us compromise," said the Northern Lion, "and give her our reproduction of an automobile horn."

"No," said the Southern Lion, "we will give her our automatic record of a Book-Advertisement; it is louder."

Then Diana trembled, indeed. But she bravely continued smiling, and said: "Thank you a thousand times for doing it once! And now please tell me what kind of Lions you are."

"Literary Lions," was their prompt and unanimous reply.

"Ah," she cried, clapping her hands with a charming gesture, "how glad I am to meet you! I have been in New York more than twenty years and never seen any one like you before! Come and sit beside me and talk."

The Lions looked at each other rather sheepishly, and glanced up and down the street, as if fearing the approach of a city ordinance. But there was no one in sight except Diana, so they shook their literary locks into a becoming disorder and sat on the steps with her, purring gently.

"Now tell me," she said, "who you are."

If she had been less beautiful they would have resented this. But, as it was, they looked sorry, and asked her if she had never read "Who's Who in America"? She shook her head, and admitted that she had not read it all through.

"Well," said her neighbor on the south, "this is rather an offhand *soiree,* and we may as well cut out proper names. But I will put you wise to the fact that I am the Magazine Lion. I got away from Roosevelt in Africa. He called me 'Mucky,' and I made tracks. Here he cannot hurt me, for they will never let that man do anything in good old New York, not even touch a Tiger."

"And I," said her neighbor on the north, "I am the Academic Lion, of whom you must have heard. My character is noted for its concealed sweetness, and my style leaves nothing to be hoped for. I am literally a man of letters, for I have seventeen degrees. Usually I look literary-lean and nobly dissatisfied, but yesterday I swallowed a British Female Novelist by accident, and that accounts for my inartistic air of cheerfulness. I won my splendid reputation by telling other Lions how they ought to have done their little tricks. But now, tired of that, I have gone into politics. This is my first public office."

Diana was somewhat confused and benumbed by these personally conducted biographies, but she was too well-bred not to appear interested.

"How lovely," she murmured, "to sit between two such Great Personages! I wonder what brought poor little Me to such an honor. And, by the way, how do you happen to be just here? What is this beautiful building behind you? Is it your Palace?"

"It is a Library," said the Academic Lion, with a superior tone.

"The biggest book-heap in America," said the Magazine Lion in his vivid way. "We have them all beaten to a finish—except the old junk-shop down in Washington."

"You forget Boston," said the Academic Lion.

"Who wouldn't?" growled the Magazine Lion.

"Do you mean to tell me," asked Diana, with her most engaging and sprightly air, "that this splendid place is a Library, all full of books, and that you are its most prominent figures, its figureheads, so to speak? How interesting! I have travelled a great deal—under the name of Pasht or Bast, in Egypt, where the Cats liked me; and under the name of Artemis in Greece; and under my own name in Italy. Believe me, I have seen all things that the moon shines upon. But I do not remember having seen Lions on a Library before. How original! How appropriate! How suggestive! But what does it suggest? What are you here for?"

"For educational purposes," said the Academic Lion.

"To catch the eye," said the Magazine Lion, "same as head-lines in a newspaper."

"I see," exclaimed Diana. "You are here to keep the people from getting at the books? How modern!"

This remark made the Academic Lion look like a Sphinx, as if he knew something but did not want to tell. But the Magazine Lion was distinctly flattered.

"Right you are," said he cheerfully, "or next door to it. We don't propose to keep the people out, only the authors. Why, when this place was publicly opened there was not a single author in the exhibit, except John Bigelow."

"Why did you not keep him out?" asked Diana.

"We were not on the spot, then," said the Lion. "Besides, there are some things that even a Lion does not dare to do."

"But I do not understand," said Diana, "precisely why authors should be kept away from a library."

The Magazine Lion laughed. "Silly little thing!" he said, with a fascinating tone of virile condescension. "An author's business is to write books, not to read them. If he reads, he grows intelligent and thoughtful and careful about his work. Those old books spoil him for the modern market. But if he just goes ahead and writes whatever comes into his head, he can do it with a bang, and everybody sits up and pays attention. That's the only way to be original. See?"

"Excuse me," broke in the Academic Lion, "but you go too far, brother. Authors should be encouraged to read, but only under critical guidance and professorial direction. Otherwise they will not be able to classify the books, and tabulate their writers, and know which ones to admire and praise. How can you expect a mere author to comprehend the faulty method of Shakespeare, or the ethical commonplaceness of Dickens and Thackeray, or the vital Ibsenism of Bernard Shaw and the other near-Ibsens, without assistance?"

"But the other people," asked Diana, "what is going to happen to them if you let them go in free and browse among the books?"

"They are less important," answered the Academic Lion. "Besides we expect soon to establish a cranial, neurological, and psychopathic examination which will determine the subliminal, temperamental needs of every applicant. Then we classify the readers in groups, and the books in lists, and the whole thing works with automatic precision."

"And I am going to make the book-lists!" said the Magazine Lion, ecstatically wagging his tail, and half-unconsciously putting his paw around the lady's waist in a spirit of pure comradeship.

But she gently slipped away, stood up, and gracefully covered a yawn with her hand.

"I am ever so much obliged to you Literary Lions for not eating me," said she. "Probably I should have disagreed with you even more than your conversation has with me. I am quite sleepy. And the moon has almost disappeared. I must be going where I can bid it good night."

So Diana rose, with shining limbs, above the housetops, and vanished toward her Garden Tower. The Lions looked disconcerted. "Old-fashioned, Victorian prude!" said one, "Brazen hussy!" said the other. And they climbed back on their Pedestals, resuming their supercilious expression. There I suppose they will stay, no matter what Diana may think of them.

THE HERO AND TIN SOLDIERS

On December twenty-fifth, 1918, that little white house in the park was certainly the happiest dwelling in Calvinton. It was simply running over with Christmas.

You see, there had come to it a most wonderful present, a surprise full of tears and laughter. Captain Walter Mayne reached home on Christmas Eve.

For a while they had thought that he would never come back at all. News had been received that he was grievously wounded in France—shot to pieces, in effect, leading his men near Chateau-Thierry. His life hung on the ragged edge of those wounds. But his wife Katharine always believed that he would pull through. So he did. But he was lacking a leg, his right arm was knocked out of commission for the present, and various other *souvenirs de la grande guerre* were inscribed upon his body.

Then word arrived that he was coming on a transport, with other wounded, to be patched up in a hospital on Staten Island. So his wife Katharine smiled her way through innumerable entanglements of red tape and went to nurse him. Then she set her steady hand to pull all the wires necessary to get him discharged and sent home. Christmas was in her heart and she would not be denied. So it came to pass that the one-legged Hero was in his own house on the happy day, and joy was bubbling all around him.

When the old Pastor entered, late in the afternoon, the Christmas-tree was twinkling with lights, the children swarming and buzzing all over the place, so that he was dazed for a moment. There were Walter's mother and his aunt and his sisters-in-law, boys and girls of various sizes, and a jubilant and entrancing baby. The Pastor took it all in, and was glad of it, but his mind was on the Hero.

Katharine, who always understood everything, whispered softly: "Walter is waiting to see you, Doctor. He is in his study, just across the hall."

Waiting? Well, what can a man whose right leg has been cut off above the knee, and who has not yet been able to get an artificial one—what can he do but wait?

The room was rather dimly lighted; brilliance is not good for the eyes of the wounded. Walter was in a long chair in the corner; his face was bronzed, drawn and lined a little by suffering; but steady and cheerful as ever, with the eager look which had made his students listen to him when he talked to them about English literature.

"My dear Walter," said the Pastor, "my dear boy, we are so glad to have you home with us again. We are very proud of you. You are our Hero."

"Thank you," said Walter, "it is mighty good to be home again. But there is no hero business about it. I only did what all the other Americans who went over there did—fought my—excuse me, my best, against the beastly Germans."

"But your leg," said the Pastor impulsively, "it is gone. Aren't you angry about that?"

Walter was silent for a moment. Then he answered.

"No, I don't think angry is the right word. You remember that story about Nathan Hale in the Revolution—'I only regret that I have but one life to give to my country.' Well, I'm glad that I had two legs to give for my country, and particularly glad that she only needed one of them."

"Tell me a bit about the fighting," said the Pastor, "I want to know what it was like—the hero-touch—you understand?"

"Not for me," said Walter, "and certainly not now. Later on I can tell you something, perhaps. But this is Christmas Day. And war? Well, Doctor, believe me, war is a horrible thing, full of grime and pain, madness, agony, hell—a thing that ought not to be. I have fought alongside of the other fellows to put an end to it, and now—"

The door swung open, and Sammy, the eldest son of the house, pranced in.

"Look, Daddy," he cried, "see what Aunt Emily has sent me for Christmas—a big box of tin soldiers!"

Mayne smiled as the little boy carefully laid the box on his knee; but there was a shadow of pain in his eyes, and he closed them for a few seconds, as if his mind were going back, somewhere, far away. Then he spoke, tenderly, but with a grave voice.

"That's fine, sonny—all those tin soldiers. But don't you think they ought to belong to me? You have lots of other toys, you know. Would you give the soldiers to me?"

The child looked up at him, puzzled for a moment; then a flash of comprehension passed over his face, and he nodded valiantly.

"Sure, Father," he said, "You're the Captain. Keep the soldiers. I'll play with the other toys," and he skipped out of the room.

Mayne's look followed him with love. Then he turned to the old Pastor and a strange expression came into his face, half whimsical and half grim.

"Doctor," he said, "will you do me a favor? Poke up that fire till it blazes. That's right. Now lay this box in the hottest part of the flames. That's right. It will soon be gone."

The elder man did what was asked, with an air of slight bewilderment, as one humors the fancies of an invalid. He wondered whether Mayne's fever had quite left him. He watched the fire bulging the lid and catching round the edges of the box. Then he heard Mayne's voice behind him, speaking very quietly.

"If ever I find my little boy *playing with tin soldiers,* I shall spank him well. No, that wouldn't be quite fair, would it? But I shall tell him why he must not do it, and *I shall make him understand that it's an impossible thing.*"

Then the old Pastor comprehended. There was no touch of fever. The one-legged Hero had come home from the wars completely well and sound in mind. So the two men sat together in love by the Christmas fire, and saw the tin soldiers melt away.

SALVAGE POINT

The Hermanns built their house at the very end of the island, five or six miles from the more or less violently rustic "summer-cottages" which adorned the hills and bluffs around the native village of Winterport.

There was a long point running out to the southward at the mouth of the great bay, rough and rocky for the most part, with little woods of pointed firs on it, some acres of pasture, and a few pockets of fertile soil lying between the stony ridges. A yellow farmhouse, with a red barn beside it, had nestled for near a hundred years in one of these hollows, buying shelter from the winter winds at the cost of an outlook over sea and shore.

It was a large price to pay. The view from the summit of the little hill a few hundred yards away was superb—a wonder even on that wonderful coast of Maine where mountain and sea meet together, forest and flood kiss each other.

But I suppose the old Yankee farmer knew what he wanted when he paid the price and snuggled his house in the hollow. I am certain the Hermanns knew what they wanted when they bought the whole point and perched their house on the very top of the hill, where all the winds of heaven might visit it as roughly as they pleased, but where nothing could rob the outlook of its ever-changing splendor and mystery, its fluent wonder and abiding charm.

You see, the Hermanns knew what they wanted because they had come through a lot of trouble. I met them when they were young—no matter how many years ago—when they were in the thick of it.

Alice Mackaye and Will Hermann had the rare luck to fall in love—a very real and great love—when they were in their early twenties. You would think that extraordinary piece of good fortune would have been enough to set them up for life, wouldn't you? But no. There was an Obstacle. And that Obstacle came very near wrecking them both.

Will Hermann was an artist and the son of an artist. The love of beauty ran in his blood. Otherwise he was poor. He earned a decent living by his painting, but each year's living depended on each year's work. Hence he was in the proletarian class.

Alice Mackaye, on the other hand, belonged to the capitalist class. I say "belonged," because that is precisely the word to describe her situation. Her father was a millionaire sugar-merchant, who lived in an ugly palace near Morristown, New Jersey, and was accustomed to have his own way in that and other States. He was the Obstacle.

He was a florid, handsome old Scotchman, orthodox in religion, shrewd in business, correct in conduct, but with no more sentiment than a hard-shell crab, and obstinate as the devil. His fixed idea was that none of his daughters should ever be carried off by a fortune-hunter. The two older girls apparently escaped this danger by making fairly wealthy matches. But Alice—come away! why should she take up with this impecunious painter? He was good-looking and had the gift of the gab, but what was that worth? If he would come into the sugar-business, where a place was waiting for him, and make good there, it would be all right. Otherwise, the affair must be broken off, absolutely, finally, and forever. From this you can see that the Obstacle was not bad-hearted, but only pig-headed.

Well, for five or six years things drifted rather miserably along this way. Will Hermann was forbidden the house at Morristown. Alice was practically a captive; her correspondence was censored. But of course, even before Marconi, wireless communication in matters of this kind has always been possible.

The trouble was that the state of affairs between them, while conventionally correct, was thoroughly unnatural and full of peril. Alice, a very good girl, obedient and tractable, was in danger of becoming a recalcitrant and sour old maid. Will, a healthy and normal young man, with no bad habits, was in danger of being driven to them by the emptiness and exasperation of his mind. The worst of it all was that both of the young people were, in accordance with a well-known law of nature, growing older with what seemed to them a frightful and unreasonable rapidity. The years crawled like snails. But the sum of them rose by leaps and bounds to an appalling total. Alice found two grey hairs in her red-gold locks. Will had to use glasses for reading fine print at night. From their point of view, decrepitude, senility, dotage stared them in the face, while the bright voyage of life which they were resolved to make only together, was threatened with shipwreck among the shoals of interminable delay.

It was at this juncture of affairs that they came to me, as fine-looking a young couple as ever I saw. They were good, as mortals go; they were loyal and upright, they wanted no scandal, no rumpus in the family, no trouble or pain for anybody else; but they wanted to belong to each other much more than they wanted to belong to any class, artistic, proletarian, or capitalist. And they were desperate because of the pertinacity of the Obstacle, whom they both respected fully as much as he deserved.

When they had stated their case, I made my answer.

"So far as I can see, the salvage of your ship of love depends entirely on yourselves. Mr. Hermann is not after a fortune, he only wants his girl; is that so? {Hermann nodded vigorously.} And Miss Mackaye does not care about being supported in the manner of living to which she has been accustomed; she only wants to live with the man whom she has chosen; is that so? {Alice blushed and nodded.} Well, then, why shouldn't you lay your course and sail ahead together? You are both of age, aren't you?"

They smiled at each other. "Yes, and a little over."

"But my father!" said Alice. "You know I honor him, and I can never deny his authority over me."

Here was the turn of the talk, the critical moment, the point where the chosen counsellor had to fall back upon the ultimate reality of his faith.

"Well," I said, "you are absolutely correct, dear daughter, in your feeling toward your father. He has earned his money and has a right to dispose of it as he will. But, you know, there is a statute of limitations in regard to the authority of parents over the *lives* of their children. You have passed the limitation. What do you want to do?"

"To be married to Will Hermann," she said, "for better for worse, for richer for poorer, I don't care. But I don't want a family quarrel, a runaway match, all that horrid newspaper talk." Here she was evidently a little excited and on the verge of tears.

"Certainly not," I hastened to reassure her, "you can't possibly have a runaway match, because there is nothing for you to run away from. There is not a single duty in your father's house which you have not fulfilled, and of which your sisters can not now relieve you. There is no authority in the world which has the right to command the sacrifice of your life to another's judgment. There is only one thing that stands in your way, and that is your claim on a large inheritance. I understand you are quite willing to let that go. You are not even 'running away' from it—that is not the word—you are ready to *jettison* it."

She looked puzzled, and murmured; "I don't exactly understand what that means."

"To jettison," I said, in that learned and dispassionate manner which is sometimes useful in relieving an emotional situation, "is a seafaring phrase. It means throwing overboard a part or the whole of a cargo in order to save the ship. As far as I can see that is the question which is up to you and your best friend at the present moment. Are you prepared to jettison the claim on a big fortune for the sake of making your voyage of life together?"

They looked at each other and a kind of radiance spread over their faces. "Surely," they answered with one voice. "But how can the marriage be arranged," asked Alice, "without a row in the family?"

"Very easily," I answered. "Both of you are over age, though you don't look it. Our good lawyer friend Harrison will help you to get the license. Fix your day for the wedding, neither secret nor notorious; invite anybody you like, and come to me on the day you have chosen. The arrangements will be made. You shall be married, all right."

So they came, and I married them, and it was a very good job.

They had some years of difficulty and uncertainty during which I caught brief glimpses of them now and then, always cheerful and happy together. In the course of time the Obstacle, being not at all bad-hearted but only pig-headed, probably relented a little, and finally was gathered to his fathers, according to the common lot of man. The older sisters behaved very well about the inheritance, and Alice was not left portionless. She brought three fine boys into the world. The house on Salvage Point was built by her and Will together.

It was there that I spent a day with them, in the summer of 1918, after many years during which we had not met. I was on naval duty, with Commander Kidd, of a certain station on the Maine coast. By invitation we put in with the motorboat S.P. 297, at Salvage Point. So it was that I met my old friends again, and knew what had become of their barque of love which I had helped to save from shipwreck.

The house on the peak of the hill was just what it ought to be; not aggressively rustic, not obtrusively classic—white pillars in front of it, and a terrace, but nothing dominating—it had the air of a very large and habitable lighthouse.

The extraordinary thing was the arrangement of the grounds. At every point one came upon some reminder of salvage. On the glorious August day when I was there, shipwreck seemed impossible: the Southern Way which opened to the Ocean was dancing with gay waves; the blue mountains of Maine were tranquil on the horizon.

"But you see," said Will Hermann, "this is really rather a dangerous point, though it is so beautiful. It is the gateway of the open sea, and there are three big ledges across it. A ship that has lost her bearings a little, or is driving in through thick weather, easily comes to grief. But there is not often a loss of life, only the ship goes to pieces. And we save the pieces."

It was true. There was a terrace west of the house, with a balustrade made of the taffrail of a wrecked brigantine. The gateway to the garden was the door of an old wheel-house. There was a pergola constructed from the timbers of a four-masted schooner that had broken up on the third ledge. The bow of the sloop *Christabel,* with the name still painted on it, was just outside the garden-gate. Everywhere you saw old anchor-bits, and rudder-posts, and knees, all silver-greyed by the weather, and fitted in to the *decor* of the place.

The prettiest thing of all was a crow's-nest from a wrecked brigantine, perched on the highest point of the hill, and looking out over the marvellous panorama of sea and shore, island and mountain. Here we sat, after a hearty luncheon with Alice and her three boys and half-a-dozen others who were with them in a kind of summer camp-school; and while we smoked our pipes, Will Hermann told this story.

"You see, Alice and I have a mania for things that have been salvaged. We don't like the idea of the wrecks, of course. But they would happen any way, whether we were here or not. And since that is so, we like to live here on the point and help save what we can. Sometimes we get a chance to do something for the crews of the little ships that come ashore—hot supper and dry clothes and so forth. But the most interesting salvage case that we ever had on the point was one in which there was really no wreck at all.

"It was a bright September afternoon ten years ago—one of those silver-blue days when there is a little quivering haze in the air everywhere, but no fog. We were sitting up here and looking out to sea. Just beyond the end of Dunker Rock a large motor-boat came in sight through the haze. She was about sixty feet long, with a low cabin forward, a cockpit aft, and a raised place for the steersman amidship—a good-looking craft, and evidently very speedy. She carried no flag or pennant. She came driving on, full tilt, straight toward us. We supposed of course she would turn east through the narrow channel to Winterport, or sheer off to the west into the Southern Way and go up the bay. But not a point did she swerve. Steady on she came, toward the three big ledges that lie out there beyond that bit of shingly beach at the end of the point.

"'I can't see any helmsman,' said Alice, 'those people must be asleep or crazy. Give them a hail through the megaphone. Perhaps you can make them hear.'

"So I yelled at the top of my lungs, and Alice waved her jersey. We might as well have hailed a comet. That boat ran straight for the ledges as if she meant to hurdle them. She came near doing it, too. Over the first she scraped, as if her heel had hit it. Over the second she shivered, hanging there for a second till a wave lifted her. On the third she bumped hard and checked her way for a moment, but the engine kept going, and finally she got herself over somehow and ran head on to the beach.

"Of course we were excited, and everybody hurried down to see what this crazy performance meant. There was not a creature on the boat, alive or dead.

"Everything was shipshape. The little craft had evidently been used for fishing. There were rough men's clothes on board, rubber boots and oilskins, fresh water and provisions, blankets in the cabin, fishing-lines and bait in the cockpit, gasolene in the tanks—a nice little outfit, all complete, and no one to run it.

"Where had she come from? There were no names on bow or stern, no papers in the cabin. Who had started her on this crazy voyage? How did she get away from them? Had they perhaps abandoned her and cast her adrift for some mysterious reason? Undoubtedly there were men—apparently three—on board when she set out. What had happened to them? A drunken quarrel? Or possibly one of the men had fallen overboard; the others had jumped in to save him; the engine had started up and the boat left them all in the lurch. Perhaps one or all of them may have had some reason for wanting to 'disappear without a trace,' so they hit upon the plan of going ashore at some lonely place and turning the boat loose to wreck herself. That would have been a stupid scheme of course, but not too stupid to be human.

"It was just a little piece of sea mystery to which we had no clew. So we debated it for an hour, and then set about the more important work of salvaging the stranded derelict. Fortunately she went ashore near the last of the ebb, and now lay comfortably in the mud, apparently little damaged except for some long scratches on her side, and a broken blade in her propeller. We dug away the mud at bow and stern, made fast a tow-line, and when the tide came in my small cruiser pulled her off easily. In the morning the mysterious stranger lay at anchor in the cove round the corner, as quiet as a China duck.

"Of course we advertised in the coast newspapers, giving a description of the boat—'came ashore,' etc.

"Three days later a boy about thirteen years old turned up at Winterport. He came from a village at the northeast corner of the bay forty miles away. He guessed the boat was his father's, but couldn't say for sure until he had seen it. So he came down to the point and identified it beyond a doubt. He told his story very simply.

"The boat belonged to his father, who was a widow-man with only one child. He used the boat for fishing, and sometimes he took Johnny with him, sometimes not. On the trips without the boy he used to stay out longer, sometimes a week or ten days. About a week ago he had started out on one of these trips with two other men. They had a dory in tow. They hadn't come back. Johnny had seen the piece in the paper. Here was the boat, for sure, but no dory. As for the rest of the story—well, that was all that Johnny had to tell us about it—the mystery was as far away as ever.

"He was a fine, sturdy little chap, with tanned face and clear blue eyes. He was rather shaken by his experience, of course, but he wouldn't cry—not for the world. We were glad to take him in for the night, while we verified his story by telegraph. It seemed the boat was practically his only inheritance, and the first question he asked, after we had gone over it, was how much we wanted him to pay for salvage.

"'Just one cent,' said Alice, taking the words out of my mouth, 'and what is more, we are going to have her repaired for you. She isn't much hurt.' So the boy stammered out the best kind of a 'thank you' that he could manage, and the look in his eyes made up for the lack of words. That was the time that he came nearest to crying. But Alice saved him by asking what he was going to do with the boat.

"He had an idea that he could run her himself, perhaps with another man to help him, for fishing in the fall, and for pleasure parties in the summer. He didn't want to cut loose from home altogether and sell the boat. Perhaps Dad might come back, some day, or send a letter. Anyway Johnny wanted to stay by a seafaring life.

"So we arranged the repairs and all that, and got a man to help on the homeward trip, and after a few days Johnny sailed off with his patrimony. That is what Alice and I consider our neatest job of salvage."

"Did it work all right?" I asked.

"Finely," said Will Hermann, "like a charm."

"And where is the lad now?"

"Bo'sun's mate on a certain destroyer somewhere off the coast of France, fighting in the U. S. Navee."

"And the father?" I inquired, being one of those old-fashioned persons who like all the loose ends of a story to be tied up. "Was anything ever heard of him?"

"That," answered my friend, carefully shaking out the ashes of his pipe beyond the crow's-nest rail, "that belongs in a different compartment of the ship."

THE BOY OF NAZARETH DREAMS

There was a Boy in Nazareth long ago whose after-life was wonderful, and whose story is written in the heart of mankind. His birth was predicted in dreams foretelling marvellous things of him, and in later years there were many true visions wherein he played a wondrous part.

Did he not also dream, in the days of his youth, while he was growing in wisdom and stature, and in favor with God and man? It would be strange indeed if his boyhood was not often visited and illumined by those swift flashes of insight and clear unveilings of hidden things, which we call dreams but which are in truth rays from "the fountain light of all our day."

The first journey that he made, his earliest visit to a great city, the three days and nights when he was lost there—surely these were times when visions must have come to him, full of mystery and wonder, yet clothed in the simple, real forms of this world, which he was learning to know. So I let my revery follow him on that unrecorded path, remembering where it led him, and imagining, in the form of dreams, what may have met him on his way.

I. THE JOURNEY TO THE CITY

There was not a lad in the country town of Nazareth, nestled high on the bosom of the Galilean hills, who did not often look eagerly southward over the plain toward the dark mountains of Samaria, and think of the great city which lay beyond them, and long for the time when he would be old enough to go with his family on pilgrimage to Jerusalem.

That journey would carry him out of childhood. It would mark the beginning of his life as a "son of the commandment," a member of the Hebrew nation. Moreover it would be an adventure—a very great and joyous adventure, which youth loves.

Palestine, in the days when Augustus Caesar was Lord of the World, was an exciting country to travel in. It was full of rovers and soldiers of fortune from many lands. It was troubled by mobs and tumults and rebellions, infested with landlopers and brigands. Jerusalem itself was not only a great city, it was a boisterous and boiling city, crowded with visitors from all parts of the world, merchants and travellers, princes and beggars, citizens of Rome and children of the Desert. There were strange sights to be seen there, and all kinds of things were sold in the markets. So while the heart of young Nazareth longed for it, the heart of older Nazareth was not without anxieties and apprehensions in regard to the first pilgrimage.

This was doubly true in the home of the Boy of whom I speak. He was the first-born, the darling of his parents, a lad beloved by all who knew him. His mother hung on him with mystical joy and hope. He was the apple of her eye. Deep in her soul she kept the memory of angelic words which had come to her while she carried him under her heart—words which made her believe that her son would be the morning-star of Israel and a light unto the Gentiles. So she cherished the Boy and watched over him with tender, unfailing care, as her most precious possession, her living, breathing, growing treasure.

When he reached the age of twelve, he was old enough to go up to the Temple and take part in the national feast of the Passover. So she clad him in the garments of youth and made him ready for the four days' pilgrimage.

It was a camping-trip, a wonder-walk, full of variety, with a spice of danger and a feast of delight.

The Boy was the joy of the journey. His keen interest in all things seen and heard was like a refreshing spring of water to the older pilgrims. They had so often travelled the same road that they had forgotten that it might be new every morning. His unwearying vigor and gladness as he ran down the hillsides, or scrambled among the rocks far above the path, or roamed through the fields filling his hands with flowers, was like a merry song that cheered the long miles of the way. He was glad to be alive, and it made the others glad to look at him.

There were sixty or seventy kinsfolk and neighbors, plain rustic men and women, in the little company that set out from Nazareth. The men carried arms to protect the caravan from robbers or marauders. As they wound slowly down the steep, stony road to the plain of Esdraelon the Boy ran ahead, making short cuts, turning aside to find a partridge's nest among the bushes, jumping from rock to rock like a young gazelle, or poising on the edge of some cliff in sheer delight of his own sure-footedness.

His body was outlined against the sky; his blue eyes (like those of his mother, who was a maid of Bethlehem) sparkled with the joy of living; his long hair was lifted and tossed by the wind of April. But his mother's look followed him anxiously, and her heart often leaped in her throat.

"My son," she said, as they took their noon-meal in the valley at the foot of dark Mount Gilboa, "you must be more careful. Your feet might slip."

"Mother," answered the Boy, "I am truly very careful. I always put my feet in the places that God has made for them—on the big, strong rocks that will not roll. It is only because I am so happy that you think I am careless."

The tents were pitched, the first night, under the walls of Bethshan, a fortified city of the Romans. Set on a knoll above the river Jordan, the town loomed big and threatening over the little camp of the Galilean pilgrims. But they kept aloof from it, because it was a city of the heathen. Its theatres and temples and palaces were accursed. The tents were indifferent to the city, and when the night opened its star-fields above them and the heavenly lights rose over the mountains of Moab and Samaria, the Boy's clear voice joined in the slumber-song of the pilgrims:

> *"I will lift up mine eyes to the hills,*
> *From whence cometh my help;*
> *My help cometh from the Lord,*
> *Who made heaven and earth.*
> *He will not suffer thy foot to stumble,*
> *He who keepeth thee will not slumber.*
> *Behold, He who guardeth Israel*
> *Will neither slumber nor sleep."*

Then they drew their woollen cloaks over their heads and rested on the ground in peace.

For two days their way led through the wide valley of the Jordan, along the level land that stretched from the mountains on either side to the rough gulch where the river was raging through its jungle. They passed through broad fields of ripe barley and ripening wheat, where the quail scuttled and piped among the thick-growing stalks. There were fruit-orchards and olive-groves on the foothills, and clear streams ran murmuring down through glistening oleander thickets. Wild flowers sprang in every untilled corner; tall spikes of hollyhocks, scarlet and blue anemones, clusters of mignonette, rock-roses, and cyclamens, purple iris in the moist places, and many-colored spathes of gladiolus growing plentifully among the wheat.

The larks sang themselves into the sky in the early morn. Hotter grew the sun and heavier the air in that long trough below the level of the sea. The song of birds melted away. Only the hawks wheeled on motionless wings above silent fields, watching for the young quail or the little rabbits, hidden among the grain.

The pilgrims plodded on in the heat. Companies of soldiers with glittering arms, merchants with laden mules jingling their bells, groups of ragged thieves and bold beggars met and jostled the peaceful travellers on the road. Once a little band of robbers, riding across the valley to the land of Moab, turned from a distance toward the Nazarenes, circled swiftly around them like hawks, whistling and calling shrilly to one another. But there was small booty in that country caravan, and the men who guarded it looked strong and tough; so the robbers whirled away as swiftly as they had come.

The Boy had stood close to his father in this moment of danger, looking on with surprise at the actions of the horsemen.

"What did those riders want?" he asked.

"All we have," answered the man.

"But it is very little," said the Boy. "Nothing but our clothes and some food for our journey. If they were hungry, why did they not ask of us?"

The man laughed. "These are not the kind that ask," he said, "they are the kind that take—what they will and when they can."

"I do not like them," said the Boy. "Their horses were beautiful, but their faces were hateful—like a jackal that I saw—in the gulley behind Nazareth one night. His eyes were burning red as fire. Those men had fires inside of them."

For the rest of that afternoon he walked more quietly and with thoughtful looks, as if he were pondering the case of men who looked like jackals and had flames within them.

At sunset, when the camp was made outside the gates of the new city of Archelaus, on a hillock among the corn-fields, he came to his mother with his hands full of the long lavender and rose and pale-blue spathes of the gladiolus-lilies.

"Look, mother," he cried, "are they not fine—like the clothes of a king?"

"What do you know of kings?" she answered, smiling. "These are only wild lilies of the field. But a great king, like Solomon, has robes of thick silk, and jewels on his neck and his fingers, and a big crown of gold on his head."

"But that must be very heavy," said the Boy, tossing his head lightly. "It must tire him to wear a crown-thing and such thick robes. Besides, I think the lilies are really prettier. They look just as if they were glad to grow in the field."

The third night they camped among the palm-groves and heavy-odored gardens of Jericho, where Herod's splendid palace rose above the trees. The fourth day they climbed the wild, steep, robber-haunted road from the Jordan valley to the highlands of Judea, and so came at sundown to their camp-ground among friends and neighbors on the closely tented slope of the Mount of Olives, over against Jerusalem.

What an evening that was for the Boy! His first sight of the holy city, the city of the great king, the city lifted up and exalted on the sides of the north, beautiful for situation, the joy of the whole earth! He had dreamed of her glory as he listened at his mother's knee to the wonder-tales of David and Solomon and the brave adventures of the fighting Maccabees. He had prayed for the peace of Jerusalem every night as he kneeled by his bed and lifted his hands toward the holy place. He had tried a thousand times to picture her strength and her splendor, her marvels and mysteries, her multitude of houses and her vast bulwarks, as he strayed among the humble cottages of Nazareth or sat in the low doorway of his own home.

Now his dream had come true. He looked into the face of Jerusalem, just across the deep, narrow valley of the Kidron, where the shadows of the evening were rising among the tombs. The huge battlemented walls, encircling the double mounts of Zion and Moriah—the vast huddle of white houses, covering hill and hollow with their flat roofs and standing so close together that the streets were hidden among them—the towers, the colonnades, the terraces—the dark bulk of the Roman castle—the marble pillars and glittering roof of the Temple in its broad court on the hilltop—it was a city of stone and ivory and gold, rising clear against the soft saffron and rose and violet of the sunset sky.

The Boy sat with his mother on the hillside while the light waned, and the lamps began to twinkle in the city, the stars to glow in the deepening blue. He questioned her eagerly—what is that black tower?—why does the big roof shine so bright?—where was King David's house?—where are we going to-morrow?

"To-morrow," she answered, "you will see. But now it is the sleep-time. Let us sing the psalm that we used to sing at night in Nazareth—but very softly, not to disturb the others—for you know this psalm is not one of the songs of the pilgrimage."

So the mother and her Child sang together with low voices:

> *"In peace will I both lay me down and sleep,*
> *For thou, Lord, makest me dwell in safety."*

The tune and the words quieted the Boy. It was like a bit of home in a far land.

II. THE GILDED TEMPLE

The next day was full of wonder and excitement. It was the first day of the Feast, and the myriad of pilgrims crowded through the gates and streets of the city, all straining toward the enclosure of the Temple, within whose walls two hundred thousand people could be gathered. On every side the Boy saw new and strange things: soldiers in their armor, and shops full of costly wares; richly dressed Sadducees with their servants following; Jews from far-away countries, and curious visitors from all parts of the world; ragged children of the city, and painted women of the street, and beggars and outcasts of the lower quarters, and rich ladies with their retinues, and priests in their snowy robes.

The family from Nazareth passed slowly through the confusion, and the Boy, bewildered by the changing scene, longed to get to the Temple. He thought everything must be quiet and holy there. But when they came into the immense outer court, with its porticos and alcoves, he found the confusion worse than ever. For there the money-changers and the buyers and sellers of animals for sacrifice were bargaining and haggling; and the thousands of people were jostling and pushing one another; and the followers of the Pharisees and the Sadducees were disputing; and on many faces he saw that strange look which speaks of a fire in the heart, so that it seemed like a meeting-place of robbers.

His father had bought a lamb for the Passover sacrifice, at one of the stalls in the outer court, and was carrying it on his shoulder. He pressed on through the crowd at the Beautiful Gate, the Boy and his mother following until they came to the Court of the Women. Here the mother stayed, for that was the law—a woman must not go farther. But the Boy was now "a son of the Commandment," and he followed his father through the Court of Israel to the entrance of the Court of the Priests. There the little lamb was given to a priest, who carried it away to the great stone altar in the middle of the court.

The Boy could not see what happened then, for the place was crowded and busy. But he heard the blowing of trumpets, and the clashing of cymbals, and the chanting of psalms. Black clouds of smoke went up from the hidden altar; the floor around was splashed and streaked with red. After a long while, as it seemed, the priest brought back the dead body of the lamb, prepared for the Passover supper.

"Is this our little lamb?" asked the Boy as his father took it again upon his shoulder.

The father nodded.

"It was a very pretty one," said the Boy. "Did it have to die?"

The father looked down at him curiously. "Surely," he said, "it had to be offered on the altar, so that we can keep our feast according to the law of Moses to-night."

"But why," persisted the Boy, "must all the lambs be killed in the Temple? Does God like that? How many do you suppose were brought to the altar to-day?"

"Tens of thousands," answered the father.

"It is a great many," said the Boy, sighing. "I wish one was enough."

He was silent and thoughtful as they made their way through the Court of the Women and found the mother and went back to the camp on the hillside. That night the family ate their Paschal feast, with their loins girded as if they were going on a journey, in memory of the long-ago flight of the Israelites from Egypt. There was the roasted lamb, with bitter herbs, and flat cakes of bread made without yeast. A cup of wine was passed around the table four times. The Boy asked his father the meaning of all these things, and the father repeated the story of the saving of the first-born sons of Israel in that far-off night of terror and death when they came out of Egypt. While the supper was going on, hymns were sung, and when it was ended they all chanted together:

"Oh, give thanks to the Lord, for He is good;
For His loving-kindness endureth for ever."

So the Boy lay down under his striped woollen cloak of blue and white and drifted toward sleep, glad that he was a son of Israel, but sorry when he thought of the thousands of little lambs and the altar floor splashed with red. He wondered if some day God would not give them another way to keep that feast.

The next day of the festival was a Sabbath, on which no work could be done. But the daily sacrifice of the Temple, and all the services and songs and benedictions in its courts, continued as usual, and there was a greater crowd than ever within its walls. As the Boy went thither with his parents they came to a place where a little house was beginning to burn, set on fire by an overturned lamp. The poor people stood by, wringing their hands and watching the flames.

"Why do they not try to save their house?" cried the Boy.

The father shook his head. "They can do nothing," he answered. "They follow the teaching of the Pharisees, who say that it is unlawful to put out a fire on the Sabbath, because it is a labor."

A little later the Boy saw a cripple with a crutch, sitting in the door of a cottage, looking very sad and lonely.

"Why does he not go with the others," asked the Boy, "and hear the music at the Temple? That would make him happier. Can't he walk?"

"Yes," answered the father, "he can hop along pretty well with his crutch on other days, but not on the Sabbath, for he would have to carry his crutch, and that would be labor."

All the time he was in the Temple, watching the procession of priests and Levites and listening to the music, the Boy was thinking what the Sabbath meant, and whether it really rested people and made them happier.

The third day of the festival was the offering of the first-fruits of the new year's harvest. That was a joyous day. A sheaf of ripe barley was reaped and carried into the Temple and presented before the high altar with incense and music. The priests blessed the people, and the people shouted and sang for gladness.

The Boy's heart bounded in his breast as he joined in the song and thought of the bright summer begun, and the birds building their nests, and the flowers clothing the hills with beautiful colors, and the wide fields of golden grain waving in the wind. He was happy all day as he walked through the busy streets with his parents, buying some things that were needed for the home in Nazareth; and he was happy at night when he lay down under an olive-tree beside the tent, for the air was warm and gentle, and he fell asleep under the tree, dreaming of what he would see and do tomorrow.

III. HOW THE BOY WAS LOST

Now comes the secret of the way he was lost—a way so simple that the wonder is that no one has ever dreamed of it before.

The three important days of the Passover were ended, and the time had come when those pilgrims who wished to return to their homes might leave Jerusalem without offense, though it was more commendable to remain through the full seven days. The people from Nazareth were anxious to be gone—they had a long road to travel—their harvests were waiting. While the Boy, tired out, was sleeping under the tree, the question of going home was talked out and decided. They would break camp at sunrise, and, joining with others of their countrymen who were tented around them, they would take the road for Galilee.

But the Boy awoke earlier than any one else the next morning. Before the dawn a linnet in the tree overhead called him with twittering songs. He was rested by his long sleep. His breath came lightly. The spirit of youth was beating in his limbs, His heart was eager for adventure. He longed for the top of a high hill—for the wide, blue sky—for the world at his feet—such a sight as he had often found in his rambles among the heights near Nazareth. Why not? He would return in time for the next visit to the Temple.

Quietly he stepped among the sleeping-tents in the dark. A footpath led through the shadowy olive-grove, up the hillside, into the open. There the light was clearer, and the breeze that runs before the daybreak was dancing through the grass. The Boy turned to the left, following along one of the sheep-trails that crossed the high, sloping pastures. Then he bore to the right, breasting the long ridge, and passed the summit, running lightly to the eastward until he came to a rounded, rocky knoll. There he sat down among the little bushes to wait for sunrise.

Far beyond the wrinkled wilderness of Tekoa, and the Dead Sea, and the mountain-wall of Moab, the rim of the sky was already tinged with silvery gray. The fading of the stars travelled slowly upward, and the brightening of the rose of dawn followed it, until all the east was softly glowing and the deep blue of the central heaven was transfused with turquoise light. Dark in the gulfs and chasms of the furrowed land the night lingered. Bright along the eastern peaks and ridges the coming day, still hidden, revealed itself in a fringe of dazzling gold, like the crest of a long mounting wave. Shoots and flashes of radiance sprang upward from the glittering edge. Streamers of rose-foam and gold-spray floated in the sky. Then over the barrier of the hills the sun surged royally-crescent, half-disk, full-orb—and overlooked the world. The luminous tide flooded the gray villages of Bethany and Bethphage, and all the emerald hills around Bethlehem were bathed in light.

The Boy sat entranced, watching the miracle by which God makes His sun to shine upon the good and the evil. How strange it was that God should do that—bestow an equal light upon those who obeyed Him and those who broke His law! Yet it was splendid, it was King-like to give in that way, with both hands. No, it was Father-like—and that was what the Boy had learned from his mother—that God who made and ruled all things was his Father. It was the name she had taught him to use in his prayers. Not in the great prayers he learned from the book—the name there was Adonai, the Lord, the Almighty. But in the little prayers that he said by himself it was "my Father!" It made the Boy feel strangely happy and strong to say that. The whole world seemed to breathe and glow around him with an invisible presence. For such a Father, for the sake of His love and favor, the Boy felt he could do anything.

More than that, his mother had told him of something special that the Father had for him to do in the world. In the evenings during the journey and when they were going home together from the Temple, she had repeated to him some of the words that the angel-voices had spoken to her heart, and some of the sayings of wise men from the East who came to visit him when he was a baby. She could not understand all the mystery of it; she did not see how it was going to be brought to pass. He was a child of poverty and lowliness; not rich, nor learned, nor powerful. But with God all things were possible. The choosing and calling of the eternal Father were more than everything else. It was fixed in her heart that somehow her Boy was sent to do a great work for Israel. He was the son of God set apart to save his people and bring back the glory of Zion. He was to fulfil the promises made in olden time and bring in the wonderful reign of the Messiah in the world—perhaps as a forerunner and messenger of the great King, or perhaps himself—ah, she did not know! But she believed in her Boy with her whole soul; and she was sure that his Father would show him what to do.

These sayings, coming amid the excitements of his first journey, his visit to the Temple, his earliest sight of the splendor and confusion and misery of the great city, had sunken all the more deeply into the Boy's mind. Excitement does not blur the impressions of youth; it sharpens them, makes them more vivid. Half-covered and hardly noticed at the time, they spring up into life when the quiet hour comes.

So the Boy remembered his mother's words while he lay watching the sunrise. It would be great to make them come true. To help everybody to feel what he felt there on the hilltop—that big, free feeling of peace and confidence and not being afraid! To make those robbers in the Jordan valley see how they were breaking the rule of the world and burning out their own hearts! To cleanse the Temple from the things that filled it with confusion and pain, and drive away the brawling buyers and sellers who were spoiling his Father's great house! To go among those poor and wretched and sorrowful folks who swarmed in Jerusalem and teach them that God was their Father too, and that they must not sin and quarrel any more! To find a better way than the priests' and the Pharisees' of making people good! To do great things for Israel—like Moses, like Joshua, like David—or like Daniel, perhaps, who prayed and was not afraid of the lions—or like Elijah and Elisha, who went about speaking to the people and healing them—

The soft tread of bare feet among the bushes behind him roused the Boy. He sprang up and saw a man with a stern face and long hair and beard looking at him mysteriously. The man was dressed in white, with a leathern girdle round his waist, into which a towel was thrust. A leathern wallet hung from his neck, and he leaned upon a long staff.

"Peace be with you, Rabbi," said the Boy, reverently bowing at the stranger's feet. But the man looked at him steadily and did not speak.

The Boy was confused by the silence. The man's eyes troubled him with their secret look, but he was not afraid.

"Who are you, sir," he asked, "and what is your will with me? Perhaps you are a master of the Pharisees or a scribe? But no—there are no broad blue fringes on your garments. Are you a priest, then?"

The man shook his head, frowning. "I despise the priests," he answered, "and I abhor their bloody and unclean sacrifices. I am Enoch the Essene, a holy one, a perfect keeper of the law. I live with those who have never defiled themselves with the eating of meat, nor with marriage, nor with wine; but we have all things in common, and we are baptized in pure water every day for the purifying of our wretched bodies, and after that we eat the daily feast of love in the kingdom of the Messiah which is at hand. Thou art called into that kingdom, son; come with me, for thou art called."

The Boy listened with astonishment. Some of the things that the man said—for instance, about the sacrifices and about the nearness of the kingdom—were already in his heart. But other things puzzled and bewildered him.

"My mother says that I am called," he answered, "but it is to serve Israel and to help the people. Where do you live, sir, and what is it that you do for the people?"

"We live among the hills of that wilderness," he answered, pointing to the south, "in the oasis of Engedi. There are palm-trees and springs of water, and we keep ourselves pure, bathing before we eat and offering our food of bread and dates as a sacrifice to God. We all work together, and none of us has anything that he calls his own. We do not go up to the Temple nor enter the synagogues. We have forsaken the uncleanness of the world and all the impure ways of men. Our only care is to keep ourselves from defilement. If we touch anything that is forbidden we wash our hands and wipe them with this towel that hangs from our girdle. We alone are serving the kingdom. Come, live with us, for I think thou art chosen."

The Boy thought for a while before he answered. "Some of it is good, my master," he said, "but the rest of it is far away from my thoughts. Is there nothing for a man to do in the world but to think of himself—either in feasting and uncleanness as the heathen do, or in fasting and purifying yourself as you do? How can you serve the kingdom if you turn away from the people? They do not see you or hear you. You are separate from them—just as if you were dead without dying. You can do nothing for them. No, I do not want to come with you and live at Engedi. I think my Father will show me something better to do."

"Your Father!" said Enoch the Essene. "Who is He?"

"Surely," answered the Boy, "He is the same as yours. He that made us and made all that we see—the great world for us to live in."

"Dust," said the man, with a darker frown—"dust and ashes! It will all perish, and thou with it. Thou art not chosen—not pure!"

With that he went away down the hill; and the Boy, surprised and grieved at his rude parting, wondered a little over the meaning of his words, and then went back as quickly as he could toward the tents.

When he came to the olive-grove they were gone! The sun was already high, and his people had departed hours ago. In the hurry and bustle of breaking camp each of the parents had supposed that the Boy was with the other, or with some of the friends and neighbors, or perhaps running along the hillside above them as he used to do. So they went their way cheerfully, not knowing that they had left their son behind. This is how it came to pass that he was lost.

IV. HOW THE BOY WENT HIS WAY

When the Boy saw what had happened he was surprised and troubled, but not frightened. He did not know what to do. He might hasten after them, but he could not tell which way to go. He was not even sure that they had gone home; for they had talked of paying a visit to their relatives in the south before returning to Nazareth; and some of the remaining pilgrims to whom he turned for news of his people said that they had taken the southern road from the Mount of Olives, going toward Bethlehem.

The Boy was at a loss, but he was not disheartened, nor even cast down. He felt that somehow all would be well with him; he would be taken care of. They would come back for him in good time. Meanwhile there were kind people here who would give him food and shelter. There were boys in the other camps with whom he could play. Best of all, he could go again to the city and the Temple. He could see more of the wonderful things there, and watch the way the people lived, and find out why so many of them seemed sad or angry, and a few proud and scornful, and almost all looked unsatisfied. Perhaps he could listen to some of the famous rabbis who taught the people in the courts of the Temple and learn from them about the things which his Father had chosen him to do.

So he went down the hill and toward the Sheep Gate by which he had always gone into the city. Outside the gate a few boys about his own age, with a group of younger children, were playing games.

"Look there," they cried—"a stranger! Let us have some fun with him. Halloo, Country, where do you come from?"

"From Galilee," answered the Boy.

"Galilee is where all the fools live," cried the children. "Where is your home? What is your name?"

He told them pleasantly, but they laughed at his country way of speaking and mimicked his pronunciation.

"Yalilean! Yalilean!" they cried. "You can't task. Can you play? Come and play with us."

So they played together. First, they had a mimic wedding-procession. Then they made believe that the bridegroom was killed by a robber, and they had a mock funeral. The Boy took always the lowest part. He was the hired mourner who followed the body, wailing; he was the flute-player who made music for the wedding-guests to dance to.

So readily did he enter into the play that the children at first were pleased with him. But they were not long contented with anything. Some of them would dance no more for the wedding; others would lament no more for the funeral. Their caprices made them quarrelsome.

"Yalilean fool," they cried, "you play it all wrong. You spoil the game. We are tired of it. Can you run? Can you throw stones?"

So they ran races; and the Boy, trained among the hills, outran the others. But they said he did not keep to the course. Then they threw stones; and the Boy threw farther and straighter than any of the rest. This made them angry.

Whispering together, they suddenly hurled a shower of stones at him. One struck his shoulder, another made a long cut on his cheek. Wiping away the blood with his sleeve, he turned silently and ran to the Sheep Gate, the other boys chasing him with loud shouts.

He darted lightly through the crowd of animals and people that thronged the gateway, turning and dodging with a sure foot among them and running up the narrow street that led to the sheep-market. The cries of his pursuers grew fainter behind him. Among the stalls of the market he wound this way and that way like a hare before the hounds. At last he had left them out of sight and hearing.

Then he ceased running and wandered blindly on through the northern quarter of the city. The sloping streets were lined with bazaars and noisy workshops. The Roman soldiers from the castle were sauntering to and fro. Women in rich attire, with ear-rings and gold chains, passed by with their slaves. Open market-places were still busy, though the afternoon trade was slackening.

But the Boy was too tired and faint with hunger and heavy at heart to take an interest in these things. He turned back toward the gate, and, missing his way a little, came to a great pool of water, walled in wit, white stone, with five porticos around it. In some of these porticos there were a few people lying upon mats. But one of the porches was empty, and here the Boy sat down.

He was worn out. His cheek was bleeding again, and the drops trickled down his neck. He went down the broad steps to the pool to wash away the blood. But he could not do it very well. His head ached too much. So he crept back to the porch, unwound his little turban, curled himself in a corner on the hard stones, his head upon his arm, and fell sound asleep.

He was awakened by a voice calling him, a hand laid upon his shoulder. He looked up and saw the face of a young woman, dark-eyed, red-lipped, only a few years older than himself. She was clad in silk, with a veil of gauze over her head, gold coins in her hair, and a phial of alabaster hanging by a gold chain around her neck. A sweet perfume like the breath of roses came from it as she moved. Her voice was soft and kind.

"Poor boy," she said, "you are wounded; some one has hurt you. What are you doing here? You look like a little brother that I had long ago. Come with me. I will take care of you."

The Boy rose and tried to go with her. But he was stiff and sore; he could hardly walk; his head was swimming. The young woman beckoned to a Nubian slave who followed her. He took the Boy in his big black arms and so carried him to a pleasant house with a garden.

There were couches and cushions there, in a marble court around a fountain. There were servants who brought towels and ointments. The young woman bathed the Boy's wound and his feet. The servants came with food, and she made him eat of the best. His eyes grew bright again, and the color came into his cheeks. He talked to her of his life in Nazareth, of the adventures of his first journey, and of the way he came to be lost.

She listened to him intently, as if there were some strange charm in his simple talk. Her eyes rested upon him with pleasure. A new look swept over her face. She leaned close to him.

"Stay with me, boy," she murmured, "for I want you. Your people are gone. You shall sleep here to-night—you shall live with me and I will be good to you—I will teach you to love me."

The Boy moved back a little and looked at her with wide eyes, as if she were saying something that he could not understand.

"But you have already been good to me, sister," he answered, "and I love you already, even as your brother did. Is your husband here? Will he come soon, so that we can all say the prayer of thanks-giving together for the food?"

Her look changed again; her eyes filled with pain and sorrow; she shrank back and turned away her face.

"I have no husband," she said. "Ah, boy, innocent boy, you do not understand. I eat the bread of shame and live in the house of wickedness. I am a sinner, a sinner of the city. How could I pray?"

With that she fell a-sobbing, rocking herself to and fro, and the tears ran through her fingers like rain. The Boy looked at her, astonished and pitiful. He moved nearer to her, after a moment, and spoke softly.

"I am very sorry, sister," he said; and as he spoke he felt her tears falling on his feet. "I am more sorry than I ever was in my life. It must be dreadful to be a sinner. But sinners can pray, for God is our Father, and fathers know how to forgive. I will stay with you and teach you some of the things my mother has taught me."

She looked up and caught his hand and kissed it. She wiped away her tears, and rose, pushing back her hair.

"No, dear little master," she said, "you shall not stay in this house—not an hour. It is not fit for you. My Nubian shall lead you back to the gate, and you will return to your friends outside of the city, and you will forget one whom you comforted for a moment."

The Boy turned back as he stood in the doorway. "No," he said. "I will not forget you. I will always remember your love and kindness. Will you learn to pray, and give up being a sinner?"

"I will try," she answered; "you have made me want to try. Go in peace. God knows what will become of me."

"God knows, sister," replied the Boy gravely. "Abide in peace."

So he went out into the dusk with the Nubian and found the camp on the hillside and a shelter in one of the friendly tents, where he slept soundly and woke refreshed in the morning.

This day he would not spend in playing and wandering. He would go straight to the Temple, to find some of the learned teachers who gave instruction there, and learn from them the wisdom that he needed in order to do his work for his Father.

As he went he thought about the things that had befallen him yesterday. Why had the man dressed in white despised him? Why had the city children mocked him and chased him away with stones? Why was the strange woman who had been so kind to him afterward so unhappy and so hopeless?

There must be something in the world that he did not understand, something evil and hateful and miserable that he had never felt in himself. But he felt it in the others, and it made him so sorry, so distressed for them, that it seemed like a heavy weight, a burden on his own heart. It was like the work of those demons, of whom his mother had told him, who entered into people and lived inside of them, like worms eating away a fruit.

Only these people of whom he was thinking did not seem to have a demon that took hold of them and drove them mad and made them foam at the mouth and cut themselves with stones, like a man he once saw in Galilee. This was something larger and more mysterious-like the hot wind that sometimes blew from the south and made people gloomy and angry—like the rank weeds that grew in certain fields, and if the sheep fed there they dropped and died.

The Boy felt that he hated this unknown, wicked, unhappy thing more than anything else in the world. He would like to save people from it. He wanted to fight against it, to drive it away. It seemed as if there were a spirit in his heart saying to him, "This is what you must do, you must fight against this evil, you must drive out the darkness, you must be a light, you must save the people—this is your Father's work for you to do."

But how? He did not know. That was what he wanted to find out. And he went into the Temple hoping that the teachers there would tell him.

He found the vast Court of the Gentiles, as it had been on his first visit, swarming with people. Jews and Syrians and foreigners of many nations were streaming into it through the eight open gates, meeting and mingling and eddying round in confused currents, bargaining and haggling with the merchants and money-changers, crowding together around some group where argument had risen to a violent dispute, drifting away again in search of some new excitement.

The morning sacrifice was ended, but the sound of music floated out from the enclosed courts in front of the altar, where the more devout worshippers were gathered. The Roman soldiers of the guard paced up and down, or leaned tranquilly upoa their spears, looking with indifference or amused contempt upon the turbulent scenes of the holy place where they were set to keep the peace and prevent the worshippers from attacking one another.

The Boy turned into the long, cool cloisters, their lofty marble columns and carved roofs, which ran around the inside of the walls. Here he found many groups of people, walking in the broad aisles between the pillars, or seated in the alcoves of Solomon's Porch around the teachers who were instructing them. From one to another of these open schools he wandered, listening eagerly to the different rabbis and doctors of the law.

Here one was reading from the Torah and explaining the laws about the food which a Jew must not eat, and the things which he must not do on the Sabbath. Here another was expounding the doctrine of the Pharisees about the purifying of the sacred vessels in the Temple; while another, a Sadducee, was disputing with him scornfully and claiming that the purification of the priests was the only important thing. "You would wash that which needs no washing," he cried, "the Golden Candlestick, one day in every week! Next you will want to wash the sun for fear an unclean ray of light may fall on the altar!"

Other teachers were reciting from the six books of the Talmud which the Pharisees were making to expound the law. Others repeated the histories of Israel, recounted the brave deeds of the Maccabees, or read from the prophecies of Enoch and Daniel. Others still were engaged in political debate: the Zealots talking fiercely of the misdeeds of the house of Herod and the outrages committed by the Romans; the Sadducees contemptuously mocking at the hopes of the revolutionists and showing that the dream of freedom for Judea was foolish. "Freedom," they said, "belongs to those who are well protected. We have the Temple and priesthood because Rome takes care of us." To this the Zealots answered angrily: "Yes, the priesthood belongs to you unbelieving Sadducees; that is why you are content with it. Look, now, at the place where you let Herod hang an accursed eagle of gold on the front of Jehovah's House."

So from group to group the Boy passed, listening intently, but hearing little to his purpose. All day long he listened, now to one, now to another, completely absorbed by what he heard, yet not satisfied. Late in the afternoon he came into the quietest part of Solomon's Porch, where two large companies were seated around their respective teachers, separated from each other by a distance of four or five columns.

As he stood on the edge of the first company, whose rabbi was a lean, dark-bearded, stern little man, the Boy was spoken to by a stranger at his side, who asked him what he sought in the Temple.

"Wisdom," answered the Boy. "I am looking for some one to give a light to my path."

"That is what I am seeking, too," said the stranger, smiling. "I am a Greek, and I desire wisdom. Let us see if we can get it from this teacher. Listen."

He made his way to the centre of the circle and stood before the stern little man.

"Master," said the Greek, "I am willing to become thy disciple if thou wilt teach me the whole law while I stand before thee thus—on one foot."

The rabbi looked at him angrily, and, lifting up his stick, smote him sharply across the leg. "That is the whole law for mockers," he cried. The stranger limped away amid the laughter of the crowd.

"But the little man was too angry; he did not see that I was in earnest," said he, as he came back to the Boy. "Now let us go to the next school and see if the master there is any better."

So they went to the second company, which was gathered around a very old man, with long, snowy beard and a gentle face. The stranger took his place as before, standing on one foot, and made the same request. The rabbi's eyes twinkled and his lips were smiling as he answered promptly:

"Do nothing to thy neighbor that thou wouldst not have him do to thee, this is the whole law; all the rest follows from this."

"Well," said the stranger, returning, "what think you of this teacher and his wisdom? Is it better?"

"It is far better," replied the Boy eagerly: "it is the best of all I have heard to-day. I am coming back to hear him to-morrow. Do you know his name?"

"I think it is Hillel," answered the Greek, "and he is a learned man, the master of the Sanhedrim. You will do well, young Jew, to listen to such a man. Socrates could not have answered me better. But now the sun is near setting. We must go our ways. Farewell."

In the tent of his friends the Boy found welcome and a supper, but no news of his parents. He told his experiences in the Temple, and the friends heard him, wondering at his discernment. They were in doubt whether to let him go again the next day; but he begged so earnestly, arguing that they could tell his parents where he was if they should come to the camp seeking him, that finally he won consent.

V. HOW THE BOY WAS FOUND

He was in Solomon's Porch long before the schools had begun to assemble. He paced up and down under the triple colonnade, thinking what questions he should ask the master.

The company that gathered around Hillel that day was smaller, but there were more scribes and doctors of the law among them, and they were speaking of the kingdom of the Messiah—the thing that lay nearest to the Boy's heart. He took his place in the midst of them, and they made room for him, for they liked young disciples and encouraged them to ask after knowledge.

It was the prophecy of Daniel that they were discussing, and the question was whether these things were written of the First Messiah or of the Second Messiah; for many of the doctors held that there must be two, and that the first would die in battle, but the second would put down all his enemies and rule over the world.

"Rabbi," asked the Boy, "if the first was really the Messiah, could not God raise him up again and send him back to rule?"

"You ask wisely, son," answered Hillel, "and I think the prophets tell us that we must hope for only one Messiah. This book of Daniel is full of heavenly words, but it is not counted among the prophets whose writings are gathered in the Scripture. Which of them have you read, and which do you love most, my son?"

"Isaiah," said the Boy, "because he says God will have mercy with everlasting-kindness. But I love Daniel, too, because he says they that turn many to righteousness shall shine as the stars for ever and ever. But I do not understand what he says about the times and a half-time and the days and the seasons before the coming of Messiah."

With this there rose a dispute among the doctors about the meaning of those sayings, and some explained them one way and some another, but Hillel sat silent. At last he said:

"It is better to hope and to wait patiently for Him than to reckon the day of His coming. For if the reckoning is wrong, and He does not come, then men despair, and no longer make ready for Him."

"How does a man make ready for Him, Rabbi?" asked the Boy.

"By prayer, son, and by study of the law, and by good works, and by sacrifices."

"But when He comes He will rule over the whole world, and how can all the world come to the Temple to sacrifice?"

"A way will be provided," answered the old man, "though I do not know how it will be. And there are offerings of the heart as well as of the altar. It is written, 'I will have mercy and not sacrifice.'"

"Will His kingdom be for the poor as well as for the rich, and for the ignorant as well as for the wise?"

{Illustration: From a painting by Holman Junt. The Finding of Christ in The Temple}

"Yes, it will be for the poor and for the rich alike. But it will not be for the ignorant, my son. For he who does not know the law cannot be pious."

"But, Rabbi," said the Boy eagerly, "will He not have mercy on them just because they are ignorant? Will He not pity them as a shepherd pities his sheep when they are silly and go astray?"

"He is not only a Shepherd," answered Hillel firmly, "but a great King. They must all keep the law, even as it is written and as the elders have taught it to us. There is no other way."

The Boy was silent for a time, while the others talked of the law, and of the Torah, and of the Talmud in which Hillel in those days was writing down the traditions of the elders. When there was an opportunity he spoke again.

"Rabbi, if most of the people should be both poor and ignorant when the Messiah came, so ignorant that they did not even know Him, wouldn't He save them just because they were poor?"

Hillel looked at the Boy with love, and hesitated before he answered.

At that moment a man and a woman came through the colonnade with hurried steps. The man stopped at the edge of the circle, astonished at what he saw. But the woman came into the centre and put her arm around the Boy.

"My boy," she cried, "why hast thou done this to us? See how sorrowful thou hast made me and thy father, looking everywhere for thee."

"Mother," he answered, "why did you look everywhere for me with sorrow? Did you not know that I would be in my Father's house? Must I not begin to think of the things my Father wants me to do?"

Thus the lost Boy was found again, and went home with, his parents to Nazareth. The old rabbi blessed him as he left the Temple.

But had he really been lost, or was he finding his way?

THE END

The Sad Shepherd,
A Christmas Story

I
DARKNESS

Out of the Valley of Gardens, where a film of new-fallen snow lay smooth as feathers on the breast of a dove, the ancient Pools of Solomon looked up into the night sky with dark, tranquil eyes, wide-open and passive, reflecting the crisp stars and the small, round moon. The full springs, overflowing on the hill-side, melted their way through the field of white in winding channels; and along their course the grass was green even in the dead of winter.

But the sad shepherd walked far above the friendly valley, in a region where ridges of gray rock welted and scarred the back of the earth, like wounds of half-forgotten strife and battles long ago. The solitude was forbidding and disquieting; the keen air that searched the wanderer had no pity in it; and the myriad glances of the night were curiously cold.

His flock straggle after him. The sheep, weather-beaten and dejected, followed the path with low heads nodding from side to side, as if they had traveled far and found little pasture. The black, lop-eared goats leaped upon the rocks, restless and ravenous, tearing down the tender branches and leaves of the dwarf oaks and wild olives. They reared up against the twisted trunks and crawled and scrambled among the boughs. It was like a company of gray downcast friends and a troop of merry little black devils following the sad shepherd afar off.

He walked looking on the ground, paying small heed to them. Now and again, when the sound of pattering feet and panting breath and the rustling and rending among the copses fell too far behind, he drew out his shepherd's pipe and blew a strain of music, shrill and plaintive, quavering and lamenting through the hollow night. He waited while the troops of gray and black scuffled and bounded and trotted near to him. Then he dropped the pipe into its place again and strode forward, looking on the ground.

The fitful, shivery wind that rasped the hill-top, fluttered the rags of his long mantle of Tyrian blue, torn by thorns and stained by travel. The rich tunic of striped silk beneath it was worn thin, and the girdle about his loins had lost all its ornaments of silver and jewels. His curling hair hung down dishevelled under a turban of fine linen, in which the gilt threads were frayed and tarnished; and his shoes of soft leather were broken by the road. On his brown fingers the places of the vanished rings were still marked in white skin. He carried not the long staff nor the heavy nail-studded rod of the shepherd, but a slender stick of carved cedar battered and scratched by hard usage, and the handle, which must once have been of precious metal, was missing.

He was a strange figure for that lonely place and that humble occupation-a branch of faded beauty from some royal garden tossed by rude winds into the wilderness-a pleasure craft adrift, buffeted and broken, on rough seas.

But he seemed to have passed beyond caring. His young face was frayed and threadbare as his garments. The splendor of the moonlight flooding the wild world meant as little to him as the hardness of the rugged track which he followed. He wrapped his tattered mantle closer around him, and strode ahead, looking on the ground.

As the path dropped from the summit of the ridge toward the Valley of Mills and passed among huge broken rocks, three men sprang at him from the shadows. He lifted his stick, but let it fall again, and a strange ghost of a smile twisted his face as they gripped him and threw him down.

"You are rough beggars," he said. "Say what you want, you are welcome to it."

"Your money, dog of a courtier," they muttered fiercely; "give us your golden collar, Herod's hound, quick, or you die!"

"The quicker the better," he answered, closing his eyes.

The bewildered flock of sheep and goats, gathered in a silent ring, stood at gaze while the robbers fumbled over their master

"This is a stray dog," said one, "he has lost his collar, there is not even the price of a mouthful of wine on him. Shall we kill him and leave him for the vultures?" "What have the vultures done for us," said another, "that we should feed them? Let us take his cloak and drive off his flock, and leave him to die in his own time."

With a kick and a curse they left him. He opened his eyes and lay quiet for a moment, with his twisted smile, watching the stars.

"You creep like snails," he said. "I thought you had marked my time tonight. But not even that is given to me for nothing. I must pay for all, it seems."

Far away, slowly scattering and receding, he heard the rustling and bleating of his frightened flock as the robbers, running and shouting, tried to drive them over the hills. Then he stood up and took the shepherd's pipe, a worthless bit of reed, from the breast of his tunic. He blew again that plaintive, piercing air, sounding it out over the ridges and distant thickets. It seemed to have neither beginning nor end; a melancholy, pleading tune that searched forever after something lost.

While he played, the sheep and the goats, slipping away from their captors by roundabout ways, hiding behind the laurel bushes, following the dark gullies, leaping down the broken cliffs, came circling back to him, one after another;

and as they came, he interrupted his playing, now and then, to call them by name. When they were nearly all assembled, he went down swiftly toward the lower valley, and they followed him, panting. At the last crook of the path on the steep hillside a straggler came after him along the cliff. He looked up and saw it outlined against the sky. Then he saw it leap, and slip, und fall beyond the path into a deep cleft.

"Little fool," he said, "fortune is kind to you! You have escaped from the big trap of life. What? You are crying for help? You are still in the trap? Then I must go down to you, little fool, for I am a fool too. But why I must do it, I know no more than you know."

He lowered himself quickly and perilously into the cleft, and found the creature with its leg broken and bleeding. It was not a sheep but a young goat. He had no cloak to wrap it in, but he took off his turban and unrolled it, and bound it around the trembling animal. Then he climbed back to the path and strode on at the head of his flock, carrying the little black kid in his arms.

There were houses in the Valley of the Mills; and in some of them lights were burning; and the drone of the mill-stones, where the women were still grinding, came out into the night like the humming of drowsy bees. As the women heard the pattering and bleating of the flock, they wondered who was passing so late. One of them, in a house where there was no mill but many lights, came to the door and looked out laughing, her face and bosom bare.

But the sad shepherd did not stay. His long shadow and the confused mass of lesser shadows behind him drifted down the white moonlight, past the yellow bars of lamplight that gleamed from the doorways. It seemed as if he were bound to go somewhere and would not delay.

Yet with all his haste to be gone, it was plain that he thought little of where he was going. For when he came to the foot of the valley, where the paths divided, he stood between them staring vacantly, without a desire to turn him this way or that. The imperative of choice halted him like a barrier. The balance of his mind hung even because both scales were empty. He could act, he could go, for his strength was untouched; but he could not choose, for his will was broken within him.

The path to the left went up toward the little town of Bethlehem, with huddled roofs and walls in silhouette along the double-crested hill. It was dark and forbidding as a closed fortress. The sad shepherd looked at it with indifferent eyes; there was nothing there to draw him. The path to the right wound through rock-strewn valleys toward the Dead Sea. But rising out of that crumpled wilderness, a mile or two away, the smooth white ribbon of a chariot-road lay upon the flank of a cone-shaped mountain and curled in loops toward its peak. There the great cone was cut squarely off, and the levelled summit was capped by a palace of marble, with round towers at the corners and flaring beacons along the walls; and the glow of an immense fire, hidden in the central court-yard, painted a false dawn in the eastern sky. All down the clean-cut mountain slopes, on terraces and blind arcades, the lights flashed from lesser pavilions and pleasure-houses.

It was the secret orchard of Herod and his friends, their trysting-place with the spirits of mirth and madness. They called it the Mountain of the Little Paradise. Rich gardens were there; and the cool water from the Pools of Solomon plashed in the fountains; and trees of the knowledge of good and evil fruited blood-red and ivory-white above them; and smooth, curving, glistening shapes, whispering softly of pleasure, lay among the flowers and glided behind the trees. All this was now hidden in the dark. Only the strange bulk of the mountain, a sharp black pyramid girdled and crowned with fire, loomed across the night-a mountain once seen never to be forgotten.

The sad shepherd remembered it well. He looked at it with the eyes of a child who has been in hell. It burned him from afar. Turning neither to the right nor to the left, he walked without a path straight out upon the plain of Bethlehem, still whitened in the hollows and on the sheltered side of its rounded hillocks by the veil of snow.

He faced a wide and empty world. To the west in sleeping Bethlehem, to the east in flaring Herodium, the life of man was infinitely far away from him. Even the stars seemed to withdraw themselves against the blue-black of the sky. They diminished and receded till they were like pin-holes in the vault above him. The moon in mid-heaven shrank into a bit of burnished silver, hard and glittering, immeasurably remote. The ragged, inhospitable ridges of Tekoa lay stretched in mortal slumber along the horizon, and between them he caught a glimpse of the sunken Lake of Death, darkly gleaming in its deep bed. There was no movement, no sound, on the plain where he walked, except the soft-padding feet of his dumb, obsequious flock.

He felt an endless isolation strike cold to his heart, against which he held the limp body of the wounded kid, wondering the while, with a half-contempt for his own foolishness, why he took such trouble to save a tiny scrap of the worthless tissue which is called life.

Even when a man does not know or care where he is going, if he steps onward he will get there. In an hour or more of walking over the plain the sad shepherd came to a sheep-fold of gray stones with a rude tower beside it. The fold was full of sheep, and at the foot of the tower a little fire of thorns was burning, around which four shepherds were crouching, wrapped in their thick woollen cloaks.

As the stranger approached they looked up, and one of them rose quickly to his feet, grasping his knotted club. But when they saw the flock that followed the sad shepherd, they stared at each other and said: "It is one of us, a keeper of sheep. But how comes he here in this raiment? It is what men wear in kings' houses."

"No," said the one who was standing, "it is what they wear when they have been thrown out of them. Look at the rags. He may be a thief and a robber with his stolen flock."

"Salute him when he comes near," said the oldest shepherd. "Are we not four to one? We have nothing to fear from a ragged traveller. Speak him fair. It is the will of God-and it costs nothing."

"Peace be with you, brother," cried the youngest shepherd; "may your mother and father be blessed."

"May your heart be enlarged," the stranger answered, "and may all your families be more blessed than mine, for I have none."

"A homeless man," said the old shepherd, "has either been robbed by his fellows, or punished by God."

"I do not know which it was," answered the stranger; "the end is the same, as you see."

"By your speech you come from Galilee. Where are you going? What are you seeking here?"

"I was going nowhere, my masters; but it was cold on the way there, and my feet turned to your fire."

"Come then, if you are a peaceable man, and warm your feet with us. Heat is a good gift; divide it and it is not less. But you shall have bread and salt too, if you will."

"May your hospitality enrich you. I am your unworthy guest. But my flock?"

"Let your flock shelter by the south wall of the fold: there is good picking there and no wind. Come you and sit with us."

So they all sat down by the fire; and the sad shepherd ate of their bread, but sparingly, like a man to whom hunger brings a need but no joy in the satisfying of it; and the others were silent for a proper time, out of courtesy. Then the oldest shepherd spoke:

"My name is Zadok the son of Eliezer, of Bethlehem. I am the chief shepherd of the flocks of the Temple, which are before you in the fold. These are my sister's sons, Jotham, and Shama, and Nathan: their father Elkanah is dead; and but for these I am a childless man."

"My name," replied the stranger, "is Ammiel the son of Jochanan, of the city of Bethsaida, by the Sea of Galilee, and I am a fatherless man."

"It is better to be childless than fatherless," said Zadok, "yet it is the will of God that children should bury their fathers. When did the blessed Jochanan die?"

"I know not whether he be dead or alive. It is three years since I looked upon his face or had word of him."

"You are an exile then? he has cast you off?"

"It was the other way," said Am-miel, looking on the ground.

At this the shepherd Shama, who had listened with doubt in his face, started up in anger. "Pig of a Galilean," he cried, "despiser of parents! breaker of the law! When I saw you coming I knew you for something vile. Why do you darken the night for us with your presence? You have reviled him who begot you. Away, or we stone you!"

Ammiel did not answer or move.

The twisted smile passed over his bowed face again as he waited to know the shepherds' will with him, even as he had waited for the robbers. But Zadok lifted his hand.

"Not so hasty, Shama-ben-Elkanah. You also break the law by judging a man unheard. The rabbis have told us that there is a tradition of the elders-a rule as holy as the law itself-that a man may deny his father in a certain way without sin. It is a strange rule, and it must be very holy or it would not be so strange. But this is the teaching of the elders: a son may say of anything for which his father asks him-a sheep, or a measure of corn, or a field, or a purse of silver-'it is Corban, a gift that I have vowed unto the Lord;' and so his father shall have no more claim upon him. Have you said 'Corban' to your father, Ammiel-ben-Jochanan? Have you made a vow unto the Lord?"

"I have said 'Corban,'" answered Ammiel, lifting his face, still shadowed by that strange smile, "but it was not the Lord who heard my vow."

"Tell us what you have done," said the old man sternly, "for we will neither judge you, nor shelter you, unless we hear your story."

"There is nothing in it," replied Ammiel indifferently. "It is an old story. But if you are curious you shall hear it. Afterward you shall deal with me as you will."

So the shepherds, wrapped in their warm cloaks, sat listening with grave faces and watchful, unsearchable eyes, while Ammiel in his tattered silk sat by the sinking fire of thorns and told his tale with a voice that had no room for hope or fear-a cool, dead voice that spoke only of things ended.

II.
NIGHTFIRE

"In my father's house I was the second son. My brother was honored and trusted in all things. He was a prudent man and profitable to the household. All that he counselled was done, all that he wished he had. My place was a narrow one. There was neither honor nor joy in it, for it was filled with daily tasks and rebukes. No one cared for me. My mother sometimes wept when I was rebuked. Perhaps she was disappointed in me. But she had no power to make things better. I felt that I was a beast of burden, fed only in order that I might be useful; and the dull life irked me like an ill-fitting harness. There was nothing in it.

"I went to my father and claimed my share of the inheritance. He was rich. He gave it to me. It did not impoverish him and it made me free. I said to him 'Corban,' and shook the dust of Bethsaida from my feet.

"I went out to look for mirth and love and joy and all that is pleasant to the eyes and sweet to the taste. If a god made me, thought I, he made me to live, and the pride of life was strong in my heart and in my flesh. My vow was offered to that well-known god. I served him in Jerusalem, in Alexandria, in Rome, for his altars are everywhere and men worship him openly or in secret.

"My money and youth made me welcome to his followers, and I spent them both freely as if they could never come to an end. I clothed myself in purple and fine linen and fared sumptuously every day. The wine of Cyprus and the dishes of Egypt and Syria were on my table. My dwelling was crowded with merry guests. They came for what I gave them. Their faces were hungry and their soft touch was like the clinging of leeches. To them I was nothing but money and youth; no longer a beast of burden-a beast of pleasure. There was nothing in it.

"From the richest fare my heart went away empty, and after the wildest banquet my soul fell drunk and solitary into sleep.

"Then I thought, Power is better than pleasure. If a man will feast and revel let him do it with the great. They will favor him, and raise him up for the service that he renders them. He will obtain place and authority in the world and gain many friends. So I joined myself to Herod."

When the sad shepherd spoke this name his listeners drew back front him as if it were a defilement to hear it. They spat upon the ground and cursed the Idumean who called himself their king.

"A slave!" Jotham cried, "a bloody tyrant and a slave from Edom! A fox, a vile beast who devours his own children! God burn him in Gehenna."

The old Zadok picked up a stone and threw it into the darkness, saying slowly, "I cast this stone on the grave of the Idumean, the blasphemer, the defiler of the Temple! God send us soon the Deliverer, the Promised One, the true King of Israel!" Ammiel made no sign, but went on with his story.

"Herod used me well,-for his own purpose. He welcomed me to his palace and his table, and gave me a place among his favorites. He was so much my friend that he borrowed my money. There were many of the nobles of Jerusalem with him, Sad-ducees, and proselytes from Rome and Asia, and women from everywhere. The law of Israel was observed in the open court, when the people were watching. But in the secret feasts there was no law but the will of Herod, and many deities were served but no god was worshipped. There the captains and the princes of Rome consorted with the high-priest and his sons by night; and there was much coming and going by hidden ways. Everybody was a borrower or a lender, a buyer or a seller of favors. It was a house of diligent madness. There was nothing in it.

"In the midst of this whirling life a great need of love came upon me and I wished to hold some one in my inmost heart.

"At a certain place in the city, within closed doors, I saw a young slave-girl dancing. She was about fifteen years old, thin and supple; she danced like a reed in the wind; but her eyes were weary as death, and her white body was marked with bruises. She stumbled, and the men laughed at her. She fell, and her mistress beat her, crying out that she would fain be rid of such a heavy-footed slave. I paid the price and took her to my dwelling.

"Her name was Tamar. She was a daughter of Lebanon. I robed her in silk and broidered linen. I nourished her with tender care so that beauty came upon her like the blossoming of an almond tree; she was a garden enclosed, breathing spices. Her eyes were like doves behind her veil, her lips were a thread of scarlet, her neck was a tower of ivory, and her breasts were as two fawns which feed among the lilies. She was whiter than milk, and more rosy than the flower of the peach, and her dancing was like the flight of a bird among the branches. So I loved her.

"She lay in my bosom as a clear stone that one has bought and polished and set in fine gold at the end of a golden chain. Never was she glad at my coming or sorry at my going. Never did she give me anything except what I took from her. There was nothing in it.

"Now whether Herod knew of the jewel that I kept in my dwelling I cannot tell. It was sure that he had his spies in all the city, and himself walked the streets by night in a disguise. On a certain day he sent for me, and had me into his secret chamber, professing great love toward me and more confidence than in any man that lived. So I must go to Rome for him, bearing a sealed letter and a private message to Caesar. All my goods would be left safely in the hands of the king, my friend, who would reward me double. There was a certain place of high authority at Jerusalem which Caesar would gladly bestow on a Jew who had done him a service. This mission would commend me to him. It was a great occasion, suited to my powers. Thus Herod fed me with fair promises, and I ran his errand. There was nothing in it.

"I stood before Caesar and gave him the letter. He read it and laughed, saying that a prince with an incurable hunger is a servant of value to an emperor. Then he asked me if there was nothing sent with the letter. I answered that there was no gift, but a message for his private ear. He drew me aside and I told him that Herod begged earnestly that his dear son, Antipater, might be sent back in haste from Rome to Palestine, for the king had great need of him.

"At this Caesar laughed again. 'To bury him, I suppose,' said he, 'with his brothers, Alexander and Aristobulus! Truly, it is better to be Herod's swine than his son. Tell the old fox he may catch his own prey.' With this he turned from me and I withdrew unrewarded, to make my way back, as best I could with an empty purse, to Palestine. I had seen the Lord of the World. There was nothing in it.

"Selling my rings and bracelets I got passage in a trading ship for Joppa. There I heard that the king was not in Jerusalem, at his Palace of the Upper City, but had gone with his friends to make merry for a month on the Mountain of the Little Paradise. On that hill-top over against us, where the lights are flaring to-night, in the banquet-hall where couches are spread for a hundred guests, I found Herod."

The listening shepherds spat upon the ground again, and Jotham muttered, "May the worms that devour his flesh never die!" But Zadok whispered, "We wait for the Lord's salvation to come out of Zion." And the sad shepherd, looking with fixed eyes at the firelit mountain far away, continued his story:

"The king lay on his ivory couch, and the sweat of his disease was heavy upon him, for he was old, and his flesh was corrupted. But his hair and his beard were dyed and perfumed and there was a wreath of roses on his head. The hall was full of nobles and great men, the sons of the high-priest were there, and the servants poured their wine in cups of gold. There was a sound of soft music; and all the men were watching a girl who danced in the middle of the hall; and the eyes of Herod were fiery, like the eyes of a fox.

"The dancer was Tamar. She glistened like the snow on Lebanon, and the redness of her was ruddier than a pomegranate, and her dancing was like the coiling of white serpents. When the dance was ended her attendants threw a veil of gauze over her and she lay among her cushions, half covered with flowers, at the feet of the king.

"Through the sound of clapping hands and shouting, two slaves led me behind the couch of Herod. His eyes narrowed as they fell upon me. I told him the message of Caesar, making it soft, as if it were a word that suffered him to catch his prey. He stroked his beard softly and his look fell on Tamar. 'I have caught it,' he murmured; 'by all the gods, I have always caught it. And my dear son, Antipater, is coming home of his own will. I have lured him, he is mine.'

"Then a look of madness crossed his face and he sprang up, with frothing lips, and struck at me. 'What is this,' he cried, 'a spy, a servant of my false son, a traitor in my banquet-hall! Who are you?' I knelt before him, protesting that he must know me; that I was his friend, his messenger; that I had left all my goods in his hands; that the girl who had danced for him was mine. At this his face changed again and he fell back on his couch, shaken with horrible laughter. 'Yours!' he cried, 'when was she yours? What is yours? I know you now, poor madman. You are Ammiel, a crazy shepherd from Galilee, who troubled us some time since. Take him away, slaves. He has twenty sheep and twenty goats among my flocks at the foot of the mountain. See to it that he gets them, and drive him away.'

"I fought against the slaves with my bare hands, but they held me. I called to Tamar, begging her to have pity on me, to speak for me, to come with me. She looked up with her eyes like doves behind her veil, but there was no knowledge of me in them. She laughed lazily, as if it were a poor comedy, and flung a broken rose-branch in my face. Then the silver cord was loosened within me, and my heart went out, and I struggled no more. There was nothing in it.

"Afterward I found myself on the road with this flock. I led them past Hebron into the south country, and so by the Vale of Eshcol, and over many hills beyond the Pools of Solomon, until my feet brought me to your fire. Here I rest on the way to nowhere."

He sat silent, and the four shepherds looked at him with amazement.

"It is a bitter tale," said Shama, "and you are a great sinner."

"I should be a fool not to know that," answered the sad shepherd, "but the knowledge does me no good."

"You must repent," said Nathan, the youngest shepherd, in a friendly voice.

"How can a man repent," answered the sad shepherd, "unless he has hope? But I am sorry for everything, and most of all for living."

"Would you not live to kill the fox Herod?" cried Jotham fiercely.

"Why should I let him out of the trap," answered the sad shepherd. "Is he not dying more slowly than I could kill him?"

"You must have faith in God," said Zadok earnestly and gravely.

"He is too far away."

"Then you must have love for your neighbor."

"He is too near. My confidence in man was like a pool by the wayside. It was shallow, but there was water in it, and sometimes a star shone there. Now the feet of many beasts have trampled through it, and the jackals have drunken of it, and there is no more water. It is dry and the mire is caked at the bottom. '

"Is there nothing good in the world?"

"There is pleasure, but I am sick of it. There is power, but I hate it. There is wisdom, but I mistrust it. Life is a game and every player is for his own hand. Mine is played. I have nothing to win or lose."

"You are young, you have many years to live."

"I am old, yet the days before me are too many."

"But you travel the road, you go forward. Do you hope for nothing?"

"I hope for nothing," said the sad shepherd. "Yet if one thing should come to me it might be the beginning of hope. If I saw in man or woman a deed of kindness without a selfish reason, and a proof of love gladly given for its own sake only, then might I turn my face toward that light. Till that comes, how can I have faith in God whom I have never seen? I have seen the world which he has made, and it brings me no faith. There is nothing in it."

"Ammiel-ben-Jochanan," said the old man sternly, "you are a son of Israel, and we have had compassion on you, according to the law. But you are an apostate, an unbeliever, and we can have no more fellowship with you, lest a curse come upon us. The company of the desperate brings misfortune. Go your way and depart from us, for our way is not yours."

So the sad shepherd thanked them for their entertainment, and took the little kid again in his arms, and went into the night, calling his flock. But the youngest shepherd Nathan followed him a few steps and said:

"There is a broken fold at the foot of the hill. It is old and small, but you may find a shelter there for your flock where the wind will not shake you. Go your way with God, brother, and see better days."

Then Ammiel went a little way down the hill and sheltered his flock in a corner of the crumbling walls. He lay among the sheep and the goats with his face upon his folded arms, and whether the time passed slowly or swiftly he did not know, for he slept.

He waked as Nathan came running and stumbling among the scattered stones.

"We have seen a vision," he cried, "a wonderful vision of angels. Did you not hear them? They sang loudly of the Hope of Israel. We are going to Bethlehem to see this thing which is come to pass. Come you and keep watch over our sheep while we are gone."

"Of angels I have seen and heard nothing," said Ammiel, "but I will guard your flocks with mine, since I am in debt to you for bread and fire."

So he brought the kid in his arms, and the weary flock straggling after him, to the south wall of the great fold again, and sat there by the embers at the foot of the tower, while the others were away. The moon rested like a ball on the edge of the western hills and rolled behind them. The stars faded in the east and the fires went out on the Mountain of the Little Paradise. Over the hills of Moab a gray flood of dawn rose slowly, and arrows of red shot far up before the sunrise.

The shepherds returned full of joy and told what they had seen.

"It was even as the angels said unto us," said Shama, "and it must be true. The King of Israel has come. The faithful shall be blessed."

"Herod shall fall," cried Jotham, lifting his clenched fist toward the dark peaked mountain. "Burn, black Idumean, in the bottomless pit, where the fire is not quenched."

Zadok spoke more quietly. "We found the new-born child of whom the angels told us wrapped in swaddling clothes and lying in a manger. The ways of God are wonderful. His salvation comes out of darkness, and we trust in the promised deliverance. But you, Ammiel-ben-Jochanan, except you believe, you shall not see it. Yet since you have kept our flocks faithfully, and because of the joy that has come to us, I give you this piece of silver to help you on your way."

But Nathan came close to the sad shepherd and touched him on the shoulder with a friendly hand, "Go you also to Bethlehem," he said in a low voice, "for it is good to see what we have seen, and we will keep your flock until you return."

"I will go," said Ammiel, looking into his face, "for I think you wish me well. But whether I shall see what you have seen, or whether I shall ever return, I know not. Farewell."

III.
DAWN

The narrow streets of Bethlehem were waking to the first stir of life as the sad shepherd came into the town with the morning, and passed through them like one walking in his sleep.

The court-yard of the great khan and the open rooms around it were crowded with travelers, rousing them from their night's rest and making ready for the day's journey. In front of the stables half hollowed in the rock beside the inn, men were saddling their horses and their beasts of burden, and there was much noise and confusion.

But beyond these, at the end of the line, there was a deeper grotto in the rock, which was used only when the nearer stalls were full. At the entrance of this an ass was tethered, and a man of middle age stood in the doorway.

The sad shepherd saluted him and told his name.

"I am Joseph the carpenter of Nazareth," replied the man. "Have you also seen the angels of whom your brother shepherds came to tell us?"

"I have seen no angels," answered Ammiel, "nor have I any brothers among the shepherds. But I would fain see what they have seen."

"It is our first-born son," said Joseph, "and the Most High has sent him to us. He is a marvellous child: great things are foretold of him. You may go in, but quietly, for the child and his mother Mary are asleep."

So the sad shepherd went in quietly. His long shadow entered before him, for the sunrise was flowing into the door of the grotto. It was made clean and put in order, and a bed of straw was laid in the corner on the ground.

The child was asleep, but the young mother was waking, for she had taken him from the manger into her lap, where her maiden veil of white was spread to receive him. And she was singing very softly as she bent over him in wonder and content.

Ammiel saluted her and kneeled down to look at the child. He saw nothing different from other young children. The mother waited for him to speak of angels, as the other shepherds had done. The sad shepherd did not speak, but only looked. And as he looked his face changed.

"You have suffered pain and danger and sorrow for his sake," he said gently.

"They are past," she answered, "and for his sake I have suffered them gladly."

"He is very little and helpless; you must bear many troubles for his sake."

"To care for him is my joy, and to bear him lightens my burden."

"He does not know you, he can do nothing for you."

"But I know him. I have carried him under my heart, he is my son and my king."

"Why do you love him?"

The mother looked up at the sad shepherd with a great reproach in her soft eyes. Then her look grew pitiful as it rested on his face.

"You are a sorrowful man," she said.

"I am a wicked man," he answered.

She shook her head gently.

"I know nothing of that," she said, "but you must be very sorrowful, since you are born of a woman and yet you ask a mother why she loves her child. I love him for love's sake, because God has given him to me."

So the mother Mary leaned over her little son again and began to croon a song as if she were alone with him.

But Ammiel was still there, watching and thinking and beginning to remember. It came back to him that there was a woman in Galilee who had wept when he was rebuked; whose eyes had followed him when he was unhappy, as if she longed to do something for him; whose voice had broken and dropped silent while she covered her tear-stained face when he went away.

His thoughts flowed swiftly and silently toward her and after her like rapid waves of light. There was a thought of her bending over a little child in her lap, singing softly for pure joy,-and the child was himself. There was a thought of her lifting a little child to the breast that had borne him as a burden and a pain, to nourish him there as a comfort and a treasure,-and the child was himself. There was a thought of her watching and tending and guiding a little child from day to day, from year to year, putting tender arms around him, bending over his first wavering steps, rejoicing in his joys, wiping away the tears from his eyes, as he had never tried to wipe her tears away,-and the child was himself. She had done everything for the child's sake, but what had the child done for her sake? And the child was himself: that was what he had come to,-after the nightfire had burned out, after the darkness had grown thin and melted in the thoughts that pulsed through it like rapid waves of light,-that was what he had come to in the early morning: himself, a child in his mother's arms.

Then he arose and went out of the grotto softly, making the threefold sign of reverence; and the eyes of Mary followed him with kind looks.

Joseph of Nazareth was still waiting outside the door.

"How was it that you did not see the angels?" he asked. "Were you not with the other shepherds?"

"No," answered Ammiel, "I was asleep. But I have seen the mother and the child. Blessed be the house that holds them."

"You are strangely clad for a shepherd," said Joseph. "Where do you come from?"

"From a far country," replied Ammiel; "from a country that you have never visited."

"Where are you going now?" asked Joseph.

"I am going home," answered Ammiel, "to my mother's and my father's house in Galilee."

"Go in peace, friend," said Joseph.

And the sad shepherd took up his battered staff, and went on his way rejoicing.

The Lost Word
I
THE POVERTY OF HERMAS

"COME down, Hermas, come down! The night is past. It is time to be stirring. Christ is born to-day. Peace be with you in His name. Make haste and come down!"

A little group of young men were standing in a street of Antioch, in the dusk of early morning, fifteen hundred years ago. It was a class of candidates who had nearly finished their two years of training for the Christian church. They had come to call their fellow-student Hermas from his lodging.

Their voices rang out cheerily through the cool air. They were full of that glad sense of life which the young feel when they awake and come to rouse one who is still sleeping. There was a note of friendly triumph in their call, as if they were exulting unconsciously in having begun the adventure of the new day before their comrade.

But Hermas was not asleep. He had been waking for hours, and the dark walls of his narrow lodging had been a prison to his restless heart. A nameless sorrow and discontent had fallen upon him, and he could find no escape from the heaviness of his own thoughts.

There is a sadness of youth into which the old cannot enter. It seems to them unreal and causeless. But it is even more bitter and burdensome than the sadness of age. There is a sting of resentment in it, a fever of angry surprise that the world should so soon be a disappointment, and life so early take on the look of a failure. It has little reason in it, perhaps, but it has all the more weariness and gloom, because the man who is oppressed by it feels dimly that it is an unnatural and an unreasonable thing, that he should be separated from the joy of his companions, and tired of living before he has fairly begun to live.

Hermas had fallen into the very depths of this strange self-pity. He was out of tune with everything around him. He had been thinking, through the dead, still night, of all that he had given up when he left the house of his father, the wealthy pagan Demetrius, to join the company of the Christians. Only two years ago he had been one of the richest young men in Antioch. Now he was one of the poorest. And the worst of it was that, though he had made the choice willingly and accepted the sacrifice with a kind of enthusiasm, he was already dissatisfied with it.

The new life was no happier than the old. He was weary of vigils and fasts, weary of studies and penances, weary of prayers and sermons. He felt like a slave in a treadmill. He knew that he must go on. His honour, his conscience, his sense of duty, bound him. He could not go back to the old careless pagan life again; for something had happened within him which made a return impossible. Doubtless he had found the true religion, but he had found it only as a task and a burden; its joy and peace had slipped away from him.

He felt disillusioned and robbed. He sat beside his hard little couch, waiting without expectancy for the gray dawn of another empty day, and hardly lifting his head at the shouts of his friends.

"Come down, Hermas, you sluggard! Come down! It is Christmas morn. Awake and be glad with us!"

"I am coming," he answered listlessly; "only have patience a moment. I have been awake since midnight, and waiting for the day."

"You hear him!" said his friends one to another. "How he puts us all to shame! He is more watchful, more eager, than any of us. Our master, John the Presbyter, does well to be proud of him. He is the best man in our class. When he is baptized the church will get a strong member."

While they were talking the door opened and Hermas stepped out. He was a figure to be remarked in any company—tall, broad-shouldered, straight-hipped, with a head proudly poised on the firm column of the neck, and short brown curls clustering over the square forehead. It was the perpetual type of vigourous and intelligent young manhood, such as may be found in every century among the throngs of ordinary men, as if to show what the flower of the race should be. But the light in his dark blue eyes was clouded and uncertain; his smooth cheeks were leaner than they should have been at twenty; and there were downward lines about his mouth which spoke of desires unsatisfied and ambitions repressed. He joined his companions with brief greetings,—a nod to one, a word to another,—and they passed together down the steep street.

Overhead the mystery of daybreak was silently transfiguring the sky. The curtain of darkness had lifted softly upward along the edge of the horizon. The ragged crests of Mount Silpius were outlined with pale rosy light. In the central vault of heaven a few large stars twinkled drowsily. The great city, still chiefly pagan, lay more than half asleep. But multitudes of the Christians, dressed in white and carrying lighted torches in their hands, were hurrying toward the Basilica of Constantine to keep the latest holy day of the church, the new festival of the birthday of their Master.

The vast, bare building was soon crowded, and the younger converts, who were not yet permitted to stand among the baptized, found it difficult to come to their appointed place between the first two pillars of the house, just within the threshold. There was some good-humoured pressing and jostling about the door; but the candidates pushed steadily forward.

"By your leave, friends, our station is beyond you. Will you let us pass? Many thanks."

A touch here, a courteous nod there, a little patience, a little persistence, and at last they stood in their place. Hermas was taller than his companions; he could look easily over their heads and survey the white sea of people stretching away through the columns, under the shadows of the high roof, as the tide spreads on a calm day into the pillared cavern of Staffa, quiet as if the ocean hardly dared to breathe. The light of many flambeaux fell, in flickering, uncertain rays, over the assembly. At the end of the vista there was a circle of clearer, steadier radiance. Hermas could see the bishop in his great chair, surrounded by the presbyters, the lofty desks on either side for the readers of the Scripture, the communion-table and the table of offerings in the middle of the church.

The call to prayer sounded down the long aisle. Thousands of hands were joyously lifted in the air, as if the sea had blossomed into waving lilies, and the "Amen" was like the murmur of countless ripples in an echoing place.

Then the singing began, led by the choir of a hundred trained voices which the Bishop Paul had founded in Antioch. Timidly, at first, the music felt its way, as the people joined with a broken and uncertain cadence, the mingling of many little waves not yet gathered into rhythm and harmony. Soon the longer, stronger billows of song rolled in, sweeping from side to side as the men and the women answered in the clear antiphony.

Hermas had often been carried on those "Tides of music's golden sea Setting toward eternity." But to-day his heart was a rock that stood motionless. The flood passed by and left him unmoved.

Looking out from his place at the foot of the pillar, he saw a man standing far off in the lofty bema. Short and slender, wasted by sickness, gray before his time, with pale cheeks and wrinkled brow, he seemed at first like a person of no significance—a reed shaken in the wind. But there was a look in his deep-set, poignant eyes, as he gathered all the glances of the multitude to himself, that belied his mean appearance and prophesied power. Hermas knew very well who it was: the man who had drawn him from his father's house, the teacher who was instructing him as a son in the Christian faith, the guide and trainer of his soul—John of Antioch, whose fame filled the city and began to overflow Asia, and who was called already Chrysostom, the golden-mouthed preacher.

Hermas had felt the magic of his eloquence many a time; and to-day, as the tense voice vibrated through the stillness, and the sentences moved onward, growing fuller and stronger, bearing argosies of costly rhetoric and treasures of homely speech in their bosom, and drawing the hearts of men with a resistless magic, Hermas knew that the preacher had never been more potent, more inspired.

He played on that immense congregation as a master on an instrument. He rebuked their sins, and they trembled. He touched their sorrows, and they wept. He spoke of the conflicts, the triumphs, the glories of their faith, and they broke out in thunders of applause. He hushed them into reverent silence, and led them tenderly, with the wise men of the East, to the lowly birthplace of Jesus.

"Do thou, therefore, likewise leave the Jewish people, the troubled city, the bloodthirsty tyrant, the pomp of the world, and hasten to Bethlehem, the sweet house of spiritual bread. For though thou be but a shepherd, and come hither, thou shalt behold the young Child in an inn. Though thou be a king, and come not hither, thy purple robe shall profit thee nothing. Though thou be one of the wise men, this shall be no hindrance to thee. Only let thy coming be to honour and adore, with trembling joy, the Son of God, to whose name be glory, on this His birthday, and forever and forever."

The soul of Hermas did not answer to the musician's touch. The strings of his heart were slack and soundless; there was no response within him. He was neither shepherd, nor king, nor wise man, only an unhappy, dissatisfied, questioning youth. He was out of sympathy with the eager preacher, the joyous hearers. In their harmony he had no part. Was it for this that he had forsaken his inheritance and narrowed his life to poverty and hardship? What was it all worth?

The gracious prayers with which the young converts were blessed and dismissed before the sacrament sounded hollow in his ears. Never had he felt so utterly lonely as in that praying throng. He went out with his companions like a man departing from a banquet where all but he had been fed.

"Farewell, Hermas," they cried, as he turned from them at the door. But he did not look back, nor wave his hand. He was alone already in his heart.

When he entered the broad Avenue of the Colonnades, the sun had already topped the eastern hills, and the ruddy light was streaming through the long double row of archways and over the pavements of crimson marble. But Hermas turned his back to the morning, and walked with his shadow before him.

The street began to swarm and whirl and quiver with the motley life of a huge city: beggars and jugglers, dancers and musicians, gilded youths in their chariots, and daughters of joy looking out from their windows, all intoxicated with the mere delight of living and the gladness of a new day. The pagan populace of Antioch—reckless, pleasure-loving, spendthrift—were preparing for the Saturnalia. But all this Hermas had renounced. He cleft his way through the crowd slowly, like a reluctant swimmer weary of breasting the tide.

At the corner of the street where the narrow, populous Lane of the Camel-drivers crossed the Colonnades, a story-teller had bewitched a circle of people around him. It was the same old tale of love and adventure that many generations have listened to; but the lively fancy of the hearers lent it new interest, and the wit of the improviser drew forth sighs of interest and shouts of laughter.

A yellow-haired girl on the edge of the throng turned, as Hermas passed, and smiled in his face. She put out her hand and caught him by the sleeve.

"Stay," she said, "and laugh a bit with us. I know who you are—the son of Demetrius. You must have bags of gold. Why do you look so black? Love is alive yet."

Hermas shook off her hand, but not ungently.

"I don't know what you mean," he said. "You are mistaken in me. I am poorer than you are."

But as he passed on, he felt the warm touch of her fingers through the cloth on his arm. It seemed as if she had plucked him by the heart.

He went out by the Western Gate, under the golden cherubim that the Emperor Titus had stolen from the ruined Temple of Jerusalem and fixed upon the arch of triumph. He turned to the left, and climbed the hill to the road that led to the Grove of Daphne.

In all the world there was no other highway as beautiful. It wound for five miles along the foot of the mountains, among gardens and villas, plantations of myrtles and mulberries, with wide outlooks over the valley of Orontes and the distant, shimmering sea.

The richest of all the dwellings was the House of the Golden Pillars, the mansion of Demetrius. He had won the favor of the apostate Emperor Julian, whose vain efforts to restore the worship of the heathen gods, some twenty years ago, had opened an easy way to wealth and power for all who would mock and oppose Christianity. Demetrius was not a sincere fanatic like his royal master; but he was bitter enough in his professed scorn of the new religion, to make him a favourite at the court where the old religion was in fashion. He had reaped a rich reward of his policy, and a strange sense of consistency made him more fiercely loyal to it than if it had been a real faith. He was proud of being called "the friend of Julian"; and when his son joined himself to the Christians, and acknowledged the unseen God, it seemed like an insult to his father's success. He drove the boy from his door and disinherited him.

The glittering portico of the serene, haughty house, the repose of the well-ordered garden, still blooming with belated flowers, seemed at once to deride and to invite the young outcast plodding along the dusty road. "This is your birthright," whispered the clambering rose-trees by the gate; and the closed portals of carven bronze said: "You have sold it for a thought—a dream."

II
A CHRISTMAS LOSS

HERMAS found the Grove of Daphne quite deserted. There was no sound in the enchanted vale but the rustling of the light winds chasing each other through the laurel thickets, and the babble of innumerable streams. Memories of the days and nights of delicate pleasure that the grove had often seen still haunted the bewildered paths and broken fountains. At the foot of a rocky eminence, crowned with the ruins of Apollo's temple, which had been mysteriously destroyed by fire just after Julian had restored and reconsecrated it, Hermas sat down beside a gushing spring, and gave himself up to sadness.

"How beautiful the world would be, how joyful, how easy to live in, without religion. These questions about unseen things, perhaps about unreal things, these restraints and duties and sacrifices—if I were only free from them all, and could only forget them all, then I could live my life as I pleased, and be happy."

"Why not?" said a quiet voice at his back.

He turned, and saw an old man with a long beard and a threadbare cloak (the garb affected by the pagan philosophers) standing behind him and smiling curiously.

"How is it that you answer that which has not been spoken?" said Hermas; "and who are you that honour me with your company?"

"Forgive the intrusion," answered the stranger; "it is not ill meant. A friendly interest is as good as an introduction."

"But to what singular circumstance do I owe this interest?"

"To your face," said the old man, with a courteous inclination. "Perhaps also a little to the fact that I am the oldest inhabitant here, and feel as if all visitors were my guests, in a way."

"Are you, then, one of the keepers of the grove? And have you given up your work with the trees to take a holiday as a philosopher?"

"Not at all. The robe of philosophy is a mere affectation, I must confess. I think little of it. My profession is the care of altars. In fact, I am that solitary priest of Apollo whom the Emperor Julian found here when he came to revive the worship of the grove, some twenty years ago. You have heard of the incident?"

"Yes," said Hermas, beginning to be interested; "the whole city must have heard of it, for it is still talked of. But surely it was a strange sacrifice that you brought to celebrate the restoration of Apollo's temple?"

"You mean the goose? Well, perhaps it was not precisely what the emperor expected. But it was all that I had, and it seemed to me not inappropriate. You will agree to that if you are a Christian, as I guess from your dress."

"You speak lightly for a priest of Apollo."

"Oh, as for that, I am no bigot. The priesthood is a professional matter, and the name of Apollo is as good as any other. How many altars do you think there have been in this grove?"

"I do not know."

"Just four-and-twenty, including that of the martyr Babylas, whose ruined chapel you see just beyond us. I have had something to do with most of them in my time. They—are transitory. They give employment to care-takers for a while. But the thing that lasts, and the thing that interests me, is the human life that plays around them. The game has been going on for centuries. It still disports itself very pleasantly on summer evenings through these shady walks.

Believe me, for I know. Daphne and Apollo were shadows. But the flying maidens and the pursuing lovers, the music and the dances, these are the realities. Life is the game, and the world keeps it up merrily. But you? You are of a sad countenance for one so young and so fair. Are you a loser in the game?"

The words and tone of the speaker fitted Hermas' mood as a key fits the lock. He opened his heart to the old man, and told him the story of his life: his luxurious boyhood in his father's house; the irresistible spell which compelled him to forsake it when he heard John's preaching of the new religion; his lonely year with the anchorites among the mountains; the strict discipline in his teacher's house at Antioch; his weariness of duty, his distaste for poverty, his discontent with worship.

"And to-day," said he, "I have been thinking that I am a fool. My life is swept as bare as a hermit's cell. There is nothing in it but a dream, a thought of God, which does not satisfy me."

The singular smile deepened on his companion's face. "You are ready, then," he suggested, "to renounce your new religion and go back to that of your father?"

"No; I renounce nothing, I accept nothing. I do not wish to think about it. I only wish to live."

"A very reasonable wish, and I think you are about to see its accomplishment. Indeed, I may even say that I can put you in the way of securing it. Do you believe in magic?"

"I have told you already that I do not know whether I believe in anything. This is not a day on which I care to make professions of faith. I believe in what I see. I want what will give me pleasure."

"Well," said the old man, soothingly, as he plucked a leaf from the laurel-tree above them and dipped it in the spring, "let us dismiss the riddles of belief. I like them as little as you do. You know this is a Castalian fountain. The Emperor Hadrian once read his fortune here from a leaf dipped in the water. Let us see what this leaf tells us. It is already turning yellow. How do you read that?"

"Wealth," said Hermas, laughing, as he looked at his mean garments.

"And here is a bud on the stem that seems to be swelling. What is that?"

"Pleasure," answered Hermas, bitterly.

"And here is a tracing of wreaths upon the surface. What do you make of that?"

"What you will," said Hermas, not even taking the trouble to look. "Suppose we say success and fame?"

"Yes," said the stranger; "it is all written here. I promise that you shall enjoy it all. But you do not need to believe in my promise. I am not in the habit of requiring faith of those whom I would serve. No such hard conditions for me! There is only one thing that I ask. This is the season that you Christians call the Christmas, and you have taken up the pagan custom of exchanging gifts. Well, if I give to you, you must give to me. It is a small thing, and really the thing you can best afford to part with: a single word—the name of Him you profess to worship. Let me take that word and all that belongs to it entirely out of your life, so that you shall never need to hear it or speak it again. You will be richer without it. I promise you everything, and this is all I ask in return. Do you consent?"

"Yes, I consent," said Hermas, mocking. "If you can take your price, a word, you can keep your promise, a dream."

The stranger laid the long, cool, wet leaf softly across the young man's eyes. An icicle of pain darted through them; every nerve in his body was drawn together there in a knot of agony.

Then all the tangle of pain seemed to be lifted out of him. A cool languor of delight flowed back through every vein, and he sank into a profound sleep.

III
PARTING, BUT NO FAREWELL

THERE is a slumber so deep that it annihilates time. It is like a fragment of eternity. Beneath its enchantment of vacancy, a day seems like a thousand years, and a thousand years might well pass as one day.

It was such a sleep that fell upon Hermas in the Grove of Daphne. An immeasurable period, an interval of life so blank and empty that he could not tell whether it was long or short, had passed over him when his senses began to stir again. The setting sun was shooting arrows of gold under the glossy laurel-leaves. He rose and stretched his arms, grasping a smooth branch above him and shaking it, to make sure that he was alive. Then he hurried back toward Antioch, treading lightly as if on air.

The ground seemed to spring beneath his feet. Already his life had changed, he knew not how. Something that did not belong to him had dropped away; he had returned to a former state of being. He felt as if anything might happen to him, and he was ready for anything. He was a new man, yet curiously familiar to himself—as if he had done with playing a tiresome part and returned to his natural state. He was buoyant and free, without a care, a doubt, a fear.

As he drew near to his father's house he saw a confusion of servants in the porch, and the old steward ran down to meet him at the gate.

"Lord, we have been seeking you everywhere. The master is at the point of death, and has sent for you. Since the sixth hour he calls your name continually. Come to him quickly, lord, for I fear the time is short."

Hermas entered the house at once; nothing could amaze him to-day. His father lay on an ivory couch in the inmost chamber, with shrunken face and restless eyes, his lean fingers picking incessantly at the silken coverlet.

"My son!" he murmured; "Hermas, my son! It is good that you have come back to me. I have missed you. I was wrong to send you away. You shall never leave me again. You are my son, my heir. I have changed everything. Hermas, my son, come nearer—close beside me. Take my hand, my son!"

The young man obeyed, and, kneeling by the couch, gathered his father's cold, twitching fingers in his firm, warm grasp.

"Hermas, life is passing—long, rich, prosperous; the last sands, I—cannot stay them. My religion, a good policy—Julian was my friend. But now he is gone—where? My soul is empty—nothing beyond—very dark—I am afraid. But you know something better. You found something that made you willing to give up your life for it—it must have been almost like dying—yet you were happy. What was it you found? See, I am giving you everything. I have forgiven you. Now forgive me. Tell me, what is it? Your secret, your faith—give it to me before I go."

At the sound of this broken pleading a strange passion of pity and love took the young man by the throat. His voice shook a little as he answered eagerly:

"Father, there is nothing to forgive. I am your son; I will gladly tell, you all that I know. I will give you the secret of faith. Father, you must believe with all your heart, and soul, and strength in—"

Where was the word—the word that he had been used to utter night and morning, the word that had meant to him more than he had ever known? What had become of it?

He groped for it in the dark room of his mind. He had thought he could lay his hand upon it in a moment, but it was gone. Some one had taken it away. Everything else was most clear to him: the terror of death; the lonely soul appealing from his father's eyes; the instant need of comfort and help. But at the one point where he looked for help he could find nothing; only an empty space. The word of hope had vanished. He felt for it blindly and in desperate haste.

"Father, wait! I have forgotten something—it has slipped away from me. I shall find it in a moment. There is hope—I will tell you presently—oh, wait!"

The bony hand gripped his like a vice; the glazed eyes opened wider. "Tell me," whispered the old man; "tell me quickly, for I must go."

The voice sank into a dull rattle. The fingers closed once more, and relaxed. The light behind the eyes went out.

Hermas, the master of the House of the Golden Pillars, was keeping watch by the dead.

IV
LOVE IN SEARCH OF A WORD

THE break with the old life was as clean as if it had been cut with a knife. Some faint image of a hermit's cell, a bare lodging in a back street of Antioch, a class-room full of earnest students, remained in Hermas' memory. Some dull echo of the voice of John the Presbyter, and the murmured sound of chanting, and the murmur of great congregations, still lingered in his ears; but it was like something that had happened to another person, something that he had read long ago, but of which he had lost the meaning.

His new life was full and smooth and rich—too rich for any sense of loss to make itself felt. There were a hundred affairs to busy him, and the days ran swiftly by as if they were shod with winged sandals.

Nothing needed to be considered, prepared for, begun. Everything was ready and waiting for him. All that he had to do was to go on with it. The estate of Demetrius was even greater than the world had supposed. There were fertile lands in Syria which the emperor had given him, marble-quarries in Phrygia, and forests of valuable timber in Cilicia; the vaults of the villa contained chests of gold and silver; the secret cabinets in the master's room were full of precious stones. The stewards were diligent and faithful. The servants of the magnificent household rejoiced at the young master's return. His table was spread; the rose-garland of pleasure was woven for his head, and his cup was already filled with the spicy wine of power.

The period of mourning for his father came at a fortunate moment, to seclude and safeguard him from the storm of political troubles and persecutions that fell upon Antioch after the insults offered by the mob to the imperial statues in the year 887. The friends of Demetrius, prudent and conservative persons, gathered around Hermas and made him welcome to their circle. Chief among them was Libanius, the sophist, his nearest neighbour, whose daughter Athenais had been the playmate of Hermas in the old days.

He had left her a child. He found her a beautiful woman. What transformation is so magical, so charming, as this? To see the uncertain lines of-youth rounded into firmness and symmetry, to discover the half-ripe, merry, changing face of the girl matured into perfect loveliness, and looking at you with calm, clear, serious eyes, not forgetting the past, but fully conscious of the changed present—this is to behold a miracle in the flesh.

"Where have you been, these two years?" said Athenais, as they walked together through the garden of lilies where they had so often played.

"In a land of tiresome dreams," answered Hermas; "but you have wakened me, and I am never going back again."

It was not to be supposed that the sudden disappearance of Hermas from among his former associates could long remain unnoticed. At first it was a mystery. There was a fear, for two or three days, that he might be lost. Some of his more intimate companions maintained that his devotion had led him out into the desert to join the anchorites. But the news of his return to the House of the Golden Pillars, and of his new life as its master, filtered quickly through the gossip of the city.

Then the church was filled with dismay and grief and reproach. Messengers and letters were sent to Hermas. They disturbed him a little, but they took no hold upon him. It seemed to him as if the messengers spoke in a strange language. As he read the letters there were words blotted out of the writing which made the full sense unintelligible.

His old companions came to reprove him for leaving them, to warn him of the peril of apostasy, to entreat him to return. It all sounded vague and futile. They spoke as if he had betrayed or offended some one; but when they came to name the object of his fear—the one whom he had displeased, and to whom he should return—he heard nothing; there was a blur of silence in their speech. The clock pointed to the hour, but the bell did not strike. At last Hermas refused to see them any more.

One day John the Presbyter stood in the atrium. Hermas was entertaining Libanius and Athenais in the banquet-hall. When the visit of the Presbyter was announced, the young master loosed a collar of gold and jewels from his neck, and gave it to his scribe.

"Take this to John of Antioch, and tell him it is a gift from his former pupil—as a token of remembrance, or to spend for the poor of the city. I will always send him what he wants, but it is idle for us to talk together any more. I do not understand what he says. I have not gone to the temple, nor offered sacrifice, nor denied his teaching. I have simply forgotten. I do not think about those things any longer. I am only living. A happy man wishes him all happiness and farewell."

But John let the golden collar fall on the marble floor. "Tell your master that we shall talk together again, after all," said he, as he passed sadly out of the hall.

The love of Athenais and Hermas was like a tiny rivulet that sinks out of sight in a cavern, but emerges again as a bright and brimming stream. The careless comradery of childhood was mysteriously changed into a complete companionship.

When Athenais entered the House of the Golden Pillars as a bride, all the music of life came with her. Hermas called the feast of her welcome "the banquet of the full chord." Day after day, night after night, week after week, month after month, the bliss of the home unfolded like a rose of a thousand leaves. When a child came to them, a strong, beautiful boy, worthy to be the heir of such a house, the heart of the rose was filled with overflowing fragrance. Happiness was heaped upon happiness. Every wish brought its own accomplishment. Wealth, honour, beauty, peace, love—it was an abundance of felicity so great that the soul of Hermas could hardly contain it.

Strangely enough, it began to press upon him, to trouble him with the very excess of joy. He felt as if there were something yet needed to complete and secure it all. There was an urgency within him, a longing to find some outlet for his feelings, he knew not how—some expression and culmination of his happiness, he knew not what.

Under his joyous demeanour a secret fire of restlessness began to burn—an expectancy of something yet to come which should put the touch of perfection on his life. He spoke of it to Athenais, as they sat together, one summer evening, in a bower of jasmine, with their boy playing at their feet. There had been music in the garden; but now the singers and lute-players had withdrawn, leaving the master and mistress alone in the lingering twilight, tremulous with inarticulate melody of unseen birds. There was a secret voice in the hour seeking vainly for utterance—a word waiting to be spoken at the centre of the charm.

"How deep is our happiness, my beloved!" said Hermas; "deeper than the sea that slumbers yonder, below the city. And yet I feel it is not quite full and perfect. There is a depth of joy that we have not yet known—a repose of happiness that is still beyond us. What is it? I have no superstitious fears, like the king who cast his signet-ring into the sea because he dreaded that some secret vengeance would fall on his unbroken good fortune. That was an idle terror. But there is something that oppresses me like an invisible burden. There is something still undone, unspoken, unfelt—something that we need to complete everything. Have you not felt it, too? Can you not lead me to it?"

"Yes," she answered, lifting her eyes to his face; "I, too, have felt it, Hermas, this burden, this need, this unsatisfied longing. I think I know what it means. It is gratitude—the language of the heart, the music of happiness. There is no perfect joy without gratitude. But we have never learned it, and the want of it troubles us. It is like being dumb with a heart full of love. We must find the word for it, and say it together. Then we shall be perfectly joined in perfect joy. Come, my dear lord, let us take the boy with us, and give thanks."

Hermas lifted the child in his arms, and turned with Athenais into the depth of the garden. There was a dismantled shrine of some forgotten fashion of worship half hidden among the luxuriant flowers. A fallen image lay beside it, face downward in the grass. They stood there, hand in hand, the boy drowsily resting on his father's shoulder—a threefold harmony of strength and beauty and innocence.

Silently the roseate light caressed the tall spires of the cypress-trees; silently the shadows gathered at their feet; silently the crystal stars looked out from the deepening arch of heaven. The very breath of being paused. It was the hour of culmination, the supreme moment of felicity waiting for its crown. The tones of Hermas were clear and low as he began, half speaking and half chanting, in the rhythm of an ancient song:

"Fair is the world, the sea, the sky, the double kingdom of day and night, in the glow of morning, in the shadow of evening, and under the dripping light of stars.

"Fairer still is life in our breasts, with its manifold music and meaning, with its wonder of seeing and hearing and feeling and knowing and being.

"Fairer and still more fair is love, that draws us together, mingles our lives in its flow, and bears them along like a river, strong and clear and swift, rejecting the stars in its bosom.

"Wide is our world; we are rich; we have all things. Life is abundant within us—a measureless deep. Deepest of all is our love, and it longs to speak.

"Come, thou final word! Come, thou crown of speech! Come, thou charm of peace! Open the gates of our hearts. Lift the weight of our joy and bear it upward.

"For all good gifts, for all perfect gifts, for love, for life, for the world, we praise, we bless, we thank—"

As a soaring bird, struck by an arrow, falls headlong from the sky, so the song of Hermas fell. At the end of his flight of gratitude there was nothing—a blank, a hollow space.

He looked for a face, and saw a void. He sought for a hand, and clasped vacancy. His heart was throbbing and swelling with passion; the bell swung to and fro within him, beating from side to side as if it would burst; but not a single note came from it. All the fulness of his feeling, that had risen upward like a living fountain, fell back from the empty sky, as cold as snow, as hard as hail, frozen and dead. There was no meaning in his happiness. No one had sent it to him. There was no one to thank for it. His felicity was a closed circle, a wall of eternal ice.

"Let us go back," he said sadly to Athenais; "the child is heavy upon my shoulder. We will lay him to sleep, and go into the library. The air grows chilly. We were mistaken. The gratitude of life is only a dream. There is no one to thank."

And in the garden it was already night.

V
RICHES WITHOUT REST

NO outward change came to the House of the Golden Pillars. Everything moved as smoothly, as delicately, as prosperously, as before. But inwardly there was a subtle, inexplicable transformation. A vague discontent—a final and inevitable sense of incompleteness, overshadowed existence from that night when Hermas realized that his joy could never go beyond itself.

The next morning the old man whom he had seen in the Grove of Daphne, but never since, appeared mysteriously at the door of the house, as if he had been sent for, and entered, to dwell there like an invited guest.

Hermas could not but make him welcome, and at first he tried to regard him with reverence and affection as the one through whom fortune had come. But it was impossible. There was a chill in the inscrutable smile of Marcion, as he called himself, that seemed to mock at reverence. He was in the house as one watching a strange experiment—tranquil, interested, ready to supply anything that might be needed for its completion, but thoroughly indifferent to the feelings of the subject; an anatomist of life, looking curiously to see how long it would continue, and how it would behave, after the heart had been removed.

In his presence Hermas was conscious of a certain irritation, a resentful anger against the calm, frigid scrutiny of the eyes that followed him everywhere, like a pair of spies, peering out over the smiling mouth and the long white beard.

"Why do you look at me so curiously?" asked Hermas, one morning, as they sat together in the library. "Do you see anything strange in me?"

"No," answered Marcion; "something familiar."

"And what is that?"

"A singular likeness to a discontented young man that I met some years ago in the Grove of Daphne."

"But why should that interest you? Surely it was to be expected."

"A thing that we expect often surprises us when we see it. Besides, my curiosity is piqued. I suspect you of keeping a secret from me."

"You are jesting with me. There is nothing in my life that you do not know. What is the secret?"

"Nothing more than the wish to have one. You are growing tired of your bargain. The game wearies you. That is foolish. Do you want to try a new part?"

The question was like a mirror upon which one comes suddenly in a half-lighted room, A quick illumination falls on it, and the passer-by is startled by the look of his own face.

"You are right," said Hermas. "I am tired. We have been going on stupidly in this house, as if nothing were possible but what my father had done before me. There is nothing original in being rich, and well fed, and well dressed. Thousands of men have tried it, and have not been very well satisfied. Let us do something new. Let us make a mark in the world."

"It is well said," nodded the old man; "you are speaking again like a man after my own heart. There is no folly but the loss of an opportunity to enjoy a new sensation."

From that day Hermas seemed to be possessed with a perpetual haste, an uneasiness that left him no repose. The summit of life had been attained, the highest possible point of felicity. Henceforward the course could only be at a level—perhaps downward. It might be brief; at the best it could not be very long. It was madness to lose a day, an hour. That would be the only fatal mistake: to forfeit anything of the bargain that he had made. He would have it, and hold it, and enjoy it all to the full. The world might have nothing better to give than it had already given; but surely it had many things that were new to bestow upon him, and Marcion should help him to find them.

Under his learned counsel the House of the Golden Pillars took on a new magnificence. Artists were brought from Corinth and Rome and Byzantium to adorn it with splendour. Its fame glittered around the world. Banquets of incredible luxury drew the most celebrated guests into its triclinium, and filled them with envious admiration. The bees swarmed and buzzed about the golden hive. The human insects, gorgeous moths of pleasure and greedy flies of appetite, parasites and flatterers and crowds of inquisitive idlers, danced and fluttered in the dazzling light that surrounded Hermas.

Everything that he touched prospered. He bought a tract of land in the Caucasus, and emeralds were discovered among the mountains. He sent a fleet of wheat-ships to Italy, and the price of grain doubled while it was on the way. He sought political favour with the emperor, and was rewarded with the governorship of the city. His name was a word to conjure with.

The beauty of Athenais lost nothing with the passing seasons, but grew more perfect, even under the inexplicable shade of dissatisfaction that sometimes veiled it as a translucent cloud that passes before the full moon. "Fair as the wife of Hermas" was a proverb in Antioch; and soon men began to add to it, "Beautiful as the son of Hermas"; for the child developed swiftly in that favouring clime. At nine years of age he was straight and strong, firm of limb and clear of eye. His brown head was on a level with his father's heart. He was the jewel of the House of the Golden Pillars; the pride of Hermas, the new Fortunatus.

That year another drop of success fell into his brimming cup. His black Numidian horses, which he had been training for three years for the world-renowned chariot-races of Antioch, won the victory over a score of rivals. Hermas received the prize carelessly from the judge's hands, and turned to drive once more around the circus, to show himself to the people. He lifted the eager boy into the chariot beside him to share his triumph.

Here, indeed, was the glory of his life—this matchless son, his brighter counterpart carved in breathing ivory, touching his arm, and balancing himself proudly on the swaying floor of the chariot. As the horses pranced around the ring, a great shout of applause filled the amphitheatre, and thousands of spectators waved their salutations of praise: "Hail, fortunate Hermas, master of success! Hail, little Hermas, prince of good luck!"

The sudden tempest of acclamation, the swift fluttering of innumerable garments in the air, startled the horses. They dashed violently forward, and plunged upon the bits. The left rein broke. They swerved to the right, swinging the chariot sideways with a grating noise, and dashing it against the stone parapet of the arena. In an instant the wheel was shattered. The axle struck the ground, and the chariot was dragged onward, rocking and staggering.

By a strenuous effort Hermas kept his place on the frail platform, clinging to the unbroken rein. But the boy was tossed lightly from his side at the first shock. His head struck the wall. And when Hermas turned to look for him, he was lying like a broken flower on the sand.

VI
GREAT FEAR AND RECOVERED JOY

THEY carried the boy in a litter to the House of the Golden Pillars, summoning the most skilful physician of Antioch to attend him. For hours the child was as quiet as death. Hermas watched the white eyelids, folded close like lily-buds at night, even as one watches for the morning. At last they opened; but the fire of fever was burning in the eyes, and the lips were moving in a wild delirium.

Hour after hour that sweet childish voice rang through the halls and chambers of the splendid, helpless house, now rising in shrill calls of distress and senseless laughter, now sinking in weariness and dull moaning. The stars waxed and waned; the sun rose and set; the roses bloomed and fell in the garden, the birds sang and slept among the jasmine-bowers. But in the heart of Hermas there was no song, no bloom, no light—only speechless anguish, and a certain fearful looking-for of desolation.

He was like a man in a nightmare. He saw the shapeless terror that was moving toward him, but he was impotent to stay or to escape it. He had done all that he could. There was nothing left but to wait.

He paced to and fro, now hurrying to the boy's bed as if he could not bear to be away from it, now turning back as if he could not endure to be near it. The people of the house, even Athenais, feared to speak to him, there was something so vacant and desperate in his face.

At nightfall, on the second of those eternal days, he shut himself in the library. The unfilled lamp had gone out, leaving a trail of smoke in the air. The sprigs of mignonette and rosemary, with which the room was sprinkled every day, were unrenewed, and scented the gloom with a close odor of decay. A costly manuscript of Theocritus was tumbled in disorder on the floor. Hermas sank into a chair like a man in whom the very spring of being is broken. Through the darkness some one drew near. He did not even lift his head. A hand touched him; a soft arm was laid over his shoulders. It was Athenais, kneeling beside him and speaking very low:

"Hermas—it is almost over—the child! His voice grows weaker hour by hour. He moans and calls for some one to help him; then he laughs. It breaks my heart. He has just fallen asleep. The moon is rising now. Unless a change comes he cannot last till sunrise. Is there nothing we can do? Is there no power that can save him? Is there no one to pity us and spare us? Let us call, let us beg for compassion and help; let us pray for his life!"

Yes; that was what he wanted—that was the only thing that could bring relief: to pray; to pour out his sorrow somewhere; to find a greater strength than his own, and cling to it and plead for mercy and help. To leave that undone was to be false to his manhood; it was to be no better than the dumb beasts when their young perish. How could he let his boy suffer and die, without an effort, a cry, a prayer?

He sank on his knees beside Athenais.

"Out of the depths—out of the depths we call for pity. The light of our eyes is fading—the child is dying. Oh, the child, the child! Spare the child's life, thou merciful—"

Not a word; only that deathly blank. The hands of Hermas, stretched out in supplication, touched the marble table. He felt the cool hardness of the polished stone beneath his fingers. A book, dislodged by his touch, fell rustling to the floor. Through the open door, faint and far off, came the footsteps of the servants, moving cautiously. The heart of Hermas was like a lump of ice in his bosom. He rose slowly to his feet, lifting Athenais with him.

"It is in vain," he said; "there is nothing for us to do. Long ago I knew something. I think it would have helped us. But I have forgotten it. It is all gone. But I would give all that I have, if I could bring it back again now, at this hour, in this time of our bitter trouble."

A slave entered the room while he was speaking, and approached hesitatingly.

"Master," he said, "John of Antioch, whom we were forbidden to admit to the house, has come again. He would take no denial. Even now he waits in the peristyle; and the old man Marcion is with him, seeking to turn him away."

"Come," said Hermas to his wife, "let us go to him; for I think I see the beginning of a way that may lead us out of this dreadful darkness."

In the central hall the two men were standing; Marcion, with disdainful eyes and sneering lips, taunting the unbidden guest to depart; John silent, quiet, patient, while the wondering slaves looked on in dismay. He lifted his searching gaze to the haggard face of Hermas.

"My son, I knew that I should see you again, even though you did not send for me. I have come to you because I have heard that you are in trouble."

"It is true," answered Hermas, passionately; "we are in trouble, desperate trouble, trouble accursed. Our child is dying. We are poor, we are destitute, we are afflicted. In all this house, in all the world, there is no one that can help us. I knew something long ago, when I was with you,—a word, a name,—in which we might have found hope. But I have lost it. I gave it to this man. He has taken it away from me forever."

He pointed to Marcion. The old man's lips curled scornfully. "A word, a name!" he sneered. "What is that, O most wise and holy Presbyter? A thing of air, an unreal thing that men make to describe their own dreams and fancies. Who would go about to rob any one of such a thing as that? It is a prize that only a fool would think of taking. Besides, the young man parted with it of his own free will. He bargained with me cleverly. I promised him wealth and pleasure and fame. What did he give in return? An empty name, which was a burden—"

"Servant of demons, be still!" The voice of John rang clear, like a trumpet, through the hall. "There is a name which none shall dare to take in vain. There is a name which none can lose without being lost. There is a name at which the devils tremble. Depart quickly, before I speak it!"

Marcion had shrunk into the shadow of one of the pillars. A bright lamp near him tottered on its pedestal and fell with a crash. In the confusion he vanished, as noiselessly as a shade.

John turned to Hermas, and his tone softened as he said: "My son, you have sinned deeper than you know. The word with which you parted so lightly is the key-word of all life and joy and peace. Without it the world has no meaning, and existence no rest, and death no refuge. It is the word that purifies love, and comforts grief, and keeps hope alive forever. It is the most precious thing that ever ear has heard, or mind has known, or heart has conceived. It is the name of Him who has given us life and breath and all things richly to enjoy; the name of Him who, though we may forget Him, never forgets us; the name of Him who pities us as you pity your suffering child; the name of Him who, though we wander far from Him, seeks us in the wilderness, and sent His Son, even as His Son has sent me this night, to breathe again that forgotten name in the heart that is perishing without it. Listen, my son, listen with all your soul to the blessed name of God our Father."

The cold agony in the breast of Hermas dissolved like a fragment of ice that melts in the summer sea. A sense of sweet release spread through him from head to foot. The lost was found. The dew of a divine peace fell on his parched soul, and the withering flower of human love lifted its head again. The light of a new hope shone on his face. He stood upright, and lifted his hands high toward heaven.

"Out of the depths have I cried unto Thee, O Lord! O my God, be merciful to me, for my soul trusteth in Thee. My God, Thou hast given; take not Thy gift away from me, O my God! Spare the life of this my child, O Thou God, my Father, my Father!"

A deep hush followed the cry. "Listen!" whispered Athenais, breathlessly.

Was it an echo? It could not be, for it came again—the voice of the child, clear and low, waking from sleep, and calling: "My father, my father!"

The Americanism of Washington

Hard is the task of the man who at this late day attempts to say anything new about Washington. But perhaps it may be possible to unsay some of the things which have been said, and which, though they were at one time new, have never at any time been strictly true.

The character of Washington, emerging splendid from the dust and tumult of those great conflicts in which he played the leading part, has passed successively into three media of obscuration, from each of which his figure, like the sun shining through vapors, has received some disguise of shape and color. First came the mist of mythology, in which we discerned the new St. George, serene, impeccable, moving through an orchard of ever-blooming cherry-trees, gracefully vanquishing dragons with a touch, and shedding fragrance and radiance around him. Out of that mythological mist we groped our way, to find ourselves beneath the rolling clouds of oratory, above which the head of the hero was pinnacled in remote grandeur, like a sphinx poised upon a volcanic peak, isolated and mysterious. That altitudinous figure still dominates the cloudy landscapes of the after-dinner orator; but the frigid, academic mind has turned away from it, and looking through the fog of criticism has descried another Washington, not really an American, not amazingly a hero, but a very decent English country gentleman, honorable, courageous, good, shrewd, slow, and above all immensely lucky.

Now here are two of the things often said about Washington which need, if I mistake not, to be unsaid: first, that he was a solitary and inexplicable phenomenon of greatness; and second, that he was not an American.

Solitude, indeed, is the last quality that an intelligent student of his career would ascribe to him. Dignified and reserved he was, undoubtedly; and as this manner was natural to him, he won more true friends by using it than if he had disguised himself in a forced familiarity and worn his heart upon his sleeve. But from first to last he was a man who did his work in the bonds of companionship, who trusted his comrades in the great enterprise even though they were not his intimates, and who neither sought nor occupied a lonely eminence of unshared glory. He was not of the jealous race of those who

"Bear, like the Turk, no brother near the throne";

nor of the temper of George III., who chose his ministers for their vacuous compliancy. Washington was surrounded by men of similar though not of equal strength—Franklin, Hamilton, Knox, Greene, the Adamses, Jefferson, Madison. He stands in history not as a lonely pinnacle like Mount Shasta, elevated above the plain

"By drastic lift of pent volcanic fires";

but as the central summit of a mountain range, with all his noble fellowship of kindred peaks about him, enhancing his unquestioned supremacy by their glorious neighborhood and their great support.

Among these men whose union in purpose and action made the strength and stability of the republic, Washington was first, not only in the largeness of his nature, the loftiness of his desires, and the vigor of his will, but also in that representative quality which makes a man able to stand as the true hero of a great people. He had an instinctive power to divine, amid the confusions of rival interests and the cries of factional strife, the new aims and hopes, the vital needs and aspirations, which were the common inspiration of the people's cause and the creative forces of the American nation. The power to understand this, the faith to believe in it, and the unselfish courage to live for it, was the central factor of Washington's life, the heart and fountain of his splendid Americanism.

It was denied during his lifetime, for a little while, by those who envied his greatness, resented his leadership, and sought to shake him from his lofty place. But he stood serene and imperturbable, while that denial, like many another blast of evil-scented wind, passed into nothingness, even before the disappearance of the party strife out of whose fermentation it had arisen. By the unanimous judgment of his countrymen for two generations after his death he was hailed as *Pater Patriae*; and the age which conferred that title was too ingenuous to suppose that the father could be of a different race from his own offspring.

But the modern doubt is more subtle, more curious, more refined in its methods. It does not spring, as the old denial did, from a partisan hatred, which would seek to discredit Washington by an accusation of undue partiality for England, and thus to break his hold upon the love of the people. It arises, rather, like a creeping exhalation, from a modern theory of what true Americanism really is: a theory which goes back, indeed, for its inspiration to Dr. Johnson's somewhat crudely expressed opinion that "the Americans were a race whom no other mortals could wish to resemble"; but which, in its later form, takes counsel with those British connoisseurs who demand of their typical American not depravity of morals but deprivation of manners, not vice of heart but vulgarity of speech, not badness but bumptiousness, and at least enough of eccentricity to make him amusing to cultivated people.

Not a few of our native professors and critics are inclined to accept some features of this view, perhaps in mere reaction from the unamusing character of their own existence. They are not quite ready to subscribe to Mr. Kipling's statement that the real American is

"Unkempt, disreputable, vast,"

I remember reading somewhere that Tennyson had an idea that Longfellow, when he met him, would put his feet upon the table. And it is precisely because Longfellow kept his feet in their proper place, in society as well as in verse, that some critics, nowadays, would have us believe that he was not a truly American poet.

Traces of this curious theory of Americanism in its application to Washington may now be found in many places. You shall hear historians describe him as a transplanted English commoner, a second edition of John Hampden. You shall read, in a famous poem, of Lincoln as

"New birth of our new soil, the *first* American."

He knew it, I say: and by what divination? By a test more searching than any mere peculiarity of manners, dress, or speech; by a touchstone able to divide the gold of essential character from the alloy of superficial characteristics; by a standard which disregarded alike Franklin's fur cap and Putnam's old felt hat, Morgan's leather leggings and Witherspoon's black silk gown and John Adams's lace ruffles, to recognize and approve, beneath these various garbs, the vital sign of America woven into the very souls of the men who belonged to her by a spiritual birthright.

For what is true Americanism, and where does it reside? Not on the tongue, nor in the clothes, nor among the transient social forms, refined or rude, which mottle the surface of human life. The log cabin has no monopoly of it, nor is it an immovable fixture of the stately pillared mansion. Its home is not on the frontier nor in the populous city, not among the trees of the wild forest nor the cultured groves of Academe. Its dwelling is in the heart. It speaks a score of dialects but one language, follows a hundred paths to the same goal, performs a thousand kinds of service in loyalty to the same ideal which is its life. True Americanism is this:

To believe that the inalienable rights of man to life, liberty, and the pursuit of happiness are given by God.

To believe that any form of power that tramples on these rights is unjust.

To believe that taxation without representation is tyranny, that government must rest upon the consent of the governed, and that the people should choose their own rulers.

To believe that freedom must be safeguarded by law and order, and that the end of freedom is fair play for all.

To believe not in a forced equality of conditions and estates, but in a true equalization of burdens, privileges, and opportunities.

To believe that the selfish interests of persons, classes, and sections must be subordinated to the welfare of the commonwealth.

To believe that union is as much a human necessity as liberty is a divine gift.

To believe, not that all people are good, but that the way to make them better is to trust the whole people.

To believe that a free state should offer an asylum to the oppressed, and an example of virtue, sobriety, and fair dealing to all nations.

To believe that for the existence and perpetuity of such a state a man should be willing to give his whole service, in property, in labor, and in life.

That is Americanism; an ideal embodying itself in a people; a creed heated white hot in the furnace of conviction and hammered into shape on the anvil of life; a vision commanding men to follow it whithersoever it may lead them. And it was the subordination of the personal self to that ideal, that creed, that vision, which gave eminence and glory to Washington and the men who stood with him.

This is the truth that emerges, crystalline and luminous, from the conflicts and confusions of the Revolution. The men who were able to surrender themselves and all their interests to the pure and loyal service of their ideal were the men who made good, the victors crowned with glory and honor. The men who would not make that surrender, who sought selfish ends, who were controlled by personal ambition and the love of gain, who were willing to stoop to crooked means to advance their own fortunes, were the failures, the lost leaders, and, in some cases, the men whose names are embalmed in their own infamy. The ultimate secret of greatness is neither physical nor intellectual, but moral. It is the capacity to lose self in the service of something greater. It is the faith to recognize, the will to obey, and the strength to follow, a star.

Washington, no doubt, was pre-eminent among his contemporaries in natural endowments. Less brilliant in his mental gifts than some, less eloquent and accomplished than others, he had a rare balance of large powers which justified Lowell's phrase of "an imperial man." His athletic vigor and skill, his steadiness of nerve restraining an intensity of passion, his undaunted courage which refused no necessary risks and his prudence which took no unnecessary ones, the quiet sureness with which he grasped large ideas and the pressing energy with which he executed small details, the breadth of his intelligence, the depth of his convictions, his power to apply great thoughts and principles to every-day affairs, and his singular superiority to current prejudices and illusions—these were gifts in combination which would have made him distinguished in any company, in any age.

But what was it that won and kept a free field for the exercise of these gifts? What was it that secured for them a long, unbroken opportunity of development in the activities of leadership, until they reached the summit of their perfection? It was a moral quality. It was the evident magnanimity of the man, which assured the people that he was no self-seeker who would betray their interests for his own glory or rob them for his own gain. It was the supreme magnanimity of the man, which made the best spirits of the time trust him implicitly, in war and peace, as one who would never forget his duty or his integrity in the sense of his own greatness.

From the first, Washington appears not as a man aiming at prominence or power, but rather as one under obligation to serve a cause. Necessity was laid upon him, and he met it willingly. After Washington's marvellous escape from death in his first campaign for the defence of the colonies, the Rev. Samuel Davies, fourth president of Princeton College, spoke of him in a sermon as "that heroic youth, Colonel Washington, whom I can but hope Providence has hitherto preserved in so signal a manner for some important service to his country." It was a prophetic voice, and Washington was not disobedient to the message. Chosen to command the Army of the Revolution in 1775, he confessed to his wife his deep reluctance to surrender the joys of home, acknowledged publicly his feeling that he was not equal to the great trust committed to him, and then, accepting it as thrown upon him "by a kind of destiny," he gave himself body and soul to its fulfilment refusing all pay beyond the mere discharge of his expenses, of which he kept a strict account, and asking no other reward than the success of the cause which he served.

"Ah, but he was a rich man," cries the carping critic; "he could afford to do it." How many rich men to-day avail themselves of their opportunity to indulge in this kind of extravagance, toiling tremendously without a salary, neglecting their own estate for the public benefit, seeing their property diminished without complaint, and coming into serious financial embarrassment, even within sight of bankruptcy, as Washington did, merely for the gratification of a desire to serve the people? This is indeed a very singular and noble form of luxury. But the wealth which makes it possible neither accounts for its existence nor detracts from its glory. It is the fruit of a manhood superior alike to riches and to poverty, willing to risk all, and to use all, for the common good.

Was it in any sense a misfortune for the people of America, even the poorest among them, that there was a man able to advance sixty-four thousand dollars out of his own purse, with no other security but his own faith in their cause, to pay his daily expenses while he was leading their armies? This unsecured loan was one of the very things, I doubt not, that helped to inspire general confidence. Even so the prophet Jeremiah purchased a field in Anathoth, in the days when Judah was captive unto Babylon, paying down the money, seventeen shekels of silver, as a token of his faith that the land would some day be delivered from the enemy and restored to peaceful and orderly habitation.

Washington's substantial pledge of property to the cause of liberty was repaid by a grateful country at the close of the war. But not a dollar of payment for the tremendous toil of body and mind, not a dollar for work "overtime," for indirect damages to his estate, for commissions on the benefits which he secured for the general enterprise, for the use of his name or the value of his counsel, would he receive.

A few years later, when his large sagacity perceived that the development of internal commerce was one of the first needs of the new country, at a time when he held no public office, he became president of a company for the extension of navigation on the rivers James and Potomac. The Legislature of Virginia proposed to give him a hundred and fifty shares of stock. Washington refused this, or any other kind of pay, saying that he could serve the people better in the enterprise if he were known to have no selfish interest in it. He was not the kind of a man to reconcile himself to a gratuity (which is the Latinized word for a "tip" offered to a person not in livery), and if the modern methods of "coming in on the ground-floor" and "taking a rake-off" had been explained and suggested to him, I suspect that he would have described them in language more notable for its force than for its elegance.

It is true, of course, that the fortune which he so willingly imperilled and impaired recouped itself again after peace was established, and his industry and wisdom made him once more a rich man for those days. But what injustice was there in that? It is both natural and right that men who have risked their all to secure for the country at large what they could have secured for themselves by other means, should share in the general prosperity attendant upon the success of their efforts and sacrifices for the common good.

I am sick of the shallow judgment that ranks the worth of a man by his poverty or by his wealth at death. Many a selfish speculator dies poor. Many an unselfish patriot dies prosperous. It is not the possession of the dollar that cankers the soul, it is the worship of it. The true test of a man is this: Has he labored for his own interest, or for the general welfare? Has he earned his money fairly or unfairly? Does he use it greedily or generously? What does it mean to him, a personal advantage over his fellow-men, or a personal opportunity of serving them?

There are a hundred other points in Washington's career in which the same supremacy of character, magnanimity focussed on service to an ideal, is revealed in conduct. I see it in the wisdom with which he, a son of the South, chose most of his generals from the North, that he might secure immediate efficiency and unity in the army. I see it in the generosity with which he praised the achievements of his associates, disregarding jealous rivalries, and ever willing to share the credit of victory as he was to bear the burden of defeat. I see it in the patience with which he suffered his fame to be imperilled for the moment by reverses and retreats, if only he might the more surely guard the frail hope of ultimate victory for his country. I see it in the quiet dignity with which he faced the Conway Cabal, not anxious to defend his own reputation and secure his own power, but nobly resolute to save the army from being crippled and the cause of liberty from being wrecked. I see it in the splendid self-forgetfulness which cleansed his mind of all temptation to take personal revenge upon those who had sought to injure him in that base intrigue. I read it in his letter of consolation and encouragement to the wretched Gates after the defeat at Camden. I hear the prolonged reechoing music of it in his letter to General Knox in 1798, in regard to military appointments, declaring his wish to "avoid feuds with those who are embarked in the same general enterprise with myself."

Listen to the same spirit as it speaks in his circular address to the governors of the different States, urging them to "forget their local prejudices and policies; to make those mutual concessions which are requisite to the general prosperity, and in some instances to sacrifice their individual advantages to the interest of the community." Watch how it guides him unerringly through the critical period of American history which lies between the success of the

Revolution and the establishment of the nation, enabling him to avoid the pitfalls of sectional and partisan strife, and to use his great influence with the people in leading them out of the confusion of a weak confederacy into the strength of an indissoluble union of sovereign States.

See how he once more sets aside his personal preferences for a quiet country life, and risks his already secure popularity, together with his reputation for consistency, by obeying the voice which calls him to be a candidate for the Presidency. See how he chooses for the cabinet and for the Supreme Court, not an exclusive group of personal friends, but men who can be trusted to serve the great cause of Union with fidelity and power—Jefferson, Randolph, Hamilton, Knox, John Jay, Wilson, Cushing, Rutledge. See how patiently and indomitably he gives himself to the toil of office, deriving from his exalted station no gain "beyond the lustre which may be reflected from its connection with a power of promoting human felicity." See how he retires, at last, to the longed-for joys of private life, confessing that his career has not been without errors of judgment, beseeching the Almighty that they may bring no harm to his country, and asking no other reward for his labors than to partake, "in the midst of my fellow-citizens, the benign influence of good laws under a free government, the ever favorite object of my heart."

Oh, sweet and stately words, revealing, through their calm reserve, the inmost secret of a life that did not flare with transient enthusiasm but glowed with unquenchable devotion to a cause! "The ever favorite object of my heart"—how quietly, how simply he discloses the source and origin of a sublime consecration, a lifelong heroism! Thus speaks the victor in calm retrospect of the long battle. But if you would know the depth and the intensity of the divine fire that burned within his breast you must go back to the dark and icy days of Valley Forge, and hear him cry in passion unrestrained: "If I know my own mind, I could offer myself a living sacrifice to the butchering enemy, provided that would contribute to the people's ease. I would be a living offering to the savage fury and die by inches to save the people."

"*The ever favorite object of my heart*!" I strike this note again and again, insisting upon it, harping upon it; for it is the key-note of the music. It is the capacity to find such an object in the success of the people's cause, to follow it unselfishly, to serve it loyally, that distinguishes the men who stood with Washington and who deserve to share his fame. I read the annals of the Revolution, and I find everywhere this secret and searching test dividing the strong from the weak, the noble from the base, the heirs of glory from the captives of oblivion and the inheritors of shame. It was the unwillingness to sink and forget self in the service of something greater that made the failures and wrecks of those tempestuous times, through which the single-hearted and the devoted pressed on to victory and honor.

Turn back to the battle of Saratoga. There were two Americans on that field who suffered under a great personal disappointment: Philip Schuyler, who was unjustly supplanted in command of the army by General Gates; and Benedict Arnold, who was deprived by envy of his due share in the glory of winning the battle. Schuyler forgot his own injury in loyalty to the cause, offered to serve Gates in any capacity, and went straight on to the end of his noble life giving all that he had to his country. But in Arnold's heart the favorite object was not his country, but his own ambition, and the wound which his pride received at Saratoga rankled and festered and spread its poison through his whole nature, until he went forth from the camp, "a leper white as snow."

What was it that made Charles Lee, as fearless a man as ever lived, play the part of a coward in order to hide his treason at the battle of Monmouth? It was the inward eating corruption of that selfish vanity which caused him to desire the defeat of an army whose command he had wished but failed to attain. He had offered his sword to America for his own glory, and when that was denied him, he withdrew the offering, and died, as he had lived, to himself.

What was it that tarnished the fame of Gates and Wilkinson and Burr and Conway? What made their lives, and those of men like them, futile and inefficient compared with other men whose natural gifts were less? It was the taint of dominant selfishness that ran through their careers, now hiding itself, now breaking out in some act of malignity or treachery. Of the common interest they were reckless, provided they might advance their own. Disappointed in that "ever favorite object of their hearts," they did not hesitate to imperil the cause in whose service they were enlisted.

Turn to other cases, in which a charitable judgment will impute no positive betrayal of trusts, but a defect of vision to recognize the claim of the higher ideal. Tory or Revolutionist a man might be, according to his temperament and conviction; but where a man begins with protests against tyranny and ends with subservience to it, we look for the cause. What was it that separated Joseph Galloway from Francis Hopkinson? It was Galloway's opinion that, while the struggle for independence might be justifiable, it could not be successful, and the temptation of a larger immediate reward under the British crown than could ever be given by the American Congress in which he had once served. What was it that divided the Rev. Jacob Duché from the Rev. John Witherspoon? It was Duché's fear that the cause for which he had prayed so eloquently in the first Continental Congress was doomed after the capture of Philadelphia, and his unwillingness to go down with that cause instead of enjoying the comfortable fruits of his native wit and eloquence in an easy London chaplaincy. What was it that cut William Franklin off from his professedly prudent and worldly wise old father, Benjamin? It was the luxurious and benumbing charm of the royal governorship of New Jersey.

"Professedly prudent" is the phrase that I have chosen to apply to Benjamin Franklin. For the one thing that is clear, as we turn to look at him and the other men who stood with Washington, is that, whatever their philosophical professions may have been, they were not controlled by prudence. They were really imprudent, and at heart willing to take all risks of poverty and death in a struggle whose cause was just though its issue was dubious. If it be rashness to commit honor and life and property to a great adventure for the general good, then these men were rash to the verge of recklessness. They refused no peril, they withheld no sacrifice, in the following of their ideal.

I hear John Dickinson saying: "It is not our duty to leave wealth to our children, but it is our duty to leave liberty to them. We have counted the cost of this contest, and we find nothing so dreadful as voluntary slavery." I see Samuel Adams, impoverished, living upon a pittance, hardly able to provide a decent coat for his back, rejecting with scorn the offer of a profitable office, wealth, a title even, to win him from his allegiance to the cause of America. I see Robert Morris, the wealthy merchant, opening his purse and pledging his credit to support the Revolution, and later devoting all his fortune and his energy to restore and establish the financial honor of the Republic, with the memorable words, "The United States may command all that I have, except my integrity." I hear the proud John Adams saying to his wife, "I have accepted a seat in the House of Representatives, and thereby have consented to my own ruin, to your ruin, and the ruin of our children"; and I hear her reply, with the tears running down her face, "Well, I am willing in this cause to run all risks with you, and be ruined with you, if you are ruined," I see Benjamin Franklin, in the Congress of 1776, already past his seventieth year, prosperous, famous, by far the most celebrated man in America, accepting without demur the difficult and dangerous mission to France, and whispering to his friend, Dr. Rush, "I am old and good for nothing, but as the store-keepers say of their remnants of cloth, 'I am but a fag-end, and you may have me for what you please.'"

Here is a man who will illustrate and prove, perhaps better than any other of those who stood with Washington, the point at which I am aiming. There was none of the glamour of romance about old Ben Franklin. He was shrewd, canny, humorous. The chivalric Southerners disliked his philosophy, and the solemn New-Englanders mistrusted his jokes. He made no extravagant claims for his own motives, and some of his ways were not distinctly ideal. He was full of prudential proverbs, and claimed to be a follower of the theory of enlightened self-interest. But there was not a faculty of his wise old head which he did not put at the service of his country, nor was there a pulse of his slow and steady heart which did not beat loyal to the cause of freedom.

He forfeited profitable office and sure preferment under the crown, for hard work, uncertain pay, and certain peril in behalf of the colonies. He followed the inexorable logic, step by step, which led him from the natural rights of his countrymen to their liberty, from their liberty to their independence. He endured with a grim humor the revilings of those whom he called "malevolent critics and bug-writers." He broke with his old and dear associates in England, writing to one of them,

"You and I were long friends; you are now my enemy and I am Yours,
B. Franklin."

He never flinched or faltered at any sacrifice of personal ease or interest to the demands of his country. His patient, skilful, laborious efforts in France did as much for the final victory of the American cause as any soldier's sword. He yielded his own opinions in regard to the method of making the treaty of peace with England, and thereby imperilled for a time his own prestige. He served as president of Pennsylvania three times, devoting all his salary to public benefactions. His influence in the Constitutional Convention was steadfast on the side of union and harmony, though in many things he differed from the prevailing party. His voice was among those who hailed Washington as the only possible candidate for the Presidency. His last public act was a petition to Congress for the abolition of slavery. At his death the government had not yet settled his accounts in its service, and his country was left apparently his debtor; which, in a sense still larger and deeper, she must remain as long as liberty endures and union triumphs in the Republic.

Is not this, after all, the root of the whole matter? Is not this the thing that is vitally and essentially true of all those great men, clustering about Washington, whose fame we honor and revere with his? They all left the community, the commonwealth, the race, in debt to them. This was their purpose and the ever-favorite object of their hearts. They were deliberate and joyful creditors. Renouncing the maxim of worldly wisdom which bids men "get all you can and keep all you get," they resolved rather to give all they had to advance the common cause, to use every benefit conferred upon them in the service of the general welfare, to bestow upon the world more than they received from it, and to leave a fair and unblotted account of business done with life which should show a clear balance in their favor.

Thus, in brief outline, and in words which seem poor and inadequate, I have ventured to interpret anew the story of Washington and the men who stood with him: not as a stirring ballad of battle and danger, in which the knights ride valiantly, and are renowned for their mighty strokes at the enemy in arms; not as a philosophic epic, in which the development of a great national idea is displayed, and the struggle of opposing policies is traced to its conclusion; but as a drama of the eternal conflict in the soul of man between self-interest in its Protean forms, and loyalty to the right, service to a cause, allegiance to an ideal.

Those great actors who played in it have passed away, but the same drama still holds the stage. The drop-curtain falls between the acts; the scenery shifts; the music alters; but the crisis and its issues are unchanged, and the parts which you and I play are assigned to us by our own choice of "the ever favorite object of our hearts."

Men tell us that the age of ideals is past, and that we are now come to the age of expediency, of polite indifference to moral standards, of careful attention to the bearing of different policies upon our own personal interests. Men tell us that the rights of man are a poetic fiction, that democracy has nothing in it to command our allegiance unless it promotes our individual comfort and prosperity, and that the whole duty of a citizen is to vote with his party and get an office for himself, or for some one who will look after him. Men tell us that to succeed means to get money, because with that all other good things can be secured. Men tell us that the one thing to do is to promote and protect the particular trade, or industry, or corporation in which we have a share: the laws of trade will work out that survival of the fittest which is the only real righteousness, and if we survive that will prove that we are fit. Men tell us that all beyond this is phantasy, dreaming, Sunday-school politics: there is nothing worth living for except to get on in the world; and nothing at all worth dying for, since the age of ideals is past.

It is past indeed for those who proclaim, or whisper, or in their hearts believe, or in their lives obey, this black gospel. And what is to follow? An age of cruel and bitter jealousies between sections and classes; of hatted and strife between the Haves and the Have-nots; of futile contests between parties which have kept their names and confused their principles, so that no man may distinguish them except as the Ins and Outs. An age of greedy privilege and sullen poverty, of blatant luxury and curious envy, of rising palaces and vanishing homes, of stupid frivolity and idiotic publicomania; in which four hundred gilded fribbles give monkey-dinners and Louis XV. revels, while four million ungilded gossips gape at them and read about them in the newspapers. An age when princes of finance buy protection from the representatives of a fierce democracy; when guardians of the savings which insure the lives of the poor, use them as a surplus to pay for the extravagances of the rich; and when men who have climbed above their fellows on golden ladders, tremble at the crack of the blackmailer's whip and come down at the call of an obscene newspaper. An age when the python of political corruption casts its "rings" about the neck of proud cities and sovereign States, and throttles honesty to silence and liberty to death. It is such an age, dark, confused, shameful, that the sceptic and the scorner must face, when they turn their backs upon those ancient shrines where the flames of faith and integrity and devotion are flickering like the deserted altar-fires of a forsaken worship.

But not for us who claim our heritage in blood and spirit from Washington and the men who stood with him,—not for us of other tribes and kindred who

"Have found a fatherland upon this shore,"

and learned the meaning of manhood beneath the shelter of liberty,—not for us, nor for our country, that dark apostasy, that dismal outlook! We see the palladium of the American ideal—goddess of the just eye, the unpolluted heart, the equal hand—standing as the image of Athene stood above the upper streams of Simois:

"It stood, and sun and moonshine rained their light
On the pure columns of its glen-built hall.
Backward and forward rolled the waves of fight
Round Troy—but while this stood Troy could not fall."

We see the heroes of the present conflict, the men whose allegiance is not to sections but to the whole people, the fearless champions of fair play. We hear from the chair of Washington a brave and honest voice which cries that our industrial problems must be solved not in the interest of capital, nor of labor, but of the whole people. We believe that the liberties which the heroes of old won with blood and sacrifice are ours to keep with labor and service.

"All that our fathers wrought With true prophetic thought, Must be
defended."
No privilege that encroaches upon those liberties is to be endured. No lawless disorder that imperils them is to be sanctioned. No class that disregards or invades them is to be tolerated.

There is a life that is worth living now, as it was worth living in the former days, and that is the honest life, the useful life, the unselfish life, cleansed by devotion to an ideal. There is a battle that is worth fighting now, as it was worth fighting then, and that is the battle for justice and equality. To make our city and our State free in fact as well as in name; to break the rings that strangle real liberty, and to keep them broken; to cleanse, so far as in our power lies, the fountains of our national life from political, commercial, and social corruption; to teach our sons and daughters, by precept and example, the honor of serving such a country as America—that is work worthy of the finest manhood and womanhood. The well born are those who are born to do that work. The well bred are those who are bred to be proud of that work. The well educated are those who see deepest into the meaning and the necessity of that work. Nor shall their labor be for naught, nor the reward of their sacrifice fail them. For high in the firmament of human destiny are set the stars of faith in mankind, and unselfish courage, and loyalty to the ideal; and while they shine, the Americanism of Washington and the men who stood with him shall never, never die.

THE END

The Unruly Sprite
A Partial Fairy Tale

There was once a man who was also a writer of books.

The merit of his books lies beyond the horizon of this tale. No doubt some of them were good, and some of them were bad, and some were merely popular. But he was all the time trying to make them better, for he was quite an honest man, and thankful that the world should give him a living for his writing. Moreover, he found great delight in the doing of it, which was something that did not enter into the world's account—a kind of daily Christmas present in addition to his wages.

But the interesting thing about the man was that he had a clan or train of little sprites attending him—small, delicate, aerial creatures, who came and went around him at their pleasure, and showed him wonderful things, and sang to him, and kept him from being discouraged, and often helped him with his work.

If you ask me what they were and where they came from, I must frankly tell you that I do not know. Neither did the man know. Neither does anybody else know.

But he had sense enough to understand that they were real—just as real as any of the other mysterious things, like microbes, and polonium, and chemical affinities, and the northern lights, by which we are surrounded. Sometimes it seemed as if the sprites were the children of the flowers that die in blooming; and sometimes as if they came in a flock with the birds from the south; and sometimes as if they rose one by one from the roots of the trees in the deep forest, or from the waves of the sea when the moon lay upon them; and sometimes as if they appeared suddenly in the streets of the city after the people had passed by and the houses had gone to sleep. They were as light as thistle-down, as unsubstantial as mists upon the mountain, as wayward and flickering as will-o'-the-wisps. But there was something immortal about them, and the man knew that the world would be nothing to him without their presence and comradeship.

Most of these attendant sprites were gentle and docile; but there was one who had a strain of wildness in him. In his hand he carried a bow, and at his shoulder a quiver of arrows, and he looked as if, some day or other, he might be up to mischief.

Now this man was much befriended by a certain lady, to whom he used to bring his stories in order that she might tell him whether they were good, or bad, or merely popular. But whatever she might think of the stories, always she like the man, and of the airy fluttering sprites she grew so fond that it almost seemed as if they were her own children. This was not unnatural, for they were devoted to her; they turned the pages of her book when she read; they made her walks through the forest pleasant and friendly; they lit lanterns for her in the dark; they brought flowers to her and sang to her, as well as to the man. Of this he was glad, because of his great friendship for the lady and his desire to see her happy.

But one day she complained to him of the sprite who carried the bow. "He is behaving badly," she said; "he teases me."

"That surprises me," said the man, "and I am distressed to hear it; for at heart he is rather good and to you he is deeply attached. But how does he tease you, dear lady? What does he do?"

"Oh, nothing," she answered, "and that is what annoys me. The others are all busy with your affairs or mine. But this idle one follows me like my shadow, and looks at me all the time. It is not at all polite. I fear he has a vacant mind and has not been well brought up."

"That may easily be," said the man, "for he came to me very suddenly one day, and I have never inquired about his education."

"But you ought to do so," said she; "it is your duty to have him taught to know his place, and not to tease, and other useful lessons."

"You are always right," said the man, "and it shall be just as you say."

On the way home he talked seriously to the sprite and told him how impolite he had been, and arranged a plan for his schooling in botany, diplomacy, music, psychology, deportment, and other useful studies.

The rest of the sprites came in to the school-room every day, to get some of the profitable lessons. The sat around quiet and orderly, so that it was quite like a kindergarten. But the principal pupil was restless and troublesome.

"You are never still," said the man, "you have an idle mind and wandering thoughts."

"No!" said the sprite, shaking his head. "It is true my mind is not on my lessons. But my thoughts do not wander at all. They always follow yours."

Then the man stopped talking, and the other sprites laughed behind their hands. But the one who had been reproved went on drawing pictures in the back of his botany book. The face in the pictures was always the same, but none of them seemed to satisfy him, for he always rubbed them out and began over again.

After several weeks of hard work the master thought his pupil must have learned something, so he gave him a holiday, and asked him what he would like to do.

"Go with you," he answered, "when you take her your new stories."

So they went together, and the lady complimented the writer on his success as an educator.

"Your pupil does you credit," said she, "he talks nicely about botany and deportment. But I am a little troubled to see him looking so pale. Perhaps you have been too severe with him. I must take him out in the garden with me every day to play a while."

"You have a kind heart," said the man, "and I hope he will appreciate it."

This agreeable and amicable life continued for some weeks, and everybody was glad that affairs had arranged themselves. But one day the lady brought a new complaint.

"He is a strange little creature, and he has begun to annoy me in the most extraordinary way." "That is bad," said the man. "What does he do now?"

"Oh, nothing," she answered, "and that is just the trouble. When I want to talk about you, he refuses, and says he does not like you as much as he used to. When I propose to play a game, he says he is tired and would rather sit under a tree and hear stories. When I tell them he says they do not suit him, they all end happily, and that is stupid. He is very perverse. But he clings to me like a bur. He is always teasing me to tell him the name of every flower in my garden and given him one of every kind."

"Is he rude about it?"

"Not exactly rude, but he is all the more annoying because he is so polite, and I always feel that he wants something different."

"He must not do that," said the man. "He must learn to want what you wish."

"But how can he learn what I wish? I do not always know that myself."

"It may be difficult," said the man, "but all the same he must learn it for your sake. I will deal with him."

So he took the unruly sprite out into the desert and gave him a sound beating with thorn branches. The blood ran down the poor little creature's arms and legs, and the teats down the man's cheeks. But the only words that he said were: "You must learn to want what she wishes —do you hear?—you must want what she wishes." At last the sprite whimpered and said: "Yes, I hear; I will wish what she wants." Then the man stopped beating him, and went back to his house, and wrote a little story that was really good.

But the sprite lay on his face in the desert for a long time, sobbing as if his heart would break. Then he fell asleep and laughed in his dreams. When he awoke it was night and the moon was shining silver. He rubbed his eyes and whispered to himself, "Now I must find out what she wants." With that he leaped up, and the moonbeams washed him white as he passed through them to the lady's house.

The next afternoon, when the man came to read her the really good story, she would not listen.

"No," she said, "I am very angry with you."

"Why?"

"You know well enough."

"Upon my honour, I do not."

"What?" cried the lady. "You profess ignorance, when he distinctly said—

"Pardon," said the man, "but who said?"

"Your unruly sprite," she answered, indignant. "He came last night outside my window, which was wide open for the moon, and shot an arrow into my breast—a little baby arrow, but it hurt. And when I cried out for the pain, he climbed up to me and kissed the place, saying that would make it well. And he swore that you made him promise to come. If that is true, I will never speak to you again."

"Then of course," said the man, "it is not true. And now what do you want me to do with this unruly sprite?"

"Get rid of him," said she firmly.

"I will," replied the man, and he bowed over her hand and went away.

He stayed for a long time—nearly a week—and when he came back he brought several sad verses with him to read. "They are very dull," said the lady; "what is the matter with you?" He confessed that he did not know, and began to talk learnedly about the Greek and Persian poets, until the lady was consumed with a fever of dulness.

"You are simply impossible!" she cried. "I wonder at myself for having chosen such a friend!"

"I am sorry indeed," said the man.

"For what?"

"For having disappointed you as a friend, and also for having lost my dear unruly sprite who kept me from being dull."

"Lost him!" exclaimed the lady. "How?"

"By now," said the man, "he must be quite dead, for I tied him to a tree in the forest five days a go and left him to starve."

"You are a brute," said the lady, "and a very stupid man. Come, take me to the tree. At least we can bury the poor sprite, and then we shall part forever."

So he took her by the hand and guided her through the woods, and they talked much of the sadness of parting forever.

When they came to the tree, there was the little sprite, with his wrists and ankles bound, lying upon the moss. His eyes were closed, and his body was white as a snowdrop. They knelt down, one on each side of him, and untied the cord. To their surprise his hands felt warm. "I believe he is not quite dead," said the lady. "Shall we try to bring him to life?" asked the man. And with that they fell to chafing his wrists and his palms. Presently he gave each of them a slight pressure of the fingers.

"Did you feel that?" cried she.

"Indeed I did," the man answered. "It shook me to the core. Would you like to take him on your lap so that I can chafe his feet?"

The lady nodded and took the soft little body on her knees and held it close to her, while the man kneeled before her rubbing the small, milk-white feet with strong and tender touches. Presently, as they were thus engaged, they heard the sprite faintly whispering, while one of his eyelids flickered:

"I think—if each of you—would kiss me—on opposite cheeks—at the same moment—those kind of movements would revive me."

The two friends looked at each other, and the man spoke first.

"He talks ungrammatically, and I think he is an incorrigible little savage, but I love him. Shall we try his idea?"

"If you love him," said the lady, "I am willing to try, provided you shut your eyes."

So they both shut their eyes and tried.

But just at that moment the unruly sprite slipped down, and put his hands behind their heads, and the two mouths that sought his cheeks met lip to lip in a kiss so warm, so long, so sweet that everything else was forgotten.

Now you can easily see that as the persons who had this strange experience were the ones who told me the tale, their forgetfulness at this point leaves it of necessity half-told. But I know from other sources that the man who was also a writer went on making books, and the lady always told him truly whether they were good, bad, or merely popular. But what the unruly sprite is doing now nobody knows.

FINIS

Days Off And Other Digressions

"A day OFF" said my Uncle Peter, settling down in his chair before the open wood-fire, with that air of complacent obstinacy which spreads over him when he is about to confess and expound his philosophy of life,—"a day off is a day that a man takes to himself."

"You mean a day of luxurious solitude," I said, "a stolen sweet of time, which he carries away into some hidden corner to enjoy alone,—a little-Jack-Horner kind of a day?"

"Not at all," said my Uncle Peter; "solitude is a thing which a man hardly ever enjoys by himself. He may practise it from a sense of duty. Or he may take refuge in it from other things that are less tolerable. But nine times out of ten he will find that he can't get a really good day to himself unless he shares it with some one else; if he takes it alone, it will be a heavy day, a chain-and-ball day,—anything but a day off."

"Just what do you mean, then?" I asked, knowing that nothing would please him better than the chance to discover his own meaning against a little background of apparent misunderstanding and opposition.

"I mean," said my Uncle Peter, in that deliberate manner which lends a flavour of deep wisdom to the most obvious remarks, "I mean that every man owes it to himself to have some days in his life when he escapes from bondage, gets away from routine, and does something which seems to have no purpose in the world, just because he wants to do it."

"Plays truant," I interjected.

"Yes, if you like to put it in that objectionable way," he answered; "but I should rather compare it to bringing flowers into the school-room, or keeping white mice in your desk, or inventing a new game for the recess. You see we are all scholars, boarding scholars, in the House of Life, from the moment when birth matriculates us to the moment when death graduates us. We never really leave the big school, no matter what we do. But my point is this: the lessons that we learn when we do not know that we are studying are often the pleasantest, and not always the least important. There is a benefit as well as a joy in finding out that you can lay down your task for a proper while without being disloyal to your duty. Play-time is a part of school-time, not a break in it. You remember what Aristotle says: '*ascholoumetha gar hina scholazomen.*'"

"My dear uncle," said I, "there is nothing out of the common in your remarks, except of course your extraordinary habit of decorating them with a Greek quotation, like an ancient coin set as a scarf-pin and stuck carelessly into a modern neck-tie. But apart from this eccentricity, everybody admits the propriety of what you have been saying. Why, all the expensive, up-to-date schools are arranged on your principle: play-hours, exercise-hours, silent-hours, social-hours, all marked in the schedule: scholars compelled and carefully guided to amuse themselves at set times and in approved fashions: athletics, dramatics, school-politics and social ethics, all organized and co-ordinated. What you flatter yourself by putting forward as an amiable heresy has become a commonplace of orthodoxy, and your liberal theory of education and life is now one of the marks of fashionable conservatism."

My Uncle Peter's face assumed the beatific expression of a man who knows that he has been completely and inexcusably misunderstood, and is therefore justified in taking as much time as he wants to make the subtlety and superiority of his ideas perfectly clear and to show how dense you have been in failing to apprehend them.

"My dear boy," said he, "it is very singular that you should miss my point so entirely. All these things that you have been saying about your modern schools illustrate precisely the opposite view from mine. They are signs of that idolatry of organization, of system, of the time-table and the schedule, which is making our modern life so tedious and exhausting. Those unfortunate school-boys and school-girls who have their amusements planned out for them and cultivate their social instincts according to rule, never know the joy of a real day off, unless they do as I say, and take it to themselves. The right kind of a school will leave room and liberty for them to do this. It will be a miniature of what life is for all of us,—a place where law reigns and independence is rewarded,—a stream of work and duty diversified by islands of freedom and repose,—a pilgrimage in which it is permitted to follow a side-path, a mountain trail, a footway through the meadow, provided the end of the journey is not forgotten and the day's march brings one a little nearer to that end."

"But will it do that," I asked, "unless one is careful to follow the straight line of the highway and march as fast as one can?"

"That depends," said my Uncle Peter, nodding his head gravely, "upon what you consider the end of the journey. If it is something entirely outside of yourself, a certain stint of work which you were created to perform; or if it is something altogether beyond yourself, a certain place or office at which you are aiming to arrive; then, of course, you must stick to the highway and hurry along.

"But suppose that the real end of your journey is something of which you yourself are a part. Suppose it is not merely to get to a certain place, but to get there in a certain condition, with the light of a sane joy in your eyes and the peace of a grateful content in your heart. Suppose it is not merely to do a certain piece of work, but to do it in a certain spirit, cheerfully and bravely and modestly, without overrating its importance or overlooking its necessity. Then, I fancy, you may find that the winding foot-path among the hills often helps you on your way as much as the high road, the day off among the islands of repose gives you a steadier hand and a braver heart to make your voyage along the stream of duty."

"You may skip the moralizing, if you please, Uncle Peter," said I, "and concentrate your mind upon giving me a reasonable account of the peculiar happiness of what you call a day off."

"Nothing could be simpler," he answered. "It is the joy of getting out of the harness that makes a horse fling up his heels, and gallop around the field, and roll over and over in the grass, when he is turned loose in the pasture. It is the impulse of pure play that makes a little bunch of wild ducks chase one another round and round on the water, and follow their leader in circles and figures of eight; there is no possible use in it, but it gratifies their instinct of freedom and makes them feel that they are not mere animal automata, whatever the natural history men may say to the contrary. It is the sense of release that a man experiences when he unbuckles the straps of his knapsack, and lays it down under a tree, and says 'You stay there till I come back for you! I'm going to rest myself by climbing this hill, just because it is not on the road-map, and because there is nothing at the top of it except the view.'

"It is this feeling of escape," he continued, in the tone of a man who has shaken off the harness of polite conversation and let himself go for a gallop around the field of monologue, "it is just this exhilarating sense of liberation that is lacking in most of our social amusements and recreations. They are dictated by fashion and directed by routine. Men get into the so-called 'round of pleasure,' and they are driven into a trot to keep up with it, just as if it were a treadmill. The only difference is that the pleasure-mill grinds no corn. Harry Bellairs was complaining to me, the other day, that after an exhausting season of cotillons in New York, he had been running his motor-car through immense fatigues in France and Italy, and had returned barely in time to do his duty by his salmon-river in Canada, work his new boat through the annual cruise of the yacht club, finish up a round of house-parties at Bar Harbor and Lenox, and get ready for the partridge-shooting in England with his friend the Duke of Bangham,—it was a dog's life, he said, and he had no time to himself at all. I rather pitied him; he looked so frayed. It seems to me that the best way for a man or a woman of pleasure to get a day off would be to do a little honest work.

"You see it is the change that makes the charm of a day off. The real joy of leisure is known only to the people who have contracted the habit of work without becoming enslaved to the vice of overwork.

"A hobby is the best thing in the world for a man with a serious vocation. It keeps him from getting muscle-bound in his own task. It helps to save him from the mistake of supposing that it is his little tick-tack that keeps the universe a-going. It leads him out, on off days, away from his own garden corner into curious and interesting regions of this wide and various earth, of which, after all, he is a citizen.

"Do you happen to know the Reverend Doctor McHook? He is a learned preacher, a devoted churchman, a faithful minister; and in addition to this he has an extra-parochial affection for ants and spiders. He can spend a happy day in watching the busy affairs of a formicary, and to observe the progress of a bit of spider-web architecture gives him a peculiar joy. There are some severe and sour-complexioned theologians who would call this devotion to objects so far outside of his parish an illicit passion. But to me it seems a blessing conferred by heavenly wisdom upon a good man, and I doubt not he escapes from many an insoluble theological puzzle, and perhaps from many an unprofitable religious wrangle, to find refreshment and invigoration in the society of his many-legged friends."

"You are moralizing again, Uncle Peter," I objected; "or at least you are getting ready to do so. Stop it; and give me a working definition of the difference between a hobby and a fad."

"Let me give you an anecdote," said he, "instead of a definition. There was a friend of mine who went to visit a famous asylum for the insane. Among the patients who were amusing themselves in the great hall, he saw an old gentleman with a long white beard, who was sitting astride of a chair, spurring its legs with his heels, holding both ends of his handkerchief which he had knotted around the back, and crying 'Get up, get up! G'long boy, steady!' with the utmost animation. 'You seem to be having a fine ride, sir,' said my friend. 'Capital,' said the old gentleman, 'this is a first-rate mount that I am riding.' 'Permit me to inquire,' asked my friend, 'whether it is a fad or a hobby?' 'Why, certainly!' replied the old gentleman, with a quizzical look. 'It is a hobby, you see, for I can get off whenever I have a mind to.' And with that he dismounted and walked into the garden.

"It is just this liberty of getting off that marks the superiority of a hobby to a fad. The game that you feel obliged to play every day at the same hour ceases to amuse you as soon as you realize that it is a diurnal duty. Regular exercise is good for the muscles, but there must be a bit of pure fun mixed with the sport that is to refresh your heart.

"A tour in Europe, carefully mapped out with an elaborate itinerary and a carefully connected timetable, may be full of instruction, but it often becomes a tax upon the spirit and a weariness to the flesh. Compulsory castles and mandatory museums and required ruins pall upon you, as you hurry from one to another, vaguely agitated by the fear that you may miss something that is marked with a star in the guide-book, and so be compelled to confess to your neighbour at the *table-d'hôte* that you have failed to see what he promptly and joyfully assures you is 'the best thing in the whole trip,' Delicate and sensitive people have been killed by taking a vacation in that way.

"I remember meeting, several years ago, a party of personally conducted tourists in Venice, at the hour which their itinerary consecrated to the enjoyment of the fine arts in the gallery of the Academy. Their personal conductor led them into one of the great rooms, and they gathered close around him, with an air of determination on their tired faces, listening to his brief, dry patter about the famous pictures that the room contained. He stood in the centre of the room holding his watch in his hand while they dispersed themselves around the walls, looking for the paintings which they ought to see, like chickens searching for scattered grains of corn. At the expiration of five minutes he clapped his hands sharply; his flock scurried back to him; and they moved on to 'do' the next room.

"I suppose that was one way of seeing Venice: but I would much rather sit at a little table on the *Riva degli Schiavoni*, with a plate of bread and cheese and a *mezzo* of Chianti before me, watching the motley crowd in the street and the many-coloured sails in the harbour; or spend a lazy afternoon in a gondola, floating through watery alley-ways that lead nowhere, and under the façades of beautiful palaces whose names I did not even care to know. Of course I should like to see a fine picture or a noble church, now and then; but only one at a time, if you please; and that one I should wish to look at as long as it said anything to me, and to revisit as often as it called me."

"That is because you have no idea of the educational uses of a vacation, Uncle Peter," said I. "You are an unsystematic person, an incorrigible idler."

"I am," he answered, without a sign of penitence, "that is precisely what I am,—in my days off. Otherwise I should not get the good of them. Even a hobby, on such days, is to be used chiefly for its lateral advantages,—the open doors of the sideshows to which it brings you, the unexpected opportunities of dismounting and tying your hobby to a tree, while you follow the trail of something strange and attractive, as Moses did when he turned aside from his shepherding on Mount Horeb and climbed up among the rocks to see the burning bush.

"The value of a favourite pursuit lies not only in its calculated results but also in its by-products. You may become a collector of almost anything in the world,—orchids, postage-stamps, flint arrowheads, cook-books, varieties of the game of cat's cradle,—and if you chase your trifle in the right spirit it will lead you into pleasant surprises and bring you acquainted with delightful or amusing people. You remember when you went with Professor Rinascimento on a Della Robbia hunt among the hill towns of Italy, and how you came by accident into that deep green valley where there are more nightingales with sweeter voices than anywhere else on earth? Your best *trouvaille* on that expedition was hidden in those undreamed-of nights of moonlight and music. And it was when you were chasing first editions of Tennyson, was it not, that you discovered your little head of a marble faun, which you vow is by Donatello, or one of his pupils? And what was it that you told me about the rare friend you found when you took a couple of days off in an ancient French town, on a flying journey from Rome to London? Believe me, dear boy, all that we win by effort and intention is sometimes overtopped by a gift that is conferred upon us out of a secret and mysterious generosity. Wordsworth was right:

"'Think you, 'mid all this mighty sum
Of things forever speaking,
That nothing of itself will come,
But we must still be seeking?'"

"You talk," said I, "as if you thought it was a man's duty to be happy."

"I do," he answered firmly, "that is precisely and definitely what I think. It is not his chief duty, nor his only duty, nor his duty all the time. But the normal man is not intended to go through this world without learning what happiness means. If he does so he misses something that he needs to complete his nature and perfect his experience. 'Tis a poor, frail plant that can not endure the wind and the rain and the winter's cold. But is it a good plant that will not respond to the quickening touch of spring and send out its sweet odours in the embracing warmth of the summer night? Suppose that you had made a house for a child, and given him a corner of the garden to keep, and set him lessons and tasks, and provided him with teachers and masters. Would you be satisfied with that child, however diligent and obedient, if you found that he was never happy, never enjoyed a holiday, never said to himself and to you, 'What a good place this is, and how glad I am to live here'?"

"Probably not," I answered, "but that is because I should be selfish enough to find a pleasure of my own in his happiness. I should like to take a day off with him, now and then, and his gladness would increase my enjoyment. There is no morality in that. It is simply natural. We are all made that way."

"Well," said my Uncle Peter, "if we are made that way we must take it into account in our philosophy of life. The fact that it is natural is not a sufficient reason for concluding that it is bad. There is an old and wonderful book which describes the creation of the world in poetic language; and when I read that description it makes me feel sure that something like this was purposely woven into the very web of life. After the six mystical days of making things and putting things in order, says this beautiful old book, the Person who had been doing it all took a day to Himself, in which He 'rested from all the things that He had created and made,' and looked at them, and saw how good they were. His work was not ended, of course, for it has been going on ever since, and will go on for ages of ages. But in the midst of it all it seemed right to Him to take a divine day off. And His example is commended to us for imitation because we are made in His likeness and have the same desire to enjoy as well as to create.

"Do you remember what the Wisest of all Masters said to his disciples when they were outworn by the weight of their work and the pressure of the crowd upon them? 'Come ye yourselves apart into a lonely place, and rest awhile.' He would never have bidden them do that, unless it had been a part of their duty to get away from their task for a little. He knew what was in man, more deeply than any one else had ever known; and so he invited his friends out among the green hills and beside the quiet waters of Galilee to the strengthening repose and the restoring joy which are only to be found in real days off."

My Uncle Peter's voice had grown very deep and gentle while he was saying these things. He sat looking far away into the rosy heart of the fire, where the bright blaze had burned itself out, and the delicate flamelets of blue and violet were playing over the glowing, crumbling logs. It seemed as if he had forgotten where we were, and gone a-wandering into some distant region of memories and dreams. I almost doubted whether to call him back; the silence was so full of comfortable and friendly intercourse.

"Well," said I, after a while, "you are an incorrigible moralist, but certainly a most unconventional one. The orthodox would never accept your philosophy. They would call you a hedonist, or something equally dreadful."

"Let them," he said, placidly.

"But tell me": I asked, "you and I have many pleasant and grateful memories, little pictures and stories, which seem like chapters in the history of this doubtful idea of yours: suppose that I should write some of them down, purely in a descriptive and narrative way, without committing myself to any opinion as to their morality; and suppose that a few of your opinions and prejudices, briefly expressed, were interspersed in the form of chapters to be skipped: would a book like that symbolize and illustrate the true inwardness of the day off? How would it do to make such a book?"

"It would do," he answered, "provided you wanted to do it, and provided you did not try to prove anything, or convince anybody, or convey any profitable instruction."

"But would any one read it?" I asked. "What do you think?"

"I think," said he, stretching his arms over his head as he rose and turned towards his den to plunge into a long evening's work, "I reckon, and calculate, and fancy, and guess that a few people, a very few, might browse through such a book in their days off."

A HOLIDAY IN A VACATION

IT was really a good little summer resort where the boy and I were pegging away at our vacation. There were the mountains conveniently arranged, with pleasant trails running up all of them, carefully marked with rustic but legible guide-posts; and there was the sea comfortably besprinkled with islands, among which one might sail around and about, day after day, not to go anywhere, but just to enjoy the motion and the views; and there were cod and haddock swimming over the outer ledges in deep water, waiting to be fed with clams at any time, and on fortunate days ridiculously accommodating in letting themselves be pulled up at the end of a long, thick string with a pound of lead and two hooks tied to it. There were plenty of places considered proper for picnics, like Jordan's Pond, and Great Cranberry Island, and the Russian Tea-house, and the Log Cabin Tea-house, where you would be sure to meet other people who also were bent on picnicking; and there were hotels and summer cottages, of various degrees of elaboration, filled with agreeable and talkable folk, most of whom were connected by occupation or marriage with the rival colleges and universities, so that their ambitions for the simple life had an academic thoroughness and regularity. There were dinner parties, and tea parties, and garden parties, and sea parties, and luncheon parties, masculine and feminine, and a horse-show at Bar Harbor, and a gymkhana at North East, and dances at all the Harbors, where Minerva met Terpischore on a friendly footing while Socrates sat out on the veranda with Midas discussing the great automobile question over their cigars.

It was all vastly entertaining and well-ordered, and you would think that any person with a properly constituted mind ought to be able to peg through a vacation in such a place without wavering. But when the boy confessed to me that he felt the need of a few "days off" in the big woods to keep him up to his duty, I saw at once that the money spent upon his education had not been wasted; for here, without effort, he announced a great psychological fact—*that no vacation is perfect without a holiday in it*. So we packed our camping-kit, made our peace with the family, tied our engagements together and cut the string below the knot, and set out to find freedom and a little fishing in the region around Lake Nicatöus.

The south-east corner of the State of Maine is a happy remnant of the ancient wilderness. The railroads will carry you around it in a day, if you wish to go that way, making a big oval of two or three hundred miles along the sea and by the banks of the Penobscot, the Mattawamkeag, and the St. Croix. But if you wisely wish to cross the oval you must ride, or go afoot, or take to your canoe; probably you will have to try all three methods of locomotion, for the country is a mixed quantity. It reminds me of what I once heard in Stockholm: that the Creator, when the making of the rest of the world was done, had a lot of fragments of land and water, forests and meadows, mountains and valleys, lakes and moors, left over; and these He threw together to make the southern part of Sweden. I like that kind of a promiscuous country. The spice of life grows there.

When we had escaped from the railroad at Enfield on the Penobscot, we slept a short night in a room over a country store, and took wagon the next morning for a twenty-five mile drive. At the somnolent little village of Burlington we found our guides waiting for us. They were sitting on the green at the cross-roads, with their paddles and axes and bundles beside them. I knew at a glance that they were ready and all right: Sam Dam, an old experienced, seasoned guide, and Harry, a good-looking young woodsman who had worked in lumber camps and on "the drive," but had never been "guiding" before. He was none the worse for that, for he belonged to the type of Maine man who has the faculty of learning things by doing them.

As we rattled along the road the farms grew poorer and sparser, until at last we came into the woods, crossed the rocky Passadumkeag River, and so over a succession of horseback hills to the landing-place on Nicatöus Stream, where the canoes were hidden in the bushes. Now load up with the bundles and boxes, the tent, the blanket-roll, the clothes-bag, the provisions—all the stuff that is known as "duffel" in New York, and "*butins*" in French Canada, and "*wangan*" in Maine—stow it all away judiciously so that the two light craft will be well balanced; and then push off, bow paddles, and let us taste the joy of a new stream! New to the boy and me, you understand; but to the guides it was old and familiar, a link in a much-travelled route. The amber water rippled merrily over the rocky bars where the river was low, and in the still reaches it spread out broad and smooth, covered with white lilies and fringed with tall grasses. All along the pleasant way Sam entertained us with memories of the stream.

"Ye see that grassy p'int, jest ahead of us? Three weeks ago I was comin' down for the mail, and there was three deer a-stannin' on that p'int, a buck and a doe and a fawn. And——"

"Up in them alders there's a little spring brook comes in. Good fishin' there in high water. But now? Well——"

"Jest beyond that bunch o' rocks last fall there was three fellers comin' down in a canoe, and a big bear come out and started 'cross river. The gun was in the case in the bottom of the canoe, and one o' the fellers had a pistol, and so———"

Beyond a doubt it was so, always has been so, and always will be so—just so, on every river travelled by canoes, until the end of time. The sportsman travels through a happy interval between memories of failure and expectation of success. But the river and the wind in the trees sing to him by the way, and there are wild flowers along the banks, and every turn in the stream makes a new picture of beauty. Thus we came leisurely and peacefully to the place where the river issued from the lake; and here we must fish awhile, for it was reported that the landlocked salmon lay in the narrow channel just above the dam.

Sure enough, no sooner had the fly crossed the current than there was a rise; and at the second cast a pretty salmon of two and a half pounds was hooked, played, and landed. Three more were taken, of which the boy got two—and his were the biggest. Fish know nothing of the respect due to age. They leaped well, those little salmon, flashing clean out of the water again and again with silvery gleams. But on the whole they did not play as strongly nor as long as their brethren (called *ouananiche*,) in the wild rapids where the Upper Saguenay breaks from Lake St. John. The same fish are always more lively, powerful, and enduring when they live in swift water, battling with the current, than when they vegetate in the quiet depths of a lake. But if a salmon must live in a luxurious home of that kind, Nicatöus is a good one, for the water is clear, the shores are clean, the islands plenty, and the bays deep and winding.

At the club-house, six miles up the lake, where we arrived at candle-lighting, we found such kindly welcome and good company that we tarried for three days in that woodland Capua, discussing the further course of our expedition. Everybody was willing to lend us aid and comfort. The sociable hermit who had summered for the last twenty years in his tiny cabin on the point gave us friendly counsel and excellent large blueberries. The matron provided us with daily bags of most delicate tea, a precaution against the native habit of "squatting" the leaves—that is, boiling and squeezing them to extract the tannin. The little lady called Katharyne (a fearless forest-maid who roamed the woods in leathern jacket and short blue skirt, followed by an enormous and admiring guide, and caught big fish everywhere) offered to lend us anything in her outfit, from a pack-basket to a darning-needle. It was cheerful to meet with such general encouragement in our small adventure. But the trouble was to decide which way to go.

Nicatöus lies near the top of a watershed about a thousand feet high. From the region round about it at least seven canoeable rivers descend to civilization. The Narraguagus and the Union on the south, the Passadumkeag on the west, the Sisladobsis and the St. Croix on the north, and the two branches of the Machias or Kowahshiscook on the east; to say nothing of the Westogus and the Hackmatack and the Mopang. Here were names to stir the fancy and paralyze the tongue. What a joy to follow one of these streams clear through its course and come out of the woods in our own craft—from Nicatöus to the sea!

It was perhaps something in the name, some wild generosity of alphabetical expenditure, that led us to the choice of the Kowahshiscook, or west branch of the Machias River. Or perhaps it was because neither of our guides had been down that stream, and so the whole voyage would be an exploration, with everybody on the same level of experience. An easy day's journey across the lake, and up Comb's Brook, where the trout were abundant, and by a two-mile carry into Horseshoe Lake, and then over a narrow hardwood ridge, brought us to Green Lake, where we camped for the night in a new log shanty.

Here we were at the topmost source—*fons et origo*—of our chosen river. This single spring, crystal-clear and ice-cold, gushing out of the hillside in a forest of spruce and yellow birch and sugar maple, gave us the clue that we must follow for a week through the wilderness.

But how changed was that transparent rivulet after it entered the lake. There the water was pale green, translucent but semi-opaque, for at a depth of two or three feet the bottom was hardly visible. The lake was filled, I believe, with some minute aquatic growth which in the course of a thousand years or so would transform it into a meadow. But meantime the mystical water was inhabited, especially around the mouth of the spring, by huge trout to whom tradition ascribed a singular and provoking disposition. They would take the bait, when the fancy moved them: but the fly they would always refuse, ignoring it with calm disdain, or slapping at it with their tails and shoving it out of their way as they played on the surface in the summer evenings. This was the mysterious reputation of the trout of Green Lake, handed down from generation to generation of anglers; and this spell we had come to break, by finding the particular fly that would be irresistible to those secret epicures and the psychological moment of the day when they could no longer resist temptation. We tried all the flies in our books; at sunset, in the twilight, by the light of the stars and the rising moon, at dawn and at sunrise. Not one trout did we capture with the fly in Green Lake. Nor could we solve the mystery of those reluctant fish. The boy made a scientific suggestion that they got plenty of food from the cloudy water, which served them as a kind of soup. My guess was that their sight was impaired so that they could not see the fly. But Sam said it was "jest pure cussedness." Many things in the world happen from that cause, and as a rule it is best not to fret over them.

The trail from Green Lake to Campbell Lake was easily found; it followed down the outlet about a mile. But it had been little used for many years and the undergrowth had almost obliterated it. Rain had been falling all the morning and the bushes were wetter than water. On such a carry travel is slow. We had three trips to make each way before we could get the stuff and the canoes over. Then a short voyage across the lake, and another mile of the same sort of portage, after which we came out with the last load, an hour before sundown, on the shore of the Big Sabeo. This lake was quite different from the others; wide and open, with smooth sand-beaches all around it. The little hills which encircled it had been burned over years ago; and the blueberry pickers had renewed the fire from year to year. The landscape was light green and yellow, beneath a low, cloudy sky; no forest in sight, except one big, black island far across the water.

The place where we came out was not attractive; but nothing is more foolish than to go on looking for a pretty camp-ground after daylight has begun to wane. When the sun comes within the width of two paddle-blades of the horizon, if you are wise you will take the first bit of level ground within reach of wood and water, and make haste to get the camp in order before dark. So we pitched our blue tent on the beach, with a screen of bushes at the back to shelter us from the wind; broke a double quantity of fir branches for our bed, to save us from the midnight misery of sand in the blankets; cut a generous supply of firewood from a dead pine-tree which stood conveniently at hand; and settled down in comfort for the night.

What could have been better than our supper, cooked in the open air and eaten by fire-light! True, we had no plates—they had been forgotten—but we never mourned for them. We made a shift to get along with the tops of some emptied tin cans and the cover of a kettle; and from these rude platters, (quite as serviceable as the porcelain of Limoges or Sèvres) we consumed our toast, and our boiled potatoes with butter, and our trout prudently brought from Horseshoe Lake, and, best of all, our bacon.

Do you remember what Charles Lamb says about roast pig? How he falls into an ecstasy of laudation, spelling the very name with small capitals, as if the lower case were too mean for such a delicacy, and breaking away from the cheap encomiums of the vulgar tongue to hail it in sonorous Latin as *princeps obsoniorum*! There is some truth in his compliments, no doubt; but they are wasteful, excessive, imprudent. For if all this praise is to be lavished on plain, fresh, immature, roast pig, what adjectives shall we find to do justice to that riper, richer, more subtle and sustaining viand, broiled bacon? On roast pig a man can not work; often he can not sleep, if he have partaken of it immoderately. But bacon "brings to its sweetness no satiety." It strengthens the arm while it satisfies the palate. Crisp, juicy, savory; delicately salt as the breeze that blows from the sea; faintly pungent as the blue smoke of incense wafted from a clean wood-fire; aromatic, appetizing, nourishing, a stimulant to the hunger which it appeases, 'tis the matured bloom and consummation of the mild little pig, spared by foresight for a nobler fate than juvenile roasting, and brought by art and man's device to a perfection surpassing nature. All the problems of woodland cookery are best saved by the baconian method. And when we say of one escaping great disaster that he has "saved his bacon," we say that the physical basis and the quintessential comfort of his life are still untouched and secure.

Steadily fell the rain all that night, plentiful, persistent, drumming on the tightened canvas over our heads, waking us now and then to pleasant thoughts of a rising stream and good water for the morrow. Breaking clouds rolled before the sunrise, and the lake was all a-glitter when we pushed away in dancing canoes to find the outlet. This is one of the problems in which the voyager learns to know something of the infinite reserve, the humorous subtlety, the hide-and-seek quality in nature. Where is it—that mysterious outlet? Behind yonder long point? Nothing here but a narrow arm of the lake. At the end of this deep bay? Nothing here but a little brook flowing in. At the back of the island? Nothing here but a landlocked lagoon. Must we make the circuit of the whole shore before we find the way out? Stop a moment. What are those two taller clumps of bushes on the edge of this broad curving meadow—down there in the corner, do you see? Turn back, go close to the shore, swing around the nearer clump, and here we are in the smooth amber stream, slipping silently, furtively, down through the meadow, as if it would steal away for a merry jest and leave us going round and round the lake till nightfall.

Easily and swiftly the canoes slide along with the little river, winding and doubling through the wide, wild field, travelling three miles to gain one. The rushes nod and glisten around us; the bending reeds whisper as we push between them, cutting across a point. Follow the stream; we know not its course, but we know that if we go with it, though it be a wayward and tricksy guide, it will bring us out—but not too soon, we hope!

Here is a lumberman's dam, broad-based, solid, and ugly, a work of infinite labour, standing lonely, deserted, here in the heart of the wilderness. Now we must carry across it. But it shall help while it hinders us. Pry up the creaking sluice-gates, sending a fresh head of water down the channel along with us, lifting us over the shallows, driving us on through the rocky places, buoyant, alert, and rejoicing, till we come again to a level meadow, and the long, calm, indolent reaches of river.

Look on the right there, under the bushes. There is a cold, still brook, slipping into the lazy river; and there we must try the truth of the tales we have heard of the plentiful trout of Machias. Let the flies fall light by the mouth of the brook, caressing, inviting. Nothing there? Then push the canoe through the interlaced alders, quietly, slowly up the narrow stream, till a wider pool lies open before you. Now let the rod swing high in the air, lifting the line above the bushes, dropping the flies as far away as you can on the dark-brown water. See how quickly the answer comes, in two swift golden flashes out of the depths of the sleeping pool. This is a pretty brace of trout, from thirty to forty ounces of thoroughbred fighting pluck, and the spirit that will not surrender. If they only knew that their strength would be doubled by acting together, they soon would tangle your line in the roots or break your rod in the alders. But all the time they are fighting against each other, making it easy to bring them up to the net and land them—a pair of beauties, evenly matched in weight and in splendour, gleaming with rich iridescent hues of orange and green and peacock-blue and crimson. A few feet beyond you find another, a smaller fish, and then one a little larger; and so you go on up the stream, threading the boat through the alders, with patience and infinite caution, carefully casting your flies when the stream opens out to invite them, till you have rounded your dozen of trout and are wisely contented. Then you go backward down the brook—too narrow for turning—and join the other canoe that waits, floating leisurely on with the river.

There is a change now in the character of the stream. The low hills that have been standing far away, come close together from either side, as if they meant to bar any further passage; and the dreamy river wakes up to wrestle its way down the narrow valley. There are no long, sleepy reaches, no wide, easy curves, now; but sharp, quick turns from one rocky ledge to another; and enormous stones piled and scattered along the river-bed; and sudden descents from level to level as if by the broad steps of a ruined, winding stairway. The water pushes, and rushes, and roars, and foams, and frets—no, it does not fret, after all, for there is always something joyous and exultant in its voice, a note of the *gaudia certaminis* by which the struggle of life is animated, a note of confident strength, sure that it can find or make a way, through all obstacles, to its goal. This is what I feel in a river, especially a little river flowing through a rough, steep country. This is what makes me love it. It seems to be thoroughly alive, and glad to be alive, and determined to go on, and certain that it will win through.

Our canoes go with the river, but no longer easily or lazily. Every step of the way must be carefully chosen; now close to the steep bank where the bushes hang over; now in mid-stream among the huge pointed rocks; now by the lowest point of a broad sunken ledge where the water sweeps smoothly over to drop into the next pool. The boy and I, using the bow paddles, are in the front of the adventure, guessing at the best channel, pushing aside suddenly to avoid treacherous stones hidden with dark moss, dashing swiftly down the long dancing rapids, with the shouting of the waves in our ears and the sprinkle of the foam in our faces.

From side to side of the wild avenue through the forest we turn and dart, zigzagging among the rocks. Thick woods shut us in on either hand, pines and hemlocks and firs and spruces, beeches and maples and yellow-birches, alders with their brown seed-cones, and mountain-ashes with their scarlet berries. All four of us know the way; there can be no doubt about that, for down the river is the only road out. But none of us knows the path; for this is a new stream, you remember, and between us and our journey's end there lie a thousand possible difficulties, accidents, and escapes.

The boy had one of them. His canoe struck on a ledge, in passing over a little fall, swung around sidewise to the current, and half filled with water; he and Harry had to leap out into the stream waist-deep. Sam and I made merry at their plight. But Nemesis was waiting for me a few miles below.

All the pools were full of fine trout. While the men were cooking lunch in a grove of balsams I waded down-stream to get another brace of fish. Stepping carefully among the rocks, I stood about thigh-deep in my rubber boots and cast across the pool. But the best bit of water was a little beyond my reach. A step further! There is a yellow bit of gravel that will give a good footing. Intent upon the flight of my flies, I took the step without care. But the yellow patch under the brown water was not gravel; it was the face of a rock polished smoother than glass. Gently, slowly, irresistibly, and with deep indignation I subsided backward into the cold pool. The rubber boots filled with water and the immersion was complete. Then I stood up and got the trout. When I returned to the camp-fire, the others laughed at me uproariously, and the boy said: "Why did you go in swimming with your clothes on? Were you expecting a party of ladies to come down the stream?"

Our tenting-places were new every night and forsaken every morning. Each of them had a charm of its own. One was under a great yellow-birch tree, close to the bank of the river. Another was on top of a bare ridge in the middle of a vast blueberry patch, where the luscious fruit, cool and fresh with the morning dew, spread an immense breakfast-table to tempt us. The most beautiful of all was at the edge of a fir-wood, with a huge rock, covered with moss and lichen, sloping down before us in a broad, open descent of thirty feet to the foaming stream. The full moon climbed into the sky as we sat around our camp-fire, and showed her face above the dark, pointed tree-tops. The winding vale was flooded with silver radiance that rested on river and rock and tree-trunk and multitudinous leafage like an enchantment of tranquillity. The curling currents and the floating foam, up and down the stream, were glistening and sparkling, ever moving, yet never losing their position. The shouting of the water melted to music, in which a thousand strange and secret voices, near and far away, blending and alternating from rapid to rapid and fall to fall, seemed like hidden choirs, answering one another from place to place. The sense of struggle, of pressure and resistance, of perpetual change, was gone; and in its stead there was a feeling of infinite quietude, of perfect balance and repose, of deep accord and amity between the watching heavens and the waiting earth, in which the conflicts of existence seemed very distant and of little meaning, and the peace of nature prophesied

"That one, far-off divine event
Towards which the whole creation moves."

Thus for six days and nights we kept company with our little river, following its guidance and enjoying all its changing moods. Sometimes it led us through a smooth country, across natural meadows, alder-fringed, where the bed of the stream was of amber sand and polished gravel, and the water rippled gently over the shallow bars, and there were deep holes underneath the hanging bushes, where the trout hid from the heat of the noon sun. Sometimes it had carved a way for itself over huge beds of solid rock, where, if the slope was gentle, we could dart arrow-like along the channel from pool to pool; but if the descent was steep and broken, we must get out of the canoes and let them down with ropes. Sometimes the course ran for miles through evergreen forests, where the fragrance of the fir-trees filled the air; and again we came out into the open regions where thousands of acres of wild blueberries were spread around us.

I call them wild because no man's hand has planted them. Yet they are cultivated after a fashion. Every two or three years a district of these hills is set on fire, and in the burned ground, the next spring, the berry-bushes come up innumerable. The following fall they are loaded so heavily with blueberries that the harvest is gathered with rakes, each of which has a cup underneath it into which the berries fall as the rake is thrust through the bushes. The land is owned by two or three large proprietors, who employ men and women to gather the crop, paying them a few cents a bushel for picking. Sometimes the proprietor leases his land to a factor, who pays a royalty on every bushel turned in at the factory in some village on the railroad or by the seashore, where the berries are canned or dried.

One day we came upon a camp of these berry-pickers by the river-side. Our first notice of their proximity was the sight of a raft with an arm-chair tied in the centre of it, stranded upon the rocks in a long, fierce rapid. Imagine how this looked to us after we had been five days in the wilderness! An arm-chair sitting up sedately in the middle of the rapids! What did it mean? Perhaps some vagrant artist had been exploring the river, and had fixed his seat there in order to paint a picture. Perhaps some lazy fisherman had found a good pool amid those boiling waters, and had arranged to take his ease while he whipped that fishy place with his flies. The mystery was solved when we rounded the next point; for there we found the berry-pickers taking their nooning in a cluster of little slab-shanties. They were friendly folks, men, women, and children, but they knew nothing about the river; had never been up farther than the place where the boys had left their raft in the high water a week ago; had never been down at all; could not tell how many falls there were below, nor whether the mouth was five or fifty miles away. They had come in by the road, which crossed the river at this point, and by the road they would go back when the berries were picked. They wanted to know whether we were prospecting for lumber or thinking of going into the berry business. We tried to explain the nature of our expedition to them, but I reckon we failed.

These were the only people that we really met on our journey, though we saw a few others far off on some bare hill. We did not encounter a single boat or canoe on the river. But we saw the deer come down to the shore, and stand shoulder-deep among the golden-rod and purple asters. We saw the ruffled grouse whir through the thickets and the wild ducks skitter down the stream ahead of us. We saw the warblers and the cedar-birds gathering in flocks for their southward flight, the muskrats making their houses ready for the winter, and the porcupines dumbly meditating and masticating among the branches of the young poplar-trees. We also had a delightful interview with a wild-cat, and almost a thrilling adventure with a bear.

The boy and I had started out from camp for an hour of evening fishing. He went down the stream some distance ahead of me, as I supposed, (though, as I afterward found, he had made a little detour and turned back). I was making my way painfully through a spruce thicket when I heard a loud crash and crackling of dead branches. "Hallo!" I cried; "have you fallen down? Are you hurt?" No answer. "Hallo, Teddy!" I shouted again; "what's the matter?" Another tremendous crash, and then dead silence.

I dropped my rod and pushed as rapidly as possible in the direction from which the sound had come. There I found a circle about fifty feet in diameter torn and trampled as if a circus had been there. The ground was trodden bare. Trees three and four inches thick were broken off. The bark of the larger trees was stripped away. The place was a ruin. A few paces away, among the bushes, there was a bear trap with some claws in it, and an iron chain attached to the middle of a clog about four feet long. The log hovel in which the trap had been set, we found later, a little way back on an old wood road. Evidently a bear had been caught there, perhaps two or three days before we came. He had dragged the trap and the chained clog down into the thicket. There he had stayed, tearing up things generally in his efforts to escape from his encumbrance, and resting quietly in the intervals of his fury. My approach had startled him and he had made the first crash that I heard. Then he lay low and listened. My second inconsiderate shout of "Hallo, *Teddy*!" had put such an enormous fear into him that he dashed through the trees, caught the foolishly chained clog across two of them, and, tearing himself loose, escaped with the loss of a couple of toes. Thus ended our almost adventure with a bear. How glad the old fellow must have been!

The moral is this: If you want a bear, you should set your trap with the clog chained at one end, not around the middle: then it will trail through the woods and not break loose. But the best way is not to want a bear.

Our last camp was just at the head of Holmes's Fall, a splendid ravine down which the river rushes in two foaming leaps. Here in the gray of the morning we lugged our canoes and our camp-kit around the cataract, and then launched away for the end of our voyage. It was full of variety, for the river was now cutting its course through a series of ridges, and every mile was broken with rapids and larger falls. There was but one other place, however, where we had to make a portage. I believe it was called Grand Falls. After that, the stream was smooth and quiet. The tall maples and ashes and elms stood along the banks as if they had been planted for a park. The first faint touch of autumn colour was beginning to illuminate their foliage. A few weeks later the river would be a long, winding avenue of gold and crimson, for every tree would redouble its splendour in the dark, unruffled water.

At one place, where there were a few cleared fields bordering on the river, we saw two or three houses and barns, and supposed we were near the end of our voyage. This was about nine o'clock in the morning; and we were glad because we calculated that we could catch the ten o'clock train for Bar Harbor. But that calculation was far astray. We skirted the cleared fields and entered the woodland again. The river flowed, broad and leisurely, in great curves half a mile long from point to point. As we rounded one cape after another we said to each other, "When we pass the next turn we shall see the village." But that inconsiderate village seemed to flee before us. Still the tall trees lined the banks in placid monotony. Still the river curved from cape to cape, each one like all the others. We paddled hard and steadily. Ten o'clock passed. Every day of our journey we had lost something—a frying-pan, a hatchet, a paddle, a ring. This day was no exception. We had lost a train. Still we pushed along against the cool wind, which always headed us, whether we turned north, or east, or south; wondering whether the village that we sought was still in the world, wondering whether the river came out anywhere, wondering—till at last we saw, across a lake-like expanse of water, the white church and the clustering houses of the far-famed Whitneyville.

It was a quaint old town, which had seen better days. The big lumber-mill that had once kept it busy was burned down, and the business had slipped away to the prosperous neighbouring town of Machias. There were nice old houses with tall pillars in front of them, now falling into decay and slipping out of plumb. There were shops that had evidently been closed for years, with not even a sign "To Let" in the windows. Our dinner was cooked for us in a boarding-house, by a brisk young lady of about fifteen years, whose mother had gone to Machias for a day in the gay world. With one exception that pleasant young lady was the only thing in Whitneyville that did not have an air of having been left behind.

The exception was the establishment of Mr. Cornelius D——, whose "General Store" beside the bridge was still open for business, and whose big white house stood under the elm-trees at the corner of the road opposite the church, with bright windows, fresh-painted walls, and plenty of flowers blooming around it. He was walking in the yard, dressed in a black broadcloth frock-coat, with a black satin necktie and a collar with pointed ends,—an old-fashioned Gladstonian garb. When I heard him speak I knew where he came from. It was the rich accent of Killarney, just as I had heard it on the Irish lakes two summers ago. But sixty years had passed since the young Cornelius had left the shores of the River Laune and come to dwell by the Kowahshiscook. He had grown up with the place; had run the lumber-mill and the first railroad that hauled the lumber from the mill down to tide-water; had become the owner of the store and the proprietor of some sixteen miles of timber-land along the river-front; had built the chief house of the village and given his children a capital education; and there he still dwelt, with his wife from Killarney, and with his tall sons and daughters about him, contented and happy, and not at all disposed to question the beneficent order of the universe. We had plenty of good talk that afternoon and evening, chiefly about the Old Country, and I had to rub up my recollections of Ross Castle and Kenmare House and all the places around Lough Leane, in order to match the old man's memory. He was interested in our expedition, too. He had often been far into the woods looking after his lumber. But I doubt whether he quite understood what it was that drew the boy and me on our idle voyage from Nicatöus to the sea.

HIS OTHER ENGAGEMENT

AMONG the annals of the Petrine Club, which has for its motto the wise words of St. Peter, "I go a-fishing," there are several profitable tales. Next to the story of Beekman De Peyster's fatal success in transforming a fairly good wife into a ferocious angler, probably the most instructive is the singular adventure that befell Bolton Chichester in taking a brief vacation while he was engaged to be married. And having already told the former story as an example of the vicissitudes of "Fisherman's Luck," I now propose to narrate the latter as a striking illustration of what may happen to a man who takes "a day off."

Chichester is known among his intimate friends as "Chinchin." This nominal appendix was given to him not in allusion to his habits of speech, for he is rather a small talker, but with reference to the prominence of that feature of his countenance which is at once the organ of utterance, the instrument of mastication, the sign of firmness, and (at least in the Gibsonian period of facial architecture) the chief point of manly beauty.

Point is an absurd word to apply to Chichester's chin. It might better be called a surface, a region, a territory. Smooth, spacious, square, kept always in perfect order and carried with a what-do-I-care-for-that air, it gives him a most distinguished appearance, and makes you think, when you meet him, that you are in the presence of a favourite matinée actor, the hero of a modern short-story, or a man of remarkable decision of character.

The last, of course, is the correct interpretation of the sign. Bolton Chichester is the most decided man that I have ever known. He can make up his mind more quickly, on a greater variety of subjects, and adhere to each determination more firmly, than all the other members of the Petrine Club put together. For this reason we always anticipated for him a large success in life, and some even predicted that he would become President of the United States—unless he made up his mind to do something else on the way to the White House. At all events, we felt sure, he would get what he wanted; and when he became decidedly attentive to Ethel Asham it was taken for granted that he would woo, win, and marry her in short order.

She was rather a difficult person, to be sure; the eldest daughter of that cryptic old millionaire, Watson Asham, who lived in New York and resided, for purposes of taxation, at West Smithfield; a graduate of Brainmore College; president of the Social Settlement of Higher Lighters; a frequent contributor in brief fiction to the Contrary Magazine; a beauty of the tea-after-tennis type; the best dancer in St. Swithin's Lenten Circle, and the most romantic creature that ever took up the cause of Progress with a large P. It would not be fair to call her strong-minded, because the adjective seems to imply some kind of a limitation in her strength. She was even stronger in her impulses than in her mind;

original in every direction; in fact, originality was a kind of convention with her. It was wonderful how many things she accomplished; but then she never lost any time; she was precise, punctual, inevitable in her sweet, feminine, self-possessed way; and her varied and surprising programme went through on schedule time, while she cherished in her heart the dream of a romance in the style of "The Prisoner of Zenda."

Naturally, such a many-sided young woman would be difficult to please; and a number of eligible young men had acquired personal knowledge of the fact. But the difficulty seemed to attract Chichester. He went at it in his bold, decided manner, with his chin forward; and he conquered. After the February campaign no one was surprised to hear, in March, that the engagement of Miss Ethel Asham to Mr. Bolton Chichester was announced, and that the wedding would occur in June.

The place was not specified. Conjectures were hazarded that it might be Dunfermline Abbey, the Castle of Chillon, Bridal Veil Falls in the Yosemite, the Natural Bridge in Virginia, or St. George's, Hanover Square. Little Pop Wilson, the well-known dialect novelist of the southeastern part of northern Kentucky, suggested that there was something to be said in favor of the Mammoth Cave—"always cool, you know. Artificial lights, pulpit rock, stalactites—all that sort of thing!" Even this was felt to be within the bounds of possibility. The one thing that was not open to doubt was that the wedding would certainly be celebrated in an original way and a romantic place, at precisely the appointed hour. If anyone had foretold that it would be broken off, and that the reason given would be "another engagement" on the part of Mr. Bolton Chichester, we should have laughed in the face of such a ridiculous prophet and advised him to take something to cool his brain.

Yet this is exactly what happened; and the secret of that other engagement is the subject of this brief, simple, but I hope not unmoral narrative.

Chichester had been with the Ashams at the residential farm-house in West Smithfield during the first fortnight of April, and had devoted the remainder of that showery month to his affairs in the city, diversified with a few afternoons of trout-fishing on Long Island: for like all the members of the Petrine Club he was a sincere angler. It was during this period that Ethel took up, in her daily correspondence with him, the question of the cruelty of angling. She was not yet quite clear in her mind upon the subject, but she wanted him to consider it seriously; and she quoted Byron, Leigh Hunt, and Aurora W. Chime's book, "The Inwardness of the Outward." Chichester promised to consider it.

The second week in May they spent together at a house-party near Portland, Maine; and he tried the landlocked salmon in Sebago Lake, twice. Ethel continued the subject of the cruelty of angling, in conversation, and illuminated her increasing conviction with references to the Reverend Wilbur Short's "Tales of Strange Things in Woods and Waters," and "Songs of the Scaly," by Alonzo Sweetbread.

"You would not allow any difference of thought or feeling to mar the perfect chord of our love, would you, Bolton dear?" she asked.

"Of course not," said Bolton.

"Then promise me faithfully that you will think about this pastime which gives so much anguish to the innocent fish—think about it very, very seriously."

"I do. I have to. It costs me seven or eight hundred a year."

"But you must think in a different way. Put yourself in the place of the fish."

"I did once. Fellow with a rod and line tried to land me in the tank at the gymnasium. Lots of fun. Never had a better fight."

"But suppose you had a hook in your mouth. How would you like that?"

"Better than the dentist's chair, I'm sure. I spent three afternoons there, last month."

"You're absurd," said Ethel, "you're perverse. Don't hold your chin up in that aggravating way. I don't believe—you—love——"

The rest of the conversation followed the usual course, which may be supplied from the pages of any of the fifteen-cent magazines, and ended with a promise on the part of Chichester that he would think again, and very, very seriously.

Meantime, you will understand, the preparations for the wedding had been going forward, in the regular way, modified, however, in one most important particular by Ethel Asham's passion for romantic originality. She insisted that the day and the place should be left entirely to her. She did not wish to have the ordinary, commonplace, fashionable wedding performance. She wanted something really and truly poetic and fitting, something to remember. She had a plan. The wedding should be in June? Yes. And she would be ready? Yes. And all the family, at least, should be there? Yes. But she asked that she might keep the secret of the precise time and the exact place as long as possible; it would make it all seem so much more spontaneous and natural.

The situation was a little peculiar, I grant you, and somewhat embarrassing to the rest of the family, including Chichester. But he took it like a man, and backed Ethel up with the utmost decision, just as if her idea was what he had always thought of and determined to do. What was his chin for, if he could not give her a firm support in a thing like this? As a matter of fact he did not care in the least where the wedding might be. A man never does. It does not seem to be his business. Ethel's paternal parent, however, had some misgivings which must be satisfied.

"Is it a church?" he growled; "none of your dusty, shabby little Higher Light shrines, eh?"

"Yes, it's a church," said Ethel solemnly, "and a very old and beautiful church."

"And a Christian ceremony," he insisted; "parson, robes, prayer-book—regular thing—no sideshow performance, eh?"

"Of course," said she, "what do you think? Do you suppose that just because I see things in an original way, I don't know what's proper? I like to hear the Swami Abikadanda talk; and I don't want a regular cut-and-dried wedding; but I'm not going to take any risks about a thing like that. The clergyman will be there, and you will give me away, and Gladys and Victoria will be the bridesmaids, and Arthur will be the best man, and Howard and Willis——"

"Well, well," grunted her father, with his chuckling laugh, "it's all right, I suppose, seeing that it's your wedding. Have it your own way while you can." For the old man had formed his idea of the significance of Chichester's chin.

So it was settled that the affair should remain unsettled for every one except Ethel; and the whole family was plunged into a cheerful state of evasion, prevarication, and downright falsification; and Chichester grinned and smoothed the left side of his chin with his forefinger and said, "What do I care for that? It's all right, I know," and everybody predicted that Ethel Asham was about to do something very original.

In the middle of June she marshalled her party for a little Canadian *giro*. There were her father and mother; and the inseparable twins, Gladys and Victoria, one of whom always laughed when the other was amused; and the three preternaturally important brothers, representing the triple-x output of Harvard, Yale and Columbia; and Aunt Euphemia van Benschoten, who had inherited the van Benschoten nose, a block on Fifth Avenue, and a pew in St. Mark's church (two of which possessions she was entitled to devise by will); and Miss Nancy Bangs, Ethel's most intimate friend; and the Reverend Oriel Bellingham Jenks, her favourite clergyman of the period; and—oh, yes! of course—there was Bolton Chichester.

It was quite a large party. They went first to Niagara, which Pop Wilson said was "premature, if not improper." Then they went down through the Thousand Islands, where Ethel pointed out the inhuman and cruel expression of the many fishermen, to which Chichester answered, "I don't know that it's cruel to catch pickerel, but it's certainly childish."

Then they descended the ridiculous rapids of Lachine, which splashed and murmured around them like a very mild surf at Shelter Island. They spent a couple of days in looking for the antiquities of Montreal, trying to find the romantic atmosphere of New France under the *ancien régime*. Then they went to Quebec, and found it.

Dear, delightful old Quebec, with her gray walls and shining tin roofs; her precipitous, headlong streets and sleepy squares and esplanades; her narrow alleys and peaceful convents; her harmless antique cannon on the parapets and her sweet-toned bells in the spires; her towering château on the heights and her long, low, queer-smelling warehouses in the lower town; her spick-and-span *caléches* and her dingy trolley-cars; her sprinkling of soldiers and sailors with Scotch accent and Irish brogue and Cockney twang, on a background of *petite bourgeoisie* speaking the quaintest of French dialects; her memories of an adventurous, glittering past and her placid contentment with the tranquil grayness of the present; her glorious daylight outlook over the vale of the St. Charles, the level shore of Montmorenci, the green Isle d'Orleans dividing the shining reaches of the broad St. Lawrence, and the blue Laurentian Mountains rolling far to the eastward—and at night, the dark bulk of the Citadel outlined against the starry blue, the trampling of many feet up and down the wooden pavement of the terrace, the chattering and the laughter, the music of the military band, and far below, the huddled housetops, the silent wharves, the lights of the great warships swinging with the tide, the intermittent ferry-boats plying to and fro, the twinkling lamps of Levis rising along the dim southern shore and reflected in the lapsing, curling, seaward-sliding waves of the great river! What city of the New World keeps so much of the charm of the Old?

The camp which Samuel de Champlain made in the wilderness three hundred years ago, has become one of the last refuges of the romantic dream and the courtly illusion, still haunted by the shades of impecunious young noblemen with velvet cloaks and feathered hats and rapiers at their hips; of delicate, high-spirited beauties braving the snowy wildwood in their silks and laces; of missionary monks, tonsured and rope-girdled, pressing with lean faces and eager eyes to plant the banner of the Church upon the shores of the West and win the fiery crown of martyrdom. Other figures follow them—gold-seekers, fur-traders, empire-builders, admirals and generals of France and England, strugglers for dominion, soldiers of fortune, makers of cunning plots, and dreamers of great enterprises—and round them all flows the confused tide of war and love, of intrigue and daring, of religious devotion and imperial plot. The massive walls of the old city have been broken, the rude palaces have vanished in fire or sunken in decay, but the past is still indomitable on Cape Diamond, and the lovers of romance can lose themselves in pleasant reveries among the winding streets and on the lofty, sun-bathed ramparts of Quebec.

It was there, in a shady corner of the Grand Battery, that Ethel disclosed to her mother and Chichester and the Reverend Father Bellingham Jenks her plan for the wedding; since, indeed, it was hardly possible to keep it a secret any longer.

"The day after to-morrow, you know," said she, "we are going to take the Saguenay boat for Tadousac. Do you know that village curving along the cliff at the base of the Mamelons; and the half-circle of the bay opening out into the big St. Lawrence, full of sunshine and blue water; and the steep, shaggy mountains of the Saguenay in the background; and the tiny old mission chapel of the Jesuit Fathers where the same bell has been ringing for nearly three hundred years? I was there the summer after I graduated; and I've never forgotten it. It's a picture and a dream. That is where I want to have my wedding. I don't believe that anybody else would have thought of it. Perhaps it's more than a hundred years since the last Indian wedding was held in that little deserted chapel; but it's all right, kept in good order, just as a relic beside the big new church. I think"—turning to the clergyman—"that it will be perfectly delightful and original to have you marry me there, at high noon, on the last day of June."

Well, of course, there was a good deal of astonishment and confusion and reluctance when this extraordinary plan came out. No one had imagined precisely this turn in Ethel's originality. Her mother was in a state of paralyzed dismay at an idea so wildly unconventional; the twins and her brothers and Miss Nancy Bangs bubbled over with practical difficulties and protests; Father Bellingham Jenks was doubtful and embarrassed. "Would it be possible—decorous—regular? The Roman Branch, you know, has not yet openly acknowledged the Anglican position in The Church. Might not objections arise—misunderstanding—refusal of permission to use the chapel? I should hesitate very much, you know!"

But Ethel carried things through with her usual sweet, sparkling high-handedness; and Chichester supported her with irresistible determination, as if he had decided on exactly this thing years ago.

"Certainly," he said, "splendid idea—entirely novel—quite correct—nothing could be better. Telegraph for one wing of the Tadousac Hotel, with drawing-rooms and private dining-room. Send down plenty of flowers and cakes and wines and whatever we need from here by boat on the twenty-ninth. Get a letter of introduction from my friend Paradol, the Minister of Fisheries and Lighthouses, to the archbishop here—letter from him to the curé at Tadousac—keys of the chapel—permission to make drawings and photographs of the interior every morning of next week. I've been at Tadousac almost every summer for the last five or six years, on the way to my salmon-fishing at the Ste. Marjorie Club. It's all perfectly easy and it shall be done."

The difficulties seemed to vanish before his masterful air, and everybody fell into line with sudden enthusiasm. Ethel smiled discreetly and moved along her pathway of inflexible originality with gentle triumph. The voyage down the river was delightful. The arrangements at the big white wooden hotel on the curving bay were rather primitive but quite comfortable; and three of the five days which were to pass before the ringing of the antique wedding-bell slipped away as if by magic.

On the fourth day, June twenty-ninth, Chichester having been assured by telegraph that all the things from Quebec had been safely shipped on the *Ste. Irenée*, was spending a morning hour with Ethel in the pavilion of the Government Fish Station at *Anse à l'Eau*, watching the great herd of captive salmon, circling round and round in restless imprisonment in their warm shallow pool. The splendid fish were growing a little dull and languid in their confined quarters, freshened only by the inflowing of a small brook, and exposed to the full glare of the sun. Many of them bore the scars of the nets in which they had been captured. Others had red wounds on the ends of their noses where they had butted against the rocks or the timbers of the dam. There were some hundreds of the fish, and every now and then a huge thirty-pounder would wallow on top of the water, or a small, lively one would spring high into the air and fall back with a sounding splash on his side. Here they must wait through the summer, the pool becoming daily hotter, more crowded, more uncomfortable, until the time came when the hatchery men would strip them of their spawn. To an angler the sight was somewhat disquieting, though he might admit the strength of the arguments for the artificial propagation of fish. But to Ethel it seemed a pretty spectacle and a striking contrast to the cruelty of angling.

"Look at them," she said, "how happy they are, and how safe! No fly-fishermen to stick a hook in their mouths and make them suffer. How can you bear to do it?"

"Well," said Chichester, "if it comes to suffering, I doubt whether the fish are conscious of any such thing, as we understand it. But even if they are, they suffer twice as much, and a thousand times as long, shut up in this hot, nasty pool, as they would in being caught in proper style."

"But think of the hook!"

"Hurts about as much as a pin-prick."

"But think of the fearful struggle, and the long, gasping agony on the shore."

"There's no fear in the struggle; it's just a trial of strength and skill, like a game of football. A fish doesn't know anything about death; so he has no fear of it. And there is no gasping on the shore; nothing but a quick rap on the head with a stick, and it's all over."

"But why should he be killed at all?"

"Well," said he, smiling, "there are reasons of taste. You eat salmon, don't you?"

"Ye-e-es," she answered a little doubtfully—then with more assurance, "but remember what Wilbur Short says in that lovely chapter on 'Communion with the Catfish': I want them brought to the table in the simplest and most painless way."

"And that is angling with the fly," said he, still more decidedly. "The fly is not swallowed like a bait. It sticks in the skin of the lip where there is least feeling. There is no torture in the play of a salmon. It's just a fair fight with an unknown opponent. Compare it with the other ways of bringing a fish to the table. If he's caught in a net he hangs there for hours, slowly strangled. If he's speared, half the time the spear slips and he struggles off badly wounded; and if the spear goes through him, he is flung out on the bank to bleed to death. Even if he escapes, he is sure to come to a pitiful end some day—perish by starvation when he gets too old to catch his food—or be torn to pieces by a seal, an otter, or a fish-hawk. Fly-fishing really offers him——"

"Never mind that," said Ethel, "what does it offer you?"

"A gentleman's sport, I suppose," he answered rather slowly. "That is, a fair and exciting effort to get something that is made for human use, in a way that involves some hardship, a little risk, a good deal of skill and patience and perseverance, and plenty of out-of-door life. I guess it must be an inheritance of the old days when people lived by the chase; but, whatever it is, almost every real man feels a certain kind of gratification in being able to get game or fish by the exertion of his own pluck or skill. Some day perhaps this will all be changed, and we shall be contented to take our exercise in the form of massage or croquet, and our food in compressed tablets. But not yet!"

Ethel shook her head and smiled rather sadly. "Bolton," she said, "you discourage me. You argue in this way because you like fishing."

"I do," he answered, promptly. "And so far as I can see, that is the principal reason why your friends, Aurora W. Chime and the Reverend Wilbur Short, and the rest of them, condemn it. They object to the evident pleasure of the fisherman more than to the imaginary suffering of the fish."

"Bolton!" she exclaimed earnestly, "that is not a fair thing to say. They are truly good and noble teachers. They live on a lofty plane and labour for the spreading of the Higher Light. You will know them when we are married. They will be far better company for you than the thoughtless fishermen in your clubs."

Bolton looked a little glum. But he behaved like a gentleman, and cheered up. "Well, well," he said, "of course—you know—your friends, my friends! I'll be glad to meet them, and hear what they have to say, and consider it all very, very seriously. I promised you that, dearest, you remember. But that reminds me—there are two of the men on the *Ste. Marjorie* now, at the club-house—Colonel Lang and the Doctor—old Harvey, you know—fine old chap. It's only twenty miles away. Couldn't we send word to them and ask them to come down for to-morrow? I'm so proud and happy about it all; I'd like to have them here, if you don't mind."

"Why, certainly," she answered, smiling with manifest pleasure, "that will be delightful. We'll send a messenger at once with a note to them. But stop a moment—I have a better plan than that! Why not drive over yourself, this afternoon, to invite them? You'll be glad to see them again; and if you stay here you'll only be in the way until to-morrow," laughed she. "Why not go over and spend the night at the club-house and come back early in the morning? That will be quite like the ancient days—the young adventurer hurrying out of the forest to meet his bride."

Bolton insisted that he couldn't think of it—didn't want to go—would much rather stay where he was. But Ethel was captivated with the novelty of the idea. She always liked her own plans. Besides, she really wished to have him out of the way for the rest of the day and the evening. There was a good deal to be done—letters to be written—a long, personal, uplifting talk with Nancy Bangs, and with Gladys, and with Victoria, and with each of her brothers separately—just half-an-hour of soul-counsel for each one: three hours altogether. She would see them in regular succession, beginning with the youngest brother, and winding up with Nancy. Then she was charmed with the picture of Bolton coming in, post haste, in the morning, as if he had just arrived from a journey across the great northern wilderness. So she carried her point, and when he had agreed to it, he found that he rather liked the plan too. It gave him something to do, a chance to practise his habit of putting things through with determination.

He sent a messenger over to *Sacré Cœur* at once, to say that he was coming and that a canoe should meet him at the landing-place on the North-East Branch. He finished up all the arrangements that remained to be made at Tadousac for the smooth running of to-morrow's affair. He ordered a good horse and a "*quatre roue*" to be ready for him at five o'clock; and having parted with Ethel in the manner appropriate even for so brief a separation, he was away for the river in due season.

The long road with its heavy stretches of sand, its incredibly steep clay hills, its ruts and bumpers over which the buckboard rocked like a boat in a choppy sea, and its succession of shadeless *habitant* houses and discouraged farms, had never seemed to him so monotonous. At eight o'clock, when it was growing dusk, and the moon rising, he reached the landing-place on the Branch, and found his canoe, with his two old canoe-men, P'tit Louis, and Vieux Louis, waiting for him. With their warm, homely greeting his spirits began to revive; and the swift run through foaming rapids and eddying pools, along the four miles of the Branch, brought him into a state of mind that was thoroughly cheerful, not to say exhilarated. There was Brackett's Camp on the point above the Forks; and there was the veteran painter-angler himself, with his white beard and his knickerbockers, standing on the shore to wave a salutation as the canoe shot by the point. There was the main river, rushing down with full waters from the northwest, and roaring past the island. There was the club-house among the white birches and the balsams on the opposite bank, with the two flags fluttering in the moonlight, and the lights twinkling from the long, low veranda. And there were half a dozen canoe-men with a lantern at the landing-steps, and old John the steward in his white apron rubbing his hands, and the Colonel and the Doctor blowing the conch and the fish-horn in merry welcome. It was all very jolly, and Chichester knew at once that he was at home.

Dinner at nine o'clock, before the big open hearth, with a friendly fire. Much chaffing and pleasant talk about the arrangements for to-morrow. A man to be sent off at daybreak to have two buckboards ready at the landing at seven for the drive to Tadousac. Then a reprehensible quantity of tobacco smoked in the book-room, and the tale of the season's angling told from the beginning with many embellishments and divagations. There were stories of good luck and bad; vituperations of the lumbermen for leaving tree-tops and broken branches in the stream to get caught among the rocks and ruin the fishing; accounts of the immense number of salmon that had been seen leaping in the estuary, waiting to come up the river. The interest centred in the story of a huge fish that had taken up his transient abode in the pool called *La Fourche*. The Colonel had pricked and lost the monster two days ago, and had seen him jump twice yesterday. The Colonel was greatly excited about it, and vowed it was the largest salmon seen in the river for ten years—"a whale, I tell you, a regular *marsouin*!" he cried, waving his hands in the air. The Doctor was provokingly sceptical about the size of the fish. But both agreed that there was one thing that must be done. Chichester must try a few casts in *La Fourche* early in the morning.

"Yes," said the Doctor, puffing slowly at his pipe, "plenty of time between daylight and breakfast—good hour for a shy, old fish—we give up our rights to you—the pool is yours—see what you can do with it—may be your last chance to try your luck—" for somehow a rumour in regard to Miss Asham's views on angling had leaked out, and Chichester's friends were inclined to make merry about it.

He rose to the fly decidedly. "I don't know about this being my last chance," said he, "but I'll take it, any way. John, give me a call at half-past three sharp, and tell the two Louis to be ready with the canoe and the rod and the big landing-net."

The little wreaths of grey mist were curling up from the river, and the fleecy western clouds were tinged with wild rose behind the wooded hills, as Chichester stepped out on the slippery rocks at the head of the pool, loosened his line, gave a couple of pulls to his reel to see that the click was all right, waved his slender rod in the air, and sent his fly out across the swift current. Once it swung around, dancing over the water, without result. The second cast carried it out a few feet further, and it curved through a wider arc, but still without result. The third cast sent it a little further still, past the edge of a big sunken rock in the current. There was a flash of silver in the amber water, a great splash on the surface, a broad tail waved in the air and vanished—an immense salmon had risen and missed the fly.

Chichester reeled in his line and sat down. His pulses were hammering, and his chin was set at the angle of solid determination. "The Colonel was right," he said, "that's an enormous fish, *and he's mine!*"

He waited the full five minutes, according to ancient rule, before making the next cast. There was a tiny wren singing among the Balm-o'-Gilead trees on the opposite shore, with a voice that rose silverly above the noise of the rapids. "Cheer up, cheer up," it seemed to say, "what's the matter with you? Don't hurry, don't worry, try it again—again—again!"

But the next cast was made in vain. There was no response. Chichester changed his fly. The result was the same. He tried three different flies in succession without effect. Then he gave the top of the pool a rest, and fished down through the smooth water at the lower end, hooking and losing a small fish. Then he came back to the big salmon again, and fished a small Durham Ranger over him without success. A number four Critchley's Fancy produced no better result. A tiny double Silver Grey brought no response. Then he looked through his fly-box in despair, and picked out an old three-nought Prince of Orange—a huge, gaudy affair with battered feathers, which he had used two years before in flood-water on the Restigouche. At least it would astonish the salmon, for it looked like a last season's picture-hat, very much the worse for wear. It lit on the ripples with a splash, and floated down stream in a dishevelled state till it reached the edge of the sunken rock. Bang! The salmon rose to that incredible fly with a rush, and went tearing across the pool.

The reel shrieked wildly as the line ran out. The rod quivered and bent almost double. Chichester had the butt pressed against his belt, the tip well up in the air, the reel-handle free from any possible touch of coat-flap or sleeve. To check that fierce rush by a hundredth part of a second meant the snapping of the delicate casting-line, or the smashing of the pliant rod-tip. He knew, as the salmon leaped clear of the water, once, twice, three times, that he was in for the fight of his life; and he dropped the point of the rod quickly at each leap to yield to the sudden strain.

The play, at first, was fast and furious. The salmon started up the stream, breasting the rapids at a lively rate, and taking out line as rapidly as the reel could run. Chichester followed along the open shore, holding his rod high with both hands, stumbling over the big rocks, wading knee-deep across a side-channel of the river, but keeping his feet somehow, until the fish paused in the lower part of the pool called *La Batture*. Here there was a chance to reel in line, and the men poled the canoe up from below, to be ready for the next turn in the contest.

The salmon was now sulking at the bottom, with his head down, balanced against the current, and boring steadily. He kept this up for a quarter of an hour, then made a rush up the pool, and a sidelong skittering leap on the surface. Coming back with a sudden turn, he threw a somersault in the air, close to the opposite shore, sank to the bottom and began jigging. Jig, jig, jig, from side to side, with short, heavy jerks, he worked his way back and forth twice the length of the pool. Chichester knew it was dangerous. Any one of these sharp blows might snap the leader or the hook. But he couldn't stop it. There was nothing to do but wait, with tense nerves, until the salmon got through jigging.

The change came suddenly. A notion to go down stream struck the salmon like a flash of lightning; without a moment's warning he took the line over his shoulder and darted into the rapids. "*Il va descendre! Vite, vite! Le canot! Au large!*" shouted the two Louis; but Chichester had already stepped into his place in the middle of the canoe, and there were still forty yards of white line left on the reel, when the narrow boat dashed away in pursuit of the fish, impelled by flashing paddles and flinging the spray to right and left. There were many large rocks half hidden in the wild white water through which they were plunging, and with a long line there was danger that the fish would take a turn around one of them and break away. It was necessary to go faster than he went, in order to retrieve as much line as possible. But paddle as fast as they could the fish kept ahead. He was not towing the boat, of course; for only an ignoramus imagines that a salmon can "tow" a boat, when the casting-line that holds him is a single strand of gut that will break under a strain of ten pounds. He was running away, and the canoe was chasing him through the roaring torrent. But he held his lead, and there were still eighty or ninety yards of line out when he rushed down the last plunge into *La Fourche*.

The situation was this: The river here is shaped like a big Y. The salmon went down the inside edge of the left-hand fork. The canoe followed him down the outside edge of the same fork. When he came to the junction it was natural to suppose that he would follow the current down the main stem of the Y. But instead of that, when the canoe dropped into the comparative stillness of the pool, the line was stretched, taut and quivering, across the foot of the left-hand fork and straight up into the current of the right-hand fork. "He's gone up the other branch," shouted Chichester, above the roar of the stream, "we must follow him! Push across the rapids! Push lively!" So the men seized their setting-poles and shoved as fast as they could across the foot of the rapids, while the rushing torrent threatened at every moment to come in over the side and swamp the canoe. There was a tugging and a trembling on the line, and it led, apparently, up the North-East Branch, past Brackett's Camp. But when the canoe reached the middle of the rapids P'tit Louis uttered an exclamation, leaned over the bow, and pulled up the end of a tree-top, the butt of which was firmly wedged among the rocks. Around the slender branches, waving and quivering in the current with life-like motion, the line was looped. The lower part of it trailed away loosely down the stream into the pool.

Chichester took in the situation in a flash of grieved insight. "Well," he said, "that is positively the worst! Good-by, Mr. Salmon. Louis, pull out that-er, er—that branch!" and he began slowly to reel in the line. But old Louis, in the stern of the canoe, had taken hold of the slack and was pulling it in hand over hand. In a second he shouted "*Arrêtez! Arrêtez! M'sieu, il n'est pas parti, il est la!*"

It was a most extraordinary affair. The spring of the flexible branch had been enough to keep the line from breaking. The salmon, resting in the comparatively still water of the pool, had remained at the end of the slack, and the hook, by some fortunate chance, held firm. It took but a moment to get the line taut and the point of the rod up again. And then the battle began anew. The salmon was refreshed by his fifteen minutes between the halves of the game. No centre in a rush-line ever played harder or faster.

He exhausted the possibilities of attack and defence in *La Fourche*, and then started down the rapids again. In the little pot-hole in mid-river, called *Pool à Michel*, he halted; but it was only for a minute. Soon he was flying down the swift water, the canoe after him, toward the fierce, foaming channel which runs between the island and the eastern bank opposite the club-house. Chichester could see the Colonel and the Doctor at the landing, waving and beckoning to him, as he darted along with the current. Intent upon carrying his fight through to a finish, he gave only a passing glance to what he thought was their friendly gesture of encouragement, took his right hand from the reel for a second to wave a greeting, and passed on, with determination written in every line of his chin, following the fish toward the sea.

Through the clear shallows of *La Pinette*, and the rapids below; through the curling depths of *Pool à Pierre*, and the rapids below; through the long, curving reach of *L'Hirondelle*, and the mad rapids below; so the battle went, and it was fight, fight, fight, and never the word "give up!" At last they came to the head of tide-water and the lake-like pool beside the old quay. Here the methods of the fish changed. There was no more leaping in the air; no more violent jigging; no more swift rushing up or down stream; but instead, there was just an obstinate adherence to the deepest water in the pool, a slow and steady circling round and round in some invisible eddy below the surface. From this he could only be moved by pressure. Now was the time to test the strength of the rod and line. The fish was lifted a few feet by main force, and the line reeled in while the rod was lowered again. Then there was another lift, and another reeling in; and so the process was repeated until he was brought close to the shore in comparatively shallow water. Even yet he did not turn over on his back, or show the white fin; but it was evident that he was through fighting.

Chichester and P'tit Louis stepped out on the shore, old Louis holding the canoe. P'tit Louis made his way carefully to a point of rock, with the wide-mouthed, long-handled net, and dipped it quietly down into the water, two or three feet deep. The fish was guided gently in toward the shore, and allowed to drop back with the smooth current until the net was around him. Then it was swiftly lifted; there was the gleam of an immense mass of silver in its meshes, an instant of furious struggle, the quick stroke of a short, heavy *baton*; and the great salmon was landed and despatched.

The hook was well set in the outside of his jaw, just underneath his chin; no wonder he played so long, with his mouth shut! Bring the spring-balance and test his weight. Forty-eight pounds, full measure, the record salmon of the river—a deep thickset fish, whose gleaming silver sides and sharp teeth proved him fresh-run from the sea! It was a signal victory for an angler to land such a fish under such conditions, and Chichester felt that fortune had been with him.

He enjoyed a quarter of an hour of great satisfaction as the men poled the canoe up-river to the club-house. But there was a shadow of anxiety, of vague misgiving, that troubled him; and he urged the men to make haste. At the landing the Colonel and the Doctor were waiting, with strange, long, inscrutable faces.

"Did you get him?" they said.

"I did," he answered; "forty-eight pounds. Hold up that fish, Louis!"

"Magnificent," they cried, "a great fish! You've done it! But, man, do you know what time it is? Five minutes to ten o'clock!"

Nearly ten, and twenty miles of rough river and road to cover before high noon. Was it possible? In a second it flashed upon Chichester what he had done, what a fearful situation he must face. "Come on, you fellows," he cried, stepping back into the canoe. "Now, Louis, shove her as you never shoved before! Ten dollars apiece if you make the upper landing in half an hour."

The other canoe followed immediately. They found the two buckboards waiting, and scrambled in, explaining to the drivers the necessity for the utmost haste. Chichester's horse was a scrawny, speedy little beast, called *Le Coq Noir*, the champion trotter of the region. "*Hé, Coq!*" shouted the driver, flourishing his whip, at the top of the first long hill; and they started off at a breakneck pace. They passed through the village of *Sacré Cœur* a mile and a half ahead of the other wagon. But on the first steep *côte* beyond the village, the inevitable happened. The buckboard went slithering down the slippery slope of clay, struck a log bridge at the bottom with a resounding thump, and broke an axle clean across. The wheel flew off, and the buckboard came to the ground, and Chichester and the driver tumbled out. The Black Cock gave a couple of leaps and then stood still, looking back with an expression of absolute dismay.

There was nothing to do but wait for the other buckboard, which arrived in ten or fifteen minutes. "Will you have the kindness to lend me your carriage?" said Chichester elaborately. "Oh, don't talk! Get out quick. You can walk!" They changed horses quickly, and Chichester took the reins and drove on. Quarter past eleven; half past; quarter to twelve—and three miles yet to go! It was barely possible to do it. And perhaps it would have been done, if at that moment the good little Black Cock had not stumbled on a loose stone, gone down almost to his knees, and recovered himself with a violent wrench—lame! Chichester was a fair runner and a good walker. But he knew that the steep sandy hills which lay between him and Tadousac could never be covered in fifteen minutes. He gave the reins to the driver, leaned back in the seat, and folded his arms.

At twenty-five minutes past twelve the buckboard passed slowly down the main street of Tadousac, bumped deliberately across the bridge, and drew up before the hotel. The little white chapel on the other side of the road was shut, deserted, sleeping in the sunlight. On the long hotel piazza were half a dozen groups of strangers, summer visitors, evidently in a state of suppressed curiosity and amusement. They fell silent as the disconsolate vehicle came to a halt, and Arthur Asham, the Harvard brother, in irreproachable morning costume and perfect form, moved forward to meet it.

"Well?" said Chichester, as he stepped out.

"Well!" answered the other; and they went a few paces together on the lawn, shaking hands politely and looking at each other with unspoken interrogations.

"I'm awfully sorry," Chichester said, "but it couldn't be helped. A chapter of accidents—I'll explain."

"My dear fellow," answered young Asham, "what good will that do? You needn't explain to me, and you can't explain to Ethel. She is in her most lofty and impossible mood. She'll never listen to you. I'm awfully sorry, too, but I fear it's all over. In fact, she has driven down to the wharf with the others to wait for the Quebec boat, which goes at one. I am staying to get the luggage together and bring it on to-morrow. She gave me this note for you. Will you read it?"

Asham politely turned away, and Chichester read:

MY DEAR MR. CHICHESTER:

Fortunate indeed is the disillusion which does not come too late. But the bridegroom who comes too late is known in time.

You may be sure that I have no resentment at what you have done; I have risen to those heights where anger is unknown. But I now see clearly what I have long felt dimly—that your soul does not keep time with the music to which my life is set. I do not know what *other engagement* kept you away. I do not ask to know. I know only that ours is at an end, and you are at liberty to return to your fishing. That you will succeed in it is the expectation of

Your well-wisher,   E. ASHAM.

Chichester's chin dropped a little as he read. For the first time in his life he looked undecided. Then he folded the note carefully, put it in the breast pocket of his coat, and turned to his companion.

"You will be going up in to-morrow's boat, I suppose. Shall we go together?"

"My dear fellow," said Arthur Asham, "really, you know—I should be delighted. But do you think it would be quite the thing?"

BOOKS THAT I LOVED AS A BOY

It is one thing," said my Uncle Peter, "to be perfectly honest. But it is quite another thing to tell the truth."

"Are you honest in that remark," I asked, "or are you merely telling the truth?"

"Both," he answered, with twinkling eyes, "for that is an abstract remark, in which species of discourse truth-telling is comparatively easy. Abstract remarks are a great relief to the lazy honest man. They spare him the trouble of meticulous investigation of unimportant facts. But a concrete remark, touching upon a number of small details, is full of traps for the truth-teller."

"You agree, then," said I, "with what the Psalmist said in his haste: 'All men are liars'?"

"Not in the least," he replied, laying down the volume which he was apparently reading when he interrupted himself. "I have leisure enough to perceive at once the falsity of that observation which the honest Psalmist recorded for our amusement. The real liars, conscious, malicious, wilful falsifiers, must always be a minority in the world, because their habits tend to bring them to an early grave or a reformatory. It is the people who want to tell the truth, and try to, but do not quite succeed, who are in the majority. Just look at this virtuous little volume which I was reading when you broke in upon me. It is called 'Books that Have Influenced Me.' A number of authors, politicians, preachers, doctors, and rich men profess to give an account of the youthful reading which has been most powerful in the development of their manly minds and characters. To judge from what they have written here you would suppose that these men were as mature and discriminating at sixteen as they are at sixty. They tell of great books, serious books, famous books. But they say little or nothing of the small, amusing books, the books full of fighting and adventure, the books of good stuff poorly written, in which every honest boy, at some time in his life, finds what he wants. They are silent, too, about the books which as a matter of fact had a tremendous influence on them—the plain, dull school-books. For my part, if you asked me what books had influenced me, I should not be telling the truth if my answer left out Webster's Spelling-Book and Greenleaf's Arithmetic, though I did not adore them extravagantly."

"That's just the point, Uncle Peter," said I, "these distinguished men were really trying to tell you about the books that delighted and inspired their youth, the books that they loved as boys."

"Well," said my Uncle Peter, "if it comes to love, and reminiscences of loving, that is precisely the region in which the exact truth is least frequently told. Maturity casts its prim and clear-cut shadow backwards upon the vague and glittering landscape of youth. Whether he speaks of books or of girls, the aged reminiscent attributes to himself a delicacy of taste, a singleness and constancy of affection, and a romantic fervour of devotion, which he might have had, but probably did not. He is not in the least to blame for drawing his fancy-picture of a young gentleman. He cannot help it. It is his involuntary tribute to the ideal. Youth dreams in the future tense; age, in the past participle.

"There is no kind of fiction more amiable and engaging than the droll legends of infancy and pious recollections of boyhood. Do you suppose that Wordsworth has given us a complete portrait of the boy that he was, in 'The Prelude'? He says not a word about the picture of his grandmother that he broke with his whip because the other children gave him a 'dare,' nor about the day when he went up into the attic with an old fencing-foil to commit suicide, nor about the girl with whom he fell in love while he was in France. Do you suppose that Stevenson's 'Memories and Portraits' represent the youthful R. L. S. with photographic accuracy and with all his frills? Not at all. Stevenson's essays are charming; and Wordsworth's poem is beautiful,—in streaks it is as fine as anything that he ever wrote: but both of these works belong to literature because they are packed full of omissions,—which Stevenson himself called 'a kind of negative exaggeration.' No, my dear boy, old Goethe found the right title for a book of reminiscences when he wrote *Wahrheit und Dichtung.*' Truth and poetry,—that is what it is bound to be. I don't know whether Goethe was as honest a man as Wordsworth and Stevenson, but I reckon he told about as much of the truth. Autobiography is usually a man's view of what his biography ought to be."

"This is rather a disquieting thought, my Uncle Peter," said I, "for it seems to leave us all adrift on a sea of illusions."

"Not if you look at it in the right way," he answered, placidly. "We can always get at a few more facts than the man himself gives us, from letters and from the dispassionate recollections of his friends. Besides, a man's view of what his life ought to have been is almost as interesting, and quite as instructive, as a mere chronicle of what it actually was. The truth is, there are two kinds of truth: one kind is——"

Crash! went the fire-irons, tumbling in brazen confusion on the red-brick hearth. When my Uncle Peter has mounted his favourite metaphysical theory, I know that nothing can make him dismount but physical violence. I apologized for the poker and the shovel and the tongs (practising a Stevensonian omission in regard to my own share in the catastrophe), arranged the offending members in their proper station on the left of the fire-place, and took the bellows to encourage the dull fire into a more concrete flame.

"I know enough about the different kinds of truth," said I, working away at the bellows. "Haven't I just been reading Professor Jacobus on 'Varieties of Religious Experience'? What I want now is something concrete; and I wish you would try to give it to me, whatever perils it may involve. Tell me something about the books that you loved as a boy. Never mind your veracity, Uncle Peter, just be honest, that will be enough."

"My veracity!" he grunted, "Humph! Impudent academic mocker, university life has destroyed your last rag of reverence. You have become a mere pivot for turning another fellow's remarks against himself. However, if you will just allow me to talk, and promise to let those fire-irons alone, I will tell you about some of the literary loves of my boyhood."

"I promise not to stir hand or tongue or foot," said I, "unless I see you sliding towards a metaphysical precipice."

"Very well," said my Uncle Peter, "I will do my best to give you the facts. And the first is this: there never was a day in my boyhood when I would not rather go a-fishing than read the best book in the world. If the choice had been given me, I never would have hesitated between climbing a mountain or paddling a canoe, and spending hours in a library. I would have liked also to hunt grizzly bears and to fight Indians,—but these were purely Platonic passions, detached from physical experience. I never realized them in hot blood.

"My native preferences were trimmed and pruned by the fortune that fixed my abode, during nine months of every year, in the city of Brooklyn, where there were no mountains to climb, no rivers to canoe, and no bears to hunt. The winter of my discontent, however, was somewhat cheered by games of football and baseball in the vacant lots on the heights above Wall Street Ferry, and by fierce battles and single combats with the tribes of 'Micks' who inhabited the regions of Furman Street and Atlantic Avenue. There was no High Court of Arbitration to suggest a peaceful solution of the difficulties out of which these conflicts arose. In fact, so far as I can remember, there was seldom a *casus belli* which could be defined and discussed. The warfare simply effervesced, like gas from a mineral spring. It was chronic, geographical, temperamental, and its everlasting continuance was suggested in the threat with which the combatants usually parted: 'wait till we ketch you alone, down our street!'

"There was also a school which claimed some hours of my attention on five days of the week. On holidays my father used to take me on the most delightful fishing excursions to the then unpolluted waters of Coney Island Creek and Sheepshead Bay; and on Monday afternoons in midwinter it was a regular thing that I should go with him to New York to ramble among the old book-shops in Nassau Street and eat oysters at Dorlon's stall, with wooden tables and sawdust-sprinkled floor, in Fulton Market. Say what you please about the friendship of books: it was worth a thousand times more to have the friendship of such a father.

"But there was still a good deal of unoccupied time on my hands between the first of October and the first of May, and having learned to read (in the old-fashioned way, by wrestling with the alphabet and plain spelling), at the age of about five years, I was willing enough to give some of my juvenile leisure to books and try to find out what they had to say about various things which interested me. I did not go to school until my tenth year, and so there was quite a long period left free for general reading, beginning with the delightful old-fashioned books of fairy tales without a moral, and closing with 'Robinson Crusoe,' 'Don Quixote,' and Plutarch's 'Lives of Illustrious Men.' In the last two books I took a real and vivid interest, though I now suspect that it was strictly limited in range. They seemed to open a new world to me, the world of the past, in which I could see men moving about and doing the most remarkable things. Both of these books appeared to me equally historical; I neither doubted the truth of their narratives nor attended to the philosophical reflections with which they were padded. The meaning of the long words I guessed at.

"My taste at this time was most indiscriminate. I could find some kind of enjoyment in almost anything that called itself a book—even a Sunday-school story, or a child's history of the world—provided only it gave something concrete for imagination to work upon. The mere process of reading, with the play of fancy that it quickened, became an agreeable pastime. I got a great deal of pleasure, and possibly some good, out of Bunyan's 'Holy War' (which I perversely preferred to 'The Pilgrim's Progress') and Livingstone's 'Missionary Journals and Researches,' and a book about the Scotch Covenanters. These volumes shortened many a Sunday. I also liked parts of 'The Compleat Angler,' but the best parts I skipped.

"With the coming of school days the time for reading was reduced, and it became necessary to make a choice among books. The natural instincts of youth asserted themselves, and I became a devotee of Captain Mayne Reid and R. M. Ballantyne, whose simple narratives of wild adventure offered a refuge from the monotony of academic life. It gave me no concern that the names of these authors were not included in the encyclopædias of literature nor commented upon in the critical reviews. I had no use for the encyclopædias or reviews; but 'The Young Voyageurs,' 'The White Chief,' 'Osceola the Seminole,' 'The Bush Boys,' 'The Coral Island,' 'Red Eric,' 'Ungava,' and 'The Gorilla Hunters' gave me unaffected delight.

"After about two years of this innocent dissipation I began to feel the desire for a better life, and turned, by my father's advice, to Sir Walter Scott. 'Ivanhoe' and 'The Pirate' pleased me immensely; 'Waverley' and 'The Heart of Midlothian' I accepted with qualifications; but the two of Scott's novels that gave me the most pleasure, I regret to state, were 'Quentin Durward' and 'Count Robert of Paris.' Then Dickens claimed me, and I yielded to the spell of 'Oliver Twist,' 'David Copperfield,' and 'Pickwick Papers.'

"By this time it had begun to dawn upon me that there was a difference among books, not only in regard to the things told, but also in regard to the way of the telling. Unconsciously I became sensitive to the magic of style, and, wandering freely through the library, was drawn to the writers whose manner and accent had a charm for me. Emerson and Carlyle I liked no better than I liked caviar; but Lamb's Essays and Irving's Sketches were fascinating. For histories of literature, thank Heaven, I never had any appetite. I preferred real books to books about books. My only idea of literature was a vivid reflection of life in the world of fancy or in the world of fact.

"In poetry, Milton's 'Comus' was about the first thing that took hold of me; I cannot tell why—perhaps it was because I liked my father's reading of it. But even he could not persuade me to anything more than a dim respect for 'Paradise Lost.' Some of Shakespeare's plays entranced me; particularly 'The Tempest,' 'Romeo and Juliet,' and 'As You Like It;' but there were others which made no real impression upon my wayward mind. Dryden and Pope and Cowper I tried in vain to appreciate; the best that I could attain to was a respectful admiration. 'The Lady of the Lake' and 'The Ancient Mariner,' on the contrary, were read without an effort and with sincere joy. The first book of poetry that I bought for myself was Tennyson's 'Enoch Arden,' and I never regretted the purchase, for it led me on, somehow or other, into the poetic studies and the real intimacy with books which enabled me to go through college without serious damage.

"I cannot remember just when I first read 'Henry Esmond;' perhaps it was about the beginning of sophomore year. But, at all events, it was then that I ceased to love books as a boy and began to love them as a man."

"And do you still love 'Henry Esmond'?" I asked.

"I do indeed," said my Uncle Peter, "and I call it the greatest of English novels. But very close to it I put 'Lorna Doone,' and 'The Heart of Midlothian,' and 'The Cloister and the Hearth,' and 'The Ordeal of Richard Feverel,' and 'John Inglesant.'"

"If you love 'John Inglesant,'" said I, "you must be getting old, Uncle Peter."

"Oh, no," he answered, comfortably lighting his pipe with a live coal of wood from the hearth, "I am only growing up."

AMONG THE QUANTOCK HILLS

MY little Dorothea was the only one of the merry crowd who cared to turn aside with me from the beaten tourist-track, and give up the sight of another English cathedral for the sake of a quiet day among the Quantock Hills. Was it the literary association of that little corner of Somersetshire with the names of Wordsworth and Coleridge that attracted her, I wonder? Or was it the promise that we would hire a dog-cart, if one could be found, and that she should be the driver all through the summer day? I confess my incompetence to decide the question. When one is fifteen years old, a live horse may be as interesting as two dead poets. Not for the world would I put Dorothea to the embarrassment of declaring which was first in her mind.

When she and I got out of the railway carriage, in the early morning, at the humble station of Watchet, (barely mentioned in the guide-book,) our travelling companions jeered gently at our enterprise. As the train rumbled away from the platform, they stuck their heads out of the window and cried, "Where are you going? And how are you going to get there?" Upon my honour, I did not know. That was just the fun of it.

But there was an inn at Watchet, though I doubt whether it had ever entertained tourists. The friendly and surprised landlady thought that she could get us a dog-cart to drive across the country; but it would take about an hour to make ready. So we strolled about the town, and saw the sights of Watchet.

They were few and simple; yet something, (perhaps the generous sunshine of the July day, or perhaps an inward glow of contentment in our hearts,) made them bright and memorable. There were the quaint, narrow streets, with their tiny shops and low stone houses. There was the coast-guard station, with its trim garden, perched on a terrace above the sea. There was the life-boat house, with its doors wide open, and the great boat, spick and span in the glory of new paint, standing ready on its rollers, and the record of splendid rescues in past years inscribed upon the walls. There was the circular basin-harbour, with the workmen slowly repairing the breakwater, and a couple of ancient looking schooners reposing on their sides in the mud at low tide. And there, back on the hill, looking down over the town and far away across the yellow waters of the Bristol Channel, was the high tower of St. Decuman's Church.

"It was from this tiny harbour," said I to Dorothea, "that a great friend of ours, the Ancient Mariner, set sail on a wonderful voyage. Do you remember?

"'The ship was cheered, the harbour cleared,
Merrily did we drop
Below the kirk, below the hill,
Below the lighthouse top.'

"That was the kirk to which he looked back as he sailed away to an unknown country."

"But, father," said Dorothea, "the Ancient Mariner was not a real person. He was only a character!"

"Are you quite sure," said I, "that a character isn't a real person? At all events, it was here that Coleridge, walking from Nether Stowey to Dulverton, saw the old sailor-man. And since Coleridge saw him, I reckon he lived, and still lives. Are we ever going to forget what he has told us?

"'He prayeth best, who loveth best
All things both great and small;
For the dear God who loveth us,
He made and loveth all.'"

Just then a most enchanting little boy and his sister, not more than five years old, came sauntering down the gray street, hand in hand. They were on their way to school, at least an hour late, round and rosy, careless and merry, manifest owners of the universe. We stopped them: they were dismayed, but resolute. We gave each of them a penny; they radiated wonder and joy. Too happy for walking, they skipped and toddled on their way, telling everyone they met, children and grown-up people, of the good fortune that had befallen them. We could see them far down the street, pausing a moment to look in at the shop-windows, or holding up their coppers while they stopped some casual passer-by and made him listen to their story—just like the Ancient Mariner.

By this time the dog-cart was ready. The landlord charged me eighteen shillings for the drive to Bridgewater, nineteen miles away, stopping where we liked, and sending back the cart with the post-boy that evening. By the look on his face I judge that he thought it was too much. But I did not. So we climbed to the high seat, Dorothea took the reins and the whip, and we set forth for a day of unguide-booked pleasure.

What good roads they have in England! Look at the piles of broken stone for repairs, stored in little niches all along the way; see how promptly and carefully every hole is filled up and every break mended; and you will understand how a small beast can pull a heavy load in this country, and why the big draught-horses wear long and do good work. A country with a fine system of roads is like a man with a good circulation of the blood; the labour of life becomes easier, effort is reduced and pleasure increased.

Bowling along the smooth road we crossed a small river at Doniford, where a man was wading the stream below the bridge and fly-fishing for trout; we passed the farmhouses of Rydon, where the steam-thresher was whirling, and the wheat was falling in golden heaps, and the pale-yellow straw was mounded in gigantic ricks; and then we climbed the hill behind St. Audries, with its pretty gray church, and manor house half hidden in the great trees of the park.

The view was one of indescribable beauty and charm; soft, tranquil woods and placid fertile fields; thatched cottages here and there, sheltered and embowered in green; far away on the shore, the village of East Quantockshead; beyond that the broad, tossing waters of the Bristol Channel; and beyond that again, thirty miles away, the silver coast of Wales and the blue mountains fading into the sky. Ships were sailing in and out, toy-like in the distance. Far to the north-west, we could see the cliffs of the Devonshire coast; to the north-east the islands of Steep Holm and Flat Holm rose from the Severn Sea; and around the point beyond them, in the little churchyard of Clevedon, I knew that the dust of Arthur Henry Hallam, whose friendship Tennyson has immortalized in "In Memoriam," was sleeping

"By the pleasant shore
And in the hearing of the wave."

High overhead the great white clouds were loitering across the deep-blue heaven. White butterflies wavered above the road. Tall foxglove spires lit the woodland shadows with rosy gleams. Bluebells and golden ragwort fringed the hedge-rows. A family of young wrens fluttered in and out of the hawthorns. A yellow-hammer, with cap of gold, warbled his sweet, common little song. The colour of the earth was warm and red; the grass was of a green so living that it seemed to be full of conscious gladness. It was a day and a scene to calm and satisfy the heart.

At Kilve, a straggling village along the road-side, I remembered Wordsworth's poem called "An Anecdote for Fathers." The little boy in the poem says that he would rather be at Kilve than at Liswyn. When his father foolishly presses him to give a reason for his preference, he invents one:

"At Kilve there was no weather-cock,
And that's the reason why."

Naturally, I looked around the village to see whether it would still answer to the little boy's description. Sure enough, there was no weather-cock in sight, not even on the church-tower.

Not far beyond Kilve we saw a white house, a mile or so away, standing among the trees to the south, at the foot of the high-rolling Quantock Hills. Our post-boy told us that it was Alfoxton, "where Muster Wudswuth used to live," but just how to get to it he did not know. So we drove into the next village of Holford and made inquiry at the "Giles' Plough Inn," a most quaint and rustic tavern with a huge ancient sign-board on the wall, representing Giles with his white horse and his brown horse and his plough. Turning right and left and right again, through narrow lanes, between cottages gay with flowers, we came to a wicket-gate beside an old stone building, and above the gate a notice warning all persons not to trespass on the grounds of Alfoxton. But the gate was on the latch, and a cottager, passing by, told us that there was a "right of way" which could not be closed—"goä straight on, and nivver feär, nubbody 'll harm ye."

A few steps brought us into the thick woods, and to the edge of a deep glen, spanned by a bridge made of a single long tree-trunk, with a hand-rail at one side. Down below us, as we stood on the swaying bridge, a stream dashed and danced and sang through the shade, among the ferns and mosses and wild flowers. The steep sides of the glen glistened with hollies and laurels, tangled and confused with blackberry bushes. Overhead was the interwoven roof of oaks and ashes and beeches. Here it was that Wordsworth, in the year 1797, when he was feeling his way back from the despair of mind which followed the shipwreck of his early revolutionary dreams, used to wander alone or with his dear sister Dorothy. And here he composed the "Lines Written in Early Spring"—almost the first notes of his new poetic power:

"I heard a thousand blended notes,
While in a grove I sat reclined,
In that sweet mood when pleasant thoughts
Bring sad thoughts to the mind.
"Through primrose tufts, in that green bower,
The periwinkle trailed its leaves;
And 'tis my faith that every flower
Enjoys the air it breathes."

Climbing up to the drive, we followed a long curving avenue toward the house. It led along the breast of the hill, with a fine view under the spreading arms of the great beeches, across the water to the Welsh mountains. On the left the woods were thick. Huge old hollies showed the ravages of age and storm. A riotous undergrowth of bushes and bracken filled the spaces between the taller trees. Doves were murmuring in the shade. Rabbits scampered across the road. In an open park at the edge of the wood, a herd of twenty or thirty fallow deer with pale spotted sides and twinkling tails trotted slowly up the slope.

Alfoxton House is a long, two-story building of white stucco, with a pillared porch facing the hills. The back looks out over a walled garden, with velvet turf and brilliant flowers and pretty evergreens, toward the sea-shore. The house has been much changed and enlarged since the days when young William Wordsworth rented it, (hardly more than a good farmhouse), for twenty-three pounds a year, and lived in it with his sister from 1797 to 1798, in order to be near his friend Coleridge at Nether Stowey. There is not a room that remains the same, though the present owner has wisely brought together as much of the old wood-work as possible into one chamber, which is known as Wordsworth's study. But the poet's real study was out of doors; and it was there that we looked for the things that he loved.

In a field beyond the house there were two splendid old ash-trees, which must have been full-grown in Wordsworth's day. We stretched ourselves among the gnarled roots, my little Dorothy and I, and fed our eyes upon the view that must have often refreshed him, while his Dorothy was leading his heart back with gentle touches toward the recovery of joy. There was the soft, dimpled landscape, in tones of silvery verdure, blue in distance, green near at hand, sloping down to the shining sea. The sky was delicate and friendly, bending close above us, with long lines of snowy clouds. There was hardly a breath of wind. Far to the east we saw the rich plain rolling away to Bridgewater and the bare line of the distant Mendip Hills. Shadows of clouds swept slowly across the land. Colours shifted and blended. On the steep hill behind us a row of trees stood out clear against the blue.

"With ships the sea was sprinkled far and nigh."

What induced Wordsworth to leave a place so beautiful? A most prosaic reason. He was practically driven out by the suspicion and mistrust of his country neighbours. A poet was a creature that they could not understand. His long rambles among the hills by day and night, regardless of the weather; his habit of talking to himself; his intimacy and his constant conferences on unknown subjects with Coleridge, whose radical ideas were no secret; his friendship with Thelwall the republican, who came to reside in the neighbourhood; the rumour that the poet had lived in France and sympathized with the Revolution—all these were dark and damning evidences to the rustic mind that there was something wrong about this long-legged, sober-faced, feckless young man. Probably he was a conspirator, plotting the overthrow of the English Government, or at least of the Tory party. So ran the talk of the country-side; and the lady who owned Alfoxton was so alarmed by it that she declined to harbour such a dangerous tenant any longer. Wordsworth went with his sister to Germany in 1798; and in the following year they found a new home at Dove Cottage, in Grasmere, among the English lakes.

On our way out to the place where we had left our equipage, we met the owner of the estate, walking with his dogs. He was much less fierce than his placard. It may have been something in Dorothea's way that mollified him, but at all events he turned and walked with us to show us the way up the "Hareknap"—the war-path of ancient armies—to a famous point of view. There we saw the Quantock Hills, rolling all around us. They were like long smooth steep billows of earth, covered with bracken, and gorse, and heather just coming into bloom. Thick woodlands hung on their sides, but above their purple shoulders the ridges were bare. They looked more than a thousand feet high. Among their cloven combes, deep-thicketed and watered with cool springs, the wild red deer still find a home. And it was here (not in Cardiganshire as the poem puts it) that Wordsworth's old huntsman, "Simon Lee," followed the chase of the stag.

It was a three-mile drive from Holford to Nether Stowey. Dorothea remarked that Coleridge and the Wordsworths must have been great walkers if this was their idea of living close together. And so they were, for that bit of road seemed to them only a prelude to a real walk of twenty or thirty miles. The exercise put them in tune for poetry, and their best thoughts came to them when they were afoot.

"The George" at Nether Stowey is a very modest inn, the entrance paved with flag-stones, the only public room a low-ceiled parlour; but its merits are far beyond its pretensions. We lunched there most comfortably on roast duck and green peas, cherry tart and cheese, and then set out to explore the village, which is closely built along the roads whose junction is marked by a little clock-tower. The market-street is paved with cobble-stones, and down one side of it runs a small brook, partly built in and covered over, but making a merry noise all the way. Coleridge speaks of it in his letters as "the dear gutter of Stowey."

Just outside of the town is the Castle Mound, a steep, grassy hill, to the top of which we climbed. There was the distinct outline of the foundations of the old castle, built in the Norman times; we could trace the moat, and the court, and all the separate rooms; but not a stone of the walls remained—only a ground-plan drawn in the turf of the hill-top. All the pride and power of the Norman barons had passed like the clouds that were sailing over the smooth ridges of the Quantocks.

Coleridge was twenty-four years old when he came to Nether Stowey with his young wife and a boy baby. Troubles had begun to gather around him; he was very poor, tormented with neuralgia, unable to find regular occupation, and estranged by a quarrel from his friend and brother-in-law, Robert Southey. Thomas Poole, a well-to-do tanner at Nether Stowey, a man of good education and noble character, a great lover of poetry and liberty, had befriended Coleridge and won his deep regard and affection. Nothing would do but that Poole should find a cottage near to his own house, where the poet could live in quietude and congenial companionship.

The cottage was found; and, in spite of Poole's misgivings about its size, and his warnings in regard to the tedium and depression of village life, Coleridge took it and moved in with his little family on the last day of the year 1796—a cold season for a "flitting!" We can imagine the young people coming down the Bridgewater road through the wintry weather with their few household goods in a cart.

The cottage was at the western end of the village; and there it stands yet, a poor, ugly house, close on the street. We went in, and after making clear to the good woman who owned it that we were not looking for lodgings, we saw all that there was to see of the dwelling. There were four rooms, two downstairs and two above. All were bare and disorderly, because, as the woman explained, house-cleaning was in progress. It was needed. She showed us a winding stair, hardly better than a ladder, which led from the lower to the upper rooms. There was no view, no garden. But in Coleridge's day there was a small plot of ground belonging to the house and running back to the large and pleasant place of his friend Poole. It was upon this little garden that the imagination of the new tenant was fixed, and there he saw, in his dream, the corn and the cabbages and the potatoes growing luxuriantly under his watchful and happy care; enough, he hoped, to feed himself and his family, and to keep a couple of what he called "snouted and grunting cousins" on the surplus. "Literature," he wrote, "though I shall never abandon it, will always be a secondary object with me. My poetic vanity and my political favour have been exhaled, and I would rather be an expert, self-maintaining gardener than a Milton, if I could not unite them both." How amusing are men's dreams—those of humility as well as those of ambition! There is a peculiarly Coleridgean touch in that last hint of uniting Milton and the market-gardener.

In fact, I doubt whether the garden ever paid expenses; but, on the other hand, the crop of poetry that sprung from Coleridge's marvellous mind was rich and splendid. It was while he lived in this poor little cottage that he produced "Osorio," "Fears in Solitude," "Ode to France," the first part of "Christabel," "Frost at Midnight," "The Nightingale," "Kubla Khan," and "The Ancient Mariner," and planned with his friend Wordsworth "Lyrical Ballads," the most epoch-making book of modern English poetry. Truly this year, from April, 1797, to April, 1798, was the *annus mirabilis* of his life. Never again was he so happy, never again did he do such good work, as when he harboured in this cottage, and slipped through the back gate to walk in the garden or read in the library of his good friend, Thomas Poole, or trudged down the road to the woods of Alfoxton to talk with the Wordsworths. He wrote lovingly of the place:

"And now, beloved Stowey, I behold
Thy Church-tower, and methinks, the four huge elms
Clustering, which mark the mansion of my friend;
And close behind them, hidden from my view,
Is my own lovely cottage, where my babe
And my babe's mother dwell in peace."

Dorothea and I were not sure that Mrs. Coleridge enjoyed the cottage as much as he did. Greta Hall, at Keswick, with its light airy rooms and its splendid view, was her next home; and when we saw it, a few weeks later, we were glad that the babe and the babe's mother had lived there.

But the afternoon was waning, and we must turn our back to the Quantocks, and take to the road again. Past the church and the manor house, with its odd little turreted summer-house, or *gazébo*, perched on the corner of the garden-wall; past a row of ancient larch-trees and a grove of Scotch pines; past smooth-rolling meadows full of cattle and sheep; past green orchards full of fruit for the famous and potent Somereset cider; past the old town of Cannington, where the fair Rosamund was born, and where, on our day, we saw the whole population in the streets, perturbed by some unknown excitement and running to and fro like mad folks; past sleepy farms and spacious parks and snug villas, we rolled along the high-road, into Bridgewater, a small city, where they make "Bath bricks," and where the statue of Admiral Blake swaggers sturdily in the market-place. There we took the train to join our friends at dinner in Bristol; and so ended our day among the Quantock Hills.

BETWEEN THE LUPIN AND THE LAUREL

NO other time of the year, on our northern Atlantic seaboard, is so alluring, so delicate and subtle in its charm, as that which follows the fading of the bright blue lupins in the meadows and along the banks of the open streams, and precedes the rosy flush of myriad laurels in full bloom on the half-wooded hillsides, and in the forest glades, and under the lofty shadow of the groves of yellow pine. Then, for a little while, the spring delays to bourgeon into summer: the woodland maid lingers at the garden gate of womanhood, reluctant to enter and leave behind the wild sweetness of freedom and uncertainty.

Winter is gone for good and all. There is no fear that he will come sneaking back with cold hands to fetch something that he has forgotten. Nature is secure of another season of love, of mating, of germination, of growth, of maturity—a fair four months in which the joyful spirit of life may have its way and work its will. The brown earth seems to thrill and quicken everywhere with new impulses which transform it into springing grass and overflowing flowers. The rivers are at their best: strong and clear and musical, the turbulence of early floods departed, the languor of later droughts not yet appearing. The shrunken woods expand; the stringent, sparkling wintry stars grow mild and liquid, shining with a tremulous and tender light; the whole world seems larger, happier, more full of untold, untried possibilities. The air vibrates with wordless promises, calls, messages, beckonings; and fairy-tales are told by all the whispering leaves.

Yet though the open season is now secure, it is not yet settled. No chance of a relapse into the winter's death, but plenty of change in the unfolding of the summer's life. There are still caprices and wayward turns in nature's moods; cold nights when the frost-elves are hovering in the upper air; windy mornings which shake and buffet the tree-tassels and light embroidered leaves; sudden heats of tranquil noon through which the sunlight pours like a flood of eager love, pressing to create new life.

Birds are still mating; and quarrelling, too. Their songs, their cries of agitation and expectancy, their call notes, their lyrical outpourings of desire are more varied and more copious than ever. All day long they are singing, and every hour on the wing, coming up from the southward, passing on to the northward, fluttering through the thickets, exploring secret places, choosing homes and building nests. In every coppice there is a running to and fro, a creeping, a scampering, and a leaping of wild creatures. At the roots of the bushes and weeds and sedges, in the soft recesses of the moss, and through the intricate tangle of withered grass-blades pierced with bright-green shoots, there is a manifold stir of insect life. In the air millions of gauzy wings are quivering, swarms of ethereal, perishable creatures rising and falling and circling in mystical dances of joy. Fish are leaping along the stream. The night breeze trembles with the shrill, piercing chorus of the innumerable hylas.

Late trees, like the ash, the white oak, the butternut, are still delaying to put forth their full foliage; veiled in tender, transparent green, or flushed with faint pink, they stand as if they were waiting for a set time; and the tiny round buds on the laurels, clustered in countless umbels of bright rose among the dark green, glistening leaves, are closed, hiding their perfect beauty until the day appointed. It is the season of the unfulfilled desire, the eager hope, the coming surprise. To-day the world is beautiful; but to-morrow, next day—who knows when?—something more beautiful is coming, something new, something perfect. This is the lure of wild nature between the lupin and the laurel.

At such a season it is hard to stay at home. The streets all seem to lead into the country, and one longs to follow their leading, out into the highway, on into the winding lane, on into the wood-road, on and on, until one comes to that mysterious and delightful ending, (told of in the familiar saying,) where the road finally dwindles into a squirrel track and runs up a tree—not an ending at all, you see, but really a beginning! For there is the tree; and if you climb it, who knows what new landscape, what lively adventure, will open before you? At any rate, you will get away from the tyranny of the commonplace, the conventional, the methodical, which transforms the rhythm of life into a logarithm. Even a small variation, a taste of surprise, will give you what you need as a spring tonic: the sense of escape, a day off.

Living in a university town, and participating with fidelity in its principal industry, I find that my own particular nightmare of monotony takes the form of examination papers—quires of them, reams of them, stacks of them—a horrid incubus, always oppressive, but then most unendurable when the book-room begins to smell musty in the morning, and the fire is unlit upon the hearth, and last night's student-lamp is stuccoed all over with tiny gnats, and the breath of the blossoming grape is wafted in at the open window, and the robins, those melodious rowdies, are whistling and piping over the lawn and through the trees in voluble mockery of the professor's task. "Come out," they say, "come out! Why do you look in a book? Double, double, toil and trouble! Give it up—tup, tup, tup! Come away and play for a day. What do you know? Let it go. You're as dry as a chip, chip, chip! Come out, won't you? will you?"

Truly, these examination questions that I framed with such pains look very dull and tedious now—a desiccation of the beautiful work of the great poets. And these answers that the boys have wrought out with such pains, on innumerable pads of sleazy white paper, how little they tell me of what the fellows really know and feel! Examination papers are "requisite and necessary," of course; I can't deny it—requisite formalities and necessary absurdities. But to turn the last page of the last pad, and mark it with a red pencil and add it to the pile of miseries past, and slip away from books to nature, from learning to life, between the lupin and the laurel—that is a pleasure doubled by release from pain.

I think a prize should be offered for the discovery of good places to take a free and natural outing within easy reach of the great city and the routine of civilized work—just-over-the-fence retreats, to which you can run off without much preparation, and from which you can come back again before your little world discovers your absence. That was the charm of Hopkinson Smith's sketch, "A Day at Laguerre's"; and an English writer who calls himself "A Son of the Marshes" has written a delightful book of interviews with birds and other wild things, which bears the attractive title, "Within an Hour of London Town." But I would make it a condition of the prize that the name of the hiding-place should not be published, lest the careless, fad-following crowd should flock thither and spoil it. Let the precious news be communicated only by word of mouth, or by letter, as a confidence and gift of friendship, so that none but the like-minded may strike the trail to the next-door remnant of Eden.

It was thus that my four friends—Friends in creed as well as in deed—told to me, one of "the world's people," toiling over my benumbing examination papers, their secret find of a little river in South Jersey, less than an hour from Philadelphia, where one could float in a canoe through mile after mile of unbroken woodland, and camp at night in a bit of wilderness as wildly fair as when the wigwams of the Lenni-Lenape were hidden among its pine groves. The Friends said that they "had a concern" to guide me to their delectable retreat, and that they hoped the "way would open" for me to come. Canoes and tents and camp-kit? "That will all be provided; it is well not to be anxious concerning these sublunary things." Mosquitoes? "Concerning this, also, thee must learn to put thy trust in Providence; yet there is a happy interval, as it were, between the fading of the hepatica and the blooming of the mosquito, when the woods of South Jersey are habitable for man, and it would be most prudent to choose this season for the exercise of providential trust regarding mosquitoes." Examination papers? Duty? "Surely thee must do what thee thinks will do most good, and follow the inward voice. And if it calls thee to stay with the examination papers, or if it calls thee to go with us, whichever way, thee will be resigned to obey." Fortunately, there was no doubt about the inward voice; it was echoing the robins; it was calling me to go out like Elijah and dwell under a juniper-tree. I replied to the Friends in the words of one of their own preachers: "I am resigned to go, or resigned to stay, but most resigned to go"; and we went.

The statue of William Penn seemed to look benignantly down upon us as we passed, bag and bundle in hand, along the regular Philadelphia shortcut which leads through the bowels of the Courthouse, from the Broad Street station to John Wanamaker's store. Philadelphians always have the air of doing something very modern, hurried, and time-saving when they lead you through that short-cut. But we were not really in a hurry; we had all the time there is; we could afford to gape a little in the shop-windows. The spasmodic Market Street trolley-car and the deliberate Camden ferry-boat were rapid enough for us. The gait of the train on the Great Sandy and Oceanic Railway was neither too fast nor too slow. Even the deserted condition of Hummingtown, where we disembarked about eleven o'clock in the morning, and found that the entire population had apparently gone to a Decoration Day ball-game, leaving post-office, telegraph station, fruit store, bakery, all closed—even this failure to meet our expectations did not put us out of humour with the universe, or call forth rude words on the degeneracy of modern times.

Our good temper was imperturbable; for had we not all "escaped as a bird from the hand of the fowler"—Master Thomas from the mastery of his famous boarding-school in Old Chester, and Friends Walter and Arthur from the uninspired scripture of their ledgers and day-books, and I from the incubation of those hideous examination papers, and the gentle Friend William from his—there! I have forgotten what particular monotony William was glad to get away from; but I know it was from something. I could read it in his face; in his pleased, communicative silence; in the air of almost reckless abandon with which he took off his straight-breasted Quaker coat, and started out in his shirt-sleeves to walk with Walter, ahead of the cart which carried our two canoes and the rest of us over to the river.

It was just an ordinary express wagon, with two long, heavy planks fastened across the top of it. On these the canoes were lashed, with their prows projecting on either flank of the huge, pachydermatous horse, who turned his head slowly from one side to the other, as he stalked along the level road, and looked back at his new environment with stolid wonder. He must have felt as if he were suffering "a sea change," and going into training for Neptune's stud. The driver sat on the dashboard between the canoes; and Master Thomas, Arthur, and I were perched upon the ends of the planks with our feet dangling over the road. It was not exactly what one would call an elegant equipage, but it rolled along.

The road was of an uncompromising straightness. It lay across the slightly undulating sandy plain like a long yellow ruler; and on each side were the neatly marked squares and parallelograms of the little truck farms, all cultivated by Italians. Their new and unabashed frame houses were freshly painted in incredible tones of carrot yellow, pea green, and radish pink. The few shade trees and the many fruit trees, with whitewashed trunks, were set out in unbending regularity of line. The women and children were working in the rows of strawberries which covered acre after acre of white sand with stripes of deep green. Some groups of people by the wayside were chattering merrily together in the language which Byron calls

"That soft bastard Latin
Which melts like kisses from a woman's mouth."

It was a scene of foreign industry and cheerfulness, a bit of little Italy transplanted. Only the landscape was distinctly not Italian, but South Jersey to the core. Yet the people seemed at home and happy in it. Perhaps prosperity made up to them for the loss of picturesqueness.

At New Prussia the road was lifted by a little ridge, and for a few minutes we travelled through another European country. Two young men were passing ball in front of a beer saloon. "Vot's der news?" said one of them in a strong German accent. We were at a loss for an answer, as it was rather a dull time in international politics; but Master Thomas began to say something about the riots in Russia. "Russia hell!" said the young man. "How's der ball-game? Vas our nine of Hummingtown ahead yet?" We could give no information on this important subject, but we perceived that New Prussia was already Americanized.

A mile or so beyond this the road dipped gently into a shallow, sparsely wooded valley and we came to a well-built stone bridge which spanned, with a single narrow arch, the little river of our voyage. It was like a big brook, flowing with deep, brown current out of a thicket, and on through a small cranberry bog below the bridge. Here we launched and loaded our canoes, and went down with the stream, through a bit of brushy woodland, till we found a good place for luncheon. For though it was long past noon and we were very hungry, we wanted to get really into the woods before we broke bread together.

Scanty woods they were, indeed; just a few scrub pines growing out of a bank of clean white sand. But we spread a rubber blanket in their thin shade, and set forth our repast of biscuits and smoked beef and olives, and fell to eating as heartily and merrily as if it had been a banquet. The yellow warblers and the song sparrows were flitting about us; and two cat-birds and a yellow-throat were singing from the thicket on the opposite shore. There were patches of snowy sand-myrtle and yellow poverty-plant growing around our table; tiny, hardy, heath-like creatures, delicately wrought with bloom as if for a king's palace; irrepressible and lovely offspring of the yearning for beauty that hides in the poorest place of earth. In a still arm of the stream, a few yards above us, was a clump of the long, naked flower-scapes of the golden-club, now half entered upon their silvery stage.

It was strange what pleasure these small gifts of blossom and song brought to us. We were in the mood which Wordsworth describes in the lines written in his pocket-copy of "The Castle of Indolence":

"There did they dwell, from earthly labour free,
As happy spirits as were ever seen;
If but a bird, to keep them company,
Or butterfly sate down, they were, I ween,
As pleased as if the same had been a Maiden-queen."

But our "earthly labour" began again when we started down the stream; for now we had fairly entered the long strip of wilderness which curtains its winding course. On either hand the thickets came down so close to the water that there were no banks left: just woods and water blending; and the dark topaz current swirling and gurgling through a clump of bushes or round the trunk of a tree, as if it did not care what path it took so long as it got through. Alders and pussy-willows, viburnums, clethras, chokecherries, swamp maples, red birches, and all sorts of trees and shrubs that are water-loving, made an intricate labyrinth for the stream to thread; and through the tangle, cat-briers, blackberries, fox grapes, and poison ivy were interlaced.

Worst of all was the poison ivy, which seemed here to deserve its other name of poison oak, for it was more like a tree than a vine, flinging its knotted branches from shore to shore, and thrusting its pallid, venomous blossoms into our faces. Walter was especially susceptible to the influence of this poison, so we put him in the middle of our canoe, and I, being a veteran and immune, took the bow-paddle. It was no easy task to guide the boat down the swift current, for it was bewilderingly crooked, twisting and turning upon itself in a way that would have made the far-famed Mæander look like a straight line. Many a time it ran us deep into the alders, or through a snarl of thorn-set vines, or crowded us under the trunk of an overhanging tree. We glimpsed the sun through the young leaves, now on our right hand, now on our left, now in front of us, and now over our shoulders. After several miles of this curliewurlie course, the incoming of the Penny Pot Stream on the left broadened the flowing trail a little. Not far below that, the Hospitality Branch poured in its abundant waters on the right, and we went floating easily down a fair, open river.

There were banks now, and they were fringed with green borders of aquatic plants, rushes, and broad spatter-docks, and flags, and arrow-heads, and marsh-marigolds, and round-leaved pond-lilies, and pointed pickerel-weed. The current was still rapid and strong, but it flowed smoothly through the straight reaches and around the wide curves. On either hand the trees grew taller and more stately. The mellow light of afternoon deepened behind them, and the rich cloud colours of approaching sunset tinged the mirror of the river with orange and rose. We floated into a strip of forest. The stream slackened and spread out, broadening into the head of a pond. On the left, there was a point of higher land, almost like a low bluff, rising ten or twelve feet above the water and covered with a grove of oaks and white pines. Here we beached our canoes and made our first camp.

A slender pole was nailed horizontally between two trees, and from this the shelter tent was stretched with its sloping roof to the breeze and its front open toward the pond. There were no balsam or hemlock boughs for the beds, so we gathered armfuls of fallen leaves and pine needles, and spread our blankets on this rude mattress. Arthur and Walter cut wood for the fire. Master Thomas and William busied themselves with the supper. There was a famous dish of scrambled eggs, and creamed potatoes, and bacon, and I know not what else. We ate till we could eat no more, and then we sat in the wide-open tent, with the camp-fire blazing in front of us, and talked of everything under the stars.

I like the Quaker speech: the gentle intimacy of their "little language," with its quaint "thees" and "thous," and the curious turn they give to their verbs, disregarding the formalities of grammar. "Will thee go," "has thee seen," "does thee like"—that is the way they speak it; an unjustifiable way, I know, but it sounds pleasantly. I like the Quaker spirit and manners, at least as I have found them in my friends: sober but not sad, plain but very considerate, genuinely simple in the very texture of their thoughts and feelings, and not averse to that quiet mirth which leaves no bitter taste behind it. One thing that I cannot understand in Charles Lamb is his confession, in the essay on "Imperfect Sympathies," that he had a prejudice against Quakers. But then I remember that one of his best bits of prose is called "A Quaker's Meeting," and one of his best poems is about the Quaker maiden, Hester Savory, and one of his best lovers and companions was the broad-brim Bernard Barton. I conclude that there must be different kinds of Quakers, as there are of other folks, and that my particular Friends belong to the tribe of Bernard and Hester, and their spiritual ancestry is in the same line with the poet Whittier.

Yet even these four are by no means of one pattern. William is the youngest of the group, but the oldest-fashioned Friend, still clinging very closely to the old doctrines and the old ritual of silent simplicity, and wearing the straight-cut, collarless coat, above which his youthful face looks strangely ascetic and serene. I can imagine him taking joyfully any amount of persecution for his faith, in the ancient days; but in these tolerant modern times, he has the air of waiting very tranquilly and with good humour for the world to see that the old ways are the best, and to come round to them again.

Walter and Arthur are Young Quakers, men of their time, diligent in business, fond of music and poetry, loyal to the society of their fathers, but more than willing to see its outward manners and customs, and even some of its ways of teaching, quietly modified to meet the needs and conditions of the present. In appearance you could hardly tell them from the world's people; yet I perceive that inwardly the meeting-house has made its indelible mark upon them in a certain poise of mind and restraint of temper, a sweet assurance of unseen things, and a mind expectant of spiritual visitations.

Master Thomas, the leader of our expedition, is a veteran school-teacher, in one of the largest and most successful of the Friends' boarding-schools. To him I think there is neither old nor new in doctrine; there is only the truth, and the only way to be sure of it is by living. He is a fervent instructor, to whom an indifferent scholar is a fascinating problem, and a pupil who "cannot understand mathematics" offers a new adventure. But part of his instruction, and the part to which he gives himself most ardently, is the knowledge and love of the great out-of-doors. Every summer he runs a guest-camp in the Adirondacks, and in the fall he gives a big camp-supper for the old pupils of his school, who come back by the hundred to renew their comradeship with "Master Thomas." It is good to have an academic title like that. Arthur and William and Walter are among his old boys, and they still call him by that name. But it is partly because he has also been their master in fire-making, and tent-pitching, and cooking, and canoe-building, and other useful arts which are not in the curriculum of book-learning.

Here, then, I have sketched the friends who sat with me before the glowing logs on that cool, starry night, within a few miles of the railroad and not far away from the roaring town, yet infinitely deep in the quietude of nature's heart. Of the talk I can remember little, except that it was free and friendly, natural and good. But one or two stories that they told me of a famous old Philadelphia Quaker, Nicholas Waln, have stuck in my memory.

His piety was tempered with a strong sense of humour, and on one occasion when he was visiting a despondent sister, he was much put out by her plaintive assertions that she was going to die. "I have no doubt," said he finally, "but that thou will; and when thou gets to heaven give my love to the Apostle Paul, and tell him I wish he would come back to earth and explain some of the hard things in his epistles." At another time he overtook a young woman Friend in worldly dress, upon which he remarked, "Satin without, and Satan within." But this time he got as good as he gave, for the young woman added, "And old Nick behind!" When it was the fashion to wear a number of capes, one above another, on a great-coat, Nicholas met a young acquaintance dressed in the mode. Taking hold of one of the capes, the old Quaker asked innocently what it was. "That is Cape Hatteras," said the pert youth. "And this?" said Nicholas, touching another. "Oh, that is Cape Henlopen," was the answer. "Then, I suppose," said Nicholas gravely, pointing to the young man's head, "this must be the lighthouse." I think that Charles Lamb, despite his imperfect sympathy with Quakers, would have liked this turn to the conversation.

Bedtime comes at last, even when you are lodging at the Sign of the Beautiful Star. There were a few quiet words read from a peace-giving book, and a few minutes of silent thought in fellowship, and then each man pulled his blanket round him and slept as if there were no troubles in the world.

Certainly there were none waiting for us in the morning; for the day rose fresh and fair, and we had nothing to do but enjoy it. After fishing for an hour or two, to supply our larder, we paddled down the pond, which presently widened into quite a lake, ending in a long, low dam with trees growing all across it. Here was the forgotten village of Watermouth, founded before the Revolution, and once the seat of a flourishing iron industry, but now stranded between two railways, six miles on either side of it, and basking on the warm sand-hills in a painless and innocent decay.

Watermouth had done nothing to deserve ill fortune. But the timber which had once been floated down its river was all cut and gone; and the bog-iron which had once been smelted in its furnaces was all used up; and the forest glass-makers and charcoal-burners who had once traded in its store had all disappeared; and the new colonies of fruit-growers and truck-farmers from Italy and Germany did not like to settle quite so far from the railway; and there was nothing left for Watermouth but to sit in the sun and doze, while one family after another melted away, and house after house closed its windows and its doors.

The manor-house stood in spacious grounds sloping gently down to the southern shore of the lake, well planted with a variety of shade trees and foreign evergreens, but overgrown with long grass and straggling weeds. Master Thomas and I landed, and strolled through the neglected lawn toward the house, in search of a possible opportunity to buy some fresh eggs. The long, pillared veranda, with its French windows opening to the floor; the wide double door giving entrance to a central hall; a score of slight and indefinable signs told us that the mansion had seen its days of comfort and elegance. But there were other signs—a pillar leaning out of plumb, a bit of railing sagging down, a board loose at the corner—which seemed to speak of the pluperfect tense. In a fragment of garden at one side, where a broken trellis led to an arbor more than half hidden by vines, we saw a lady, clad in black, walking slowly among the bewildered roses and clumps of hemerocallis, stooping now and then to pluck a flower or tenderly to lift and put aside a straggling branch.

"This is plainly the mistress of the house," said Master Thomas; "does thee think that we could make bold to speak with her upon the subject of fresh eggs?"

"I think," said I, "that with thy friendly tact thee could speak with anybody upon any subject."

"But my coat?" said Master Thomas, for he had left it in the boat.

"'Tis a warm day, Master Thomas," I answered, "and doubtless the lady will know that thee has a coat, when she hears thee speak. But in any event, it is wise not to think too much of these mundane things. Let us go up."

So we made our salutations, stated our names and our occupations, and described the voyage which had brought us to Watermouth, in a way that led naturally to an explanation of our present need and desire for fresh eggs: though indeed it was hardly necessary to be explicit on that point, for our little tin pail betrayed us as foragers. The lady in black received us with gracious dignity, identified and placed us without difficulty (indeed she knew some relation of each of us), and gave us hospitable assurance that our wants in the matter of eggs could easily be satisfied. Meantime we must come up to the house with her and rest ourselves.

Rest was not an imperative necessity for us just then, but we were glad to see the interior of the old mansion. There was the long drawing-room, with its family portraits running back into the eighteenth century—one of them an admirable painting by Sully—and the library, with its tall book-shelves, now empty, and engravings and autographs hanging on the walls. The lady in black was rather sad; for her father, a distinguished publicist and man of letters, had built this house; and her grandfather, a great iron-master, had owned most of the land hereabouts; and the roots and tendrils of her memory were all entwined about the place; but now she was dismantling it and closing it up, preparatory to going away, perhaps to selling it.

By this time the tin pail had come in, filled with the nutritious fruit of the industrious and faithful hen. So we said farewell to the lady in black, with suitable recognition of her courtesy and kindness, and not without some silent reflections on the mutability of human affairs. Here had been a fine estate, a great family, a prosperous industry firmly established, now fading away like smoke. But I do not believe the lady in black will ever disappear entirely from Watermouth while she lives; for is there not the old meeting-house, a hundred years old (with the bees' nest in the weather-boarding), for her to watch over, and care for, and worship in?

The young men were waiting for us below the dam. Here was a splendid water-power running away almost idle. For the great iron forge, with its massive stone buildings, standing (if the local tradition is correct) on the site where the first American cannon-balls had been cast for the Revolutionary War, and where that shrewd Rhode Islander, Gen. Nathanael Greene, had invested some of the money he made in army contracts, had been put out of business many years ago by the development of iron-making in North Jersey and Pennsylvania. An attempt was made to turn it into a wood-pulp factory; but that had failed because the refractory yellow pine was full of hard knots that refused to let themselves be ground into pulp. Now a feeble little saw-mill was running from time to time in one corner of the huge edifice; and the greater part of the river out of work was foaming and roaring in wasteful beauty over the gates of the dam.

It was here, on the slopes of the open fields and on the dry sides of the long embankment, that we saw the faded remnants of the beauty with which the lupins had surrounded Watermouth a few days ago. The innumerable plants with their delicate palmate leaves were still fresh and vigorous; no drought can wither them even in the dryest soil, for their roots reach down to the hidden waters. But their winged blossoms, with which a little while since they had "blued the earth," as Thoreau says, were now almost all gone; as if a countless flock of blue butterflies had taken flight and vanished. Only here and there one could see little groups of belated flowers, scraps of the cœrulean colour, like patches of deep-blue sky seen through the rents in a drifting veil of clouds.

But the river called us away from the remembrance of the lupins to follow the promise of the laurels. How charming was the curve of that brown, foam-flecked stream, as it rushed swiftly down, from pool to pool, under the ancient, overhanging elms and willows and sycamores! We gave ourselves to the current, and darted swiftly past the row of weather-beaten houses on the left bank, into the heart of the woods again.

Here the forest was dense, lofty, overarching. The tall silver maple, the black ash, the river birch, the swamp white oak, the sweet gum and the sour gum, and a score of other trees closed around the course of the stream as it swept along with full, swirling waters. The air was full of a diffused, tranquil green light, subdued yet joyous, through which flakes and beams of golden sunshine flickered and sifted downward, as if they were falling into some strange, ethereal medium—something half liquid and half aërial, midway between an atmosphere and the still depths of a fairy sea.

The spirit of enchantment was in the place; brooding in the delicate, luminous midday twilight; hushing the song of the strong-flowing river to a humming murmur; casting a spell of beautiful immobility on the slender flower-stalks and fern-fronds and trailing shrubberies of the undergrowth, while the young leaves of the tree-tops, far overhead, were quivering and dancing in the sunlight and the breeze. Here Oberon and Titania might sleep beneath a bower of motionless royal Osmunda. Here Puck might have a noon-tide council with Peaseblossom, Cobweb, Moth, and Mustardseed, holding forth to them in whispers, beneath the green and purple sounding-board of a Jack-in-the-Pulpit. Here, even in this age of reason, the mystery of nature wove its magic round the curious mind of man,

"Annihilating all that's made,
To a green thought in a green shade."

Do you remember how old Andrew Marvell goes on from those two lovely lines, in his poem?

"Here at the fountain's sliding foot,
Or at some fruit-tree's mossy root,
Casting the body's vest aside,
My soul into the boughs does glide;
There, like a bird, it sits and sings,
Then whets and claps its silver wings,
And, till prepared for longer flight,
Waves in its plumes the various light."

There were many beautiful shrubs and bushes coming into bloom around us as we drifted down the stream. Two of the fairest bore the names of nymphs. One was called after Leucothoë, "the white goddess," and its curved racemes of tiny white bells hanging over the water were worthy emblems of that pure queen who leaped into the sea with her babe in her arms to escape from the frenzy of Athamas. The other was named for Andromeda; and the great Linnæus, who gave the name, thus describes his thought in giving it: "*Andromeda polifolia* was now in its highest beauty, decorating the marshy grounds in a most agreeable manner. The flowers are quite blood-red before they expand, but when full-grown the corolla is of a flesh-colour. As I contemplated it, I could not help thinking of Andromeda as described by the poets; and the more I meditated upon their descriptions, the more applicable they seemed to the little plant before me. Andromeda is represented by them as a virgin of most exquisite and unrivalled charms.... This plant is always fixed on some little turfy hillock in the midst of the swamps, as Andromeda herself was chained to the rock in the sea, which bathed her feet as the fresh water does the roots of the plant. Dragons and venomous serpents surrounded her, as toads and other reptiles frequent the abode of her vegetable resembler. As the distressed virgin cast down her face through excessive affliction, so does this rosy coloured flower hang its head.... At length comes Perseus in the shape of summer, dries up the surrounding water and destroys the monsters."

But more lovely than any of the shrubs along the river was that small tree known as the sweet bay or the swamp laurel. Of course it is not a laurel at all, but a magnolia (*Magnolia glauca*), and its glistening leaves, dark green above, silvery beneath, are set around the large, solitary flowers at the ends of the branches, like backgrounds of malachite, to bring out the perfection of a blossom carved in fresh ivory. What creamy petals are these, so thick, so tenderly curved around the cone-like heart of the flower's fertility! They are warm within, so that your finger can feel the soft glow in the centre of the blossoms. But it is not for you to penetrate into the secret of their love mystery. Leave that to the downy bee, the soft-winged moth, the flying beetle, who, seeking their own pleasure, carry the life-bestowing pollen from flower to flower. Your heavy hand would bruise the soft flesh and discolor its purity. Be content to feast your eyes upon its beauty, and breathe its wonderful fragrance, floating on the air like the breath of love in the south and wild summer.

About the middle of the afternoon, after passing through miles of enchanted forest, unbroken by sign of human habitation, we

"Came unto a land
In which it seemed always afternoon."

Low-rolling ridges of gravel, clothed with pine and oak, came down along the river. The bank on the right rose higher, and, at a sharp angle in the stream, lifted itself into a bluff-like point. Opposite was the serpentine course of the Dead River, coiling through an open marsh-meadow. Below the junction of the two streams our own river flowed swiftly, through a straight reach, to the mouth of the still lagoon where Mare Run came in.

Here we made our second camp, on the point, among the pines and the hollies. For here, at last, we were in the heart of the region of laurels, which we had come to see. All along the river we had found some of them, just beginning to open their flowers, here and there. But above and below the mouth of the Dead River the banks and ridges, under the high shadow of the pines, were crowded with shining clumps of the *Kalmia latifolia*, and something in the soil and exposure, or perhaps even the single day of warm sunshine that had passed since we began our voyage, had brought them already into the young flood of bloom.

I have seen the flame azaleas at their bright hour of consummation in the hill country of central Georgia—lakes of tranquil and splendid fire spreading far away through the rough-barked colonnades of the pineries. I have seen the thickets of great rhododendrons on the mountains of Pennsylvania in coronation week, when the magic of June covered their rich robes of darkest green with countless sceptres, crowns, and globes of white bloom divinely tinged with rose: superb, opulent, imperial flowers. I have seen the Magnolia Gardens near Charleston when their Arabian Nights' dream of colour was unfolding beneath the dark cypresses and moss-bannered live-oaks. I have seen the tulip and hyacinth beds of Holland rolled like a gorgeous carpet on the meadows beneath the feet of Spring; and the royal gardens of Kew in the month when the rose is queen of all the flowers; but never have I seen an efflorescence more lovely, more satisfying to the eye, than that of the high laurel along the shores of the unknown little river in South Jersey.

Cool, pure, and virginal in their beauty, the innumerable clusters of pink and white blossoms thronged the avenues of the pine woods, and ranged themselves along the hillsides and sloping banks, and trooped down by cape and promontory to reflect their young loveliness in the flowing stream. It was as if some quiet and shadowy region of solitude had been suddenly invaded by companies of maidens attired for a holiday and joyously confident of their simple charms. The dim woodland was illumined with the blush of conscious pleasure.

Seen at a distance the flower clusters look like big hemispheres of flushed snow. But examine them closely and you see that each of the rounded umbels is compounded of many separate blossoms—shallow, half-translucent cups poised on slender stems of pale green. The cup is white, tinted more or less deeply with rose-pink, the colour brightest along the rim and on the outside. The edge is scalloped into five points, and on the outer surface there are ten tiny projections around the middle of the cup. Looking within, you find that each of these is a little red hollow made to receive the crimson tip of a curving anther, cunningly bent like a spring, so that the least touch may loosen it and scatter the pollen. There is no flower in the world more exquisitely fashioned than this. It is the emblem of a rustic maid in the sweet prime of her morning.

We were well content with our day's voyage and our parting camp on the river. We had done no harm; no accident had befallen us; we had seen many lovely things and heard music from warbler and vireo, thrush and wren, all day long. Even now a wood thrush closed his last descant in flute-like notes across the river. Night began silently to weave her dusky veil upon the vast loom of the forest. The pink glow had gone from the flower-masses around us; whitely they glimmered through the deepening shadows, and stood like gentle ghosts against the dark. To-morrow we must paddle down to the village where the railroad crosses the river, and hurry back to civilization and work. But to-night we were still very far off; and we should sleep at the foot of a pine-tree, beneath the stars, among the virgin laurels.

LITTLE RED TOM

⁂MY Uncle Peter was much interested in the war which broke out, not long ago, among the professional nature-writers. He said that it was a civil war, and therefore a philosopher was bound to be regardful of it, because a civil war always involved subtle problems of psychology. He also said that it was a most uncivil war, and that the picturesque violence of the language employed on both sides was intrinsically noteworthy to a philologist, and therefore he felt obliged to follow it with care. When the Chief Magistrate of his native country took a hand in it, my Uncle Peter claimed that it had become a subject of national importance and that no true patriot could be indifferent to it. Finally he admitted, in a moment of confidence, that the real reason for his interest was the fact that so many of his friends were engaged in the strife, on both sides, and were being badly pummeled; and that he would like to take some part in it himself. I asked him what part. He answered that he proposed to himself the part of peace-maker. I pointed out that this part is usually the most perilous and painful. He said that this should not deter him from doing his duty, and he added that he thought he could do it in such a way that no one could tell that he was doing it. A week later he brought me the following paper, which he called

THE TRAGEDY OF LITTLE RED TOM:
A Contribution to the Fight About Nature-Books.

He was the youngest of the family, a late-comer at the feast of life. Yet the rose-garlands on the table were not faded when he arrived, and the welcome that he received was not colder, indeed it was probably several degrees warmer, because he was so tardy, so young, so tiny.

There was room for him in the household circle; joyous affection and merry murmurs of contentment greeted his coming. His older brothers never breathed a word of jealousy or unkindness toward him. He grew peacefully under the shelter of mother-love; and it would have been difficult to foresee, in the rosy promise of his youth, the crimson tragedy in which his life ended.

How dull, how insensible to such things, most men and women are! They go on their way, busily and happily, doing their work, seeking their daily food, enjoying their human pleasures, and never troubling themselves about the hidden and inarticulate sorrows of the universe. The hunter hunts, and the fisher fishes, with inconsiderate glee. A man kills a troublesome insect, he eats a juicy berry or a succulent oyster, without thinking of what his victims must feel.

But there are some tender and sensitive souls who are too fine for these callous joys. They no longer imagine that human emotions are confined to man. They reflect that every plant and every animal is doomed to die in some way which the average man would regard as distinctly unpleasant. To them the sight of a chicken-house is full of sorrowful suggestion, and a walk through a vegetable garden is like a funeral procession. They meditate upon the tragic side of all existence; and to them there will be nothing strange in this story of the tragedy of Little Red Tom.

You have guessed that he was called "red" on account of his colour. It was a family trait. All his brothers had it; and strange to say they were proud of it.

Most people are so foolish that they speak with ridicule, or even with contempt of this colour, when it is personally evolved. Have you ever asked yourself why it is that the cold world alludes derisively to a "red-headed boy," or a "red-headed girl"? The language is different when the locks are of another hue. Then it is a "black-haired boy," or a "golden-haired girl." Is not the very word "red-headed," with its implied slur upon an innocent and gorgeous colour, an unconscious evidence of the unreasonable prejudice and hard insensibility of the human race?

Not so the family of Tom. The redder they grew the happier they were, and the more pride their mother took in them. But she herself was green. And so was little Tom, like all his brothers, when he made his first appearance in the world—green—very green.

Nestled against his mother's side, sheltered by her embracing arms, safe and happy in the quietude of her maternal care, he must have looked out upon the passing show with wonder and pleasure, while she instilled into him the lessons of wisdom and the warnings of destiny.

"Grow, my little one," we can imagine her saying to him, in her mysterious wordless language, "your first duty is to grow. Look at your brothers, how big and round and fat they are! I can hardly lift them. They did what I told them, and see what they have become. All by growing! Simple process! Even a babe can understand it. Grow, my Tommykin, grow! But don't try to grow red; first, you must grow big."

It is quite sure, and evident to every imaginative observer of nature, that Tommy's mother *must* have told him something like this, for this is precisely what he did—obedient, docile, clever little creature! How else could he have learned it, if she had not taught him? Who can trace the subtle avenues by which intelligence is communicated from the old to the young, the treasured lore of the ages handed down from one generation to another? But when we see the result, when the little one begins to do what its parents and grandparents have done, is it not evident that the teaching must have been given, though in some way beyond our ken? If Tommy's mother had not taught him, there is at least an even chance that he would have tried to grow red before he grew big. But he laid her lesson to heart, and day by day, week by week, his rotundity expanded, while his verdancy remained.

It was a very beautiful life that they lived in the garden; and if the thoughts and feelings that unfolded there could be known, perhaps they would seem even more wonderful than the things which the old German gardener cultivated. Away at one end were the beds of old-fashioned flowers: hollyhocks and phlox and stocks, coreopsis and calliopsis, calendula and campanula, fox-gloves and monks-hoods and lady-slippers. At the other end were the strawberry-bed and the asparagus-bed. In between, there were long rows of all kinds of vegetables and small fruits and fragrant herbs.

Who can tell what ideas and emotions were stirring in those placid companies of leguminous comrades? What aspirations toward a loftier life in the climbing beans? What high spirits in the corn? What light and airy dreams on the asparagus-bed? What philosophy among the sage? Imagine what great schemes were hatching among the egg-plants, and what hot feelings stung the peppers when the raspberries crowded them!

Tommy, from his central place in the garden must have felt the agitation of this mimic world around him. Many a time, no doubt, he was tempted to give himself up to one or another of the contiguous influences, and throw himself into the social tide for "one glorious hour of crowded life." But his mother always held him back.

"No, my Tommykin, stay with me. It is not for you to climb a pole like a bean or wave in the wind like an asparagus stalk, or rasp your neighbours like a raspberry. Be modest, be natural, be true to yourself. Stay with me and grow fat."

When the sunshine of the long July days flooded the garden, glistening on the silken leaves of the corn, wilting the potato-blossoms, unfolding the bright yellow flowers of the okra and the melon, Tom would fain have pushed himself out into the full tide of light and heat. But his mother bent tenderly over him.

"Not yet, my child; it is not time for you to bear the heat of the day. A little shade is good for you. Let me cover you. It is too soon for you to be sunburned."

When the plumping afternoon showers came down, refreshing leaf and root of every plant, Tom shrank from the precipitate inundation.

"Mother, I'm all wet. I want to come in out of the rain."

But the mother knew what was good for him. So she held him out bravely while the streaming drops washed him; and she taught him how to draw in the moisture which she gathered for his nourishment.

In late August a change began to come over his complexion. His verdant brilliancy was "sicklied o'er with a pale cast of thought," whitish, yellowish, nondescript. A foolish human mother would have been alarmed and would have hurried to the medicine closet for a remedy for biliousness. Not so Tom's wise parent. She knew that the time had come for him to grow red. She let him have his own way now about being out in the sunshine. She even thrust him gently forth into the full light, withdrawing the shelter that she had cast around him. Slowly, gradually, but surely the bright crimson hue spread over him, until the illumination was complete, and the mother felt that he was the most beautiful of her children—not the largest, but round and plump and firm and glowing red as a ruby.

Then the mother-heart knew that the perils of life were near at hand for Little Red Tom. Many of his brothers had already been torn from her by the cruel hand of fate and had disappeared into the unknown.

"Where have they gone to?" wondered Tom. But his mother could not tell him. All that she could do was to warn him of the unseen dangers that surrounded him, and prepare him to meet them.

"Listen, my child, and do as I tell you. When you hear a step on the garden path, that means danger; and when a thing with wings flies around me and comes near to you, that means danger too. But I will teach you how to avoid it. I will give you three signs.

"The first sign is a rustling noise that I will make when a bird comes near to you. That means *droop*. Let yourself down behind the wire netting that I lean on, and then the bird will be afraid to come close enough to peck at you. The second sign is a trembling that you will feel in my arms when the gardener comes along the walk. That means *snuggle*. Hide yourself as close to me as you can. The third sign—well, I will tell you the third sign to-morrow evening, for now I am tired."

In the early morning of a bright September day, while the dew was still heavy on the leaves and the grass, and the gossamer cobwebs glistened with little diamonds, a hungry robin flew into the garden, and Tom heard the signal "*Droop!*" So he let himself down behind the woven wire, and the robin put his head on one side and looked at Tom greedily, and flew on to find a breakfast elsewhere.

A little before noon, when the sun was shining broadly and the silken tassels of the corn were shrivelling up into make-believe tobacco for bad little boys to smoke, there was a heavy step on the garden walk, and Tom felt the signal "*Snuggle!*" Then he hugged as close as he could to his mother's side, and the gardener with his sharp knife cut off all Tom's surviving brothers and put them into a box full of vegetables. But he did not see Tom, hidden close and safe.

How glad the mother must have been, and how much Tom must have loved her as he remembered all her wise lessons! It was a long beautiful afternoon that they spent together, filled with pleasant reminiscences, touched by no shadow of gloom, no dream of parting. A golden afternoon—the last!

Just before sunset, a fair creature, clothed in white, came into the garden. She moved for a while among the flowers, her yellow hair gleaming in the low rays of the sun, her eyes bluer than forget-me-nots. Who could think that such a creature could be cruel or heartless? Who could dream that she would pursue her pleasure at the cost of pain to the innocent? Who could imagine that she would take life to feed her own?

Gently and daintily she came down the garden walk, past the raspberry patch, past the tall rows of corn, past the egg-plants and the peppers, with steps so light that the ground hardly felt them, with bright eyes glancing from side to side—yes, with all these, and also with a remorseless purpose in her heart and a basket half full of cut flowers on her arm.

No signal to *droop* or *snuggle* came to Tom. The third signal—ah, that he had not yet learned! So he basked his rosy sides in the sunlight as the lovely apparition drew near to him. She looked at him with delight. She put out her delicate hand to embrace him. Then, without a tremor, she tore him ruthlessly from his mother's grasp, from the home that he loved, and dropped him into her basket.

"Oh, you little red beauty!" she cried. "You are just what I wanted to fill up my tomato salad."

That night, as she sat at supper, with her father and mother and brother and sisters, she was smiling and serene, for the table was well furnished, and the feast was merry. There was white bread that had been ground from thousands of innocent blades of wheat, once waving in the sunlight, and a juicy fish that had been lured and unwillingly drawn from the crystal waters. There was a brace of grouse that had been snatched away from their feeding-grounds among the spicy berries in the woods. And there was poor Little Red Tom, in the centre of the salad, surrounded by crisp lettuce leaves and dressed to the queen's taste.

Are there not some who would have shed tears at that sight, and lamented even while they ate? But do you suppose the young girl was one of that kind? Do you imagine that she thought she had played a part in a tragedy? Not a bit of it. She was simply grateful that her salad was so good, and glad that the others liked it.

SILVERHORNS

THE railway station of Bathurst, New Brunswick, did not look particularly merry at two o'clock of a late September morning. There was an easterly haar driving in from the *Baie des Chaleurs* and the darkness was so saturated with chilly moisture that an honest downpour of rain would have been a relief. Two or three depressed and somnolent travellers yawned in the waiting-room, which smelled horribly of smoky lamps. The telegraph instrument in the ticket-office clicked spasmodically for a minute, and then relapsed into a gloomy silence. The imperturbable station-master was tipped back against the wall in a wooden armchair, with his feet on the table, and his mind sunk in an old Christmas number of *The Cowboy Magazine*. The express-agent, in the baggage-room, was going over his last week's way-bills and accounts by the light of a lantern, trying to locate an error, and sighing profanely to himself as he failed to find it. A wooden trunk tied with rope, a couple of dingy canvas bags, a long box marked "Fresh Fish! Rush!" and two large leather portmanteaus with brass fittings were piled on the luggage-truck at the far end of the platform; and beside the door of the waiting-room, sheltered by the overhanging eaves, was a neat travelling bag, with a gun-case and a rod-case leaning against the wall. The wet rails glittered dimly northward and southward away into the night. A few blurred lights glimmered from the village across the bridge.

Dudley Hemenway had observed all these features of the landscape with silent dissatisfaction, as he smoked steadily up and down the platform, waiting for the Maritime Express. It is usually irritating to arrive at the station on time for a train on the Intercolonial Railway. The arrangement is seldom mutual; and sometimes yesterday's train does not come along until to-morrow afternoon. Moreover, Hemenway was inwardly discontented with the fact that he was coming out of the woods instead of going in. "Coming out" always made him a little unhappy, whether his expedition had been successful or not. He did not like the thought that it was all over; and he had the very bad habit, at such times, of looking ahead and computing the slowly lessening number of chances that were left to him.

"Sixty odd years—I may live to be that old and keep my shooting sight," he said to himself. "That would give me a couple of dozen more camping trips. It's a short allowance. I wonder if any of them will be more lucky than this one. This makes the seventh year I've tried to get a moose; and the odd trick has gone against me every time."

He tossed away the end of his cigar, which made a little trail of sparks as it rolled along the sopping platform, and turned to look in through the window of the ticket-office. Something in the agent's attitude of literary absorption aggravated him. He went round to the door and opened it.

"Don't you know or care when this train is coming?"

"Nope," said the man placidly.

"Well, when? What's the matter with her? When is she due?"

"Doo twenty minits ago," said the man. "Forty minits late down to Noocastle. Git here quatter to three, ef nothin' more happens."

"But what has happened already? What's wrong with the beastly old road, anyhow?"

"Freight-car skipped the track," said the man "up to Charlo. Everythin' hung up an' kinder goin' slow till they git the line clear. Dunno nothin' more."

With this conclusive statement the agent seemed to disclaim all responsibility for the future of impatient travellers, and dropped his mind back into the magazine again. Hemenway lit another cigar and went into the baggage-room to smoke with the expressman. It was nearly three o'clock when they heard the far-off shriek of the whistle sounding up from the south; then, after an interval, the puffing of the engine on the up-grade; then the faint ringing of the rails, the increasing clatter of the train, and the blazing headlight of the locomotive swept slowly through the darkness, past the platform. The engineer was leaning on one arm, with his head out of the cab-window, and as he passed he nodded and waved his hand to Hemenway. The conductor also nodded and hurried into the ticket-office, where the tick-tack of a conversation by telegraph was soon under way. The black porter of the Pullman car was looking out from the vestibule, and when he saw Hemenway his sleepy face broadened into a grin reminiscent of many generous tips.

"Howdy, Mr. Hennigray." he cried; "glad to see yo' ag'in, sah! I got yo' section alright, sah! Lemme take yo' things, sah! Train gwine to stop hy'eh fo' some time yet, I reckon."

"Well, Charles," said Hemenway, "you take my things and put them in the car. Careful with that gun now! The Lord only knows how much time this train's going to lose. I'm going ahead to see the engineer."

Angus McLeod was a grizzle-bearded Scotchman who had run a locomotive on the Intercolonial ever since the road was cut through the woods from New Brunswick to Quebec. Everyone who travelled often on that line knew him, and all who knew him well enough to get below his rough crust, liked him for his big heart.

"Hallo, McLeod," said Hemenway as he came up through the darkness, "is that you?"

"It's nane else," answered the engineer as he stepped down from his cab and shook hands warmly. "Hoo are ye, Dud, an' whaur hae ye been murderin' the innocent beasties noo? Hae ye killt yer moose yet? Ye've been chasin' him these mony years."

"Not much murdering," replied Hemenway. "I had a queer trip this time—away up the Nepissiguit, with old McDonald. You know him, don't you?"

"Fine do I ken Rob McDonald, an' a guid mon he is. Hoo was it that ye couldna slaughter stacks o' moose wi' him to help ye? Did ye see nane at all?"

"Plenty, and one with the biggest horns in the world! But that's a long story, and there's no time to tell it now."

"Time to burrrn, Dud, nae fear o' it! 'Twill be an hour afore the line's clear to Charlo an' they lat us oot o' this. Come awa' up into the cab. mon, an' tell us yer tale.' Tis couthy an' warm in the cab, an' I'm willin' to leesten to yer bluidy advaintures."

So the two men clambered up into the engineer's seat. Hemenway gave McLeod his longest and strongest cigar, and filled his own briarwood pipe. The rain was now pattering gently on the roof of the cab. The engine hissed and sizzled patiently in the darkness. The fragrant smoke curled steadily from the glowing tip of the cigar; but the pipe went out half a dozen times while Hemenway was telling the story of Silverhorns.

"We went up the river to the big rock, just below Indian Falls. There we made our main camp, intending to hunt on Forty-two Mile Brook. There's quite a snarl of ponds and bogs at the head of it, and some burned hills over to the west, and it's very good moose country.

"But some other party had been there before us, and we saw nothing on the ponds, except two cow moose and a calf. Coming out the next morning we got a fine deer on the old wood road—a beautiful head. But I have plenty of deer-heads already."

"Bonny creature!" said McLeod. "An' what did ye do wi' it, when ye had murdered it?"

"Ate it, of course. I gave the head to Billy Boucher, the cook. He said he could get ten dollars for it. The next evening we went to one of the ponds again, and Injun Pete tried to 'call' a moose for me. But it was no good. McDonald was disgusted with Pete's calling; said it sounded like the bray of a wild ass of the wilderness. So the next day we gave up calling and travelled the woods over toward the burned hills.

"In the afternoon McDonald found an enormous moose-track; he thought it looked like a bull's track, though he wasn't quite positive. But then, you know, a Scotchman never likes to commit himself, except about theology or politics."

"Humph!" grunted McLeod in the darkness, showing that the stroke had counted.

"Well, we went on, following that track through the woods, for an hour or two. It was a terrible country, I tell you: tamarack swamps, and spruce thickets, and windfalls, and all kinds of misery. Presently we came out on a bare rock on the burned hillside, and there, across a ravine, we could see the animal lying down, just below the trunk of a big dead spruce that had fallen. The beast's head and neck were hidden by some bushes, but the fore-shoulder and side were in clear view, about two hundred and fifty yards away. McDonald seemed to be inclined to think that it was a bull and that I ought to shoot. So I shot, and knocked splinters out of the spruce log. We could see them fly. The animal got up quickly, and looked at us for a moment, shaking her long ears; then the huge, unmitigated cow vamoosed into the brush. McDonald remarked that it was 'a varra fortunate shot, almaist providaintial!' And so it was; for if it had gone six inches lower, and the news had gotten out at Bathurst, it would have cost me a fine of two hundred dollars."

"Ye did weel, Dud," puffed McLeod; "varra weel indeed—for the coo!"

"After that," continued Hemenway, "of course my nerve was a little shaken, and we went back to the main camp on the river, to rest over Sunday. That was all right, wasn't it, Mac?"

"Aye!" replied McLeod, who was a strict member of the Presbyterian church at Moncton. "That was surely a varra safe thing to do. Even a hunter, I'm thinkin', wouldna like to be breakin' twa commandments in the ane day—the foorth and the saxth!"

"Perhaps not. It's enough to break one, as you do once a fortnight when you run your train into Rivière du Loup Sunday morning. How's that, you old Calvinist?"

"Dudley, ma son," said the engineer, "dinna airgue a point that ye canna understond. There's guid an' suffeecient reasons for the train. But ye'll ne'er be claimin' that moose-huntin' is a wark o' neecessity or maircy?"

"No, no, of course not; but then, you see, barring Sundays, we felt that it was necessary to do all we could to get a moose, just for the sake of our reputations. Billy, the cook, was particularly strong about it. He said that an old woman in Bathurst, a kind of fortune-teller, had told him that he was going to have '*la bonne chance*' on this trip. He wanted to try his own mouth at 'calling.' He had never really done it before. But he had been practising all winter in imitation of a tame cow moose that Johnny Moreau had, and he thought he could make the sound '*b'en bon*.' So he got the birch-bark horn and gave us a sample of his skill. McDonald told me privately that it was 'nae sa bad; a deal better than Pete's feckless bellow.' We agreed to leave the Indian to keep the camp (after locking up the whiskey-flask in my bag), and take Billy with us on Monday to 'call' at Hogan's Pond.

"It's a small bit of water, about three-quarters of a mile long and four hundred yards across, and four miles back from the river. There is no trail to it, but a blazed line runs part of the way, and for the rest you follow up the little brook that runs out of the pond. We stuck up our shelter in a hollow on the brook, half a mile below the pond, so that the smoke of our fire would not drift over the hunting-ground, and waited till five o'clock in the afternoon. Then we went up to the pond, and took our position in a clump of birch-trees on the edge of the open meadow that runs round the east shore. Just at dark Billy began to call, and it was beautiful. You know how it goes. Three short grunts, and then a long ooooo-aaaa-ooooh, winding up with another grunt! It sounded lonelier than a love-sick hippopotamus on the house-top. It rolled and echoed over the hills as if it would wake the dead.

"There was a fine moon shining, nearly full, and a few clouds floating by. Billy called, and called, and called again. The air grew colder and colder; light frost on the meadow-grass; our teeth were chattering, fingers numb.

"Then we heard a bull give a short bawl, away off to the southward. Presently we could hear his horns knock against the trees, far up on the hill. McDonald whispered, 'He's comin',' and Billy gave another call.

"But it was another bull that answered, back of the north end of the pond, and pretty soon we could hear him rapping along through the woods. Then everything was still. 'Call agen,' says McDonald, and Billy called again.

"This time the bawl came from another bull, on top of the western hill, straight across the pond. It seemed to start up the other two bulls, and we could hear all three of them thrashing along, as fast as they could come, towards the pond. 'Call agen, a wee one,' says McDonald, trembling with joy. And Billy called a little, seducing call, with two grunts at the end.

"Well, sir, at that, a cow and a calf came rushing down through the brush not two hundred yards away from us, and the three bulls went splash into the water, one at the south end, one at the north end, and one on the west shore. 'Lord,' whispers McDonald, 'it's a meenadgerie!'"

"Dud," said the engineer, getting down to open the furnace door a crack, "this is mair than murder ye're comin' at; it's a buitchery—or else it's juist a pack o' lees."

"I give you my word," said Hemenway, "it's all true as the catechism. But let me go on. The cow and the calf only stayed in the water a few minutes, and then ran back through the woods. But the three bulls went sloshing around in the pond as if they were looking for something. We could hear them, but we could not see any of them, for the sky had clouded up, and they kept far away from us. Billy tried another short call, but they did not come any nearer. McDonald whispered that he thought the one in the south end might be the biggest, and he might be feeding, and the two others might be young bulls, and they might be keeping away because they were afraid of the big one. This seemed reasonable; and I said that I was going to crawl around the meadow to the south end. 'Keep near a tree,' says Mac; and I started.

"There was a deep trail, worn by animals, through the high grass; and in this I crept along on my hands and knees. It was very wet and muddy. My boots were full of cold water. After ten minutes I came to a little point running out into the pond, and one young birch growing on it. Under this I crawled, and rising up on my knees looked over the top of the grass and bushes.

"There, in a shallow bay, standing knee-deep in the water, and rooting up the lily-stems with his long, pendulous nose, was the biggest and blackest bull moose in the world. As he pulled the roots from the mud and tossed up his dripping head I could see his horns—four and a half feet across, if they were an inch, and the palms shining like tea-trays in the moonlight. I tell you, old Silverhorns was the most beautiful monster I ever saw.

"But he was too far away to shoot by that dim light, so I left my birch-tree and crawled along toward the edge of the bay. A breath of wind must have blown across me to him, for he lifted his head, sniffed, grunted, came out of the water, and began to trot slowly along the trail which led past me. I knelt on one knee and tried to take aim. A black cloud came over the moon. I couldn't see either of the sights on the gun. But when the bull came opposite to me, about fifty yards off, I blazed away at a venture.

"He reared straight up on his hind legs—it looked as if he rose fifty feet in the air—wheeled, and went walloping along the trail, around the south end of the pond. In a minute he was lost in the woods. Good-by, Silverhorns!"

"Ye tell it weel," said McLeod, reaching out for a fresh cigar, "fegs! Ah doot Sir Walter himsel' couldna impruve upon it. An, sae thot's the way ye didna murder puir Seelverhorrns? It's a tale I'm joyfu' to be hearin'."

"Wait a bit," Hemenway answered. "That's not the end, by a long shot. There's worse to follow. The next morning we returned to the pond at daybreak, for McDonald thought I might have wounded the moose. We searched the bushes and the woods when he went out very carefully, looking for drops of blood on his trail."

"Bluid!" groaned the engineer. "Hech, mon, wouldna that come nigh to mak' ye greet, to find the beast's red bluid splashed ower the leaves, and think o' him staggerin' on thro' the forest, drippin' the heart oot o' him wi' every step?"

"But we didn't find any blood, you old sentimentalist. That shot in the dark was a clear miss. We followed the trail by broken bushes and footprints, for half a mile, and then came back to the pond and turned to go down through the edge of the woods to the camp.

"It was just after sunrise. I was walking a few yards ahead, McDonald next, and Billy last. Suddenly he looked around to the left, gave a low whistle and dropped to the ground, pointing northward. Away at the head of the pond, beyond the glitter of the sun on the water, the big blackness of Silverhorns' head and body was pushing through the bushes, dripping with dew.

"Each of us flopped down behind the nearest shrub as if we had been playing squat-tag. Billy had the birch-bark horn with him, and he gave a low, short call. Silverhorns heard it, turned, and came parading slowly down the western shore, now on the sand-beach, now splashing through the shallow water. We could see every motion and hear every sound. He marched along as if he owned the earth, swinging his huge head from side to side and grunting at each step.

"You see, we were just in the edge of the woods, strung along the south end of the pond, Billy nearest the west shore, where the moose was walking, McDonald next, and I last, perhaps fifteen yards farther to the east. It was a fool arrangement, but we had no time to think about it. McDonald whispered that I should wait until the moose came close to us and stopped.

"So I waited. I could see him swagger along the sand and step out around the fallen logs. The nearer he came the bigger his horns looked; each palm was like an enormous silver fish-fork with twenty prongs. Then he went out of my sight for a minute as he passed around a little bay in the southwest corner, getting nearer and nearer to Billy. But I could still hear his steps distinctly—slosh, slosh, slosh—thud, thud, thud (the grunting had stopped)—closer came the sound, until it was directly behind the dense green branches of a fallen balsam-tree, not twenty feet away from Billy. Then suddenly the noise ceased. I could hear my own heart pounding at my ribs, but nothing else. And of Silverhorns not hair nor hide was visible. It looked as if he must be a Boojum, and had the power to

"'Softly and silently vanish away.'

"Billy and Mac were beckoning to me fiercely and pointing to the green balsam-top. I gripped my rifle and started to creep toward them. A little twig, about as thick as the tip of a fishing-rod, cracked under my knee. There was a terrible crash behind the balsam, a plunging through the underbrush and a rattling among the branches, a lumbering gallop up the hill through the forest, and Silverhorns was gone into the invisible.

"He had stopped behind the tree because he smelled the grease on Billy's boots. As he stood there, hesitating, Billy and Mac could see his shoulder and his side through a gap in the branches—a dead-easy shot. But so far as I was concerned, he might as well have been in Alaska. I told you that the way we had placed ourselves was a fool arrangement. But McDonald would not say anything about it, except to express his conviction that *it was not predestinated we should get that moose*."

"Ah didna ken auld Rob had sae much theology aboot him," commented McLeod. "But noo I'm thinkin' ye went back to yer main camp, an' lat puir Seelverhorrns live oot his life?"

"Not much, did we! For now we knew that he wasn't badly frightened by the adventure of the night before, and that we might get another chance at him. In the afternoon it began to rain; and it poured for forty-eight hours. We cowered in our shelter before a smoky fire, and lived on short rations of crackers and dried prunes—it was a hungry time."

"But wasna there slathers o' food at the main camp? Ony fule wad ken enough to gae doon to the river an' tak' a guid fill-up."

"But that wasn't what we wanted. It was Silverhorns. Billy and I made McDonald stay, and Thursday afternoon, when the clouds broke away, we went back to the pond to have a last try at turning our luck.

"This time we took our positions with great care, among some small spruces on a point that ran out from the southern meadow. I was farthest to the west; McDonald (who had also brought his gun) was next; Billy, with the horn, was farthest away from the point where he thought the moose would come out. So Billy began to call, very beautifully. The long echoes went bellowing over the hills. The afternoon was still and the setting sun shone through a light mist, like a ball of red gold.

"Fifteen minutes after sundown Silverhorns gave a loud bawl from the western ridge and came crashing down the hill. He cleared the bushes two or three hundred yards to our left with a leap, rushed into the pond, and came wading around the south shore toward us. The bank here was rather high, perhaps four feet above the water, and the mud below it was deep, so that the moose sank in to his knees. I give you my word, as he came along there was nothing visible to Mac and me except his ears and his horns. Everything else was hidden below the bank.

"There were we behind our little spruce-trees. And there was Silverhorns, standing still now, right in front of us. And all that Mac and I could see were those big ears and those magnificent antlers, appearing and disappearing as he lifted and lowered his head. It was a fearful situation. And there was Billy, with his birch-bark hooter, forty yards below us—he could see the moose perfectly.

"I looked at Mac, and he looked at me. He whispered something about predestination. Then Billy lifted his horn and made ready to give a little soft grunt, to see if the moose wouldn't move along a bit, just to oblige us. But as Billy drew in his breath, one of those tiny fool flies that are always blundering around a man's face flew straight down his throat. Instead of a call he burst out with a furious, strangling fit of coughing. The moose gave a snort, and a wild leap in the water, and galloped away under the bank, the way he had come. Mac and I both fired at his vanishing ears and horns, but of course——"

"All aboooard!" The conductor's shout rang along the platform.

"Line's clear," exclaimed McLeod, rising. "Noo we'll be off! Wull ye stay here wi' me, or gang awa' back to yer bed?"

"Here," answered Hemenway, not budging from his place on the bench.

The bell clanged, and the powerful machine puffed out on its flaring way through the night. Faster and faster came the big explosive breaths, until they blended in a long steady roar, and the train was sweeping northward at forty miles an hour. The clouds had broken; the night had grown colder; the gibbous moon gleamed over the vast and solitary landscape. It was a different thing to Hemenway, riding in the cab of the locomotive, from an ordinary journey in the passenger-car or an unconscious ride in the sleeper. Here he was on the crest of motion, at the fore-front of speed, and the quivering engine with the long train behind it seemed like a living creature leaping along the track. It responded to the labour of the fireman and the touch of the engineer almost as if it could think and feel. Its pace quickened without a jar; its great eye pierced the silvery space of moonlight with a shaft of blazing yellow; the rails sang before it and trembled behind it; it was an obedient and joyful monster, conquering distance and devouring darkness.

On the wide level barrens beyond the Tete-a-Gouche River the locomotive reached its best speed, purring like a huge cat and running smoothly. McLeod leaned back on his bench with a satisfied air.

"She's doin' fine, the nicht," said he. "Ah'm thinkin', whiles, o' yer auld Seelverhorrns. Whaur is he noo? Awa' up on Hogan's Pond, gallantin' around i' the licht o' the mune wi' a lady moose, an' the gladness juist bubblin' in his hairt. Ye're no sorry that he's leevin' yet, are ye, Dud?"

"Well," answered Hemenway slowly, between the puffs of his pipe, "I can't say I'm sorry that he's alive and happy, though I'm not glad that I lost him. But he did his best, the old rogue; he played a good game, and he deserved to win. Where he is now nobody can tell. He was travelling like a streak of lightning when I last saw him. By this time he may be——"

"What's yon?" cried McLeod, springing up. Far ahead, in the narrow apex of the converging rails, stood a black form, motionless, mysterious. McLeod grasped the whistle-cord. The black form loomed higher in the moonlight and was clearly silhouetted against the horizon—a big moose standing across the track. They could see his grotesque head, his shadowy horns, his high, sloping shoulders. The engineer pulled the cord. The whistle shrieked loud and long.

The moose turned and faced the sound. The glare of the headlight fascinated, challenged, angered him. There he stood defiant, front feet planted wide apart, head lowered, gazing steadily at the unknown enemy that was rushing toward him. He was the monarch of the wilderness. There was nothing in the world that he feared, except those strange-smelling little beasts on two legs who crept around through the woods and shot fire out of sticks. This was surely not one of those treacherous animals, but some strange new creature that dared to shriek at him and try to drive him out of its way. He would not move. He would try his strength against this big yellow-eyed beast.

"Losh!" cried McLeod; "he's gaun' to fecht us!" and he dropped the cord, grabbed the levers, and threw the steam off and the brakes on hard. The heavy train slid groaning and jarring along the track. The moose never stirred. The fire smouldered in his small narrow eyes. His black crest was bristling. As the engine bore down upon him, not a rod away, he reared high in the air, his antlers flashing in the blaze, and struck full at the headlight with his immense fore feet. There was a shattering of glass, a crash, a heavy shock, and the train slid on through the darkness, lit only by the moon.

Thirty or forty yards beyond, the momentum was exhausted and the engine came to a stop. Hemenway and McLeod clambered down and ran back, with the other trainmen and a few of the passengers. The moose was lying in the ditch beside the track, stone dead and frightfully shattered. But the great head and the vast, spreading antlers were intact.

"Seelver-horrns, sure eneugh!" said McLeod, bending over him. "He was crossin' frae the Nepissiguit to the Jacquet; but he didna get across. Weel, Dud, are ye glad? Ye hae killt yer first moose!"

"Yes," said Hemenway, "it's my first moose. But it's your first moose, too. And I think it's our last. Ye gods, what a fighter!"

NOTIONS ABOUT NOVELS

"YOU must write a novel," said my Uncle Peter to the young Man of Letters. "The novel is the literary form in which the psychological conditions of interest are most easily discovered and met. It appeals directly to the reader's self-consciousness, and invites him to fancy how fine a figure he would cut in more picturesque circumstances than his own. When it simplifies great events, as Stevenson said it must, it produces the feeling of power; and when it dignifies the commonplace, as Schopenhauer said it ought to, it produces the sense of importance. People like to imagine themselves playing on a large stage. The most humdrum of men would be pleased to act a hero's part, if it could be done without risk or effort; and the plainest of women has the capacity to enjoy, at least in fancy, a greater variety in the affair of love than real life is likely to furnish. Novels give these unsatisfied souls their opportunity. That is why fiction is so popular. You must take advantage of the laws of the human mind if you want to be a successful author. Write a novel."

This protracted remark was patiently received by the little company of friends, who were sitting on a rocky eminence of the York Harbor Golf Links (near the seventh hole, which was called, for obvious reasons,

"Götterdämmerung"). My Uncle Peter's right to make long speeches was conceded. In him they did not seem criminal, because they were evidently necessary. Moreover, in this case, the majority agreed with him, and therefore were not tempted to interrupt.

"A novel," said the Publisher, "will bear ten times as much advertising as any other kind of book. This is a fact."

"A novel," said the Critic, "is the most highly developed type of literature. Therefore, it is the fittest to survive. This is a theory. And I should like——"

But the Critic did not share the Philosopher's long-speech prerogative. His audience was inclined to limit him to the time when he could be pungent.

The Business Man broke in upon him: "A novel is good because it is just plain reading—no theories or explanations—or at least, if there are any, you can skip them."

"Novels," said the Doctor of Divinity solemnly, "are valuable because they give an insight into life. I deprecate the vice of excessive novel-reading in young persons. But for myself I wish that there were more really interesting novels to read. Most of the old ones I have read already."

A smile flickered around the circle. "What do you call old?" asked the Cynic. "Have you read 'The Vulgarities of Antoinette'?"

"Nonsense," said the Publisher; "some novels grow as old in a twelvemonth as others do in a decade. A book is not really aged until it ceases to be advertised. 'The Celestial Triplets,' for example. But fortunately it is a poor year that does not produce at least three new novelists of distinction."

"For my part," said the True Story Teller, seated on her throne among the rocks and dispensing gentle influence like the silent sweetness of the summer afternoon, "for my part, I am not sure that fiction is the only kind of literature worth reading. Essays, biography, history and poetry still have their attractions for me. But what I should like to know is what made one kind of novel so popular yesterday, and what puts another kind in its place to-day, and what kind is likely to last forever? What gives certain novels their amazing vogue?"

"A new public," answered the Cynic. "Popular education has done it. Fifty years ago thinking and reading went together. But nowadays reading is the most familiar amusement of the thoughtless. It is the new public that buys four hundred thousand copies of a novel in a single year."

"A striking explanation," said the Critic, "but, you know, De Quincey said practically the same thing more than fifty years ago in his essay on Oliver Goldsmith. Yet the sale of 'The Prude of Pimlico' exceeds the sale of the leading novel of De Quincey's day by at least five hundred per cent. How do you explain that?"

"Very simply," said the Cynic. "A thousand *per centum* increase in the new public; stock of intelligence still more freely watered."

"But you are not answering my question about the different kinds of novels," said the lady. "Tell me why the types of fiction change."

"Fashion, dear lady," replied the Cynic. "It is like tight sleeves and loose sleeves. People feel comfortable when they wear what everybody is wearing and read what everybody is reading. The art of modern advertising is an appeal to the instinct of imitation. Our friend the Publisher has become a millionaire by discovering that the same law governs the sale of books and of dry-goods."

"Not at all," interrupted the Critic; "your explanation is too crude for satire and too shallow for science. There is a regular evolution in fiction. First comes the external type, the novel of plot; then the internal type, the novel of character; then the social type, the novel of problem and purpose. The development proceeds from outward to inward, from objective to subjective, from simplicity to complexity."

"But," said the lady, "if I remember rightly, the facts happened the other way. 'Pamela' and 'Joseph Andrews' and 'Caleb Williams' are character novels; 'Waverley' and 'Ivanhoe' are adventure novels. Kingsley wrote 'Yeast' and 'Alton Locke' before 'Westward Ho!' and 'Hypatia.' 'Bleak House' and 'Uncle Tom's Cabin' are older than 'Lorna Doone' and 'David Balfour.' The day before yesterday it was all character-sketching, mainly Scotch; the day before that it was all problem-solving, chiefly religious; yesterday it was all adventure-seeking, called historical because it seems highly improbable; and to-day it is a mixture of automobile-journeys and slum-life. It looks to me as if there must be somebody always ready to read some kind of fiction, but his affections are weather-cocky."

"I don't object to a few characters in a novel," said the Man of Business, "provided they do something interesting."

"Right," said the Publisher; "the public always knows what is interesting, provided it is properly pointed out. Now here is a little list of our most profitable new books: a story of a beautiful Cow-boy, a Kentucky love-tale, a narrative of the Second Crusade, a romance about an imaginary princess and two motor-cars, a modern society story with vivid descriptions of the principal New York restaurants and Monte Carlo—all of these have passed the forty-thousand line. We send out the list with a statement to that effect, and advise people not to lose the chance of reading books that have aroused so much interest."

"It seems to me," put in the Doctor of Divinity, "that some of the modern books do not give me as much insight into life as I should like. I perused 'The Prisoner on a Bender' the other day without getting a single illustration for a sermon. But I continue to read novels from a sense of duty, to keep in touch with my young people."

"I think," began my Uncle Peter (and this solemn announcement made everyone attentive), "I think you have failed to discern a certain law of periodicity which governs the formal variations of fiction. This periodicity is natural to the human mind, and it also has relations to profound social movements. The popularity of the novels of Fielding, Richardson, and Smollett, whose characters were mainly drawn from humble life, was due to the rise of the same spirit of democracy that produced the American and French Revolutions. The reaction to the romantic and historical novel, under Scott and his followers, was a revival of the aristocratic spirit. It took a historical form because the past had been made vivid to the popular imagination by the great historians of the eighteenth century. The purpose novels, which took the lead in the middle of the nineteenth century, were another reaction, and came out of the social ferment of the times. The general pictures of society and manners which followed were written for a public that was fairly well-to-do and contented with itself. The later realistic studies of life in its lowest forms were the offspring of the scientific spirit. And the latest reaction to the novel of adventure, with its emphasis on daring and virility, is connected with the remarkable revival of imperialism. But while fiction is specifically the most transient of forms, generically it is the most permanent. Therefore, our young Man of Letters must write a novel. That is what the public wants."

"Yes," cried the Publisher, "a novel of adventure in Cromwell's time. That period is up, just now, and has not been worked out."

"A novel of purpose," said the Critic; "that is the highest type of fiction."

"A novel of character," said the Cynic. "A change in fashion is due. Take the President of a Trust for your hero, and make him repent under the pressure of the Social Boycott. The public loves surprises."

"Why not write the Great American Novel?" said the Doctor of Divinity. "I have heard several demands for it."

"A good love story," said the Man of Business, "or perhaps a detective story, would be the best thing to sell."

"The one point on which your friends seem agreed," said the True Story Teller, with a smile, "is that the public gives you an order for a novel."

"Well, you know, I have written one already," answered the young Man of Letters, very quietly.

"Why didn't you tell us?" chorused the others. "Why haven't you published it?"

He hesitated a moment before answering: "It did not seem to me good enough."

"My young friend," said the Publisher, with his most impressive and benevolent air, "we have your welfare at heart. You may write essays and stories and poems as a recreation, or for some future age. But this is the day of the novel, and you are wasting your chance unless you publish one as soon as possible. Touch your novel up, or give it to me as it is. You will certainly make a big thing out of it."

"Perhaps," said the young Man of Letters, thoughtfully; "but what if I would rather write the things that please me most, and try to do good work?"

My Uncle Peter looked at him half-quizzically, yet with a smile of benevolent approval, and conferred upon him the honour and reward of escorting the True Story Teller home in his canoe that evening, across the swirling river, where the molten gold of sunset ran slowly to the sea.

SOME REMARKS ON GULLS
WITH A FOOT-NOTE ON A FISH
I
CITY GULLS

THE current estimate of the sea-gull as an intellectual force is compressed into the word "gullibility"—a verbal monument of contempt. But when we think how many things the gull does that we cannot do—how he has mastered the arts of flying and floating, so that he is equally at home in the air and on the water; how cleverly he adapts himself to his environment, keeping warm among the ice-floes in winter and cool when all the rest of the folks at the summer watering-places are sweltering in the heat; how well he holds his own against the encroachments of that grasping animal, man, who has driven so many other wild creatures to the wall, and over it into extinction; how prudently he accepts and utilizes all the devices of civilization which suit him, (such as steamship-lanes across the Atlantic, and dumping-scows in city harbors, and fish-oil factories on the seashore), without becoming in the least civilized himself—in short, when we consider how he succeeds in doing what every wise person is trying to do, living his own proper life amid various and changing circumstances, it seems as if we might well reform the spelling of that supercilious word, and write it "gull-ability."

But probably the gull would show no more relish for the compliment than he has hitherto shown distaste for the innuendo; both of them being inedible, and he of a happy disposition, indifferent to purely academic opinions of his rank and station in the universe. Imagine a gull being disquieted because some naturalist solemnly averred that a hawk or a swallow was a better master of the art of flight; or a mocking-bird falling into a mood of fierce resentment or nervous depression because some professor of music declared that the hermit thrush had a more spontaneous and inspired song! The gull goes a-flying in his own way and the mocking-bird sits a-singing his roundelay, original or imitated, just as it comes to him; and neither of them is angry or depressed when a critic makes odious comparisons, because they are both doing the best that they know with "a whole and happy heart." Not so with poets, orators, and other human professors of the high-flying and cantatory arts. They are often perturbed and acerbated, and sometimes diverted from their proper course by the winds of adverse comment.

When Cicero Tomlinson began his career as a public speaker he showed a very pretty vein of humour, which served to open his hearers' minds with honest laughter to receive his plain and forcible arguments. But someone remarked that his speaking lacked dignity and weight; so he loaded himself with the works of Edmund Burke; and now he discusses the smallest subject with a ponderosity suited to the largest. The charm of Alfred Tennyson Starling's early lyrics was unmistakable. But in an evil day a newspaper announced that his poetry smelled of the lamp and was deficient in virility. Alfred took it painfully to heart, and fell into a violent state of Whitmania. Have you seen his patient imitations of the long-lined, tumultuous one?

After all, the surest way to be artificial is to try to be natural according to some other man's recipe.

One reason why the wild children of nature attract our eyes, and give us an inward, subtle satisfaction in watching them, is because they seem so confident that their own way of doing things is, for them at least, the best way. They let themselves go, on the air, in the water, over the hills, among the trees, and do not ask for admiration or correction from people who are differently built. The sea-gulls flying over a busy port of commerce, or floating at ease on the discoloured, choppy, churned-up waves of some great river,

"Bordered by cities, and hoarse
With a thousand cries,"

are unconscious symbols of nature's self-reliance and content with her ancient methods. Not a whit have they changed their manner of flight, their comfortable, rocking-chair seat upon the water, their creaking, eager voice of hunger and excitement, since the days when the port was a haven of solitude, and the river was crossed only by the red man's canoe passing from forest to forest. They are untroubled by the fluctuations of trade, the calms and tempests which afflict the stock market, the hot waves and cold waves of politics. They do not fash themselves about the fashions—except, perhaps, that silly and barbarous one of adorning the headgear of women with the remains of dead gulls. They do not ask whether life is worth living, but launch themselves boldly upon the supposition that it is, and seem to find it interesting, various, and highly enjoyable, even among wharves, steamboats, and factory chimneys.

My first acquaintance with these untamed visitors of the metropolis was

"When that I was a littel tine boy,"

and lived on the Heights of Brooklyn. A nurse, whose hateful official relation was mitigated by many amiable personal qualities—she was a rosy Irish girl—had the happy idea of going, now and then, for a "day off" and a breath of fresh air, on one of the ferry-boats that ply the waters of Manhattan. Sometimes she took one of the ordinary ferries that went straight over to New York and back again; but more often she chose a boat that proposed a longer and more adventurous voyage—to Hoboken, or Hunter's Point, or Staten Island. We would make the trip to and fro several times, but Biddy never paid, so far as my memory goes, more than one fare. By what arrangement or influence she made the deckhands considerately blind to this repetition of the journey without money and without price, I neither knew nor cared, being altogether engaged with playing about the deck and admiring the wonders of the vasty deep.

The other boats were wonderful, especially the big sailing-ships, which were far more numerous then than they are now. The steam tugs, with their bluff, pushing, hasty manners, were very attractive, and I wondered why all of them had a gilt eagle, instead of a gull, on top of the wheel-house. A little rowboat, tossing along the edge of the wharves, or pushing out bravely for Governor's Island, seemed to be full of perilous adventure. But most wonderful of all were the sea-gulls, flying and floating all over the East River and the North River and the bay.

Where did they come from? It was easy to see where they got their living; they were "snappers-up of unconsidered trifles" from every passing vessel whose cabin-boy threw the rubbish overboard. If you could succeed in getting off the peel of an orange in two or three big pieces, or if you could persuade yourself to leave a reasonably large core of an apple, or, best of all, if you had the limp skin of a yellow banana, you cast the forbidden fruit into the water, and saw how quickly one of the gulls would pick it up, and how beautifully the others would fight him for it. Evidently gulls have a wider range of diet than little boys; also they have never been told that it is wrong to fight.

"How greedy they are! What makes some of them white and some of them gray? They must be different kinds; or else the gray ones are the father and mother gulls. But if that is so, it is funny that the white ones are the best fliers and seem able to take things away from the gray ones. How would you like to fly like that? They swoop around and go just where they want to. Perhaps that is the way the angels fly; only of course the angels are much larger, and very much more particular about what they eat. Isn't it queer that all the gulls have eyes just alike—black and shiny and round, just like little shoe-buttons? How funnily they swim! They sit right down on the water as if it wasn't wet. Don't you wish you could do that? Look how they tuck up their pinky feet under them when they fly, and how they turn their heads from side to side, looking for something good to eat. See, there's a great big flock all together in the water, over yonder, must be a thousand hundred. Now they all fly up at once, like when you tear a newspaper into little scraps and throw a handful out of the window. Where do you suppose they go at night? Perhaps they sleep on the water. That must be fun! Do they have gulls in Ireland, Biddy, and are all their eyes black and shiny?"

"Sure!" says Biddy. "An' they do be a hundred toimes bigger an' foiner than these wans. The feathers o' thim shoines in the sun loike silver and gowld, an' their oyes is loike jools, an' they do be floying fasther then the ships can sail. If ye was only seein' some o' thim rale Oirish gulls, ye'd think no more o' these little wans!"

This increases your determination to go to the marvellous green island some day; but it does not in the least diminish your admiration for the gulls of Manhattan. In the summer, when you go to the seaside and watch the

"Gray spirits of the sea and of the shore"

sailing over the white beach or floating on the blue waves of the unsullied ocean, you wonder whether these country gulls are happier than the city gulls. That they are different you are sure, and also that they must have less variety in their diet, hardly any banana-skins and orange-peel at all. But then they have more fish, and probably more fun in catching them.

These are memories of old times—the ancient days before the Great Invasion of the English Sparrows—the good old days when orioles and robins still built their nests in Brooklyn trees, and Brooklyn streets still resounded to the musical cries of the hucksters: "Radishees! *new* radishees!" or "Ole clo' an' bottles! any *ole* clo' to sell!" or "Shad O! *fre-e-sh* shad!" In that golden age we played football around the old farmhouse on Montague Terrace, coasted down the hill to Fulton Ferry, and made an occasional expedition to Manhattan to observe the strange wigwams and wild goats of the tribe of squatters who inhabited the rocky country south of the newly discovered Central Park. *Eheu fugaces!*

There was a long interval of years after that when the sea-gulls of the harbour did not especially interest me. But now again, of late, I have begun to find delight in them. Conscience, awakened by responsibility, no longer permits those surreptitiously repeated voyages without a repeated fare. But I go through the gate at the end of each voyage, and consider twelve cents a reasonable price for the pleasure of travelling up and down the North River for an hour and watching the city gulls in their winter holiday.

I know a little more about them now. They are almost all herring gulls, although occasionally a stray bird of another species may be seen. The dark-gray ones are the young. They grow lighter and more innocent-looking as they grow older, until they are pure white, except the back and the top of the wings, which are of the softest pearl gray. The head and neck, in winter, are delicately pencilled with dusky lines. The bill is bright yellow and rather long, with the upper part curved and slightly hooked, for a good hold on slippery little fish. The foot has three long toes in front and a foolish little short one behind. The web between the front toes goes down to the tips; but it makes only a small paddle, after all, and when it comes to swimming, the loon and the duck and several other birds can easily distance the gull. It is as a floater that he excels in water sports; he rides the waves more lightly and gracefully than any other creature.

"The gull, high floating like a sloop unladen,
Lets the loose water waft him as it will;
The duck, round-breasted as a rustic maiden,
Paddles and plunges, busy, busy, still."

But it is when the gull rises into the air, where, indeed, he seems to spend most of his time, that you perceive the perfection of his design as a master of motion. The spread of his wings is more than twice the length of his body, and every feather of those long, silvery-pearly, crescent fans seems instinct with the passion and the skill of flight. He rises and falls without an effort; he swings and turns from side to side with balancing motions like a skater; he hangs suspended in the air immovable as if he were held there by some secret force of levitation; he dives suddenly head foremost and skims along the water, feet dangling and wings flapping, to snatch a bit of food from the surface with his crooked golden bill. If the morsel is too large for him to swallow, look how quickly three or four other gulls will follow him, trying to take it away. How he turns and twists and dodges, and how cleverly they head him off and hang on his airy trail, like winged hounds, giving tongue with thin and querulous voices, half laughing and half crying and altogether hungry. He cannot say a word, for his mouth is full. He gulps hastily at his booty, trying to get it down before the others catch him. But it is too big for his gullet, and he drops it in the very act and article of happy deglutition. The largest and whitest of his pursuers scoops up the morsel almost before it touches the waves, and flaps away to enjoy his piratical success in some quiet retreat.

What a variety of cooking the gulls enjoy from the steamships and sailing-vessels of various nationalities which visit Manhattan! French cooks, Italian, German, Spanish, English, Swedish—cooks of all races minister to their appetites. Whenever a panful of scraps is thrown out from the galley, a flock of gulls may be seen fluttering over their fluent *table d'hôte*. Their shrill, quavering cries of joy and expectancy sound as if the machinery of their emotions were worked by rusty pulleys; their sharp eyes glisten, and their great wings flap and whirl together in a confusion of white and gray. It is said that they do useful service as scavengers of the harbor. No doubt; but to me they commend themselves chiefly as visible embodiments and revelations of the mystery, wonder, and gladness of flight.

What do we know about it, after all? We call this long-winged fellow *Larus argerdatus smithsonianus*. We find that his normal temperature is about two degrees higher than ours, and that he breathes faster, and that his bones are lighter, and that his body is full of air-sacs, fitting him to fly. But how does he do it? How does he poise himself on an invisible ledge of air,

"Motionless as a cloud ...
That heareth not the loud winds when they call,
And moveth altogether if it move at all?"

How does he sail after a ship, with wings outspread, against the wind, never seeming to move a feather? You understand how a kite mounts upon the breeze: the string holds it from going back, so it must go up. But where is the string that holds the gull?

I like these city gulls because they come to us in winter, when the gypsy part of our nature is most in need of comforting reminders that the world is not yet entirely dead or civilized. A man that I know once wrote a poem about them, and sent it to a magazine. It was evidently an out-of-door poem and so the editor put it in the midsummer number,—when you might cross the ferry a hundred times without seeing a single gull. They do not begin to come to town until October; and it is well on into November before their social season begins. In March and April they begin to flit again, and by May they are all away northward, to the inland lakes among the mountains, or to the rocky islands of the Maine coast. Let us follow them.

II
A GULL PARADISE

IN the waters south of Cape Cod, where blue-fish and other gamy surface swimmers are found, the gulls are often useful guides to the fisherman. When he sees a great flock of them fluttering over the water, he suspects that the objects of his pursuit are there, feeding from below on the squid, the shiners, or the skip-jack, on which the gulls are feeding from above. So the fisherman sails as fast as possible in that direction, wishing to drag his trolls through the school of fish while they are still hungry. But in the colder waters around the island of Mount Desert, where the blue-fish have never come and the mackerel have gone away, the sign of the fluttering gulls does not indicate fish to be caught, but fish which have already been caught, and which some other fisherman is cleaning for the market as he hurries home. The gulls follow his boat and glean from the waves behind it. They are commentators now, not prophets.

In these blue and frigid deeps the real sport of angling is unknown. There is instead a rather childish, but amusing, game of salt-water grab-bag. You let down a heavy lump of lead and two big hooks baited with clams into thirty, forty, or sixty feet of water. Then you wait until something nudges the line. Then you give the line a quick jerk, and pull in, hand over hand, and see what you have drawn from the grab-bag. It may be a silly, but nutritious cod, gaping in surprise at this curious termination of his involuntary rise in the world; or a silvery haddock, staring at you with round, reproachful eyes; or a pollock, handsome but worthless; or a shiny, writhing dog-fish, whose villainy is written in every line of his degenerate, chinless face. It may be that spiny gargoyle of the sea, a sculpin; or a soft and stupid bake from the mud-flats. It may be any one of the grotesque products of Neptune's vegetable garden, a sea-cucumber, a sea-carrot, or a sea-cabbage. Or it may be nothing at all. When you have made your grab, and deposited the result, if it be edible, in the barrel which stands in the middle of the boat, you try another grab, and that's the whole story.

It is astonishing how much amusement apparently sane men can get out of such a simple game as this. The interest lies, first, in the united effort to fill the barrel, and second, in the rivalry among the fishermen as to which of them shall take in the largest cod or the greatest number of haddock, these being regarded as prize packages. The sculpin and the sea vegetables may be compared to comic valentines, which expose the recipient to ridicule. The dog-fish are like tax notices and assessments; the man who gets one of them gets less than nothing, for they count against the catcher. It is quite as much a game of chance as politics or poker. You do not know on which side of the boat the good fish are hidden. You cannot tell the difference between the nibble of a cod and the bite of a dog-fish. You have no idea what is coming to you, until you have hauled in almost all of your line and caught sight of your allotment wriggling and whirling in the blue water. Sometimes you get twins.

The barrel is nearly full. Let us stop fishing and drifting. Hoist the jib, and trim in the main-sheet. The boat ceases to rock lazily on the tide. The life of the wind enters into her, and she begins to step over the waves and to cut through them, sending bright showers of spray from her bow, and leaving a swirling, bubbling, foaming wake astern. Were there ever waters so blue, or woods so green, or rocky shores so boldly and variously cut, or mountains so clear in outline and so jewel-like in shifting colors, as these of Mount Desert? Was there ever an air which held a stronger, sweeter cordial, fragrant with blended odours of the forest and the sea, soothing, exhilarating, and life-renewing?

Here is the place to see it all, and to drain the full cup of delight; not a standpoint, but a sailing-line just beyond Baker's Island: a voyager's field of vision, shifting, changing, unfolding, as new bays and islands come into view, and new peaks arise, and new valleys open in the line of emerald and amethyst and carnelian and tourmaline hills. You can count all the summits: Newport, and Green, and Pemetic, and Sargent, and Brown, and Dog, and Western. The lesser hills, the Bubbles, Bald Mountain, Flying Mountain, and the rest, detach themselves one after another and stand out from their background of green and gray. How rosy the cliffs of Otter and Seal Harbor glow in the sunlight! How magically the great white flower of foam expands and closes on the sapphire water as the long waves, one by one, pass over the top of the big rock between us and Islesford! This is a bird's-eye view: not a high-flying bird, circling away up in the sky, or perched upon some lofty crag, as Tennyson describes the eagle:—

"Close to the sun in lonely lands,
Ringed with the azure world he stands;
The wrinkled sea beneath him crawls,
He watches from his mountain-walls;"

but a to-and-fro-travelling bird, keeping close to sea and shore. It is a gull's-eye view—just as the flocks of herring gulls see it every day, passing back and forth from their seaward nesting-place to their favourite feeding-ground at Bar Harbor. There they go now, flapping southward with the breeze. We will go with them to their island home, and eat our dinner while they are digesting theirs.

Great and Little Duck Islands lie about ten miles off shore from Seal Harbor. Their name suggests that they were once the haunt of various kinds of sea-fowl. But the ducks have been almost, if not quite, exterminated; and the herring gulls would probably have gone the same way, but for the exertions of the Audubon Society, which have resulted in the reservation of the islands as a breeding-ground under governmental protection. It has taken a long time to awaken the American people to the fact that the wild and beautiful creatures of earth and air and sea are a precious part of the common inheritance, and that their needless and heedless destruction, by pot-hunters or plume-hunters or silly shooters who are not happy unless they are destroying something, is a crime against the commonwealth which must be punished or prevented. The people are not yet wide awake, but they are beginning to get their eyes open; and the State of Maine, which was once the Butchers' Happy Hunting Ground, is now a leader in the enactment and enforcement of good game laws.

There is only one place on the shore of Great Duck where you can land comfortably when the wind has any northing in it, and that is a little cove among the rocks, below a fisherman's shanty, on the lower end of the island. Here there are a few cleared acres; some low stone walls dividing abandoned fields; the cellar of a vanished house, and a ruined fireplace and chimney; a little enclosure, overgrown with bushes and weeds, marking a lonely, forgotten burial-ground.

There are few gulls to be seen at this end of the island; it is a tranquil, forsaken place where we can sit beside our fire of driftwood and eat our broiled fish and bread, and smoke an after-dinner pipe of peace. A grassy foot-path leads down the fields, and across a salt-meadow, and along a high sea-wall of rocks and pebbles cast up by the storms, and so by a rude wood-road through a forest of spruce-trees to the higher part of the island. It rises perhaps a hundred feet or more above the sea, with a steep shore built of huge sloping ledges of flat rock. On the seaward point is the lighthouse, with the three dwelling-houses of the keepers, all precisely alike, immaculately neat and trim, surrounded by a long picket fence, and presenting a front of indomitable human order and discipline to the tumultuous and unruly ocean, which heaves away untamed and unbroken to the shores of Spain and Brittany.

The chief keeper of the light, Captain Stanley, who has been with it since it was first kindled twenty years ago, is also the warden of the sea-gulls. All around us, in the air, on the green slopes of the island, on the broad gray granite ledges, on the dancing blue waves, his feathered flocks are scattered, and their innumerable laughter and shrill screaming confuse the ear. The spruce-trees on the top of the island and the eastward slopes are almost all dead; their fallen trunks and branches and up-turned roots cover the little hillocks and hollows in all directions. The gulls' nests are hidden away among this gray *débris*, or in crevices among the rocks, sheltered as much as possible from the wind and the rain.

They are not very wonderful from an architectural point of view, being nothing more than rough little circles of dried twigs and grass matted together, with perhaps a bit of seaweed or moss for padding in the case of a parent with luxurious tastes. Three eggs in a nest is the rule, and all that the average mother-gulls wants is a place where she can hold them together and keep them warm until they are hatched. The young birds are præcocial; they emerge from the shell with a full suit of downy feathers, and are able to walk after a fashion, and to swim pretty well, almost from the day of their second and completed birth. The young of altricial birds, like orioles, and bluebirds, and thrushes, being born naked and helpless, have a reason for loving their nest-homes, so carefully and delicately built to shelter their nude infancy. But the young gull cares not for "a local habitation and a name." All that he wants of home is a father and mother, nimble and assiduous in bringing food to him while he flops around, practising his legs and his wings.

It is August now, and the eggs are gone, shells and all. Almost all of the young gulls are accomplished swimmers and fair fliers by this time, and I suppose the majority of the brood can go with their parents to the nearer harbours and along the island shores to forage for themselves. But there are a few backward or lazy children—perhaps a hundred—still hanging around the places where they chipped the egg, hiding among the roots of the trees or crouching beside the rocks. What quaint, ungainly creatures they are! Big-headed, awkward, dusky, like gnomes or goblins, they hop and scuffle away as you come near them, stumbling over the tangled dead branches and the tussocks of grass, with outspread wings and clumsy motions. Follow one a little while and he will take refuge in a hole under a fallen tree, or between two big stones, squatting there without much apparent fright while you pat his back or gently scratch his head. But you must be careful not to follow the youngsters who are near the edge of the sea when there is a surf running, for if you alarm them they will plunge into the water and be bruised and wounded, perhaps killed, by the breakers throwing them against the rocks.

Wild animals, like polecats and minks, who would be likely to prey upon the young birds, are not allowed to reside on the island; and it is too far to swim from the mainland. But I wonder why large hawks and other birds of prey do not resort to this place as a marine restaurant. Perhaps a young gull is too big, or too tough, or too high-flavoured a dish for them. Possibly the old gulls know how to fight for their offspring. I suppose that enough of the adult birds are always on hand for defence, although during a good part of the day the majority of the flock are away at the feeding-grounds.

I opened the gate of the light-house enclosure and went in. Three little children who were playing in the garden came shyly up to me, each silently offering a flower. The keeper of the light, who is a most intelligent man and an ardent Audubonite, asked me into his sitting-room and told me a lot about his gulls.

In the spring, the first of them come back in March, sometimes arriving in a snowstorm. They keep to the shore most of the time, but fuss around a little, pulling old nests to pieces or making new ones. About the first of May, they move up to the centre of the island. There are three or four thousand of them, and not quite half as many nests. By the middle of May the first egg may be expected, and in the second week of June the first gray chick puts out his big head. A week later the brood is all hatched and the parental troubles begin.

"The old birds," says Mr. Stanley, "do not fail to provide food for their young, although as the birds get large the old ones have to go sometimes many miles to do it, but, as a general thing, there is plenty for them. I have watched them coming back at night, appearing very tired, flying very low, one behind the other. They would light near where the young should be and call, and the chicks would rush up to the old bird and pick its bill; after the proper time the old bird will stretch out its neck, and up will come a mess of almost everything, from bread to sea-cucumbers, livers, fish (all the small kind). If there is anything left after the feast the old bird will swallow it again. Woe betide the young bird that belongs to a neighbour, who tries to fill up at the wrong place! I have seen a young bird killed by one blow from the old bird's bill, his head torn in two. As the young birds grow, the old birds bring them larger fish to swallow. We have a few old birds who know the time we feed the hens, and when that time draws near they are on hand to dine with the hens."

By the latter part of August, having done their duties, the old birds, the white ones, begin to leave the island. The dingy youngsters are slower to forsake their Eden of innocence, lingering on beside the unsullied waters and beneath the crystalline skies until the frosts of late September warn them that winter is at hand. Then the last of the colony take flight, winging their way southward leisurely and comfortably, putting in at many a port where fish are cleaned and scraps are thrown overboard, until they arrive at their chosen harbour by some populous and smoke-clouded city, and learn to dodge the steamboats and swim in troubled waters.

So the Gull Paradise is deserted by all but its guardians. The school district of Duck Island—the smallest in the United States—resumes its activities; the school-house is open, the teacher raps on the desk, and the fourteen children of the keepers apply themselves to the knowledge that is dried in books.

III
IN THE GULLS' BATH-TUB

OVER our cottage we saw them flying inland every morning about ten or eleven o'clock; in groups of three or four; in companies of twelve or twenty; sometimes a solitary bird, hurrying a little as if he were belated. Over our cottage we saw them flying seaward every afternoon, one or two at a time, and then, at last, a larger company all together. The trail through the woods, up along the lovely mountain-brook, led us in the same direction as the gulls' path through the air. A couple of miles of walking underneath green boughs brought us to the shores of Jordan Pond, lying in a deep gorge between the mountains of rock with the rounded, forest-clad Bubbles at its head, and the birches, and maples, and poplars, and hemlocks fringing its clean, stony shores. Then we understood what brought the gulls up from the sea every day. They came for a fresh-water bath and a little fun in the woods.

Look at them, gathered like a flotilla, in the centre of the pond. They are not feeding; they are not attending to any business of importance; they are not even worrying about their young; they are not doing anything at all but "bath-ing" themselves, as my little lad used to say, in this clear, cool, unsalted water, and having the best time in the world. See how they swim lazily this way or that way, as the fancy strikes them. See how they duck their heads, and stretch their long wings in the air, and splash the water over one another; how they preen their feathers and rise on the surface, shaking themselves. Here comes a trio of late starters, flying up from the sea. They hover overhead a moment, crying out to the crowd below, which answers them with a general shout and a flutter of excitement. Didn't you hear what they said?

"Hello, fellows! How's the water?"

"Bully! Just right—come in quick's you can!" So the new arrivals swoop down, spreading out their tails like fans, and dangling their feet under them, and settling in the centre of the crowd amid general hilarity.

How long the gulls stay at their bath I do not know. Probably some of the busy and conscientious ones just hurry in for a dip and hurry back again. Others, of a more pleasure-loving temperament, make the trip more than once, like a boy I knew, whose proud boast it was that he had gone in swimming seven times in one afternoon. The very idle and self-indulgent ones, I reckon, spend nearly the whole day in their spacious and well-fitted bath-tub.

The mountain lake has been turned into a reservoir for the neighbouring village of Seal Harbor. But the gulls do not know that, I am sure; nor would anyone else who judged by outward appearances suspect that such a transformation had taken place. For the dam at the outlet is made of rough stones, very low, almost unnoticeable; and the water has not been raised enough to kill any of the trees or spoil the shore. Jordan Pond, which was named for a commonplace lumberman who used to cut timber on its banks, and which has, so far as I know, no tradition or legend of any kind connected with it, is still as wild, as lovely, as perfect in its lonely charm as if it were consecrated and set apart to the memory of a score of old romances.

At the lower end, in an open space of slightly rising ground, there is an ancient farmhouse which has been extended and piazzaed and made into a rustic place of entertainment. Here the fashionable summer-folk of the various harbours come to drink afternoon tea and to eat famous dinners of broiled chicken, baked potatoes, and pop-overs. The proprietor has learned from the modern author and advertiser the secret of success; avoid versatility and stick to the line in which the public know you. Having won a reputation on pop-overs and chickens, he continues to turn them out with diligence and fidelity, like short-stories of a standard pattern.

I asked him if there was any fishing in the lake. He said that there was plenty of fishing; but he said it in a tone which made me doubtful about his meaning. "What kind of fish were there?" "Trout by nature, and landlocked salmon by artificial planting." "Could we fish for them?" "Sure; but as for catching anything big enough to keep—well, he did not want to encourage us. It was two or three years since any good fish had been caught in the lake, though there had been plenty of fishing. But in old times men used to come over from Hull's Cove, fishing through the ice, and they caught"—then followed the usual piscatorial legends of antiquity.

But the Gypsy girl and I were not to be disheartened by historical comparisons. We insisted on putting our living luck to the proof, and finding out for ourselves what kind of fish were left in Jordan Pond. We had a couple of four-ounce rods, one of which I fitted up with a troll, while she took the oars in a round-bottomed, snub-nosed white boat, and rowed me slowly around the shore. The water was very clear; at a depth of twenty feet we could see every stone and stick on the bottom—and no fish! We tried a little farther out, where the water was deeper. My guide was a merry rower and the voyage was delightful, but we caught nothing.

Let us set up the other rod, while we are trolling, and try a few casts with the fly as we move along. I will put the trolling-rod behind me, leaning over the back-board; if a fish should strike, he would hook himself and I could pick up the rod and land him. Now we will straighten out a leader and choose some flies—a silver doctor and a queen of the water—how would those do? Or perhaps a royal coachman would be—Chrrr-p! goes the reel. I turn hastily around, just in time to see the trolling-rod vanish over the stern of the boat. Stop, stop! Back water—hard as you can! Too late! There goes my best-beloved little rod, with a reel and fifty yards of line, settling down in the deep water, almost out of sight, and slowly following the flight of that invisible fish, who has hooked himself and my property at the same time.

This is a piece of bad luck. Shall we let the day end with this? "Never," says the Gypsy. "Adventures ought to be continued till they end with good luck. We will put a long line on the other rod, and try that beautiful little phantom minnow, the silver silk one that came from Scotland. There must be some good fish in the pond, since they are big enough to run away with your tackle."

Round and round the shore she rows, past the points of broken rocks, underneath the rugged bluffs, skirting all the shelving bays. Faintly falls the evening breeze, and behind the western ridge of Jordan Mountain suddenly the sun drops down. Look, the gulls have all gone home. Creeping up the rosy side of Pemetic, see old Jordan's silhouette sketched in shadow by the sun. Hark, was that a coaching horn, sounding up from Wildwood Road? There's the whistle of the boat coming round the point at Seal. How it sinks into the silence, fading gradually away. Twilight settles slowly down, all around the wooded shore, and across the opal lake—

Chr-r-r-r! sings the reel. The line tightens. The little rod, firmly gripped in my hand, bends into a bow of beauty, and a hundred feet behind us a splendid silver salmon leaps into the air. "What is it?" cries the Gypsy, "a fish?" It is a fish, indeed, a noble ouananiche, and well hooked. Now if the gulls were here, who grab little fish suddenly and never give them a chance, or if the mealy-mouthed sentimentalists were here, who like their fish slowly strangled to death in nets, they should see a fairer method of angling.

The weight of the fish is twenty times that of the rod against which he matches himself. The tiny hook is caught painlessly in the gristle of his jaw. The line is long and light. He has the whole lake to play in, and he uses almost all of it, running, leaping, sounding the deep water, turning suddenly to get a slack line. The Gypsy, tremendously excited, manages the boat with perfect skill, rowing this way and that way, advancing or backing water to meet the tactics of the fish, and doing the most important part of the work.

After half an hour the ouananiche begins to grow tired and can be reeled in near to the boat. We can see him distinctly as he gleams in the dark water. It is time to think of landing him. Then we remember, with a flash of despair, that we have no landing-net! To lift him from the water by the line would break it in an instant. There is not a foot of the rocky shore smooth enough to beach him on. Our caps are far too small to use as a net for such a fish. What to do? We must row around with him gently and quietly for another ten minutes until he is quite weary and tame. Now let me draw him softly in toward the boat, slip my fingers under his gills to get a firm hold, and lift him quickly over the gunwale before he can gasp or kick. A tap on the head with the empty rod-case—there he is—the prettiest landlocked salmon that I ever saw, plump, round, perfectly shaped and coloured, and just six and a half pounds in weight, the record fish of Jordan Pond!

Do you think that the Gypsy and I wept over our lost rod, or were ashamed of our flannel shirts and tweeds, as we sat down to our broiled chickens and pop-overs that evening, on the piazza of the tea-house, among the white frocks and Tuxedo jackets of the diners-out? No, for there was our prize lying in state on the floor beside our table. "And we caught him," said she, "in the gulls' bath-tub!"

LEVIATHAN

THE village of Samaria in the central part of the State of Connecticut resembled the royal city of Israel, after which it was named, in one point only. It was perched upon the top of a hill, encircled by gentle valleys which divided it from an outer ring of hills still more elevated, almost mountainous. But, except this position in the centre of the stage, you would find nothing theatrical or striking about the little New England hill-town: no ivory palaces to draw down the denunciations of a minor prophet, no street of colonnades to girdle the green eminence with its shining pillars, not even a dirty picturesqueness such as now distinguishes the forlorn remnant of the once haughty city of Omri and of Herod.

Neat, proper, reserved, not to say conventional, the Connecticut Samaria concealed its somewhat chilly architectural beauties beneath a veil of feathery elms and round-topped maples. It was not until you had climbed the hill from the clump of houses and shops which had grown up around the railway station,—a place of prosperous ugliness and unabashed modernity,—that you perceived the respectable evidences of what is called in America "an ancient town." The village green, and perhaps a half dozen of the white wooden houses which fronted it with their prim porticoes, were possibly a little more than a hundred years old. The low farmhouse, which showed its gambrel-roof and square brick chimney a few rods down the northern road, was a relic of colonial days. The stiff white edifice with its pointed steeple, called in irreverent modern phrase the "Congo" church, claimed an equal antiquity; but it had been so often repaired and "improved" to suit the taste of various epochs, that the traces of Sir Christopher Wren in its architecture were quite confused by the admixture of what one might describe as the English Sparrow style.

The other buildings on the green, or within sight of it along the roads north, south, east, and west, had been erected or built-over at different periods, by prosperous inhabitants or returning natives who wished to have a summer cottage in their birth-place. These structures, although irreproachable in their moral aspect, indicated that the development of the builder's art in Samaria had not followed any known historical scheme, but had been conducted along sporadic lines of imitation, and interrupted at least once by a volcanic outbreak of the style named, for some inscrutable reason, after Queen Anne. On the edges of the hill, looking off in various directions over the encircling vale, and commanding charming views of the rolling ridges which lay beyond, were the houses of the little summer colony of artists, doctors, lawyers and merchants. Two or three were flamboyant, but for the most part they blended rather gently with the landscape, and were of a modesty which gave their owners just ground for pride.

The countenance of the place was placid. It breathed an air of repose and satisfaction, a spirit which when it refers to outward circumstances is called contentment, and when it refers to oneself is called complacency. The Samaritans, in fact, did not think ill of themselves, and of their village they thought exceeding well. There was nothing in its situation, its looks, its customs which they would have wished to alter; and when a slight change came, a new house, a pathway on the other side of the green, an iron fence around the graveyard, a golf-links in addition to the tennis-courts, a bridge-whist afternoon to supplement the croquet club, by an unconscious convention its novelty was swiftly eliminated and in a short time it became one of the "old traditions." Decidedly a place of peace was Samaria in Connecticut,—a place in which "the struggle for life" and the rivalries and contests of the great outside world were known only by report. Yet, being human, it had its own inward strifes; and of one of these I wish to tell the tale.

In the end this internal conflict centred about Leviathan; but in the beginning I believe that it was of an ecclesiastical nature. At all events it did not run its course without a manifest admixture of the *odium theologicum*, and it came near to imperilling the cause of Christian unity in Samaria.

The Episcopal Church was really one of the more recent old institutions of the village. It stood beside the graveyard, just around the corner from the village green; and the type of its wooden architecture, which was profoundly early Gothic and was painted of a burnt-umber hue sprinkled with sand to imitate brownstone, indicated that it must have been built in the Upjohn Period, about the middle of the nineteenth century. But Samaria, without the slightest disloyalty to the principles of the Puritans, had promptly adopted and assimilated the Episcopal form of worship. The singing by a voluntary quartette of mixed voices, the hours of service, even the sermons, were all of the Samaritan type. The old rector, Dr. Snodgrass, a comfortably stout and evangelical man, lived for forty years on terms of affectionate intimacy with three successive ministers of the Congregational Church, the deacons of which shared with his vestrymen the control of the village councils.

The summer residents divided their attendance impartially between the two houses of worship. Even in the distribution of parts in the amateur theatricals which were given every year by the villagers in the town hall at the height of the season, no difference was made between the adherents of the ancient faith of Connecticut and the followers of the more recently introduced order of Episcopacy. When old Dr. Snodgrass died and was buried, the Rev. Cotton Mather Hopkins, who was an energetic widower of perhaps thirty-five years, made an eloquent address at his funeral, comparing him to the prophet Samuel, the apostle John, and a green bay tree whose foundations are built upon the rock. In short, all was tranquil in the ecclesiastical atmosphere of Samaria. There was not a cloud upon the horizon.

The air changed with the arrival of the new rector, the Rev. Willibert Beauchamp Jones, B.D., from the Divinity School of St. Jerome at Oshkosh. He was a bachelor, not only of divinity but also in the social sense; a plump young man of eight and twenty summers, with an English accent, a low-crowned black felt hat, blue eyes, a cherubic smile, and very high views on liturgics. He was full of the best intentions toward the whole world, a warm advocate of the reunion of Christendom on his platform, and a man of sincere enthusiasm who regarded Samaria as a missionary field and was prepared to consecrate his life to it. The only point in which he was not true to the teachings of his professors at St. Jerome's was the celibacy of the parish clergy. Here he held that the tradition of the Greek Church was to be preferred to that of the Roman, and felt in his soul that the priesthood and matrimony were not inconsistent. In fact, he was secretly ambitious to prove their harmony in his own person. He was a very social young man, and firm in his resolution to be kind and agreeable to everybody, even to those who were outside of the true fold.

Mr. Hopkins called on him without delay and was received with cordiality amounting to *empressement*. The two men talked together in the friendliest manner of interests that they had in common, books, politics, and out-of-door sports, to which both of them were addicted. Mr. Jones offered to lend Mr. Hopkins any of the new books, with which his library was rather well stocked, and promised to send over the *Pall Mall Review*, to which he was a subscriber, every week. Mr. Hopkins told Mr. Jones the name of the best washerwoman in the village, one of his own new parishioners, as it happened, and proposed to put him up at once for membership in the Golf Club. In fact the conversation went off most harmoniously.

"It was extraordinarily kind of you to call so early, my dear fellow," said Jones as he followed his guest to the door of the little rectory. "I take it as a mark of Christian brotherhood; and naturally, as a clergyman, I want to be as close as possible to every one who is working in any way for the good of the place where my parish lies."

"Of course!" answered Hopkins. "That's all right. I guess you won't have any trouble about Christian brotherhood in Samaria. Good-bye till Monday afternoon."

But as he walked across the green, the skirts of his black frock-coat flapping in the September breeze, and his brown Fedora hat set at a reflective angle on the back of his head, he pondered a little over the precise significance of his *confrère's* last remark, which had not altogether pleased him. Was there a subtle shade of difference between those who were working "in any way" for the good of Samaria, and the "clergyman" who felt bound to be on good terms with them?

On Monday afternoon they had appointed to take a country walk together, and Hopkins, who was a lean, long-legged, wiry fellow, with a deep chest, gray eyes, and a short, crisp brown beard and moustache, led the way at a lively pace over hill and dale around Lake Marapaug and back,—fourteen miles in three hours. Jones was rather red when they returned to the front gate of the rectory about five o'clock, and he wiped his beaded forehead with his handkerchief as he invited his comrade to come in and have a cup of tea.

"No, thank you," said Hopkins, "I'm just ready for a bit of work in my study, now. Nice little stroll, wasn't it? I want you to know the country about here, and the people too. You mustn't feel strange in this Puritan region where my church has been established so long. We'll soon make you feel at home. Good-bye."

An hour later, when Jones had sipped his tea, he looked up from an article in the *Pall Mall Review* and began to wonder whether Hopkins had meant anything in particular by that last remark.

"He's an awfully good chap, to be sure, but just a bit set in his way. I fancy he has some odd notions. Well, perhaps I shall be able to put him right, if I am patient and friendly. It is rather plain that I shall have a lot of missionary work to do here among these dissenters."

So he turned to his bookshelves and took down a volume on *The Primitive Diaconate and the Reconstruction of Christendom*. Meantime Hopkins was in his study making notes for a series of sermons on "The Scriptural Polity of the Early New England Churches."

Well, you can see from this how the great Leviathan conflict began. Two men meeting with good intentions, both anxious, even determined, to be the best of friends, yet each unconsciously pressing upon the other the only point of difference between them. Now add to this a pair of consciences aggravated by the sense of official responsibilities, and a number of ladies who were alike in cherishing for one or the other of these two men a warm admiration, amounting in several cases, shall I say, to a sentimental adoration, and you have a collection of materials not altogether favourable to a peaceful combination.

My business, however, is with Leviathan, and therefore I do not propose to narrate the development of the rivalry between these two excellent men. How Mr. Jones introduced an early morning service, and Mr. Hopkins replied with an afternoon musical vespers: how a vested choir of boys was installed in the brown church, and a cornet and a harp appeared in the gallery of the white church: how candles were lighted in the Episcopalian apse, (whereupon Erastus Whipple resigned from the vestry because he said he knew that he was "goin' to act ugly"), and a stereopticon threw illuminated pictures of Palestine upon the wall behind the Congregational pulpit (which induced Abijah Lemon to refuse to pass the plate the next Sunday, because he said he "wa'nt goin' to take up no collection for a peep-show in meetin'"): how a sermon beside the graveyard on "the martyrdom of King Charles I," was followed, on the green, by a discourse on "the treachery of Charles II": how Mrs. Slicer and Mrs. Cutter crossed each other in the transfer of their church relations, because the Slicer boys were not asked to sing in the vested choir, and because Orlando Cutter was displaced as cornetist by a young man from Hitchfield: how the Jonesites learned to speak of themselves as "churchmen" and of their neighbours as "adherents of other religious bodies," while the Hopkinsians politely inquired as to the hours at which "mass was celebrated" in the brown edifice and were careful to speak of their own services as "Divine worship": how Mr. Jones went so far, in his Washington's Birthday Speech, as to compliment the architectural effect of "the old meeting-house on the green, that venerable monument of an earnest period of dissent," to which Mr. Hopkins made the retort courteous by giving thanks, in his prayer on the same occasion, for "the gracious memories of fraternal intercourse which still hallowed the little brown chapel beside the cemetery": how all these strokes and counterstrokes were given and exchanged in a decorous and bloodless religious war which enlivened a Samaritan autumn and winter almost to the point of effervescence: and how they were prevented from doing any great harm by the general good feeling and the constitutional sense of humour of the village, it is not my purpose, I say, to relate in detail.

The fact is, the incipient fermentation passed away almost as naturally and suddenly as it began. Old Cap'n Elihu Gray, who had made a tidy fortune in his voyages to the East Indies and retired to enjoy it in a snug farmhouse beside the Lirrapaug River, a couple of miles below the village, was reputed to be something of a freethinker, but he used to come up, every month, to one or other of the two churches to sample a sermon. His summary of the controversy which threatened the peace of Samaria, seemed to strike the common-sense of his fellow-townsmen in the place where friendly laughter lies.

"Wa'al," said he, puffing a meditative pipe, "I've seen folks pray to cows and jest despise folks 'at prayed to elephants. 'N I've seen folks whose r'ligion wouldn't 'low 'em to eat pig's meat fight with folks whose r'ligion wouldn't 'low 'em to eat meat 't all. But I never seen reel Christians dispise other reel Christians for prayin' at seven in the mornin' 'stead of at eleven, nor yet fight 'bout the difference 'tween a passel o' boys singin' in white nightgowns an' half-a-dozen purty young gals tunin' their voices to a pipe-organ an' a harp o' sollum saound. I don't 'low there is eny devil, but ef ther' wuz, guess that's the kind o' fight 'd make him grin."

This opinion appeared to reach down to the fundamental saving grace of humour in the Samaritan mind. The vestry persuaded the Reverend Willibert that the time was not yet ripe for candles; and the board of deacons induced the Reverend Cotton Mather to substitute a course of lectures on the Women of the Bible for the stereopticon exhibitions. Hostilities gently frothed themselves away and subsided. Decoration Day was celebrated in Samaria, according to the Hitchfield *Gazette*, "by a notable gathering in the Town Hall, at which the Rev. Jones offered an eloquent extemporaneous prayer and the Rev. Hopkins pronounced an elegant oration on the Civil War, after which the survivors partook of a banquet at the Hancock Hotel."

But the rivalry between the two leaders, sad to say, did not entirely disappear with the peaceful reconciliation and commingling of their forces. On the contrary, it was as if a general engagement had been abandoned and both the opposing companies had resolved themselves into the happy audience of a single combat. It was altogether a friendly and chivalrous contest, you understand,—nothing bitter or malicious about it,—but none the less it was a *duel a l'outrance*, a struggle for the mastery between two men whom nature had made rivals, and for whom circumstances had prepared the arena in the double sphere of love and angling.

Hopkins had become known, during the seven years of his residence at Samaria, as the best trout-fisherman of the village, and indeed of all the tributary region. With the black bass there were other men who were his equals, and perhaps one or two, like Judge Ward, who spent the greater part of his summer vacation sitting under an umbrella in a boat on Lake Marapaug, and Jags Witherbee, the village ne'er-do-weel, who were his superiors. But with the delicate, speckled, evasive trout he was easily first. He knew all the cold, foaming, musical brooks that sang their way down from the hills. He knew the spring-holes in the Lirrapaug River where the schools of fish assembled in the month of May, waiting to go up the brooks in the warm weather. He knew the secret haunts and lairs of the large fish where they established themselves for the whole season and took toll of the passing minnows. He knew how to let his line run with the current so that it would go in under the bushes without getting entangled, and sink to the bottom of the dark pools, beneath the roots of fallen trees, without the hook catching fast. He knew how to creep up to a stream that had hollowed out a way under the bank of a meadow, without shaking the boggy ground. He had a trick with a detachable float, made from a quill and a tiny piece of cork, that brought him many a fish from the centre of a mill-pond. He knew the best baits for every season,—worms, white grubs, striped minnows, miller's thumbs, bumble-bees, grasshoppers, young field-mice,—and he knew where to find them.

For it must be confessed that Cotton Mather was a confirmed bait-fisherman. Confession is not the word that he would have used with reference to the fact; he would have called it a declaration of principles, and would have maintained that he was a follower of the best, the most skilful, the most productive, the fairest, the truly Apostolic method of fishing.

Jones, on the other hand, was not a little shocked when he discovered in the course of conversation that his colleague, who was in many respects such a good sportsman, was addicted to fishing with bait. For his own angling education had been acquired in a different school,—among the clear streams of England, the open rivers of Scotland, the carefully preserved waters of Long Island. He had been taught that the artificial fly was the proper lure for a true angler to use.

For coarse fish like perch and pike, a bait was permissible. For middle-class fish, like bass, which would only rise to the fly during a brief and uncertain season, a trolling-spoon or an artificial minnow might be allowed. But for fish whose blood, though cold, was noble,—for game fish of undoubted rank like the salmon and the trout, the true angler must use only the lightest possible tackle, the most difficult possible methods, the cleanest and prettiest possible lure,—to wit, the artificial fly. Moreover, he added his opinion that in the long run, taking all sorts of water and weather together, and fishing through the season, a man can take more trout with the fly than with the bait,—that is, of course, if he understands the art of fly-fishing.

You perceive at once that here was a very pretty ground for conflict between the two men, after the ecclesiastical battle had been called off. Their community of zeal as anglers only intensified their radical opposition as to the authoritative and orthodox mode of angling. In the close season, when the practice of their art was forbidden, they discussed its theory with vigour; and many were the wit-combats between these two champions, to which the Samaritans listened in the drug-store-and-post-office that served them in place of a Mermaid Tavern. There was something of Shakspere's quickness and elegance in Willibert's methods; but Cotton Mather had the advantage in learning and in weight of argument.

"It is unhistorical," he said, "to claim that there is only one proper way to catch fish. The facts are against you."

"But surely, my dear fellow," replied Willibert, "there is one best way, and that must be the proper way on which all should unite."

"I don't admit that," said the other, "variety counts for something. Besides, it is up to you to prove that fly-fishing is the best way."

"Well," answered Willibert, "I fancy that would be easy enough. All the authorities are on my side. Doesn't every standard writer on angling say that fly-fishing is the perfection of the art?"

"Not at all," Cotton Mather replied, with some exultation, "Izaak Walton's book is all about bait-fishing, except two or three pages on the artificial fly, which were composed for him by Thomas Barker, a retired confectioner. But suppose all the books were on your side. There are ten thousand men who love fishing and know about fishing, to one who writes about it. The proof of the angler is the full basket."

At this Willibert looked disgusted. "You mistake quantity for quality. It's better to take one fish prettily and fairly than to fill your basket in an inferior way. Would you catch trout with a net?"

Cotton Mather admitted that he would not.

"Well, then, why not carry your discrimination a little farther and reject the coarse bait-hook, and the stiff rod, and the heavy line? Fly-tackle appeals to the æsthetic taste,—the slender, pliant rod with which you land a fish twenty times its weight, the silken line, the gossamer leader, the dainty fly of bright feathers concealing the tiny hook!"

"Concealing!" broke in the advocate of the bait, "that is just the spirit of the whole art of fly-fishing. It's all a deception. The slender rod is made of split cane that will bend double before it breaks; the gossamer leader is of drawn-gut carefully tested to stand a heavier strain than the rod can put upon it. The trout thinks he can smash your tackle, but you know he can't, and you play with him half-an-hour to convince him that you are right. And after all, when you've landed him, he hasn't had even a taste of anything good to eat to console him for being caught,—nothing but a little bunch of feathers which he never would look at if he knew what it was. Don't you think that fly-fishing is something of a piscatorial immorality?"

"Not in the least," answered Willibert, warming to his work, "it is a legitimate appeal, not to the trout's lower instinct, his mere physical hunger, but to his curiosity, his sense of beauty, his desire for knowledge. He takes the fly, not because it looks like an edible insect, for nine times out of ten it doesn't, but because it's pretty and he wants to know what it is. When he has found out, you give him a fair run for his money and bring him to basket with nothing more than a pin-prick in his lip. But what does the bait-fisher do? He deceives the trout into thinking that a certain worm or grub or minnow is wholesome, nourishing, digestible, fit to be swallowed. In that deceptive bait he has hidden a big, heavy hook which sticks deep in the trout's gullet and by means of which the disappointed fish is forcibly and brutally dragged to land. It lacks refinement. It is primitive, violent, barbaric, and so simple that any unskilled village lad can do it as well as you can."

"I think not," said Cotton Mather, now on the defensive, "just let the village-lad try it. Why, the beauty of real bait-fishing is that it requires more skill than any other kind of angling. To present your bait to the wary old trout without frightening him; to make it move in the water so that it shall seem alive and free"; ("deception," murmured Willibert), "to judge the proper moment after he has taken it when you should strike, and how hard; to draw him safely away from the weeds and roots among which he has been lying; all this takes quite a little practice and some skill,—a good deal more, I reckon, than hooking and playing a trout on the clear surface of the water when you can see every motion."

"Ah, there you are," cried Willibert, "that's the charm of fly-fishing! It's all open and above-board. The long, light cast of the fly, 'fine and far off,' the delicate drop of the feathers upon the water, the quick rise of the trout and the sudden gleam of his golden side as he turns, the electric motion of the wrist by which you hook him,—that is the magic of sport."

"Yes," replied the other, "I'll admit there's something in it, but bait-fishing is superior. You take a long pool, late in the season; water low and clear; fish lying in the middle; you can't get near them. You go to the head of the pool in the rapids and stir up the bottom so as to discolour the water a little——"

"Deceptive," interrupted Willibert, "and decidedly immoral!"

"Only a little," continued Cotton Mather, "a very little! Then you go down to the bottom of the pool with a hand-line——"

"A hand-line!" murmured the listener, half-shuddering in feigned horror.

"Yes, a hand-line," the speaker went on firmly, "a long, light hand-line, without a sinker, baited with a single, clean angle-worm, and loosely coiled in your left hand. You cast the hook with your right hand, and it falls lightly without a splash, a hundred feet up stream. Then you pull the line in very gently, just fast enough to keep it from sinking to the bottom. When the trout bites, you strike him and land him by hand, without the help of rod or landing-net or any other mechanical device. Try this once, and you will see whether it is easier than throwing the fly. I reckon this was the way the Apostle Peter fished when he was told to 'go to the sea, and cast a hook, and take up the fish that first cometh up.' It is the only true Apostolic method of fishing."

"But, my dear fellow," answered the other, "the text doesn't say that it was a bait-hook. It may have been a fly-hook. Indeed the text rather implies that, for it speaks of the fish as 'coming up,' and that means rising to the fly."

"Wa'al," said Cap'n Gray, rising slowly and knocking out the ashes of his pipe on the edge of his chair, "I can't express no jedgment on the merits of this debate, seein' I've never been much of a fisher. But ef I wuz, my fust ch'ice'd be to git the fish, an' enny way that got 'em I'd call good."

The arrival of the Springtime, releasing the streams from their imprisonment of ice, and setting the trout to leaping in every meadow-brook and all along the curving reaches of the swift Lirrapaug, transferred this piscatorial contest from the region of discourse to the region of experiment. The rector proved himself a competitor worthy of the minister's mettle. Although at first he was at some disadvantage on account of his slight acquaintance with the streams, he soon overcame this by diligent study; and while Hopkins did better work on the brooks that were overhung with trees and bushes, Jones was more effective on the open river and in the meadow-streams just at sundown. They both made some famous baskets that year, and were running neck and neck in the angling field, equal in success.

But in the field of love, I grieve to say, their equality was of another kind. Both of them were seriously smitten with the beauty of Lena Gray, the old Captain's only daughter, who had just come home from Smith College, with a certificate of graduation, five charming new hats, and a considerable knowledge of the art of amateur dramatics. She was cast for the part of leading lady in Samaria's play that summer, and Mr. Jones and Mr. Hopkins were both secretly ambitious for the post of stage-manager. But it fell to Orlando Cutter, who lived on the farm next to the Grays. The disappointed candidates consoled themselves by the size of the bouquets which they threw to the heroine at the close of the third act. One was of white roses and red carnations; the other was of pink roses and lilies of the valley. The flowers that she carried when she answered the final curtain-call, curiously enough, were damask roses and mignonette. A minute observer would have noticed that there was a fine damask rose-bush growing in the Cutter's back garden.

There was no dispute of methods between Jones and Hopkins in the amatorial realm, like that which divided them in matters piscatorial. They were singularly alike in attitude and procedure. Both were very much in earnest; both expressed their earnestness by offerings presented to the object of their devotions; both hesitated to put their desires and hopes into words, because they could not do it in any but a serious way, and they feared to invite failure by a premature avowal. So, as I said, they stood in love upon an equal footing, but not an equality of success; rather one of doubt, delay and dissatisfaction. Miss Gray received their oblations with an admirable impartiality. She liked their books, their candy, their earnest conversation, their mild clerical jokes, without giving any indication which of them she liked best. As her father's daughter she was free from ecclesiastical entanglements; but of course she wanted to go to church, so she attended the Episcopal service at eleven o'clock and became a member of Mr. Hopkins's Bible Class which met at twelve thirty. Orlando Cutter usually drove home with her when the class was over.

You can imagine how eagerly and gravely Cotton Mather and Willibert considered the best means of advancing their respective wishes in regard to this young lady; how they sought for some gift which should not be too costly for her to accept with propriety, and yet sufficiently rare and distinguished to indicate her supreme place in their regards. They had sent her things to read and things to eat; they had drawn upon Hitchfield in the matter of flowers. Now each of them was secretly casting about in his mind for some unique thing to offer, which might stand out from trivial gifts, not by its cost, but by its individuality, by the impossibility of any other person's bringing it, and so might prepare the way for a declaration.

By a singular, yet not unnatural, coincidence, the solution presented itself to the imagination of each of them (separately and secretly of course) in the form of Leviathan.

I feel that a brief word of explanation is necessary here. Every New England village that has any trout-fishing in its vicinity has also a legend of a huge trout, a great-grandfather of fishes, præternaturally wise and wary, abnormally fierce and powerful, who lives in some particular pool of the principal stream, and is seen, hooked, and played by many anglers but never landed. Such a traditional trout there was at Samaria. His lair was in a deep hole of the Lirrapaug, beside an overhanging rock, and just below the mouth of the little spring-brook that divided the Gray's farm from the Cutter's. But this trout was not only traditional, he was also real. Small boys had fished for him, and described vividly the manner in which their hooks had been carried away,—but that does not count. Jags Witherbee declared that he had struggled with him for nearly an hour, only to fall exhausted in the rapids below the pool while the trout executed a series of somersaults in the direction of Simsville,—but that does not count. What really counts is that two reputable clergymen testified that they had seen him. He rose once to Jones's fly when he was fishing up the river after dusk, and Hopkins had seen him chase a minnow up the brook just before sunrise. The latter witness averred that the fish made a wake like a steamboat, and the former witness estimated his weight at a little short of five pounds,—both called him Leviathan, and desired to draw him out with a hook.

Now the thought that secretly occurred to each of these worthy young men, as I say, not unnaturally, but with a strange simultaneousness which no ordinary writer of fiction would dare to invent, was this: "Catch Leviathan on the last day of the trout-season and present him to Miss Gray. That will be a famous gift, and no one else can duplicate it."

The last day of the season was July 31st. Long before daybreak the Rev. Cotton Mather Hopkins stole away from the manse, slipping through the darkness noiselessly, and taking the steep path by Bushy Brook towards the valley of the Lirrapaug. In one pocket was his long, light, hand-line, carefully coiled, with a selected sneck-bend hook of tempered steel made fast to the line by the smallest and firmest of knots. In the other pocket was a box of choice angle-worms, dug from the garden two days before, and since that time kept in moss and sprinkled with milk to make them clean and rosy. It was his plan to go down stream a little way below the rock-pool, wait for daylight, and then fish up the pool slowly until he reached Leviathan's lair and caught him. It was a good plan.

The day came gently and serenely; a touch of gray along the eastern horizon; a fading of the deep blue overhead, a paling of the stars, a flush of orange in the east; then silver and gold on the little floating clouds, and amber and rose along the hill-tops; then lances of light showing over the edge of the world and a cool flood of diffused radiance flowing across field and river. It was at this moment, before there was a shadow to be found in the scene, that the bait-fisherman stepped into the rapid below the pool and began to wade slowly and cautiously upward along the eastern bank. Not a ripple moved before him; his steps fell on the rocky bottom as if he had been shod with velvet. The long line shot out from his swinging hand and the bait fell lightly on the pool,—too far away yet to reach the rock. Another cast follows, and still another, but without any result. The rock is now reached, but the middle of it projects a little into the pool, and makes a bend or bay which is just out of sight from the point where the fisherman stands. He gathers his line in his left hand again and makes another cast. It is a beauty. The line uncoils itself without a hitch and the bait curves around the corner, settling down beside the rock as if a bit of sand had fallen from the top of the bank.

But what is that dark figure kneeling on the eastern bank at the head of the pool? It is the form of Willibert Beauchamp Jones, B.D. He has assumed this attitude of devotion in order that Leviathan may not see him from afar; but it also serves unconsciously to hide him from the fisherman at the foot of the pool. Willibert is casting the fly very beautifully, very delicately, very accurately, across the mouth of the spring-brook towards the upper end of the rock.

The tiny royal coachman falls like a snowflake on the water, and the hare's ear settles like a bit of thistledown two feet beyond it. Nearer and nearer the flies come to the rock, until at last they cover the place where the last cast of the hand-line fell. There is a flash of purple and gold in the water, a great splash on the surface,—Leviathan has risen; Willibert has struck him; the royal coachman is fast in his upper lip.

At the same instant the fisherman at the lower end of the pool feels a tightening of his line. He gives it a quick twitch with his right hand, and prepares to pull in with his left. Leviathan has taken the bait; Cotton Mather has struck; the hook is well fastened in the roof of the fish's mouth and the sport begins.

Willibert leaps to his feet and moves towards the end of the point. Cotton Mather, feeling the heavy strain on his line, wades out towards the deeper part of the pool. The two fishermen behold each other, in the moment of their common triumph, and they perceive what lies between them.

"Excuse me," said Hopkins, "but that is my fish. He must have taken my bait before he rose to the fly, and I'll be much obliged to you if you'll let go of him."

"I beg your pardon," replied Jones, "but it's quite evident that he rose to my fly before you felt him bite at your bait; and as I struck him first and hooked him first, he is my fish and I'll thank you to leave him alone."

It was a pretty situation. Each fisherman realized that he was called upon to do his best and yet unable to get ahead of the other without danger to his own success,—no time for argument surely! Yet I think they would have argued, and that with fierceness, had it not been for a sudden interruption.

"Good morning, gentlemen!" said the voice of Orlando Cutter, as he stepped from the bushes at the mouth of the brook, with a landing-net in his hand, "I see you are out early to-day. I came down myself to have a try for the big fish, and Miss Gray was good enough to come with me."

The rosy, laughing face of the girl emerged from the willows. "Good morning, good morning," she cried. "Why it's quite a party, isn't it? But how wet you both are, Mr. Hopkins and Mr. Jones,—did you fall in the water? And you look vexed, too! What is the matter? Oh, I see, both your lines are caught fast in the bottom of the pool,—no, they are tangled together"—(at this the fish gave a mighty splash and a rush towards the shore,)—"oh, Orlando, it's a fish, and such a beauty!"

The trout, bewildered and exhausted by the double strain upon him, floundered a little and moved into the shallow water at the mouth of the brook. Orlando stepped down and quietly slipped the landing-net under him.

"I see it is a fish," he said, "and it seems to be caught with a bait and a fly, but it certainly is landed with a net. So in that case, gentlemen, as your claims seem to be divided, I will take the liberty of disengaging both your hooks, and of begging Miss Gray to accept this Leviathan, as—may I tell them?—she has just accepted me."

By this time the newly risen sun was shining upon the ripples of the Lirrapaug River and upon the four people who stood on the bank shaking hands and exchanging polite remarks. His glowing face was bright with that cheerful air of humourous and sympathetic benevolence with which he seems to look upon all our human experiences of disappointment and success.

The weary anglers found some physical comfort, at least, in the cool glasses of milk which Miss Gray poured for them as they sat on the verandah of the farmhouse. On their way up the hill, by the pleasant path which followed Bushy Brook, these two brethren who were so much of one mind in their devotion to their fishing and who differed only in regard to the method to be pursued, did not talk much, but they felt themselves nearer to each other than ever before. Something seemed to weave between them the delicate and firm bonds of a friendship strengthened by a common aim and chastened by a common experience of disappointment. They could afford to be silent together because they were now true comrades. I shall always maintain that both of them received a great benefit from Leviathan.

THE ART OF LEAVING OFF

IT was a hot August Sunday, one of those days on which art itself must not be made too long lest it should shorten life. A little company of us had driven down from our hotel on the comparatively breezy hill to attend church in the village. The majority chose to pay their devotions at the big yellow meeting-house, where the preacher was reputed a man of eloquence; but my Uncle Peter drew me with him to the modest gray chapel, at the far end of the street, which was temporarily under the care of a student in the winter-school of theology, who was wisely spending his vacation in the summer-school of life. Some happy inspiration led the young man to select one of Lyman Abbott's shortest and simplest sermons,—itself a type of the mercy which it commended,—and frankly read it to us instead of pronouncing a discourse of his own. The result of this was that we came out of chapel at a quarter past eleven in a truly grateful and religious frame of mind.

But our comrades were still detained in the yellow meeting-house; and while the stage-coach waited for them in the glaring fervour of noon, my Uncle Peter and I climbed down from our seats and took refuge on the grass, in the shadow of the roundhead maples that stood guard along the north wall of the Puritan sanctuary. The windows were open. We could see the rhythmic motion of the fan-drill in the pews. The pulpit was not visible; but from that unseen eminence a strident, persistent voice flowed steadily, expounding the necessity and uses of "a baptism of fire," with a monotonous variety of application. Fire was needful for the young, for the middle-aged, for the old, and for those, if any, who occupied the intermediate positions. It was needful for the rich and for the poor, for the ignorant and for the learned, for church-members, for those who were "well-wishers" but not "professors," and for hardened sinners,—for everybody in fact: and if any class or condition of human creatures were omitted in the exhaustive analysis, the preacher led us to apprehend that he was only holding them in reserve, and that presently he would include them in the warm and triumphant application of his subject. He was one of those preachers who say it all, and make no demands upon the intelligence of their hearers.

Meantime the brown-and-yellow grasshoppers crackled over the parched fields, and the locusts rasped their one-stringed fiddles in the trees, and the shrunken little river complained faintly in its bed, and all nature was sighing, not for fire, but for water and cool shade. But still the ardent voice continued its fuliginous exhortations, until the very fans grew limp, and the flowers in the hats of the village girls seemed to wilt with fervent heat.

My Uncle Peter and I were brought up in that old-fashioned school of manners which discouraged the audible criticism of religious exercises. But we could not help thinking.

"He has just passed 'Secondly,'" said I, "and that leaves two more main heads, and a practical conclusion of either three or five points."

My Uncle Peter said nothing in answer to this. After a while he remarked in an abstract, disconnected way: "I wonder why no school of divinity has ever established a professorship of the Art of Leaving Off."

"The thing is too simple," I replied; "theological seminaries do not concern themselves with the simplicities."

"And yet," said he, "the simplest things are often the most difficult and always the most important. The proverb says that 'well begun is half done.' But the other half is harder and more necessary,—to get a thing well ended. It is the final word that is most effective, and it is something quite different from the last word. Many a talker, in the heat of his discussion and his anxiety to have the last word, runs clear past the final word and never gets back to it again."

"Talking," said I, "is only a small part of life, and not of much consequence."

"I don't agree with you," he answered. "The tongue is but a little member, yet behold how great a fire it kindles. Talking, rightly considered, is the expression and epitome of life itself. All the other arts are but varieties of talking. And in this matter of the importance of the final touch, the point at which one leaves off, talking is just a symbol of everything else that we do. It is the last step that costs, says the proverb; and I would like to add, it is the last step that counts."

"Be concrete," I begged, "I like you best that way."

"Well," he continued, "take the small art of making artificial flies for fishing. The knot that is hardest to tie is that which finishes off the confection, and binds the feathers and the silk securely to the hook, gathering up the loose ends and concealing them with invisible firmness. I remember, when I first began to tie flies, I never could arrive at this final knot, but kept on and on, winding the thread around the hook and making another half-hitch to fasten the ones that were already made, until the alleged fly looked like a young ostrich with a sore throat.

"Or take the art of sailing a boat. You remember Fanny Adair? She had a sublime confidence in herself that amounted to the first half of genius. She observed that, given a wind and a sail and a rudder, any person of common sense could make a boat move along. So she invited a small party of equally inexperienced friends to go out with her in a cat-boat on Newport harbour. The wind was blowing freshly and steadily towards the wharf, and neither the boat-keeper nor I suspected any lack in Fanny's competence as she boldly grasped the tiller and started out in fine style, beating merrily to and fro across the bay. I went up town and came back at the appointed hour of six o'clock to meet the party. The wind was still blowing freshly and steadily, straight onto the wharf, but they had not returned. They were beating up and down, now skimming near to the landing, now darting away from it. We called them to come in. I saw a look of desperation settle on Fanny's face. She slacked away the main-sheet, put the boat before the wind, held the tiller straight, and ran down upon the wharf with a crash that cracked the mast and tumbled the passengers over like ten-pins in a strike. 'I knew I could sail the old thing,' said Fanny, 'but I didn't think it would be so hard to stop her!'"

"I see what you mean," said I. "Isn't the same difficulty often experienced by after-dinner speakers and lecturers, and speculators on the stock-market, and moral reformers, and academic co-ordinators of the social system of the universe?"

"It is," he answered. "They can sail the sea of theory splendidly, but they don't know how to make a landing. Yet that is really the thing that everybody ought to learn. No voyage is successful unless you deliver the goods. Even in a pleasure-voyage there must be a fit time and place for leaving off. There is a psychological moment at which the song has made its most thrilling impression, and the music should cease. There is an instant of persuasion at which the argument has had its force, and there it should break off, just when the nail is driven home, and before the hammer begins to bruise the wood. The art lies in discovering this moment of cessation and using it to the best advantage. That is the fascination of the real 'short story' as told by Hawthorne, or Poe, or Stevenson, or Cable, or De Maupassant, or Miss Jewett, or Margaret Deland. It reaches the point of interest and stops. The impression is not blurred. It is like a well-cut seal: small, but clear and sharp. You take the imprint of it distinctly. Stockton's story of 'The Lady or the Tiger' would not gain anything by an addition on the natural history of tigers or the psychological peculiarities of ladies.

"That is what is meant by the saying that 'brevity is the soul of wit,'—the thing that keeps it alive. A good joke prolonged degenerates into teasing; and a merry jest with explanations becomes funereal. When a man repeats the point of his story it is already broken off. Somebody said of Mr. Gladstone's oratory that it was 'good, but copious.' Canaries sing well, but the defect of their music is its abundance. I prefer the hermit-thrush to the nightingale, not because the thrush's notes are sweeter, but because he knows when to leave off, and let his song vanish, at the exquisite moment, into the silence of mysterious twilight."

"You seem to be proving," I said, "what most men will admit without argument, that 'enough is as good as a feast.'"

"On the contrary," he replied, "I am arguing against that proverb. Enough is not as good as a feast. It is far better. There is something magical and satisfying in the art of leaving off. Good advice is infinitely more potent when it is brief and earnest than when it dribbles into vague exhortations. Many a man has been worried into vice by well-meant but wearisome admonitions to be virtuous. A single word of true friendly warning or encouragement is more eloquent than volumes of nagging pertinacity, and may safely be spoken and left to do its work. After all when we are anxious to help a friend into the right path, there is not much more or better that we can say than what Sir Walter Scott said, when he was a-dying, to his son-in-law Lockhart: 'Be a good man, my dear, be a good man.' The life must say the rest."

"You are talking as seriously," said I, "as if you were a preacher and we were in a church."

"Are we not?" said he, very quietly. "When we are thinking and talking of the real meaning of life it seems to me that we are in the Temple. Let me go on a moment longer with my talk. We often fancy, in this world, that beautiful and pleasant things would satisfy us better if they could be continued, without change, forever. We regret the ending of a good 'day off.' We are sorry to be 'coming out of the woods' instead of 'going in.' And that regret is perfectly natural and all right. It is part of the condition on which we receive our happiness. The mistake lies in wishing to escape from it by a petrification of our joys. The stone forest in Arizona will never decay, but it is no place for a man to set up his tents forever.

"The other day, a friend was admiring the old-fashioned house where I live. "Tis *a good camp*,' said I, 'plenty of wood and water, and I hope it's on the right trail.'

"Many of our best friends have gone ahead of us on that trail. Why should we hold back? The fairest things in the world and the finest are always in transition: the bloom of tender Spring disappearing in the dark verdure of Summer; the week of meadow-rue and nodding lilies passing as silently as it came; the splendid hues of the autumnal hills fading like the colours on a bubble; the dear child, whose innocence and simplicity are a daily joy to you, growing up into a woman. Would you keep her a child forever, her head always a little lower than your heart? Would you stand where you are to-day, always doing the same things, always repeating the same experiences, never leaving off? Then be thankful that the Wisdom and Goodness by which this passing show is ordered will not suffer you to indulge your foolish wish. The wisest men and women are not those who cling tenaciously to one point of life, with desperate aversion to all change, but those who travel cheerfully through its mutations, finding in every season, in every duty, in every pleasure, a time to begin and a time to cease, and moving on with willing adaptation through the conclusion of each chapter to the end of the book.

"And concerning that *Finis* of the volume, which is printed in such sober, black, italic type, I remember a good saying of old Michel de Montaigne in one of his essays,—not the exact words, but the soul of his remarks. He says that we cannot judge whether a man has been truly fortunate in life until we have seen him act with tranquillity and contentment in the last scene of his comedy, which is undoubtedly the most difficult. For himself, he adds, his chief study and desire is that he may well behave himself at his last gasp, that is quietly and constantly. It is a good saying; for life has no finer lesson to teach us than how to leave off."

"I wish you would promise me one thing," said I to my Uncle Peter: "that you will not leave off before I do."

"Ah," he answered, "that is the one thing that no man can promise another. We can promise not to break friendship, not to cut loose, not to cease loving, not to forget. Isn't that enough?"

He stood up reverently and bared his head. The music of the long-metre doxology was floating through the open windows.

"Listen," he said. "If that is true, what more do we need? We are all in His hand."

Little Rivers, A Book of Essays in Profitable Idleness

DEDICATION

To one who wanders by my side
As cheerfully as waters glide;
Whose eyes are brown as woodland streams,
And very fair and full of dreams;
Whose heart is like a mountain spring,
Whose thoughts like merry rivers sing:
To her—my little daughter Brooke—
I dedicate this little book.

PRELUDE
AN ANGLER'S WISH IN TOWN

*When tulips bloom in Union Square,
And timid breaths of vernal air
Are wandering down the dusty town,
Like children lost in Vanity Fair;
When every long, unlovely row
Of westward houses stands aglow
And leads the eyes toward sunset skies,
Beyond the hills where green trees grow;
Then weary is the street parade,
And weary books, and weary trade:
I'm only wishing to go a-fishing;
For this the month of May was made.*

*I guess the pussy-willows now
Are creeping out on every bough
Along the brook; and robins look
For early worms behind the plough.
The thistle-birds have changed their dun
For yellow coats to match the sun;
And in the same array of flame
The Dandelion Show's begun.
The flocks of young anemones
Are dancing round the budding trees:
Who can help wishing to go a-fishing
In days as full of joy as these?*

*I think the meadow-lark's clear sound
Leaks upward slowly from the ground,
While on the wing the bluebirds ring
Their wedding-bells to woods around:
The flirting chewink calls his dear
Behind the bush; and very near,
Where water flows, where green grass grows,
Song-sparrows gently sing, "Good cheer:"
And, best of all, through twilight's calm
The hermit-thrush repeats his psalm:
How much I'm wishing to go a-fishing
In days so sweet with music's balm!*

*'Tis not a proud desire of mine;
I ask for nothing superfine;
No heavy weight, no salmon great,
To break the record, or my line:
Only an idle little stream,
Whose amber waters softly gleam,
Where I may wade, through woodland shade,
And cast the fly, and loaf, and dream:
Only a trout or two, to dart
From foaming pools, and try my art:
No more I'm wishing—old-fashioned fishing,
And just a day on Nature's heart.*
1894.

LITTLE RIVERS

"*There's no music like a little river's. It plays the same tune (and that's the favourite) over and over again, and yet does not weary of it like men fiddlers. It takes the mind out of doors; and though we should be grateful for good houses, there is, after all, no house like God's out-of-doors. And lastly, sir, it quiets a man down like saying his prayers.*"——
ROBERT LOUIS STEVENSON: *Prince Otto.*

LITTLE RIVERS

A river is the most human and companionable of all inanimate things. It has a life, a character, a voice of its own, and is as full of good fellowship as a sugar-maple is of sap. It can talk in various tones, loud or low, and of many subjects, grave and gay. Under favourable circumstances it will even make a shift to sing, not in a fashion that can be reduced to notes and set down in black and white on a sheet of paper, but in a vague, refreshing manner, and to a wandering air that goes;

"*Over the hills and far away.*"

For real company and friendship, there is nothing outside of the animal kingdom that is comparable to a river.

I will admit that a very good case can be made out in favour of some other objects of natural affection. For example, a fair apology has been offered by those ambitious persons who have fallen in love with the sea. But, after all, that is a formless and disquieting passion. It lacks solid comfort and mutual confidence. The sea is too big for loving, and too uncertain. It will not fit into our thoughts. It has no personality because it has so many. It is a salt abstraction. You might as well think of loving a glittering generality like "the American woman." One would be more to the purpose.

Mountains are more satisfying because they are more individual. It is possible to feel a very strong attachment for a certain range whose outline has grown familiar to our eyes, or a clear peak that has looked down, day after day, upon our joys and sorrows, moderating our passions with its calm aspect. We come back from our travels, and the sight of such a well-known mountain is like meeting an old friend unchanged. But it is a one-sided affection. The mountain is voiceless and imperturbable; and its very loftiness and serenity sometimes make us the more lonely.

Trees seem to come closer to our life. They are often rooted in our richest feelings, and our sweetest memories, like birds, build nests in their branches. I remember, the last time that I saw James Russell Lowell, (only a few weeks before his musical voice was hushed,) he walked out with me into the quiet garden at Elmwood to say good-bye. There was a great horse-chestnut tree beside the house, towering above the gable, and covered with blossoms from base to summit,—a pyramid of green supporting a thousand smaller pyramids of white. The poet looked up at it with his gray, pain-furrowed face, and laid his trembling hand upon the trunk. "I planted the nut," said he, "from which this tree grew. And my father was with me and showed me how to plant it."

Yes, there is a good deal to be said in behalf of tree-worship; and when I recline with my friend Tityrus beneath the shade of his favourite oak, I consent in his devotions. But when I invite him with me to share my orisons, or wander alone to indulge the luxury of grateful, unlaborious thought, my feet turn not to a tree, but to the bank of a river, for there the musings of solitude find a friendly accompaniment, and human intercourse is purified and sweetened by the flowing, murmuring water. It is by a river that I would choose to make love, and to revive old friendships, and to play with the children, and to confess my faults, and to escape from vain, selfish desires, and to cleanse my mind from all the false and foolish things that mar the joy and peace of living. Like David's hart, I pant for the water-brooks. There is wisdom in the advice of Seneca, who says, "Where a spring rises, or a river flows, there should we build altars and offer sacrifices."

The personality of a river is not to be found in its water, nor in its bed, nor in its shore. Either of these elements, by itself, would be nothing. Confine the fluid contents of the noblest stream in a walled channel of stone, and it ceases to be a stream; it becomes what Charles Lamb calls "a mockery of a river—a liquid artifice—a wretched conduit." But take away the water from the most beautiful river-banks, and what is left? An ugly road with none to travel it; a long, ghastly scar on the bosom of the earth.

The life of a river, like that of a human being, consists in the union of soul and body, the water and the banks. They belong together. They act and react upon each other. The stream moulds and makes the shore; hollowing out a bay here, and building a long point there; alluring the little bushes close to its side, and bending the tall slim trees over its current; sweeping a rocky ledge clean of everything but moss, and sending a still lagoon full of white arrow-heads and rosy knotweed far back into the meadow. The shore guides and controls the stream; now detaining and now advancing it; now bending it in a hundred sinuous curves, and now speeding it straight as a wild-bee on its homeward flight; here hiding the water in a deep cleft overhung with green branches, and there spreading it out, like a mirror framed in daisies, to reflect the sky and the clouds; sometimes breaking it with sudden turns and unexpected falls into a foam of musical laughter, sometimes soothing it into a sleepy motion like the flow of a dream.

Is it otherwise with the men and women whom we know and like? Does not the spirit influence the form, and the form affect the spirit? Can we divide and separate them in our affections?

I am no friend to purely psychological attachments. In some unknown future they may be satisfying, but in the present I want your words and your voice with your thoughts, your looks and your gestures to interpret your feelings. The warm, strong grasp of Greatheart's hand is as dear to me as the steadfast fashion of his friendships; the lively, sparkling eyes of the master of Rudder Grange charm me as much as the nimbleness of his fancy; and the firm poise of the Hoosier Schoolmaster's shaggy head gives me new confidence in the solidity of his views of life. I like the pure tranquillity of Isabel's brow as well as her—

"*most silver flow*
Of subtle-pacèd counsel in distress."

The soft cadences and turns in my lady Katrina's speech draw me into the humour of her gentle judgments of men and things. The touches of quaintness in Angelica's dress, her folded kerchief and smooth-parted hair, seem to partake of herself, and enhance my admiration for the sweet order of her thoughts and her old-fashioned ideals of love and duty. Even so the stream and its channel are one life, and I cannot think of the swift, brown flood of the Batiscan without its shadowing primeval forests, or the crystalline current of the Boquet without its beds of pebbles and golden sand and grassy banks embroidered with flowers.

Every country—or at least every country that is fit for habitation—has its own rivers; and every river has its own quality; and it is the part of wisdom to know and love as many as you can, seeing each in the fairest possible light, and receiving from each the best that it has to give. The torrents of Norway leap down from their mountain home with plentiful cataracts, and run brief but glorious races to the sea. The streams of England move smoothly through green fields and beside ancient, sleepy towns. The Scotch rivers brawl through the open moorland and flash along steep Highland glens. The rivers of the Alps are born in icy caves, from which they issue forth with furious, turbid waters; but when their anger has been forgotten in the slumber of some blue lake, they flow down more softly to see the vineyards of France and Italy, the gray castles of Germany, the verdant meadows of Holland. The mighty rivers of the

West roll their yellow floods through broad valleys, or plunge down dark cañons. The rivers of the South creep under dim arboreal archways hung with banners of waving moss. The Delaware and the Hudson and the Connecticut are the children of the Catskills and the Adirondacks and the White Mountains, cradled among the forests of spruce and hemlock, playing through a wild woodland youth, gathering strength from numberless tributaries to bear their great burdens of lumber and turn the wheels of many mills, issuing from the hills to water a thousand farms, and descending at last, beside new cities, to the ancient sea.

Every river that flows is good, and has something worthy to be loved. But those that we love most are always the ones that we have known best,—the stream that ran before our father's door, the current on which we ventured our first boat or cast our first fly, the brook on whose banks we first picked the twinflower of young love. However far we may travel, we come back to Naaman's state of mind: "Are not Abana and Pharpar, rivers of Damascus, better than all the waters of Israel?"

It is with rivers as it is with people: the greatest are not always the most agreeable, nor the best to live with. Diogenes must have been an uncomfortable bedfellow: Antinoüs was bored to death in the society of the Emperor Hadrian: and you can imagine much better company for a walking-trip than Napoleon Bonaparte. Semiramis was a lofty queen, but I fancy that Ninus had more than one bad quarter-of-an-hour with her: and in "the spacious times of great Elizabeth" there was many a milkmaid whom the wise man would have chosen for his friend, before the royal red-haired virgin. "I confess," says the poet Cowley, "I love Littleness almost in all things. A little convenient Estate, a little cheerful House, a little Company, and a very little Feast, and if I were ever to fall in Love again, (which is a great Passion, and therefore, I hope, I have done with it,) it would be, I think, with Prettiness, rather than with Majestical Beauty. I would neither wish that my Mistress, nor my Fortune, should be a *Bona Roba*, as *Homer* uses to describe his Beauties, like a daughter of great *Jupiter* for the stateliness and largeness of her Person, but as *Lucretius* says:

'*Parvula, pumilio, Χαρίτων μία, tota merum sal.*'"

Now in talking about women it is prudent to disguise a prejudice like this, in the security of a dead language, and to intrench it behind a fortress of reputable authority. But in lowlier and less dangerous matters, such as we are now concerned with, one may dare to speak in plain English. I am all for the little rivers. Let those who will, chant in heroic verse the renown of Amazon and Mississippi and Niagara, but my prose shall flow—or straggle along at such a pace as the prosaic muse may grant me to attain—in praise of Beaverkill and Neversink and Swiftwater, of Saranac and Raquette and Ausable, of Allegash and Aroostook and Moose River. "Whene'er I take my walks abroad," it shall be to trace the clear Rauma from its rise on the *fjeld* to its rest in the *fjord*; or to follow the Ericht and the Halladale through the heather. The Ziller and the Salzach shall be my guides through the Tyrol; the Rotha and the Dove shall lead me into the heart of England. My sacrificial flames shall be kindled with birch-bark along the wooded stillwaters of the Penobscot and the Peribonca, and my libations drawn from the pure current of the Ristigouche and the Ampersand, and my altar of remembrance shall rise upon the rocks beside the falls of Seboomok.

I will set my affections upon rivers that are not too great for intimacy. And if by chance any of these little ones have also become famous, like the Tweed and the Thames and the Arno, I at least will praise them, because they are still at heart little rivers.

If an open fire is, as Charles Dudley Warner says, the eye of a room; then surely a little river may be called the mouth, the most expressive feature, of a landscape. It animates and enlivens the whole scene. Even a railway journey becomes tolerable when the track follows the course of a running stream.

What charming glimpses you catch from the window as the train winds along the valley of the French Broad from Asheville, or climbs the southern Catskills beside the Æsopus, or slides down the Pusterthal with the Rienz, or follows the Glommen and the Gula from Christiania to Throndhjem. Here is a mill with its dripping, lazy wheel, the type of somnolent industry; and there is a white cascade, foaming in silent pantomime as the train clatters by; and here is a long, still pool with the cows standing knee-deep in the water and swinging their tails in calm indifference to the passing world; and there is a lone fisherman sitting upon a rock, rapt in contemplation of the point of his rod. For a moment you become a partner of his tranquil enterprise. You turn around, you crane your neck to get the last sight of his motionless angle. You do not know what kind of fish he expects to catch, nor what species of bait he is using, but at least you pray that he may have a bite before the train swings around the next curve. And if perchance your wish is granted, and you see him gravely draw some unknown, reluctant, shining reward of patience from the water, you feel like swinging your hat from the window and crying out "Good luck!"

Little rivers seem to have the indefinable quality that belongs to certain people in the world,—the power of drawing attention without courting it, the faculty of exciting interest by their very presence and way of doing things.

The most fascinating part of a city or town is that through which the water flows. Idlers always choose a bridge for their place of meditation when they can get it; and, failing that, you will find them sitting on the edge of a quay or embankment, with their feet hanging over the water. What a piquant mingling of indolence and vivacity you can enjoy by the river-side! The best point of view in Rome, to my taste, is the Ponte San Angelo; and in Florence or Pisa I never tire of loafing along the Lung' Arno. You do not know London until you have seen it from the Thames. And you will miss the charm of Cambridge unless you take a little boat and go drifting on the placid Cam, beneath the bending trees, along the backs of the colleges.

But the real way to know a little river is not to glance at it here or there in the course of a hasty journey, nor to become acquainted with it after it has been partly civilised and spoiled by too close contact with the works of man.

You must go to its native haunts; you must see it in youth and freedom; you must accommodate yourself to its pace, and give yourself to its influence, and follow its meanderings whithersoever they may lead you.

Now, of this pleasant pastime there are three principal forms. You may go as a walker, taking the river-side path, or making a way for yourself through the tangled thickets or across the open meadows. You may go as a sailor, launching your light canoe on the swift current and committing yourself for a day, or a week, or a month, to the delightful uncertainties of a voyage through the forest. You may go as a wader, stepping into the stream and going down with it, through rapids and shallows and deeper pools, until you come to the end of your courage and the daylight. Of these three ways I know not which is best. But in all of them the essential thing is that you must be willing and glad to be led; you must take the little river for your guide, philosopher, and friend.

And what a good guidance it gives you. How cheerfully it lures you on into the secrets of field and wood, and brings you acquainted with the birds and the flowers. The stream can show you, better than any other teacher, how nature works her enchantments with colour and music.

Go out to the Beaver-kill

"*In the tassel-time of spring,*"

and follow its brimming waters through the budding forests, to that corner which we call the Painter's Camp. See how the banks are all enamelled with the pale hepatica, the painted trillium, and the delicate pink-veined spring beauty. A little later in the year, when the ferns are uncurling their long fronds, the troops of blue and white violets will come dancing down to the edge of the stream, and creep venturously out to the very end of that long, moss-covered log in the water. Before these have vanished, the yellow crow-foot and the cinquefoil will appear, followed by the star-grass and the loose-strife and the golden St. John's-wort. Then the unseen painter begins to mix the royal colour on his palette, and the red of the bee-balm catches your eye. If you are lucky, you may find, in midsummer, a slender fragrant spike of the purple-fringed orchis, and you cannot help finding the universal self-heal. Yellow returns in the drooping flowers of the jewel-weed, and blue repeats itself in the trembling hare-bells, and scarlet is glorified in the flaming robe of the cardinal-flower. Later still, the summer closes in a splendour of bloom, with gentians and asters and goldenrod.

You never get so close to the birds as when you are wading quietly down a little river, casting your fly deftly under the branches for the wary trout, but ever on the lookout for all the various pleasant things that nature has to bestow upon you. Here you shall come upon the cat-bird at her morning bath, and hear her sing, in a clump of pussy-willows, that low, tender, confidential song which she keeps for the hours of domestic intimacy. The spotted sandpiper will run along the stones before you, crying, "*wet-feet, wet-feet!*" and bowing and teetering in the friendliest manner, as if to show you the way to the best pools. In the thick branches of the hemlocks that stretch across the stream, the tiny warblers, dressed in a hundred colours, chirp and twitter confidingly above your head; and the Maryland yellow-throat, flitting through the bushes like a little gleam of sunlight, calls "*witchery, witchery, witchery!*" That plaintive, forsaken, persistent note, never ceasing, even in the noonday silence, comes from the wood-pewee, drooping upon the bough of some high tree, and complaining, like Mariana in the moated grange, "*weary, weary, wéary!*"

When the stream runs out into the old clearing, or down through the pasture, you find other and livelier birds,—the robin, with his sharp, saucy call and breathless, merry warble; the bluebird, with his notes of pure gladness, and the oriole, with his wild, flexible whistle; the chewink, bustling about in the thicket, talking to his sweetheart in French, "*chérie, chérie!*" and the song-sparrow, perched on his favourite limb of a young maple, close beside the water, and singing happily, through sunshine and through rain. This is the true bird of the brook, after all: the winged spirit of cheerfulness and contentment, the patron saint of little rivers, the fisherman's friend. He seems to enter into your sport with his good wishes, and for an hour at a time, while you are trying every fly in your book, from a black gnat to a white miller, to entice the crafty old trout at the foot of the meadow-pool, the song-sparrow, close above you, will be chanting patience and encouragement. And when at last success crowns your endeavour, and the parti-coloured prize is glittering in your net, the bird on the bough breaks out in an ecstasy of congratulation: "*catch 'im, catch 'im, catch 'im; oh, what a pretty fellow! sweet!*"

There are other birds that seem to have a very different temper. The blue-jay sits high up in the withered-pine tree, bobbing up and down, and calling to his mate in a tone of affected sweetness, "*salúte-her, salúte-her,*" but when you come in sight he flies away with a harsh cry of "*thief, thief, thief!*" The kingfisher, ruffling his crest in solitary pride on the end of a dead branch, darts down the stream at your approach, winding up his reel angrily as if he despised you for interrupting his fishing. And the cat-bird, that sang so charmingly while she thought herself unobserved, now tries to scare you away by screaming "*snake, snake!*"

As evening draws near, and the light beneath the trees grows yellower, and the air is full of filmy insects out for their last dance, the voice of the little river becomes louder and more distinct. The true poets have often noticed this apparent increase in the sound of flowing waters at nightfall. Gray, in one of his letters, speaks of "hearing the murmur of many waters not audible in the daytime." Wordsworth repeats the same thought almost in the same words:

"*A soft and lulling sound is heard*
Of streams inaudible by day."

And Tennyson, in the valley of Cauteretz, tells of the river

"*Deepening his voice with deepening of the night.*"

It is in this mystical hour that you will hear the most celestial and entrancing of all bird-notes, the songs of the thrushes,—the hermit, and the wood-thrush, and the veery. Sometimes, but not often, you will see the singers. I remember once, at the close of a beautiful day's fishing on the Swiftwater, I came out, just after sunset, into a little open space in an elbow of the stream. It was still early spring, and the leaves were tiny. On the top of a small sumac, not thirty feet away from me, sat a veery. I could see the pointed spots upon his breast, the swelling of his white throat, and the sparkle of his eyes, as he poured his whole heart into a long liquid chant, the clear notes rising and falling, echoing and interlacing in endless curves of sound,

"*Orb within orb, intricate, wonderful.*"

Other bird-songs can be translated into words, but not this. There is no interpretation. It is music,—as Sidney Lanier defines it,—

"*Love in search of a word.*"

But it is not only to the real life of birds and flowers that the little rivers introduce you. They lead you often into familiarity with human nature in undress, rejoicing in the liberty of old clothes, or of none at all. People do not mince along the banks of streams in patent-leather shoes or crepitating silks. Corduroy and home-spun and flannel are the stuffs that suit this region; and the frequenters of these paths go their natural gaits, in calf-skin or rubber boots, or barefooted. The girdle of conventionality is laid aside, and the skirts rise with the spirits.

A stream that flows through a country of upland farms will show you many a pretty bit of *genre* painting. Here is the laundry-pool at the foot of the kitchen garden, and the tubs are set upon a few planks close to the water, and the farmer's daughters, with bare arms and gowns tucked up, are wringing out the clothes. Do you remember what happened to Ralph Peden in *The Lilac Sunbonnet* when he came on a scene like this? He tumbled at once into love with Winsome Charteris,—and far over his head.

And what a pleasant thing it is to see a little country lad riding one of the plough-horses to water, thumping his naked heels against the ribs of his stolid steed, and pulling hard on the halter as if it were the bridle of Bucephalus! Or perhaps it is a riotous company of boys that have come down to the old swimming-hole, and are now splashing and gambolling through the water like a drove of white seals very much sun-burned. You had hoped to catch a goodly trout in that hole, but what of that? The sight of a harmless hour of mirth is better than a fish, any day.

Possibly you will overtake another fisherman on the stream. It may be one of those fabulous countrymen, with long cedar poles and bed-cord lines, who are commonly reported to catch such enormous strings of fish, but who rarely, so far as my observation goes, do anything more than fill their pockets with fingerlings. The trained angler, who uses the finest tackle, and drops his fly on the water as accurately as Henry James places a word in a story, is the man who takes the most and the largest fish in the long run. Perhaps the fisherman ahead of you is such an one,—a man whom you have known in town as a lawyer or a doctor, a merchant or a preacher, going about his business in the hideous respectability of a high silk hat and a long black coat. How good it is to see him now in the freedom of a flannel shirt and a broad-brimmed gray felt with flies stuck around the band.

In Professor John Wilson's *Essays Critical and Imaginative*, there is a brilliant description of a bishop fishing, which I am sure is drawn from the life: "Thus a bishop, sans wig and petticoat, in a hairy cap, black jacket, corduroy breeches and leathern leggins, creel on back and rod in hand, sallying from his palace, impatient to reach a famous salmon-cast ere the sun leave his cloud, ... appears not only a pillar of his church, but of his kind, and in such a costume is manifestly on the high road to Canterbury and the Kingdom-Come." I have had the good luck to see quite a number of bishops, parochial and diocesan, in that style, and the vision has always dissolved my doubts in regard to the validity of their claim to the true apostolic succession.

Men's "little ways" are usually more interesting, and often more instructive than their grand manners. When they are off guard, they frequently show to better advantage than when they are on parade. I get more pleasure out of Boswell's *Johnson* than I do out of *Rasselas* or *The Rambler*. The *Little Flowers of St. Francis* appear to me far more precious than the most learned German and French analyses of his character. There is a passage in Jonathan Edwards' *Personal Narrative*, about a certain walk that he took in the fields near his father's house, and the blossoming of the flowers in the spring, which I would not exchange for the whole of his dissertation *On the Freedom of the Will*. And the very best thing of Charles Darwin's that I know is a bit from a letter to his wife: "At last I fell asleep," says he, "on the grass, and awoke with a chorus of birds singing around me, and squirrels running up the tree, and some woodpeckers laughing; and it was as pleasant and rural a scene as ever I saw; and I did not care one penny how any of the birds or beasts had been formed."

Little rivers have small responsibilities. They are not expected to bear huge navies on their breast or supply a hundred-thousand horse-power to the factories of a monstrous town. Neither do you come to them hoping to draw out Leviathan with a hook. It is enough if they run a harmless, amiable course, and keep the groves and fields green and fresh along their banks, and offer a happy alternation of nimble rapids and quiet pools,

"*With here and there a lusty trout,
And here and there a grayling.*"

When you set out to explore one of these minor streams in your canoe, you have no intention of epoch-making discoveries, or thrilling and world-famous adventures. You float placidly down the long stillwaters, and make your way patiently through the tangle of fallen trees that block the stream, and run the smaller falls, and carry your boat around the larger ones, with no loftier ambition than to reach a good camp-ground before dark and to pass the intervening hours pleasantly, "without offence to God or man." It is an agreeable and advantageous frame of mind for one who has done his fair share of work in the world, and is not inclined to grumble at his wages. There are few moods in which we are more susceptible of gentle instruction; and I suspect there are many tempers and attitudes, often called virtuous, in which the human spirit appears to less advantage in the sight of Heaven.

It is not required of every man and woman to be, or to do, something great; most of us must content ourselves with taking small parts in the chorus. Shall we have no little lyrics because Homer and Dante have written epics? And because we have heard the great organ at Freiburg, shall the sound of Kathi's zither in the alpine hut please us no more? Even those who have greatness thrust upon them will do well to lay the burden down now and then, and congratulate themselves that they are not altogether answerable for the conduct of the universe, or at least not all the time. "I reckon," said a cowboy to me one day, as we were riding through the Bad Lands of Dakota, "there's some one bigger than me, running this outfit. He can 'tend to it well enough, while I smoke my pipe after the round-up."

There is such a thing as taking ourselves and the world too seriously, or at any rate too anxiously. Half of the secular unrest and dismal, profane sadness of modern society comes from the vain idea that every man is bound to be a critic of life, and to let no day pass without finding some fault with the general order of things, or projecting some plan for its improvement. And the other half comes from the greedy notion that a man's life does consist, after all, in the abundance of the things that he possesses, and that it is somehow or other more respectable and pious to be always at work making a larger living, than it is to lie on your back in the green pastures and beside the still waters, and thank God that you are alive.

Come, then, my gentle reader, (for by this time you have discovered that this chapter is only a preface in disguise,—a declaration of principles or the want of them, an apology or a defence, as you choose to take it,) and if we are agreed, let us walk together; but if not, let us part here without ill-will.

You shall not be deceived in this book. It is nothing but a handful of rustic variations on the old tune of "Rest and be thankful," a record of unconventional travel, a pilgrim's scrip with a few bits of blue-sky philosophy in it. There is, so far as I know, very little useful information and absolutely no criticism of the universe to be found in this volume. So if you are what Izaak Walton calls "a severe, sour-complexioned man," you would better carry it back to the bookseller, and get your money again, if he will give it to you, and go your way rejoicing after your own melancholy fashion.

But if you care for plain pleasures, and informal company, and friendly observations on men and things, (and a few true fish-stories,) then perhaps you may find something here not unworthy your perusal. And so I wish that your winter fire may burn clear and bright while you read these pages; and that the summer days may be fair, and the fish may rise merrily to your fly, whenever you follow one of these little rivers.

1895.

A LEAF OF SPEARMINT
RECOLLECTIONS OF A BOY AND A ROD

"It puzzles me now, that I remember all these young impressions so, because I took no heed of them at the time whatever; and yet they come upon me bright, when nothing else is evident in the gray fog of experience."——
R. D. BLACKMORE: *Lorna Doone.*
A LEAF OF SPEARMINT

Of all the faculties of the human mind, memory is the one that is most easily "led by the nose." There is a secret power in the sense of smell which draws the mind backward into the pleasant land of old times.

If you could paint a picture of Memory, in the symbolical manner of Quarles's *Emblems*, it should represent a man travelling the highway with a dusty pack upon his shoulders, and stooping to draw in a long, sweet breath from the small, deep-red, golden-hearted flowers of an old-fashioned rose-tree straggling through the fence of a neglected garden. Or perhaps, for a choice of emblems, you would better take a yet more homely and familiar scent: the cool fragrance of lilacs drifting through the June morning from the old bush that stands between the kitchen door and the well; the warm layer of pungent, aromatic air that floats over the tansy-bed in a still July noon; the drowsy dew of odour that falls from the big balm-of-Gilead tree by the roadside as you are driving homeward through the twilight of August; or, best of all, the clean, spicy, unexpected, unmistakable smell of a bed of spearmint—that is the bed whereon Memory loves to lie and dream!

Why not choose mint as the symbol of remembrance? It is the true spice-tree of our Northern clime, the myrrh and frankincense of the land of lingering snow. When its perfume rises, the shrines of the past are unveiled, and the magical rites of reminiscence begin.

I.

You are fishing down the Swiftwater in the early Spring. In a shallow pool, which the drought of summer will soon change into dry land, you see the pale-green shoots of a little plant thrusting themselves up between the pebbles, and just beginning to overtop the falling water. You pluck a leaf of it as you turn out of the stream to find a comfortable place for lunch, and, rolling it between your fingers to see whether it smells like a good salad for your bread and cheese, you discover suddenly that it is new mint. For the rest of that day you are bewitched; you follow a stream that runs through the country of Auld Lang Syne, and fill your creel with the recollections of a boy and a rod.

And yet, strangely enough, you cannot recall the boy himself at all distinctly. There is only the faintest image of him on the endless roll of films that has been wound through your mental camera: and in the very spots where his small figure should appear, it seems as if the pictures were always light-struck. Just a blur, and the dim outline of a new cap, or a well-beloved jacket with extra pockets, or a much-hated pair of copper-toed shoes—that is all you can see.

But the people that the boy saw, the companions who helped or hindered him in his adventures, the sublime and marvellous scenes among the Catskills and the Adirondacks and the Green Mountains, in the midst of which he lived and moved and had his summer holidays—all these stand out sharp and clear, as the "Bab Ballads" say,

"*Photographically lined
On the tablets of your mind.*"

And most vivid do these scenes and people become when the vague and irrecoverable boy who walks among them carries a rod over his shoulder, and you detect the soft bulginess of wet fish about his clothing, and perhaps the tail of a big one emerging from his pocket. Then it seems almost as if these were things that had really happened, and of which you yourself were a great part.

The rod was a reward, yet not exactly of merit. It was an instrument of education in the hand of a father less indiscriminate than Solomon, who chose to interpret the text in a new way, and preferred to educate his child by encouraging him in pursuits which were harmless and wholesome, rather than by chastising him for practices which would likely enough never have been thought of, if they had not been forbidden. The boy enjoyed this kind of father at the time, and later he came to understand, with a grateful heart, that there is no richer inheritance in all the treasury of unearned blessings. For, after all, the love, the patience, the kindly wisdom of a grown man who can enter into the perplexities and turbulent impulses of a boy's heart, and give him cheerful companionship, and lead him on by free and joyful ways to know and choose the things that are pure and lovely and of good report, make as fair an image as we can find of that loving, patient Wisdom which must be above us all if any good is to come out of our childish race.

Now this was the way in which the boy came into possession of his undreaded rod. He was by nature and heredity one of those predestined anglers whom Izaak Walton tersely describes as "born so." His earliest passion was fishing. His favourite passage in Holy Writ was that place where Simon Peter throws a line into the sea and pulls out a great fish at the first cast.

But hitherto his passion had been indulged under difficulties—with improvised apparatus of cut poles, and flabby pieces of string, and bent pins, which always failed to hold the biggest fish; or perhaps with borrowed tackle, dangling a fat worm in vain before the noses of the staring, supercilious sunfish that poised themselves in the clear water around the Lake House dock at Lake George; or, at best, on picnic parties across the lake, marred by the humiliating presence of nurses, and disturbed by the obstinate refusal of old Horace, the boatman, to believe that the boy could bait his own hook, but sometimes crowned with the delight of bringing home a whole basketful of yellow perch and goggle-eyes. Of nobler sport with game fish, like the vaulting salmon and the merry, pugnacious trout, as yet the boy had only dreamed. But he had heard that there were such fish in the streams that flowed down from the mountains around Lake George, and he was at the happy age when he could believe anything—if it was sufficiently interesting.

There was one little river, and only one, within his knowledge and the reach of his short legs. It was a tiny, lively rivulet that came out of the woods about half a mile away from the hotel, and ran down cater-cornered through a sloping meadow, crossing the road under a flat bridge of boards, just beyond the root-beer shop at the lower end of the village. It seemed large enough to the boy, and he had long had his eye upon it as a fitting theatre for the beginning of a real angler's life. Those rapids, those falls, those deep, whirling pools with beautiful foam on them like soft, white custard, were they not such places as the trout loved to hide in?

You can see the long hotel piazza, with the gossipy groups of wooden chairs standing vacant in the early afternoon; for the grown-up people are dallying with the ultimate nuts and raisins of their mid-day dinner. A villainous clatter of innumerable little vegetable-dishes comes from the open windows of the pantry as the boy steals past the kitchen end of the house, with Horace's lightest bamboo pole over his shoulder, and a little brother in skirts and short white stockings tagging along behind him.

When they come to the five-rail fence where the brook runs out of the field, the question is, Over or under? The lowlier method seems safer for the little brother, as well as less conspicuous for persons who desire to avoid publicity until their enterprise has achieved success. So they crawl beneath a bend in the lowest rail,—only tearing one tiny three-cornered hole in a jacket, and making some juicy green stains on the white stockings,—and emerge with suppressed excitement in the field of the cloth of buttercups and daisies.

What an afternoon—how endless and yet how swift! What perilous efforts to leap across the foaming stream at its narrowest points; what escapes from quagmires and possible quicksands; what stealthy creeping through the grass to the edge of a likely pool, and cautious dropping of the line into an unseen depth, and patient waiting for a bite, until the restless little brother, prowling about below, discovers that the hook is not in the water at all, but lying on top of a dry stone,—thereby proving that patience is not the only virtue—or, at least, that it does a better business when it has a small vice of impatience in partnership with it!

How tired the adventurers grow as the day wears away; and as yet they have taken nothing! But their strength and courage return as if by magic when there comes a surprising twitch at the line in a shallow, unpromising rapid, and with a jerk of the pole a small, wiggling fish is whirled through the air and landed thirty feet back in the meadow.

"For pity's sake, don't lose him! There he is among the roots of the blue flag."

"I've got him! How cold he is—how slippery—how pretty! Just like a piece of rainbow!"

"Do you see the red spots? Did you notice how gamy he was, little brother; how he played? It is a trout, for sure; a real trout, almost as long as your hand."

So the two lads tramp along up the stream, chattering as if there were no rubric of silence in the angler's code. Presently another simple-minded troutling falls a victim to their unpremeditated art; and they begin already, being human, to wish for something larger. In the very last pool that they dare attempt—a dark hole under a steep bank, where the brook issues from the woods—the boy drags out the hoped-for prize, a splendid trout, longer than a new lead-pencil. But he feels sure that there must be another, even larger, in the same place. He swings his line out carefully over the water, and just as he is about to drop it in, the little brother, perched on the sloping brink, slips on the smooth pine-needles, and goes sliddering down into the pool up to his waist. How he weeps with dismay, and how funnily his dress sticks to him as he crawls out! But his grief is soon assuaged by the privilege of carrying the trout strung on an alder twig; and it is a happy, muddy, proud pair of urchins that climb over the fence out of the field of triumph at the close of the day.

What does the father say, as he meets them in the road? Is he frowning or smiling under that big brown beard? You cannot be quite sure. But one thing is clear: he is as much elated over the capture of the real trout as any one. He is ready to deal mildly with a little irregularity for the sake of encouraging pluck and perseverance. Before the three comrades have reached the hotel, the boy has promised faithfully never to take his little brother off again without asking leave; and the father has promised that the boy shall have a real jointed fishing-rod of his own, so that he will not need to borrow old Horace's pole any more.

At breakfast the next morning the family are to have a private dish; not an every-day affair of vulgar, bony fish that nurses can catch, but trout—three of them! But the boy looks up from the table and sees the adored of his soul, Annie V——, sitting at the other end of the room, and faring on the common food of mortals. Shall she eat the ordinary breakfast while he feasts on dainties? Do not other sportsmen send their spoils to the ladies whom they admire? The waiter must bring a hot plate, and take this largest trout to Miss V—— (Miss Annie, not her sister—make no mistake about it).

The face of Augustus is as solemn as an ebony idol while he plays his part of Cupid's messenger. The fair Annie affects surprise; she accepts the offering rather indifferently; her curls drop down over her cheeks to cover some small confusion. But for an instant the corner of her eye catches the boy's sidelong glance, and she nods perceptibly, whereupon his mother very inconsiderately calls attention to the fact that yesterday's escapade has sun-burned his face dreadfully.

Beautiful Annie V——, who, among all the unripened nymphs that played at hide-and-seek among the maples on the hotel lawn, or waded with white feet along the yellow beach beyond the point of pines, flying with merry shrieks into the woods when a boat-load of boys appeared suddenly around the corner, or danced the lancers in the big, bare parlours before the grown-up ball began—who in all that joyous, innocent bevy could be compared with you for charm or daring? How your dark eyes sparkled, and how the long brown ringlets tossed around your small head, when you stood up that evening, slim and straight, and taller by half a head than your companions, in the lamp-lit room where the children were playing forfeits, and said, "There is not one boy here that *dares* to kiss *me*!" Then you ran out on the dark porch, where the honeysuckle vines grew up the tall, inane Corinthian pillars.

Did you blame the boy for following? And were you very angry, indeed, about what happened,—until you broke out laughing at his cravat, which had slipped around behind his ear? That was the first time he ever noticed how much sweeter the honeysuckle smells at night than in the day. It was his entrance examination in the school of nature—human and otherwise. He felt that there was a whole continent of newly discovered poetry within him, and worshipped his Columbus disguised in curls. Your boy is your true idealist, after all, although (or perhaps because) he is still uncivilised.

II.

The arrival of the rod, in four joints, with an extra tip, a brass reel, and the other luxuries for which a true angler would willingly exchange the necessaries of life, marked a new epoch in the boy's career. At the uplifting of that wand, as if it had been in the hand of another Moses, the waters of infancy rolled back, and the way was opened into the promised land, whither the tyrant nurses, with all their proud array of baby-chariots, could not follow. The way was open, but not by any means dry. One of the first events in the dispensation of the rod was the purchase of a pair of high rubber boots. Inserted in this armour of modern infantry, and transfigured with delight, the boy clumped through all the little rivers within a circuit of ten miles from Caldwell, and began to learn by parental example the yet unmastered art of complete angling.

But because some of the streams were deep and strong, and his legs were short and slender, and his ambition was even taller than his boots, the father would sometimes take him up pickaback, and wade along carefully through the perilous places—which are often, in this world, the very places one longs to fish in. So, in your remembrance, you can see the little rubber boots sticking out under the father's arms, and the rod projecting over his head, and the bait dangling down unsteadily into the deep holes, and the delighted boy hooking and playing and basketing his trout high in the air. How many of our best catches in life are made from some one else's shoulders!

From this summer the whole earth became to the boy, as Tennyson describes the lotus country, "a land of streams." In school-days and in town he acknowledged the sway of those mysterious and irresistible forces which produce tops at one season, and marbles at another, and kites at another, and bind all boyish hearts to play mumble-the-peg at the due time more certainly than the stars are bound to their orbits. But when vacation came, with its annual exodus from the city, there was only one sign in the zodiac, and that was Pisces.

No country seemed to him tolerable without trout, and no landscape beautiful unless enlivened by a young river. Among what delectable mountains did those watery guides lead his vagrant steps, and with what curious, mixed, and sometimes profitable company did they make him familiar!

There was one exquisite stream among the Alleghanies, called Lycoming Creek, beside which the family spent a summer in a decadent inn, kept by a tremulous landlord who was always sitting on the steps of the porch, and whose most memorable remark was that he had "a misery in his stomach." This form of speech amused the boy, but he did not in the least comprehend it. It was the description of an unimaginable experience in a region which was as yet known to him only as the seat of pleasure. He did not understand how any one could be miserable when he could catch trout from his own dooryard.

The big creek, with its sharp turns from side to side of the valley, its hemlock-shaded falls in the gorge, and its long, still reaches in the "sugar-bottom," where the maple-trees grew as if in an orchard, and the superfluity of grasshoppers made the trout fat and dainty, was too wide to fit the boy. But nature keeps all sizes in her stock, and a smaller stream, called Rocky Run, came tumbling down opposite the inn, as if made to order for juvenile use.

How well you can follow it, through the old pasture overgrown with alders, and up past the broken-down mill-dam and the crumbling sluice, into the mountain-cleft from which it leaps laughing! The water, except just after a rain-storm, is as transparent as glass—old-fashioned window-glass, I mean, in small panes, with just a tinge of green in it, like the air in a grove of young birches. Twelve feet down in the narrow chasm below the falls, where the water is full of tiny bubbles, like Apollinaris, you can see the trout poised, with their heads up-stream, motionless, but quivering a little, as if they were strung on wires.

The bed of the stream has been scooped out of the solid rock. Here and there banks of sand have been deposited, and accumulations of loose stone disguise the real nature of the channel. Great boulders have been rolled down the alleyway and left where they chanced to stick; the stream must get around them or under them as best it can. But there are other places where everything has been swept clean; nothing remains but the primitive strata, and the flowing water merrily tickles the bare ribs of mother earth. Whirling stones, in the spring floods, have cut well-holes in the rock, as round and even as if they had been made with a drill, and sometimes you can see the very stone that sunk the well lying at the bottom. There are long, straight, sloping troughs through which the water runs like a mill-race. There are huge basins into which the water rumbles over a ledge, as if some one were pouring it very steadily out of a pitcher, and from which it glides away without a ripple, flowing over a smooth pavement of rock which shelves down from the shallow foot to the deep head of the pool.

The boy wonders how far he dare wade out along that slippery floor. The water is within an inch of his boot-tops now. But the slope seems very even, and just beyond his reach a good fish is rising. Only one step more, and then, like the wicked man in the psalm, his feet begin to slide. Slowly, and standing bolt upright, with the rod held high above his head, as if it must on no account get wet, he glides forward up to his neck in the ice-cold bath, gasping with amazement. There have been other and more serious situations in life into which, unless I am mistaken, you have made an equally unwilling and embarrassed entrance, and in which you have been surprised to find yourself not only up to your neck, but over,—and you are a lucky man if you have had the presence of mind to stand still for a moment, before wading out, and make sure at least of the fish that tempted you into your predicament.

But Rocky Run, they say, exists no longer. It has been blasted by miners out of all resemblance to itself, and bewitched into a dingy water-power to turn wheels for the ugly giant, Trade. It is only in the valley of remembrance that its current still flows like liquid air; and only in that country that you can still see the famous men who came and went along the banks of the Lycoming when the boy was there.

There was Collins, who was a wondrous adept at "daping, dapping, or dibbling" with a grasshopper, and who once brought in a string of trout which he laid out head to tail on the grass before the house in a line of beauty forty-seven feet long. A mighty bass voice had this Collins also, and could sing, "Larboard Watch, Ahoy!" "Down in a Coal-Mine," and other profound ditties in a way to make all the glasses on the table jingle; but withal, as you now suspect, rather a fishy character, and undeserving of the unqualified respect which the boy had for him. And there was Dr. Romsen, lean, satirical, kindly, a skilful though reluctant physician, who regarded it as a personal injury if any one in the party fell sick in summer time; and a passionately unsuccessful hunter, who would sit all night in the crotch of a tree beside an alleged deer-lick, and come home perfectly satisfied if he had heard a hedgehog grunt. It was he who called attention to the discrepancy between the boy's appetite and his size by saying loudly at a picnic, "I wouldn't grudge you what you eat, my boy, if I could only see that it did you any good,"—which remark was not forgiven until the doctor redeemed his reputation by pronouncing a serious medical opinion, before a council of mothers, to the effect that it did not really hurt a boy to get his feet wet. That was worthy of Galen in his most inspired moment. And there was hearty, genial Paul Merit, whose mere company was an education in good manners, and who could eat eight hard-boiled eggs for supper without ruffling his equanimity; and the tall, thin, grinning Major, whom an angry Irishwoman once described as "like a comb, all back and teeth;" and many more were the comrades of the boy's father, all of whom he admired, (and followed when they would let him,) but none so much as the father himself, because he was the wisest, kindest, and merriest of all that merry crew, now dispersed to the uttermost parts of the earth and beyond.

Other streams played a part in the education of that happy boy: the Kaaterskill, where there had been nothing but the ghosts of trout for the last thirty years, but where the absence of fish was almost forgotten in the joy of a first introduction to Dickens, one very showery day, when dear old Ned Mason built a smoky fire in a cave below Haines's Falls, and, pulling *The Old Curiosity Shop* out of his pocket, read aloud about Little Nell until the tears ran down the cheeks of reader and listener—the smoke was so thick, you know: and the Neversink, which flows through John Burroughs's country, and past one house in particular, perched on a high bluff, where a very dreadful old woman come out and throws stones at "city fellers fishin' through her land" (as if any one wanted to touch her land! It was the water that ran over it, you see, that carried the fish with it, and they were not hers at all): and the stream at Healing Springs, in the Virginia mountains, where the medicinal waters flow down into a lovely wild brook without injuring the health of the trout in the least, and where the only drawback to the angler's happiness is the abundance of rattlesnakes—but a boy does not mind such things as that; he feels as if he were immortal. Over all these streams memory skips lightly, and strikes a trail through the woods to the Adirondacks, where the boy made his first acquaintance with navigable rivers,—that is to say, rivers which are traversed by canoes and hunting-skiffs, but not yet defiled by steamboats,—and slept, or rather lay awake, for the first time on a bed of balsam-boughs in a tent.

III.

The promotion from all-day picnics to a two weeks' camping-trip is like going from school to college. By this time a natural process of evolution has raised the first rod to something lighter and more flexible,—a fly-rod, so to speak, but not a bigoted one,—just a serviceable, unprejudiced article, not above using any kind of bait that may be necessary to catch the fish. The father has received the new title of "governor," indicating not less, but more authority, and has called in new instructors to carry on the boy's education: real Adirondack guides—old Sam Dunning and one-eyed Enos, the last and laziest of the Saranac Indians. Better men will be discovered for later trips, but none more amusing, and none whose woodcraft seems more wonderful than that of this queerly matched team, as they make the first camp in a pelting rain-storm on the shore of Big Clear Pond. The pitching of the tents is a lesson in architecture, the building of the camp-fire a victory over damp nature, and the supper of potatoes and bacon and fried trout a veritable triumph of culinary art.

At midnight the rain is pattering persistently on the canvas; the fronts flaps are closed and tied together; the lingering fire shines through them, and sends vague shadows wavering up and down: the governor is rolled up in his blankets, sound asleep. It is a very long night for the boy.

What is that rustling noise outside the tent? Probably some small creature, a squirrel or a rabbit. Rabbit stew would be good for breakfast. But it sounds louder now, almost loud enough to be a fox,—there are no wolves left in the Adirondacks, or at least only a very few. That is certainly quite a heavy footstep prowling around the provision-box. Could it be a panther,—they step very softly for their size,—or a bear perhaps? Sam Dunning told about catching one in a trap just below here. (Ah, my boy, you will soon learn that there is no spot in all the forests created by a bountiful Providence so poor as to be without its bear story.) Where was the rifle put? There it is, at the foot of the tent-pole. Wonder if it is loaded?

"*Waugh-ho! Waugh-ho-o-o-o!*"

The boy springs from his blankets like a cat, and peeps out between the tent-flaps. There sits Enos, in the shelter of a leaning tree by the fire, with his head thrown back and a bottle poised at his mouth. His lonely eye is cocked up at a great horned owl on the branch above him. Again the sudden voice breaks out:

"*Whoo! whoo! whoo cooks for you all?*"

Enos puts the bottle down, with a grunt, and creeps off to his tent.

"De debbil in dat owl," he mutters. "How he know I cook for dis camp? How he know 'bout dat bottle? Ugh!"

There are hundreds of pictures that flash into light as the boy goes on his course, year after year, through the woods. There is the luxurious camp on Tupper's Lake, with its log cabins in the spruce-grove, and its regiment of hungry men who ate almost a deer a day; and there is the little bark shelter on the side of Mount Marcy, where the governor and the boy, with baskets full of trout from the Opalescent River, are spending the night, with nothing but a fire to keep them warm. There is the North Bay at Moosehead, with Joe La Croix (one more Frenchman who thinks he looks like Napoleon) posing on the rocks beside his canoe, and only reconciled by his vanity to the wasteful pastime of taking photographs while the big fish are rising gloriously out at the end of the point. There is the small spring-hole beside the Saranac River, where Pliny Robbins and the boy caught twenty-three noble trout, weighing from one to three pounds apiece, in the middle of a hot August afternoon, and hid themselves in the bushes whenever they heard a party coming down the river, because they did not care to attract company; and there are the Middle

Falls, where the governor stood on a long spruce log, taking two-pound fish with the fly, and stepping out at every cast a little nearer to the end of the log, until it slowly tipped with him, and he settled down into the river.

Among such scenes as these the boy pursued his education, learning many things that are not taught in colleges; learning to take the weather as it comes, wet or dry, and fortune as it falls, good or bad; learning that a meal which is scanty fare for one becomes a banquet for two—provided the other is the right person; learning that there is some skill in everything, even in digging bait, and that what is called luck consists chiefly in having your tackle in good order; learning that a man can be just as happy in a log shanty as in a brownstone mansion, and that the very best pleasures are those that do not leave a bad taste in the mouth. And in all this the governor was his best teacher and his closest comrade.

Dear governor, you have gone out of the wilderness now, and your steps will be no more beside these remembered little rivers—no more, forever and forever. You will not come in sight around any bend of this clear Swiftwater stream where you made your last cast; your cheery voice will never again ring out through the deepening twilight where you are lingering for your disciple to catch up with you; he will never again hear you call: "Hallo, my boy! What luck? Time to go home!" But there is a river in the country where you have gone, is there not?—a river with trees growing all along it—evergreen trees; and somewhere by those shady banks, within sound of clear running waters, I think you will be dreaming and waiting for your boy, if he follows the trail that you have shown him even to the end.

1895.

AMPERSAND

"It is not the walking merely, it is keeping yourself in tune for a walk, in the spiritual and bodily condition in which you can find entertainment and exhilaration in so simple and natural a pastime. You are eligible to any good fortune when you are in a condition to enjoy a walk. When the air and water taste sweet to you, how much else will taste sweet! When the exercise of your limbs affords you pleasure, and the play of your senses upon the various objects and shows of Nature quickens and stimulates your spirit, your relation to the world and to yourself is what it should be,—simple, and direct, and wholesome."——

JOHN BURROUGHS: *Pepacton*.

AMPERSAND

The right to the name of Ampersand, like the territory of Gaul in those *Commentaries* which Julius Cæsar wrote for the punishment of school-boys, is divided into three parts. It belongs to a mountain, and a lake, and a little river.

The mountain stands in the heart of the Adirondack country, just near enough to the thoroughfare of travel for thousands of people to see it every year, and just far enough from the beaten track to be unvisited except by a very few of the wise ones, who love to turn aside. Behind the mountain is the lake, which no lazy man has ever seen. Out of the lake flows the stream, winding down a long, untrodden forest valley, to join the Stony Creek waters and empty into the Raquette River.

Which of the three Ampersands has the prior claim to the name, I cannot tell. Philosophically speaking, the mountain ought to be regarded as the head of the family, because it was undoubtedly there before the others. And the lake was probably the next on the ground, because the stream is its child. But man is not strictly just in his nomenclature; and I conjecture that the little river, the last-born of the three, was the first to be christened Ampersand, and then gave its name to its parent and grand-parent. It is such a crooked stream, so bent and curved and twisted upon itself, so fond of turning around unexpected corners and sweeping away in great circles from its direct course, that its first explorers christened it after the eccentric supernumerary of the alphabet which appears in the old spelling-books as &—and *per se*, and.

But in spite of this apparent subordination to the stream in the matter of a name, the mountain clearly asserts its natural authority. It stands up boldly; and not only its own lake, but at least three others, the Lower Saranac, Round Lake, and Lonesome Pond, lie at its foot and acknowledge its lordship. When the cloud is on its brow, they are dark. When the sunlight strikes it, they smile. Wherever you may go over the waters of these lakes you shall see Mount Ampersand looking down at you, and saying quietly, "This is my domain."

I never look at a mountain which asserts itself in this fashion without desiring to stand on the top of it. If one can reach the summit, one becomes a sharer in the dominion. The difficulties in the way only add to the zest of the victory. Every mountain is, rightly considered, an invitation to climb. And as I was resting for a month one summer at Bartlett's, Ampersand challenged me daily.

Did you know Bartlett's in its palmy time? It was the homeliest, quaintest, coziest place in the Adirondacks. Away back in the *ante-bellum* days Virgil Bartlett had come into the woods, and built his house on the bank of the Saranac River, between the Upper Saranac and Round Lake. It was then the only dwelling within a circle of many miles. The deer and bear were in the majority. At night one could sometimes hear the scream of the panther or the howling of wolves. But soon the wilderness began to wear the traces of a conventional smile. The desert blossomed a little—if not as the rose, at least as the gilly-flower. Fields were cleared, gardens planted; half a dozen log cabins were scattered along the river; and the old house, having grown slowly and somewhat irregularly for twenty years, came out, just before the time of which I write, in a modest coat of paint and a broad-brimmed piazza. But Virgil himself, the creator of the oasis—well known of hunters and fishermen, dreaded of lazy guides and quarrelsome lumbermen,—"Virge," the irascible, kind-hearted, indefatigable, was there no longer. He had made his last clearing, and fought his last fight; done his last favour to a friend, and thrown his last adversary out of the tavern door. His last log had gone down the river. His camp-fire had burned out. Peace to his ashes. His wife, who had often played the part of Abigail toward travellers who had unconsciously incurred the old man's mistrust, now reigned in his stead; and there was great abundance of maple-syrup on every man's flapjack.

The charm of Bartlett's for the angler was the stretch of rapid water in front of the house. The Saranac River, breaking from its first resting-place in the Upper Lake, plunged down through a great bed of rocks, making a chain of short falls and pools and rapids, about half a mile in length. Here, in the spring and early summer, the speckled trout—brightest and daintiest of all fish that swim—used to be found in great numbers. As the season advanced, they moved away into the deep water of the lakes. But there were always a few stragglers left, and I have taken them in the rapids at the very end of August. What could be more delightful than to spend an hour or two, in the early morning or evening of a hot day, in wading this rushing stream, and casting the fly on its clear waters? The wind blows softly down the narrow valley, and the trees nod from the rocks above you. The noise of the falls makes constant music in your ears. The river hurries past you, and yet it is never gone.

The same foam-flakes seem to be always gliding downward, the same spray dashing over the stones, the same eddy coiling at the edge of the pool. Send your fly in under those cedar branches, where the water swirls around by that old log. Now draw it up toward the foam. There is a sudden gleam of dull gold in the white water. You strike too soon. Your line comes back to you. In a current like this, a fish will almost always hook himself. Try it again. This time he takes the fly fairly, and you have him. It is a good fish, and he makes the slender rod bend to the strain. He sulks for a moment as if uncertain what to do, and then with a rush darts into the swiftest part of the current. You can never stop him there. Let him go. Keep just enough pressure on him to hold the hook firm, and follow his troutship down the stream as if he were a salmon. He slides over a little fall, gleaming through the foam, and swings around in the next pool. Here you can manage him more easily; and after a few minutes' brilliant play, a few mad dashes for the current, he comes to the net, and your skilful guide lands him with a quick, steady sweep of the arm. The scales credit him with an even pound, and a better fish than this you will hardly take here in midsummer.

"On my word, master," says the appreciative Venator, in Walton's *Angler*, "this is a gallant trout; what shall we do with him?" And honest Piscator, replies: "Marry! e'en eat him to supper; we'll go to my hostess from whence we came; she told me, as I was going out of door, that my brother Peter, and who is this but Romeyn of Keeseville? a good angler and a cheerful companion, had sent word he would lodge there to-night, and bring a friend with him. My hostess has two beds, *and I know you and I have the best*; we'll rejoice with my brother Peter and his friend, tell tales, or sing ballads, or make a catch, or find some harmless sport to content us, and pass away a little time without offence to God or man."

Ampersand waited immovable while I passed many days in such innocent and healthful pleasures as these, until the right day came for the ascent. Cool, clean, and bright, the crystal morning promised a glorious noon, and the mountain almost seemed to beckon us to come up higher. The photographic camera and a trustworthy lunch were stowed away in the pack-basket. The backboard was adjusted at a comfortable angle in the stern seat of our little boat. The guide held the little craft steady while I stepped into my place; then he pushed out into the stream, and we went swiftly down toward Round Lake.

A Saranac boat is one of the finest things that the skill of man has ever produced under the inspiration of the wilderness. It is a frail shell, so light that a guide can carry it on his shoulders with ease, but so dexterously fashioned that it rides the heaviest waves like a duck, and slips through the water as if by magic. You can travel in it along the shallowest rivers and across the broadest lakes, and make forty or fifty miles a day, if you have a good guide.

Everything depends, in the Adirondacks, as in so many other regions of life, upon your guide. If he is selfish, or surly, or stupid, you will have a bad time. But if he is an Adirondacker of the best old-fashioned type,—now unhappily growing more rare from year to year,—you will find him an inimitable companion, honest, faithful, skilful and cheerful. He is as independent as a prince, and the gilded youths and finicking fine ladies who attempt to patronise him are apt to make but a sorry show before his solid and undisguised contempt. But deal with him man to man, and he will give you a friendly, loyal service which money cannot buy, and teach you secrets of woodcraft and lessons in plain, self-reliant manhood more valuable than all the learning of the schools. Such a guide was mine, rejoicing in the Scriptural name of Hosea, but commonly called, in brevity and friendliness, "Hose."

As we entered Round Lake on this fair morning, its surface was as smooth and shining as a mirror. It was too early yet for the tide of travel which sends a score of boats up and down this thoroughfare every day; and from shore to shore the water was unruffled, except by a flock of sheldrakes which had been feeding near Plymouth Rock, and now went skittering off into Weller Bay with a motion between flying and swimming, leaving a long wake of foam behind them.

At such a time as this you can see the real colour of these Adirondack lakes. It is not blue, as romantic writers so often describe it, nor green, like some of those wonderful Swiss lakes; although of course it reflects the colour of the trees along the shore; and when the wind stirs it, it gives back the hue of the sky, blue when it is clear, gray when the clouds are gathering, and sometimes as black as ink under the shadow of storm. But when it is still, the water itself is like that river which one of the poets has described as

"Flowing with a smooth brown current."

And in this sheet of burnished bronze the mountains and islands were reflected perfectly, and the sun shone back from it, not in broken gleams or a wide lane of light, but like a single ball of fire, moving before us as we moved.

But stop! What is that dark speck on the water, away down toward Turtle Point? It has just the shape and size of a deer's head. It seems to move steadily out into the lake. There is a little ripple, like a wake, behind it. Hose turns to look at it, and then sends the boat darting in that direction with long, swift strokes. It is a moment of pleasant excitement, and we begin to conjecture whether the deer is a buck or a doe, and whose hounds have driven it in. But when Hose turns to look again, he slackens his stroke, and says: "I guess we needn't to hurry; he won't get away. It's astonishin' what a lot of fun a man can get in the course of a natural life a-chasin' chumps of wood."

We landed on a sand beach at the mouth of a little stream, where a blazed tree marked the beginning of the Ampersand trail. This line through the forest was made years ago by that ardent sportsman and lover of the Adirondacks, Dr. W. W. Ely, of Rochester. Since that time it has been shortened and improved a little by other travellers, and also not a little blocked and confused by the lumbermen and the course of Nature. For when the lumbermen go into the woods, they cut roads in every direction, leading nowhither, and the unwary wanderer is thereby led aside from the right way, and entangled in the undergrowth. And as for Nature, she is entirely opposed to continuance of paths through her forest. She covers them with fallen leaves, and hides them with thick bushes. She drops great trees across them, and blots them out with windfalls. But the blazed line—a succession of broad axe-marks on the trunks of the trees, just high enough to catch the eye on a level—cannot be so easily obliterated, and this, after all, is the safest guide through the woods.

Our trail led us at first through a natural meadow, overgrown with waist-high grass, and very spongy to the tread. Hornet-haunted also was this meadow, and therefore no place for idle dalliance or unwary digression, for the sting of the hornet is one of the saddest and most humiliating surprises of this mortal life.

Then through a tangle of old wood-roads my guide led me safely, and we struck one of the long ridges which slope gently from the lake to the base of the mountain. Here walking was comparatively easy, for in the hard-wood timber there is little underbrush. The massive trunks seemed like pillars set to uphold the level roof of green. Great yellow birches, shaggy with age, stretched their knotted arms high above us; sugar-maples stood up straight and proud under their leafy crowns; and smooth beeches—the most polished and park-like of all the forest trees—offered opportunities for the carving of lovers' names in a place where few lovers ever come.

The woods were quiet. It seemed as if all living creatures had deserted them. Indeed, if you have spent much time in our Northern forests, you must have often wondered at the sparseness of life, and felt a sense of pity for the apparent loneliness of the squirrel that chatters at you as you pass, or the little bird that hops noiselessly about in the thickets. The midsummer noontide is an especially silent time. The deer are asleep in some wild meadow. The partridge has gathered her brood for their midday nap. The squirrels are perhaps counting over their store of nuts in a hollow tree, and the hermit-thrush spares his voice until evening. The woods are close—not cool and fragrant as the foolish romances describe them—but warm and still; for the breeze which sweeps across the hilltop and ruffles the lake does not penetrate into these shady recesses, and therefore all the inhabitants take the noontide as their hour of rest. Only the big woodpecker—he of the scarlet head and mighty bill—is indefatigable, and somewhere unseen is "tapping the hollow beechtree," while a wakeful little bird,—I guess it is the black-throated green warbler,—prolongs his dreamy, listless ditty,— *'te-dé-terit-scā,— 'te-dé-us-wait*.

After about an hour of easy walking, our trail began to ascend more sharply. We passed over the shoulder of a ridge and around the edge of a fire-slash, and then we had the mountain fairly before us. Not that we could see anything of it, for the woods still shut us in, but the path became very steep, and we knew that it was a straight climb; not up and down and round about did this most uncompromising trail proceed, but right up, in a direct line for the summit.

Now this side of Ampersand is steeper than any Gothic roof I have ever seen, and withal very much encumbered with rocks and ledges and fallen trees. There were places where we had to haul ourselves up by roots and branches, and places where we had to go down on our hands and knees to crawl under logs. It was breathless work, but not at all dangerous or difficult. Every step forward was also a step upward; and as we stopped to rest for a moment, we could see already glimpses of the lake below us. But at these I did not much care to look, for I think it is a pity to spoil the surprise of a grand view by taking little snatches of it beforehand. It is better to keep one's face set to the mountain, and then, coming out from the dark forest upon the very summit, feel the splendour of the outlook flash upon one like a revelation.

The character of the woods through which we were now passing was entirely different from those of the lower levels. On these steep places the birch and maple will not grow, or at least they occur but sparsely. The higher slopes and sharp ridges of the mountains are always covered with soft-wood timber. Spruce and hemlock and balsam strike their roots among the rocks, and find a hidden nourishment. They stand close together; thickets of small trees spring up among the large ones; from year to year the great trunks are falling one across another, and the undergrowth is thickening around them, until a spruce forest seems to be almost impassable. The constant rain of needles and the crumbling of the fallen trees form a rich, brown mould, into which the foot sinks noiselessly. Wonderful beds of moss, many feet in thickness, and softer than feathers, cover the rocks and roots. There are shadows never broken by the sun, and dark, cool springs of icy water hidden away in the crevices. You feel a sense of antiquity here which you can never feel among the maples and birches. Longfellow was right when he filled his forest primeval with "murmuring pines and hemlocks."

The higher one climbs, the darker and gloomier and more rugged the vegetation becomes. The pine-trees soon cease to follow you; the hemlocks disappear, and the balsams can go no farther. Only the hardy spruce keeps on bravely, rough and stunted, with branches matted together and pressed down flat by the weight of the winter's snow, until finally, somewhere about the level of four thousand feet above the sea, even this bold climber gives out, and the weather-beaten rocks of the summit are clad only with mosses and Alpine plants.

Thus it is with mountains, as perhaps with men, a mark of superior dignity to be naturally bald.

Ampersand, falling short by a thousand feet of the needful height, cannot claim this distinction. But what Nature has denied, human labour has supplied. Under the direction of the Adirondack Survey, some years ago, several acres of trees were cut from the summit; and when we emerged, after the last sharp scramble, upon the very crest of the mountain, we were not shut in by a dense thicket, but stood upon a bare ridge of granite in the centre of a ragged clearing.

I shut my eyes for a moment, drew a few long breaths of the glorious breeze, and then looked out upon a wonder and a delight beyond description.

A soft, dazzling splendour filled the air. Snowy banks and drifts of cloud were floating slowly over a wide and wondrous land. Vast sweeps of forest, shining waters, mountains near and far, the deepest green and the palest blue, changing colours and glancing lights, and all so silent, so strange, so far away, that it seemed like the landscape of a dream. One almost feared to speak, lest it should vanish.

Right below us the Lower Saranac and Lonesome Pond, Round Lake and the Weller Ponds, were spread out like a map. Every point and island was clearly marked. We could follow the course of the Saranac River in all its curves and windings, and see the white tents of the haymakers on the wild meadows. Far away to the northeast stretched the level fields of Bloomingdale. But westward all was unbroken wilderness, a great sea of woods as far as the eye could reach. And how far it can reach from a height like this! What a revelation of the power of sight! That faint blue outline far in the north was Lyon Mountain, nearly thirty miles away as the crow flies. Those silver gleams a little nearer were the waters of St. Regis. The Upper Saranac was displayed in all its length and breadth, and beyond it the innumerable waters of Fish Creek were tangled among the dark woods. The long ranges of the hills about the Jordan bounded the western horizon, and on the southwest Big Tupper Lake was sleeping at the base of Mount Morris. Looking past the peak of Stony Creek Mountain, which rose sharp and distinct in a line with Ampersand, we could trace the path of the Raquette River from the distant waters of Long Lake down through its far-stretched valley, and catch here and there a silvery link of its current.

But when we turned to the south and east, how wonderful and how different was the view! Here was no widespread and smiling landscape with gleams of silver scattered through it, and soft blue haze resting upon its fading verge, but a wild land of mountains, stern, rugged, tumultuous, rising one beyond another like the waves of a stormy ocean,—Ossa piled upon Pelion,—McIntyre's sharp peak, and the ragged crest of the Gothics, and, above all, Marcy's dome-like head, raised just far enough above the others to assert his royal right as monarch of the Adirondacks.

But grandest of all, as seen from this height, was Mount Seward,—a solemn giant of a mountain, standing apart from the others, and looking us full in the face. He was clothed from base to summit in a dark, unbroken robe of forest. *Ou-kor-lah*, the Indians called him—the Great Eye; and he seemed almost to frown upon us in defiance. At his feet, so straight below us that it seemed almost as if we could cast a stone into it, lay the wildest and most beautiful of all the Adirondack waters—Ampersand Lake.

On its shore, some five-and-twenty years ago, the now almost forgotten Adirondack Club had their shanty—the successor of "the Philosophers' Camp" on Follensbee Pond. Agassiz, Appleton, Norton, Emerson, Lowell, Hoar, Gray, John Holmes, and Stillman, were among the company who made their resting-place under the shadow of Mount Seward. They had bought a tract of forest land completely encircling the pond, cut a rough road to it through the woods, and built a comfortable log cabin, to which they purposed to return summer after summer. But the civil war broke out, with all its terrible excitement and confusion of hurrying hosts: the club existed but for two years, and the little house in the wilderness was abandoned. In 1878, when I spent three weeks at Ampersand, the cabin was in ruins, and surrounded by an almost impenetrable growth of bushes. The only philosophers to be seen were a family of what the guides quaintly call "quill pigs." The roof had fallen to the ground; raspberry-bushes thrust themselves through the yawning crevices between the logs; and in front of the sunken door-sill lay a rusty, broken iron stove, like a dismantled altar on which the fire had gone out forever.

After we had feasted upon the view as long as we dared, counted the lakes and streams, and found that we could see without a glass more than thirty, and recalled the memories of "good times" which came to us from almost every point of the compass, we unpacked the camera, and proceeded to take some pictures.

If you are a photographer, and have anything of the amateur's passion for your art, you will appreciate my pleasure and my anxiety. Never before, so far as I knew, had a camera been set up on Ampersand. I had but eight plates with me. The views were all very distant and all at a downward angle. The power of the light at this elevation was an unknown quantity. And the wind was sweeping vigorously across the open summit of the mountain. I put in my smallest stop, and prepared for short exposures.

My instrument was a thing called a Tourograph, which differs from most other cameras in having the plate-holder on top of the box. The plates are dropped into a groove below, and then moved into focus, after which the cap is removed and the exposure made.

I set my instrument for Ampersand Pond, sighted the picture through the ground glass, and measured the focus. Then I waited for a quiet moment, dropped the plate, moved it carefully forward to the proper mark, and went around to take off the cap. I found that I already had it in my hand, *and the plate had been exposed for about thirty seconds with a sliding focus*!

I expostulated with myself. I said: "You are excited; you are stupid; you are unworthy of the name of photographer. Light-writer! You ought to write with a whitewash-brush!" The reproof was effectual, and from that moment all went well. The plates dropped smoothly, the camera was steady, the exposure was correct. Six good pictures were made, to recall, so far as black and white could do it, the delights of that day.

It has been my good luck to climb many of the peaks of the Adirondacks—Dix, the Dial, Hurricane, the Giant of the Valley, Marcy, and Whiteface—but I do not think the outlook from any of them is so wonderful and lovely as that from little Ampersand; and I reckon among my most valuable chattels the plates of glass on which the sun has traced for me (who cannot draw) the outlines of that loveliest landscape.

The downward journey was swift. We halted for an hour or two beside a trickling spring, a few rods below the summit, to eat our lunch. Then, jumping, running, and sometimes sliding, we made the descent, passed in safety by the dreaded lair of the hornet, and reached Bartlett's as the fragrance of the evening pancake was softly diffused through the twilight. Mark that day, Memory, with a double star in your catalogue!

1885.

A HANDFUL OF HEATHER

"*Scotland is the home of romance because it is the home of Scott, Burns, Black, Macdonald, Stevenson, and Barrie—and of thousands of men like that old Highlander in kilts on the tow-path, who loves what they have written. I would wager he has a copy of Burns in his sporran, and has quoted him half a dozen times to the grim Celt who is walking with him. Those old boys don't read for excitement or knowledge, but because they love their land and their people and their religion—and their great writers simply express their emotions for them in words they can understand. You and I come over here, with thousands of our countrymen, to borrow their emotions.*"——
ROBERT BRIDGES: *Overheard in Arcady.*

A HANDFUL OF HEATHER

My friend the Triumphant Democrat, fiercest of radicals and kindest of men, expresses his scorn for monarchical institutions (and his invincible love for his native Scotland) by tenanting, summer after summer, a famous castle among the heathery Highlands. There he proclaims the most uncompromising Americanism in a speech that grows more broadly Scotch with every week of his emancipation from the influence of the clipped, commercial accent of New York, and casts contempt on feudalism by playing the part of lord of the manor to such a perfection of high-handed beneficence that the people of the glen are all become his clansmen, and his gentle lady would be the patron saint of the district—if the republican theology of Scotland could only admit saints among the elect.

Every year he sends trophies of game to his friends across the sea—birds that are as toothsome and wild-flavoured as if they had not been hatched under the tyranny of the game-laws. He has a pleasant trick of making them grateful to the imagination as well as to the palate by packing them in heather. I'll warrant that Aaron's rod bore no bonnier blossoms than these stiff little bushes—and none more magical. For every time I take up a handful of them they transport me to the Highlands, and send me tramping once more, with knapsack and fishing-rod, over the braes and down the burns.

I.
BELL-HEATHER.

Some of my happiest meanderings in Scotland have been taken under the lead of a book. Indeed, for travel in a strange country there can be no better courier. Not a guide-book, I mean, but a real book, and, by preference, a novel.

Fiction, like wine, tastes best in the place where it was grown. And the scenery of a foreign land (including architecture, which is artificial landscape) grows less dreamlike and unreal to our perception when we people it with familiar characters from our favourite novels. Even on a first journey we feel ourselves among old friends. Thus to read *Romola* in Florence, and *Les Misérables* in Paris, and *Lorna Doone* on Exmoor, and *The Heart of Midlothian* in

Edinburgh, and *David Balfour* in the Pass of Glencoe, and *The Pirate* in the Shetland Isles, is to get a new sense of the possibilities of life. All these things have I done with much inward contentment; and other things of like quality have I yet in store; as, for example, the conjunction of *The Bonnie Brier-Bush* with Drumtochty, and *The Little Minister* with Thrums, and *The Raiders* with Galloway. But I never expect to pass pleasanter days than those I spent with *A Princess of Thule* among the Hebrides.

For then, to begin with, I was young; which is an unearned increment of delight sure to be confiscated by the envious years and never regained. But even youth itself was not to be compared with the exquisite felicity of being deeply and desperately in love with Sheila, the clear-eyed heroine of that charming book. In this innocent passion my gray-haired comrades, Howard Crosby, the Chancellor of the University of New York, and my father, an ex-Moderator of the Presbyterian General Assembly, were ardent but generous rivals.

How great is the joy and how fascinating the pursuit of such an ethereal affection! It enlarges the heart without embarrassing the conscience. It is a cup of pure gladness with no bitterness in its dregs. It spends the present moment with a free hand, and yet leaves no undesirable mortgage upon the future. King Arthur, the founder of the Round Table, expressed a conviction, according to Tennyson, that the most important element in a young knight's education is "the maiden passion for a maid." Surely the safest form in which this course in the curriculum may be taken is by falling in love with a girl in a book. It is the only affair of the kind into which a young fellow can enter without responsibility, and out of which he can always emerge, when necessary, without discredit. And as for the old fellow who still keeps up this education of the heart, and worships his heroine with the ardour of a John Ridd and the fidelity of a Henry Esmond, I maintain that he is exempt from all the penalties of declining years. The man who can love a girl in a book may be old, but never aged.

So we sailed, lovers all three, among the Western Isles, and whatever ship it was that carried us, her figurehead was always the Princess Sheila. Along the ruffled blue waters of the sounds and lochs that wind among the roots of unpronounceable mountains, and past the dark hills of Skye, and through the unnumbered flocks of craggy islets where the sea-birds nest, the spell of the sweet Highland maid drew us, and we were pilgrims to the *Ultima Thule* where she lived and reigned.

The Lewis, with its tail-piece, the Harris, is quite a sizable island to be appended to such a country as Scotland. It is a number of miles long, and another number of miles wide, and it has a number of thousand inhabitants—I should say as many as three-quarters of an inhabitant to the square mile—and the conditions of agriculture and the fisheries are extremely interesting and quarrelsome. All these I duly studied at the time, and reported in a series of intolerably dull letters to the newspaper which supplied a financial basis for my sentimental journey. They are full of information; but I have been amused to note, after these many years, how wide they steer of the true motive and interest of the excursion. There is not even a hint of Sheila in any of them. Youth, after all, is a shamefaced and secretive season; like the fringed polygala, it hides its real blossom underground.

It was Sheila's dark-blue dress and sailor hat with the white feather that we looked for as we loafed through the streets of Stornoway, that quaint metropolis of the herring-trade, where strings of fish alternated with boxes of flowers in the windows, and handfuls of fish were spread upon the roofs to dry just as the sliced apples are exposed upon the kitchen-sheds of New England in September, and dark-haired women were carrying great creels of fish on their shoulders, and groups of sunburned men were smoking among the fishing-boats on the beach and talking about fish, and sea-gulls were floating over the houses with their heads turning from side to side and their bright eyes peering everywhere for unconsidered trifles of fish, and the whole atmosphere of the place, physical, mental, and moral, was pervaded with fish. It was Sheila's soft, sing-song Highland speech that we heard through the long, luminous twilight in the pauses of that friendly chat on the balcony of the little inn where a good fortune brought us acquainted with Sam Bough, the mellow Edinburgh painter. It was Sheila's low sweet brow, and long black eyelashes, and tender blue eyes, that we saw before us as we loitered over the open moorland, a far-rolling sea of brown billows, reddened with patches of bell-heather, and brightened here and there with little lakes lying wide open to the sky. And were not these peat-cutters, with the big baskets on their backs, walking in silhouette along the ridges, the people that Sheila loved and tried to help; and were not these crofters' cottages with thatched roofs, like beehives, blending almost imperceptibly with the landscape, the dwellings into which she planned to introduce the luxury of windows; and were not these Standing Stones of Callernish, huge tombstones of a vanished religion, the roofless temple from which the Druids paid their westernmost adoration to the setting sun as he sank into the Atlantic—was not this the place where Sheila picked the bunch of wild flowers and gave it to her lover? There is nothing in history, I am sure, half so real to us as some of the things in fiction. The influence of an event upon our character is little affected by considerations as to whether or not it ever happened.

There were three churches in Stornoway, all Presbyterian, of course, and therefore full of pious emulation. The idea of securing an American preacher for an August Sabbath seemed to fall upon them simultaneously, and to offer the prospect of novelty without too much danger. The brethren of the U. P. congregation, being a trifle more gleg than the others, arrived first at the inn, and secured the promise of a morning sermon from Chancellor Howard Crosby. The session of the Free Kirk came in a body a little later, and to them my father pledged himself for the evening sermon. The senior elder of the Established Kirk, a snuff-taking man and very deliberate, was the last to appear, and to his request for an afternoon sermon there was nothing left to offer but the services of the young probationer in theology. I could see that it struck him as a perilous adventure. Questions about "the fundamentals" glinted in his watery eye. He crossed and uncrossed his legs with solemnity, and blew his nose so frequently in a huge red silk handkerchief that it seemed like a signal of danger. At last he unburdened himself of his hesitations.

"Ah'm not saying that the young man will not be orthodox—ahem! But ye know, sir, in the Kirk, we are not using hymns, but just the pure Psawms of Daffit, in the meetrical fairsion. And ye know, sir, they are ferry tifficult in the reating, whatefer, for a young man, and one that iss a stranger. And if his father will just be coming with him in the pulpit, *to see that nothing iss said amiss, that will be ferry comforting to the congregation.*"

So the dear governor swallowed his laughter gravely and went surety for his son. They appeared together in the church, a barnlike edifice, with great galleries half-way between the floor and the roof. Still higher up, the pulpit stuck like a swallow's nest against the wall. The two ministers climbed the precipitous stair and found themselves in a box so narrow that one must stand perforce, while the other sat upon the only seat. In this "ride and tie" fashion they went through the service. When it was time to preach, the young man dropped the doctrines as discreetly as possible upon the upturned countenances beneath him. I have forgotten now what it was all about, but there was a quotation from the Song of Solomon, ending with "Sweet is thy voice, and thy countenance is comely." And when it came to that, the probationer's eyes (if the truth must be told) went searching through that sea of faces for one that should be familiar to his heart, and to which he might make a personal application of the Scripture passage—even the face of Sheila.

There are rivers in the Lewis, at least two of them, and on one of these we had the offer of a rod for a day's fishing. Accordingly we cast lots, and the lot fell upon the youngest, and I went forth with a tall, red-legged gillie, to try for my first salmon. The Whitewater came singing down out of the moorland into a rocky valley, and there was a merry curl of air on the pools, and the silver fish were leaping from the stream. The gillie handled the big rod as if it had been a fairy's wand, but to me it was like a giant's spear. It was a very different affair from fishing with five ounces of split bamboo on a Long Island trout-pond. The monstrous fly, like an awkward bird, went fluttering everywhere but in the right direction. It was the mercy of Providence that preserved the gillie's life. But he was very patient and forbearing, leading me on from one pool to another, as I spoiled the water and snatched the hook out of the mouth of rising fish, until at last we found a salmon that knew even less about the niceties of salmon-fishing than I did. He seized the fly firmly, before I could pull it away, and then, in a moment, I found myself attached to a creature with the strength of a whale and the agility of a flying-fish. He led me rushing up and down the bank like a madman. He played on the surface like a whirlwind, and sulked at the bottom like a stone. He meditated, with ominous delay, in the middle of the deepest pool, and then, darting across the river, flung himself clean out of water and landed far up on the green turf of the opposite shore. My heart melted like a snowflake in the sea, and I thought that I had lost him forever. But he rolled quietly back into the water with the hook still set in his nose. A few minutes afterwards I brought him within reach of the gaff, and my first salmon was glittering on the grass beside me.

Then I remembered that William Black had described this very fish in *A Princess of Thule*. I pulled the book from my pocket, and, lighting a pipe, sat down to read that delightful chapter over again. The breeze played softly down the valley. The warm sunlight was filled with the musical hum of insects and the murmur of falling waters. I thought how much pleasanter it would have been to learn salmon-fishing, as Black's hero did, from the Maid of Borva, than from a red-headed gillie. But, then, his salmon, after leaping across the stream, got away; whereas mine was safe. A man cannot have everything in this world. I picked a spray of rosy bell-heather from the bank of the river, and pressed it between the leaves of the book in memory of Sheila.

II.
COMMON HEATHER.

It is not half as far from Albany to Aberdeen as it is from New York to London. In fact, I venture to say that an American on foot will find himself less a foreigner in Scotland than in any other country in the Old World. There is something warm and hospitable—if he knew the language well enough he would call it *couthy*—in the greeting that he gets from the shepherd on the moor, and the conversation that he holds with the farmer's wife in the stone cottage, where he stops to ask for a drink of milk and a bit of oat-cake. He feels that there must be a drop of Scotch somewhere in his mingled blood, or at least that the texture of his thought and feelings has been partly woven on a Scottish loom—perhaps the Shorter Catechism, or Robert Burns's poems, or the romances of Sir Walter Scott. At all events, he is among a kindred and comprehending people. They do not speak English in the same way that he does—through the nose—but they think very much more in his mental dialect than the English do. They are independent and wide awake, curious and full of personal interest. The wayside mind in Inverness or Perth runs more to muscle and less to fat, has more active vanity and less passive pride, is more inquisitive and excitable and sympathetic—in short, to use a symbolist's description, it is more apt to be red-headed—than in Surrey or Somerset. Scotchmen ask more questions about America, but fewer foolish ones. You will never hear them inquiring whether there is any good bear-hunting in the neighbourhood of Boston, or whether Shakespeare is much read in the States. They have a healthy respect for our institutions, and have quite forgiven (if, indeed, they ever resented) that little affair in 1776. They are all born Liberals. When a Scotchman says he is a Conservative, it only means that he is a Liberal with hesitations.

And yet in North Britain the American pedestrian will not find that amused and somewhat condescending toleration for his peculiarities, that placid willingness to make the best of all his vagaries of speech and conduct, that he finds in South Britain. In an English town you may do pretty much what you like on a Sunday, even to the extent of wearing a billycock hat to church, and people will put up with it from a country-man of Buffalo Bill and the Wild

West Show. But in a Scotch village, if you whistle in the street on a Lord's Day, though it be a Moody and Sankey tune, you will be likely to get, as I did, an admonition from some long-legged, grizzled elder:

"Young man, do ye no ken it 's the Sawbath Day?"

I recognised the reproof of the righteous, an excellent oil which doth not break the head, and took it gratefully at the old man's hands. For did it not prove that he regarded me as a man and a brother, a creature capable of being civilised and saved?

It was in the gray town of Dingwall that I had this bit of pleasant correction, as I was on the way to a fishing tramp through Sutherlandshire. This northwest corner of Great Britain is the best place in the whole island for a modest and impecunious angler. There are, or there were a few years ago, wild lochs and streams which are still practically free, and a man who is content with small things can pick up some very pretty sport from the highland inns, and make a good basket of memorable experiences every week.

The inn at Lairg, overlooking the narrow waters of Loch Shin, was embowered in honeysuckles, and full of creature comfort. But there were too many other men with rods there to suit my taste. "The feesh in this loch," said the boatman, "iss not so numerous ass the feeshermen, but more wise. There iss not one of them that hass not felt the hook, and they know ferry well what side of the fly has the forkit tail."

At Altnaharra, in the shadow of Ben Clebrig, there was a cozy little house with good fare, and abundant trout-fishing in Loch Naver and Loch Meadie. It was there that I fell in with a wandering pearl-peddler who gathered his wares from the mussels in the moorland streams. They were not of the finest quality, these Scotch pearls, but they had pretty, changeable colours of pink and blue upon them, like the iridescent light that plays over the heather in the long northern evenings. I thought it must be a hard life for the man, wading day after day in the ice-cold water, and groping among the coggly, sliddery stones for the shellfish, and cracking open perhaps a thousand before he could find one pearl. "Oh, yess," said he, "and it iss not an easy life, and I am not saying that it will be so warm and dry ass liffing in a rich house. But it iss the life that I am fit for, and I hef my own time and my thoughts to mysel', and that is a ferry goot thing; and then, sir, I haf found the Pearl of Great Price, and I think upon that day and night."

Under the black, shattered peaks of Ben Laoghal, where I saw an eagle poising day after day as if some invisible centripetal force bound him forever to that small circle of air, there was a loch with plenty of brown trout and a few *salmo ferox*; and down at Tongue there was a little river where the sea-trout sometimes come up with the tide.

Here I found myself upon the north coast, and took the road eastward between the mountains and the sea. It was a beautiful region of desolation. There were rocky glens cutting across the road, and occasionally a brawling stream ran down to the salt water, breaking the line of cliffs with a little bay and a half-moon of yellow sand. The heather covered all the hills. There were no trees, and but few houses. The chief signs of human labour were the rounded piles of peat, and the square cuttings in the moor marking the places where the subterranean wood-choppers had gathered their harvests. The long straths were once cultivated, and every patch of arable land had its group of cottages full of children. The human harvest has always been the richest and most abundant that is raised in the Highlands; but unfortunately the supply exceeded the demand; and so the crofters were evicted, and great flocks of sheep were put in possession of the land; and now the sheep-pastures have been changed into deer-forests; and far and wide along the valleys and across the hills there is not a trace of habitation, except the heaps of stones and the clumps of straggling bushes which mark the sites of lost homes. But what is one country's loss is another country's gain. Canada and the United States are infinitely the richer for the tough, strong, fearless, honest men that were dispersed from these lonely straths to make new homes across the sea.

It was after sundown when I reached the straggling village of Melvich, and the long day's journey had left me weary. But the inn, with its red-curtained windows, looked bright and reassuring. Thoughts of dinner and a good bed comforted my spirit—prematurely. For the inn was full. There were but five bedrooms and two parlours. The gentlemen who had the neighbouring shootings occupied three bedrooms and a parlour; the other two bedrooms had just been taken by the English fishermen who had passed me in the road an hour ago in the mail-coach (oh! why had I not suspected that treacherous vehicle?); and the landlord and his wife assured me, with equal firmness and sympathy, that there was not another cot or pair of blankets in the house. I believed them, and was sinking into despair when Sandy M'Kaye appeared on the scene as my angel of deliverance. Sandy was a small, withered, wiry man, dressed in rusty gray, with an immense white collar thrusting out its points on either side of his chin, and a black stock climbing over the top of it. I guessed from his speech that he had once lived in the lowlands. He had hoped to be engaged as a gillie by the shooting party, but had been disappointed. He had wanted to be taken by the English fishermen, but another and younger man had stepped in before him. Now Sandy saw in me his Predestinated Opportunity, and had no idea of letting it post up the road that night to the next village. He cleared his throat respectfully and cut into the conversation.

"Ah'm thinkin' the gentleman micht find a coomfortaible lodgin' wi' the weedow Macphairson a wee bittie doon the road. Her dochter is awa' in Ameriky, an' the room is a verra fine room, an' it is a peety to hae it stannin' idle, an' ye wudna mind the few steps to and fro tae yir meals here, sir, wud ye? An' if ye 'ill gang wi' me efter dinner, 'a 'll be prood to shoo ye the hoose."

So, after a good dinner with the English fishermen, Sandy piloted me down the road through the thickening dusk. I remember a hoodie crow flew close behind us with a choking, ghostly cough that startled me. The Macpherson cottage was a snug little house of stone, with fuchsias and roses growing in the front yard: and the widow was a douce old lady, with a face like a winter apple in the month of April, wrinkled, but still rosy. She was a little doubtful about entertaining strangers, but when she heard I was from America she opened the doors of her house and her heart. And when, by a subtle cross examination that would have been a credit to the wife of a Connecticut deacon, she discovered the fact that her lodger was a minister, she did two things, with equal and immediate fervour; she brought out the big Bible and asked him to conduct evening worship, and she produced a bottle of old Glenlivet and begged him to "guard against takkin' cauld by takkin' a glass of speerits."

It was a very pleasant fortnight at Melvich. Mistress Macpherson was so motherly that "takkin' cauld" was reduced to a permanent impossibility. The other men at the inn proved to be very companionable fellows, quite different from the monsters of insolence that my anger had imagined in the moment of disappointment. The shooting party kept the table abundantly supplied with grouse and hares and highland venison; and there was a piper to march up and down before the window and play while we ate dinner—a very complimentary and disquieting performance. But there are many occasions in life when pride can be entertained only at the expense of comfort.

Of course Sandy was my gillie. It was a fine sight to see him exhibiting the tiny American trout-rod, tied with silk ribbons in its delicatecase, to the other gillies and exulting over them. Every morning he would lead me away through the heather to some lonely loch on the shoulders of the hills, from which we could look down upon the Northern Sea and the blue Orkney Isles far away across the Pentland Firth. Sometimes we would find a loch with a boat on it, and drift up and down, casting along the shores. Sometimes, in spite of Sandy's confident predictions, no boat could be found, and then I must put on the Mackintosh trousers and wade out over my hips into the water, and circumambulate the pond, throwing the flies as far as possible toward the middle, and feeling my way carefully along the bottom with the long net-handle, while Sandy danced on the bank in an agony of apprehension lest his Predestinated Opportunity should step into a deep hole and be drowned. It was a curious fact in natural history that on the lochs with boats the trout were in the shallow water, but in the boatless lochs they were away out in the depths. "Juist the total depraivity o' troots," said Sandy, "an' terrible fateegin'."

Sandy had an aversion to commit himself to definite statements on any subject not theological. If you asked him how long the morning's tramp would be, it was "no verra long, juist a bit ayant the hull yonner." And if, at the end of the seventh mile, you complained that it was much too far, he would never do more than admit that "it micht be shorter." If you called him to rejoice over a trout that weighed close upon two pounds, he allowed that it was "no bad—but there's bigger anes i' the loch gin we cud but wile them oot." And at lunch-time, when we turned out a full basket of shining fish on the heather, the most that he would say, while his eyes snapped with joy and pride, was, "Aweel, we canna complain, the day."

Then he would gather an armful of dried heather-stems for kindling, and dig out a few roots and crooked limbs of the long-vanished forest from the dry, brown, peaty soil, and make our camp-fire of prehistoric wood—just for the pleasant, homelike look of the blaze—and sit down beside it to eat our lunch. Heat is the least of the benefits that man gets from fire. It is the sign of cheerfulness and good comradeship. I would not willingly satisfy my hunger, even in a summer nooning, without a little flame burning on a rustic altar to consecrate and enliven the feast. When the bread and cheese were finished and the pipes were filled with Virginia tobacco, Sandy would begin to tell me, very solemnly and respectfully, about the mistakes I had made in the fishing that day, and mourn over the fact that the largest fish had not been hooked. There was a strong strain of pessimism in Sandy, and he enjoyed this part of the sport immensely.

But he was at his best in the walk home through the lingering twilight, when the murmur of the sea trembled through the air, and the incense of burning peat floated up from the cottages, and the stars blossomed one by one in the pale-green sky. Then Sandy dandered on at his ease down the hills, and discoursed of things in heaven and earth. He was an unconscious follower of the theology of the Reverend John Jasper, of Richmond, Virginia, and rejected the Copernican theory of the universe as inconsistent with the history of Joshua. "Gin the sun doesna muve," said he, "what for wad Joshua be tellin' him to stond steel? 'A wad suner beleeve there was a mistak' in the veesible heevens than ae fault in the Guid Buik." Whereupon we held long discourse of astronomy and inspiration; but Sandy concluded it with a philosophic word which left little to be said: "Aweel, yon teelescope is a wonnerful deescovery; but 'a dinna think the less o' the Baible."

III.
WHITE HEATHER.

Memory is a capricious and arbitrary creature. You never can tell what pebble she will pick up from the shore of life to keep among her treasures, or what inconspicuous flower of the field she will preserve as the symbol of

"Thoughts that do often lie too deep for tears."

She has her own scale of values for these mementos, and knows nothing of the market price of precious stones or the costly splendour of rare orchids. The thing that pleases her is the thing that she will hold fast. And yet I do not doubt that the most important things are always the best remembered; only we must learn that the real importance of what we see and hear in the world is to be measured at last by its meaning, its significance, its intimacy with the heart of our heart and the life of our life. And when we find a little token of the past very safely and imperishably kept among our recollections, we must believe that memory has made no mistake. It is because that little thing has entered into our experience most deeply, that it stays with us and we cannot lose it.

You have half forgotten many a famous scene that you travelled far to look upon. You cannot clearly recall the sublime peak of Mont Blanc, the roaring curve of Niagara, the vast dome of St. Peter's. The music of Patti's crystalline voice has left no distinct echo in your remembrance, and the blossoming of the century-plant is dimmer than the shadow of a dream. But there is a nameless valley among the hills where you can still trace every curve of the stream, and see the foam-bells floating on the pool below the bridge, and the long moss wavering in the current. There is a rustic song of a girl passing through the fields at sunset, that still repeats its far-off cadence in your listening ears. There is a small flower trembling on its stem in some hidden nook beneath the open sky, that never withers through all the changing years; the wind passes over it, but it is not gone—it abides forever in your soul, an amaranthine blossom of beauty and truth.

White heather is not an easy flower to find. You may look for it among the highlands for a day without success. And when it is discovered, there is little outward charm to commend it. It lacks the grace of the dainty bells that hang so abundantly from the *Erica Tetralix*, and the pink glow of the innumerable blossoms of the common heather. But then it is a symbol. It is the Scotch *Edelweiss*. It means sincere affection, and unselfish love, and tender wishes as pure as prayers. I shall always remember the evening when I found the white heather on the moorland above Glen Ericht. Or, rather, it was not I that found it (for I have little luck in the discovery of good omens, and have never plucked a four-leaved clover in my life), but my companion, the gentle Mistress of the Glen, whose hair was as white as the tiny blossoms, and yet whose eyes were far quicker than mine to see and name every flower that bloomed in those lofty, widespread fields.

Ericht Water is formed by the marriage of two streams, one flowing out of Strath Ardle and the other descending from Cairn Gowar through the long, lonely Pass of Glenshee. The Ericht begins at the bridge of Cally, and its placid, beautiful glen, unmarred by railway or factory, reaches almost down to Blairgowrie. On the southern bank, but far above the water, runs the high road to Braemar and the Linn of Dee. On the other side of the river, nestling among the trees, is the low white manor-house,

"*An ancient home of peace.*"

It is a place where one who had been wearied and perchance sore wounded in the battle of life might well desire to be carried, as Arthur to the island valley of Avilion, for rest and healing.

I have no thought of renewing the conflicts and cares that filled that summer with sorrow. There were fightings without and fears within; there was the surrender of an enterprise that had been cherished since boyhood, and the bitter sense of irremediable weakness that follows such a reverse; there was a touch of that wrath with those we love, which, as Coleridge says,

"*Doth work like madness in the brain;*"

flying across the sea from these troubles, I had found my old comrade of merrier days sentenced to death, and caught but a brief glimpse of his pale, brave face as he went away into exile. At such a time the sun and the light and the moon and the stars are darkened, and the clouds return after rain. But through those clouds the Mistress of the Glen came to meet me—a stranger till then, but an appointed friend, a minister of needed grace, an angel of quiet comfort. The thick mists of rebellion, mistrust, and despair have long since rolled away, and against the background of the hills her figure stands out clearly, dressed in the fashion of fifty years ago, with the snowy hairgathered close beneath her widow's cap, and a spray of white heather in her outstretched hand.

There were no other guests in the house by the river during those still days in the noontide hush of midsummer. Every morning, while the Mistress was busied with her household cares and letters, I would be out in the fields hearing the lark sing, and watching the rabbits as they ran to and fro, scattering the dew from the grass in a glittering spray. Or perhaps I would be angling down the river, with the swift pressure of the water around my knees, and an inarticulate current of cooling thoughts flowing on and on through my brain like the murmur of the stream. Every afternoon there were long walks with the Mistress in the old-fashioned garden, where wonderful roses were blooming; or through the dark, fir-shaded den where the wild burn dropped down to join the river; or out upon the high moor under the waning orange sunset. Every night there were luminous and restful talks beside the open fire in the library, when the words came clear and calm from the heart, unperturbed by the vain desire of saying brilliant things, which turns so much of our conversation into a combat of wits instead of an interchange of thoughts. Talk like this is possible only between two. The arrival of a third person sets the lists for a tournament, and offers the prize for a verbal victory. But where there are only two, the armour is laid aside, and there is no call to thrust and parry.

One of the two should be a good listener, sympathetic, but not silent, giving confidence in order to attract it—and of this art a woman is the best master. But its finest secrets do not come to her until she has passed beyond the uncertain season of compliments and conquests, and entered into the serenity of a tranquil age.

What is this foolish thing that men say about the impossibility of true intimacy and converse between the young and the old? Hamerton, for example, in his book on *Human Intercourse*, would have us believe that a difference in years is a barrier between hearts. For my part, I have more often found it an open door, and a security of generous and tolerant welcome for the young soldier, who comes in tired and dusty from the battle-field, to tell his story of defeat or victory in the garden of still thoughts where old age is resting in the peace of honourable discharge. I like what Robert Louis Stevenson says about it in his essay on *Talk and Talkers*.

"Not only is the presence of the aged in itself remedial, but their minds are stored with antidotes, wisdom's simples, plain considerations overlooked by youth. They have matter to communicate, be they never so stupid. Their talk is not merely literature, it is great literature; classic by virtue of the speaker's detachment; studded, like a book of travel, with things we should not otherwise have learnt.... Where youth agrees with age, not where they differ, wisdom lies; and it is when the young disciple finds his heart to beat in tune with his gray-haired teacher's that a lesson may be learned."

The conversation of the Mistress of the Glen shone like the light and distilled like the dew, not only by virtue of what she said, but still more by virtue of what she was. Her face was a good counsel against discouragement; and the cheerful quietude of her demeanour was a rebuke to all rebellious, cowardly, and discontented thoughts. It was not the striking novelty or profundity of her commentary on life that made it memorable, it was simply the truth of what she said and the gentleness with which she said it. Epigrams are worth little for guidance to the perplexed, and less for comfort to the wounded. But the plain, homely sayings which come from a soul that has learned the lesson of patient courage in the school of real experience, fall upon the wound like drops of balsam, and like a soothing lotion upon the eyes smarting and blinded with passion.

She spoke of those who had walked with her long ago in her garden, and for whose sake, now that they had all gone into the world of light, every flower was doubly dear. Would it be a true proof of loyalty to them if she lived gloomily or despondently because they were away? She spoke of the duty of being ready to welcome happiness as well as to endure pain, and of the strength that endurance wins by being grateful for small daily joys, like the evening light, and the smell of roses, and the singing of birds. She spoke of the faith that rests on the Unseen Wisdom and Love like a child on its mother's breast, and of the melting away of doubts in the warmth of an effort to do some good in the world. And if that effort has conflict, and adventure, and confused noise, and mistakes, and even defeats mingled with it, in the stormy years of youth, is not that to be expected? The burn roars and leaps in the den; the stream chafes and frets through the rapids of the glen; the river does not grow calm and smooth until it nears the sea. Courage is a virtue that the young cannot spare; to lose it is to grow old before the time; it is better to make a thousand mistakes and suffer a thousand reverses than to refuse the battle. Resignation is the final courage of old age; it arrives in its own season; and it is a good day when it comes to us. Then there are no more disappointments; for we have learned that it is even better to desire the things that we have than to have the things that we desire. And is not the best of all our hopes—the hope of immortality—always before us? How can we be dull or heavy while we have that new experience to look forward to? It will be the most joyful of all our travels and adventures. It will bring us our best acquaintances and friendships. But there is only one way to get ready for immortality, and that is to love this life, and live it as bravely and cheerfully and faithfully as we can.

So my gentle teacher with the silver hair showed me the treasures of her ancient, simple faith; and I felt that no sermons, nor books, nor arguments can strengthen the doubting heart so deeply as just to come into touch with a soul which has proved the truth of that plain religion whose highest philosophy is "Trust in the Lord and do good." At the end of the evening the household was gathered for prayers, and the Mistress kneeled among her servants, leading them, in her soft Scottish accent, through the old familiar petitions for pardon for the errors of the day, and refreshing sleep through the night and strength for the morrow. It is good to be in a land where the people are not ashamed to pray. I have shared the blessing of Catholics at their table in lowly huts among the mountains of the Tyrol, and knelt with Covenanters at their household altar in the glens of Scotland; and all around the world, where the spirit of prayer is, there is peace. The genius of the Scotch has made many contributions to literature, but none I think, more precious, and none that comes closer to the heart, than the prayer which Robert Louis Stevenson wrote for his family in distant Samoa, the night before he died:—

"We beseech thee, Lord, to behold us with favour, folk of many families and nations, gathered together in the peace of this roof: weak men and women subsisting under the covert of thy patience. Be patient still; suffer us yet a while longer—with our broken promises of good, with our idle endeavours against evil—suffer us a while longer to endure, and (if it may be) help us to do better. Bless to us our extraordinary mercies; if the day come when these must be taken, have us play the man under affliction. Be with our friends, be with ourselves. Go with each of us to rest; if any awake, temper to them the dark hours of watching; and when the day returns to us—our sun and comforter—call us with morning faces, eager to labour, eager to be happy, if happiness shall be our portion, and, if the day be marked to sorrow, strong to endure it. We thank thee and praise thee; and, in the words of Him to whom this day is sacred, close our oblation."

The man who made that kindly human prayer knew the meaning of white heather. And I dare to hope that I too have known something of its meaning, since that evening when the Mistress of the Glen picked the spray and gave it to me on the lonely moor. "And now," she said, "you will be going home across the sea; and you have been welcome here, but it is time that you should go, for there is the place where your real duties and troubles and joys are waiting for you. And if you have left any misunderstandings behind you, you will try to clear them up; and if there have been any quarrels, you will heal them. Carry this little flower with you. It's not the bonniest blossom in Scotland, but it's the dearest, for the message that it brings. And you will remember that love is not getting, but giving; not a wild dream of pleasure, and a madness of desire—oh no, love is not that—it is goodness, and honour, and peace, and pure living—yes, love is that; and it is the best thing in the world, and the thing that lives longest. And that is what I am wishing for you and yours with this bit of white heather."

1893.

THE RISTIGOUCHE FROM A HORSE-YACHT

"Dr. Paley was ardently attached to this amusement; so much so, that when the Bishop of Durham inquired of him when one of his most important works would be finished, he said, with great simplicity and good humour, 'My Lord, I shall work steadily at it when the fly-fishing season is over.'"——
SIR HUMPHRY DAVY: *Salmonia*.

THE RISTIGOUCHE FROM A HORSE-YACHT

The boundary line between the Province of Quebec and New Brunswick, for a considerable part of its course, resembles the name of the poet Keats; it is "writ in water." But like his fame, it is water that never fails,—the limpid current of the river Ristigouche.

The railway crawls over it on a long bridge at Metapedia, and you are dropped in the darkness somewhere between midnight and dawn. When you open your window-shutters the next morning, you see that the village is a disconsolate hamlet, scattered along the track as if it had been shaken by chance from an open freight-car; it consists of twenty houses, three shops, and a discouraged church perched upon a little hillock like a solitary mourner on the anxious seat. The one comfortable and prosperous feature in the countenance of Metapedia is the house of the Ristigouche Salmon Club—an old-fashioned mansion, with broad, white piazza, looking over rich meadow-lands. Here it was that I found my friend Favonius, president of solemn societies, pillar of church and state, ingenuously arrayed in gray knickerbockers, a flannel shirt, and a soft hat, waiting to take me on his horse-yacht for a voyage up the river.

Have you ever seen a horse-yacht? Sometimes it is called a scow; but that sounds common. Sometimes it is called a house-boat; but that is too English. What does it profit a man to have a whole dictionary full of language at his service, unless he can invent a new and suggestive name for his friend's pleasure-craft? The foundation of the horse-yacht—if a thing that floats may be called fundamental—is a flat-bottomed boat, some fifty feet long and ten feet wide, with a draft of about eight inches. The deck is open for fifteen feet aft of the place where the bowsprit ought to be; behind that it is completely covered by a house, cabin, cottage, or whatever you choose to call it, with straight sides and a peaked roof of a very early Gothic pattern. Looking in at the door you see, first of all, two cots, one on either side of the passage; then an open space with a dining-table, a stove, and some chairs; beyond that a pantry with shelves, and a great chest for provisions. A door at the back opens into the kitchen, and from that another door opens into a sleeping-room for the boatmen. A huge wooden tiller curves over the stern of the boat, and the helmsman stands upon the kitchen-roof. Two canoes are floating behind, holding back, at the end of their long tow-ropes, as if reluctant to follow so clumsy a leader. This is an accurate description of the horse-yacht. If necessary it could be sworn to before a notary public. But I am perfectly sure that you might read this page through without skipping a word, and if you had never seen the creature with your own eyes, you would have no idea how absurd it looks and how comfortable it is.

While we were stowing away our trunks and bags under the cots, and making an equitable division of the hooks upon the walls, the motive power of the yacht stood patiently upon the shore, stamping a hoof, now and then, or shaking a shaggy head in mild protest against the flies. Three more pessimistic-looking horses I never saw. They were harnessed abreast, and fastened by a prodigious tow-rope to a short post in the middle of the forward deck. Their driver was a truculent, brigandish, bearded old fellow in long boots, a blue flannel shirt, and a black sombrero. He sat upon the middle horse, and some wild instinct of colour had made him tie a big red handkerchief around his shoulders, so that the eye of the beholder took delight in him. He posed like a bold, bad robber-chief. But in point of fact I believe he was the mildest and most inoffensive of men. We never heard him say anything except at a distance, to his horses, and we did not inquire what that was.

Well, as I have said, we were haggling courteously over those hooks in the cabin, when the boat gave a lurch. The bow swung out into the stream. There was a scrambling and clattering of iron horse-shoes on the rough shingle of the bank; and when we looked out of doors, our house was moving up the river with the boat under it.

The Ristigouche is a noble stream, stately and swift and strong. It rises among the dense forests in the northern part of New Brunswick—a moist upland region, of never-failing springs and innumerable lakes—and pours a flood of clear, cold water one hundred and fifty miles northward and eastward through the hills into the head of the Bay of Chaleurs. There are no falls in its course, but rapids everywhere. It is steadfast but not impetuous, quick but not turbulent, resolute and eager in its desire to get to the sea, like the life of a man who has a purpose,

"Too great for haste, too high for rivalry."

The wonder is where all the water comes from. But the river is fed by more than six thousand square miles of territory. From both sides the little brooks come dashing in with their supply. At intervals a larger stream, reaching away back among the mountains like a hand with many fingers to gather

"The filtered tribute of the rough woodland,"

delivers its generous offering to the main current.

The names of the chief tributaries of the Ristigouche are curious. There is the headstrong Metapedia, and the crooked Upsalquitch, and the Patapedia, and the Quatawamkedgwick. These are words at which the tongue balks at first, but you soon grow used to them and learn to take anything of five syllables with a rush, as a hunter takes a five-barred gate, trusting to fortune that you will come down with the accent in the right place.

For six or seven miles above Metapedia the river has a breadth of about two hundred yards, and the valley slopes back rather gently to the mountains on either side. There is a good deal of cultivated land, and scattered farm-houses appear. The soil is excellent. But it is like a pearl cast before an obstinate, unfriendly climate. Late frosts prolong the winter. Early frosts curtail the summer. The only safe crops are grass, oats, and potatoes. And for half the year all the cattle must be housed and fed to keep them alive. This lends a melancholy aspect to agriculture. Most of the farmers look as if they had never seen better days. With few exceptions they are what a New Englander would call "slack-twisted and shiftless." Their barns are pervious to the weather, and their fences fail to connect. Sleds and ploughs rust together beside the house, and chickens scratch up the front-door yard. In truth, the people have been somewhat demoralised by the conflicting claims of different occupations; hunting in the fall, lumbering in the winter and spring, and working for the American sportsmen in the brief angling season, are so much more attractive and offer so much larger returns of ready money, that the tedious toil of farming is neglected. But for all that, in the bright days of midsummer, these green fields sloping down to the water, and pastures high up among the trees on the hillsides, look pleasant from a distance, and give an inhabited air to the landscape.

At the mouth of the Upsalquitch we passed the first of the fishing-lodges. It belongs to a sage angler from Albany who saw the beauty of the situation, years ago, and built a habitation to match it. Since that time a number of gentlemen have bought land fronting on good pools, and put up little cottages of a less classical style than Charles Cotton's "Fisherman's Retreat" on the banks of the river Dove, but better suited to this wild scenery, and more convenient to live in. The prevailing pattern is a very simple one; it consists of a broad piazza with a small house in the middle of it. The house bears about the same proportion to the piazza that the crown of a Gainsborough hat does to the brim. And the cost of the edifice is to the cost of the land as the first price of a share in a bankrupt railway is to the assessments which follow the reorganisation. All the best points have been sold, and real estate on the Ristigouche has been bid up to an absurd figure. In fact, the river is over-populated and probably over-fished. But we could hardly find it in our hearts to regret this, for it made the upward trip a very sociable one. At every lodge that was open, Favonius (who knows everybody) had a friend, and we must slip ashore in a canoe to leave the mail and refresh the inner man.

An angler, like an Arab, regards hospitality as a religious duty. There seems to be something in the craft which inclines the heart to kindness and good-fellowship. Few anglers have I seen who were not pleasant to meet, and ready to do a good turn to a fellow-fisherman with the gift of a killing fly or the loan of a rod. Not their own particular and well-proved favourite, of course, for that is a treasure which no decent man would borrow; but with that exception the best in their store is at the service of an accredited brother. One of the Ristigouche proprietors I remember, whose name bespoke him a descendant of Caledonia's patron saint. He was fishing in front of his own door when we came up, with our splashing horses, through the pool; but nothing would do but he must up anchor and have us away with him into the house to taste his good cheer. And there were his daughters with their books and needlework, and the photographs which they had taken pinned up on the wooden walls, among Japanese fans and bits of bright-coloured stuff in which the soul of woman delights, and, in a passive, silent way, the soul of man also. Then, after we had discussed the year's fishing, and the mysteries of the camera, and the deep question of what makes some negatives too thin and others too thick, we must go out to see the big salmon which one of the ladies had caught a few days before, and the large trout swimming about in their cold spring. It seemed to me, as we went on our way, that there could hardly be a more wholesome and pleasant summer-life for well-bred young women than this, or two amusements more innocent and sensible than photography and fly-fishing.

It must be confessed that the horse-yacht as a vehicle of travel is not remarkable in point of speed. Three miles an hour is not a very rapid rate of motion. But then, if you are not in a hurry, why should you care to make haste?

The wild desire to be forever racing against old Father Time is one of the kill-joys of modern life. That ancient traveller is sure to beat you in the long run, and as long as you are trying to rival him, he will make your life a burden. But if you will only acknowledge his superiority and profess that you do not approve of racing after all, he will settle down quietly beside you and jog along like the most companionable of creatures. That is a pleasant pilgrimage in which the journey itself is part of the destination.

As soon as one learns to regard the horse-yacht as a sort of moving house, it appears admirable. There is no dust or smoke, no rumble of wheels, or shriek of whistles. You are gliding along steadily through an ever-green world; skirting the silent hills; passing from one side of the river to the other when the horses have to swim the current to find a good foothold on the bank. You are on the water, but not at its mercy, for your craft is not disturbed by the heaving of rude waves, and the serene inhabitants do not say "I am sick." There is room enough to move about without falling overboard. You may sleep, or read, or write in your cabin, or sit upon the floating piazza in an arm-chair and smoke the pipe of peace, while the cool breeze blows in your face and the musical waves go singing down to the sea.

There was one feature about the boat, which commended itself very strongly to my mind. It was possible to stand upon the forward deck and do a little trout-fishing in motion. By watching your chance, when the corner of a good pool was within easy reach, you could send out a hasty line and cajole a sea-trout from his hiding-place. It is true that the tow-ropes and the post made the back cast a little awkward; and the wind sometimes blew the flies up on the roof of the cabin; but then, with patience and a short line the thing could be done. I remember a pair of good trout that rose together just as we were going through a boiling rapid; and it tried the strength of my split-bamboo rod to bring those fish to the net against the current and the motion of the boat.

When nightfall approached we let go the anchor (to wit, a rope tied to a large stone on the shore), ate our dinner "with gladness and singleness of heart" like the early Christians, and slept the sleep of the just, lulled by the murmuring of the waters, and defended from the insidious attacks of the mosquito by the breeze blowing down the river and the impregnable curtains over our beds. At daybreak, long before Favonius and I had finished our dreams, we were under way again; and when the trampling of the horses on some rocky shore wakened us, we could see the steep hills gliding past the windows and hear the rapids dashing against the side of the boat, and it seemed as if we were still dreaming.

At Cross Point, where the river makes a long loop around a narrow mountain, thin as a saw and crowned on its jagged edge by a rude wooden cross, we stopped for an hour to try the fishing. It was here that I hooked two mysterious creatures, each of which took the fly when it was below the surface, pulled for a few moments in a sullen way and then apparently melted into nothingness. It will always be a source of regret to me that the nature of these fish must remain unknown. While they were on the line it was the general opinion that they were heavy trout; but no sooner had they departed, than I became firmly convinced, in accordance with a psychological law which holds good all over the world, that they were both enormous salmon. Even the Turks have a proverb which says, "Every fish that escapes appears larger than it is." No one can alter that conviction, because no one can logically refute it. Our best blessings, like our largest fish, always depart before we have time to measure them.

The Slide Pool is in the wildest and most picturesque part of the river, about thirty-five miles above Metapedia. The stream, flowing swiftly down a stretch of rapids between forest-clad hills, runs straight toward the base of an eminence so precipitous that the trees can hardly find a foothold upon it, and seem to be climbing up in haste on either side of the long slide which leads to the summit. The current, barred by the wall of rock, takes a great sweep to the right, dashing up at first in angry waves, then falling away in oily curves and eddies, until at last it sleeps in a black deep, apparently almost motionless, at the foot of the hill. It was here, on the upper edge of the stream, opposite to the slide, that we brought our floating camp to anchor for some days. What does one do in such a watering-place?

Let us take a "specimen day." It is early morning, or to be more precise, about eight of the clock, and the white fog is just beginning to curl and drift away from the surface of the river. Sooner than this it would be idle to go out. The preternaturally early bird in his greedy haste may catch the worm; but the salmon never take the fly until the fog has lifted; and in this the scientific angler sees, with gratitude, a remarkable adaptation of the laws of nature to the tastes of man. The canoes are waiting at the front door. We step into them and push off, Favonius going up the stream a couple of miles to the mouth of the Patapedia, and I down, a little shorter distance, to the famous Indian House Pool. The slim boat glides easily on the current, with a smooth buoyant motion, quickened by the strokes of the paddles in the bow and the stern. We pass around two curves in the river and find ourselves at the head of the pool. Here the man in the stern drops the anchor, just on the edge of the bar where the rapid breaks over into the deeper water. The long rod is lifted; the fly unhooked from the reel; a few feet of line pulled through the rings, and the fishing begins.

First cast,—to the right, straight across the stream, about twenty feet: the current carries the fly down with a semicircular sweep, until it comes in line with the bow of the canoe. Second cast,—to the left, straight across the stream, with the same motion: the semicircle is completed, and the fly hangs quivering for a few seconds at the lowest point of the arc. Three or four feet of line are drawn from the reel. Third cast to the right; fourth cast to the left. Then a little more line. And so, with widening half-circles, the water is covered, gradually and very carefully, until at length the angler has as much line out as his two-handed rod can lift and swing. Then the first "drop" is finished; the man in the stern quietly pulls up the anchor and lets the boat drift down a few yards; the same process is repeated on the second drop; and so on, until the end of the run is reached and the fly has passed over all the good water. This seems like a very regular and somewhat mechanical proceeding as one describes it, but in the performance it is rendered intensely interesting by the knowledge that at any moment it is liable to be interrupted.

This morning the interruption comes early. At the first cast of the second drop, before the fly has fairly lit, a great flash of silver darts from the waves close by the boat. Usually a salmon takes the fly rather slowly, carrying it under water before he seizes it in his mouth. But this one is in no mood for deliberation. He has hooked himself with a rush, and the line goes whirring madly from the reel as he races down the pool. Keep the point of the rod low; he must have his own way now. Up with the anchor quickly, and send the canoe after him, bowman and sternman paddling with swift strokes. He has reached the deepest water; he stops to think what has happened to him; we have passed around and below him; and now, with the current to help us, we can begin to reel in. Lift the point of the rod, with a strong, steady pull. Put the force of both arms into it. The tough wood will stand the strain. The fish must be moved; he must come to the boat if he is ever to be landed. He gives a little and yields slowly to the pressure. Then suddenly he gives too much, and runs straight toward us. Reel in now as swiftly as possible, or else he will get a slack on the line and escape. Now he stops, shakes his head from side to side, and darts away again across the pool, leaping high out of water. Don't touch the reel! Drop the point of the rod quickly, for if he falls on the leader he will surely break it. Another leap, and another! Truly he is "a merry one," and it will go hard with us to hold him. But those great leaps have exhausted his strength, and now he follows the rod more easily. The men push the boat back to the shallow side of the pool until it touches lightly on the shore. The fish comes slowly in, fighting a little and making a few short runs; he is tired and turns slightly on his side; but even yet he is a heavy weight on the line, and it seems a wonder that so slight a thing as the leader can guide and draw him. Now he is close to the boat. The boatman steps out on a rock with his gaff. Steadily now and slowly, lift the rod, bending it backward. A quick sure stroke of the steel! a great splash! and the salmon is lifted upon the shore. How he flounces about on the stones. Give him the *coup de grace* at once, for his own sake as well as for ours. And now look at him, as he lies there on the green leaves. Broad back; small head tapering to a point; clean, shining sides with a few black spots on them; it is a fish fresh-run from the sea, in perfect condition, and that is the reason why he has given such good sport.

We must try for another before we go back. Again fortune favours us, and at eleven o'clock we pole up the river to the camp with two good salmon in the canoe. Hardly have we laid them away in the ice-box, when Favonius comes dropping down from Patapedia with three fish, one of them a twenty-four pounder. And so the morning's work is done.

In the evening, after dinner, it was our custom to sit out on the deck, watching the moonlight as it fell softly over the black hills and changed the river into a pale flood of rolling gold. The fragrant wreaths of smoke floated lazily away on the faint breeze of night. There was no sound save the rushing of the water and the crackling of the camp-fire on the shore. We talked of many things in the heavens above, and the earth beneath, and the waters under the earth; touching lightly here and there as the spirit of vagrant converse led us. Favonius has the good sense to talk about himself occasionally and tell his own experience. The man who will not do that must always be a dull companion. Modest egoism is the salt of conversation: you do not want too much of it; but if it is altogether omitted, everything tastes flat. I remember well the evening when he told me the story of the Sheep of the Wilderness.

"I was ill that summer," said he, "and the doctor had ordered me to go into the woods, but on no account to go without plenty of fresh meat, which was essential to my recovery. So we set out into the wild country north of Georgian Bay, taking a live sheep with us in order to be sure that the doctor's prescription might be faithfully followed. It was a young and innocent little beast, curling itself up at my feet in the canoe, and following me about on shore like a dog. I gathered grass every day to feed it, and carried it in my arms over the rough portages. It ate out of my hand and rubbed its woolly head against my leggings. To my dismay, I found that I was beginning to love it for its own sake and without any ulterior motives. The thought of killing and eating it became more and more painful to me, until at length the fatal fascination was complete, and my trip became practically an exercise of devotion to that sheep. I carried it everywhere and ministered fondly to its wants. Not for the world would I have alluded to mutton in its presence. And when we returned to civilisation I parted from the creature with sincere regret and the consciousness that I had humoured my affections at the expense of my digestion. The sheep did not give me so much as a look of farewell, but fell to feeding on the grass beside the farm-house with an air of placid triumph."

After hearing this touching tale, I was glad that no great intimacy had sprung up between Favonius and the chickens which we carried in a coop on the forecastle head, for there is no telling what restrictions his tender-heartedness might have laid upon our larder. But perhaps a chicken would not have given such an opening for misplaced affection as a sheep. There is a great difference in animals in this respect. I certainly never heard of any one falling in love with a salmon in such a way as to regard it as a fond companion. And this may be one reason why no sensible person who has tried fishing has ever been able to see any cruelty in it.

Suppose the fish is not caught by an angler, what is his alternative fate? He will either perish miserably in the struggles of the crowded net, or die of old age and starvation like the long, lean stragglers which are sometimes found in the shallow pools, or be devoured by a larger fish, or torn to pieces by a seal or an otter. Compared with any of these miserable deaths, the fate of a salmon who is hooked in a clear stream and after a glorious fight receives the happy despatch at the moment when he touches the shore, is a sort of euthanasia. And, since the fish was made to be man's food, the angler who brings him to the table of destiny in the cleanest, quickest, kindest way is, in fact, his benefactor.

There were some days, however, when our benevolent intentions toward the salmon were frustrated; mornings when they refused to rise, and evenings when they escaped even the skilful endeavours of Favonius. In vain did he try every fly in his book, from the smallest "Silver Doctor" to the largest "Golden Eagle." The "Black Dose" would not move them. The "Durham Ranger" covered the pool in vain. On days like this, if a stray fish rose, it was hard to land him, for he was usually but slightly hooked.

I remember one of these shy creatures which led me a pretty dance at the mouth of Patapedia. He came to the fly just at dusk, rising very softly and quietly, as if he did not really care for it but only wanted to see what it was like. He went down at once into deep water, and began the most dangerous and exasperating of all salmon-tactics, moving around in slow circles and shaking his head from side to side, with sullen pertinacity. This is called "jigging," and unless it can be stopped, the result is fatal.

I could not stop it. That salmon was determined to jig. He knew more than I did.

The canoe followed him down the pool. He jigged away past all three of the inlets of the Patapedia, and at last, in the still, deep water below, after we had laboured with him for half an hour, and brought him near enough to see that he was immense, he calmly opened his mouth and the fly came back to me void. That was a sad evening, in which all the consolations of philosophy were needed.

Sunday was a very peaceful day in our camp. In the Dominion of Canada, the question "to fish or not to fish" on the first day of the week is not left to the frailty of the individual conscience. The law on the subject is quite explicit, and says that between six o'clock on Saturday evening and six o'clock on Monday morning all nets shall be taken up and no one shall wet a line. The Ristigouche Salmon Club has its guardians stationed all along the river, and they are quite as inflexible in seeing that their employers keep this law as the famous sentinel was in refusing to let Napoleon pass without the countersign. But I do not think that these keen sportsmen regard it as a hardship; they are quite willing that the fish should have "an off day" in every week, and only grumble because some of the net-owners down at the mouth of the river have brought political influence to bear in their favour and obtained exemption from the rule. For our part, we were nothing loath to hang up our rods, and make the day different from other days.

In the morning we had a service in the cabin of the boat, gathering a little congregation of guardians and boatmen, and people from a solitary farm-house by the river. They came in *pirogues*—long, narrow boats hollowed from the trunk of a tree; the black-eyed, brown-faced girls sitting back to back in the middle of the boat, and the men standing up bending to their poles. It seemed a picturesque way of travelling, although none too safe.

In the afternoon we sat on deck and looked at the water. What a charm there is in watching a swift stream! The eye never wearies of following its curls and eddies, the shadow of the waves dancing over the stones, the strange, crinkling lines of sunlight in the shallows. There is a sort of fascination in it, lulling and soothing the mind into a quietude which is even pleasanter than sleep, and making it almost possible to do that of which we so often speak, but which we never quite accomplish—"think about nothing." Out on the edge of the pool, we could see five or six huge salmon, moving slowly from side to side, or lying motionless like gray shadows. There was nothing to break the silence except the thin clear whistle of the white-throated sparrow far back in the woods. This is almost the only bird-song that one hears on the river, unless you count the metallic "*chr-r-r-r*" of the kingfisher as a song.

Every now and then one of the salmon in the pool would lazily roll out of water, or spring high into the air and fall back with a heavy splash. What is it that makes salmon leap? Is it pain or pleasure? Do they do it to escape the attack of another fish, or to shake off a parasite that clings to them, or to practise jumping so that they can ascend the falls when they reach them, or simply and solely out of exuberant gladness and joy of living? Any one of these reasons would be enough to account for it on week-days. On Sunday I am quite sure they do it for the trial of the fisherman's faith.

But how should I tell all the little incidents which made that lazy voyage so delightful? Favonius was the ideal host, for on water, as well as on land, he knows how to provide for the liberty as well as for the wants of his guests. He understands also the fine art of conversation, which consists of silence as well as speech. And when it comes to angling, Izaak Walton himself could not have been a more profitable teacher by precept or example. Indeed, it is a curious thought, and one full of sadness to a well-constituted mind, that on the Ristigouche "I. W." would have been at sea, for the beloved father of all fishermen passed through this world without ever catching a salmon. So ill does fortune match with merit here below.

At last the days of idleness were ended. We could not,

"*Fold our tents like the Arabs,*
And as silently steal away;"

but we took down the long rods, put away the heavy reels, made the canoes fast to the side of the house, embarked the three horses on the front deck, and then dropped down with the current, swinging along through the rapids, and drifting slowly through the still places, now grounding on a hidden rock, and now sweeping around a sharp curve, until at length we saw the roofs of Metapedia and the ugly bridge of the railway spanning the river. There we left our floating house, awkward and helpless, like some strange relic of the flood, stranded on the shore. And as we climbed the bank we looked back and wondered whether Noah was sorry when he said good-bye to his ark.

1888.

ALPENROSEN AND GOAT'S MILK

"Nay, let me tell you, there be many that have forty times our estates, that would give the greatest part of it to be healthful and cheerful like us; who, with the expense of a little money, have ate, and drank, and laughed, and angled, and sung, and slept securely; and rose next day, and cast away care, and sung, and laughed, and angled again; which are blessings rich men cannot purchase with all their money."——
IZAAK WALTON: *The Complete Angler.*
ALPENROSEN AND GOAT'S MILK

A great deal of the pleasure of life lies in bringing together things which have no connection. That is the secret of humour—at least so we are told by the philosophers who explain the jests that other men have made—and in regard to travel, I am quite sure that it must be illogical in order to be entertaining. The more contrasts it contains, the better.

Perhaps it was some philosophical reflection of this kind that brought me to the resolution, on a certain summer day, to make a little journey, as straight as possible, from the sea-level streets of Venice to the lonely, lofty summit of a Tyrolese mountain, called, for no earthly reason that I can discover, the Gross-Venediger.

But apart from the philosophy of the matter, which I must confess to passing over very superficially at the time, there were other and more cogent reasons for wanting to go from Venice to the Big Venetian. It was the first of July, and the city on the sea was becoming tepid. A slumbrous haze brooded over canals and palaces and churches. It was difficult to keep one's conscience awake to Baedeker and a sense of moral obligation; Ruskin was impossible, and a picture-gallery was a penance. We floated lazily from one place to another, and decided that, after all, it was too warm to go in. The cries of the gondoliers, at the canal corners, grew more and more monotonous and dreamy. There was danger of our falling fast asleep and having to pay by the hour for a day's repose in a gondola. If it grew much warmer, we might be compelled to stay until the following winter in order to recover energy enough to get away. All the signs of the times pointed northward, to the mountains, where we should see glaciers and snow-fields, and pick Alpenrosen, and drink goat's milk fresh from the real goat.

I.

The first stage on the journey thither was by rail to Belluno—about four or five hours. It is a sufficient commentary on railway travel that the most important thing about it is to tell how many hours it takes to get from one place to another.

We arrived in Belluno at night, and when we awoke the next morning we found ourselves in a picturesque little city of Venetian aspect, with a piazza and a campanile and a Palladian cathedral, surrounded on all sides by lofty hills. We were at the end of the railway and at the beginning of the Dolomites.

Although I have a constitutional aversion to scientific information given by unscientific persons, such as clergymen and men of letters, I must go in that direction far enough to make it clear that the word Dolomite does not describe a kind of fossil, nor a sect of heretics, but a formation of mountains lying between the Alps and the Adriatic. Draw a diamond on the map, with Brixen at the northwest corner, Lienz at the northeast, Belluno at the southeast, and Trent at the southwest, and you will have included the region of the Dolomites, a country so picturesque, so interesting, so full of sublime and beautiful scenery, that it is equally a wonder and a blessing that it has not been long since completely overrun by tourists and ruined with railways. It is true, the glaciers and snow-fields are limited; the waterfalls are comparatively few and slender, and the rivers small; the loftiest peaks are little more than ten thousand feet high. But, on the other hand, the mountains are always near, and therefore always imposing. Bold, steep, fantastic masses of naked rock, they rise suddenly from the green and flowery valleys in amazing and endless contrast; they mirror themselves in the tiny mountain lakes like pictures in a dream.

I believe the guide-book says that they are formed of carbonate of lime and carbonate of magnesia in chemical composition; but even if this be true, it need not prejudice any candid observer against them. For the simple and fortunate fact is that they are built of such stone that wind and weather, keen frost and melting snow and rushing water have worn and cut and carved them into a thousand shapes of wonder and beauty. It needs but little fancy to see in them walls and towers, cathedrals and campaniles, fortresses and cities, tinged with many hues from pale gray to deep red, and shining in an air so soft, so pure, so cool, so fragrant, under a sky so deep and blue and a sunshine so genial, that it seems like the happy union of Switzerland and Italy.

The great highway through this region from south to north is the Ampezzo road, which was constructed in 1830, along the valleys of the Piave, the Boite, and the Rienz—the ancient line of travel and commerce between Venice and Innsbruck. The road is superbly built, smooth and level. Our carriage rolled along so easily that we forgot and forgave its venerable appearance and its lack of accommodation for trunks. We had been persuaded to take four horses, as our luggage seemed too formidable for a single pair. But in effect our concession to apparent necessity turned out to be a mere display of superfluous luxury, for the two white leaders did little more than show their feeble paces, leaving the gray wheelers to do the work. We had the elevating sense of travelling four-in-hand, however—a satisfaction to which I do not believe any human being is altogether insensible.

At Longarone we breakfasted for the second time, and entered the narrow gorge of the Piave. The road was cut out of the face of the rock. Below us the long lumber-rafts went shooting down the swift river. Above, on the right, were the jagged crests of Monte Furlon and Premaggiore, which seemed to us very wonderful, because we had not yet learned how jagged the Dolomites can be. At Perarolo, where the Boite joins the Piave, there is a lump of a mountain in the angle between the rivers, and around this we crawled in long curves until we had risen a thousand feet, and arrived at the same Hotel Venezia, where we were to dine.

While dinner was preparing, the Deacon and I walked up to Pieve di Cadore, the birthplace of Titian. The house in which the great painter first saw the colours of the world is still standing, and tradition points out the very room in which he began to paint. I am not one of those who would inquire too closely into such a legend as this. The cottage may have been rebuilt a dozen times since Titian's day; not a scrap of the original stone or plaster may remain; but beyond a doubt the view that we saw from the window is the same that Titian saw. Now, for the first time, I could understand and appreciate the landscape-backgrounds of his pictures. The compact masses of mountains, the bold, sharp forms, the hanging rocks of cold gray emerging from green slopes, the intense blue aerial distances—these all had seemed to be unreal and imaginary—compositions of the studio. But now I knew that, whether Titian painted out-of-doors, like our modern impressionists, or not, he certainly painted what he had seen, and painted it as it is.

The graceful brown-eyed boy who showed us the house seemed also to belong to one of Titian's pictures. As we were going away, the Deacon, for lack of copper, rewarded him with a little silver piece, a half-lira, in value about ten cents. A celestial rapture of surprise spread over the child's face, and I know not what blessings he invoked upon us. He called his companions to rejoice with him, and we left them clapping their hands and dancing.

Driving after one has dined has always a peculiar charm. The motion seems pleasanter, the landscape finer than in the morning hours. The road from Cadore ran on a high level, through sloping pastures, white villages, and bits of larch forest. In its narrow bed, far below, the river Boite roared as gently as Bottom's lion. The afternoon sunlight touched the snow-capped pinnacle of Antelao and the massive pink wall of Sorapis on the right; on the left, across the valley, Monte Pelmo's vast head and the wild crests of La Rochetta and Formin rose dark against the glowing sky. The peasants lifted their hats as we passed, and gave us a pleasant evening greeting. And so, almost without knowing it, we slipped out of Italy into Austria, and drew up before a bare, square stone building with the double black eagle, like a strange fowl split for broiling, staring at us from the wall, and an inscription to the effect that this was the Royal and Imperial Austrian Custom-house.

The officer saluted us so politely that we felt quite sorry that his duty required him to disturb our luggage. "The law obliged him to open one trunk; courtesy forbade him to open more." It was quickly done; and, without having to make any contribution to the income of His Royal and Imperial Majesty, Francis Joseph, we rolled on our way, through the hamlets of Acqua Bona and Zuel, into the Ampezzan metropolis of Cortina, at sundown.

The modest inn called "The Star of Gold" stood facing the public square, just below the church, and the landlady stood facing us in the doorway, with an enthusiastic welcome—altogether a most friendly and entertaining landlady, whose one desire in life seemed to be that we should never regret having chosen her house instead of "The White Cross," or "The Black Eagle."

"O ja!" she had our telegram received; and would we look at the rooms? Outlooking on the piazza, with a balcony from which we could observe the Festa of to-morrow. She hoped they would please us. "Only come in; accommodate yourselves."

It was all as she promised; three little bedrooms, and a little salon opening on a little balcony; queer old oil-paintings and framed embroideries and tiles hanging on the walls; spotless curtains, and board floors so white that it would have been a shame to eat off them without spreading a cloth to keep them from being soiled.

"These are the rooms of the Baron Rothschild when he comes here always in the summer—with nine horses and nine servants—the Baron Rothschild of Vienna."

I assured her that we did not know the Baron, but that should make no difference. We would not ask her to reduce the price on account of a little thing like that.

She did not quite grasp this idea, but hoped that we would not find the pension too dear at a dollar and fifty-seven and a half cents a day each, with a little extra for the salon and the balcony. "The English people all please themselves here—there comes many every summer—English Bishops and their families."

I inquired whether there were many Bishops in the house at that moment.

"No, just at present—she was very sorry—none."

"Well, then," I said, "it is all right. We will take the rooms."

Good Signora Barbaria, you did not speak the American language, nor understand those curious perversions of thought which pass among the Americans for humour; but you understood how to make a little inn cheerful and home-like; yours was a very simple and agreeable art of keeping a hotel. As we sat in the balcony after supper, listening to the capital playing of the village orchestra, and the Tyrolese songs with which they varied their music, we thought within ourselves that we were fortunate to have fallen upon the Star of Gold.

II.

Cortina lies in its valley like a white shell that has rolled down into a broad vase of malachite. It has about a hundred houses and seven hundred inhabitants, a large church and two small ones, a fine stone campanile with excellent bells, and seven or eight little inns. But it is more important than its size would signify, for it is the capital of the district whose lawful title is *Magnifica Comunità di Ampezzo*—a name conferred long ago by the Republic of Venice. In the fifteenth century it was Venetian territory; but in 1516, under Maximilian I., it was joined to Austria; and it is now one of the richest and most prosperous communes of the Tyrol. It embraces about thirty-five hundred people, scattered in hamlets and clusters of houses through the green basin with its four entrances, lying between the peaks of Tofana, Cristallo, Sorapis, and Nuvolau. The well-cultivated grain fields and meadows, the smooth alps filled with fine cattle, the well-built houses with their white stone basements and balconies of dark brown wood and broad overhanging roofs, all speak of industry and thrift. But there is more than mere agricultural prosperity in this valley. There is a fine race of men and women—intelligent, vigorous, and with a strong sense of beauty. The outer walls of the annex of the Hotel Aquila Nera are covered with frescoes of marked power and originality, painted by the son of the innkeeper. The art schools of Cortina are famous for their beautiful work in gold and silver filigree, and wood-inlaying. There are nearly two hundred pupils in these schools, all peasants' children, and they produce results, especially in *intarsia*, which are admirable. The village orchestra, of which I spoke a moment ago, is trained and led by a peasant's son, who has never had a thorough musical education. It must have at least twenty-five members, and as we heard them at the Festa they seemed to play with extraordinary accuracy and expression.

This Festa gave us a fine chance to see the people of the Ampezzo all together. It was the annual jubilation of the district; and from all the outlying hamlets and remote side valleys, even from the neighbouring vales of Agordo and

Auronzo, across the mountains, and from Cadore, the peasants, men and women and children, had come in to the *Sagro* at Cortina. The piazza—which is really nothing more than a broadening of the road behind the church—was quite thronged. There must have been between two and three thousand people.

The ceremonies of the day began with general church-going. The people here are honestly and naturally religious. I have seen so many examples of what can only be called "sincere and unaffected piety," that I cannot doubt it. The church, on Cortina's feast-day, was crowded to the doors with worshippers, who gave every evidence of taking part not only with the voice, but also with the heart, in the worship.

Then followed the public unveiling of a tablet, on the wall of the little Inn of the Anchor, to the memory of Giammaria Ghedini, the founder of the art-schools of Cortina. There was music by the band; and an oration by a native Demosthenes (who spoke in Italian so fluent that it ran through one's senses like water through a sluice, leaving nothing behind), and an original *Canto* sung by the village choir, with a general chorus, in which they called upon the various mountains to "reëcho the name of the beloved master John-Mary as a model of modesty and true merit," and wound up with—

"Hurrah for John-Mary! Hurrah for his art!
Hurrah for all teachers as skilful as he!
Hurrah for us all, who have now taken part
In singing together in do ... re ... mi."

It was very primitive, and I do not suppose that the celebration was even mentioned in the newspapers of the great world; but, after all, has not the man who wins such a triumph as this in the hearts of his own people, for whom he has made labour beautiful with the charm of art, deserved better of fame than many a crowned monarch or conquering warrior? We should be wiser if we gave less glory to the men who have been successful in forcing their fellow-men to die, and more glory to the men who have been successful in teaching their fellow-men how to live.

But the Festa of Cortina did not remain all day on this high moral plane. In the afternoon came what our landlady called *"allerlei Dummheiten."* There was a grand lottery for the benefit of the Volunteer Fire Department. The high officials sat up in a green wooden booth in the middle of the square, and called out the numbers and distributed the prizes. Then there was a greased pole with various articles of an attractive character tied to a large hoop at the top—silk aprons, and a green jacket, and bottles of wine, and half a smoked pig, and a coil of rope, and a purse. The gallant firemen voluntarily climbed up the pole as far as they could, one after another, and then involuntarily slid down again exhausted, each one wiping off a little more of the grease, until at last the lucky one came who profited by his forerunners' labours, and struggled to the top to snatch the smoked pig. After that it was easy.

Such is success in this unequal world; the man who wipes off the grease seldom gets the prize.

Then followed various games, with tubs of water; and coins fastened to the bottom of a huge black frying-pan, to be plucked off with the lips; and pots of flour to be broken with sticks; so that the young lads of the village were ducked and blackened and powdered to an unlimited extent, amid the hilarious applause of the spectators. In the evening there was more music, and the peasants danced in the square, the women quietly and rather heavily, but the men with amazing agility, slapping the soles of their shoes with their hands, or turning cart-wheels in front of their partners. At dark the festivities closed with a display of fireworks; there were rockets and bombs and pin-wheels; and the boys had tiny red and blue lights which they held until their fingers were burned, just as boys do in America; and there was a general hush of wonder as a particularly brilliant rocket swished into the dark sky; and when it burst into a rain of serpents, the crowd breathed out its delight in a long-drawn "Ah-h-h-h!" just as the crowd does everywhere. We might easily have imagined ourselves at a Fourth of July celebration in Vermont, if it had not been for the costumes.

The men of the Ampezzo Valley have kept but little that is peculiar in their dress. Men are naturally more progressive than women, and therefore less picturesque. The tide of fashion has swept them into the international monotony of coat and vest and trousers—pretty much the same, and equally ugly, all over the world. Now and then you may see a short jacket with silver buttons, or a pair of knee-breeches; and almost all the youths wear a bunch of feathers or a tuft of chamois' hair in their soft green hats. But the women of the Ampezzo—strong, comely, with golden brown complexions, and often noble faces—are not ashamed to dress as their grandmothers did. They wear a little round black felt hat with rolled rim and two long ribbons hanging down at the back. Their hair is carefully braided and coiled, and stuck through and through with great silver pins. A black bodice, fastened with silver clasps, is covered in front with the ends of a brilliant silk kerchief, laid in many folds around the shoulders. The white shirt-sleeves are very full and fastened up above the elbow with coloured ribbon. If the weather is cool, the women wear a short black jacket, with satin yoke and high puffed sleeves. But, whatever the weather may be, they make no change in the large, full dark skirts, almost completely covered with immense silk aprons, by preference light blue. It is not a remarkably brilliant dress, compared with that which one may still see in some districts of Norway or Sweden, but upon the whole it suits the women of the Ampezzo wonderfully.

For my part, I think that when a woman has found a dress that becomes her, it is a waste of time to send to Paris for a fashion-plate.

III.

When the excitement of the Festa had subsided, we were free to abandon ourselves to the excursions in which the neighbourhood of Cortina abounds, and to which the guide-book earnestly calls every right-minded traveller. A walk through the light-green shadows of the larchwoods to the tiny lake of Ghedina, where we could see all the four dozen trout swimming about in the clear water and catching flies; a drive to the Belvedere, where there are superficial refreshments above and profound grottos below; these were trifles, though we enjoyed them. But the great mountains encircling us on every side, standing out in clear view with that distinctness and completeness of vision which is one charm of the Dolomites, seemed to summon us to more arduous enterprises. Accordingly, the Deacon and I selected the easiest one, engaged a guide, and prepared for the ascent.

Monte Nuvolau is not a perilous mountain. I am quite sure that at my present time of life I should be unwilling to ascend a perilous mountain unless there were something extraordinarily desirable at the top, or remarkably disagreeable at the bottom. Mere risk has lost the attractions which it once had. As the father of a family I felt bound to abstain from going for amusement into any place which a Christian lady might not visit with propriety and safety. Our preparation for Nuvolau, therefore, did not consist of ropes, ice-irons, and axes, but simply of a lunch and two long sticks.

Our way led us, in the early morning, through the clustering houses of Lacedel, up the broad, green slope that faces Cortina on the west, to the beautiful Alp Pocol. Nothing could exceed the pleasure of such a walk in the cool of the day, while the dew still lies on the short, rich grass, and the myriads of flowers are at their brightest and sweetest. The infinite variety and abundance of the blossoms is a continual wonder. They are sown more thickly than the stars in heaven, and the rainbow itself does not show so many tints. Here they are mingled like the threads of some strange embroidery; and there again nature has massed her colours; so that one spot will be all pale blue with innumerable forget-me-nots, or dark blue with gentians; another will blush with the delicate pink of the Santa Lucia or the deeper red of the clover; and another will shine yellow as cloth of gold. Over all this opulence of bloom the larks were soaring and singing. I never heard so many as in the meadows about Cortina. There was always a sweet spray of music sprinkling down out of the sky, where the singers poised unseen. It was like walking through a shower of melody.

From the Alp Pocol, which is simply a fair, lofty pasture, we had our first full view of Nuvolau, rising bare and strong, like a huge bastion, from the dark fir-woods. Through these our way led onward now for seven miles, with but a slight ascent. Then turning off to the left we began to climb sharply through the forest. There we found abundance of the lovely Alpenrosen, which do not bloom on the lower ground. Their colour is a deep, glowing pink, and when a Tyrolese girl gives you one of these flowers to stick in the band of your hat, you may know that you have found favour in her eyes.

Through the wood the cuckoo was calling—the bird which reverses the law of good children, and insists on being heard, but not seen.

When the forest was at an end we found ourselves at the foot of an alp which sloped steeply up to the Five Towers of Averau. The effect of these enormous masses of rock, standing out in lonely grandeur, like the ruins of some forsaken habitation of giants, was tremendous. Seen from far below in the valley their form was picturesque and striking; but as we sat beside the clear, cold spring which gushes out at the foot of the largest tower, the Titanic rocks seemed to hang in the air above us as if they would overawe us into a sense of their majesty. We felt it to the full; yet none the less, but rather the more, could we feel at the same time the delicate and ethereal beauty of the fringed gentianella and the pale Alpine lilies scattered on the short turf beside us.

We had now been on foot about three hours and a half. The half hour that remained was the hardest. Up over loose, broken stones that rolled beneath our feet, up over great slopes of rough rock, up across little fields of snow where we paused to celebrate the Fourth of July with a brief snowball fight, up along a narrowing ridge with a precipice on either hand, and so at last to the summit, 8600 feet above the sea.

It is not a great height, but it is a noble situation. For Nuvolau is fortunately placed in the very centre of the Dolomites, and so commands a finer view than many a higher mountain. Indeed, it is not from the highest peaks, according to my experience, that one gets the grandest prospects, but rather from those of middle height, which are so isolated as to give a wide circle of vision, and from which one can see both the valleys and the summits. Monte Rosa itself gives a less imposing view than the Görner Grat.

It is possible, in this world, to climb too high for pleasure.

But what a panorama Nuvolau gave us on that clear, radiant summer morning—a perfect circle of splendid sight! On one side we looked down upon the Five Towers; on the other, a thousand feet below, the Alps, dotted with the huts of the herdsmen, sloped down into the deep-cut vale of Agordo. Opposite to us was the enormous mass of Tofana, a pile of gray and pink and saffron rock. When we turned the other way, we faced a group of mountains as ragged as the crests of a line of fir-trees, and behind them loomed the solemn head of Pelmo. Across the broad vale of the Boite, Antelao stood beside Sorapis, like a campanile beside a cathedral, and Cristallo towered above the green pass of the Three Crosses. Through that opening we could see the bristling peaks of the Sextenthal. Sweeping around in a wider circle from that point, we saw, beyond the Dürrenstein, the snow-covered pile of the Gross-Glockner; the crimson bastions of the Rothwand appeared to the north, behind Tofana; then the white slopes that hang far away above the Zillerthal; and, nearer, the Geislerspitze, like five fingers thrust into the air; behind that, the distant Oetzthaler Mountain, and just a single white glimpse of the highest peak of the Ortler by the Engadine; nearer still we saw the vast fortress of the Sella group and the red combs of the Rosengarten; Monte Marmolata, the Queen of the

Dolomites, stood before us revealed from base to peak in a bridal dress of snow; and southward we looked into the dark rugged face of La Civetta, rising sheer out of the vale of Agordo, where the Lake of Alleghe slept unseen. It was a sea of mountains, tossed around us into a myriad of motionless waves, and with a rainbow of colours spread among their hollows and across their crests. The cliffs of rose and orange and silver gray, the valleys of deepest green, the distant shadows of purple and melting blue, and the dazzling white of the scattered snow-fields seemed to shift and vary like the hues on the inside of a shell. And over all, from peak to peak, the light, feathery clouds went drifting lazily and slowly, as if they could not leave a scene so fair.

There is barely room on the top of Nuvolau for the stone shelter-hut which a grateful Saxon baron has built there as a sort of votive offering for the recovery of his health among the mountains. As we sat within and ate our frugal lunch, we were glad that he had recovered his health, and glad that he had built the hut, and glad that we had come to it. In fact, we could almost sympathise in our cold, matter-of-fact American way with the sentimental German inscription which we read on the wall:—

Von Nuvolau's hohen Wolkenstufen
Lass mich, Natur, durch deine Himmel rufen—
An deiner Brust gesunde, wer da krank!
So wird zum Völkerdank *mein* Sachsendank.

We refrained, however, from shouting anything through Nature's heaven, but went lightly down, in about three hours, to supper in the Star of Gold.

IV.

When a stern necessity forces one to leave Cortina, there are several ways of departure. We selected the main highway for our trunks, but for ourselves the Pass of the Three Crosses; the Deacon and the Deaconess in a mountain waggon, and I on foot. It should be written as an axiom in the philosophy of travel that the easiest way is best for your luggage, and the hardest way is best for yourself.

All along the rough road up to the Pass, we had a glorious outlook backward over the Val d' Ampezzo, and when we came to the top, we looked deep down into the narrow Val Buona behind Sorapis. I do not know just when we passed the Austrian border, but when we came to Lake Misurina we found ourselves in Italy again. My friends went on down the valley to Landro, but I in my weakness, having eaten of the trout of the lake for dinner, could not resist the temptation of staying over-night to catch one for breakfast.

It was a pleasant failure. The lake was beautiful, lying on top of the mountain like a bit of blue sky, surrounded by the peaks of Cristallo, Cadino, and the Drei Zinnen. It was a happiness to float on such celestial waters and cast the hopeful fly. The trout were there; they were large; I saw them; they also saw me; but, alas! I could not raise them. Misurina is, in fact, what the Scotch call "a dour loch," one of those places which are outwardly beautiful, but inwardly so demoralised that the trout will not rise.

When we came ashore in the evening, the boatman consoled me with the story of a French count who had spent two weeks there fishing, and only caught one fish. I had some thoughts of staying thirteen days longer, to rival the count, but concluded to go on the next morning, over Monte Pian and the Cat's Ladder to Landro.

The view from Monte Pian is far less extensive than that from Nuvolau; but it has the advantage of being very near the wild jumble of the Sexten Dolomites. The Three Shoemakers and a lot more of sharp and ragged fellows are close by, on the east; on the west, Cristallo shows its fine little glacier, and Rothwand its crimson cliffs; and southward Misurina gives to the view a glimpse of water, without which, indeed, no view is complete. Moreover, the mountain has the merit of being, as its name implies, quite gentle. I met the Deacon and the Deaconess at the top, they having walked up from Landro. And so we crossed the boundary line together again, seven thousand feet above the sea, from Italy into Austria. There was no custom-house.

The way down, by the Cat's Ladder, I travelled alone. The path was very steep and little worn, but even on the mountain-side there was no danger of losing it, for it had been blazed here and there, on trees and stones, with a dash of blue paint. This is the work of the invaluable DÖAV—which is, being interpreted, the German-Austrian Alpine Club. The more one travels in the mountains, the more one learns to venerate this beneficent society, for the shelter-huts and guide-posts it has erected, and the paths it has made and marked distinctly with various colours. The Germans have a genius for thoroughness. My little brown guide-book, for example, not only informed me through whose back yard I must go to get into a certain path, but it told me that in such and such a spot I should find quite a good deal (*ziemlichviel*) of Edelweiss, and in another a small echo; it advised me in one valley to take provisions and dispense with a guide, and in another to take a guide and dispense with provisions, adding varied information in regard to beer, which in my case was useless, for I could not touch it. To go astray under such auspices would be worse than inexcusable.

Landro we found a very different place from Cortina. Instead of having a large church and a number of small hotels, it consists entirely of one large hotel and a very tiny church. It does not lie in a broad, open basin, but in a narrow valley, shut in closely by the mountains. The hotel, in spite of its size, is excellent, and a few steps up the valley is one of the finest views in the Dolomites. To the east opens a deep, wild gorge, at the head of which the pinnacles of the Drei Zinnen are seen; to the south the Dürrensee fills the valley from edge to edge, and reflects in its pale waters the huge bulk of Monte Cristallo. It is such a complete picture, so finished, so compact, so balanced, that one might think a painter had composed it in a moment of inspiration. But no painter ever laid such colours on his canvas as those which are seen here when the cool evening shadows have settled upon the valley, all gray and green, while the mountains shine above in rosy Alpenglow, as if transfigured with inward fire.

There is another lake, about three miles north of Landro, called the Toblacher See, and there I repaired the defeat of Misurina. The trout at the outlet, by the bridge, were very small, and while the old fisherman was endeavouring to catch some of them in his new net, which would not work, I pushed my boat up to the head of the lake, where the stream came in. The green water was amazingly clear, but the current kept the fish with their heads up stream; so that one could come up behind them near enough for a long cast, without being seen. As my fly lighted above them and came gently down with the ripple, I saw the first fish turn and rise and take it. A motion of the wrist hooked him, and he played just as gamely as a trout in my favourite Long Island pond. How different the colour, though, as he came out of the water. This fellow was all silvery, with light pink spots on his sides. I took seven of his companions, in weight some four pounds, and then stopped because the evening light was failing.

How pleasant it is to fish in such a place and at such an hour! The novelty of the scene, the grandeur of the landscape, lend a strange charm to the sport. But the sport itself is so familiar that one feels at home—the motion of the rod, the feathery swish of the line, the sight of the rising fish—it all brings back a hundred woodland memories, and thoughts of good fishing comrades, some far away across the sea, and, perhaps, even now sitting around the forest camp-fire in Maine or Canada, and some with whom we shall keep company no more until we cross the greater ocean into that happy country whither they have preceded us.

V.

Instead of going straight down the valley by the high road, a drive of an hour, to the railway in the Pusterthal, I walked up over the mountains to the east, across the Plätzwiesen, and so down through the Pragserthal. In one arm of the deep fir-clad vale are the Baths of Alt-Prags, famous for having cured the Countess of Görz of a violent rheumatism in the fifteenth century. It is an antiquated establishment, and the guests, who were walking about in the fields or drinking their coffee in the balcony, had a fifteenth century look about them—venerable but slightly ruinous. But perhaps that was merely a rheumatic result.

All the waggons in the place were engaged. It is strange what an aggravating effect this state of affairs has upon a pedestrian who is bent upon riding. I did not recover my delight in the scenery until I had walked about five miles farther, and sat down on the grass, beside a beautiful spring, to eat my lunch.

What is there in a little physical rest that has such magic to restore the sense of pleasure? A few moments ago nothing pleased you—the bloom was gone from the peach; but now it has come back again—you wonder and admire. Thus cheerful and contented I trudged up theright arm of the valley to the Baths of Neu-Prags, less venerable, but apparently more popular than Alt-Prags, and on beyond them, through the woods, to the superb Pragser-Wildsee, a lake whose still waters, now blue as sapphire under the clear sky, and now green as emerald under gray clouds, sleep encircled by mighty precipices. Could anything be a greater contrast with Venice? There the canals alive with gondolas, and the open harbour bright with many-coloured sails; here, the hidden lake, silent and lifeless, save when

"*A leaping fish*
Sends through the tarn a lonely cheer."

Tired, and a little foot-sore, after nine hours' walking, I came into the big railway hotel at Toblach that night. There I met my friends again, and parted from them and the Dolomites the next day, with regret. For they were "stepping westward;" but in order to get to the Gross-Venediger I must make a détour to the east, through the Pusterthal, and come up through the valley of the Isel to the great chain of mountains called the Hohe Tauern.

At the junction of the Isel and the Drau lies the quaint little city of Lienz, with its two castles—the square, double-towered one in the town, now transformed into the offices of the municipality, and the huge mediæval one on a hill outside, now used as a damp restaurant and dismal beer-cellar. I lingered at Lienz for a couple of days, in the ancient hostelry of the Post. The hallways were vaulted like a cloister, the walls were three feet thick, the kitchen was in the middle of the house on the second floor, so that I looked into it every time I came from my room, and ordered dinner direct from the cook. But, so far from being displeased with these peculiarities, I rather liked the flavour of them; and then, in addition, the landlady's daughter, who was managing the house, was a person of most engaging manners, and there was trout and grayling fishing in a stream near by, and the neighbouring church of Dolsach contained the beautiful picture of the Holy Family, which Franz Defregger painted for his native village.

The peasant women of Lienz have one very striking feature in their dress—a black felt hat with a broad, stiff brim and a high crown, smaller at the top than at the base. It looks a little like the traditional head-gear of the Pilgrim Fathers, exaggerated. There is a solemnity about it which is fatal to feminine beauty.

I went by the post-waggon, with two slow horses and ten passengers, fifteen miles up the Iselthal, to Windisch-Matrei, a village whose early history is lost in the mist of antiquity, and whose streets are pervaded with odours which must have originated at the same time with the village. One wishes that they also might have shared the fate of its early history. But it is not fair to expect too much of a small place, and Windisch-Matrei has certainly a beautiful situation and a good inn. There I took my guide—a wiry and companionable little man, whose occupation in the lower world was that of a maker and merchant of hats—and set out for the Pragerhütte, a shelter on the side of the Gross-Venediger.

The path led under the walls of the old Castle of Weissenstein, and then in steep curves up the cliff which blocks the head of the valley, and along a cut in the face of the rock, into the steep, narrow Tauernthal, which divides the Glockner group from the Venediger. How entirely different it was from the region of the Dolomites! There the variety of colour was endless and the change incessant; here it was all green grass and trees and black rocks, with glimpses of snow. There the highest mountains were in sight constantly; here they could only be seen from certain points in the valley. There the streams played but a small part in the landscape; here they were prominent, the main river raging and foaming through the gorge below, while a score of waterfalls leaped from the cliffs on either side and dashed down to join it.

The peasants, men, women and children, were cutting the grass in the perpendicular fields; the woodmen were trimming and felling the trees in the fir-forests; the cattle-tenders were driving their cows along the stony path, or herding them far up on the hillsides. It was a lonely scene, and yet a busy one; and all along the road was written the history of the perils and hardships of the life which now seemed so peaceful and picturesque under the summer sunlight.

These heavy crosses, each covered with a narrow, pointed roof and decorated with a rude picture, standing beside the path, or on the bridge, or near the mill—what do they mean? They mark the place where a human life has been lost, or where some poor peasant has been delivered from a great peril, and has set up a memorial of his gratitude.

Stop, traveller, as you pass by, and look at the pictures. They have little more of art than a child's drawing on a slate; but they will teach you what it means to earn a living in these mountains. They tell of the danger that lurks on the steep slopes of grass, where the mowers have to go down with ropes around their waists, and in the beds of the streams where the floods sweep through in the spring, and in the forests where the great trees fall and crush men like flies, and on the icy bridges where a slip is fatal, and on the high passes where the winter snow-storm blinds the eyes and benumbs the limbs of the traveller, and under the cliffs from which avalanches slide and rocks roll. They show you men and women falling from waggons, and swept away by waters, and overwhelmed in land-slips. In the corner of the picture you may see a peasant with the black cross above his head—that means death. Or perhaps it is deliverance that the tablet commemorates—and then you will see the miller kneeling beside his mill with a flood rushing down upon it, or a peasant kneeling in his harvest-field under an inky-black cloud, or a landlord beside his inn in flames, or a mother praying beside her sick children; and above appears an angel, or a saint, or the Virgin with her Child.

Read the inscriptions, too, in their quaint German. Some of them are as humourous as the epitaphs in New England graveyards. I remember one which ran like this:

Here lies Elias Queer,
Killed in his sixtieth year;
Scarce had he seen the light of day
When a waggon-wheel crushed his life away.
And there is another famous one which says:
Here perished the honoured and virtuous
maiden,
G. V.

This tablet was erected by her only son.

But for the most part a glance at these *Marterl und Taferl*, which are so frequent on all the mountain-roads of the Tyrol, will give you a strange sense of the real pathos of human life. If you are a Catholic, you will not refuse their request to say a prayer for the departed; if you are a Protestant, at least it will not hurt you to say one for those who still live and suffer and toil among such dangers.

After we had walked for four hours up the Tauernthal, we came to the Matreier-Tauernhaus, an inn which is kept open all the year for the shelter of travellers over the high pass that crosses the mountain-range at this point, from north to south. There we dined. It was a bare, rude place, but the dish of juicy trout was garnished with flowers, each fish holding a big pansy in its mouth, and as the maid set them down before me she wished me "a good appetite," with the hearty old-fashioned Tyrolese courtesy which still survives in these remote valleys. It is pleasant to travel in a land where the manners are plain and good. If you meet a peasant on the road he says, "God greet you!" if you give a child a couple of kreuzers he folds his hands and says, "God reward you!" and the maid who lights you to bed says, "Good-night, I hope you will sleep well!"

Two hours more of walking brought us through Ausser-gschlöss and Inner-gschlöss, two groups of herdsmen's huts, tenanted only in summer, at the head of the Tauernthal. Mid-way between them lies a little chapel, cut into the solid rock for shelter from the avalanches. This lofty vale is indeed rightly named; for it is shut off from the rest of the world. The portal is a cliff down which the stream rushes in foam and thunder. On either hand rises a mountain wall. Within, the pasture is fresh and green, sprinkled with Alpine roses, and the pale river flows swiftly down between the rows of dark wooden houses. At the head of the vale towers the Gross-Venediger, with its glaciers and snow-fields dazzling white against the deep blue heaven. The murmur of the stream and the tinkle of the cow-bells and the jödelling of the herdsmen far up the slopes, make the music for the scene.

The path from Gschlöss leads straight up to the foot of the dark pyramid of the Kesselkopf, and then in steep endless zig-zags along the edge of the great glacier. I saw, at first, the pinnacles of ice far above me, breaking over the face of the rock; then, after an hour's breathless climbing, I could look right into the blue crevasses; and at last, after another hour over soft snow-fields and broken rocks, I was at the Pragerhut, perched on the shoulder of the mountain, looking down upon the huge river of ice.

It was a magnificent view under the clear light of evening. Here in front of us, the Venediger with all his brother-mountains clustered about him; behind us, across the Tauern, the mighty chain of the Glockner against the eastern sky.

This is the frozen world. Here the Winter, driven back into his stronghold, makes his last stand against the Summer, in perpetual conflict, retreating by day to the mountain-peak, but creeping back at night in frost and snow to regain a little of his lost territory, until at last the Summer is wearied out, and the Winter sweeps down again to claim the whole valley for his own.

VI.

In the Pragerhut I found mountain comfort. There were bunks along the wall of the guestroom, with plenty of blankets. There was good store of eggs, canned meats, and nourishing black bread. The friendly goats came bleating up to the door at nightfall to be milked. And in charge of all this luxury there was a cheerful peasant-wife with her brown-eyed daughter, to entertain travellers. It was a pleasant sight to see them, as they sat down to their supper with my guide; all three bowed their heads and said their "grace before meat," the guide repeating the longer prayer and the mother and daughter coming in with the responses. I went to bed with a warm and comfortable feeling about my heart. It was a good ending for the day. In the morning, if the weather remained clear, the alarm-clock was to wake us at three for the ascent to the summit.

But can it be three o'clock already. The gibbous moon still hangs in the sky and casts a feeble light over the scene. Then up and away for the final climb. How rough the path is among the black rocks along the ridge! Now we strike out on the gently rising glacier, across the crust of snow, picking our way among the crevasses, with the rope tied about our waists for fear of a fall. How cold it is! But now the gray light of morning dawns, and now the beams of sunrise shoot up behind the Glockner, and now the sun itself glitters into sight. The snow grows softer as we toil up the steep, narrow comb between the Gross-Venediger and his neighbour the Klein-Venediger. At last we have reached our journey's end. See, the whole of the Tyrol is spread out before us in wondrous splendour, as we stand on this snowy ridge; and at our feet the Schlatten glacier, like a long, white snake, curls down into the valley.

There is still a little peak above us; an overhanging horn of snow which the wind has built against the mountain-top. I would like to stand there, just for a moment. The guide protests it would be dangerous, for if the snow should break it would be a fall of a thousand feet to the glacier on the northern side. But let us dare the few steps upward. How our feet sink! Is the snow slipping? Look at the glacier! What is happening? It is wrinkling and curling backward on us, serpent-like. Its head rises far above us. All its icy crests are clashing together like the ringing of a thousand bells. We are falling! I fling out my arm to grasp the guide—and awake to find myself clutching a pillow in the bunk. The alarm-clock is ringing fiercely for three o'clock. A driving snow-storm is beating against the window. The ground is white. Peer through the clouds as I may, I cannot even catch a glimpse of the vanished Gross-Venediger.

AU LARGE

"Wherever we strayed, the same tranquil leisure enfolded us; day followed day in an order unbroken and peaceful as the unfolding of the flowers and the silent march of the stars. Time no longer ran like the few sands in a delicate hour-glass held by a fragile human hand, but like a majestic river fed by fathomless seas.... We gave ourselves up to the sweetness of that unmeasured life, without thought of yesterday or to-morrow; we drank the cup to-day held to our lips, and knew that so long as we were athirst that draught would not be denied us."——
HAMILTON W. MABIE: *Under the Trees.*
AU LARGE

There is magic in words, surely, and many a treasure besides Ali Baba's is unlocked with a verbal key. Some charm in the mere sound, some association with the pleasant past, touches a secret spring. The bars are down; the gate is open; you are made free of all the fields of memory and fancy—by a word.

Au large! Envoyez au large! is the cry of the Canadian voyageurs as they thrust their paddles against the shore and push out on the broad lake for a journey through the wilderness. *Au large!* is what the man in the bow shouts to the man in the stern when the birch canoe is running down the rapids, and the water grows too broken, and the rocks too thick, along the river-bank. Then the frail bark must be driven out into the very centre of the wild current, into the midst of danger to find safety, dashing, like a frightened colt, along the smooth, sloping lane bordered by white fences of foam.

Au large! When I hear that word, I hear also the crisp waves breaking on pebbly beaches, and the big wind rushing through innumerable trees, and the roar of headlong rivers leaping down the rocks. I see long reaches of water sparkling in the sun, or sleeping still between evergreen walls beneath a cloudy sky; and the gleam of white tents on the shore; and the glow of firelight dancing through the woods. I smell the delicate vanishing perfume of forest flowers; and the incense of rolls of birch-bark, crinkling and flaring in the camp-fire; and the soothing odour of balsam-boughs piled deep for woodland beds—the veritable and only genuine perfume of the land of Nod. The thin shining veil of the Northern lights waves and fades and brightens over the night sky; at the sound of the word, as at the ringing of a bell, the curtain rises. *Scene, the Forest of Arden; enter a party of hunters.*

It was in the Lake St. John country, two hundred miles north of Quebec, that I first heard my rustic incantation; and it seemed to fit the region as if it had been made for it. This is not a little pocket wilderness like the Adirondacks, but something vast and primitive. You do not cross it, from one railroad to another, by a line of hotels. You go into it by one river as far as you like, or dare; and then you turn and come back again by another river, making haste to get out before your provisions are exhausted. The lake itself is the cradle of the mighty Saguenay: an inland sea, thirty miles across and nearly round, lying in the broad limestone basin north of the Laurentian Mountains. The southern and eastern shores have been settled for twenty or thirty years; and the rich farm-land yields abundant crops of wheat and oats and potatoes to a community of industrious *habitants*, who live in little modern villages, named after the saints and gathered as closely as possible around big gray stone churches, and thank the good Lord that he has given them a climate at least four or five degrees milder than Quebec. A railroad, built through a region of granite hills, which will never be tamed to the plough, links this outlying settlement to the civilised world; and at the end of the railroad the Hotel Roberval, standing on a hill above the lake, offers to the pampered tourist electric lights, and spring-beds, and a wide veranda from which he can look out across the water into the face of the wilderness.

Northward and westward the interminable forest rolls away to the shores of Hudson's Bay and the frozen wastes of Labrador. It is an immense solitude. A score of rivers empty into the lake; little ones like the Pikouabi and La Pipe, and middle-sized ones like the Ouiatchouan and La Belle Rivière, and big ones like the Mistassini and the Peribonca; and each of these streams is the clue to a labyrinth of woods and waters. The canoe-man who follows it far enough will find himself among lakes that are not named on any map; he will camp on virgin ground, and make the acquaintance of unsophisticated fish; perhaps even, like the maiden in the fairy-tale, he will meet with the little bear, and the middle-sized bear, and the great big bear.

Damon and I set out on such an expedition shortly after the nodding lilies in the Connecticut meadows had rung the noon-tide bell of summer, and when the raspberry bushes along the line of the Quebec and Lake St. John Railway had spread their afternoon collation for birds and men. At Roberval we found our four guides waiting for us, and the steamboat took us all across the lake to the Island House, at the northeast corner. There we embarked our tents and blankets, our pots and pans, and bags of flour and potatoes and bacon and other delicacies, our rods and guns, and last, but not least, our axes (without which man in the woods is a helpless creature), in two birch-bark canoes, and went flying down the Grande Décharge.

It is a wonderful place, this outlet of Lake St. John. All the floods of twenty rivers are gathered here, and break forth through a net of islands in a double stream, divided by the broad Ile d'Alma, into the Grande Décharge and the Petite Décharge. The southern outlet is small, and flows somewhat more quietly at first. But the northern outlet is a huge confluence and tumult of waters. You see the set of the tide far out in the lake, sliding, driving, crowding, hurrying in with smooth currents and swirling eddies, toward the corner of escape. By the rocky cove where the Island House peers out through the fir-trees, the current already has a perceptible slope. It begins to boil over hidden stones in the middle, and gurgles at projecting points of rock. A mile farther down there is an islet where the stream quickens, chafes, and breaks into a rapid. Behind the islet it drops down in three or four foaming steps. On the outside it makes one long, straight rush into a line of white-crested standing waves.

As we approached, the steersman in the first canoe stood up to look over the course. The sea was high. Was it too high? The canoes were heavily loaded. Could they leap the waves? There was a quick talk among the guides as we slipped along, undecided which way to turn. Then the question seemed to settle itself, as most of these woodland questions do, as if some silent force of Nature had the casting-vote. "*Sautez, sautez!*" cried Ferdinand, "*envoyez au large!*" In a moment we were sliding down the smooth back of the rapid, directly toward the first big wave. The rocky shore went by us like a dream; we could feel the motion of the earth whirling around with us. The crest of the billow in front curled above the bow of the canoe. "*Arrét', arrét', doucement!*" A swift stroke of the paddle checked the canoe, quivering and prancing like a horse suddenly reined in. The wave ahead, as if surprised, sank and flattened for a second. The canoe leaped through the edge of it, swerved to one side, and ran gayly down along the fringe of the line of billows, into quieter water.

Every one feels the exhilaration of such a descent. I know a lady who almost cried with fright when she went down her first rapid, but before the voyage was ended she was saying:—

"*Count that day lost whose low, descending sun*
Sees no fall leaped, no foaming rapid run."

It takes a touch of danger to bring out the joy of life.

Our guides began to shout, and joke each other, and praise their canoes.

"You grazed that villain rock at the corner," said Jean; "didn't you know where it was?"

"Yes, after I touched it," cried Ferdinand; "but you took in a bucket of water, and I suppose your *m'sieu'* is sitting on a piece of the river. Is it not?"

This seemed to us all a very merry jest, and we laughed with the same inextinguishable laughter which a practical joke, according to Homer, always used to raise in Olympus. It is one of the charms of life in the woods that it brings back the high spirits of boyhood and renews the youth of the world. Plain fun, like plain food, tastes good out-of-doors. Nectar is the sweet sap of a maple-tree. Ambrosia is only another name for well-turned flapjacks. And all the immortals, sitting around the table of golden cedar-slabs, make merry when the clumsy Hephaistos, playing the part of Hebe, stumbles over a root and upsets the plate of cakes into the fire.

The first little rapid of the Grande Décharge was only the beginning. Half a mile below we could see the river disappear between two points of rock. There was a roar of conflict, and a golden mist hanging in the air, like the smoke of battle. All along the place where the river sank from sight, dazzling heads of foam were flashing up and falling back, as if a horde of water-sprites were vainly trying to fight their way up to the lake. It was the top of the *grande chûte*, a wild succession of falls and pools where no boat could live for a moment. We ran down toward it as far as the water served, and then turned off among the rocks on the left hand, to take the portage.

These portages are among the troublesome delights of a journey in the wilderness. To the guides they mean hard work, for everything, including the boats, must be carried on their backs. The march of the canoes on dry land is a curious sight. Andrew Marvell described it two hundred years ago when he was poetizing beside the little river Wharfe in Yorkshire:—

"*And now the salmon-fishers moist*
Their leathern boats begin to hoist,
And like antipodes in shoes
Have shod their heads in their canoes.
How tortoise-like, but none so slow,
These rational amphibii go!"

But the sportsman carries nothing, except perhaps his gun, or his rod, or his photographic camera; and so for him the portage is only a pleasant opportunity to stretch his legs, cramped by sitting in the canoe, and to renew his acquaintance with the pretty things that are in the woods.

We sauntered along the trail, Damon and I, as if school were out and would never keep again. How fresh and tonic the forest seemed as we plunged into its bath of shade. There were our old friends the cedars, with their roots twisted across the path; and the white birches, so trim in youth and so shaggy in age; and the sociable spruces and balsams, crowding close together, and interlacing their arms overhead. There were the little springs, trickling through the moss; and the slippery logs laid across the marshy places; and the fallen trees, cut in two and pushed aside,—for this was a much-travelled portage.

Around the open spaces, the tall meadow-rue stood dressed in robes of fairy white and green. The blue banners of the *fleur-de-lis* were planted beside the springs. In shady corners, deeper in the wood, the fragrant pyrola lifted its scape of clustering bells, like a lily of the valley wandered to the forest. When we came to the end of the portage, a perfume like that of cyclamens in Tyrolean meadows welcomed us, and searching among the loose grasses by the water-side we found the exquisite purple spikes of the lesser fringed orchis, loveliest and most ethereal of all the woodland flowers save one. And what one is that? Ah, my friend, it is your own particular favourite, the flower, by whatever name you call it, that you plucked long ago when you were walking in the forest with your sweetheart,—

"*Im wunderschönen Monat Mai*
Als alle Knospen sprangen."

We launched our canoes again on the great pool at the foot of the first fall,—a broad sweep of water a mile long and half a mile wide, full of eddies and strong currents, and covered with drifting foam. There was the old camp-ground on the point, where I had tented so often with my lady Greygown, fishing for ouananiche, the famous land-locked salmon of Lake St. John. And there were the big fish, showing their back fins as they circled lazily around in the eddies, as if they were waiting to play with us. But the goal of our day's journey was miles away, and we swept along with the stream, now through a rush of quick water, boiling and foaming, now through a still place like a lake, now through

"*Fairy crowds*
Of islands, that together lie,
As quietly as spots of sky
Among the evening clouds."

The beauty of the shores was infinitely varied, and unspoiled by any sign of the presence of man. We met no company except a few kingfishers, and a pair of gulls who had come up from the sea to spend the summer, and a large flock of wild ducks, which the guides call "Betseys," as if they were all of the gentler sex. In such a big family of girls we supposed that a few would not be missed, and Damon bagged two of the tenderest for our supper.

In the still water at the mouth of the Rivière Mistook, just above the Rapide aux Cèdres, we went ashore on a level wooded bank to make our first camp and cook our dinner. Let me try to sketch our men as they are busied about the fire.

They are all French Canadians of unmixed blood, descendants of the men who came to New France with Samuel de Champlain, that incomparable old woodsman and life-long lover of the wilderness. Ferdinand Larouche is our *chef*—there must be a head in every party for the sake of harmony—and his assistant is his brother François. Ferdinand is a stocky little fellow, a "sawed off" man, not more than five feet two inches tall, but every inch of him is pure vim. He can carry a big canoe or a hundred-weight of camp stuff over a mile portage without stopping to take breath. He is a capital canoe-man, with prudence enough to balance his courage, and a fair cook, with plenty of that quality which is wanting in the ordinary cook of commerce—good humour. Always joking, whistling, singing, he brings the atmosphere of a perpetual holiday along with him. His weather-worn coat covers a heart full of music. He has two talents which make him a marked man among his comrades. He plays the fiddle to the delight of all the balls and weddings through the country-side; and he speaks English to the admiration and envy of the other guides. But like all men of genius he is modest about his accomplishments. "H'I not spik good h'English—h'only for camp—fishin', cookin', dhe voyage—h'all dhose t'ings." The aspirates puzzle him. He can get through a slash of fallen timber more easily than a sentence full of "this" and "that." Sometimes he expresses his meaning queerly. He was telling me once about his farm, "not far off here, in dhe Rivière au Cochon, river of dhe pig, you call 'im. H'I am a widow, got five sons, t'ree of dhem are girls." But he usually ends by falling back into French, which, he assures you, you speak to perfection, "much better than the Canadians; the French of Paris in short—M'sieu' has been in Paris?" Such courtesy is born in the blood, and is irresistible. You cannot help returning the compliment and assuring him that his English is remarkable, good enough for all practical purposes, better than any of the other guides can speak. And so it is.

François is a little taller, a little thinner, and considerably quieter than Ferdinand. He laughs loyally at his brother's jokes, and sings the response to his songs, and wields a good second paddle in the canoe.

Jean—commonly called Johnny—Morel is a tall, strong man of fifty, with a bushy red beard that would do credit to a pirate. But when you look at him more closely, you see that he has a clear, kind blue eye and a most honest, friendly face under his slouch hat. He has travelled these woods and waters for thirty years, so that he knows the way through them by a thousand familiar signs, as well as you know the streets of the city. He is our pathfinder.

The bow paddle in his canoe is held by his son Joseph, a lad not quite fifteen, but already as tall, and almost as strong as a man. "He is yet of the youth," said Johnny, "and he knows not the affairs of the camp. This trip is for him the first—it is his school—but I hope he will content you. He is good, M'sieu', and of the strongest for his age. I have educated already two sons in the bow of my canoe. The oldest has gone to *Pennsylvanie*; he peels the bark there for the tanning of leather. The second had the misfortune of breaking his leg, so that he can no longer kneel to paddle. He has descended to the making of shoes. Joseph is my third pupil. And I have still a younger one at home waiting to come into my school."

A touch of family life like that is always refreshing, and doubly so in the wilderness. For what is fatherhood at its best, everywhere, but the training of good men to take the teacher's place when his work is done? Some day, when Johnny's rheumatism has made his joints a little stiffer and his eyes have lost something of their keenness, he will be wielding the second paddle in the boat, and going out only on the short and easy trips. It will be young Joseph that steers the canoe through the dangerous places, and carries the heaviest load over the portages, and leads the way on the long journeys.

It has taken me longer to describe our men than it took them to prepare our frugal meal: a pot of tea, the woodsman's favourite drink, (I never knew a good guide that would not go without whisky rather than without tea,) a few slices of toast and juicy rashers of bacon, a kettle of boiled potatoes, and a relish of crackers and cheese. We were in a hurry to be off for an afternoon's fishing, three or four miles down the river, at the Ile Maligne.

The island is well named, for it is the most perilous place on the river, and has a record of disaster and death. The scattered waters of the Discharge are drawn together here into one deep, narrow, powerful stream, flowing between gloomy shores of granite. In mid-channel the wicked island shows its scarred and bristling head, like a giant ready to dispute the passage. The river rushes straight at the rocky brow, splits into two currents, and raves away on both sides of the island in a double chain of furious falls and rapids.

In these wild waters we fished with immense delight and fair success, scrambling down among the huge rocks along the shore, and joining the excitement of an Alpine climb with the placid pleasures of angling. At nightfall we were at home again in our camp, with half a score of ouananiche, weighing from one to four pounds each.

Our next day's journey was long and variegated. A portage of a mile or two across the Ile d'Alma, with a cart to haul our canoes and stuff, brought us to the Little Discharge, down which we floated for a little way, and then hauled through the village of St. Joseph to the foot of the Carcajou, or Wildcat Falls. A mile of quick water was soon passed, and we came to the junction of the Little Discharge with the Grand Discharge at the point where the picturesque club-house stands in a grove of birches beside the big Vache Caille Falls. It is lively work crossing the pool here, when the water is high and the canoes are heavy; but we went through the labouring seas safely, and landed some distance below, at the head of the Rapide Gervais, to eat our lunch. The water was too rough to run down with loaded boats, so Damon and I had to walk about three miles along the river-bank, while the men went down with the canoes.

On our way beside the rapids, Damon geologised, finding the marks of ancient glaciers, and bits of iron-ore, and pockets of sand full of infinitesimal garnets, and specks of gold washed from the primitive granite; and I fished, picking up a pair of ouananiche in foam-covered nooks among the rocks. The swift water was almost passed when we embarked again and ran down the last slope into a long dead-water.

The shores, at first bold and rough, covered with dense thickets of second-growth timber, now became smoother and more fertile. Scattered farms, with square, unpainted houses, and long, thatched barns, began to creep over the hills toward the river. There was a hamlet, called St. Charles, with a rude little church and a campanile of logs. The curé, robed in decent black and wearing a tall silk hat of the vintage of 1860, sat on the veranda of his trim presbytery, looking down upon us, like an image of propriety smiling at Bohemianism. Other craft appeared on the river. A man and his wife paddling an old dugout, with half a dozen children packed in amidships; a crew of lumbermen, in a sharp-nosed bateau, picking up stray logs along the banks; a couple of boatloads of young people returning merrily from a holiday visit; a party of berry-pickers in a flat-bottomed skiff; all the life of the country-side was in evidence on the river. We felt quite as if we had been "in the swim" of society, when at length we reached the point where the Rivière des Aunes came tumbling down a hundred-foot ladder of broken black rocks. There we pitched our tents in a strip of meadow by the water-side, where we could have the sound of the falls for a slumber-song all night and the whole river for a bath at sunrise.

A sparkling draught of crystal weather was poured into our stirrup-cup in the morning, as we set out for a drive of fifteen miles across country to the Rivière à l'Ours, a tributary of the crooked, unnavigable river of Alders. The canoes and luggage were loaded on a couple of *charrettes*, or two-wheeled carts. But for us and the guides there were two *quatre-roues*, the typical vehicles of the century, as characteristic of Canada as the carriole is of Norway. It is a two-seated buckboard, drawn by one horse, and the back seat is covered with a hood like an old-fashioned poke bonnet. The road is of clay and always rutty. It runs level for a while, and then jumps up a steep ridge and down again, or into a deep gully and out again. The *habitant's* idea of good driving is to let his horse slide down the hill and gallop up. This imparts a spasmodic quality to the motion, like Carlyle's style.

The native houses are strung along the road. The modern pattern has a convex angle in the roof, and dormer-windows; it is a rustic adaptation of the Mansard. The antique pattern, which is far more picturesque, has a concave curve in the roof, and the eaves project like eyebrows, shading the flatness of the face. Paint is a rarity. The prevailing colour is the soft gray of weather-beaten wood. Sometimes, in the better class of houses, a gallery is built across the front and around one side, and a square of garden is fenced in, with dahlias and hollyhocks and marigolds, and perhaps a struggling rose-bush, and usually a small patch of tobacco growing in one corner. Once in a long while you may see a balm-of-Gilead tree, or a clump of sapling poplars, planted near the door.

How much better it would have been if the farmer had left a few of the noble forest-trees to shade his house. But then, when the farmer came into the wilderness he was not a farmer, he was first of all a wood-chopper. He regarded the forest as a stubborn enemy in possession of his land. He attacked it with fire and axe and exterminated it, instead of keeping a few captives to hold their green umbrellas over his head when at last his grain fields should be smiling around him and he should sit down on his doorstep to smoke a pipe of home-grown tobacco.

In the time of adversity one should prepare for prosperity. I fancy there are a good many people unconsciously repeating the mistake of the Canadian farmer—chopping down all the native growths of life, clearing the ground of all the useless pretty things that seem to cumber it, sacrificing everything to utility and success. We fell the last green tree for the sake of raising an extra hill of potatoes; and never stop to think what an ugly, barren place we may have to sit in while we eat them. The ideals, the attachments—yes, even the dreams of youth are worth saving. For the artificial tastes with which age tries to make good their loss grow very slowly and cast but a slender shade.

Most of the Canadian farmhouses have their ovens out-of-doors. We saw them everywhere; rounded edifices of clay, raised on a foundation of logs, and usually covered with a pointed roof of boards. They looked like little family chapels—and so they were; shrines where the ritual of the good housewife was celebrated, and the gift of daily bread, having been honestly earned, was thankfully received.

At one house we noticed a curious fragment of domestic economy. Half a pig was suspended over the chimney, and the smoke of the summer fire was turned to account in curing the winter's meat. I guess the children of that family had a peculiar fondness for the parental roof-tree. We saw them making mud-pies in the road, and imagined that they looked lovingly up at the pendent porker, outlined against the sky,—a sign of promise, prophetic of bacon.

About noon the road passed beyond the region of habitation into a barren land, where blueberries were the only crop, and partridges took the place of chickens. Through this rolling gravelly plain, sparsely wooded and glowing with the tall magenta bloom of the fireweed, we drove toward the mountains, until the road went to seed and we could follow it no longer. Then we took to the water and began to pole our canoes up the River of the Bear. It was a clear, amber-coloured stream, not more than ten or fifteen yards wide, running swift and strong, over beds of sand and rounded pebbles. The canoes went wallowing and plunging up the narrow channel, between thick banks of alders, like clumsy sea-monsters. All the grace with which they move under the strokes of the paddle, in large waters, was gone. They looked uncouth and predatory, like a pair of seals that I once saw swimming far up the river Ristigouche in chase of fish. From the bow of each canoe the landing-net stuck out as a symbol of destruction—after the fashion of the Dutch admiral who nailed a broom to his masthead. But it would have been impossible to sweep the trout out of that little river by any fair method of angling, for there were millions of them; not large, but lively, and brilliant, and fat; they leaped in every bend of the stream. We trailed our flies, and made quick casts here and there, as we went along. It was fishing on the wing. And when we pitched our tents in a hurry at nightfall on the low shore of Lac Sâle, among the bushes where firewood was scarce and there were no *sapins* for the beds, we were comforted for the poorness of the camp-ground by the excellence of the trout supper.

It was a bitter cold night for August. There was a skin of ice on the water-pail at daybreak. We were glad to be up and away for an early start. The river grew wilder and more difficult. There were rapids, and ruined dams built by the lumbermen years ago. At these places the trout were larger, and so plentiful that it was easy to hook two at a cast. It came on to rain furiously while we were eating our lunch. But we did not seem to mind it any more than the fish did. Here and there the river was completely blocked by fallen trees. The guides called it *bouchée*, "corked," and leaped out gayly into the water with their axes to "un-cork" it. We passed through some pretty lakes, unknown to the map-makers, and arrived, before sundown, at the Lake of the Bear, where we were to spend a couple of days. The lake was full of floating logs, and the water, raised by the heavy rains and the operations of the lumbermen, was several feet above its usual level. Nature's landing-places were all blotted out, and we had to explore halfway around the shore before we could get out comfortably. We raised the tents on a small shoulder of a hill, a few rods above the water; and a glorious camp-fire of birch logs soon made us forget our misery as though it had not been.

The name of the Lake of the Beautiful Trout made us desire to visit it. The portage was said to be only fifty acres long (the *arpent* is the popular measure of distance here), but it passed over a ridge of newly burned land, and was so entangled with ruined woods and desolate of birds and flowers that it seemed to us at least five miles. The lake was charming—a sheet of singularly clear water, of a pale green tinge, surrounded by wooded hills. In the translucent depths trout and pike live together, but whether in peace or not I cannot tell. Both of them grow to an enormous size, but the pike are larger and have more capacious jaws. One of them broke my tackle and went off with a silver spoon in his mouth, as if he had been born to it. Of course the guides vowed that they saw him as he passed under the canoe, and declared that he must weigh thirty or forty pounds. The spectacles of regret always magnify.

The trout were coy. We took only five of them, perfect specimens of the true *Salvelinus fontinalis*, with square tails, and carmine spots on their dark, mottled sides; the largest weighed three pounds and three-quarters, and the others were almost as heavy.

On our way back to the camp we found the portage beset by innumerable and bloodthirsty foes. There are four grades of insect malignity in the woods. The mildest is represented by the winged idiot that John Burroughs' little boy called a "blunderhead." He dances stupidly before your face, as if lost in admiration, and finishes his pointless tale by getting in your eye, or down your throat. The next grade is represented by the midges. "Bite 'em no see 'em," is the Indian name for these invisible atoms of animated pepper which settle upon you in the twilight and make your skin burn like fire. But their hour is brief, and when they depart they leave not a bump behind. One step lower in the scale we find the mosquito, or rather he finds us, and makes his poisoned mark upon our skin. But after all, he has his good qualities. The mosquito is a gentlemanly pirate. He carries his weapon openly, and gives notice of an attack. He respects the decencies of life, and does not strike below the belt, or creep down the back of your neck. But the black fly is at the bottom of the moral scale. He is an unmitigated ruffian, the plug-ugly of the woods. He looks like a tiny, immature house-fly, with white legs as if he must be innocent. But, in fact, he crawls like a serpent and bites like a dog. No portion of the human frame is sacred from his greed. He takes his pound of flesh anywhere, and does not scruple to take the blood with it. As a rule you can defend yourself, to some degree, against him, by wearing a head-net, tying your sleeves around your wrists and your trousers around your ankles, and anointing yourself with grease, flavoured with pennyroyal, for which cleanly and honest scent he has a coarse aversion. But sometimes, especially on burned land, about the middle of a warm afternoon, when a rain is threatening, the horde of black flies descend in force and fury knowing that their time is short. Then there is no escape. Suits of chain armour, Nubian ointments of far-smelling potency, would not save you. You must do as our guides did on the portage, submit to fate and walk along in heroic silence, like Marco Bozzaris "bleeding at every pore,"—or do as Damon and I did, break into ejaculations and a run, until you reach a place where you can light a smudge and hold your head over it.

"And yet," said my comrade, as we sat coughing and rubbing our eyes in the painful shelter of the smoke, "there are worse trials than this in the civilised districts: social enmities, and newspaper scandals, and religious persecutions. The blackest fly I ever saw is the Reverend ——" but here his voice was fortunately choked by a fit of coughing.

A couple of wandering Indians—descendants of the *Montagnais*, on whose hunting domain we were travelling—dropped in at our camp that night as we sat around the fire. They gave us the latest news about the portages on our further journey; how far they had been blocked with fallen trees, and whether the water was high or low in the rivers—just as a visitor at home would talk about the effect of the strikes on the stock market, and the prospects of the newest organization of the non-voting classes for the overthrow of Tammany Hall. Every phase of civilisation or barbarism creates its own conversational currency. The weather, like the old Spanish dollar, is the only coin that passes everywhere.

But our Indians did not carry much small change about them. They were dark, silent chaps, soon talked out; and then they sat sucking their pipes before the fire, (as dumb as their own wooden effigies in front of a tobacconist's shop,) until the spirit moved them, and they vanished in their canoe down the dark lake. Our own guides were very different. They were as full of conversation as a spruce-tree is of gum. When all shallower themes were exhausted they would discourse of bears and canoes and lumber and fish, forever. After Damon and I had left the fire and rolled ourselves in the blankets in our own tent, we could hear the men going on and on with their simple jests and endless tales of adventure, until sleep drowned their voices.

It was the sound of a French *chanson* that woke us early on the morning of our departure from the Lake of the Bear. A gang of lumbermen were bringing a lot of logs through the lake. Half-hidden in the cold gray mist that usually betokens a fine day, and wet to the waist from splashing about after their unwieldy flock, these rough fellows were singing at their work as cheerfully as a party of robins in a cherrytree at sunrise. It was like the miller and the two girls whom Wordsworth saw dancing in their boats on the Thames:

"*They dance not for me,*
Yet mine is their glee!
Thus pleasure is spread through the earth
In stray gifts to be claimed by whoever shall find;
Thus a rich loving-kindness, redundantly kind,
Moves all nature to gladness and mirth."

But our later thoughts of the lumbermen were not altogether grateful, when we arrived that day, after a mile of portage, at the little Rivière Blanche, upon which we had counted to float us down to Lac Tchitagama, and found that they had stolen all its water to float their logs down the Lake of the Bear. The poor little river was as dry as a theological novel. There was nothing left of it except the bed and the bones; it was like a Connecticut stream in the middle of August. All its pretty secrets were laid bare; all its music was hushed. The pools that lingered among the rocks seemed like big tears; and the voice of the forlorn rivulets that trickled in here and there, seeking the parent stream, was a voice of weeping and complaint.

For us the loss meant a hard day's work, scrambling over slippery stones, and splashing through puddles, and forcing a way through the tangled thickets on the bank, instead of a pleasant two hours' run on a swift current. We ate our dinner on a sandbank in what was once the middle of a pretty pond; and entered, as the sun was sinking, a narrow wooded gorge between the hills, completely filled by a chain of small lakes, where travelling became easy and pleasant. The steep shores, clothed with cedar and black spruce and dark-blue fir-trees, rose sheer from the water; the passage from lake to lake was a tiny rapid a few yards long, gurgling through mossy rocks; at the foot of the chain there was a longer rapid, with a portage beside it. We emerged from the dense bush suddenly and found ourselves face to face with Lake Tchitagama.

How the heart expands at such a view! Nine miles of shining water lay stretched before us, opening through the mountains that guarded it on both sides with lofty walls of green and gray, ridge over ridge, point beyond point, until the vista ended in

"*Yon orange sunset waning slow.*"

At a moment like this one feels a sense of exultation. It is a new discovery of the joy of living. And yet, my friend and I confessed to each other, there was a tinge of sadness, an inexplicable regret mingled with our joy. Was it the thought of how few human eyes had even seen that lovely vision? Was it the dim foreboding that we might never see it again? Who can explain the secret pathos of Nature's loveliness? It is a touch of melancholy inherited from our mother Eve. It is an unconscious memory of the lost Paradise. It is the sense that even if we should find another Eden, we would not be fit to enjoy it perfectly, nor stay in it forever.

Our first camp on Tchitagama was at the sunrise end of the lake, in a bay paved with small round stones, laid close together and beaten firmly down by the waves. There, and along the shores below, at the mouth of a little river that foamed in over a ledge of granite, and in the shadow of cliffs of limestone and feldspar, we trolled and took many fish: pike of enormous size, fresh-water sharks, devourers of nobler game, fit only to kill and throw away; huge old trout of six or seven pounds, with broad tails and hooked jaws, fine fighters and poor food; stupid, wide-mouthed chub—*ouitouche*, the Indians call them—biting at hooks that were not baited for them; and best of all, high-bred ouananiche, pleasant to capture and delicate to eat.

Our second camp was on a sandy point at the sunset end of the lake—a fine place for bathing, and convenient to the wild meadows and blueberry patches, where Damon went to hunt for bears. He did not find any; but once he heard a great noise in the bushes, which he thought was a bear; and he declared that he got quite as much excitement out of it as if it had had four legs and a mouthful of teeth.

He brought back from one of his expeditions an Indian letter, which he had found in a cleft stick by the river. It was a sheet of birch-bark with a picture drawn on it in charcoal; five Indians in a canoe paddling up the river, and one in another canoe pointing in another direction; we read it as a message left by a hunting party, telling their companions not to go on up the river, because it was already occupied, but to turn off on a side stream.

There was a sign of a different kind nailed to an old stump behind our camp. It was the top of a soap-box, with an inscription after this fashion:

AD. MEYER & B. LEVIT
Soap Mfrs. N. Y.
Camped here July 18—
1 Trout 17-1/2 pounds. II Ouan
anisHes 18-1/2 pounds. One
Pike 147-1/2 lbs.

There was a combination of piscatorial pride and mercantile enterprise in this quaint device, that took our fancy. It suggested also a curious question of psychology in regard to the inhibitory influence of horses and fish upon the human nerve of veracity. We named the place "Point Ananias."

And yet, in fact, it was a wild and lonely spot, and not even the Hebrew inscription could spoil the sense of solitude that surrounded uswhen the night came, and the storm howled across the lake, and the darkness encircled us with a wall that only seemed the more dense and impenetrable as the firelight blazed and leaped within the black ring.

"How far away is the nearest house, Johnny?"

"I don't know; fifty miles, I suppose."

"And what would you do if the canoes were burned, or if a tree fell and smashed them?"

"Well, I'd say a *Pater noster*, and take bread and bacon enough for four days, and an axe, and plenty of matches, and make a straight line through the woods. But it wouldn't be a joke, M'sieu', I can tell you."

The river Peribonca, into which Lake Tchitagama flows without a break, is the noblest of all the streams that empty into Lake St. John. It is said to be more than three hundred miles long, and at the mouth of the lake it is perhaps a thousand feet wide, flowing with a deep, still current through the forest. The dead-water lasted for several miles;

then the river sloped into a rapid, spread through a net of islands, and broke over a ledge in a cataract. Another quiet stretch was followed by another fall, and so on, along the whole course of the river.

We passed three of these falls in the first day's voyage (by portages so steep and rough that an Adirondack guide would have turned gray at the sight of them), and camped at night just below the Chûte du Diable, where we found some ouananiche in the foam. Our tents were on an islet, and all around we saw the primeval, savage beauty of a world unmarred by man.

The river leaped, shouting, down its double stairway of granite, rejoicing like a strong man to run a race. The afterglow in the western sky deepened from saffron to violet among the tops of the cedars, and over the cliffs rose the moonlight, paling the heavens but glorifying the earth. There was something large and generous and untrammelled in the scene, recalling one of Walt Whitman's rhapsodies:—

"Earth of departed sunsets! Earth of the mountains
misty-topped!
Earth of the vitreous pour of the full moon just
tinged with blue!
Earth of shine and dark, mottling the tide of the
river!"

All the next day we went down with the current. Regiments of black spruce stood in endless files like grenadiers, each tree capped with a thick tuft of matted cones and branches. Tall white birches leaned out over the stream, Narcissus-like, as if to see their own beauty in the moving mirror. There were touches of colour on the banks, the ragged pink flowers of the Joe-Pye-weed (which always reminds me of a happy, good-natured tramp), and the yellow eardrops of the jewel-weed, and the intense blue of the closed gentian, that strange flower which, like a reticent heart, never opens to the light. Sometimes the river spread out like a lake, between high bluffs of sand fully a mile apart; and again it divided into many channels, winding cunningly down among the islands as if it were resolved to slip around the next barrier of rock without a fall. There were eight of these huge natural dams in the course of that day's journey. Sometimes we followed one of the side canals, and made the portage at a distance from the main cataract; and sometimes we ran with the central current to the very brink of the chûte, darting aside just in time to escape going over. At the foot of the last fall we made our camp on a curving beach of sand, and spent the rest of the afternoon in fishing.

It was interesting to see how closely the guides could guess at the weight of the fish by looking at them. The ouananiche are much longer in proportion to their weight than trout, and a novice almost always overestimates them. But the guides were not deceived. "This one will weigh four pounds and three-quarters, and this one four pounds, but that one not more than three pounds; he is meagre, M'sieu', *but* he is meagre." When we went ashore and tried the spring balance (which every angler ought to carry with him, as an aid to his conscience), the guides guess usually proved to be within an ounce or two of the fact. Any one of the senses can be educated to do the work of the others. The eyes of these experienced fishermen were as sensitive to weight as if they had been made to use as scales.

Below the last fall the Peribonca flows for a score of miles with an unbroken, ever-widening stream, through low shores of forest and bush and meadow. Near its mouth the Little Peribonca joins it, and the immense flood, nearly two miles wide, pours into Lake St. John. Here we saw the first outpost of civilisation—a huge unpainted storehouse, where supplies are kept for the lumbermen and the new settlers. Here also we found the tiny, lame steam launch that was to carry us back to the Hotel Roberval. Our canoes were stowed upon the roof of the cabin, and we embarked for the last stage of our long journey.

As we came out of the river-mouth, the opposite shore of the lake was invisible, and a stiff "Nor'wester" was rolling big waves across the bar. It was like putting out into the open sea. The launch laboured and puffed along for four or five miles, growing more and more asthmatic with every breath. Then there was an explosion in the engine-room. Some necessary part of the intestinal machinery had blown out. There was a moment of confusion. The captain hurried to drop the anchor, and the narrow craft lay rolling in the billows.

What to do? The captain shrugged his shoulders like a Frenchman. "Wait here, I suppose." But how long? "Who knows? Perhaps till to-morrow; perhaps the day after. They will send another boat to look for us in the course of time."

But the quarters were cramped; the weather looked ugly; if the wind should rise, the cranky launch would not be a safe cradle for the night. Damon and I preferred the canoes, for they at least would float if they were capsized. So we stepped into the frail, buoyant shells of bark once more, and danced over the big waves toward the shore. We made a camp on a wind-swept point of sand, and felt like shipwrecked mariners. But it was a gilt-edged shipwreck. For our larder was still full, and as if to provide us with the luxuries as well as the necessities of life, Nature had spread an inexhaustible dessert of the largest and most luscious blueberries around our tents.

After supper, strolling along the beach, we debated the best way of escape; whether to send one of our canoes around the eastern shore of the lake that night, to meet the steamer at the Island House and bring it to our rescue; or to set out the next morning, and paddle both canoes around the western end of the lake, thirty miles, to the Hotel Roberval. While we were talking, we came to a dry old birch-tree, with ragged, curling bark. "Here is a torch," cried Damon, "to throw light upon the situation." He touched a match to it, and the flames flashed up the tall trunk until it was transformed into a pillar of fire. But the sudden illumination burned out, and our counsels were wrapt again in darkness and uncertainty, when there came a great uproar of steam-whistles from the lake. They must be signalling for us. What could it mean?

We fired our guns, leaped into a canoe, leaving two of the guides to break camp, and paddled out swiftly into the night. It seemed an endless distance before we found the feeble light where the crippled launch was tossing at anchor. The captain shouted something about a larger steamboat and a raft of logs, out in the lake, a mile or two beyond. Presently we saw the lights, and the orange glow of the cabin windows. Was she coming, or going, or standing still? We paddled on as fast as we could, shouting and firing off a revolver until we had no more cartridges. We were resolved not to let that mysterious vessel escape us, and threw ourselves with energy into the novel excitement of chasing a steamboat in the dark.

Then the lights began to swing around; the throbbing of paddle-wheels grew louder and louder; she was evidently coming straight toward us. At that moment it flashed upon us that, while she had plenty of lights, we had none! We were lying, invisible, right across her track. The character of the steamboat chase was reversed. We turned and fled, as the guides say, *à quatre pattes*, into illimitable space, trying to get out of the way of our too powerful friend. It makes considerable difference, in the voyage of life, whether you chase the steamboat, or the steamboat chases you.

Meantime our other canoe had approached unseen. The steamer passed safely between the two boats, slackening speed as the pilot caught our loud halloo! She loomed up above us like a man-of-war, and as we climbed the ladder to the main-deck we felt that we had indeed gotten out of the wilderness. My old friend, Captain Savard, made us welcome. He had been sent out, much to his disgust, to catch a runaway boom of logs and tow it back to Roberval; it would be an all night affair; but we must take possession of his stateroom and make ourselves comfortable; he would certainly bring us to the hotel in time for breakfast. So he went off on the upper deck, and we heard him stamping about and yelling to his crew as they struggled to get their unwieldy drove of six thousand logs in motion.

All night long we assisted at the lumbermen's difficult enterprise. We heard the steamer snorting and straining at her clumsy, stubborn convoy. The hoarse shouts of the crew, disguised in a mongrel dialect which made them (perhaps fortunately) less intelligible and more forcible, mingled with our broken dreams.

But it was, in fact, a fitting close of our voyage. For what were we doing? It was the last stage of the woodman's labour. It was the gathering of a wild herd of the houses and churches and ships and bridges that grow in the forests, and bringing them into the fold of human service. I wonder how often the inhabitant of the snug Queen Anne cottage in the suburbs remembers the picturesque toil and varied hardship that it has cost to hew and drag his walls and floors and pretty peaked roofs out of the backwoods. It might enlarge his home, and make his musings by the winter fireside less commonplace, to give a kindly thought now and then to the long chain of human workers through whose hands the timber of his house has passed, since it first felt the stroke of the axe in the snow-bound winter woods, and floated, through the spring and summer, on far-off lakes and little rivers, *au large*.

1894.

TROUT-FISHING IN THE TRAUN

"Those who wish to forget painful thoughts do well to absent themselves for a time from the ties and objects that recall them; but we can be said only to fulfil our destiny in the place that gave us birth. I should on this account like well enough to spend the whole of my life in travelling abroad, if I could anywhere borrow another life to spend afterwards at home."——

WILLIAM HAZLITT: *On Going a Journey.*

TROUT-FISHING IN THE TRAUN

The peculiarity of trout-fishing in the Traun is that one catches principally grayling. But in this it resembles some other pursuits which are not without their charm for minds open to the pleasures of the unexpected—for example, reading George Borrow's *The Bible in Spain* with a view to theological information, or going to the opening night at the Academy of Design with the intention of looking at pictures.

Moreover, there are really trout in the Traun, *rari nantes in gurgite*; and in some places more than in others; and all of high spirit, though few of great size. Thus the angler has his favourite problem: Given an unknown stream and two kinds of fish, the one better than the other; to find the better kind, and determine the hour at which they will rise. This is sport.

As for the little river itself, it has so many beauties that one does not think of asking whether it has any faults. Constant fulness, and crystal clearness, and refreshing coolness of living water, pale green like the jewel that is called *aqua marina*, flowing over beds of clean sand and bars of polished gravel, and dropping in momentary foam from rocky ledges, between banks that are shaded by groves of fir and ash and poplar, or through dense thickets of alder and willow, or across meadows of smooth verdure sloping up to quaint old-world villages—all these are features of the ideal little river.

I have spoken of these personal qualities first, because a truly moral writer ought to make more of character than of position. A good river in a bad country would be more worthy of affection than a bad river in a good country. But the Traun has also the advantages of an excellent worldly position. For it rises all over the Salzkammergut, the summer hunting-ground of the Austrian Emperor, and flows through that most picturesque corner of his domain from end to end. Under the desolate cliffs of the Todtengebirge on the east, and below the shining ice-fields of the Dachstein on the south, and from the green alps around St. Wolfgang on the west, the translucent waters are gathered in little tarns, and shot through roaring brooks, and spread into lakes of wondrous beauty, and poured through growing streams, until at last they are all united just below the summer villa of his Kaiserly and Kingly Majesty, Francis Joseph, and flow away northward, through the rest of his game-preserve, into the Traunsee. It is an imperial playground, and such as I would consent to hunt the chamois in, if an inscrutable Providence had made me a kingly kaiser, or even a plain king or an unvarnished kaiser. But, failing this, I was perfectly content to spend a few idle days in fishing for trout and catching grayling, at such times and places as the law of the Austrian Empire allowed.

For it must be remembered that every stream in these over-civilised European countries belongs to somebody, by purchase or rent. And all the fish in the stream are supposed to belong to the person who owns or rents it. They do not know their master's voice, neither will they follow when he calls. But they are theoretically his. To this legal fiction the untutored American must conform. He must learn to clothe his natural desires in the raiment of lawful sanction, and take out some kind of a license before he follows his impulse to fish.

It was in the town of Aussee, at the junction of the two highest branches of the Traun, that this impulse came upon me, mildly irresistible. The full bloom of mid-July gayety in that ancient watering-place was dampened, but not extinguished, by two days of persistent and surprising showers. I had exhausted the possibilities of interest in the old Gothic church, and felt all that a man should feel in deciphering the mural tombstones of the families who were exiled for their faith in the days of the Reformation. The throngs of merry Hebrews from Vienna and Buda-Pesth, amazingly arrayed as mountaineers and milk-maids, walking up and down the narrow streets under umbrellas, had Cleopatra's charm of an infinite variety; but custom staled it. The woodland paths, winding everywhere through the plantations of fir-trees and provided with appropriate names on wooden labels, and benches for rest and conversation at discreet intervals, were too moist for even the nymphs to take delight in them. The only creatures that suffered nothing by the rain were the two swift, limpid Trauns, racing through the woods, like eager and unabashed lovers, to meet in the middle of the village. They were as clear, as joyous, as musical as if the sun were shining. The very sight of their opalescent rapids and eddying pools was an invitation to that gentle sport which is said to have the merit of growing better as the weather grows worse.

I laid this fact before the landlord of the hotel of the Erzherzog Johann, as poetically as I could, but he assured me that it was of no consequence without an invitation from the gentleman to whom the streams belonged; and he had gone away for a week. The landlord was such a good-natured person, and such an excellent sleeper, that it was impossible to believe that he could have even the smallest inaccuracy upon his conscience. So I bade him farewell, and took my way, four miles through the woods, to the lake from which one of the streams flowed.

It was called the Gründlsee. As I do not know the origin of the name, I cannot consistently make any moral or historical reflections upon it. But if it has never become famous, it ought to be, for the sake of a cozy and busy little Inn, perched on a green hill beside the lake and overlooking the whole length of it, from the groups of toy villas at the foot to the heaps of real mountains at the head. This Inn kept a thin but happy landlord, who provided me with a blue license to angle, for the inconsiderable sum of fifteen cents a day. This conferred the right of fishing not only in the Gründlsee, but also in the smaller tarn of Toplitz, a mile above it, and in the swift stream which unites them. It all coincided with my desire as if by magic. A row of a couple of miles to the head of the lake, and a walk through the forest, brought me to the smaller pond; and as the afternoon sun was ploughing pale furrows through the showers, I waded out on a point of reeds and cast the artful fly in the shadow of the great cliffs of the Dead Mountains.

It was a fit scene for a lone fisherman. But four sociable tourists promptly appeared to act as spectators and critics. Fly-fishing usually strikes the German mind as an eccentricity which calls for remonstrance. After one of the tourists had suggestively narrated the tale of seven trout which he had caught in another lake, *with worms*, on the previous Sunday, they went away for a row, (with salutations in which politeness but thinly veiled their pity,) and left me still whipping the water in vain. Nor was the fortune of the day much better in the stream below. It was a long and wet wade for three fish too small to keep. I came out on the shore of the lake, where I had left the row-boat, with an empty bag and a feeling of damp discouragement.

There was still an hour or so of daylight, and a beautiful place to fish where the stream poured swirling out into the lake. A rise, and a large one, though rather slow, awakened my hopes. Another rise, evidently made by a heavy fish, made me certain that virtue was about to be rewarded. The third time the hook went home. I felt the solid weight of the fish against the spring of the rod, and that curious thrill which runs up the line and down the arm, changing, somehow or other, into a pleasurable sensation of excitement as it reaches the brain. But it was only for a moment; and then came that foolish, feeble shaking of the line from side to side which tells the angler that he has hooked a great, big, leather-mouthed chub—a fish which Izaak Walton says "the French esteem so mean as to call him Un Vilain." Was it for this that I had come to the country of Francis Joseph?

I took off the flies and put on one of those phantom minnows which have immortalised the name of a certain Mr. Brown. The minnow swung on a long line as the boat passed back and forth across the current, once, twice, three times—and on the fourth circle there was a sharp strike. The rod bent almost double, and the reel sang shrilly to the first rush of the fish. He ran; he doubled; he went to the bottom and sulked; he tried to go under the boat; he did all that a game fish can do, except leaping. After twenty minutes he was tired enough to be lifted gently into the boat by a hand slipped around his gills, and there he was, a *lachs-forelle* of three pounds' weight: small pointed head; silver sides mottled with dark spots; square, powerful tail and large fins—a fish not unlike the land-locked salmon of the Saguenay, but more delicate.

Half an hour later he was lying on the grass in front of the Inn. The waiters paused, with their hands full of dishes, to look at him; and the landlord called his guests, including my didactic tourists, to observe the superiority of the trout of the Gründlsee. The maids also came to look; and the buxom cook, with her spotless apron and bare arms akimbo, was drawn from her kitchen, and pledged her culinary honour that such a *pracht-kerl* should be served up in her very best style. The angler who is insensible to this sort of indirect flattery through his fish does not exist. Even the most indifferent of men thinks more favourably of people who know a good trout when they see it, and sits down to his supper with kindly feelings. Possibly he reflects, also, upon the incident as a hint of the usual size of the fish in that neighbourhood. He remembers that he may have been favoured in this case beyond his deserts by good-fortune, and resolving not to put too heavy a strain upon it, considers the next place where it would be well for him to angle.

Hallstatt is about ten miles below Aussee. The Traun here expands into a lake, very dark and deep, shut in by steep and lofty mountains. The railway runs along the eastern shore. On the other side, a mile away, you see the old town, its white houses clinging to the cliff like lichens to the face of a rock. The guide-book calls it "a highly original situation." But this is one of the cases where a little less originality and a little more reasonableness might be desired, at least by the permanent inhabitants. A ledge under the shadow of a precipice makes a trying winter residence. The people of Hallstatt are not a blooming race: one sees many dwarfs and cripples among them. But to the summer traveller the place seems wonderfully picturesque. Most of the streets are flights of steps. The high-road has barely room to edge itself through among the old houses, between the window-gardens of bright flowers. On the hottest July day the afternoon is cool and shady. The gay, little skiffs and long, open gondolas are flitting continually along the lake, which is the main street of Hallstatt.

The incongruous, but comfortable, modern hotel has a huge glass veranda, where you can eat your dinner and observe human nature in its transparent holiday disguises. I was much pleased and entertained by a family, or confederacy, of people attired as peasants—the menwith feathered hats, green stockings, and bare knees—the women with bright skirts, bodices, and silk neckerchiefs—who were always in evidence, rowing gondolas with clumsy oars, meeting the steamboat at the wharf several times a day, and filling the miniature garden of the hotel with rustic greetings and early Salzkammergut attitudes. After much conjecture, I learned that they were the family and friends of a newspaper editor from Vienna. They had the literary instinct for local colour.

The fishing at Hallstatt is at Obertraun. There is a level stretch of land above the lake, where the river flows peaceably, and the fish have leisure to feed and grow. It is leased to a peasant, who makes a business of supplying the hotels with fish. He was quite willing to give permission to an angler; and I engaged one of his sons, a capital young fellow, whose natural capacities for good fellowship were only hampered by a most extraordinary German dialect, to row me across the lake, and carry the net and a small green barrel full of water to keep the fish alive, according to the custom of the country. The first day we had only four trout large enough to put into the barrel; the next day I think there were six; the third day, I remember very well, there were ten. They were pretty creatures, weighing from half a pound to a pound each, and coloured as daintily as bits of French silk, in silver gray with faint pink spots.

There was plenty to do at Hallstatt in the mornings. An hour's walk from the town there was a fine waterfall, three hundred feet high. On the side of the mountain above the lake was one of the salt-mines for which the region is celebrated. It has been worked for ages by many successive races, from the Celt downward. Perhaps even the men of the Stone Age knew of it, and came hither for seasoning to make the flesh of the cave-bear and the mammoth more palatable. Modern pilgrims are permitted to explore the long, wet, glittering galleries with a guide, and slide down the smooth wooden rollers which join the different levels of the mines. This pastime has the same fascination as sliding down the balusters; and it is said that even queens and princesses have been delighted with it. This is a touching proof of the fundamental simplicity and unity of our human nature.

But by far the best excursion from Hallstatt was an all-day trip to the Zwieselalp—a mountain which seems to have been especially created as a point of view. From the bare summit you look right into the face of the huge, snowy Dachstein, with the wild lake of Gosau gleaming at its foot; and far away on the other side your vision ranges over a confusion of mountains, with all the white peaks of the Tyrol stretched along the horizon. Such a wide outlook as this helps the fisherman to enjoy the narrow beauties of his little rivers. No sport is at its best without interruption and contrast. To appreciate wading, one ought to climb a little on odd days.

Ischl is about ten or twelve miles below Hallstatt, in the valley of the Traun. It is the fashionable summer-resort of Austria. I found it in the high tide of amusement. The shady esplanade along the river was crowded with brave women and fair men, in gorgeous raiment; the hotels were overflowing; and there were various kinds of music and entertainments at all hours of day and night. But all this did not seem to affect the fishing.

The landlord of the Königin Elizabeth, who is also the Burgomaster and a gentleman of varied accomplishments and no leisure, kindly furnished me with a fishing license in the shape of a large pink card. There were many rules printed upon it: "All fishes under nine inches must be gently restored to the water. No instrument of capture must be used except the angle in the hand. The card of legitimation must be produced and exhibited at the polite request of any of the keepers of the river." Thus duly authorised and instructed, I sallied forth to seek my pastime according to the law.

The easiest way, in theory, was to take the afternoon train up the river to one of the villages, and fish down a mile or two in the evening, returning by the eight o'clock train. But in practice the habits of the fish interfered seriously with the latter part of this plan.

On my first day I had spent several hours in the vain effort to catch something better than small grayling. The best time for the trout was just approaching, as the broad light faded from the stream; already they were beginning to feed, when I looked up from the edge of a pool and saw the train rattling down the valley below me. Under the circumstances the only thing to do was to go on fishing. It was an even pool with steep banks, and the water ran through it very straight and swift, some four feet deep and thirty yards across. As the tail-fly reached the middle of the water, a fine trout literally turned a somersault over it, but without touching it. At the next cast he was ready, taking it with a rush that carried him into the air with the fly in his mouth. He weighed three-quarters of a pound. The next one was equally eager in rising and sharp in playing, and the third might have been his twin sister or brother. So, after casting for hours and taking nothing in the most beautiful pools, I landed three trout from one unlikely place in fifteen minutes. That was because the trout's supper-time had arrived. So had mine. I walked over to the rambling old inn at Goisern, sought the cook in the kitchen, and persuaded her, in spite of the lateness of the hour, to boil the largest of the fish for my supper, after which I rode peacefully back to Ischl by the eleven o'clock train.

For the future I resolved to give up the illusory idea of coming home by rail, and ordered a little one-horse carriage to meet me at some point on the high-road every evening at nine o'clock. In this way I managed to cover the whole stream, taking a lower part each day, from the lake of Hallstatt down to Ischl.

There was one part of the river, near Laufen, where the current was very strong and waterfally, broken by ledges of rock. Below these it rested in long, smooth reaches, much beloved by the grayling. There was no difficulty in getting two or three of them out of each run.

The grayling has a quaint beauty. His appearance is æsthetic, like a fish in a pre-Raphaelite picture. His colour, in midsummer, is a golden gray, darker on the back, and with a few black spots just behind his gills, like patches put on to bring out the pallor of his complexion. He smells of wild thyme when he first comes out of the water, wherefore St. Ambrose of Milan complimented him in courtly fashion: "*Quid specie tua gratius? Quid odore fragrantius? Quod mella fragrant, hoc tuo corpore spiras.*" But the chief glory of the grayling is the large iridescent fin on his back. You see it cutting the water as he swims near the surface; and when you have him on the bank it arches over him like a rainbow. His mouth is under his chin, and he takes the fly gently, by suction. He is, in fact, and to speak plainly, something of a sucker; but then he is a sucker idealised and refined, the flower of the family. Charles Cotton, the ingenious young friend of Walton, was all wrong in calling the grayling "one of the deadest-hearted fishes in the world." He fights and leaps and whirls, and brings his big fin to bear across the force of the current with a variety of tactics that would put his more aristocratic fellow-citizen, the trout, to the blush. Twelve of these pretty fellows, with a brace of good trout for the top, filled my big creel to the brim. And yet, such is the inborn hypocrisy of the human heart that I always pretended to myself to be disappointed because there were not more trout, and made light of the grayling as a thing of naught.

The pink fishing license did not seem to be of much use. Its exhibition was demanded only twice. Once a river guardian, who was walking down the stream with a Belgian Baron and encouraging him to continue fishing, climbed out to me on the end of a long embankment, and with proper apologies begged to be favoured with a view of my document. It turned out that his request was a favour to me, for it discovered the fact that I had left my fly-book, with the pink card in it, beside an old mill, a quarter of a mile up the stream.

Another time I was sitting beside the road, trying to get out of a very long, wet, awkward pair of wading-stockings, an occupation which is unfavourable to tranquillity of mind, when a man came up to me in the dusk and accosted me with an absence of politeness which in German amounted to an insult.

"Have you been fishing?"

"Why do you want to know?"

"Have you any right to fish?"

"What right have you to ask?"

"I am a keeper of the river. Where is your card?"

"It is in my pocket. But pardon my curiosity, where is *your* card?"

This question appeared to paralyse him. He had probably never been asked for his card before. He went lumbering off in the darkness, muttering "My card? Unheard of! *My* card!"

The routine of angling at Ischl was varied by an excursion to the Lake of St. Wolfgang and the Schafberg, an isolated mountain on whose rocky horn an inn has been built. It stands up almost like a bird-house on a pole, and commands a superb prospect; northward, across the rolling plain and the Bavarian forest; southward, over a tumultuous land of peaks and precipices. There are many lovely lakes in sight; but the loveliest of all is that which takes its name from the old saint who wandered hither from the country of the "furious Franks" and built his peaceful hermitage on the Falkenstein. What good taste some of those old saints had!

There is a venerable church in the village, with pictures attributed to Michael Wohlgemuth, and a chapel which is said to mark the spot where St. Wolfgang, who had lost his axe far up the mountain, found it, like Longfellow's arrow, in an oak, and "still unbroke." The tree is gone, so it was impossible to verify the story. But the saint's well is there, in a pavilion; with a bronze image over it, and a profitable inscription to the effect that the poorer pilgrims, "who have come unprovided with either money or wine, should be jolly well contented to find the water so fine." There is also a famous echo farther up the lake, which repeats six syllables with accuracy. It is a strange coincidence that there are just six syllables in the name of "der heilige Wolfgang." But when you translate it into English, the inspiration of the echo seems to be less exact. The sweetest thing about St. Wolfgang was the abundance of purple cyclamens, clothing the mountain meadows, and filling the air with delicate fragrance like the smell of lilacs around a New England farmhouse in early June.

There was still one stretch of the river above Ischl left for the last evening's sport. I remember it so well: the long, deep place where the water ran beside an embankment of stone, and the big grayling poised on the edge of the shadow, rising and falling on the current as a kite rises and falls on the wind and balances back to the same position; the murmur of the stream and the hissing of the pebbles underfoot in the rapids as the swift water rolled them over and over; the odour of the fir-trees, and the streaks of warm air in quiet places, and the faint whiffs of wood-smoke wafted from the houses, and the brown flies dancing heavily up and down in the twilight; the last good pool, where the river was divided, the main part making a deep, narrow curve to the right, and the lesser part bubbling into it over a bed of stones with half-a-dozen tiny waterfalls, with a fine trout lying at the foot of each of them and rising merrily as the white fly passed over him—surely it was all very good, and a memory to be grateful for. And when the basket was full, it was pleasant to put off the heavy wading-shoes and the long rubber-stockings, and ride homeward in an open carriage through the fresh night air. That is as near to sybaritic luxury as a man should care to come.

The lights in the cottages are twinkling like fire-flies, and there are small groups of people singing and laughing down the road. The honest fisherman reflects that this world is only a place of pilgrimage, but after all there is a good deal of cheer on the journey, if it is made with a contented heart. He wonders who the dwellers in the scattered houses may be, and weaves romances out of the shadows on the curtained windows. The lamps burning in the wayside shrines tell him stories of human love and patience and hope, and of divine forgiveness. Dream-pictures of life float before him, tender and luminous, filled with a vague, soft atmosphere in which the simplest outlines gain a strange significance. They are like some of Millet's paintings—"The Sower," or "The Sheepfold,"—there is very little detail in them; but sometimes a little means so much.

Then the moon slips up into the sky from behind the eastern hills, and the fisherman begins to think of home, and of the foolish, fond old rhymes about those whom the moon sees far away, and the stars that have the power to fulfil wishes—as if the celestial bodies knew or cared anything about our small nerve-thrills which we call affection and desires! But if there were Some One above the moon and stars who did know and care, Some One who could see the places and the people that you and I would give so much to see, Some One who could do for them all of kindness that you and I fain would do, Some One able to keep our beloved in perfect peace and watch over the little children sleeping in their beds beyond the sea—what then? Why, then, in the evening hour, one might have thoughts of home that would go across the ocean by way of heaven, and be better than dreams, almost as good as prayers.

1892.

AT THE SIGN OF THE BALSAM BOUGH

"Come live with me, and be my love,
And we will all the pleasures prove
That valleys, groves, or hills, or field,
Or woods and steepy mountains yield.
"There we will rest our sleepy heads,
And happy hearts, on balsam beds;
And every day go forth to fish
In foamy streams for ouananiche."
Old Song with a New Ending.

AT THE SIGN OF THE BALSAM BOUGH

It has been asserted, on high philosophical authority, that woman is a problem. She is more; she is a cause of problems to others. This is not a theoretical statement. It is a fact of experience.

Every year, when the sun passes the summer solstice, the

"Two souls with but a single thought,"

of whom I am so fortunate as to be one, are summoned by that portion of our united mind which has at once the right of putting the question and of casting the deciding vote, to answer this conundrum: How can we go abroad without crossing the ocean, and abandon an interesting family of children without getting completely beyond their reach, and escape from the frying-pan of housekeeping without falling into the fire of the summer hotel? This apparently insoluble problem we usually solve by going to camp in Canada.

It is indeed a foreign air that breathes around us as we make the harmless, friendly voyage from Point Levis to Quebec. The boy on the ferry-boat, who cajoles us into buying a copy of *Le Moniteur* containing last month's news, has the address of a true though diminutive Frenchman. The landlord of the quiet little inn on the outskirts of the town welcomes us with Gallic effusion as well-known guests, and rubs his hands genially before us, while he escorts us to our apartments, groping secretly in his memory to recall our names. When we walk down the steep, quaint streets to revel in the purchase of moccasins and water-proof coats and camping supplies, we read on a wall the familiar but transformed legend, *L'enfant pleurs, il veut son Camphoria,* and remember with joy that no infant who weeps in French can impose any responsibility upon us in these days of our renewed honeymoon.

But the true delight of the expedition begins when the tents have been set up, in the forest back of Lake St. John, and the green branches have been broken for the woodland bed, and the fire has been lit under the open sky, and, the livery of fashion being all discarded, I sit down at a log table to eat supper with my lady Greygown. Then life seems simple and amiable and well worth living. Then the uproar and confusion of the world die away from us, and we hear only the steady murmur of the river and the low voice of the wind in the tree-tops. Then time is long, and the only art that is needful for its enjoyment is short and easy. Then we taste true comfort, while we lodge with Mother Green at the Sign of the Balsam Bough.

I.
UNDER THE WHITE BIRCHES.

Men may say what they will in praise of their houses, and grow eloquent upon the merits of various styles of architecture, but, for our part, we are agreed that there is nothing to be compared with a tent. It is the most venerable and aristocratic form of human habitation. Abraham and Sarah lived in it, and shared its hospitality with angels. It is exempt from the base tyranny of the plumber, the paper-hanger, and the gas-man. It is not immovably bound to one dull spot of earth by the chains of a cellar and a system of water-pipes. It has a noble freedom of locomotion. It follows the wishes of its inhabitants, and goes with them, a travelling home, as the spirit moves them to explore the wilderness. At their pleasure, new beds of wild flowers surround it, new plantations of trees overshadow it, and new avenues of shining water lead to its ever-open door. What the tent lacks in luxury it makes up in liberty: or rather let us say that liberty itself is the greatest luxury.

Another thing is worth remembering—a family which lives in a tent never can have a skeleton in the closet.

But it must not be supposed that every spot in the woods is suitable for a camp, or that a good tenting-ground can be chosen without knowledge and forethought. One of the requisites, indeed, is to be found everywhere in the St. John region; for all the lakes and rivers are full of clear, cool water, and the traveller does not need to search for a spring. But it is always necessary to look carefully for a bit of smooth ground on the shore, far enough above the water to be dry, and slightly sloping, so that the head of the bed may be higher than the foot. Above all, it must be free from big stones and serpentine roots of trees. A root that looks no bigger than an inch-worm in the daytime assumes the proportions of a boa-constrictor at midnight—when you find it under your hip-bone. There should also be plenty of evergreens near at hand for the beds. Spruce will answer at a pinch; it has an aromatic smell; but it is too stiff and humpy. Hemlock is smoother and more flexible; but the spring soon wears out of it. The balsam-fir, with its elastic branches and thick flat needles, is the best of all. A bed of these boughs a foot deep is softer than a mattress and as fragrant as a thousand Christmas-trees. Two things more are needed for the ideal camp-ground—an open situation, where the breeze will drive away the flies and mosquitoes, and an abundance of dry firewood within easy reach. Yes, and a third thing must not be forgotten; for, says my lady Greygown:

"I shouldn't feel at home in camp unless I could sit in the door of the tent and look out across flowing water."

All these conditions are met in our favourite camping place below the first fall in the Grande Décharge. A rocky point juts out into the river and makes a fine landing for the canoes. There is a dismantled fishing-cabin a few rods back in the woods, from which we can borrow boards for a table and chairs. A group of cedars on the lower edge of the point opens just wide enough to receive and shelter our tent. At a good distance beyond ours, the guides' tent is pitched; and the big camp-fire burns between the two dwellings. A pair of white-birches lift their leafy crowns far above us, and after them we name the place *Le Camp aux Bouleaux*.

"Why not call trees people?—since, if you come to live among them year after year, you will learn to know many of them personally, and an attachment will grow up between you and them individually." So writes that *Doctor Amabilis* of woodcraft, W. C. Prime, in his book, *Among the Northern Hills*, and straightway launches forth into eulogy on the white-birch. And truly it is an admirable, lovable, and comfortable tree, beautiful to look upon and full of various uses. Its wood is strong to make paddles and axe handles, and glorious to burn, blazing up at first with a flashing flame, and then holding the fire in its glowing heart all through the night. Its bark is the most serviceable of all the products of the wilderness. In Russia, they say, it is used in tanning, and gives its subtle, sacerdotal fragrance to Russia leather. But here, in the woods, it serves more primitive ends. It can be peeled off in a huge roll from some giant tree and fashioned into a swift canoe to carry man over the waters. It can be cut into square sheets to roof his shanty in the forest. It is the paper on which he writes his woodland despatches, and the flexible material which he bends into drinking-cups of silver lined with gold. A thin strip of it wrapped around the end of a candle and fastened in a cleft stick makes a practicable chandelier. A basket for berries, a horn to call the lovelorn moose through the autumnal woods, a canvas on which to draw the outline of great and memorable fish—all these and many other indispensable luxuries are stored up for the skilful woodsman in the birch bark.

Only do not rob or mar the tree, unless you really need what it has to give you. Let it stand and grow in virgin majesty, ungirdled and unscarred, while the trunk becomes a firm pillar of the forest temple, and the branches spread abroad a refuge of bright green leaves for the birds of the air. Nature never made a more excellent piece of handiwork. "And if," said my lady Greygown, "I should ever become a dryad, I would choose to be transformed into a white-birch. And then, when the days of my life were numbered, and the sap had ceased to flow, and the last leaf had fallen, and the dry bark hung around me in ragged curls and streamers, some wandering hunter would come in the wintry night and touch a lighted coal to my body, and my spirit would flash up in a fiery chariot into the sky."

The chief occupation of our idle days on the Grande Décharge was fishing. Above the camp spread a noble pool, more than two miles in circumference, and diversified with smooth bays and whirling eddies, sand beaches and rocky islands. The river poured into it at the head, foaming and raging down a long *chûte*, and swept out of it just in front of our camp in a merry, musical rapid. It was full of fish of various kinds—long-nosed pickerel, wall-eyed pike, and stupid chub. But the prince of the pool was the fighting ouananiche, the little salmon of St. John.

Here let me chant thy praise, thou noblest and most high-minded fish, the cleanest feeder, the merriest liver, the loftiest leaper, and the bravest warrior of all creatures that swim! Thy cousin, the trout, in his purple and gold with crimson spots, wears a more splendid armour than thy russet and silver mottled with black, but thine is the kinglier nature. His courage and skill compared with thine

"Are as moonlight unto sunlight, and as water unto wine."

The old salmon of the sea who begot thee, long ago, in these inland waters, became a backslider, descending again to the ocean, and grew gross and heavy with coarse feeding. But thou, unsalted salmon of the foaming floods, not land-locked, as men call thee, but choosing of thine own free-will to dwell on a loftier level, in the pure, swift current of a living stream, hast grown in grace and risen to a higher life. Thou art not to be measured by quantity, but by quality, and thy five pounds of pure vigour will outweigh a score of pounds of flesh less vitalised by spirit. Thou feedest on the flies of the air, and thy food is transformed into an aerial passion for flight, as thou springest across the pool, vaulting toward the sky. Thine eyes have grown large and keen by peering through the foam, and the feathered hook that can deceive thee must be deftly tied and delicately cast. Thy tail and fins, by ceaseless conflict with the rapids, have broadened and strengthened, so that they can flash thy slender body like a living arrow up the fall. As Lancelot among the knights, so art thou among the fish, the plain-armoured hero, the sunburnt champion of all the water-folk.

Every morning and evening, Greygown and I would go out for ouananiche, and sometimes we caught plenty and sometimes few, but we never came back without a good catch of happiness. There were certain places where the fish liked to stay. For example, we always looked for one at the lower corner of a big rock, very close to it, where he could poise himself easily on the edge of the strong downward stream. Another likely place was a straight run of water, swift, but not too swift, with a sunken stone in the middle. The ouananiche does not like crooked, twisting water. An even current is far more comfortable, for then he discovers just how much effort is needed to balance against it, and keeps up the movement mechanically, as if he were half asleep. But his favourite place is under one of the floating islands of thick foam that gather in the corners below the falls. The matted flakes give a grateful shelter from the sun, I fancy, and almost all game-fish love to lie in the shade; but the chief reason why the ouananiche haunt the drifting white mass is because it is full of flies and gnats, beaten down by the spray of the cataract, and sprinkled all through the foam like plums in a cake. To this natural confection the little salmon, lurking in his corner, plays the part of Jack Horner all day long, and never wearies.

"See that *belle brou* down below there!" said Ferdinand, as we scrambled over the huge rocks at the foot of the falls; "there ought to be salmon there *en masse*." Yes, there were the sharp noses picking out the unfortunate insects, and the broad tails waving lazily through the foam as the fish turned in the water. At this season of the year, when summer is nearly ended, and every ouananiche in the Grande Décharge has tasted feathers and seen a hook, it is useless to attempt to delude them with the large gaudy flies which the fishing-tackle-maker recommends. There are only two successful methods of angling now. The first of these I tried, and by casting delicately with a tiny brown trout-fly tied on a gossamer strand of gut, captured a pair of fish weighing about three pounds each. They fought against the spring of the four-ounce rod for nearly half an hour before Ferdinand could slip the net around them. But there was another and a broader tail still waving disdainfully on the outer edge of the foam. "And now," said the gallant Ferdinand, "the turn is to madame, that she should prove her fortune—attend but a moment, madame, while I seek the *sauterelle*."

This was the second method: the grasshopper was attached to the hook, and casting the line well out across the pool, Ferdinand put the rod into Greygown's hands. She stood poised upon a pinnacle of rock, like patience on a monument, waiting for a bite. It came. There was a slow, gentle pull at the line, answered by a quick jerk of the rod, and a noble fish flashed into the air. Four pounds and a half at least! He leaped again and again, shaking the drops from his silvery sides. He rushed up the rapids as if he had determined to return to the lake, and down again as if he had changed his plans and determined to go to the Saguenay. He sulked in the deep water and rubbed his nose against the rocks. He did his best to treat that treacherous grasshopper as the whale served Jonah. But Greygown, through all her little screams and shouts of excitement, was steady and sage. She never gave the fish an inch of slack line; and at last he lay glittering on the rocks, with the black St. Andrew's crosses clearly marked on his plump sides, and the iridescent spots gleaming on his small, shapely head. "*Une belle!*" cried Ferdinand, as he held up the fish in triumph, "and it is madame who has the good fortune. She understands well to take the large fish—is it not?" Greygown stepped demurely down from her pinnacle, and as we drifted down the pool in the canoe, under the mellow evening sky, her conversation betrayed not a trace of the pride that a victorious fisherman would have shown. On the contrary, she insisted that angling was an affair of chance—which was consoling, though I knew it was not altogether true—and that the smaller fish were just as pleasant to catch and better to eat, after all. For a generous rival, commend me to a woman. And if I must compete, let it be with one who has the grace to dissolve the bitter of defeat in the honey of a mutual self-congratulation.

We had a garden, and our favourite path through it was the portage leading around the falls. We travelled it very frequently, making an excuse of idle errands to the steamboat-landing on the lake, and sauntering along the trail as if school were out and would never keep again. It was the season of fruits rather than of flowers. Nature was reducing the decorations of her table to make room for the banquet. She offered us berries instead of blossoms.

There were the light coral clusters of the dwarf cornel set in whorls of pointed leaves; and the deep blue bells of the *Clintonia borealis* (which the White Mountain people call the bear-berry, and I hope the name will stick, for it smacks of the woods, and it is a shame to leave so free and wild a plant under the burden of a Latin name); and the gray, crimson-veined berries for which the Canada Mayflower had exchanged its feathery white bloom; and the ruby drops of the twisted stalk hanging like jewels along its bending stem. On the three-leaved table which once carried the gay flower of the wake-robin, there was a scarlet lump like a red pepper escaped to the forest and run wild. The partridge-vine was full of rosy provision for the birds. The dark tiny leaves of the creeping snow-berry were all sprinkled over with delicate drops of spicy foam. There were a few belated raspberries, and, if we chose to go out into the burnt ground, we could find blueberries in plenty.

But there was still bloom enough to give that festal air without which the most abundant feast seems coarse and vulgar. The pale gold of the loosestrife had faded, but the deeper yellow of the goldenrod had begun to take its place. The blue banners of the fleur-de-lis had vanished from beside the springs, but the purple of the asters was appearing. Closed gentians kept their secret inviolate, and bluebells trembled above the rocks. The quaint pinkish-white flowers of the turtle-head showed in wet places, and instead of the lilac racemes of the purple-fringed orchis, which had disappeared with midsummer, we found now the slender braided spikes of the lady's-tresses, latest and lowliest of the orchids, pale and pure as nuns of the forest, and exhaling a celestial fragrance. There is a secret pleasure in finding these delicate flowers in the rough heart of the wilderness. It is like discovering the veins of poetry in the character of a guide or a lumberman. And to be able to call the plants by name makes them a hundredfold more sweet and intimate. Naming things is one of the oldest and simplest of human pastimes. Children play at it with their dolls and toy animals. In fact, it was the first game ever played on earth, for the Creator who planted the garden eastward in Eden knew well what would please the childish heart of man, when He brought all the new-made creatures to Adam, "to see what he would call them."

Our rustic bouquet graced the table under the white-birches, while we sat by the fire and watched our four men at the work of the camp—Joseph and Raoul chopping wood in the distance; François slicing juicy rashers from the flitch of bacon; and Ferdinand, the *chef*, heating the frying-pan in preparation for supper.

"Have you ever thought," said Greygown, in a contented tone of voice, "that this is the only period of our existence when we attain to the luxury of a French cook?"

"And one with the grand manner, too," I replied, "for he never fails to ask what it is that madame desires to eat to-day, as if the larder of Lucullus were at his disposal, though he knows well enough that the only choice lies between broiled fish and fried fish, or bacon with eggs and a rice omelet. But I like the fiction of a lordly ordering of the repast. How much better it is than having to eat what is flung before you at a summer boarding-house by a scornful waitress!"

"Another thing that pleases me," continued my lady, "is the unbreakableness of the dishes. There are no nicks in the edges of the best plates here; and, oh! it is a happy thing to have a home without bric-à-brac. There is nothing here that needs to be dusted."

"And no engagements for to-morrow," I ejaculated. "Dishes that can't be broken, and plans that can—that's the ideal of housekeeping."

"And then," added my philosopher in skirts, "it is certainly refreshing to get away from all one's relations for a little while."

"But how do you make that out?" I asked, in mild surprise. "What are you going to do with me?"

"Oh," said she, with a fine air of independence, "I don't count you. You are not a relation, only a connection by marriage."

"Well, my dear," I answered, between the meditative puffs of my pipe, "it is good to consider the advantages of our present situation. We shall soon come into the frame of mind of the Sultan of Morocco when he camped in the Vale of Rabat. The place pleased him so well that he staid until the very pegs of his tent took root and grew up into a grove of trees around his pavilion."

II.
KENOGAMI.

The guides were a little restless under the idle régime of our lazy camp, and urged us to set out upon some adventure. Ferdinand was like the uncouth swain in Lycidas. Sitting upon the bundles of camp equipage on the shore, and crying,—

"*To-morrow to fresh woods and pastures new,*"
he led us forth to seek the famous fishing grounds on Lake Kenogami.

We skirted the eastern end of Lake St. John in our two canoes, and pushed up La Belle Rivière to Hebertville, where all the children turned out to follow our procession through the village. It was like the train that tagged after the Pied Piper of Hamelin. We embarked again, surrounded by an admiring throng, at the bridge where the main street crossed a little stream, and paddled up it, through a score of back yards and a stretch of reedy meadows, where the wild and tame ducks fed together, tempting the sportsman to sins of ignorance. We crossed the placid Lac Vert, and after a carry of a mile along the high-road toward Chicoutimi, turned down a steep hill and pitched our tents on a crescent of silver sand, with the long, fair water of Kenogami before us.

It is amazing to see how quickly these woods-men can make a camp. Each one knew precisely his share of the enterprise. One sprangto chop a dry spruce log into fuel for a quick fire, and fell a harder tree to keep us warm through the night. Another stripped a pile of boughs from a balsam for the beds. Another cut the tent-poles from a neighbouring thicket. Another unrolled the bundles and made ready the cooking utensils. As if by magic, the miracle of the camp was accomplished.—

"*The bed was made, the room was fit,*
By punctual eve the stars were lit"—
but Greygown always insists upon completing that quotation from Stevenson in her own voice; for this is the way it ends,—

"*When we put up, my ass and I,*
At God's green caravanserai."

Our permanent camp was another day's voyage down the lake, on a beach opposite the Point Ausable. There the water was contracted to a narrow strait, and in the swift current, close to the point, the great trout had fixed their spawning-bed from time immemorial. It wasthe first week in September, and the magnates of the lake were already assembling—the Common Councilmen and the Mayor and the whole Committee of Seventy. There were giants in that place, rolling lazily about, and chasing each other on the surface of the water. "Look, M'sieu'!" cried François, in excitement, as we lay at anchor in the gray morning twilight; "one like a horse has just leaped behind us; I assure you, big like a horse!"

But the fish were shy and dour. Old Castonnier, the guardian of the lake, lived in his hut on the shore, and flogged the water, early and late, every day with his home-made flies. He was anchored in his dugout close beside us, and grinned with delight as he saw his over-educated trout refuse my best casts. "They are here, M'sieu', for you can see them," he said, by way of discouragement, "but it is difficult to take them. Do you not find it so?"

In the back of my fly-book I discovered a tiny phantom minnow—a dainty affair of varnished silk, as light as a feather—and quietlyattached it to the leader in place of the tail-fly. Then the fun began.

One after another the big fish dashed at that deception, and we played and netted them, until our score was thirteen, weighing altogether thirty-five pounds, and the largest five pounds and a half. The guardian was mystified and disgusted. He looked on for a while in silence, and then pulled up anchor and clattered ashore. He must have made some inquiries and reflections during the day, for that night he paid a visit to our camp. After telling bear stories and fish stories for an hour or two by the fire, he rose to depart, and tapping his fore-finger solemnly upon my shoulder, delivered himself as follows:—

"You can say a proud thing when you go home, M'sieu'—that you have beaten the old Castonnier. There are not many fishermen who can say that. But," he added, with confidential emphasis, "*c'était votre sacré p'tit poisson qui a fait cela.*"

That was a touch of human nature, my rusty old guardian, more welcome to me than all the morning's catch. Is there not always a "confounded little minnow" responsible for our failures? Did you ever see a school-boy tumble on the ice without stooping immediately to re-buckle the strap of his skates? And would not Ignotus have painted a masterpiece if he could have found good brushes and a proper canvas? Life's shortcomings would be bitter indeed if we could not find excuses for them outside of ourselves. And as for life's successes—well, it is certainly wholesome to remember how many of them are due to a fortunate position and the proper tools.

Our tent was on the border of a coppice of young trees. It was pleasant to be awakened by a convocation of birds at sunrise, and to watch the shadows of the leaves dance out upon our translucent roof of canvas.

All the birds in the bush are early, but there are so many of them that it is difficult to believe that every one can be rewarded with a worm. Here in Canada those little people of the air who appear as transient guests of spring and autumn in the Middle States, are in their summer home and breeding-place. Warblers, named for the magnolia and the myrtle, chestnut-sided, bay-breasted, blue-backed, and black-throated, flutter and creep along the branches with simple lisping music. Kinglets, ruby-crowned and golden-crowned, tiny, brilliant sparks of life, twitter among the trees, breaking occasionally into clearer, sweeter songs. Companies of redpolls and crossbills pass chirping through the thickets, busily seeking their food. The fearless, familiar chickadee repeats his name merrily, while he leads his family to explore every nook and cranny of the wood. Cedar wax-wings, sociable wanderers, arrive in numerous flocks. The Canadians call them "*récollets,*" because they wear a brown crest of the same colour as the hoods of the monks who came with the first settlers to New France. They are a songless tribe, although their quick, reiterated call as they take to flight has given them the name of chatterers. The beautiful tree-sparrows and the pine-siskins are more melodious, and the slate-coloured juncos, flitting about the camp, are as garrulous as chippy-birds. All these varied notes come and go through the tangle of morning dreams. And now the noisy blue-jay is calling *"Thief—thief—thief!"* in the distance, and a pair of great pileated woodpeckers with crimson crests are laughing loudly in the swamp over some family joke. But listen! what is that harsh creaking note? It is the cry of the Northern shrike, of whom tradition says that he catches little birds and impales them on sharp thorns. At the sound of his voice the concert closes suddenly and the singers vanish into thin air. The hour of music is over; the commonplace of day has begun. And there is my lady Greygown, already up and dressed, standing by the breakfast-table and laughing at my belated appearance.

But the birds were not our only musicians at Kenogami. French Canada is one of the ancestral homes of song. Here you can still listen to those quaint ballads which were sung centuries ago in Normandie and Provence. *"A la Claire Fontaine," "Dans Paris y a-t-une Brune plus Belle que le Jour," "Sur le Pont d'Avignon," "En Roulant ma Boule," "La Poulette Grise,"* and a hundred other folk-songs linger among the peasants and voyageurs of these northern woods. You may hear

*"Malbrouck s'en va-t-en guerre—
Mironton, mironton, mirontaine,"*
and
*"Isabeau s'y promène
Le long de son jardin,"*

chanted in the farmhouse or the lumber shanty, to the tunes which have come down from an unknown source, and never lost their echo in the hearts of the people.

Our Ferdinand was a perfect fountain of music. He had a clear tenor voice, and solaced every task and shortened every voyage with melody. "A song, Ferdinand, a jolly song," the other men would say, as the canoes went sweeping down the quiet lake. And then the leader would strike up a well-known air, and his companions would come in on the refrain, keeping time with the stroke of their paddles. Sometimes it would be a merry ditty:

*"My father had no girl but me,
And yet he sent me off to sea;
Leap, my little Cécilia."*
Or perhaps it was:
*"I've danced so much the livelong day,—
Dance, my sweetheart, let's be gay,—
I've fairly danced my shoes away,—
Till evening.
Dance, my pretty, dance once more;
Dance, until we break the floor."*

But more frequently the song was touched with a plaintive pleasant melancholy. The minstrel told how he had gone into the woods and heard the nightingale, and she had confided to him that lovers are often unhappy. The story of *La Belle Françoise* was repeated in minor cadences—how her sweetheart sailed away to the wars, and when he came back the village church bells were ringing, and he said to himself that Françoise had been faithless, and the chimes were for her marriage; but when he entered the church it was her funeral that he saw, for she had died of love. It is strange how sorrow charms us when it is distant and visionary. Even when we are happiest we enjoy making music

"Of old, unhappy, far-off things."

"What is that song which you are singing, Ferdinand?" asks the lady, as she hears him humming behind her in the canoe.

"Ah, madame, it is the *chanson* of a young man who demands of his *blonde* why she will not marry him. He says that he has waited long time, and the flowers are falling from the rose-tree, and he is very sad."

"And does she give a reason?"

"Yes, madame—that is to say, a reason of a certain sort; she declares that she is not quite ready; he must wait until the rose-tree adorns itself again."

"And what is the end—do they get married at last?"

"But I do not know, madame. The *chanson* does not go so far. It ceases with the complaint of the young man. And it is a very uncertain affair—this affair of the heart—is it not?"

Then, as if he turned from such perplexing mysteries to something plain and sure and easy to understand, he breaks out into the jolliest of all Canadian songs:

*"My bark canoe that flies, that flies,
Hola! my bark canoe!"*

III.
THE ISLAND POOL.

Among the mountains there is a gorge. And in the gorge there is a river. And in the river there is a pool. And in the pool there is an island. And on the island, for four happy days, there was a camp.

It was by no means an easy matter to establish ourselves in that lonely place. The river, though not remote from civilisation, is practically inaccessible for nine miles of its course by reason of the steepness of its banks, which are long, shaggy precipices, and the fury of its current, in which no boat can live. We heard its voice as we approached through the forest, and could hardly tell whether it was far away or near.

There is a perspective of sound as well as of sight, and one must have some idea of the size of a noise before one can judge of its distance. A mosquito's horn in a dark room may seem like a trumpet on the battlements; and the tumult of a mighty stream heard through an unknown stretch of woods may appear like the babble of a mountain brook close at hand.

But when we came out upon the bald forehead of a burnt cliff and looked down, we realised the grandeur and beauty of the unseen voice that we had been following. A river of splendid strength went leaping through the chasm five hundred feet below us, and at the foot of two snow-white falls, in an oval of dark topaz water, traced with curves of floating foam, lay the solitary island.

The broken path was like a ladder. "How shall we ever get down?" sighed Greygown, as we dropped from rock to rock; and at the bottom she looked up sighing, "I know we never can get back again." There was not a foot of ground on the shores level enough for a tent. Our canoe ferried us over, two at a time, to the island. It was about a hundred paces long, composed of round, coggly stones, with just one patch of smooth sand at the lower end. There was not a tree left upon it larger than an alder-bush. The tent-poles must be cut far up on the mountain-sides, and every bough for our beds must be carried down the ladder of rocks. But the men were gay at their work, singing like mocking-birds. After all, the glow of life comes from friction with its difficulties. If we cannot find them at home, we sally abroad and create them, just to warm up our mettle.

The ouananiche in the island pool were superb, astonishing, incredible. We stood on the cobble-stones at the upper end, and cast our little flies across the sweeping stream, and for three days the fish came crowding in to fill the barrel of pickled salmon for our guides' winter use; and the score rose,—twelve, twenty-one, thirty-two; and the size of the "biggest fish" steadily mounted—four pounds, four and a half, five, five and three-quarters. "Precisely almost six pounds," said Ferdinand, holding the scales; "but we may call him six, M'sieu', for if it had been to-morrow that we had caught him, he would certainly have gained the other ounce." And yet, why should I repeat the fisherman's folly of writing down the record of that marvellous catch? We always do it, but we know that it is a vain thing. Few listen to the tale, and none accept it. Does not Christopher North, reviewing the *Salmonia* of Sir Humphry Davy, mock and jeer unfeignedly at the fish stories of that most reputable writer? But, on the very next page, old Christopher himself meanders on into a perilous narrative of the day when he caught a whole cart-load of trout in a Highland loch. Incorrigible, happy inconsistency! Slow to believe others, and full of sceptical inquiry, fond man never doubts one thing—that somewhere in the world a tribe of gentle readers will be discovered to whom his fish stories will appear credible.

One of our days on the island was Sunday—a day of rest in a week of idleness. We had a few books; for there are some in existence which will stand the test of being brought into close contact with nature. Are not John Burroughs' cheerful, kindly essays full of woodland truth and companionship? Can you not carry a whole library of musical philosophy in your pocket in Matthew Arnold's volume of selections from Wordsworth? And could there be a better sermon for a Sabbath in the wilderness than Mrs. Slosson's immortal story of *Fishin' Jimmy*?

But to be very frank about the matter, the camp is not stimulating to the studious side of my mind. Charles Lamb, as usual, has said what I feel: "I am not much a friend to out-of-doors reading. I cannot settle my spirits to it."

There are blueberries growing abundantly among the rocks—huge clusters of them, bloomy and luscious as the grapes of Eshcol. The blueberry is nature's compensation for the ruin of forest fires. It grows best where the woods have been burned away and the soil is too poor to raise another crop of trees. Surely it is an innocent and harmless pleasure to wander along the hillsides gathering these wild fruits, as the Master and His disciples once walked through the fields and plucked the ears of corn, never caring what the Pharisees thought of that new way of keeping the Sabbath.

And here is a bed of moss beside a dashing rivulet, inviting us to rest and be thankful. Hark! There is a white-throated sparrow, on a little tree across the river, whistling his afternoon song

"*In linkèd sweetness long drawn out.*"

Down in Maine they call him the Peabody-bird, because his notes sound to them like *Old mān—Péabody, péabody, péabody*. In New Brunswick the Scotch settlers say that he sings *Lōst—lōst—Kénnedy, kénnedy, kénnedy*. But here in his northern home I think we can understand him better. He is singing again and again, with a cadence that never wearies, "*Sweet—sweet—Cánada, cánada, cánada!*" The Canadians, when they came across the sea, remembering the nightingale of southern France, baptised this little gray minstrel their *rossignol*, and the country ballads are full of his praise. Every land has its nightingale, if we only have the heart to hear him. How distinct his voice is—how personal, how confidential, as if he had a message for us!

There is a breath of fragrance on the cool shady air beside our little stream, that seems familiar. It is the first week of September. Can it be that the twin-flower of June, the delicate *Linnæa borealis*, is blooming again? Yes, here is the threadlike stem lifting its two frail pinkbells above the bed of shining leaves. How dear an early flower seems when it comes back again and unfolds its beauty in a St. Martin's summer! How delicate and suggestive is the faint, magical odour! It is like a renewal of the dreams of youth.

"And need we ever grow old?" asked my lady Greygown, as she sat that evening with the twin-flower on her breast, watching the stars come out along the edge of the cliffs, and tremble on the hurrying tide of the river. "Must we grow old as well as gray? Is the time coming when all life will be commonplace and practical, and governed by a dull 'of course'? Shall we not always find adventures and romances, and a few blossoms returning, even when the season grows late?"

"At least," I answered, "let us believe in the possibility, for to doubt it is to destroy it. If we can only come back to nature together every year, and consider the flowers and the birds, and confess our faults and mistakes and our unbelief under these silent stars, and hear the river murmuring our absolution, we shall die young, even though we live long: we shall have a treasure of memories which will be like the twin-flower, always a double blossom on a single stem, and carry with us into the unseen world something which will make it worth while to be immortal."

1894.

A SONG AFTER SUNDOWN
THE WOOD-NOTES OF THE VEERY

The moonbeams over Arno's vale in silver flood were pouring,
When first I heard the nightingale a long-lost love deploring:
So passionate, so full of pain, it sounded strange and eerie,
I longed to hear a simpler strain, the wood-notes of the veery.
The laverock sings a bonny lay, above the Scottish heather,
It sprinkles from the dome of day like light and love together;
He drops the golden notes to greet his brooding mate, his dearie;
I only know one song more sweet, the vespers of the veery.
In English gardens green and bright, and rich in fruity treasure,
I've heard the blackbird with delight repeat his merry measure;
The ballad was a lively one, the tune was loud and cheery,
And yet with every setting sun I listened for the veery.
O far away, and far away, the tawny thrush is singing,
New England woods at close of day with that clear chant are ringing;
And when my light of life is low, and heart and flesh are weary,
I fain would hear, before I go, the wood-notes of the veery.

1895.

Fisherman's Luck

Has it ever fallen in your way to notice the quality of the greetings that belong to certain occupations?

There is something about these salutations in kind which is singularly taking and grateful to the ear. They are as much better than an ordinary "good day" or a flat "how are you?" as a folk-song of Scotland or the Tyrol is better than the futile love-ditty of the drawing-room. They have a spicy and rememberable flavour. They speak to the imagination and point the way to treasure-trove.

There is a touch of dignity in them, too, for all they are so free and easy—the dignity of independence, the native spirit of one who takes for granted that his mode of living has a right to make its own forms of speech. I admire a man who does not hesitate to salute the world in the dialect of his calling.

How salty and stimulating, for example, is the sailorman's hail of "Ship ahoy!" It is like a breeze laden with briny odours and a pleasant dash of spray. The miners in some parts of Germany have a good greeting for their dusky trade. They cry to one who is going down the shaft, "Gluck auf!" All the perils of an underground adventure and all the joys of seeing the sun again are compressed into a word. Even the trivial salutation which the telephone has lately created and claimed for its peculiar use—"Hello, hello"—seems to me to have a kind of fitness and fascination. It is like a thoroughbred bulldog, ugly enough to be attractive. There is a lively, concentrated, electric air about it. It makes courtesy wait upon dispatch, and reminds us that we live in an age when it is necessary to be wide awake.

I have often wished that every human employment might evolve its own appropriate greeting. Some of them would be queer, no doubt; but at least they would be an improvement on the wearisome iteration of "Good-evening" and "Good-morning," and the monotonous inquiry, "How do you do?"—a question so meaningless that it seldom tarries for an answer. Under the new and more natural system of etiquette, when you passed the time of day with a man you would know his business, and the salutations of the market-place would be full of interest.

As for my chosen pursuit of angling (which I follow with diligence when not interrupted by less important concerns), I rejoice with every true fisherman that it has a greeting all its own and of a most honourable antiquity. There is no written record of its origin. But it is quite certain that since the days after the Flood, when Deucalion

> *"Did first this art invent*
> *Of angling, and his people taught the same,"*

two honest and good-natured anglers have never met each other by the way without crying out, "What luck?"

Here, indeed, is an epitome of the gentle art. Here is the spirit of it embodied in a word and paying its respects to you with its native accent. Here you see its secret charms unconsciously disclosed. The attraction of angling for all the ages of man, from the cradle to the grave, lies in its uncertainty. 'Tis an affair of luck.

No amount of preparation in the matter of rods and lines and hooks and lures and nets and creels can change its essential character. No excellence of skill in casting the delusive fly or adjusting the tempting bait upon the hook can make the result secure. You may reduce the chances, but you cannot eliminate them. There are a thousand points at which fortune may intervene. The state of the weather, the height of the water, the appetite of the fish, the presence or absence of other anglers—all these indeterminable elements enter into the reckoning of your success. There is no combination of stars in the firmament by which you can forecast the piscatorial future. When you go a-fishing, you just take your chances; you offer yourself as a candidate for anything that may be going; you try your luck.

There are certain days that are favourites among anglers, who regard them as propitious for the sport. I know a man who believes that the fish always rise better on Sunday than on any other day in the week. He complains bitterly of this supposed fact, because his religious scruples will not allow him to take advantage of it. He confesses that he has sometimes thought seriously of joining the Seventh-Day Baptists.

Among the Pennsylvania Dutch, in the Alleghany Mountains, I have found a curious tradition that Ascension Day is the luckiest in the year for fishing. On that morning the district school is apt to be thinly attended, and you must be on the stream very early if you do not wish to find wet footprints on the stones ahead of you.

But in fact, all these superstitions about fortunate days are idle and presumptuous. If there were such days in the calendar, a kind and firm Providence would never permit the race of man to discover them. It would rob life of one of its principal attractions, and make fishing altogether too easy to be interesting.

Fisherman's luck is so notorious that it has passed into a proverb. But the fault with that familiar saying is that it is too short and too narrow to cover half the variations of the angler's possible experience. For if his luck should be bad, there is no portion of his anatomy, from the crown of his head to the soles of his feet, that may not be thoroughly wet. But if it should be good, he may receive an unearned blessing of abundance not only in his basket, but also in his head and his heart, his memory and his fancy. He may come home from some obscure, ill-named, lovely stream—some Dry Brook, or Southwest Branch of Smith's Run—with a creel full of trout, and a mind full of grateful recollections of flowers that seemed to bloom for his sake, and birds that sang a new, sweet, friendly message to his tired soul. He may climb down to "Tommy's Rock" below the cliffs at Newport (as I have done many a day with my lady Greygown), and, all unnoticed by the idle, weary promenaders in the path of fashion, haul in a basketful of blackfish, and at the same time look out across the shining sapphire waters and inherit a wondrous good fortune of dreams—

> *"Have glimpses that will make him less forlorn;*
> *Have sight of Proteus rising from the sea,*
> *Or hear old Triton blow his wreathed horn."*

But all this, you must remember, depends upon something secret and incalculable, something that we can neither command nor predict. It is an affair of gift, not of wages. Fish (and the other good things which are like sauce to the catching of them) cast no shadow before. Water is the emblem of instability. No one can tell what he shall draw out of it until he has taken in his line. Herein are found the true charm and profit of angling for all persons of a pure and childlike mind.

Look at those two venerable gentlemen floating in a skiff upon the clear waters of Lake George. One of them is a successful statesman, an ex-President of the United States, a lawyer versed in all the curious eccentricities of the "lawless science of the law." The other is a learned doctor of medicine, able to give a name to all diseases from which men have imagined that they suffered, and to invent new ones for those who are tired of vulgar maladies. But all their learning is forgotten, their cares and controversies are laid aside, in "innocuous desuetude." The Summer School of Sociology is assembled. The Medical Congress is in session.

But they care not—no, not so much as the value of a single live bait. The sun shines upon them with a fervent heat, but it irks them not. The rain descends, and the winds blow and beat upon them, but they are unmoved. They are securely anchored here in the lee of Sabbath-Day Point.

What enchantment binds them to that inconsiderable spot? What magic fixes their eyes upon the point of a fishing-rod, as if it were the finger of destiny? It is the enchantment of uncertainty: the same natural magic that draws the little suburban boys in the spring of the year, with their strings and pin-hooks, around the shallow ponds where dace and redfins hide; the same irresistible charm that fixes a row of city gamins, like ragged and disreputable fish-crows, on the end of a pier where blear-eyed flounders sometimes lurk in the muddy water. Let the philosopher explain it as he will. Let the moralist reprehend it as he chooses. There is nothing that attracts human nature more powerfully than the sport of tempting the unknown with a fishing-line.

Those ancient anglers have set out upon an exodus from the tedious realm of the definite, the fixed, the must-certainly-come-to-pass. They are on a holiday in the free country of peradventure. They do not know at this moment whether the next turn of Fortune's reel will bring up a perch or a pickerel, a sunfish or a black bass. It may be a hideous catfish or a squirming eel, or it may be a lake-trout, the grand prize in the Lake George lottery. There they sit, those gray-haired lads, full of hope, yet equally prepared for resignation; taking no thought for the morrow, and ready to make the best of to-day; harmless and happy players at the best of all games of chance.

"In other words," I hear some severe and sour-complexioned reader say, "in plain language, they are a pair of old gamblers."

Yes, if it pleases you to call honest men by a bad name. But they risk nothing that is not their own; and if they lose, they are not impoverished. They desire nothing that belongs to other men; and if they win, no one is robbed. If all gambling were like that, it would be difficult to see the harm in it. Indeed, a daring moralist might even assert, and prove by argument, that so innocent a delight in the taking of chances is an aid to virtue.

Do you remember Martin Luther's reasoning on the subject of "excellent large pike"? He maintains that God would never have created them so good to the taste, if He had not meant them to be eaten. And for the same reason I conclude that this world would never have been left so full of uncertainties, nor human nature framed so as to find a peculiar joy and exhilaration in meeting them bravely and cheerfully, if it had not been divinely intended that most of our amusement and much of our education should come from this source.

"Chance" is a disreputable word, I know. It is supposed by many pious persons to be improper and almost blasphemous to use it. But I am not one of those who share this verbal prejudice. I am inclined rather to believe that it is a good word to which a bad reputation has been given. I feel grateful to that admirable "psychologist who writes like a novelist," Mr. William James, for his brilliant defence of it. For what does it mean, after all, but that some things happen in a certain way which might have happened in another way? Where is the immorality, the irreverence, the atheism in such a supposition? Certainly God must be competent to govern a world in which there are possibilities of various kinds, just as well as one in which every event is inevitably determined beforehand. St. Peter and the other fishermen-disciples on the Lake of Galilee were perfectly free to cast their net on either side of the ship. So far as they could see, so far as any one could see, it was a matter of chance where they chose to cast it. But it was not until they let it down, at the Master's word, on the right side that they had good luck. And not the least element of their joy in the draft of fishes was that it brought a change of fortune.

Leave the metaphysics of the question on the table for the present. As a matter of fact, it is plain that our human nature is adapted to conditions variable, undetermined, and hidden from our view. We are not fitted to live in a world where a + b always equals c, and there is nothing more to follow. The interest of life's equation arrives with the appearance of x, the unknown quantity. A settled, unchangeable, clearly foreseeable order of things does not suit our constitution. It tends to melancholy and a fatty heart. Creatures of habit we are undoubtedly; but it is one of our most fixed habits to be fond of variety. The man who is never surprised does not know the taste of happiness, and unless the unexpected sometimes happens to us, we are most grievously disappointed.

Much of the tediousness of highly civilized life comes from its smoothness and regularity. To-day is like yesterday, and we think that we can predict to-morrow. Of course we cannot really do so. The chances are still there. But we have covered them up so deeply with the artificialities of life that we lose sight of them. It seems as if everything in our neat little world were arranged, and provided for, and reasonably sure to come to pass. The best way of escape from this TAEDIUM VITAE is through a recreation like angling, not only because it is so evidently a matter of luck, but also because it tempts us into a wilder, freer life. It leads almost inevitably to camping out, which is a wholesome and sanitary imprudence.

It is curious and pleasant, to my apprehension, to observe how many people in New England, one of whose States is called "the land of Steady Habits," are sensible of the joy of changing them,—out of doors. These good folk turn out from their comfortable farm-houses and their snug suburban cottages to go a-gypsying for a fortnight among the mountains or beside the sea. You see their white tents gleaming from the pine-groves around the little lakes, and catch glimpses of their bathing-clothes drying in the sun on the wiry grass that fringes the sand-dunes. Happy fugitives from the bondage of routine! They have found out that a long journey is not necessary to a good vacation. You may reach the Forest of Arden in a buckboard. The Fortunate Isles are within sailing distance in a dory. And a voyage on the river Pactolus is open to any one who can paddle a canoe.

I was talking—or rather listening—with a barber, the other day, in the sleepy old town of Rivermouth. He told me, in one of those easy confidences which seem to make the razor run more smoothly, that it had been the custom of his family, for some twenty years past, to forsake their commodious dwelling on Anchor Street every summer, and emigrate six miles, in a wagon to Wallis Sands, where they spent the month of August very merrily under canvas. Here was a sensible household for you! They did not feel bound to waste a year's income on a four weeks' holiday. They were not of those foolish folk who run across the sea, carefully carrying with them the same tiresome mind that worried them at home. They got a change of air by making an alteration of life. They escaped from the land of Egypt by stepping out into the wilderness and going a-fishing.

The people who always live in houses, and sleep on beds, and walk on pavements, and buy their food from butchers and bakers and grocers, are not the most blessed inhabitants of this wide and various earth. The circumstances of their existence are too mathematical and secure for perfect contentment. They live at second or third hand. They are boarders in the world. Everything is done for them by somebody else.

It is almost impossible for anything very interesting to happen to them. They must get their excitement out of the newspapers, reading of the hairbreadth escapes and moving accidents that befall people in real life. What do these tame ducks really know of the adventure of living? If the weather is bad, they are snugly housed. If it is cold, there is a furnace in the cellar. If they are hungry, the shops are near at hand. It is all as dull, flat, stale, and unprofitable as adding up a column of figures. They might as well be brought up in an incubator.

But when man abides in tents, after the manner of the early patriarchs, the face of the world is renewed. The vagaries of the clouds become significant. You watch the sky with a lover's look, eager to know whether it will smile or frown. When you lie at night upon your bed of boughs and hear the rain pattering on the canvas close above your head, you wonder whether it is a long storm or only a shower.

The rising wind shakes the tent-flaps. Are the pegs well driven down and the cords firmly fastened? You fall asleep again and wake later, to hear the rain drumming still more loudly on the tight cloth, and the big breeze snoring through the forest, and the waves plunging along the beach. A stormy day? Well, you must cut plenty of wood and keep the camp-fire glowing, for it will be hard to start it up again, if you let it get too low. There is little use in fishing or hunting in such a storm. But there is plenty to do in the camp: guns to be cleaned, tackle to be put in order, clothes to be mended, a good story of adventure to be read, a belated letter to be written to some poor wretch in a summer hotel, a game of hearts or cribbage to be played, or a hunting-trip to be planned for the return of fair weather. The tent is perfectly dry. A little trench dug around it carries off the surplus water, and luckily it is pitched with the side to the lake, so that you get the pleasant heat of the fire without the unendurable smoke. Cooking in the rain has its disadvantages. But how good the supper tastes when it is served up on a tin plate, with an empty box for a table and a roll of blankets at the foot of the bed for a seat!

A day, two days, three days, the storm may continue, according to your luck. I have been out in the woods for a fortnight without a drop of rain or a sign of dust. Again, I have tented on the shore of a big lake for a week, waiting for an obstinate tempest to pass by.

Look now, just at nightfall: is there not a little lifting and breaking of the clouds in the west, a little shifting of the wind toward a better quarter? You go to bed with cheerful hopes. A dozen times in the darkness you are half awake, and listening drowsily to the sounds of the storm. Are they waxing or waning? Is that louder pattering a new burst of rain, or is it only the plumping of the big drops as they are shaken from the trees? See, the dawn has come, and the gray light glimmers through the canvas. In a little while you will know your fate.

Look! There is a patch of bright yellow radiance on the peak of the tent. The shadow of a leaf dances over it. The sun must be shining. Good luck! and up with you, for it is a glorious morning.

The woods are glistening as fresh and fair as if they had been new-created overnight. The water sparkles, and tiny waves are dancing and splashing all along the shore. Scarlet berries of the mountain-ash hang around the lake. A pair of kingfishers dart back and forth across the bay, in flashes of living blue. A black eagle swings silently around his circle, far up in the cloudless sky. The air is full of pleasant sounds, but there is no noise. The world is full of joyful life, but there is no crowd and no confusion. There is no factory chimney to darken the day with its smoke, no trolley-car to split the silence with its shriek and smite the indignant ear with the clanging of its impudent bell. No lumberman's axe has robbed the encircling forests of their glory of great trees. No fires have swept over the hills and left behind them the desolation of a bristly landscape. All is fresh and sweet, calm and clear and bright.

'Twas rather a rude jest of Nature, that tempest of yesterday. But if you have taken it in good part, you are all the more ready for her caressing mood to-day. And now you must be off to get your dinner—not to order it at a shop, but to look for it in the woods and waters. You are ready to do your best with rod or gun. You will use all the skill you have as hunter or fisherman. But what you shall find, and whether you shall subsist on bacon and biscuit, or feast on trout and partridges, is, after all, a matter of luck.

I profess that it appears to me not only pleasant, but also salutary, to be in this condition. It brings us home to the plain realities of life; it teaches us that a man ought to work before he eats; it reminds us that, after he has done all he can, he must still rely upon a mysterious bounty for his daily bread. It says to us, in homely and familiar words, that life was meant to be uncertain, that no man can tell what a day will bring forth, and that it is the part of wisdom to be prepared for disappointments and grateful for all kinds of small mercies.

There is a story in that fragrant book, THE LITTLE FLOWERS OF ST. FRANCIS, which I wish to transcribe here, without tying a moral to it, lest any one should accuse me of preaching.

"Hence says the quaint old chronicler, having assigned to his companions the other parts of the world, St. Francis, taking Brother Maximus as his comrade, set forth toward the province of France. And coming one day to a certain town, and being very hungry, they begged their bread as they went, according to the rule of their order, for the love of God. And St. Francis went through one quarter of the town, and Brother Maximus through another. But forasmuch as St. Francis was a man mean and low of stature, and hence was reputed a vile beggar by such as knew him not, he only received a few scanty crusts and mouthfuls of dry bread. But to Brother Maximus, who was large and well favoured, were given good pieces and big, and an abundance of bread, yea, whole loaves. Having thus begged, they met together without the town to eat, at a place where there was a clear spring and a fair large stone, upon which each spread forth the gifts that he had received. And St. Francis, seeing that the pieces of bread begged by Brother Maximus were bigger and better than his own, rejoiced greatly, saying, 'Oh, Brother Maximus, we are not worthy of so great a treasure.' As he repeated these words many times, Brother Maximus made answer: 'Father, how can you talk of treasures when there is such great poverty and such lack of all things needful? Here is neither napkin nor knife, neither board nor trencher, neither house nor table, neither man-servant nor maid-servant.' St. Francis replied: 'And this is what I reckon a great treasure, where naught is made ready by human industry, but all that is here is prepared by Divine Providence, as is plainly set forth in the bread which we have begged, in the table of fair stone, and in the spring of clear water. And therefore I would that we should pray to God that He teach us with all our hearts to love the treasure of holy poverty, which is so noble a thing, and whose servant is God the Lord.'"

I know of but one fairer description of a repast in the open air; and that is where we are told how certain poor fishermen, coming in very weary after a night of toil (and one of them very wet after swimming ashore), found their Master standing on the bank of the lake waiting for them. But it seems that he must have been busy in their behalf while he was waiting; for there was a bright fire of coals burning on the shore, and a goodly fish broiling thereon, and bread to eat with it. And when the Master had asked them about their fishing, he said, "Come, now, and get your breakfast." So they sat down around the fire, and with his own hands he served them with the bread and the fish.

Of all the banquets that have ever been given upon earth, that is the one in which I would rather have had a share.

But it is now time that we should return to our fishing. And let us observe with gratitude that almost all of the pleasures that are connected with this pursuit—its accompaniments and variations, which run along with the tune and weave an embroidery of delight around it—have an accidental and gratuitous quality about them. They are not to be counted upon beforehand. They are like something that is thrown into a purchase by a generous and open-handed dealer, to make us pleased with our bargain and inclined to come back to the same shop.

If I knew, for example, before setting out for a day on the brook, precisely what birds I should see, and what pretty little scenes in the drama of woodland life were to be enacted before my eyes, the expedition would lose more than half its charm. But, in fact, it is almost entirely a matter of luck, and that is why it never grows tiresome.

The ornithologist knows pretty well where to look for the birds, and he goes directly to the places where he can find them, and proceeds to study them intelligently and systematically. But the angler who idles down the stream takes them as they come, and all his observations have a flavour of surprise in them.

He hears a familiar song,—one that he has often heard at a distance, but never identified,—a loud, cheery, rustic cadence sounding from a low pine-tree close beside him. He looks up carefully through the needles and discovers a hooded warbler, a tiny, restless creature, dressed in green and yellow, with two white feathers in its tail, like the ends of a sash, and a glossy little black bonnet drawn closely about its golden head. He will never forget that song again. It will make the woods seem homelike to him, many a time, as he hears it ringing through the afternoon, like the call of a small country girl playing at hide-and-seek: "See ME; here I BE."

Another day he sits down on a mossy log beside a cold, trickling spring to eat his lunch. It has been a barren day for birds. Perhaps he has fallen into the fault of pursuing his sport too intensely, and tramped along the stream looking for nothing but fish. Perhaps this part of the grove has really been deserted by its feathered inhabitants, scared away by a prowling hawk or driven out by nest-hunters. But now, without notice, the luck changes. A surprise-party of redstarts breaks into full play around him. All through the dark-green shadow of the hemlocks they flash like little candles—CANDELITAS, the Cubans call them. Their brilliant markings of orange and black, and their fluttering, airy, graceful movements, make them most welcome visitors. There is no bird in the bush easier to recognize or pleasanter to watch. They run along the branches and dart and tumble through the air in fearless chase of invisible flies and moths. All the time they keep unfolding and furling their rounded tails, spreading them out and waving them and closing them suddenly, just as the Cuban girls manage their fans. In fact, the redstarts are the tiny fantail pigeons of the forest.

There are other things about the birds, besides their musical talents and their good looks, that the fisherman has a chance to observe on his lucky days. He may sea something of their courage and their devotion to their young.

I suppose a bird is the bravest creature that lives, in spite of its natural timidity. From which we may learn that true courage is not incompatible with nervousness, and that heroism does not mean the absence of fear, but the conquest of it. Who does not remember the first time that he ever came upon a hen-partridge with her brood, as he was strolling through the woods in June? How splendidly the old bird forgets herself in her efforts to defend and hide her young!

Smaller birds are no less daring. One evening last summer I was walking up the Ristigouche from Camp Harmony to fish for salmon at Mowett's Rock, where my canoe was waiting for me. As I stepped out from a thicket on to the shingly bank of the river, a spotted sandpiper teetered along before me, followed by three young ones. Frightened at first, the mother flew out a few feet over the water. But the piperlings could not fly, having no feathers; and they crept under a crooked log. I rolled the log over very gently and took one of the cowering creatures into my hand—a tiny, palpitating scrap of life, covered with soft gray down, and peeping shrilly, like a Liliputian chicken. And now the mother was transformed. Her fear was changed into fury. She was a bully, a fighter, an Amazon in feathers. She flew at me with loud cries, dashing herself almost into my face. I was a tyrant, a robber, a kidnapper, and she called heaven to witness that she would never give up her offspring without a struggle. Then she changed her tactics and appealed to my baser passions. She fell to the ground and fluttered around me as if her wing were broken. "Look!" she seemed to say, "I am bigger than that poor little baby. If you must eat something, eat me! My wing is lame. I can't fly. You can easily catch me. Let that little bird go!" And so I did; and the whole family disappeared in the bushes as if by magic. I wondered whether the mother was saying to herself, after the manner of her sex, that men are stupid things, after all, and no match for the cleverness of a female who stoops to deception in a righteous cause.

Now, that trivial experience was what I call a piece of good luck—for me, and, in the event, for the sandpiper. But it is doubtful whether it would be quite so fresh and pleasant in the remembrance, if it had not also fallen to my lot to take two uncommonly good salmon on that same evening, in a dry season.

Never believe a fisherman when he tells you that he does not care about the fish he catches. He may say that he angles only for the pleasure of being out-of-doors, and that he is just as well contented when he takes nothing as when he makes a good catch. He may think so, but it is not true. He is not telling a deliberate falsehood. He is only assuming an unconscious pose, and indulging in a delicate bit of self-flattery. Even if it were true, it would not be at all to his credit.

Watch him on that lucky day when he comes home with a full basket of trout on his shoulder, or a quartette of silver salmon covered with green branches in the bottom of the canoe. His face is broader than it was when he went out, and there is a sparkle of triumph in his eye. "It is naught, it is naught," he says, in modest depreciation of his triumph. But you shall see that he lingers fondly about the place where the fish are displayed upon the grass, and does not fail to look carefully at the scales when they are weighed, and has an attentive ear for the comments of admiring spectators. You shall find, moreover, that he is not unwilling to narrate the story of the capture—how the big fish rose short, four times, to four different flies, and finally took a small Black Dose, and played all over the pool, and ran down a terribly stiff rapid to the next pool below, and sulked for twenty minutes, and had to be stirred up with stones, and made such a long fight that, when he came in at last, the hold of the hook was almost worn through, and it fell out of his mouth as he touched the shore. Listen to this tale as it is told, with endless variations, by every man who has brought home a fine fish, and you will perceive that the fisherman does care for his luck, after all.

And why not? I am no friend to the people who receive the bounties of Providence without visible gratitude. When the sixpence falls into your hat, you may laugh. When the messenger of an unexpected blessing takes you by the hand and lifts you up and bids you walk, you may leap and run and sing for joy, even as the lame man, whom St. Peter healed, skipped piously and rejoiced aloud as he passed through the Beautiful Gate of the Temple. There is no virtue in solemn indifference. Joy is just as much a duty as beneficence is. Thankfulness is the other side of mercy.

When you have good luck in anything, you ought to be glad. Indeed, if you are not glad, you are not really lucky.

But boasting and self-glorification I would have excluded, and most of all from the behaviour of the angler. He, more than other men, is dependent for his success upon the favour of an unseen benefactor. Let his skill and industry be never so great, he can do nothing unless LA BONNE CHANCE comes to him.

I was once fishing on a fair little river, the P'tit Saguenay, with two excellent anglers and pleasant companions, H. E. G—— and C. S. D——. They had done all that was humanly possible to secure good sport. The stream had been well preserved. They had boxes full of beautiful flies, and casting-lines imported from England, and a rod for every fish in the river. But the weather was "dour," and the water "drumly," and every day the lumbermen sent a "drive" of ten thousand spruce logs rushing down the flooded stream. For three days we had not seen a salmon, and on the fourth, despairing, we went down to angle for sea-trout in the tide of the greater Saguenay. There, in the salt water, where men say the salmon never take the fly, H. E. G——, fishing with a small trout-rod, a poor, short line, and an ancient red ibis of the common kind, rose and hooked a lordly salmon of at least five-and-thirty pounds. Was not this pure luck?

Pride is surely the most unbecoming of all vices in a fisherman. For though intelligence and practice and patience and genius, and many other noble things which modesty forbids him to mention, enter into his pastime, so that it is, as Izaak Walton has firmly maintained, an art; yet, because fortune still plays a controlling hand in the game, its net results should never be spoken of with a haughty and vain spirit. Let not the angler imitate Timoleon, who boasted of his luck and lost it. It is tempting Providence to print the record of your wonderful catches in the sporting newspapers;

or at least, if it must be done, there should stand at the head of the column some humble, thankful motto, like "NON NOBIS, DOMINE." Even Father Izaak, when he has a fish on his line, says, with a due sense of human limitations, "There is a trout now, and a good one too, IF I CAN BUT HOLD HIM!"

This reminds me that we left H. E. G——, a few sentences back, playing his unexpected salmon, on a trout-rod, in the Saguenay. Four times that great fish leaped into the air; twice he suffered the pliant reed to guide him toward the shore, and twice ran out again to deeper water. Then his spirit awoke within him: he bent the rod like a willow wand, dashed toward the middle of the river, broke the line as if it had been pack-thread, and sailed triumphantly away to join the white porpoises that were tumbling in the tide. "WHE-E-EW," they said, "WHE-E-EW! PSHA-A-AW!" blowing out their breath in long, soft sighs as they rolled about like huge snowballs in the black water. But what did H. E. G—— say? He sat him quietly down upon a rock and reeled in the remnant of his line, uttering these remarkable and Christian words: "Those porpoises," said he, "describe the situation rather mildly. But it was good fun while it lasted."

Again I remembered a saying of Walton: "Well, Scholar, you must endure worse luck sometimes, or you will never make a good angler."

Or a good man, either, I am sure. For he who knows only how to enjoy, and not to endure, is ill-fitted to go down the stream of life through such a world as this.

I would not have you to suppose, gentle reader, that in discoursing of fisherman's luck I have in mind only those things which may be taken with a hook. It is a parable of human experience. I have been thinking, for instance, of Walton's life as well as of his angling: of the losses and sufferings that he, the firm Royalist, endured when the Commonwealth men came marching into London town; of the consoling days that were granted to him, in troublous times, on the banks of the Lea and the Dove and the New River, and the good friends that he made there, with whom he took sweet counsel in adversity; of the little children who played in his house for a few years, and then were called away into the silent land where he could hear their voices no longer. I was thinking how quietly and peaceably he lived through it all, not complaining nor desponding, but trying to do his work well, whether he was keeping a shop or writing books, and seeking to prove himself an honest man and a cheerful companion, and never scorning to take with a thankful heart such small comforts and recreations as came to him.

It is a plain, homely, old-fashioned meditation, reader, but not unprofitable. When I talk to you of fisherman's luck, I do not forget that there are deeper things behind it. I remember that what we call our fortunes, good or ill, are but the wise dealings and distributions of a Wisdom higher, and a Kindness greater, than our own. And I suppose that their meaning is that we should learn, by all the uncertainties of our life, even the smallest, how to be brave and steady and temperate and hopeful, whatever comes, because we believe that behind it all there lies a purpose of good, and over it all there watches a providence of blessing.

In the school of life many branches of knowledge are taught. But the only philosophy that amounts to anything, after all, is just the secret of making friends with our luck.

THE THRILLING MOMENT

"In angling, as in all other recreations into which excitement enters, we have to be on our guard, so that we can at any moment throw a weight of self-control into the scale against misfortune; and happily we can study to some purpose, both to increase our pleasure in success and to lessen our distress caused by what goes ill. It is not only in cases of great disasters, however, that the angler needs self-control. He is perpetually called upon to use it to withstand small exasperations."

—SIR EDWARD GREY: *Fly-Fishing.*

Every moment of life, I suppose, is more or less of a turning-point. Opportunities are swarming around us all the time, thicker than gnats at sundown. We walk through a cloud of chances, and if we were always conscious of them they would worry us almost to death.

But happily our sense of uncertainty is soothed and cushioned by habit, so that we can live comfortably with it. Only now and then, by way of special excitement, it starts up wide awake. We perceive how delicately our fortune is poised and balanced on the pivot of a single incident. We get a peep at the oscillating needle, and, because we have happened to see it tremble, we call our experience a crisis.

The meditative angler is not exempt from these sensational periods. There are times when all the uncertainty of his chosen pursuit seems to condense itself into one big chance, and stand out before him like a salmon on the top wave of a rapid. He sees that his luck hangs by a single strand, and he cannot tell whether it will hold or break. This is his thrilling moment, and he never forgets it.

Mine came to me in the autumn of 1894, on the banks of the Unpronounceable River, in the Province of Quebec. It was the last day, of the open season for ouananiche, and we had set our hearts on catching some good fish to take home with us. We walked up from the mouth of the river, four preposterously long and rough miles, to the famous fishing-pool, "LA PLACE DE PECHE A BOIVIN." It was a noble day for walking; the air was clear and crisp, and all the hills around us were glowing with the crimson foliage of those little bushes which God created to make burned lands look beautiful. The trail ended in a precipitous gully, down which we scrambled with high hopes, and fishing-rods unbroken, only to find that the river was in a condition which made angling absurd if not impossible.

There must have been a cloud-burst among the mountains, for the water was coming down in flood. The stream was bank-full, gurgling and eddying out among the bushes, and rushing over the shoal where the fish used to lie, in a brown torrent ten feet deep. Our last day with the land-locked salmon seemed destined to be a failure, and we must wait eight months before we could have another. There were three of us in the disappointment, and we shared it according to our temperaments.

Paul virtuously resolved not to give up while there was a chance left, and wandered down-stream to look for an eddy where he might pick up a small fish. Ferdinand, our guide, resigned himself without a sigh to the consolation of eating blueberries, which he always did with great cheerfulness. But I, being more cast down than either of my comrades, sought out a convenient seat among the rocks, and, adapting my anatomy as well as possible to the irregularities of nature's upholstery, pulled from my pocket AN AMATEUR ANGLER'S DAYS IN DOVE DALE, and settled down to read myself into a Christian frame of mind.

Before beginning, my eyes roved sadly over the pool once more. It was but a casual glance. It lasted only for an instant. But in that fortunate fragment of time I distinctly saw the broad tail of a big ouananiche rise and disappear in the swift water at the very head of the pool.

Immediately the whole aspect of affairs was changed. Despondency vanished, and the river glittered with the beams of rising hope.

Such is the absurd disposition of some anglers. They never see a fish without believing that they can catch him; but if they see no fish, they are inclined to think that the river is empty and the world hollow.

I said nothing to my companions. It would have been unkind to disturb them with expectations which might never be realized. My immediate duty was to get within casting distance of that salmon as soon as possible.

The way along the shore of the pool was difficult. The bank was very steep, and the rocks by the river's edge were broken and glibbery. Presently I came to a sheer wall of stone, perhaps thirty feet high, rising directly from the deep water.

There was a tiny ledge or crevice running part of the way across the face of this wall, and by this four-inch path I edged along, holding my rod in one hand, and clinging affectionately with the other to such clumps of grass and little bushes as I could find. There was one small huckleberry plant to which I had a particular attachment. It was fortunately a firm little bush, and as I held fast to it I remembered Tennyson's poem which begins

"Flower in the crannied wall,"

and reflected that if I should succeed in plucking out this flower, "root and all," it would probably result in an even greater increase of knowledge than the poet contemplated.

The ledge in the rock now came to an end. But below me in the pool there was a sunken reef; and on this reef a long log had caught, with one end sticking out of the water, within jumping distance. It was the only chance. To go back would have been dangerous. An angler with a large family dependent upon him for support has no right to incur unnecessary perils.

Besides, the fish was waiting for me at the upper end of the pool!

So I jumped; landed on the end of the log; felt it settle slowly down; ran along it like a small boy on a seesaw, and leaped off into shallow water just as the log rolled from the ledge and lunged out into the stream.

It went wallowing through the pool and down the rapid like a playful hippopotamus. I watched it with interest and congratulated myself that I was no longer embarked upon it. On that craft a voyage down the Unpronounceable River would have been short but far from merry. The "all ashore" bell was not rung early enough. I just got off, with not half a second to spare.

But now all was well, for I was within reach of the fish. A little scrambling over the rocks brought me to a point where I could easily cast over him. He was lying in a swift, smooth, narrow channel between two large stones. It was a snug resting-place, and no doubt he would remain there for some time. So I took out my fly-book and prepared to angle for him according to the approved rules of the art.

Nothing is more foolish in sport than the habit of precipitation. And yet it is a fault to which I am singularly subject. As a boy, in Brooklyn, I never came in sight of the Capitoline Skating Pond, after a long ride in the horse-cars, without breaking into a run along the board walk, buckling on my skates in a furious hurry, and flinging myself impetuously upon the ice, as if I feared that it would melt away before I could reach it. Now this, I confess, is a grievous defect, which advancing years have not entirely cured; and I found it necessary to take myself firmly, as it were, by the mental coat-collar, and resolve not to spoil the chance of catching the only ouananiche in the Unpronounceable River by undue haste in fishing for him.

I carefully tested a brand-new leader, and attached it to the line with great deliberation and the proper knot. Then I gave my whole mind to the important question of a wise selection of flies.

It is astonishing how much time and mental anxiety a man can spend on an apparently simple question like this. When you are buying flies in a shop it seems as if you never had half enough. You keep on picking out a half-dozen of each new variety as fast as the enticing salesman shows them to you. You stroll through the streets of Montreal or

Quebec and drop in at every fishing-tackle dealer's to see whether you can find a few more good flies. Then, when you come to look over your collection at the critical moment on the bank of a stream, it seems as if you had ten times too many. And, spite of all, the precise fly that you need is not there.

You select a couple that you think fairly good, lay them down beside you in the grass, and go on looking through the book for something better. Failing to satisfy yourself, you turn to pick up those that you have laid out, and find that they have mysteriously vanished from the face of the earth.

Then you struggle with naughty words and relapse into a condition of mental palsy.

Precipitation is a fault. But deliberation, for a person of precipitate disposition, is a vice.

The best thing to do in such a case is to adopt some abstract theory of action without delay, and put it into practice without hesitation. Then if you fail, you can throw the responsibility on the theory.

Now, in regard to flies there are two theories. The old, conservative theory is, that on a bright day you should use a dark, dull fly, because it is less conspicuous. So I followed that theory first and put on a Great Dun and a Dark Montreal. I cast them delicately over the fish, but he would not look at them.

Then I perverted myself to the new, radical theory which says that on a bright day you must use a light, gay fly, because it is more in harmony with the sky, and therefore less noticeable. Accordingly I put on a Professor and a Parmacheene Belle; but this combination of learning and beauty had no attraction for the ouananiche.

Then I fell back on a theory of my own, to the effect that the ouananiche have an aversion to red, and prefer yellow and brown. So I tried various combinations of flies in which these colours predominated.

Then I abandoned all theories and went straight through my book, trying something from every page, and winding up with that lure which the guides consider infallible,—"a Jock o' Scott that cost fifty cents at Quebec." But it was all in vain. I was ready to despair.

At this psychological moment I heard behind me a voice of hope,—the song of a grasshopper: not one of those fat-legged, green-winged imbeciles that feebly tumble in the summer fields, but a game grasshopper,—one of those thin-shanked, brown-winged fellows that leap like kangaroos, and fly like birds, and sing KRI-KAREE-KAREE-KRI in their flight.

It is not really a song, I know, but it sounds like one; and, if you had heard that Kri-karee carolling as I chased him over the rocks, you would have been sure that he was mocking me.

I believed that he was the predestined lure for that ouananiche; but it was hard to persuade him to fulfill his destiny. I slapped at him with my hat, but he was not there. I grasped at him on the bushes, and brought away "nothing but leaves." At last he made his way to the very edge of the water and poised himself on a stone, with his legs well tucked in for a long leap and a bold flight to the other side of the river. It was my final opportunity. I made a desperate grab at it and caught the grasshopper.

My premonition proved to be correct. When that Kri-karee, invisibly attached to my line, went floating down the stream, the ouananiche was surprised. It was the fourteenth of September, and he had supposed the grasshopper season was over. The unexpected temptation was too strong for him. He rose with a rush, and in an instant I was fast to the best land-locked salmon of the year.

But the situation was not without its embarrassments. My rod weighed only four and a quarter ounces; the fish weighed between six and seven pounds. The water was furious and headstrong. I had only thirty yards of line and no landing-net.

"HOLA! FERDINAND!" I cried. "APPORTE LA NETTE, VITE! A BEAUTY! HURRY UP!"

I thought it must be an hour while he was making his way over the hill, through the underbrush, around the cliff. Again and again the fish ran out my line almost to the last turn. A dozen times he leaped from the water, shaking his silvery sides. Twice he tried to cut the leader across a sunken ledge. But at last he was played out, and came in quietly towards the point of the rock. At the same moment Ferdinand appeared with the net.

Now, the use of the net is really the most difficult part of angling. And Ferdinand is the best netsman in the Lake St. John country. He never makes the mistake of trying to scoop a fish in motion. He does not grope around with aimless, futile strokes as if he were feeling for something in the dark. He does not entangle the dropper-fly in the net and tear the tail-fly out of the fish's mouth. He does not get excited.

He quietly sinks the net in the water, and waits until he can see the fish distinctly, lying perfectly still and within reach. Then he makes a swift movement, like that of a mower swinging the scythe, takes the fish into the net head-first, and lands him without a slip.

I felt sure that Ferdinand was going to do the trick in precisely this way with my ouananiche. Just at the right instant he made one quick, steady swing of the arms, and—the head of the net broke clean off the handle and went floating away with the fish in it!

All seemed to be lost. But Ferdinand was equal to the occasion. He seized a long, crooked stick that lay in a pile of driftwood on the shore, sprang into the water up to his waist, caught the net as it drifted past, and dragged it to land, with the ultimate ouananiche, the prize of the season, still glittering through its meshes.

This is the story of my most thrilling moment as an angler.

But which was the moment of the deepest thrill?

Was it when the huckleberry bush saved me from a watery grave, or when the log rolled under my feet and started down the river? Was it when the fish rose, or when the net broke, or when the long stick captured it?

No, it was none of these. It was when the Kri-karee sat with his legs tucked under him on the brink of the stream. That was the turning-point. The fortunes of the day depended on the comparative quickness of the reflex action of his neural ganglia and mine. That was the thrilling moment.

I see it now. A crisis is really the commonest thing in the world. The reason why life sometimes seems dull to us is because we do not perceive the importance and the excitement of getting bait.

TALKABILITY
A PRELUDE AND THEME WITH VARIATIONS
"He praises a meditative life, and with evident sincerity: but we feel that he liked nothing so well as good talk."
—JAMES RUSSELL LOWELL: Walton.
I. PRELUDE—ON AN OLD, FOOLISH MAXIM

The inventor of the familiar maxim that "fishermen must not talk" is lost in the mists of antiquity, and well deserves his fate. For a more foolish rule, a conventionality more obscure and aimless in its tyranny, was never imposed upon an innocent and honourable occupation, to diminish its pleasure and discount its profits. Why, in the name of all that is genial, should anglers go about their harmless sport in stealthy silence like conspirators, or sit together in a boat, dumb, glum, and penitential, like naughty schoolboys on the bench of disgrace? 'Tis an Omorcan superstition; a rule without a reason; a venerable, idiotic fashion invented to repress lively spirits and put a premium on stupidity.

For my part, I incline rather to the opinion of the Neapolitan fishermen who maintain that a certain amount of noise, of certain kinds, is likely to improve the fishing, and who have a particular song, very sweet and charming, which they sing to draw the fishes around them. It is narrated, likewise, of the good St. Brandan, that on his notable voyage from Ireland in search of Paradise, he chanted the service for St. Peter's day so pleasantly that a subaqueous audience of all sorts and sizes was attracted, insomuch that the other monks began to be afraid, and begged the abbot that he would sing a little lower, for they were not quite sure of the intention of the congregation. Of St. Anthony of Padua it is said that he even succeeded in persuading the fishes, in great multitudes, to listen to a sermon; and that when it was ended (it must be noted that it was both short and cheerful) they bowed their heads and moved their bodies up and down with every mark of fondness and approval of what the holy father had spoken.

If we can believe this, surely we need not be incredulous of things which seem to be no less, but rather more, in harmony with the course of nature. Creatures who are sensible to the attractions of a sermon can hardly be indifferent to the charm of other kinds of discourse. I can easily imagine a company of grayling wishing to overhear a conversation between I. W. and his affectionate (but somewhat prodigal) son and servant, Charles Cotton; and surely every intelligent salmon in Scotland might have been glad to hear Christopher North and the Ettrick Shepherd bandy jests and swap stories. As for trout,—was there one in Massachusetts that would not have been curious to listen to the intimate opinions of Daniel Webster as he loafed along the banks of the Marshpee,—or is there one in Pennsylvania to-day that might not be drawn with interest and delight to the feet of Joseph Jefferson, telling how he conceived and wrote RIP VAN WINKLE on the banks of a trout-stream?

Fishermen must be silent? On the contrary, it is far more likely that good talk may promote good fishing.

All this, however, goes upon the assumption that fish can hear, in the proper sense of the word. And this, it must be confessed, is an assumption not yet fully verified. Experienced anglers and students of fishy ways are divided upon the question. It is beyond a doubt that all fishes, except the very lowest forms, have ears. But then so have all men; and yet we have the best authority for believing that there are many who "having ears, hear not."

The ears of fishes, for the most part, are inclosed in their skull, and have no outward opening. Water conveys sound, as every country boy knows who has tried the experiment of diving to the bottom of the swimming-hole and knocking two big stones together. But I doubt whether any country boy, engaged in this interesting scientific experiment, has heard the conversation of his friends on the bank who were engaged in hiding his clothes.

There are many curious and more or less venerable stories to the effect that fishes may be trained to assemble at the ringing of a bell or the beating of a drum. Lucian, a writer of the second century, tells of a certain lake wherein many sacred fishes were kept, of which the largest had names given to them, and came when they were called. But Lucian was not a man of especially good reputation, and there is an air of improbability about his statement that the LARGEST fishes came. This is not the custom of the largest fishes.

In the present century there was a tale of an eel in a garden-well, in Scotland, which would come to be fed out of a spoon when the children called him by his singularly inappropriate name of Rob Roy. This seems a more likely story than Lucian's; at all events it comes from a more orthodox atmosphere. But before giving it full credence, I should like to know whether the children, when they called "Rob Roy!" stood where the eel could see the spoon.

On the other side of the question, we may quote Mr. Ronalds, also a Scotchman, and the learned author of THE FLY-FISHER'S ENTOMOLOGY, who conducted a series of experiments which proved that even trout, the most fugacious of fish, are not in the least disturbed by the discharge of a gun, provided the flash is concealed. Mr. Henry P. Wells, the author of THE AMERICAN SALMON ANGLER, says that he has "never been able to make a sound in the air which seemed to produce the slightest effect upon trout in the water."

So the controversy on the hearing of fishes continues, and the conclusion remains open. Every man is at liberty to embrace that side which pleases him best. You may think that the finny tribes are as sensitive to sound as Fine Ear, in the German fairy-tale, who could hear the grass grow. Or you may hold the opposite opinion, that they are

"Deafer than the blue-eyed cat."

But whichever theory you adopt, in practice, if you are a wise fisherman, you will steer a middle course, between one thing which must be left undone and another thing which should be done. You will refrain from stamping on the bank, or knocking on the side of the boat, or dragging the anchor among the stones on the bottom; for when the water vibrates the fish are likely to vanish. But you will indulge as freely as you please in pleasant discourse with your comrade; for it is certain that fishing is never hindered, and may even be helped, in one way or another, by good talk.

I should therefore have no hesitation in advising any one to choose, for companionship on an angling expedition, long or short, a person who has the rare merit of being TALKABLE.

II. THEME—ON A SMALL, USEFUL VIRTUE

"Talkable" is not a new adjective. But it needs a new definition, and the complement of a corresponding noun. I would fain set down on paper some observations and reflections which may serve to make its meaning clear, and render due praise to that most excellent quality in man or woman,—especially in anglers,—the small but useful virtue of TALKABILITY.

Robert Louis Stevenson uses the word "talkable" in one of his essays to denote a certain distinction among the possible subjects of human speech. There are some things, he says in effect, about which you can really talk; and there are other things about which you cannot properly talk at all, but only dispute, or harangue, or prose, or moralize, or chatter.

After mature consideration I have arrived at the opinion that this distinction among the themes of speech is an illusion. It does not exist. All subjects, "the foolish things of the world, and the weak things of the world, and base things of the world, yea, and things that are not," may provide matter for good talk, if only the right people are engaged in the enterprise. I know a man who can make a description of the weather as entertaining as a tune on the violin; and even on the threadbare theme of the waywardness of domestic servants, I have heard a discreet woman play the most diverting and instructive variations.

No, the quality of talkability does not mark a distinction among things; it denotes a difference among people. It is not an attribute unequally distributed among material objects and abstract ideas. It is a virtue which belongs to the mind and moral character of certain persons. It is a reciprocal human quality; active as well as passive; a power of bestowing and receiving.

An amiable person is one who has a capacity for loving and being loved. An affable person is one who is ready to speak and to be spoken to,—as, for example, Milton's "affable archangel" Raphael; though it must be confessed that he laid the chief emphasis on the active side of his affability. A "clubable" person (to use a word which Dr. Samuel Johnson invented but did not put into his dictionary) is one who is fit for the familiar give and take of club-life. A talkable person, therefore, is one whose nature and disposition invite the easy interchange of thoughts and feelings, one in whose company it is a pleasure to talk or to be talked to.

Now this good quality of talkability is to be distinguished, very strictly and inflexibly, from the bad quality which imitates it and often brings it into discredit. I mean the vice of talkativeness. That is a selfish, one-sided, inharmonious affair, full of discomfort, and productive of most unchristian feelings.

You may observe the operations of this vice not only in human beings, but also in birds. All the birds in the bush can make some kind of a noise; and most of them like to do it; and some of them like it a great deal and do it very much. But it is not always for edification, nor are the most vociferous and garrulous birds commonly the most pleasing. A parrot, for instance, in your neighbour's back yard, in the summer time, when the windows are open, is not an aid to the development of Christian character. I knew a man who had to stay in the city all summer, and in the autumn was asked to describe the character and social standing of a new family that had moved into his neighbourhood. Were they "nice people," well-bred, intelligent, respectable? "Well," said he, "I don't know what your standards are, and would prefer not to say anything libellous; but I'll tell you in a word,—they are the kind of people that keep a parrot."

Then there is the English Sparrow! What an insufferable chatterbox, what an incurable scold, what a voluble and tiresome blackguard is this little feathered cockney. There is not a sweet or pleasant word in all his vocabulary.

I am convinced that he talks altogether of scandals and fights and street-sweepings.

The kingdom of ornithology is divided into two departments,—real birds and English sparrows. English sparrows are not real birds; they are little beasts.

There was a church in Brooklyn which was once covered with a great and spreading vine, in which the sparrows built innumerable nests. These ungodly little birds kept up such a din that it was impossible to hear the service of the sanctuary. The faithful clergy strained their voices to the verge of ministerial sore throat, but the people had no peace in their devotions until the vine was cut down, and the Anglican intruders were evicted.

A talkative person is like an English sparrow,—a bird that cannot sing, and will sing, and ought to be persuaded not to try to sing. But a talkable person has the gift that belongs to the wood thrush and the veery and the wren, the oriole and the white-throat and the rose-breasted grosbeak, the mockingbird and the robin (sometimes); and the brown thrush; yes, the brown thrush has it to perfection, if you can catch him alone,—the gift of being interesting, charming, delightful, in the most off-hand and various modes of utterance.

Talkability is not at all the same thing as eloquence. The eloquent man surprises, overwhelms, and sometimes paralyzes us by the display of his power. Great orators are seldom good talkers. Oratory in exercise is masterful and jealous, and intolerant of all interruptions. Oratory in preparation is silent, self-centred, uncommunicative. The painful truth of this remark may be seen in the row of countenances along the president's table at a public banquet about nine o'clock in the evening. The bicycle-face seems unconstrained and merry by comparison with the after-dinner-speech-face. The flow of table-talk is corked by the anxious conception of post-prandial oratory.

Thackeray, in one of his ROUNDABOUT PAPERS, speaks of "the sin of tall-talking," which, he says, "is the sin of schoolmasters, governesses, critics, sermoners, and instructors of young or old people." But this is not in accord with my observation. I should say it was rather the sin of dilettanti who are ambitious of that high-stepping accomplishment which is called "conversational ability."

This has usually, to my mind, something set and artificial about it, although in its most perfect form the art almost succeeds in concealing itself. But, at all events, "conversation" is talk in evening dress, with perhaps a little powder and a touch of rouge. 'T is like one of those wise virgins who are said to look their best by lamplight. And doubtless this is an excellent thing, and not without its advantages. But for my part, commend me to one who loses nothing by the early morning illumination,—one who brings all her attractions with her when she comes down to breakfast,—she is a very pleasant maid.

Talk is that form of human speech which is exempt from all duties, foreign and domestic. It is the nearest thing in the world to thinking and feeling aloud. It is necessarily not for publication,—solely an evidence of good faith and mutual kindness. You tell me what you have seen and what you are thinking about, because you take it for granted that it will interest and entertain me; and you listen to my replies and the recital of my adventures and opinions, because you know I like to tell them, and because you find something in them, of one kind or another, that you care to hear. It is a nice game, with easy, simple rules, and endless possibilities of variation. And if we go into it with the right spirit, and play it for love, without heavy stakes, the chances are that if we happen to be fairly talkable people we shall have one of the best things in the world,—a mighty good talk.

What is there in this anxious, hide-bound, tiresome existence of ours, more restful and remunerative? Montaigne says, "The use of it is more sweet than of any other action of life; and for that reason it is that, if I were compelled to choose, I should sooner, I think, consent to lose my sight than my hearing and speech." The very aimlessness with which it proceeds, the serene disregard of all considerations of profit and propriety with which it follows its wandering course, and brings up anywhere or nowhere, to camp for the night, is one of its attractions. It is like a day's fishing, not valuable chiefly for the fish you bring home, but for the pleasant country through which it leads you, and the state of personal well-being and health in which it leaves you, warmed, and cheered, and content with life and friendship.

The order in which you set out upon a talk, the path which you pursue, the rules which you observe or disregard, make but little difference in the end. You may follow the advice of Immanuel Kant if you like, and begin with the weather and the roads, and go on to current events, and wind up with history, art, and philosophy. Or you may reverse the order if you prefer, like that admirable talker Clarence King, who usually set sail on some highly abstract paradox, such as "Civilization is a nervous disease," and landed in a tale of adventure in Mexico or the Rocky Mountains. Or you may follow the example of Edward Eggleston, who started in at the middle and worked out at either end, and sometimes at both. It makes no difference. If the thing is in you at all, you will find good matter for talk anywhere along the route. Hear what Montaigne says again: "In our discourse all subjects are alike to me; let there be neither weight nor depth, 't is all one; there is yet grace and pertinence; all there is tented with a mature and constant judgment, and mixed with goodness, freedom, gayety, and friendship."

How close to the mark the old essayist sends his arrow! He is right about the essential qualities of good talk. They are not merely intellectual. They are moral. Goodness of heart, freedom of spirit, gayety of temper, and friendliness of disposition,—these are four fine things, and doubtless as acceptable to God as they are agreeable to men. The talkability which springs out of these qualities has its roots in a good soil. On such a plant one need not look for the poison berries of malign discourse, nor for the Dead Sea apples of frivolous mockery. But fair fruit will be there, pleasant to the sight and good for food, brought forth abundantly according to the season.

III. VARIATIONS—ON A PLEASANT PHRASE FROM MONTAIGNE

Montaigne has given as our text, "Goodness, freedom, gayety, and friendship,"—these are the conditions which produce talkability. And on this fourfold theme we may embroider a few variations, by way of exposition and enlargement.

GOODNESS is the first thing and the most needful. An ugly, envious, irritable disposition is not fitted for talk. The occasions for offence are too numerous, and the way into strife is too short and easy. A touch of good-natured combativeness, a fondness for brisk argument, a readiness to try a friendly bout with any comer, on any ground, is a decided advantage in a talker. It breaks up the offensive monotony of polite concurrence, and makes things lively. But quarrelsomeness is quite another affair, and very fatal.

I am always a little uneasy in a discourse with the Reverend Bellicosus Macduff. It is like playing golf on links liable to earthquakes. One never knows when the landscape will be thrown into convulsions. Macduff has a tendency to regard a difference of opinion as a personal insult. If he makes a bad stroke he seems to think that the way to retrieve it is to deliver the next one on the head of the other player. He does not tarry for the invitation to lay on; and before you know what has happened you find yourself in a position where you are obliged to cry, "Hold, enough!" and to be liberally damned without any bargain to that effect. This is discouraging, and calculated to make one wish that human intercourse might be put, as far as Macduff is concerned, upon the gold basis of silence.

On the other hand, what a delight it was to talk with that old worthy, Chancellor Howard Crosby. He was a fighting man for four or five generations hack, Dutch on one side, English on the other. But there was not one little drop of gall in his blood. His opinions were fixed to a degree; he loved to do battle for them; he never changed them—at least never in the course of the same discussion. He admired and respected a gallant adversary, and urged him on, with quips and puns and daring assaults and unqualified statements, to do his best. Easy victories were not to his taste. Even if he joined with you in laying out some common falsehood for burial, you might be sure that before the affair was concluded there would be every prospect of what an Irishman would call "an elegant wake." If you stood up against him on one of his favorite subjects of discussion you must be prepared for hot work. You would have to take off your coat. But when the combat was over he would be the man to help you on with it again; and you would walk home together arm in arm, through the twilight, smoking the pipe of peace. Talk like that does good. It quickens the beating of the heart, and leaves no scars upon it.

But this manly spirit, which loves

"To drink delight of battle with its peers,"

is a very different thing from that mean, bad, hostile temper which loves to inflict wounds and injuries just for the sake of showing power, and which is never so happy as when it is making some one wince. There are such people in the world, and sometimes their brilliancy tempts us to forget their malignancy. But to have much converse with them is as if we should make playmates of rattlesnakes for their grace of movement and swiftness of stroke.

I knew a man once (I will not name him even with an initial) who was malignant to the core. Learned, industrious, accomplished, he kept all his talents at the service of a perfect genius for hatred. If you crossed his path but once, he would never cease to curse you. The grave might close over you, but he would revile your epitaph and mock at your memory. It was not even necessary that you should do anything to incur his enmity. It was enough to be upright and sincere and successful, to waken the wrath of this Shimei. Integrity was an offence to him, and excellence of any kind filled him with spleen. There was no good cause within his horizon that he did not give a bad word to, and no decent man in the community whom he did not try either to use or to abuse. To listen to him or to read what he had written was to learn to think a little worse of every one that he mentioned, and worst of all of him. He had the air of a gentleman, the vocabulary of a scholar, the style of a Junius, and the heart of a Thersites.

Talk, in such company, is impossible. The sense of something evil, lurking beneath the play of wit, is like the knowledge that there are snakes in the grass. Every step must be taken with fear. But the real pleasure of a walk through the meadow comes from the feeling of security, of ease, of safe and happy abandon to the mood of the moment. This ungirdled and unguarded felicity in mutual discourse depends, after all, upon the assurance of real goodness in your companion. I do not mean a stiff impeccability of conduct. Prudes and Pharisees are poor comrades. I mean simply goodness of heart, the wholesome, generous, kindly quality which thinketh no evil, rejoiceth not in iniquity, hopeth all things, endureth all things, and wisheth well to all men. Where you feel this quality you can let yourself go, in the ease of hearty talk.

FREEDOM is the second note that Montaigne strikes, and it is essential to the harmony of talking. Very careful, prudent, precise persons are seldom entertaining in familiar speech. They are like tennis players in too fine clothes. They think more of their costume than of the game.

A mania for absolutely correct pronunciation is fatal. The people who are afflicted with this painful ailment are as anxious about their utterance as dyspeptics about their diet. They move through their sentences as delicately as Agag walked. Their little airs of nicety, their starched cadences and frilled phrases seem as if they had just been taken out of a literary bandbox. If perchance you happen to misplace an accent, you shall see their eyebrows curl up like an interrogation mark, and they will ask you what authority you have for that pronunciation. As if, forsooth, a man could not talk without book-license! As if he must have a permit from some dusty lexicon before he can take a good word into his mouth and speak it out like the people with whom he has lived!

The truth is that the man who is very particular not to commit himself, in pronunciation or otherwise, and talks as if his remarks were being taken down in shorthand, and shudders at the thought of making a mistake, will hardly be able to open your heart or let out the best that is in his own.

Reserve and precision are a great protection to overrated reputations; but they are death to talk.

In talk it is not correctness of grammar nor elegance of enunciation that charms us; it is spirit, VERVE, the sudden turn of humour, the keen, pungent taste of life. For this reason a touch of dialect, a flavour of brogue, is delightful. Any dialect is classic that has conveyed beautiful thoughts. Who that ever talked with the poet Tennyson, when he let himself go, over the pipes, would miss the savour of his broad-rolling Lincolnshire vowels, now heightening the humour, now deepening the pathos, of his genuine manly speech? There are many good stories lingering in the memories of those who knew Dr. James McCosh, the late president of Princeton University,—stories too good, I fear, to get into a biography; but the best of them, in print, would not have the snap and vigour of the poorest of them, in talk, with his own inimitable Scotch-Irish brogue to set it forth.

A brogue is not a fault. It is a beauty, an heirloom, a distinction. A local accent is like a landed inheritance; it marks a man's place in the world, tells where he comes from. Of course it is possible to have too much of it. A man does not need to carry the soil of his whole farm around with him on his boots. But, within limits, the accent of a native region is delightful. 'T is the flavour of heather in the grouse, the taste of wild herbs and evergreen-buds in the venison. I like the maple-sugar tang of the Vermonter's sharp-edged speech; the round, full-waisted r's of Pennsylvania and Ohio; the soft, indolent vowels of the South. One of the best talkers now living is a schoolmaster from Virginia, Colonel Gordon McCabe. I once crossed the ocean with him on a stream of stories that reached from Liverpool to New York. He did not talk in the least like a book. He talked like a Virginian.

When Montaigne mentions GAYETY as the third clement of satisfying discourse, I fancy he does not mean mere fun, though that has its value at the right time and place. But there is another quality which is far more valuable and always fit. Indeed it underlies the best fun and makes it wholesome. It is cheerfulness, the temper which makes the best of things and squeezes the little drops of honey even out of thistle-blossoms. I think this is what Montaigne meant. Certainly it is what he had.

Cheerfulness is the background of all good talk. A sense of humour is a means of grace. With it I have heard a pleasant soul make even that most perilous of all subjects, the description of a long illness, entertaining. The various physicians moved through the recital as excellent comedians, and the medicines appeared like a succession of timely jests.

There is no occasion upon which this precious element of talkability comes out stronger than when we are on a journey. Travel with a cheerless and easily discouraged companion is an unadulterated misery. But a cheerful comrade is better than a waterproof coat and a foot-warmer.

I remember riding once with my lady Graygown fifteen miles through a cold rainstorm, in an open buckboard, over the worst road in the world, from LAC A LA BELLE RIVIERE to the Metabetchouan River. Such was the cheerfulness of her ejaculations (the only possible form of talk) that we arrived at our destination as warm and merry as if we had been sitting beside a roaring camp-fire.

But after all, the very best thing in good talk, and the thing that helps it most, is FRIENDSHIP. How it dissolves the barriers that divide us, and loosens all constraint, and diffuses itself like some fine old cordial through all the veins of life—this feeling that we understand and trust each other, and wish each other heartily well! Everything into which it really comes is good. It transforms letter-writing from a task into a pleasure. It makes music a thousand times more sweet. The people who play and sing not at us, but TO us,—how delightful it is to listen to them! Yes, there is a talkability that can express itself even without words. There is an exchange of thought and feeling which is happy alike in speech and in silence. It is quietness pervaded with friendship.

Having come thus far in the exposition of Montaigne, I shall conclude with an opinion of my own, even though I cannot quote a sentence of his to back it.

The one person of all the world in whom talkability is most desirable, and talkativeness least endurable, is a wife.

A WILD STRAWBERRY

"Such is the story of the Boblink; once spiritual, musical, admired, the joy of the meadows, and the favourite bird of spring; finally a gross little sensualist who expiates his sensuality in the larder. His story contains a moral, worthy the attention of all little birds and little boys; warning them to keep to those refined and intellectual pursuits which raised him to so high a pitch of popularity during the early part of his career; but to eschew all tendency to that gross and dissipated indulgence, which brought this mistaken little bird to an untimely end."

—WASHINGTON IRVING: Wolfert's Roost.

The Swiftwater brook was laughing softly to itself as it ran through a strip of hemlock forest on the edge of the Woodlings' farm. Among the evergreen branches overhead the gayly-dressed warblers,—little friends of the forest,—were flitting to and fro, lisping their June songs of contented love: milder, slower, lazier notes than those in which they voiced the amorous raptures of May. Prince's Pine and golden loose-strife and pink laurel and blue hare-bells and purple-fringed orchids, and a score of lovely flowers were all abloom. The late spring had hindered some; the sudden heats of early summer had hastened others; and now they seemed to come out all together, as if Nature had suddenly tilted up her cornucopia and poured forth her treasures in spendthrift joy.

I lay on a mossy bank at the foot of a tree, filling my pipe after a frugal lunch, and thinking how hard it would be to find in any quarter of the globe a place more fair and fragrant than this hidden vale among the Alleghany Mountains. The perfume of the flowers of the forest is more sweet and subtle than the heavy scent of tropical blossoms. No lily-field in Bermuda could give a fragrance half so magical as the fairy-like odour of these woodland slopes, soft carpeted with the green of glossy vines above whose tiny leaves, in delicate profusion,

"The slight Linnaea hangs its twin-born heads."

Nor are there any birds in Africa, or among the Indian Isles, more exquisite in colour than these miniature warblers, showing their gold and green, their orange and black, their blue and white, against the dark background of the rhododendron thicket.

But how seldom we put a cup of pleasure to our lips without a dash of bitters, a touch of faultfinding. My drop of discontent, that day, was the thought that the northern woodland, at least in June, yielded no fruit to match its beauty and its fragrance.

There is good browsing among the leaves of the wood and the grasses of the meadow, as every well-instructed angler knows. The bright emerald tips that break from the hemlock and the balsam like verdant flames have a pleasant savour to the tongue. The leaves of the sassafras are full of spice, and the bark of the black-birch twigs holds a fine cordial. Crinkle-root is spicy, but you must partake of it delicately, or it will bite your tongue. Spearmint and peppermint never lose their charm for the palate that still remembers the delights of youth. Wild sorrel has an agreeable, sour, shivery flavour. Even the tender stalk of a young blade of grass is a thing that can be chewed by a person of childlike mind with much contentment.

But, after all, these are only relishes. They whet the appetite more than they appease it. There should be something to eat, in the June woods, as perfect in its kind, as satisfying to the sense of taste, as the birds and the flowers are to the senses of sight and hearing and smell. Blueberries are good, but they are far away in July. Blackberries are luscious when they are fully ripe, but that will not be until August. Then the fishing will be over, and the angler's hour of need will be past. The one thing that is lacking now beside this mountain stream is some fruit more luscious and dainty than grows in the tropics, to melt upon the lips and fill the mouth with pleasure.

But that is what these cold northern woods will not offer. They are too reserved, too lofty, too puritanical to make provision for the grosser wants of humanity. They are not friendly to luxury.

Just then, as I shifted my head to find a softer pillow of moss after this philosophic and immoral reflection, Nature gave me her silent answer. Three wild strawberries, nodding on their long stems, hung over my face. It was an invitation to taste and see that they were good.

The berries were not the round and rosy ones of the meadow, but the long, slender, dark crimson ones of the forest. One, two, three; no more on that vine; but each one as it touched my lips was a drop of nectar and a crumb of ambrosia, a concentrated essence of all the pungent sweetness of the wildwood, sapid, penetrating, and delicious. I tasted the odour of a hundred blossoms and the green shimmering of innumerable leaves and the sparkle of sifted sunbeams and the breath of highland breezes and the song of many birds and the murmur of flowing streams,—all in a wild strawberry.

Do you remember, in THE COMPLEAT ANGLER, a remark which Isaak Walton quotes from a certain "Doctor Boteler" about strawberries? "Doubtless," said that wise old man, "God could have made a better berry, but doubtless God never did."

Well, the wild strawberry is the one that God made.

I think it would have been pleasant to know a man who could sum up his reflections upon the important question of berries in such a pithy saying as that which Walton repeats. His tongue must have been in close communication with his heart. He must have had a fair sense of that sprightly humour without which piety itself is often insipid.

I have often tried to find out more about him, and some day I hope I shall. But up to the present, all that the books have told me of this obscure sage is that his name was William Butler, and that he was an eminent physician, sometimes called "the Aesculapius of his age." He was born at Ipswich, in 1535, and educated at Clare Hall, Cambridge; in the neighbourhood of which town he appears to have spent the most of his life, in high repute as a practitioner of physic. He had the honour of doctoring King James the First after an accident on the hunting field, and must have proved himself a pleasant old fellow, for the king looked him up at Cambridge the next year, and spent an hour in his lodgings. This wise physician also invented a medicinal beverage called "Doctor Butler's Ale." I do not quite like the sound of it, but perhaps it was better than its name. This much is sure, at all events: either it was really a harmless drink, or else the doctor must have confined its use entirely to his patients; for he lived to the ripe age of eighty-three years.

Between the time when William Butler first needed the services of a physician, in 1535, and the time when he last prescribed for a patient, in 1618, there was plenty of trouble in England. Bloody Queen Mary sat on the throne; and there were all kinds of quarrels about religion and politics; and Catholics and Protestants were killing one another in the name of God. After that the red-haired Elizabeth, called the Virgin Queen, wore the crown, and waged triumphant war and tempestuous love. Then fat James of Scotland was made king of Great Britain; and Guy Fawkes tried to blow him up with gunpowder, and failed; and the king tried to blow out all the pipes in England with his COUNTERBLAST AGAINST TOBACCO; but he failed too. Somewhere about that time, early in the seventeenth century, a very small event happened. A new berry was brought over from Virginia,—FRAGRARIA VIRGINIANA,—and then, amid wars and rumours of wars, Doctor Butler's happiness was secure. That new berry was so much richer and sweeter and more generous than the familiar FRAGRARIA VESCA of Europe, that it attracted the sincere interest of all persons of good taste. It inaugurated a new era in the history of the strawberry. The long lost masterpiece of Paradise was restored to its true place in the affections of man.

Is there not a touch of merry contempt for all the vain controversies and conflicts of humanity in the grateful ejaculation with which the old doctor greeted that peaceful, comforting gift of Providence?

"From this time forward," he seems to say, "the fates cannot beggar me, for I have eaten strawberries. With every Maytime that visits this distracted island, the white blossoms with hearts of gold will arrive. In every June the red drops of pleasant savour will hang among the scalloped leaves. The children of this world may wrangle and give one another wounds that even my good ale cannot cure. Nevertheless, the earth as God created it is a fair dwelling and full of comfort for all who have a quiet mind and a thankful heart. Doubtless God might have made a better world, but doubtless this is the world He made for us; and in it He planted the strawberry."

Fine old doctor! Brave philosopher of cheerfulness! The Virginian berry should have been brought to England sooner, or you should have lived longer, at least to a hundred years, so that you might have welcomed a score of strawberry-seasons with gratitude and an epigram.

Since that time a great change has passed over the fruit which Doctor Butler praised so well. That product of creative art which Divine wisdom did not choose to surpass, human industry has laboured to improve. It has grown immensely in size and substance. The traveller from America who steams into Queenstown harbour in early summer is presented (for a consideration) with a cabbage-leaf full of pale-hued berries, sweet and juicy, any one of which would outbulk a dozen of those that used to grow in Virginia when Pocahontas was smitten with the charms of Captain John Smith. They are superb, those light-tinted Irish strawberries. And there are wonderful new varieties developed in the gardens of New Jersey and Rhode Island, which compare with the ancient berries of the woods and meadows as Leviathan with a minnow. The huge crimson cushions hang among the plants so thick that they seem like bunches of fruit with a few leaves attached for ornament. You can satisfy your hunger in such a berry-patch in ten minutes, while out in the field you must pick for half an hour, and in the forest thrice as long, before you can fill a small tin cup.

Yet, after all, it is questionable whether men have really bettered God's CHEF D'OEUVRE in the berry line. They have enlarged it and made it more plentiful and more certain in its harvest. But sweeter, more fragrant, more poignant in its flavour? No. The wild berry still stands first in its subtle gusto.

Size is not the measure of excellence. Perfection lies in quality, not in quantity. Concentration enhances pleasure, gives it a point so that it goes deeper.

Is not a ten-inch trout better than a ten-foot sturgeon? I would rather read a tiny essay by Charles Lamb than a five-hundred page libel on life by a modern British novelist who shall be nameless. Flavour is the priceless quality. Style is the thing that counts and is remembered, in literature, in art, and in berries.

No JOCUNDA, nor TRIUMPH, nor VICTORIA, nor any other high-titled fruit that ever took the first prize at an agricultural fair, is half so delicate and satisfying as the wild strawberry that dropped into my mouth, under the hemlock tree, beside the Swiftwater.

A touch of surprise is essential to perfect sweetness.

To get what you have been wishing for is pleasant; but to get what you have not been sure of, makes the pleasure tingle. A new door of happiness is opened when you go out to hunt for something and discover it with your own eyes. But there is an experience even better than that. When you have stupidly forgotten (or despondently forgone) to look about you for the unclaimed treasures and unearned blessings which are scattered along the by-ways of life, then, sometimes by a special mercy, a small sample of them is quietly laid before you so that you cannot help seeing it, and it brings you back to a sense of the joyful possibilities of living.

How full of enjoyment is the search after wild things,—wild birds, wild flowers, wild honey, wild berries! There was a country club on Storm King Mountain, above the Hudson River, where they used to celebrate a festival of flowers every spring. Men and women who had conservatories of their own, full of rare plants and costly orchids, came together to admire the gathered blossoms of the woodlands and meadows. But the people who had the best of the entertainment were the boys and girls who wandered through the thickets and down the brooks, pushed their way into the tangled copses and crept venturesomely across the swamps, to look for the flowers. Some of the seekers may have had a few gray hairs; but for that day at least they were all boys and girls. Nature was as young as ever, and they were all her children. Hand touched hand without a glove. The hidden blossoms of friendship unfolded. Laughter and merry shouts and snatches of half-forgotten song rose to the lips. Gay adventure sparkled in the air. School was out and nobody listened for the bell. It was just a day to live, and be natural, and take no thought for the morrow.

There is great luck in this affair of looking for flowers. I do not see how any one who is prejudiced against games of chance can consistently undertake it.

For my own part, I approve of garden flowers because they are so orderly and so certain; but wild flowers I love, just because there is so much chance about them. Nature is all in favour of certainty in great laws and of uncertainty in small events. You cannot appoint the day and the place for her flower-shows. If you happen to drop in at the right moment she will give you a free admission. But even then it seems as if the table of beauty had been spread for the joy of a higher visitor, and in obedience to secret orders which you have not heard.

Have you ever found the fringed gentian?

> *"Just before the snows,*
> *There came a purple creature*
> *That lavished all the hill:*

*And summer hid her forehead,
And mockery was still.*

*The frosts were her condition:
The Tyrian would not come
Until the North evoked her,—
'Creator, shall I bloom?'"*

There are strange freaks of fortune in the finding of wild flowers, and curious coincidences which make us feel as if some one were playing friendly tricks on us. I remember reading, one evening in May, a passage in a good book called THE PROCESSION OF THE FLOWERS, in which Colonel Higginson describes the singular luck that a friend of his enjoyed, year after year, in finding the rare blossoms of the double rueanemone. It seems that this man needed only to take a walk in the suburbs of any town, and he would come upon a bed of these flowers, without effort or design. I envied him his good fortune, for I had never discovered even one of them. But the next morning, as I strolled out to fish the Swiftwater, down below Billy Lerns's spring-house I found a green bank in the shadow of the wood all bespangled with tiny, trembling, twofold stars,—double rueanemones, for luck! It was a favourable omen, and that day I came home with a creel full of trout.

The theory that Adam lived out in the woods for some time before he was put into the garden of Eden "to dress it and to keep it" has an air of probability. How else shall we account for the arboreal instincts that cling to his posterity?

There is a wilding strain in our blood that all the civilization in the world will not eradicate. I never knew a real boy—or, for that matter, a girl worth knowing—who would not rather climb a tree, any day, than walk up a golden stairway.

It is a touch of this instinct, I suppose, that makes it more delightful to fish in the most insignificant of free streams than in a carefully stocked and preserved pond, where the fish are brought up by hand and fed on minced liver. Such elaborate precautions to ensure good luck extract all the spice from the sport of angling. Casting the fly in such a pond, if you hooked a fish, you might expect to hear the keeper say, "Ah, that is Charles, we will play him and put him back, if you please, sir; for the master is very fond of him,"—or, "Now you have got hold of Edward; let us land him and keep him; he is three years old this month, and just ready to be eaten." It would seem like taking trout out of cold storage.

Who could find any pleasure in angling for the tame carp in the fish-pool of Fontainebleau? They gather at the marble steps, those venerable, courtly fish, to receive their rations; and there are veterans among them, in ancient livery, with fringes of green moss on their shoulders, who could tell you pretty tales of being fed by the white hands of maids of honour, or even of nibbling their crumbs of bread from the jewelled fingers of a princess.

There is no sport in bringing pets to the table. It may be necessary sometimes; but the true sportsman would always prefer to leave the unpleasant task of execution to menial hands, while he goes out into the wild country to capture his game by his own skill,—if he has good luck. I would rather run some risk in this enterprise (even as the young Tobias did, when the voracious pike sprang at him from the waters of the Tigris, and would have devoured him but for the friendly instruction of the piscatory Angel, who taught Tobias how to land the monster),—I would far rather take any number of chances in my sport than have it domesticated to the point of dulness.

The trim plantations of trees which are called "forests" in certain parts of Europe—scientifically pruned and tended, counted every year by uniformed foresters, and defended against all possible depredations—are admirable and useful in their way; but they lack the mystic enchantment of the fragments of native woodland which linger among the Adirondacks and the White Mountains, or the vast, shaggy, sylvan wildernesses which hide the lakes and rivers of Canada. These Laurentian Hills lie in No Man's Land. Here you do not need to keep to the path, for there is none. You may make your own trail, whithersoever fancy leads you; and at night you may pitch your tent under any tree that looks friendly and firm.

Here, if anywhere, you shall find Dryads, and Naiads, and Oreads. And if you chance to see one, by moonlight, combing her long hair beside the glimmering waterfall, or slipping silently, with gleaming shoulders, through the grove of silver birches, you may call her by the name that pleases you best. She is all your own discovery. There is no social directory in the wilderness.

One side of our nature, no doubt, finds its satisfaction in the regular, the proper, the conventional. But there is another side of our nature, underneath, that takes delight in the strange, the free, the spontaneous. We like to discover what we call a law of Nature, and make our calculations about it, and harness the force which lies behind it for our own purposes. But we taste a different kind of joy when an event occurs which nobody has foreseen or counted upon. It seems like an evidence that there is something in the world which is alive and mysterious and untrammelled.

The weather-prophet tells us of an approaching storm. It comes according to the programme. We admire the accuracy of the prediction, and congratulate ourselves that we have such a good meteorological service. But when, perchance, a bright, crystalline piece of weather arrives instead of the foretold tempest, do we not feel a secret sense of pleasure which goes beyond our mere comfort in the sunshine? The whole affair is not as easy as a sum in simple addition, after all,—at least not with our present knowledge. It is a good joke on the Weather Bureau. "Aha, Old Probabilities!" we say, "you don't know it all yet; there are still some chances to be taken!"

Some day, I suppose, all things in the heavens above, and in the earth beneath, and in the hearts of the men and women who dwell between, will be investigated and explained. We shall live a perfectly ordered life, with no accidents, happy or unhappy. Everybody will act according to rule, and there will be no dotted lines on the map of human existence, no regions marked "unexplored." Perhaps that golden age of the machine will come, but you and I will hardly live to see it. And if that seems to you a matter for tears, you must do your own weeping, for I cannot find it in my heart to add a single drop of regret.

The results of education and social discipline in humanity are fine. It is a good thing that we can count upon them. But at the same time let us rejoice in the play of native traits and individual vagaries. Cultivated manners are admirable, yet there is a sudden touch of inborn grace and courtesy that goes beyond them all. No array of accomplishments can rival the charm of an unsuspected gift of nature, brought suddenly to light. I once heard a peasant girl singing down the Traunthal, and the echo of her song outlives, in the hearing of my heart, all memories of the grand opera.

The harvest of the gardens and the orchards, the result of prudent planting and patient cultivation, is full of satisfaction. We anticipate it in due season, and when it comes we fill our mouths and are grateful. But pray, kind Providence, let me slip over the fence out of the garden now and then, to shake a nut-tree that grows untended in the wood. Give me liberty to put off my black coat for a day, and go a-fishing on a free stream, and find by chance a wild strawberry.

LOVERS AND LANDSCAPE

"He insisted that the love that was of real value in the world was n't interesting, and that the love that was interesting was n't always admirable. Love that happened to a person like the measles or fits, and was really of no particular credit to itself or its victims, was the sort that got into the books and was made much of; whereas the kind that was attained by the endeavour of true souls, and that had wear in it, and that made things go right instead of tangling them up, was too much like duty to make satisfactory reading for people of sentiment."—E. S. MARTIN: My Cousin Anthony.

The first day of spring is one thing, and the first spring day is another. The difference between them is sometimes as great as a month.

The first day of spring is due to arrive, if the calendar does not break down, about the twenty-first of March, when the earth turns the corner of Sun Alley and starts for Summer Street. But the first spring day is not on the time-table at all. It comes when it is ready, and in the latitude of New York this is usually not till after All Fools' Day.

About this time,—

> *"When chinks in April's windy dome*
> *Let through a day of June,*
> *And foot and thought incline to roam,*
> *And every sound's a tune,"*—

it is the habit of the angler who lives in town to prepare for the labours of the approaching season by longer walks or bicycle-rides in the parks, or along the riverside, or in the somewhat demoralized Edens of the suburbs. In the course of these vernal peregrinations and circumrotations, I observe that lovers of various kinds begin to occupy a notable place in the landscape.

The burnished dove puts a livelier iris around his neck, and practises fantastic bows and amourous quicksteps along the verandah of the pigeon-house and on every convenient roof. The young male of the human species, less gifted in the matter of rainbows, does his best with a gay cravat, and turns the thoughts which circulate above it towards the securing or propitiating of a best girl.

The objects of these more or less brilliant attentions, doves and girls, show a becoming reciprocity, and act in a way which leads us to infer (so far as inferences hold good in the mysterious region of female conduct) that they are not seriously displeased. To a rightly tempered mind, pleasure is a pleasant sight. And the philosophic observer who could look upon this spring spectacle of the lovers with any but friendly feelings would be indeed what the great Dr. Samuel Johnson called "a person not to be envied."

Far be it from me to fall into such a desiccated and supercilious mood. My small olive-branch of fancy will be withered, in truth, and ready to drop budless from the tree, when I cease to feel a mild delight in the billings and cooings of the little birds that separate from the flocks to fly together in pairs, or in the uninstructive but mutually satisfactory converse which Strephon holds with Chloe while they dally along the primrose path.

I am glad that even the stony and tumultuous city affords some opportunities for these amiable observations. In the month of April there is hardly a clump of shrubbery in the Central Park which will not serve as a trysting-place for yellow warblers and catbirds just home from their southern tours. At the same time, you shall see many a bench, designed for the accommodation of six persons, occupied at the sunset hour by only two, and apparently so much too small for them that they cannot avoid a little crowding.

These are infallible signs. Taken in conjunction with the eruption of tops and marbles among the small boys, and the purchase of fishing-tackle and golf-clubs by the old boys, they certify us that the vernal equinox has arrived, not only in the celestial regions, but also in the heart of man.

I have been reflecting of late upon the relation of lovers to the landscape, and questioning whether art has given it quite the same place as that which belongs to it in nature. In fiction, for example, and in the drama, and in music, I have some vague misgivings that romantic love has come to hold a more prominent and a more permanent position than it fills in real life.

This is dangerous ground to venture upon, even in the most modest and deprecatory way. The man who expresses an opinion, or even a doubt, on this subject, contrary to the ruling traditions, will have a swarm of angry critics buzzing about him. He will be called a heretic, a heathen, a cold-blooded freak of nature. As for the woman who hesitates to subscribe all the thirty-nine articles of romantic love, if such a one dares to put her reluctance into words, she is certain to be accused either of unwomanly ambition or of feminine disappointment.

Let us make haste, then, to get back for safety to the ornithological aspect of the subject. Here there can be no penalties for heresy. And here I make bold to avow my conviction that the pairing season is not the only point of interest in the life of the birds; nor is the instinct by which they mate altogether and beyond comparison the noblest passion that stirs their feathered breasts.

'T is true, the time of mating is their prettiest season; but it is very short. How little we should know of the drama of their airy life if we had eyes only for this brief scene! Their finest qualities come out in the patient cares that protect the young in the nest, in the varied struggles for existence through the changing year, and in the incredible heroisms of the annual migrations. Herein is a parable.

It may be observed further, without fear of rebuke, that the behaviour of the different kinds of birds during the prevalence of romantic love is not always equally above reproach. The courtship of English sparrows—blustering, noisy, vulgar—is a sight to offend the taste of every gentle on-looker. Some birds reiterate and vociferate their love-songs in a fashion that displays their inconsiderateness as well as their ignorance of music. This trait is most marked in domestic fowls. There was a guinea-cock, once, that chose to do his wooing close under the window of a farm-house where I was lodged. He had no regard for my hours of sleep or meditation. His amatory click-clack prevented the morning and wrecked the tranquillity of the evening. It was odious, brutal,—worse, it was absolutely thoughtless. Herein is another parable.

Let us admit cheerfully that lovers have a place in the landscape and lend a charm to it. This does not mean that they are to take up all the room there is. Suppose, for example, that a pair of them, on Goat Island, put themselves in such a position as to completely block out your view of Niagara. You cannot regard them with gratitude. They even become a little tedious. Or suppose that you are visiting at a country-house, and you find that you must not enjoy the moonlight on the verandah because Augustus and Amanda are murmuring in one corner, and that you must not go into the garden because Louis and Lizzie are there, and that you cannot have a sail on the lake because Richard and Rebecca have taken the boat.

Of course, unless you happen to be a selfish old curmudgeon, you rejoice, by sympathy, in the happiness of these estimable young people. But you fail to see why it should cover so much ground.

Why should they not pool their interests, and all go out in the boat, or all walk in the garden, or all sit on the verandah? Then there would be room for somebody else about the place.

In old times you could rely upon lovers for retirement. But nowadays their role seems to be a bold ostentation of their condition. They rely upon other people to do the timid, shrinking part. Society, in America, is arranged principally for their convenience; and whatever portion of the landscape strikes their fancy, they preempt and occupy. All this goes upon the presumption that romantic love is really the only important interest in life.

This train of thought was illuminated, the other night, by an incident which befell me at a party. It was an assembly of men, drawn together by their common devotion to the sport of canoeing. There were only three or four of the gentler sex present (as honorary members), and only one of whom it could be suspected that she was at that time a victim or an object of the tender passion. In the course of the evening, by way of diversion to our disputations on keels and centreboards, canvas and birch-bark, cedar-wood and bass-wood, paddles and steering-gear, a fine young Apollo, with a big, manly voice, sang us a few songs. But he did not chant the joys of weathering a sudden squall, or running a rapid feather-white with foam, or floating down a long, quiet, elm-bowered river. Not all. His songs were full of sighs and yearnings, languid lips and sheep's-eyes. His powerful voice informed us that crowns of thorns seemed like garlands of roses, and kisses were as sweet as samples of heaven, and various other curious sensations were experienced; and at the end of every stanza the reason was stated, in tones of thunder—

"Because I love you, dear."

Even if true, it seemed inappropriate. How foolish the average audience in a drawing-room looks while it is listening to passionate love-ditties! And yet I suppose the singer chose these songs, not from any malice aforethought, but simply because songs of this kind are so abundant that it is next to impossible to find anything else in the shops.

In regard to novels, the situation is almost as discouraging. Ten love-stories are printed to one of any other kind. We have a standing invitation to consider the tribulations and difficulties of some young man or young woman in finding a mate. It must be admitted that the subject has its capabilities of interest. Nature has her uses for the lover, and she gives him an excellent part to play in the drama of life. But is this tantamount to saying that his interest is perennial and all-absorbing, and that his role on the stage is the only one that is significant and noteworthy?

Life is much too large to be expressed in the terms of a single passion. Friendship, patriotism, parental tenderness, filial devotion, the ardour of adventure, the thirst for knowledge, the ecstasy of religion,—these all have their dwelling in the heart of man. They mould character. They control conduct. They are stars of destiny shining in the inner firmament. And if art would truly hold the mirror up to nature, it must reflect these greater and lesser lights that rule the day and the night.

How many of the plays that divert and misinform the modern theatre-goer turn on the pivot of a love-affair, not always pure, but generally simple! And how many of those that are imported from France proceed upon the theory that the Seventh is the only Commandment, and that the principal attraction of life lies in the opportunity of breaking it! The matinee-girl is not likely to have a very luminous or truthful idea of existence floating around in her pretty little head.

But, after all, the great plays, those that take the deepest hold upon the heart, like HAMLET and KING LEAR, MACBETH and OTHELLO, are not love-plays. And the most charming comedies, like THE WINTER'S TALE, and THE RIVALS, and RIP VAN WINKLE, are chiefly memorable for other things than love-scenes.

Even in novels, love shows at its best when it does not absorb the whole plot. LORNA DOONE is a lovers' story, but there is a blessed minimum of spooning in it, and always enough of working and fighting to keep the air clear and fresh. THE HEART OF MIDLOTHIAN, and HYPATIA, and ROMOLA, and THE CLOISTER AND THE HEARTH, and JOHN INGLESANT, and THE THREE MUSKETEERS, and NOTRE DAME, and PEACE AND WAR, and QUO VADIS,—these are great novels because they are much more than tales of romantic love. As for HENRY ESMOND, (which seems to me the best of all,) certainly "love at first sight" does not play the finest role in that book.

There are good stories of our own day—pathetic, humourous, entertaining, powerful—in which the element of romantic love is altogether subordinate, or even imperceptible. THE RISE OF SILAS LAPHAM does not owe its deep interest to the engagement of the very charming young people who enliven it. MADAME DELPHINE and OLE 'STRACTED are perfect stories of their kind. I would not barter THE JUNGLE BOOKS for a hundred of THE BRUSHWOOD BOY.

The truth is that love, considered merely as the preference of one person for another of the opposite sex, is not "the greatest thing in the world." It becomes great only when it leads on, as it often does, to heroism and self-sacrifice and fidelity. Its chief value for art (the interpreter) lies not in itself, but in its quickening relation to the other elements of life. It must be seen and shown in its due proportion, and in harmony with the broader landscape.

Do you believe that in all the world there is only one woman specially created for each man, and that the order of the universe will be hopelessly askew unless these two needles find each other in the haystack? You believe it for yourself, perhaps; but do you believe it for Tom Johnson? You remember what a terrific disturbance he made in the summer of 189-, at Bar Harbor, about Ellinor Brown, and how he ran away with her in September. You have also seen them together (occasionally) at Lenox and Newport, since their marriage. Are you honestly of the opinion that if Tom had not married Ellinor, these two young lives would have been a total wreck?

Adam Smith, in his book on THE MORAL SENTIMENTS, goes so far as to say that "love is not interesting to the observer because it is AN AFFECTION OF THE IMAGINATION, into which it is difficult for a third party to enter." Something of the same kind occurred to me in regard to Tom and Ellinor. Yet I would not have presumed to suggest this thought to either of them. Nor would I have quoted in their hearing the melancholy and frigid prediction of Ralph Waldo Emerson, to the effect that they would some day discover "that all which at first drew them together—those once sacred features, that magical play of charm—was deciduous."

DECIDUOUS, indeed? Cold, unpleasant, botanical word! Rather would I prognosticate for the lovers something perennial,

"A sober certainty of waking bliss,"

to survive the evanescence of love's young dream. Ellinor should turn out to be a woman like the Lady Elizabeth Hastings, of whom Richard Steele wrote that "to love her was a liberal education." Tom should prove that he had in him the lasting stuff of a true man and a hero. Then it would make little difference whether their conjunction had been eternally prescribed in the book of fate or not. It would be evidently a fit match, made on earth and illustrative of heaven.

But even in the making of such a match as this, the various stages of attraction, infatuation, and appropriation should not be displayed too prominently before the world, nor treated as events of overwhelming importance and enduring moment. I would not counsel Tom and Ellinor, in the midsummer of their engagement, to have their photographs taken together in affectionate attitudes.

The pictures of an imaginary kind which deal with the subject of romantic love are, almost without exception, fatuous and futile. The inanely amatory, with their languishing eyes, weary us. The endlessly osculatory, with their protracted salutations, are sickening. Even when an air of sentimental propriety is thrown about them by some such title as "Wedded" or "The Honeymoon," they fatigue us. For the most part, they remind me of the remark which the Commodore made upon a certain painting of Jupiter and Io which hangs in the writing-room of the Contrary Club.

"Sir," said that gently piercing critic, "that picture is equally unsatisfactory to the artist, to the moralist, and to the voluptuary."

Nevertheless, having made a clean breast of my misgivings and reservations on the subject of lovers and landscape, I will now confess that the whole of my doubts do not weigh much against my unreasoned faith in romantic love. At heart I am no infidel, but a most obstinate believer and devotee. My seasons of skepticism are transient. They are connected with a torpid liver and aggravated by confinement to a sedentary life and enforced abstinence from angling. Out-of-doors, I return to a saner and happier frame of mind.

As my wheel rolls along the Riverside Drive in the golden glow of the sunset, I rejoice that the episode of Charles Henry and Matilda Jane has not been omitted from the view. This vast and populous city, with all its passing show of life, would be little better than a waste, howling wilderness if we could not catch a glimpse, now and then, of young people falling in love in the good old-fashioned way. Even on a trout-stream, I have seen nothing prettier than the sight upon which I once came suddenly as I was fishing down the Neversink.

A boy was kneeling beside the brook, and a girl was giving him a drink of water out of her rosy hands. They stared with wonder and compassion at the wet and solitary angler, wading down the stream, as if he were some kind of a mild lunatic. But as I glanced discreetly at their small tableau, I was not unconscious of the new joy that came into the landscape with the presence of

"A lover and his lass."

I knew how sweet the water tasted from that kind of a cup. I also have lived in Arcadia, and have not forgotten the way back.

A FATAL SUCCESS

"What surprises me in her behaviour," said he, "is its thoroughness. Woman seldom does things by halves, but often by doubles."

—SOLOMON SINGLEWITZ: *The Life of Adam.*

Beekman De Peyster was probably the most passionate and triumphant fisherman in the Petrine Club. He angled with the same dash and confidence that he threw into his operations in the stock-market. He was sure to be the first man to get his flies on the water at the opening of the season. And when we came together for our fall meeting, to compare notes of our wanderings on various streams and make up the fish-stories for the year, Beekman was almost always "high hook." We expected, as a matter of course, to hear that he had taken the most and the largest fish.

It was so with everything that he undertook. He was a masterful man. If there was an unusually large trout in a river, Beekman knew about it before any one else, and got there first, and came home with the fish. It did not make him unduly proud, because there was nothing uncommon about it. It was his habit to succeed, and all the rest of us were hardened to it.

When he married Cornelia Cochrane, we were consoled for our partial loss by the apparent fitness and brilliancy of the match. If Beekman was a masterful man, Cornelia was certainly what you might call a mistressful woman. She had been the head of her house since she was eighteen years old. She carried her good looks like the family plate; and when she came into the breakfast-room and said good-morning, it was with an air as if she presented every one with a check for a thousand dollars. Her tastes were accepted as judgments, and her preferences had the force of laws. Wherever she wanted to go in the summer-time, there the finger of household destiny pointed. At Newport, at Bar Harbour, at Lenox, at Southampton, she made a record. When she was joined in holy wedlock to Beekman De Peyster, her father and mother heaved a sigh of satisfaction, and settled down for a quiet vacation in Cherry Valley.

It was in the second summer after the wedding that Beekman admitted to a few of his ancient Petrine cronies, in moments of confidence (unjustifiable, but natural), that his wife had one fault.

"It is not exactly a fault," he said, "not a positive fault, you know. It is just a kind of a defect, due to her education, of course. In everything else she's magnificent. But she does n't care for fishing. She says it's stupid,—can't see why any one should like the woods,—calls camping out the lunatic's diversion. It's rather awkward for a man with my habits to have his wife take such a view. But it can be changed by training. I intend to educate her and convert her. I shall make an angler of her yet."

And so he did.

The new education was begun in the Adirondacks, and the first lesson was given at Paul Smith's. It was a complete failure.

Beekman persuaded her to come out with him for a day on Meacham River, and promised to convince her of the charm of angling. She wore a new gown, fawn-colour and violet, with a picture-hat, very taking. But the Meacham River trout was shy that day; not even Beekman could induce him to rise to the fly. What the trout lacked in confidence the mosquitoes more than made up. Mrs. De Peyster came home much sunburned, and expressed a highly unfavourable opinion of fishing as an amusement and of Meacham River as a resort.

"The nice people don't come to the Adirondacks to fish," said she; "they come to talk about the fishing twenty years ago. Besides, what do you want to catch that trout for? If you do, the other men will say you bought it, and the hotel will have to put in a new one for the rest of the season."

The following year Beekman tried Moosehead Lake. Here he found an atmosphere more favourable to his plan of education. There were a good many people who really fished, and short expeditions in the woods were quite fashionable. Cornelia had a camping-costume of the most approved style made by Dewlap on Fifth Avenue,—pearl-gray with linings of rose-silk,—and consented to go with her husband on a trip up Moose River. They pitched their tent the first evening at the mouth of Misery Stream, and a storm came on. The rain sifted through the canvas in a fine spray, and Mrs. De Peyster sat up all night in a waterproof cloak, holding an umbrella. The next day they were back at the hotel in time for lunch.

"It was horrid," she told her most intimate friend, "perfectly horrid. The idea of sleeping in a shower-bath, and eating your breakfast from a tin plate, just for sake of catching a few silly fish! Why not send your guides out to get them for you?"

But, in spite of this profession of obstinate heresy, Beekman observed with secret joy that there were signs, before the end of the season, that Cornelia was drifting a little, a very little but still perceptibly, in the direction of a change of heart. She began to take an interest, as the big trout came along in September, in the reports of the catches made by the different anglers. She would saunter out with the other people to the corner of the porch to see the fish weighed and spread out on the grass. Several times she went with Beekman in the canoe to Hardscrabble Point, and showed distinct evidences of pleasure when he caught large trout. The last day of the season, when he returned from a successful expedition to Roach River and Lily Bay, she inquired with some particularity about the results of his sport; and in the evening, as the company sat before the great open fire in the hall of the hotel, she was heard to use this information with considerable skill in putting down Mrs. Minot Peabody of Boston, who was recounting the details of her husband's catch at Spencer Pond. Cornelia was not a person to be contented with the back seat, even in fish-stories.

When Beekman observed these indications he was much encouraged, and resolved to push his educational experiment briskly forward to his customary goal of success.

"Some things can be done, as well as others," he said in his masterful way, as three of us were walking home together after the autumnal dinner of the Petrine Club, which he always attended as a graduate member. "A real fisherman never gives up. I told you I'd make an angler out of my wife; and so I will. It has been rather difficult. She is 'dour' in rising. But she's beginning to take notice of the fly now. Give me another season, and I'll have her landed."

Good old Beekman! Little did he think—But I must not interrupt the story with moral reflections.

The preparations that he made for his final effort at conversion were thorough and prudent. He had a private interview with Dewlap in regard to the construction of a practical fishing-costume for a lady, which resulted in something more reasonable and workmanlike than had ever been turned out by that famous artist. He ordered from Hook and Catchett a lady's angling-outfit of the most enticing description,—a split-bamboo rod, light as a girl's wish, and strong as a matron's will; an oxidized silver reel, with a monogram on one side, and a sapphire set in the handle for good luck; a book of flies, of all sizes and colours, with the correct names inscribed in gilt letters on each page. He surrounded his favourite sport with an aureole of elegance and beauty. And then he took Cornelia in September to the Upper Dam at Rangeley.

She went reluctant. She arrived disgusted. She stayed incredulous. She returned—Wait a bit, and you shall hear how she returned.

The Upper Dam at Rangeley is the place, of all others in the world, where the lunacy of angling may be seen in its incurable stage. There is a cosy little inn, called a camp, at the foot of a big lake. In front of the inn is a huge dam of gray stone, over which the river plunges into a great oval pool, where the trout assemble in the early fall to perpetuate their race. From the tenth of September to the thirtieth, there is not an hour of the day or night when there are no boats floating on that pool, and no anglers trailing the fly across its waters. Before the late fishermen are ready to come in at midnight, the early fishermen may be seen creeping down to the shore with lanterns in order to begin before cock-crow. The number of fish taken is not large,—perhaps five or six for the whole company on an average day,—but the size is sometimes enormous,—nothing under three pounds is counted,—and they pervade thought and conversation at the Upper Dam to the exclusion of every other subject. There is no driving, no dancing, no golf, no tennis. There is nothing to do but fish or die.

At first, Cornelia thought she would choose the latter alternative. But a remark of that skilful and morose old angler, McTurk, which she overheard on the verandah after supper, changed her mind.

"Women have no sporting instinct," said he. "They only fish because they see men doing it. They are imitative animals."

That same night she told Beekman, in the subdued tone which the architectural construction of the house imposes upon all confidential communications in the bedrooms, but with resolution in every accent, that she proposed to go fishing with him on the morrow.

"But not on that pool, right in front of the house, you understand. There must be some other place, out on the lake, where we can fish for three or four days, until I get the trick of this wobbly rod. Then I'll show that old bear, McTurk, what kind of an animal woman is."

Beekman was simply delighted. Five days of diligent practice at the mouth of Mill Brook brought his pupil to the point where he pronounced her safe.

"Of course," he said patronizingly, "you have 'nt learned all about it yet. That will take years. But you can get your fly out thirty feet, and you can keep the tip of your rod up. If you do that, the trout will hook himself, in rapid water, eight times out of ten. For playing him, if you follow my directions, you 'll be all right. We will try the pool tonight, and hope for a medium-sized fish."

Cornelia said nothing, but smiled and nodded. She had her own thoughts.

At about nine o'clock Saturday night, they anchored their boat on the edge of the shoal where the big eddy swings around, put out the lantern and began to fish. Beekman sat in the bow of the boat, with his rod over the left side;

Cornelia in the stern, with her rod over the right side. The night was cloudy and very black. Each of them had put on the largest possible fly, one a "Bee-Pond" and the other a "Dragon;" but even these were invisible. They measured out the right length of line, and let the flies drift back until they hung over the shoal, in the curly water where the two currents meet.

There were three other boats to the left of them. McTurk was their only neighbour in the darkness on the right. Once they heard him swearing softly to himself, and knew that he had hooked and lost a fish.

Away down at the tail of the pool, dimly visible through the gloom, the furtive fisherman, Parsons, had anchored his boat. No noise ever came from that craft. If he wished to change his position, he did not pull up the anchor and let it down again with a bump. He simply lengthened or shortened his anchor rope. There was no click of the reel when he played a fish. He drew in and paid out the line through the rings by hand, without a sound. What he thought when a fish got away, no one knew, for he never said it. He concealed his angling as if it had been a conspiracy. Twice that night they heard a faint splash in the water near his boat, and twice they saw him put his arm over the side in the darkness and bring it back again very quietly.

"That's the second fish for Parsons," whispered Beekman, "what a secretive old Fortunatus he is! He knows more about fishing than any man on the pool, and talks less."

Cornelia did not answer. Her thoughts were all on the tip of her own rod. About eleven o'clock a fine, drizzling rain set in. The fishing was very slack. All the other boats gave it up in despair; but Cornelia said she wanted to stay out a little longer, they might as well finish up the week.

At precisely fifty minutes past eleven, Beekman reeled up his line, and remarked with firmness that the holy Sabbath day was almost at hand and they ought to go in.

"Not till I've landed this trout," said Cornelia.

"What? A trout! Have you got one?"

"Certainly; I've had him on for at least fifteen minutes. I'm playing him Mr. Parsons' way. You might as well light the lantern and get the net ready; he's coming in towards the boat now."

Beekman broke three matches before he made the lantern burn; and when he held it up over the gunwale, there was the trout sure enough, gleaming ghostly pale in the dark water, close to the boat, and quite tired out. He slipped the net over the fish and drew it in,—a monster.

"I'll carry that trout, if you please," said Cornelia, as they stepped out of the boat; and she walked into the camp, on the last stroke of midnight, with the fish in her hand, and quietly asked for the steelyard.

Eight pounds and fourteen ounces,—that was the weight. Everybody was amazed. It was the "best fish" of the year. Cornelia showed no sign of exultation, until just as John was carrying the trout to the ice-house. Then she flashed out:—"Quite a fair imitation, Mr. McTurk,—is n't it?"

Now McTurk's best record for the last fifteen years was seven pounds and twelve ounces.

So far as McTurk is concerned, this is the end of the story. But not for the De Peysters. I wish it were. Beekman went to sleep that night with a contented spirit. He felt that his experiment in education had been a success. He had made his wife an angler.

He had indeed, and to an extent which he little suspected. That Upper Dam trout was to her like the first taste of blood to the tiger. It seemed to change, at once, not so much her character as the direction of her vital energy. She yielded to the lunacy of angling, not by slow degrees, (as first a transient delusion, then a fixed idea, then a chronic infirmity, finally a mild insanity,) but by a sudden plunge into the most violent mania. So far from being ready to die at Upper Dam, her desire now was to live there—and to live solely for the sake of fishing—as long as the season was open.

There were two hundred and forty hours left to midnight on the thirtieth of September. At least two hundred of these she spent on the pool; and when Beekman was too exhausted to manage the boat and the net and the lantern for her, she engaged a trustworthy guide to take Beekman's place while he slept. At the end of the last day her score was twenty-three, with an average of five pounds and a quarter. His score was nine, with an average of four pounds. He had succeeded far beyond his wildest hopes.

The next year his success became even more astonishing. They went to the Titan Club in Canada. The ugliest and most inaccessible sheet of water in that territory is Lake Pharaoh. But it is famous for the extraordinary fishing at a certain spot near the outlet, where there is just room enough for one canoe. They camped on Lake Pharaoh for six weeks, by Mrs. De Peyster's command; and her canoe was always the first to reach the fishing-ground in the morning, and the last to leave it in the evening.

Some one asked him, when he returned to the city, whether he had good luck.

"Quite fair," he tossed off in a careless way; "we took over three hundred pounds."

"To your own rod?" asked the inquirer, in admiration.

"No-o-o," said Beekman, "there were two of us."

There were two of them, also, the following year, when they joined the Natasheebo Salmon Club and fished that celebrated river in Labrador. The custom of drawing lots every night for the water that each member was to angle over the next day, seemed to be especially designed to fit the situation. Mrs. De Peyster could fish her own pool and her husband's too. The result of that year's fishing was something phenomenal. She had a score that made a paragraph in the newspapers and called out editorial comment. One editor was so inadequate to the situation as to entitle the article in which he described her triumph "The Equivalence of Woman." It was well-meant, but she was not at all pleased with it.

She was now not merely an angler, but a "record" angler of the most virulent type. Wherever they went, she wanted, and she got, the pick of the water. She seemed to be equally at home on all kinds of streams, large and small. She would pursue the little mountain-brook trout in the early spring, and the Labrador salmon in July, and the huge speckled trout of the northern lakes in September, with the same avidity and resolution. All that she cared for was to get the best and the most of the fishing at each place where she angled. This she always did.

And Beekman,—well, for him there were no more long separations from the partner of his life while he went off to fish some favourite stream. There were no more home-comings after a good day's sport to find her clad in cool and dainty raiment on the verandah, ready to welcome him with friendly badinage. There was not even any casting of the fly around Hardscrabble Point while she sat in the canoe reading a novel, looking up with mild and pleasant interest when he caught a larger fish than usual, as an older and wiser person looks at a child playing some innocent game. Those days of a divided interest between man and wife were gone. She was now fully converted, and more. Beekman and Cornelia were one; and she was the one.

The last time I saw the De Peysters he was following her along the Beaverkill, carrying a landing-net and a basket, but no rod. She paused for a moment to exchange greetings, and then strode on down the stream. He lingered for a few minutes longer to light a pipe.

"Well, old man," I said, "you certainly have succeeded in making an angler of Mrs. De Peyster."

"Yes, indeed," he answered,—"have n't I?" Then he continued, after a few thoughtful puffs of smoke, "Do you know, I 'm not quite so sure as I used to be that fishing is the best of all sports. I sometimes think of giving it up and going in for croquet."

FISHING IN BOOKS

> *"SIMPSON.—Have you ever seen any American books on angling, Fisher?"*
>
> *"FISHER.—No, I do not think there are any published. Brother Jonathan is not yet sufficiently civilized to produce anything original on the gentle art. There is good trout-fishing in America, and the streams, which are all free, are much less fished than in our Island, 'from the small number of gentlemen,' as an American writer says, 'who are at leisure to give their time to it.'"*
>
> —WILLIAM ANDREW CHATTO: The Angler's Souvenir (London, 1835).

That wise man and accomplished scholar, Sir Henry Wotton, the friend of Izaak Walton and ambassador of King James I to the republic of Venice, was accustomed to say that "he would rather live five May months than forty Decembers." The reason for this preference was no secret to those who knew him. It had nothing to do with British or Venetian politics. It was simply because December, with all its domestic joys, is practically a dead month in the angler's calendar.

His occupation is gone. The better sort of fish are out of season. The trout are lean and haggard: it is no trick to catch them and no treat to eat them. The salmon, all except the silly kelts, have run out to sea, and the place of their habitation no man knoweth. There is nothing for the angler to do but wait for the return of spring, and meanwhile encourage and sustain his patience with such small consolations in kind as a friendly Providence may put within his reach.

Some solace may be found, on a day of crisp, wintry weather, in the childish diversion of catching pickerel through the ice. This method of taking fish is practised on a large scale and with elaborate machinery by men who supply the market. I speak not of their commercial enterprise and its gross equipage, but of ice-fishing in its more sportive and desultory form, as it is pursued by country boys and the incorrigible village idler.

You choose for this pastime a pond where the ice is not too thick, lest the labour of cutting through should be discouraging; nor too thin, lest the chance of breaking in should be embarrassing. You then chop out, with almost any kind of a hatchet or pick, a number of holes in the ice, making each one six or eight inches in diameter, and placing them about five or six feet apart. If you happen to know the course of a current flowing through the pond, or the location of a shoal frequented by minnows, you will do well to keep near it. Over each hole you set a small contrivance called a "tilt-up." It consists of two sticks fastened in the middle, at right angles to each other. The stronger of the two is laid across the opening in the ice. The other is thus balanced above the aperture, with a baited hook and line attached to one end, while the other end is adorned with a little flag. For choice, I would have the flags red. They look gayer, and I imagine they are more lucky.

When you have thus baited and set your tilt-ups,—twenty or thirty of them,—you may put on your skates and amuse yourself by gliding to and fro on the smooth surface of the ice, cutting figures of eight and grapevines and diamond twists, while you wait for the pickerel to begin their part of the performance. They will let you know when they are ready.

A fish, swimming around in the dim depths under the ice, sees one of your baits, fancies it, and takes it in. The moment he tries to run away with it he tilts the little red flag into the air and waves it backward and forward. "Be quick!" he signals all unconsciously; "here I am; come and pull me up!"

When two or three flags are fluttering at the same moment, far apart on the pond, you must skate with speed and haul in your lines promptly.

How hard it is, sometimes, to decide which one you will take first! That flag in the middle of the pond has been waving for at least a minute; but the other, in the corner of the bay, is tilting up and down more violently: it must be a larger fish. Great Dagon! There's another red signal flying, away over by the point! You hesitate, you make a few strokes in one direction, then you whirl around and dart the other way. Meantime one of the tilt-ups, constructed with too short a cross-stick, has been pulled to one side, and disappears in the hole. One pickerel in the pond carries a flag. Another tilt-up ceases to move and falls flat upon the ice. The bait has been stolen. You dash desperately toward the third flag and pull in the only fish that is left,—probably the smallest of them all!

A surplus of opportunities does not insure the best luck.

A room with seven doors—like the famous apartment in Washington's headquarters at Newburgh—is an invitation to bewilderment. I would rather see one fair opening in life than be confused by three dazzling chances.

There was a good story about fishing through the ice which formed part of the stock-in-conversation of that ingenious woodsman, Martin Moody, Esquire, of Big Tupper Lake. "'T was a blame cold day," he said, "and the lines friz up stiffer 'n a fence-wire, jus' as fast as I pulled 'em in, and my fingers got so dum' frosted I could n't bait the hooks. But the fish was thicker and hungrier 'n flies in June. So I jus' took a piece of bait and held it over one o' the holes. Every time a fish jumped up to git it, I 'd kick him out on the ice. I tell ye, sir, I kicked out more 'n four hundred pounds of pick'rel that morning. Yaas, 't was a big lot, I 'low, but then 't was a cold day! I jus' stacked 'em up solid, like cordwood."

Let us now leave this frigid subject! Iced fishing is but a chilling and unsatisfactory imitation of real sport. The angler will soon turn from it with satiety, and seek a better consolation for the winter of his discontent in the entertainment of fishing in books.

Angling is the only sport that boasts the honour of having given a classic to literature.

Izaak Walton's success with THE COMPLEAT ANGLER was a fine illustration of fisherman's luck. He set out, with some aid from an adept in fly-fishing and cookery, named Thomas Barker, to produce a little "discourse of fish and fishing" which should serve as a useful manual for quiet persons inclined to follow the contemplative man's recreation. He came home with a book which has made his name beloved by ten generations of gentle readers, and given him a secure place in the Pantheon of letters,—not a haughty eminence, but a modest niche, all his own, and ever adorned with grateful offerings of fresh flowers.

This was great luck. But it was well-deserved, and therefore it has not been grudged or envied.

Walton was a man so peaceful and contented, so friendly in his disposition, and so innocent in all his goings, that only three other writers, so far as I know, have ever spoken ill of him.

One was that sour-complexioned Cromwellian trooper, Richard Franck, who wrote in 1658 an envious book entitled NORTHERN MEMOIRS, CALCULATED FOR THE MERIDIAN OF SCOTLAND, ETC., TO WHICH IS ADDED THE CONTEMPLATIVE AND PRACTICAL ANGLER. In this book the furious Franck first pays Walton the flattery of imitation, and then further adorns him with abuse, calling THE COMPLEAT ANGLER "an indigested octavo, stuffed with morals from Dubravius and others," and more than hinting that the father of anglers knew little or nothing of "his uncultivated art." Walton was a Churchman and a Loyalist, you see, while Franck was a Commonwealth man and an Independent.

The second detractor of Walton was Lord Byron, who wrote

"The quaint, old, cruel coxcomb in his gullet
Should have a hook, and a small trout to pull it."

But Byron is certainly a poor authority on the quality of mercy. His contempt need not cause an honest man overwhelming distress. I should call it a complimentary dislike.

The third author who expressed unpleasant sentiments in regard to Walton was Leigh Hunt. Here, again, I fancy that partizan prejudice had something to do with the dislike. Hunt was a radical in politics and religion. Moreover there was a feline strain in his character, which made it necessary for him to scratch somebody now and then, as a relief to his feelings.

Walton was a great quoter. His book is not "stuffed," as Franck jealously alleged, but it is certainly well sauced with piquant references to other writers, as early as the author of the Book of Job, and as late as John Dennys, who betrayed to the world THE SECRETS OF ANGLING in 1613. Walton further seasoned his book with fragments of information about fish and fishing, more or less apocryphal, gathered from Aelian, Pliny, Plutarch, Sir Francis Bacon, Dubravius, Gesner, Rondeletius, the learned Aldrovandus, the venerable Bede, the divine Du Bartas, and many others. He borrowed freely for the adornment of his discourse, and did not scorn to make use of what may be called LIVE QUOTATIONS,—that is to say, the unpublished remarks of his near contemporaries, caught in friendly conversation, or handed down by oral tradition.

But these various seasonings did not disguise, they only enhanced, the delicate flavour of the dish which he served up to his readers. This was all of his own taking, and of a sweetness quite incomparable.

I like a writer who is original enough to water his garden with quotations, without fear of being drowned out. Such men are Charles Lamb and James Russell Lowell and John Burroughs.

Walton's book is as fresh as a handful of wild violets and sweet lavender. It breathes the odours of the green fields and the woods. It tastes of simple, homely, appetizing things like the "syllabub of new verjuice in a new-made haycock" which the milkwoman promised to give Piscator the next time he came that way. Its music plays the tune of A CONTENTED HEART over and over again without dulness, and charms us into harmony with

"A noise like the sound of a hidden brook
In the leafy month of June,
That to the sleeping woods all night
Singeth a quiet tune."

Walton has been quoted even more than any of the writers whom he quotes. It would be difficult, even if it were not ungrateful, to write about angling without referring to him. Some pretty saying, some wise reflection from his pages, suggests itself at almost every turn of the subject.

And yet his book, though it be the best, is not the only readable one that his favourite recreation has begotten. The literature of angling is extensive, as any one may see who will look at the list of the collection presented by Mr. John Bartlett to Harvard University, or study the catalogue of the piscatorial library of Mr. Dean Sage, of Albany, who himself has contributed an admirable book on THE RISTIGOUCHE.

Nor is this literature altogether composed of dry and technical treatises, interesting only to the confirmed anglimaniac, or to the young novice ardent in pursuit of practical information. There is a good deal of juicy reading in it.

Books about angling should be divided (according to De Quincey's method) into two classes,—the literature of knowledge, and the literature of power.

The first class contains the handbooks on rods and tackle, the directions how to angle for different kinds of fish, and the guides to various fishing-resorts. The weakness of these books is that they soon fall out of date, as the manufacture of tackle is improved, the art of angling refined, and the fish in once-famous waters are educated or exterminated.

Alas, how transient is the fashion of this world, even in angling! The old manuals with their precise instruction for trimming and painting trout-rods eighteen feet long, and their painful description of "oyntments" made of nettle-juice, fish-hawk oil, camphor, cat's fat, or assafoedita, (supposed to allure the fish,) are altogether behind the age. Many of the flies described by Charles Cotton and Thomas Barker seem to have gone out of style among the trout. Perhaps familiarity has bred contempt. Generation after generation of fish have seen these same old feathered confections floating on the water, and learned by sharp experience that they do not taste good. The blase trout demand something new, something modern. It is for this reason, I suppose, that an altogether original fly, unheard of, startling, will often do great execution in an over-fished pool.

Certain it is that the art of angling, in settled regions, is growing more dainty and difficult. You must cast a longer, lighter line; you must use finer leaders; you must have your flies dressed on smaller hooks.

And another thing is certain: in many places (described in the ancient volumes) where fish were once abundant, they are now like the shipwrecked sailors in Vergil his Aeneid,—

"rari nantes in gurgite vasto."

The floods themselves are also disappearing. Mr. Edmund Clarence Stedman was telling me, the other day, of the trout-brook that used to run through the Connecticut village when he nourished a poet's youth. He went back to visit the stream a few years since, and it was gone, literally vanished from the face of earth, stolen to make a watersupply for the town, and used for such base purposes as the washing of clothes and the sprinkling of streets.

I remember an expedition with my father, some twenty years ago, to Nova Scotia, whither we set out to realize the hopes kindled by an ANGLER'S GUIDE written in the early sixties. It was like looking for tall clocks in the farmhouses around Boston. The harvest had been well gleaned before our arrival, and in the very place where our visionary author located his most famous catch we found a summer hotel and a sawmill.

'T is strange and sad, how many regions there are where "the fishing was wonderful forty years ago"!

The second class of angling books—the literature of power—includes all (even those written with some purpose of instruction) in which the gentle fascinations of the sport, the attractions of living out-of-doors, the beauties of stream and woodland, the recollections of happy adventure, and the cheerful thoughts that make the best of a day's luck, come clearly before the author's mind and find some fit expression in his words. Of such books, thank Heaven, there is a plenty to bring a Maytide charm and cheer into the fisherman's dull December. I will name, by way of random tribute from a grateful but unmethodical memory, a few of these consolatory volumes.

First of all comes a family of books that were born in Scotland and smell of the heather.

Whatever a Scotchman's conscience permits him to do, is likely to be done with vigour and a fiery mind. In trade and in theology, in fishing and in fighting, he is all there and thoroughly kindled.

There is an old-fashioned book called THE MOOR AND THE LOCH, by John Colquhoun, which is full of contagious enthusiasm. Thomas Tod Stoddart was a most impassioned angler, (though over-given to strong language,) and in his ANGLING REMINISCENCES he has touched the subject with a happy hand,—happiest when he breaks into poetry and tosses out a song for the fisherman. Professor John Wilson of the University of Edinburgh held the chair of Moral Philosophy in that institution, but his true fame rests on his well-earned titles of A. M. and F. R. S.,—Master of Angling, and Fisherman Royal of Scotland. His RECREATIONS OF CHRISTOPHER NORTH, albeit their humour is sometimes too boisterously hammered in, are genial and generous essays, overflowing with passages of good-fellowship and pedestrian fancy. I would recommend any person in a dry and melancholy state of mind to read his paper on "Streams," in the first volume of ESSAYS CRITICAL AND IMAGINATIVE. But it must be said, by way of warning to those with whom dryness is a matter of principle, that all Scotch fishing-books are likely to be sprinkled with Highland Dew.

Among English anglers, Sir Humphry Davy is one of whom Christopher North speaks rather slightingly. Nevertheless his SALMONIA is well worth reading, not only because it was written by a learned man, but because it exhales the spirit of cheerful piety and vital wisdom. Charles Kingsley was another great man who wrote well about angling. His CHALK-STREAM STUDIES are clear and sparkling. They cleanse the mind and refresh the heart and put us more in love with living. Of quite a different style are the MAXIMS AND HINTS FOR AN ANGLER, AND MISERIES OF FISHING, which were written by Richard Penn, a grandson of the founder of Pennsylvania. This is a curious and rare little volume, professing to be a compilation from the "Common Place Book of the Houghton Fishing Club," and dealing with the subject from a Pickwickian point of view. I suppose that William Penn would have thought his grandson a frivolous writer.

But he could not have entertained such an opinion of the Honourable Robert Boyle, of whose OCCASIONAL REFLECTIONS no less than twelve discourses treat "of Angling Improved to Spiritual Uses." The titles of some of these discourses are quaint enough to quote. "Upon the being called upon to rise early on a very fair morning." "Upon the mounting, singing, and lighting of larks." "Upon fishing with a counterfeit fly." "Upon a danger arising from an unseasonable contest with the steersman." "Upon one's drinking water out of the brim of his hat." With such good texts it is easy to endure, and easier still to spare, the sermons.

Englishmen carry their love of travel into their anglimania, and many of their books describe fishing adventures in foreign parts. RAMBLES WITH A FISHING-ROD, by E. S. Roscoe, tells of happy days in the Salzkammergut and the Bavarian Highlands and Normandy. FISH-TAILS AND A FEW OTHERS, by Bradnock Hall, contains some delightful chapters on Norway. THE ROD IN INDIA, by H. S. Thomas, narrates wonderful adventures with the Mahseer and the Rohu and other pagan fish.

But, after all, I like the English angler best when he travels at home, and writes of dry-fly fishing in the Itchen or the Test, or of wet-fly fishing in Northumberland or Sutherlandshire. There is a fascinating booklet that appeared quietly, some years ago, called AN AMATEUR ANGLER'S DAYS IN DOVE DALE. It runs as easily and merrily and kindly as a little river, full of peace and pure enjoyment. Other books of the same quality have since been written by the same pen,—DAYS IN CLOVER, FRESH WOODS, BY MEADOW AND STREAM. It is no secret, I believe, that the author is Mr. Edward Marston, the senior member of a London publishing-house. But he still clings to his retiring pen-name of "The Amateur Angler," and represents himself, by a graceful fiction, as all unskilled in the art. An instance of similar modesty is found in Mr. Andrew Lang, who entitles the first chapter of his delightful ANGLING SKETCHES (without which no fisherman's library is complete), "Confessions of a Duffer." This an engaging liberty which no one else would dare to take.

The best English fish-story pure and simple, that I know, is "Crocker's Hole," by H. D. Black-more, the creator of LORNA DOONE.

Let us turn now to American books about angling. Of these the merciful dispensations of Providence have brought forth no small store since Mr. William Andrew Chatto made the ill-natured remark which is pilloried at the head of this chapter. By the way, it seems that Mr. Chatto had never heard of "The Schuylkill Fishing Company," which was founded on that romantic stream near Philadelphia in 1732, nor seen the AUTHENTIC HISTORICAL MEMOIR of that celebrated and amusing society.

I am sorry for the man who cannot find pleasure in reading the appendix of THE AMERICAN ANGLER'S BOOK, by Thaddeus Norris; or the discursive pages of Frank Forester's FISH AND FISHING; or the introduction and notes of that unexcelled edition of Walton which was made by the Reverend Doctor George W. Bethune; or SUPERIOR FISHING and GAME FISH OF THE NORTH, by Mr. Robert B. Roosevelt; or Henshall's BOOK OF THE BLACK BASS; or the admirable disgressions of Mr. Henry P. Wells, in his FLY-RODS AND FLY-TACKLE, and THE AMERICAN SALMON ANGLER. Dr. William C. Prime has never put his profound knowledge of the art of angling into a manual of technical instruction; but he has written of the delights of the sport in OWL CREEK LETTERS, and in I GO A-FISHING, and in some of the chapters of ALONG NEW ENGLAND ROADS and AMONG NEW ENGLAND HILLS, with a persuasive skill that has created many new anglers, and made many old ones grateful. It is a fitting coincidence of heredity that his niece, Mrs. Annie Trumbull Slosson, is the author of the most tender and pathetic of all angling stories, FISHIN' JIMMY.

But it is not only in books written altogether from his peculiar point of view and to humour his harmless insanity, that the angler may find pleasant reading about his favourite pastime. There are excellent bits of fishing scattered all through the field of good literature. It seems as if almost all the men who could write well had a friendly feeling for the contemplative sport.

Plutarch, in THE LIVES OF THE NOBLE GRECIANS AND ROMANS, tells a capital fish-story of the manner in which the Egyptian Cleopatra fooled that far-famed Roman wight, Marc Antony, when they were angling together on the Nile. As I recall it, from a perusal in early boyhood, Antony was having very bad luck indeed; in fact he had taken nothing, and was sadly put out about it. Cleopatra, thinking to get a rise out of him, secretly told one of her attendants to dive over the opposite side of the barge and fasten a salt fish to the Roman general's hook. The attendant was much pleased with this commission, and, having executed it, proceeded to add a fine stroke of his own; for when he had made the fish fast on the hook, he gave a great pull to the line and held on tightly. Antony was much excited and began to haul violently at his tackle.

"By Jupiter!" he exclaimed, "it was long in coming, but I have a colossal bite now."

"Have a care," said Cleopatra, laughing behind her sunshade, "or he will drag you into the water. You must give him line when he pulls hard."

"Not a denarius will I give!" rudely responded Antony. "I mean to have this halibut or Hades!"

At this moment the man under the boat, being out of breath, let the line go, and Antony, falling backward, drew up the salted herring.

"Take that fish off the hook, Palinurus," he proudly said. "It is not as large as I thought, but it looks like the oldest one that has been caught to-day."

Such, in effect, is the tale narrated by the veracious Plutarch. And if any careful critic wishes to verify my quotation from memory, he may compare it with the proper page of Langhorne's translation; I think it is in the second volume, near the end.

Sir Walter Scott, who once described himself as

*"No fisher,
But a well-wisher
To the game,"*

has an amusing passage of angling in the third chapter of REDGAUNTLET. Darsie Latimer is relating his adventures in Dumfriesshire. "By the way," says he, "old Cotton's instructions, by which I hoped to qualify myself for the gentle society of anglers, are not worth a farthing for this meridian. I learned this by mere accident, after I had waited four mortal hours. I shall never forget an impudent urchin, a cowherd, about twelve years old, without either brogue or bonnet, barelegged, with a very indifferent pair of breeches,—how the villain grinned in scorn at my landing-net, my plummet, and the gorgeous jury of flies which I had assembled to destroy all the fish in the river. I was induced at last to lend the rod to the sneering scoundrel, to see what he would make of it; and he not only half-filled my basket in an hour, but literally taught me to kill two trouts with my own hand."

Thus ancient and well-authenticated is the superstition of the angling powers of the barefooted country-boy,—in fiction.

Sir Edward Bulwer Lytton, in that valuable but over-capitalized book, MY NOVEL, makes use of Fishing for Allegorical Purposes. The episode of John Burley and the One-eyed Perch not only points a Moral but adorns the Tale.

In the works of R. D. Blackmore, angling plays a less instructive but a pleasanter part. It is closely interwoven with love. There is a magical description of trout-fishing on a meadow-brook in ALICE LORRAINE. And who that has read LORNA DOONE, (pity for the man or woman that knows not the delight of that book!) can ever forget how young John Ridd dared his way up the gliddery water-slide, after loaches, and found Lorna in a fair green meadow adorned with flowers, at the top of the brook?

I made a little journey into the Doone Country once, just to see that brook and to fish in it. The stream looked smaller, and the water-slide less terrible, than they seemed in the book. But it was a mighty pretty place after all; and I suppose that even John Ridd, when he came back to it in after years, found it shrunken a little.

All the streams were larger in our boyhood than they are now, except, perhaps, that which flows from the sweetest spring of all, the fountain of love, which John Ridd discovered beside the Bagworthy River,—and I, on the willow-shaded banks of the Patapsco, where the Baltimore girls fish for gudgeons,—and you? Come, gentle reader, is there no stream whose name is musical to you, because of a hidden spring of love that you once found on its shore? The waters of that fountain never fail, and in them alone we taste the undiminished fulness of immortal youth.

The stories of William Black are enlivened with fish, and he knew, better than most men, how they should be taken. Whenever he wanted to get two young people engaged to each other, all other devices failing, he sent them out to angle together. If it had not been for fishing, everything in A PRINCESS OF THULE and WHITE HEATHER would have gone wrong.

But even men who have been disappointed in love may angle for solace or diversion. I have known some old bachelors who fished excellently well; and others I have known who could find, and give, much pleasure in a day on the stream, though they had no skill in the sport. Of this class was Washington Irving, with an extract from whose SKETCH BOOK I will bring this rambling dissertation to an end.

"Our first essay," says he, "was along a mountain brook among the highlands of the Hudson; a most unfortunate place for the execution of those piscatory tactics which had been invented along the velvet margins of quiet English rivulets. It was one of those wild streams that lavish, among our romantic solitudes, unheeded beauties enough to fill the sketch-book of a hunter of the picturesque. Sometimes it would leap down rocky shelves, making small cascades, over which the trees threw their broad balancing sprays, and long nameless weeds hung in fringes from the impending banks, dripping with diamond drops. Sometimes it would brawl and fret along a ravine in the matted shade of a forest, filling it with murmurs; and, after this termagant career, would steal forth into open day, with the most placid, demure face imaginable; as I have seen some pestilent shrew of a housewife, after filling her home with uproar and ill-humour, come dimpling out of doors, swimming and courtesying, and smiling upon all the world.

"How smoothly would this vagrant brook glide, at such times, through some bosom of green meadow-land among the mountains, where the quiet was only interrupted by the occasional tinkling of a bell from the lazy cattle among the clover, or the sound of a woodcutter's axe from the neighbouring forest!

"For my part, I was always a bungler at all kinds of sport that required either patience or adroitness, and had not angled above half an hour before I had completely 'satisfied the sentiment,' and convinced myself of the truth of Izaak Walton's opinion, that angling is something like poetry,—a man must be born to it. I hooked myself instead of the fish; tangled my line in every tree; lost my bait; broke my rod; until I gave up the attempt in despair, and passed the day under the trees, reading old Izaak, satisfied that it was his fascinating vein of honest simplicity and rural feeling that had bewitched me, and not the passion for angling."

A NORWEGIAN HONEYMOON

"The best rose-bush, after all, is not that which has the fewest thorns, but that which bears the finest roses."

—SOLOMON SINGLEWITZ: *The Life of Adam.*

I

It was not all unadulterated sweetness, of course. There were enough difficulties in the way to make it seem desirable; and a few stings of annoyance, now and then, lent piquancy to the adventure. But a good memory, in dealing with the past, has the art of straining out all the beeswax of discomfort, and storing up little jars of pure hydromel. As we look back at our six weeks in Norway, we agree that no period of our partnership in experimental honeymooning has yielded more honey to the same amount of comb.

Several considerations led us to the resolve of taking our honeymoon experimentally rather than chronologically. We started from the self-evident proposition that it ought to be the happiest time in married life.

"It is perfectly ridiculous," said my lady Graygown, "to suppose that a thing like that can be fixed by the calendar. It may possibly fall in the first month after the wedding, but it is not likely. Just think how slightly two people know each other when they get married. They are in love, of course, but that is not at all the same as being well acquainted. Sometimes the more love, the less acquaintance! And sometimes the more acquaintance, the less love! Besides, at first there are always the notes of thanks for the wedding-presents to be written, and the letters of congratulation to be answered, and it is awfully hard to make each one sound a little different from the others and perfectly natural. Then, you know, everybody seems to suspect you of the folly of being newly married. You run across your friends everywhere, and they grin when they see you. You can't help feeling as if a lot of people were watching you through opera-glasses, or taking snap-shots at you with a kodak. It is absurd to imagine that the first month must be the real honeymoon. And just suppose it were,—what bad luck that would be! What would there be to look forward to?"

Every word that fell from her lips seemed to me like the wisdom of Diotima.

"You are right," I cried; "Portia could not hold a candle to you for clear argument. Besides, suppose two people are imprudent enough to get married in the first week of December, as we did!—what becomes of the chronological honeymoon then? There is no fishing in December, and all the rivers of Paradise, at least in our latitude, are frozen up. No, my lady, we will discover our month of honey by the empirical method. Each year we will set out together to seek it in a solitude for two; and we will compare notes on moons, and strike the final balance when we are sure that our happiest experiment has been completed."

We are not sure of that, even yet. We are still engaged, as a committee of two, in our philosophical investigation, and we decline to make anything but a report of progress. We know more now than we did when we first went honeymooning in the city of Washington. For one thing, we are certain that not even the far-famed rosemary-fields of Narbonne, or the fragrant hillsides of the Corbieres, yield a sweeter harvest to the busy-ness of the bees than the Norwegian meadows and mountain-slopes yielded to our idleness in the summer of 1888.

II

The rural landscape of Norway, on the long easterly slope that leads up to the watershed among the mountains of the western coast, is not unlike that of Vermont or New Hampshire. The railway from Christiania to the Randsfjord carried us through a hilly country of scattered farms and villages. Wood played a prominent part in the scenery. There were dark stretches of forest on the hilltops and in the valleys; rivers filled with floating logs; sawmills beside the waterfalls; wooden farmhouses painted white; and rail-fences around the fields. The people seemed sturdy, prosperous, independent. They had the familiar habit of coming down to the station to see the train arrive and depart.

We might have fancied ourselves on a journey through the Connecticut valley, if it had not been for the soft sing-song of the Norwegian speech and the uniform politeness of the railway officials.

What a room that was in the inn at Randsfjord where we spent our first night out! Vast, bare, primitive, with eight windows to admit the persistent nocturnal twilight; a sea-like floor of blue-painted boards, unbroken by a single island of carpet; and a castellated stove in one corner: an apartment for giants, with two little beds for dwarfs on opposite shores of the ocean. There was no telephone; so we arranged a system of communication with a fishing-line, to make sure that the sleepy partner should be awake in time for the early boat in the morning.

The journey up the lake took seven hours, and reminded us of a voyage on Lake George; placid, picturesque, and pervaded by summer boarders. Somewhere on the way we had lunch, and were well fortified to take the road when the steamboat landed us at Odnaes, at the head of the lake, about two o'clock in the afternoon.

There are several methods in which you may drive through Norway. The government maintains posting-stations at the farms along the main travelled highways, where you can hire horses and carriages of various kinds. There are also English tourist agencies which make a business of providing travellers with complete transportation. You may try either of these methods alone, or you may make a judicious mixture.

Thus, by an application of the theory of permutations and combinations, you have your choice among four ways of accomplishing a driving-tour. First, you may engage a carriage and pair, with a driver, from one of the tourist agencies, and roll through your journey in sedentary ease, provided your horses do not go lame or give out. Second, you may rely altogether upon the posting-stations to send you on your journey; and this is a very pleasant, lively way, provided there is not a crowd of travellers on the road before you, who take up all the comfortable conveyances and leave you nothing but a jolting cart or a ramshackle KARIOL of the time of St. Olaf. Third, you may rent an easy-riding vehicle (by choice a well-hung gig) for the entire trip, and change ponies at the stations as you drive along; this is the safest way. The fourth method is to hire your horseflesh at the beginning for the whole journey, and pick up your vehicles from place to place. This method is theoretically possible, but I do not know any one who has tried it.

Our gig was waiting for us at Odnaes. There was a brisk little mouse-coloured pony in the shafts; and it took but a moment to strap our leather portmanteau on the board at the back, perch the postboy on top of it, and set out for our first experience of a Norwegian driving-tour.

The road at first was level and easy; and we bowled along smoothly through the valley of the Etnaelv, among drooping birch-trees and green fields where the larks were singing. At Tomlevolden, ten miles farther on, we reached the first station, a comfortable old farmhouse, with a great array of wooden outbuildings. Here we had a chance to try our luck with the Norwegian language in demanding "en hest, saa straxt som muligt." This was what the guide-book told us to say when we wanted a horse.

There is great fun in making a random cast on the surface of a strange language. You cannot tell what will come up. It is like an experiment in witchcraft. We should not have been at all surprised, I must confess, if our preliminary incantation had brought forth a cow or a basket of eggs.

But the good people seemed to divine our intentions; and while we were waiting for one of the stable-boys to catch and harness the new horse, a yellow-haired maiden inquired, in very fair English, if we would not be pleased to have a cup of tea and some butter-bread; which we did with great comfort.

The SKYDSGUT, or so-called postboy, for the next stage of the journey, was a full-grown man of considerable weight. As he climbed to his perch on our portmanteau, my lady Graygown congratulated me on the prudence which had provided that one side of that receptacle should be of an inflexible stiffness, quite incapable of being crushed; otherwise, asked she, what would have become of her Sunday frock under the pressure of this stern necessity of a postboy?

But I think we should not have cared very much if all our luggage had been smashed on this journey, for the road now began to ascend, and the views over the Etnadal, with its winding river, were of a breadth and sweetness most consoling. Up and up we went, curving in and out through the forest, crossing wild ravines and shadowy dells, looking back at every turn on the wide landscape bathed in golden light. At the station of Sveen, where we changed horse and postboy again, it was already evening. The sun was down, but the mystical radiance of the northern twilight illumined the sky. The dark fir-woods spread around us, and their odourous breath was diffused through the cool, still air. We were crossing the level summit of the plateau, twenty-three hundred feet above the sea. Two tiny woodland lakes gleamed out among the trees. Then the road began to slope gently towards the west, and emerged suddenly on the edge of the forest, looking out over the long, lovely vale of Valders, with snow-touched mountains on the horizon, and the river Baegna shimmering along its bed, a thousand feet below us.

What a heart-enlarging outlook! What a keen joy of motion, as the wheels rolled down the long incline, and the sure-footed pony swung between the shafts and rattled his hoofs merrily on the hard road! What long, deep breaths of silent pleasure in the crisp night air! What wondrous mingling of lights in the afterglow of sunset, and the primrose bloom of the first stars, and faint foregleamings of the rising moon creeping over the hill behind us! What perfection of companionship without words, as we rode together through a strange land, along the edge of the dark!

When we finished the thirty-fifth mile, and drew up in the courtyard of the station at Frydenlund, Graygown sprang out, with a little sigh of regret.

"Is it last night," she cried, "or to-morrow morning? I have n't the least idea what time it is; it seems as if we had been travelling in eternity."

"It is just ten o'clock," I answered, "and the landlord says there will be a hot supper of trout ready for us in five minutes."

It would be vain to attempt to give a daily record of the whole journey in which we made this fair beginning. It was a most idle and unsystematic pilgrimage. We wandered up and down, and turned aside when fancy beckoned. Sometimes we hurried on as fast as the horses would carry us, driving sixty or seventy miles a day; sometimes we loitered and dawdled, as if we did not care whether we got anywhere or not. If a place pleased us, we stayed and tried the fishing. If we were tired of driving, we took to the water, and travelled by steamer along a fjord, or hired a rowboat to cross from point to point. One day we would be in a good little hotel, with polyglot guests, and serving-maids in stagey Norse costumes,—like the famous inn at Stalheim, which commands the amazing panorama of the Naerodal. Another day we would lodge in a plain farmhouse like the station at Nedre Vasenden, where eggs and fish were the staples of diet, and the farmer's daughter wore the picturesque peasants' dress, with its tall cap, without any dramatic airs. Lakes and rivers, precipices and gorges, waterfalls and glaciers and snowy mountains were our daily repast. We drove over five hundred miles in various kinds of open wagons, KARIOLS for one, and STOLKJAERRES for two, after we had left our comfortable gig behind us. We saw the ancient dragon-gabled church of Burgund; and the delightful, showery town of Bergen; and the gloomy cliffs of the Geiranger-Fjord laced with filmy cataracts; and the bewitched crags of the Romsdal; and the wide, desolate landscape of Jerkin; and a hundred other unforgotten scenes. Somehow or other we went, (around and about, and up and down, now on wheels, and now on foot, and now in a boat,) all the way from Christiania to Throndhjem. My lady Graygown could give you the exact itinerary, for she has been well brought up, and always keeps a diary. All I know is, that we set out from one city and arrived at the other, and we gathered by the way a collection of instantaneous photographs. I am going to turn them over now, and pick out a few of the clearest pictures.

III

Here is the bridge over the Naeselv at Fagernaes. Just below it is a good pool for trout, but the river is broad and deep and swift. It is difficult wading to get out within reach of the fish. I have taken half a dozen small ones and come to the end of my cast. There is a big one lying out in the middle of the river, I am sure. But the water already rises to my hips; another step will bring it over the top of my waders, and send me downstream feet uppermost.

"Take care!" cries Graygown from the grassy bank, where she sits placidly crocheting some mysterious fabric of white yarn.

She does not see the large rock lying at the bottom of the river just beyond me. If I can step on that, and stand there without being swept away, I can reach the mid-current with my flies. It is a long stride and a slippery foothold, but by good luck "the last step which costs" is accomplished. The tiny black and orange hackle goes curling out over the stream, lights softly, and swings around with the current, folding and expanding its feathers as if it were alive. The big trout takes it promptly the instant it passes over him; and I play him and net him without moving from my perilous perch.

Graygown waves her crochet-work like a flag, "Bravo!" she cries. "That's a beauty, nearly two pounds! But do be careful about coming back; you are not good enough to take any risks yet."

The station at Skogstad is a solitary farmhouse lying far up on the bare hillside, with its barns and out-buildings grouped around a central courtyard, like a rude fortress. The river travels along the valley below, now wrestling its way through a narrow passage among the rocks, now spreading out at leisure in a green meadow. As we cross the bridge, the crystal water is changed to opal by the sunset glow, and a gentle breeze ruffles the long pools, and the trout are rising freely. It is the perfect hour for fishing. Would Graygown dare to drive on alone to the gate of the fortress, and blow upon the long horn which doubtless hangs beside it, and demand admittance and a lodging, "in the name of the great Jehovah and the Continental Congress,"—while I angle down the river a mile or so?

Certainly she would. What door is there in Europe at which the American girl is afraid to knock? "But wait a moment. How do you ask for fried chicken and pancakes in Norwegian? KYLLING OG PANDEKAGE? How fierce it sounds! All right now. Run along and fish."

The river welcomes me like an old friend. The tune that it sings is the same that the flowing water repeats all around the world. Not otherwise do the lively rapids carry the familiar air, and the larger falls drone out a burly bass, along the west branch of the Penobscot, or down the valley of the Bouquet. But here there are no forests to conceal the course of the stream. It lies as free to the view as a child's thought. As I follow on from pool to pool, picking out a good trout here and there, now from a rocky corner edged with foam, now from a swift gravelly run, now from a snug hiding-place that the current has hollowed out beneath the bank, all the way I can see the fortress far above me on the hillside.

I am as sure that it has already surrendered to Graygown as if I could discern her white banner of crochet-work floating from the battlements.

Just before dark, I climb the hill with a heavy basket of fish. The castle gate is open. The scent of chicken and pancakes salutes the weary pilgrim. In a cosy little parlour, adorned with fluffy mats and pictures framed in pine-cones, lit by a hanging lamp with glass pendants, sits the mistress of the occasion, calmly triumphant and plying her crochet-needle.

There is something mysterious about a woman's fancy-work. It seems to have all the soothing charm of the tobacco-plant, without its inconveniences. Just to see her tranquillity, while she relaxes her mind and busies her fingers with a bit of tatting or embroidery or crochet, gives me a sense of being domesticated, a "homey" feeling, anywhere in the wide world.

If you ever go to Norway, you must be sure to see the Loenvand. You can set out from the comfortable hotel at Faleide, go up the Indvik Fjord in a rowboat, cross over a two-mile hill on foot or by carriage, spend a happy day on the lake, and return to your inn in time for a late supper. The lake is perhaps the most beautiful in Norway. Long and narrow, it lies like a priceless emerald of palest green, hidden and guarded by jealous mountains. It is fed by huge glaciers, which hang over the shoulders of the hills like ragged cloaks of ice.

As we row along the shore, trolling in vain for the trout that live in the ice-cold water, fragments of the tattered cloth-of-silver far above us, on the opposite side, are loosened by the touch of the summer sun, and fall from the precipice. They drift downward, at first, as noiselessly as thistledowns; then they strike the rocks and come crashing towards the lake with the hollow roar of an avalanche.

At the head of the lake we find ourselves in an enormous amphitheatre of mountains. Glaciers are peering down upon us. Snow-fields glare at us with glistening eyes. Black crags seem to bend above us with an eternal frown. Streamers of foam float from the forehead of the hills and the lips of the dark ravines. But there is a little river of cold, pure water flowing from one of the rivers of ice, and a pleasant shelter of young trees and bushes growing among the debris of shattered rocks; and there we build our camp-fire and eat our lunch.

Hunger is a most impudent appetite. It makes a man forget all the proprieties. What place is there so lofty, so awful, that he will not dare to sit down in it and partake of food? Even on the side of Mount Sinai, the elders of Israel spread their out-of-door table, "and did eat and drink."

I see the Tarn of the Elk at this moment, just as it looked in the clear sunlight of that August afternoon, ten years ago. Far down in a hollow of the desolate hills it nestles, four thousand feet above the sea. The moorland trail hangs high above it, and, though it is a mile away, every curve of the treeless shore, every shoal and reef in the light green water is clearly visible. With a powerful field-glass one can almost see the large trout for which the pond is famous.

The shelter-hut on the bank is built of rough gray stones, and the roof is leaky to the light as well as to the weather. But there are two beds in it, one for my guide and one for me; and a practicable fireplace, which is soon filled with a blaze of comfort. There is also a random library of novels, which former fishermen have thoughtfully left behind them. I like strong reading in the wilderness. Give me a story with plenty of danger and wholesome fighting in it,— "The Three Musketeers," or "Treasure Island," or "The Afghan's Knife." Intricate studies of social dilemmas and tales of mild philandering seem bloodless and insipid.

The trout in the Tarn of the Elk are large, undoubtedly, but they are also few in number and shy in disposition. Either some of the peasants have been fishing over them with the deadly "otter," or else they belong to that variety of the trout family known as TRUTTA DAMNOSA,—the species which you can see but cannot take. We watched these aggravating fish playing on the surface at sunset; we saw them dart beneath our boat in the early morning; but not until a driving snowstorm set in, about noon of the second day, did we succeed in persuading any of them to take the fly. Then they rose, for a couple of hours, with amiable perversity. I caught five, weighing between two and four pounds each, and stopped because my hands were so numb that I could cast no longer.

Now for a long tramp over the hills and home. Yes, home; for yonder in the white house at Drivstuen, with fuchsias and geraniums blooming in the windows, and a pretty, friendly Norse girl to keep her company, my lady is waiting for me. See, she comes running out to the door, in the gathering dusk, with a red flower in her hair, and hails me with the fisherman's greeting. WHAT LUCK?

Well, THIS luck, at all events! I can show you a few good fish, and sit down with you to a supper of reindeer-venison and a quiet evening of music and talk.

Shall I forget thee, hospitable Stuefloten, dearest to our memory of all the rustic stations in Norway? There are no stars beside thy name in the pages of Baedeker. But in the book of our hearts a whole constellation is thine.

The long, low, white farmhouse stands on a green hill at the head of the Romsdal. A flourishing crop of grass and flowers grows on the stable-roof, and there is a little belfry with a big bell to call the labourers home from the fields. In the corner of the living-room of the old house there is a broad fireplace built across the angle. Curious cupboards are tucked away everywhere. The long table in the dining-room groans thrice a day with generous fare. There are as many kinds of hot bread as in a Virginia country-house; the cream is thick enough to make a spoon stand up in amazement; once, at dinner, we sat embarrassed before six different varieties of pudding.

In the evening, when the saffron light is beginning to fade, we go out and walk in the road before the house, looking down the long mystical vale of the Rauma, or up to the purple western hills from which the clear streams of the Ulvaa flow to meet us.

Above Stuefloten the Rauma lingers and meanders through a smoother and more open valley, with broad beds of gravel and flowery meadows. Here the trout and grayling grow fat and lusty, and here we angle for them, day after day, in water so crystalline that when one steps into the stream one hardly knows whether to expect a depth of six inches or six feet.

Tiny English flies and leaders of gossamer are the tackle for such water in midsummer. With this delicate outfit, and with a light hand and a long line, one may easily outfish the native angler, and fill a twelve-pound basket every fair day. I remember an old Norwegian, an inveterate fisherman, whose footmarks we saw ahead of us on the stream all through an afternoon. Footmarks I call them; and so they were, literally, for there were only the prints of a single foot to be seen on the banks of sand, and between them, a series of small, round, deep holes.

"What kind of a bird made those marks, Frederik?" I asked my faithful guide.

"That is old Pedersen," he said, "with his wooden leg. He makes a dot after every step. We shall catch him in a little while."

Sure enough, about six o'clock we saw him standing on a grassy point, hurling his line, with a fat worm on the end of it, far across the stream, and letting it drift down with the current. But the water was too fine for that style of fishing, and the poor old fellow had but a half dozen little fish. My creel was already overflowing, so I emptied out all of the grayling into his bag, and went on up the river to complete my tale of trout before dark.

And when the fishing is over, there is Graygown with the wagon, waiting at the appointed place under the trees, beside the road. The sturdy white pony trots gayly homeward. The pale yellow stars blossom out above the hills again, as they did on that first night when we were driving down into the Valders. Frederik leans over the back of the seat, telling us marvellous tales, in his broken English, of the fishing in a certain lake among the mountains, and of the reindeer-shooting on the fjeld beyond it.

"It is sad that you go to-morrow," says he "but you come back another year, I think, to fish in that lake, and to shoot those reindeer."

Yes, Frederik, we are coming back to Norway some day, perhaps,—who can tell? It is one of the hundred places that we are vaguely planning to revisit. For, though we did not see the midnight sun there, we saw the honeymoon most distinctly. And it was bright enough to take pictures by its light.

WHO OWNS THE MOUNTAINS?

"My heart is fixed firm and stable in the belief that ultimately the sunshine and the summer, the flowers and the azure sky, shall become, as it were, interwoven into man's existence. He shall take from all their beauty and enjoy their glory."—RICHARD JEFFERIES: The Life of the Fields.

It was the little lad that asked the question; and the answer also, as you will see, was mainly his.

We had been keeping Sunday afternoon together in our favourite fashion, following out that pleasant text which tells us to "behold the fowls of the air." There is no injunction of Holy Writ less burdensome in acceptance, or more profitable in obedience, than this easy out-of-doors commandment. For several hours we walked in the way of this precept, through the untangled woods that lie behind the Forest Hills Lodge, where a pair of pigeon-hawks had their nest; and around the brambly shores of the small pond, where Maryland yellow-throats and song-sparrows were settled; and under the lofty hemlocks of the fragment of forest across the road, where rare warblers flitted silently among the tree-tops. The light beneath the evergreens was growing dim as we came out from their shadow into the widespread glow of the sunset, on the edge of a grassy hill, overlooking the long valley of the Gale River, and uplooking to the Franconia Mountains.

It was the benediction hour. The placid air of the day shed a new tranquillity over the consoling landscape. The heart of the earth seemed to taste a repose more perfect than that of common days. A hermit-thrush, far up the vale, sang his vesper hymn; while the swallows, seeking their evening meal, circled above the river-fields without an effort, twittering softly, now and then, as if they must give thanks. Slight and indefinable touches in the scene, perhaps the mere absence of the tiny human figures passing along the road or labouring in the distant meadows, perhaps the blue curls of smoke rising lazily from the farmhouse chimneys, or the family groups sitting under the maple-trees before the door, diffused a sabbath atmosphere over the world.

Then said the lad, lying on the grass beside me, "Father, who owns the mountains?"

I happened to have heard, the day before, of two or three lumber companies that had bought some of the woodland slopes; so I told him their names, adding that there were probably a good many different owners, whose claims taken all together would cover the whole Franconia range of hills.

"Well," answered the lad, after a moment of silence, "I don't see what difference that makes. Everybody can look at them."

They lay stretched out before us in the level sunlight, the sharp peaks outlined against the sky, the vast ridges of forest sinking smoothly towards the valleys, the deep hollows gathering purple shadows in their bosoms, and the little foothills standing out in rounded promontories of brighter green from the darker mass behind them.

Far to the east, the long comb of Twin Mountain extended itself back into the untrodden wilderness. Mount Garfield lifted a clear-cut pyramid through the translucent air. The huge bulk of Lafayette ascended majestically in front of us, crowned with a rosy diadem of rocks. Eagle Cliff and Bald Mountain stretched their line of scalloped peaks across the entrance to the Notch. Beyond that shadowy vale, the swelling summits of Cannon Mountain rolled away to meet the tumbling waves of Kinsman, dominated by one loftier crested billow that seemed almost ready to curl and break out of green silence into snowy foam. Far down the sleeping Landaff valley the undulating dome of Moosilauke trembled in the distant blue.

They were all ours, from crested cliff to wooded base. The solemn groves of firs and spruces, the plumed sierras of lofty pines, the stately pillared forests of birch and beech, the wild ravines, the tremulous thickets of silvery poplar, the bare peaks with their wide outlooks, and the cool vales resounding with the ceaseless song of little rivers,—we knew and loved them all; they ministered peace and joy to us; they were all ours, though we held no title deeds and our ownership had never been recorded.

What is property, after all? The law says there are two kinds, real and personal. But it seems to me that the only real property is that which is truly personal, that which we take into our inner life and make our own forever, by understanding and admiration and sympathy and love. This is the only kind of possession that is worth anything.

A gallery of great paintings adorns the house of the Honourable Midas Bond, and every year adds a new treasure to his collection. He knows how much they cost him, and he keeps the run of the quotations at the auction sales, congratulating himself as the price of the works of his well-chosen artists rises in the scale, and the value of his art treasures is enhanced. But why should he call them his? He is only their custodian. He keeps them well varnished, and framed in gilt. But he never passes through those gilded frames into the world of beauty that lies behind the painted canvas. He knows nothing of those lovely places from which the artist's soul and hand have drawn their inspiration. They are closed and barred to him. He has bought the pictures, but he cannot buy the key. The poor art student who wanders through his gallery, lingering with awe and love before the masterpieces, owns them far more truly than Midas does.

Pomposus Silverman purchased a rich library a few years ago. The books were rare and costly. That was the reason why Pomposus bought them. He was proud to feel that he was the possessor of literary treasures which were not to be found in the houses of his wealthiest acquaintances. But the threadbare Bucherfreund, who was engaged at a slender salary to catalogue the library and take care of it, became the real proprietor. Pomposus paid for the books, but Bucherfreund enjoyed them.

I do not mean to say that the possession of much money is always a barrier to real wealth of mind and heart. Nor would I maintain that all the poor of this world are rich in faith and heirs of the kingdom. But some of them are. And if some of the rich of this world (through the grace of Him with whom all things are possible) are also modest in their tastes, and gentle in their hearts, and open in their minds, and ready to be pleased with unbought pleasures, they simply share in the best things which are provided for all.

I speak not now of the strife that men wage over the definition and the laws of property. Doubtless there is much here that needs to be set right. There are men and women in the world who are shut out from the right to earn a living, so poor that they must perish for want of daily bread, so full of misery that there is no room for the tiniest seed of joy in their lives. This is the lingering shame of civilization. Some day, perhaps, we shall find the way to banish it. Some day, every man shall have his title to a share in the world's great work and the world's large joy.

But meantime it is certain that, where there are a hundred poor bodies who suffer from physical privation, there are a thousand poor souls who suffer from spiritual poverty. To relive this greater suffering there needs no change of laws, only a change of heart.

What does it profit a man to be the landed proprietor of countless acres unless he can reap the harvest of delight that blooms from every rood of God's earth for the seeing eye and the loving spirit? And who can reap that harvest so closely that there shall not be abundant gleaning left for all mankind? The most that a wide estate can yield to its legal owner is a living. But the real owner can gather from a field of goldenrod, shining in the August sunlight, an unearned increment of delight.

We measure success by accumulation. The measure is false. The true measure is appreciation. He who loves most has most.

How foolishly we train ourselves for the work of life! We give our most arduous and eager efforts to the cultivation of those faculties which will serve us in the competitions of the forum and the market-place. But if we were wise, we should care infinitely more for the unfolding of those inward, secret, spiritual powers by which alone we can become the owners of anything that is worth having. Surely God is the great proprietor. Yet all His works He has given away. He holds no title-deeds. The one thing that is His, is the perfect understanding, the perfect joy, the perfect love, of all things that He has made. To a share in this high ownership He welcomes all who are poor in spirit. This is the earth which the meek inherit. This is the patrimony of the saints in light.

"Come, laddie," I said to my comrade, "let us go home. You and I are very rich. We own the mountains. But we can never sell them, and we don't want to."

A LAZY, IDLE BROOK

"Perpetual devotion to what a man calls his business is only to be sustained by perpetual neglect of many other things. And it is not by any means certain that a man's business is the most important thing he has to do."
—ROBERT LOUIS STEVENSON: *An Apology for Idlers.*

I. A CASUAL INTRODUCTION

On the South Shore of Long Island, all things incline to a natural somnolence. There are no ambitious mountains, no braggart cliffs, no hasty torrents, no hustling waterfalls in that land,

"In which it seemeth always afternoon."

The salt meadows sleep in the summer sun; the farms and market-gardens yield a placid harvest to a race of singularly unhurried tillers of the soil; the low hills rise with gentle slopes, not caring to get too high in the world, only far enough to catch a pleasant glimpse of the sea and a breath of fresh air; the very trees grow leisurely, as if they felt that they had "all the time there is." And from this dreamy land, close as it lies to the unresting ocean, the tumult of the breakers and the foam of ever-turning tides are shut off by the languid lagoons of the Great South Bay and a long range of dunes, crested with wire-grass, bay-bushes, and wild-roses.

In such a country you could not expect a little brook to be noisy, fussy, energetic. If it were not lazy, it would be out of keeping.

But the actual and undisguised idleness of this particular brook was another affair, and one in which it was distinguished among its fellows. For almost all the other little rivers of the South Shore, lazy as they may be by nature, yet manage to do some kind of work before they finish the journey from their crystal-clear springs into the brackish waters of the bay. They turn the wheels of sleepy gristmills, while the miller sits with his hands in his pockets underneath the willow-trees. They fill reservoirs out of which great steam-engines pump the water to quench the thirst of Brooklyn. Even the smaller streams tarry long enough in their seaward sauntering to irrigate a few cranberry-bogs and so provide that savoury sauce which makes the Long Island turkey a fitter subject for Thanksgiving.

But this brook of which I speak did none of these useful things. It was absolutely out of business.

There was not a mill, nor a reservoir, nor a cranberry-bog, on all its course of a short mile. The only profitable affair it ever undertook was to fill a small ice-pond near its entrance into the Great South Bay. You could hardly call this a very energetic enterprise. It amounted to little more than a good-natured consent to allow itself to be used by the winter for the making of ice, if the winter happened to be cold enough. Even this passive industry came to nothing; for the water, being separated from the bay only by a short tideway under a wooden bridge on the south country road, was too brackish to freeze easily; and the ice, being pervaded with weeds, was not much relished by the public. So the wooden ice-house, innocent of paint, and toned by the weather to a soft, sad-coloured gray, stood like an improvised ruin among the pine-trees beside the pond.

It was through this unharvested ice-pond, this fallow field of water, that my lady Graygown and I entered on acquaintance with our lazy, idle brook. We had a house, that summer, a few miles down the bay. But it was a very small house, and the room that we like best was out of doors. So we spent much time in a sailboat,—by name "The Patience,"—making voyages of exploration into watery corners and byways. Sailing past the wooden bridge one day, when a strong east wind had made a very low tide, we observed the water flowing out beneath the road with an eddying current. We were interested to discover where such a stream came from. But the sailboat could not go under the bridge, nor even make a landing on the shore without risk of getting aground. The next day we came back in a rowboat to follow the clue of curiosity. The tide was high now, and we passed with the reversed current under the bridge, almost bumping our heads against the timbers. Emerging upon the pond, we rowed across its shallow, weed-encumbered waters, and were introduced without ceremony to one of the most agreeable brooks that we had ever met.

It was quite broad where it came into the pond,—a hundred feet from side to side,—bordered with flags and rushes and feathery meadow grasses. The real channel meandered in sweeping curves from bank to bank, and the water, except in the swifter current, was filled with an amazing quantity of some aquatic moss. The woods came straggling down on either shore. There were fallen trees in the stream here and there. On one of the points an old swamp-maple, with its decrepit branches and its leaves already touched with the hectic colours of decay, hung far out over the water which was undermining it, looking and leaning downward, like an aged man who bends, half-sadly and half-willingly, towards the grave.

But for the most part the brook lay wide open to the sky, and the tide, rising and sinking somewhat irregularly in the pond below, made curious alternations in its depth and in the swiftness of its current. For about half a mile we navigated this lazy little river, and then we found that rowing would carry us no farther, for we came to a place where the stream issued with a livelier flood from an archway in a thicket.

This woodland portal was not more than four feet wide, and the branches of the small trees were closely interwoven overhead. We shipped the oars and took one of them for a paddle. Stooping down, we pushed the boat through the archway and found ourselves in the Fairy Dell. It was a long, narrow bower, perhaps four hundred feet from end to end, with the brook dancing through it in a joyous, musical flow over a bed of clean yellow sand and white pebbles. There were deep places in the curves where you could hardly touch bottom with an oar, and shallow places in the straight runs where the boat would barely float. Not a ray of unbroken sunlight leaked through the green roof of this winding corridor; and all along the sides there were delicate mosses and tall ferns and wildwood flowers that love the shade.

At the upper end of the bower our progress in the boat was barred by a low bridge, on a forgotten road that wound through the pine-woods. Here I left my lady Graygown, seated on the shady corner of the bridge with a book, swinging her feet over the stream, while I set out to explore its further course. Above the wood-road there were no more fairy dells, nor easy-going estuaries. The water came down through the most complicated piece of underbrush that I have ever encountered. Alders and swamp maples and pussy-willows and gray birches grew together in a wild confusion. Blackberry bushes and fox-grapes and cat-briers trailed and twisted themselves in an incredible tangle. There was only one way to advance, and that was to wade in the middle of the brook, stooping low, lifting up the pendulous alder-branches, threading a tortuous course, now under and now over the innumerable obstacles, as a darning-needle is pushed in and out through the yarn of a woollen stocking.

It was dark and lonely in that difficult passage. The brook divided into many channels, turning this way and that way, as if it were lost in the woods. There were huge clumps of OSMUNDA REGALIS spreading their fronds in tropical profusion. Mouldering logs were covered with moss. The water gurgled slowly into deep corners under the banks. Catbirds and blue jays fluttered screaming from the thickets. Cotton-tailed rabbits darted away, showing the white flag of fear. Once I thought I saw the fuscous gleam of a red fox stealing silently through the brush. It would have been no surprise to hear the bark of a raccoon, or see the eyes of a wildcat gleaming through the leaves.

For more than an hour I was pushing my way through this miniature wilderness of half a mile; and then I emerged suddenly, to find myself face to face with—a railroad embankment and the afternoon express, with its parlour-cars, thundering down to Southampton!

It was a strange and startling contrast. The explorer's joy, the sense of adventure, the feeling of wildness and freedom, withered and crumpled somewhat preposterously at the sight of the parlour-cars. My scratched hands and wet boots and torn coat seemed unkempt and disreputable. Perhaps some of the well-dressed people looking out at the windows of the train were the friends with whom we were to dine on Saturday. BATECHE! What would they say to such a costume as mine? What did I care what they said!

But, all the same, it was a shock, a disenchantment, to find that civilization, with all its absurdities and conventionalities, was so threateningly close to my new-found wilderness. My first enthusiasm was not a little chilled as I walked back, along an open woodland path, to the bridge where Graygown was placidly reading. Reading, I say, though her book was closed, and her brown eyes were wandering over the green leaves of the thicket, and the white clouds drifting, drifting lazily across the blue deep of the sky.

II. A BETTER ACQUAINTANCE

On the voyage home, she gently talked me out of my disappointment, and into a wiser frame of mind.

It was a surprise, of course, she admitted, to find that our wilderness was so little, and to discover the trail of a parlour-car on the edge of Paradise. But why not turn the surprise around, and make it pleasant instead of disagreeable? Why not look at the contrast from the side that we liked best?

It was not necessary that everybody should take the same view of life that pleased us. The world would not get on very well without people who preferred parlour-cars to canoes, and patent-leather shoes to India-rubber boots, and ten-course dinners to picnics in the woods. These good people were unconsciously toiling at the hard and necessary work of life in order that we, of the chosen and fortunate few, should be at liberty to enjoy the best things in the world.

Why should we neglect our opportunities, which were also our real duties? The nervous disease of civilization might prevail all around us, but that ought not to destroy our grateful enjoyment of the lucid intervals that were granted to us by a merciful Providence.

Why should we not take this little untamed brook, running its humble course through the borders of civilized life and midway between two flourishing summer resorts,—a brook without a single house or a cultivated field on its banks, as free and beautiful and secluded as if it flowed through miles of trackless forest,—why not take this brook as a sign that the ordering of the universe had a "good intention" even for inveterate idlers, and that the great Arranger of the world felt some kindness for such gipsy-hearts as ours? What law, human or divine, was there to prevent us from making this stream our symbol of deliverance from the conventional and commonplace, our guide to liberty and a quiet mind?

So reasoned Graygown with her

> "most silver flow
> Of subtle-paced counsel in distress."

And, according to her word, so did we. That lazy, idle brook became to us one of the best of friends; the pathfinder of happiness on many a bright summer day; and, through long vacations, the faithful encourager of indolence.

Indolence in the proper sense of the word, you understand. The meaning which is commonly given to it, as Archbishop Trench pointed out in his suggestive book about WORDS AND THEIR USES, is altogether false. To speak of indolence as if it were a vice is just a great big verbal slander.

Indolence is a virtue. It comes from two Latin words, which mean freedom from anxiety or grief. And that is a wholesome state of mind. There are times and seasons when it is even a pious and blessed state of mind. Not to be in a hurry; not to be ambitious or jealous or resentful; not to feel envious of anybody; not to fret about to-day nor worry about to-morrow,—that is the way we ought all to feel at some time in our lives; and that is the kind of indolence in which our brook faithfully encouraged us.

'T is an age in which such encouragement is greatly needed. We have fallen so much into the habit of being always busy that we know not how nor when to break it off with firmness. Our business tags after us into the midst of our pleasures, and we are ill at ease beyond reach of the telegraph and the daily newspaper. We agitate ourselves amazingly about a multitude of affairs,—the politics of Europe, the state of the weather all around the globe, the marriages and festivities of very rich people, and the latest novelties in crime, none of which are of vital interest to us. The more earnest souls among us are cultivating a vicious tendency to Summer Schools, and Seaside Institutes of Philosophy, and Mountaintop Seminaries of Modern Languages.

We toil assiduously to cram something more into those scrap-bags of knowledge which we fondly call our minds. Seldom do we rest tranquil long enough to find out whether there is anything in them already that is of real value,—any native feeling, any original thought, which would like to come out and sun itself for a while in quiet.

For my part, I am sure that I stand more in need of a deeper sense of contentment with life than of a knowledge of the Bulgarian tongue, and that all the paradoxes of Hegel would not do me so much good as one hour of vital sympathy with the careless play of children. The Marquis du Paty de l'Huitre may espouse the daughter and heiress of the Honourable James Bulger with all imaginable pomp, if he will. CA NE M'INTRIGUE POINT DU TOUT. I would rather stretch myself out on the grass and watch yonder pair of kingbirds carrying luscious flies to their young ones in the nest, or chasing away the marauding crow with shrill cries of anger.

What a pretty battle it is, and in a good cause, too! Waste no pity on that big black ruffian. He is a villain and a thief, an egg-stealer, an ogre, a devourer of unfledged innocents. The kingbirds are not afraid of him, knowing that he is a coward at heart. They fly upon him, now from below, now from above. They buffet him from one side and from the other. They circle round him like a pair of swift gunboats round an antiquated man-of-war. They even perch upon his back and dash their beaks into his neck and pluck feathers from his piratical plumage. At last his lumbering flight has carried him far enough away, and the brave little defenders fly back to the nest, poising above it on quivering wings for a moment, then dipping down swiftly in pursuit of some passing insect. The war is over. Courage has had its turn. Now tenderness comes into play. The young birds, all ignorant of the passing danger, but always conscious of an insatiable hunger, are uttering loud remonstrances and plaintive demands for food. Domestic life begins again, and they that sow not, neither gather into barns, are fed.

Do you suppose that this wondrous stage of earth was set, and all the myriad actors on it taught to play their parts, without a spectator in view? Do you think that there is anything better for you and me to do, now and then, than to sit down quietly in a humble seat, and watch a few scenes in the drama? Has it not something to say to us, and do we not understand it best when we have a peaceful heart and free from dolor? That is what IN-DOLENCE means, and there are no better teachers of it then the light-hearted birds and untoiling flowers, commended by the wisest of all masters to our consideration; nor can we find a more pleasant pedagogue to lead us to their school than a small, merry brook.

And this was what our chosen stream did for us. It was always luring us away from an artificial life into restful companionship with nature.

Suppose, for example, we found ourselves growing a bit dissatisfied with the domestic arrangements of our little cottage, and coveting the splendours of a grander establishment. An afternoon on the brook was a good cure for that folly. Or suppose a day came when there was an imminent prospect of many formal calls. We had an important engagement up the brook; and while we kept it we could think with satisfaction of the joy of our callers when they discovered that they could discharge their whole duty with a piece of pasteboard. This was an altruistic pleasure. Or suppose that a few friends were coming to supper, and there were no flowers for the supper-table. We could easily have bought them in the village. But it was far more to our liking to take the children up the brook, and come back with great bunches of wild white honeysuckle and blue flag, or posies of arrowheads and cardinal-flowers. Or suppose that I was very unwisely and reluctantly labouring at some serious piece of literary work, promised for the next number of THE SCRIBBLER'S REVIEW; and suppose that in the midst of this labour the sad news came to me that the fisherman had forgotten to leave any fish at our cottage that morning. Should my innocent babes and my devoted wife be left to perish of starvation while I continued my poetical comparison of the two Williams, Shakspeare and Watson? Inhuman selfishness! Of course it was my plain duty to sacrifice my inclinations, and get my fly-rod, and row away across the bay, with a deceptive appearance of cheerfulness, to catch a basket of trout in—

III. THE SECRETS OF INTIMACY

THERE! I came within eight letters of telling the name of the brook, a thing that I am firmly resolved not to do. If it were an ordinary fishless little river, or even a stream with nothing better than grass-pike and sunfish in it, you should have the name and welcome. But when a brook contains speckled trout, and when their presence is known to a very few persons who guard the secret as the dragon guarded the golden apples of the Hesperides, and when the size of the trout is large beyond the dreams of hope,—well, when did you know a true angler who would willingly give away the name of such a brook as that? You may find an encourager of indolence in almost any stream of the South Side, and I wish you joy of your brook. But if you want to catch trout in mine you must discover it for yourself, or perhaps go with me some day, and solemnly swear secrecy.

That was the way in which the freedom of the stream was conferred upon me. There was a small boy in the village, the son of rich but respectable parents, and an inveterate all-round sportsman, aged fourteen years, with whom I had formed a close intimacy. I was telling him about the pleasure of exploring the idle brook, and expressing the opinion that in bygone days, (in that mythical "forty years ago" when all fishing was good), there must have been trout in it. A certain look came over the boy's face. He gazed at me solemnly, as if he were searching the inmost depths of my character before he spoke.

"Say, do you want to know something?"

I assured him that an increase of knowledge was the chief aim of my life.

"Do you promise you won't tell?"

I expressed my readiness to be bound to silence by the most awful pledge that the law would sanction.

"Wish you may die?"

I not only wished that I might die, but was perfectly certain that I would die.

"Well, what's the matter with catching trout in that brook now? Do you want to go with me next Saturday? I saw four or five bully ones last week, and got three."

On the appointed day we made the voyage, landed at the upper bridge, walked around by the woodpath to the railroad embankment, and began to worm our way down through the tangled wilderness. Fly-fishing, of course, was out of the question. The only possible method of angling was to let the line, baited with a juicy "garden hackle," drift down the current as far as possible before you, under the alder-branches and the cat-briers, into the holes and corners of the stream. Then, if there came a gentle tug on the rod, you must strike, to one side or the other, as the branches might allow, and trust wholly to luck for a chance to play the fish. Many a trout we lost that day,—the largest ones, of course,—and many a hook was embedded in a sunken log, or hopelessly entwined among the boughs overhead. But when we came out at the bridge, very wet and disheveled, we had seven pretty fish, the heaviest about half a pound. The Fairy Dell yielded a brace of smaller ones, and altogether we were reasonably happy as we took up the oars and pushed out upon the open stream.

But if there were fish above, why should there not be fish below? It was about sunset, the angler's golden hour. We were already committed to the crime of being late for supper. It would add little to our guilt and much to our pleasure to drift slowly down the middle of the brook and cast the artful fly in the deeper corners on either shore. So I took off the vulgar bait-hook and put on a delicate leader with a Queen of the Water for a tail-fly and a Yellow Sally for a dropper,—innocent little confections of feathers and tinsel, dressed on the tiniest hooks, and calculated to tempt the appetite or the curiosity of the most capricious trout.

For a long time the whipping of the water produced no result, and it seemed as if the dainty style of angling were destined to prove less profitable than plain fishing with a worm. But presently we came to an elbow of the brook, just above the estuary, where there was quite a stretch of clear water along the lower side, with two half-sunken logs sticking out from the bank, against which the current had drifted a broad raft of weeds. I made a long cast, and sent the tail-fly close to the edge of the weeds. There was a swelling ripple on the surface of the water, and a noble fish darted from under the logs, dashed at the fly, missed it, and whirled back to his shelter.

"Gee!" said the boy, "that was a whacker! He made a wake like a steamboat."

It was a moment for serious thought. What was best to be done with that fish? Leave him to settle down for the night and come back after him another day? Or try another cast for him at once? A fish on Saturday evening is worth two on Monday morning. I changed the Queen of the Water for a Royal Coachman tied on a number fourteen hook,—white wings, peacock body with a belt of crimson silk,—and sent it out again, a foot farther up the stream and a shade closer to the weeds. As it settled on the water, there was a flash of gold from the shadow beneath the logs, and a quick turn of the wrist made the tiny hook fast in the fish. He fought wildly to get back to the shelter of his logs, but the four ounce rod had spring enough in it to hold him firmly away from that dangerous retreat. Then he splurged up and down the open water, and made fierce dashes among the grassy shallows, and seemed about to escape a dozen times. But at last his force was played out; he came slowly towards the boat, turning on his side, and I netted him in my hat.

"Bully for us;" said the boy, "we got him! What a dandy!"

It was indeed one of the handsomest fish that I have ever taken on the South Side,—just short of two pounds and a quarter,—small head, broad tail, and well-rounded sides coloured with orange and blue and gold and red. A pair of the same kind, one weighing two pounds and the other a pound and three quarters, were taken by careful fishing down the lower end of the pool, and then we rowed home through the dusk, pleasantly convinced that there is no virtue more certainly rewarded than the patience of anglers, and entirely willing to put up with a cold supper and a mild reproof for the sake of sport.

Of course we could not resist the temptation to show those fish to the neighbours. But, equally of course, we evaded the request to give precise information as to the precise place where they were caught. Indeed, I fear that there must have been something confused in our description of where we had been on that afternoon. Our carefully selected language may have been open to misunderstanding. At all events, the next day, which was the Sabbath, there was a row of eager but unprincipled anglers sitting on a bridge OVER ANOTHER STREAM, and fishing for trout with worms and large expectations, but without visible results.

The boy and I agreed that if this did not teach a good moral lesson it was not our fault.

I obtained the boy's consent to admit the partner of my life's joys and two of our children to the secret of the brook, and thereafter, when we visited it, we took the fly-rod with us. If by chance another boat passed us in the estuary, we were never fishing, but only gathering flowers, or going for a picnic, or taking photographs. But when the uninitiated ones had passed by, we would get out the rod again, and try a few more casts.

One day in particular I remember, when Graygown and little Teddy were my companions. We really had no hopes of angling, for the hour was mid-noon, and the day was warm and still. But suddenly the trout, by one of those unaccountable freaks which make their disposition so interesting and attractive, began to rise all about us in a bend of the stream.

"Look!" said Teddy; "wherever you see one of those big smiles on the water, I believe there's a fish!"

Fortunately the rod was at hand. Graygown and Teddy managed the boat and the landing-net with consummate skill. We landed no less than a dozen beautiful fish at that most unlikely hour and then solemnly shook hands all around.

There is a peculiar pleasure in doing a thing like this, catching trout in a place where nobody thinks of looking for them, and at an hour when everybody believes they cannot be caught. It is more fun to take one good fish out of an old, fished-out stream, near at hand to the village, than to fill a basket from some far-famed and well-stocked water. It is the unexpected touch that tickles our sense of pleasure. While life lasts, we are always hoping for it and expecting it. There is no country so civilized, no existence so humdrum, that there is not room enough in it somewhere for a lazy, idle brook, an encourager of indolence, with hope of happy surprises.

THE OPEN FIRE

"It is a vulgar notion that a fire is only for heat. A chief value of it is, however, to look at. And it is never twice the same."
—CHARLES DUDLEY WARNER: *Backlog Studies.*

I. LIGHTING UP

Man is the animal that has made friends with the fire.

All the other creatures, in their natural state, are afraid of it. They look upon it with wonder and dismay. It fascinates them, sometimes, with its glittering eyes in the night. The squirrels and the hares come pattering softly towards it through the underbrush around the new camp. The fascinated deer stares into the blaze of the jack-light while the hunter's canoe creeps through the lily-pads. But the charm that masters them is one of dread, not of love. It is the witchcraft of the serpent's lambent look. When they know what it means, when the heat of the fire touches them, or even when its smell comes clearly to their most delicate sense, they recognize it as their enemy, the Wild Huntsman whose red hounds can follow, follow for days without wearying, growing stronger and more furious with every turn of the chase. Let but a trail of smoke drift down the wind across the forest, and all the game for miles and miles will catch the signal for fear and flight.

Many of the animals have learned how to make houses for themselves. The CABANE of the beaver is a wonder of neatness and comfort, much preferable to the wigwam of his Indian hunter. The muskrat knows how thick and high to build the dome of his waterside cottage, in order to protect himself against the frost of the coming winter and the floods of the following spring. The woodchuck's house has two or three doors; and the squirrel's dwelling is provided with a good bed and a convenient storehouse for nuts and acorns. The sportive otters have a toboggan slide in front of their residence; and the moose in winter make a "yard," where they can take exercise comfortably and find shelter for sleep. But there is one thing lacking in all these various dwellings,—a fireplace.

Man is the only creature that dares to light a fire and to live with it. The reason? Because he alone has learned how to put it out.

It is true that two of his humbler friends have been converted to fire-worship. The dog and the cat, being half-humanized, have begun to love the fire. I suppose that a cat seldom comes so near to feeling a true sense of affection as when she has finished her saucer of bread and milk, and stretched herself luxuriously underneath the kitchen stove, while her faithful mistress washes up the dishes. As for a dog, I am sure that his admiring love for his master is never greater than when they come in together from the hunt, wet and tired, and the man gathers a pile of wood in front of the tent, touches it with a tiny magic wand, and suddenly the clear, consoling flame springs up, saying cheerfully, "Here we are, at home in the forest; come into the warmth; rest, and eat, and sleep." When the weary, shivering dog sees this miracle, he knows that his master is a great man and a lord of things.

After all, that is the only real open fire. Wood is the fuel for it. Out-of-doors is the place for it. A furnace is an underground prison for a toiling slave. A stove is a cage for a tame bird. Even a broad hearthstone and a pair of glittering andirons—the best ornament of a room—must be accepted as an imitation of the real thing. The veritable open fire is built in the open, with the whole earth for a fireplace and the sky for a chimney.

To start a fire in the open is by no means as easy as it looks. It is one of those simple tricks that every one thinks he can perform until he tries it.

To do it without trying,—accidentally and unwillingly,—that, of course, is a thing for which any fool is fit. You knock out the ashes from your pipe on a fallen log; you toss the end of a match into a patch of grass, green on top, but dry as punk underneath; you scatter the dead brands of an old fire among the moss,—a conflagration is under way before you know it.

A fire in the woods is one thing; a comfort and a joy. Fire in the woods is another thing; a terror, an uncontrollable fury, a burning shame.

But the lighting up of a proper fire, kindly, approachable, serviceable, docile, is a work of intelligence. If, perhaps, you have to do it in the rain, with a single match, it requires no little art and skill.

There is plenty of wood everywhere, but not a bit to burn. The fallen trees are waterlogged. The dead leaves are as damp as grief. The charred sticks that you find in an old fireplace are absolutely incombustible. Do not trust the handful of withered twigs and branches that you gather from the spruce-trees. They seem dry, but they are little better for your purpose than so much asbestos. You make a pile of them in some apparently suitable hollow, and lay a few larger sticks on top. Then you hastily scratch your solitary match on the seat of your trousers and thrust it into the pile of twigs. What happens? The wind whirls around in your stupid little hollow, and the blue flame of the sulphur spirts and sputters for an instant, and then goes out. Or perhaps there is a moment of stillness; the match flares up bravely;

the nearest twigs catch fire, crackling and sparkling; you hurriedly lay on more sticks; but the fire deliberately dodges them, creeps to the corner of the pile where the twigs are fewest and dampest, snaps feebly a few times, and expires in smoke. Now where are you? How far is it to the nearest match?

If you are wise, you will always make your fire before you light it. Time is never saved by doing a thing badly.

II. THE CAMP-FIRE

In the making of fires there is as much difference as in the building of houses. Everything depends upon the purpose that you have in view. There is the camp-fire, and the cooking-fire, and the smudge-fire, and the little friendship-fire,—not to speak of other minor varieties. Each of these has its own proper style of architecture, and to mix them is false art and poor economy.

The object of the camp-fire is to give heat, and incidentally light, to your tent or shanty. You can hardly build this kind of a fire unless you have a good axe and know how to chop. For the first thing that you need is a solid backlog, the thicker the better, to hold the heat and reflect it into the tent. This log must not be too dry, or it will burn out quickly. Neither must it be too damp, else it will smoulder and discourage the fire. The best wood for it is the body of a yellow birch, and, next to that, a green balsam. It should be five or six feet long, and at least two and a half feet in diameter. If you cannot find a tree thick enough, cut two or three lengths of a smaller one; lay the thickest log on the ground first, about ten or twelve feet in front of the tent; drive two strong stakes behind it, slanting a little backward; and lay the other logs on top of the first, resting against the stakes.

Now you are ready for the hand-chunks, or andirons. These are shorter sticks of wood, eight or ten inches thick, laid at right angles to the backlog, four or five feet apart. Across these you are to build up the firewood proper.

Use a dry spruce-tree, not one that has fallen, but one that is dead and still standing, if you want a lively, snapping fire. Use a hard maple or a hickory if you want a fire that will burn steadily and make few sparks. But if you like a fire to blaze up at first with a splendid flame, and then burn on with an enduring heat far into the night, a young white birch with the bark on is the tree to choose. Six or eight round sticks of this laid across the hand-chunks, with perhaps a few quarterings of a larger tree, will make a glorious fire.

But before you put these on, you must be ready to light up. A few splinters of dry spruce or pine or balsam, stood endwise against the backlog, or, better still, piled up in a pyramid between the hand-chunks; a few strips of birch-bark; and one good match,—these are all that you want. But be sure that your match is a good one. It is better to see to this before you go into the brush. Your comfort, even your life, may depend on it.

"AVEC CES ALLUMETTES-LA," said my guide at LAC ST. JEAN one day, as he vainly tried to light his pipe with a box of parlour matches from the hotel,—AVEC CES GNOGNOTTES D'ALLUMETTES ON POURRA MOURIR AU BOIS!"

In the woods, the old-fashioned brimstone match of our grandfathers—the match with a brown head and a stout stick and a dreadful smell—is the best. But if you have only one, do not trust even that to light your fire directly. Use it first to touch off a roll of birch-bark which you hold in your hand. Then, when the bark is well alight, crinkling and curling, push it under the heap of kindlings, give the flame time to take a good hold, and lay your wood over it, a stick at a time, until the whole pile is blazing. Now your fire is started. Your friendly little red-haired gnome is ready to serve you through the night.

He will dry your clothes if you are wet. He will cheer you up if you are despondent. He will diffuse an air of sociability through the camp, and draw the men together in a half circle for storytelling and jokes and singing. He will hold a flambeau for you while you spread your blankets on the boughs and dress for bed. He will keep you warm while you sleep,—at least till about three o'clock in the morning, when you dream that you are out sleighing in your pajamas, and wake up with a shiver.

"HOLA, FERDINAND, FRANCOIS!" you call out from your bed, pulling the blankets over your ears; "RAMANCHEZ LE FEU, S'IL VOUS PLAIT. C'EST UN FREITE DE CHIEN."

III. THE COOKING-FIRE

Of course such a fire as I have been describing can be used for cooking, when it has burned down a little, and there is a bed of hot embers in front of the backlog. But a correct kitchen fire should be constructed after another fashion. What you want now is not blaze, but heat, and that not diffused, but concentrated. You must be able to get close to your fire without burning your boots or scorching your face.

If you have time and the material, make a fireplace of big stones. But not of granite, for that will split with the heat, and perhaps fly in your face.

If you are in a hurry and there are no suitable stones at hand, lay two good logs nearly parallel with each other, a foot or so apart, and build your fire between them. For a cooking-fire, use split wood in short sticks. Let the first supply burn to glowing coals before you begin. A frying-pan that is lukewarm one minute and red-hot the next is the abomination of desolation. If you want black toast, have it made before a fresh, sputtering, blazing heap of wood.

In fires, as in men, an excess of energy is a lack of usefulness. The best work is done without many sparks. Just enough is the right kind of a fire and a feast.

To know how to cook is not a very elegant accomplishment. Yet there are times and seasons when it seems to come in better than familiarity with the dead languages, or much skill upon the lute.

You cannot always rely on your guides for a tasteful preparation of food. Many of them are ignorant of the difference between frying and broiling, and their notion of boiling a potato or a fish is to reduce it to a pulp. Now and then you find a man who has a natural inclination to the culinary art, and who does very well within familiar limits.

Old Edouard, the Montaignais Indian who cooked for my friends H. E. G. and C. S. D. last summer on the STE. MARGUERITE EN BAS, was such a man. But Edouard could not read, and the only way he could tell the nature of the canned provisions was by the pictures on the cans. If the picture was strange to him, there was no guessing what he would do with the contents of the can. He was capable of roasting strawberries, and serving green peas cold for dessert. One day a can of mullagatawny soup and a can of apricots were handed out to him simultaneously and without explanations. Edouard solved the problem by opening both cans and cooking them together. We had a new soup that day, MULLAGATAWNY AUX APRICOTS. It was not as bad as it sounds. It tasted somewhat like chutney.

The real reason why food that is cooked over an open fire tastes so good to us is because we are really hungry when we get it. The man who puts up provisions for camp has a great advantage over the dealers who must satisfy the pampered appetite of people in houses. I never can get any bacon in New York like that which I buy at a little shop in Quebec to take into the woods. If I ever set up in the grocery business, I shall try to get a good trade among anglers. It will be easy to please my customers.

The reputation that trout enjoy as a food-fish is partly due to the fact that they are usually cooked over an open fire. In the city they never taste as good. It is not merely a difference in freshness. It is a change in the sauce. If the truth must be told, even by an angler, there are at least five salt-water fish which are better than trout,—to eat. There is none better to catch.

IV. THE SMUDGE-FIRE

But enough of the cooking-fire. Let us turn now to the subject of the smudge, known in Lower Canada as LA BOUCANE. The smudge owes its existence to the pungent mosquito, the sanguinary black-fly, and the peppery midge,—LE MARINGOUIN, LA MOUSTIQUE, ET LE BRULOT. To what it owes its English name I do not know; but its French name means simply a thick, nauseating, intolerable smoke.

The smudge is called into being for the express purpose of creating a smoke of this kind, which is as disagreeable to the mosquito, the black-fly, and the midge as it is to the man whom they are devouring. But the man survives the smoke, while the insects succumb to it, being destroyed or driven away. Therefore the smudge, dark and bitter in itself, frequently becomes, like adversity, sweet in its uses. It must be regarded as a form of fire with which man has made friends under the pressure of a cruel necessity.

It would seem as if it ought to be the simplest affair in the world to light up a smudge. And so it is—if you are not trying.

An attempt to produce almost any other kind of a fire will bring forth smoke abundantly. But when you deliberately undertake to create a smudge, flames break from the wettest timber, and green moss blazes with a furious heat. You hastily gather handfuls of seemingly incombustible material and throw it on the fire, but the conflagration increases. Grass and green leaves hesitate for an instant and then flash up like tinder. The more you put on, the more your smudge rebels against its proper task of smudging. It makes a pleasant warmth, to encourage the black-flies; and bright light to attract and cheer the mosquitoes. Your effort is a brilliant failure.

The proper way to make a smudge is this. Begin with a very little, lowly fire. Let it be bright, but not ambitious. Don't try to make a smoke yet.

Then gather a good supply of stuff which seems likely to suppress fire without smothering it. Moss of a certain kind will do, but not the soft, feathery moss that grows so deep among the spruce-trees. Half-decayed wood is good; spongy, moist, unpleasant stuff, a vegetable wet blanket. The bark of dead evergreen trees, hemlock, spruce, or balsam, is better still. Gather a plentiful store of it. But don't try to make a smoke yet.

Let your fire burn a while longer; cheer it up a little. Get some clear, resolute, unquenchable coals aglow in the heart of it. Don't try to make a smoke yet.

Now pile on your smouldering fuel. Fan it with your hat. Kneel down and blow it, and in ten minutes you will have a smoke that will make you wish you had never been born.

That is the proper way to make a smudge. But the easiest way is to ask your guide to make it for you.

If he makes it in an old iron pot, so much the better, for then you can move it around to the windward when the breeze veers, and carry it into your tent without risk of setting everything on fire, and even take it with you in the canoe while you are fishing.

Some of the pleasantest pictures in the angler's gallery of remembrance are framed in the smoke that rises from a smudge.

With my eyes shut, I can call up a vision of eight birch-bark canoes floating side by side on Moosehead Lake, on a fair June morning, fifteen years ago. They are anchored off Green Island, riding easily on the long, gentle waves. In the stern of each canoe there is a guide with a long-handled net; in the bow, an angler with a light fly-rod; in the middle, a smudge-kettle, smoking steadily. In the air to the windward of the little fleet hovers a swarm of flies drifting down on the shore breeze, with bloody purpose in their breasts, but baffled by the protecting smoke. In the water to the leeward plays a school of speckled trout, feeding on the minnows that hang around the sunken ledges of rock. As a larger wave than usual passes over the ledges, it lifts the fish up, and you can see the big fellows, three, and four, and even five pounds apiece, poising themselves in the clear brown water. A long cast will send the fly over one of them. Let it sink a foot. Draw it up with a fluttering motion. Now the fish sees it, and turns to catch it. There is a yellow gleam in the depth, a sudden swirl on the surface; you strike sharply, and the trout is matching his strength against the spring of your four ounces of split bamboo.

You can guess at his size, as he breaks water, by the breadth of his tail: a pound of weight to an inch of tail,—that is the traditional measure, and it usually comes pretty close to the mark, at least in the case of large fish. But it is never safe to record the weight until the trout is in the canoe. As the Canadian hunters say, "Sell not the skin of the bear while he carries it."

Now the breeze that blows over Green Island drops away, and the smoke of the eight smudge-kettles falls like a thick curtain. The canoes, the dark shores of Norcross Point, the twin peaks of Spencer Mountain, the dim blue summit of Katahdin, the dazzling sapphire sky, the flocks of fleece-white clouds shepherded on high by the western wind, all have vanished. With closed eyes I see another vision, still framed in smoke,—a vision of yesterday.

It is a wild river flowing into the Gulf of St. Lawrence, on the COTE NORD, far down towards Labrador. There is a long, narrow, swift pool between two parallel ridges of rock. Over the ridge on the right pours a cataract of pale yellow foam. At the bottom of the pool, the water slides down into a furious rapid, and dashes straight through an impassable gorge half a mile to the sea. The pool is full of salmon, leaping merrily in their delight at coming into their native stream. The air is full of black-flies, rejoicing in the warmth of the July sun. On a slippery point of rock, below the fall, are two anglers, tempting the fish and enduring the flies. Behind them is an old HABITANT raising a mighty column of smoke.

Through the cloudy pillar which keeps back the Egyptian host, you see the waving of a long rod. A silver-gray fly with a barbed tail darts out across the pool, swings around with the current, well under water, and slowly works past the big rock in the centre, just at the head of the rapid. Almost past it, but not quite: for suddenly the fly disappears; the line begins to run out; the reel sings sharp and shrill; a salmon is hooked.

But how well is he hooked? That is the question. This is no easy pool to play a fish in. There is no chance to jump into a canoe and drop below him, and get the current to help you in drowning him. You cannot follow him along the shore. You cannot even lead him into quiet water, where the gaffer can creep near to him unseen and drag him in with a quick stroke. You must fight your fish to a finish, and all the advantages are on his side. The current is terribly strong. If he makes up his mind to go downstream to the sea, the only thing you can do is to hold him by main force; and then it is ten to one that the hook tears out or the leader breaks.

It is not in human nature for one man to watch another handling a fish in such a place without giving advice. "Keep the tip of your rod up. Don't let your reel overrun. Stir him up a little, he 's sulking. Don't let him 'jig,' or you'll lose him. You 're playing him too hard. There, he 's going to jump again. Drop your tip. Stop him, quick! he 's going down the rapid!"

Of course the man who is playing the salmon does not like this. If he is quick-tempered, sooner or later he tells his counsellor to shut up. But if he is a gentle, early-Christian kind of a man, wise as a serpent and harmless as a dove, he follows the advice that is given to him, promptly and exactly. Then, when it is all ended, and he has seen the big fish, with the line over his shoulder, poised for an instant on the crest of the first billow of the rapid, and has felt the leader stretch and give and SNAP!—then he can have the satisfaction, while he reels in his slack line, of saying to his friend, "Well, old man, I did everything just as you told me. But I think if I had pushed that fish a little harder at the beginning, AS I WANTED TO, I might have saved him."

But really, of course, the chances were all against it. In such a pool, most of the larger fish get away. Their weight gives them a tremendous pull. The fish that are stopped from going into the rapid, and dragged back from the curling wave, are usually the smaller ones. Here they are,—twelve pounds, eight pounds, six pounds, five pounds and a half, FOUR POUNDS! Is not this the smallest salmon that you ever saw? Not a grilse, you understand, but a real salmon, of brightest silver, hall-marked with St. Andrew's cross.

Now let us sit down for a moment and watch the fish trying to leap up the falls. There is a clear jump of about ten feet, and above that an apparently impossible climb of ten feet more up a ladder of twisting foam. A salmon darts from the boiling water at the bottom of the fall like an arrow from a bow. He rises in a beautiful curve, fins laid close to his body and tail quivering; but he has miscalculated his distance. He is on the downward curve when the water strikes him and tumbles him back. A bold little fish, not more than eighteen inches long, makes a jump at the side of the fall, where the water is thin, and is rolled over and over in the spray. A larger salmon rises close beside us with a tremendous rush, bumps his nose against a jutting rock, and flops back into the pool. Now comes a fish who has made his calculations exactly. He leaves the pool about eight feet from the foot of the fall, rises swiftly, spreads his fins, and curves his tail as if he were flying, strikes the water where it is thickest just below the brink, holds on desperately, and drives himself, with one last wriggle, through the bending stream, over the edge, and up the first step of the foaming stairway. He has obeyed the strongest instinct of his nature, and gone up to make love in the highest fresh water that he can reach.

The smoke of the smudge-fire is sharp and tearful, but a man can learn to endure a good deal of it when he can look through its rings at such scenes as these.

V. THE LITTLE FRIENDSHIP-FIRE

There are times and seasons when the angler has no need of any of the three fires of which we have been talking. He sleeps in a house. His breakfast and dinner are cooked for him in a kitchen. He is in no great danger from black-flies or mosquitoes. All he needs now, as he sets out to spend a day on the Neversink, or the Willowemoc, or the Shepaug, or the Swiftwater, is a good lunch in his pocket, and a little friendship-fire to burn pleasantly beside him while he eats his frugal fare and prolongs his noonday rest.

This form of fire does less work than any other in the world. Yet it is far from being useless; and I, for one, should be sorry to live without it. Its only use is to make a visible centre of interest where there are two or three anglers eating their lunch together, or to supply a kind of companionship to a lone fisherman. It is kindled and burns for no other purpose than to give you the sense of being at home and at ease. Why the fire should do this, I cannot tell, but it does.

You may build your friendship-fire in almost any way that pleases you; but this is the way in which you shall build it best. You have no axe, of course, so you must look about for the driest sticks that you can find. Do not seek them close beside the stream, for there they are likely to be water-soaked; but go back into the woods a bit and gather a good armful of fuel. Then break it, if you can, into lengths of about two feet, and construct your fire in the following fashion.

Lay two sticks parallel, and put between them a pile of dried grass, dead leaves, small twigs, and the paper in which your lunch was wrapped. Then lay two other sticks crosswise on top of your first pair. Strike your match and touch your kindlings. As the fire catches, lay on other pairs of sticks, each pair crosswise to the pair that is below it, until you have a pyramid of flame. This is "a Micmac fire" such as the Indians make in the woods.

Now you can pull off your wading-boots and warm your feet at the blaze. You can toast your bread if you like. You can even make shift to broil one of your trout, fastened on the end of a birch twig if you have a fancy that way. When your hunger is satisfied, you shake out the crumbs for the birds and the squirrels, pick up a stick with a coal at the end to light your pipe, put some more wood on your fire, and settle down for an hour's reading if you have a book in your pocket, or for a good talk if you have a comrade with you.

The stream of time flows swift and smooth, by such a fire as this. The moments slip past unheeded; the sun sinks down his western arch; the shadows begin to fall across the brook; it is time to move on for the afternoon fishing. The fire has almost burned out. But do not trust it too much. Throw some sand over it, or bring a hatful of water from the brook to pour on it, until you are sure that the last glowing ember is extinguished, and nothing but the black coals and the charred ends of the sticks are left.

Even the little friendship-fire must keep the law of the bush. All lights out when their purpose is fulfilled!

VI. ALTARS OF REMEMBRANCE

It is a question that we have often debated, in the informal meetings of our Petrine Club: Which is pleasanter,—to fish an old stream, or a new one?

The younger members are all for the "fresh woods and pastures new." They speak of the delight of turning off from the high-road into some faintly-marked trail; following it blindly through the forest, not knowing how far you have to go; hearing the voice of waters sounding through the woodland; leaving the path impatiently and striking straight across the underbrush; scrambling down a steep bank, pushing through a thicket of alders, and coming out suddenly, face to face with a beautiful, strange brook. It reminds you, of course, of some old friend. It is a little like the Beaverkill, or the Ausable, or the Gale River. And yet it is different. Every stream has its own character and disposition. Your new acquaintance invites you to a day of discoveries. If the water is high, you will follow it down, and have easy fishing. If the water is low, you will go upstream, and fish "fine and far-off." Every turn in the avenue which the little river has made for you opens up a new view,—a rocky gorge where the deep pools are divided by white-footed falls; a lofty forest where the shadows are deep and the trees arch overhead; a flat, sunny stretch where the stream is spread out, and pebbly islands divide the channels, and the big fish are lurking at the sides in the sheltered corners under the bushes. From scene to scene you follow on, delighted and expectant, until the night suddenly drops its veil, and then you will be lucky if you can find your way home in the dark!

Yes, it is all very good, this exploration of new streams. But, for my part, I like still better to go back to a familiar little river, and fish or dream along the banks where I have dreamed and fished before. I know every bend and curve: the sharp turn where the water runs under the roots of the old hemlock-tree; the snaky glen, where the alders stretch their arms far out across the stream; the meadow reach, where the trout are fat and silvery, and will only rise about sunrise or sundown, unless the day is cloudy; the Naiad's Elbow, where the brook rounds itself, smooth and dimpled, to embrace a cluster of pink laurel-bushes. All these I know; yes, and almost every current and eddy and backwater I know long before I come to it. I remember where I caught the big trout the first year I came to the stream; and where I lost a bigger one. I remember the pool where there were plenty of good fish last year, and wonder whether they are there now.

Better things than these I remember: the companions with whom I have followed the stream in days long past; the rendezvous with a comrade at the place where the rustic bridge crosses the brook; the hours of sweet converse beside the friendship-fire; the meeting at twilight with my lady Graygown and the children, who have come down by the wood-road to walk home with me.

Surely it is pleasant to follow an old stream. Flowers grow along its banks which are not to be found anywhere else in the wide world. "There is rosemary, that 's for remembrance; and there is pansies, that 's for thoughts!"

One May evening, a couple of years since, I was angling in the Swiftwater, and came upon Joseph Jefferson, stretched out on a large rock in midstream, and casting the fly down a long pool. He had passed the threescore years and ten, but he was as eager and as happy as a boy in his fishing.

"You here!" I cried. "What good fortune brought you into these waters?"

"Ah," he answered, "I fished this brook forty-five years ago. It was in the Paradise Valley that I first thought of Rip Van Winkle. I wanted to come back again for the sake of old times."

But what has all this to do with an open fire? I will tell you. It is at the places along the stream, where the little flames of love and friendship have been kindled in bygone days, that the past returns most vividly. These are the altars of remembrance.

It is strange how long a small fire will leave its mark. The charred sticks, the black coals, do not decay easily. If they lie well up the hank, out of reach of the spring floods, they will stay there for years. If you have chanced to build a rough fireplace of stones from the brook, it seems almost as if it would last forever.

There is a mossy knoll beneath a great butternut-tree on the Swiftwater where such a fireplace was built four years ago; and whenever I come to that place now I lay the rod aside, and sit down for a little while by the fast-flowing water, and remember.

This is what I see: A man wading up the stream, with a creel over his shoulder, and perhaps a dozen trout in it; two little lads in gray corduroys running down the path through the woods to meet him, one carrying a frying-pan and a kettle, the other with a basket of lunch on his arm. Then I see the bright flames leaping up in the fireplace, and hear the trout sizzling in the pan, and smell the appetizing odour. Now I see the lads coming back across the foot-bridge that spans the stream, with a bottle of milk from the nearest farmhouse. They are laughing and teetering as they balance along the single plank. Now the table is spread on the moss. How good the lunch tastes! Never were there such pink-fleshed trout, such crisp and savoury slices of broiled bacon. Douglas, (the beloved doll that the younger lad shamefacedly brings out from the pocket of his jacket,) must certainly have some of it. And after the lunch is finished, and the bird's portion has been scattered on the moss, we creep carefully on our hands and knees to the edge of the brook, and look over the bank at the big trout that is poising himself in the amber water. We have tried a dozen times to catch him, but never succeeded. The next time, perhaps—

Well, the fireplace is still standing. The butternut-tree spreads its broad branches above the stream. The violets and the bishop's-caps and the wild anemones are sprinkled over the banks. The yellow-throat and the water-thrush and the vireos still sing the same tunes in the thicket. And the elder of the two lads often comes back with me to that pleasant place and shares my fisherman's luck beside the Swiftwater.

But the younger lad?

Ah, my little Barney, you have gone to follow a new stream,—clear as crystal,—flowing through fields of wonderful flowers that never fade. It is a strange river to Teddy and me; strange and very far away. Some day we shall see it with you; and you will teach us the names of those blossoms that do not wither. But till then, little Barney, the other lad and I will follow the old stream that flows by the woodland fireplace,—your altar.

Rue grows here. Yes, there is plenty of rue. But there is also rosemary, that 's for remembrance! And close beside it I see a little heart's-ease.

A SLUMBER SONG FOR THE FISHERMAN'S CHILD

Furl your sail, my little boatie;
Here 's the haven, still and deep,
Where the dreaming tides, in-streaming,
Up the channel creep.
See, the sunset breeze is dying;
Hark, the plover, landward flying,
Softly down the twilight crying;
Come to anchor, little boatie,
In the port of Sleep.

Far away, my little boatie,
Roaring waves are white with foam;
Ships are striving, onward driving,
Day and night they roam.
Father 's at the deep-sea trawling,
In the darkness, rowing, hauling,
While the hungry winds are calling,—
God protect him, little boatie,
Bring him safely home!

Not for you, my little boatie,
Is the wide and weary sea;
You 're too slender, and too tender,
You must rest with me.
All day long you have been straying
Up and down the shore and playing;
Come to port, make no delaying!
Day is over, little boatie,
Night falls suddenly.

Furl your sail, my little boatie;
Fold your wings, my tired dove.
Dews are sprinkling, stars are twinkling
Drowsily above.
Cease from sailing, cease from rowing;
Rock upon the dream-tide, knowing
Safely o'er your rest are glowing,
All the night, my little boatie,

Harbour-lights of love.

The complete Poems of Henry Van Dyke

SONGS OUT OF DOORS

EARLY VERSES
THE AFTER-ECHO
How long the echoes love to play

Around the shore of silence, as a wave
Retreating circles down the sand!
One after one, with sweet delay,
The mellow sounds that cliff and island gave,
Have lingered in the crescent bay,
Until, by lightest breezes fanned,
They float far off beyond the dying day
And leave it still as death.
But hark,—
Another singing breath
Comes from the edge of dark;
A note as clear and slow
As falls from some enchanted bell,
Or spirit, passing from the world below,
That whispers back, Farewell.
So in the heart,
When, fading slowly down the past,
Fond memories depart,
And each that leaves it seems the last;
Long after all the rest are flown,
Returns a solitary tone,—
The after-echo of departed years,—
And touches all the soul to tears.
1871.

DULCIORA
A tear that trembles for a little while
Upon the trembling eyelid, till the world
Wavers within its circle like a dream,
Holds more of meaning in its narrow orb
Than all the distant landscape that it blurs.
A smile that hovers round a mouth beloved,
Like the faint pulsing of the Northern Light,
And grows in silence to an amber dawn
Born in the sweetest depths of trustful eyes,
Is dearer to the soul than sun or star.
A joy that falls into the hollow heart
From some far-lifted height of love unseen,
Unknown, makes a more perfect melody
Than hidden brooks that murmur in the dusk,
Or fall athwart the cliff with wavering gleam.
Ah, not for their own sake are earth and sky
And the fair ministries of Nature dear,
But as they set themselves unto the tune
That fills our life; as light mysterious
Flows from within and glorifies the world.
For so a common wayside blossom, touched
With tender thought, assumes a grace more sweet
Than crowns the royal lily of the South;
And so a well-remembered perfume seems
The breath of one who breathes in Paradise.
1872.

THREE ALPINE SONNETS
I
THE GLACIER
At dawn in silence moves the mighty stream,
The silver-crested waves no murmur make;
But far away the avalanches wake
The rumbling echoes, dull as in a dream;
Their momentary thunders, dying, seem
To fall into the stillness, flake by flake,
And leave the hollow air with naught to break
The frozen spell of solitude supreme.
At noon unnumbered rills begin to spring
Beneath the burning sun, and all the walls
Of all the ocean-blue crevasses ring
With liquid lyrics of their waterfalls;
As if a poet's heart had felt the glow
Of sovereign love, and song began to flow.
Zermatt, 1872.

II
THE SNOW-FIELD
White Death had laid his pall upon the plain,
And crowned the mountain-peaks like monarchs dead;
The vault of heaven was glaring overhead
With pitiless light that filled my eyes with pain;
And while I vainly longed, and looked in vain
For sign or trace of life, my spirit said,
"Shall any living thing that dares to tread
This royal lair of Death escape again?"
But even then I saw before my feet
A line of pointed footprints in the snow:
Some roving chamois, but an hour ago,
Had passed this way along his journey fleet,
And left a message from a friend unknown
To cheer my pilgrim-heart, no more alone.
Zermatt, 1872.

III
MOVING BELLS
I love the hour that comes, with dusky hair
And dewy feet, along the Alpine dells,
To lead the cattle forth. A thousand bells
Go chiming after her across the fair
And flowery uplands, while the rosy flare
Of sunset on the snowy mountain dwells,
And valleys darken, and the drowsy spells
Of peace are woven through the purple air.
Dear is the magic of this hour: she seems
To walk before the dark by falling rills,
And lend a sweeter song to hidden streams;
She opens all the doors of night, and fills
With moving bells the music of my dreams,
That wander far among the sleeping hills.
Gstaad, August, 1909.

MATINS

Flowers rejoice when night is done,
Lift their heads to greet the sun;
Sweetest looks and odours raise,
In a silent hymn of praise.
So my heart would turn away
From the darkness to the day;
Lying open in God's sight
Like a flower in the light.

THE PARTING AND THE COMING GUEST

Who watched the worn-out Winter die?
Who, peering through the window-pane
At nightfall, under sleet and rain
Saw the old graybeard totter by?
Who listened to his parting sigh,
The sobbing of his feeble breath,
His whispered colloquy with Death,
And when his all of life was done
Stood near to bid a last good-bye?
Of all his former friends not one
Saw the forsaken Winter die.
Who welcomed in the maiden Spring?
Who heard her footfall, swift and light
As fairy-dancing in the night?
Who guessed what happy dawn would bring
The flutter of her bluebird's wing,
The blossom of her mayflower-face
To brighten every shady place?
One morning, down the village street,
"Oh, here am I," we heard her sing,—
And none had been awake to greet
The coming of the maiden Spring.
But look, her violet eyes are wet
With bright, unfallen, dewy tears;
And in her song my fancy hears
A note of sorrow trembling yet.
Perhaps, beyond the town, she met
Old Winter as he limped away
To die forlorn, and let him lay
His weary head upon her knee,
And kissed his forehead with regret
For one so gray and lonely,—see,
Her eyes with tender tears are wet.
And so, by night, while we were all at rest,
I think the coming sped the parting guest.
1873.

IF ALL THE SKIES

If all the skies were sunshine,
Our faces would be fain
To feel once more upon them
The cooling plash of rain.
If all the world were music,
Our hearts would often long
For one sweet strain of silence.
To break the endless song.
If life were always merry,
Our souls would seek relief,
And rest from weary laughter
In the quiet arms of grief.

WINGS OF A DOVE
I
At sunset, when the rosy light was dying
Far down the pathway of the west,
I saw a lonely dove in silence flying,
To be at rest.
Pilgrim of air, I cried, could I but borrow
Thy wandering wings, thy freedom blest,
I'd fly away from every careful sorrow,
And find my rest.
II
But when the filmy veil of dusk was falling,
Home flew the dove to seek his nest,
Deep in the forest where his mate was calling
To love and rest.
Peace, heart of mine! no longer sigh to wander;
Lose not thy life in barren quest.
There are no happy islands over yonder;
Come home and rest.
1874.

THE FALL OF THE LEAVES
I
In warlike pomp, with banners flowing,
The regiments of autumn stood:
I saw their gold and scarlet glowing
From every hillside, every wood.
Above the sea the clouds were keeping
Their secret leaguer, gray and still;
They sent their misty vanguard creeping
With muffled step from hill to hill.
All day the sullen armies drifted
Athwart the sky with slanting rain;
At sunset for a space they lifted,
With dusk they settled down again.
II
At dark the winds began to blow
With mutterings distant, low;
From sea and sky they called their strength
Till with an angry, broken roar,
Like billows on an unseen shore,
Their fury burst at length.
I heard through the night
The rush and the clamour;
The pulse of the fight
Like blows of Thor's hammer;
The pattering flight
Of the leaves, and the anguished
Moan of the forest vanquished.
At daybreak came a gusty song:
"Shout! the winds are strong.
The little people of the leaves are fled.
Shout! The Autumn is dead!"
III
The storm is ended! The impartial sun
Laughs down upon the battle lost and won,
And crowns the triumph of the cloudy host
In rolling lines retreating to the coast.
But we, fond lovers of the woodland shade,
And grateful friends of every fallen leaf,
Forget the glories of the cloud-parade,
And walk the ruined woods in quiet grief.

For ever so our thoughtful hearts repeat
On fields of triumph dirges of defeat;
And still we turn on gala-days to tread
Among the rustling memories of the dead.
1874.

A SNOW-SONG

Does the snow fall at sea?
Yes, when the north winds blow,
When the wild clouds fly low,
Out of each gloomy wing,
Silently glimmering,
Over the stormy sea
Falleth the snow.
Does the snow hide the sea?
Nay, on the tossing plains
Never a flake remains;
Drift never resteth there;
Vanishing everywhere,
Into the hungry sea
Falleth the snow.
What means the snow at sea?
Whirled in the veering blast,
Thickly the flakes drive past;
Each like a childish ghost
Wavers, and then is lost;
In the forgetful sea
Fadeth the snow.
1875.

ROSLIN AND HAWTHORNDEN

Fair Roslin Chapel, how divine
The art that reared thy costly shrine!
Thy carven columns must have grown
By magic, like a dream in stone.
Yet not within thy storied wall
Would I in adoration fall,
So gladly as within the glen
That leads to lovely Hawthornden.

A long-drawn aisle, with roof of green
And vine-clad pillars, while between,
The Esk runs murmuring on its way,
In living music night and day.
Within the temple of this wood
The martyrs of the covenant stood,
And rolled the psalm, and poured the prayer,
From Nature's solemn altar-stair.
Edinburgh, 1877.

SONGS OUT OF DOORS
LATER POEMS
WHEN TULIPS BLOOM

I

When tulips bloom in Union Square,
And timid breaths of vernal air
Go wandering down the dusty town,
Like children lost in Vanity Fair;
When every long, unlovely row
Of westward houses stands aglow,
And leads the eyes to sunset skies
Beyond the hills where green trees grow;

Then weary seems the street parade,
And weary books, and weary trade:
I'm only wishing to go a-fishing;
For this the month of May was made.

II

I guess the pussy-willows now
Are creeping out on every bough
Along the brook; and robins look
For early worms behind the plough.
The thistle-birds have changed their dun,
For yellow coats, to match the sun;
And in the same array of flame
The Dandelion Show's begun.
The flocks of young anemones
Are dancing round the budding trees:
Who can help wishing to go a-fishing
In days as full of joy as these?

III

I think the meadow-lark's clear sound
Leaks upward slowly from the ground,
While on the wing the bluebirds ring
Their wedding-bells to woods around.
The flirting chewink calls his dear
Behind the bush; and very near,
Where water flows, where green grass grows,
Song-sparrows gently sing, "Good cheer."
And, best of all, through twilight's calm
The hermit-thrush repeats his psalm.
How much I'm wishing to go a-fishing
In days so sweet with music's balm!

IV

'Tis not a proud desire of mine;
I ask for nothing superfine;
No heavy weight, no salmon great,
To break the record, or my line.
Only an idle little stream,
Whose amber waters softly gleam,
Where I may wade through woodland shade,
And cast the fly, and loaf, and dream:
Only a trout or two, to dart
From foaming pools, and try my art:
'Tis all I'm wishing—old-fashioned fishing,
And just a day on Nature's heart.
1894.

THE WHIP-POOR-WILL

Do you remember, father,—
It seems so long ago,—
The day we fished together
Along the Pocono?
At dusk I waited for you,
Beside the lumber-mill,
And there I heard a hidden bird
That chanted, "whip-poor-will,"
"Whippoorwill! whippoorwill!"
Sad and shrill,—"whippoorwill!"
The place was all deserted;
The mill-wheel hung at rest;
The lonely star of evening
Was throbbing in the west;

The veil of night was falling;
The winds were folded still;
And everywhere the trembling air
Re-echoed "whip-poor-will!"
"Whippoorwill! whippoorwill!"
Sad and shrill,—"whippoorwill!"
You seemed so long in coming,
I felt so much alone;
The wide, dark world was round me,
And life was all unknown;
The hand of sorrow touched me,
And made my senses thrill
With all the pain that haunts the strain
Of mournful whip-poor-will.
"Whippoorwill! whippoorwill!"
Sad and shrill,—"whippoorwill!"
What knew I then of trouble?
An idle little lad,
I had not learned the lessons
That make men wise and sad.
I dreamed of grief and parting,
And something seemed to fill
My heart with tears, while in my ears
Resounded "whip-poor-will."
"Whippoorwill! whippoorwill!"
Sad and shrill,—"whippoorwill!"
'Twas but a cloud of sadness,
That lightly passed away;
But I have learned the meaning
Of sorrow, since that day.
For nevermore at twilight,
Beside the silent mill,
I'll wait for you, in the falling dew,
And hear the whip-poor-will.
"Whippoorwill! whippoorwill!"
Sad and shrill,—"whippoorwill!"
But if you still remember
In that fair land of light,
The pains and fears that touch us
Along this edge of night,
I think all earthly grieving,
And all our mortal ill,
To you must seem like a sad boy's dream.
Who hears the whip-poor-will.
"Whippoorwill! whippoorwill!"
A passing thrill,—"whippoorwill!"
1894.

THE LILY OF YORROW

Deep in the heart of the forest the lily of Yorrow is growing;
Blue is its cup as the sky, and with mystical odour o'erflowing;
Faintly it falls through the shadowy glades when the south wind is blowing.
Sweet are the primroses pale and the violets after a shower;
Sweet are the borders of pinks and the blossoming grapes on the bower;
Sweeter by far is the breath of that far-away woodland flower.
Searching and strange in its sweetness, it steals like a perfume enchanted
Under the arch of the forest, and all who perceive it are haunted,
Seeking and seeking for ever, till sight of the lily is granted.
Who can describe how it grows, with its chalice of lazuli leaning
Over a crystalline spring, where the ferns and the mosses are greening?
Who can imagine its beauty, or utter the depth of its meaning?
Calm of the journeying stars, and repose of the mountains olden,
Joy of the swift-running rivers, and glory of sunsets golden,
Secrets that cannot be told in the heart of the flower are holden.
Surely to see it is peace and the crown of a life-long endeavour;
Surely to pluck it is gladness,—but they who have found it can never
Tell of the gladness and peace: they are hid from our vision for ever.
'Twas but a moment ago that a comrade was walking near me:
Turning aside from the pathway he murmured a greeting to cheer me,—
Then he was lost in the shade, and I called but he did not hear me.
Why should I dream he is dead, and bewail him with passionate sorrow?
Surely I know there is gladness in finding the lily of Yorrow:
He has discovered it first, and perhaps I shall find it to-morrow.
1894.

THE VEERY

The moonbeams over Arno's vale in silver flood were pouring,
When first I heard the nightingale a long-lost love deploring.
So passionate, so full of pain, it sounded strange and eerie;
I longed to hear a simpler strain,—the wood-notes of the veery.
The laverock sings a bonny lay above the Scottish heather;
It sprinkles down from far away like light and love together;
He drops the golden notes to greet his brooding mate, his dearie;
I only know one song more sweet,—the vespers of the veery.
In English gardens, green and bright and full of fruity treasure,
I heard the blackbird with delight repeat his merry measure:
The ballad was a pleasant one, the tune was loud and cheery,
And yet, with every setting sun, I listened for the veery.

But far away, and far away, the tawny thrush is singing;
New England woods, at close of day, with that clear chant are ringing:
And when my light of life is low, and heart and flesh are weary,
I fain would hear, before I go, the wood-notes of the veery.
1895.

THE SONG-SPARROW
There is a bird I know so well,
It seems as if he must have sung
Beside my crib when I was young;
Before I knew the way to spell
The name of even the smallest bird,
His gentle-joyful song I heard.
Now see if you can tell, my dear,
What bird it is that, every year,
Sings "Sweet—sweet—sweet—very merry cheer."
He comes in March, when winds are strong,
And snow returns to hide the earth;
But still he warms his heart with mirth,
And waits for May. He lingers long
While flowers fade; and every day
Repeats his small, contented lay;
As if to say, we need not fear
The season's change, if love is here
With "Sweet—sweet—sweet—very merry cheer."
He does not wear a Joseph's-coat
Of many colours, smart and gay;
His suit is Quaker brown and gray,
With darker patches at his throat.
And yet of all the well-dressed throng
Not one can sing so brave a song.
It makes the pride of looks appear
A vain and foolish thing, to hear
His "Sweet—sweet—sweet—very merry cheer."
A lofty place he does not love,
But sits by choice, and well at ease,
In hedges, and in little trees
That stretch their slender arms above
The meadow-brook; and there he sings
Till all the field with pleasure rings;
And so he tells in every ear,
That lowly homes to heaven are near
In "Sweet—sweet—sweet—very merry cheer."
I like the tune, I like the words;
They seem so true, so free from art,
So friendly, and so full of heart,
That if but one of all the birds
Could be my comrade everywhere,
My little brother of the air,
I'd choose the song-sparrow, my dear,
Because he'd bless me, every year,
With "Sweet—sweet—sweet—very merry cheer."
1895.

THE MARYLAND YELLOW-THROAT
When May bedecks the naked trees
With tassels and embroideries,
And many blue-eyed violets beam
Along the edges of the stream,
I hear a voice that seems to say,
Now near at hand, now far away,
"Witchery—witchery—witchery."
An incantation so serene,
So innocent, befits the scene:
There's magic in that small bird's note—
See, there he flits—the Yellow-throat;
A living sunbeam, tipped with wings,
A spark of light that shines and sings
"Witchery—witchery—witchery."
You prophet with a pleasant name,
If out of Mary-land you came,
You know the way that thither goes
Where Mary's lovely garden grows:
Fly swiftly back to her, I pray,
And try to call her down this way,
"Witchery—witchery—witchery!"
Tell her to leave her cockle-shells,
And all her little silver bells
That blossom into melody,
And all her maids less fair than she.
She does not need these pretty things,
For everywhere she comes, she brings
"Witchery—witchery—witchery!"
The woods are greening overhead,
And flowers adorn each mossy bed;
The waters babble as they run—
One thing is lacking, only one:
If Mary were but here to-day,
I would believe your charming lay,
"Witchery—witchery—witchery!"
Along the shady road I look—
Who's coming now across the brook?
A woodland maid, all robed in white—
The leaves dance round her with delight,
The stream laughs out beneath her feet—
Sing, merry bird, the charm's complete,
"Witchery—witchery—witchery!"
1895.

A NOVEMBER DAISY
Afterthought of summer's bloom!
Late arrival at the feast,
Coming when the songs have ceased
And the merry guests departed,
Leaving but an empty room,
Silence, solitude, and gloom,—
Are you lonely, heavy-hearted;
You, the last of all your kind,
Nodding in the autumn-wind;
Now that all your friends are flown,
Blooming late and all alone?
Nay, I wrong you, little flower,
Reading mournful mood of mine
In your looks, that give no sign
Of a spirit dark and cheerless!
You possess the heavenly power
That rejoices in the hour.
Glad, contented, free, and fearless,
Lift a sunny face to heaven
When a sunny day is given!
Make a summer of your own,

Blooming late and all alone!
Once the daisies gold and white
Sea-like through the meadow rolled:
Once my heart could hardly hold
All its pleasures. I remember,
In the flood of youth's delight
Separate joys were lost to sight.
That was summer! Now November
Sets the perfect flower apart;
Gives each blossom of the heart
Meaning, beauty, grace unknown,—
Blooming late and all alone.
November, 1899.

THE ANGLER'S REVEILLE

What time the rose of dawn is laid across the lips of night,
And all the little watchman-stars have fallen asleep in light,
'Tis then a merry wind awakes, and runs from tree to tree,
And borrows words from all the birds to sound the reveille.
This is the carol the Robin throws
Over the edge of the valley;
Listen how boldly it flows,
Sally on sally:
Tirra-lirra,
Early morn,
New born!
Day is near,
Clear, clear.
Down the river
All a-quiver,
Fish are breaking;
Time for waking,
Tup, tup, tup!
Do you hear?
All clear—
Wake up!
The phantom flood of dreams has ebbed and vanished with the dark,
And like a dove the heart forsakes the prison of the ark;
Now forth she fares thro' friendly woods and diamond-fields of dew,
While every voice cries out "Rejoice!" as if the world were new.
This is the ballad the Bluebird sings,
Unto his mate replying,
Shaking the tune from his wings
While he is flying:
Surely, surely, surely,
Life is dear
Even here.
Blue above,
You to love,
Purely, purely, purely.
There's wild azalea on the hill, and iris down the dell,
And just one spray of lilac still abloom beside the well;
The columbine adorns the rocks, the laurel buds grow pink,
Along the stream white arums gleam, and violets bend to drink.
This is the song of the Yellow-throat,
Fluttering gaily beside you;
Hear how each voluble note
Offers to guide you:
Which way, sir?
I say, sir,
Let me teach you,
I beseech you!
Are you wishing
Jolly fishing?
This way, sir!
I'll teach you.
Then come, my friend, forget your foes and leave your fears behind,
And wander forth to try your luck, with cheerful, quiet mind;
For be your fortune great or small, you take what God will give,
And all the day your heart will say, "'Tis luck enough to live."
This is the song the Brown Thrush flings
Out of his thicket of roses;
Hark how it bubbles and rings,
Mark how it closes:
Luck, luck,
What luck?
Good enough for me,
I'm alive, you see!
Sun shining,
No repining;
Never borrow
Idle sorrow;
Drop it!
Cover it up!
Hold your cup!
Joy will fill it,
Don't spill it,
Steady, be ready,
Good luck!
1899.

THE RUBY-CROWNED KINGLET

I

Where's your kingdom, little king?
Where the land you call your own,
Where your palace and your throne?
Fluttering lightly on the wing
Through the blossom-world of May,
Whither lies your royal way,
Little king?
Far to northward lies a land
Where the trees together stand
Closely as the blades of wheat
When the summer is complete.
Rolling like an ocean wide
Over vale and mountainside,
Balsam, hemlock, spruce and pine,—
All those mighty trees are mine.
There's a river flowing free,—
All its waves belong to me.
There's a lake so clear and bright
Stars shine out of it all night;
Rowan-berries round it spread

Like a belt of coral red.
Never royal garden planned
Fair as my Canadian land!
There I build my summer nest,
There I reign and there I rest,
While from dawn to dark I sing,
Happy kingdom! Lucky king!
II
Back again, my little king!
Is your happy kingdom lost
To the rebel knave, Jack Frost?
Have you felt the snow-flakes sting?
Houseless, homeless in October,
Whither now? Your plight is sober,
Exiled king!
Far to southward lie the regions
Where my loyal flower-legions
Hold possession of the year,
Filling every month with cheer.
Christmas wakes the winter rose;
New Year daffodils unclose;
Yellow jasmine through the wood
Flows in February flood,
Dropping from the tallest trees
Golden streams that never freeze.
Thither now I take my flight
Down the pathway of the night,
Till I see the southern moon
Glisten on the broad lagoon,
Where the cypress' dusky green,
And the dark magnolia's sheen,
Weave a shelter round my home.
There the snow-storms never come;
There the bannered mosses gray
Like a curtain gently sway,
Hanging low on every side
Round the covert where I bide,
Till the March azalea glows,
Royal red and heavenly rose,
Through the Carolina glade
Where my winter home is made.
There I hold my southern court,
Full of merriment and sport:
There I take my ease and sing,
Happy kingdom! Lucky king!
III
Little boaster, vagrant king,
Neither north nor south is yours,
You've no kingdom that endures!
Wandering every fall and spring,
With your ruby crown so slender,
Are you only a Pretender,
Landless king?
Never king by right divine
Ruled a richer realm than mine!
What are lands and golden crowns,
Armies, fortresses and towns,
Jewels, sceptres, robes and rings,—
What are these to song and wings?
Everywhere that I can fly,
There I own the earth and sky;
Everywhere that I can sing.

There I'm happy as a king.
1900.

SCHOOL
I put my heart to school
In the world where men grow wise:
"Go out," I said, "and learn the rule;
Come back when you win a prize."
My heart came back again:
"Now where is the prize?" I cried.—
"The rule was false, and the prize was pain,
And the teacher's name was Pride."
I put my heart to school
In the woods where veeries sing
And brooks run clear and cool,
In the fields where wild flowers spring.
"And why do you stay so long
My heart, and where do you roam?"
The answer came with a laugh and a song,—
"I find this school is home."
April, 1901.

INDIAN SUMMER
A silken curtain veils the skies,
And half conceals from pensive eyes
The bronzing tokens of the fall;
A calmness broods upon the hills,
And summer's parting dream distils
A charm of silence over all.
The stacks of corn, in brown array,
Stand waiting through the tranquil day,
Like tattered wigwams on the plain;
The tribes that find a shelter there
Are phantom peoples, forms of air,
And ghosts of vanished joy and pain.
At evening when the crimson crest
Of sunset passes down the West,
I hear the whispering host returning;
On far-off fields, by elm and oak,
I see the lights, I smell the smoke,—
The Camp-fires of the Past are burning.
Tertius and Henry van Dyke.
November, 1903.

SPRING IN THE NORTH
I
Ah, who will tell me, in these leaden days,
Why the sweet Spring delays,
And where she hides,—the dear desire
Of every heart that longs
For bloom, and fragrance, and the ruby fire
Of maple-buds along the misty hills,
And that immortal call which fills
The waiting wood with songs?
The snow-drops came so long ago,
It seemed that Spring was near!
But then returned the snow
With biting winds, and earth grew sere,
And sullen clouds drooped low
To veil the sadness of a hope deferred:
Then rain, rain, rain, incessant rain
Beat on the window-pane,

Through which I watched the solitary bird
That braved the tempest, buffeted and tossed
With rumpled feathers down the wind again.
Oh, were the seeds all lost
When winter laid the wild flowers in their tomb?
I searched the woods in vain
For blue hepaticas, and trilliums white,
And trailing arbutus, the Spring's delight,
Starring the withered leaves with rosy bloom.
But every night the frost
To all my longing spoke a silent nay,
And told me Spring was far away.
Even the robins were too cold to sing,
Except a broken and discouraged note,—
Only the tuneful sparrow, on whose throat
Music has put her triple finger-print,
Lifted his head and sang my heart a hint,—
"Wait, wait, wait! oh, wait a while for Spring!"

II
But now, Carina, what divine amends
For all delay! What sweetness treasured up,
What wine of joy that blends
A hundred flavours in a single cup,
Is poured into this perfect day!
For look, sweet heart, here are the early flowers
That lingered on their way,
Thronging in haste to kiss the feet of May,
Entangled with the bloom of later hours,—
Anemones and cinque-foils, violets blue
And white, and iris richly gleaming through
The grasses of the meadow, and a blaze
Of butter-cups and daisies in the field,
Filling the air with praise,
As if a chime of golden bells had pealed!
The frozen songs within the breast
Of silent birds that hid in leafless woods,
Melt into rippling floods
Of gladness unrepressed.
Now oriole and bluebird, thrush and lark,
Warbler and wren and vireo,
Mingle their melody; the living spark
Of Love has touched the fuel of desire,
And every heart leaps up in singing fire.
It seems as if the land
Were breathing deep beneath the sun's caress,
Trembling with tenderness,
While all the woods expand,
In shimmering clouds of rose and gold and green,
To veil a joy too sacred to be seen.

III
Come, put your hand in mine,
True love, long sought and found at last,
And lead me deep into the Spring divine
That makes amends for all the wintry past.
For all the flowers and songs I feared to miss
Arrive with you;
And in the lingering pressure of your kiss
My dreams come true;
And in the promise of your generous eyes
I read the mystic sign
Of joy more perfect made
Because so long delayed,

And bliss enhanced by rapture of surprise.
Ah, think not early love alone is strong;
He loveth best whose heart has learned to wait:
Dear messenger of Spring that tarried long,
You're doubly dear because you come so late.

SPRING IN THE SOUTH
Now in the oak the sap of life is welling,
Tho' to the bough the rusty leafage clings;
Now on the elm the misty buds are swelling;
Every little pine-wood grows alive with wings;
Blue-jays are fluttering, yodeling and crying,
Meadow-larks sailing low above the faded grass,
Red-birds whistling clear, silent robins flying,—
Who has waked the birds up? What has come to pass?
Last year's cotton-plants, desolately bowing,
Tremble in the March-wind, ragged and forlorn;
Red are the hillsides of the early ploughing,
Gray are the lowlands, waiting for the corn.
Earth seems asleep, but she is only feigning;
Deep in her bosom thrills a sweet unrest;
Look where the jasmine lavishly is raining
Jove's golden shower into Danäe's breast!
Now on the plum-tree a snowy bloom is sifted,
Now on the peach-tree, the glory of the rose,
Far o'er the hills a tender haze is drifted,
Full to the brim the yellow river flows.
Dark cypress boughs with vivid jewels glisten,
Greener than emeralds shining in the sun.
Whence comes the magic? Listen, sweetheart, listen!
The mocking-bird is singing: Spring is begun.
Hark, in his song no tremor of misgiving!
All of his heart he pours into his lay,—
"Love, love, love, and pure delight of living:
Winter is forgotten: here's a happy day!"
Fair in your face I read the flowery presage,
Snowy on your brow and rosy on your mouth:
Sweet in your voice I hear the season's message,—
Love, love, love, and Spring in the South!
1904.

A NOON SONG
There are songs for the morning and songs for the night,
For sunrise and sunset, the stars and the moon;
But who will give praise to the fulness of light,
And sing us a song of the glory of noon?
Oh, the high noon, the clear noon,
The noon with golden crest;
When the blue sky burns, and the great sun turns
With his face to the way of the west!
How swiftly he rose in the dawn of his strength!
How slowly he crept as the morning wore by!
Ah, steep was the climbing that led him at length
To the height of his throne in the wide summer sky.
Oh, the long toil, the slow toil,
The toil that may not rest,
Till the sun looks down from his journey's crown,
To the wonderful way of the west!
Then a quietness falls over meadow and hill,
The wings of the wind in the forest are furled,
The river runs softly, the birds are all still,
The workers are resting all over the world.

Oh, the good hour, the kind hour,
The hour that calms the breast!
Little inn half-way on the road of the day,
Where it follows the turn to the west!
There's a plentiful feast in the maple-tree shade,
The lilt of a song to an old-fashioned tune,
The talk of a friend, or the kiss of a maid,
To sweeten the cup that we drink to the noon.
Oh, the deep noon, the full noon,
Of all the day the best!
When the blue sky burns, and the great sun turns
To his home by the way of the west!
1906.

LIGHT BETWEEN THE TREES
Long, long, long the trail
Through the brooding forest-gloom,
Down the shadowy, lonely vale
Into silence, like a room
Where the light of life has fled,
And the jealous curtains close
Round the passionless repose
Of the silent dead.
Plod, plod, plod away,
Step by step in mouldering moss;
Thick branches bar the day
Over languid streams that cross
Softly, slowly, with a sound
Like a smothered weeping,
In their aimless creeping
Through enchanted ground.
"Yield, yield, yield thy quest,"
Whispers through the woodland deep;
"Come to me and be at rest;
I am slumber, I am sleep."
Then the weary feet would fail,
But the never-daunted will
Urges "Forward, forward still!
Press along the trail!"
Breast, breast, breast the slope
See, the path is growing steep.
Hark! a little song of hope
Where the stream begins to leap.
Though the forest, far and wide,
Still shuts out the bending blue,
We shall finally win through,
Cross the long divide.
On, on, on we tramp!
Will the journey never end?
Over yonder lies the camp;
Welcome waits us there, my friend.
Can we reach it ere the night?
Upward, upward, never fear!
Look, the summit must be near;
See the line of light!
Red, red, red the shine
Of the splendour in the west,
Glowing through the ranks of pine,
Clear along the mountain-crest!
Long, long, long the trail
Out of sorrow's lonely vale;
But at last the traveller sees
Light between the trees!
March, 1904.

THE HERMIT THRUSH
O wonderful! How liquid clear
The molten gold of that ethereal tone,
Floating and falling through the wood alone,
A hermit-hymn poured out for God to hear!
O holy, holy, holy! Hyaline,
Long light, low light, glory of eventide!
Love far away, far up,—up,—love divine!
Little love, too, for ever, ever near,
Warm love, earth love, tender love of mine,
In the leafy dark where you hide,
You are mine,—mine,—mine!
Ah, my belovèd, do you feel with me
The hidden virtue of that melody,
The rapture and the purity of love,
The heavenly joy that can not find the word?
Then, while we wait again to hear the bird,
Come very near to me, and do not move,—
Now, hermit of the woodland, fill anew
The cool, green cup of air with harmony,
And we will drink the wine of love with you.
May, 1908.

TURN O' THE TIDE
The tide flows in to the harbour,—
The bold tide, the gold tide, the flood o' the sunlit sea,—
And the little ships riding at anchor,
Are swinging and slanting their prows to the ocean, panting
To lift their wings to the wide wild air,
And venture a voyage they know not where,—
To fly away and be free!
The tide runs out of the harbour,—
The low tide, the slow tide, the ebb o' the moonlit bay,—
And the little ships rocking at anchor,
Are rounding and turning their bows to the landward, yearning
To breathe the breath of the sun-warmed strand,
To rest in the lee of the high hill land,—
To hold their haven and stay!

My heart goes round with the vessels,—
My wild heart, my child heart, in love with the sea and the land,—
And the turn o' the tide passes through it,
In rising and falling with mystical currents, calling
At morn, to range where the far waves foam,
At night, to a harbour in love's true home,
With the hearts that understand!
Seal Harbour, August 12, 1911.

SIERRA MADRE
O Mother mountains! billowing far to the snow-lands,
Robed in aërial amethyst, silver, and blue,
Why do ye look so proudly down on the lowlands?
What have their groves and gardens to do with you?
Theirs is the languorous charm of the orange and myrtle,
Theirs are the fruitage and fragrance of Eden of old,—
Broad-boughed oaks in the meadows fair and fertile,

Dark-leaved orchards gleaming with globes of gold.
You, in your solitude standing, lofty and lonely,
Bear neither garden nor grove on your barren breasts;
Rough is the rock-loving growth of your canyons, and only
Storm-battered pines and fir-trees cling to your crests.
Why are ye throned so high, and arrayed in splendour
Richer than all the fields at your feet can claim?
What is your right, ye rugged peaks, to the tender
Queenly promise and pride of the mother-name?
Answered the mountains, dim in the distance dreaming:
"Ours are the forests that treasure the riches of rain;
Ours are the secret springs and the rivulets gleaming
Silverly down through the manifold bloom of the plain.
"Vain were the toiling of men in the dust of the dry land,
Vain were the ploughing and planting in waterless fields,
Save for the life-giving currents we send from the sky-land,
Save for the fruit our embrace with the storm-cloud yields."
O mother mountains, Madre Sierra, I love you!
Rightly you reign o'er the vale that your bounty fills—
Kissed by the sun, or with big, bright stars above you,—
I murmur your name and lift up mine eyes to the hills.

Pasadena, March, 1913.

THE GRAND CANYON
DAYBREAK

What makes the lingering Night so cling to thee?
Thou vast, profound, primeval hiding-place
Of ancient secrets,—gray and ghostly gulf
Cleft in the green of this high forest land,
And crowded in the dark with giant forms!
Art thou a grave, a prison, or a shrine?
A stillness deeper than the dearth of sound
Broods over thee: a living silence breathes
Perpetual incense from thy dim abyss.
The morning-stars that sang above the bower
Of Eden, passing over thee, are dumb
With trembling bright amazement; and the Dawn
Steals through the glimmering pines with naked feet,
Her hand upon her lips, to look on thee!
She peers into thy depths with silent prayer
For light, more light, to part thy purple veil.
O Earth, swift-rolling Earth, reveal, reveal,—
Turn to the East, and show upon thy breast
The mightiest marvel in the realm of Time!
'Tis done,—the morning miracle of light,—
The resurrection of the world of hues
That die with dark, and daily rise again
With every rising of the splendid Sun!
Be still, my heart! Now Nature holds her breath
To see the solar flood of radiance leap
Across the chasm, and crown the western rim
Of alabaster with a far-away
Rampart of pearl, and flowing down by walls
Of changeful opal, deepen into gold
Of topaz, rosy gold of tourmaline,
Crimson of garnet, green and gray of jade,
Purple of amethyst, and ruby red,
Beryl, and sard, and royal porphyry;

Until the cataract of colour breaks
Upon the blackness of the granite floor.
How far below! And all between is cleft
And carved into a hundred curving miles
Of unimagined architecture! Tombs,
Temples, and colonnades are neighboured there
By fortresses that Titans might defend,
And amphitheatres where Gods might strive.
Cathedrals, buttressed with unnumbered tiers
Of ruddy rock, lift to the sapphire sky
A single spire of marble pure as snow;
And huge aërial palaces arise
Like mountains built of unconsuming flame.
Along the weathered walls, or standing deep
In riven valleys where no foot may tread,
Are lonely pillars, and tall monuments
Of perished æons and forgotten things.
My sight is baffled by the wide array
Of countless forms: my vision reels and swims
Above them, like a bird in whirling winds.
Yet no confusion fills the awful chasm;
But spacious order and a sense of peace
Brood over all. For every shape that looms
Majestic in the throng, is set apart
From all the others by its far-flung shade,
Blue, blue, as if a mountain-lake were there.
How still it is! Dear God, I hardly dare
To breathe, for fear the fathomless abyss
Will draw me down into eternal sleep.
What force has formed this masterpiece of awe?
What hands have wrought these wonders in the waste?
O river, gleaming in the narrow rift
Of gloom that cleaves the valley's nether deep,—
Fierce Colorado, prisoned by thy toil,
And blindly toiling still to reach the sea,—
Thy waters, gathered from the snows and springs
Amid the Utah hills, have carved this road
Of glory to the Californian Gulf.
But now, O sunken stream, thy splendour lost,
'Twixt iron walls thou rollest turbid waves,
Too far away to make their fury heard!
At sight of thee, thou sullen labouring slave
Of gravitation,—yellow torrent poured
From distant mountains by no will of thine,
Through thrice a hundred centuries of slow
Fallings and liftings of the crust of Earth,—
At sight of thee my spirit sinks and fails.
Art thou alone the Maker? Is the blind
Unconscious power that drew thee dumbly down
To cut this gash across the layered globe,
The sole creative cause of all I see?
Are force and matter all? The rest a dream?
Then is thy gorge a canyon of despair,
A prison for the soul of man, a grave
Of all his dearest daring hopes! The world
Wherein we live and move is meaningless,
No spirit here to answer to our own!
The stars without a guide: The chance-born Earth
Adrift in space, no Captain on the ship:
Nothing in all the universe to prove
Eternal wisdom and eternal love!
And man, the latest accident of Time,—

Who thinks he loves, and longs to understand,
Who vainly suffers, and in vain is brave,
Who dupes his heart with immortality,—
Man is a living lie,—a bitter jest
Upon himself,—a conscious grain of sand
Lost in a desert of unconsciousness,
Thirsting for God and mocked by his own thirst.
Spirit of Beauty, mother of delight,
Thou fairest offspring of Omnipotence
Inhabiting this lofty lone abode,
Speak to my heart again and set me free
From all these doubts that darken earth and heaven!
Who sent thee forth into the wilderness
To bless and comfort all who see thy face?
Who clad thee in this more than royal robe
Of rainbows? Who designed these jewelled thrones
For thee, and wrought these glittering palaces?
Who gave thee power upon the soul of man
To lift him up through wonder into joy?
God! let the radiant cliffs bear witness, God!
Let all the shining pillars signal, God!
He only, on the mystic loom of light,
Hath woven webs of loveliness to clothe
His most majestic works: and He alone
Hath delicately wrought the cactus-flower
To star the desert floor with rosy bloom.
O Beauty, handiwork of the Most High,
Where'er thou art He tells his Love to man,
And lo, the day breaks, and the shadows flee!
Now, far beyond all language and all art
In thy wild splendour, Canyon marvellous,
The secret of thy stillness lies unveiled
In wordless worship! This is holy ground;
Thou art no grave, no prison, but a shrine.
Garden of Temples filled with Silent Praise,
If God were blind thy Beauty could not be!
February 24-26, 1913.

THE HEAVENLY HILLS OF HOLLAND

The heavenly hills of Holland,—
How wondrously they rise
Above the smooth green pastures
Into the azure skies!
With blue and purple hollows,
With peaks of dazzling snow,
Along the far horizon
The clouds are marching slow.
No mortal foot has trodden
The summits of that range,
Nor walked those mystic valleys
Whose colours ever change;
Yet we possess their beauty,
And visit them in dreams,
While ruddy gold of sunset
From cliff and canyon gleams.
In days of cloudless weather
They melt into the light;
When fog and mist surround us
They're hidden from our sight;
But when returns a season
Clear shining after rain,

While the northwest wind is blowing,
We see the hills again.
The old Dutch painters loved them,
Their pictures show them fair,—
Old Hobbema and Ruysdael,
Van Goyen and Vermeer.
Above the level landscape,
Rich polders, long-armed mills,
Canals and ancient cities,—
Float Holland's heavenly hills.
The Hague, November, 1916.

FLOOD-TIDE OF FLOWERS
IN HOLLAND

The laggard winter ebbed so slow
With freezing rain and melting snow,
It seemed as if the earth would stay
Forever where the tide was low,
In sodden green and watery gray.
But now from depths beyond our sight,
The tide is turning in the night,
And floods of colour long concealed
Come silent rising toward the light,
Through garden bare and empty field.
And first, along the sheltered nooks,
The crocus runs in little brooks
Of joyance, till by light made bold
They show the gladness of their looks
In shining pools of white and gold.
The tiny scilla, sapphire blue,
Is gently seeping in, to strew
The earth with heaven; and sudden rills
Of sunlit yellow, sweeping through,
Spread into lakes of daffodils.
The hyacinths, with fragrant heads,
Have overflowed their sandy beds,
And fill the earth with faint perfume,
The breath that Spring around her sheds.
And now the tulips break in bloom!
A sea, a rainbow-tinted sea,
A splendour and a mystery,
Floods o'er the fields of faded gray:
The roads are full of folks in glee,
For lo,—to-day is Easter Day!
April, 1916.

ODE
GOD OF THE OPEN AIR

I
Thou who hast made thy dwelling fair
With flowers below, above with starry lights
And set thine altars everywhere,—
On mountain heights,
In woodlands dim with many a dream,
In valleys bright with springs,
And on the curving capes of every stream:
Thou who hast taken to thyself the wings
Of morning, to abide
Upon the secret places of the sea,
And on far islands, where the tide
Visits the beauty of untrodden shores,
Waiting for worshippers to come to thee

In thy great out-of-doors!
To thee I turn, to thee I make my prayer,
God of the open air.

II

Seeking for thee, the heart of man
Lonely and longing ran,
In that first, solitary hour,
When the mysterious power
To know and love the wonder of the morn
Was breathed within him, and his soul was born;
And thou didst meet thy child,
Not in some hidden shrine,
But in the freedom of the garden wild,
And take his hand in thine,—
There all day long in Paradise he walked,
And in the cool of evening with thee talked.

III

Lost, long ago, that garden bright and pure,
Lost, that calm day too perfect to endure,
And lost the child-like love that worshipped and was sure!
For men have dulled their eyes with sin,
And dimmed the light of heaven with doubt,
And built their temple walls to shut thee in,
And framed their iron creeds to shut thee out.
But not for thee the closing of the door,
O Spirit unconfined!
Thy ways are free
As is the wandering wind,
And thou hast wooed thy children, to restore
Their fellowship with thee,
In peace of soul and simpleness of mind.

IV

Joyful the heart that, when the flood rolled by,
Leaped up to see the rainbow in the sky;
And glad the pilgrim, in the lonely night,
For whom the hills of Haran, tier on tier,
Built up a secret stairway to the height
Where stars like angel eyes were shining clear.
From mountain-peaks, in many a land and age,
Disciples of the Persian seer
Have hailed the rising sun and worshipped thee;
And wayworn followers of the Indian sage
Have found the peace of God beneath a spreading tree.

V

But One, but One,—ah, Son most dear,
And perfect image of the Love Unseen,—
Walked every day in pastures green,
And all his life the quiet waters by,
Reading their beauty with a tranquil eye.
To him the desert was a place prepared
For weary hearts to rest;
The hillside was a temple blest;
The grassy vale a banquet-room
Where he could feed and comfort many a guest.
With him the lily shared
The vital joy that breathes itself in bloom;
And every bird that sang beside the nest
Told of the love that broods o'er every living thing.
He watched the shepherd bring
His flock at sundown to the welcome fold,
The fisherman at daybreak fling
His net across the waters gray and cold,
And all day long the patient reaper swing
His curving sickle through the harvest-gold.
So through the world the foot-path way he trod,
Breathing the air of heaven in every breath;
And in the evening sacrifice of death
Beneath the open sky he gave his soul to God.
Him will I trust, and for my Master take;
Him will I follow; and for his dear sake,
God of the open air,
To thee I make my prayer.

VI

From the prison of anxious thought that greed has builded,
From the fetters that envy has wrought and pride has gilded,
From the noise of the crowded ways and the fierce confusion,
From the folly that wastes its days in a world of illusion,
(Ah, but the life is lost that frets and languishes there!)
I would escape and be free in the joy of the open air.

By the breadth of the blue that shines in silence o'er me,
By the length of the mountain-lines that stretch before me,
By the height of the cloud that sails, with rest in motion,
Over the plains and the vales to the measureless ocean,
(Oh, how the sight of the greater things enlarges the eyes!)
Draw me away from myself to the peace of the hills and skies.

While the tremulous leafy haze on the woodland is spreading,
And the bloom on the meadow betrays where May has been treading;
While the birds on the branches above, and the brooks flowing under,
Are singing together of love in a world full of wonder,
(Lo, in the magic of Springtime, dreams are changed into truth!)
Quicken my heart, and restore the beautiful hopes of youth.

By the faith that the wild-flowers show when they bloom unbidden,
By the calm of the river's flow to a goal that is hidden,
By the strength of the tree that clings to its deep foundation,
By the courage of birds' light wings on the long migration,
(Wonderful spirit of trust that abides in Nature's breast!)
Teach me how to confide, and live my life, and rest.

For the comforting warmth of the sun that my body embraces,
For the cool of the waters that run through the shadowy places,
For the balm of the breezes that brush my face with their fingers,
For the vesper-hymn of the thrush when the twilight lingers,
For the long breath, the deep breath, the breath of a heart without care,—
I will give thanks and adore thee, God of the open air!

VII

These are the gifts I ask
Of thee, Spirit serene:
Strength for the daily task,
Courage to face the road,
Good cheer to help me bear the traveller's load,
And, for the hours of rest that come between,
An inward joy in all things heard and seen.
These are the sins I fain
Would have thee take away:
Malice, and cold disdain,
Hot anger, sullen hate,
Scorn of the lowly, envy of the great,
And discontent that casts a shadow gray
On all the brightness of the common day.
These are the things I prize
And hold of dearest worth:
Light of the sapphire skies,
Peace of the silent hills,
Shelter of forests, comfort of the grass,
Music of birds, murmur of little rills,
Shadows of cloud that swiftly pass,
And, after showers,
The smell of flowers
And of the good brown earth,—
And best of all, along the way, friendship and mirth.
So let me keep
These treasures of the humble heart
In true possession, owning them by love;
And when at last I can no longer move
Among them freely, but must part
From the green fields and from the waters clear,
Let me not creep
Into some darkened room and hide
From all that makes the world so bright and dear;
But throw the windows wide
To welcome in the light;
And while I clasp a well-belovèd hand,
Let me once more have sight
Of the deep sky and the far-smiling land,—
Then gently fall on sleep,
And breathe my body back to Nature's care,
My spirit out to thee, God of the open air.
1904.

NARRATIVE POEMS
THE TOILING OF FELIX
A LEGEND ON A NEW SAYING OF JESUS

In the rubbish heaps of the ancient city of Oxyrhynchus, near the River Nile, a party of English explorers, in the winter of 1897, discovered a fragment of a papyrus book, written in the second or third century, and hitherto unknown. This single leaf contained parts of seven short sentences of Christ, each introduced by the words, "Jesus says." It is to the fifth of these Sayings of Jesus that the following poem refers.

THE TOILING OF FELIX
I
PRELUDE

Hear a word that Jesus spake
Nineteen hundred years ago,
Where the crimson lilies blow
Round the blue Tiberian lake:
There the bread of life He brake,
Through the fields of harvest walking
With His lowly comrades, talking
Of the secret thoughts that feed
Weary souls in time of need.
Art thou hungry? Come and take;
Hear the word that Jesus spake!
'Tis the sacrament of labour, bread and wine divinely blest;
Friendship's food and sweet refreshment, strength and courage, joy and rest.
But this word the Master said
Long ago and far away,
Silent and forgotten lay
Buried with the silent dead,
Where the sands of Egypt spread
Sea-like, tawny billows heaping
Over ancient cities sleeping,
While the River Nile between
Rolls its summer flood of green
Rolls its autumn flood of red:
There the word the Master said,
Written on a frail papyrus, wrinkled, scorched by fire, and torn,
Hidden by God's hand was waiting for its resurrection morn.
Now at last the buried word
By the delving spade is found,
Sleeping in the quiet ground.
Now the call of life is heard:
Rise again, and like a bird,
Fly abroad on wings of gladness
Through the darkness and the sadness,
Of the toiling age, and sing
Sweeter than the voice of Spring,
Till the hearts of men are stirred
By the music of the word,—
Gospel for the heavy-laden, answer to the labourer's cry:
"Raise the stone, and thou shall find me; cleave the wood and there am I."

II
LEGEND

Brother-men who look for Jesus, long to see Him close and clear,
Hearken to the tale of Felix, how he found the Master near.
Born in Egypt, 'neath the shadow of the crumbling gods of night,
He forsook the ancient darkness, turned his young heart toward the Light.
Seeking Christ, in vain he waited for the vision of the Lord;
Vainly pondered many volumes where the creeds of men were stored;
Vainly shut himself in silence, keeping vigil night and day;
Vainly haunted shrines and churches where the Christians came to pray.

One by one he dropped the duties of the common life of care,
Broke the human ties that bound him, laid his spirit waste and bare,
Hoping that the Lord would enter that deserted dwelling-place,
And reward the loss of all things with the vision of His face.

Still the blessed vision tarried; still the light was unrevealed;
Still the Master, dim and distant, kept His countenance concealed.
Fainter grew the hope of finding, wearier grew the fruitless quest;
Prayer and penitence and fasting gave no comfort, brought no rest.

Lingering in the darkened temple, ere the lamp of faith went out,
Felix knelt before the altar, lonely, sad, and full of doubt.

"Hear me, O my Lord and Master," from the altar-step he cried,
"Let my one desire be granted, let my hope be satisfied!

"Only once I long to see Thee, in the fulness of Thy grace:
Break the clouds that now enfold Thee, with the sunrise of Thy face!

"All that men desire and treasure have I counted loss for Thee;
Every hope have I forsaken, save this one, my Lord to see.

"Loosed the sacred bands of friendship, solitary stands my heart;
Thou shalt be my sole companion when I see Thee as Thou art.

"From Thy distant throne in glory, flash upon my inward sight,
Fill the midnight of my spirit with the splendour of Thy light.

"All Thine other gifts and blessings, common mercies, I disown;
Separated from my brothers, I would see Thy face alone.

"I have watched and I have waited as one waiteth for the morn:
Still the veil is never lifted, still Thou leavest me forlorn.

"Now I seek Thee in the desert, where the holy hermits dwell;
There, beside the saint Serapion, I will find a lonely cell.

"There at last Thou wilt be gracious; there Thy presence, long-concealed,
In the solitude and silence to my heart shall be revealed.

"Thou wilt come, at dawn or twilight, o'er the rolling waves of sand;
I shall see Thee close beside me, I shall touch Thy pierced hand.

"Lo, Thy pilgrim kneels before Thee; bless my journey with a word;
Tell me now that if I follow, I shall find Thee, O my Lord!"

Felix listened: through the darkness, like a murmur of the wind,
Came a gentle sound of stillness: "Never faint, and thou shalt find."

Long and toilsome was his journey through the heavy land of heat,
Egypt's blazing sun above him, blistering sand beneath his feet.
Patiently he plodded onward, from the pathway never erred,
Till he reached the river-headland called the Mountain of the Bird.

There the tribes of air assemble, once a year, their noisy flock,
Then, departing, leave a sentinel perched upon the highest rock.
Far away, on joyful pinions, over land and sea they fly;
But the watcher on the summit lonely stands against the sky.

There the eremite Serapion in a cave had made his bed;
There the faithful bands of pilgrims sought his blessing, brought him bread.
Month by month, in deep seclusion, hidden in the rocky cleft,
Dwelt the hermit, fasting, praying; once a year the cave he left.
On that day a happy pilgrim, chosen out of all the band,
Won a special sign of favour from the holy hermit's hand.

Underneath the narrow window, at the doorway closely sealed,
While the afterglow of sunset deepened round him, Felix kneeled.

"Man of God, of men most holy, thou whose gifts cannot be priced!
Grant me thy most precious guerdon; tell me how to find the Christ."

Breathless, Felix bent and listened, but no answering voice he heard;
Darkness folded, dumb and deathlike, round the Mountain of the Bird.
Then he said, "The saint is silent; he would teach my soul to wait:
I will tarry here in patience, like a beggar at his gate."

Near the dwelling of the hermit Felix found a rude abode,
In a shallow tomb deserted, close beside the pilgrim-road.

So the faithful pilgrims saw him waiting there without complaint,—
Soon they learned to call him holy, fed him as they fed the saint.
Day by day he watched the sunrise flood the distant plain with gold,
While the River Nile beneath him, silvery coiling, sea-ward rolled.

Night by night he saw the planets range their glittering court on high,
Saw the moon, with queenly motion, mount her throne and rule the sky.

Morn advanced and midnight fled, in visionary pomp attired;
Never morn and never midnight brought the vision long-desired.

Now at last the day is dawning when Serapion makes his gift;
Felix kneels before the threshold, hardly dares his eyes to lift.

Now the cavern door uncloses, now the saint above him stands,
Blesses him without a word, and leaves a token in his hands.
'Tis the guerdon of thy waiting! Look, thou happy pilgrim, look!
Nothing but a tattered fragment of an old papyrus book.
Read! perchance the clue to guide thee hidden in the words may lie:
"Raise the stone, and thou shalt find me; cleave the wood, and there am I."
Can it be the mighty Master spake such simple words as these?
Can it be that men must seek Him at their toil 'mid rocks and trees?
Disappointed, heavy-hearted, from the Mountain of the Bird
Felix mournfully descended, questioning the Master's word.
Not for him a sacred dwelling, far above the haunts of men:
He must turn his footsteps backward to the common life again.
From a quarry near the river, hollowed out amid the hills,
Rose the clattering voice of labour, clanking hammers, clinking drills.
Dust, and noise, and hot confusion made a Babel of the spot:
There, among the lowliest workers, Felix sought and found his lot.
Now he swung the ponderous mallet, smote the iron in the rock—
Muscles quivering, tingling, throbbing—blow on blow and shock on shock;
Now he drove the willow wedges, wet them till they swelled and split,
With their silent strength, the fragment, sent it thundering down the pit.
Now the groaning tackle raised it; now the rollers made it slide;
Harnessed men, like beasts of burden, drew it to the river-side.
Now the palm-trees must be riven, massive timbers hewn and dressed;
Rafts to bear the stones in safety on the rushing river's breast.
Axe and auger, saw and chisel, wrought the will of man in wood:
'Mid the many-handed labour Felix toiled, and found it good.
Every day the blood ran fleeter through his limbs and round his heart;
Every night he slept the sweeter, knowing he had done his part.
Dreams of solitary saintship faded from him; but, instead,
Came a sense of daily comfort in the toil for daily bread.

Far away, across the river, gleamed the white walls of the town
Whither all the stones and timbers day by day were floated down.
There the workman saw his labour taking form and bearing fruit,
Like a tree with splendid branches rising from a humble root.
Looking at the distant city, temples, houses, domes, and towers,
Felix cried in exultation: "All that mighty work is ours.

"Every toiler in the quarry, every builder on the shore,
Every chopper in the palm-grove, every raftsman at the oar,
"Hewing wood and drawing water, splitting stones and cleaving sod,
All the dusty ranks of labour, in the regiment of God,

"March together toward His triumph, do the task His hands prepare:
Honest toil is holy service; faithful work is praise and prayer."
While he bore the heat and burden Felix felt the sense of rest
Flowing softly like a fountain, deep within his weary breast;
Felt the brotherhood of labour, rising round him like a tide,
Overflow his heart and join him to the workers at his side.
Oft he cheered them with his singing at the breaking of the light,
Told them tales of Christ at noonday, taught them words of prayer at night.
Once he bent above a comrade fainting in the mid-day heat,
Sheltered him with woven palm-leaves, gave him water, cool and sweet.
Then it seemed, for one swift moment, secret radiance filled the place;
Underneath the green palm-branches flashed a look of Jesus' face.
Once again, a raftsman, slipping, plunged beneath the stream and sank;
Swiftly Felix leaped to rescue, caught him, drew him toward the bank—
Battling with the cruel river, using all his strength to save—
Did he dream? or was there One beside him walking on the wave?
Now at last the work was ended, grove deserted, quarry stilled;

Felix journeyed to the city that his hands had helped to build.
In the darkness of the temple, at the closing hour of day,
As of old he sought the altar, as of old he knelt to pray:
"Hear me, O Thou hidden Master! Thou hast sent a word to me;
It is written—Thy commandment—I have kept it faithfully
"Thou hast bid me leave the visions of the solitary life,
Bear my part in human labour, take my share in human strife.
"I have done Thy bidding, Master; raised the rock and felled the tree,
Swung the axe and plied the hammer, working every day for Thee.
"Once it seemed I saw Thy presence through the bending palm-leaves gleam;
Once upon the flowing water—Nay, I know not; 'twas a dream!
"This I know: Thou hast been near me: more than this I dare not ask.
Though I see Thee not, I love Thee. Let me do Thy humblest task!"

Through the dimness of the temple slowly dawned a mystic light;
There the Master stood in glory, manifest to mortal sight:

Hands that bore the mark of labour, brow that bore the print of care;
Hands of power, divinely tender; brow of light, divinely fair.
"Hearken, good and faithful servant, true disciple, loyal friend!
Thou hast followed me and found me; I will keep thee to the end.
"Well I know thy toil and trouble; often weary, fainting, worn,
I have lived the life of labour, heavy burdens I have borne.
"Never in a prince's palace have I slept on golden bed,
Never in a hermit's cavern have I eaten unearned bread.
"Born within a lowly stable, where the cattle round me stood,
Trained a carpenter in Nazareth, I have toiled, and found it good.
"They who tread the path of labour follow where my feet have trod;
They who work without complaining do the holy will of God.
"Where the many toil together, there am I among my own;
Where the tired workman sleepeth, there am I with him alone.
"I, the peace that passeth knowledge, dwell amid the daily strife;
I, the bread of heaven, am broken in the sacrament of life.

"Every task, however simple, sets the soul that does it free;
Every deed of love and mercy, done to man, is done to me.

"Thou hast learned the open secret; thou hast come to me for rest;
With thy burden, in thy labour, thou art Felix, doubly blest.
"Nevermore thou needest seek me; I am with thee everywhere;
Raise the stone, and thou shall find me; cleave the wood, and I am there."

III
ENVOY

The legend of Felix is ended, the toiling of Felix is done;
The Master has paid him his wages, the goal of his journey is won;
He rests, but he never is idle; a thousand years pass like a day,
In the glad surprise of that Paradise where work is sweeter than play.

Yet often the King of that country comes out from His tireless host,
And walks in this world of the weary as if He loved it the most;
For here in the dusty confusion, with eyes that are heavy and dim,
He meets again the labouring men who are looking and longing for Him.

He cancels the curse of Eden, and brings them a blessing instead:
Blessed are they that labour, for Jesus partakes of their bread.
He puts His hand to their burdens, He enters their homes at night:
Who does his best shall have as a guest the Master of life and light.

And courage will come with His presence, and patience return at His touch,
And manifold sins be forgiven to those who love Him much;
The cries of envy and anger will change to the songs of cheer,
The toiling age will forget its rage when the Prince of Peace draws near.

This is the gospel of labour, ring it, ye bells of the kirk!
The Lord of Love came down from above, to live with the men who work.
This is the rose that He planted, here in the thorn-curst soil:
Heaven is blest with perfect rest, but the blessing of Earth is toil.
1898.

VERA
I
A silent world,—yet full of vital joy
Uttered in rhythmic movements manifold,
And sunbeams flashing on the face of things
Like sudden smilings of divine delight,—
A world of many sorrows too, revealed

In fading flowers and withering leaves and dark
Tear-laden clouds, and tearless, clinging mists
That hung above the earth too sad to weep,—
A world of fluent change, and changeless flow,
And infinite suggestion of new thought,
Reflected in the crystal of the heart,—
A world of many meanings but no words,
A silent world was Vera's home.
For her
The inner doors of sound were closely sealed
The outer portals, delicate as shells
Suffused with faintest rose of far-off morn,
Like underglow of daybreak in the sea,—
The ear-gates of the garden of her soul,
Shaded by drooping tendrils of brown hair,—
Waited in vain for messengers to pass,
And thread the labyrinth with flying feet,
And swiftly knock upon the inmost door,
And enter in, and speak the mystic word.
But through those gates no message ever came.
Only with eyes did she behold and see,—
With eyes as luminous and bright and brown
As waters of a woodland river,—eyes
That questioned so they almost seemed to speak,
And answered so they almost seemed to hear,—
Only with wondering eyes did she behold
The silent splendour of a living world.
She saw the great wind ranging freely down
Interminable archways of the wood,
While tossing boughs and bending tree-tops hailed
His coming: but no sea-toned voice of pines,
No roaring of the oaks, no silvery song
Of poplars or of birches, followed him.
He passed; they waved their arms and clapped their hands;
There was no sound.
The torrents from the hills
Leaped down their rocky pathways, like wild steeds
Breaking the yoke and shaking manes of foam.
The lowland brooks coiled smoothly through the fields,
And softly spread themselves in glistening lakes
Whose ripples merrily danced among the reeds.
The standing waves that ever keep their place
In the swift rapids, curled upon themselves,
And seemed about to break and never broke;
And all the wandering waves that fill the sea
Came buffeting in along the stony shore,
Or plunging in along the level sands,
Or creeping in along the winding creeks
And inlets. Yet from all the ceaseless flow
And turmoil of the restless element
Came neither song of joy nor sob of grief;
For there were many waters, but no voice.
Silent the actors all on Nature's stage
Performed their parts before her watchful eyes,
Coming and going, making war and love,
Working and playing, all without a sound.
The oxen drew their load with swaying necks;
The cows came sauntering home along the lane;
The nodding sheep were led from field to fold
In mute obedience. Down the woodland track
The hounds with panting sides and lolling tongues
Pursued their flying prey in noiseless haste.
The birds, the most alive of living things,
Mated, and built their nests, and reared their young,
And swam the flood of air like tiny ships
Rising and falling over unseen waves,
And, gathering in great navies, bore away
To North or South, without a note of song.

All these were Vera's playmates; and she loved
To watch them, wondering oftentimes how well
They knew their parts, and how the drama moved
So swiftly, smoothly on from scene to scene
Without confusion. But she sometimes dreamed
There must be something hidden in the play
Unknown to her, an utterance of life
More clear than action and more deep than looks.
And this she felt most deeply when she watched
Her human comrades and the throngs of men,
Who met and parted oft with moving lips
That had a meaning more than she could see.
She saw a lover bend above a maid,
With moving lips; and though he touched her not
A sudden rose of joy bloomed in her face.
She saw a hater stand before his foe
And move his lips; whereat the other shrank
As if he had been smitten on the mouth.
She saw the regiments of toiling men
Marshalled in ranks and led by moving lips.
And once she saw a sight more strange than all:
A crowd of people sitting charmed and still
Around a little company of men
Who touched their hands in measured, rhythmic time
To curious instruments; a woman stood
Among them, with bright eyes and heaving breast,
And lifted up her face and moved her lips.
Then Vera wondered at the idle play,
But when she looked around, she saw the glow
Of deep delight on every face, as if
Some visitor from a celestial world
Had brought glad tidings. But to her alone
No angel entered, for the choir of sound
Was vacant in the temple of her soul,
And worship lacked her golden crown of song.
So when by vision baffled and perplexed
She saw that all the world could not be seen,
And knew she could not know the whole of life
Unless a hidden gate should be unsealed,
She felt imprisoned. In her heart there grew
The bitter creeping plant of discontent,
The plant that only grows in prison soil,
Whose root is hunger and whose fruit is pain.
The springs of still delight and tranquil joy
Were drained as dry as desert dust to feed
That never-flowering vine, whose tendrils clung
With strangling touch around the bloom of life
And made it wither. Vera could not rest
Within the limits of her silent world;
Along its dumb and desolate paths she roamed
A captive, looking sadly for escape.
Now in those distant days, and in that land
Remote, there lived a Master wonderful,
Who knew the secret of all life, and could,

With gentle touches and with potent words,
Open all gates that ever had been sealed,
And loose all prisoners whom Fate had bound.
Obscure he dwelt, not in the wilderness,
But in a hut among the throngs of men,
Concealed by meekness and simplicity.
And ever as he walked the city streets,
Or sat in quietude beside the sea,
Or trod the hillsides and the harvest fields,
The multitude passed by and knew him not.
But there were some who knew, and turned to him
For help; and unto all who asked, he gave.
Thus Vera came, and found him in the field,
And knew him by the pity in his face.
She knelt to him and held him by one hand,
And laid the other hand upon her lips
In mute entreaty. Then she lifted up
The coils of hair that hung about her neck,
And bared the beauty of the gates of sound,—
Those virgin gates through which no voice had passed,—
She made them bare before the Master's sight,
And looked into the kindness of his face
With eyes that spoke of all her prisoned pain,
And told her great desire without a word.
The Master waited long in silent thought,
As one reluctant to bestow a gift,
Not for the sake of holding back the thing
Entreated, but because he surely knew
Of something better that he fain would give
If only she would ask it. Then he stooped
To Vera, smiling, touched her ears and spoke:
"Open, fair gates, and you, reluctant doors,
Within the ivory labyrinth of the ear,
Let fall the bar of silence and unfold!
Enter, you voices of all living things,
Enter the garden sealed,—but softly, slowly,
Not with a noise confused and broken tumult,—
Come in an order sweet as I command you,
And bring the double gift of speech and hearing."
Vera began to hear. At first the wind
Breathed a low prelude of the birth of sound,
As if an organ far away were touched
By unseen fingers; then the little stream
That hurried down the hillside, swept the harp
Of music into merry, tinkling notes;
And then the lark that poised above her head
On wings a-quiver, overflowed the air
With showers of song; and one by one the tones
Of all things living, in an order sweet,
Without confusion and with deepening power,
Entered the garden sealed. And last of all
The Master's voice, the human voice divine,
Passed through the gates and called her by her name,
And Vera heard.

II

What rapture of new life
Must come to one for whom a silent world
Is suddenly made vocal, and whose heart
By the same magic is awaked at once,
Without the learner's toil and long delay,
Out of a night of dumbly moving dreams,
Into a day that overflows with music!
This joy was Vera's; and to her it seemed
As if a new creative morn had risen
Upon the earth, and after the full week
When living things unfolded silently,
And after the long, quiet Sabbath day,
When all was still, another day had dawned,
And through the calm expectancy of heaven
A secret voice had said, "Let all things speak."
The world responded with an instant joy;
And all the unseen avenues of sound
Were thronged with varying forms of viewless life.
To every living thing a voice was given
Distinct and personal. The forest trees
Were not more varied in their shades of green
Than in their tones of speech; and every bird
That nested in their branches had a song
Unknown to other birds and all his own.
The waters spoke a hundred dialects
Of one great language; now with pattering fall
Of raindrops on the glistening leaves, and now
With steady roar of rivers rushing down
To meet the sea, and now with rhythmic throb
And measured tumult of tempestuous waves,
And now with lingering lisp of creeping tides,—
The manifold discourse of many waters.
But most of all the human voice was full
Of infinite variety, and ranged
Along the scale of life's experience
With changing tones, and notes both sweet and sad,
All fitted to express some unseen thought,
Some vital motion of the hidden heart.
So Vera listened with her new-born sense
To all the messengers that passed the gates,
In measureless delight and utter trust,
Believing that they brought a true report
From every living thing of its true life,
And hoping that at last they would make clear
The mystery and the meaning of the world.
But soon there came a trouble in her joy,
A note discordant that dissolved the chord
And broke the bliss of hearing into pain.
Not from the harsher sounds and voices wild
Of anger and of anguish, that reveal
The secret strife in nature, and confess
The touch of sorrow on the heart of life,—
From these her trouble came not. For in these,
However sad, she felt the note of truth,
And truth, though sad, is always musical.
The raging of the tempest-ridden sea,
The crash of thunder, and the hollow moan
Of winds complaining round the mountain-crags,
The shrill and quavering cry of birds of prey,
The fiercer roar of conflict-loving beasts,—
All these wild sounds are potent in their place
Within life's mighty symphony; the charm
Of truth attunes them, and the hearing ear
Finds pleasure in their rude sincerity.
Even the broken and tumultuous noise
That rises from great cities, where the heart
Of human toil is beating heavily
With ceaseless murmurs of the labouring pulse,

*Is not a discord; for it speaks to life
Of life unfeigned, and full of hopes and fears,
And touched through all the trouble of its notes
With something real and therefore glorious.
One voice alone of all that sound on earth,
Is hateful to the soul, and full of pain,—
The voice of falsehood. So when Vera heard
This mocking voice, and knew that it was false;
When first she learned that human lips can speak
The thing that is not, and betray the ear
Of simple trust with treachery of words;
The joy of hearing withered in her heart.
For now she felt that faithless messengers
Could pass the open and unguarded gates
Of sound, and bring a message all untrue,
Or half a truth that makes the deadliest lie,
Or idle babble, neither false nor true,
But hollow to the heart, and meaningless.
She heard the flattering voices of deceit,
That mask the hidden purposes of men
With fair attire of favourable words,
And hide the evil in the guise of good:
The voices vain and decorous and smooth,
That fill the world with empty-hearted talk;
The foolish voices, wandering and confused,
That never clearly speak the thing they would,
But ramble blindly round their true intent
And tangle sense in hopeless coils of sound,—
All these she heard, and with a deep mistrust
Began to doubt the value of her gift.
It seemed as if the world, the living world,
Sincere, and vast, and real, were still concealed,
And she, within the prison of her soul,
Still waiting silently to hear the voice
Of perfect knowledge and of perfect peace.
So with the burden of her discontent
She turned to seek the Master once again,
And found him sitting in the market-place,
Half-hidden in the shadow of a porch,
Alone among the careless crowd.
She spoke:
"Thy gift was great, dear Master, and my heart
Has thanked thee many times because I hear
But I have learned that hearing is not all;
For underneath the speech of men, there flows
Another current of their hidden thoughts;
Behind the mask of language I perceive
The eyes of things unsaid.
Touch me again,
O Master, with thy liberating hand,
And free me from the bondage of deceit.
Open another gate, and let me hear
The secret thoughts and purposes of men;
For only thus my heart will be at rest,
And only thus, at last, I shall perceive
The mystery and the meaning of the world."
The Master's face was turned aside from her;
His eyes looked far away, as if he saw
Something beyond her sight; and yet she knew
That he was listening; for her pleading voice
No sooner ceased than he put forth his hand
To touch her brow, and very gently spoke:*

*"Thou seekest for thyself a wondrous gift,—
The opening of the second gate, a gift
That many wise men have desired in vain:
But some have found it,—whether well or ill
For their own peace, they have attained the power
To hear unspoken thoughts of other men.
And thou hast begged this gift? Thou shalt receive,—
Not knowing what thou seekest,—it is thine:
The second gate is open! Thou shalt hear
All that men think and feel within their hearts:
Thy prayer is granted, daughter, go thy way!
But if thou findest sorrow on this path,
Come back again,—there is a path to peace."*

III

*Beyond our power of vision, poets say,
There is another world of forms unseen,
Yet visible to purer eyes than ours.
And if the crystal of our sight were clear,
We should behold the mountain-slopes of cloud,
The moving meadows of the untilled sea,
The groves of twilight and the dales of dawn,
And every wide and lonely field of air,
More populous than cities, crowded close
With living creatures of all shapes and hues.
But if that sight were ours, the things that now
Engage our eyes would seem but dull and dim
Beside the wonders of our new-found world,
And we should be amazed and overwhelmed
Not knowing how to use the plenitude
Of vision.
So in Vera's soul, at first,
The opening of the second gate of sound
Let in confusion like a whirling flood.
The murmur of a myriad-throated mob;
The trampling of an army through a place
Where echoes hide; the sudden, whistling flight
Of an innumerable flock of birds
Along the highway of the midnight sky;
The many-whispered rustling of the reeds
Beneath the passing feet of all the winds;
The long-drawn, inarticulate, wailing cry
Of million-pebbled beaches when the lash
Of stormy waves is drawn across their back,—
All these were less bewildering than to hear
What now she heard at once: the tangled sound
Of all that moves within the minds of men.
For now there was no measured flow of words
To mark the time; nor any interval
Of silence to repose the listening ear.
But through the dead of night, and through the calm
Of weary noon-tide, through the solemn hush
That fills the temple in the pause of praise,
And through the breathless awe in rooms of death,
She heard the ceaseless motion and the stir
Of never-silent hearts, that fill the world
With interwoven thoughts of good and ill,
With mingled music of delight and grief,
With songs of love, and bitter cries of hate,
With hymns of faith, and dirges of despair,
And murmurs deeper and more vague than all,—
Thoughts that are born and die without a name,*

Or rather, never die, but haunt the soul,
With sad persistence, till a name is given.
These Vera heard, at first with mind perplexed
And half-benumbed by the disordered sound.
But soon a clearer sense began to pierce
The cloudy turmoil with discerning power.
She learned to know the tones of human thought
As plainly as she knew the tones of speech.
She could divide the evil from the good,
Interpreting the language of the mind,
And tracing every feeling like a thread
Within the mystic web the passions weave
From heart to heart around the living world.

But when at last the Master's second gift
Was perfected within her, and she heard
And understood the secret thoughts of men,
A sadness fell upon her, and the load
Of insupportable knowledge pressed her down
With weary wishes to know more, or less.
For all she knew was like a broken word
Inscribed upon the fragment of a ring;
And all she heard was like a broken strain
Preluding music that is never played.

Then she remembered in her sad unrest
The Master's parting word,—"a path to peace,"—
And turned again to seek him with her grief.
She found him in a hollow of the hills,
Beside a little spring that issued forth
Beneath the rocks and filled a mossy cup
With never-failing water. There he sat,
With waiting looks that welcomed her afar.
"I know that thou hast heard, my child," he said,
"For all the wonder of the world of sound
Is written in thy face. But hast thou heard,
Among the many voices, one of peace?
And is thy heart that hears the secret thoughts,
The hidden wishes and desires of men,
Content with hearing? Art thou satisfied?"
"Nay, Master," she replied, "thou knowest well
That I am not at rest, nor have I heard
The voice of perfect peace; but what I hear
Brings me disquiet and a troubled mind.
The evil voices in the souls of men,
Voices of rage and cruelty and fear
Have not dismayed me; for I have believed
The voices of the good, the kind, the true,
Are more in number and excel in strength.
There is more love than hate, more hope than fear,
In the deep throbbing of the human heart.
But while I listen to the troubled sound,
One thing torments me, and destroys my rest
And presses me with dull, unceasing pain.
For out of all the minds of all mankind,
There rises evermore a questioning voice
That asks the meaning of this mighty world
And finds no answer,—asks, and asks again,
With patient pleading or with wild complaint,
But wakens no response, except the sound
Of other questions, wandering to and fro,
From other souls in doubt. And so this voice

Persists above all others that I hear,
And binds them up together into one,
Until the mingled murmur of the world
Sounds through the inner temple of my heart
Like an eternal question, vainly asked
By every human soul that thinks and feels.
This is the heaviness that weighs me down,
And this the pain that will not let me rest.
Therefore, dear Master, shut the gates again,
And let me live in silence as before!
Or else,—and if there is indeed a gate
Unopened yet, through which I might receive
An answer in the voice of perfect peace—"

She ceased; and in her upward faltering tone
The question echoed.
Then the Master said:
"There is another gate, not yet unclosed.
For through the outer portal of the ear
Only the outer voice of things may pass;
And through the middle doorway of the mind
Only the half-formed voice of human thoughts,
Uncertain and perplexed with endless doubt;
But through the inmost gate the spirit hears
The voice of that great Spirit who is Life.
Beneath the tones of living things He breathes
A deeper tone than ever ear hath heard;
And underneath the troubled thoughts of men
He thinks forever, and His thought is peace.
Behold, I touch thee once again, my child:
The third and last of those three hidden gates
That closed around thy soul and shut thee in,
Is open now, and thou shalt truly hear."
Then Vera heard. The spiritual gate
Was opened softly as a full-blown flower
Unfolds its heart to welcome in the dawn,
And on her listening face there shone a light
Of still amazement and completed joy
In the full gift of hearing.
What she heard
I cannot tell; nor could she ever tell
In words; because all human words are vain.
There is no speech nor language, to express
The secret messages of God, that make
Perpetual music in the hearing heart.
Below the voice of waters, and above
The wandering voice of winds, and underneath
The song of birds, and all the varying tones
Of living things that fill the world with sound,
God spoke to her, and what she heard was peace.

So when the Master questioned, "Dost thou hear?"
She answered, "Yea, at last I hear." And then
He asked her once again, "What hearest thou?
What means the voice of Life?" She answered, "Love!
For love is life, and they who do not love
Are not alive. But every soul that loves,
Lives in the heart of God and hears Him speak."

1898.

ANOTHER CHANCE

A DRAMATIC LYRIC

Come, give me back my life again, you heavy-handed Death!
Uncrook your fingers from my throat, and let me draw my breath.
You do me wrong to take me now—too soon for me to die—
Ah, loose me from this clutching pain, and hear the reason why.
I know I've had my forty years, and wasted every one;
And yet, I tell you honestly, my life is just begun;
I've walked the world like one asleep, a dreamer in a trance;
But now you've gripped me wide awake—I want another chance.
My dreams were always beautiful, my thoughts were high and fine;
No life was ever lived on earth to match those dreams of mine.
And would you wreck them unfulfilled? What folly, nay, what crime!
You rob the world, you waste a soul; give me a little time.
You'll hear me? Yes, I'm sure you will, my hope is not in vain:
I feel the even pulse of peace, the sweet relief from pain;
The black fog rolls away from me; I'm free once more to plan:
Another chance is all I need to prove myself a man!
The world is full of warfare 'twixt the evil and the good;
I watched the battle from afar as one who understood
The shouting and confusion, the bloody, blundering fight—
How few there are that see it clear, how few that wage it right!
The captains flushed with foolish pride, the soldiers pale with fear,
The faltering flags, the feeble fire from ranks that swerve and veer,
The wild mistakes, the dismal doubts, the coward hearts that flee—
The good cause needs a nobler knight to win the victory.

A man whose soul is pure and strong, whose sword is bright and keen,
Who knows the splendour of the fight and what its issues mean;
Who never takes one step aside, nor halts, though hope be dim,
But cleaves a pathway thro' the strife, and bids men follow him.
No blot upon his stainless shield, no weakness in his arm;
No sign of trembling in his face to break his valour's charm:
A man like this could stay the flight and lead the wavering line;
Ah, give me but a year of life—I'll make that glory mine!

Religion? Yes, I know it well; I've heard its prayers and creeds,
And seen men put them all to shame with poor, half-hearted deeds.
They follow Christ, but far away; they wander and they doubt.
I'll serve him in a better way, and live his precepts out.
You see, I waited just for this; I could not be content
To own a feeble, faltering faith with human weakness blent.
Too many runners in the race move slowly, stumble, fall;
But I will run so straight and swift I shall outstrip them all.
Oh, think what it will mean to men, amid their foolish strife,
To see the clear, unshadowed light of one true Christian life,
Without a touch of selfishness, without a taint of sin,—
With one short month of such a life a new world would begin!

And love!—I often dream of that—the treasure of the earth;
How little they who use the coin have realised its worth!
'Twill pay all debts, enrich all hearts, and make all joys secure.
But love, to do its perfect work, must be sincere and pure.
My heart is full of virgin gold. I'll pour it out and spend
My hidden wealth with open hand on all who call me friend.
Not one shall miss the kindly deed, the largess of relief,
The generous fellowship of joy, the sympathy of grief.
I'll say the loyal, helpful things that make life sweet and fair,
I'll pay the gratitude I owe for human love and care.
Perhaps I've been at fault sometimes—I'll ask to be forgiven,
And make this little room of mine seem like a bit of heaven.
For one by one I'll call my friends to stand beside my bed;
I'll speak the true and tender words so often left unsaid;
And every heart shall throb and glow, all coldness melt away
Around my altar-fire of love—ah, give me but one day!

What's that? I've had another day, and wasted it again?
A priceless day in empty dreams, another chance in vain?
Thou fool—this night—it's very dark—the last—this choking breath—
One prayer—have mercy on a dreamer's soul—God, this is death!

A LEGEND OF SERVICE

It pleased the Lord of Angels (praise His name!)
To hear, one day, report from those who came
With pitying sorrow, or exultant joy,
To tell of earthly tasks in His employ.
For some were grieved because they saw how slow
The stream of heavenly love on earth must flow;
And some were glad because their eyes had seen,
Along its banks, fresh flowers and living green.
At last, before the whiteness of the throne
The youngest angel, Asmiel, stood alone;
Nor glad, nor sad, but full of earnest thought,
And thus his tidings to the Master brought

"Lord, in the city Lupon I have found
Three servants of thy holy name, renowned
Above their fellows. One is very wise,
With thoughts that ever range beyond the skies;
And one is gifted with the golden speech
That makes men gladly hear when he will teach;
And one, with no rare gift or grace endued,
Has won the people's love by doing good.
With three such saints Lupon is trebly blest;
But, Lord, I fain would know, which loves Thee best?"
Then spake the Lord of Angels, to whose look
The hearts of all are like an open book:
"In every soul the secret thought I read,
And well I know who loves me best indeed.
But every life has pages vacant still,
Whereon a man may write the thing he will;
Therefore I read the record, day by day,
And wait for hearts untaught to learn my way.
But thou shalt go to Lupon, to the three
Who serve me there, and take this word from me:
Tell each of them his Master bids him go
Alone to Spiran's huts, across the snow;
There he shall find a certain task for me:
But what, I do not tell to them nor thee.
Give thou the message, make my word the test,
And crown for me the one who loves me best."
Silent the angel stood, with folded hands,
To take the imprint of his Lord's commands;
Then drew one breath, obedient and elate,
And passed the self-same hour, through Lupon's gate.
First to the Temple door he made his way;
And there, because it was a holy-day,
He saw the folk in thousands thronging, stirred
By ardent thirst to hear the preacher's word.
Then, while the people whispered Bernol's name,
Through aisles that hushed behind him Bernol came;
Strung to the keenest pitch of conscious might,
With lips prepared and firm, and eyes alight.
One moment at the pulpit step he knelt
In silent prayer, and on his shoulder felt
The angel's hand:—"The Master bids thee go
Alone to Spiran's huts, across the snow,
To serve Him there." Then Bernol's hidden face
Went white as death, and for about the space
Of ten slow heart-beats there was no reply;
Till Bernol looked around and whispered, "Why?"
But answer to his question came there none;
The angel sighed, and with a sigh was gone.
Within the humble house where Malvin spent
His studious years, on holy things intent,
Sweet stillness reigned; and there the angel found
The saintly sage immersed in thought profound,
Weaving with patient toil and willing care
A web of wisdom, wonderful and fair:
A seamless robe for Truth's great bridal meet,
And needing but one thread to be complete.
Then Asmiel touched his hand, and broke the thread
Of fine-spun thought, and very gently said,
"The One of whom thou thinkest bids thee go
Alone to Spiran's huts, across the snow,
To serve Him there." With sorrow and surprise
Malvin looked up, reluctance in his eyes.

The broken thought, the strangeness of the call,
The perilous passage of the mountain-wall,
The solitary journey, and the length
Of ways unknown, too great for his frail strength,
Appalled him. With a doubtful brow
He scanned the doubtful task, and muttered "How?"
But Asmiel answered, as he turned to go,
With cold, disheartened voice, "I do not know."
Now as he went, with fading hope, to seek
The third and last to whom God bade him speak,
Scarce twenty steps away whom should he meet
But Fermor, hurrying cheerful down the street,
With ready heart that faced his work like play,
And joyed to find it greater every day!
The angel stopped him with uplifted hand,
And gave without delay his Lord's command:
"He whom thou servest here would have thee go
Alone to Spiran's huts, across the snow,
To serve Him there." Ere Asmiel breathed again
The eager answer leaped to meet him, "When?"
The angel's face with inward joy grew bright,
And all his figure glowed with heavenly light;
He took the golden circlet from his brow
And gave the crown to Fermor, answering, "Now!
For thou hast met the Master's hidden test,
And I have found the man who loves Him best.
Not thine, nor mine, to question or reply
When He commands us, asking 'how?' or 'why?'
He knows the cause; His ways are wise and just;
Who serves the King must serve with perfect trust."
February, 1902.

THE WHITE BEES
I
LEGEND

Long ago Apollo called to Aristæus, youngest of the shepherds,
Saying, "I will make you keeper of my bees."
Golden were the hives and golden was the honey; golden, too, the music
Where the honey-makers hummed among the trees.

Happy Aristæus loitered in the garden, wandered in the orchard,
Careless and contented, indolent and free;
Lightly took his labour, lightly took his pleasure, till the fated moment
When across his pathway came Eurydice.
Then her eyes enkindled burning love within him; drove him wild with longing
For the perfect sweetness of her flower-like face;
Eagerly he followed, while she fled before him, over mead and mountain,
On through field and forest, in a breathless race.
But the nymph, in flying, trod upon a serpent; like a dream she vanished;
Pluto's chariot bore her down among the dead!
Lonely Aristæus, sadly home returning, found his garden empty,
All the hives deserted, all the music fled.
Mournfully bewailing,—"Ah, my honey-makers, where have you departed?"

Far and wide he sought them over sea and shore;
Foolish is the tale that says he ever found them, brought them home in triumph,—
Joys that once escape us fly for evermore.
Yet I dream that somewhere, clad in downy whiteness, dwell the honey-makers,
In aërial gardens that no mortal sees:
And at times returning, lo, they flutter round us, gathering mystic harvest,—
So I weave the legend of the long-lost bees.

II
THE SWARMING OF THE BEES
Who can tell the hiding of the white bees' nest?
Who can trace the guiding of their swift home flight?
Far would be his riding on a life-long quest:
Surely ere it ended would his beard grow white.
Never in the coming of the rose-red Spring,
Never in the passing of the wine-red Fall,
May you hear the humming of the white bee's wing
Murmur o'er the meadow ere the night bells call.
Wait till winter hardens in the cold gray sky,
Wait till leaves are fallen and the brooks all freeze,
Then above the gardens where the dead flowers lie,
Swarm the merry millions of the wild white bees.
Out of the high-built airy hive,
Deep in the clouds that veil the sun,
Look how the first of the swarm arrive;
Timidly venturing, one by one,
Down through the tranquil air,
Wavering here and there,
Large, and lazy in flight,—
Caught by a lift of the breeze,
Tangled among the naked trees,—
Dropping then, without a sound,
Feather-white, feather-light,
To their rest on the ground.
Thus the swarming is begun.
Count the leaders, every one
Perfect as a perfect star
Till the slow descent is done.
Look beyond them, see how far
Down the vistas dim and gray,
Multitudes are on the way.
Now a sudden brightness
Dawns within the sombre day,
Over fields of whiteness;
And the sky is swiftly alive
With the flutter and the flight
Of the shimmering bees, that pour
From the hidden door of the hive
Till you can count no more.
Now on the branches of hemlock and pine
Thickly they settle and cluster and swing,
Bending them low; and the trellised vine
And the dark elm-boughs are traced with a line
Of beauty wherever the white bees cling.
Now they are hiding the wrecks of the flowers,
Softly, softly, covering all,
Over the grave of the summer hours
Spreading a silver pall.
Now they are building the broad roof ledge,
Into a cornice smooth and fair,
Moulding the terrace, from edge to edge,
Into the sweep of a marble stair.
Wonderful workers, swift and dumb,
Numberless myriads, still they come,
Thronging ever faster, faster, faster!
Where is their queen? Who is their master?
The gardens are faded, the fields are frore,—
What is the honey they toil to store
In the desolate day, where no blossoms gleam?
Forgetfulness and a dream!
But now the fretful wind awakes;
I hear him girding at the trees;
He strikes the bending boughs, and shakes
The quiet clusters of the bees
To powdery drift;
He tosses them away,
He drives them like spray;
He makes them veer and shift
Around his blustering path.
In clouds blindly whirling,
In rings madly swirling,
Full of crazy wrath,
So furious and fast they fly
They blur the earth and blot the sky
In wild, white mirk.
They fill the air with frozen wings
And tiny, angry, icy stings;
They blind the eyes, and choke the breath,
They dance a maddening dance of death
Around their work,
Sweeping the cover from the hill,
Heaping the hollows deeper still,
Effacing every line and mark,
And swarming, storming in the dark
Through the long night;
Until, at dawn, the wind lies down
Weary of fight;
The last torn cloud, with trailing gown,
Passes the open gates of light;
And the white bees are lost in flight.
Look how the landscape glitters wide and still,
Bright with a pure surprise!
The day begins with joy, and all past ill,
Buried in white oblivion, lies
Beneath the snow-drifts under crystal skies.
New hope, new love, new life, new cheer,
Flow in the sunrise beam,—
The gladness of Apollo when he sees,
Upon the bosom of the wintry year,
The honey-harvest of his wild white bees,
Forgetfulness and a dream!

III
LEGEND
Listen, my beloved, while the silver morning, like a tranquil vision,
Fills the world around us and our hearts with peace;
Quiet is the close of Aristæus' legend, happy is the ending—
Listen while I tell you how he found release.

Many months he wandered far away in sadness, desolately thinking
Only of the vanished joys he could not find;
Till the great Apollo, pitying his shepherd, loosed him from the burden
Of a dark, reluctant, backward-looking mind.
Then he saw around him all the changeful beauty of the changing seasons,
In the world-wide regions where his journey lay;
Birds that sang to cheer him, flowers that bloomed beside him, stars that shone to guide him,—
Traveller's joy was plenty all along the way!
Everywhere he journeyed strangers made him welcome, listened while he taught them
Secret lore of field and forest he had learned:
How to train the vines and make the olives fruitful; how to guard the sheepfolds;
How to stay the fever when the dog-star burned.
Friendliness and blessing followed in his footsteps; richer were the harvests,
Happier the dwellings, wheresoe'er he came;
Little children loved him, and he left behind him, in the hour of parting,
Memories of kindness and a god-like name.
So he travelled onward, desolate no longer, patient in his seeking,
Reaping all the wayside comfort of his quest;
Till at last in Thracia, high upon Mount Hæmus, far from human dwelling,
Weary Aristæus laid him down to rest.

Then the honey-makers, clad in downy whiteness, fluttered soft around him,
Wrapt him in a dreamful slumber pure and deep.
This is life, beloved: first a sheltered garden, then a troubled journey,
Joy and pain of seeking,—and at last we sleep!
    1905.

NEW YEAR'S EVE
I
The other night I had a dream, most clear
And comforting, complete
In every line, a crystal sphere,
And full of intimate and secret cheer.
Therefore I will repeat
That vision, dearest heart, to you,
As of a thing not feigned, but very true,
Yes, true as ever in my life befell;
And you, perhaps, can tell
Whether my dream was really sad or sweet.
II
The shadows flecked the elm-embowered street
I knew so well, long, long ago;
And on the pillared porch where Marguerite
Had sat with me, the moonlight lay like snow.
But she, my comrade and my friend of youth,
Most gaily wise,
Most innocently loved,—
She of the blue-gray eyes
That ever smiled and ever spoke the truth,—
From that familiar dwelling, where she moved
Like mirth incarnate in the years before,
Had gone into the hidden house of Death.
I thought the garden wore
White mourning for her blessed innocence,
And the syringa's breath
Came from the corner by the fence
Where she had made her rustic seat,
With fragrance passionate, intense,
As if it breathed a sigh for Marguerite.
My heart was heavy with a sense
Of something good for ever gone. I sought
Vainly for some consoling thought,
Some comfortable word that I could say
To her sad father, whom I visited again
For the first time since she had gone away.
The bell rang shrill and lonely,—then
The door was opened, and I sent my name
To him,—but ah! 'twas Marguerite who came!
There in the dear old dusky room she stood
Beneath the lamp, just as she used to stand,
In tender mocking mood.
"You did not ask for me," she said,
"And so I will not let you take my hand;
But I must hear what secret talk you planned
With father. Come, my friend, be good,
And tell me your affairs of state:
Why you have stayed away and made me wait
So long. Sit down beside me here,—
And, do you know, it seems a year
Since we have talked together,—why so late?"
Amazed, incredulous, confused with joy
I hardly dared to show,
And stammering like a boy,
I took the place she showed me at her side;
And then the talk flowed on with brimming tide
Through the still night,
While she with influence light
Controlled it, as the moon the flood.
She knew where I had been, what I had done,
What work was planned, and what begun;
My troubles, failures, fears she understood,
And touched them with a heart so kind,
That every care was melted from my mind,
And every hope grew bright,
And life seemed moving on to happy ends.
(Ah, what self-beggared fool was he
That said a woman cannot be
The very best of friends?)
Then there were memories of old times,
Recalled with many a gentle jest;
And at the last she brought the book of rhymes
We made together, trying to translate
The Songs of Heine (hers were always best).
"Now come," she said,
"To-night we will collaborate
Again; I'll put you to the test.
Here's one I never found the way to do,—
The simplest are the hardest ones, you know,—
I give this song to you."
And then she read:
Mein Kind, wir waren Kinder,
Zwei Kinder, jung und froh.

But all the while, a silent question stirred
Within me, though I dared not speak the word:
"Is it herself, and is she truly here,
And was I dreaming when I heard
That she was dead last year?
Or was it true, and is she but a shade
Who brings a fleeting joy to eye and ear,
Cold though so kind, and will she gently fade
When her sweet ghostly part is played
And the light-curtain falls at dawn of day?"
But while my heart was troubled by this fear
So deeply that I could not speak it out,
Lest all my happiness should disappear,
I thought me of a cunning way
To hide the question and dissolve the doubt.
"Will you not give me now your hand,
Dear Marguerite," I asked, "to touch and hold,
That by this token I may understand
You are the same true friend you were of old?"
She answered with a smile so bright and calm
It seemed as if I saw the morn arise
In the deep heaven of her eyes;
And smiling so, she laid her palm
In mine. Dear God, it was not cold
But warm with vital heat!
"You live!" I cried, "you live, dear Marguerite!"
When I awoke; but strangely comforted,
Although I knew again that she was dead.

III
Yes, there's the dream! And was it sweet or sad?
Dear mistress of my waking and my sleep,
Present reward of all my heart's desire,
Watching with me beside the winter fire,
Interpret now this vision that I had.
But while you read the meaning, let me keep
The touch of you: for the Old Year with storm
Is passing through the midnight, and doth shake
The corners of the house,—and oh! my heart would break
Unless both dreaming and awake
My hand could feel your hand was warm, warm, warm!
1905.

THE VAIN KING
In robes of Tyrian blue the King was drest,
A jewelled collar shone upon his breast,
A giant ruby glittered in his crown:
Lord of rich lands and many a splendid town,
In him the glories of an ancient line
Of sober kings, who ruled by right divine,
Were centred; and to him with loyal awe
The people looked for leadership and law.
Ten thousand knights, the safeguard of the land,
Were like a single sword within his hand;
A hundred courts, with power of life and death,
Proclaimed decrees of justice by his breath;
And all the sacred growths that men had known
Of order and of rule upheld his throne.
Proud was the King: yet not with such a heart
As fits a man to play a royal part.
Not his the pride that honours as a trust
The right to rule, the duty to be just:
Not his the dignity that bends to bear
The monarch's yoke, the master's load of care,
And labours like the peasant at his gate,
To serve the people and protect the State.
Another pride was his, and other joys:
To him the crown and sceptre were but toys,
With which he played at glory's idle game,
To please himself and win the wreaths of fame.
The throne his fathers held from age to age,
To his ambition seemed a fitting stage
Built for King Martin to display at will,
His mighty strength and universal skill.
No conscious child, that, spoiled with praising, tries
At every step to win admiring eyes,
No favourite mountebank, whose acting draws
From gaping crowds the thunder of applause,
Was vainer than the King: his only thirst
Was to be hailed, in every race, the first.
When tournament was held, in knightly guise
The King would ride the lists and win the prize;
When music charmed the court, with golden lyre
The King would take the stage and lead the choir;
In hunting, his the lance to slay the boar;
In hawking, see his falcon highest soar;
In painting, he would wield the master's brush;
In high debate,—"the King is speaking! Hush!"
Thus, with a restless heart, in every field
He sought renown, and made his subjects yield.
But while he played the petty games of life
His kingdom fell a prey to inward strife;
Corruption through the court unheeded crept,
And on the seat of honour justice slept.
The strong trod down the weak; the helpless poor
Groaned under burdens grievous to endure;
The nation's wealth was spent in vain display,
And weakness wore the nation's heart away.
Yet think not Earth is blind to human woes—
Man has more friends and helpers than he knows;
And when a patient people are oppressed,
The land that bore them feels it in her breast.
Spirits of field and flood, of heath and hill,
Are grieved and angry at the spreading ill;
The trees complain together in the night,
Voices of wrath are heard along the height,
And secret vows are sworn, by stream and strand,
To bring the tyrant low and free the land.
But little recked the pampered King of these;
He heard no voice but such as praise and please.
Flattered and fooled, victor in every sport,
One day he wandered idly with his court
Beside the river, seeking to devise
New ways to show his skill to wondering eyes.
There in the stream a patient angler stood,
And cast his line across the rippling flood.
His silver spoil lay near him on the green:
"Such fish," the courtiers cried, "were never seen!
Three salmon longer than a cloth-yard shaft—
This man must be the master of his craft!"
"An easy art!" the jealous King replied:
"Myself could learn it better, if I tried,
And catch a hundred larger fish a week—
Wilt thou accept the challenge, fellow? Speak!"

The angler turned, came near, and bent his knee:
"'Tis not for kings to strive with such as me;
Yet if the King commands it, I obey.
But one condition of the strife I pray:
The fisherman who brings the least to land
Shall do whate'er the other may command."
Loud laughed the King: "A foolish fisher thou!
For I shall win, and rule thee then as now."
Then to Prince John, a sober soul, sedate
And slow, King Martin left the helm of State,
While to the novel game with eager zest
He all his time and all his powers addressed.
Sure such a sight was never seen before!
In robe and crown the monarch trod the shore;
His golden hooks were decked with feathers fine,
His jewelled reel ran out a silken line.
With kingly strokes he flogged the crystal stream;
Far-off the salmon saw his tackle gleam;
Careless of kings, they eyed with calm disdain
The gaudy lure, and Martin fished in vain.
On Friday, when the week was almost spent,
He scanned his empty creel with discontent,
Called for a net, and cast it far and wide,
And drew—a thousand minnows from the tide!
Then came the angler to conclude the match,
And at the monarch's feet spread out his catch—
A hundred salmon, greater than before.
"I win!" he cried: "the King must pay the score."
Then Martin, angry, threw his tackle down:
"Rather than lose this game I'd lose my crown!"
"Nay, thou hast lost them both," the angler said;
And as he spoke a wondrous light was shed
Around his form; he dropped his garments mean,
And in his place the River-god was seen.
"Thy vanity has brought thee in my power,
And thou must pay the forfeit at this hour:
For thou hast shown thyself a royal fool,
Too proud to angle, and too vain to rule,
Eager to win in every trivial strife,—
Go! Thou shalt fish for minnows all thy life!"
Wrathful, the King the magic sentence heard;
He strove to answer, but he only chirr-r-ed:
His royal robe was changed to wings of blue,
His crown a ruby crest,—away he flew!

So every summer day along the stream
The vain King-fisher darts, an azure gleam,
And scolds the angler with a mocking scream.
April, 1904.

THE FOOLISH FIR-TREE
A tale that the poet Rückert told
To German children, in days of old;
Disguised in a random, rollicking rhyme
Like a merry mummer of ancient time,
And sent, in its English dress, to please
The little folk of the Christmas trees.

A little fir grew in the midst of the wood
Contented and happy, as young trees should.
His body was straight and his boughs were clean;
And summer and winter the bountiful sheen
Of his needles bedecked him, from top to root,
In a beautiful, all-the-year, evergreen suit.
But a trouble came into his heart one day,
When he saw that the other trees were gay
In the wonderful raiment that summer weaves
Of manifold shapes and kinds of leaves:
He looked at his needles so stiff and small,
And thought that his dress was the poorest of all.
Then jealousy clouded the little tree's mind,
And he said to himself, "It was not very kind
To give such an ugly old dress to a tree!
If the fays of the forest would only ask me,
I'd tell them how I should like to be dressed,—
In a garment of gold, to bedazzle the rest!"
So he fell asleep, but his dreams were bad.
When he woke in the morning, his heart was glad;
For every leaf that his boughs could hold
Was made of the brightest beaten gold.
I tell you, children, the tree was proud;
He was something above the common crowd;
And he tinkled his leaves, as if he would say
To a pedlar who happened to pass that way,
"Just look at me! Don't you think I am fine?
And wouldn't you like such a dress as mine?"
"Oh, yes!" said the man, "and I really guess
I must fill my pack with your beautiful dress."
So he picked the golden leaves with care,
And left the little tree shivering there.
"Oh, why did I wish for golden leaves?"
The fir-tree said, "I forgot that thieves
Would be sure to rob me in passing by.
If the fairies would give me another try,
I'd wish for something that cost much less,
And be satisfied with glass for my dress!"
Then he fell asleep; and, just as before,
The fairies granted his wish once more.
When the night was gone, and the sun rose clear,
The tree was a crystal chandelier;
And it seemed, as he stood in the morning light,
That his branches were covered with jewels bright.
"Aha!" said the tree. "This is something great!"
And he held himself up, very proud and straight;
But a rude young wind through the forest dashed,
In a reckless temper, and quickly smashed
The delicate leaves. With a clashing sound
They broke into pieces and fell on the ground,
Like a silvery, shimmering shower of hail,
And the tree stood naked and bare to the gale.
Then his heart was sad; and he cried, "Alas
For my beautiful leaves of shining glass!
Perhaps I have made another mistake
In choosing a dress so easy to break.
If the fairies only would hear me again
I'd ask them for something both pretty and plain:
It wouldn't cost much to grant my request,—
In leaves of green lettuce I'd like to be dressed!"
By this time the fairies were laughing, I know;
But they gave him his wish in a second; and so
With leaves of green lettuce, all tender and sweet,
The tree was arrayed, from his head to his feet.
"I knew it!" he cried, "I was sure I could find
The sort of a suit that would be to my mind.

There's none of the trees has a prettier dress,
And none as attractive as I am, I guess."
But a goat, who was taking an afternoon walk,
By chance overheard the fir-tree's talk.
So he came up close for a nearer view;—
"My salad!" he bleated, "I think so too!
You're the most attractive kind of a tree,
And I want your leaves for my five-o'clock tea."
So he ate them all without saying grace,
And walked away with a grin on his face;
While the little tree stood in the twilight dim,
With never a leaf on a single limb.
Then he sighed and groaned; but his voice was weak—
He was so ashamed that he could not speak.
He knew at last he had been a fool,
To think of breaking the forest rule,
And choosing a dress himself to please,
Because he envied the other trees.
But it couldn't be helped, it was now too late,
He must make up his mind to a leafless fate!
So he let himself sink in a slumber deep,
But he moaned and he tossed in his troubled sleep,
Till the morning touched him with joyful beam,
And he woke to find it was all a dream.
For there in his evergreen dress he stood,
A pointed fir in the midst of the wood!
His branches were sweet with the balsam smell,
His needles were green when the white snow fell.
And always contented and happy was he,—
The very best kind of a Christmas tree.

"GRAN' BOULE"
A SEAMAN'S TALE OF THE SEA

We men hat go down for a livin' in ships to the sea,—
We love it a different way from you poets that 'bide on the land.
We are fond of it, sure! But, you take it as comin' from me,
There's a fear and a hate in our love that a landsman can't understand.
Oh, who could help likin' the salty smell, and the blue
Of the waves that are lazily breathin' as if they dreamed in the sun?
She's a Sleepin' Beauty, the sea,—but you can't tell what she'll do;
And the seamen never trust her,—they know too well what she's done!
She's a wench like one that I saw in a singin'-play,—
Carmen they called her,—Lord, what a life her lovers did lead!
She'd cuddle and kiss you, and sing you and dance you away;
And then,—she'd curse you, and break you, and throw you down like a weed.
You may chance it awhile with the girls like that, if you please;
But you want a woman to trust when you settle down with a wife;
And a seaman's thought of growin' old at his ease
Is a snug little house on the land to shelter the rest of his life.

So that was old Poisson's dream,—did you know the Cap'?
A brown little Frenchman, clever, and brave, and quick as a fish,—
Had a wife and kids on the other side of the map,—
And a rose-covered cottage for them and him was his darlin' wish.
"I 'ave sail," says he, in his broken-up Frenchy talk,
"Mos' forty-two year; I 'ave go on all part of de worl' dat ees wet.
I'm seeck of de boat and de water. I rader walk
Wid ma Josephine in one garden; an' eef we get tire', we set!
"You see dat bateau, Sainte Brigitte? I bring 'er dh'are
From de Breton coas', by gar, jus' feefteen year bifore.
She ole w'en she come on Kebec, but Holloway Frères
Dey buy 'er, an' hire me run 'er along dat dam' Nort' Shore.
"Dose engine one leetl' bit cranky,—too ole, you see,—
She roll and peetch in de wave'. But I lak' 'er pretty well;
An' dat sheep she lak' 'er captaine, sure, dat's me!
Wit' forty ton coal in de bunker, I tek' dat sheep t'rou' hell.

"But I don' wan' risk it no more; I had bonne chance:
I save already ten t'ousan' dollar', dat's plenty I s'pose!
Nex' winter I buy dat house wid de garden on France
An' I tell adieu to de sea, and I leev' on de lan' in ripose."
All summer he talked of his house,—you could see the flowers
Abloom, and the pear-trees trained on the garden-wall so trim,
And the Captain awalkin' and smokin' away the hours,—
He thought he had done with the sea, but the sea hadn't done with him!

It was late in the fall when he made the last regular run,
Clear down to the Esquimault Point and back with his rickety ship;
She hammered and pounded a lot, for the storms had begun;
But he drove her,—and went for his season's pay at the end of the trip.
Now the Holloway Brothers are greedy and thin little men,
With their eyes set close together, and money's their only God;
So they told the Cap' he must run the "Bridget" again,
To fetch a cargo from Moisie, two thousand quintals of cod.
He said the season was over. They said: "Not yet.
You finish the whole of your job, old man, or you don't draw a cent!"
(They had the "Bridget" insured for all they could get.)
And the Captain objected, and cursed, and cried. But he went.
They took on the cargo at Moisie, and folks beside,—
Three traders, a priest, and a couple of nuns, and a girl
For a school at Quebec,—when the Captain saw her he sighed,
And said: "Ma littl' Fifi got hair lak' dat, all curl!"

The snow had fallen a foot, and the wind was high,

320

When the "Bridget" butted her way thro' the billows on Moisie bar.
The darkness grew with the gale, not a star in the sky,
And the Captain swore: "We mus' make Sept Isles to-night, by gar!"
He couldn't go back, for he didn't dare to turn;
The sea would have thrown the ship like a mustang noosed with a rope;
For the monstrous waves were leapin' high astern,
And the shelter of Seven Island Bay was the only hope.
There's a bunch of broken hills half sunk in the mouth
Of the bay, with their jagged peaks afoam; and the Captain thought
He could pass to the north; but the sea kept shovin' him south,
With her harlot hands, in the snow-blind murk, till she had him caught.
She had waited forty years for a night like this,—
Did he think he could leave her now, and live in a cottage, the fool?
She headed him straight for the island he couldn't miss;
And heaved his boat in the dark,—and smashed it against Gran' Boule.
How the Captain and half of the people clambered ashore,
Through the surf and the snow in the gloom of that horrible night,
There's no one ever will know. For two days more
The death-white shroud of the tempest covered the island from sight.
How they suffered, and struggled, and died, will never be told;
We discovered them all at last when we reached Gran' Boule with a boat;
The drowned and the frozen were lyin' stiff and cold,
And the poor little girl with the curls was wrapped in the Captain's coat.
Go write your song of the sea as the landsmen do,
And call her your "great sweet mother," your "bride," and all the rest;
She was made to be loved,—but remember, she won't love you,—
The men who trust her the least are the sailors who know her the best.

HEROES OF THE "TITANIC"
Honour the brave who sleep
Where the lost "Titanic" lies,
The men who knew what a man must do
When he looks Death in the eyes.
"Women and children first,"—
Ah, strong and tender cry!
The sons whom women had borne and nursed,
Remembered,—and dared to die.
The boats crept off in the dark:
The great ship groaned: and then,—
O stars of the night, who saw that sight,
Bear witness, These were men!
November 9, 1912.

THE STANDARD-BEARER
I

"How can I tell," Sir Edmund said,
"Who has the right or the wrong o' this thing?
Cromwell stands for the people's cause,
Charles is crowned by the ancient laws;
English meadows are sopping red,
Englishmen striking each other dead,—
Times are black as a raven's wing.
Out of the ruck and the murk I see
Only one thing!
The King has trusted his banner to me,
And I must fight for the King."

II
Into the thick of the Edgehill fight
Sir Edmund rode with a shout; and the ring
Of grim-faced, hard-hitting Parliament men
Swallowed him up,—it was one against ten!
He fought for the standard with all his might,
Never again did he come to sight—
Victor, hid by the raven's wing!
After the battle had passed we found
Only one thing,—
The hand of Sir Edmund gripped around
The banner-staff of his King.
1914.

THE PROUD LADY
When Stävoren town was in its prime
And queened the Zuyder Zee,
Her ships went out to every clime
With costly merchantry.
A lady dwelt in that rich town,
The fairest in all the land;
She walked abroad in a velvet gown,
With many rings on her hand.
Her hair was bright as the beaten gold,
Her lips as coral red,
Her roving eyes were blue and bold,
And her heart with pride was fed.
For she was proud of her father's ships,
As she watched them gaily pass;
And pride looked out of her eyes and lips
When she saw herself in the glass.
"Now come," she said to the captains ten,
Who were ready to put to sea,
"Ye are all my men and my father's men,
And what will ye do for me?"
"Go north and south, go east and west,
And get me gifts," she said.
"And he who bringeth me home the best,
With that man will I wed."
So they all fared forth, and sought with care
In many a famous mart,
For satins and silks and jewels rare,
To win that lady's heart.
She looked at them all with never a thought,
And careless put them by;
"I am not fain of the things ye brought,
Enough of these have I."
The last that came was the head of the fleet,
His name was Jan Borel;
He bent his knee at the lady's feet,—

In truth he loved her well.
"I've brought thee home the best i' the world,
A shipful of Danzig corn!"
She stared at him long; her red lips curled,
Her blue eyes filled with scorn.
"Now out on thee, thou feckless kerl,
A loon thou art," she said.
"Am I a starving beggar girl?
Shall I ever lack for bread?"
"Go empty all thy sacks of grain
Into the nearest sea,
And never show thy face again
To make a mock of me."
Young Jan Borel, he answered naught,
But in the harbour cast
The sacks of golden corn he brought,
And groaned when fell the last.
Then Jan Borel, he hoisted sail,
And out to sea he bore;
He passed the Helder in a gale
And came again no more.
But the grains of corn went drifting down
Like devil-scattered seed,
To sow the harbour of the town
With a wicked growth of weed.
The roots were thick and the silt and sand
Were gathered day by day,
Till not a furlong out from land
A shoal had barred the way.
Then Stävoren town saw evil years,
No ships could out or in,
The boats lay rotting at the piers,
And the mouldy grain in the bin.
The grass-grown streets were all forlorn,
The town in ruin stood,
The lady's velvet gown was torn,
Her rings were sold for food.
Her father had perished long ago,
But the lady held her pride,
She walked with a scornful step and slow,
Till at last in her rags she died.
Yet still on the crumbling piers of the town,
When the midnight moon shines free,
A woman walks in a velvet gown
And scatters corn in the sea.
917.

LYRICS OF
LABOUR AND ROMANCE
A MILE WITH ME

O who will walk a mile with me
Along life's merry way?
A comrade blithe and full of glee,
Who dares to laugh out loud and free,
And let his frolic fancy play,
Like a happy child, through the flowers gay
That fill the field and fringe the way
Where he walks a mile with me.
And who will walk a mile with me
Along life's weary way?
A friend whose heart has eyes to see
The stars shine out o'er the darkening lea,
And the quiet rest at the end o' the day,—
A friend who knows, and dares to say,
The brave, sweet words that cheer the way
Where he walks a mile with me.
With such a comrade, such a friend,
I fain would walk till journeys end,
Through summer sunshine, winter rain,
And then?—Farewell, we shall meet again!

THE THREE BEST THINGS
I
WORK

Let me but do my work from day to day,
In field or forest, at the desk or loom,
In roaring market-place or tranquil room;
Let me but find it in my heart to say,
When vagrant wishes beckon me astray,
"This is my work; my blessing, not my doom;
Of all who live, I am the one by whom
This work can best be done in the right way."
Then shall I see it not too great, nor small,
To suit my spirit and to prove my powers;
Then shall I cheerful greet the labouring hours,
And cheerful turn, when the long shadows fall
At eventide, to play and love and rest,
Because I know for me my work is best.

II
LOVE

Let me but love my love without disguise,
Nor wear a mask of fashion old or new,
Nor wait to speak till I can hear a clue,
Nor play a part to shine in others' eyes,
Nor bow my knees to what my heart denies;
But what I am, to that let me be true,
And let me worship where my love is due,
And so through love and worship let me rise.
For love is but the heart's immortal thirst
To be completely known and all forgiven,
Even as sinful souls that enter Heaven:
So take me, dear, and understand my worst,
And freely pardon it, because confessed,
And let me find in loving thee, my best.

III
LIFE

Let me but live my life from year to year,
With forward face and unreluctant soul;
Not hurrying to, nor turning from, the goal;
Not mourning for the things that disappear
In the dim past, nor holding back in fear
From what the future veils; but with a whole
And happy heart, that pays its toll
To Youth and Age, and travels on with cheer.
So let the way wind up the hill or down,
O'er rough or smooth, the journey will be joy:
Still seeking what I sought when but a boy,
New friendship, high adventure, and a crown,
My heart will keep the courage of the quest,
And hope the road's last turn will be the best.

RELIANCE

Not to the swift, the race:
Not to the strong, the fight:
Not to the righteous, perfect grace
Not to the wise, the light.
But often faltering feet
Come surest to the goal;
And they who walk in darkness meet
The sunrise of the soul.
A thousand times by night
The Syrian hosts have died;
A thousand times the vanquished right
Hath risen, glorified.
The truth the wise men sought
Was spoken by a child;
The alabaster box was brought
In trembling hands defiled.
Not from my torch, the gleam,
But from the stars above:
Not from my heart, life's crystal stream,
But from the depths of Love.

DOORS OF DARING

The mountains that inclose the vale
With walls of granite, steep and high,
Invite the fearless foot to scale
Their stairway toward the sky.
The restless, deep, dividing sea
That flows and foams from shore to shore,
Calls to its sunburned chivalry,
"Push out, set sail, explore!"
The bars of life at which we fret,
That seem to prison and control,
Are but the doors of daring, set
Ajar before the soul.
Say not, "Too poor," but freely give;
Sigh not, "Too weak," but boldly try;
You never can begin to live
Until you dare to die.

THE CHILD IN THE GARDEN

When to the garden of untroubled thought
I came of late, and saw the open door,
And wished again to enter, and explore
The sweet, wild ways with stainless bloom inwrought,
And bowers of innocence with beauty fraught,
It seemed some purer voice must speak before
I dared to tread that garden loved of yore,
That Eden lost unknown and found unsought.
Then just within the gate I saw a child,—
A stranger-child, yet to my heart most dear;
He held his hands to me, and softly smiled
With eyes that knew no shade of sin or fear:
"Come in," he said, "and play awhile with me;
I am the little child you used to be."

LOVE'S REASON

For that thy face is fair I love thee not;
Nor yet because thy brown benignant eyes
Have sudden gleams of gladness and surprise,
Like woodland brooks that cross a sunlit spot:
Nor for thy body, born without a blot,
And loveliest when it shines with no disguise
Pure as the star of Eve in Paradise,—
For all these outward things I love thee not:

But for a something in thy form and face,
Thy looks and ways, of primal harmony;
A certain soothing charm, a vital grace
That breathes of the eternal womanly,
And makes me feel the warmth of Nature's breast,
When in her arms, and thine, I sink to rest.

THE ECHO IN THE HEART

It's little I can tell
About the birds in books;
And yet I know them well,
By their music and their looks:
When May comes down the lane,
Her airy lovers throng
To welcome her with song,
And follow in her train:
Each minstrel weaves his part
In that wild-flowery strain,
And I know them all again
By their echo in my heart.
It's little that I care
About my darling's place
In books of beauty rare,
Or heraldries of race:
For when she steps in view,
It matters not to me
What her sweet type may be,
Of woman, old or new.
I can't explain the art,
But I know her for my own,
Because her lightest tone
Wakes an echo in my heart.

"UNDINE"

'Twas far away and long ago,
When I was but a dreaming boy,
This fairy tale of love and woe
Entranced my heart with tearful joy;
And while with white Undine I wept
Your spirit,—ah, how strange it seems,—
Was cradled in some star, and slept,
Unconscious of her coming dreams.

"RENCONTRE"

Oh, was I born too soon, my dear, or were you born too late,
That I am going out the door while you come in the gate?
For you the garden blooms galore, the castle is en fête;
You are the coming guest, my dear,—for me the horses wait.
I know the mansion well, my dear, its rooms so rich and wide;
If you had only come before I might have been your guide,
And hand in hand with you explore the treasures that they hide;
But you have come to stay, my dear, and I prepare to ride.

Then walk with me an hour, my dear, and pluck the reddest rose
Amid the white and crimson store with which your garden glows,—
A single rose,—I ask no more of what your love bestows;
It is enough to give, my dear,—a flower to him who goes.

The House of Life is yours, my dear, for many and many a day,
But I must ride the lonely shore, the Road to Far Away:
So bring the stirrup-cup and pour a brimming draught, I pray,
And when you take the road, my dear, I'll meet you on the way.

LOVE IN A LOOK
Let me but feel thy look's embrace,
Transparent, pure, and warm,
And I'll not ask to touch thy face,
Or fold thee in mine arm.
For in thine eyes a girl doth rise,
Arrayed in candid bliss,
And draws me to her with a charm
More close than any kiss.
A loving-cup of golden wine,
Songs of a silver brook,
And fragrant breaths of eglantine,
Are mingled in thy look.
More fair they are than any star,
Thy topaz eyes divine—
And deep within their trysting-nook
Thy spirit blends with mine.

MY APRIL LADY
When down the stair at morning
The sunbeams round her float,
Sweet rivulets of laughter
Are rippling in her throat;
The gladness of her greeting
Is gold without alloy;
And in the morning sunlight
I think her name is Joy.
When in the evening twilight
The quiet book-room lies,
We read the sad old ballads,
While from her hidden eyes
The tears are falling, falling,
That give her heart relief;
And in the evening twilight,
I think her name is Grief.
My little April lady,
Of sunshine and of showers
She weaves the old spring magic,
And my heart breaks in flowers!
But when her moods are ended,
She nestles like a dove;
Then, by the pain and rapture,
I know her name is Love.

A LOVER'S ENVY
I envy every flower that blows
Along the meadow where she goes,
And every bird that sings to her,
And every breeze that brings to her
The fragrance of the rose.
I envy every poet's rhyme
That moves her heart at eventime,
And every tree that wears for her
Its brightest bloom, and bears for her
The fruitage of its prime.
I envy every Southern night
That paves her path with moonbeams white,
And silvers all the leaves for her,
And in their shadow weaves for her
A dream of dear delight.
I envy none whose love requires
Of her a gift, a task that tires:
I only long to live to her,
I only ask to give to her,
All that her heart desires.

FIRE-FLY CITY
Like a long arrow through the dark the train is darting,
Bearing me far away, after a perfect day of love's delight:
Wakeful with all the sad-sweet memories of parting,
I lift the narrow window-shade and look out on the night.
Lonely the land unknown, and like a river flowing,
Forest and field and hill are gliding backward still athwart my dream;
Till in that country strange, and ever stranger growing,
A magic city full of lights begins to glow and gleam.
Wide through the landscape dim the lamps are lit in millions;
Long avenues unfold clear-shining lines of gold across the green;
Clusters and rings of light, and luminous pavilions,—
Oh, who will tell the city's name, and what these wonders mean?
Why do they beckon me, and what have they to show me?
Crowds in the blazing street, mirth where the feasters meet, kisses and wine:
Many to laugh with me, but never one to know me:
A cityful of stranger-hearts and none to beat with mine!
Look how the glittering lines are wavering and lifting,—
Softly the breeze of night scatters the vision bright: and, passing fair,
Over the meadow-grass and through the forest drifting,
The Fire-Fly City of the Dark is lost in empty air!

THE GENTLE TRAVELLER
"Through many a land your journey ran,
And showed the best the world can boast:
Now tell me, traveller, if you can,
The place that pleased you most."
She laid her hands upon my breast,
And murmured gently in my ear,
"The place I loved and liked the best
Was in your arms, my dear!"

NEPENTHE
Yes, it was like you to forget,
And cancel in the welcome of your smile
My deep arrears of debt,
And with the putting forth of both your hands

To sweep away the bars my folly set
Between us—bitter thoughts, and harsh demands,
And reckless deeds that seemed untrue
To love, when all the while
My heart was aching through and through
For you, sweet heart, and only you.
Yet, as I turned to come to you again,
I thought there must be many a mile
Of sorrowful reproach to cross,
And many an hour of mutual pain
To bear, until I could make plain
That all my pride was but the fear of loss,
And all my doubt the shadow of despair
To win a heart so innocent and fair;
And even that which looked most ill
Was but the fever-fret and effort vain
To dull the thirst which you alone could still.
But as I turned, the desert miles were crossed,
And when I came, the weary hours were sped!
For there you stood beside the open door,
Glad, gracious, smiling as before,
And with bright eyes and tender hands outspread
Restored me to the Eden I had lost.
Never a word of cold reproof,
No sharp reproach, no glances that accuse
The culprit whom they hold aloof,—
Ah, 'tis not thus that other women use
The empire they have won!
For there is none like you, beloved,—none
Secure enough to do what you have done.
Where did you learn this heavenly art,—
You sweetest and most wise of all that live,—
With silent welcome to impart
Assurance of the royal heart
That never questions where it would forgive?

None but a queen could pardon me like this!
My sovereign lady, let me lay
Within each rosy palm a loyal kiss
Of penitence, then close the fingers up,
Thus—thus! Now give the cup
Of full nepenthe in your crimson mouth,
And come—the garden blooms with bliss,
The wind is in the south,
The rose of love with dew is wet—
Dear, it was like you to forget!

DAY AND NIGHT
How long is the night, brother,
And how long is the day?
Oh, the day's too short for a happy task,
And the day's too short for play;
And the night's too short for the bliss of love,
For look, how the edge of the sky grows gray,
While the stars die out in the blue above,
And the wan moon fades away.
How short is the day, brother,
And how short is the night?
Oh, the day's too long for a heavy task,
And long, long, long is the night,
When the wakeful hours are filled with pain,
And the sad heart waits for the thing it fears,

And sighs for the dawn to come again,—
The night is a thousand years!
How long is a life, dear God,
And how fast does it flow?
The measure of life is a flame in the soul:
It is neither swift nor slow.
But the vision of time is the shadow cast
By the fleeting world on the body's wall;
When it fades there is neither future nor past,
But love is all in all.

HESPER
Her eyes are like the evening air,
Her voice is like a rose,
Her lips are like a lovely song,
That ripples as it flows,
And she herself is sweeter than
The sweetest thing she knows.
A slender, haunting, twilight form
Of wonder and surprise,
She seemed a fairy or a child,
Till, deep within her eyes,
I saw the homeward-leading star
Of womanhood arise.

ARRIVAL
Across a thousand miles of sea, a hundred leagues of land,
Along a path I had not traced and could not understand,
I travelled fast and far for this,—to take thee by the hand.

A pilgrim knowing not the shrine where he would bend his knee,
A mariner without a dream of what his port would be,
So fared I with a seeking heart until I came to thee.
O cooler than a grove of palm in some heat-weary place,
O fairer than an isle of calm after the wild sea race,
The quiet room adorned with flowers where first I saw thy face!
Then furl the sail, let fall the oar, forget the paths of foam!
The fate that made me wander far at last has brought me home
To thee, dear haven of my heart, and I no more will roam.

DEPARTURE
Oh, why are you shining so bright, big Sun,
And why is the garden so gay?
Do you know that my days of delight are done,
Do you know I am going away?
If you covered your face with a cloud, I'd dream
You were sorry for me in my pain,
And the heavily drooping flowers would seem
To be weeping with me in the rain.
But why is your head so low, sweet heart,
And why are your eyes overcast?
Are you crying because you know we must part,
Do you think this embrace is our last?
Then kiss me again, and again, and again,
Look up as you bid me good-bye!
For your face is too dear for the stain of a tear,
And your smile is the sun in my sky.

THE BLACK BIRDS

I

Once, only once, I saw it clear,—
That Eden every human heart has dreamed
A hundred times, but always far away!
Ah, well do I remember how it seemed,
Through the still atmosphere
Of that enchanted day,
To lie wide open to my weary feet:
A little land of love and joy and rest,
With meadows of soft green,
Rosy with cyclamen, and sweet
With delicate breath of violets unseen,—
And, tranquil 'mid the bloom
As if it waited for a coming guest,
A little house of peace and joy and love
Was nested like a snow-white dove.

II

From the rough mountain where I stood,
Homesick for happiness,
Only a narrow valley and a darkling wood
To cross, and then the long distress
Of solitude would be forever past,—
I should be home at last.
But not too soon! oh, let me linger here
And feed my eyes, hungry with sorrow,
On all this loveliness, so near,
And mine to-morrow!

III

Then, from the wood, across the silvery blue,
A dark bird flew,
Silent, with sable wings.
Close in his wake another came,—
Fragments of midnight floating through
The sunset flame,—
Another and another, weaving rings
Of blackness on the primrose sky,—
Another, and another, look, a score,
A hundred, yes, a thousand rising heavily
From that accursed, dumb, and ancient wood,
They boiled into the lucid air
Like smoke from some deep caldron of despair!
And more, and more, and ever more,
The numberless, ill-omened brood
Flapping their ragged plumes,
Possessed the landscape and the evening light
With menaces and glooms.
Oh, dark, dark, dark they hovered o'er the place
Where once I saw the little house so white
Amid the flowers, covering every trace
Of beauty from my troubled sight,—
And suddenly it was night!

IV

At break of day I crossed the wooded vale;
And while the morning made
A trembling light among the tree-tops pale,
I saw the sable birds on every limb,
Clinging together closely in the shade,
And croaking placidly their surly hymn.
But, oh, the little land of peace and love
That those night-loving wings had poised above,—
Where was it gone?
Lost, lost, forevermore!
Only a cottage, dull and gray,
In the cold light of dawn,
With iron bars across the door:
Only a garden where the drooping head
Of one sad rose, foreboding its decay,
Hung o'er a barren bed:
Only a desolate field that lay
Untilled beneath the desolate day,—
Where Eden seemed to bloom I found but these!
So, wondering, I passed along my way,
With anger in my heart, too deep for words,
Against that grove of evil-sheltering trees,
And the black magic of the croaking birds.

WITHOUT DISGUISE

If I have erred in showing all my heart,
And lost your favour by a lack of pride;
If standing like a beggar at your side
With naked feet, I have forgot the art
Of those who bargain well in passion's mart,
And win the thing they want by what they hide;
Be mine the fault as mine the hope denied,
Be mine the lover's and the loser's part.
The sin, if sin it was, I do repent,
And take the penance on myself alone;
Yet after I have borne the punishment,
I shall not fear to stand before the throne
Of Love with open heart, and make this plea:
"At least I have not lied to her nor Thee!"

AN HOUR

You only promised me a single hour:
But in that hour I journeyed through a year
Of life: the joy of finding you,—the fear
Of losing you again,—the sense of power
To make you all my own,—the sudden shower
Of tears that came because you were more dear
Than words could ever tell you,—then,—the clear
Soft rapture when I plucked love's crimson flower.
An hour,—a year,—I felt your bosom rise
And fall with mystic tides, and saw the gleam
Of undiscovered stars within your eyes,—
A year,—an hour? I knew not, for the stream
Of love had carried me to Paradise,
Where all the forms of Time are like a dream.

"RAPPELLE-TOI"

Remember, when the timid light
Through the enchanted hall of dawn is gleaming;
Remember, when the pensive night
Beneath her silver-sprinkled veil walks dreaming;
When pleasure calls thee and thy heart beats high,
When tender joys through evening shades draw nigh,
Hark, from the woodland deeps
A gentle whisper creeps,
Remember!
Remember, when the hand of fate

My life from thine forevermore has parted;
When sorrow, exile, and the weight
Of lonely years have made me heavy-hearted;
Think of my loyal love, my last adieu;
Absence and time are naught, if we are true;
Long as my heart shall beat,
To thine it will repeat,
Remember!
Remember, when the cool, dark tomb
Receives my heart into its quiet keeping,
And some sweet flower begins to bloom
Above the grassy mound where I am sleeping;
Ah then, my face thou nevermore shalt see,
But still my soul will linger close to thee,
And in the holy place of night,
The litany of love recite,—
Remember!
Freely rendered from the French of Alfred de Musset.

LOVE'S NEARNESS

I think of thee when golden sunbeams glimmer
Across the sea;
And when the waves reflect the moon's pale shimmer
I think of thee.
I see thy form when down the distant highway
The dust-clouds rise;
In darkest night, above the mountain by-way
I see thine eyes.
I hear thee when the ocean-tides returning
Aloud rejoice;
And on the lonely moor in silence yearning
I hear thy voice.
I dwell with thee; though thou art far removed,
Yet thou art near.
The sun goes down, the stars shine out,—Beloved
If thou wert here!
From the German of Goethe, 1898.

TWO SONGS OF HEINE
I
"EIN FICHTENBAUM"

A fir-tree standeth lonely
On a barren northern height,
Asleep, while winter covers
His rest with robes of white.
In dreams, he sees a palm-tree
In the golden morning-land;
She droops alone and silent
In burning wastes of sand.

II
"DU BIST WIE EINE BLUME"

Fair art thou as a flower
And innocent and shy:
I look on thee and sorrow;
I grieve, I know not why.

I long to lay, in blessing,
My hand upon thy brow,
And pray that God may keep thee
As fair and pure as now.
1872.

EIGHT ECHOES FROM THE POEMS OF AUGUSTE ANGELLIER
I
THE IVORY CRADLE

The cradle I have made for thee
Is carved of orient ivory,
And curtained round with wavy silk
More white than hawthorn-bloom or milk.
A twig of box, a lilac spray,
Will drive the goblin-horde away;
And charm thy childlike heart to keep
Her happy dream and virgin sleep.
Within that pure and fragrant nest,
I'll rock thy gentle soul to rest,
With tender songs we need not fear
To have a passing angel hear.
Ah, long and long I fain would hold
The snowy curtain's guardian fold
Around thy crystal visions, born
In clearness of the early morn.
But look, the sun is glowing red
With triumph in his golden bed;
Aurora's virgin whiteness dies
In crimson glory of the skies.
The rapid flame will burn its way
Through these white curtains, too, one day;
The ivory cradle will be left
Undone, and broken, and bereft.

II
DREAMS

Often I dream your big blue eyes,
Though loth their meaning to confess,
Regard me with a clear surprise
Of dawning tenderness.
Often I dream you gladly hear
The words I hardly dare to breathe,—
The words that falter in their fear
To tell what throbs beneath.
Often I dream your hand in mine
Falls like a flower at eventide,
And down the path we leave a line
Of footsteps side by side.
But ah, in all my dreams of bliss,
In passion's hunger, fever's drouth,
I never dare to dream of this:
My lips upon your mouth.
And so I dream your big blue eyes,
That look on me with tenderness,
Grow wide, and deep, and sad, and wise,
And dim with dear distress.

III
THE GARLAND OF SLEEP

A wreath of poppy flowers,
With leaves of lotus blended,
Is carved on Life's facade of hours,
From night to night suspended.

Along the columned wall,
From birth's low portal starting,
It flows, with even rise and fall,

To death's dark door of parting.

How short each measured arc,
How brief the columns' number!
The wreath begins and ends in dark,
And leads from sleep to slumber.
The marble garland seems,
With braided leaf and bloom,
To deck the palace of our dreams
As if it were a tomb.

IV
TRANQUIL HABIT
Dear tranquil Habit, with her silent hands,
Doth heal our deepest wounds from day to day
With cooling, soothing oil, and firmly lay
Around the broken heart her gentle bands.
Her nursing is as calm as Nature's care;
She doth not weep with us; yet none the less
Her quiet fingers weave forgetfulness,—
We fall asleep in peace when she is there.
Upon the mirror of the mind her breath
Is like a cloud, to hide the fading trace
Of that dear smile, of that remembered face,
Whose presence were the joy and pang of death.
And he who clings to sorrow overmuch,
Weeping for withered grief, has cause to bless,
More than all cries of pity and distress,—
Dear tranquil Habit, thy consoling touch!

V
THE OLD BRIDGE
On the old, old bridge, with its crumbling stones
All covered with lichens red and gray,
Two lovers were talking in sweet low tones:
And we were they!

As he leaned to breathe in her willing ear
The love that he vowed would never die,
He called her his darling, his dove most dear:
And he was I!
She covered her face from the pale moonlight
With her trembling hands, but her eyes looked through,
And listened and listened with long delight:
And she was you!
On the old, old bridge, where the lichens rust,
Two lovers are learning the same old lore;
He tells his love, and she looks her trust:
But we,—no more!

VI
EYES AND LIPS
1
Our silent eyes alone interpreted
The new-born feeling in the heart of each:
In yours I read your sorrow without speech,
Your lonely struggle in their tears unshed.
Behind their dreamy sweetness, as a veil,
I saw the moving lights of trouble shine;
And then my eyes were brightened as with wine,
My spirit reeled to see your face grow pale!
Our deepening love, that is not yet allowed
Another language than the eyes, doth learn
To speak it perfectly: above the crowd
Our looks exchange avowals and desires,—
Like wave-divided beacon lights that burn,
And talk to one another by their fires.
2
When I embrace her in a fragrant shrine
Of climbing roses, my first kiss shall fall
On you, sweet eyes, that mutely told me all,—
Through you my soul will rise to make her mine.
Upon your drooping lids, blue-veined and fair,
The touch of tenderness I first will lay,
You springs of joy, lights of my gloomy day,
Whose dear discovered secret bade me dare!
And when you open, eyes of my fond dove,
Your look will shine with new delight, made sure
By this forerunner of a faithful love.
Tis just, dear eyes, so pensive and so pure,
That you should bear the sealing kisses true
Of love unhoped that came to me through you.
3
his was my thought; but when beneath the rose
That hides the lonely bench where lovers rest,
In friendly dusk I held her on my breast
For one brief moment,—while I saw you close,
Dear, yielding eyes, as if your lids, blue-veined
And pure, were meekly fain at last to bear
The proffered homage of my wistful prayer,—
In that high moment, by your grace obtained,
Forgetting your avowals, your alarms,
Your anguish and your tears, sweet weary eyes,
Forgetting that you gave her to my arms,
I broke my promise; and my first caress,
Ungrateful, sought her lips in sweet surprise,—
Her lips, which breathed a word of tenderness!

VII
AN EVOCATION
When first upon my brow I felt your kiss,
A sudden splendour filled me, like the ray
That promptly runs to crown the hills with bliss
Of purple dawn before the golden day,
And ends the gloom it crosses at one leap.
My brow was not unworthy your caress;
For some foreboding joy had bade me keep
From all affront the place your lips would bless.
Yet when your mouth upon my mouth did lay
The royal touch, no rapture made me thrill,
But I remained confused, ashamed, and still.
Beneath your kiss, my queen without a stain,
I felt,—like ghosts who rise at Judgment Day,—
A throng of ancient kisses vile and vain!

VIII
RESIGNATION
1
Well, you will triumph, dear and noble friend!
The holy love that wounded you so deep
Will bring you balm, and on your heart asleep
The fragrant dew of healing will descend.
Your children,—ah, how quickly they will grow
Between us, like a wall that fronts the sun,
Lifting a screen with rosy buds o'errun,
To hide the shaded path where I must go.
You'll walk in light; and dreaming less and less
Of him who droops in gloom beyond the wall,

*Your mother-soul will fill with happiness
When first you hear your grandchild's babbling call,
Beneath the braided bloom of flower and leaf
That We has wrought to veil your vanished grief.*
2
*Then I alone shall suffer! I shall bear
The double burden of our grief alone,
While I enlarge my soul to take your share
Of pain and hold it close beside my own.
Our love is torn asunder; but the crown
Of thorns that love has woven I will make
My relic sacrosanct, and press it down
Upon my bleeding heart that will not break.
Ah, that will be the depth of solitude!
For my regret, that evermore endures,
Will know that new-born hope has conquered yours;
And when the evening comes, no gentle brood
Of wondering children, gathered at my side,
Will soothe away the tears I cannot hide.
Freely rendered from the French, 1911.*

RAPPEL D'AMOUR
*Come home, my love, come home!
The twilight is falling,
The whippoorwill calling,
The night is very near,
And the darkness full of fear,
Come home to my arms, come home!
Come home, my love, come home!
In folly we parted,
And now, lonely hearted,
I know you look in vain
For a love like mine again;
Come home to my arms, come home!
Come home, dear love, come home!
I've much to forgive you,
And more yet to give you.
I'll put a little light
In the window every night,—
Come home to my arms, come home.*

THE RIVER OF DREAMS
*The river of dreams runs quietly down
From its hidden home in the forest of sleep,
With a measureless motion calm and deep;
And my boat slips out on the current brown,
In a tranquil bay where the trees incline
Far over the waves, and creepers twine
Far over the boughs, as if to steep
Their drowsy bloom in the tide that goes
By a secret way that no man knows,
Under the branches bending,
Under the shadows blending,
And the body rests, and the passive soul
Is drifted along to an unseen goal,
While the river of dreams runs down.
The river of dreams runs gently down,
With a leisurely flow that bears my bark
Out of the visionless woods of dark,
Into a glory that seems to crown
Valley and hill with light from far,
Clearer than sun or moon or star,
Luminous, wonderful, weird, oh, mark
How the radiance pulses everywhere,
In the shadowless vault of lucid air!
Over the mountains shimmering,
Up from the fountains glimmering,—
Tis the mystical glow of the inner light,
That shines in the very noon of night,
While the river of dreams runs down.
The river of dreams runs murmuring down,
Through the fairest garden that ever grew;
And now, as my boat goes drifting through,
A hundred voices arise to drown
The river's whisper, and charm my ear
With a sound I have often longed to hear,—
A magical music, strange and new,
The wild-rose ballad, the lilac-song,
The virginal chant of the lilies' throng,
Blue-bells silverly ringing,
Pansies merrily singing,—
For all the flowers have found their voice;
And I feel no wonder, but only rejoice,
While the river of dreams runs down.
The river of dreams runs broadening down,
Away from the peaceful garden-shore,
With a current that deepens more and more,
By the league-long walls of a mighty town;
And I see the hurrying crowds of men
Gather like clouds and dissolve again;
But never a face I have seen before.
They come and go, they shift and change,
Their ways and looks are wild and strange,—
This is a city haunted,
A multitude enchanted!
At the sight of the throng I am dumb with fear,
And never a sound from their lips I hear,
While the river of dreams runs down.
The river of dreams runs darkly down
Into the heart of a desolate land,
With ruined temples half-buried in sand,
And riven hills, whose black brows frown
Over the shuddering, lonely wave.
The air grows dim with the dust of the grave;
No sign of life on the dreary strand;
No ray of light on the mountain's crest;
And a weary wind that cannot rest
Comes down the valley creeping,
Lamenting, wailing, weeping,—
I strive to cry out, but my fluttering breath
Is choked with the clinging fog of death,
While the river of dreams runs down.
The river of dreams runs trembling down,
Out of the valley of nameless fear,
Into a country calm and clear,
With a mystical name of high renown,—
A name that I know, but may not tell,—
And there the friends that I loved so well,
Old companions forever dear,
Come beckoning down to the river shore,
And hail my boat with the voice of yore.
Fair and sweet are the places
Where I see their unchanged faces!
And I feel in my heart with a secret thrill,*

That the loved and lost are living still,
While the river of dreams runs down.
The river of dreams runs dimly down
By a secret way that no man knows;
But the soul lives on while the river flows
Through the gardens bright and the forests brown;
And I often think that our whole life seems
To be more than half made up of dreams.
The changing sights and the passing shows,
The morning hopes and the midnight fears,
Are left behind with the vanished years;
Onward, with ceaseless motion,
The life-stream flows to the ocean,
While we follow the tide, awake or asleep,
Till we see the dawn on Love's great deep,
And the shadows melt, and the soul is free,—
The river of dreams has reached the sea.
1900.

SONGS OF HEARTH AND ALTAR
A HOME SONG

I read within a poet's book
A word that starred the page:
"Stone walls do not a prison make,
Nor iron bars a cage!"
Yes, that is true, and something more:
You'll find, where'er you roam,
That marble floors and gilded walls
Can never make a home.
But every house where Love abides,
And Friendship is a guest,
Is surely home, and home-sweet-home:
For there the heart can rest.

"LITTLE BOATIE"
A SLUMBER-SONG FOR THE FISHERMAN'S CHILD

Furl your sail, my little boatie;
Here's the haven still and deep,
Where the dreaming tides in-streaming
Up the channel creep.
Now the sunset breeze is dying;
Hear the plover, landward flying,
Softly down the twilight crying;
Come to anchor, little boatie,
In the port of Sleep.
Far away, my little boatie,
Roaring waves are white with foam;
Ships are striving, onward driving,
Day and night they roam.
Father's at the deep-sea trawling,
In the darkness, rowing, hauling,
While the hungry winds are calling,—
God protect him, little boatie,
Bring him safely home!
Not for you, my little boatie,
Is the wide and weary sea;
You're too slender, and too tender,
You must bide with me.
All day long you have been straying
Up and down the shore and playing;
Come to harbour, no delaying!
Day is over, little boatie,
Night falls suddenly.
Furl your sail, my little boatie,
Fold your wings, my weary dove.
Dews are sprinkling, stars are twinkling
Drowsily above.
Cease from sailing, cease from rowing;
Rock upon the dream-tide, knowing
Safely o'er your rest are glowing,
All the night, my little boatie,
Harbour-lights of love.
1897.

A MOTHER'S BIRTHDAY

Lord Jesus, Thou hast known
A mother's love and tender care:
And Thou wilt hear,
While for my own
Mother most dear
I make this birthday prayer.
Protect her life, I pray,
Who gave the gift of life to me;
And may she know,
From day to day,
The deepening glow
Of joy that comes from Thee.
As once upon her breast
Fearless and well content I lay,
So let her heart,
On Thee at rest,
Feel fear depart
And trouble fade away.
Ah, hold her by the hand,
As once her hand held mine;
And though she may
Not understand
Life's winding way,
Lead her in peace divine.

I cannot pay my debt
For all the love that she has given;
But Thou, love's Lord,
Wilt not forget
Her due reward,—
Bless her in earth and heaven.

TRANSFORMATION

Only a little shrivelled seed,
It might be flower, or grass, or weed;
Only a box of earth on the edge
Of a narrow, dusty window-ledge;
Only a few scant summer showers;
Only a few clear shining hours;
That was all. Yet God could make
Out of these, for a sick child's sake,
A blossom-wonder, fair and sweet
As ever broke at an angel's feet.
Only a life of barren pain,
Wet with sorrowful tears for rain,
Warmed sometimes by a wandering gleam
Of joy, that seemed but a happy dream;

A life as common and brown and bare
As the box of earth in the window there;
Yet it bore, at last, the precious bloom
Of a perfect soul in that narrow room;
Pure as the snowy leaves that fold
Over the flower's heart of gold.

RENDEZVOUS
I count that friendship little worth
Which has not many things untold,
Great longings that no words can hold,
And passion-secrets waiting birth.
Along the slender wires of speech
Some message from the heart is sent;
But who can tell the whole that's meant?
Our dearest thoughts are out of reach.
I have not seen thee, though mine eyes
Hold now the image of thy face;
In vain, through form, I strive to trace
The soul I love: that deeper lies.
A thousand accidents control
Our meeting here. Clasp hand in hand,
And swear to meet me in that land
Where friends hold converse soul to soul.

GRATITUDE
"Do you give thanks for this?—or that?" No, God be thanked
I am not grateful
In that cold, calculating way, with blessings ranked
As one, two, three, and four,—that would be hateful.
I only know that every day brings good above
My poor deserving;
I only feel that in the road of Life true Love
Is leading me along and never swerving.
Whatever gifts and mercies to my lot may fall,
I would not measure
As worth a certain price in praise, or great or small;
But take and use them all with simple pleasure.
For when we gladly eat our daily bread, we bless
The Hand that feeds us;
And when we tread the road of Life in cheerfulness,
Our very heart-beats praise the Love that leads us.

PEACE
With eager heart and will on fire,
I strove to win my great desire.
"Peace shall be mine," I said; but life
Grew bitter in the barren strife.
My soul was weary, and my pride
Was wounded deep; to Heaven I cried,
"God grant me peace or I must die;"
The dumb stars glittered no reply.

Broken at last, I bowed my head,
Forgetting all myself, and said,
"Whatever comes, His will be done;"
And in that moment peace was won.

SANTA CHRISTINA
Saints are God's flowers, fragrant souls
That His own hand hath planted,
Not in some far-off heavenly place,
Or solitude enchanted,
But here and there and everywhere,—
In lonely field, or crowded town,
God sees a flower when He looks down.
Some wear the lily's stainless white,
And some the rose of passion,
And some the violet's heavenly blue,
But each in its own fashion,
With silent bloom and soft perfume,
Is praising Him who from above
Beholds each lifted face of love.
One such I knew,—and had the grace
To thank my God for knowing:
The beauty of her quiet life
Was like a rose in blowing,
So fair and sweet, so all-complete
And all unconscious, as a flower,
That light and fragrance were her dower.
No convent-garden held this rose,
Concealed like secret treasure;
No royal terrace guarded her
For some sole monarch's pleasure.
She made her shrine, this saint of mine,
In a bright home where children played;
And there she wrought and there she prayed.

In sunshine, when the days were glad,
She had the art of keeping
The clearest rays, to give again
In days of rain and weeping;
Her blessed heart could still impart
Some portion of its secret grace,
And charity shone in her face.
In joy she grew from year to year;
And sorrow made her sweeter;
And every comfort, still more kind;
And every loss, completer.
Her children came to love her name,—
"Christina,"—'twas a lip's caress;
And when they called, they seemed to bless.
No more they call, for she is gone
Too far away to hear them;
And yet they often breathe her name
As if she lingered near them;
They cannot reach her with love's speech,
But when they say "Christina" now
'Tis like a prayer or like a vow:
A vow to keep her life alive
In deeds of pure affection,
So that her love shall find in them
A daily resurrection;
A constant prayer that they may wear
Some touch of that supernal light
With which she blossoms in God's sight.

THE BARGAIN
What shall I give for thee,
Thou Pearl of greatest price?
For all the treasures I possess
Would not suffice.

I give my store of gold;
It is but earthly dross:
But thou wilt make me rich, beyond
All fear of loss.
Mine honours I resign;
They are but small at best:
Thou like a royal star wilt shine
Upon my breast.
My worldly joys I give,
The flowers with which I played;
Thy beauty, far more heavenly fair,
Shall never fade.

Dear Lord, is that enough?
Nay, not a thousandth part.
Well, then, I have but one thing more:
Take Thou my heart.

TO THE CHILD JESUS
I
THE NATIVITY

Could every time-worn heart but see Thee once again,
A happy human child, among the homes of men,
The age of doubt would pass,—the vision of Thy face
Would silently restore the childhood of the race.

II
THE FLIGHT INTO EGYPT

Thou wayfaring Jesus, a pilgrim and stranger,
Exiled from heaven by love at thy birth,
Exiled again from thy rest in the manger,
A fugitive child 'mid the perils of earth,—
Cheer with thy fellowship all who are weary,
Wandering far from the land that they love;
Guide every heart that is homeless and dreary,
Safe to its home in thy presence above.

BITTER-SWEET

Just to give up, and trust
All to a Fate unknown,
Plodding along life's road in the dust,
Bounded by walls of stone;
Never to have a heart at peace;
Never to see when care will cease;
Just to be still when sorrows fall—
This is the bitterest lesson of all.
Just to give up, and rest
All on a Love secure,
Out of a world that's hard at the best,
Looking to heaven as sure;
Ever to hope, through cloud and fear,
In darkest night, that the dawn is near;
Just to wait at the Master's feet—
Surely, now, the bitter is sweet.

HYMN OF JOY
TO THE MUSIC OF BEETHOVEN'S NINTH SYMPHONY

Joyful, joyful, we adore Thee,
God of glory, Lord of love;
Hearts unfold like flowers before Thee,
Praising Thee their sun above.
Melt the clouds of sin and sadness;
Drive the dark of doubt away;
Giver of immortal gladness,
Fill us with the light of day!
All Thy works with joy surround Thee,
Earth and heaven reflect Thy rays,
Stars and angels sing around Thee,
Centre of unbroken praise:
Field and forest, vale and mountain,
Blooming meadow, flashing sea,
Chanting bird and flowing fountain,
Call us to rejoice in Thee.
Thou art giving and forgiving,
Ever blessing, ever blest,
Well-spring of the joy of living,
Ocean-depth of happy rest!
Thou our Father, Christ our Brother,—
All who live in love are Thine:
Teach us how to love each other,
Lift us to the Joy Divine.
Mortals join the mighty chorus,
Which the morning stars began;
Father-love is reigning o'er us,
Brother-love binds man to man.
Ever singing march we onward,
Victors in the midst of strife;
Joyful music lifts us sunward
In the triumph song of life.
1908.

SONG OF A PILGRIM-SOUL

March on, my soul, nor like a laggard stay!
March swiftly on. Yet err not from the way
Where all the nobly wise of old have trod,—
The path of faith, made by the sons of God.

Follow the marks that they have set beside
The narrow, cloud-swept track, to be thy guide:
Follow, and honour what the past has gained,
And forward still, that more may be attained.

Something to learn, and something to forget:
Hold fast the good, and seek the better yet:
Press on, and prove the pilgrim-hope of youth:
The Creeds are milestones on the road to Truth.

ODE TO PEACE
I
IN EXCELSIS

Two dwellings, Peace, are thine.
One is the mountain-height,
Uplifted in the loneliness of light
Beyond the realm of shadows,—fine,
And far, and clear,—where advent of the night
Means only glorious nearness of the stars,
And dawn unhindered breaks above the bars
That long the lower world in twilight keep.
Thou sleepest not, and hast no need of sleep,
For all thy cares and fears have dropped away;
The night's fatigue, the fever-fret of day,
Are far below thee; and earth's weary wars,
In vain expense of passion, pass

Before thy sight like visions in a glass,—
Or like the wrinkles of the storm that creep
Across the sea and leave no trace
Of trouble on that immemorial face,—
So brief appear the conflicts, and so slight
The wounds men give, the things for which they fight!
Here hangs a fortress on the distant steep,—
A lichen clinging to the rock.
There sails a fleet upon the deep,—
A wandering flock
Of snow-winged gulls. And yonder, in the plain,
A marble palace shines,—a grain
Of mica glittering in the rain.
Beneath thy feet the clouds are rolled
By voiceless winds: and far between
The rolling clouds, new shores and peaks are seen,
In shimmering robes of green and gold,
And faint aerial hue
That silent fades into the silent blue.
Thou, from thy mountain-hold,
All day in tranquil wisdom looking down
On distant scenes of human toil and strife,
All night, with eyes aware of loftier life
Uplifted to the sky where stars are sown,
Dost watch the everlasting fields grow white
Unto the harvest of the sons of light,
And welcome to thy dwelling-place sublime
The few strong souls that dare to climb
The slippery crags, and find thee on the height.

II
DE PROFUNDIS
But in the depth thou hast another home,
For hearts less daring, or more frail.
Thou dwellest also in the shadowy vale;
And pilgrim-souls that roam
With weary feet o'er hill and dale,
Bearing the burden and the heat
Of toilful days,
Turn from the dusty ways
To find thee in thy green and still retreat.
Here is no vision wide outspread
Before the lonely and exalted seat
Of all-embracing knowledge. Here, instead,
A little cottage, and a garden-nook,
With outlooks brief and sweet
Across the meadows, and along the brook,—
A little stream that nothing knows
Of the great sea to which it gladly flows,—
A little field that bears a little wheat
To make a portion of earth's daily bread.
The vast cloud-armies overhead
Are marshalled, and the wild wind blows
Its trumpet, but thou canst not tell
Whence comes the wind nor where it goes;
Nor dost thou greatly care, since all is well.
Thy daily task is done,
And now the wages of repose are won.
Here friendship lights the fire, and every heart,
Sure of itself and sure of all the rest,
Dares to be true, and gladly takes its part
In open converse, bringing forth its best:
And here is music, melting every chain
Of lassitude and pain:
And here, at last, is sleep with silent gifts,—
Kind sleep, the tender nurse who lifts
The soul grown weary of the waking world,
And lays it, with its thoughts all furled,
Its fears forgotten, and its passions still,
On the deep bosom of the Eternal Will.

THREE PRAYERS FOR SLEEP AND WAKING
I
BEDTIME
Ere thou sleepest gently lay
Every troubled thought away:
Put off worry and distress
As thou puttest off thy dress:
Drop thy burden and thy care
In the quiet arms of prayer.

Lord, Thou knowest how I live,
All I've done amiss forgive:
All of good I've tried to do,
Strengthen, bless, and carry through,
All I love in safety keep,
While in Thee I fall asleep.

II
NIGHT WATCH
If slumber should forsake
Thy pillow in the dark,
Fret not thyself to mark
How long thou liest awake.
There is a better way;
Let go the strife and strain,
Thine eyes will close again,
If thou wilt only pray.
Lord, Thy peaceful gift restore,
Give my body sleep once more:
While I wait my soul will rest
Like a child upon Thy breast.

III
NEW DAY
Ere thou risest from thy bed,
Speak to God Whose wings were spread
O'er thee in the helpless night:
Lo, He wakes thee now with light!
Lift thy burden and thy care
In the mighty arms of prayer.

Lord, the newness of this day
Calls me to an untried way:
Let me gladly take the road,
Give me strength to bear my load,
Thou my guide and helper be—
I will travel through with Thee.
The Mission Inn, California, Easter, 1913.

PORTRAIT AND REALITY
If on the closed curtain of my sight
My fancy paints thy portrait far away,

I see thee still the same, by night or day;
Crossing the crowded street, or moving bright
'Mid festal throngs, or reading by the light
Of shaded lamp some friendly poet's lay,
Or shepherding the children at their play,—
The same sweet self, and my unchanged delight.
But when I see thee near, I recognize
In every dear familiar way some strange
Perfection, and behold in April guise
The magic of thy beauty that doth range
Through many moods with infinite surprise,—
Never the same, and sweeter with each change.

THE WIND OF SORROW
The fire of love was burning, yet so low
That in the peaceful dark it made no rays,
And in the light of perfect-placid days
The ashes hid the smouldering embers' glow.
Vainly, for love's delight, we sought to throw
New pleasures on the pyre to make it blaze:
In life's calm air and tranquil-prosperous ways
We missed the radiant heat of long ago.
Then in the night, a night of sad alarms,
Bitter with pain and black with fog of fears
That drove us trembling to each other's arms,
Across the gulf of darkness and salt tears
Into life's calm the wind of sorrow came,
And fanned the fire of love to clearest name.

HIDE AND SEEK
I
All the trees are sleeping, all the winds are still,
All the fleecy flocks of cloud, gone beyond the hill;
Through the noon-day silence, down the woods of June,
Hark, a little hunter's voice, running with a tune.
"Hide and seek!
When I speak,
You must answer me:
Call again,
Merry men,
Coo-ee, coo-ee, coo-ee!"
Now I hear his footsteps rustling in the grass:
Hidden in my leafy nook, shall I let him pass?
Just a low, soft whistle,—quick the hunter turns,
Leaps upon me laughing loud, rolls me in the ferns.
"Hold him fast,
Caught at last!
Now you're it, you see.
Hide your eye,
Till I cry,
Coo-ee, coo-ee, coo-ee!"

II
Long ago he left me, long and long ago;
Now I wander thro' the world, seeking high and low.
Hidden safe and happy, in some pleasant place,—
If I could but hear his voice, soon I'd see his face!
Far away,
Many a day,
Where can Barney be?
Answer, dear,
Don't you hear?
Coo-ee, coo-ee, coo-ee!
Birds that every spring-time sung him full of joy,
Flowers he loved to pick for me, mind me of my boy.
Somewhere he is waiting till my steps come nigh;
Love may hide itself awhile, but love can never die.
Heart, be glad,
The little lad
Will call again to thee:
"Father dear,
Heaven is here,
Coo-ee, coo-ee, coo-ee!"
1898.

AUTUMN IN THE GARDEN
When the frosty kiss of Autumn in the dark
Makes its mark
On the flowers, and the misty morning grieves
Over fallen leaves;
Then my olden garden, where the golden soil
Through the toil
Of a hundred years is mellow, rich, and deep,
Whispers in its sleep.
'Mid the crumpled beds of marigold and phlox,
Where the box
Borders with its glossy green the ancient walks,
There's a voice that talks
Of the human hopes that bloomed and withered here
Year by year,—
And the dreams that brightened all the labouring hours.
Fading as the flowers.
Yet the whispered story does not deepen grief;
But relief
For the loneliness of sorrow seems to flow
From the Long-Ago,
When I think of other lives that learned, like mine,
To resign,
And remember that the sadness of the fall
Comes alike to all.
What regrets, what longings for the lost were theirs!
And what prayers
For the silent strength that nerves us to endure
Things we cannot cure!
Pacing up and down the garden where they paced,
I have traced
All their well-worn paths of patience, till I find
Comfort in my mind.
Faint and far away their ancient griefs appear:
Yet how near
Is the tender voice, the careworn, kindly face,
Of the human race!
Let us walk together in the garden, dearest heart,—
Not apart!
They who know the sorrows other lives have known
Never walk alone.
October, 1903.

THE MESSAGE
Waking from tender sleep,
My neighbour's little child
Put out his baby hand to me,
Looked in my face, and smiled.
It seems as if he came

Home from a happy land,
To bring a message to my heart
And make me understand.
Somewhere, among bright dreams,
A child that once was mine
Has whispered wordless love to him,
And given him a sign.
Comfort of kindly speech,
And counsel of the wise,
Have helped me less than what I read
In those deep-smiling eyes.
Sleep sweetly, little friend,
And dream again of heaven:
With double love I kiss your hand,—
Your message has been given.
November, 1903.

DULCIS MEMORIA
Long, long ago I heard a little song,
(Ah, was it long ago, or yesterday?)
So lowly, slowly wound the tune along,
That far into my heart it found the way:
A melody consoling and endearing;
And now, in silent hours, I'm often hearing
The small, sweet song that does not die away.
Long, long ago I saw a little flower—
(Ah, was it long ago, or yesterday?)
So fair of face and fragrant for an hour,
That something dear to me it seemed to say,—
A wordless joy that blossomed into being;
And now, in winter days, I'm often seeing
The friendly flower that does not fade away.
Long, long ago we had a little child,—
(Ah, was it long ago, or yesterday?)
Into his mother's eyes and mine he smiled
Unconscious love; warm in our arms he lay.
An angel called! Dear heart, we could not hold him;
Yet secretly your arms and mine infold him—
Our little child who does not go away.
Long, long ago? Ah, memory, make it clear—
(It was not long ago, but yesterday.)
So little and so helpless and so dear—
Let not the song be lost, the flower decay!
His voice, his waking eyes, his gentle sleeping:
The smallest things are safest in thy keeping,—
Sweet memory, keep our child with us alway.
November, 1903.

THE WINDOW
All night long, by a distant bell
The passing hours were notched
On the dark, while her breathing rose and fell;
And the spark of life I watched
In her face was glowing, or fading,—who could tell?—
And the open window of the room,
With a flare of yellow light,
Was peering out into the gloom,
Like an eye that searched the night.
Oh, what do you see in the dark, little window, and why do you peer?
"I see that the garden is crowded with creeping forms of fear:
Little white ghosts in the locust-tree, wave in the night-wind's breath,
And low in the leafy laurels the lurking shadow of death."
Sweet, clear notes of a waking bird
Told of the passing away
Of the dark,—and my darling may have heard;
For she smiled in her sleep, while the ray
Of the rising dawn spoke joy without a word,
Till the splendour born in the east outburned
The yellow lamplight, pale and thin,
And the open window slowly turned
To the eye of the morning, looking in.
Oh, what do you see in the room, little window, that makes you so bright?
"I see that a child is asleep on her pillow, soft and white:
With the rose of life on her lips, the pulse of life in her breast,
And the arms of God around her, she quietly takes her rest."
Neuilly, June, 1909.

CHRISTMAS TEARS
The day returns by which we date our years:
Day of the joy of giving,—that means love;
Day of the joy of living,—that means hope;
Day of the Royal Child,—and day that brings
To older hearts the gift of Christmas tears!
Look, how the candles twinkle through the tree,
The children shout when baby claps his hands,
The room is full of laughter and of song!
Your lips are smiling, dearest,—tell me why
Your eyes are brimming full of Christmas tears?
Was it a silent voice that joined the song?
A vanished face that glimmered once again
Among the happy circle round the tree?
Was it an unseen hand that touched your cheek
And brought the secret gift of Christmas tears?
Not dark and angry like the winter storm
Of selfish grief,—but full of starry gleams,
And soft and still that others may not weep,—
Dews of remembered happiness descend
To bless us with the gift of Christmas tears.
Ah, lose them not, dear heart,—life has no pearls
More pure than memories of joy love-shared.
See, while we count them one by one with prayer,
The Heavenly hope that lights the Christmas tree
Has made a rainbow in our Christmas tears!
1912.

DOROTHEA
1888-1912
A deeper crimson in the rose,
A deeper blue in sky and sea,
And ever, as the summer goes,
A deeper loss in losing thee!
A deeper music in the strain
Of hermit-thrush from lonely tree;
And deeper grows the sense of gain
My life has found in having thee.
A deeper love, a deeper rest,
A deeper joy in all I see;
And ever deeper in my breast

A silver song that comes from thee!
Seal Harbour, August 1, 1912.

EPIGRAMS, GREETINGS, AND INSCRIPTIONS
FOR KATRINA'S SUN-DIAL
IN HER GARDEN OF YADDO

Hours fly,
Flowers die
New days,
New ways,
Pass by.
Love stays.
Time is
Too Slow for those who Wait,
Too Swift for those who Fear,
Too Long for those who Grieve,
Too Short for those who Rejoice;
But for those who Love,
Time is not.

FOR KATRINA'S WINDOW
IN HER TOWER OF YADDO

This is the window's message,
In silence, to the Queen:
"Thou hast a double kingdom
And I am set between:
Look out and see the glory,
On hill and plain and sky:
Look in and see the light of love
That nevermore shall die!"

L'ENVOI
Window in the Queen's high tower,
This shall be thy magic power!
Shut the darkness and the doubt,
Shut the storm and conflict, out;
Wind and hail and snow and rain
Dash against thee all in vain.
Let in nothing from the night,—
Let in every ray of light!

FOR THE FRIENDS AT HURSTMONT
THE HOUSE
The cornerstone in Truth is laid,
The guardian walls of Honour made,
The roof of Faith is built above,
The fire upon the hearth is Love:
Though rains descend and loud winds call,
This happy house shall never fall.

THE HEARTH
When the logs are burning free,
Then the fire is full of glee:
When each heart gives out its best,
Then the talk is full of zest:
Light your fire and never fear,
Life was made for love and cheer.

THE DOOR
The lintel low enough to keep out pomp and pride:
The threshold high enough to turn deceit aside:
The fastening strong enough from robbers to defend:
This door will open at a touch to welcome every friend.

THE DIAL
Time can never take
What Time did not give;
When my shadows have all passed,
You shall live.

THE SUN-DIAL AT MORVEN
FOR BAYARD AND HELEN STOCKTON
Two hundred years of blessing I record
For Morven's house, protected by the Lord:
And still I stand among old-fashioned flowers
To mark for Morven many sunlit hours.

THE SUN-DIAL AT WELLS COLLEGE
FOR THE CLASS OF 1904
The shadow by my finger cast
Divides the future from the past:
Before it, sleeps the unborn hour,
In darkness, and beyond thy power:
Behind its unreturning line,
The vanished hour, no longer thine:
One hour alone is in thy hands,—
The NOW on which the shadow stands.
March, 1904.

TO MARK TWAIN
I
AT A BIRTHDAY FEAST
With memories old and wishes new
We crown our cups again,
And here's to you, and here's to you
With love that ne'er shall wane!
And may you keep, at sixty-seven,
The joy of earth, the hope of heaven,
And fame well-earned, and friendship true,
And peace that comforts every pain,
And faith that fights the battle through,
And all your heart's unbounded wealth,
And all your wit, and all your health,—
Yes, here's a hearty health to you,
And here's to you, and here's to you,
Long life to you, Mark Twain.
November 30, 1902.

II
AT THE MEMORIAL MEETING
We knew you well, dear Yorick of the West,
The very soul of large and friendly jest!
You loved and mocked the broad grotesque of things
In this new world where all the folk are kings.
Your breezy humour cleared the air, with sport
Of shams that haunt the democratic court;
For even where the sovereign people rule,
A human monarch needs a royal fool.
Your native drawl lent flavour to your wit;
Your arrows lingered but they always hit;
Homeric mirth around the circle ran,
But left no wound upon the heart of man.
We knew you kind in trouble, brave in pain;
We saw your honour kept without a stain;

We read this lesson of our Yorick's years,—
True wisdom comes with laughter and with tears.
November 30, 1910.

STARS AND THE SOUL
(TO CHARLES A. YOUNG, ASTRONOMER)

"Two things," the wise man said, "fill me with awe:
The starry heavens and the moral law."
Nay, add another wonder to thy roll,—
The living marvel of the human soul!
Born in the dust and cradled in the dark,
It feels the fire of an immortal spark,
And learns to read, with patient, searching eyes,
The splendid secret of the unconscious skies.
For God thought Light before He spoke the word;
The darkness understood not, though it heard:
But man looks up to where the planets swim,
And thinks God's thoughts of glory after Him.
What knows the star that guides the sailor's way,
Or lights the lover's bower with liquid ray,
Of toil and passion, danger and distress,
Brave hope, true love, and utter faithfulness?
But human hearts that suffer good and ill,
And hold to virtue with a loyal will,
Adorn the law that rules our mortal strife
With star-surpassing victories of life.
So take our thanks, dear reader of the skies,
Devout astronomer, most humbly wise,
For lessons brighter than the stars can give,
And inward light that helps us all to live.

TO JULIA MARLOWE
(READING KEATS' ODE ON A GRECIAN URN)

Long had I loved this "Attic shape," the brede
Of marble maidens round this urn divine:
But when your golden voice began to read,
The empty urn was filled with Chian wine.

TO JOSEPH JEFFERSON

May 4th, 1898.—To-day, fishing down the Swiftwater, I found Joseph Jefferson on a big rock in the middle of the brook, casting the fly for trout. He said he had fished this very stream three-and-forty years ago; and near by, in the Paradise Valley, he wrote his famous play.—Leaf from my Diary.

We met on Nature's stage,
And May had set the scene,
With bishop-caps standing in delicate ranks,
And violets blossoming over the banks,
While the brook ran full between.
The waters rang your call,
With frolicsome waves a-twinkle,—
They knew you as boy, and they knew you as man,
And every wave, as it merrily ran,
Cried, "Enter Rip van Winkle!"

THE MOCKING-BIRD

In mirth he mocks the other birds at noon,
Catching the lilt of every easy tune;
But when the day departs he sings of love,—
His own wild song beneath the listening moon.

THE EMPTY QUATRAIN

A flawless cup: how delicate and fine
The flowing curve of every jewelled line!
Look, turn it up or down, 'tis perfect still,—
But holds no drop of life's heart-warming wine.

PAN LEARNS MUSIC
FOR A SCULPTURE BY SARA GREENE

Limber-limbed, lazy god, stretched on the rock,
Where is sweet Echo, and where is your flock?
What are you making here? "Listen," said Pan,—
"Out of a river-reed music for man!"

THE SHEPHERD OF NYMPHS

The nymphs a shepherd took
To guard their snowy sheep;
He led them down along the brook,
And guided them with pipe and crook,
Until he fell asleep.
But when the piping stayed,
Across the flowery mead
The milk-white nymphs ran out afraid:
O Thyrsis, wake! Your flock has strayed,—
The nymphs a shepherd need.

ECHOES FROM THE GREEK ANTHOLOGY
I
STARLIGHT

With two bright eyes, my star, my love,
Thou lookest on the stars above:
Ah, would that I the heaven might be
With a million eyes to look on thee.
Plato.

II
ROSELEAF

A little while the rose,
And after that the thorn;
An hour of dewy morn,
And then the glamour goes.
Ah, love in beauty born,
A little while the rose!
Unknown.

III
PHOSPHOR—HESPER

O morning star, farewell!
My love I now must leave;
The hours of day I slowly tell,
And turn to her with the twilight bell,—
O welcome, star of eve!
Meleager.

IV
SEASONS

Sweet in summer, cups of snow,
Cooling thirsty lips aglow;
Sweet to sailors winter-bound,
Spring arrives with garlands crowned;
Sweeter yet the hour that covers
With one cloak a pair of lovers,

Living lost in golden weather,
While they talk of love together.
Asclepiades.

V
THE VINE AND THE GOAT
Although you eat me to the root,
I yet shall bear enough of fruit
For wine to sprinkle your dim eyes,
When you are made a sacrifice.
Euenus.

VI
THE PROFESSOR
Seven pupils, in the class
Of Professor Callias,
Listen silent while he drawls,—
Three are benches, four are walls.

Unknown.

ONE WORLD
"The worlds in which we live are two:
The world 'I am' and the world 'I do,'"

The worlds in which we live at heart are one,
The world "I am," the fruit of "I have done";
And underneath these worlds of flower and fruit,
The world "I love,"—the only living root.

JOY AND DUTY
"Joy is a Duty,"—so with golden lore
The Hebrew rabbis taught in days of yore,
And happy human hearts heard in their speech
Almost the highest wisdom man can reach.
But one bright peak still rises far above,
And there the Master stands whose name is Love,
Saying to those whom weary tasks employ:
"Life is divine when Duty is a Joy."

THE PRISON AND THE ANGEL
Self is the only prison that can ever bind the soul;
Love is the only angel who can bid the gates unroll;
And when he comes to call thee, arise and follow fast;
His way may lie through darkness, but it leads to light at last.

THE WAY
Who seeks for heaven alone to save his soul,
May keep the path, but will not reach the goal;
While he who walks in love may wander far,
But God will bring him where the Blessed are.

LOVE AND LIGHT
There are many kinds of love, as many kinds of light,
And every kind of love makes a glory in the night.
There is love that stirs the heart, and love that gives it rest,
But the love that leads life upward is the noblest and the best.

FACTA NON VERBA
Deeds not Words: I say so too!
And yet I find it somehow true,
A word may help a man in need,
To nobler act and braver deed.

FOUR THINGS
Four things a man must learn to do
If he would make his record true:
To think without confusion clearly;
To love his fellow-men sincerely;
To act from honest motives purely;
To trust in God and Heaven securely.

THE GREAT RIVER
"In la sua volontade è nostra pace."
O mighty river! strong, eternal Will,
Wherein the streams of human good and ill
Are onward swept, conflicting, to the sea!
The world is safe because it floats in Thee.

INSCRIPTION FOR A TOMB IN ENGLAND
Read here, O friend unknown,
Our grief, of her bereft;
Yet think not tears alone
Within our hearts are left.
The gifts she came to give,
Her heavenly love and cheer,
Have made us glad to live
And die without a fear.
1912.

THE TALISMAN
What is Fortune, what is Fame?
Futile gold and phantom name,—
Riches buried in a cave,
Glory written on a grave.
What is Friendship? Something deep
That the heart can spend and keep:
Wealth that greatens while we give,
Praise that heartens us to live.
Come, my friend, and let us prove
Life's true talisman is love!
By this charm we shall elude
Poverty and solitude.
January 21, 1914.

THORN AND ROSE
Far richer than a thornless rose
Whose branch with beauty never glows,
Is that which every June adorns
With perfect bloom among its thorns.
Merely to live without a pain
Is little gladness, little gain,
Ah, welcome joy tho' mixt with grief,—
The thorn-set flower that crowns the leaf.
June 20, 1914.

"THE SIGNS"
Dedicated to the Zodiac Club
Who knows how many thousand years ago
The twelvefold Zodiac was made to show
The course of stars above and men below?
The great sun plows his furrow by its "lines":
From all its "houses" mystic meaning shines:
Deep lore of life is written in its "signs."

Aries—Sacrifice.
Snow-white and sacred is the sacrifice
That Heaven demands for what our heart doth prize:
The man who fears to suffer, ne'er can rise.
Taurus—Strength.
Rejoice, my friend, if God has made you strong:
Put forth your force to move the world along:
Yet never shame your strength to do a wrong.

Gemini—Brotherhood.
Bitter his life who lives for self alone,
Poor would he be with riches and a throne:
But friendship doubles all we are and own.
Cancer—The Wisdom of Retreat.
Learn from the crab, O runner fresh and fleet,
Sideways to move, or backward, when discreet;
Life is not all advance,—sometimes retreat!
Leo—Fire.
The sign of Leo is the sign of fire.
Hatred we hate: but no man should desire
A heart too cold to flame with righteous ire.
Virgo—Love.
Mysterious symbol, words are all in vain
To tell the secret power by which you reign.
The more we love, the less we can explain.
Libra—Justice.
Examine well the scales with which you weigh;
Let justice rule your conduct every day;
For when you face the Judge you'll need fair play.
Scorpio—Self-Defense.
There's not a creature in the realm of night
But has the wish to live, likewise the right:
Don't tread upon the scorpion, or he'll fight.
Sagittarius—The Archer.
Life is an arrow, therefore you must know
What mark to aim at, how to use the bow,—
Then draw it to the head and let it go!
Capricornus—The Goat.
The goat looks solemn, yet he likes to run,
And leap the rocks, and gambol in the sun:
The truly wise enjoy a little fun.
Aquarius—Water.
"Like water spilt upon the ground,"—alas,
Our little lives flow swiftly on and pass;
Yet may they bring rich harvests and green grass!
Pisces—The Fishes.
Last of the sacred signs, you bring to me
A word of hope, a word of mystery,—
We all are swimmers in God's mighty sea.
February 28, 1918.

PRO PATRIA
PATRIA

I would not even ask my heart to say
If I could love another land as well
As thee, my country, had I felt the spell
Of Italy at birth, or learned to obey
The charm of France, or England's mighty sway.
I would not be so much an infidel
As once to dream, or fashion words to tell,
What land could hold my heart from thee away.
For like a law of nature in my blood,

America, I feel thy sovereignty,
And woven through my soul thy vital sign.
My life is but a wave and thou the flood;
I am a leaf and thou the mother-tree;
Nor should I be at all, were I not thine.
June, 1904.

AMERICA

I love thine inland seas,
Thy groves of giant trees,
Thy rolling plains;
Thy rivers' mighty sweep,
Thy mystic canyons deep,
Thy mountains wild and steep,
All thy domains;
Thy silver Eastern strands,
Thy Golden Gate that stands
Wide to the West;
Thy flowery Southland fair,
Thy sweet and crystal air,—
O land beyond compare,
Thee I love best!
March, 1906.

THE ANCESTRAL DWELLINGS

Dear to my heart are the ancestral dwellings of America,
Dearer than if they were haunted by ghosts of royal splendour;
They are simple enough to be great in their friendly dignity,—
Homes that were built by the brave beginners of a nation.

I love the old white farmhouses nestled in New England valleys,
Ample and long and low, with elm-trees feathering over them:
Borders of box in the yard, and lilacs, and old-fashioned roses,
A fan-light above the door, and little square panes in the windows,
The wood-shed piled with maple and birch and hickory ready for winter,
The gambrel-roof with its garret crowded with household relics,—
All the tokens of prudent thrift and the spirit of self-reliance.
I love the weather-beaten, shingled houses that front the ocean;
They seem to grow out of the rocks, there is something indomitable about them:
Their backs are bowed, and their sides are covered with lichens;
Soft in their colour as gray pearls, they are full of a patient courage.
Facing the briny wind on a lonely shore they stand undaunted,
While the thin blue pennant of smoke from the square-built chimney
Tells of a haven for man, with room for a hearth and a cradle.

I love the stately southern mansions with their tall white columns,
They look through avenues of trees, over fields where the cotton is growing;
I can see the flutter of white frocks along their shady porches,
Music and laughter float from the windows, the yards are full of hounds and horses.
Long since the riders have ridden away, yet the houses have not forgotten,
They are proud of their name and place, and their doors are always open,
For the thing they remember best is the pride of their ancient hospitality.
In the towns I love the discreet and tranquil Quaker dwellings,
With their demure brick faces and immaculate marble doorsteps;
And the gabled houses of the Dutch, with their high stoops and iron railings,
(I can see their little brass knobs shining in the morning sunlight);
And the solid self-contained houses of the descendants of the Puritans,
Frowning on the street with their narrow doors and dormer-windows;
And the triple-galleried, many-pillared mansions of Charleston,
Standing open sideways in their gardens of roses and magnolias.
Yes, they are all dear to my heart, and in my eyes they are beautiful;
For under their roofs were nourished the thoughts that have made the nation;
The glory and strength of America come from her ancestral dwellings.
July, 1909.

HUDSON'S LAST VOYAGE
THE SHALLOP ON HUDSON BAY
June 22, 1611

One sail in sight upon the lonely sea,
And only one! For never ship but mine
Has dared these waters. We were first,
My men, to battle in between the bergs
And floes to these wide waves. This gulf is mine;
I name it! and that flying sail is mine!
And there, hull-down below that flying sail,
The ship that staggers home is mine, mine, mine!
My ship Discoverie!
The sullen dogs
Of mutineers, the bitches' whelps that snatched
Their food and bit the hand that nourished them,
Have stolen her. You ingrate Henry Greene,
I picked you from the gutter of Houndsditch,
And paid your debts, and kept you in my house,
And brought you here to make a man of you!
You Robert Juet, ancient, crafty man,
Toothless and tremulous, how many times
Have I employed you as a master's mate
To give you bread? And you Abacuck Prickett,

You sailor-clerk, you salted puritan,
You knew the plot and silently agreed,
Salving your conscience with a pious lie!
Yes, all of you—hounds, rebels, thieves! Bring back
My ship!
Too late,—I rave,—they cannot hear
My voice: and if they heard, a drunken laugh
Would be their answer; for their minds have caught
The fatal firmness of the fool's resolve,
That looks like courage but is only fear.
They'll blunder on, and lose my ship, and drown;
Or blunder home to England and be hanged.
Their skeletons will rattle in the chains
Of some tall gibbet on the Channel cliffs,
While passing mariners look up and say:
"Those are the rotten bones of Hudson's men
Who left their captain in the frozen North!"
O God of justice, why hast Thou ordained
Plans of the wise and actions of the brave
Dependent on the aid of fools and cowards?
Look,—there she goes,—her topsails in the sun
Gleam from the ragged ocean edge, and drop
Clean out of sight! So let the traitors go
Clean out of mind! We'll think of braver things!
Come closer in the boat, my friends. John King,
You take the tiller, keep her head nor'west.
You Philip Staffe, the only one who chose
Freely to share our little shallop's fate,
Rather than travel in the hell-bound ship,—
Too good an English sailor to desert
Your crippled comrades,—try to make them rest
More easy on the thwarts. And John, my son,
My little shipmate, come and lean your head
Against my knee. Do you remember still
The April morn in Ethelburga's church,
Five years ago, when side by side we kneeled
To take the sacrament with all our men,
Before the Hopewell left St. Catherine's docks
On our first voyage? It was then I vowed
My sailor-soul and yours to search the sea
Until we found the water-path that leads
From Europe into Asia.
I believe
That God has poured the ocean round His world,
Not to divide, but to unite the lands.
And all the English captains that have dared
In little ships to plough uncharted waves,—
Davis and Drake, Hawkins and Frobisher,
Raleigh and Gilbert,—all the other names,—
Are written in the chivalry of God
As men who served His purpose. I would claim
A place among that knighthood of the sea;
And I have earned it, though my quest should fail!
For, mark me well, the honour of our life
Derives from this: to have a certain aim
Before us always, which our will must seek
Amid the peril of uncertain ways.
Then, though we miss the goal, our search is crowned
With courage, and we find along our path
A rich reward of unexpected things.
Press towards the aim: take fortune as it fares!
I know not why, but something in my heart

Has always whispered, "Westward seek your goal!"
Three times they sent me east, but still I turned
The bowsprit west, and felt among the floes
Of ruttling ice along the Greenland coast,
And down the rugged shore of Newfoundland,
And past the rocky capes and wooded bays
Where Gosnold sailed,—like one who feels his way
With outstretched hand across a darkened room,—
I groped among the inlets and the isles,
To find the passage to the Land of Spice.
I have not found it yet,—but I have found
Things worth the finding!
Son, have you forgot
Those mellow autumn days, two years ago,
When first we sent our little ship Half-Moon,—
The flag of Holland floating at her peak,—
Across a sandy bar, and sounded in
Among the channels, to a goodly bay
Where all the navies of the world could ride?
A fertile island that the redmen called
Manhattan, lay above the bay: the land
Around was bountiful and friendly fair.
But never land was fair enough to hold
The seaman from the calling of the sea.
And so we bore to westward of the isle,
Along a mighty inlet, where the tide
Was troubled by a downward-flowing flood
That seemed to come from far away,—perhaps
From some mysterious gulf of Tartary?
Inland we held our course; by palisades
Of naked rock; by rolling hills adorned
With forests rich in timber for great ships;
Through narrows where the mountains shut us in
With frowning cliffs that seemed to bar the stream;
And then through open reaches where the banks
Sloped to the water gently, with their fields
Of corn and lentils smiling in the sun.
Ten days we voyaged through that placid land,
Until we came to shoals, and sent a boat
Upstream to find,—what I already knew,—
We travelled on a river, not a strait.
But what a river! God has never poured
A stream more royal through a land more rich.
Even now I see it flowing in my dream,
While coming ages people it with men
Of manhood equal to the river's pride.
I see the wigwams of the redmen changed
To ample houses, and the tiny plots
Of maize and green tobacco broadened out
To prosperous farms, that spread o'er hill and dale
The many-coloured mantle of their crops.
I see the terraced vineyard on the slope
Where now the fox-grape loops its tangled vine,
And cattle feeding where the red deer roam,
And wild-bees gathered into busy hives
To store the silver comb with golden sweet;
And all the promised land begins to flow
With milk and honey. Stately manors rise
Along the banks, and castles top the hills,
And little villages grow populous with trade,
Until the river runs as proudly as the Rhine,—
The thread that links a hundred towns and towers!

Now looking deeper in my dream, I see
A mighty city covering the isle
They call Manhattan, equal in her state
To all the older capitals of earth,—
The gateway city of a golden world,—
A city girt with masts, and crowned with spires,
And swarming with a million busy men,
While to her open door across the bay
The ships of all the nations flock like doves.
My name will be remembered there, the world
Will say, "This river and this isle were found
By Henry Hudson, on his way to seek
The Northwest Passage."
Yes, I seek it still,—
My great adventure and my guiding star!
For look ye, friends, our voyage is not done;
We hold by hope as long as life endures!
Somewhere among these floating fields of ice,
Somewhere along this westward widening bay,
Somewhere beneath this luminous northern night,
The channel opens to the Farthest East,—
I know it,—and some day a little ship
Will push her bowsprit in, and battle through!
And why not ours,—to-morrow,—who can tell?
The lucky chance awaits the fearless heart!
These are the longest days of all the year;
The world is round and God is everywhere,
And while our shallop floats we still can steer.
So point her up, John King, nor'west by north
We'll keep the honour of a certain aim
Amid the peril of uncertain ways,
And sail ahead, and leave the rest to God.
July, 1909.

SEA-GULLS OF MANHATTAN

Children of the elemental mother,
Born upon some lonely island shore
Where the wrinkled ripples run and whisper,
Where the crested billows plunge and roar;
Long-winged, tireless roamers and adventurers,
Fearless breasters of the wind and sea,
In the far-off solitary places
I have seen you floating wild and free!

Here the high-built cities rise around you;
Here the cliffs that tower east and west,
Honeycombed with human habitations,
Have no hiding for the sea-bird's nest:
Here the river flows begrimed and troubled;
Here the hurrying, panting vessels fume,
Restless, up and down the watery highway,
While a thousand chimneys vomit gloom.
Toil and tumult, conflict and confusion,
Clank and clamour of the vast machine
Human hands have built for human bondage—
Yet amid it all you float serene;
Circling, soaring, sailing, swooping lightly
Down to glean your harvest from the wave;
In your heritage of air and water,
You have kept the freedom Nature gave.
Even so the wild-woods of Manhattan
Saw your wheeling flocks of white and gray;

Even so you fluttered, followed, floated,
Round the Half-Moon creeping up the bay;
Even so your voices creaked and chattered.
Laughing shrilly o'er the tidal rips,
While your black and beady eyes were glistening
Round the sullen British prison-ships.
Children of the elemental mother,
Fearless floaters 'mid the double blue,
From the crowded boats that cross the ferries
Many a longing heart goes out to you.
Though the cities climb and close around us,
Something tells us that our souls are free,
While the sea-gulls fly above the harbour,
While the river flows to meet the sea!
December, 1905.

A BALLAD OF CLAREMONT HILL
The roar of the city is low,
Muffled by new-fallen snow,
And the sign of the wintry moon is small and round and still.
Will you come with me to-night,
To see a pleasant sight
Away on the river-side, at the edge of Claremont Hill?
"And what shall we see there,
But streets that are new and bare,
And many a desolate place that the city is coming to fill;
And a soldier's tomb of stone,
And a few trees standing alone—
Will you walk for that through the cold, to the edge of Claremont Hill?"
But there's more than that for me,
In the place that I fain would see:
There's a glimpse of the grace that helps us all to bear life's ill,
A touch of the vital breath
That keeps the world from death,
A flower that never fades, on the edge of Claremont Hill.
For just where the road swings round,
In a narrow strip of ground,
Where a group of forest trees are lingering fondly still,
There's a grave of the olden time,
When the garden bloomed in its prime,
And the children laughed and sang on the edge of Claremont Hill.
The marble is pure and white,
And even in this dim light,
You may read the simple words that are written there if you will;
You may hear a father tell
Of the child he loved so well,
A hundred years ago, on the edge of Claremont Hill.
The tide of the city has rolled
Across that bower of old,
And blotted out the beds of the rose and the daffodil;
But the little playmate sleeps,
And the shrine of love still keeps
A record of happy days, on the edge of Claremont Hill.
The river is pouring down
To the crowded, careless town,
Where the intricate wheels of trade are grinding on like a mill;
But the clamorous noise and strife
Of the hurrying waves of life
Flow soft by this haven of peace on the edge of Claremont Hill.
And after all, my friend,
When the tale of our years shall end,
Be it long or short, or lowly or great, as God may will,
What better praise could we hear,
Than this of the child so dear:
You have made my life more sweet, on the edge of Claremont Hill?
December, 1896.

URBS CORONATA
(Song for the City College of New York)
O youngest of the giant brood
Of cities far-renowned;
In wealth and glory thou hast passed
Thy rivals at a bound;
Thou art a mighty queen, New York;
And how wilt thou be crowned?
"Weave me no palace-wreath of Pride,"
The royal city said;
"Nor forge of frowning fortress-walls
A helmet for my head;
But let me wear a diadem
Of Wisdom's towers instead."
She bowed herself, she spent herself,
She wrought her will forsooth,
And set upon her island height
A citadel of Truth,
A house of Light, a home of Thought,
A shrine of noble Youth.

Stand here, ye City College towers,
And look both up and down;
Remember all who wrought for you
Within the toiling town;
Remember all their hopes for you,
And be the City's Crown.
June, 1908.

MERCY FOR ARMENIA
I
THE TURK'S WAY
Stand back, ye messengers of mercy! Stand
Far off, for I will save my troubled folk
In my own way. So the false Sultan spoke;
And Europe, hearkening to his base command,
Stood still to see him heal his wounded land.
Through blinding snows of winter and through smoke
Of burning towns, she saw him deal the stroke
Of cruel mercy that his hate had planned.
Unto the prisoners and the sick he gave
New tortures, horrible, without a name;
Unto the thirsty, blood to drink; a sword
Unto the hungry; with a robe of shame
He clad the naked, making life abhorred;
He saved by slaughter, and denied a grave.

II
AMERICA'S WAY

But thou, my country, though no fault be thine
For that red horror far across the sea;
Though not a tortured wretch can point to thee,
And curse thee for the selfishness supine
Of those great Powers that cowardly combine
To shield the Turk in his iniquity;
Yet, since thy hand is innocent and free,
Arise, and show the world the way divine!
Thou canst not break the oppressor's iron rod,
But thou canst help and comfort the oppressed;
Thou canst not loose the captive's heavy chain,
But thou canst bind his wounds and soothe his pain.
Armenia calls thee, Sovereign of the West,
To play the Good Samaritan for God.
1896.

SICILY, DECEMBER, 1908
O garden isle, beloved by Sun and Sea,
Whose bluest billows kiss thy curving bays,
Whose light infolds thy hills with golden rays,
Filling with fruit each dark-leaved orange-tree,
What hidden hatred hath the Earth for thee,
That once again, in these dark, dreadful days,
Breaks forth in trembling rage, and swiftly lays
Thy beauty waste in wreck and agony!
Is Nature, then, a strife of jealous powers,
And man the plaything of unconscious fate?
Not so, my troubled heart! God reigns above,
And man is greatest in his darkest hours.
Walking amid the cities desolate,
Behold the Son of God in human love!
Tertius and Henry van Dyke.

"COME BACK AGAIN, JEANNE D'ARC"
The land was broken in despair,
The princes quarrelled in the dark,
When clear and tranquil, through the troubled air
Of selfish minds and wills that did not dare,
Your star arose, Jeanne d'Arc.
O virgin breast with lilies white,
O sun-burned hand that bore the lance,
You taught the prayer that helps men to unite,
You brought the courage equal to the fight,
You gave a heart to France!
Your king was crowned, your country free,
At Rheims you had your soul's desire:
And then, at Rouen, maid of Domrémy,
The black-robed judges gave your victory
The martyr's crown of fire.
And now again the times are ill,
And doubtful leaders miss the mark;
The people lack the single faith and will
To make them one,—your country needs you still,—
Come back again, Jeanne d'Arc!
O woman-star, arise once more
And shine to bid your land advance:
The old heroic trust in God restore,
Renew the brave, unselfish hopes of yore,
And give a heart to France!
Paris, July, 1909.

NATIONAL MONUMENTS

Count not the cost of honour to the dead!
The tribute that a mighty nation pays
To those who loved her well in former days
Means more than gratitude for glories fled;
For every noble man that she hath bred,
Lives in the bronze and marble that we raise,
Immortalised by art's immortal praise,
To lead our sons as he our fathers led.
These monuments of manhood strong and high
Do more than forts or battle-ships to keep
Our dear-bought liberty. They fortify
The heart of youth with valour wise and deep;
They build eternal bulwarks, and command
Immortal hosts to guard our native land.
February, 1905.

THE MONUMENT OF FRANCIS MAKEMIE
(Presbyter of Christ in America, 1683-1708)
To thee, plain hero of a rugged race,
We bring the meed of praise too long delayed!
Thy fearless word and faithful work have made
For God's Republic firmer resting-place
In this New World: for thou hast preached the grace
And power of Christ in many a forest glade,
Teaching the truth that leaves men unafraid
Of frowning tyranny or death's dark face.
Oh, who can tell how much we owe to thee,
Makemie, and to labour such as thine,
For all that makes America the shrine
Of faith untrammelled and of conscience free?
Stand here, gray stone, and consecrate the sod
Where rests this brave Scotch-Irish man of God!
April, 1908.

THE STATUE OF SHERMAN BY ST. GAUDENS
This is the soldier brave enough to tell
The glory-dazzled world that 'war is hell':
Lover of peace, he looks beyond the strife,
And rides through hell to save his country's life.
April, 1904.

"AMERICA FOR ME"
'Tis fine to see the Old World, and travel up and down
Among the famous palaces and cities of renown,
To admire the crumbly castles and the statues of the kings,—
But now I think I've had enough of antiquated things.
So it's home again, and home again, America for me!
My heart is turning home again, and there I long to be,
In the land of youth and freedom beyond the ocean bars,
Where the air is full of sunlight and the flag is full of stars.
Oh, London is a man's town, there's power in the air;
And Paris is a woman's town, with flowers in her hair;
And it's sweet to dream in Venice, and it's great to study Rome;
But when it comes to living there is no place like home.
I like the German fir-woods, in green battalions drilled;
I like the gardens of Versailles with flashing fountains filled;
But, oh, to take your hand, my dear, and ramble for a day

In the friendly western woodland where Nature has her way!
I know that Europe's wonderful, yet something seems to lack:
The Past is too much with her, and the people looking back.
But the glory of the Present is to make the Future free,—
We love our land for what she is and what she is to be.
Oh, it's home again, and home again, America for me!
I want a ship that's westward bound to plough the rolling sea,
To the blessèd Land of Room Enough beyond the ocean bars,
Where the air is full of sunlight and the flag is full of stars.
June, 1909.

THE BUILDERS
ODE FOR THE HUNDRED AND FIFTIETH ANNIVERSARY OF PRINCETON COLLEGE
October 21, 1896

I

Into the dust of the making of man
Spirit was breathed when his life began,
Lifting him up from his low estate,
With masterful passion, the wish to create.
Out of the dust of his making, man
Fashioned his works as the ages ran;
Fortress, and palace, and temple, and tower,
Filling the world with the proof of his power.
Over the dust that awaits him, man,
Building the walls that his pride doth plan,
Dreams they will stand in the light of the sun
Bearing his name till Time is done.

II

The monuments of mortals
Are as the glory of the grass;
Through Time's dim portals
A voiceless, viewless wind doth pass,
The blossoms fall before it in a day,
The forest monarchs year by year decay,
And man's great buildings slowly fade away.
One after one,
They pay to that dumb breath
The tribute of their death,
And are undone.
The towers incline to dust,
The massive girders rust,
The domes dissolve in air,
The pillars that upbear
The lofty arches crumble, stone by stone,
While man the builder looks about him in despair,
For all his works of pride and power are overthrown.

III

A Voice came from the sky:
"Set thy desires more high.
Thy buildings fade away
Because thou buildest clay.
Now make the fabric sure
With stones that will endure!
Hewn from the spiritual rock,
The immortal towers of the soul
At Death's dissolving touch shall mock,
And stand secure while æons roll."

IV

Well did the wise in heart rejoice
To hear the summons of that Voice,
And patiently begin
The builder's work within,
Houses not made with hands,
Nor founded on the sands.
And thou, Reverèd Mother, at whose call
We come to keep thy joyous festival,
And celebrate thy labours on the walls of Truth
Through sevenscore years and ten of thine eternal youth—
A master builder thou,
And on thy shining brow,
Like Cybele, in fadeless light dost wear
A diadem of turrets strong and fair.

V

I see thee standing in a lonely land,
But late and hardly won from solitude,
Unpopulous and rude,—
On that far western shore I see thee stand,
Like some young goddess from a brighter strand,
While in thine eyes a radiant thought is born,
Enkindling all thy beauty like the morn.
Sea-like the forest rolled, in waves of green,
And few the lights that glimmered, leagues between.
High in the north, for fourscore years alone
Fair Harvard's earliest beacon-tower had shone
When Yale was lighted, and an answering ray
Flashed from the meadows by New Haven Bay.
But deeper spread the forest, and more dark,
Where first Neshaminy received the spark
Of sacred learning to a woodland camp,
And Old Log College glowed with Tennant's lamp.
Thine, Alma Mater, was the larger sight,
That saw the future of that trembling light,
And thine the courage, thine the stronger will,
That built its loftier home on Princeton Hill.
"New light!" men cried, and murmured that it came
From an unsanctioned source with lawless flame;
It shone too free, for still the church and school
Must only shine according to their rule.
But Princeton answered, in her nobler mood,
"God made the light, and all the light is good.
There is no war between the old and new;
The conflict lies between the false and true.
The stars, that high in heaven their courses run,
In glory differ, but their light is one.
The beacons, gleaming o'er the sea of life,
Are rivals but in radiance, not in strife.
Shine on, ye sister-towers, across the night!
I too will build a lasting house of light."

VI

Brave was that word of faith and bravely was it kept:
With never-wearying zeal that faltered not, nor slept,
Our Alma Mater toiled, and while she firmly laid
The deep foundation-walls, at all her toil she prayed.
And men who loved the truth because it made them free,
And clearly saw the twofold Word of God agree,
Reading from Nature's book and from the Bible's page

By the same inward ray that grows from age to age,
Were built like living stones that beacon to uplift,
And drawing light from heaven gave to the world the gift.
Nor ever, while they searched the secrets of the earth,
Or traced the stream of life through mystery to its birth,
Nor ever, while they taught the lightning-flash to bear
The messages of man in silence through the air,
Fell from their home of light one false, perfidious ray
To blind the trusting heart, or lead the life astray.
But still, while knowledge grew more luminous and broad
It lit the path of faith and showed the way to God.

VII

Yet not for peace alone
Labour the builders.
Work that in peace has grown
Swiftly is overthrown,
When in the darkening skies
Storm-clouds of wrath arise,
And through the cannon's crash,
War's deadly lightning-flash
Smites and bewilders.
Ramparts of strength must frown
Round every placid town
And city splendid;
All that our fathers wrought
With true prophetic thought,
Must be defended!

VIII

But who could raise protecting walls for thee,
Thou young, defenceless land of liberty?
Or who could build a fortress strong enough,
Or stretch a mighty bulwark long enough
To hold thy far-extended coast
Against the overweening host
That took the open path across the sea,
And like a tempest poured
Their desolating horde,
To quench thy dawning light in gloom of tyranny?
Yet not unguarded thou wert found
When on thy shore with sullen sound
The blaring trumpets of an unjust king
Proclaimed invasion. From the ground,
In freedom's darkest hour, there seemed to spring
Unconquerable walls for her defence;
Not trembling, like those battlements of stone
That fell when Joshua's horns were blown;
But firm and stark the living rampart rose,
To meet the onset of imperious foes
With a long line of brave, unyielding men.
This was thy fortress, well-defended land,
And on these walls, the patient, building hand
Of Princeton laboured with the force of ten.
Her sons were foremost in the furious fight;
Her sons were firmest to uphold the right
In council-chambers of the new-born State,
And prove that he who would be free must first be great
In heart, and high in thought, and strong
In purpose not to do or suffer wrong.
Such were the men, impregnable to fear,
Whose souls were framed and fashioned here;
And when war shook the land with threatening shock,
The men of Princeton stood like muniments of rock.

Nor has the breath of Time
Dissolved that proud array
Of never-broken strength:
For though the rocks decay,
And all the iron bands
Of earthly strongholds are unloosed at length,
And buried deep in gray oblivion's sands;
The work that heroes' hands
Wrought in the light of freedom's natal day
Shall never fade away,
But lifts itself, sublime
Into a lucid sphere,
For ever calm and clear,
Preserving in the memory of the fathers' deed,
A never-failing fortress for their children's need.
There we confirm our hearts to-day, and read
On many a stone the signature of fame,
The builder's mark, our Alma Mater's name.

IX

Bear with us then a moment, while we turn
From all the present splendours of this place—
The lofty towers that like a dream have grown
Where once old Nassau Hall stood all alone—
Back to that ancient time, with hearts that burn
In filial gratitude, to trace
The glory of our mother's best degree,
In that "high son of Liberty,"
Who like a granite block,
Riven from Scotland's rock,
Stood loyal here to keep Columbia free.
Born far away beyond the ocean's tide,
He found his fatherland upon this side;
And every drop of ardent blood that ran
Through his great heart, was true American.
He held no fealty to a distant throne,
But made his new-found country's cause his own.
In peril and distress,
In toil and weariness,
When darkness overcast her
With shadows of disaster,
And voices of confusion
Proclaimed her hope delusion,
Robed in his preacher's gown,
He dared the danger down;
Like some old prophet chanting an inspired rune
In freedom's councils rang the voice of Witherspoon.
And thou, my country, write it on thy heart:
Thy sons are they who nobly take thy part;
Who dedicates his manhood at thy shrine,
Wherever born, is born a son of thine.
Foreign in name, but not in soul, they come
To find in thee their long desired home;
Lovers of liberty and haters of disorder,
They shall be built in strength along thy border.
Dream not thy future foes
Will all be foreign-born!
Turn thy clear look of scorn
Upon thy children who oppose
Their passions wild and policies of shame
To wreck the righteous splendour of thy name.
Untaught and overconfident they rise,

With folly on their lips, and envy in their eyes:
Strong to destroy, but powerless to create,
And ignorant of all that made our fathers great,
Their hands would take away thy golden crown,
And shake the pillars of thy freedom down
In Anarchy's ocean, dark and desolate.
O should that storm descend,
What fortress shall defend
The land our fathers wrought for,
The liberties they fought for?
What bulwark shall secure
Her shrines of law, and keep her founts of justice pure?
Then, ah then,
As in the olden days,
The builders must upraise
A rampart of indomitable men.
And once again,
Dear Mother, if thy heart and hand be true,
There will be building work for thee to do;
Yea, more than once again,
Thou shalt win lasting praise,
And never-dying honour shall be thine,
For setting many stones in that illustrious line,
To stand unshaken in the swirling strife,
And guard their country's honour as her life.

X

Softly, my harp, and let me lay the touch
Of silence on these rudely clanging strings;
For he who sings
Even of noble conflicts overmuch,
Loses the inward sense of better things;
And he who makes a boast
Of knowledge, darkens that which counts the most,—
The insight of a wise humility
That reverently adores what none can see.
The glory of our life below
Comes not from what we do, or what we know,
But dwells forevermore in what we are.
There is an architecture grander far
Than all the fortresses of war,
More inextinguishably bright
Than learning's lonely towers of light.
Framing its walls of faith and hope and love
In souls of men, it lifts above
The frailty of our earthly home
An everlasting dome;
The sanctuary of the human host,
The living temple of the Holy Ghost.

XI

If music led the builders long ago,
When Arthur planned the halls of Camelot,
And made the royal city grow,
Fair as a flower in that forsaken spot;
What sweeter music shall we bring,
To weave a harmony divine
Of prayer and holy thought
Into the labours of this loftier shrine,
This consecrated hill,
Where through so many a year
Our Alma Mater's hand hath wrought,
With toil serene and still,
And heavenly hope, to rear

Eternal dwellings for the Only King?
Here let no martial trumpets blow,
Nor instruments of pride proclaim
The loud exultant notes of fame!
But let the chords be clear and low,
And let the anthem deeper grow,
And let it move more solemnly and slow;
For only such an ode
Can seal the harmony
Of that deep masonry
Wherein the soul of man is framed for God's abode.

XII

O Thou whose boundless love bestows
The joy of earth, the hope of Heaven,
And whose unchartered mercy flows
O'er all the blessings Thou hast given;
Thou by whose light alone we see;
And by whose truth our souls set free
Are made imperishably strong;
Hear Thou the solemn music of our song.
Grant us the knowledge that we need
To solve the questions of the mind,
And light our candle while we read,
To keep our hearts from going blind;
Enlarge our vision to behold
The wonders Thou hast wrought of old;
Reveal thyself in every law,
And gild the towers of truth with holy awe.
Be Thou our strength if war's wild gust
Shall rage around us, loud and fierce;
Confirm our souls and let our trust
Be like a shield that none can pierce;
Renew the courage that prevails,
The steady faith that never fails,
And make us stand in every fight
Firm as a fortress to defend the right.
O God, control us as Thou wilt,
And guide the labour of our hand;
Let all our work be surely built
As Thou, the architect, hast planned;
But whatso'er thy power shall make
Of these frail lives, do not forsake
Thy dwelling: let thy presence rest
For ever in the temple of our breast.

**SPIRIT OF THE EVERLASTING BOY
ODE FOR THE HUNDREDTH ANNIVERSARY
OF LAWRENCEVILLE SCHOOL**

June 11, 1910

I

The British bard who looked on Eton's walls,
Endeared by distance in the pearly gray
And soft aerial blue that ever falls
On English landscape with the dying day,
Beheld in thought his boyhood far away,
Its random raptures and its festivals
Of noisy mirth,
The brief illusion of its idle joys,
And mourned that none of these can stay
With men, whom life inexorably calls
To face the grim realities of earth.

His pensive fancy pictured there at play
From year to year the careless bands of boys,
Unconscious victims kept in golden state,
While haply they await
The dark approach of disenchanting Fate,
To hale them to the sacrifice
Of Pain and Penury and Grief and Care,
Slow-withering Age, or Failure's swift despair.
Half-pity and half-envy dimmed the eyes
Of that old poet, gazing on the scene
Where long ago his youth had flowed serene,
And all the burden of his ode was this:
"Where ignorance is bliss,
'Tis folly to be wise."

II

But not for us, O plaintive elegist,
Thine epicedial tone of sad farewell
To joy in wisdom and to thought in youth!
Our western Muse would keep her tryst
With sunrise, not with sunset, and foretell
In boyhood's bliss the dawn of manhood's truth.

III

O spirit of the everlasting boy,
Alert, elate,
And confident that life is good,
Thou knockest boldly at the gate,
In hopeful hardihood,
Eager to enter and enjoy
Thy new estate.
Through the old house thou runnest everywhere,
Bringing a breath of folly and fresh air.
Ready to make a treasure of each toy,
Or break them all in discontented mood;
Fearless of Fate,
Yet strangely fearful of a comrade's laugh;
Reckless and timid, hard and sensitive;
In talk a rebel, full of mocking chaff,
At heart devout conservative;
In love with love, yet hating to be kissed;
Inveterate optimist,
And judge severe,
In reason cloudy but in feeling clear;
Keen critic, ardent hero-worshipper,
Impatient of restraint in little ways,
Yet ever ready to confer
On chosen leaders boundless power and praise;
Adventurous spirit burning to explore
Untrodden paths where hidden danger lies,
And homesick heart looking with wistful eyes
Through every twilight to a mother's door;
Thou daring, darling, inconsistent boy,
How dull the world would be
Without thy presence, dear barbarian,
And happy lord of high futurity!
Be what thou art, our trouble and our joy,
Our hardest problem and our brightest hope!
And while thine elders lead thee up the slope
Of knowledge, let them learn from teaching thee
That vital joy is part of nature's plan,
And he who keeps the spirit of the boy
Shall gladly grow to be a happy man.

IV

What constitutes a school?
Not ancient halls and ivy-mantled towers,
Where dull traditions rule
With heavy hand youth's lightly springing powers;
Not spacious pleasure courts,
And lofty temples of athletic fame,
Where devotees of sports
Mistake a pastime for life's highest aim;
Not fashion, nor renown
Of wealthy patronage and rich estate;
No, none of these can crown
A school with light and make it truly great.
But masters, strong and wise,
Who teach because they love the teacher's task,
And find their richest prize
In eyes that open and in minds that ask;
And boys, with heart aglow
To try their youthful vigour on their work,
Eager to learn and grow,
And quick to hate a coward or a shirk:
These constitute a school,—
A vital forge of weapons keen and bright,
Where living sword and tool
Are tempered for true toil or noble fight!
But let not wisdom scorn
The hours of pleasure in the playing fields:
There also strength is born,
And every manly game a virtue yields.
Fairness and self-control,
Good-humour, pluck, and patience in the race,
Will make a lad heart-whole
To win with honour, lose without disgrace.
Ah, well for him who gains
In such a school apprenticeship to life:
With him the joy of youth remains
In later lessons and in larger strife!

V

On Jersey's rolling plain, where Washington,
In midnight marching at the head
Of ragged regiments, his army led
To Princeton's victory of the rising sun;
Here in this liberal land, by battle won
For Freedom and the rule
Of equal rights for every child of man,
Arose a democratic school,
To train a virile race of sons to bear
With thoughtful joy the name American,
And serve the God who heard their father's prayer.
No cloister, dreaming in a world remote
From that real world wherein alone we live;
No mimic court, where titled names denote
A dignity that only worth can give;
But here a friendly house of learning stood,
With open door beside the broad highway,
And welcomed lads to study and to play
In generous rivalry of brotherhood.
A hundred years have passed, and Lawrenceville,
In beauty and in strength renewed,
Stands with her open portal still,
And neither time nor fortune brings
To her deep spirit any change of mood,
Or faltering from the faith she held of old.

Still to the democratic creed she clings:
That manhood needs nor rank nor gold
To make it noble in our eyes;
That every boy is born with royal right,
From blissful ignorance to rise
To joy more lasting and more bright,
In mastery of body and of mind,
King of himself and servant of mankind.

VI

Old Lawrenceville,
Thy happy bell
Shall ring to-day,
O'er vale and hill,
O'er mead and dell,
While far away,
With silent thrill,
The echoes roll
Through many a soul,
That knew thee well,
In boyhood's day,
And loves thee still.
Ah, who can tell
How far away,
Some sentinel
Of God's good will,
In forest cool,
Or desert gray,
By lonely pool,
Or barren hill,
Shall faintly hear,
With inward ear,
The chiming bell,
Of his old school,
Through darkness pealing;
And lowly kneeling,
Shall feel the spell
Of grateful tears
His eyelids fill;
And softly pray
To Him who hears:
God bless old Lawrenceville!

TEXAS
A DEMOCRATIC ODE *

I
THE WILD-BEES

All along the Brazos river,
All along the Colorado,
In the valleys and the lowlands
Where the trees were tall and stately,
In the rich and rolling meadows
Where the grass was full of wild-flowers,
Came a humming and a buzzing,
Came the murmur of a going
To and fro among the tree-tops,
Far and wide across the meadows.
And the red-men in their tepees
Smoked their pipes of clay and listened.
"What is this?" they asked in wonder;
"Who can give the sound a meaning?
Who can understand the language
Of this going in the tree-tops?"

Then the wisest of the Tejas
Laid his pipe aside and answered:
"O my brothers, these are people,
Very little, winged people,
Countless, busy, banded people,
Coming humming through the timber.
These are tribes of bees, united
By a single aim and purpose,
To possess the Tejas' country,
Gather harvest from the prairies,
Store their wealth among the timber.
These are hive and honey makers,
Sent by Manito to warn us
That the white men now are coming,
With their women and their children.
Not the fiery filibusters
Passing wildly in a moment,
Like a flame across the prairies,
Like a whirlwind through the forest,
Leaving empty lands behind them!
Not the Mexicans and Spaniards,
Indolent and proud hidalgos,
Dwelling in their haciendas,
Dreaming, talking of tomorrow,
While their cattle graze around them,
And their fickle revolutions
Change the rulers, not the people!
Other folk are these who follow
When the wild-bees come to warn us;
These are hive and honey makers,
These are busy, banded people,
Roaming far to swarm and settle,
Working every day for harvest,
Fighting hard for peace and order,
Worshipping as queens their women,
Making homes and building cities
Full of riches and of trouble.
All our hunting-grounds must vanish,
All our lodges fall before them,
All our customs and traditions,
All our happy life of freedom,
Fade away like smoke before them.
Come, my brothers, strike your tepees,
Call your women, load your ponies!
Let us take the trail to westward,
Where the plains are wide and open,
Where the bison-herds are gathered
Waiting for our feathered arrows.
We will live as lived our fathers,
Gleaners of the gifts of nature,
Hunters of the unkept cattle,
Men whose women run to serve them.
If the toiling bees pursue us,
If the white men seek to tame us,
We will fight them off and flee them,
Break their hives and take their honey,
Moving westward, ever westward,
There to live as lived our fathers."
So the red-men drove their ponies,
With the tent-poles trailing after,
Out along the path to sunset,
While along the river valleys

Swarmed the wild-bees, the forerunners;
And the white men, close behind them,
Men of mark from old Missouri,
Men of daring from Kentucky,
Tennessee, Louisiana,
Men of many States and races,
Bringing wives and children with them,
Followed up the wooded valleys,
Spread across the rolling prairies,
Raising homes and reaping harvests.
Rude the toil that tried their patience,
Fierce the fights that proved their courage,
Rough the stone and tough the timber
Out of which they built their order!
Yet they never failed nor faltered,
And the instinct of their swarming
Made them one and kept them working,
Till their toil was crowned with triumph,
And the country of the Tejas
Was the fertile land of Texas.

II
THE LONE STAR

Behold a star appearing in the South,
A star that shines apart from other stars,
Ruddy and fierce like Mars!
Out of the reeking smoke of cannon's mouth
That veils the slaughter of the Alamo,
Where heroes face the foe,
One man against a score, with blood-choked breath
Shouting the watchword, "Victory or Death—"
Out of the dreadful cloud that settles low
On Goliad's plain,
Where thrice a hundred prisoners lie slain
Beneath the broken word of Mexico—
Out of the fog of factions and of feuds
That ever drifts and broods
Above the bloody path of border war,
Leaps the Lone Star!
What light is this that does not dread the dark?
What star is this that fights a stormy way
To San Jacinto's field of victory?
It is the fiery spark
That burns within the breast
Of Anglo-Saxon men, who can not rest
Under a tyrant's sway;
The upward-leading ray
That guides the brave who give their lives away
Rather than not be free!
O question not, but honour every name,
Travis and Crockett, Bowie, Bonham, Ward,
Fannin and King, and all who drew the sword
And dared to die for Texan liberty!
Yea, write them all upon the roll of fame,
But no less love and equal honour give
To those who paid the longer sacrifice—
Austin and Houston, Burnet, Rusk, Lamar
And all the stalwart men who dared to live
Long years of service to the lonely star.
Great is the worth of such heroic souls:
Amid the strenuous turmoil of their deeds,
They clearly speak of something that controls

The higher breeds of men by higher needs
Than bees, content with honey in their hives!
Ah, not enough the narrow lives
On profitable toil intent!
And not enough the guerdons of success
Garnered in homes of affluent selfishness!
A noble discontent
Cries for a wider scope
To use the wider wings of human hope;
A vision of the common good
Opens the prison-door of solitude;
And, once beyond the wall,
Breathing the ampler air,
The heart becomes aware
That life without a country is not life at all.
A country worthy of a freeman's love;
A country worthy of a good man's prayer;
A country strong, and just, and brave, and fair,—
A woman's form of beauty throned above
The shrine where noble aspirations meet—
To live for her is great, to die is sweet!
Heirs of the rugged pioneers
Who dreamed this dream and made it true,
Remember that they dreamed for you.
They did not fear their fate
In those tempestuous years,
But put their trust in God, and with keen eyes,
Trained in the open air for looking far,
They saw the many-million-acred land
Won from the desert by their hand,
Swiftly among the nations rise,—
Texas a sovereign State,
And on her brow a star!

III
THE CONSTELLATION

How strange that the nature of light is a thing beyond our ken,
And the flame of the tiniest candle flows from a fountain sealed!
How strange that the meaning of life, in the little lives of men,
So often baffles our search with a mystery unrevealed!
But the larger life of man, as it moves in its secular sweep,
Is the working out of a Sovereign Will whose ways appear;
And the course of the journeying stars on the dark blue boundless deep,
Is the place where our science rests in the reign of law most clear.
I would read the story of Texas as if it were written on high;
I would look from afar to follow her path through the calms and storms;
With a faith in the worldwide sway of the Reason that rules in the sky,
And gathers and guides the starry host in clusters and swarms.
When she rose in the pride of her youth, she seemed to be moving apart,

As a single star in the South, self-limited, self-possessed;
But the law of the constellation was written deep in her heart,
And she heard when her sisters called, from the North and the East and the West.
They were drawn together and moved by a common hope and aim—
The dream of a sign that should rule a third of the heavenly arch;
The soul of a people spoke in their call, and Texas came
To enter the splendid circle of States in their onward march.

So the glory gathered and grew and spread from sea to sea,
And the stars of the great republic lent each other light;
For all were bound together in strength, and each was free—
Suddenly broke the tempest out of the ancient night!
It came as a clash of the force that drives and the force that draws;
And the stars were riven asunder, the heavens were desolate,
While brother fought with brother, each for his country's cause:
But the country of one was the Nation, the country of other the State.
Oh, who shall measure the praise or blame in a strife so vast?
And who shall speak of traitors or tyrants when all were true?
We lift our eyes to the sky, and rejoice that the storm is past,
And we thank the God of all that the Union shines in the blue.
Yea, it glows with the glory of peace and the hope of a mighty race,
High over the grave of broken chains and buried hates;
And the great, big star of Texas is shining clear in its place
In the constellate symbol and sign of the free United States.

IV
AFTER THE PIONEERS

After the pioneers—
Big-hearted, big-handed lords of the axe and the plow and the rifle,
Tan-faced tamers of horses and lands, themselves remaining tameless,
Full of fighting, labour and romance, lovers of rude adventure—
After the pioneers have cleared the way to their homes and graves on the prairies:
After the State-builders—
Zealous and jealous men, dreamers, debaters, often at odds with each other,
All of them sure it is well to toil and to die, if need be,
Just for the sake of founding a country to leave to their children—
After the builders have done their work and written their names upon it:

After the civil war—
Wildest of all storms, cruel and dark and seemingly wasteful,
Tearing up by the root the vines that were splitting the old foundations,
Washing away with a rain of blood and tears the dust of slavery,
After the cyclone has passed and the sky is fair to the far horizon;
After the era of plenty and peace has come with full hands to Texas,
Then—what then?
Is it to be the life of an indolent heir, fat-witted and self-contented,
Dwelling at ease in the house that others have builded,
Boasting about the country for which he has done nothing?
Is it to be an age of corpulent, deadly-dull prosperity,
Richer and richer crops to nourish a race of Philistines,
Bigger and bigger cities full of the same confusion and sorrow,
The people increasing mightily but no increase of the joy?
Is this what the forerunners wished and toiled to win for you,
This the reward of war and the fruitage of high endeavor,
This the goal of your hopes and the vision that satisfies you?
Nay, stand up and answer—I can read what is in your hearts—
You, the children of those who followed the wild-bees,
You, the children of those who served the Lone Star,
Now that the hives are full and the star is fixed in the constellation,
I know that the best of you still are lovers of sweetness and light!
You hunger for honey that comes from invisible gardens;
Pure, translucent, golden thoughts and feelings and inspirations,
Sweetness of all the best that has bloomed in the mind of man.
You rejoice in the light that is breaking along the borders of science;
The hidden rays that enable a man to look through a wall of stone;
The unseen, fire-filled wings that carry his words across the ocean;
The splendid gift of flight that shines, half-captured, above him;
The gleam of a thousand half-guessed secrets, just ready to be discovered!
You dream and devise great things for the coming race—
Children of yours who shall people and rule the domain of Texas;
They shall know, they shall comprehend more than their fathers,
They shall grow in the vigour of well-rounded manhood and womanhood,
Riper minds, richer hearts, finer souls, the only true wealth of a nation—
The league-long fields of the State are pledged to ensure this harvest!

*Your old men have dreamed this dream and your young
  men have seen this vision.
The age of romance has not gone, it is only beginning;
Greater words than the ear of man has heard are waiting
  to be spoken,
Finer arts than the eyes of man have seen are sleeping to
  be awakened:
Science exploring the scope of the world,
Poetry breathing the hope of the world,
Music to measure and lead the onward march of man!
Come, ye honoured and welcome guests from the elder
  nations,
Princes of science and arts and letters,
Look on the walls that embody the generous dream of one
  of the old men of Texas,
Enter these halls of learning that rise in the land of the
  pioneer's log-cabin,
Read the confessions of faith that are carved on the stones
  around you:
Faith in the worth of the smallest fact and the laws that
  govern the starbeams,
Faith in the beauty of truth and the truth of perfect
  beauty,
Faith in the God who creates the souls of men by
  knowledge and love and worship.
This is the faith of the New Democracy—
Proud and humble, patiently pressing forward,
Praising her heroes of old and training her future
  leaders,
Seeking her crown in a nobler race of men and women—
After the pioneers, sweetness and light!
October, 1912.*

* *Read at the Dedication of the Rice Institute, Houston,
Texas, October, 1912.*

WHO FOLLOW THE FLAG
PHI BETA KAPPA ODE
HARVARD UNIVERSITY
June 30, 1910

I

*All day long in the city's canyon-street,
With its populous cliffs alive on either side,
I saw a river of marching men like a tide
Flowing after the flag: and the rhythmic beat
Of the drums, and the bugles' resonant blare
Metred the tramp, tramp, tramp of a myriad feet,
While the red-white-and-blue was fluttering everywhere,
And the heart of the crowd kept time to a martial air:
O brave flag, O bright flag, O flag to lead the free!
The glory of thy silver stars,
Engrailed in blue above the bars
Of red for courage, white for truth,
Has brought the world a second youth
And drawn a hundred million hearts to follow after thee.*

II

*Old Cambridge saw thee first unfurled,
By Washington's far-reaching hand,
To greet, in Seventy-six, the wintry morn
Of a new year, and herald to the world
Glad tidings from a Western land,—
A people and a hope new-born!
The double cross then filled thine azure field,
In token of a spirit loath to yield
The breaking ties that bound thee to a throne.
But not for long thine oriflamme could bear
That symbol of an outworn trust in kings.
The wind that bore thee out on widening wings
Called for a greater sign and all thine own,—
A new device to speak of heavenly laws
And lights that surely guide the people's cause.
Oh, greatly did they hope, and greatly dare,
Who bade the stars in heaven fight for them,
And set upon their battle-flag a fair
New constellation as a diadem!
Along the blood-stained banks of Brandywine
The ragged troops were rallied to this sign;
Through Saratoga's woods it fluttered bright
Amid the perils of the hard-won fight;
O'er Yorktown's meadows broad and green
It hailed the glory of the final scene;
And when at length Manhattan saw
The last invaders' line of scarlet coats
Pass Bowling Green, and fill the waiting boats
And sullenly withdraw,
The flag that proudly flew
Above the battered line of buff and blue,
Marching, with rattling drums and shrilling pipes,
Along the Bowery and down Broadway,
Was this that leads the great parade to-day,—
The glorious banner of the stars and stripes.
First of the flags of earth to dare
A heraldry so high;
First of the flags of earth to bear
The blazons of the sky;
Long may thy constellation glow,
Foretelling happy fate;
Wider thy starry circle grow,
And every star a State!*

III

*Pass on, pass on, ye flashing files
Of men who march in militant array;
Ye thrilling bugles, throbbing drums,
Ring out, roll on, and die away;
And fade, ye crowds, with the fading day!
Around the city's lofty piles
Of steel and stone
The lilac veil of dusk is thrown,
Entangled full of sparks of fairy light;
And the never-silent heart of the city hums
To a homeward-turning tune before the night.
But far above, on the sky-line's broken height,
From all the towers and domes outlined
In gray and gold along the city's crest,
I see the rippling flag still take the wind
With a promise of good to come for all mankind.*

IV

*O banner of the west,
No proud and brief parade,
That glorifies a nation's holiday
With show of troops for warfare dressed,
Can rightly measure or display
The mighty army thou hast made*

Loyal to guard thy more than royal sway.
Millions have come across the sea
To find beneath thy shelter room to grow;
Millions were born beneath thy folds and know
No other flag but thee.
And other, darker millions bore the yoke
Of bondage in thy borders till the voice
Of Lincoln spoke,
And sent thee forth to set the bondmen free.
Rejoice, dear flag, rejoice!
Since thou hast proved and passed that bitter strife,
Richer thy red with blood of heroes wet,
Purer thy white through sacrificial life,
Brighter thy blue wherein new stars are set.
Thou art become a sign,
Revealed in heaven to speak of things divine:
Of Truth that dares
To slay the lie it sheltered unawares;
Of Courage fearless in the fight,
Yet ever quick its foemen to forgive;
Of Conscience earnest to maintain its right
And gladly grant the same to all who live.
Thy staff is deeply planted in the fact
That nothing can ennoble man
Save his own act,
And naught can make him worthy to be free
But practice in the school of liberty.
The cords are two that lift thee to the sky:
Firm faith in God, the King who rules on high;
And never-failing trust
In human nature, full of faults and flaws,
Yet ever answering to the inward call
That bids it set the "ought" above the "must,"
In all its errors wiser than it seems,
In all its failures full of generous dreams,
Through endless conflict rising without pause
To self-dominion, charactered in laws
That pledge fair-play alike to great and small,
And equal rights for each beneath the rule of all.
These are thy halyards, banner bold,
And while these hold,
Thy brightness from the sky shall never fall,
Thy broadening empire never know decrease,—
Thy strength is union and thy glory peace.

V

Look forth across thy widespread lands,
O flag, and let thy stars to-night be eyes
To see the visionary hosts
Of men and women grateful to be thine,
That joyfully arise
From all thy borders and thy coasts,
And follow after thee in endless line!
They lift to thee a forest of saluting hands;
They hail thee with a rolling ocean-roar
Of cheers; and as the echo dies,
There comes a sweet and moving song
Of treble voices from the childish throng
Who run to thee from every school-house door.
Behold thine army! Here thy power lies:
The men whom freedom has made strong,
And bound to follow thee by willing vows;
The women greatened by the joys
Of motherhood to rule a happy house;
The vigorous girls and boys,
Whose eager faces and unclouded brows
Foretell the future of a noble race,
Rich in the wealth of wisdom and true worth!
While millions such as these to thee belong,
What foe can do thee wrong,
What jealous rival rob thee of thy place
Foremost of all the flags of earth?

VI

My vision darkens as the night descends;
And through the mystic atmosphere
I feel the creeping coldness that portends
A change of spirit in my dream
The multitude that moved with song and cheer
Have vanished, yet a living stream
Flows on and follows still the flag,
But silent now, with leaden feet that lag
And falter in the deepening gloom,—
A weird battalion bringing up the rear.
Ah, who are these on whom the vital bloom
Of life has withered to the dust of doom?
These little pilgrims prematurely worn
And bent as if they bore the weight of years?
These childish faces, pallid and forlorn,
Too dull for laughter and too hard for tears?
Is this the ghost of that insane crusade
That led ten thousand children long ago,
A flock of innocents, deceived, betrayed,
Yet pressing on through want and woe
To meet their fate, faithful and unafraid?
Nay, for a million children now
Are marching in the long pathetic line,
With weary step and early wrinkled brow;
And at their head appears no holy sign
Of hope in heaven;
For unto them is given
No cross to carry, but a cross to drag.
Before their strength is ripe they bear
The load of labour, toiling underground
In dangerous mines and breathing heavy air
Of crowded shops; their tender lives are bound
To service of the whirling, clattering wheels
That fill the factories with dust and noise;
They are not girls and boys,
But little "hands" who blindly, dumbly feed
With their own blood the hungry god of Greed.
Robbed of their natural joys,
And wounded with a scar that never heals,
They stumble on with heavy-laden soul,
And fall by thousands on the highway lined
With little graves; or reach at last their goal
Of stunted manhood and embittered age,
To brood awhile with dark and troubled mind,
Beside the smouldering fire of sullen rage,
On life's unfruitful work and niggard wage.
Are these the regiments that Freedom rears
To serve her cause in coming years?
Nay, every life that Avarice doth maim
And beggar in the helpless days of youth,
Shall surely claim
A just revenge, and take it without ruth;

*And every soul denied the right to grow
Beneath the flag, shall be its secret foe.
Bow down, dear land, in penitence and shame!
Remember now thine oath, so nobly sworn,
To guard an equal lot
For every child within thy borders born!
These are thy children whom thou hast forgot:
They have the bitter right to live, but not
The blessed right to look for happiness.
O lift thy liberating hand once more,
To loose thy little ones from dark duress;
The vital gladness to their hearts restore
In healthful lessons and in happy play;
And set them free to climb the upward way
That leads to self-reliant nobleness.
Speak out, my country, speak at last,
As thou hast spoken in the past,
And clearly, bravely say:
"I will defend
The coming race on whom my hopes depend:
Beneath my flag and on my sacred soil
No child shall bear the crushing yoke of toil."
VII*

*Look up, look up, ye downcast eyes!
The night is almost gone:
Along the new horizon flies
The banner of the dawn;
The eastern sky is banded low
With white and crimson bars,
While far above the morning glow
The everlasting stars.
O bright flag, O brave flag, O flag to lead the free!
The hand of God thy colours blent,
And heaven to earth thy glory lent,
To shield the weak, and guide the strong
To make an end of human wrong,
And draw a countless human host to follow after thee!*

STAIN NOT THE SKY
*Ye gods of battle, lords of fear,
Who work your iron will as well
As once ye did with sword and spear,
With rifled gun and rending shell,—
Masters of sea and land, forbear
The fierce invasion of the inviolate air!
With patient daring man hath wrought
A hundred years for power to fly;
And will you make his winged thought
A hovering horror in the sky,
Where flocks of human eagles sail,
Dropping their bolts of death on hill and dale?
Ah no, the sunset is too pure,
The dawn too fair, the noon too bright
For wings of terror to obscure
Their beauty, and betray the night
That keeps for man, above his wars,
The tranquil vision of untroubled stars.
Pass on, pass on, ye lords of fear!
Your footsteps in the sea are red,
And black on earth your paths appear
With ruined homes and heaps of dead.
Pass on to end your transient reign,
And leave the blue of heaven without a stain.
The wrong ye wrought will fall to dust,
The right ye shielded will abide;
The world at last will learn to trust
In law to guard, and love to guide;
And Peace of God that answers prayer
Will fall like dew from the inviolate air.
March 5, 1914.*

PEACE-HYMN OF THE REPUBLIC
*O Lord our God, Thy mighty hand
Hath made our country free;
From all her broad and happy land
May praise arise to Thee.
Fulfill the promise of her youth,
Her liberty defend;
By law and order, love and truth,
America befriend!
The strength of every State increase
In Union's golden chain;
Her thousand cities fill with peace,
Her million fields with grain.
The virtues of her mingled blood
In one new people blend;
By unity and brotherhood,
America befriend!
O suffer not her feet to stray;
But guide her untaught might,
That she may walk in peaceful day,
And lead the world in light.
Bring down the proud, lift up the poor,
Unequal ways amend;
By justice, nation-wide and sure,
America befriend!
Thro' all the waiting land proclaim
Thy gospel of good-will;
And may the music of Thy name
In every bosom thrill.
O'er hill and vale, from sea to sea.
Thy holy reign extend;
By faith and hope and charity,
America befriend!*

THE RED FLOWER
AND
GOLDEN STARS
*These verses were written during the terrible world-war, and immediately after. The earlier ones had to be unsigned because America was still "neutral" and I held a diplomatic post. The rest of them were printed after I had resigned, and was free to speak out, and to take active service in the Navy, when America entered the great conflict for liberty and peace on earth.
Avalon, February 22, 1920.*

THE RED FLOWER
*June, 1914
In the pleasant time of Pentecost,
By the little river Kyll,
I followed the angler's winding path
Or waded the stream at will,*

And the friendly fertile German land
Lay round me green and still.

But all day long on the eastern bank
Of the river cool and clear,
Where the curving track of the double rails
Was hardly seen though near,
The endless trains of German troops
Went rolling down to Trier.
They packed the windows with bullet heads
And caps of hodden gray;
They laughed and sang and shouted loud
When the trains were brought to a stay;
They waved their hands and sang again
As they went on their iron way.
No shadow fell on the smiling land,
No cloud arose in the sky;
I could hear the river's quiet tune
When the trains had rattled by;
But my heart sank low with a heavy sense
Of trouble,—I knew not why.
Then came I into a certain field
Where the devil's paint-brush spread
'Mid the gray and green of the rolling hills
A flaring splotch of red,—
An evil omen, a bloody sign,
And a token of many dead.
I saw in a vision the field-gray horde
Break forth at the devil's hour,
And trample the earth into crimson mud
In the rage of the Will to Power,—
All this I dreamed in the valley of Kyll,
At the sign of the blood-red flower.

A SCRAP OF PAPER
"Will you go to war just for a scrap of paper?"—
Question of the German Chancellor to the British
Ambassador, August 5, 1914.
A mocking question! Britain's answer came
Swift as the light and searching as the flame.
"Yes, for a scrap of paper we will fight
Till our last breath, and God defend the right!
"A scrap of paper where a name is set
Is strong as duty's pledge and honor's debt.
"A scrap of paper holds for man and wife
The sacrament of love, the bond of life.
"A scrap of paper may be Holy Writ
With God's eternal word to hallow it.
"A scrap of paper binds us both to stand
Defenders of a neutral neighbor land.
"By God, by faith, by honor, yes! We fight
To keep our name upon that paper white."
September, 1914.

STAND FAST
Stand fast, Great Britain!
Together England, Scotland, Ireland stand
One in the faith that makes a mighty land,—
True to the bond you gave and will not break
And fearless in the fight for conscience' sake!
Against the Giant Robber clad in steel,
With blood of trampled Belgium on his heel,
Striding through France to strike you down at last,
Britain, stand fast!
Stand fast, brave land!
The Huns are thundering toward the citadel;
They prate of Culture but their path is Hell;
Their light is darkness, and the bloody sword
They wield and worship is their only Lord.
O land where reason stands secure on right,
O land where freedom is the source of light,
Against the mailed Barbarians' deadly blast,
Britain, stand fast!
Stand fast, dear land!
Thou island mother of a world-wide race,
Whose children speak thy tongue and love thy face,
Their hearts and hopes are with thee in the strife,
Their hands will break the sword that seeks thy life;
Fight on until the Teuton madness cease;
Fight bravely on, until the word of peace
Is spoken in the English tongue at last,—
Britain, stand fast!
September, 1914.

LIGHTS OUT
(1915)
"Lights out" along the land,
"Lights out" upon the sea.
The night must put her hiding hand
O'er peaceful towns where children sleep,
And peaceful ships that darkly creep
Across the waves, as if they were not free.
The dragons of the air,
The hell-hounds of the deep,
Lurking and prowling everywhere,
Go forth to seek their helpless prey,
Not knowing whom they maim or slay—
Mad harvesters, who care not what they reap.
Out with the tranquil lights,
Out with the lights that burn
For love and law and human rights!
Set back the clock a thousand years:
All they have gained now disappears,
And the dark ages suddenly return.
Kaiser, who loosed wild death,
And terror in the night,
God grant you draw no quiet breath,
Until the madness you began
Is ended, and long-suffering man,
Set free from war lords, cries, "Let there be Light."
October, 1915.
Read at the meeting of the American Academy, Boston,
November, 1915.

REMARKS ABOUT KINGS
"God said I am tired of kings."—EMERSON.
God said, "I am tired of kings,"—
But that was a long while ago!
And meantime man said, "No,—
I like their looks in their robes and rings."
So he crowned a few more,
And they went on playing the game as before,
Fighting and spoiling things.
Man said, "I am tired of kings!

Sons of the robber-chiefs of yore,
They make me pay for their lust and their war;
I am the puppet, they pull the strings;
The blood of my heart is the wine they drink.
I will govern myself for awhile I think,
And see what that brings!"
Then God, who made the first remark,
Smiled in the dark.
October, 1915.
Read at the meeting of the American Academy, Boston,
November, 1915.

MIGHT AND RIGHT
If Might made Right, life were a wild-beasts' cage;
If Right made Might, this were the golden age;
But now, until we win the long campaign,
Right must gain Might to conquer and to reign.
July 1, 1915.

THE PRICE OF PEACE
Peace without Justice is a low estate,—
A coward cringing to an iron Fate!
But Peace through Justice is the great ideal,—
We'll pay the price of war to make it real.
December 28, 1916.

STORM-MUSIC
O Music hast thou only heard
The laughing river, the singing bird,
The murmuring wind in the poplar-trees,—
Nothing but Nature's melodies?
Nay, thou hearest all her tones,
As a Queen must hear!
Sounds of wrath and fear,
Mutterings, shouts, and moans,
Madness, tumult, and despair,—
All she has that shakes the air
With voices fierce and wild!
Thou art a Queen and not a dreaming child,—
Put on thy crown and let us hear thee reign
Triumphant in a world of storm and strain!
Echo the long-drawn sighs
Of the mounting wind in the pines;
And the sobs of the mounting waves that rise
In the dark of the troubled deep
To break on the beach in fiery lines.
Echo the far-off roll of thunder,
Rumbling loud
And ever louder, under
The blue-black curtain of cloud,
Where the lightning serpents gleam.
Echo the moaning
Of the forest in its sleep
Like a giant groaning
In the torment of a dream.
Now an interval of quiet
For a moment holds the air
In the breathless hush
Of a silent prayer.
Then the sudden rush
Of the rain, and the riot
Of the shrieking, tearing gale
Breaks loose in the night,
With a fusillade of hail!
Hear the forest fight,
With its tossing arms that crack and clash
In the thunder's cannonade,
While the lightning's forked flash
Brings the old hero-trees to the ground with a crash!
Hear the breakers' deepening roar,
Driven like a herd of cattle
In the wild stampede of battle,
Trampling, trampling, trampling, to overwhelm the shore!
Is it the end of all?
Will the land crumble and fall?
Nay, for a voice replies
Out of the hidden skies,
"Thus far, O sea, shalt thou go,
So long, O wind, shalt thou blow:
Return to your bounds and cease,
And let the earth have peace!"
O Music, lead the way—
The stormy night is past,
Lift up our hearts to greet the day,
And the joy of things that last.
The dissonance and pain
That mortals must endure,
Are changed in thine immortal strain
To something great and pure.
True love will conquer strife,
And strength from conflict flows,
For discord is the thorn of life
And harmony the rose.
May, 1916.

THE BELLS OF MALINES
August 17, 1914
The gabled roofs of old Malines
Are russet red and gray and green,
And o'er them in the sunset hour
Looms, dark and huge, St. Rombold's tower.
High in that rugged nest concealed,
The sweetest bells that ever pealed,
The deepest bells that ever rung,
The lightest bells that ever sung,
Are waiting for the master's hand
To fling their music o'er the land.
And shall they ring to-night, Malines?
In nineteen hundred and fourteen,
The frightful year, the year of woe,
When fire and blood and rapine flow
Across the land from lost Liége,
Storm-driven by the German rage?
The other carillons have ceased:
Fallen is Hasselt, fallen Diest,
From Ghent and Bruges no voices come,
Antwerp is silent, Brussels dumb!
But in thy belfry, O Malines,
The master of the bells unseen
Has climbed to where the keyboard stands,—
To-night his heart is in his hands!
Once more, before invasion's hell
Breaks round the tower he loves so well,

Once more he strikes the well-worn keys,
And sends aërial harmonies
Far-floating through the twilight dim
In patriot song and holy hymn.
O listen, burghers of Malines!
Soldier and workman, pale béguine,
And mother with a trembling flock
Of children clinging to thy frock,—
Look up and listen, listen all!
What tunes are these that gently fall
Around you like a benison?
"The Flemish Lion," "Brabançonne,"
"O brave Liége," and all the airs
That Belgium in her bosom bears.
Ring up, ye silvery octaves high,
Whose notes like circling swallows fly;
And ring, each old sonorous bell,—
"Jesu," "Maria," "Michaël!"
Weave in and out, and high and low,
The magic music that you know,
And let it float and flutter down
To cheer the heart of the troubled town.
Ring out, "Salvator," lord of all,—
"Roland" in Ghent may hear thee call!
O brave bell-music of Malines,
In this dark hour how much you mean!
The dreadful night of blood and tears
Sweeps down on Belgium, but she hears
Deep in her heart the melody
Of songs she learned when she was free.
She will not falter, faint, nor fail,
But fight until her rights prevail
And all her ancient belfries ring
"The Flemish Lion," "God Save the King!"

JEANNE D'ARC RETURNS *
1914-1916
What hast thou done, O womanhood of France,
Mother and daughter, sister, sweetheart, wife,
What hast thou done, amid this fateful strife,
To prove the pride of thine inheritance
In this fair land of freedom and romance?
I hear thy voice with tears and courage rife,—
Smiling against the swords that seek thy life,—
Make answer in a noble utterance:
"I give France all I have, and all she asks.
Would it were more! Ah, let her ask and take:
My hands to nurse her wounded, do her tasks,—
My feet to run her errands through the dark,—
My heart to bleed in triumph for her sake,—
And all my soul to follow thee, Jeanne d'Arc!"
April 16, 1916.
* This sonnet belongs with the poem on page 309,
"Come Back Again, Jeanne D'Arc."

THE NAME OF FRANCE
Give us a name to fill the mind
With the shining thoughts that lead mankind,
The glory of learning, the joy of art,—
A name that tells of a splendid part
In the long, long toil and the strenuous fight
Of the human race to win its way
From the feudal darkness into the day
Of Freedom, Brotherhood, Equal Right,—
A name like a star, a name of light.
I give you France!
Give us a name to stir the blood
With a warmer glow and a swifter flood,
At the touch of a courage that conquers fear,—
A name like the sound of a trumpet, clear,
And silver-sweet, and iron-strong,
That calls three million men to their feet,
Ready to march, and steady to meet
The foes who threaten that name with wrong,—
A name that rings like a battle-song.
I give you France!
Give us a name to move the heart
With the strength that noble griefs impart,
A name that speaks of the blood outpoured
To save mankind from the sway of the sword,—
A name that calls on the world to share
In the burden of sacrificial strife
When the cause at stake is the world's free life
And the rule of the people everywhere,—
A name like a vow, a name like a prayer.
I give you France!

The Hague, September, 1916.

AMERICA'S PROSPERITY
They tell me thou art rich, my country: gold
In glittering flood has poured into thy chest;
Thy flocks and herds increase, thy barns are pressed
With harvest, and thy stores can hardly hold
Their merchandise; unending trains are rolled
Along thy network rails of East and West;
Thy factories and forges never rest;
Thou art enriched in all things bought and sold!
But dost thou prosper? Better news I crave.
O dearest country, is it well with thee
Indeed, and is thy soul in health?
A nobler people, hearts more wisely brave,
And thoughts that lift men up and make them free,—
These are prosperity and vital wealth!
The Hague, October 1, 1916.

THE GLORY OF SHIPS
The glory of ships is an old, old song,
since the days when the sea-rovers ran,
In their open boats through the roaring surf,
and the spread of the world began;
The glory of ships is a light on the sea,
and a star in the story of man.
When Homer sang of the galleys of Greece
that conquered the Trojan shore,
And Solomon lauded the barks of Tyre
that brought great wealth to his door,
'Twas little they knew, those ancient men,
what would come of the sail and the oar.
The Greek ships rescued the West from the East,
when they harried the Persians home;
And the Roman ships were the wings of strength
that bore up the empire, Rome;
And the ships of Spain found a wide new world,
far over the fields of foam.
Then the tribes of courage at last saw clear

that the ocean was not a bound,
But a broad highway, and a challenge to seek
for treasure as yet unfound;
So the fearless ships fared forth to the search,
in joy that the globe was round.
Their hulls were heightened, their sails spread out,
they grew with the growth of their quest;
They opened the secret doors of the East,
and the golden gates of the West;
And many a city of high renown
was proud of a ship on its crest.
The fleets of England and Holland and France
were at strife with each other and Spain;
And battle and storm sent a myriad ships
to sleep in the depths of the main;
But the seafaring spirit could never be drowned,
and it filled up the fleets again.
They greatened and grew, with the aid of steam,
to a wonderful, vast array,
That carries the thoughts and the traffic of men
into every harbor and bay;
And now in the world-wide work of the ships
'tis England that leads the way.
O well for the leading that follows the law
of a common right on the sea!
But ill for the leader who tries to hold
what belongs to mankind in fee!
The way of the ships is an open way,
and the ocean must ever be free!
Remember, O first of the maritime folk,
how the rise of your greatness began.
It will live if you safeguard the round-the-world road
from the shame of a selfish ban;
For the glory of ships is a light on the sea,
and a star in the story of man!
September 12, 1916.

MARE LIBERUM
I
You dare to say with perjured lips,
"We fight to make the ocean free"?
You, whose black trail of butchered ships
Bestrews the bed of every sea
Where German submarines have wrought
Their horrors! Have you never thought,—
What you call freedom, men call piracy!

II

Unnumbered ghosts that haunt the wave,
Where you have murdered, cry you down;
And seamen whom you would not save,
Weave now in weed-grown depths a crown
Of shame for your imperious head,
A dark memorial of the dead
Women and children whom you sent to drown.

III
Nay, not till thieves are set to guard
The gold, and corsairs called to keep
O'er peaceful commerce watch and ward,
And wolves to herd the helpless sheep,
Shall men and women look to thee,
Thou ruthless Old Man of the Sea,
To safeguard law and freedom on the deep!

IV
In nobler breeds we put our trust:
The nations in whose sacred lore
The "Ought" stands out above the "Must,"
And honor rules in peace and war.
With these we hold in soul and heart,
With these we choose our lot and part,
Till Liberty is safe on sea and shore.
London Times, February 12, 1917.

"LIBERTY ENLIGHTENING THE WORLD"
Thou warden of the western gate, above Manhattan Bay,
The fogs of doubt that hid thy face are driven clean away:
Thine eyes at last look far and clear, thou liftest high thy hand
To spread the light of liberty world-wide for every land.
No more thou dreamest of a peace reserved alone for thee,
While friends are fighting for thy cause beyond the guardian sea:
The battle that they wage is thine; thou fallest if they fall;
The swollen flood of Prussian pride will sweep unchecked o'er all.
O cruel is the conquer-lust in Hohenzollern brains:
The paths they plot to gain their goal are dark with shameful stains;
No faith they keep, no law revere, no god but naked Might;
They are the foemen of mankind. Up, Liberty, and smite!
Britain, and France, and Italy, and Russia newly born,
Have waited for thee in the night. Oh, come as comes the morn!
Serene and strong and full of faith, America, arise,
With steady hope and mighty help to join thy brave Allies.
O dearest country of my heart, home of the high desire,
Make clean thy soul for sacrifice on Freedom's altar-fire:
For thou must suffer, thou must fight, until the warlords cease,
And all the peoples lift their heads in liberty and peace.
London Times, April 12, 1917.

THE OXFORD THRUSHES
February, 1917
I never thought again to hear
The Oxford thrushes singing clear,
Amid the February rain,
Their sweet, indomitable strain.
A wintry vapor lightly spreads
Among the trees, and round the beds
Where daffodil and jonquil sleep;
Only the snowdrop wakes to weep.
It is not springtime yet. Alas,
What dark, tempestuous days must pass,
Till England's trial by battle cease,
And summer comes again with peace.
The lofty halls, the tranquil towers,
Where Learning in untroubled hours
Held her high court, serene in fame,
Are lovely still, yet not the same.
The novices in fluttering gown
No longer fill the ancient town;

But fighting men in khaki drest,
And in the Schools the wounded rest.
Ah, far away, 'neath stranger skies
Full many a son of Oxford lies,
And whispers from his warrior grave,
"I died to keep the faith you gave."
The mother mourns, but does not fail,
Her courage and her love prevail
O'er sorrow, and her spirit hears
The promise of triumphant years.
Then sing, ye thrushes, in the rain
Your sweet indomitable strain.
Ye bring a word from God on high
And voices in our hearts reply.

HOMEWARD BOUND
Home, for my heart still calls me;
Home, through the danger zone;
Home, whatever befalls me,
I will sail again to my own!
Wolves of the sea are hiding
Closely along the way,
Under the water biding
Their moment to rend and slay.
Black is the eagle that brands them,
Black are their hearts as the nights
Black is the hate that sends them
To murder but not to fight.
Flower of the German Culture,
Boast of the Kaiser's Marine,
Choose for your emblem the vulture,
Cowardly, cruel, obscene!
Forth from her sheltered haven
Our peaceful ship glides slow,
Noiseless in flight as a raven,
Gray as a hoodie crow.
She doubles and turns in her bearing,
Like a twisting plover she goes;
The way of her westward faring
Only the captain knows.
In a lonely bay concealing
She lingers for days, and slips
At dusk from her covert, stealing
Thro' channels feared by the ships.
Brave are the men, and steady,
Who guide her over the deep,—
British mariners, ready
To face the sea-wolf's leap.
Lord of the winds and waters,
Bring our ship to her mark,
Safe from this game of hide-and-seek
With murderers in the dark!
On the S.S. Baltic, May, 1917.

THE WINDS OF WAR-NEWS
The winds of war-news change and veer:
Now westerly and full of cheer,
Now easterly, depressing, sour
With tidings of the Teutons' power.
But thou, America, whose heart
With brave Allies has taken part,
Be not a weathercock to change
With these wild winds that shift and range.
Be thou a compass ever true,
Through sullen clouds or skies of blue,
To that great star which rules the night,—
The star of Liberty and Right.
Lover of peace, oh set thy soul,
Thy strength, thy wealth, thy conscience whole,
To win the peace thine eyes foresee,—
The triumph of Democracy.
December 19, 1917.

RIGHTEOUS WRATH
There are many kinds of anger, as many kinds of fire;
And some are fierce and fatal with murderous desire;
And some are mean and craven, revengeful, sullen, slow,
They hurt the man that holds them more than they hurt his foe.
And yet there is an anger that purifies the heart:
The anger of the better against the baser part,
Against the false and wicked, against the tyrant's sword,
Against the enemies of love, and all that hate the Lord.
O cleansing indignation, O flame of righteous wrath,
Give me a soul to feel thee and follow in thy path!
Save me from selfish virtue, arm me for fearless fight,
And give me strength to carry on, a soldier of the Right!
January, 1918.

THE PEACEFUL WARRIOR
I have no joy in strife,
Peace is my great desire;
Yet God forbid I lose my life
Through fear to face the fire.
A peaceful man must fight
For that which peace demands,—
Freedom and faith, honor and right,
Defend with heart and hands.
Farewell, my friendly books;
Farewell, ye woods and streams;
The fate that calls me forward looks
To a duty beyond dreams.
Oh, better to be dead
With a face turned to the sky,
Than live beneath a slavish dread
And serve a giant lie.
Stand up, my heart, and strive
For the things most dear to thee!
Why should we care to be alive
Unless the world is free?

May, 1918.

FROM GLORY UNTO GLORY
AMERICAN FLAG SONG
1776
O dark the night and dim the day
When first our flag arose;
It fluttered bravely in the fray
To meet o'erwhelming foes.
Our fathers saw the splendor shine,
They dared and suffered all;
They won our freedom by the sign—
The holy sign, the radiant sign—

Of the stars that never fall.
Chorus
All hail to thee, Young Glory!
Among the flags of earth
We'll ne'er forget the story
Of thy heroic birth.

1861
O wild the later storm that shook
The pillars of the State,
When brother against brother took
The final arms of fate.
But union lived and peace divine
Enfolded brothers all;
The flag floats o'er them with the sign—
The loyal sign, the equal sign—
Of the stars that never fall.
Chorus
All hail to thee, Old Glory!
Of thee our heart's desire
Foretells a golden story,
For thou hast come through fire.

1917
O fiercer than all wars before
That raged on land or sea,
The Giant Robber's world-wide war
For the things that shall not be!
Thy sister banners hold the line;
To thee, dear flag, they call;
And thou hast joined them with the sign—
The heavenly sign, the victor sign—
Of the stars that never fall.
Chorus

All hail to thee, New Glory!
We follow thee unfurled
To write the larger story
Of Freedom for the World.
September 4, 1918.

BRITAIN, FRANCE, AMERICA
The rough expanse of democratic sea
Which parts the lands that live by liberty
Is no division; for their hearts are one.
To fight together till their cause is won.
For land and water let us make our pact,
And seal the solemn word with valiant act:
No continent is firm, no ocean pure,
Until on both the rights of man are sure.
April, 1917.

THE RED CROSS
Sign of the Love Divine
That bends to bear the load
Of all who suffer, all who bleed,
Along life's thorny road:
Sign of the Heart Humane,
That through the darkest fight
Would bring to wounded friend and foe
A ministry of light:
O dear and holy sign,
Lead onward like a star!
The armies of the just are thine,

And all we have and are.
October 20, 1918.
For the Red Cross Christmas Roll Call.

EASTER ROAD
1918
Under the cloud of world-wide war,
While earth is drenched with sorrow,
I have no heart for idle merrymaking,
Or for the fashioning of glad raiment.
I will retrace the divine footmarks,
On the Road of the first Easter.
Down through the valley of utter darkness
Dripping with blood and tears;
Over the hill of the skull, the little hill of great anguish,
The ambuscade of Death.
Into the no-man's-land of Hades
Bearing despatches of hope to spirits in prison,
Mortally stricken and triumphant
Went the faithful Captain of Salvation.
Then upward, swiftly upward,—
Victory, liberty, glory,
The feet that were wounded walked in the tranquil garden,
Bathed in dew and the light of deathless dawn.
O my soul, my comrades, soldiers of freedom,
Follow the pathway of Easter, for there is no other,
Follow it through to peace, yea, follow it fighting.
This Armageddon is not darker than Calvary.
The day will break when the Dragon is vanquished;
He that exalteth himself as God shall be cast down,
And the Lords of war shall fall,
And the long, long terror be ended,
Victory, justice, peace enduring!
They that die in this cause shall live forever,
And they that live shall never die,
They shall rejoice together in the Easter of a new world.
March 31, 1918.

AMERICA'S WELCOME HOME
Oh, gallantly they fared forth in khaki and in blue,
America's crusading host of warriors bold and true;
They battled for the rights of man beside our brave Allies,
And now they're coming home to us with glory in their eyes.
Oh, it's home again, and home again, America for me!
Our hearts are turning home again and there we long to be,
In our beautiful big country beyond the ocean bars,
Where the air is full of sunlight and the flag is full of stars.
Our boys have seen the Old World as none have seen before.
They know the grisly horror of the German gods of war:
The noble faith of Britain and the hero-heart of France,
The soul of Belgium's fortitude and Italy's romance.
They bore our country's great word across the rolling sea,
"America swears brotherhood with all the just and free."
They wrote that word victorious on fields of mortal strife,
And many a valiant lad was proud to seal it with his life.

Oh, welcome home in Heaven's peace, dear spirits of the dead!
And welcome home ye living sons America hath bred!
The lords of war are beaten down, your glorious task is done;
You fought to make the whole world free, and the victory is won.
Now it's home again, and home again, our hearts are turning west,
Of all the lands beneath the sun America is best.
We're going home to our own folks, beyond the ocean bars,
Where the air is full of sunlight and the flag is full of stars.
November 11, 1918.
A sequel to "America For Me," written in 1909. Page 314.

THE SURRENDER OF THE GERMAN FLEET

Ship after ship, and every one with a high-resounding name,
From the robber-nest of Heligoland the German war-fleet came;
Not victory or death they sought, but a rendezvous of shame.
Sing out, sing out,
A joyful shout,
Ye lovers of the sea!
The "Kaiser" and the "Kaiserin,"
The "König" and the "Prinz,"
The potentates of piracy,
Are coming to surrender,
And the ocean shall be free.
They never dared the final fate of battle on the blue;
Their sea-wolves murdered merchantmen and mocked the drowning crew;
They stained the wave with martyr-blood,—but we sent our transports through!

What flags are these that dumbly droop from the gaff o' the mainmast tall?
The black of the Kaiser's iron cross, the red of the Empire's fall!
Come down, come down, ye pirate flags. Yea, strike your colors all.
The Union Jack and the Tricolor and the Starry Flag o' the West
Shall guard the fruit of Freedom's war and the victory confest,
The flags of the brave and just and free shall rule on the ocean's breast.
Sing out, sing out,
A mighty shout,
Ye lovers of the sea!
The "Kaiser" and the "Kaiserin,"
The "König" and the "Prinz,"
The robber-lords of death and sin,
Have come to their surrender,
And the ocean shall be free!
November 20, 1918.

GOLDEN STARS

I
It was my lot of late to travel far
Through all America's domain,
A willing, gray-haired servitor
Bearing the Fiery Cross of righteous war.
And everywhere, on mountain, vale and plain,
In crowded street and lonely cottage door,
I saw the symbol of the bright blue star.
Millions of stars! Rejoice, dear land, rejoice
That God hath made thee great enough to give
Beneath thy starry flag unfurled
A gift to all the world,—
Thy living sons that Liberty might live.

II
It seems but yesterday they sallied forth
Boys of the east, the west, the south, the north,
High-hearted, keen, with laughter and with song,
Fearless of lurking danger on the sea,
Eager to fight in Flanders or in France
Against the monstrous German wrong,
And sure of victory!
Brothers in soul with British and with French
They held their ground in many a bloody trench;
And when the swift word came—
Advance!
Over the top they went through waves of flame,—
Confident, reckless, irresistible,
Real Americans,—
Their rush was never stayed
Until the foe fell back, defeated and dismayed.
O land that bore them, write upon thy roll
Of battles won
To liberate the human soul,
Château Thierry and Saint Mihiel
And the fierce agony of the Argonne;
Yea, count among thy little rivers, dear
Because of friends whose feet have trodden there,
The Marne, the Meuse, and the Moselle.

III
Now the vile sword
In Potsdam forged and bathed in hell,
Is beaten down, the victory given
To the sword forged in faith and bathed in heaven.
Now home again our heroes come:
Oh, welcome them with bugle and with drum,
Ring bells, blow whistles, make a joyful noise
Unto the Lord,
And welcome home our blue-star boys,
Whose manhood has made known
To all the world America,
Unselfish, brave and free, the Great Republic,
Who lives not to herself alone.

IV
But many a lad we hold
Dear in our heart of hearts
Is missing from the home-returning host.
Ah, say not they are lost,
For they have found and given their life
In sacrificial strife:
Their service stars have changed from blue to gold!
That sudden rapture took them far away,

Yet are they here with us to-day,
Even as the heavenly stars we cannot see
Through the bright veil of sunlight,
Shed their influence still
On our vexed life, and promise peace
From God to all men of good will.

V

What wreaths shall we entwine
For our dear boys to deck their holy shrine?
Mountain-laurel, morning-glory,
Goldenrod and asters blue,
Purple loosestrife, prince's-pine,
Wild-azalea, meadow-rue,
Nodding-lilies, columbine,—
All the native blooms that grew
In these fresh woods and pastures new,
Wherein they loved to ramble and to play.
Bring no exotic flowers:
America was in their hearts,
And they are ours
For ever and a day.

VI

O happy warriors, forgive the tear
Falling from eyes that miss you:
Forgive the word of grief from mother-lips
That ne'er on earth shall kiss you;
Hear only what our hearts would have you hear,—
Glory and praise and gratitude and pride
From the dear country in whose cause you died.
Now you have run your race and won your prize,
Old age shall never burden you, the fears
And conflicts that beset our lingering years
Shall never vex your souls in Paradise.
Immortal, young, and crowned with victory,
From life's long battle you have found release.
And He who died for all on Calvary
Has welcomed you, brave soldiers of the cross,
Into eternal Peace.

VII

Come, let us gird our loins and lift our load,
Companions who are left on life's rough road,
And bravely take the way that we must tread
To keep true faith with our beloved dead.
To conquer war they dared their lives to give,
To safeguard peace our hearts must learn to live.
Help us, dear God, our forward faith to hold!
We want a better world than that of old.
Lead us on paths of high endeavor,
Toiling upward, climbing ever,
Ready to suffer for the right,
Until at last we gain a loftier height,
More worthy to behold
Our guiding stars, our hero-stars of gold.
Ode for the Memorial Service,
Princeton University, December 15, 1918.

IN THE BLUE HEAVEN

In the blue heaven the clouds will come and go,
Scudding before the gale, or drifting slow
As galleons becalmed in Sundown Bay:
And through the air the birds will wing their way
Soaring to far-off heights, or flapping low,
Or darting like an arrow from the bow;
And when the twilight comes the stars will show,
One after one, their tranquil bright array
In the blue heaven.
But ye who fearless flew to meet the foe,
Eagles of freedom,—nevermore, we know,
Shall we behold you floating far away.
Yet clouds and birds and every starry ray
Will draw our heart to where your spirits glow
In the blue Heaven.
For the American Aviators who died in the war.
March, 1919.

A SHRINE IN THE PANTHEON
FOR THE UNNAMED SOLDIERS WHO DIED IN FRANCE

Universal approval has been accorded the proposal made in the French Chamber that the ashes of an unnamed French soldier, fallen for his country, shall be removed with solemn ceremony to the Pantheon. In this way it is intended to honor by a symbolic ceremony the memory of all who lie in unmarked graves.

Here the great heart of France,
Victor in noble strife,
Doth consecrate a Poilu's tomb
To those who saved her life!
Brave son without a name,
Your country calls you home,
To rest among her heirs of fame,
Beneath the Pantheon's dome!
Now from the height of Heaven,
The souls of heroes look;
Their names, ungraven on this stone,
Are written in God's book.
Women of France, who mourn
Your dead in unmarked ground,
Come hither! Here the man you loved
In the heart of France is found!

IN PRAISE OF POETS
MOTHER EARTH

Mother of all the high-strung poets and singers departed,
Mother of all the grass that weaves over their graves the glory of the field,
Mother of all the manifold forms of life, deep-bosomed, patient, impassive,
Silent brooder and nurse of lyrical joys and sorrows!
Out of thee, yea, surely out of the fertile depth below thy breast,
Issued in some strange way, thou lying motionless, voiceless,
All these songs of nature, rhythmical, passionate, yearning,
Coming in music from earth, but not unto earth returning.

Dust are the blood-red hearts that beat in time to these measures,
Thou hast taken them back to thyself, secretly, irresistibly
Drawing the crimson currents of life down, down, down

Deep into thy bosom again, as a river is lost in the sand.
But the souls of the singers have entered into the songs that revealed them,—
Passionate songs, immortal songs of joy and grief and love and longing,
Floating from heart to heart of thy children, they echo above thee:
Do they not utter thy heart, the voices of those that love thee?
Long hadst thou lain like a queen transformed by some old enchantment
Into an alien shape, mysterious, beautiful, speechless,
Knowing not who thou wert, till the touch of thy Lord and Lover
Wakened the man-child within thee to tell thy secret.
All of thy flowers and birds and forests and flowing waters
Are but the rhythmical forms to reveal the life of the spirit;
Thou thyself, earth-mother, in mountain and meadow and ocean,
Holdest the poem of God, eternal thought and emotion.
December, 1905.

MILTON
I
Lover of beauty, walking on the height
Of pure philosophy and tranquil song;
Born to behold the visions that belong
To those who dwell in melody and light;
Milton, thou spirit delicate and bright!
What drew thee down to join the Roundhead throng
Of iron-sided warriors, rude and strong,
Fighting for freedom in a world half night?

Lover of Liberty at heart wast thou,
Above all beauty bright, all music clear:
To thee she bared her bosom and her brow,
Breathing her virgin promise in thine ear,
And bound thee to her with a double vow,—
Exquisite Puritan, grave Cavalier!

II
The cause, the cause for which thy soul resigned
Her singing robes to battle on the plain,
Was won, O poet, and was lost again;
And lost the labour of thy lonely mind
On weary tasks of prose. What wilt thou find
To comfort thee for all the toil and pain?
What solace, now thy sacrifice is vain
And thou art left forsaken, poor, and blind?
Like organ-music comes the deep reply:
"The cause of truth looks lost, but shall be won.
For God hath given to mine inward eye
Vision of England soaring to the sun.
And granted me great peace before I die,
In thoughts of lowly duty bravely done."

III
O bend again above thine organ-board,
Thou blind old poet longing for repose!
Thy Master claims thy service not with those
Who only stand and wait for His reward;
He pours the heavenly gift of song restored
Into thy breast, and bids thee nobly close
A noble life, with poetry that flows
In mighty music of the major chord.
Where hast thou learned this deep, majestic strain,
Surpassing all thy youthful lyric grace,
To sing of Paradise? Ah, not in vain
The griefs that won at Dante's side thy place,
And made thee, Milton, by thy years of pain,
The loftiest poet of the English race!
1908.

WORDSWORTH
Wordsworth, thy music like a river rolls
Among the mountains, and thy song is fed
By living springs far up the watershed;
No whirling flood nor parching drought controls
The crystal current: even on the shoals
It murmurs clear and sweet; and when its bed
Deepens below mysterious cliffs of dread,
Thy voice of peace grows deeper in our souls.

But thou in youth hast known the breaking stress
Of passion, and hast trod despair's dry ground
Beneath black thoughts that wither and destroy.
Ah, wanderer, led by human tenderness
Home to the heart of Nature, thou hast found
The hidden Fountain of Recovered Joy.
October, 1906.

KEATS
The melancholy gift Aurora gained
From Jove, that her sad lover should not see
The face of death, no goddess asked for thee,
My Keats! But when the scarlet blood-drop stained
Thy pillow, thou didst read the fate ordained,—
Brief life, wild love, a flight of poesy!
And then,—a shadow fell on Italy:
Thy star went down before its brightness waned.
Yet thou hast won the gift Tithonus missed:
Never to feel the pain of growing old,
Nor lose the blissful sight of beauty's truth,
But with the ardent lips Urania kissed
To breathe thy song, and, ere thy heart grew cold,
Become the Poet of Immortal Youth.
August, 1906.

SHELLEY
Knight-errant of the Never-ending Quest,
And Minstrel of the Unfulfilled Desire;
For ever tuning thy frail earthly lyre
To some unearthly music, and possessed
With painful passionate longing to invest
The golden dream of Love's immortal fire
With mortal robes of beautiful attire,
And fold perfection to thy throbbing breast!

What wonder, Shelley, that the restless wave
Should claim thee and the leaping flame consume
Thy drifted form on Viareggio's beach?
These were thine elements,—thy fitting grave.
But still thy soul rides on with fiery plume,

Thy wild song rings in ocean's yearning speech!
August, 1906.

ROBERT BROWNING
How blind the toil that burrows like the mole,
In winding graveyard pathways underground,
For Browning's lineage! What if men have found
Poor footmen or rich merchants on the roll
Of his forbears? Did they beget his soul?
Nay, for he came of ancestry renowned
Through all the world,—the poets laurel-crowned
With wreaths from which the autumn takes no toll.
The blazons on his coat-of-arms are these:
The flaming sign of Shelley's heart on fire,
The golden globe of Shakespeare's human stage,
The staff and scrip of Chaucer's pilgrimage,
The rose of Dante's deep, divine desire,
The tragic mask of wise Euripides.
November, 1906.

TENNYSON
In Lucem Transitus, October, 1892
From the misty shores of midnight, touched with splendours of the moon,
To the singing tides of heaven, and the light more clear than noon,
Passed a soul that grew to music till it was with God in tune.
Brother of the greatest poets, true to nature, true to art;
Lover of Immortal Love, uplifter of the human heart;
Who shall cheer us with high music, who shall sing, if thou depart?
Silence here—for love is silent, gazing on the lessening sail;
Silence here—for grief is voiceless when the mighty minstrels fail;
Silence here—but far beyond us, many voices crying, Hail!

"IN MEMORIAM"
The record of a faith sublime,
And hope, through clouds, far-off discerned;
The incense of a love that burned
Through pain and doubt defying Time:
The story of a soul at strife
That learned at last to kiss the rod,
And passed through sorrow up to God,
From living to a higher life:
A light that gleams across the wave
Of darkness, down the rolling years,
Piercing the heavy mist of tears—
A rainbow shining o'er a grave.

VICTOR HUGO
1802-1902
Heart of France for a hundred years,
Passionate, sensitive, proud, and strong,
Quick to throb with her hopes and fears,
Fierce to flame with her sense of wrong!
You, who hailed with a morning song
Dream-light gilding a throne of old:
You, who turned when the dream grew cold,
Singing still, to the light that shone
Pure from Liberty's ancient throne,
Over the human throng!
You, who dared in the dark eclipse,—
When the pygmy heir of a giant name
Dimmed the face of the land with shame,—
Speak the truth with indignant lips,
Call him little whom men called great,
Scoff at him, scorn him, deny him,
Point to the blood on his robe of state,
Fling back his bribes and defy him!
You, who fronted the waves of fate
As you faced the sea from your island home,
Exiled, yet with a soul elate,
Sending songs o'er the rolling foam,
Bidding the heart of man to wait
For the day when all should see
Floods of wrath from the frowning skies
Fall on an Empire founded in lies,
And France again be free!
You, who came in the Terrible Year
Swiftly back to your broken land,
Now to your heart a thousand times more dear,—
Prayed for her, sung to her, fought for her,
Patiently, fervently wrought for her,
Till once again,
After the storm of fear and pain,
High in the heavens the star of France stood clear!
You, who knew that a man must take
Good and ill with a steadfast soul,
Holding fast, while the billows roll
Over his head, to the things that make
Life worth living for great and small,
Honour and pity and truth,
The heart and the hope of youth,
And the good God over all!
You, to whom work was rest,
Dauntless Toiler of the Sea,
Following ever the joyful quest
Of beauty on the shores of old Romance,
Bard of the poor of France,
And warrior-priest of world-wide charity!
You who loved little children best
Of all the poets that ever sung,
Great heart, golden heart,
Old, and yet ever young,
Minstrel of liberty,
Lover of all free, winged things,
Now at last you are free,—
Your soul has its wings!
Heart of France for a hundred years,
Floating far in the light that never fails you,
Over the turmoil of mortal hopes and fears
Victor, forever victor, the whole world hails you!
March, 1902.

LONGFELLOW
In a great land, a new land, a land full of labour and riches and confusion,
Where there were many running to and fro, and shouting, and striving together,

In the midst of the hurry and the troubled noise, I heard the voice of one singing.
"What are you doing there, O man, singing quietly amid all this tumult?
This is the time for new inventions, mighty shoutings, and blowings of the trumpet."
But he answered, "I am only shepherding my sheep with music."
So he went along his chosen way, keeping his little flock around him;
And he paused to listen, now and then, beside the antique fountains,
Where the faces of forgotten gods were refreshed with musically falling waters;

Or he sat for a while at the blacksmith's door, and heard the cling-clang of the anvils;
Or he rested beneath old steeples full of bells, that showered their chimes upon him;
Or he walked along the border of the sea, drinking in the long roar of the billows;
Or he sunned himself in the pine-scented shipyard, amid the tattoo of the mallets;
Or he leaned on the rail of the bridge, letting his thoughts flow with the whispering river;
He hearkened also to ancient tales, and made them young again with his singing.
Then a flaming arrow of death fell on his flock, and pierced the heart of his dearest!
Silent the music now, as the shepherd entered the mystical temple of sorrow:
Long he tarried in darkness there: but when he came out he was singing.
And I saw the faces of men and women and children silently turning toward him;
The youth setting out on the journey of life, and the old man waiting beside the last mile-stone;
The toiler sweating beneath his load; and the happy mother rocking her cradle;
The lonely sailor on far-off seas; and the gray-minded scholar in his book-room;
The mill-hand bound to a clacking machine; and the hunter in the forest;
And the solitary soul hiding friendless in the wilderness of the city;
Many human faces, full of care and longing, were drawn irresistibly toward him,
By the charm of something known to every heart, yet very strange and lovely,
And at the sound of his singing wonderfully all their faces were lightened.
"Why do you listen, O you people, to this old and world-worn music?
This is not for you, in the splendour of a new age, in the democratic triumph!
Listen to the clashing cymbals, the big drums, the brazen trumpets of your poets."
But the people made no answer, following in their hearts the simpler music:
For it seemed to them, noise-weary, nothing could be better worth the hearing
Than the melodies which brought sweet order into life's confusion.
So the shepherd sang his way along, until he came unto a mountain:
And I know not surely whether the mountain was called Parnassus,
But he climbed it out of sight, and still I heard the voice of one singing.
January, 1907.

THOMAS BAILEY ALDRICH
I
BIRTHDAY VERSES, 1906

Dear Aldrich, now November's mellow days
Have brought another Festa round to you,
You can't refuse a loving-cup of praise
From friends the fleeting years have bound to you.
Here come your Marjorie Daw, your dear Bad Boy,
Prudence, and Judith the Bethulian,
And many more, to wish you birthday joy,
And sunny hours, and sky cerulean!
Your children all, they hurry to your den,
With wreaths of honour they have won for you,
To merry-make your threescore years and ten.
You, old? Why, life has just begun for you!

There's many a reader whom your silver songs
And crystal stories cheer in loneliness.
What though the newer writers come in throngs?
You're sure to keep your charm of only-ness.
You do your work with careful, loving touch,—
An artist to the very core of you,—
You know the magic spell of "not-too-much":
We read,—and wish that there was more of you.
And more there is: for while we love your books
Because their subtle skill is part of you;
We love you better, for our friendship looks
Behind them to the human heart of you.

II
MEMORIAL SONNET, 1908

This is the house where little Aldrich read
The early pages of Life's wonder-book
With boyish pleasure: in this ingle-nook
He watched the drift-wood fire of Fancy shed
Bright colour on the pictures blue and red:
Boy-like he skipped the longer words, and took
His happy way, with searching, dreamful look
Among the deeper things more simply said.
Then, came his turn to write: and still the flame
Of Fancy played through all the tales he told,
And still he won the laurelled poet's fame
With simple words wrought into rhymes of gold.
Look, here's the face to which this house is frame,—
A man too wise to let his heart grow old!

EDMUND CLARENCE STEDMAN
(Read at His Funeral, January 21, 1908)
Oh, quick to feel the lightest touch
Of beauty or of truth,
Rich in the thoughtfulness of age,
The hopefulness of youth,

The courage of the gentle heart,
The wisdom of the pure,
The strength of finely tempered souls
To labour and endure!
The blue of springtime in your eyes
Was never quenched by pain;
And winter brought your head the crown
Of snow without a stain.
The poet's mind, the prince's heart,
You kept until the end,
Nor ever faltered in your work,
Nor ever failed a friend.
You followed, through the quest of life,
The light that shines above
The tumult and the toil of men,
And shows us what to love.
Right loyal to the best you knew,
Reality or dream,
You ran the race, you fought the fight,
A follower of the Gleam.
We lay upon your folded hands
The wreath of asphodel;
We speak above your peaceful face
The tender word Farewell!
For well you fare, in God's good care,
Somewhere within the blue,
And know, to-day, your dearest dreams
Are true,—and true,—and true!

TO JAMES WHITCOMB RILEY
ON HIS "BOOK OF JOYOUS CHILDREN"

Yours is a garden of old-fashioned flowers;
Joyous children delight to play there;
Weary men find rest in its bowers,
Watching the lingering light of day there.
Old-time tunes and young love-laughter
Ripple and run among the roses;
Memory's echoes, murmuring after,
Fill the dusk when the long day closes.
Simple songs with a cadence olden—
These you learned in the Forest of Arden:
Friendly flowers with hearts all golden—
These you borrowed from Eden's garden.
This is the reason why all men love you;
Truth to life is the finest art:
Other poets may soar above you—
You keep close to the human heart.
December, 1903.

RICHARD WATSON GILDER
IN MEMORIAM

Soul of a soldier in a poet's frame,
Heart of a hero in a body frail;
Thine was the courage clear that did not quail
Before the giant champions of shame
Who wrought dishonour to the city's name;
And thine the vision of the Holy Grail
Of Love, revealed through Music's lucid veil,
Filling thy life with heavenly song and flame.
Pure was the light that lit thy glowing eye,
And strong the faith that held thy simple creed.
Ah, poet, patriot, friend, to serve our need
Thou leavest two great gifts that will not die:
Above the city's noise, thy lyric cry,—
Amid the city's strife, thy noble deed.
November, 1909.

THE VALLEY OF VAIN VERSES

The grief that is but feigning,
And weeps melodious tears
Of delicate complaining
From self-indulgent years;
The mirth that is but madness,
And has no inward gladness
Beneath its laughter straining,
To capture thoughtless ears;
The love that is but passion
Of amber-scented lust;
The doubt that is but fashion;
The faith that has no trust;
These Thamyris disperses,
In the Valley of Vain Verses
Below the Mount Parnassian,—
And they crumble into dust.

MUSIC
I
PRELUDE
1

Daughter of Psyche, pledge of that wild night
When, pierced with pain and bitter-sweet delight,
She knew her Love and saw her Lord depart,
Then breathed her wonder and her woe forlorn
Into a single cry, and thou wast born!
Thou flower of rapture and thou fruit of grief;
Invisible enchantress of the heart;
Mistress of charms that bring relief
To sorrow, and to joy impart
A heavenly tone that keeps it undefined,—
Thou art the child
Of Amor, and by right divine
A throne of love is thine,
Thou flower-folded, golden-girdled, star-crowned Queen,
Whose bridal beauty mortal eyes have never seen!

2

Thou art the Angel of the pool that sleeps,
While peace and joy lie hidden in its deeps,
Waiting thy touch to make the waters roll
In healing murmurs round the weary soul.
Ah, when wilt thou draw near,
Thou messenger of mercy robed in song?
My lonely heart has listened for thee long;
And now I seem to hear
Across the crowded market-place of life,
Thy measured foot-fall, ringing light and clear
Above unmeaning noises and unruly strife.
In quiet cadence, sweet and slow,
Serenely pacing to and fro,
Thy far-off steps are magical and dear,—
Ah, turn this way, come close and speak to me!
From this dull bed of languor set my spirit free,
And bid me rise, and let me walk awhile with thee.

II

INVOCATION

Where wilt thou lead me first?
In what still region
Of thy domain,
Whose provinces are legion,
Wilt thou restore me to myself again,
And quench my heart's long thirst?
I pray thee lay thy golden girdle down,
And put away thy starry crown:
For one dear restful hour
Assume a state more mild.
Clad only in thy blossom-broidered gown
That breathes familiar scent of many a flower,
Take the low path that leads through pastures green;
And though thou art a Queen,
Be Rosamund awhile, and in thy bower,
By tranquil love and simple joy beguiled,
Sing to my soul, as mother to her child.

III
PLAY SONG

O lead me by the hand,
And let my heart have rest,
And bring me back to childhood land,
To find again the long-lost band
Of playmates blithe and blest.

Some quaint, old-fashioned air,
That all the children knew,
Shall run before us everywhere,
Like a little maid with flying hair,
To guide the merry crew.
Along the garden ways
We chase the light-foot tune,
And in and out the flowery maze,
With eager haste and fond delays,
In pleasant paths of June.
For us the fields are new,
For us the woods are rife
With fairy secrets, deep and true,
And heaven is but a tent of blue
Above the game of life.
The world is far away:
The fever and the fret,
And all that makes the heart grow gray,
Is out of sight and far away,
Dear Music, while I hear thee play
That olden, golden roundelay,
"Remember and forget!"

IV
SLEEP SONG

Forget, forget!
The tide of life is turning;
The waves of light ebb slowly down the west:
Along the edge of dark some stars are burning
To guide thy spirit safely to an isle of rest.
A little rocking on the tranquil deep
Of song, to soothe thy yearning,
A little slumber and a little sleep,
And so, forget, forget!
Forget, forget,—
The day was long in pleasure;
Its echoes die away across the hill;
Now let thy heart beat time to their slow measure,
That swells, and sinks, and faints, and falls, till all is still.
Then, like a weary child that loves to keep
Locked in its arms some treasure,
Thy soul in calm content shall fall asleep,
And so forget, forget.
Forget, forget,—
And if thou hast been weeping,
Let go the thoughts that bind thee to thy grief:
Lie still, and watch the singing angels, reaping
The golden harvest of thy sorrow, sheaf by sheaf;
Or count thy joys like flocks of snow-white sheep
That one by one come creeping
Into the quiet fold, until thou sleep,
And so forget, forget!
Forget, forget,—
Thou art a child and knowest
So little of thy life! But music tells
The secret of the world through which thou goest
To work with morning song, to rest with evening bells:
Life is in tune with harmony so deep
That when the notes are lowest
Thou still canst lay thee down in peace and sleep,
For God will not forget.

V
HUNTING SONG

Out of the garden of playtime, out of the bower of rest,
Fain would I follow at daytime, music that calls to a quest.
Hark, how the galloping measure
Quickens the pulses of pleasure;
Gaily saluting the morn
With the long, clear note of the hunting-horn,
Echoing up from the valley,
Over the mountain side,—
Rally, you hunters, rally,
Rally, and ride!
Drink of the magical potion music has mixed with her wine,
Full of the madness of motion, joyful, exultant, divine!
Leave all your troubles behind you,
Ride where they never can find you,
Into the gladness of morn,
With the long, clear note of the hunting-horn,
Swiftly o'er hillock and hollow,
Sweeping along with the wind,—
Follow, you hunters, follow,
Follow and find!
What will you reach with your riding? What is the charm of the chase?
Just the delight and the striding swing of the jubilant pace.
Danger is sweet when you front her,—
In at the death, every hunter!
Now on the breeze the mort is borne
In the long, clear note of the hunting-horn,
Winding merrily, over and over,—
Come, come, come!
Home again, Ranger! home again, Rover!
Turn again, home!

VI
DANCE-MUSIC
1
Now let the sleep-tune blend with the play-tune,
Weaving the mystical spell of the dance;
Lighten the deep tune, soften the gay tune,
Mingle a tempo that turns in a trance.
Half of it sighing, half of it smiling,
Smoothly it swings, with a triplicate beat;
Calling, replying, yearning, beguiling,
Wooing the heart and bewitching the feet.
Every drop of blood
Rises with the flood,
Rocking on the waves of the strain;
Youth and beauty glide
Turning with the tide—
Music making one out of twain,
Bearing them away, and away, and away,
Like a tone and its terce—
Till the chord dissolves, and the dancers stay,
And reverse.
Violins leading, take up the measure,
Turn with the tune again,—clarinets clear
Answer their pleading,—harps full of pleasure
Sprinkle their silver like light on the mere.
Semiquaver notes,
Merry little motes,
Tangled in the haze
Of the lamp's golden rays,
Quiver everywhere
In the air,
Like a spray,—
Till the fuller stream of the might of the tune,
Gliding like a dream in the light of the moon,
Bears them all away, and away, and away,
Floating in the trance of the dance.
2
Then begins a measure stately,
Languid, slow, serene;
All the dancers move sedately,
Stepping leisurely and straitly,
With a courtly mien;
Crossing hands and changing places,
Bowing low between,
While the minuet inlaces
Waving arms and woven paces,—
Glittering damaskeen.
Where is she whose form is folden
In its royal sheen?
From our longing eyes withholden
By her mystic girdle golden,
Beauty sought but never seen,
Music walks the maze, a queen.

VII
WAR-MUSIC
Break off! Dance no more!
Danger is at the door.
Music is in arms.
To signal war's alarms.

Hark, a sudden trumpet calling
Over the hill!
Why are you calling, trumpet, calling?
What is your will?
Men, men, men!
Men who are ready to fight
For their country's life, and the right
Of a liberty-loving land to be
Free, free, free!
Free from a tyrant's chain,
Free from dishonor's stain,
Free to guard and maintain
All that her fathers fought for,
All that her sons have wrought for,
Resolute, brave, and free!
Call again, trumpet, call again,
Call up the men!
Do you hear the storm of cheers
Mingled with the women's tears
And the tramp, tramp, tramp of marching feet?
Do you hear the throbbing drum
As the hosts of battle come
Keeping time, time, time to its beat?
O Music give a song
To make their spirit strong
For the fury of the tempest they must meet.
The hoarse roar
Of the monster guns;
And the sharp bark
Of the lesser guns;
The whine of the shells,
The rifles' clatter
Where the bullets patter,
The rattle, rattle, rattle
Of the mitrailleuse in battle,
And the yells
Of the men who charge through hells
Where the poison gas descends,
And the bursting shrapnel rends
Limb from limb
In the dim
Chaos and clamor of the strife
Where no man thinks of his life
But only of fighting through,
Blindly fighting through, through!
'Tis done
At last!
The victory won,
The dissonance of warfare past!
O Music mourn the dead
Whose loyal blood was shed,
And sound the taps for every hero slain;
Then lead into the song
That made their spirit strong,
And tell the world they did not die in vain.
Thank God we can see, in the glory of morn,
The invincible flag that our fathers defended;
And our hearts can repeat what the heroes have sworn,
That war shall not end till the war-lust is ended.
Then the bloodthirsty sword shall no longer be lord
Of the nations oppressed by the conqueror's horde,
But the banners of Liberty proudly shall wave
O'er the world of the free and the lands of the brave.
May, 1916.

VIII
THE SYMPHONY

Music, they do thee wrong who say thine art
Is only to enchant the sense.
For every timid motion of the heart,
And every passion too intense
To bear the chain of the imperfect word,
And every tremulous longing, stirred
By spirit winds that come we know not whence
And go we know not where,
And every inarticulate prayer
Beating about the depths of pain or bliss,
Like some bewildered bird
That seeks its nest but knows not where it is,
And every dream that haunts, with dim delight,
The drowsy hour between the day and night,
The wakeful hour between the night and day,—
Imprisoned, waits for thee,
Impatient, yearns for thee,
The queen who comes to set the captive free!
Thou lendest wings to grief to fly away,
And wings to joy to reach a heavenly height;
And every dumb desire that storms within the breast
Thou leadest forth to sob or sing itself to rest.
All these are thine, and therefore love is thine.
For love is joy and grief,
And trembling doubt, and certain-sure belief,
And fear, and hope, and longing unexpressed,
In pain most human, and in rapture brief
Almost divine.
Love would possess, yet deepens when denied;
And love would give, yet hungers to receive;
Love like a prince his triumph would achieve;
And like a miser in the dark his joys would hide.
Love is most bold,
He leads his dreams like armèd men in line;
Yet when the siege is set, and he must speak,
Calling the fortress to resign
Its treasure, valiant love grows weak,
And hardly dares his purpose to unfold.
Less with his faltering lips than with his eyes
He claims the longed-for prize:
Love fain would tell it all, yet leaves the best untold.
But thou shalt speak for love. Yea, thou shalt teach
The mystery of measured tone,
The Pentecostal speech
That every listener heareth as his own.
For on thy head the cloven tongues of fire,—
Diminished chords that quiver with desire,
And major chords that glow with perfect peace,—
Have fallen from above;
And thou canst give release
In music to the burdened heart of love.
Sound with the 'cellos' pleading, passionate strain
The yearning theme, and let the flute reply
In placid melody, while violins complain,
And sob, and sigh,
With muted string;
Then let the oboe half-reluctant sing
Of bliss that trembles on the verge of pain,
While 'cellos plead and plead again,
With throbbing notes delayed, that would impart
To every urgent tone the beating of the heart.
So runs the andante, making plain
The hopes and fears of love without a word.
Then comes the adagio, with a yielding theme
Through which the violas flow soft as in a dream,
While horns and mild bassoons are heard
In tender tune, that seems to float
Like an enchanted boat
Upon the downward-gliding stream,
Toward the allegro's wide, bright sea
Of dancing, glittering, blending tone,
Where every instrument is sounding free,
And harps like wedding-chimes are rung, and trumpets blown
Around the barque of love
That rides, with smiling skies above,
A royal galley, many-oared,
Into the happy harbour of the perfect chord.

IX
IRIS

Light to the eye and Music to the ear,—
These are the builders of the bridge that springs
From earth's dim shore of half-remembered things
To reach the heavenly sphere
Where nothing silent is and nothing dark.
So when I see the rainbow's arc
Spanning the showery sky, far-off I hear
Music, and every colour sings:
And while the symphony builds up its round
Full sweep of architectural harmony
Above the tide of Time, far, far away I see
A bow of colour in the bow of sound.
Red as the dawn the trumpet rings;
Blue as the sky, the choir of strings
Darkens in double-bass to ocean's hue,
Rises in violins to noon-tide's blue,
With threads of quivering light shot through and through;
Green as the mantle that the summer flings
Around the world, the pastoral reeds in tune
Embroider melodies of May and June.
Purer than gold,
Yea, thrice-refinèd gold,
And richer than the treasures of the mine,
Floods of the human voice divine
Along the arch in choral song are rolled.
So bends the bow complete:
And radiant rapture flows
Across the bridge, so full, so strong, so sweet,
That the uplifted spirit hardly knows
Whether the Music-Light that glows
Within the arch of tones and colours seven,
Is sunset-peace of earth or sunrise-joy of Heaven.

X
SEA AND SHORE

Music, I yield to thee
As swimmer to the sea,
I give my spirit to the flood of song!
Bear me upon thy breast
In rapture and at rest,

Bathe me in pure delight and make me strong;
From strife and struggle bring release,
And draw the waves of passion into tides of peace.
Remembered songs most dear
In living songs I hear,
While blending voices gently swing and sway,
In melodies of love,
Whose mighty currents move
With singing near and singing far away;
Sweet in the glow of morning light,
And sweeter still across the starlit gulf of night.
Music, in thee we float,
And lose the lonely note
Of self in thy celestial-ordered strain,
Until at last we find
The life to love resigned
In harmony of joy restored again;
And songs that cheered our mortal days
Break on the shore of light in endless hymns of praise.
December, 1901—May, 1903—May, 1916.

MASTER OF MUSIC
(In memory of Theodore Thomas, 1905)
Glory architect, glory of painter, and sculptor, and bard,
Living forever in temple and picture and statue and song,—
Look how the world with the lights that they lit is illumined and starred;
Brief was the flame of their life, but the lamps of their art burn long!
Where is the Master of Music, and how has he vanished away?
Where is the work that he wrought with his wonderful art in the air?
Gone,—it is gone like the glow on the cloud at the close of the day!
The Master has finished his work and the glory of music is—where?
Once, at the wave of his wand, all the billows of musical sound
Followed his will, as the sea was ruled by the prophet of old:
Now that his hand is relaxed, and his rod has dropped to the ground,
Silent and dark are the shores where the marvellous harmonies rolled!

Nay, but not silent the hearts that were filled by that life-giving sea;
Deeper and purer forever the tides of their being will roll,
Grateful and joyful, O Master, because they have listened to thee;
The glory of music endures in the depths of the human soul.

THE PIPES O' PAN
Great Nature had a million words,
In tongues of trees and songs of birds,
But none to breathe the heart of man,
Till Music filled the pipes o' Pan.

1909.

TO A YOUNG GIRL SINGING
Oh, what do you know of the song, my dear,
And how have you made it your own?
You have caught the turn of the melody clear,
And you give it again with a golden tone,
Till the wonder-word and the wedded note
Are flowing out of your beautiful throat
With a liquid charm for every ear:
And they talk of your art,—but for you alone
The song is a thing, unheard, unknown;
You only have learned it by rote.
But when you have lived for awhile, my dear,
I think you will learn it anew!
For a joy will come, or a grief, or a fear,
That will alter the look of the world for you;
And the lyric you learned as a bit of art,
Will wake to life as a wonderful part
Of the love you feel so deep and true;
And the thrill of a laugh or the throb of a tear,
Will come with your song to all who hear;
For then you will know it by heart.

April, 1911.

THE OLD FLUTE
The time will come when I no more can play
This polished flute: the stops will not obey
My gnarled fingers; and the air it weaves
In modulations, like a vine with leaves
Climbing around the tower of song, will die
In rustling autumn rhythms, confused and dry.
My shortened breath no more will freely fill
This magic reed with melody at will;
My stiffened lips will try and try in vain
To wake the liquid, leaping, dancing strain;
The heavy notes will falter, wheeze, and faint,
Or mock my ear with shrillness of complaint.
Then let me hang this faithful friend of mine
Upon the trunk of some old, sacred pine,
And sit beneath the green protecting boughs
To hear the viewless wind, that sings and soughs
Above me, play its wild, aerial lute,
And draw a ghost of music from my flute!
So will I thank the gods; and most of all
The Delian Apollo, whom men call
The mighty master of immortal sound,—
Lord of the billows in their chanting round,
Lord of the winds that fill the wood with sighs,
Lord of the echoes and their sweet replies,
Lord of the little people of the air
That sprinkle drops of music everywhere,
Lord of the sea of melody that laves
The universe with never silent waves,—
Him will I thank that this brief breath of mine
Has caught one cadence of the song divine;
And these frail fingers learned to rise and fall
In time with that great tune which throbs thro' all;
And these poor lips have lent a lilt of joy
To songless men whom weary tasks employ!
My life has had its music, and my heart
In harmony has borne a little part,

*And now I come with quiet, grateful breast
To Death's dim hall of silence and of rest.
Freely rendered from the French of Auguste Angellier,
1911.*

THE FIRST BIRD O' SPRING
TO OLIVE WHEELER

*Winter on Mount Shasta,
April down below;
Golden hours of glowing sun,
Sudden showers of snow!
Under leafless thickets
Early wild-flowers cling;
But, oh, my dear, I'm fain to hear
The first bird o' Spring!
Alders are in tassel,
Maples are in bud;
Waters of the blue McCloud
Shout in joyful flood;
Through the giant pine-trees
Flutters many a wing;
But, oh, my dear, I long to hear
The first bird o' Spring!
Candle-light and fire-light
Mingle at "the Bend;"
'Neath the roof of Bo-hai-pan
Light and shadow blend.
Sweeter than a wood-thrush
A maid begins to sing;
And, oh, my dear, I'm glad to hear
The first bird o' Spring!*

The Bend, California, April 29, 1913.

The house of Rimmon

A DRAMA IN FOUR ACTS
DRAMATIS PERSONÆ

Benhadad: King of Damascus.
Rezon: High Priest of the House of Rimmon.
Saballidin: A Noble.
Hazael } Courtiers.
Izdubhar
Rakhaz
Shumakim: The King's Fool.
Elisha: Prophet of Israel.
NAAMAN: Captain of the Armies of Damascus.
RUAHMAH: A Captive Maid of Israel.
Tsarpi: Wife to Naaman.
Khamma } Attendants of Tsarpi.
Nubta
Soldiers, Servants, Citizens, etc., etc.

Scene: Damascus and the Mountains of Samaria.

Time: 850 B. C.

ACT I
Scene I

Night, in the garden of Naaman at Damascus. At the left the palace, with softly gleaming lights and music coming from the open latticed windows. The garden is full of oleanders, roses, pomegranates, abundance of crimson flowers; the air is heavy with their fragrance: a fountain at the right is plashing gently: behind it is an arbour covered with vines. Near the centre of the garden stands a small, hideous image of the god Rimmon. Beyond the arbour rises the lofty square tower of the House of Rimmon, which casts a shadow from the moon across the garden. The background is a wide, hilly landscape, with the snow-clad summit of Mount Herman in the distance.
Enter by the palace door, the lady Tsarpi, robed in red and gold, and followed by her maids, Khamma and Nubta. She remains on the terrace: they go down into the garden, looking about, and returning to her.

Khamma:
There's no one here; the garden is asleep.
Nubta:
The flowers are nodding, all the birds abed,—
Nothing awake except the watchful stars!
Khamma:
The stars are sentinels discreet and mute:
How many things they know and never tell!
Tsarpi: Impatiently.
Unlike the stars, how many things you tell
And do not know! When comes your master home?
Nubta:
Lady, his armour-bearer brought us word,—
At moonset, not before.
Tsarpi:
He haunts the camp
And leaves me much alone; yet I can pass
The time of absence not unhappily,
If I but know the time of his return.
An hour of moonlight yet! Khamma, my mirror!
These curls are ill arranged, this veil too low,—
So,—that is better, careless maids! Withdraw,—
But bring me word if Naaman appears!
Khamma:
Mistress, have no concern; for when we hear
The clatter of his horse along the street,
We'll run this way and lead your dancers down
With song and laughter,—you shall know in time.
Exeunt Khamma and Nubta laughing, Tsarpi descends the steps.
Tsarpi:
My guest is late; but he will surely come!
The man who burns to drain the cup of love,
The priest whose greed of glory never fails,
Both, both have need of me, and he will come.
And I,—what do I need? Why everything
That helps my beauty to a higher throne;
All that a priest can promise, all a man
Can give, and all a god bestow, I need:
This may a woman win, and this will I.
Enter Rezon quietly from the shadow of the trees. He stands behind Tsarpi and listens, smiling, to her last words. Then he drops his mantle of leopard-skin, and lifts his high priest's rod of bronze, shaped at one end like a star.
Rezon:
Tsarpi!
Tsarpi: Bowing low before him.
The mistress of the house of Naaman
Salutes the master of the House of Rimmon.
Rezon:
Rimmon receives you with his star of peace,
For you were once a handmaid of his altar.
He lowers the star-point of the rod, which glows for a moment with rosy light above her head.
And now the keeper of his temple asks
The welcome of the woman for the man.
Tsarpi: Giving him her hand, but holding off his embrace.
No more,—till I have heard what brings you here
By night, within the garden of the one
Who scorns you most and fears you least in all
Damascus.
Rezon:
Trust me, I repay his scorn
With double hatred,—Naaman, the man
Who stands against the nobles and the priests,
This powerful fool, this impious devotee
Of liberty, who loves the people more
Than he reveres the city's ancient god:
This frigid husband who sets you below
His dream of duty to a horde of slaves:
This man I hate, and I will humble him.
Tsarpi:
I think I hate him too. He stands apart
From me, ev'n while he holds me in his arms,

*By something that I cannot understand.
He swears he loves his wife next to his honour!
Next? That's too low! I will be first or nothing.*
Rezon:
*With me you are the first, the absolute!
When you and I have triumphed you shall reign;
And you and I will bring this hero down.*
Tsarpi:
But how? For he is strong.
Rezon:
*By this, the hand
Of Tsarpi; and by this, the rod of Rimmon.*
Tsarpi:
Your plan?
Rezon:
*You know the host of Nineveh
Is marching now against us. Envoys come
To bid us yield before a hopeless war.
Our king is weak: the nobles, being rich,
Would purchase peace to make them richer still:
Only the people and the soldiers, led
By Naaman, would fight for liberty.
Blind fools! To-day the envoys came to me,
And talked with me in secret. Promises,
Great promises! For every noble house
That urges peace, a noble recompense:
The King, submissive, kept in royal state
And splendour: most of all, honour and wealth
Shall crown the House of Rimmon, and his priest,—
Yea, and his priestess! For we two will rise
Upon the city's fall. The common folk
Shall suffer; Naaman shall sink with them
In wreck; but I shall rise, and you shall rise
Above me! You shall climb, through incense-smoke,
And days of pomp, and nights of revelry,
Unto the topmost room in Rimmon's tower,
The secret, lofty room, the couch of bliss,
And the divine embraces of the god.*
Tsarpi: *Throwing out her arms in exultation.*
All, all I wish! What must I do for this?
Rezon:
Turn Naaman away from thoughts of war.
Tsarpi:
*But if I fail? His will is proof against
The lure of kisses and the wile of tears.*
Rezon:
*Where woman fails, woman and priest succeed.
Before the King decides, he must consult
The oracle of Rimmon. This my hands
Prepare,—and you shall read the signs prepared
In words of fear to melt the brazen heart
Of Naaman.*
Tsarpi:
But if it flame instead?
Rezon:
*I know a way to quench that flame. The cup,
The parting cup your hand shall give to him!
What if the curse of Rimmon should infect
That sacred wine with poison, secretly
To work within his veins, week after week
Corrupting all the currents of his blood,
Dimming his eyes, wasting his flesh? What then?*

*Would he prevail in war? Would he come back
To glory, or to shame? What think you?*
Tsarpi:
*I?—
I do not think; I only do my part.
But can the gods bless this?*
Rezon:
*The gods can bless
Whatever they decree; their will makes right;
And this is for the glory of the House
Of Rimmon,—and for thee, my queen. Come, come!
The night grows dark: we'll perfect our alliance.
Rezon draws her with him, embracing her, through the
shadows of the garden. Ruahmah, who has been sleeping
in the arbour, has been awakened during the dialogue,
and has been dimly visible in her white dress, behind the
vines. She parts them and comes out, pushing back her
long, dark hair from her temples.*
Ruahmah:
*What have I heard? O God, what shame is this
Plotted beneath Thy pure and silent stars!
Was it for this that I was brought away
A captive from the hills of Israel
To serve the heathen in a land of lies?
Ah, treacherous, shameful priest! Ah, shameless wife
Of one too noble to suspect thy guilt!
The very greatness of his generous heart
Betrays him to their hands. What can I do!
Nothing,—a slave,—hated and mocked by all
My fellow-slaves! O bitter prison-life!
I smother in this black, betraying air
Of lust and luxury; I faint beneath
The shadow of this House of Rimmon. God
Have mercy! Lead me out to Israel.
To Israel!
Music and laughter heard within the palace. The doors
fly open and a flood of men and women, dancers, players,
flushed with wine, dishevelled, pour down the steps,
Khamma and Nubta with them. They crown the image
with roses and dance around it. Ruahmah is discovered
crouching beside the arbour. They drag her out beside the
image.*
Nubta:
*Look! Here's the Hebrew maid,—
She's homesick; let us comfort her!*
Khamma: *They put their arms around her.*
*Yes, dancing is the cure for homesickness.
We'll make her dance.*
Ruahmah: *She slips away.*
*I pray you, let me go!
I cannot dance, I do not know your measures.*
Khamma:
Then sing for us,—a song of Israel!
Ruahmah:
*How can I sing the songs of Israel
In this strange country? O my heart would break!*
A Servant:
*A stubborn and unfriendly maid! We'll whip her.
They circle around her, striking her with rose-
branches; she sinks to her knees, covering her face with
her bare arms, which bleed.*
Nubta:

Look, look! She kneels to Rimmon, she is tamed.
Ruahmah: *Springing up and lifting her arms.*
Nay, not to this dumb idol, but to Him
Who made Orion and the seven stars!
All:
She raves,—she mocks at Rimmon! Punish her!
The fountain! Wash her blasphemy away!
They push her toward the fountain, laughing and shouting. In the open door of the palace Naaman appears, dressed in blue and silver, bareheaded and unarmed. He comes to the top of the steps and stands for a moment, astonished and angry.
Naaman:
Silence! What drunken rout is this? Begone,
Ye barking dogs and mewing cats! Out, all!
Poor child, what have they done to thee?
Exeunt all except Ruahmah, who stands with her face covered by her hands. Naaman comes to her, laying his hand on her shoulder.
Ruahmah: *Looking up in his face.*
Nothing,
My lord and master! They have harmed me not.
Naaman: *Touching her arm.*
Dost call this nothing?
Ruahmah:
Since my lord is come!
Naaman:
I do not know thy face,—who art thou, child?
Ruahmah:
The handmaid of thy wife.
Naaman:
Whence comest thou?
Thy voice is like thy mistress, but thy looks
Have something foreign. Tell thy name, thy land.
Ruahmah:
Ruahmah is my name, a captive maid,
The daughter of a prince in Israel,
Where once, in olden days, I saw my lord
Ride through our highlands, when Samaria
Was allied with Damascus to defeat
Our common foe.
Naaman:
And thou rememberest this?
Ruahmah:
As clear as yesterday! Master, I saw
Thee riding on a snow-white horse beside
Our king; and all we joyful little maids
Strewed boughs of palm along the victors' way,
For you had driven out the enemy,
Broken; and both our lands were friends and free.
Naaman: *Sadly.*
Well, they are past, those noble days! The days
When nations would imperil all to keep
Their liberties, are only memories now.
The common cause is lost,—and thou art brought,
The captive of some mercenary raid,
Some skirmish of a gold-begotten war,
To serve within my house. Dost thou fare well?
Ruahmah:
Master, thou seest.
Naaman:
Yes, I see! My child,

Why do they hate thee so?
Ruahmah:
I do not know,
Unless because I will not bow to Rimmon.
Naaman:
Thou needest not. I fear he is a god
Who pities not his people, will not save.
My heart is sick with doubt of him. But thou
Shalt hold thy faith,—I care not what it is,—
Worship thy god; but keep thy spirit free.
He takes the amulet from his neck and gives it to her.
Here, take this chain and wear it with my seal,
None shall molest the maid who carries this.
Thou hast found favour in thy master's eyes;
Hast thou no other gift to ask of me?
Ruahmah: *Earnestly.*
My lord, I do entreat thee not to go
To-morrow to the council. Seek the King
And speak with him in secret; but avoid
The audience-hall.
Naaman:
Why, what is this? Thy wits
Are wandering. My honour is engaged
To speak for war, to lead in war against
The Assyrian Bull and save Damascus.
Ruahmah: *With confused earnestness.*
Then, lord, if thou must go, I pray thee speak,—
I know not how,—but so that all must hear.
With magic of unanswerable words
Persuade thy foes. Yet watch,—beware,—
Naaman:
Of what?
Ruahmah: *Turning aside.*
I am entangled in my speech,—no light,—
How shall I tell him? He will not believe.
O my dear lord, thine enemies are they
Of thine own house. I pray thee to beware,—
Beware,—of Rimmon!
Naaman:
Child, thy words are wild:
Thy troubles have bewildered all thy brain.
Go, now, and fret no more; but sleep, and dream
Of Israel! For thou shalt see thy home
Among the hills again.
Ruahmah:
Master, good-night.
And may thy slumber be as sweet and deep
As if thou camped at snowy Hermon's foot,
Amid the music of his waterfalls.
There friendly oak-trees bend their boughs above
The weary head, pillowed on earth's kind breast,
And unpolluted breezes lightly breathe
A song of sleep among the murmuring leaves.
There the big stars draw nearer, and the sun
Looks forth serene, undimmed by city's mirk
Or smoke of idol-temples, to behold
The waking wonder of the wide-spread world.
There life renews itself with every morn
In purest joy of living. May the Lord
Deliver thee, dear master, from the nets
Laid for thy feet, and lead thee out along
The open path, beneath the open sky!

Exit Ruahmah: Naaman stands looking after her.

Scene II
Time: The following morning

The audience-hall in Benhadad's palace. The sides of the hall are lined with lofty columns: the back opens toward the city, with descending steps: the House of Rimmon with its high tower is seen in the background. The throne is at the right in front: opposite is the royal door of entrance, guarded by four tall sentinels. Enter at the rear between the columns, Rakhaz, Saballidin, Hazael, Izdubhar.

Izdubhar: *An excited old man.*
The city is all in a turmoil. It boils like a pot of lentils. The people are foaming and bubbling round and round like beans in the pottage.

Hazael: *A lean, crafty man.*
Fear is a hot fire.

Rakhaz: *A fat, pompous man.*
Well may they fear, for the Assyrians are not three days distant. They are blazing along like a waterspout to chop Damascus down like a pitcher of spilt milk.

Saballidin: *Young and frank.*
Cannot Naaman drive them back?

Rakhaz: *Puffing and blowing.*
Ho! Naaman? Where have you been living? Naaman is a broken reed whose claws have been cut. Build no hopes on that foundation, for it will run away and leave you all adrift in the conflagration.

Saballidin:
He clatters like a windmill. What would he say, Hazael?

Hazael:
Naaman can do nothing without the command of the King; and the King fears to order the army to march without the approval of the gods. The High Priest is against it. The House of Rimmon is for peace with Asshur.

Rakhaz:
Yes, and all the nobles are for peace. We are the men whose wisdom lights the rudder that upholds the chariot of state. Would we be rich if we were not wise? Do we not know better than the rabble what medicine will silence this fire that threatens to drown us?

Izdubhar:
But if the Assyrians come, we shall all perish; they will despoil us all.

Hazael:
Not us, my lord, only the common people. The envoys have offered favourable terms to the priests, and the nobles, and the King. No palace, no temple, shall be plundered. Only the shops, and the markets, and the houses of the multitude shall be given up to the Bull. He will eat his supper from the pot of lentils, not from our golden plate.

Rakhaz:
Yes, and all who speak for peace in the council shall be enriched; our heads shall be crowned with seats of honour in the procession of the Assyrian king. He needs wise counsellors to help him guide the ship of empire onto the solid rock of prosperity. You must be with us, my lords Izdubhar and Saballidin, and let the stars of your wisdom roar loudly for peace.

Izdubhar:
He talks like a tablet read upside down,—a wild ass braying in the wilderness. Yet there is policy in his words.

Saballidin:
I know not. Can a kingdom live without a people or an army? If we let the Bull in to sup on the lentils, will he not make his breakfast in our vineyards?

Enter other courtiers following Shumakim, a hump-backed jester, in blue, green and red, a wreath of poppies around his neck and a flagon in his hand. He walks unsteadily, and stutters in his speech.

Hazael:
Here is Shumakim, the King's fool, with his legs full of last night's wine.

Shumakim: *Balancing himself in front of them and chuckling.*
Wrong, my lords, very wrong! This is not last night's wine, but a draught the King's physician gave me this morning for a cure. It sobers me amazingly! I know you all, my lords: any fool would know you. You, master, are a statesman; and you are a politician; and you are a patriot.

Rakhaz:
Am I a statesman? I felt something of the kind about me. But what is a statesman?

Shumakim:
A politician that is stuffed with big words; a fat man in a mask; one that plays a solemn tune on a sackbut full o' wind.

Hazael:
And what is a politician?

Shumakim:
A statesman that has dropped his mask and cracked his sackbut. Men trust him for what he is, and he never deceives them, because he always lies.

Izdubhar:
Why do you call me a patriot?

Shumakim:
Because you know what is good for you; you love your country as you love your pelf. You feel for the common people,—as the wolf feels for the sheep.

Saballidin:
And what am I?

Shumakim:
A fool, master, just a plain fool; and there is hope of thee for that reason. Embrace me, brother, and taste this; but not too much,—it will intoxicate thee with sobriety.

The hall has been slowly filling with courtiers and soldiers; a crowd of people begin to come up the steps at the rear, where they are halted by a chain guarded by servants of the palace. A bell tolls; the royal door is thrown open; the aged King totters across the hall and takes his seat on the throne with the four tall sentinels standing behind him. All bow down shading their eyes with their hands.

Benhadad:
The hour of royal audience is come.
I'll hear the envoys. Are my counsellors
At hand? Where are the priests of Rimmon's house?
Gongs sound. Rezon comes in from the side, followed by a procession of priests in black and yellow. The

courtiers bow; the King rises; Rezon takes his stand on the steps of the throne at the left of the King.
Benhadad:
Where is my faithful servant Naaman,
The captain of my host?
Trumpets sound from the city. The crowd on the steps divide; the chain is lowered; Naaman enters, followed by six soldiers. He is dressed in chain-mail with a silver helmet and a cloak of blue. He uncovers, and kneels on the steps of the throne at the King's right.
Naaman:
My lord the King,
The bearer of thy sword is here.

Benhadad: *Giving Naaman his hand, and sitting down.*
Welcome,
My strong right arm that never me failed yet!
I am in doubt,—but stay thou close to me
While I decide this cause. Where are the envoys?
Let them appear and give their message.

Enter the Assyrian envoys; one in white and the other in red; both with the golden Bull's head embroidered on their robes. They come from the right, rear, bow slightly before the throne, and take the centre of the hall.

White Envoy: *Stepping forward.*
Greeting from Shalmaneser, Asshur's son,
Who rules the world from Nineveh,
Unto Benhadad, monarch in Damascus!
The conquering Bull has led his army forth;
The south has fallen before him, and the west
His feet have trodden; Hamath is laid waste;
He pauses at your gate, invincible,—
To offer peace. The princes of your court,
The priests of Rimmon's house, and you, the King,
If you pay homage to your Overlord,
Shall rest secure, and flourish as our friends.
Assyria sends to you this gilded yoke;
Receive it as the sign of proffered peace.
He lays a yoke on the steps of the throne.
Benhadad:
What of the city? Said your king no word
Of our Damascus, and the many folk
That do inhabit her and make her great?
What of the soldiers who have fought for us?
White Envoy:
Of these my royal master did not speak.
Benhadad:
Strange silence! Must we give them up to him?
Is this the price at which he offers us
The yoke of peace? What if we do refuse?
Red Envoy: *Stepping forward.*
Then ruthless war! War to the uttermost.
No quarter, no compassion, no escape!
The Bull will gore and trample in his fury
Nobles and priests and king,—none shall be spared!
Before the throne we lay our second gift;
This bloody horn, the symbol of red war.
He lays a long bull's horn, stained with blood, on the steps of the throne.
White Envoy:
Our message is delivered. We return
Unto our master. He will wait three days
To know your royal choice between his gifts.
Keep which you will and send the other back.
The red bull's horn your youngest page may bring;
But with the yoke, best send your mightiest army!

The Envoys retire, amid confused murmurs of the people, the King silent, his head, sunken on his breast.
Benhadad:
Proud words, a bitter message, hard to endure!
We are not now that force which feared no foe:
Our old allies have left us. Can we face the Bull
Alone, and beat him back? Give me your counsel.
Many speak at once, confusedly.
What babblement is this? Were ye born at Babel?
Give me clear words and reasonable speech.
Rakhaz: *Pompously.*
O King, I am a reasonable man!
And there be some who call me very wise
And prudent; but of this I will not speak,
For I am also modest. Let me plead,
Persuade, and reason you to choose for peace.
This golden yoke may be a bitter draught,
But better far to fold it in our arms,
Than risk our cargoes in the savage horn
Of war. Shall we imperil all our wealth,
Our valuable lives? Nobles are few,
Rich men are rare, and wise men rarer still;
The precious jewels on the tree of life,
Wherein the common people are but bricks
And clay and rubble. Let the city go,
But save the corner-stones that float the ship!
Have I not spoken well?
Benhadad: *Shaking his head.*
Excellent well!
Most eloquent! But misty in the meaning.
Hazael: *With cold decision.*
Then let me speak, O King, in plainer words!
The days of independent states are past:
The tide of empire sweeps across the earth;
Assyria rides it with resistless power
And thunders on to subjugate the world.
Oppose her, and we fight with Destiny;
Submit to her demands, and we shall ride
With her to victory. Therefore accept
The golden yoke, Assyria's gift of peace.
Naaman: *Starting forward eagerly.*
There is no peace beneath a conqueror's yoke!
For every state that barters liberty
To win imperial favour, shall be drained
Of her best blood, henceforth, in endless wars
To make the empire greater. Here's the choice,
My King, we fight to keep our country free,
Or else we fight forevermore to help
Assyria bind the world as we are bound.
I am a soldier, and I know the hell
Of war! But I will gladly ride through hell
To save Damascus. Master, bid me ride!
Ten thousand chariots wait for your command;
And twenty thousand horsemen strain the leash
Of patience till you let them go; a throng

*Of spearmen, archers, swordsmen, like the sea
Chafing against a dike, roar for the onset!
O master, let me launch your mighty host
Against the Bull,—we'll bring him to his knees!
Cries of "war!" from the soldiers and the people;
"peace!" from the courtiers and the priests. The King
rises, turning toward Naaman, and seems about to speak.
Rezon lifts his rod.*
Rezon:
*Shall not the gods decide when mortals doubt?
Rimmon is master of the city's fate;
We read his will, by our most ancient-faith,
In omens and in signs of mystery.
Must we not hearken to his high commands?*
Benhadad: *Sinking back on the throne, submissively.*
*I am the faithful son of Rimmon's House.
Consult the oracle. But who shall read?*
Rezon:
*Tsarpi, the wife of Naaman, who served
Within the temple in her maiden years,
Shall be the mouth-piece of the mighty god,
To-day's high-priestess. Bring the sacrifice!
Gongs and cymbals sound: enter priests carrying an
altar on which a lamb is bound. The altar is placed in the
centre of the hall. Tsarpi follows the priests, covered with
a long transparent veil of black, sown with gold stars;
Ruahmah, in white, bears her train. Tsarpi stands before
the altar, facing it, and lifts her right hand holding a knife.
Ruahmah steps back, near the throne, her hands crossed
on her breast, her head bowed. The priests close in
around Tsarpi and the altar. The knife is seen to strike
downward. Gongs and cymbals sound: cries of "Rimmon,
hear us!" The circle of priests opens, and Tsarpi turns
slowly to face the King.*
Tsarpi: *Monotonously.*
*Black is the blood of the victim,
Rimmon is unfavourable,
Asratu is unfavourable;
They will not war against Asshur,
They will make a league with the God of Nineveh.
Evil is in store for Damascus,
A strong enemy will lay waste the land.
Therefore make peace with the Bull;
Hearken to the voice of Rimmon.
She turns again to the altar, and the priests close in
around her. Rezon lifts his rod toward the tower of the
temple. A flash of lightning followed by thunder; smoke
rises from the altar; all except Naaman and Ruahmah
cover their faces. The circle of priests opens again, and
Tsarpi comes forward slowly, chanting.*
Chant:
*Hear the words of Rimmon! Thus your Maker
speaketh:
I, the god of thunder, riding on the whirlwind,
I, the god of lightning leaping from the storm-cloud,
I will smite with vengeance him who dares defy me!
He who leads Damascus into war with Asshur,
Conquering or conquered, bears my curse upon him.
Surely shall my arrow strike his heart in secret,
Burn his flesh with fever, turn his blood to poison.
Brand him with corruption, drive him into darkness;
He shall surely perish by the doom of Rimmon.*

*All are terrified and look toward Naaman, shuddering.
Ruahmah alone seems not to heed the curse, but stands
with her eyes fixed on Naaman.*
Ruahmah:
*Be not afraid! There is a greater God
Shall cover thee with His almighty wings:
Beneath his shield and buckler shalt thou trust.*
Benhadad:
Repent, my son, thou must not brave this curse.
Naaman:
*My King, there is no curse as terrible
As that which lights a bosom-fire for him
Who gives away his honour, to prolong
A craven life whose every breath is shame!
If I betray the men who follow me,
The city that has put her trust in me,
What king can shield me from my own deep scorn
What god release me from that self-made hell?
The tender mercies of Assyria
I know; and they are cruel as creeping tigers.
Give up Damascus, and her streets will run
Rivers of innocent blood; the city's heart,
That mighty, labouring heart, wounded and crushed
Beneath the brutal hooves of the wild Bull,
Will cry against her captain, sitting safe
Among the nobles, in some pleasant place.
I shall be safe,—safe from the threatened wrath
Of unknown gods, but damned forever by
The men I know,—that is the curse I fear.*
Benhadad:
*Speak not so high, my son. Must we not bow
Our heads before the sovereignties of heaven?
The unseen rulers are Divine.*
Naaman:
*O King,
I am unlearned in the lore of priests;
Yet well I know that there are hidden powers
About us, working mortal weal and woe
Beyond the force of mortals to control.
And if these powers appear in love and truth,
I think they must be gods, and worship them.
But if their secret will is manifest
In blind decrees of sheer omnipotence,
That punish where no fault is found, and smite
The poor with undeserved calamity,
And pierce the undefended in the dark
With arrows of injustice, and foredoom
The innocent to burn in endless pain,
I will not call this fierce almightiness
Divine. Though I must bear, with every man,
The burden of my life ordained, I'll keep
My soul unterrified, and tread the path
Of truth and honour with a steady heart!
Have ye not heard, my lords? The oracle
Proclaims to me, to me alone, the doom
Of vengeance if I lead the army out.
"Conquered or conquering!" I grip that chance!
Damascus free, her foes all beaten back,
The people saved from slavery, the King
Upheld in honour on his ancient throne,—
O what's the cost of this? I'll gladly pay
Whatever gods there be, whatever price*

They ask for this one victory. Give me
This gilded sign of shame to carry back;
I'll shake it in the face of Asshur's king,
And break it on his teeth.
        Benhadad: Rising.
Then go, my never-beaten captain, go!
And may the powers that hear thy solemn vow
Forgive thy rashness for Damascus' sake,
Prosper thy fighting, and remit thy pledge.
        Rezon: Standing beside the altar.
The pledge, O King, this man must seal his pledge
At Rimmon's altar. He must take the cup
Of soldier-sacrament, and bind himself
By thrice-performed libation to abide
The fate he has invoked.
        Naaman: Slowly.
            And so I will.
He comes down the steps, toward the altar, where
Rezon is filling the cup which Tsarpi holds. Ruahmah
throws herself before Naaman, clasping his knees.
        Ruahmah: Passionately and wildly.
My lord, I do beseech you, stay! There's death
Within that cup. It is an offering
To devils. See, the wine blazes like fire,
It flows like blood, it is a cursed cup,
Fulfilled of treachery and hate.
Dear master, noble master, touch it not!
        Naaman:
Poor maid, thy brain is still distraught. Fear not,
But let me go! Here, treat her tenderly!
        Gives her into the hands of Saballidin.
Can harm befall me from the wife who bears
My name? I take the cup of fate from her.
I greet the unknown powers; Pours libation.
            I will perform my vow; Again.
            I will abide my fate; Again.
I pledge my life to keep Damascus free.
        He drains the cup, and lets it fall.
            CURTAIN.

ACT II
Time: A week later

The fore-court of the House of Rimmon. At the back the broad steps and double doors of the shrine; above them the tower of the god, its summit invisible. Enter various groups of citizens, talking, laughing, shouting: Rakhaz, Hazael, Shumakim and others.
        First Citizen:
Great news, glorious news, the Assyrians are beaten!

        Second Citizen:
Naaman is returning, crowned with victory. Glory to our noble captain!
        Third Citizen:
No, he is killed. I had it from one of the camp-followers who saw him fall at the head of the battle. They are bringing his body to bury it with honour. O sorrowful victory!
        Rakhaz:
Peace, my good fellows, you are ignorant, you have not been rightly informed, I will misinform you. The accounts of Naaman's death are overdrawn. He was killed, but his life has been preserved. One of his wounds was mortal, but the other three were curable, and by these the physicians have saved him.
        Shumakim: Balancing himself before Rakhaz in pretended admiration.
O wonderful! Most admirable logic! One mortal, and three curable, therefore he must recover as it were, by three to one. Rakhaz, do you know that you are a marvelous man?
        Rakhaz:
Yes, I know it, but I make no boast of my knowledge.
        Shumakim:
Too modest, for in knowing this you know more than any other in Damascus!
Enter, from the right, Saballidin in armour: from the left, Tsarpi with her attendants, among whom is Ruahmah.
        Hazael:
Here is Saballidin, we'll question him;
He was enflamed by Naaman's wild words,
And rode with him to battle. Give us news,
Of your great captain! Is he safe and well?
When will he come? Or will he come at all?
        All gather around him listening eagerly.
        Saballidin:
He comes but now, returning from the field
Where he hath gained a crown of deathless fame!
Three times he led the charge; three times he fell
Wounded, and the Assyrians beat us back.
Yet every wound was but a spur to urge
His valour onward. In the last attack
He rode before us as the crested wave
That leads the flood; and lo, our enemies
Were broken like a dam of river-reeds.
The flying King encircled by his guard
Was lodged like driftwood on a little hill.
Then Naaman, who led our foremost band
Of whirlwind riders, hammered through the hedge
Of spearmen, brandishing the golden yoke.
"Take back this gift," he cried; and shattered it
On Shalmaneser's helmet. So the fight
Dissolved in universal rout; the King,
His chariots and his horsemen fled away;
Our captain stood the master of the field,
And saviour of Damascus! Now he brings,
First to the King, report of this great triumph.
        Shouts of joy and applause.
        Ruahmah: Coming close to Saballidin.
But what of him who won it? Fares he well?
My mistress would receive some word of him.
        Saballidin:
Hath she not heard?
        Ruahmah:
But one brief message came:
A letter saying, "We have fought and conquered,"
No word of his own person. Fares he well?
        Saballidin:
Alas, most ill! For he is like a man
Consumed by some strange sickness: wasted, wan,—
His eyes are dimmed so that he scarce can see;
His ears are dulled; his fearless face is pale
As one who walks to meet a certain doom
Yet will not flinch. It is most pitiful,—

But you shall see.
Ruahmah:
Yea, we shall see a man
Who dared to face the wrath of evil powers
Unknown, and hazard all to save his country.
Enter Benhadad with courtiers.
Benhadad:
Where is my faithful servant Naaman,
The captain of my host?
Saballidin:
My lord, he comes.
Trumpet sounds. Enter company of soldiers in armour. Then four soldiers bearing captured standards of Asshur. Naaman follows, very pale, armour dinted and stained; he is blind, and guides himself by cords from the standards on each side, but walks firmly. The doors of the temple open slightly, and Rezon appears at the top of the steps. Naaman lets the cords fall, and gropes his way for a few paces.
Naaman: Kneeling.
Where is my King?
Master, the bearer of thy sword returns.
The golden yoke thou gavest me I broke
On him who sent it. Asshur's Bull hath fled
Dehorned. The standards of his host are thine!
Damascus is all thine, at peace, and free!
Benhadad: Holding out his arms.
Thou art a mighty man of valour! Come,
And let me fold thy courage to my heart.
Rezon: Lifting his rod.
Forbear, O King! Stand back from him, all men!
By the great name of Rimmon I proclaim
This man a leper! See, upon his brow,
This little mark, the death-white seal of doom!
That tiny spot will spread, eating his flesh,
Gnawing his fingers bone from bone, until
The impious heart that dared defy the gods
Dissolves in the slow death which now begins.
Unclean! unclean! Henceforward he is dead:
No human hand shall touch him, and no home
Of men shall give him shelter. He shall walk
Only with corpses of the selfsame death
Down the long path to a forgotten tomb.
Avoid, depart, I do adjure you all,
Leave him to god,—the leper Naaman!
All shrink back horrified. Rezon retires into the temple; the crowd melts away, wailing; Tsarpi is among the first to go, followed by her attendants, except Ruahmah, who crouches, with her face covered, not far from Naaman.
Benhadad: Lingering and turning back.
Alas, my son! O Naaman, my son!
Why did I let thee go? I must obey.
Who can resist the gods? Yet none shall take
Thy glorious title, captain of my host!
I will provide for thee, and thou shalt dwell
With guards of honour in a house of mine
Always. Damascus never shall forget
What thou hast done! O miserable words
Of crowned impotence! O mockery of power
Given to kings who cannot even defend
Their dearest from the secret wrath of heaven!
O Naaman, my son, my son! *Exit.*

Naaman: Slowly passing his hand over his eyes, and looking up.
Am I alone
With thee, inexorable one, whose pride
Offended takes this horrible revenge?
I must submit my mortal flesh to thee,
Almighty, but I will not call thee god!
Yet thou hast found the way to wound my soul
Most deeply through the flesh; and I must find
The way to let my wounded soul escape!
Drawing his sword.
Come, my last friend, thou art more merciful
Than Rimmon. Why should I endure the doom
He sends me? Irretrievably cut off
From all dear intercourse of human love,
From all the tender touch of human hands,
From all brave comradeship with brother-men,
With eyes that see no faces through this dark,
With ears that hear all voices far away,
Why should I cling to misery, and grope
My long, long way from pain to pain, alone?
Ruahmah: At his feet.
Nay, not alone, dear lord, for I am here;
And I will never leave thee, nor forsake thee!
Naaman:
What voice is that? The silence of my tomb
Is broken by a ray of music,—whose?
Ruahmah: Rising.
The one who loves thee best in all the world.
Naaman:
Why that should be,—O dare I dream it true?
Tsarpi, my wife? Have I misjudged thy heart
As cold and proud? How nobly thou forgivest!
Thou com'st to hold me from the last disgrace,—
The coward's flight into the dark. Go back
Unstained, my sword! Life is endurable
While there is one alive on earth who loves us.
Ruahmah:
My lord,—my lord,—O listen! You have erred,—
You do mistake me now,—this dream—
Naaman:
Ah, wake me not! For I can conquer death
Dreaming this dream. Let me at last believe,
Though gods are cruel, a woman can be kind.
Grant me but this! For see,—I ask so little,—
Only to know that thou art faithful,
That thou art near me, though I touch thee not,—
O this will hold me up, though it be given
From pity more than love.
Ruahmah: Trembling, and speaking slowly.
Not so, my lord!
My pity is a stream; my pride of thee
Is like the sea that doth engulf the stream;
My love for thee is like the sovereign moon
That rules the sea. The tides that fill my soul
Flow unto thee and follow after thee;
And where thou goest I will go; and where
Thou diest I will die,—in the same hour.
She lays her hand on his arm. He draws back.
Naaman:
O touch me not! Thou shalt not share my doom.
Ruahmah:

Entreat me not to go. I will obey
In all but this; but rob me not of this,—
The only boon that makes life worth the living,—
To walk beside thee day by day, and keep
Thy foot from stumbling; to prepare thy food
When thou art hungry, music for thy rest,
And cheerful words to comfort thy black hour;
And so to lead thee ever on, and on,
Through darkness, till we find the door of hope.
Naaman:
What word is that? The leper has no hope.
Ruahmah:
Dear lord, the mark upon thy brow is yet
No broader than my little finger-nail.
Thy force is not abated, and thy step
Is firm. Wilt thou surrender to the enemy
Before thy strength is touched? Why, let me put
A drop of courage from my breast in thine!
There is a hope for thee. The captive maid
Of Israel who dwelt within thy house
Knew of a god very compassionate,
Long-suffering, slow to anger, one who heals
The sick, hath pity on the fatherless,
And saves the poor and him who has no helper.
His prophet dwells nigh to Samaria;
And I have heard that he hath brought the dead
To life again. We'll go to him. The King,
If I beseech him, will appoint a guard
Of thine own soldiers and Saballidin,
Thy friend, to convoy us upon our journey.
He'll give us royal letters to the King
Of Israel to make our welcome sure;
And we will take the open road, beneath
The open sky, to-morrow, and go on
Together till we find the door of hope.
Come, come with me!
She grasps his hand.
Naaman: *Drawing back.*
Thou must not touch me!
Ruahmah: *Unclasping her girdle and putting the end*
in his hand.
Take my girdle, then!
Naaman: *Kissing the clasp of the girdle.*
I do begin to think there is a God,
Since love on earth can work such miracles!
CURTAIN.

ACT III
Time: A month later: dawn
Scene I

Naaman's tent, on high ground among the mountains near Samaria: the city below. In the distance, a wide and splendid landscape. Saballidin and soldiers on guard below the tent. Enter Ruahmah in hunter's dress, with a lute slung from her shoulder.
Ruahmah:
Peace and good health to you, Saballidin.
Good morrow to you all. How fares my lord?
Saballidin:
The curtains of his tent are folded still:
They have not moved since we returned, last night,
And told him what befell us in the city.
Ruahmah:
Told him! Why did you make report to him
And not to me? Am I not captain here,
Intrusted by the King's command with care
Of Naaman until he is restored?
'Tis mine to know the first of good or ill
In this adventure: mine to shield his heart
From every arrow of adversity.
What have you told him? Speak!
Saballidin:
Lady, we feared
To bring our news to you. For when the King
Of Israel had read our monarch's letter,
He rent his clothes, and cried, "Am I a god,
To kill and make alive, that I should heal
A leper? Ye have come with false pretence,
Damascus seeks a quarrel with me. Go!"
But when we told our lord, he closed his tent,
And there remains enfolded in his grief.
I trust he sleeps; 'twere kind to let him sleep!
For now he doth forget his misery,
And all the burden of his hopeless woe
Is lifted from him by the gentle hand
Of slumber. Oh, to those bereft of hope
Sleep is the only blessing left,—the last
Asylum of the weary, the one sign
Of pity from impenetrable heaven.
Waking is strife; sleep is the truce of God!
Ah, lady, wake him not. The day will be
Full long for him to suffer, and for us
To turn our disappointed faces home
On the long road by which we must return.
Ruahmah:
Return! Who gave you that command? Not I!
The King made me the leader of this quest,
And bound you all to follow me, because
He knew I never would return without
The thing for which he sent us. I'll go on
Day after day, unto the uttermost parts
Of earth, if need be, and beyond the gates
Of morning, till I find that which I seek,—
New life for Naaman. Are ye ashamed
To have a woman lead you? Then go back
And tell the King, "This huntress went too far
For us to follow: she pursues the trail
Of hope alone, refusing to forsake
The quarry: we grew weary of the chase;
And so we left her and retraced our steps,
Like faithless hounds, to sleep beside the fire."
Did Naaman forsake his soldiers thus
When you went forth to hunt the Assyrian Bull?
Your manly courage is less durable
Than woman's love, it seems. Go, if you will,—
Who bids me now farewell?
Soldiers:
Not I, not I!
Saballidin:
Lady, lead on, we'll follow you forever!
Ruahmah:
Why, now you speak like men! Brought you no word
Out of Samaria, except that cry
Of impotence and fear from Israel's King?

Saballidin:
I do remember while he spoke with us
A rustic messenger came in, and cried
"Elisha saith, bring Naaman to me
At Dothan, he shall surely know there is
A God in Israel."
Ruahmah:
What said the King?
Saballidin:
He only shouted "Go!" more wildly yet,
And rent his clothes again, as if he were
Half-maddened by a coward's fear, and thought
Only of how he might be rid of us.
What comfort could there be for him, what hope
For us, in the rude prophet's misty word?
Ruahmah:
It is the very word for which I prayed!
My trust was not in princes; for the crown,
The sceptre, and the purple robe are not
Significant of vital power. The man
Who saves his brother-men is he who lives
His life with Nature, takes deep hold on truth,
And trusts in God. A prophet's word is more
Than all the kings on earth can speak. How far
Is Dothan?
Soldier:
Lady, 'tis but three hours' ride
Along the valley southward.
Ruahmah:
Near! so near?
I had not thought to end my task so soon!
Prepare yourselves with speed to take the road.
I will awake my lord.
Exeunt all but Saballidin and Ruahmah. She goes
toward the tent.
Saballidin:
Ruahmah, stay! She turns back.
I've been your servant in this doubtful quest,
Obedient, faithful, loyal to your will,—
What have I earned by this?
Ruahmah:
The gratitude
Of him we both desire to serve: your friend,—
My master and my lord.
Saballidin:
No more than this?
Ruahmah:
Yes, if you will, take all the thanks my hands
Can hold, my lips can speak.
Saballidin:
I would have more.
Ruahmah:
My friend, there's nothing more to give to you.
My service to my lord is absolute.
There's not a drop of blood within my veins
But quickens at the very thought of him;
And not a dream of mine but he doth stand
Within its heart and make it bright. No man
To me is other than his friend or foe.
You are his friend, and I believe you true!
Saballidin:
I have been true to him,—now, I am true
To you.
Ruahmah:
Why, then, be doubly true to him.
O let us match our loyalties, and strive
Between us who shall win the higher crown!
Men boast them of a friendship stronger far
Than love of woman. Prove it! I'll not boast,
But I'll contend with you on equal terms
In this brave race: and if you win the prize
I'll hold you next to him: and if I win
He'll hold you next to me; and either way
We'll not be far apart. Do you accept
My challenge?
Saballidin:
Yes! For you enforce my heart
By honour to resign its great desire,
And love itself to offer sacrifice
Of all disloyal dreams on its own altar.
Yet love remains; therefore I pray you, think
How surely you must lose in our contention.
For I am known to Naaman: but you
He blindly takes for Tsarpi. 'Tis to her
He gives his gratitude: the praise you win
Endears her name.
Ruahmah:
Her name? Why, what is that?
A name is but an empty shell, a mask
That does not change the features of the face
Beneath it. Can a name rejoice, or weep,
Or hope? Can it be moved by tenderness
To daily services of love, or feel the warmth
Of dear companionship? How many things
We call by names that have no meaning! Kings
That cannot rule; and gods that are not good;
And wives that do not love! It matters not
What syllables he utters when he calls,
'Tis I who come,—'tis I who minister
Unto my lord, and mine the living heart
That feels the comfort of his confidence,
The thrill of gladness when he speaks to me,—
I do not hear the name!
Saballidin:
And yet, be sure
There's danger in this error,—and no gain!
Ruahmah:
I seek no gain: I only tread the path
Marked for me daily by the hand of love.
And if his blindness spared my lord one pang
Of sorrow in his black, forsaken hour,—
And if this error makes his burdened heart
More quiet, and his shadowed way less dark,
Whom do I rob? Not her who chose to stay
At ease in Rimmon's House! Surely not him!
Only myself! And that enriches me.
Why trouble we the master? Let it go,—
To-morrow he must know the truth,—and then
He shall dispose of me e'en as he will!
Saballidin:
To-morrow?
Ruahmah:
Yes, for I will tarry here,
While you conduct him to Elisha's house

*To find the promised healing. I forebode
A sudden danger from the craven King
Of Israel, or else a secret ambush
From those who hate us in Damascus. Go,
But leave me twenty men: this mountain-pass
Protects the road behind you. Make my lord
Obey the prophet's word, whatever he commands,
And come again in peace. Farewell!*

Exit Saballidin. Ruahmah goes toward the tent, then pauses and turns back. She takes her lute and sings.
Song
*Above the edge of dark appear the lances of the sun;
Along the mountain-ridges clear his rosy heralds run;
    The vapours down the valley go
    Like broken armies, dark and low.
    Look up, my heart, from every hill
    In folds of rose and daffodil
    The sunrise banners flow.
O fly away on silent wing, ye boding owls of night!
O welcome little birds that sing the coming-in of light!
    For new, and new, and ever-new,
    The golden bud within the blue;
    And every morning seems to say:
    "There's something happy on the way,
    And God sends love to you!"*
Naaman: *Appearing at the entrance of his tent.*
*O let me ever wake to music! For the soul
Returns most gently then, and finds its way
By the soft, winding clue of melody,
Out of the dusky labyrinth of sleep,
Into the light. My body feels the sun
Though I behold naught that his rays reveal.
Come, thou who art my daydawn and my sight,
Sweet eyes, come close, and make the sunrise mine!*
Ruahmah: *Coming near.*
*A fairer day, dear lord, was never born
In Paradise! The sapphire cup of heaven
Is filled with golden wine: the earth, adorned
With jewel-drops of dew, unveils her face
A joyful bride, in welcome to her king.
And look! He leaps upon the Eastern hills
All ruddy fire, and claims her with a kiss.
Yonder the snowy peaks of Hermon float
Unmoving as a wind-dropt cloud. The gulf
Of Jordan, filled with violet haze, conceals
The river's winding trail with wreaths of mist.
Below us, marble-crowned Samaria thrones
Upon her emerald hill amid the Vale
Of Barley, while the plains to northward change
Their colour like the shimmering necks of doves.
The lark springs up, with morning on her wings,
To climb her singing stairway in the blue,
And all the fields are sprinkled with her joy!*
Naaman:
*Thy voice is magical: thy words are visions!
I must content myself with them, for now
My only hope is lost: Samaria's King
Rejects our monarch's message,—hast thou heard?
"Am I a god that I should cure a leper?"
He sends me home unhealed, with angry words,
Back to Damascus and the lingering death.*

Ruahmah:
*What matter where he sends? No god is he
To slay or make alive. Elisha bids
You come to him at Dothan, there to learn
There is a God in Israel.*
Naaman:
*I fear
That I am grown mistrustful of all gods;
Their secret counsels are implacable.*
Ruahmah:
*Fear not! There's One who rules in righteousness
High over all.*
Naaman:
What knowest thou of Him?
Ruahmah:
*Oh, I have heard,—the maid of Israel,—
Rememberest thou? She often said her God
Was merciful and kind, and slow to wrath,
And plenteous in forgiveness, pitying us
Like as a father pitieth his children.*
Naaman:
*If there were such a God, I'd worship Him
Forever!*
Ruahmah:
*Then make haste to hear the word
His prophet promises to speak to thee!
Obey it, my dear lord, and thou shalt find
Healing and peace. The light shall fill thine eyes.
Thou wilt not need my leading any more,—
Nor me,—for thou wilt see me, all unveiled,—
I tremble at the thought.*
Naaman:
*Why, what is this?
Why shouldst thou tremble? Art thou not mine own?*
Ruahmah: *Turning to him and speaking in broken words.*
*I am,—thy handmaid,—all and only thine,—
The very pulses of my heart are thine!
Feel how they throb to comfort thee to-day—
To-day! Because it is thy time of trouble.*

She takes his hand and puts it to her forehead and her lips, but before she can lay it upon her heart, he draws away from her.
Naaman:
*Thou art too dear to injure with a kiss,—
How should I take a gift may bankrupt thee,
Or drain the fragrant chalice of thy love
With lips that may be fatal? Tempt me not
To sweet dishonour; strengthen me to wait
Until thy prophecy is all fulfilled,
And I can claim thee with a joyful heart.*
Ruahmah: *Turning away.*
*Thou wilt not need me then,—and I shall be
No more than the faint echo of a song
Heard half asleep. We shall go back to where
We stood before this journey.*
Naaman:
*Never again!
For thou art changed by some deep miracle.
The flower of womanhood hath bloomed in thee,—
Art thou not changed?*

Ruahmah:
Yea, I am changed,—and changed
Again,—bewildered,—till there's nothing clear
To me but this: I am the instrument
In an Almighty hand to rescue thee
From death. This will I do,—and afterward—
A trumpet is blown without.
Hearken, the trumpet sounds, the chariot waits.
Away, dear lord, follow the road to light!
Scene II *
The house of Elisha, upon a terraced hillside. A low stone cottage with vine-trellises and flowers; a flight of steps, at the foot of which is Naaman's chariot. He is standing in it; Saballidin beside it. Two soldiers come down the steps.
First Soldier:
We have delivered my lord's greeting and his message.
Second Soldier:
Yes, and near lost our noses in the doing of it! For the servant slammed the door in our faces. A most unmannerly reception!
First Soldier:
But I take that as a good omen. It is a mark of holy men to keep ill-conditioned servants. Look, the door opens, the prophet is coming.
Second Soldier:
No, by my head, it is that notable mark of his master's holiness, that same lantern-jawed lout of a servant.
Gehazi loiters down the steps and comes to Naaman with a slight obeisance.
Gehazi:
My master, the prophet of Israel, sends word to
Naaman the Syrian,—are you he?—"Go wash in Jordan
seven times and be healed."
Gehazi turns and goes slowly up the steps.
Naaman:
What insolence is this? Am I a man
To be put off with surly messengers?
Has not Damascus rivers more renowned
Than this rude muddy Jordan? Crystal streams,
Abana! Pharpar! flowing smoothly through
A paradise of roses? Might I not
Have bathed in them and been restored at ease?
Come up, Saballidin, and guide me home!
Saballidin:
Bethink thee, master, shall we lose our quest
Because a servant is uncouth? The road
That seeks the mountain leads us through the vale.
The prophet's word is friendly after all;
For had it been some mighty task he set,
Thou wouldst perform it. How much rather then
This easy one? Hast thou not promised her
Who waits for thy return? Wilt thou go back
To her unhealed?
Naaman:
No! not for all my pride!
I'll make myself most humble for her sake,
And stoop to anything that gives me hope
Of having her. Make haste, Saballidin,
Bring me to Jordan. I will cast myself
Into that river's turbulent embrace
A hundred times, until I save my life
Or lose it!
Exeunt. The light fades: musical interlude. The light increases again with ruddy sunset shining on the door of Elisha's house. The prophet appears and looks off, shading his eyes with his hand as he descends the steps. Trumpet blows,—Naaman's call;—sound of horses galloping and men shouting. Naaman enters joyously, followed by Saballidin and soldiers, with gifts.
Naaman:
Behold a man delivered from the grave
By thee! I rose from Jordan's waves restored
To youth and vigour, as the eagle mounts
Upon the sunbeam and renews his strength!
O mighty prophet deign to take from me
These gifts too poor to speak my gratitude;
Silver and gold and jewels, damask robes,—
Elisha: Interrupting.
As thy soul liveth I will not receive
A gift from thee, my son! Give all to Him
Whose mercy hath redeemed thee from thy plague.
Naaman:
He is the only God! I worship Him!
Grant me a portion of the blessed soil
Of this most favoured land where I have found
His mercy; in Damascus will I build
An altar to His name, and praise Him there
Morning and night. There is no other God
In all the world.
Elisha:
Thou needst not
This load of earth to build a shrine for Him;
Yet take it if thou wilt. But be assured
God's altar is in every loyal heart,
And every flame of love that kindles there
Ascends to Him and brightens with His praise.
There is no other God! But evil Powers
Make war against Him in the darkened world;
And many temples have been built to them.
Naaman:
I know them well! Yet when my master goes
To worship in the House of Rimmon, I
Must enter with him; for he trusts me, leans
Upon my hand; and when he bows himself
I cannot help but make obeisance too,—
But not to Rimmon! To my country's King
I'll bow in love and honour. Will the Lord
Pardon thy servant in this thing?
Elisha:
My son,
Peace has been granted thee. 'Tis thine to find
The only way to keep it. Go in peace.

Naaman:
Thou hast not answered me,—may I bow down?
Elisha:
The answer must be thine. The heart that knows
The perfect peace of gratitude and love,
Walks in the light and needs no other rule.
When next thou comest into Rimmon's House,
Thy heart will tell thee how to go in peace.
CURTAIN.

Note that this scene is not intended to be put upon the stage, the effect of the action upon the drama being given at the beginning of Act IV.

ACT IV
Scene I

The interior of Naaman's tent, at night. Ruahmah alone, sleeping on the ground. A vision appears to her through the curtains of the tent: Elisha standing on the hillside at Dothan: Naaman, restored to sight, comes in and kneels before him. Elisha blesses him, and he goes out rejoicing. The vision of the prophet turns to Ruahmah and lifts his hand in warning.

Elisha:
Daughter of Israel, what dost thou here?
Thy prayer is granted. Naaman is healed:
Mar not true service with a selfish thought.
Nothing remains for thee to do, except
Give thanks, and go whither the Lord commands.
Obey,—obey! Ere Naaman returns
Thou must depart to thine own house in Shechem.
The vision vanishes.
Ruahmah: *Waking and rising slowly.*
A dream, a dream, a messenger of God!
O dear and dreadful vision, art thou true?
Then am I glad with all my broken heart.
Nothing remains,—nothing remains but this,—
Give thanks, obey, depart,—and so I do.
Farewell, my master's sword! Farewell to you,
My amulet! I lay you on the hilt
His hand shall clasp again: bid him farewell
For me, since I must look upon his face
No more for ever!—Hark, what sound was that?
Enter soldier hurriedly.
Soldier:
Mistress, an arméd troop, footmen and horse,
Mounting the hill!
Ruahmah:
My lord returns in triumph.
Soldier:
Not so, for these are enemies; they march
In haste and silence, answering not our cries.
Ruahmah:
Our enemies? Then hold your ground,—on guard!
Fight! fight! Defend the pass, and drive them down.

Exit soldier. Ruahmah draws Naaman's sword from the scabbard and hurries out of the tent. Confused noise of fighting outside. Three or four soldiers are driven in by a troop of men in disguise. Ruahmah follows: she is beaten to her knees, and her sword is broken.
Rezon: *Throwing aside the cloth which covers his face.*
Hold her! So, tiger-maid, we've found your lair
And trapped you. Where is Naaman,
Your master?
Ruahmah: *Rising, her arms held by two of Rezon's followers.*
He is far beyond your reach.
Rezon:
Brave captain! He has saved himself, the leper,
And left you here?
Ruahmah:
The leper is no more.
Rezon:
What mean you?
Ruahmah:
He has gone to meet his God.
Rezon:
Dead? Dead? Behold how Rimmon's wrath is swift!
Damascus shall be mine; I'll terrify
The King with this, and make my terms. But no!
False maid, you sweet-faced harlot, you have lied
To save him,—speak.
Ruahmah:
I am not what you say,
Nor have I lied, nor will I ever speak
A word to you, vile servant of a traitor-god.
Rezon:
Break off this little flute of blasphemy,
This ivory neck,—twist it, I say!
Give her a swift despatch after her leper!
But stay,—if he still lives he'll follow her,
And so we may ensnare him. Harm her not!
Bind her! Away with her to Rimmon's House!
Is all this carrion dead? There's one that moves,—
A spear,—fasten him down! All quiet now?
Then back to our Damascus! Rimmon's face
Shall be made bright with sacrifice.
Exeunt, forcing Ruahmah with them. Musical interlude. A wounded soldier crawls from a dark corner of the tent and finds the chain with Naaman's seal, which has fallen to the ground in the struggle.
Wounded Soldier:
The signet of my lord, her amulet!
Lost, lost! Ah, noble lady,—let me die
With this upon my breast.
The tent is dark. Enter Naaman and his company in haste, with torches.
Naaman:
What bloody work
Is here? God, let me live to punish him
Who wrought this horror! Treacherously slain
At night, by unknown hands, my brave companions:
Tsarpi, my best beloved, light of my soul,
Put out in darkness! O my broken lamp
Of life, where art thou? Nay, I cannot find her.
Wounded Soldier: *Raising himself on his arm.*
Master!
Naaman: *Kneels beside him.*
One living? Quick, a torch this way!
Lift up his head,—so,—carefully!
Courage, my friend, your captain is beside you.
Call back your soul and make report to him.
Wounded Soldier:
Hail, captain! O my captain,—here!
Naaman:
Be patient,—rest in peace,—the fight is done.
Nothing remains but render your account.
Wounded Soldier:
They fell upon us suddenly,—we fought
Our fiercest,—every man,—our lady fought
Fiercer than all. They beat us down,—she's gone.
Rezon has carried her away a captive. See,—
Her amulet,—I die for you, my captain.

Naaman: He gently lays the dead soldier on the ground, and rises.
Farewell. This last report was brave; but strange
Beyond my thought! How came the High Priest here?
And what is this? my chain, my seal! But this
Has never been in Tsarpi's hand. I gave
This signet to a captive maid one night,—
A maid of Israel. How long ago?
Ruahmah was her name,—almost forgotten!
So long ago,—how comes this token here?
What is this mystery, Saballidin?
Saballidin:
Ruahmah is her name who brought you hither.
Naaman:
Where then is Tsarpi?
Saballidin:
In Damascus.
She left you when the curse of Rimmon fell,—
Took refuge in his House,—and there she waits
Her lord's return,—Rezon's return.
Naaman:
'Tis false!
Saballidin:
The falsehood is in her. She hath been friend
With Rezon in his priestly plot to win
Assyria's favour,—friend to his design
To sell his country to enrich his temple,—
And friend to him in more,—I will not name it.
Naaman:
Nor will I credit it. Impossible!
Saballidin:
Did she not plead with you against the war,
Counsel surrender, seek to break your will?
Naaman:
She did not love my work, a soldier's task.
She never seemed to be at one with me
Until I was a leper.
Saballidin:
From whose hand
Did you receive the sacred cup?
Naaman:
From hers.
Saballidin:
And from that hour the curse began to work.
Naaman:
But did she not have pity when she saw
Me smitten? Did she not beseech the King
For letters and a guard to make this journey?
Has she not been the fountain of my hope,
My comforter and my most faithful guide
In this adventure of the dark? All this
Is proof of perfect love that would have shared
A leper's doom rather than give me up.
Can I doubt her who dared to love like this?
Saballidin:
O master, doubt her not,—but know her name;
Ruahmah! It was she alone who wrought
This wondrous work of love. She won the King
To furnish forth this company. She led
Our march, kept us in heart, fought off despair,
Watched over you as if you were her child,
Prepared your food, your cup, with her own hands,
Sang you asleep at night, awake at dawn,—
Naaman: Interrupting.
Enough! I do remember every hour
Of that sweet comradeship! And now her voice
Wakens the echoes in my lonely breast.
Shall I not see her, thank her, speak her name?
Ruahmah! Let me live till I have looked
Into her eyes and called her my Ruahmah!
To his soldiers.
Away! away! I burn to take the road
That leads me back to Rimmon's House,—
But not to bow,—by God, never to bow!

Scene II
Time: Three days later

Inner court of the House of Rimmon; a temple with huge pillars at each side. In the right foreground the seat of the King; at the left, of equal height, the seat of the High Priest. In the background a broad flight of steps, rising to a curtain of cloudy gray, embroidered with two gigantic hands holding thunderbolts. The temple is in half darkness at first. Enter Khamma and Nubta, robed as Kharimati, or religious dancers, in gowns of black gauze with yellow embroideries and mantles.

Khamma:
All is ready for the rites of worship; our lady will play a great part in them. She has put on her Tyrian robes, and all her ornaments.
Nubta:
That is a sure sign of a religious purpose. She is most devout, our lady Tsarpi!
Khamma:
A favourite of Rimmon, too! The High Priest has assured her of it. He is a great man,—next to the King, now that Naaman is gone.
Nubta:
But if Naaman should come back, healed of the leprosy?
Khamma:
How can he come back? The Hebrew slave that went away with him, when they caught her, said that he was dead. The High Priest has shut her up in the prison of the temple, accusing her of her master's death.
Nubta:
Yet I think he does not believe it, for I heard him telling our mistress what to do if Naaman should return.
Khamma:
What, then?
Nubta:
She will claim him as her husband. Was she not wedded to him before the god? That is a sacred bond. Only the High Priest can loose it. She will keep her hold on Naaman for the sake of the House of Rimmon. A wife knows her husband's secrets, she can tell—
Enter Shumakim, with his flagon, walking unsteadily.
Khamma:
Hush! here comes the fool Shumakim. He is never sober.
Shumakim: Laughing.
Are there two of you? I see two, but that is no proof. I think there is only one, but beautiful enough for two. What were you talking to yourself about, fairest one!

Khamma:
*About the lady Tsarpi, fool, and what she would do if
her husband returned.*
Shumakim:
*Fie! fie! That is no talk for an innocent fool to hear.
Has she a husband?*
Nubta:
*You know very well that she is the wife of Lord
Naaman.*
Shumakim:
*I remember that she used to wear his name and his
jewels. But I thought he had exchanged her,—for a
leprosy.*
Khamma:
*You must have heard that he went away to Samaria to
look for healing. Some say that he died on the journey; but
others say he has been cured, and is on his way home to
his wife.*
Shumakim:
*It may be, for this is a mad world, and men never know
when they are well off,—except us fools. But he must come
soon if he would find his wife as he parted from her,—or
the city where he left it. The Assyrians have returned with
a greater army, and this time they will make an end of us.
There is no Naaman now, and the Bull will devour
Damascus like a bunch of leeks, flowers and all,—flowers
and all, my double-budded fair one! Are you not afraid?*
Nubta:
We belong to the House of Rimmon. He will protect us.
Shumakim:
*What? The mighty one who hides behind the curtain
there, and tells his secrets to Rezon? No doubt he will take
care of you, and of himself. Whatever game is played, the
gods never lose. But for the protection of the common
people and the rest of us fools, I would rather have
Naaman at the head of an army than all the sacred images
between here and Babylon.*
Khamma:
*You are a wicked old man. You mock the god. He will
punish you.*
Shumakim: Bitterly.
*How can he punish me? Has he not already made me a
fool? Hark, here comes my brother the High Priest, and
my brother the King. Rimmon made us all; but nobody
knows who made Rimmon, except the High Priest; and he
will never tell.*
*Gongs and cymbals sound. Enter Rezon with priests,
and the King with courtiers. They take their seats. A
throng of Khali and Kharimati come in, Tsarpi presiding;
a sacred dance is performed with torches, burning
incense, and chanting, in which Tsarpi leads.*
Chant
*Hail, mighty Rimmon, ruler of the whirl-storm,
Hail, shaker of mountains, breaker-down of forests,
Hail, thou who roarest terribly in the darkness,
Hail, thou whose arrows flame across the heavens!
Hail, great destroyer, lord of flood and tempest,
In thine anger almighty, in thy wrath eternal,
Thou who delightest in ruin, maker of desolations,
Immeru, Addu, Berku, Rimmon!
See we tremble before thee, low we bow at thine altar,
Have mercy upon us, be favourable unto us,
Save us from our enemy, accept our sacrifice,
Barku, Immeru, Addu, Rimmon!
Silence follows, all bowing down.*
Rezon:
*O King, last night the counsel from above
Was given in answer to our divination.
Ambassadors must go forthwith to crave
Assyria's pardon, and a second offer
Of the same terms of peace we did reject
Not long ago.*
Benhadad:
*Dishonour! Yet I see
No other way! Assyria will refuse,
Or make still harder terms. Disaster, shame
For this gray head, and ruin for Damascus!*
Rezon:
*Yet may we trust Rimmon will favour us,
If we adhere devoutly to his worship.
He will incline his brother-god, the Bull,
To spare us, if we supplicate him now
With costly gifts. Therefore I have prepared
A sacrifice: Rimmon shall be well pleased
With the red blood that bathes his knees to-night!*
Benhadad:
*My mind is dark with doubt,—I do forebode
Some horror! Let me go,—I am an old man,—
If Naaman my captain were alive!
But he is dead,—the glory is departed!
He rises, trembling, to leave the throne. Trumpet
sounds,—Naaman's call;—enter Naaman, followed by
soldiers; he kneels at the foot of the throne.*
Benhadad: Half-whispering.
*Art thou a ghost escaped from Allatu?
How didst thou pass the seven doors of death?
O noble ghost I am afraid of thee,
And yet I love thee,—let me hear thy voice!*
Naaman:
*No ghost, my King, but one who lives to serve
Thee and Damascus with his heart and sword
As in the former days. The only God
Has healed my leprosy: my life is clean
To offer to my country and my King.*
Benhadad: Starting toward him.
O welcome to thy King! Thrice welcome!
*Rezon: Leaving his seat and coming toward Naaman.
Stay!
The leper must appear before the priest,
The only one who can pronounce him clean.
Naaman turns; they stand looking each other in the
face.
Yea,—thou art cleansed: Rimmon hath pardoned
thee,—
In answer to the daily prayers of her
Whom he restores to thine embrace,—thy wife.
Tsarpi comes slowly toward Naaman.*
Naaman:
*From him who rules this House will I receive
Nothing! I seek no pardon from his priest,
No wife of mine among his votaries!*
Tsarpi: Holding out her hands.
Am I not yours? Will you renounce our vows?
Naaman:

The vows were empty,—never made you mine
In aught but name. A wife is one who shares
Her husband's thought, incorporates his heart
With hers by love, and crowns him with her trust.
She is God's remedy for loneliness,
And God's reward for all the toil of life.
This you have never been to me,—and so
I give you back again to Rimmon's House
Where you belong. Claim what you will of mine,—
Not me! I do renounce you,—or release you,—
According to the law. If you demand
A further cause than what I have declared,
I will unfold it fully to the King.
        Rezon: Interposing hurriedly.
No need of that! This duteous lady yields
To your caprice as she has ever done:
She stands a monument of loyalty
        And woman's meekness.
                Naaman:
                Let her stand for that!
Adorn your temple with her piety!
But you in turn restore to me the treasure
You stole at midnight from my tent.
        Rezon:
What treasure! I have stolen none from you.
        Naaman:
The very jewel of my soul,—Ruahmah!
My King, the captive maid of Israel,
To whom thou didst commit my broken life
With letters to Samaria,—my light,
My guide, my saviour in this pilgrimage,—
        Dost thou remember?
                Benhadad:
                I recall the maid,—
But dimly,—for my mind is old and weary,
She was a fearless maid, I trusted her
And gave thee to her charge. Where is she now?
        Naaman:
This robber fell upon my camp by night,—
While I was with Elisha at the Jordan,—
Slaughtered my soldiers, carried off the maid,
And holds her somewhere in imprisonment.
O give this jewel back to me, my King,
And I will serve thee with a grateful heart
For ever. I will fight for thee, and lead
Thine armies on to glorious victory
Over all foes! Thou shalt no longer fear
The host of Asshur, for thy throne shall stand
Encompassed with a wall of dauntless hearts,
And founded on a mighty people's love,
And guarded by the God of righteousness.
        Benhadad:
I feel the flame of courage at thy breath
Leap up among the ashes of despair.
Thou hast returned to save us! Thou shalt have
The maid; and thou shalt lead my host again!
Priest, I command you give her back to him.
        Rezon:
O master, I obey thy word as thou
Hast ever been obedient to the voice
Of Rimmon. Let thy fiery captain wait
Until the sacrifice has been performed,

And he shall have the jewel that he claims.
Must we not first placate the city's god
With due allegiance, keep the ancient faith,
And pay our homage to the Lord of Wrath?

Benhadad: Sinking back upon his throne in fear.
I am the faithful son of Rimmon's House,—
And lo, these many years I worship him!
My thoughts are troubled,—I am very old,
But still a King! O Naaman, be patient!
Priest, let the sacrifice be offered.
The High Priest lifts his rod. Gongs and cymbals
sound. The curtain is rolled back, disclosing the image of
Rimmon; a gigantic and hideous idol, with a cruel human
face, four horns, the mane of a lion, and huge paws
stretched in front of him enclosing a low altar of black
stone. Ruahmah stands on the altar, chained, her arms are
bare and folded on her breast. The people prostrate
themselves in silence, with signs of astonishment and
        horror.
                Rezon:
Behold the sacrifice! Bow down, bow down!
        Naaman: Stabbing him.
Bow thou, black priest! Down,—down to hell!
Ruahmah! do not die! I come to thee.
Naaman rushes toward her, attacked by the priests,
crying "Sacrilege! Kill him!" But the soldiers stand on the
steps and beat them back. He springs upon the altar and
clasps her by the hand. Tumult and confusion. The King
rises and speaks with a loud voice, silence follows.
        Benhadad:
Peace, peace! The King commands all weapons down!
O Naaman, what wouldst thou do? Beware
Lest thou provoke the anger of a god.
        Naaman:
There is no God but one, the Merciful,
Who gave this perfect woman to my soul
That I might learn through her to worship Him,
And know the meaning of immortal Love.
        Benhadad: Agitated.
Yet she is consecrated, bound, and doomed
To sacrificial death; but thou art sworn
To live and lead my host,—Hast thou not sworn?
        Naaman:
Only if thou wilt keep thy word to me!
Break with this idol of iniquity
Whose shadow makes a darkness in the land;
Give her to me who gave me back to thee;
And I will lead thine army to renown
And plant thy banners on the hill of triumph.
But if she dies, I die with her, defying Rimmon.
Cries of "Spare them! Release her! Give us back our
Captain!" and "Sacrilege! Let them die!" Then silence,
        all turning toward the King.
        Benhadad:
Is this the choice? Must we destroy the bond
Of ancient faith, or slay the city's living hope!
I am an old, old man,—and yet the King!
Must I decide?—O let me ponder it!
His head sinks upon his breast. All stand eagerly
        looking at him.
                Naaman:

*Ruahmah, my Ruahmah! I have come
To thee at last! And art thou satisfied?
Ruahmah: Looking into his face.
Belovéd, my belovéd, I am glad
Of all, and glad for ever, come what may.
Nothing can harm me,—since my lord is come!*

APPENDIX
CARMINA FESTIVA
THE LITTLE-NECK CLAM

A modern verse-sequence, showing how a native American subject, strictly realistic, may be treated in various manners adapted to the requirements of different magazines, thus combining Art-for-Art's-Sake with Writing-for-the-Market. Read at the First Dinner of the American Periodical Publishers' Association, in Washington, April, 1904.

I

THE ANTI-TRUST CLAM
For McClure's Magazine
*The clam that once, on Jersey's banks,
Was like the man who dug it, free,
Now slave-like thro' the market clanks
In chains of corporate tyranny.
The Standard Fish-Trust of New York
Holds every clam-bank in control;
And like base Beef and menial Pork,
The free-born Clam has lost its soul.
No more the bivalve treads the sands
In freedom's rapture, free from guilt:
It follows now the harsh commands
Of Morgiman and Rockabilt.
Rise, freemen, rise! Your wrath is just!
Call on the Sherman Act to dam
The floods of this devouring Trust,
And liberate the fettered Clam.*

II
THE WHITMANIAC CLAM
For the Bookman
*Not Dante when he wandered by the river Arno,
Not Burns who plowed the banks and braes of bonnie Ayr,
Not even Shakspere on the shores of Avon,—ah, no!
Not one of those great bards did taste true Poet's Fare.
But Whitman, loafing in Long Island and New Jersey,
Found there the sustenance of mighty ode and psalm,
And while his rude emotions swam around in verse, he
Fed chiefly on the wild, impassioned, sea-born clam.
Thus in his work we feel the waves' bewildering motion,
And winds from mighty mud-flats, weird and wild:
His clam-filled bosom answered to the voice of ocean,
And rose and fell responsively with every tide.*

III
IL MERCATORE ITALIANO DELLA CLAMMA
For the Century Magazine
*"Clam O! Fres' Clam!" How strange it sounds and sweet,
The Dago's cry along the New York street!
"Dago" we call him, like the thoughtless crowd;
And yet this humble man may well be proud
To hail from Petrarch's land, Boccaccio's home,—
Firenze, Gubbio, Venezia, Rome,—
From fair Italia, whose enchanted soil
Transforms the lowly cotton-seed to olive-oil.
To me his chant, with alien accent sung,
Brings back an echo of great Virgil's tongue:
It seems to cry against the city's woe,
In liquid Latin syllables,—Clamo!
As thro' the crowded street his cart he jams
And cries aloud, ah, think of more than clams!
Receive his secret plaint with pity warm,
And grant Italia's plea for Tenement-House Reform!*

IV
THE SOCIAL CLAM
For the Smart Set
*Fair Phyllis is another's bride:
Therefore I like to sit beside
Her at a very smart set dinner,
And whisper love, and try to win her.
The little-necks,—in number six,—
That from their pearly shells she picks
And swallows whole,—ah, is it selfish
To wish my heart among those shell-fish?
"But Phyllis is another's wife;
And if she should absorb thy life
'Twould leave thy bosom vacant."—Well,
I'd keep at least the empty shell!*

V
THE RECREANT CLAM
For the Outlook
*Low dost thou lie amid the languid ooze,
Because thy slothful spirit doth refuse
The bliss of battle and the strain of strife.
Rise, craven clam, and lead the strenuous life!*

A FAIRY TALE
For the Mark Twain Dinner, December 5, 1905
*Some three-score years and ten ago
A prince was born at Florida, Mo.;
And though he came incognito,
With just the usual yells of woe,
The watchful fairies seemed to know
Precisely what the row meant;
For when he was but five days old,
(December fifth as I've been told,)
They pattered through the midnight cold,
And came around his crib, to hold
A "Council of Endowment."
"I give him Wit," the eldest said,
And stooped above the little bed,
To touch his forehead round and red.
"Within this bald, unfurnished head,
Where wild luxuriant locks shall spread
And wave in years hereafter,
I kindle now the lively spark,
That still shall flash by day and dark,
And everywhere he goes shall mark
His way with light and laughter."*

The fairies laughed to think of it
That such a rosy, wrinkled bit
Of flesh should be endowed with Wit!
But something serious seemed to hit
The mind of one, as if a fit
Of fear had come upon her.
"I give him Truth," she quickly cried,
"That laughter may not lead aside
To paths where scorn and falsehood hide,—
I give him Truth and Honour!"
"I give him Love," exclaimed the third;
And as she breathed the mystic word,
I know not if the baby heard,
But softly in his dream he stirred,
And twittered like a little bird,
And stretched his hands above him.
The fairy's gift was sealed and signed
With kisses twain the deed to bind:
"A heart of love to human-kind,
And human-kind to love him!"
"Now stay your giving!" cried the Queen.
"These gifts are passing rich I ween;
And if reporters should be mean
Enough to spy upon this scene,
'Twould make all other babies green
With envy at the rumour.
Yet since I love this child, forsooth,
I'll mix your gifts, Wit, Love and Truth,
With spirits of Immortal Youth,
And call the mixture Humour!"
The fairies vanished with their glittering train;
But here's the Prince with all their gifts,—Mark Twain.

THE BALLAD OF THE SOLEMN ASS
Recited at the Century Club, New York: Twelfth Night.
1906

Come all ye good Centurions and wise men of the times,
You've made a Poet Laureate, now you must hear his rhymes.
Extend your ears and I'll respond by shortening up my tale:—
Man cannot live by verse alone, he must have cakes and ale.
So while you wait for better things and muse on schnapps and salad,
I'll try my Pegasus his wings and sing a little ballad:
A legend of your ancestors, the Wise Men of the East,
Who brought among their baggage train a quaint and curious beast.

Their horses were both swift and strong, and we should think it lucky
If we could buy, by telephone, such horses from Kentucky;
Their dromedaries paced along, magnificent and large,
Their camels were as stately as if painted by La Farge.
But this amazing little ass was never satisfied,
He made more trouble every day than all the rest beside:
His ears were long, his legs were short, his eyes were bleared and dim,
But nothing in the wide, wide world was good enough for him.
He did not like the way they went, but lifted up his voice
And said that any other way would be a better choice.
He braced his feet and stood his ground, and made the wise men wait,
While with his heels at all around he did recalcitrate.

It mattered not how fair the land through which the road might run,
He found new causes for complaint with every Morning Sun:
And when the shades of twilight fell and all the world grew nappy,
They tied him to his Evening Post, but still he was not happy.
He thought his load was far too large, he thought his food was bad,
He thought the Star a poor affair, he thought the Wise Men mad:
He did not like to hear them laugh,—'twas childish to be jolly;
And if perchance they sang a hymn,—'twas sentimental folly!
So day by day this little beast performed his level best
To make their life, in work and play, a burden to the rest:
And when they laid them down at night, he would not let them sleep,
But criticized the Universe with hee-haws loud and deep.
One evening, as the Wise Men sat before their fire-lit tent,
And ate and drank and talked and sang, in grateful merriment,
The solemn donkey butted in, in his most solemn way,
And broke the happy meeting up with a portentous bray.

"Now by my head," Balthazar said (his real name was Choate),
"We've had about enough of this! I'll put it to the vote.
I move the donkey be dismissed; let's turn him out to grass,
And travel on our cheerful way, without the solemn ass."
The vote was aye! and with a whack the Wise Men drove him out;
But still he wanders up and down, and all the world about;
You'll know him by his long, sad face and supercilious ways,
And likewise by his morning kicks and by his evening brays.
But while we sit at Eagle Roost and make our Twelfth Night cheer,
Full well we know the solemn ass will not disturb us here:
For pleasure rules the roost to-night, by order of the King,

388

And every one must play his part, and laugh, and likewise sing.
The road of life is long, we know, and often hard to find,
And yet there's many a pleasant turn for men of cheerful mind:
We've done our day's work honestly, we've earned the right to rest,
We'll take a cup of friendship now and spice it with a jest.
A silent health to absent friends, their memories are bright!
A hearty health to all who keep the feast with us to-night!
A health to dear Centuria, oh, may she long abide!
A health, a health to all the world,—and the solemn ass, outside!

A BALLAD OF SANTA CLAUS
For the St. Nicholas Society of New York
Among the earliest saints of old, before the first Hegira,
I find the one whose name we hold, St. Nicholas of Myra:
The best-beloved name, I guess, in sacred nomenclature,—
The patron-saint of helpfulness, and friendship, and good-nature.
A bishop and a preacher too, a famous theologian,
He stood against the Arian crew and fought them like a Trojan:
But when a poor man told his need and begged an alms in trouble,
He never asked about his creed, but quickly gave him double.
Three pretty maidens, so they say, were longing to be married;
But they were paupers, lack-a-day, and so the suitors tarried.
St. Nicholas gave each maid a purse of golden ducats chinking,
And then, for better or for worse, they wedded quick as winking.

Once, as he sailed, a storm arose; wild waves the ship surrounded;
The sailors wept and tore their clothes, and shrieked "We'll all be drownded!"
St. Nicholas never turned a hair; serenely shone his halo;
He simply said a little prayer, and all the billows lay low.
The wicked keeper of an inn had three small urchins taken,
And cut them up in a pickle-bin, and salted them for bacon.
St. Nicholas came and picked them out, and put their limbs together,—
They lived, they leaped, they gave a shout, "St. Nicholas forever!"
And thus it came to pass, you know, that maids without a nickel,
And sailor-lads when tempest blow, and children in a pickle,
And every man that's fatherly, and every kindly matron,
In choosing saints would all agree to call St. Nicholas patron.
He comes again at Christmas-time and stirs us up to giving;
He rings the merry bells that chime good-will to all the living;
He blesses every friendly deed and every free donation;
He sows the secret, golden seed of love through all creation.
Our fathers drank to Santa Claus, the sixth of each December,
And still we keep his feast because his virtues we remember.
Among the saintly ranks he stood, with smiling human features,
And said, "Be good! But not too good to love your fellow-creatures!"
December 6, 1907.

ARS AGRICOLARIS
An Ode for the "Farmer's Dinner," University Club, New York, January 23, 1913
All hail, ye famous Farmers!
Ye vegetable-charmers,
Who know the art of making barren earth
Smile with prolific mirth
And bring forth twins or triplets at a birth!
Ye scientific fertilizers of the soil,
And horny-handed sons of toil!
To-night from all your arduous cares released,
With manly brows no longer sweat-impearled,
Ye hold your annual feast,
And like the Concord farmers long ago,
Ye meet above the "Bridge" below,
And draw the cork heard round the world!
What memories are yours! What tales
Of triumph have your tongues rehearsed,
Telling how ye have won your first
Potatoes from the stubborn mead,
(Almost as many as ye sowed for seed!)
And how the luscious cabbages and kails
Have bloomed before you in their bed
At seven dollars a head!
And how your onions took a prize
For bringing tears into the eyes
Of a hard-hearted cook! And how ye slew
The Dragon Cut-worm at a stroke!
And how ye broke,
Routed, and put to flight the horrid crew
Of vile potato-bugs and Hessian flies!
And how ye did not quail
Before th' invading armies of San José Scale,
But met them bravely with your little pail
Of poison, which ye put upon each tail
O' the dreadful beasts and made their courage fail!
And how ye did acquit yourselves like men
In fields of agricultural strife, and then,

Like generous warriors, sat you down at ease
And gently to your gardener said, "Let us have
Pease!"
But were there Pease? Ah, no, dear Farmers, no!
The course of Nature is not ordered so.
For when we want a vegetable most,
She holds it back;
And when we boast
To our week-endly friends
Of what we'll give them on our farm, alack,
Those things the old dam, Nature, never sends.
O Pease in bottles, Sparrow-grass in jars,
How often have ye saved from scars
Of shame, and deep embarrassment,
The disingenuous farmer-gent,
To whom some wondering guest has cried,
"How do you raise such Pease and Sparrow-grass?"
Whereat the farmer-gent has not denied
The compliment, but smiling has replied,
"To raise such things you must have lots of glass."
From wiles like these, true Farmers, hold aloof;
Accept no praise unless you have the proof.
If niggard Nature should withhold the green
And sugary Pea, welcome the humble Bean.
Even the easy Radish, and the Beet,
If grown by your own toil are extra sweet.
Let malefactors of great wealth and banker-felons
Rejoice in foreign artichokes, imported melons;
But you, my Farmers, at your frugal board
Spread forth the fare your Sabine Farms afford.
Say to Mæcenas, when he is your guest,
"No peaches! try this turnip, 'tis my best."
Thus shall ye learn from labors in the field
What honesty a farmer's life may yield,
And like G. Washington in early youth,
Though cherries fail, produce a crop of truth.
But think me not too strict, O followers of the plough;
Some place for fiction in your lives I would allow.
In January when the world is drear,
And bills come in, and no results appear,
And snow-storms veil the skies,
And ice the streamlet clogs,
Then may you warm your heart with pleasant lies
And revel in the seedsmen's catalogues!
What visions and what dreams are these
Of cauliflower obese,—
Of giant celery, taller than a mast,—
Of strawberries
Like red pincushions, round and vast,—
Of succulent and spicy gumbo,—
Of cantaloupes, as big as Jumbo,—
Of high-strung beans without the strings,—
And of a host of other wild, romantic things!
Why, then, should Doctor Starr declare
That modern habits mental force impair?
And why should H. Marquand complain
That jokes as good as his will never come again?
And why should Bridges wear a gloomy mien
About the lack of fiction for his Magazine?
The seedsman's catalogue is all we need
To stir our dull imaginations
To new creations,
And lead us, by the hand
Of Hope, into a fairy-land.
So dream, my friendly Farmers, as you will;
And let your fancy all your garners fill
With wondrous crops; but always recollect
That Nature gives us less than we expect.
Scorn not the city where you earn the wealth
That, spent upon your farms, renews your health;
And tell your wife, whene'er the bills have shocked her,
"A country-place is cheaper than a doctor."
May roses bloom for you, and may you find
Your richest harvest in a tranquil mind.

ANGLER'S FIRESIDE SONG
Oh, the angler's path is a very merry way,
And his road through the world is bright;
For he lives with the laughing stream all day,
And he lies by the fire at night.
Sing hey nonny, ho nonny
And likewise well-a-day!
The angler's life is a very jolly life
And that's what the anglers say!
Oh, the angler plays for the pleasure of the game,
And his creel may be full or light,
But the tale that he tells will be just the same
When he lies by the fire at night.
Sing hey nonny, ho nonny
And likewise well-a-day!
We love the fire and the music of the lyre,
And that's what the anglers say!
To the San Francisco Fly-Casting Club, April, 1913.

HOW SPRING COMES TO SHASTA JIM
I never seen no "red gods"; I dunno wot's a "lure";
But if it's sumpin' takin', then Spring has got it sure;
An' it doesn't need no Kiplins, ner yet no London Jacks,
To make up guff about it, w'ile settin' in their shacks.
It's sumpin' very simple 'at happens in the Spring,
But it changes all the lookin's of every blessed thing;
The buddin' woods look bigger, the mounting twice as high,
But the house looks kindo smaller, tho I couldn't tell ye why.
It's cur'ous wot a show-down the month of April makes,
Between the reely livin', an' the things 'at's only fakes!
Machines an' barns an' buildin's, they never give no sign;
But the livin' things look lively w'en Spring is on the line.
She doesn't come too suddin, ner she doesn't come too slow;
Her gaits is some cayprishus, an' the next ye never know,—
A single-foot o' sunshine, a buck o' snow er hail,—
But don't be disapp'inted, fer Spring ain't goin' ter fail.
She's loopin' down the hillside,—the driffs is fadin' out.
She's runnin' down the river,—d'ye see them risin' trout?
She's loafin' down the canyon,—the squaw-bed's growin' blue,
An' the teeny Johnny-jump-ups is jest a-peekin' thru.
A thousan' miles o' pine-trees, with Douglas firs between,

Is waitin' fer her fingers to freshen up their green;
With little tips o' brightness the firs 'ill sparkle thick,
An' every yaller pine-tree, a giant candle-stick!
The underbrush is risin' an' spreadin' all around,
Jest like a mist o' greenness 'at hangs above the ground;
A million manzanitas 'ill soon be full o' pink;
So saddle up, my sonny,—it's time to ride, I think!
We'll ford er swim the river, becos there ain't no bridge;
We'll foot the gulches careful, an' lope along the ridge;
We'll take the trail to Nowhere, an' travel till we tire,
An' camp beneath a pine-tree, an' sleep beside the fire.
We'll see the blue-quail chickens, an' hear 'em pipin' clear;
An' p'raps we'll sight a brown-bear, er else a bunch o' deer;
But nary a heathen goddess or god 'ill meet our eyes;
For why? There isn't any! They're jest a pack o' lies!
Oh, wot's the use o' "red gods," an' "Pan," an' all that stuff?
The natcheral facts o' Springtime is wonderful enuff!
An' if there's Someone made 'em, I guess He understood,
To be alive in Springtime would make a man feel good.
California, 1913.

A BUNCH OF TROUT-FLIES
For Archie Rutledge
Here's a half-a-dozen flies,
Just about the proper size
For the trout of Dickey's Run,—
Luck go with them every one!
Dainty little feathered beauties,
Listen now and learn your duties:
Not to tangle in the box;
Not to catch on logs or rocks,
Boughs that wave or weeds that float,
Nor in the angler's "pants" or coat!
Not to lure the glutton frog
From his banquet in the bog;
Nor the lazy chub to fool,
Splashing idly round the pool;
Nor the sullen hornèd pout
From the mud to hustle out!
None of this vulgarian crew,
Dainty flies, is game for you.
Darting swiftly through the air
Guided by the angler's care,
Light upon the flowing stream
Like a wingèd fairy dream;
Float upon the water dancing,
Through the lights and shadows glancing,
Till the rippling current brings you,
And with quiet motion swings you,
Where a speckled beauty lies
Watching you with hungry eyes.
Here's your game and here's your prize!
Hover near him, lure him, tease him,
Do your very best to please him,
Dancing on the water foamy,
Like the frail and fair Salome,
Till the monarch yields at last;
Rises, and you have him fast!
Then remember well your duty,—
Do not lose, but land, your booty;
For the finest fish of all is
Salvelinus Fontinalis.
So, you plumed illusions, go,
Let my comrade Archie know
Every day he goes a-fishing
I'll be with him in well-wishing.
Most of all when lunch is laid
In the dappled orchard shade,
With Will, Corinne, and Dixie too,
Sitting as we used to do
Round the white cloth on the grass
While the lazy hours pass,
And the brook's contented tune
Lulls the sleepy afternoon,—
Then's the time my heart will be
With that pleasant company!

June 17, 1913.

Made in the USA
San Bernardino, CA
30 November 2019